INTERACTIVE CASEBOOK SERIES℠

THE FIRST AMENDMENT

A Contemporary Approach

Alan E. Garfield
DISTINGUISHED PROFESSOR OF LAW,
WIDENER UNIVERSITY DELAWARE LAW SCHOOL

Rodney A. Smolla
PRESIDENT AND PROFESSOR OF LAW,
VERMONT LAW AND GRADUATE SCHOOL

WEST ACADEMIC

The publisher is not engaged in rendering legal or other professional advice, and this publication is not a substitute for the advice of an attorney. If you require legal or other expert advice, you should seek the services of a competent attorney or other professional.

Interactive Casebook Series is a servicemark registered in the U.S. Patent and Trademark Office.

860 Blue Gentian Road, Suite 350
Eagan, MN 55121
1-877-888-1330

Published in the United States of America

ISBN: 978-1-68561-243-6

For Phyllis, Hannah, and Danny

–A.E.G.

For my family

–R.A.S.

Preface

This casebook is a survey of First Amendment jurisprudence. In the pages that follow, you will learn how judges have interpreted the First Amendment of the U.S. Constitution to implement its commitments to protect freedom of speech and religion. The material is certain to challenge you. The cases can be complex, the policy choices confounding, and the doctrine prone to shifting. But the vital importance of the subject ensures an engaging and rewarding course of study.

The two rights under consideration—freedom of speech and freedom of religion—are essential components of human autonomy. Speech, after all, is the primary means through which individuals communicate and interact with others. And religion, for many if not most, is how individuals define their place in the universe and find meaning and purpose. A society committed to human dignity is inconceivable without protection of these rights.

But the freedoms of speech and religion do more than foster individual human autonomy. They are also essential prerequisites for *communities* to flourish. Consider the importance of freedom of speech in furthering the core value, enshrined in the Declaration of Independence, that people have the right to govern themselves rather than be subject to the whims of a monarch or dictator. If this worthy vision is to be realized, citizens must have access to information and the freedom to discuss the merits of government policies and elected officials. This makes freedom of speech a crucial cornerstone of representative government. As Justice Benjamin Cardozo explained, it is "the matrix, the indispensable condition, of nearly every other form of freedom."

Freedom of religion plays a different, but equally important, role in enabling communities to flourish. It is inevitable that members of any sizable community will have diverse religious beliefs. And given the fervor with which these beliefs are often held, it is essential for a society to thread the needle of honoring religious differences without allowing them to erupt into religious strife. History is littered with societies that failed to meet this challenge. But properly calibrated protection for religious liberty offers the hope of avoiding this fate. In this manner, the protection of religious freedom can be a lubricant that facilitates peaceful coexistence in a pluralistic society.

These are theoretical justifications for protecting speech and religion. They are not practical rules for implementing that protection. In American constitutional law, those rules emerge not from philosophical tractates, but from the piecemeal case-by-case resolution of disputes by judges. It is through this slow common law process that the doctrinal framework for implementing First Amendment values is assembled and continues to evolve.

In generating this corpus of jurisprudence, judges have wrestled with everything from the broad theoretical question of why speech and religion should receive special protection to the practical question of what constitutes "speech" or "religion." The latter might not sound daunting, but it can be surprisingly nuanced. Is it obvious, for instance, whether computer code or a custom-designed wedding cake is speech, or whether fortune telling or the "First Church of Marijuana" (we did not make that up) is a religion?

Even when judges acknowledge that speech or religious interests are implicated, they often must mediate between these interests and competing societal interests that call for restraining these liberties. Consider, for example, whether our societal commitment to equality justifies the suppression of hate speech, or whether our concern for safety justifies the suppression of bombmaking instructions. On the religion front, consider whether religious adherents should be exempt from antidiscrimination laws so they can refuse service to same-sex couples, or whether a state can prohibit religious adherents from attending services during a life-threatening pandemic.

These are a sampling of the issues you will encounter in this casebook. We tried to make the material accessible by providing background information for cases so you can better understand and critically evaluate them. We sought to bring the cases to life with related stories and images. You will not have to imagine the Ten Commandments monument on public property or a proposed Texas license plate with a Confederate flag. You will see for yourself what the judges were contending with. To help you master the material, we have included explanatory charts and numerous exercises to test your newly acquired knowledge. Each chapter also ends with a link to assessment questions to reinforce your learning.

Please note that the excerpted court opinions have been heavily edited for brevity and clarity. The result is a highly "cleaned up" style in which internal citations and footnotes are typically omitted. We have not used ellipses to indicate where material has been omitted, but we have used brackets to indicate when text has been inserted. Our goal was to capture the important elements of cases, while making the opinions more accessible and the reading load lighter. While we have tried to stay faithful to the substance of the cases, you should always return to the original sources when preparing your own work product.

It may take a village to raise a child, but it takes a megalopolis to write a casebook. To thank everyone who played a role in this work's creation is impossible. We want to pay tribute, however, to all the scholars, past and present, whose contributions to the field have enriched our own understanding of the subject. If there are any insights in this book where we see further than those scholars, it is only because we stood on their shoulders. Likewise, we are grateful to the generations of students whom we have taught and who, through their questions, insights, and even confusion, have helped us spot stumbling blocks on the path to learning and motivated us to forever be thinking about how best to present the material.

We are deeply grateful to the professionals at West Academic who made this book possible. Senior Acquisitions Editor Jon Harkness embraced our vision for the book and graciously shepherded the project from proposal to print. The wonderful design team led by Michele Bassett and including Whitney Esson and Megan Hoffman used their magic to convert a bland manuscript into an elegant text. The authors are also grateful to their superb copy editor, Jen McCreary, whose discerning eye caught a multitude of imperfections that the bleary-eyed authors glossed over.

We are also deeply appreciative of the scholars who graciously gave their time to offer feedback on parts of the book. They include Wayne Batchis, John Culhane, Jeffrey Dunoff, Martin Gilens, Barry McDonald, Laura Ray, Stephen Wermiel, and John Wladis. Their comments improved the book and did nothing to harm it. The authors instead bear full responsibility for any imperfections.

Professor Garfield would like to thank the librarians at his law school, Margaret Adams, Christy D'Antonio, and Janet Lindenmuth, as well as his superb research assistants, Heather Romansky and Victoria Swiacki. He is also deeply grateful for the administrative assistance and good counsel of Connie Sweeney and Debbe Patrick. His siblings, Jeff and Diane, as well as good friends, including Jean Eggen, Claudia and Alan Silverman, Andy Strauss, and Audrey Wladis, provided the moral support to help him persevere through the book writing process. Finally, Professor Garfield is eternally grateful to his wife, Phyllis Rubin, whose love, support, and editorial assistance ensured that he stayed grounded, nourished, and succinct, and to their wonderful children, Hannah and Danny, who provide them with an endless source of joy and pride.

As this casebook goes to press, we are entering an era in which the values embodied in the First Amendment are under severe strain. New technologies, such as deep fakes and artificially generated text and images, are making it increasingly difficult to distinguish fact from fiction. At the same time, algorithms running social media routinely direct users toward heat rather than light, and the vast diversity of media outlets makes it easy for people to live in information echo chambers that reinforce but never challenge their assumptions.

We hope that this book will help readers appreciate the bedrock importance of a healthy marketplace of ideas to the success of our democracy. Ideally, the book will inspire some to become leaders—as lawyers, judges, public officials, journalists, educators, and, most importantly, as citizens—in the never-ending work to ensure that our union, as promised in the Constitution's Preamble, continues to secure "the Blessings of Liberty to ourselves and our Posterity."

May 2024

ALAN GARFIELD
Wilmington, Delaware

RODNEY SMOLLA
South Royalton, Vermont

Summary of Contents

Content-Based Regulations of Speech: When Speech Is Regulated Because of a Speaker's Message

Additional Speech-Related Rights: The Right Not to Speak, the Right to Associate for Expressive Purposes, and Freedom of the Press

Part III. Freedom of Religion

Table of Contents

Content-Based Regulations of Speech: When Speech Is Regulated Because of a Speaker's Message

Additional Speech-Related Rights: The Right Not to Speak, the Right to Associate for Expressive Purposes, and Freedom of the Press

Chapter 16 *When Government Interferes with Freedom of the Press: Access to Government Information, Gag Orders, Newsgathering, and Confidential Sources* 723

Part III. Freedom of Religion

Table of Cases

The principal cases are in bold type.

THE FIRST AMENDMENT

A Contemporary Approach

Part I

Introduction to the First Amendment

Chapter One

Introduction:
The Big Picture

Nothing cuts to the core of an individual's humanity more than the ability to express oneself and to define one's belief about the nature of existence. The Framers of the U.S. Constitution recognized this fact. In the First Amendment to the Constitution, they provided protection for both freedom of speech and freedom of religion.

But enshrining these values in our national charter was merely the starting point to making these values a reality. The hard work came later, and continues to this day, as our society wrestles with how to translate these values into concrete legal principles.

This casebook surveys the current state of these legal principles, as they have been derived from the First Amendment, that our society has developed for protecting freedom of speech and religious liberty. Its focus will be on U.S. Supreme Court opinions interpreting the First Amendment. Judges are the primary expositors of the Constitution's meaning, and Supreme Court justices sit atop the judicial pyramid. We will pay particular attention to how the Court has balanced constitutional commitments to speech and religion against other societal values ranging from safety and equality to aesthetics and tranquility.

Before you embark on this journey, you need a grounding in the First Amendment's text, as well as the Supreme Court's role in interpreting that text.

A. Meet the First Amendment

When the Framers signed the Constitution in Philadelphia on September 17, 1787, the document did not protect freedom of speech or religion. The Framers were certainly aware of the dangers of government censorship and religious persecution. The histories of Great Britain and continental Europe were ample testaments to these dangers. The Framers were also familiar with earlier rights-bearing documents with provisions protecting freedom of speech or religion. For example, the Virginia Declaration of Rights, which predated even the Declaration of Independence, provided that "all men are equally entitled to the free exercise of religion" and described freedom of the press as "one of the great bulwarks of liberty" that could "never be restrained but by despotic governments."[1]

Conventional wisdom offers two explanations for the Framers' surprising failure to include freedom of speech and religion, as well as other fundamental rights, in the original Constitution. First, the Framers believed that the government created by the Constitution would have only limited and specifically enumerated powers. Consequently, if the Constitution did not give Congress the power to abridge speech, there was no need for a provision prohibiting Congress from doing so. As Alexander Hamilton explained, "why declare that things shall not be done which there is no power to do?"[2] Second, the Framers were concerned that listing some rights in the Constitution would imply that other rights did not exist.[3]

The lack of adequate rights protection in the Constitution led to objections during the ratification process. Some states appealed for the newly created legislature to promptly propose a bill of rights. That task fell to James Madison, who had been elected to represent Virginia in the House of Representatives. Madison had played a leading role at the Constitutional Convention and had been a member of the Virginia Convention of Delegates that had adopted the Virginia Declaration of Rights. Madison drafted 17 proposed amendments to the Constitution that were passed by the House. The Senate modified and consolidated these into 12 amendments, which, after congressional approval, were sent to the states for ratification. Ten were quickly ratified and became part of the Constitution in 1791. Collectively, they are referred to as the Bill of Rights.

This casebook focuses on the first of these 10 amendments to the U.S. Constitution. Here is the First Amendment's complete text:

> Congress shall make no law respecting an establishment of religion, or prohibiting the free exercise thereof; or abridging the freedom of speech, or of the press; or the right of the people peaceably to assemble, and to petition the Government for a redress of grievances.

If you are unfamiliar with the First Amendment's various provisions, you're in good company. A 2006 national survey by the McCormick Tribune Freedom Museum found that only one in 1,000 Americans could name all five of the freedoms guar-

---

1 The text of the Virginia Declaration of Rights is *available at* https://www.archives.gov/founding-docs/virginia-declaration-of-rights. See a copy of the original document at https://edu.lva.virginia.gov/dbva/items/show/184.

2 Alexander Hamilton, The Federalist Papers No. 84, *available at* https://founders.archives.gov/documents/Hamilton/01-04-02-0247.

3 When the Bill of Rights amendments were later proposed, the Framers tried to alleviate this concern by providing in the Ninth Amendment that the "enumeration in the Constitution, of certain rights, shall not be construed to deny or disparage others retained by the people."

anteed in the First Amendment.[4] By contrast, one in five Americans could name all five members of the cartoon Simpsons family. Certainly, it is easier to remember Homer, Marge, Lisa, Bart, and Maggie than Freedom of Religion, Freedom of Speech, Freedom of the Press, Freedom of Assembly, and Freedom to Petition for Redress of Grievances.

In fairness to the American public, the lion's share of First Amendment jurisprudence has been about only some of these rights. There is little jurisprudence about the right to petition the government. Even the Press Clause, which you might think would be a rich source of jurisprudence, has been largely undeveloped by the Supreme Court. And the right to peaceably assemble has been mostly addressed through jurisprudence under the Free Speech Clause. In the annals of constitutional jurisprudence, these three clauses have not obtained the prominence of a Lisa, Bart, or Maggie. The vast bulk of First Amendment jurisprudence is focused on the two religion clauses (the Establishment Clause and the Free Exercise Clause) and the Free Speech Clause. Cases interpreting those clauses fill the pages of this book.

Before immersing ourselves in the material on freedom of speech and religion, let us start with a brief tour of the First Amendment's various provisions. For some of the less frequently litigated clauses, this may be all you'll read about them in this casebook.

1. The Religion Clauses

The First Amendment begins with two clauses addressing freedom of religion: the Establishment Clause and the Free Exercise Clause ("Congress shall make no law respecting an establishment of religion, or prohibiting the free exercise thereof"). While these clauses expressly apply only to "Congress," they have been interpreted, as have the other First Amendment clauses, to apply to all branches of the federal government, as well as to state and local governments. So, for example, the Establishment Clause would be implicated if Congress placed a Latin cross, a widely recognized symbol of Christianity, on the top of the Capitol Building, if a state legislature placed a similar cross atop its legislative hall, and if a public elementary school placed a comparable cross above the school entrance. We will discuss how these clauses came to be applied to all levels of government in later chapters.

Here is a sampling of the issues you will wrestle with when we explore the Establishment and Free Exercise Clauses in Chapters 17 to 19.

---

[4] Gerry Doyle, *About those First Amendment rights, Doh!*, Chicago Trib., Mar. 1, 2006, *available at* https://www.chicagotribune.com/news/ct-xpm-2006-03ws-01-0603010312-story.html; *Simpsons Outpace Constitution*, CBS News, Mar. 1, 2006, *available at* https://www.cbsnews.com/news/simpsons-outpace-us-constitution/.

a. The Establishment Clause

The Supreme Court's Establishment Clause jurisprudence focuses on government actions that benefit religion, such as funding, endorsement, or favoritism. All justices have agreed that the clause—"Congress shall make no law respecting an establishment of religion"—was intended to prevent the creation of a national church, such as the Church of England. Beyond that, there is little consensus about the extent to which the Establishment Clause limits other government actions favoring religion.

Some Supreme Court justices want as much separation of church and state as possible. They quote from a letter written by Thomas Jefferson that said the religion clauses were meant to build "a wall of separation between church and state."[5] These justices think that government funds should not be used to support religious institutions, prayers should not be permitted in public schools, and religious displays, like Ten Commandment monuments, should not be allowed on government property.

Justices who favor separation believe that religious institutions should rely on their members for financial support. They worry that government support for religion corrupts religious institutions by making them beholden to their government benefactors. They also fear that having religious groups compete for government support will generate religious conflict. These judges emphasize that one of the primary purposes of the Establishment Clause was to avoid religious tensions, which the Framers knew had caused centuries of strife in Europe.

These justices also worry that government favoritism toward one religion makes the adherents of other religions feel like second-class citizens. They are therefore concerned by government actions that appear to endorse one religion over others or even religion over secularism. As Justice Sandra Day O'Connor explained, the Establishment Clause was meant to prohibit government "from making adherence to a religion relevant in any way to a person's standing in the political community."[6]

Justices on the opposite end of the spectrum believe that the government can acknowledge and accommodate religion without violating the Establishment Clause. These judges emphasize that Americans are a religious people, that religion played an important role in our nation's history (just try taking Christ's body out of Corpus Christi or Saint Francis out of San Francisco), and that religion provides the moral foundation for our country. Justice Antonin Scalia, for example, said, "Those who wrote the Constitution believed that morality was essential to the well-being of society and that encouragement of religion was the best way to foster morality."[7] These judges are more accepting of religious displays on government property and more willing to permit prayers in public schools, and they would allow government support for

---

5 *Reynolds v. United States*, 98 U.S. 145, 164 (1878); *Everson v. Board of Educ.*, 330 U.S. 1, 16 (1947).

6 *Lynch v. Donnelly*, 465 U.S. 668, 687 (1984) (O'Connor, J., concurring).

7 *McCreary County v. ACLU of Ky.*, 545 U.S. 844, 887 (2005) (Scalia, J., dissenting).

religious institutions as long as the money is distributed to a wide range of charitable and educational organizations.

Justices over the years have ranged from "high separationists" to "low separationists" to those in between. The justices' varying attitudes about the appropriate level of church/state separation have produced a muddled jurisprudence. Be prepared for a little cognitive dissonance as you read the justices' opinions. Whether you are pleased or displeased with any given opinion will likely depend on how high you think the wall between church and state should be.

b. The Free Exercise Clause

The Free Exercise Clause—"Congress shall make no law . . . prohibiting the free exercise [of religion]"—addresses situations when government actions burden religion. All justices have agreed that the government cannot mandate what people should believe or compel people to affirmatively espouse a belief in a god or a religious tenet. Free exercise problems more commonly arise when laws interfere with believers' ability to practice their religion. To take an example from a famous case, consider the dilemma for Native American Church members if the government makes it illegal to use peyote but their religion requires the use of peyote for religious rituals. If the church members stop using peyote, they violate their faith. If they use peyote, they violate the law. Free exercise jurisprudence asks whether the government must accommodate people in this situation by granting them an exemption from the law.

Here, too, justices have been split over how to apply this clause. All justices have agreed that the government cannot deliberately discriminate against religious practice. For example, the government could not ban the use of wine for Catholic Communion while permitting it for all other uses. The justices have taken a dim view of such discrimination, which might explain why laws blatantly discriminating against religious practice are rare.

The more common situation is when a nondiscriminatory or "neutral" law incidentally interferes with an individual's religious practice. That was the case with the law criminalizing the use of peyote. The law was a "neutral law of general applicability"—it was not targeted at the Native American Church and applied to people generally. The free exercise issue was whether the Constitution required the government to exempt Native American Church members from this neutral law.

Given the facts of the peyote case, you might be sympathetic to the church members' claim. The potential harm of allowing these individuals to use small amounts of peyote for ritualistic purposes might seem small, and the law's burden on their religious practice might seem great. But coming up with a general rule for when religious adherents should be exempted from neutral laws of general applicability is trickier than this one case suggests. For example, should the Constitution require the government to exempt religious adherents from laws that forbid polygamous marriages or that require vaccinations? Should a religious baker be exempted from an antidiscrimination law because it would violate his faith to make a wedding cake for a same-sex couple?

2. The Free Speech Clause

The First Amendment provides that "Congress shall make no law . . . abridging the freedom of speech." You likely know that this clause protects Americans' right to express virtually any idea, no matter how controversial, offensive, hateful, or foolish. At the same time, the Supreme Court has never interpreted the Free Speech Clause to bar all abridgments of speech, even if the words "no law" suggest an absolute prohibition. Instead, the Court has allowed the government to regulate speech in a variety of ways, from laws regulating the placement of signs to criminalizing the distribution of obscene literature. The challenge has been figuring out which abridgements of speech are constitutional and which abridgments are not.

We will begin our study of the Free Speech Clause in the next chapter, so we will keep our discussion of it here brief.

3. The Press Clause

The First Amendment couples its protection for freedom of speech with protection for freedom of the press. The latter right follows on the heels of the former: "Congress shall make no law . . . abridging the freedom of speech, or of the press." The central interpretive question involving the Press Clause is whether it provides the press with greater protection than it already receives under the Free Speech Clause.

Advocates for press freedom contend that the media plays a vital role in our society. The press can inform and educate the public and help protect against government abuse by investigating and reporting on the actions of government officials. Noteworthy examples include journalists Bob Woodward and Carl Bernstein's dogged investigation of the Watergate burglary, which eventually led to President Nixon's resignation, and television coverage of the civil rights movement, which helped propel the passage of federal civil rights legislation.

Recognizing the importance of a free press, Thomas Jefferson said, "were it left to me to decide whether we should have a government without newspapers, or newspapers without a government, I should not hesitate a moment to prefer the latter."[8] Yet the same Jefferson, equally aware of the press' potential failings, cynically

---

[8] Letter from Thomas Jefferson to Edward Carrington (Jan. 16, 1787), *available at* https://founders.archives.gov/documents/Jefferson/01-11-02-0047.

commented, "the man who never looks into a newspaper is better informed than he who reads them."[9]

Even if one acknowledges the importance of a free press, there remains the interpretive question of whether the Press Clause should provide the media with greater freedoms than those enjoyed by all Americans under the Free Speech Clause. Thus far, the Supreme Court has said it does not.

Perhaps the Court believes there is no need to give the press any special immunity because free speech protections are sufficiently robust. The Court may also have been reluctant to extend special protections to the press because doing so would require the justices to define who qualifies as a member of the "press."[10] That is a far knottier problem than you might think. Everyone might agree that *The New York Times* and CBS News are the press, but what about a person who does her own investigations and writes news stories on a personal blog? What about a freelance photographer who captures news images and sells them to established media outlets?

Instead of sorting out this thorny issue, the Supreme Court has declined to give the Press Clause substantive meaning, focusing instead on the rights given to both the press and all other citizens under the Free Speech Clause. Nevertheless, Chapter 16 will focus on First Amendment issues that are particularly relevant to the press, such as whether the amendment shields reporters from having to disclose their sources and whether it provides a right to access government information.

4. The Right to Peaceably Assemble Clause

The right to peaceably assemble is closely related to the right of free speech. People often assemble so that they can more effectively communicate with each other or convey a collective message to a wider audience.

Rather than generate a separate jurisprudence about the right to assemble, the Supreme Court has largely addressed issues concerning this right in its free speech jurisprudence. So, for example, free speech jurisprudence addresses issues about the government's ability to regulate public rallies and parades and the right of people to associate with others for the purpose of communicating a collective message.[11]

---

9 Letter from Thomas Jefferson to John Norvell (June 11, 1807), *available at* https://founders.archives.gov/documents/Jefferson/99-01-02-5737.

10 See Sonja West, *Press Exceptionalism*, 127 Harv. L. Rev. 2434, 2436 (2014) (acknowledging that, "[t]o recognize unique press protections, the Court must figure out who or what the press is," and offering factors for making this determination).

11 John D. Inazu, *The Forgotten Freedom of Assembly*, 84 Tul. L. Rev. 565, 566 (2010) ("One might, with good reason, contend that the right of assembly has been subsumed into the rights of speech and association," but advocating for increased attention to assembly as a separate right). *See also* Tabatha Abu El-Haj, *The Neglected Right of Assembly*, 56 U.C.L.A. L. Rev. 543 (2009) (contending that "the right of

5. The Right to Petition Clause

The right to petition the government for a redress of grievances traces back to the Magna Carta, the "Great Charter" signed by England's King John in 1215, which gave English barons the right to declare a grievance and "claim immediate redress."[12] Five centuries later, American colonists cited King George's failure to respond to their petitions as a justification for declaring independence from Great Britain. "We have petitioned for redress in the most humble terms," the Declaration of Independence said, but "our repeated petitions have been answered only by repeated injury."[13]

In 2011, the Supreme Court observed that the right to free speech and the right to petition often overlap but are nevertheless distinct:

> Both speech and petition are integral to the democratic process, although not necessarily in the same way. The right to petition allows citizens to express their ideas, hopes, and concerns to their government and their elected representatives, whereas the right to speak fosters the public exchange of ideas that is integral to deliberative democracy as well as to the whole realm of ideas and human affairs.[14]

The Court has acknowledged that there "may arise cases where the special concerns of the Petition Clause" dictate a "distinct analysis" from that required by the Free Speech Clause.[15] To date, however, the right to petition has not been richly developed.[16]

---

assembly should not be collapsed into the right of free expression" and that doing so has given the government undue power to regulate assemblies through permit requirements and conditions).

12 Magna Carta, § 61, *available at* https://www.nationalarchives.gov.uk/education/resources/magna-carta/british-library-magna-carta-1215-runnymede/.

13 Declaration of Independence, *available at* https://www.archives.gov/founding-docs/declaration-transcript.

14 *Borough of Duryea v. Guarnieri*, 564 U.S. 379, 388 (2011).

15 *Id.* at 389.

16 For a brief description of the right to petition from the National Constitution Center, *see* John Inazu and Burt Neuborne, *Right to Assemble and Petition*, National Constitution Center, *available* here (observing that "the modern Supreme Court has all but read the venerable right to petition out of the Bill of Rights, effectively holding that it has been rendered obsolete by an expanding Free Speech Clause," but noting that the right to petition and freedom of speech are not synonymous and an "energized" right to petition could make legislators more responsive to their constituents). For an example of a scholarly effort to reenergize the right to petition, *see* Maggie McKinley, *Lobbying and the Petition Clause*, 68 Stan. L. Rev. 1131 (2016).

Points for Discussion

1. **Can you hear Madison's music?** Professor Burt Neuborne finds music in the way James Madison organized the rights in the First Amendment. He notes that Madison did not create these rights out of whole cloth; he had access to earlier documents protecting similar rights. But Madison's genius, Neuborne says, was to combine these rights into a single text and organize them in a manner that chronologically tracks the evolution of a democratic idea from its conception in an individual's mind, to its dissemination to the public, and culminating in the idea's presentation to a legislative body that can enact the idea into law:

> Madison deploys the foundational concepts in his First Amendment on a disciplined inside-to-outside axis, beginning in the two religion clauses with freedom of thought, progressing through three ascending levels of individual interaction with the community—free expression of an idea by an individual, mass dissemination of the idea by a free press, and collective action in support of the idea by the people—and culminating in the petition clause with the introduction of the idea into the formal process of democratic lawmaking. In short, a chronological description of the arc of a democratic idea—from conception to codification. No document in the history of self-government prefigures such a carefully drawn, chronologically organized blueprint of democracy in action.

Burt Neuborne, Madison's Music: On Reading of the First Amendment 17–18 (2015).

2. **Football and the First Amendment.** A case we will be studying in Chapter 19 concerns a public high school football coach who felt compelled to say a prayer at the 50-yard line after each game. At times, players or community members would join him as he prayed. The school administration told the coach to stop his post-game prayers on the field. When the coach refused to comply, he was fired. The coach sued, claiming that his First Amendment rights were violated. You have been only briefly introduced to the clauses of the First Amendment, but can you identify which ones might be relevant to a judge deciding this case?

Do the clauses you identified uniformly favor a ruling for either the coach or the school, or do some favor the coach and some favor the school? If the latter is true, how is a judge supposed to decide which First Amendment provision should be given priority?

B. The Supreme Court's Role in Interpreting the First Amendment

The First Amendment may reflect core societal values, but it gives little guidance for how to implement them. To say that government should "make no law respecting an establishment of religion" does not answer the questions of whether there can be a National Christmas Tree, whether government can give public funds to religious universities to erect science buildings, or whether our currency can say "In God We Trust." (By the way, is it really a good idea to associate religion with, of all things, money?) Neither is the prohibition that government should "make no law . . . prohibiting the free exercise [of religion]" especially illuminating. This seeming prohibition on any interference with religious practice could not possibly mean that religious adherents may engage in human sacrifice or force young children into unwanted marriages. Similarly, the Free Speech Clause's command that "no law" may abridge speech cannot be taken literally. Surely, the government can punish perjury, solicitation of murder, parades in the middle of the night, and painting graffiti on public buildings.

It is tempting to think that judges can resolve constitutional issues by merely searching the Constitution's text for answers. For some narrowly defined issues (perhaps the age a person must be to serve in the House of Representatives[17]), the process might be that straightforward. But that is not the case for most constitutional issues. For while the Constitution contains many words (around 4,500), the vast bulk of constitutional jurisprudence concerns only a handful of short phrases, such as "due process," "equal protection," "commerce among the several states," and "unreasonable searches and seizures." Each of these "majestic generalities,"[18] as Justice Robert Jackson referred to them, has generated enough jurisprudence to fill a library. The same is true for the succinctly stated rights in the First Amendment.

In our constitutional system, the primary job of interpreting the Constitution, including the First Amendment, has been given to judges. That is because judges have the power of "judicial review," or the power to declare laws unconstitutional. This power is not enumerated in the Constitution. Instead, it is derived from the Supreme Court's opinion in *Marbury v. Madison*, in which Chief Justice John Marshall famously declared, "It is emphatically the province and duty of the judicial department to say what the law is."[19]

---

17 Even this seemingly simple rule has required further clarification. For example, must a person be 25 years old before running for a seat in the House of Representatives or only 25 years old at the time the person would hold office? The latter is the rule. *See* Congressional Research Serv., *Qualifications of Members of Congress* 11 (Jan. 15, 2015), *available at* https://sgp.fas.org/crs/misc/R41946.pdf.

18 *West Virginia State Bd. of Educ. v. Barnette*, 319 U.S. 624, 639 (1943).

19 *Marbury v. Madison*, 5 U.S. 137, 177 (1803).

William Marbury (L) and James Madison (R)

Marbury painting by Rembrandt Peale, Collection of the Supreme Court of the United States

Madison painting by Gilbert Stuart, Collection of the National Gallery of Art

Supreme Court justices are not the only judges who can declare laws unconstitutional—so can lower federal court judges and state court judges. The key difference is that the Supreme Court is the highest court in the land. There is no appeal from the Supreme Court. If the Court decides that a law is unconstitutional, whether it be a law punishing flag burning or a law limiting corporate campaign expenditures, the only way to overturn the Court's ruling, other than the justices reversing themselves, is to amend the Constitution.[20]

The Constitution has been amended to overturn Supreme Court decisions on four occasions.[21] But amending the Constitution is a heavy lift. A proposed amend-

[20] A notable exception to this rule is that Congress, through ordinary legislation, can override a Supreme Court decision that a state or local law violates the dormant Commerce Clause. The Court has said that this is because Congress has plenary power to regulate interstate commerce. *See generally* Erwin Chemerinsky, Constitutional Law: Principles and Policies 510 (7th ed. 2023).

Of course, the justices can always reverse an earlier Supreme Court opinion. The public was vividly reminded of this in 2022 when the Court reversed the two leading decisions establishing a woman's right to obtain an abortion. *Dobbs v. Jackson Women's Health Org.*, 142 S. Ct. 2228 (2022). The justices are usually reluctant to overturn precedent, but they have certainly done so—perhaps most famously when *Brown v. Board of Education*, 347 U.S. 483 (1954), reversed *Plessy v. Ferguson*, 163 U.S. 537 (1896). Often, the impetus for these reversals is a change in the makeup of the Court. That was the case with the 2022 reversal of the *Roe v. Wade* abortion precedent after the appointment of three new justices during the Trump administration. Congress has the power to expedite this change by expanding the number of seats on the Court. President Franklin Delano Roosevelt encouraged Congress to do so in the 1930s when the Court was striking down his New Deal legislation. Congress did not change the Court's size at Roosevelt's urging, and there has been a reluctance to do so in subsequent years because doing so would threaten the Court's independence. Nevertheless, after the Supreme Court's reversal of *Roe v. Wade*, some critics of the Court's current direction have encouraged Congress to expand the Court's size.

[21] The Eleventh Amendment overturned *Chisholm v. Georgia*, 2 U.S. 419 (1793), which had allowed states to be sued in federal court by citizens of other states or foreign countries. The Fourteenth Amend-

ment needs to pass both houses of Congress by a two-thirds vote and must then be ratified by three-quarters of the states, typically by a state's legislature.[22] Note that this is three-quarters of the states and not three-quarters of the population. California might have 40 million residents and Wyoming half a million, but each counts as one state when ratifying a proposed amendment. You can appreciate the difficulty of amending the Constitution when you realize that the Constitution is over 200 years old but has had only 27 amendments. Of those amendments, 10 (the Bill of Rights) were enacted shortly after the Constitution was ratified, and three were enacted in response to the Civil War. And let's not forget that two amendments were needed to institute, and then abolish, Prohibition.

The difficulty of overriding the justices' constitutional opinions casts in stark relief the central question underlying all constitutional law jurisprudence. Chief Justice John Roberts stated this question bluntly when he dissented in *Obergefell v. Hodges*, the 2015 decision in which a slim five-justice majority held that same-sex couples have a constitutional right to marry. After excoriating the majority for ordering "the transformation of a social institution that has formed the basis of human society for millennia," Chief Justice Roberts put the question front and center:

Just who do we think we are?[23]

Indeed, the first words of the Constitution are "We the People," not "We the Supreme Court Justices." In a democracy, you expect the people, through their elected representatives, to set policy. You don't expect policy to be made by unelected, life-tenured judges. Yet, through their power of judicial review, Supreme Court justices can and do overturn laws enacted by elected officials, and it takes only five justices (a bare majority of the Court) to do so. Just five justices declared flag burning protected speech, even though their opinion so incensed the people's elected representatives that members of Congress considered passing a constitutional amendment to overturn the decision. Similarly, just five justices decided the landmark *Citizens United* case, which struck down on First Amendment grounds a democratically enacted law that limited corporate expenditures on political campaigns.[24] Can you understand why Yale law

---

ment overturned *Dred Scott v. Sandford*, 60 U.S. 393 (1857), which held that African Americans could never be citizens of the United States. The Sixteenth Amendment overturned *Pollock v. Farmers' Loan & Trust Co.*, 157 U.S. 429 (1895), which held that Congress could not enact a personal income tax. The Twenty-sixth Amendment overturned *Oregon v. Mitchell*, 400 U.S. 112 (1970), which that held that Congress did not have the power to lower the voting age in state and local elections from 21 years to 18.

22 U.S. Const., Art. V. Although it has never been done, an amendment can also be proposed by a constitutional convention called by the legislatures of two-thirds of the states. Such an amendment would also have to be ratified by three-quarters of the states. There has been a movement in recent years to use this alterative mechanism for proposing amendments. *See* Carl Hulse, *A Second Constitutional Convention? Some Republicans Want to Force One*, N.Y. Times, Sept. 4, 2022, *available at* https://www.nytimes.com/2022/09/04/us/politics/constitutional-convention-republican-states.html.

23 *Obergefell v. Hodges*, 576 U.S. 644, 687 (2015) (Roberts, C.J., dissenting).

24 *Citizens United v. Federal Election Comm'n*, 558 U.S. 310 (2010).

professor Alexander Bickel described judicial review as a "deviant institution in the American democracy"?[25]

Even if judicial review is a deviant institution, most Americans likely realize that this counter-majoritarian check on the democratic process is sometimes desirable. For example, one common justification for judicial review is that a pure democratic process can lead to a tyranny of the majority. A dominant racial group could wield its power to convince legislators to enact laws that benefited its group over others. Similarly, a dominant religious group could push for laws that favored its adherents over those of minority faiths.

All justices have recognized that it is appropriate for them to sometimes use their power of judicial review to protect minority groups (in the First Amendment context, this can mean protecting unpopular speakers or members of minority faiths). But protecting minorities from the tyranny of the majority cannot fully resolve how the justices should exercise their power. The justices cannot always favor minority rights—that would turn democracy on its head by allowing the minority tail to wag the majority dog. Constitutional law is instead about balancing majority will and minority rights. So, for example, a minority religious group might want to conduct human sacrifices, but the Supreme Court would surely allow the majority to "tyrannize" this minority by prosecuting its adherents for murder. Similarly, a minority group of people might enjoy sharing its collections of child pornography, but, as you'll learn, if the members of this group get caught, the only thing they might be sharing is a jail cell.

If protecting minorities from majority suppression cannot explain everything the justices do when interpreting the Constitution, what can? Are these nine unelected judges merely imposing their will on the rest of society? That is precisely what Justice Scalia accused the five-justice majority in *Obergefell* of doing: "Today's decree says that my Ruler, and the Ruler of 320 million Americans coast-to-coast, is a majority of the nine lawyers on the Supreme Court."[26] He said the majority's opinion "robs the People of the most important liberty they asserted in the Declaration of Independence and won in the Revolution of 1776: the freedom to govern themselves."[27]

Justice Scalia and Chief Justice Roberts may have decried the use of judicial review in the same-sex marriage case, but neither had qualms about joining the five-justice majority in *Citizens United* when it overturned a democratically enacted law limiting corporate campaign expenditures. Yet why did that decision not rob the people of their right to govern themselves and the *Obergefell* decision did? Is it just that one opinion coincided with Chief Justice Roberts' and Justice Scalia's personal

---

[25] Alexander Bickel, The Least Dangerous Branch 18 (2d ed. 1986).

[26] *Obergefell v. Hodges*, 576 U.S. at 713 (Scalia, J., dissenting).

[27] *Id.* at 714.

values and the other did not? Of course, the same could be asked of the justices who reached the opposite conclusions in those cases.

All justices, regardless of their jurisprudential philosophy, are disinclined to leave the impression that they are deciding cases based on their personal predilections. They want to say they are applying the law, not making it. As Chief Justice Roberts explained during his confirmation hearings, judges are supposed to be neutral umpires whose job is "to call balls and strikes, and not to pitch or bat."[28]

But what exactly is controlling the justices' discretion when they are interpreting the Constitution? Is it the Constitution's text? As you study the First Amendment, consider how much guidance the text provides judges, although you probably already realize that its guidance is limited. Certainly, the First Amendment can serve as a fixed North Star that directs judges toward protecting religious and expressive liberty. But when it comes to resolving real world conflicts, the text is largely unhelpful. It is not a Google Maps for constitutional adjudication.

If the text provides only vague guidance, perhaps the Framers' intent or the original meaning of the Constitution's words can fill in the remaining gap. Some justices claim to adhere to this "originalist" approach to interpreting the Constitution. In response to the question "Who do we think we are?," they claim that they are not deciding cases based on their personal predilections but instead are interpreting the Constitution according to its original intent or meaning. To discern this meaning, these justices examine documents and societal practices from the time a constitutional provision was written. You will encounter justices using this approach in the cases involving the religion clauses. It is less common in the Court's free speech jurisprudence.

When you read opinions with originalist reasoning, ask yourself whether you find the reasoning persuasive. Do you think it is possible to discover the original meaning or intent of a constitutional provision that was drafted long ago and ratified by numerous people? Even if it is, do you think that 21st-century Americans should be bound by 18th-century values?

If you are dubious about an originalist approach to constitutional interpretation, you might be in the same camp as a non-originalist justice like Justice William Brennan, who warned against a "too literal quest for the advice of the Founding Fathers."[29] In the context of interpreting the Establishment Clause, Justice Brennan concluded that "the historical record is at best ambiguous, and statements can readily be found to support either side of the proposition."[30] Justice Robert Jackson expressed a similar

---

[28] Chief Justice Roberts Statement—Nomination Process, *available at* https://www.uscourts.gov/educational-resources/educational-activities/chief-justice-roberts-statement-nomination-process.

[29] *School Dist. of Abington Twp. v. Schempp*, 374 U.S. 203, 237 (1963) (Brennan, J., concurring).

[30] *Id.*

sentiment when describing the challenges of discerning the Framers' intent about executive power: "Just what our forefathers did envision, or would have envisioned had they foreseen modern conditions, must be divined from materials almost as enigmatic as the dreams Joseph was called upon to interpret for Pharaoh."[31]

But if neither the text nor the original intent or meaning controls the justices' discretion, what does? For non-originalist justices who believe that the Constitution is a "living" document, what is reining in their discretion when they decide how the Constitution evolves? Here is what Justice Anthony Kennedy said in the majority opinion in *Obergefell*, the decision that Chief Justice Roberts and Justice Scalia so harshly criticized:

> The identification and protection of fundamental rights is an enduring part of the judicial duty to interpret the Constitution. That responsibility, however, has not been reduced to any formula. Rather, it requires courts to exercise reasoned judgment in identifying interests of the person so fundamental that the State must accord them its respect. That process is guided by many of the same considerations relevant to analysis of other constitutional provisions that set forth broad principles rather than specific requirements. History and tradition guide and discipline this inquiry but do not set its outer boundaries. That method respects our history and learns from it without allowing the past alone to rule the present.[32]

Note how Justice Kennedy, like most justices who believe in a "living" Constitution, does not dismiss the importance of history and tradition. But he also says that history and tradition cannot set the "outer boundaries" of what the Constitution means. The justices, he says, must consider history "without allowing the past alone to rule the present." Indeed, he believes that the Framers themselves intended for the Constitution to evolve in response to the insights of future generations:

> The nature of injustice is that we may not always see it in our own times. The generations that wrote and ratified the Bill of Rights and the Fourteenth Amendment did not presume to know the extent of freedom in all of its dimensions, and so they entrusted to future generations a charter protecting the right of all persons to enjoy liberty as we learn its meaning.[33]

Yet what constrains the justices' discretion as they discover new liberties unforeseen by the Framers? Justice Kennedy suggested that this constraint comes from the justices exercising "reasoned judgment," but does that standard really limit judicial discretion? Is the sky the limit? Can the justices consider principles of natural law,

31 *Youngstown Sheet & Tube Co. v. Sawyer*, 343 U.S. 579, 634 (1952) (Jackson, J., concurring).
32 *Obergefell*, 576 U.S. at 663–64.
33 *Id.* at 664.

morality, "evolving standards of decency,"[34] democratic theory, surveys of American public opinion, comparative law, or their own gut instincts? Justice Stephen Breyer contended that the justices should use a "pragmatic" approach that identifies fundamental values embedded in a constitutional right and then balances those values against competing societal interests.[35]

There is no consensus on how the Constitution should be interpreted. The topic has been debated by the justices and scholars ever since the Constitution was ratified and is certain to continue being debated. As you read the judicial opinions collected in this casebook, you might sometimes find a majority opinion persuasive and sometimes a dissenting opinion. Over time, you might develop your own philosophy for how the Constitution should be interpreted. That could be handy if a future president calls and offers to appoint you to the Supreme Court. (That might sound crazy, but today's law students will become tomorrow's lawyers, and some lawyers, albeit a miniscule few, will get that call.)

Points for Discussion

1. **Do you know who the justices are?** The photograph below shows the members of the Supreme Court at the beginning of the October 2022 term. Can you identify each of them? Try doing a little research to figure out when each justice was appointed. Article III of the Constitution provides that justices will hold their offices "during good Behaviour," which has been interpreted to mean that they have life tenure. The only way to involuntarily remove a justice is through impeachment.

Fred Schilling, Collection of the Supreme Court of the United States

[34] *Roper v. Simmons*, 543 U.S. 551, 561 (2005).

[35] Stephen Breyer, Making Our Democracy Work 80, 162–64 (2010).

2. **Justice Brennan and the most important rule of constitutional law.** When Justice Brennan met his new law clerks each year, he would ask them to identify the most important rule of constitutional law. The clerks would flounder around making guesses—the Free Speech Clause, the Equal Protection Clause, the Due Process Clause—until Justice Brennan finally cut them off by holding up his hand with all five fingers extended. Why did he think that the most important rule of constitutional law was the number five? To find out, *see* Stephen Wermiel, *Justice Brennan and His Law Clerks*, 98 Marquette L. Rev. 367, 381 (2014).

You Be the Legislator!

To amend or not to amend, that is this question

Imagine that you are a member of the House of Representatives and that you take great pride in being responsive to your constituents. Imagine that during your years of service, the Supreme Court issued opinions that were highly unpopular with the voters in your district. These decisions protected flag burning as speech, protected hate speech, struck down limits on corporate campaign expenditures, and prohibited prayer in public schools. Now imagine that, after each decision was issued, a member of Congress proposed a bill to amend the Constitution to overturn the Court's opinion. You know that it is difficult to amend the Constitution and that these efforts are unlikely to succeed, but that does not preclude you from voting in favor of these proposed amendments.

How would you decide whether to vote for the proposed amendments? Would you automatically support an amendment if the majority of your constituents supported it? Would you never support an amendment because you believe that the legislative branch should defer to the judicial branch on matters of constitutional law? Or would you have your own personal standard for when it is appropriate to amend the Constitution to overturn a Supreme Court decision, and if so, what factors would you consider? Would you, for example, vote for a proposal to amend the Constitution in any of examples mentioned above?

C. Be Prepared for a Wild Ride

The time has come to dive into First Amendment jurisprudence. You should be prepared for a wild ride, so buckle up. We will explore free speech cases on topics ranging from pharmaceutical advertising to nude dancing, funeral protests to violent video games, and cross burnings to campaign expenditures. When studying religious liberty cases, we will encounter religious adherents who refuse to pay Social Security taxes or provide contraceptive care for their employees while others insist on their right to use hallucinogenic drugs and enter polygamous marriages.

If at any time during this journey you feel overwhelmed, angry, or confused, just take a deep breath and recite the following words from Justice John Harlan: "That the air may at times seem filled with verbal cacophony is not a sign of weakness but of strength."[36]

Test Your Knowledge

To assess your understanding of the material in this chapter, click here to take a quiz.

[36] *Cohen v. California*, 403 U.S. 15, 25 (1971).

Part II

Freedom of Speech

Chapter Two

Why Protect Speech?

Lessons from History and Theory

The Framers manifested their appreciation for freedom of speech when they added the First Amendment to the Constitution. Two centuries later, Americans continue to recognize the importance of this right. In a 2021 survey, 63% of respondents characterized freedom of speech as "extremely important," 28% said it was "very important," and 7% considered it "moderately important."[1]

But why is freedom of speech so important? After all, the government restrains people's liberties all the time. There is no constitutional right to be a barber, experiment with hallucinogenic drugs, or drive without a seatbelt. These liberties might give people meaning, pleasure, or income, or at least a sense that the government cannot tell them what to do, yet the government is largely free to regulate or even criminalize these activities. So why should the liberty of speaking be any different?

This chapter considers that question by examining historical and theoretical reasons for protecting speech. This is not a mere academic exercise. If we are to sensibly protect speech, we need some sense of why we are doing so. Otherwise, we will have no means of gauging what is at stake when we confront questions of when, if ever, speech may be abridged to further competing societal interests.

A. Historical Reasons for Protecting Freedom of Speech: The "Perfectly Logical" Tendency to Suppress Speech

If you grew up in the United States, where freedom of speech is robustly protected, you might assume that this represents the natural order of things. You would be understandably, but woefully, mistaken. The history of the world is not one of governments affording people generous speech protection. To the contrary, it is a history of people in power—whether monarchs, religious authorities, Communist politburo members, or autocrats—suppressing speech they disliked or perceived as a threat to their power.

---

1 Knight Found., Free Expression in America Post-2020: A Landmark Survey of American's Views on Speech Rights, *available at* https://knightfoundation.org/wp-content/uploads/2022/01/KF_Free_Expression_2022.pdf.

This is not to say that there was no appreciation or protection for freedom speech until the modern era. At various times and places, free speech did flourish for at least some members of a community. In his book about the history of free speech, Danish lawyer and scholar Jacob Mchangama noted that this was true for segments of society in ancient Athens, the late Roman Republic, and the Abbasid Caliphate in the 9th century. But Mchangama also acknowledged that the *yin* of free speech inevitably triggers the *yang* of government censorship: "The leaders of any political system—no matter how enlightened—inevitably convince themselves that *now* freedom of speech has gone too far."[2] Historic examples of governments' censoring speech are legion. Some famous cases include the trial of Socrates, Roman persecution of Christians, Galileo's being charged with heresy, the deportation of dissidents to the Soviet Gulag, and the targeting of intellectuals during China's Cultural Revolution.[3]

That people in power would suppress speech they dislike is hardly surprising. As Justice Oliver Wendell Holmes famously observed, it is "perfectly logical" for them to do so:

> Persecution for the expression of opinions seems to me perfectly logical. If you have no doubt of your premises or your power and want a certain result with all your heart you naturally express your wishes in law and sweep away all opposition. To allow opposition by speech seems to indicate that you think the speech impotent, as when a man says that he has squared the circle, or that you do not care whole-heartedly for the result, or that you doubt either your power or your premises.[4]

One need not be a historian to confirm the wisdom of Justice Holmes' observation. Even today, most people live in countries where freedom of speech is the exception and not the rule. The Varieties of Democracy (V-Dem) Institute, for example, which uses empirical data to measure the state of global democracy, concluded in a 2023 report that 72% of the world's population, or 5.7 billion people, live in autocracies, a 46% increase from 10 years ago.[5] Included in this group are 2.2 billion people living in "closed autocracies," which the report defines as countries that lack multiparty elections and have an "absence of fundamental democratic components such as freedom of expression, freedom of association, and free and fair elections."[6] Among these countries is China, the world's second most populous nation, as well as Iran, Vietnam, and Myanmar. The remaining 3.5 billion people living in autocracies are in "electoral autocracies," which are defined as countries that have multiparty elections

---

2 Jacob Mchangama, Free Speech: A History from Socrates to Social Media 2 (2022) (emphasis in original).

3 You can read about the trials of both Socrates and Galileo at Professor Douglas Linder's web collection of famous trials, *available at* https://famous-trials.com/.

4 *Abrams v. United States*, 250 U.S. 616, 630 (1919) (Holmes, J., dissenting).

5 Varieties of Democracy Inst., Democracy Report 2023: Defiance in the Face of Autocratization 12, *available at* https://www.v-dem.net/publications/democracy-reports/.

6 *Id.* at 11–12.

but still lack the fundamental prerequisites of a healthy democracy, including freedom of speech, expression, and association. This group includes the world's most populous country, India, as well as other countries with sizable populations, such as Nigeria, Pakistan, Russia, the Philippines, and Turkey.[7]

Those who follow international news can easily find headlines to substantiate the V-Dem report. One prominent example is China's aggressive use of a national security law in 2020 to all but extinguish the robust freedoms of speech and press that had long been enjoyed by Hong Kong residents. As one observer noted, the law "effectively criminalizes any dissent and adopts extremely broad definitions for crimes such as terrorism, subversion, secession, and collusion with foreign powers."[8] Liberal democracies in the United States and Western Europe reacted to China's clampdown on civil liberties by seeking to cultivate stronger relations with China's neighbor India. But, as Human Rights Watch has reported, "[Indian] Prime Minister Narendra Modi's Hindu-nationalist Bharatiya Janata Party has mimicked many of the same abuses that have enabled Chinese state repression—systematic discrimination against religious minorities, stifling of peaceful dissent, and use of technology to suppress free expression—to tighten its grip on power."[9]

Meanwhile, in Europe, Russia's invasion of Ukraine has been described by the nonprofit research institute Freedom House as "the gravest challenge to peace, freedom, and democracy in Europe since the end of the Cold War."[10] Freedom House, which also tracks the state of civil liberties and democracy globally, added that the war in Ukraine has been accompanied by a "dramatic loss of civil liberties within Russia itself," where the government has "forced the few remaining independent media outlets and NGOs to close down or go into exile, and imposed heavy prison sentences on prominent dissidents as well as ordinary citizens who dared to express opposition to the war."[11]

Many free speech advocates, including Jacob Mchangama, have even sounded the alarm about a rising threat to freedom of speech in the liberal democracies of Western Europe and the United States. These countries might perceive their motivations for limiting free speech as well-intentioned: to protect minority groups from hate speech, to counter disinformation, and to curtail the disruptive effects of algorithm-driven social media platforms. But as Mchangama warns, "To impose silence and call it

---

7 *Id.* at 12–13.

8 Lindsay Maizland, Council on Foreign Relations, *Hong Kong's Freedoms: What China Promised and How It's Cracking Down* (last updated May 19, 2022), *available at* https://www.cfr.org/backgrounder/hong-kong-freedoms-democracy-protests-china-crackdown#:~:text=In%202020%2C%20Beijing%20imposed%20a,of%20the%20press%20and%20speech.

9 Tirana Hassan, *A New Model for Global Leadership on Human Rights* (keynote essay for Human Rights Watch World Report 2023), *available at* https://www.hrw.org/world-report/2023.

10 Freedom House, Nations in Transit 2023: War Deepens a National Divide 2, *available at* https://freedomhouse.org/report/nations-transit/2023/war-deepens-regional-divide.

11 *Id.* at 9.

tolerance does not make it so."[12] From his long view of history, even well-intentioned efforts to limit speech lead to nations that are "less free, democratic, and equal and more ignorant, autocratic, and oppressive."[13]

Nobel Peace Prize Awarded to Two Journalists

In 2021, the Nobel Prize Committee raised global awareness about the growing threat to freedom of speech, and particularly to freedom of the press, when it awarded the Nobel Peace Prize to two journalists for their fearless reporting in the face of relentless government persecution. Here is how Berit Reiss-Anderson, the chair of the Norwegian Nobel Committee, described the honorees:

> Maria Ressa uses freedom of expression to expose abuse of power, use of violence and growing authoritarianism in her native country, the Philippines. In 2012, she co-founded *Rappler*, an online news website for investigative journalism, of which she is the president. Maria Ressa is a fearless defender of freedom of expression. *Rappler* has focused critical attention on the Duterte regime's controversial, murderous anti-drug campaign. The campaign has death tolls so high that it resembles a civil war. Ms. Ressa and *Rappler* have also documented how social media is used to spread fake news, harass opponents and manipulate public discourse.
>
> Dmitry Muratov stands out as one of the most prominent defenders of freedom of speech in Russia today. He is one of the founders of *Novaya Gazeta* and has been its editor-in-chief since 1995. *Novaya Gazeta* is the most independent newspaper in Russia today, with a fundamentally critical attitude towards power. The newspaper's fact-based journalism and professional integrity have made it an important source of information on aspects of Russian society rarely mentioned by other media.
>
> Both laureates have been the object of ridicule, harassment, threats and violence as a result of their work. Being a journalist is for many a high-risk occupation. Six journalists working for *Novaya Gazeta* have been killed. In the Philippines, a total of 87 journalists have died in the line of duty since 1992. Maria Ressa has received death threats on public TV from the Philippine President.

(Reiss-Anderson's speech is available here.)

---

12 Mchangama, *supra* note 2, at 8.

13 *Id.*

In March 2022, Novaya Gazeta suspended its operations in Russia after the government threatened to send journalists to jail for publishing stories about the war in Ukraine that deviated from the Kremlin's characterization of the war. James C. McKinley, Jr., *Russia Media Regulator Moves to Revoke the License of Novaya Gazeta, an Independent News Agency*, N.Y. Times, July, 28, 2002, available here.

Maria Ressa (L) and Dmitry Muratov (R)
Courtesy of © Geir Anders Rybakken Ørslien/Nobel Prize Outreach

See It

In its 2023 World Press Freedom Index, Reporters without Borders ranked the world's countries based on the degree of freedom available to journalists. You can see the index here.

Does it surprise you that the United States is ranked #45 in the index?

You might also want to explore this interactive map developed by Freedom House that tracks the status of freedom and democracy in countries around the world.

Points for Discussion

1. **The "perfect logic" for suppressing speech.** Why did Justice Holmes think it is perfectly logical for governments to suppress speech they dislike? Can you think of examples, either historic or contemporary, of governments' suppressing unwanted speech?

2. **Has the U.S. government suppressed unpopular speech?** Can you think of examples in American history when the federal government or state governments suppressed speech they disfavored? Can you think of any contemporary examples?

3. **Is there currently suppression of speech in liberal democracies?** Mchangama and others have contended that free speech is under attack not only in authoritarian countries but also in the liberal democracies of Europe and North America. What are these critics referring to? Can you come up with any examples of attacks on freedom of speech in the United States? Are these attacks coming from liberals or conservatives, or both? Do you agree with the critics that the limits being imposed on free speech are dangerous and undesirable, or do you think that the limits are an appropriate use of government power to regulate speech to further other important societal interests?

1. English History: Devices the Crown and Parliament Used to Control Speech

The Framers of the U.S. Constitution were deeply influenced by the history, jurisprudence, and philosophical traditions of England. Those who drafted and advocated for the adoption of the First Amendment were keenly aware of both England's historical suppression of speech as well as the struggles and victories of those who fought for greater speech protection.

The two features of English speech regulation that had the greatest influence on the Framers, and subsequently on Supreme Court justices interpreting the First

Amendment, were the English system of licensing publications and its prosecution of speakers for seditious libel.

a. Licensing of Publications: When Government Permission Was Needed to Publish

People in power, whether secular or religious authorities, often feel threatened when new technologies make it easier to disseminate information. If they can control the technology, it can be harnessed for the propagandistic purpose of bolstering public support for the regime. If they are unable to control it, the technology can be used to spread information that challenges the regime's authority.

Such was the dilemma faced by the Crown in England after the introduction of the printing press. In 1538, King Henry VIII's solution was to set up a licensing system in which publications had to be approved by the king's Privy Council.[14] A century later, in 1643, Parliament took up the mantle of government censorship by enacting a law that required all books and pamphlets to be approved by government-appointed licensors.[15]

This licensing system did not go unchallenged. Author and poet John Milton famously condemned the licensing system in his unlicensed publication *Areopagitica*. In an oft-quoted line that presaged the "marketplace of ideas" theory for protecting speech, he wrote:

> Though all the winds of doctrine were let loose to play upon the earth, so Truth be in the field, we do injuriously, by licensing and prohibiting, to misdoubt her strength. Let her and Falsehood grapple; who ever knew Truth put to the worse, in a free and open encounter?[16]

Several years after the Glorious Revolution in 1688, when Parliament asserted greater authority over the Crown, the licensing scheme was allowed to lapse. Historians contend that this decision had more to do with dissatisfaction with the effectiveness of the licensing regime than a newfound commitment to freedom of speech.[17]

---

14 Fred S. Siebert, Freedom of the Press in England 1476–1776: The Rise and Decline of Government Control 48–49 (1952). *See also* Michael L. Meyerson, *The Neglected History of the Prior Restraint Doctrine: Rediscovering the Link between the First Amendment and the Separation of Powers*, 34 Ind. L. Rev. 295, 298 (2001).

15 Meyerson, *supra* note 14, at 303.

16 John Milton, Areopagitica, A Speech for the Liberty of Unlicensed Printing to the Parliament of England (1644), available at https://milton.host.dartmouth.edu/reading_room/areopagitica/text.shtml.

17 Siebert, *supra* note 14, at 261. In describing the House of Commons' reasoning for letting the licensing law lapse, Lord T.B. Macaulay observed, "On the great question of principle, on the question whether the liberty of unlicensed printing be, on the whole, a blessing or a curse to society, not a word is said." T.B. Macaulay, IV History of England 123 (1906), *available at* https://ia600503.us.archive.org/4/items/macaulayshistory04maca/macaulayshistory04maca.pdf.

Nevertheless, the common law tradition came to embody a general revulsion to the idea of having to obtain government permission before being able to speak, or what we refer to today as prior restraints. William Blackstone, the author of a highly influential 18th-century treatise on English common law, captured this sentiment when he wrote, "The liberty of the press [consists] in laying no previous restraints upon publications."[18] Two centuries later, the U.S. Supreme Court enshrined this principle into First Amendment jurisprudence by ruling that "any system of prior restraints of expression comes to this Court bearing a heavy presumption against its constitutional validity."[19] You will learn more about this in subsequent chapters.

A Comparative Perspective

For a contemporary example of a country trying to control the dissemination of information through a new technology, consider China's ongoing effort to regulate public access to the internet. This is colloquially referred to as the "Great Firewall of China" (as opposed to the physical Great Wall of China). You can read about the Great Chinese Firewall here.

b. Seditious Libel: When Criticizing Government Was a Crime

Even after the licensing scheme lapsed, the English government continued to vigorously employ a second device for curtailing speech critical of government. This was the law of seditious libel, which criminally punished statements critical of government officials as well as impersonal attacks on government itself. In a 1704 opinion, Lord Holt explained the logic behind punishing seditious libel:

> If men should not be called upon to account for possessing the people with an ill opinion of the Government, no Government can subsist; for it is very necessary for every Government, that the people should have a good opinion of it. And nothing can be worse to any Government than to endeavour to procure animosities as to the management of it. This has been always look'd upon as a crime, and no Government can be safe unless it be punished.[20]

Seditious libel was thought to be so pernicious that even truthful criticism of the government was punishable. Truthful statements were considered more dangerous than false ones because the government could not refute them. Thus, a common

---

18 4 William Blackstone, Commentaries on the Laws of England 151 (1765).

19 *New York Times Co. v. United States*, 403 U.S. 713, 714 (1971).

20 *Queen v. Tutchin*, 90 Eng. Rep. 1133 (Q.B. 1704).

reframe in seditious libel jurisprudence was "the greater the truth, the greater the libel."

Blackstone's treatise on the laws of England reflected the country's discordant treatment of free speech; prior restraints on speech were anathema, but punishment for speech after its publication was perfectly acceptable:

> The liberty of the press is indeed essential to the nature of a free state; but this consists of laying no previous restraints upon publications, and not in freedom from censure for criminal matter when published. . . . To subject the press to the restrictive power of the licenser, as was formerly done . . . is to subject all freedom of sentiment to the prejudices of one man, and make him the arbitrary and infallible judge of all controverted points in learning, religion, and government. But to punish (as the law does at present) any dangerous or offensive writings, which, when published, shall on a fair and impartial trial be adjudged of a pernicious tendency, is necessary for the preservation of peace and good order, of government and religion, the only solid foundation of civil liberty.[21]

A Comparative Perspective

Prosecutions for seditious libel are alive and well in some countries. Thailand has a notoriously harsh lèse-majesté ("injured majesty") law that makes it a crime to criticize senior members of the royal family. Here is a 2021 *New York Times* story about a former Thai civil servant who posted audio clips on social media that were perceived as critical of the monarchy. She was sentenced to 43 years in prison.

2. Across the Atlantic: Free Speech in the Colonies

Parliament allowed the English system of licensing publications to lapse in 1695, but prosecutions for seditious libel continued unabated. There were prosecutions for seditious libel in the colonies, but they appear to have been rare. This might have been attributable to the most famous prosecution in the colonies, which resulted in a resounding defeat for the government.

The case concerned John Peter Zenger, a German immigrant who worked as printer in New York. Zenger had published statements, written by others, that were critical of the governor general of New York, William Cosby. Zenger was charged and tried for seditious libel in 1735. Even though truth was not a defense in seditious libel

21 Blackstone, *supra* note 18, at 151–52.

cases, Zenger's lawyer, Andrew Hamilton, encouraged the jury to ignore the judge's instructions. The jury followed this advice and acquitted Zenger. This exercise in "jury nullification" was not surprising because the public viewed Zenger as a local hero and Cosby as a despised bureaucrat. The case became a cause célèbre in the colonies and likely explains colonial governments' reluctance to pursue additional seditious libel prosecutions.

The Zenger trial is often hailed as an early indicator of America's devotion to freedom of speech. But a society's commitment to free speech is best measured by its willingness to defend unpopular speakers, not a beloved speaker like Zenger. By that measure, the American public has often come up short. Indeed, in the decades following the Zenger trial, as tensions rose between the colonies and England, Americans showed little tolerance for "royalist" speakers who favored continued allegiance to Britain.[22]

See It

A year after Zenger's acquittal, James Alexander wrote a widely distributed account of the trial, *A Brief Narrative of the Case and Trial of John Peter Zenger*. You can see it here.

3. Enshrining Protection for Free Speech in the Constitution: The Adoption of the First Amendment

As we learned in Chapter 1, the Constitution that was drafted in Philadelphia in 1787 did not protect free speech or a free press.[23] Anti-Federalists cited the absence of protection for these rights as a reason for not ratifying the Constitution. As one Anti-Federalist publication proclaimed, "If the liberty of the press be an inherent political right, let it be so declared, that no despot however great shall dare to gain say it."[24] This obstacle was overcome by an agreement that the newly assembled Congress would propose amendments to the Constitution to protect individual liberties.

While the Framers enshrined protection for freedom of speech and press in the First Amendment, it is not at all clear what they intended to accomplish by doing so. Some historians have argued that the Framers merely intended to adopt Black-

[22] Leonard W. Levy, Emergence of a Free Press 173–183 (1985).

[23] The one limited exception was the Speech and Debate Clause in Article I, which provides that, "for any Speech or Debate in either House, they [members of Congress] shall not be questioned in any other Place." U.S. Const., Art. I, § 6, cl. 1. This clause ensures that senators and representatives can speak freely as they do their legislative work because they cannot be held legally accountable for their statements. The clause derives from a comparable provision protecting parliamentarians in the English Bill of Rights of 1689, which provided that "the freedom of speech and debates or proceedings in Parliament ought not to be impeached or questioned in any court or place out of Parliament." See https://avalon.law.yale.edu/17th_century/england.asp. You can read about the Speech and Debate Clause at https://constitution.congress.gov/browse/essay/artI-S6-C1-3-1/ALDE_00013300/.

[24] The Pennsylvania Herald and General Advertiser, Oct. 27, 1787, at 334. *See also* Herbert J. Storing, What the Antif-Federalists Were For 64–65 (1981).

stone's narrow definition of freedom of speech, which provided protection against prior restraints but not against punishment for speech after it was published.[25] Other historians claimed that the Framers intended to adopt a more robust vision of free speech that protected against *both* prior restraints and subsequent punishments.[26]

The most significant evidence against an expansive interpretation was Congress' enactment, less than a decade after the First Amendment's adoption, of the Sedition Act of 1798. The law, pushed through by the Federalist party, was purportedly intended to address the prospect of an impending war with France, but it was practically used to persecute members of the Republican Party, the Federalists' political rivals.[27] The Sedition Act made it a crime to print or publish "any false, scandalous and malicious writing" against the federal government, Congress, or the president. Unlike the English law of seditious libel, truth was a defense under the Sedition Act, but this concession did not prevent the Federalists from successfully using the law to prosecute Republicans. The Sedition Act expired on the last day of Federalist President John Adams' term, conveniently ensuring that the Republicans, after Thomas Jefferson defeated Adams in the election of 1800, could not use the law against Federalists.[28]

Whatever the Framers may have intended in adopting the First Amendment—assuming a singular intent existed and could be identified—there is no doubt that the First Amendment has since been interpreted to protect against both prior restraints and subsequent punishments. This was not obviously the case when the Supreme Court first began to wrestle with the First Amendment in the early 20th century. In one of the Court's early decisions, *Patterson v. Colorado*, Justice Holmes suggested that the "main purpose" of the First Amendment was "to prevent all such previous restraints upon publication" and not to "prevent the subsequent punishment of such as may be deemed contrary to the public welfare."[29] But Justice Holmes changed his tune 12 years later in *Schenck v. United States* when he observed, "It well may be that the prohibition of laws abridging the freedom of speech is not confined to previous restraints."[30] Twenty-three years later the Court made its position unequivocally clear: "The protection of the First Amendment is not limited to the Blackstonian idea that freedom of the press means only freedom from restraint prior to publication."[31]

The Sedition Act expired in 1801, and the Supreme Court never ruled on its constitutionality. It is unclear how the Court would have ruled in the early 19th

25 Levy, *supra* note 22. *But see* David Rabban, *An Ahistorical Historian: Leonard Levy on Freedom of Expression in Early American History*, 37 Stan. L. Rev. 795 (1985).

26 Zechariah Chafee Jr., Free Speech in the United States 18–20 (1941).

27 Geoffrey R. Stone, Perilous Times: Free Speech in War Time 67 (2004).

28 *Id.*

29 *Patterson v. Colorado*, 205 U.S. 454, 462 (1907).

30 *Schenck v. United States*, 249 U.S. 47, 51 (1919).

31 *Chaplinsky v. New Hampshire*, 315 U.S. 568, 572 n.3 (1942).

century, but Justice William Brennan made it clear in 1964 that the law had not passed the test of time:

> Although the Sedition Act was never tested in this Court, the attack upon its validity has carried the day in the court of history. Fines levied in its prosecution were repaid by Act of Congress on the ground that it was unconstitutional. Jefferson, as President, pardoned those who had been convicted and sentenced under the Act and remitted their fines. The invalidity of the Act has also been assumed by Justices of this Court. These views reflect a broad consensus that the Act, because of the restraint it imposed upon criticism of government and public officials, was inconsistent with the First Amendment.[32]

B. The Theory Behind Freedom of Speech: What's so Special About Speech?

The founding generation took a major step toward protecting freedom of speech by enshrining this value in the nation's foundational charter. But it has been the task of judges to give concrete meaning to this commitment. To fulfill that role, judges have had to wrestle with the initial question of why speech deserves special protection. There is no single or correct answer to that question. But over time, judges and scholars have identified several prominent theories for why speech, as opposed to other human activities, should be protected. This section surveys those theories.

A Treasure Hunt for Theories

Looking for gold in Justice Brandeis' concurrence in Whitney v. California

Before considering the various theories for why speech deserves protection, it is worth pausing to read a famous passage from Justice Louis Brandeis' 1927 concurrence in *Whitney v. California*, 274 U.S. 357 (1927). You will read the *Whitney* opinion in Chapter 5, but it is helpful to examine one of its paragraphs here because Justice Brandeis used it to succinctly explain why the Framers protected freedom of speech. In doing so, Justice Brandeis alluded to many of the primary theories for why speech deserves special protection. Take a moment to read the passage and see how many theories you can find.

> Those who won our independence believed that the final end of the state was to make men free to develop their faculties; and that in its government the deliberative forces should prevail over the arbitrary. They

---

32 *Sullivan*, 376 U.S. at 276.

> valued liberty both as an end and as a means. They believed liberty to be the secret of happiness and courage to be the secret of liberty. They believed that freedom to think as you will and to speak as you think are means indispensable to the discovery and spread of political truth; that without free speech and assembly discussion would be futile; that with them, discussion affords ordinarily adequate protection against the dissemination of noxious doctrine; that the greatest menace to freedom is an inert people; that public discussion is a political duty; and that this should be a fundamental principle of the American government. They recognized the risks to which all human institutions are subject. But they knew that order cannot be secured merely through fear of punishment for its infraction; that it is hazardous to discourage thought, hope and imagination; that fear breeds repression; that repression breeds hate; that hate menaces stable government; that the path of safety lies in the opportunity to discuss freely supposed grievances and proposed remedies; and that the fitting remedy for evil counsels is good ones. Believing in the power of reason as applied through public discussion, they eschewed silence coerced by law—the argument of force in its worst form. Recognizing the occasional tyrannies of governing majorities, they amended the Constitution so that free speech and assembly should be guaranteed.

What did you find? What do you think Justice Brandeis meant when he said the Framers valued liberty "both as an end and a means"? Do some of his theories value speech as a means to some other end? Do some value speech as an end in itself?

1. The Pursuit of Truth: Is an Open Marketplace of Ideas the Best Test of the Truth?

Recall Justice Holmes' observation about how it was perfectly logical for people in power to suppress speech they disliked: "If you have no doubt of your premises or your power and want a certain result with all your heart you naturally express your wishes in law and sweep away all opposition." So why, then, would any regime, including our own, choose to protect speech? Justice Holmes found the answer in the annals of collective human experience:

> When men have realized that time has upset many fighting faiths, they may come to believe even more than they believe the very foundations of their own conduct that the ultimate good desired is better reached by free trade in ideas—that the best test of truth is the power of the thought to get

> itself accepted in the competition of the market, and that truth is the only ground upon which their wishes safely can be carried out. That at any rate is the theory of our Constitution. It is an experiment, as all life is an experiment. Every year if not every day we have to wager our salvation upon some prophecy based upon imperfect knowledge.[33]

Can you think of any "fighting faiths" that people fought and died for but were later exposed as false ideas? If so, would you draw the same lesson from this history as Justice Holmes did—that it is better to pursue truth through an open marketplace of ideas than to let the government declare the truth and banish any conflicting ideas? Did you notice how Justice Brandeis' concurrence in *Whitney* similarly contended that freedom of speech was "indispensable to the discovery and spread of political truth"?

Justice Holmes did not create the "marketplace of ideas" theory out of whole cloth. Indeed, we learned about how John Milton advocated for a free and open encounter between truth and falsehood back in 1644. Two centuries after Milton, English philosopher John Stuart Mill further refined the argument for an open marketplace of ideas in his classic essay *On Liberty*:

> The opinion which it is attempted to suppress by authority may possibly be true. Those who desire to suppress it, of course deny its truth; but they are not infallible. They have no authority to decide the question for all mankind, and exclude every other person from the means of judging. . . . Complete liberty of contradicting and disproving our opinion, is the very condition which justifies us in assuming its truth for purposes of action; and on no other terms can a being with human faculties have any rational assurance of being right.[34]

The core premise of the marketplace theory is that it is preferable to give people access to ideas than to permit the government to decide which ideas people may express or hear. This premise has played a major if not dominant role in shaping First Amendment jurisprudence. It has prompted the Supreme Court to protect ideas even when they seemed dangerous, misguided, or offensive, and even when most people would prefer that the ideas be censored. As the Court has explained: "Under the First Amendment there is no such thing as a false idea. However pernicious an opinion may seem, we depend for its correction not on the conscience of judges and juries but on the competition of other ideas."[35]

This absolutist prohibition on government censorship of ideas could be called the First Amendment's "neutrality principle."[36] Under this principle, all ideas are cre-

---

[33] *Abrams*, 250 U.S. at 630.

[34] John Stuart Mill, On Liberty 32, 35 (1859), *available at* https://www.gutenberg.org/files/34901/34901-h/34901-h.htm.

[35] *Gertz v. Robert Welch, Inc.*, 418 U.S. 323, 339–40 (1974).

[36] Rodney A. Smolla, Smolla & Nimmer on Freedom of Speech § 4.6 (2023).

ated equal in the eyes of the First Amendment—even those ideas that are universally condemned or that seem to run counter to other constitutional principles. As Justice Brennan observed in one of the most oft-quoted passages in First Amendment jurisprudence, "If there is a bedrock principle underlying the First Amendment, it is that the Government may not prohibit the expression of an idea simply because society finds the idea itself offensive or disagreeable."[37]

Points for Discussion

1. **Is truth certain to prevail in an open marketplace of ideas?** Do you agree with Milton that truth will always prevail in a free and open encounter with falsehood? Does history justify this assumption? Note how Justice Holmes described the marketplace of ideas as the "best test" of truth and not the "test" of truth. Is there a distinction between these two?

2. **Do you trust people to be good consumers in the marketplace of ideas?** Underlying the marketplace theory is the notion that it is better to allow people to have access to ideas than to let the government decide which ideas people may express or hear. As Justice Robert Jackson explained: "It is not the function of our Government to keep the citizen from falling into error; it is the function of the citizen to keep the Government from falling into error. We could justify any censorship only when the censors are better shielded against error than the censored." *American Commc'ns Ass'n v. Douds*, 339 U.S. 382, 442–43 (1950) (Jackson, J., concurring and dissenting).

   Based on your own experience, are you confident that your fellow citizens will be good consumers of information in the marketplace of ideas? Does this theory assume that people will be rational and discerning consumers of information? Is that likely to be the case? Are people as easily swayed by emotion, prejudice, and willful ignorance as they are by cool-headed logic and dispassionate objectivity? If you are doubtful that citizens will be discerning consumers in the marketplace of ideas, would you prefer a system in which the government initially decides which ideas are worthy of being considered by the public?

3. **Are there some ideas that should be banned from the marketplace?** Supreme Court justices have largely subscribed to the marketplace theory for protecting speech. The theory is best captured in the Court's oft-repeated statement that "under the First Amendment there is no such thing as a false idea." *Gertz v. Robert Welch, Inc.*, 418 U.S. 323, 339 (1974). Do you agree that there is no such thing as a false idea? Aren't there some ideas that we can all agree are "bad" or "false" and should be kept out of the marketplace? How about the idea that genocide

[37] *Texas v. Johnson*, 491 U.S. 397, 414 (1989).

is good? On the day of the attack on the Capitol Building on January 6, 2021, one of the protesters wore a shirt that said "6MWE." This was shorthand for "Six Million Wasn't Enough." It is a reference to the fact that Hitler killed 6 million Jews during the Holocaust and, quite obviously, suggests that Hitler should have killed more. Is that an idea that should be permitted into the marketplace?

Even if we are confident that an idea like "genocide is good" will eventually be proven false in an open marketplace of ideas, can we afford to wait for this to happen? Consider this observation from legal scholar Harry H. Wellington about German demonization of Jews during the Holocaust: "Truth may win, and in the long run it may almost always win, but millions of Jews were deliberately and systematically murdered in a very short period of time." Harry H. Wellington, *On Freedom of Expression*, 88 Yale L.J. 1105, 1132 (1979).

4. **Should the First Amendment protect false statements of fact?** Even if there is no such thing as a false idea under the First Amendment, should the First Amendment protect false statements of fact? John Stuart Mill suggested in *On Liberty* that false statements should be protected because their collision with true statements gives people a sharper awareness of the truth:

> The peculiar evil of silencing the expression of an opinion is, that it is robbing the human race; posterity as well as the existing generation; those who dissent from the opinion, still more than those who hold it. If the opinion is right, they are deprived of the opportunity of exchanging error for truth; if wrong, they lose, what is almost as great a benefit, the clearer perception and livelier impression of truth, produced by its collision with error.

Do you agree that there is a benefit in giving people access to false statements of fact? Justice Brennan, quoting from Mill, made this argument in his 1964 opinion in *New York Times Co. v. Sullivan*, 376 U.S. 254, 279, n.19 (1964). A decade later, Justice Lewis Powell rejected this argument in *Gertz*. He acknowledged that "there is no such thing as a false idea" under the First Amendment but said "there is no constitutional value in false statements of fact."

Are you with Justice Brennan or Justice Powell? Whichever way you lean, do you think it is always possible to separate false facts from false ideas? Was former President Donald Trump's statement that Joe Biden stole the 2020 presidential election a false statement of fact that the government should have been able to suppress, or was it a false idea that deserved First Amendment protection? What about statements during the Covid-19 pandemic that vaccines were dangerous or statements denying that human activity is causing global warming? Should the government be able to suppress these statements, or would that be giving the government the power to declare the "truth" and suppress any speech that conflicted with the government's declaration? *See Hoeg v. Newsom*, 652 F. Supp. 3d 1172 (E.D. Cal. 2023) (enjoining enforcement of California law that expanded the definition of "unprofessional conduct" to include physician's dissemination of misinformation about Covid-19).

5. **The Court's refusal to find false statements of fact categorically unprotected.** In *United States v. Alvarez*, 567 U.S. 709 (2012), the defendant was prosecuted under the federal Stolen Valor Act, which made it crime to falsely claim that one had received a military honor. The law applied regardless of whether the statement misled anyone or was used to obtain a material advantage. As Justice Anthony Kennedy explained, "The Act by its plain terms applies to a false statement made at any time, in any place, to any person." The defendant challenged the constitutionality of the act, and the government responded by encouraging the Court to uphold the law by declaring false statements of fact categorically unprotected. Justice Kennedy, in a plurality opinion joined by Chief Justice John Roberts and Justices Ruth Bader Ginsburg and Sonia Sotomayor, declined this invitation. Citing the George Orwell classic *Nineteen Eighty-Four*, Justice Kennedy said, "Our constitutional tradition stands against the idea that we need Oceania's Ministry of Truth." As Justice Kennedy explained:

> Were the Court to hold that the interest in truthful discourse alone is sufficient to sustain a ban on speech, absent any evidence that the speech was used to gain a material advantage, it would give government a broad censorial power unprecedented in this Court's cases or in our constitutional tradition. The mere potential for the exercise of that power casts a chill, a chill the First Amendment cannot permit if free speech, thought, and discourse are to remain a foundation of our freedom.
>
> The remedy for speech that is false is speech that is true. This is the ordinary course in a free society. The response to the unreasoned is the rational; to the uninformed, the enlightened; to the straight-out lie, the simple truth.

In an opinion concurring in the judgment that was joined by Justice Elena Kagan, Justice Stephen Breyer gave another reason for not finding false statements of fact categorically unprotected. He noted that sometimes false statements can be beneficial:

> False factual statements can serve useful human objectives, for example: in social contexts, where they may prevent embarrassment, protect privacy, shield a person from prejudice, provide the sick with comfort,

> or preserve a child's innocence; in public contexts, where they may stop a panic or otherwise preserve calm in the face of danger; and even in technical, philosophical, and scientific contexts, where (as Socrates' methods suggest) examination of a false statement (even if made deliberately to mislead) can promote a form of thought that ultimately helps realize the truth.

In his dissenting opinion, which was joined by Justices Antonin Scalia and Clarence Thomas, Justice Samuel Alito similarly conceded that there are "circumstances in which false factual statements enjoy a degree of instrumental constitutional protection":

> There are broad areas in which any attempt by the state to penalize purportedly false speech would present a grave and unacceptable danger of suppressing truthful speech. Laws restricting false statements about philosophy, religion, history, the social sciences, the arts, and other matters of public concern would present such a threat. The point is not that there is no such thing as truth or falsity in these areas or that the truth is always impossible to ascertain, but rather that it is perilous to permit the state to be the arbiter of truth.

After the Court issued the *Alvarez* decision, Congress amended the Stolen Valor Act so that it now applies only when a false claim of receiving a military honor is used to obtain a material advantage. As this revision suggests, false statements of fact can be punished when they lead to concrete harm. For example, fraudulent statements can be the basis for a defamation claim or justification for rescinding a contract. You will also learn that the government has broad leeway to regulate false and misleading advertisements.

6. **Are all false statements of fact alike?** Should the government be able to punish a car dealer's false statement that a vehicle had a six-cylinder engine when in fact it had only four cylinders? If so, is that statement different from a statement that the 2020 presidential election was stolen or that Covid-19 vaccines do more harm than good? Should the government be able to shut down a website that promotes the idea that the Holocaust never happened? Can a public university deny tenure to a science professor who claims that climate change is not real?

   If your sense is that not all false statements of fact are alike and that the government should have more leeway to regulate some false statements than others, can you articulate a rule for identifying which falsehoods should receive less First Amendment protection and which should not? In his book *Liars: Falsehoods and Free Speech in an Age of Deception* 3–4 (2021), Professor Cass R. Sunstein tries to create a framework for making this distinction. He starts with a general rule that "falsehoods ought not to be censored or regulated" and warns that public officials empowered to act as "truth police" inevitably "end up punishing dissent." But he qualifies his rule with an exception: "False statements are not constitutionally protected if the government can show that they threaten to cause serious harm that cannot be avoided through a more speech-protective route." Can you think of falsehoods that fall into Sunstein's exception? Would your decision to exclude a falsehood from protection depend on the speaker's state of mind (such as whether the speaker knew that his statement was false or was merely negligent about the statement's truth or falsity)? Would your answer to that question in turn depend on the type of punishment that would be imposed on the speaker (such as criminal sanctions, civil sanctions, or injunctive relief)?

7. **Having doubts about the "marketplace of ideas" theory? How about a competing "order and morality" theory?** If, in answering Question 1 in these Points for Discussion, you were doubtful that truth would always prevail in an open marketplace of ideas; and if, in answering Question 2, you were dubious that citizens would be discerning consumers in the marketplace of ideas; and if, in answering Question 3, you started thinking that some ideas are not worthy of First Amendment protection, then consider the merits of an alternative that we'll call the "order and morality" theory. Under this concept, the government would have greater leeway to regulate ideas that are widely considered to be both harmful and unworthy of First Amendment protection. Candidates for exclusion from protection might include hate speech, sexist speech, profanity, and graphically violent works. The name for the theory derives from the 1942 case *Chaplinsky v. New Hampshire*, 315 U.S. 568 (1942), in which the Court approved of the government's power to regulate speech when:

> such utterances are no essential part of any exposition of ideas, and are of such slight social value as a step to truth that any benefit that may be derived from them is clearly outweighed by the social interest in order and morality.

This order and morality theory, because it allows government censorship of some ideas, is at loggerheads with the marketplace of ideas theory. The two are dueling visions of when speech may be regulated. One could argue that the order and morality theory was the dominant theory in the Supreme Court's jurisprudence from the World War I era, when the justices first began wrestling with free speech issues, through the 1950s. Evidence of it can be found in not just the *Chaplinsky* opinion, but in cases like *Beauharnais v. Illinois*, 343 U.S. 250 (1952), which upheld what today would be called a hate speech law, and *Roth v. United States*, 354 U.S. 476 (1957), which upheld the government's power to regulate obscene speech. Even the Court's early incitement jurisprudence, which adopted the seemingly speech-protective "clear and present danger" test, usually culminated in the Court's upholding a defendant's conviction.

In the 1960s, the Supreme Court started to heavily favor the marketplace of ideas theory. Nevertheless, remnants of the order and morality theory are still evident in the Court's jurisprudence. This is true in the justices' continued refusal to protect obscene speech. It is also present in the Court's willingness to tolerate greater speech regulation in special settings, such as student speech in public schools.

As you wade through the materials in this casebook on hateful, sexist, violent, and profane speech, you might ask yourself what you would do if you were a Supreme Court justice. Would you be inclined to steer the Court's jurisprudence back toward the order and morality pole, or would you be inclined to stay the course toward the marketplace of ideas pole? If you're inclined toward the former, what justifies your confidence that the government will not abuse its power if given greater discretion to regulate speech?

Expect to feel the push and pull between the marketplace of ideas and order and morality theories as you work through the remaining materials on freedom of speech.

8. **Does the marketplace of ideas need to be regulated like an economic market?** In economic markets, we regulate to ensure that parties do not obtain monopoly power over a market. Should there be similar anti-monopoly rules for the marketplace of ideas? Should the government be able to tell a broadcaster or newspaper that it must provide space on its platform for alternative viewpoints? Should the government be able to regulate the news feed on Facebook to ensure that it is politically balanced? And what about the distorting influence of money in political campaigns? Should the government be able to limit campaign expenditures to ensure that wealthy candidates do not drown out the voices of less wealthy candidates? These topics will be explored in Chapter 12 when we consider whether the government may regulate speech to ensure a vibrant marketplace of ideas.

2. Facilitating Effective Self-Governance: How Can People Rule if They Are Not Informed?

Justice Holmes assumed that it was perfectly logical for those in power to suppress speech that threatens their power. But what if those in power are the people themselves?

The core premise of the Declaration of Independence was that governments derive their power from the people:

> We hold these truths to be self-evident, that all men are created equal, that they are endowed by their Creator with certain unalienable Rights, that among these are Life, Liberty and the pursuit of Happiness. That to secure

> these rights, Governments are instituted among Men, deriving their just powers from the consent of the governed, That whenever any Form of Government becomes destructive of these ends, it is the Right of the People to alter or to abolish it, and to institute new Government, laying its foundation on such principles and organizing its powers in such form, as to them shall seem most likely to effect their Safety and Happiness.

The Constitution crystallized this notion of popular sovereignty in the first three words of its preamble: "We the People." As Chief Justice Thurgood Marshall explained in *McCulloch v. Maryland*: "The government of the Union is, emphatically, and truly, a government of the people. In form and in substance it emanates from them."[38] President Abraham Lincoln echoed this point in the Gettysburg Address when he said that the fallen soldiers had not died in vain but to ensure that "government of the people, by the people, for the people, shall not perish from the earth."

Of course, for much of American history, these lofty words were belied by the facts on the ground. Even the Constitution's inclusive reference to "We the People" did not prevent the Framers from adopting a document that protected slavery and failed to give women the right to vote.[39] To the contrary, it took long, hard struggles and a civil war to correct these imperfections.

For present purposes, it is worth pondering the implications of popular sovereignty for freedom of speech. If a government derives from the people and exists to serve their interests, then presumably people need to be able to identify their policy preferences and communicate these preferences to their elected representatives. Yet people can do this effectively only if they have access to information, the ability to process this information, and a vehicle, such as voting, for expressing their views. Freedom of speech, which guarantees the right to express and receive information, would seem to be an essential component of this democratic process. As philosopher Alexander Meiklejohn explained, the First Amendment is "not a Law of Nature or of Reason" but rather "a deduction from the basic American agreement that public issues shall be decided by universal suffrage."[40]

Without access to information, particularly information about the functioning of government, it would be impossible for citizens to fulfill their civic duties. As James Madison explained, popular sovereignty cannot succeed if people do not have access to information:

> A popular Government, without popular information, or the means of acquiring it, is but a Prologue to a Farce or a Tragedy; or, perhaps both. Knowledge will forever govern ignorance: And a people who mean to be

---

38 *McCulloch v. Maryland*, 17 U.S. 316, 404–05 (1819).

39 Paul Finkelman, *How the Proslavery Constitution Led to the Civil War*, 43 Rutgers L. Rev. 405 (2013).

40 Alexander Meiklejohn, Free Speech and Its Relation to Self-Government 26–27 (1948).

> their own Governors, must arm themselves with the power which knowledge gives.[41]

The Supreme Court has fully embraced the self-governance rationale for protecting freedom of speech. As Justice Brennan explained, "the First Amendment embodies more than a commitment to free expression and communicative interchange for their own sakes; it has a *structural* role to play in securing and fostering our republican system of self-government."[42]

The Supreme Court has manifested its commitment to the self-governance rationale through its repeated statements about the vaunted status of "political speech." As Chief Justice John Roberts observed, "speech on public issues occupies the highest rung of the hierarchy of First Amendment values and is entitled to special protection."[43] This is because "speech concerning public affairs is more than self-expression; it is the essence of self-government."[44]

Points for Discussion

1. **Should the First Amendment protect only political speech?** If the core justification for protecting freedom of speech is to facilitate effective self-governance, should the First Amendment protect only speech that is relevant to citizens' roles as self-governors? Robert Bork, who taught at Yale Law School and later became a federal judge, used this logic to contend that the First Amendment should protect only political speech. He acknowledged that many types of speech could influence a person's political perspectives. But he warned that, "if the dialectical progression is not to become an analogical stampede, the protection of the First Amendment must be cut off when it reaches the outer limits of political speech." Robert Bork, *Neutral Principles and Some First Amendment Problems*, 47 Ind. L.J. 1, 27 (1971). Do you agree with Bork that the First Amendment should protect only political speech? Do you think that judges can make a principled distinction between political speech and other forms of speech? In answering these questions, consider Pablo Picasso's observation that "Art is a lie that makes us realize the truth." Do novels, movies, music, and other artistic creations affect how people understand the world and thereby affect their political orientation?

2. **Will protecting all speech water down the protection for political speech?** Notwithstanding its statements about the vaunted status of political speech, the Supreme Court has repeatedly held that the First Amendment protects not just

---

41 The Writings of James Madison 103 (Gaillard Hunt ed. 1910).

42 *Richmond Newspapers, Inc. v. Virginia*, 448 U.S. 555, 587 (1980) (Brennan, J., concurring).

43 *Snyder v. Phelps*, 562 U.S. 443, 452 (2011) *quoting Connick v. Myers*, 461 U.S. 138, 145 (1983).

44 *Id.*

political speech but the vast array of human expression. For example, in *Brown v. Entertainment Merchants Association*, 564 U.S. 786, 790 (2011), the Court held that the First Amendment protected video games:

> The Free Speech Clause exists principally to protect discourse on public matters, but we have long recognized that it is difficult to distinguish politics from entertainment, and dangerous to try. "Everyone is familiar with instances of propaganda through fiction. What is one man's amusement, teaches another's doctrine." Like the protected books, plays, and movies that preceded them, video games communicate ideas—and even social messages—through many familiar literary devices (such as characters, dialogue, plot, and music) and through features distinctive to the medium (such as the player's interaction with the virtual world). That suffices to confer First Amendment protection. Under our Constitution, "esthetic and moral judgments about art and literature are for the individual to make, not for the Government to decree, even with the mandate or approval of a majority."

This observation might have pleased Picasso, but is there a danger in interpreting the First Amendment to cover everything from core political speech to Grand Theft Auto? Is it possible that public pressure to regulate violent or sexual speech in entertainment products will cause the Court to water down its protection for all speech, including political speech?

3. **What does the self-governance theory suggest about the obligations of citizens?** It is easy to imagine an idealized version of how self-governance and freedom of speech work in tandem. Citizens use their freedom to seek out reliable information about political issues and the performance of elected officials. They engage in thoughtful debates with their fellow citizens, especially before elections, to sharpen their understanding of the issues and the candidates. Finally, after this process of information gathering and deliberative discourse, they use the insights they have gained to intelligently exercise their right to vote. Do you think that this description reflects how Americans approach their civic responsibilities, or is there a sizable gap between how people act in an idealized world and how they act in the real world? Do you think that Justice Brandeis was concerned about this gap when he warned in his *Whitney* concurrence that "the greatest menace to freedom is an inert people" and that "public discussion is a political duty"?

The Supreme Court has ruled that there is no constitutional right to education. *San Antonio Indep. Sch. Dist. v. Rodriguez*, 411 U.S. 1 (1973). Is that holding in tension with a First Amendment vision of citizens being informed and intelligent participants in the political process? The plaintiffs in *Rodriguez* insisted that education is "essential to the effective exercise of First Amendment freedoms and to intelligent utilization of the right to vote." The Supreme Court conceded that these were "desirable goals" that should be "pursued by a people whose thoughts and beliefs are freed from governmental interference," but it nevertheless said they were "not values to be implemented by judicial intrusion into otherwise legitimate state activities."

4. **The First Amendment as a check on political power.** Professor Vincent Blasi has offered an additional theory for protecting the freedoms of speech, press, and assembly that focuses on how these freedoms provide a critical check on abuses of government power. He refers to this as the First Amendment's "checking value." Blasi provides two examples of this checking function during the Nixon administration: anti-war protests that prevented the administration from further escalating the Vietnam War, and dogged press reporting that helped uncover the Watergate abuses. He writes:

> These incidents in our recent political experience are so familiar that it is easy to underestimate their importance. In the last decade, the First Amendment has had at least as much impact on American life by facilitating a process by which countervailing forces check the misuse of official power as by protecting the dignity of the individual, maintaining a diverse society in the face of conformist pressures, promoting the quest for scientific and philosophic truth, or fostering a regime of "self-government" in which large numbers of ordinary citizens take an active part in political affairs.

Vincent Blasi, *The Checking Value in First Amendment Theory*, 2 Am. Bar Found. Research J. 3, 527 (1977). Does the First Amendment's ability to fulfill this checking function depend on public access to information about how public officials use their power? If it does, should the First Amendment be interpreted to imply a right of public access to government information? We will explore that topic in Chapter 16 when we study freedom of the press.

The effectiveness of the checking function would also seem to depend on the existence of a vibrant press to report on government abuses. Should that make us concerned about the steep decline in regional and local news outlets covering state, county, and city governments? *See* Steve Waldman, *Our local-news situation is even worse than we think*, Colum. Journalism Rev., Feb. 25, 2022, available here.

3. The Inherent Value of Human Expression: Should Speech Be Protected Because Self-Expression Is What Makes Us Human?

The marketplace of ideas and self-governance theories protect speech because it leads to some other societal good: the discovery of truth or better self-governance. But is there an argument for protecting speech even if it lacks a secondary benefit? In other words, should freedom of speech, as Justice Brandeis suggested in his *Whitney* concurrence, be valued "both as an end and as a means"?

The most prominent theory for protecting speech as an end in itself is the "autonomy" theory. Underlying this theory is the notion that freedom of speech is inherently valuable because speech, more than any other human activity, is the vehicle through which people manifest their humanity. Professor Thomas Emerson described speech as the means by which people achieve self-fulfillment:

> The right to freedom of expression is justified first of all as the right of an individual purely in his capacity as an individual. It derives from the widely accepted premise of Western thought that the proper end of man is the realization of his character and potentialities as a human being. Man is distinguishable from other animals principally by the qualities of his mind. He has powers of imagination, insight and feeling. It is through development of these powers that man finds his meaning and his place in the world.[45]

Justice Marshall captured the autonomy theory when he observed how the First Amendment "serves not only the needs of the polity but also those of the human spirit—a spirit that demands self-expression."[46] Justice Brandeis may have intended a similar message when he said in his *Whitney* concurrence that the Framers "believed liberty to be the secret of happiness."

Under the autonomy theory, people should be free to express themselves—no matter how stupid, foolish, hateful, or offensive their expression might be—because expressing themselves is how they manifest their personalities. Like all liberties, there might be limits on how far this self-expression may go. But the notion is that, absent an important justification for suppressing this expression, it should be permitted.

---

[45] Thomas I. Emerson, *Toward a General Theory of the First Amendment*, 72 Yale L.J. 879 (April 1963). *See also* Martin H. Redish, *The Value of Free Speech*, 130 U. Penn. L. Rev. 591 (1982); C. Edwin Baker, Human Liberty and Freedom of Speech (1989).

[46] *Procunier v. Martinez*, 416 U.S. 396, 427 (1974) (Marshall, J. concurring).

Points for Discussion

1. **Why is self-expression more important for human realization than any other activity?** The autonomy principle assumes that speech is more closely tied to an individual's ability to achieve self-fulfillment than other forms of human activity. But is that a fair assumption? Robert Bork expressed doubt that any principled distinction exists:

   > Two benefits [of speech]—development of individual faculties and the achievement of pleasure—are or may be found, for both speaker and hearer, in all varieties of speech, from political discourse to shop talk to salacious literature. But the important point is that these benefits do not distinguish speech from any other human activity. An individual may develop his faculties or derive pleasure from trading on the stock market, following his profession as a river port pilot, working as a barmaid, engaging in sexual activity, playing tennis, rigging prices or in any of thousands of other endeavors.

   Robert H. Bork, *Neutral Principles and Some First Amendment Problems*, 47 Ind. L.J. 1, 25 (1971). Is Bork correct, or is there something unique about speech that distinguishes it from the myriad other ways people might find meaning or satisfaction?

2. **What if your fulfillment is my oppression?** What if some people express their humanity by denigrating other people's humanity, such as through hate speech or misogynistic language? Which group's humanity should take preference?

4. The Eclectic Approach: Why Choose When You Can Have Them All?

The Supreme Court has never settled on a specific theory as the exclusive reason for protecting speech. To the contrary, all the theories make regular appearances in the Court's jurisprudence. The justices apparently have found value in each of the theories and have not seen any reason why they should be mutually exclusive. Still, individual justices might find some theories more compelling than others, and their preferences might influence how they rule on First Amendment issues.

Is the justices' refusal to settle on a single theory a sign of intellectual weakness, or is there no logical reason for requiring speech protection to be based on a single rationale? Before answering this question, you might consider how the various theories often complement, rather than compete with, each other. For example, an open marketplace of ideas can simultaneously help people discover the truth, improve their ability to perform as citizens, and give them freedom to express their personalities.

Given the Freedom, What Will People Do with It?

The theories for protecting freedom of speech tend to assume people will use their freedom wisely, by seeking out the truth or becoming better informed and engaged citizens. But is that what people actually do with this freedom? Let's take a brief moment to ponder that question by looking at what people do as both consumers and producers of expression.

CONSUMING EXPRESSION: When people go into the marketplace of ideas, do they seek out quality information from reliable sources? Or are they drawn to expression that is titillating, sensational, polarizing, snarky, or outlandish? If people know that producing quality information requires substantial resources, are they willing to pay for it?

Even if people have the desire and determination to be intelligent consumers in the marketplace of ideas, how easy is it for them to do so? Consider, for example, this description of how emerging artificial intelligence (AI) technologies could hamper voters' ability to educate themselves about candidates and issues:

> AI may worsen the flood of misinformation and disinformation now typical of election season. AI equips illiberal nonstate actors and autocracies with an array of comparatively low-cost, unmanned tools by which adversaries may pry the electorate further apart, fueling caustic polarization and internal destabilization. Political bots, deepfakes, and other AI-generated visuals have already scrambled pre-election information ecosystems in democracies across the globe. AI's capacity to rapidly generate "pink slime," news sites comprised completely of fake news, exhibits its potential to turbocharge preexisting election interference tactics.

Norman Eisen, Nicol Turner Lee, Colby Galliher, and Jonathan Katz, *AI can strengthen U.S. democracy—and weaken it*, Brookings Inst. (Nov. 21, 2023), available here.

PRODUCING EXPRESSION: The internet created a whole new world in which individuals are able to widely disseminate their ideas at little or no cost. What have people done with this newfound freedom? Have they used it to express the best of themselves, the worst of themselves, or both? On the one hand, there are infinite ways in which people use the internet to bring joy, comfort, and insight to others. On the other hand, there are infinite ways in which people use the internet to harass, troll, dox, demean, threaten, and mislead others. On the latter point, consider a 2021 Pew Research poll in which 41% of U.S. adults said they experienced online harassment and 25% said they experienced severe harassment. You can read the study here.

If you have mixed feelings about how people use their freedom of speech, does that make you think some other system might be preferable? Or maybe you think about freedom of speech the way Winston Churchill thought about democracy: "No one pretends that democracy is perfect or all-wise. Indeed it has been said that democracy is the worst form of Government except for all those other forms that have been tried from time to time."

Even if you apply Churchill's reasoning to freedom of speech, are there nevertheless different ways in which a country could manifest its commitment to free speech? After all, there are different types of democracies (from Churchill's parliamentary democracy to our own presidential democracy). There are similarly wide variations in how countries with even strong free speech traditions protect speech.

As we explore how our own country protects speech, we will occasionally consider how other liberal democracies have done so. As you will discover, these countries often make different choices about how to balance free speech interests against other societal interests, such as security, equality, or morality. In these instances, you might ask yourself if you think our country or another country has made a better choice.

Test Your Knowledge

To assess your understanding of the material in this chapter, click here to take a quiz.

Chapter Three

Seeking Guidance from the Text:
Parsing the Free Speech Clause

The Framers enshrined protection for freedom of speech in our nation's foundational charter. But articulating this ideal was not the same as making it a reality. The challenge of translating this value into workable legal principles came afterward and continues to this day. Much of this work has been done by Supreme Court justices.

Imagine that you were one of those justices. Time and again you would be asked to decide how the Free Speech Clause should be applied to specific factual contexts. How would you go about making your decisions?

Most likely, your starting point would be the text of the Constitution. For freedom of speech, that means these 10 words:

> Congress shall make no law . . . abridging the freedom of speech

Let us parse these words to see how much guidance, or lack thereof, they give to judges trying to apply them.

A. "Congress": Who Is Restrained by the Free Speech Clause?

The Free Speech Clause expressly prohibits "Congress" from abridging speech. It says nothing about whether officials in the federal executive or judicial branches may abridge speech. It is also silent about abridgements of speech by state and local government officials.

A strict textualist could fairly contend that the Free Speech Clause should mean what it says: that only Congress is restrained by the clause. But, if you were on the Supreme Court, would you interpret the clause so narrowly? Or would you interpret it to apply to all levels and branches of government notwithstanding the text's plain meaning?

As you are about to learn, the Supreme Court has taken the more expansive approach.

1. Application of the Free Speech Clause to Federal, State, and Local Governments: Incorporation of the Free Speech Clause into the Fourteenth Amendment

The initial conundrum raised by the First Amendment's first word, "Congress," is whether this reference to a single branch of the federal government should preclude judges from applying the amendment to the other branches of the federal government. Some scholars, albeit a minority, believe that it should.[1] They believe that the First Amendment is a restraint on Congress and Congress alone, and that is true for all the amendment's provisions.

While these scholars have a strong textualist argument for their position, they have not succeeded in winning judicial adherents. To the contrary, the conventional wisdom among judges is that the First Amendment applies to all branches of the federal government.[2] So, for example, the Supreme Court has stated that "courts, too, are bound by the First Amendment"[3] and has indicated that judicial orders enjoining speech are presumptively unconstitutional.[4] Similarly, the Court has assumed that members of the executive branch are bound by the First Amendment.[5]

The application of the First Amendment to state and local governments presented a different conundrum for the Supreme Court. That was because the Court ruled in 1833 that the Bill of Rights applied to only the federal government. In *Barron v. Mayor of Baltimore*, Chief Justice John Marshall concluded that the Bill of Rights provisions were intended to restrain the government created by the Constitution—the federal

---

1 Gary Lawson & Guy Seidman, The Constitution of Empire 42–43 (2004); Nicholas Quinn Rosenkranz, *The Objects of the Constitution*, 63 Stan. L. Rev. 1005 (2011); Nicholas Quinn Rosenkranz, *The Subjects of the Constitution*, 62 Stan. L. Rev. 1209, 1253 (2010) [hereinafter Rosenkranz, *Subjects*]. For thoughtful responses to this scholarship, *see* Sonja R. West, *Suing the President for First Amendment Violations*, 71 Okla. L. Rev. 321 (2018); Daniel J. Hemel, *Executive Action and the First Amendment's First Word*, 40 Pepp. L. Rev. 601 (2013).

2 Rosenkranz, *Subjects*, at 1254–55 (observing that the word "Congress" is "not ambiguous" and is "one of the few words that the Constitution itself actually defines," yet noting that the Supreme Court and the academy "seem determined to treat this most determinate word of the First Amendment as if it were an inkblot").

3 *Citizens United v. Federal Election Comm'n*, 558 U.S. 310, 326 (2010).

4 *See, e.g., New York Times Co. v. United States*, 403 U.S. 713 (1971) (overturning federal court's temporary injunction on publication).

5 For example, in *Hein v. Freedom from Religion Foundation, Inc.*, 551 U.S. 587 (2007), the Court assumed a faith-based initiative initiated by President George W. Bush was subject to the Establishment Clause even though the case was decided on standing grounds. Similarly, in *Federal Communications Commission v. Pacifica Foundation*, 438 U.S. 726 (1978), the Court took it as given that the First Amendment applied to the FCC's actions. Of course, in many cases the actions of an executive agency have been authorized by a federal statute and therefore can be traced back to Congress. *See, e.g.*, Hemel, *supra* note 1, at 610.

government—and not state and local governments.[6] Protection against violations by state and local governments were expected to come from state laws and constitutions.

Pressure for change arose in the late 19th and early 20th centuries when the Supreme Court no longer found this immunity for state and local governments tolerable. Slowly, and incrementally, the Court began to hold that provisions in the Bill of Rights applied indirectly to state and local governments through the Fourteenth Amendment, which was added to the Constitution after the Civil War and expressly restrains state governments.

The casual reader of the Fourteenth Amendment[7] could be forgiven for thinking that the Supreme Court would have accomplished this feat by using the Fourteenth Amendment's Privileges or Immunities Clause: "No State shall make or enforce any law which shall abridge the privileges or immunities of citizens of the United States." After all, what could possibly be better candidates for these "privileges or immunities" than the rights protected by the Bill of Rights? But, in an 1872 case, the Supreme Court interpreted the Privileges or Immunities Clause so narrowly as to render it largely superfluous. As a dissenting judge lamented, the majority reduced the clause to a "vain and idle enactment."[8]

With that avenue closed, the Supreme Court eventually turned to the Due Process Clause of the Fourteenth Amendment as the vehicle for applying the Bill of Rights provisions to state governments. The Due Process Clause, which says "nor shall any State deprive any person of life, liberty, or property, without due process of law," was an awkward choice for incorporating substantive rights, like freedom of speech, because the clause focuses on procedure ("due process") and not substance. Despite the awkward fit, the Supreme Court seized upon the word "liberty" in the Due Process Clause and held that this term can "incorporate" substantive rights, including those found in the Bill of Rights. When a Bill of Rights provision is incorporated into the Fourteenth Amendment, it typically operates as a restraint on state governments in the same way that it does for the federal government. And because local governments are political subdivisions of states, they are also restrained by these incorporated rights.

The Supreme Court's decision to incorporate both the freedoms of speech and press into the Fourteenth Amendment occurred with little fanfare in 1925 in *Gitlow v. New York*. A single sentence did the trick:

---

6 *Barron v. Mayor of Balt.*, 32 U.S. 243 (1833).

7 U.S. Const., amend. XIV, § 1 ("All persons born or naturalized in the United States, and subject to the jurisdiction thereof, are citizens of the United States and of the State wherein they reside. No State shall make or enforce any law which shall abridge the privileges or immunities of citizens of the United States; nor shall any State deprive any person of life, liberty, or property, without due process of law; nor deny to any person within its jurisdiction the equal protection of the laws.").

8 *Slaughter-House Cases, Butchers' Benevolent Ass'n v. Crescent City Live-Stock Landing & Slaughter-House Co.*, 83 U.S. 36, 96 (1872) (Field, J., dissenting).

> For present purposes we may and do assume that freedom of speech and of the press—which are protected by the First Amendment from abridgment by Congress—are among the fundamental personal rights and "liberties" protected by the due process clause of the Fourteenth Amendment from impairment by the States.[9]

The upshot of this jurisprudence is that the Free Speech Clause is a restraint on all levels of government, from Congress down to a local police department, library, or public elementary school. For example, a 2021 Supreme Court opinion concerned a public high school student's claim that her school violated her First Amendment rights by suspending her from the cheerleading squad because she had posted profane messages on Snapchat.[10] As you will learn in Chapter 11, the student prevailed.

In First Amendment cases involving state or local government actors, judges will often clarify that the First Amendment is being applied indirectly to these actors through the Fourteenth Amendment. But judges sometimes skip this step and discuss the cases as if the First Amendment applied directly (*e.g.*, "the high school administrators violated the student's First Amendment rights"). For brevity's sake, this casebook will also sometimes use this shorthand. But you should remain cognizant of the fact that any application of the First Amendment to state and local government occurs through the First Amendment's incorporation into the Fourteenth Amendment.

2. The Free Speech Clause Does Not, with Rare Exceptions, Apply to Private Actors: A Company Town, a Shopping Mall, and a Private School

Except for the Thirteenth Amendment's bar on owning slaves, the restraints in the Constitution apply to only government actors. The jurisprudence describes this as the "state action" requirement.

Put simply, if the government punishes a person because of her speech, the First Amendment is implicated. But if Walmart or Holiday Inn does the same, the First Amendment is not implicated. This means that Facebook is free to regulate speech on its platform without having to worry about the First Amendment. It means that the National Football League can discipline players for kneeling during the National Anthem even if this act of kneeling is a form of expressive conduct.[11]

There are instances when courts treat private actors as state actors, but they are few and far between. They typically arise in two contexts: when a private party per-

9 *Gitlow v. New York*, 268 U.S. 652, 666 (1925).

10 *Mahanoy Area Sch. Dist. v. B.L.*, 141 S. Ct. 2038 (2021).

11 There is an open question about whether the Green Bay Packers, owned through a peculiar public corporation that is effectively the city of Green Bay, might be a state actor.

forms a public function and when government involvement with a private party makes it appropriate to treat the private party as a state actor.

a. Public Function Exception: When a Private Party Performs a Function Traditionally and Exclusively Performed by Government

The first exception is when a private actor is performing a function that has traditionally and exclusively been performed by government. The classic example in the First Amendment context is *Marsh v. Alabama,* 326 U.S. 501 (1946), a case concerning a small Alabama town called Chickasaw that was privately owned by the Gulf Shipbuilding Corporation. The corporation owned the buildings, the sidewalks, and the streets in Chickasaw, including the town's shopping district. The case arose when Gulf prohibited a Jehovah's Witness from distributing literature in the town. When the Jehovah's Witness refused to leave, she was arrested and ultimately charged with violating an Alabama trespass law.

At first blush, this case would not seem to trigger the First Amendment. The decision to prevent the Jehovah's Witness from distributing literature was made by a private actor, Gulf Shipbuilding, and not a state actor. Nevertheless, the Court held that the corporation was constrained by the First Amendment. As the owner of the town, the Court reasoned, Gulf was effectively acting like a municipal government and should be treated as such:

> We do not agree that the corporation's property interests settle the question. The State urges in effect that the corporation's right to control the inhabitants of Chickasaw is coextensive with the right of a homeowner to regulate the conduct of his guests. We cannot accept that contention. Ownership does not always mean absolute dominion. The more an owner, for his advantage, opens up his property for use by the public in general, the more do his rights become circumscribed by the statutory and constitutional rights of those who use it.
>
> Whether a corporation or a municipality owns or possesses the town the public in either case has an identical interest in the functioning of the community in such manner that the channels of communication remain free. As we have heretofore stated, the town of Chickasaw does not function differently from any other town. The "business block" serves as the community shopping center and is freely accessible and open to the people in the area and those passing through. The managers appointed by the corporation cannot curtail the liberty of press and religion of these people consistently with the purposes of the Constitutional guarantees, and a state statute, as the one here involved, which enforces such action by criminally punishing those who attempt to distribute religious literature clearly violates the First and Fourteenth Amendments to the Constitution.

The facts of the *Marsh* case present the quintessential example of a private actor's performing a function that has traditionally and exclusively been performed by a government. But there is language in the decision suggesting an even more capacious understanding of the public function exception to the state action doctrine. In saying that the more an owner "opens up his property for use by the public," the more the owner is constrained by the "constitutional rights of those who use it," the Court implied that the public function exception could apply to any business that was open to the public.

This more expansive interpretation of *Marsh* briefly carried the day when the Supreme Court held in *Amalgamated Food Employees Union v. Logan Valley Plaza*, 391 U.S. 308 (1968), that the First Amendment required the owners of a private shopping center to allow labor picketers into the mall to protest at a store. The Court concluded that the shopping center "is clearly the functional equivalent of the business district of Chickasaw involved in *Marsh*."

As the following case reveals, this expansive interpretation of the public function exception was short-lived. The facts in the case largely mirrored those in *Logan Valley*: union members claiming a First Amendment right to picket in a private shopping mall.

Hudgens v. National Labor Relations Board

Supreme Court of the United States, 1976
424 U.S. 507

MR. JUSTICE STEWART delivered the opinion of the Court.

It is, of course, a commonplace that the constitutional guarantee of free speech is a guarantee only against abridgment by government, federal or state. Thus, while statutory or common law may in some situations extend protection or provide redress against a private corporation or person who seeks to abridge the free expression of others, no such protection or redress is provided by the Constitution itself.

This elementary proposition is little more than a truism. But even truisms are not always unexceptionably true, and an exception to this one was recognized almost 30 years ago in *Marsh v. Alabama*. In *Marsh*, a Jehovah's Witness who had distributed literature without a license on a sidewalk in Chickasaw, Ala., was convicted of criminal trespass. Chickasaw was a so-called company town, wholly owned by the Gulf Shipbuilding Corp.

The Court pointed out that if the "title" to Chickasaw had "belonged not to a private but to a municipal corporation and had appellant been arrested for violating a municipal ordinance rather than a ruling by those appointed by the corporation to manage a company town it would have been clear that appellant's conviction must be reversed." Concluding that Gulf's "property interests" should not be allowed to lead to a different result in Chickasaw, which did "not function differently from any other town," the Court invoked the First and Fourteenth Amendments to reverse the appellant's conviction.

It was the *Marsh* case that in 1968 provided the foundation for the Court's decision in *Logan Valley*. The Court's opinion reviewed the *Marsh* case in detail, emphasized the similarities between the business block in Chickasaw, Ala., and the Logan Valley shopping center and unambiguously concluded: "The shopping center here is clearly the functional equivalent of the business district of Chickasaw involved in *Marsh*."

There were three dissenting opinions in the *Logan Valley* case, one of them by the author of the Court's opinion in *Marsh*, Mr. Justice Black. His disagreement with the Court's reasoning was total:

> The question is, under what circumstances can private property be treated as though it were public? The answer that *Marsh* gives is when that property has taken on all the attributes of a town, i.e., "residential buildings, streets, a system of sewers, a sewage disposal plant and a business block on which business places are situated." I can find nothing in *Marsh* which indicates that if one of these features is present, *e.g.*, a business district, this is sufficient for the Court to confiscate a part of an owner's private property and give its use to people who want to picket on it.
>
> To hold that store owners are compelled by law to supply picketing areas for pickets to drive store customers away is to create a court-made law wholly disregarding the constitutional basis on which private ownership of property rests in this country.

Four years later, the Court had occasion to reconsider the *Logan Valley* doctrine in *Lloyd Corp. v. Tanner*, 407 U.S. 551 (1972). That case involved a shopping center covering some 50 acres in downtown Portland, Ore. On a November day in 1968 five young people entered the mall of the shopping center and distributed handbills protesting the then ongoing American military operations in Vietnam. [*Authors' note*: The lower courts, relying on *Logan Valley*, held that the activists had a First Amendment right to enter the mall, but the Supreme Court reversed.]

The Court in its *Lloyd* opinion did not say that it was overruling the *Logan Valley* decision. Indeed, a substantial portion of the Court's opinion in *Lloyd* was devoted to pointing out the differences between the two cases. But the fact is that the reasoning of the Court's opinion in *Lloyd* cannot be squared with the reasoning of the Court's opinion in *Logan Valley*:

> Respondents contend that the property of a large shopping center is "open to the public," serves the same purposes as a "business district" of a municipality, and therefore has been dedicated to certain types of public use. The argument is that such a center has sidewalks, streets, and parking areas which are functionally similar to facilities customarily provided by municipalities. It is then asserted that all members of the public, whether invited as customers or not, have the same right of free speech as they would have on the similar public facilities in the streets of a city or town.
>
> The argument reaches too far. The Constitution by no means requires such an attenuated doctrine of dedication of private property to public use. The closest decision in theory, *Marsh*, involved the assumption by a private enterprise of all of the attributes of a state-created municipality and the exercise by that enterprise of semi-official municipal functions as a delegate of the State. In effect, the owner of the company town was performing the full spectrum of municipal powers and stood in the shoes of the State. In the instant case there is no comparable assumption or exercise of municipal functions or power.

We conclude, in short, that under the present state of the law the constitutional guarantee of free expression has no part to play in a case such as this.

MR. JUSTICE MARSHALL, with whom MR. JUSTICE BRENNAN joins, dissenting.

In the final analysis, the Court's rejection of any role for the First Amendment in the privately owned shopping center complex stems, I believe, from an overly formalistic view of the relationship between the institution of private ownership of property and the First Amendment's guarantee of freedom of speech. No one would seriously question the legitimacy of the values of privacy and individual autonomy traditionally associated with privately owned property. But property that is privately owned is not always held for private use, and when a property owner opens his property to public use the force of those values diminishes. A degree of privacy is necessarily surrendered; thus, the privacy interest that petitioner retains when he leases space to 60 retail businesses and invites the public onto his land for the transaction of business with other members of the public is small indeed.

The interest of members of the public in communicating with one another on subjects relating to the businesses that occupy a modern shopping center is substantial. Not only employees with a labor dispute, but also consumers with complaints against business establishments, may look to the location of a retail store as the only reasonable avenue for effective communication with the public. As far as these groups are concerned, the shopping center owner has assumed the traditional role of the state in its control of historical First Amendment forums. [*Logan Valley*] recognized the vital role the First Amendment has to play in such cases, and I believe that this Court errs when it holds otherwise.

[Justice Powell's concurrence, which was joined by Chief Justice Burger, is omitted, as is Justice White's opinion concurring in the result. Justice Stevens did not participate in the case.]

Points for Discussion

1. **The critical importance of the public/private distinction.** Because the First Amendment applies to only government actors (referred to as "state" actors), the determination of whether a public or private actor is suppressing speech is critical. If a public actor is suppressing speech, the First Amendment is implicated. If a private actor is suppressing speech, the First Amendment is irrelevant. Thus, the *Marsh* opinion, as recounted in *Hudgens*, noted that there would have been a clear violation of the Jehovah's Witness's First Amendment rights if Chickasaw had been a public municipality. That's because, as you will learn in Chapters 11 and 13, people have a First Amendment right to hand out literature on publicly owned streets, parks, and sidewalks (what are called "traditional public forums"). By contrast, private property owners are free to exclude whatever speech they want without First Amendment restraints.

   Marsh, however, was a rare decision in which the Court treated a private property owner as a state actor. Why did the *Marsh* Court conclude that the owner of the private town should be treated as a government actor, and why did the *Hudgens* Court refuse to extend the logic of *Marsh* to the owners of private shopping centers?

   Do you think that *Hudgens* reached the correct result? If the idea of public forums is that people in a free society need places where they can gather and engage in grassroots communications (through leafletting, soapbox speeches, and rallies), then is it important for people to be able to do so in places like private shopping malls? What if society has changed so that people no longer gather in city centers or public parks but instead gather in local malls?

2. **When the distinction between public and private is elusive.** Even a government official can be a private actor when not performing his or her official duties. So, for example, a police officer on duty is not free to arrest anyone whose speech the officer dislikes. But, while at home, the officer is free to kick people off his property because he dislikes their speech. This distinction might seem clear, but sometimes it can be elusive.

Consider the case of Donald Trump's Twitter (now called X) account, @realDonaldTrump. Trump created his account long before he became president. As the U.S. Court of Appeals for the Second Circuit explained, "No one disputes that before he became President the Account was a purely private one or that once he leaves office the Account will presumably revert to its private status." But after Trump became president, he registered the account in the name of "Donald J. Trump, 45th President of the United States of America, Washington, D.C." and both Trump and his aides described his tweets as official presidential statements. Indeed, Trump used the account to make such significant announcements as the appointment of a new FBI director, the firing of the president's chief of staff, and the sale of sophisticated weaponry to Japan and South Korea.

During his presidency, Trump blocked users on this Twitter account because he disliked their comments. When he did so, was he a private actor managing a private account, or had he turned his account into a government-controlled public forum that was subject to the First Amendment?

The Second Circuit concluded that the latter had occurred:

> The salient issues in this case arise from the decision of the President to use a relatively new type of social media platform to conduct official business and to interact with the public. We do not consider or decide whether an elected official violates the Constitution by excluding persons from a wholly private social media account. Nor do we consider or decide whether private social media companies are bound by the First Amendment when policing their platforms. We do conclude, however, that the First Amendment does not permit a public official who utilizes a social media account for all manner of official purposes to exclude persons from an otherwise-open online dialogue because they expressed views with which the official disagrees.

Knight First Amendment Inst. v. Trump, 928 F.3d 226, 230 (2d Cir. 2019). After Trump left office, the Supreme Court vacated the Second Circuit's opinion and ordered the lower court to dismiss the case as moot. *Biden v. Knight First Amendment Inst.*, 141 S. Ct. 1220 (2021).

Do you think the Second Circuit reached the correct decision? Although the Supreme Court did not issue a ruling in the Trump Twitter case, the Court did take two cases in its October 2023 term that considered whether public officials are state actors when they block users from the officials' social media accounts. *Lindke v. Freed*, 2024 WL 1120880 (2024); *O'Connor-Ratcliff v. Garnier*, 2024 WL 1120878 (2024). Writing for a unanimous Court in *Lindke*, Justice Amy Coney Barrett announced the test for determining when a government official's social media posts will be attributable to the State: "We hold that such speech is attributable to the State only if the official (1) possessed actual authority to speak on the State's behalf, and (2) purported to exercise that authority when he spoke on social media." Both cases were remanded to the lower courts for further proceedings in accordance with the Court's newly announced standard.

3. **Should the First Amendment apply to social media companies like Twitter and Facebook?** Large social media companies such as Facebook and Twitter/X have increasingly become the forums through which public discourse occurs. That, in turn, has given these companies considerable power to influence this discourse. For example, Trump's ability to communicate with his followers was greatly hampered after Facebook and Twitter removed him from their platforms amid concerns that he had incited the January 6, 2021, attack on the Capitol.

   Justice Clarence Thomas alluded to the outsized influence of these companies in a concurring opinion that accompanied the Supreme Court order vacating the Second Circuit opinion in the Trump Twitter case. Justice Thomas thought it especially ironic that Trump's Twitter account could be characterized as a government-controlled forum when Twitter, a private company unrestrained by the First Amendment, could terminate Trump's account at its discretion:

   > Respondents have a point that some aspects of Mr. Trump's account resemble a constitutionally protected public forum. But it seems rather odd to say that something is a government forum when a private company has unrestricted authority to do away with it.

   Justice Thomas used this observation to suggest that the more significant First Amendment issue had to do with the power of the social media companies:

   > The Second Circuit feared that then-President Trump cut off speech by using the features that Twitter made available to him. But if the aim is to ensure that speech is not smothered, then the more glaring concern must perforce be the dominant digital platforms themselves. As Twitter made clear, the right to cut off speech lies most powerfully in the hands of private digital platforms. The extent to which that power matters for purposes of the First Amendment and the extent to which that power could lawfully be modified raise interesting and important questions. This petition, unfortunately, affords us no opportunity to confront them.

   Does Justice Thomas have a point? Should social media companies' immense power over public discourse matter for First Amendment purposes? If these companies are the modern-day equivalent of the town square, should they be subject to First Amendment restraints? Are the companies the tech version of the company-owned town in *Marsh* that was bound by the First Amendment?

Before jumping to any conclusion, it is worth considering the costs and benefits of subjecting social media companies to First Amendment constraints. On the positive side, imposing First Amendment restraints could prevent the companies from skewing public discourse in favor of their (or their management's) political preferences. On the negative side, First Amendment restraints would hamper the companies' ability to remove speech from their platforms, even if the speech was offensive, hateful, or misinformed. Professor Noah Feldman captured this tradeoff in an article he wrote in response to the Second Circuit's opinion in the Trump Twitter case:

> On the surface, this apparent expansion of free speech may seem sensible, even exciting. After all, if social media is where we do our political talking, it would seem logical to bring the Constitution to bear there.
>
> The problem, however, is that applying the First Amendment to social media will make it harder or even impossible for the platforms to limit fake news, online harassment and hate speech—precisely the serious social ills that the world is calling on them to address.

Noah Feldman, *Are You Sure You Want a Right to Trump's Twitter Account?*, N.Y. Times, June 5, 2018.

b. Entanglement Exception: When Government Involvement Makes It Appropriate to Treat a Private Party as a State Actor

The second exception to the state action requirement applies when a private actor is sufficiently entangled with government that it is appropriate to treat the private actor as a state actor. This is especially true when the government authorizes, encourages, or facilitates the private actor's conduct.[12]

If this entanglement exception was interpreted expansively, it could turn all private actions into state action. After all, all property, contract, and tort causes of action are creations of state law that are enforced by public officials such as judges and law enforcement officers. Indeed, when reading the background to *Marsh*, you might have thought that the state action issue was open and shut because the Jehovah's Witness had been arrested and charged under Alabama state law for trespass. The subsequent shopping center cases, however, imply that the First Amendment is not triggered when an ordinary private property owner, as opposed to the owner of an entire town, orders a trespasser off his property, even if the trespasser is subsequently arrested and charged by state actors for trespass.[13]

---

[12] *See generally* Erwin Chemerinsky, Constitutional Law: Principles and Policies 589 (7th ed. 2023).

[13] *Hudgens*, 424 U.S. at 509 (noting that the shopping center manager informed the picketers that "if they did not leave they would be arrested for trespassing"). The Court had an opportunity to decide whether the enforcement of a trespass law at the behest of a private property owner constituted state action when it considered a series of cases involving trespass actions brought against African Americans

The question, then, is how much government involvement with a private actor is sufficient to justify treating a private actor as a state actor. Is it enough that a private actor receives government funding, is regulated by the government, or provides a public service? Is it enough that a private company operates as a type of business organization that is a creation of state law?

While some older Supreme Court opinions suggested that government regulation or funding could turn a private actor into a state actor, more recent opinions have made it clear that this will rarely be the case. A good illustration of the current rules is found in the next case.

Rendell-Baker v. Kohn

Supreme Court of the United States, 1982
457 U.S. 830

CHIEF JUSTICE BURGER delivered the opinion of the Court.

We granted certiorari to decide whether a private school, whose income is derived primarily from public sources and which is regulated by public authorities, acted under color of state law when it discharged certain employees.

Respondent Kohn is the director of the New Perspectives School, a nonprofit institution located on privately owned property in Brookline, Massachusetts. The school was founded as a private institution and is operated by a board of directors, none of whom are public officials or are chosen by public officials. The school specializes in dealing with students who have experienced difficulty completing public high schools; many have drug, alcohol, or behavioral problems, or other special needs. In recent years, nearly all of the students at the school have been referred to it by the Brookline or Boston School Committees, or by the Drug Rehabilitation Division of the Massachusetts Department of Mental Health. The school issues high school diplomas certified by the Brookline School Committee.

When students are referred to the school by Brookline or Boston under Chapter 766 of the Massachusetts Acts of 1972, the School Committees in those cities pay for the students' education. The school also receives funds from a number of other state and federal agencies. In recent years, public funds have accounted for at least 90%, and in one year 99%, of respondent school's operating budget. There were approximately 50 students at the school in those years and none paid tuition.

---

who engaged in sit-ins at private restaurants. While the Court overturned the convictions in these cases, it did so on narrower grounds that avoided the larger constitutional question. *See, e.g., Bell v. Maryland*, 378 U.S. 226 (1964). *See generally* Christopher W. Schmidt, *The Sit-Ins and the State Action Doctrine*, 18 Wm. & Mary Bill Rts. J. 767 (2010) (describing the Court's unwillingness to adopt a more expansive interpretation of the state action doctrine in the sit-in cases).

To be eligible for tuition funding under Chapter 766, the school must comply with a variety of regulations, many of which are common to all schools. The State has issued detailed regulations concerning matters ranging from recordkeeping to student-teacher ratios. Concerning personnel policies, the Chapter 766 regulations require the school to maintain written job descriptions and written statements describing personnel standards and procedures, but they impose few specific requirements.

The school is also regulated by Boston and Brookline as a result of its Chapter 766 funding. By its contract with the Boston School Committee, which refers to the school as a "contractor," the school must agree to carry out the individualized plan developed for each student referred to the school by the Committee. The contract specifies that school employees are not city employees.

The school also has a contract with the State Drug Rehabilitation Division. Like the contract with the Boston School Committee, that agreement refers to the school as a "contractor." It provides for reimbursement for services provided for students referred to the school by the Drug Rehabilitation Division, and includes requirements concerning the services to be provided. Except for general requirements, such as an equal employment opportunity requirement, the agreement does not cover personnel policies.

While five of the six petitioners were teachers at the school, petitioner Rendell-Baker was a vocational counselor hired under a grant from the federal Law Enforcement Assistance Administration, whose funds are distributed in Massachusetts through the State Committee on Criminal Justice. As a condition of the grant, the Committee on Criminal Justice must approve the school's initial hiring decisions. The purpose of this requirement is to insure that the school hires vocational counselors who meet the qualifications described in the school's grant proposal to the Committee; the Committee does not interview applicants for counselor positions.

[*Authors' note:* This case was brought after the school administrators fired the vocational counselor Rendell-Baker and later five teachers after disputes arose between the employees and the administration. The employees claimed that their terminations violated the First Amendment and brought an action under 42 U.S.C. § 1983, which allows parties to bring civil actions for constitutional violations by state or local government actors.]

The core issue presented in this case is not whether petitioners were discharged because of their speech or without adequate procedural protections, but whether the school's action in discharging them can fairly be seen as state action. If the action of the respondent school is not state action, our inquiry ends.

In *Blum v. Yaretsky*, 457 U.S. 991(1982), the Court analyzed the state action requirement of the Fourteenth Amendment. The Court considered whether certain nursing homes were state actors for the purpose of determining whether decisions regarding transfers of patients could be fairly attributed to the State, and hence be subjected to Fourteenth Amendment due process requirements. The challenged transfers primarily involved decisions, made by physicians and nursing home administrators, to move patients from "skilled nursing facilities" to less expensive "health related facilities." Like the New Perspectives School, the nursing homes were privately owned and operated. The Court held that, "a State normally can be held responsible for a private decision only when it has exercised coercive power or has provided such significant encouragement, either overt or covert, that the choice must in law be deemed to be that of the State." In determining that the transfer decisions were not actions of the State, the Court considered each of the factors alleged by petitioners here to make the discharge decisions of the New Perspectives School fairly attributable to the State.

First, the nursing homes, like the school, depended on the State for funds; the State subsidized the operating and capital costs of the nursing homes, and paid the medical expenses of more than 90% of the patients. Here the Court of Appeals concluded that the fact that virtually all of the school's income was derived from government funding was the strongest factor to support a claim of state action. But in *Blum*, we held that the similar dependence of the nursing homes did not make the acts of the physicians and nursing home administrators acts of the State, and we conclude that the school's receipt of public funds does not make the discharge decisions acts of the State.

The school, like the nursing homes, is not fundamentally different from many private corporations whose business depends primarily on contracts to build roads, bridges, dams, ships, or submarines for the government. Acts of such private contractors do not become acts of the government by reason of their significant or even total engagement in performing public contracts.

A second factor considered in *Blum* was the extensive regulation of the nursing homes by the State. There the State was indirectly involved in the transfer decisions challenged in that case because a primary goal of the State in regulating nursing homes was to keep costs down by transferring patients from intensive treatment centers to less expensive facilities when possible. Both state and federal regulations encouraged the nursing homes to transfer patients to less expensive facilities when appropriate. The nursing homes were extensively regulated in many other ways as well. The Court relied on *Jackson v. Metropolitan Edison Co.*, 419 U.S. 345 (1974), where we held that state regulation, even if "extensive and detailed," did not make a utility's actions state action.

Here the decisions to discharge the petitioners were not compelled or even influenced by any state regulation. Indeed, in contrast to the extensive regulation of the school generally, the various regulators showed relatively little interest in the school's personnel matters. The most intrusive personnel regulation promulgated by the various government agencies was the requirement that the Committee on Criminal Justice had the power to approve persons hired as vocational counselors. Such a regulation is not sufficient to make a decision to discharge, made by private management, state action.

The third factor asserted to show that the school is a state actor is that it performs a "public function." However, our holdings have made clear that the relevant question is not simply whether a private group is serving a "public function." We have held that the question is whether the function performed has been "traditionally the *exclusive* prerogative of the State." There can be no doubt that the education of maladjusted high school students is a public function, but that is only the beginning of the inquiry. Chapter 766 of the Massachusetts Acts of 1972 demonstrates that the State intends to provide services for such students at public expense. That legislative policy choice in no way makes these services the exclusive province of the State. Indeed, the Court of Appeals noted that until recently the State had not undertaken to provide education for students who could not be served by traditional public schools. That a private entity performs a function which serves the public does not make its acts state action.

We hold that petitioners have not stated a claim for relief under 42 U.S.C. § 1983; accordingly, the judgment of the Court of Appeals for the First Circuit is *Affirmed.*

JUSTICE WHITE, concurring in the judgments.

For me, the critical factor is the absence of any allegation that the employment decision was itself based upon some rule of conduct or policy put forth by the State. As the majority states, "in contrast to the extensive regulation of the school generally, the various regulators showed relatively little interest in the school's personnel matters." The employment decision remains, therefore, a private decision not fairly attributable to the State.

JUSTICE MARSHALL, with whom JUSTICE BRENNAN joins, dissenting.

In my view, this holding simply cannot be justified. The State has delegated to the New Perspectives School its statutory duty to educate children with special needs. The school receives almost all of its funds from the State, and is heavily regulated. This nexus between the school and the State is so substantial that the school's action must be considered state action. I therefore dissent.

Points for Discussion

1. **Why did the Court treat the New Perspectives School as a private actor?** The New Perspectives School received the bulk of its funding from the government,

was heavily regulated by government, and provided a public service. Why didn't the Court find that the school was sufficiently entangled with government that it should be treated as a state actor? What type of government involvement does the Court suggest is required before a private actor can be deemed a state actor?

2. **Judicial enforcement of tort actions based on speech constitutes state action.** As previously noted, judicial enforcement of private contract, property, or tort rights does not automatically trigger constitutional restraints. The most famous exception is *Shelley v. Kraemer*, 334 U.S. 1 (1948), which held that judicial enforcement of racially restrictive covenants constituted state action. There is also an important exception to this rule in the First Amendment context. If a private party brings a tort action in which the cause of action is based on a defendant's speech, the judicial enforcement of the tort is considered state action that triggers the First Amendment. The Court announced this rule in *New York Times Co. v. Sullivan*, 376 U.S. 254 (1964). You will learn about this rule when you study the interaction of First Amendment jurisprudence and tort law in Chapter 9.

3. **Can the government avoid First Amendment limits by delegating its power to a private actor?** New York requires cable television operators to set aside channels for public access. The cable companies are expected to operate these channels unless the local government chooses to do so or designates a private party to operate the channels. In *Manhattan Community Access Corp. v. Halleck*, 139 S. Ct. 1921 (2019), the Court addressed a fact pattern in which Time Warner, which operated a cable system in Manhattan, set aside channels for public access. New York City chose not to operate the channels itself and instead delegated this responsibility to a private nonprofit corporation called Manhattan Neighborhood Network (MNN). The plaintiffs, producers of public access programming, sued MNN claiming that the corporation violated their First Amendment rights by refusing to air their programs. The issue was whether MNN was a state actor subject to First Amendment constraints.

   Justice Brett Kavanaugh, writing for the majority, concluded that MNN was not a state actor:

   > A private entity such as MNN who opens its property for speech by others is not transformed by that fact alone into a state actor. In operating the public access channels, MNN is a private actor, not a state actor, and MNN therefore is not subject to First Amendment constraints on its editorial discretion.

   Justice Kavanaugh rejected the argument that MNN was performing a public function because operating public access channels "has not traditionally and exclusively been performed by government." He similarly rejected the argument that MNN was a state actor because it was regulated by the government: "Put simply, being regulated by the State does not make one a state actor."

Justice Sonia Sotomayor, writing for three other justices, dissented. Here is how she summarized her reasoning:

> This is a case about an organization appointed by the government to administer a constitutional public forum. (It is not, as the Court suggests, about a private property owner that simply opened up its property to others.) New York City secured a property interest in public-access television channels when it granted a cable franchise to a cable company. State regulations require those public-access channels to be made open to the public on terms that render them a public forum. The City contracted out the administration of that forum to a private organization, petitioner Manhattan Community Access Corporation (MNN). By accepting that agency relationship, MNN stepped into the City's shoes and thus qualifies as a state actor, subject to the First Amendment like any other.

Do you think that the majority or the dissent has the better argument?

4. **Is there a point at which government cajoling of social media companies turns the companies into state actors?** During the Covid pandemic, the Biden administration was in constant communication with social media companies and aggressively advocated for them to take down postings with misinformation about Covid and the Covid vaccines. In response to this advocacy, social media companies took down postings and terminated accounts associated with the spread of misinformation. Is there a point at which this aggressive government advocacy can cross the line from cajoling into coercion, and, if so, where should that line be drawn? If the government action crossed the line into coercion, should the social media companies' removal of postings be treated as government actions that are subject to First Amendment constraints? *Missouri v. Biden*, 2023 WL 4335270 (W.D. La. July 4, 2023), *aff'd in part and rev'd in part*, 83 F.4th 350 (5th Cir. 2023), *cert. granted sub nom. Murthy v. Missouri*, 144 S. Ct. 7 (2023).

5. **Other means of ensuring that private actors protect freedom of speech.** The fact that the First Amendment does not apply to private actors does not preclude other laws from requiring these actors to respect free speech interests. Here are two possibilities:

   a. **Restraints imposed by state constitutions.** In addition to the federal constitution, all 50 states have their own constitutions, and all, in one fashion or another, provide some protection for freedom of speech, press, or assembly. *See* Fifty State Statutory Survey: Right to Assemble/Protest. State courts, which have the final word on the meaning of state constitutions, could interpret these provisions to place restraints on private actors. For example, the California Supreme Court held that the free speech clause in the state constitution gave the public a right to access privately owned shopping centers for speech purposes even though the U.S. Supreme Court held three years earlier that the public did not have a comparable right under the U.S. Constitution. *Robins v. PruneYard Shopping Ctr.*, 592 P.2d 341 (Cal. 1979). Here is the provision in the California Constitution that the court relied on: "Every person may freely speak, write and publish his or her sentiments on all subjects, being responsible for the abuse of this right. A law may not restrain or abridge liberty of speech or press."

State constitutions may give people greater rights than they have under the U.S. Constitution as long as those rights do not conflict with a provision in the U.S. Constitution. That was an issue after the California Supreme Court granted the public a right to access private shopping centers in the *Robins* case. The owner of a private mall claimed that this ruling violated the owner's free speech rights under the First Amendment of the U.S. Constitution because the public would assume that the owner endorsed the messages being circulated in its mall. In essence, the mall owner was saying that California was forcing the owner to say something it did not want to say (what you will soon learn is called "compelled speech").

The U.S. Supreme Court acknowledged that compelling a person to speak can violate the First Amendment. But the Court concluded that California was not forcing the mall owner to speak because mall visitors would not associate the circulated messages with the owner:

> The views expressed by members of the public in passing out pamphlets or seeking signatures for a petition will not likely be identified with those of the owner. [The owner] can expressly disavow any connection with the message by simply posting signs in the area where the speakers or handbillers stand. Such signs, for example, could disclaim any sponsorship of the message and could explain that the persons are communicating their own messages by virtue of state law.

PruneYard Shopping Ctr. v. Robins, 447 U.S. 74, 87 (1980).

b. **Statutory protection of freedom of speech.** Legislators, on federal, state, and local levels, can enact laws that require private actors to protect speech interests in certain contexts. For example, there are numerous statutes that protect whistleblowers who expose wrongdoing. Similarly, even though the First Amendment applies to only public and not private universities, California has a state statute that requires private universities in the state to abide by the same First Amendment rules that apply to public universities. A California state court used this statute to strike down a hate speech regulation at the privately owned Stanford University. *Corry v. Leland Stanford Junior Univ.*, No. 740309 (Cal. Super. Ct., Santa Clara Cnty. Feb. 27, 1995).

A notable and controversial law that provides protection for speech beyond that afforded by the First Amendment is Section 230 of the Communications Decency Act. 47 U.S.C.A. § 230. This statutory provision gives online platforms broad protection against tort liability for publishing content provided by their users. Congress recognized that it was impossible for social media companies to screen the millions of postings by their users and that the companies would face immense liability if they could be held liable for the content of these postings. To avoid the chilling effect of this potential liability, Congress enacted Section 230 to limit the companies' liability. The merits of Section 230 immunity and the precise scope of this immunity are the subject of considerable debate. *See* Rodney Smolla, 3 Smolla & Nimmer on Freedom of Speech § 23.12 (2023). In Chapter 9, you will learn about important, but less expansive, First Amendment limits on tort liability.

6. **Can legislation ensure that social media companies adequately protect speech interests?** Even if the First Amendment does not apply to social media companies because they are private actors, could legislators nevertheless enact laws that require these companies to comply with First Amendment principles? For example, the state of Florida, in response to purported claims that social media companies were liberally biased, enacted a law that prohibited the companies from de-platforming political candidates, prioritizing messages about candidates, or removing any content posted by a "journalistic enterprise." *NetChoice, LLC v. Attorney Gen., State of Fla.*, 34 F.4th 1196, 1203 (11th Cir. 2022). Does this sound like a legitimate effort to correct distortions in the marketplace of ideas caused by private media companies or an illegitimate effort to interfere with the editorial control at these companies? We will explore this issue in Chapter 12 when we discuss the government's ability to regulate speech to promote a vibrant marketplace of ideas.

B. "Speech": What Is Protected by the Free Speech Clause?

The First Amendment says that Congress shall make no law abridging the freedom of "speech." But what, exactly, is "speech"?

The most obvious examples of speech would be written or spoken words. This would include not only the initial expression of these words but also their further dissemination, whether through physical copies such as leaflets or books or through electronic dissemination such as radio or television broadcasts or the posting of works on the internet.

Pictures are said to be worth a thousand words. Does that mean that images are also speech? The short answer is yes. For example, we learned in Chapter 2 that the First Amendment protects works of entertainment such as movies, television shows, and video games. Justice David Souter has said that the First Amendment protects art and music even when they do not convey any discernible "particularized message." So, for example, he said the First Amendment "unquestionably shielded [the] painting of Jackson Pollock, music of Arnold Schoenberg, or Jabberwocky verse of Lewis Carroll."[14]

Jackson Pollock, *Number 1* (1949)
© 2023 The Pollock-Krasner Foundation/Artists Rights Society (ARS), New York[15]

If words and images are considered speech, what about expressive conduct? Of course, speaking, writing, and painting are a form of conduct, but here we are referring to conduct that is not inherently expressive.

Consider the example of burning the national flag. Certainly, this conduct could be expressive, such as burning a flag at an anti-war rally. But burning a flag is not

14 *Hurley v. Irish-American Gay, Lesbian & Bisexual Grp. of Boston*, 515 U.S. 557, 569 (1995).

15 The Museum of Contemporary Art, Los Angeles/Photo by Brian Forest. Enamel and metallic paint on canvas 63 x 102 1/2 in. (160.02 x 260.35 cm). The Rita and Taft Schreiber Collection. Given in loving memory of her husband, Taft Schreiber, by Rita Schreiber.

necessarily expressive. Imagine shivering campers tossing a flag into a campfire as extra kindling.

The Supreme Court has acknowledged that conduct can be considered speech when it is expressive. The Court refers to conduct that communicates as either "expressive conduct" or "symbolic speech." In *United States v. O'Brien*, 391 U.S. 367, 376 (1968), a case concerning the burning of draft cards during the Vietnam War, the Court accepted that the First Amendment protects symbolic speech but also rejected "the view that an apparently limitless variety of conduct can be labeled 'speech' whenever the person engaging in the conduct intends thereby to express an idea." Instead, the Court typically uses the test from *Spence v. Washington*, 418 U.S. 405 (1974), to determine whether conduct is entitled to First Amendment protection. The *Spence* case concerned a defendant who taped a peace symbol to an American flag. Under the *Spence* test, conduct will be considered expressive if the person engaged in the conduct intended to convey a message and those viewing the conduct would be likely to understand the message. Both must be true for conduct to be considered speech.

We will explore expressive conduct in depth when we get to Chapter 14. But you will see examples of expressive conduct in earlier chapters, so be prepared to use the *Spence* test.

You Be the Lawyer!

Make arguments for and against finding the following to be speech

In many First Amendment cases, it is obvious that a party is engaged in speech. But that is not always the case. Imagine that you are a lawyer who is confronted by the following hypothetical fact patterns. In each case, try to come up with arguments for why a party's conduct should be considered speech, as well as counterarguments for why it should not be considered speech. For now, focus only on whether the conduct should be considered speech and not on whether, if the conduct is speech, the government should be able to regulate it.

Edible Speech?

An evangelical Christian baker refuses to make wedding cakes for same-sex couples even though a state law prohibits businesses from discriminating against customers based on their sexual orientation. The baker says that forcing him to make a wedding cake for a same-sex couple would compel him to convey a message—approval of same-sex marriages—that he does not wish to communicate.

The baker considers himself to be an artist. He specializes in making personalized wedding cakes for couples. Before he designs a cake, he first interviews the couple. He then meticulously sculpts and paints a cake to capture the specific characteristics of the couple who commissioned the cake.

In addition to making these customized wedding cakes, the baker makes and sells conventional wedding cakes that are not personalized for any couple. Samples of these cakes are on display in the bakery for customers to select and place an order.

The baker refuses to sell either the personally designed or the conventional wedding cakes to same-sex couples. He claims that selling either type of cake would force him convey a message of approval for same-sex marriages.

What arguments can be made for and against finding that selling these cakes to same-sex couples constitutes speech? Is the strength of the baker's argument stronger or weaker if a cake is personalized or standardized?

Erotic Speech?

An adult entertainment establishment wants to have female dancers who are completely naked. State law, however, requires female dancers to wear, at a minimum, pasties and G-strings. The owner of the establishment claims that the law is violating the free speech rights of the establishment and the dancers.

What arguments can be made for and against finding that nude dancing is speech?

Now assume a different fact pattern. A woman likes to sunbathe at the beach in the nude. She thinks this gives her a better tan and is the natural thing to do. State law, however, forbids public nudity. The woman challenges the law, claiming that its application to her nude sunbathing violates the First Amendment.

What arguments can be made for and against finding nude sunbathing to be speech?

Binary Speech?

Cody Wilson, the founder of the Texas-based nonprofit Defense Distributed, wanted to post computer code that, if fed to a 3D printer, could produce an operational .38 caliber handgun or an AR-15 assault rifle. The government sought to prevent Wilson from posting the code. Wilson claimed that the code was speech and that prohibiting him from posting it violated the First Amendment.

What arguments can be made for and against finding the posting of this computer code to be speech? For some guidance, try consulting Kyle Langvardt, *The Replicator and the First Amendment*, 25 Fordham Intell. Prop. Media & Ent. L.J. 59 (2014); Lee Tien, *Publishing Software as a Speech Act*, 15 Berkeley Tech. L.J. 629 (2000); and Robert Post, *Encryption Source Code and the First Amendment*, 15 Berkeley Tech. L.J. 713 (2000).

C. "Abridging": When Has Freedom of Speech Been Abridged?

The Free Speech Clause is implicated only if the government abridges speech. But what constitutes an abridgement of speech?

The most obvious example of a government abridgment of speech is when the government criminally punishes someone for speaking. This is true regardless of whether the punishment takes the form of jail time or a monetary fine. The Supreme Court has also held that imposing tort liability in a civil case is an abridgment of speech if the liability is based on a defendant's speech.

Those are straightforward examples of how the government can abridge speech, but speech abridgements can also occur in more subtle ways. Here are a few important examples you will encounter in future chapters:

- **When government compels speech.** In the typical First Amendment case, the government abridges speech by preventing or inhibiting a party from speaking. But the Supreme Court has also recognized that freedom of speech can be abridged when the government compels a person to speak. A classic example is *Wooley v. Maynard*, 430 U.S. 705 (1977), in which a Jehovah's Witness couple was criminally charged for covering over the state motto, "Live Free or Die," on the couple's New Hampshire license plate. For religious reasons, the couple did not want their car to be a "mobile billboard" for conveying this message, but New Hampshire law made it a crime to cover the motto. In ruling for the couple, the Supreme Court clarified that freedom of speech includes both "the right to speak freely and the right to refrain from speaking at all." By compelling the couple to communicate the message "Live Free or Die," New Hampshire had violated the couple's right not to speak. You will see examples of compelled speech throughout this casebook and will study the topic in depth in Chapter 15.

- **When government interferes with freedom of association.** The Supreme Court has said that individuals not only have the right to speak, but also have the right to associate with others for expressive purposes. This "right of association" is not expressly mentioned in the First Amendment, but the Court has nevertheless said that the right is implied. It is easy to appreciate why. As the Court explained in *NAACP v. Alabama*, 357 U.S. 449 (1958), "effective advocacy of both public and private points of view, particularly controversial ones, is undeniably enhanced by group association." The right of association protects the ability of people to form organizations to collectively convey their messages, such as the Sierra Club, the National Rifle Association, or political parties such as the Democratic and Republican parties.

  The right of association is abridged when the government interferes with people's ability to associate for expressive purposes. It can also be abridged when the government compels an association to accept members whom the association claims will interfere with its message. For example, the Boy Scouts claimed that forcing it to accept a gay scoutmaster would interfere with the organization's message that it is inappropriate to be gay. We will study both freedom of association and freedom not to associate in Chapter 15.

- **When government conditions government benefits on surrendering free speech rights ("unconstitutional conditions").** The Supreme Court has said that speech can be abridged when the government conditions receipt of a benefit on surrendering First Amendment rights. To take an egregious example, imagine that a state refused to give welfare recipients their benefits unless they agreed not to criticize the governor. There is no constitutional right to welfare benefits so the state could have never provided the benefits in the first place. But the state still could not condition receipt of the benefits on the recipients' surrendering their First Amendment rights. The Supreme Court refers to this as an "unconstitutional condition" and treats it as an abridgment of speech. We will explore this topic in Chapter 12 when we discuss First Amendment limits on government funding.

Compelling speech, interfering with freedom of association, and conditioning benefits on surrendering speech rights are just some examples of the myriad ways in which government actions can abridge speech. In any given case, the key factor to focus on is whether the government has, in one form or another, interfered with or inhibited a person's ability to speak.

Is Forcing Law Schools to Accommodate Military Recruiters an Abridgment of Speech?

Ready to test your First Amendment chops? The following case was heard a decade before the Supreme Court held that gays and lesbians had a constitutional right to marry in *Obergefell v. Hodges*, 576 U.S. 644 (2015). From 1993 until 2011, the Department of Defense adopted a policy concerning gay service members that was colloquially referred to as "don't ask, don't tell." The policy prohibited gay service members from engaging in homosexual sex or disclosing their sexual orientation ("don't tell"). At the same time, it forbade the military from inquiring about a service member's sexual orientation ("don't ask") unless it had evidence that the service member had engaged in actions prohibited by the policy.

Several law schools that objected to the policy decided to register their displeasure by barring military recruiters from using the schools' facilities to meet with students. Congress responded with the Solomon Amendment, which provided that institutions of higher education that denied military recruiters the same access as other recruiters would lose some of their federal funding.

The law schools, through an association called the Forum for Academic & Institutional Rights, brought a lawsuit claiming that the Solomon Amendment violated their First Amendment rights. The schools lost at the district court, won at the court of appeals, and then lost 8–0 at the Supreme Court. (Justice Samuel Alito did not participate in the case.)

Before you read the case, try to anticipate both the law schools' arguments and the Supreme Court's response. Recall that the Solomon Amendment said that schools that failed to give military recruiters the same access as other recruiters would lose federal funding. What arguments could the schools make that the Solomon Amendment not only implicated their free speech rights but also abridged those rights? What arguments could the government make that the Solomon Amendment did not violate the schools' First Amendment rights? Once you've tried to figure this out by yourself (or with some classmates), you can plunge into the case.

Rumsfeld v. Forum for Academic & Institutional Rights, Inc.

Supreme Court of the United States, 2006
547 U.S. 47

CHIEF JUSTICE ROBERTS delivered the opinion of the Court.

When law schools began restricting the access of military recruiters to their students because of disagreement with the Government's policy on homosexuals in the military, Congress responded by enacting the Solomon Amendment. That provision specifies that if any part of an institution of higher education denies military recruiters access equal to that provided other recruiters, the entire institution would lose certain federal funds. The law schools responded by suing, alleging that the Solomon Amendment infringed their First Amendment freedoms of speech and association. The District Court disagreed but was reversed by a divided panel of the Court of Appeals for the Third Circuit, which ordered the District Court to enter a preliminary injunction against enforcement of the Solomon Amendment. We granted certiorari.

Respondent Forum for Academic and Institutional Rights, Inc. (FAIR), is an association of law schools and law faculties. Its declared mission is "to promote academic freedom, support educational institutions in opposing discrimination and vindicate the rights of institutions of higher education." FAIR members have adopted policies expressing their opposition to discrimination based on, among other factors, sexual orientation. They would like to restrict military recruiting on their campuses because they object to the policy Congress has adopted with respect to homosexuals in the military. The Solomon Amendment, however, forces institutions to choose between enforcing their nondiscrimination policy against military recruiters in this way and continuing to receive specified federal funding.

The Government and FAIR agree on what this statute requires: In order for a law school and its university to receive federal funding, the law school must offer military recruiters the same access to its campus and students that it provides to the nonmilitary recruiter receiving the most favorable access.

Other decisions recognize a limit on Congress' ability to place conditions on the receipt of funds. We recently held that "the government may not deny a benefit to a person on a basis that infringes his constitutionally protected freedom of speech even if he has no entitlement to that benefit." Under this principle, known as the unconstitutional conditions doctrine, the Solomon Amendment would be unconstitutional if Congress could not directly require universities to provide military recruiters equal access to their students.

This case does not require us to determine when a condition placed on university funding becomes an unconstitutional condition. It is clear that a funding condition cannot be unconstitutional if it could be constitutionally imposed directly. Because the First Amendment would not prevent Congress from directly imposing the Solomon Amendment's access requirement, the statute does not place an unconstitutional condition on the receipt of federal funds.

The Solomon Amendment neither limits what law schools may say nor requires them to say anything. Law schools remain free under the statute to express whatever views they may have on the military's congressionally mandated employment policy, all the while retaining eligibility for federal funds. As a general matter, the Solomon Amendment regulates conduct, not speech. It affects what law schools must *do*—afford equal access to military recruiters—not what they may or may not *say*.

Nevertheless, the Third Circuit concluded that the Solomon Amendment violates law schools' freedom of speech in a number of ways. First, in assisting military recruiters, law schools provide some services, such as sending e-mails and distributing flyers, that clearly involve speech. The Court of Appeals held that in supplying these services law schools are unconstitutionally compelled to speak the Government's message. Second, military recruiters are, to some extent, speaking while they are on campus. The Court of Appeals held that, by forcing law schools to permit the military on campus to express its message, the Solomon Amendment unconstitutionally requires law schools to host or accommodate the military's speech. Third, although the Court of Appeals thought that the Solomon Amendment regulated speech, it held in the alternative that, if the statute regulates conduct, this conduct is expressive and regulating it unconstitutionally infringes law schools' right to engage in expressive conduct. We consider each issue in turn.

Some of this Court's leading First Amendment precedents have established the principle that freedom of speech prohibits the government from telling people what they must say. In *West Virginia Bd. of Ed. v. Barnette,* 319 U.S. 624, 642 (1943), we held unconstitutional a state law requiring schoolchildren to recite the Pledge of Allegiance and to salute the flag. And in *Wooley v. Maynard,* 430 U.S. 705, 717 (1977), we held unconstitutional another that required New Hampshire motorists to display the state motto—"Live Free or Die"—on their license plates.

The Solomon Amendment does not require any similar expression by law schools. Nonetheless, recruiting assistance provided by the schools often includes elements of speech. For example, schools may send e-mails or post notices on bulletin boards on an employer's behalf. Law schools offering such services to other recruiters must also send e-mails and post notices on behalf of the military to comply with the Solomon Amendment. As FAIR points out, these compelled statements of fact ("The U.S. Army recruiter will meet interested students in Room 123 at 11 a.m."), like compelled statements of opinion, are subject to First Amendment scrutiny.

This sort of recruiting assistance, however, is a far cry from the compelled speech in *Barnette* and *Wooley*. The Solomon Amendment, unlike the laws at issue in those cases, does not dictate the content of the speech at all, which is only "compelled" if, and to the extent, the school provides such speech for other recruiters. There is nothing in this case approaching a Government-mandated pledge or motto that the school must endorse.

The compelled speech to which the law schools point is plainly incidental to the Solomon Amendment's regulation of conduct, and "it has never been deemed an abridgment of freedom of speech or press to make a course of conduct illegal merely because the conduct was in part initiated, evidenced, or carried out by means of language, either spoken, written, or printed." Congress, for example, can prohibit employers from discriminating in hiring on the basis of race. The fact that this will require an employer to take down a sign reading "White Applicants Only" hardly means that the law should be analyzed as one regulating the employer's speech rather than conduct. Compelling a law school that sends scheduling e-mails for other recruiters to send one for a military recruiter is simply not the same as forcing a student to pledge allegiance, or forcing a Jehovah's Witness to display the motto "Live Free or Die," and it trivializes the freedom protected in *Barnette* and *Wooley* to suggest that it is.

Our compelled-speech cases are not limited to the situation in which an individual must personally speak the government's message. We have also in a number of instances limited the government's ability to force one speaker to host or accommodate another speaker's message. Relying on these precedents, the Third Circuit concluded that the Solomon Amendment unconstitutionally compels law schools to accommodate the military's message "by requiring schools to include military recruiters in the interviews and recruiting receptions the schools arrange."

The compelled-speech violation in each of our prior cases, however, resulted from the fact that the complaining speaker's own message was affected by the speech it was forced to accommodate. In this case, accommodating the military's message does not affect the law schools' speech, because the schools are not speaking when they host interviews and recruiting receptions. A law school's decision to allow recruiters on campus is not inherently expressive. A law school's recruiting services is not compelled speech because the accommodation does not sufficiently interfere with any message of the school.

The schools respond that if they treat military and nonmilitary recruiters alike in order to comply with the Solomon Amendment, they could be viewed as sending the message that they see nothing wrong with the military's policies, when they do. We rejected a similar argument in *PruneYard Shopping Center v. Robins,* 447 U.S. 74 (1980). In that case, we upheld a state law requiring a shopping center owner to allow certain expressive activities by others on its property. We explained that there was little likelihood that the views of those engaging in the expressive activities would be identified with the owner, who remained free to disassociate himself from those views and who was "not being compelled to affirm a belief in any governmentally prescribed position or view."

The same is true here. Nothing about recruiting suggests that law schools agree with any speech by recruiters, and nothing in the Solomon Amendment restricts what the law schools may say about the military's policies. We have held that high school students can appreciate the difference between speech a school sponsors and speech the school permits because legally required to do so, pursuant to an equal access policy. Surely students have not lost that ability by the time they get to law school.

Having rejected the view that the Solomon Amendment impermissibly regulates *speech,* we must still consider whether the expressive nature of the *conduct* regulated by the statute brings that conduct within the First Amendment's protection. In *O'Brien,* we recognized that some forms of "symbolic speech" were deserving of First Amendment protection. But we rejected the view that "conduct can be labeled 'speech' whenever the person engaging in the conduct intends thereby to express an idea." Instead, we have extended First Amendment protection only to conduct that is inherently expressive. In *Texas v. Johnson,* 491 U.S. 397, 406 (1989), for example, we applied *O'Brien* and held that burning the American flag was sufficiently expressive to warrant First Amendment protection.

Unlike flag burning, the conduct regulated by the Solomon Amendment is not inherently expressive. Prior to the adoption of the Solomon Amendment's equal access requirement, law schools "expressed" their disagreement with the military by treating military recruiters differently from other recruiters. But these actions were expressive only because the law schools accompanied their conduct with speech explaining it. For example, the point of requiring military interviews to be conducted on the undergraduate campus is not "overwhelmingly apparent." An observer who sees military recruiters interviewing away from the law school has no way of knowing whether the law school is expressing its disapproval of the military, all the law school's interview rooms are full, or the military recruiters decided for reasons of their own that they would rather interview someplace else.

The expressive component of a law school's actions is not created by the conduct itself but by the speech that accompanies it. The fact that such explanatory speech is necessary is strong evidence that the conduct at issue here is not so inherently expressive that it warrants protection under *O'Brien.* If combining speech and conduct were enough to create expressive conduct, a regulated party could always transform conduct into "speech" simply by talking about it. For instance, if an individual announces that he intends to express his disapproval of the Internal Revenue Service by refusing to pay his income taxes, we would have to apply *O'Brien* to determine whether the Tax Code violates the First Amendment. Neither *O'Brien* nor its progeny supports such a result.

The Solomon Amendment does not violate law schools' freedom of speech, but the First Amendment's protection extends beyond the right to speak. We have recognized a First Amendment right to associate for the purpose of speaking, which we have termed a "right of expressive association." The reason we have extended First Amendment protection in this way is clear: The right to speak is often exercised most effectively by combining one's voice with the voices of others. If the government were free to restrict individuals' ability to join together and speak, it could essentially silence views that the First Amendment is intended to protect.

FAIR argues that the Solomon Amendment violates law schools' freedom of expressive association. According to FAIR, law schools' ability to express their message that discrimination on the basis of sexual orientation is wrong is significantly affected by the presence of military recruiters on campus and the schools' obligation to assist them. Relying heavily on our decision in [*Boy Scouts of America v. Dale*, 530 U.S. 640 (2000)], the Court of Appeals agreed.

In *Dale,* we held that the Boy Scouts' freedom of expressive association was violated by New Jersey's public accommodations law, which required the organization to accept a homosexual as a scoutmaster. After determining that the Boy Scouts was an expressive association, that "the forced inclusion of Dale would significantly affect its expression," and that the State's interests did not justify this intrusion, we concluded that the Boy Scouts' First Amendment rights were violated.

The Solomon Amendment, however, does not similarly affect a law school's associational rights. To comply with the statute, law schools must allow military recruiters on campus and assist them in whatever way the school chooses to assist other employers. Law schools therefore "associate" with military recruiters in the sense that they interact with them. But recruiters are not part of the law school. Recruiters are, by definition, outsiders who come onto campus for the limited purpose of trying to hire students—not to become members of the school's expressive association. This distinction is critical. Unlike the public accommodations law in *Dale,* the Solomon Amendment does not force a law school "to accept members it does not desire." The law schools *say* that allowing military recruiters equal access impairs their own expression by requiring them to associate with the recruiters, but just as saying conduct is undertaken for expressive purposes cannot make it symbolic speech, so too a speaker cannot "erect a shield" against laws requiring access "simply by asserting" that mere association "would impair its message."

The Solomon Amendment has no effect on a law school's associational rights. Students and faculty are free to associate to voice their disapproval of the military's message; nothing about the statute affects the composition of the group by making group membership less desirable. The Solomon Amendment therefore does not violate a law school's First Amendment rights. A military recruiter's mere presence on campus does not violate a law school's right to associate, regardless of how repugnant the law school considers the recruiter's message.

In this case, FAIR has attempted to stretch a number of First Amendment doctrines well beyond the sort of activities these doctrines protect. The law schools object to having to treat military recruiters like other recruiters, but that regulation of conduct does not violate the First Amendment.

Because Congress could require law schools to provide equal access to military recruiters without violating the schools' freedoms of speech or association, the Court of Appeals erred in holding that the Solomon Amendment likely violates the First Amendment. We therefore reverse the judgment of the Third Circuit and remand the case for further proceedings consistent with this opinion.

Points for Discussion

1. **Why did the law schools lose?** Can you articulate the various arguments the law schools made for why the Solomon Amendment abridged their First Amendment rights? Can you then articulate why the Supreme Court rejected these arguments?

2. **An example of a government action abridging speech: denying the incentive to speak.** In *United States v. National Treasury Employees Union*, 513 U.S. 454 (1995), the Court considered a federal law that "broadly prohibits federal employees from accepting any compensation for making speeches or writing articles," regardless of whether "the speech or article [or] the person or group paying for it has any connection with the employee's official duties." For example, the law would prohibit a mail handler for the Postal Service from receiving an honorarium for speaking about the Quaker religion.

   Although this law did not bar the federal employees from speaking, the Court nevertheless found that it abridged their free speech rights by denying them the incentive to speak:

   > Although [the law] neither prohibits any speech nor discriminates among speakers based on the content or viewpoint of their messages, its prohibition on compensation unquestionably imposes a significant burden on expressive activity. Publishers compensate authors because compensation provides a significant incentive toward more expression. By denying respondents that incentive, the honoraria ban induces

> them to curtail their expression if they wish to continue working for the Government.

While we are on the topic of denying economic incentives to speak, you might want to consider whether the government can force a convicted criminal to disgorge any compensation he receives for selling the story of his crime. *See Simon & Schuster, Inc. v. Members of N.Y. State Crime Victims Bd.*, 502 U.S. 105 (1991).

3. **An example of a government action not abridging speech: censuring an elected official with no consequences attached.** In *Houston Community College System v. Wilson*, 595 U.S. 468 (2022), the board of trustees of a community college system adopted a resolution censuring one of its board members, David Wilson, for conduct that was "not consistent with the best interests of the College" and "not only inappropriate, but reprehensible." No other punishment was imposed on the board member. Wilson sued, claiming that the censure resolution violated his First Amendment rights because it was issued in retaliation for his speech.

In rejecting Wilson's argument, the Court first noted that history was not on his side. To the contrary, there is a longstanding tradition in this country of elected bodies' censuring their members, and there was no evidence that "a purely verbal censure analogous to Mr. Wilson's has ever been widely considered offensive to the First Amendment." The Court also noted that contemporary jurisprudence requires a plaintiff in a First Amendment retaliation case to show that the government took an "adverse action" in response to his speech. Under the circumstances of the case, the Court concluded that Wilson had failed to show that the board's censure constituted a "materially adverse" action triggering the First Amendment:

> The censure at issue before us was a form of speech by elected representatives. It concerned the public conduct of another elected representative. Everyone involved was an equal member of the same deliberative body. As it comes to us, too, the censure did not prevent Mr. Wilson from doing his job, it did not deny him any privilege of office, and Mr. Wilson does not allege it was defamatory. At least in these circumstances, we do not see how the Board's censure could have materially deterred an elected official like Mr. Wilson from exercising his own right to speak.

The Court was careful to point out that verbal reprimands or censures in other contexts could give rise to a First Amendment retaliation claim, such as government reprimands or censures of students, employees, or licensees.

D. "No Law": Which Abridgments of Speech Are Unconstitutional?

The First Amendment could not be clearer. It states that Congress shall make "no law" abridging the freedom of speech, and you learned earlier in this chapter that this prohibition extends beyond Congress to all levels of government.

But can "no law" really mean "no law"?

The short answer is no. Indeed, if you reflect even briefly upon the question, it quickly becomes apparent that the government can and does abridge speech. There are laws punishing perjury and false advertising. Tort law imposes liability for defaming another or disclosing a person's intimate private facts. And there are myriad laws restricting speech for purposes of ensuring tranquility (*e.g.*, no rallies in the middle of the night), order (*e.g.*, no parades in the middle of a highway), and aesthetics (*e.g.*, no billboards on top of suburban homes).

In a landmark 1919 opinion, Justice Oliver Wendell Holmes dismantled the argument for an absolutist interpretation of the First Amendment with a single sentence: "The most stringent protection of free speech would not protect a man in falsely shouting fire in a theatre and causing a panic."[16]

But where does that leave us? If some abridgments of speech are constitutional and others are not, how are judges supposed to separate the wheat of lawful abridgments from the chaff of unlawful ones? That topic will occupy us for the remaining chapters on freedom of speech.

Point for Discussion

1. **Justice Hugo Black's absolutism and its limits.** Justice Hugo Black famously contended that the First Amendment's command that "no law" shall abridge speech meant exactly what it said: that the government may never abridge speech. Justice Black's absolutism might seem admirable for its unwavering commitment to free speech, but is it feasible in practice?

   Indeed, Justice Black himself voted to uphold some abridgments of speech. For example, in two Vietnam era cases, he voted to uphold the conviction of a defendant who wore a jacket that said "Fuck the Draft" and to uphold a public school's suspension of students who wore black armbands to protest the war. How did Justice Black square his votes in these cases with his absolutist view of the First Amendment? You might consider that question when we get to those cases.

16 *Schenck v. United States*, 249 U.S. 47, 52 (1919).

Test Your Knowledge

To assess your understanding of the material in this chapter, click here to take a quiz.

Chapter Four

When Is an Abridgment of Speech Unlawful?

A Roadmap for Analyzing Free Speech Cases

How are judges supposed to decide whether an abridgment of speech violates the First Amendment? If they followed the literal meaning of the Free Speech Clause—"Congress shall make no law . . . abridging the freedom of speech"—they would find all abridgments of speech unconstitutional. But such an absolutist approach, as the previous chapter observed, seems neither feasible nor desirable. The justices are unlikely to hold that the government cannot punish perjurers or people who spray-paint government buildings. The unequivocal command that "no law" shall abridge speech captures the gravity with which the Framers viewed abridgments of speech. But it is not a workable principle in practice.

If the text is unilluminating, where else can judges find guidance for resolving free speech cases? A judge committed to an "originalist" interpretation of the Constitution would say that they should seek guidance from either the Framers' intent or the original public meaning of the First Amendment's words. We will encounter Supreme Court justices using this approach in some of the Court's religious liberty opinions. It is less common in the Court's free speech cases.[1] Commentators suggest that this is because the legislative history behind the Free Speech Clause is too sparse to provide meaningful guidance. Those who adopted the First Amendment certainly manifested an appreciation for freedom of speech. But a distant general appreciation is not sufficient to answer specific contemporary questions.

Without adequate guidance from either the text or history, Supreme Court justices have instead developed their own method for determining which abridgments of speech are unconstitutional. Rather than relying on an ad hoc process in which

[1] A diehard originalist like Justice Clarence Thomas does occasionally make originalist arguments in free speech cases, but other justices have not tended to follow his lead. For example, in *Mahanoy Area School District v. B.L.*, 141 S. Ct. 2038, 2059 (2021) (Thomas, J., dissenting), Justice Thomas lamented the Court's failure to consider the state of students' free speech rights at the time the Fourteenth Amendment was ratified (because the First Amendment applied to the defendant school district through its incorporation into the Fourteenth Amendment).

each fact pattern is considered in isolation, the justices instead have built a complex framework of rules to help guide them in their decision making. This framework did not come into existence all at once. To the contrary, it has evolved over many decades, beginning with the Court's inaugural First Amendment opinions in the early 20th century. This can create confusion because earlier decisions sometimes use terminology that differs from more recent opinions. Adding to this confusion is the fact that the framework continues to evolve. Each new Supreme Court opinion on freedom of speech alters the framework. These alterations are usually modest and incremental, but sometimes they make major structural changes.

This chapter provides a roadmap of the Supreme Court's framework for analyzing free speech issues. The map seeks to give you the big picture of the framework—the forest and not the trees. The remaining chapters on freedom of speech will fill in the details about individual trees.

Before beginning this journey, it is important to emphasize that this roadmap comes into play only if a party first alleges that (1) the government (2) has abridged (3) his or her freedom of speech. In other words, the issues covered in the previous chapter about *who* the First Amendment restrains, *what* the Free Speech Clause protects, and *when* speech has been abridged are all preliminary questions that need to be answered before a court will consider whether an abridgment of speech is unconstitutional. If the government has not abridged speech, the First Amendment has not been implicated, and no further analysis is necessary.

This chapter organizes the framework for analyzing free speech cases around two core questions: Why is the government regulating speech, and how is the government regulating speech?

A. Why Is the Government Regulating Speech? Because of Its Message or Regardless of Its Message: Content-Based vs. Content-Neutral Regulations of Speech

In free speech jurisprudence, as in other areas of constitutional law, the primary determinant of whether a law is likely to be upheld is the level of scrutiny the Supreme Court applies in assessing the law's constitutionality. Some laws are subject to "strict scrutiny," the Court's most demanding level of review. Under strict scrutiny, the government has the burden of proving that a law is necessary to further a compelling governmental interest. The government is rarely able to satisfy this demanding standard, and the vast bulk of laws reviewed under strict scrutiny are found unconstitutional.

At the opposite end of the spectrum is "rational basis" review. Under this test, the person challenging a law bears the burden of proving that the law is not rationally related to furthering a legitimate government interest. While the requirements of being "rationally related" to a "legitimate" interest might sound rigorous, they have been interpreted in a manner that has rendered them largely toothless. Consequently, rational basis review tends to be highly deferential to the government, and almost all laws subjected to it are upheld. Justice David Souter described rational basis scrutiny as "a paradigm of judicial restraint."[2]

heightened

Between strict scrutiny and rational basis review is the appropriately named "intermediate scrutiny." Under this level of scrutiny, the government bears the burden of showing that a law is substantially related to furthering an important or significant governmental interest. We will flesh out these terms later in this chapter. Suffice it to say for now that laws reviewed under intermediate scrutiny, as you have likely surmised, are neither given a free pass nor routinely struck down. Instead, they have a reasonable chance of being either upheld or struck down depending on the specific nature of the law and the context in which the law is being applied.[3]

In its First Amendment jurisprudence, the Supreme Court mostly uses either strict or intermediate scrutiny to determine whether laws abridging speech are constitutional. Unlike in other areas of constitutional law, the Court rarely uses the rational basis test in free speech cases. The Court's reluctance to use this test suggests the seriousness with which the Court views abridgments of speech. The justices have determined that almost all laws abridging freedom of speech should get heightened scrutiny—whether strict or intermediate—and not the highly deferential rational basis review.

The key question underlying many First Amendment cases is which level of scrutiny—strict or intermediate—should be used to evaluate any given abridgment of speech. The choice of scrutiny will greatly influence the likelihood of whether the government action will be upheld.

As you are about to learn, the primary determinant of whether a court will use strict or intermediate scrutiny is whether a government regulation of speech is classified as content-based or content-neutral. Content-based regulations are evaluated under strict scrutiny and are usually, though not always, struck down. Content-neutral regulations are evaluated under intermediate scrutiny and are sometimes upheld and sometimes struck down depending on the specific law and facts.

As the name implies, content-based regulations of speech regulate speech because of its content or message. This is true of both a law that bans speech on an entire

---

2 *United States v. Lopez*, 514 U.S. 549, 604 (1995) (Souter, J., dissenting).

3 In a 2021 opinion, the Supreme Court clarified that there is a fourth level of review, called "exacting scrutiny," which is less demanding than strict scrutiny but more demanding than intermediate scrutiny. This level of scrutiny applies in only limited contexts, so we will not focus on it in this broad overview of First Amendment jurisprudence. We will discuss it later in the chapter.

subject area (*e.g.*, no one may publicly discuss the topic of abortion) and a law that restricts the expression of viewpoints on one side of an issue but not the other (*e.g.*, no one may express views supporting abortion rights, but people may express views opposing abortion rights). The former is referred to as "subject matter" regulation of speech and the latter as "viewpoint discrimination." Both are considered content-based, receive strict scrutiny, and are very likely to be struck down. The Supreme Court is especially leery of laws that discriminate based on viewpoint and treats these laws as virtually per se unconstitutional.[4]

The Court applies rigorous scrutiny to content-based laws because these laws raise the specter of government censorship. As the Court explained in *Turner Broadcasting System v. FCC*, "Laws of this sort pose the inherent risk that the Government seeks not to advance a legitimate regulatory goal, but to suppress unpopular ideas or information or manipulate the public debate through coercion rather than persuasion."[5]

The Court's skepticism of content-based laws was captured in *Police Department of Chicago v. Mosley*,[6] a case concerning a Chicago ordinance that prohibited demonstrations or picketing within 150 feet of a primary or secondary school while the school was in session but made an exception for peaceful labor picketing of a school involved in a labor dispute. In explaining its reasoning for striking down the ordinance, the Court emphasized that the ability to demonstrate near a school turned on the content of the picketer's message:

> The central problem with Chicago's ordinance is that it describes permissible picketing in terms of its subject matter. Peaceful picketing on the subject of a school's labor-management dispute is permitted, but all other peaceful picketing is prohibited. The operative distinction is the message on a picket sign. But, above all else, the First Amendment means that government has no power to restrict expression because of its message, its ideas, its subject matter, or its content. To permit the continued building of our politics and culture, and to assure self-fulfillment for each individual, our people are guaranteed the right to express any thought, free from government censorship. The essence of this forbidden censorship is content control. Any restriction on expressive activity because of its content would completely undercut the "profound national commitment to the principle that debate on public issues should be uninhibited, robust, and wide-open."

---

4 *Rosenberger v. Rector and Visitors of Univ. of Va.*, 515 U.S. 819, 829–30 (1995) ("When the government targets not subject matter but particular views taken by speakers on a subject, the violation of the First Amendment is all the more blatant. Viewpoint discrimination is thus an egregious form of content discrimination.").

5 *Turner Broad. Sys. v. Federal Commc'ns Comm'n*, 512 U.S. 622, 641 (1994).

6 *Police Dep't of Chicago v. Mosley*, 408 U.S. 92 (1972).

In contrast to content-based laws, content-neutral laws regulate speech without regard to its message. For example, imagine a law that prohibited the posting of signs on the walls of government buildings. This law, which was likely enacted to combat visual clutter and protect the appearance of government buildings, is content-neutral. It bans the posting of signs on government buildings regardless of their message. The signs might be praising the government or criticizing it, advertising chewing gum or an upcoming rock concert, or offering a reward to anyone who finds a lost dog. All these signs are prohibited under this content-neutral regulation.

The Supreme Court applies the more forgiving intermediate scrutiny to content-neutral laws. This likely reflects the justices' recognition that governments need flexibility to regulate speech for purposes of order, tranquility, and aesthetics. For example, governments would understandably want to forbid people from handing out leaflets in the middle of a highway or holding rallies in the middle of the night. At the same time, the intermediate scrutiny test does not give content-neutral laws a free pass. That is because the justices recognize that even content-neutral laws can severely affect free speech interests. Just imagine a law that prohibited all leafletting, rallies, and parades.

The differing levels of scrutiny applied to content-based and content-neutral regulations make the initial determination of whether a law is content-based or content-neutral a vitally important aspect of any First Amendment analysis. In many cases, it is readily apparent how a law should be classified. A law that punishes people for criticizing a president's climate change policy is clearly content-based. A law that forbids late night rallies in a public park will almost certainly be considered content-neutral absent an underlying illicit motive.

But sometimes the classification of a speech regulation is more elusive. In these instances, the justices have had to struggle with, and sometimes disagree about, how to determine whether a law is content-based or content-neutral. Should the answer, for example, depend solely on whether the law "on its face" (meaning the text of the law) treats speech differently based on its content, or is the critical question whether the law raises the specter of government censorship (*i.e.*, that the government is trying to suppress a particular message or idea)? Conversely, what should the Court do if the text of a law is facially neutral, but there is evidence that the law was enacted to suppress the content of speech? Imagine, for example, a law that banned any expressive activities within 150 feet of an abortion clinic entrance. This law is facially content-neutral. It applies to any expression—pro-life, pro-choice, pro-chocolate—occurring within 150 feet of an abortion clinic. But what if the only speech that typically occurs outside of abortion clinics is anti-abortion speech, and the legislative history indicates that the legislators enacted the law to suppress this speech?

Even when the justices agree that a law is content-based, they do not always agree that the law should automatically receive strict scrutiny. Some justices believe that content-based laws should be subject to strict scrutiny only when there is evidence that the government was trying to suppress certain ideas or viewpoints. If the specter of government censorship is absent, these justices would apply intermediate scrutiny even to a law that makes content-based distinctions about which speech is regulated.

The justices' struggles over how to classify speech regulations and which regulations should receive strict scrutiny were on full display in a case concerning a seemingly innocuous city ordinance about the placement of signs.

Reed v. Town of Gilbert

Supreme Court of the United States, 2015
576 U.S. 155

JUSTICE THOMAS delivered the opinion of the Court.

The town of Gilbert, Arizona (or Town), has adopted a comprehensive code governing the manner in which people may display outdoor signs. The Sign Code identifies various categories of signs based on the type of information they convey, then subjects each category to different restrictions. One of the categories is "Temporary Directional Signs Relating to a Qualifying Event," loosely defined as signs directing the public to a meeting of a nonprofit group. The Code imposes more stringent restrictions on these signs than it does on signs conveying other messages. We hold that these provisions are content-based regulations of speech that cannot survive strict scrutiny.

The Sign Code prohibits the display of outdoor signs anywhere within the Town without a permit, but it then exempts 23 categories of signs from that requirement. These exemptions include everything from bazaar signs to flying banners. Three categories of exempt signs are particularly relevant here.

The first is "Ideological Signs." This category includes any "sign communicating a message or ideas for noncommercial purposes." Of the three categories discussed here, the Code treats ideological signs most favorably, allowing them to be up to 20 square feet in area and to be placed in all "zoning districts" without time limits.

The second category is "Political Signs." This includes any "temporary sign designed to influence the outcome of an election called by a public body." The Code treats these signs less favorably than ideological signs. The Code allows the placement of political signs up to 16 square feet on residential property and up to 32 square feet on nonresidential property, undeveloped municipal property, and "rights-of-way." These signs may be displayed up to 60 days before a primary election and up to 15 days following a general election.

The third category is "Temporary Directional Signs Relating to a Qualifying Event." This includes any "Temporary Sign intended to direct pedestrians, motorists, and other passersby to a 'qualifying event.' " A "qualifying event" is defined as any "assembly, gathering, activity, or meeting sponsored, arranged, or promoted by a religious, charitable, community service, educational, or other similar non-profit organization." The Code treats temporary directional signs even less favorably than political signs. Temporary directional signs may be no larger than six square feet. They may be placed on private property or on a public right-of-way, but no more than four signs may be placed on a single property at any time. And, they may be displayed no more than 12 hours before the "qualifying event" and no more than 1 hour afterward.

Petitioners Good News Community Church (Church) and its pastor, Clyde Reed, wish to advertise the time and location of their Sunday church services. The Church is a small, cash-strapped entity that owns no building, so it holds its services at elementary schools or other locations in or near the Town. In order to inform the public about its services, which are held in a variety of different locations, the Church began placing 15 to 20 temporary signs around the Town, frequently in the public right-of-way abutting the street. The signs typically displayed the Church's name, along with the time and location of the upcoming service. Church members would post the signs early in the day on Saturday and then remove them around midday on Sunday. The display of these signs requires little money and manpower, and thus has proved to be an economical and effective way for the Church to let the community know where its services are being held each week.

The temporary directional sign at issue in *Reed v. Town of Gilbert*

This practice caught the attention of the Town's Sign Code compliance manager, who twice cited the Church for violating the Code. The first citation noted that the Church exceeded the time limits for displaying its temporary directional signs.

The second citation referred to the same problem, along with the Church's failure to include the date of the event on the signs. Town officials even confiscated one of the Church's signs, which Reed had to retrieve from the municipal offices.

Petitioners filed a complaint in the United States District Court for the District of Arizona, arguing that the Sign Code abridged their freedom of speech in violation of the First and Fourteenth Amendments. The District Court granted summary judgment in favor of the Town. The Court of Appeals affirmed, holding that the Code's sign categories were content neutral. The court concluded that "the distinctions between Temporary Directional Signs, Ideological Signs, and Political Signs are based on objective factors relevant to Gilbert's creation of the specific exemption from the permit requirement and do not otherwise consider the substance of the sign." Relying on this Court's decision in *Hill v. Colorado,* 530 U.S. 703 (2000), the Court of Appeals concluded that the Sign Code is content neutral. As the court explained, "Gilbert did not adopt its regulation of speech because it disagreed with the message conveyed" and its "interests in regulating temporary signs are unrelated to the content of the sign." Accordingly, the court believed that the Code was "content-neutral as that term has been defined by the Supreme Court." In light of that determination, it applied a lower level of scrutiny to the Sign Code and concluded that the law did not violate the First Amendment.

We granted certiorari and now reverse.

The First Amendment, applicable to the States through the Fourteenth Amendment, prohibits the enactment of laws "abridging the freedom of speech." Under that Clause, a government, including a municipal government vested with state authority, "has no power to restrict expression because of its message, its ideas, its subject matter, or its content." Content-based laws—those that target speech based on its communicative content—are presumptively unconstitutional and may be justified only if the government proves that they are narrowly tailored to serve compelling state interests.

Government regulation of speech is content based if a law applies to particular speech because of the topic discussed or the idea or message expressed. This commonsense meaning of the phrase "content based" requires a court to consider whether a regulation of speech "on its face" draws distinctions based on the message a speaker conveys. Some facial distinctions based on a message are obvious, defining regulated speech by particular subject matter, and others are more subtle, defining regulated speech by its function or purpose. Both are distinctions drawn based on the message a speaker conveys, and, therefore, are subject to strict scrutiny.

Our precedents have also recognized a separate and additional category of laws that, though facially content neutral, will be considered content-based regulations of speech: laws that cannot be "justified without reference to the content of the regulated speech," or that were adopted by the government "because of disagreement with the message the speech conveys." Those laws, like those that are content based on their face, must also satisfy strict scrutiny.

The Town's Sign Code is content based on its face. It defines "Temporary Directional Signs" on the basis of whether a sign conveys the message of directing the public to church or some other "qualifying event." It defines "Political Signs" on the basis of whether a sign's message is "designed to influence the outcome of an election." And it defines "Ideological Signs" on the basis of whether a sign "communicates a message or ideas" that do not fit within the Code's other categories. It then subjects each of these categories to different restrictions.

The restrictions in the Sign Code that apply to any given sign thus depend entirely on the communicative content of the sign. If a sign informs its reader of the time and place a book club will discuss John Locke's Two Treatises of Government, that sign will be treated differently from a sign expressing the view that one should vote for one of Locke's followers in an upcoming election, and both signs will be treated differently from a sign expressing an ideological view rooted in Locke's theory of government. More to the point, the Church's signs inviting people to attend its worship services are treated differently from signs conveying other types of ideas. On its face, the Sign Code is a content-based regulation of speech. We thus have no need to consider the government's justifications or purposes for enacting the Code to determine whether it is subject to strict scrutiny.

In reaching the contrary conclusion, the Court of Appeals offered several theories to explain why the Town's Sign Code should be deemed content neutral. None is persuasive.

The Court of Appeals first determined that the Sign Code was content neutral because the Town "did not adopt its regulation of speech based on disagreement with the message conveyed," and its justifications for regulating temporary directional signs were "unrelated to the content of the sign." In its brief to this Court, the United States similarly contends that a sign regulation is content neutral—even if it expressly draws distinctions based on the sign's communicative content—if those distinctions can be "justified without reference to the content of the regulated speech."

But this analysis skips the crucial first step in the content-neutrality analysis: determining whether the law is content neutral on its face. A law that is content based on its face is subject to strict scrutiny regardless of the government's benign motive, content-neutral justification, or lack of "animus toward the ideas contained" in the regulated speech. We have thus made clear that "illicit legislative intent is not the *sine qua non* of a violation of the First Amendment," and a party opposing the government "need adduce no evidence of an improper censorial motive." Although "a content-based purpose may be sufficient in certain circumstances to show that a regulation is content based, it is not necessary." In other words, an innocuous justification cannot transform a facially content-based law into one that is content neutral.

That is why we have repeatedly considered whether a law is content neutral on its face *before* turning to the law's justification or purpose. Because strict scrutiny applies either when a law is content based on its face or when the purpose and justification for the law are content based, a court must evaluate each question before it concludes that the law is content neutral and thus subject to a lower level of scrutiny.

The Court of Appeals and the United States misunderstand our decision in *Ward v. Rock Against Racism*, 491 U.S. 781 (1989), as suggesting that a government's purpose is relevant even when a law is content based on its face. That is incorrect. *Ward* had nothing to say about facially content-based restrictions because it involved a facially content-*neutral* ban on the use, in a city-owned music venue, of sound amplification systems not provided by the city. In that context, we looked to governmental motive, including whether the government had regulated speech "because of disagreement" with its message, and whether the regulation was "justified without reference to the content of the speech." But *Ward's* framework "applies only if a statute is content neutral." Its rules thus operate "to protect speech," not "to restrict it."

The First Amendment requires no less. Innocent motives do not eliminate the danger of censorship presented by a facially content-based statute, as future government officials may one day wield such statutes to suppress disfavored speech. That is why the First Amendment expressly targets the operation of the laws—*i.e.,* the "abridg[ement] of speech"—rather than merely the motives of those who enacted them. "The vice of content-based legislation is not that it is always used for invidious, thought-control purposes, but that it lends itself to use for those purposes."

The Court of Appeals next reasoned that the Sign Code was content neutral because it "does not mention any idea or viewpoint, let alone single one out for differential treatment." It reasoned that, for the purpose of the Code provisions, "it makes no difference which candidate is supported, who sponsors the event, or what ideological perspective is asserted."

The Town seizes on this reasoning, insisting that "content based" is a term of art that "should be applied flexibly" with the goal of protecting "viewpoints and ideas from government censorship or favoritism." In the Town's view, a sign regulation that "does not censor or favor particular viewpoints or ideas" cannot be content based. The Sign Code allegedly passes this test because its treatment of temporary directional signs does not raise any concerns that the government is "endorsing or suppressing ideas or viewpoints," and the provisions for political signs and ideological signs "are neutral as to particular ideas or viewpoints" within those categories.

This analysis conflates two distinct but related limitations that the First Amendment places on government regulation of speech. Government discrimination among viewpoints—or the regulation of speech based on "the specific motivating ideology or the opinion or perspective of the speaker"—is a "more blatant" and "egregious form of content discrimination." But it is well established that "the First Amendment's hostility to content-based regulation extends not only to restrictions on particular viewpoints, but also to prohibition of public discussion of an entire topic."

Thus, a speech regulation targeted at specific subject matter is content based even if it does not discriminate among viewpoints within that subject matter. For example, a law banning the use of sound trucks for political speech—and only political speech—would be a content-based regulation, even if it imposed no limits on the political viewpoints that could be expressed. The Town's Sign Code likewise singles out specific subject matter for differential treatment, even if it does not target viewpoints within that subject matter. Ideological messages are given more favorable treatment than messages concerning a political candidate, which are themselves given more favorable treatment than messages announcing an assembly of like-minded individuals. That is a paradigmatic example of content-based discrimination.

b/c it targets a specific content makes it content-based

Finally, the Court of Appeals characterized the Sign Code's distinctions as turning on "the content-neutral elements of who is speaking through the sign and whether and when an event is occurring." That analysis is mistaken on both factual and legal grounds.

To start, the Sign Code's distinctions are not speaker based. The restrictions for political, ideological, and temporary event signs apply equally no matter who sponsors them.

In any case, the fact that a distinction is speaker based does not, as the Court of Appeals seemed to believe, automatically render the distinction content neutral. Because "speech restrictions based on the identity of the speaker are all too often simply a means to control content," we have insisted that "laws favoring some speakers over others demand strict scrutiny when the legislature's speaker preference reflects a content preference."

Because the Town's Sign Code imposes content-based restrictions on speech, those provisions can stand only if they survive strict scrutiny, "which requires the Government to prove that the restriction furthers a compelling interest and is narrowly tailored to achieve that interest." Thus, it is the Town's burden to demonstrate that the Code's differentiation between temporary directional signs and other types of signs, such as political signs and ideological signs, furthers a compelling governmental interest and is narrowly tailored to that end.

has to survive strict scrutiny

The Town cannot do so. It has offered only two governmental interests in support of the distinctions the Sign Code draws: preserving the Town's aesthetic appeal and traffic safety. Assuming for the sake of argument that those are compelling governmental interests, the Code's distinctions fail as hopelessly underinclusive.

Starting with the preservation of aesthetics, temporary directional signs are "no greater an eyesore," than ideological or political ones. Yet the Code allows unlimited proliferation of larger ideological signs while strictly limiting the number, size, and duration of smaller directional ones. The Town cannot claim that placing strict limits on temporary directional signs is necessary to beautify the Town while at the same time allowing unlimited numbers of other types of signs that create the same problem.

The Town similarly has not shown that limiting temporary directional signs is necessary to eliminate threats to traffic safety, but that limiting other types of signs is not. The Town has offered no reason to believe that directional signs pose a greater threat to safety than do ideological or political signs. If anything, a sharply worded ideological sign seems more likely to distract a driver than a sign directing the public to a nearby church meeting.

In light of this underinclusiveness, the Town has not met its burden to prove that its Sign Code is narrowly tailored to further a compelling government interest. Because a "law cannot be regarded as protecting an interest of the highest order, and thus as justifying a restriction on truthful speech, when it leaves appreciable damage to that supposedly vital interest unprohibited," the Sign Code fails strict scrutiny.

Our decision today will not prevent governments from enacting effective sign laws. The Town asserts that an "absolutist" content-neutrality rule would render "virtually all distinctions in sign laws subject to strict scrutiny," but that is not the case. Not "all distinctions" are subject to strict scrutiny, only *content-based* ones are. Laws that are *content neutral* are instead subject to lesser scrutiny.

The Town has ample content-neutral options available to resolve problems with safety and aesthetics. For example, its current Code regulates many aspects of signs that have nothing to do with a sign's message: size, building materials, lighting, moving parts, and portability. And on public property, the Town may go a long way toward entirely forbidding the posting of signs, so long as it does so in an evenhanded, content-neutral manner.

We reverse the judgment of the Court of Appeals and remand the case for proceedings consistent with this opinion.

JUSTICE ALITO, with whom JUSTICE KENNEDY and JUSTICE SOTOMAYOR join, concurring.

I join the opinion of the Court but add a few words of further explanation.

As the Court shows, the regulations at issue in this case are replete with content-based distinctions, and as a result they must satisfy strict scrutiny. This does not mean, however, that municipalities are powerless to enact and enforce reasonable sign regulations. I will not attempt to provide anything like a comprehensive list, but here are some rules that would not be content based:

- Rules regulating the size of signs. These rules may distinguish among signs based on any content-neutral criteria, including any relevant criteria listed below.

- Rules regulating the locations in which signs may be placed. These rules may distinguish between free-standing signs and those attached to buildings.

- Rules distinguishing between lighted and unlighted signs.

- Rules distinguishing between signs with fixed messages and electronic signs with messages that change.

- Rules that distinguish between the placement of signs on private and public property.

- Rules distinguishing between the placement of signs on commercial and residential property.

- Rules distinguishing between on-premises and off-premises signs.

- Rules restricting the total number of signs allowed per mile of roadway.

- Rules imposing time restrictions on signs advertising a one-time event. Rules of this nature do not discriminate based on topic or subject and are akin to rules restricting the times within which oral speech or music is allowed.

Properly understood, today's decision will not prevent cities from regulating signs in a way that fully protects public safety and serves legitimate esthetic objectives.

JUSTICE BREYER, concurring in the judgment.

I join Justice Kagan's separate opinion. Like Justice Kagan I believe that categories alone cannot satisfactorily resolve the legal problem before us. The First Amendment requires greater judicial sensitivity both to the Amendment's expressive objectives and to the public's legitimate need for regulation than a simple recitation of categories, such as "content discrimination" and "strict scrutiny," would permit. In my view, the category "content discrimination" is better considered in many contexts, including here, as a rule of thumb, rather than as an automatic "strict scrutiny" trigger, leading to almost certain legal condemnation.

To use content discrimination to trigger strict scrutiny sometimes makes perfect sense. There are cases in which the Court has found content discrimination an unconstitutional method for suppressing a viewpoint. And there are cases where the Court has found content discrimination to reveal that rules governing a traditional public forum are, in fact, not a neutral way of fairly managing the forum in the interest of all speakers. In these types of cases, strict scrutiny is often appropriate, and content discrimination has thus served a useful purpose.

But content discrimination, while helping courts to identify unconstitutional suppression of expression, cannot and should not *always* trigger strict scrutiny. To use the presence of content discrimination automatically to trigger strict scrutiny and thereby call into play a strong presumption against constitutionality goes too far. That is because virtually all government activities involve speech, many of which involve the regulation of speech. Regulatory programs almost always require content discrimination. And to hold that such content discrimination triggers strict scrutiny is to write a recipe for judicial management of ordinary government regulatory activity.

Consider a few examples of speech regulated by government that inevitably involve content discrimination, but where a strong presumption against constitutionality has no place. Consider governmental regulation of securities (requirements for content that must be included in a registration statement); of energy conservation labeling-practices, (requirements for content that must be included on labels of certain consumer electronics); of prescription drugs, (requiring a prescription drug label to bear the symbol "Rx only"); of doctor-patient confidentiality (requiring confidentiality of certain medical records, but allowing a physician to disclose that the patient has HIV to the patient's spouse or sexual partner); of commercial airplane briefings (requiring pilots to ensure that each passenger has been briefed on flight procedures, such as seatbelt fastening); of signs at petting zoos (requiring petting zoos to post a sign at every exit "strongly recommending that persons wash their hands upon exiting the petting zoo area"); and so on.

I recognize that the Court could escape the problem by watering down the force of the presumption against constitutionality that "strict scrutiny" normally carries with it. But, in my view, doing so will weaken the First Amendment's protection in instances where "strict scrutiny" should apply in full force.

The better approach is to generally treat content discrimination as a strong reason weighing against the constitutionality of a rule where a traditional public forum, or where viewpoint discrimination, is threatened, but elsewhere treat it as a rule of thumb, finding it a helpful, but not determinative legal tool, in an appropriate case, to determine the strength of a justification. I would use content discrimination as a supplement to a more basic analysis, which, tracking most of our First Amendment cases, asks whether the regulation at issue works harm to First Amendment interests that is disproportionate in light of the relevant regulatory objectives. Answering this question requires examining the seriousness of the harm to speech, the importance of the countervailing objectives, the extent to which the law will achieve those objectives, and whether there are other, less restrictive ways of doing so. Admittedly, this approach does not have the simplicity of a mechanical use of categories. But it does permit the government to regulate speech in numerous instances where the voters have authorized the government to regulate and where courts should hesitate to substitute judicial judgment for that of administrators.

Here, regulation of signage along the roadside, for purposes of safety and beautification is at issue. There is no traditional public forum nor do I find any general effort to censor a particular viewpoint. Consequently, the specific regulation at issue does not warrant "strict scrutiny." Nonetheless, for the reasons that Justice Kagan sets forth, I believe that the Town of Gilbert's regulatory rules violate the First Amendment. I consequently concur in the Court's judgment only.

JUSTICE KAGAN, with whom JUSTICE GINSBURG and JUSTICE BREYER join, concurring in the judgment.

Countless cities and towns across America have adopted ordinances regulating the posting of signs, while exempting certain categories of signs based on their subject matter. For example, some municipalities generally prohibit illuminated signs in residential neighborhoods, but lift that ban for signs that identify the address of a home or the name of its owner or occupant. In other municipalities, safety signs such as "Blind Pedestrian Crossing" and "Hidden Driveway" can be posted without a permit, even as other permanent signs require one. Elsewhere, historic site markers—for example, "George Washington Slept Here"—are also exempt from general regulations. And similarly, the federal Highway Beautification Act limits signs along interstate highways unless, for instance, they direct travelers to "scenic and historical attractions" or advertise free coffee.

Given the Court's analysis, many sign ordinances of that kind are now in jeopardy. Although the majority insists that applying strict scrutiny to all such ordinances is "essential" to protecting First Amendment freedoms, I find it challenging to understand why that is so. This Court's decisions articulate two important and related reasons for subjecting content-based speech regulations to the most exacting standard of review. The first is "to preserve an uninhibited marketplace of ideas in which truth will ultimately prevail." The second is to ensure that the government has not regulated speech "based on hostility—or favoritism—towards the underlying message expressed." Yet the subject-matter exemptions included in many sign ordinances do not implicate those concerns. Allowing residents, say, to install a light bulb over "name and address" signs but no others does not distort the marketplace of ideas. Nor does that different treatment give rise to an inference of impermissible government motive.

We apply strict scrutiny to facially content-based regulations of speech, in keeping with the rationales just described, when there is any "realistic possibility that official suppression of ideas is afoot." That is always the case when the regulation facially differentiates on the basis of viewpoint. It is also the case (except in non-public or limited public forums) when a law restricts "discussion of an entire topic" in public debate. We have stated that "if the marketplace of ideas is to remain free and open, governments must not be allowed to choose which issues are worth discussing or debating." And we have recognized that such subject-matter restrictions, even though viewpoint-neutral on their face, may "suggest an attempt to give one side of a debatable public question an advantage in expressing its views to the people." Subject-matter regulation, in other words, may have the intent or effect of favoring some ideas over others. When that is realistically possible—when the restriction "raises the specter that the Government may effectively drive certain ideas or viewpoints from the marketplace"—we insist that the law pass the most demanding constitutional test.

But when that is not realistically possible, we may do well to relax our guard so that "entirely reasonable" laws imperiled by strict scrutiny can survive. To do its intended work, of course, the category of content-based regulation triggering strict scrutiny must sweep more broadly than the actual harm; that category exists to create a buffer zone guaranteeing that the government cannot favor or disfavor certain viewpoints. But that buffer zone need not extend forever. We can administer our content-regulation doctrine with a dose of common sense, so as to leave standing laws that in no way implicate its intended function.

And indeed we have done just that: Our cases have been far less rigid than the majority admits in applying strict scrutiny to facially content-based laws—including in cases just like this one. In *City of Ladue v. Gilleo,* 512 U.S. 43 (1994), the Court assumed *arguendo* that a sign ordinance's exceptions for address signs, safety signs, and for-sale signs in residential areas did not trigger strict scrutiny. We did not need to, and so did not, decide the level-of-scrutiny question because the law's breadth made it unconstitutional under any standard.

The majority could easily have taken *Ladue*'s tack here. The Town of Gilbert's defense of its sign ordinance—most notably, the law's distinctions between directional signs and others—does not pass strict scrutiny, or intermediate scrutiny, or even the laugh test. The Town, for example, provides no reason at all for prohibiting more than four directional signs on a property while placing no limits on the number of other types of signs. Similarly, the Town offers no coherent justification for restricting the size of directional signs to 6 square feet while allowing other signs to reach 20 square feet. The absence of any sensible basis for these and other distinctions dooms the Town's ordinance under even the intermediate scrutiny that the Court typically applies to "time, place, or manner" speech regulations. Accordingly, there is no need to decide in this case whether strict scrutiny applies to every sign ordinance in every town across this country containing a subject-matter exemption.

I suspect this Court and others will regret the majority's insistence today on answering that question in the affirmative. As the years go by, courts will discover that thousands of towns have such ordinances, many of them "entirely reasonable." And as the challenges to them mount, courts will have to invalidate one after the other. (This Court may soon find itself a veritable Supreme Board of Sign Review.) And courts will strike down those democratically enacted local laws even though no one—certainly not the majority—has ever explained why the vindication of First Amendment values requires that result. Because I see no reason why such an easy case calls for us to cast a constitutional pall on reasonable regulations quite unlike the law before us, I concur only in the judgment.

Points for Discussion

1. **The justices' disagreement over when to apply strict scrutiny to laws that make distinctions based on content.** All the justices who wrote opinions in *Reed*—Justices Thomas, Alito, Breyer, and Kagan—agreed that the Gilbert town ordinance was unconstitutional. But note how Justice Breyer's and Justice Kagan's concurring opinions agreed with only the conclusion of Justice Thomas' majority opinion and not with its reasoning. Can you state the rule Justice Thomas articulated for when content-based regulations should be subject to strict scrutiny and why both Justice Breyer and Justice Kagan thought that Justice Thomas' rule was problematic? Can you articulate the alternative rules Justices Breyer and Kagan would use for making this decision? Whose rules seem easier to apply? Whose rules seem more sensible?

2. **Subject matter and viewpoint discrimination.** Justices Thomas, Breyer, and Kagan all agreed that laws that discriminate based on the viewpoint being expressed should be subject to strict scrutiny. This accords with the Supreme

Court's longstanding aversion to such laws. As the Court explained in *Rosenberger v. University of Virginia*, 515 U.S. 819, 829 (1995), "viewpoint discrimination is an egregious form of content discrimination." Because viewpoint-discriminatory laws reflect the most pernicious form of government censorship, the Supreme Court has said that these laws are virtually per se unconstitutional.

Justices Thomas, Breyer, and Kagan disagreed, however, over whether content-based laws that regulate a subject area should automatically receive strict scrutiny. Both Justice Breyer and Justice Kagan acknowledged that subject matter regulations could be a subterfuge for government efforts to discriminate against a particular viewpoint and conceded that such laws should receive strict scrutiny. But they did not think that this was always the case, and they thought that automatically applying strict scrutiny to every law that regulates speech based on subject matter would threaten to invalidate many legitimate regulations. What examples did they offer when making this point? Are they correct that Justice Thomas' more rigid approach for determining which laws are subject to strict scrutiny will put these laws in jeopardy?

3. **The many ways in which a law can be content-based.** Justice Thomas noted that there are multiple ways in which a law can be considered content-based, which he described as a regulation that "applies to particular speech because of the topic discussed or the idea or message expressed." The first and most obvious way is if a law "on its face" draws "distinctions based on the message a speaker conveys." This is sometimes obvious, he said, but it can be more subtle, such as when a law defines the regulated speech "by its function or purpose." What do you think he meant by this?

   In addition, he said that even facially neutral laws will be considered content-based and receive strict scrutiny if they "cannot be justified without reference to the content of the regulated speech" or if they "were adopted by the government because of disagreement with the message the speech conveyed." Can you articulate what each of these factors entails? What did Justice Thomas mean when he said that a law cannot be "justified without reference to the content of the regulated speech"?

   Finally, Justice Thomas noted that laws that regulate who may speak will often be considered content-based. He explained that "speech restrictions based on the identity of the speaker are all too often simply a means to control content" and that these laws should be subjected to strict scrutiny if "the legislature's speaker preference reflects a content preference." Imagine, for example, that the Chicago ordinance in the *Mosley* case discussed above had stated that no one may picket within 150 feet of a school except for members of the teachers' union. Would that have made the law content-neutral, or would this speaker-based distinction merely be a proxy for the same content-based distinction that the Court denounced in its decision?

4. **The debate continues in another signage case.** Seven years after the *Reed* case, the Court addressed another signage regulation, and once again the justices were deeply divided over whether the law should be subjected to strict scrutiny. *City of Austin v. Reagan Nat'l Advert.*, 596 U.S. 61 (2022). The case concerned an Austin, Texas, law that treated signs differently based on whether they were advertising the sale of goods or services that were being sold on the premises where the sign was located (what the Court referred as "on-premises" signs) and signs that advertised the sale of goods or services that were being sold at places other than the property where the sign was located ("off-premises" signs). The Court noted that there was a longstanding tradition of federal, state, and local laws treating on- and off-premises signs differently.

   The Austin law regulated on-premises signage more leniently than off-premises signage. The law was challenged by the owner of billboards whose off-premises advertising was subject to the more restrictive regulations.

   The sole issue before the Supreme Court was whether the law was facially content-based or content-neutral. The majority of the Court, in an opinion by Justice Sonia Sotomayor, held that the law was facially content-neutral. This prompted a sharp dissent from Justice Thomas, the author of the *Reed* decision, who claimed that the majority "misinterprets *Reed*'s clear rule for content-based restrictions and replaces it with an incoherent and malleable standard."

   The U.S. Court of Appeals for the Fifth Circuit, which found the Austin law to be facially content-based, interpreted *Reed* to mean that a law is content-based if a person must read the message on the sign to determine if the law applied. Since the application of the Austin law required one to read a sign to determine whether it was advertising on- or off-premises goods or services, the Court of Appeals held that the law was facially content-based.

   In rejecting the Fifth Circuit's reasoning, Justice Sotomayor offered this explanation:

   > In this case, enforcing the City's challenged sign code provisions requires reading a billboard to determine whether it directs readers to the property on which it stands or to some other, offsite location. Unlike the sign code at issue in *Reed*, however, the City's provisions at issue here do not single out any topic or subject matter for differential treatment. A sign's substantive message itself is irrelevant to the application of the provisions; there are no content-discriminatory classifications for political messages, ideological messages, or directional messages

> concerning specific events, including those sponsored by religious and nonprofit organizations. The message on the sign matters only to the extent that it informs the sign's relative location. The on-/off-premises distinction is therefore similar to ordinary [content-neutral] time, place, or manner restrictions. *Reed* does not require the application of strict scrutiny to this kind of location-based regulation.

By contrast, Justice Thomas thought that the Austin law was clearly content-based under the standard he had announced in *Reed*:

> In *Reed*, we held that a speech regulation is content based—and thus presumptively invalid—if it "draws distinctions based on the message a speaker conveys." Under *Reed*, Austin's off-premises restriction is content based. It discriminates against certain signs based on the message they convey—*e.g.*, whether they promote an on- or off-site event, activity, or service.

Where do you come out in this debate? Do you favor Justice Thomas' formalist approach for deciding when strict scrutiny should be applied or Justice Sotomayor's realist approach? Stated more bluntly, do you think it makes sense to subject on-premises/off-premises sign regulations to the rigors of strict scrutiny?

1. The Rules for Evaluating Content-Based Regulations of Speech: The Elements of Strict Scrutiny

While it is often easy to determine whether a regulation of speech is content-based, the *Reed* and *City of Austin* cases are reminders that the distinction is sometimes elusive and that the justices even disagree about whether strict scrutiny should apply to all content-based regulations of speech. Nevertheless, it is important to recognize that Justice Thomas wrote the legally binding majority opinion in *Reed* and that the *City of Austin* decision did not disturb *Reed*'s core holding that "content-based laws—those that target speech based on its communicative content—are presumptively unconstitutional and may be justified only if the government proves that they are narrowly tailored to serve compelling state interests." *City of Austin* also reaffirmed Justice Thomas' observation in *Reed* that both viewpoint-discriminatory regulations and subject matter regulations are content-based and are subject to strict scrutiny. And it reaffirmed that even a facially content-neutral law will be treated as content-based if the legislature's underlying purpose in enacting the law was to discriminate against speech based on its content.

For now, let's assume that a law has been classified as a content-based regulation of speech. As you know, this means that the law will be subject to strict scrutiny. But what, exactly, does that entail?

In *Reed*, Justice Thomas said that strict scrutiny means that content-based laws are "presumptively unconstitutional" and will be upheld only "if the government proves that they are narrowly tailored to serve compelling state interests." Let's unpack each of those elements.

First, note that the government has the burden of proof in strict scrutiny cases. Content-based laws are presumptively unconstitutional. The government bears the burden of overriding this presumption by convincing a court that its abridgment of speech is justified.

Second, note what the government must prove to carry this burden. It must show that the law is "narrowly tailored" to serve a "compelling" state interest. This looks to both the "end" of the law and the "means" used to achieve the end. The "end" aspect requires the government to show that the law serves a "compelling" governmental interest. There is no quantitative measure for when an interest is compelling, but the Supreme Court's choice of the word "compelling" suggests that the interest must be exceedingly important.

The "means" aspect requires the government to show that the law is narrowly tailored to further the government's compelling interest. To satisfy this requirement, the government must use the least speech-restrictive means to further its purpose. If there is an alternative way to achieve the government's purpose that suppresses less speech, the law is unconstitutional. In other words, there must be a perfect fit, or at least a nearly perfect fit, between the means used and the end to be achieved.

As we learned earlier, content-based regulations can be characterized as either viewpoint-discriminatory or subject matter regulations. Both are reviewed under strict scrutiny, and both are extremely likely to be found unconstitutional. But the Supreme Court is especially troubled by viewpoint-discriminatory laws, which the Court views as the most egregious form of content-based regulation.[7] These laws are considered highly suspect and are almost certain to be struck down.[8]

Ready to apply these rules? Here are two cases where the application of the rules is relatively straightforward.

---

7 *Rosenberger*, 515 U.S. at 829–30.

8 *Matal v. Tam*, 582 U.S. 218, 234 (2017) ("the First Amendment forbids the government to regulate speech in ways that favor some viewpoints or ideas at the expense of others") (citing *Lamb's Chapel v. Center Moriches Union Free Sch. Dist.*, 508 U.S. 384, 394 (1993)).

Burson v. Freeman

Supreme Court of the United States, 1992
504 U.S. 191

JUSTICE BLACKMUN announced the judgment of the Court and delivered an opinion, in which THE CHIEF JUSTICE, JUSTICE WHITE, and JUSTICE KENNEDY join.

The question presented is whether a provision of the Tennessee Code, which prohibits the solicitation of votes and the display or distribution of campaign materials within 100 feet of the entrance to a polling place, violates the First and Fourteenth Amendments.

The State of Tennessee has carved out an election-day "campaign-free zone" through § 2–7–111(b) of its election code. That section reads in pertinent part:

law

> Within the appropriate boundary as established in subsection (a) [100 feet from the entrances], and the building in which the polling place is located, the display of campaign posters, signs or other campaign materials, distribution of campaign materials, and solicitation of votes for or against any person or political party or position on a question are prohibited.

Violation of § 2–7–111(b) is a Class C misdemeanor punishable by a term of imprisonment not greater than 30 days or a fine not to exceed $50, or both. Tenn.Code Ann. §§ 2–19–119 and 40–35–111(e)(3).

Respondent Mary Rebecca Freeman has been a candidate for office in Tennessee, has managed local campaigns, and has worked actively in statewide elections. In 1987, she was the treasurer for the campaign of a city-council candidate in Metropolitan Nashville-Davidson County.

Asserting that §§ 2–7–111(b) and 2–19–119 limited her ability to communicate with voters, respondent brought a facial challenge to these statutes in Davidson County Chancery Court. She sought a declaratory judgment that the provisions were unconstitutional under both the United States and the Tennessee Constitutions. She also sought a permanent injunction against their enforcement.

The First Amendment provides that "Congress shall make no law abridging the freedom of speech." This Court in *Thornhill v. Alabama,* 310 U.S. 88, 95 (1940), said: "The freedom of speech which is secured by the First Amendment against abridgment by the United States, is among the fundamental personal rights and liberties which are secured to all persons by the Fourteenth Amendment against abridgment by a State."

The Tennessee restriction under consideration is not a facially content-neutral time, place, or manner restriction. Whether individuals may exercise their free speech rights near polling places depends entirely on whether their speech is related to a political campaign. This Court has held that the First Amendment's hostility to content-based regulation extends not only to a restriction on a particular viewpoint, but also to a prohibition of public discussion of an entire topic.

As a facially content-based restriction on political speech in a public forum, § 2–7–111(b) must be subjected to exacting scrutiny: The State must show that the regulation is necessary to serve a compelling state interest and that it is narrowly drawn to achieve that end.

Tennessee asserts that its campaign-free zone serves two compelling interests. First, the State argues that its regulation serves its compelling interest in protecting the right of its citizens to vote freely for the candidates of their choice. Second, Tennessee argues that its restriction protects the right to vote in an election conducted with integrity and reliability.

The interests advanced by Tennessee obviously are compelling ones. This Court has recognized that the right to vote freely for the candidate of one's choice is of the essence of a democratic society. Indeed, no right is more precious in a free country than that of having a voice in the election of those who make the laws under which, as good citizens, we must live. Other rights, even the most basic, are illusory if the right to vote is undermined.

Accordingly, this Court has concluded that a State has a compelling interest in protecting voters from confusion and undue influence.

The Court also has recognized that a State indisputably has a compelling interest in preserving the integrity of its election process. The Court thus has upheld generally applicable and evenhanded restrictions that protect the integrity and reliability of the electoral process itself. In other words, it has recognized that a State has a compelling interest in ensuring that an individual's right to vote is not undermined by fraud in the election process.

To survive strict scrutiny, however, a State must do more than assert a compelling state interest—it must demonstrate that its law is necessary to serve the asserted interest. While we readily acknowledge that a law rarely survives such scrutiny, an examination of the evolution of election reform, both in this country and abroad, demonstrates the necessity of restricted areas in or around polling places.

An examination of the history of election regulation in this country reveals a persistent battle against two evils: voter intimidation and election fraud. After an unsuccessful experiment with an unofficial ballot system, all 50 States, together with numerous other Western democracies, settled on the same solution: a secret ballot secured in part by a restricted zone around the voting compartments. We find that this widespread and time-tested consensus demonstrates that some restricted zone is necessary in order to serve the States' compelling interests in preventing voter intimidation and election fraud.

The real question then is *how large* a restricted zone is permissible or sufficiently tailored. Respondent and the dissent argue that Tennessee's 100-foot boundary is not narrowly drawn to achieve the State's compelling interest in protecting the right to vote. We disagree.

We do not think that the minor geographic limitation prescribed by § 2–7–111(b) constitutes such a significant impingement. Thus, we simply do not view the question whether the 100-foot boundary line could be somewhat tighter as a question of "constitutional dimension." Reducing the boundary to 25 feet, as suggested by the Tennessee Supreme Court, is a difference only in degree, not a less restrictive alternative in kind. As was pointed out in the dissenting opinion in the Tennessee Supreme Court, it "takes approximately 15 seconds to walk 75 feet." The State of Tennessee has decided that these last 15 seconds before its citizens enter the polling place should be their own, as free from interference as possible. We do not find that this is an unconstitutional choice.

In conclusion, we reaffirm that it is the rare case in which we have held that a law survives strict scrutiny. This, however, is such a rare case. Here, the State, as recognized administrator of elections, has asserted that the exercise of free speech rights conflicts with another fundamental right, the right to cast a ballot in an election free from the taint of intimidation and fraud. A long history, a substantial consensus, and simple common sense show that some restricted zone around polling places is necessary to protect that fundamental right. Given the conflict between these two rights, we hold that requiring solicitors to stand 100 feet from the entrances to polling places does not constitute an unconstitutional compromise.

The judgment of the Tennessee Supreme Court is reversed, and the case is remanded for further proceedings not inconsistent with this opinion.

JUSTICE KENNEDY, concurring.

There is a narrow area in which the First Amendment permits freedom of expression to yield to the extent necessary for the accommodation of another constitutional right. That principle can apply here without danger that the general rule permitting no content restriction will be engulfed by the analysis; for under the statute the State acts to protect the integrity of the polling place where citizens exercise the right to vote. Voting is one of the most fundamental and cherished liberties in our democratic system of government. The State is not using this justification to suppress legitimate expression. With these observations, I concur in the opinion of Justice Blackmun and the judgment of the Court.

Justice Stevens, with whom Justice O'Connor and Justice Souter join, dissenting.

I fully agree with the plurality that Tennessee must show that its "regulation is necessary to serve a compelling state interest and that it is narrowly drawn to achieve that end." I do not agree, however, that Tennessee has made anything approaching such a showing.

The evidence introduced at trial to demonstrate the necessity for Tennessee's campaign-free zone was exceptionally thin. Although the State's sole witness explained the need for special restrictions *inside* the polling place itself, she offered no justification for a ban on political expression *outside* the polling place. On this record it is far from surprising that the Tennessee Supreme Court—which surely is more familiar with the State's electoral practices and traditions than we are—concluded that the 100-foot ban outside the polling place was not justified by regulatory concerns. This conclusion is bolstered by Tennessee law, which indicates that normal police protection is completely adequate to maintain order in the area more than *10* feet from the polling place.

Tennessee's content-based discrimination is particularly problematic because such a regulation will inevitably favor certain groups of candidates. As the testimony in this case illustrates, several groups of candidates rely heavily on last-minute campaigning. Candidates with fewer resources, candidates for lower visibility offices, and "grassroots" candidates benefit disproportionately from last-minute campaigning near the polling place.

In my opinion, the presence of campaign workers outside a polling place is, in most situations, a minor nuisance. But we have long recognized that "the fact that society may find speech offensive is not a sufficient reason for suppressing it." Although we often pay homage to the electoral process, we must be careful not to confuse sanctity with silence. The hubbub of campaign workers outside a polling place may be a nuisance, but it is also the sound of a vibrant democracy.

In silencing that sound, Tennessee "trenches upon an area in which the importance of First Amendment protections is at its zenith." For that reason, Tennessee must shoulder the burden of demonstrating that its restrictions on political speech are no broader than necessary to protect orderly access to the polls. It has not done so.

I therefore respectfully dissent.

[Justice Scalia's opinion concurring in the judgment is omitted. Justice Thomas did not participate in the case.]

Points for Discussion

1. **Why did the plurality think that the Tennessee law was content-based?** Why didn't the Court treat the Tennessee law as a content-neutral time, place, or manner regulation since the law was regulating the "place" where electioneering was prohibited (*i.e.*, within 100 feet of a polling place's entrance)? Would a law that prohibited speaking about socialism in New York City's Central Park be a content-based law or a content-neutral time, place, or manner law?

2. **Did the plurality find any compelling state interests to justify the Tennessee law?** To pass strict scrutiny, the government must have a compelling interest or reason for its content-based regulation of speech. Did Justice Blackmun find any compelling interests to justify the Tennessee law?

3. **Did the plurality find that the Tennessee law was narrowly tailored to achieving the state's interest?** Even if the government has a compelling justification for a content-based law, the law must still be narrowly tailored to achieve that interest. Did Justice Blackmun think that the Tennessee law was narrowly tailored? If so, why?

4. **Why did three justices dissent?** In his dissent, which was joined by Justices O'Connor and Souter, Justice Stevens said that he "fully agree[d] with the plurality that Tennessee must show that its regulation is necessary to serve a compelling state interest and that it is narrowly drawn to achieve that end." Why did he think that Tennessee had failed to satisfy this test?

5. **It is rare for a law to pass strict scrutiny.** Don't let the result in *Burson* fool you. As Justice Blackmun emphasized at the end of his opinion, it is "the rare case in which we have held that a law survives strict scrutiny." In the vast majority of cases, content-based laws reviewed under strict scrutiny are struck down.

Sable Communications of California, Inc. v. FCC

Supreme Court of the United States, 1989
492 U.S. 115

[*Authors' note:* As you will learn, the Supreme Court has said that certain categories of speech are not protected by the First Amendment. The government may regulate the content of these categories without the regulation being subject to strict scrutiny. One of these categories, which is relevant to this case, is obscene speech that graphically depicts sexual conduct. Because obscene speech is not protected by the First Amendment, even adults may be denied access to it. By contrast, sexual material that is not explicit enough to be considered obscene, which is sometimes referred to as "indecent" speech, is protected by the First Amendment. Because indecent speech is protected by the First Amendment, laws regulating the content of indecent speech are subject to strict scrutiny.]

JUSTICE WHITE delivered the opinion of the Court.

The issue before us is the constitutionality of § 223(b) of the Communications Act of 1934. The statute, as amended in 1988, imposes an outright ban on indecent as well as obscene interstate commercial telephone messages. The District Court upheld the prohibition against obscene interstate telephone communications for commercial purposes, but enjoined the enforcement of the statute insofar as it applied to indecent messages. We affirm the District Court in both respects.

In 1983, Sable Communications, Inc., began offering sexually oriented prerecorded telephone messages (popularly known as "dial-a-porn") through the Pacific Bell telephone network. In 1988, Sable brought suit in District Court seeking declaratory and injunctive relief against enforcement of the recently amended § 223(b).

The District Court upheld § 223(b)'s prohibition of obscene telephone messages as constitutional. We agree with that judgment. In contrast to the prohibition on indecent communications, there is no constitutional barrier to the ban on obscene dial-a-porn recordings. We have repeatedly held that the protection of the First Amendment does not extend to obscene speech. The cases before us today do not require us to decide what is obscene or what is indecent but rather to determine whether Congress is empowered to prohibit transmission of obscene telephonic communications.

The District Court concluded that while the Government has a legitimate interest in protecting children from exposure to indecent dial-a-porn messages, § 223(b) was not sufficiently narrowly drawn to serve that purpose and thus violated the First Amendment. We agree.

Sexual expression which is indecent but not obscene is protected by the First Amendment; and the federal parties do not submit that the sale of such materials to adults could be criminalized solely because they are indecent. The Government may, however, regulate the content of constitutionally protected speech in order to promote a compelling interest if it chooses the least restrictive means to further the articulated interest. We have recognized that there is a compelling interest in protecting the physical and psychological well-being of minors. This interest extends to shielding minors from the influence of literature that is not obscene by adult standards. The Government may serve this legitimate interest, but to withstand constitutional scrutiny, "it must do so by narrowly drawn regulations designed to serve those interests without unnecessarily interfering with First Amendment freedoms. It is not enough to show that the Government's ends are compelling; the means must be carefully tailored to achieve those ends.

In *Butler v. Michigan,* 352 U.S. 380 (1957), a unanimous Court reversed a conviction under a statute which made it an offense to make available to the general public materials found to have a potentially harmful influence on minors. The Court found the law to be insufficiently tailored since it denied adults their free speech rights by allowing them to read only what was acceptable for children. As Justice Frankfurter said in that case, "surely this is to burn the house to roast the pig." In our judgment, this case, like *Butler,* presents us with "legislation not reasonably restricted to the evil with which it is said to deal."

The federal parties argue that the total ban on indecent commercial telephone communications is justified because nothing less could prevent children from gaining access to such messages. We find the argument quite unpersuasive. The FCC, after lengthy proceedings, determined that its credit card, access code, and scrambling rules were a satisfactory solution to the problem of keeping indecent dial-a-porn messages out of the reach of minors. The Court of Appeals, after careful consideration, agreed that these rules represented a "feasible and effective" way to serve the Government's compelling interest in protecting children.

Under our precedents, § 223(b), in its present form, has the invalid effect of limiting the content of adult telephone conversations to that which is suitable for children to hear. It is another case of "burning the house to roast the pig."

Because the statute's denial of adult access to telephone messages which are indecent but not obscene far exceeds that which is necessary to limit the access of minors to such messages, we hold that the ban does not survive constitutional scrutiny.

JUSTICE SCALIA, concurring.

I join the Court's opinion because I think it correct that a wholesale prohibition upon adult access to indecent speech cannot be adopted merely because the FCC's alternate proposal could be circumvented by as few children as the evidence suggests. But where a reasonable person draws the line in this balancing process—that is, how few children render the risk unacceptable—depends in part upon what mere "indecency" (as opposed to "obscenity") includes.

[Justice Brennan's opinion concurring in part and dissenting in part, which was joined by Justice Marshall and Justice Stevens, is omitted.]

Points for Discussion

1. **Was the Communications Act's regulation of indecent phone calls content-based or content-neutral?** Did the Court treat the indecency provision in the Communications Act as a content-based or content-neutral regulation of speech? Can you explain why the Court reached the conclusion it did?

2. **Did the Court think that the indecency regulation served a compelling government interest?** If the indecency regulation was content-based, the government needed a compelling reason to justify it. Did the Court think that the government had one? If so, what was it?

3. **Did the Court find that the indecency regulation was narrowly tailored to achieve the government's interest?** Even if the government has a compelling justification for a content-based law, the law must still be narrowly tailored to achieve that interest. Did the Court think that the indecency regulation law was narrowly tailored? If so, why? If not, why not? What did the Court mean when it said this is another case of "burning the house to roast the pig"?

Exceptions to the General Rule: When Content-Based Regulation of Speech Does Not Trigger Strict Scrutiny

If you think you have mastered the art of analyzing content-based regulations of speech, think again. What good would a rule be without exceptions, and there are important exceptions to the general rule that content-based regulations of speech are subject to strict scrutiny. We will be fleshing out these exceptions in subsequent chapters, but here is quick preview:

- **Exception #1: Regulations of unprotected categories of speech.** The Supreme Court has long declared that there are certain categories of speech that are not protected by the First Amendment. Because these categories are unprotected, the government may regulate their content without the regulations' being subject to strict scrutiny. This is referred to as the Court's "categorical" approach to the First Amendment. Its origin traces back to *Chaplinsky v. New Hampshire*, 315 U.S. 568 (1942), which you will read in Chapter 5. *Chaplinsky* announced that some categories of speech are unprotected because they "are of such slight social value as a step to truth that any benefit that may be derived from them is clearly outweighed by the social interest in order and morality."

Some of the most widely recognized categories of unprotected speech are incitement, fighting words, speech provoking a hostile audience, true threats, obscenity, child pornography, and defamation. You will be studying these categories in depth in Chapters 5 through 9. An outlier to this general framework is "commercial speech," which is neither fully protected nor fully unprotected. You will learn about commercial speech in Chapter 10.

The *Sable Communications* case provided a good example of how an unprotected category of speech affects a court's analysis. Recall how the federal law in that case banned both "obscene" and "indecent" phone messages. Because indecent speech is protected by the First Amendment, the Court subjected the law's content-based regulation of indecent speech to strict scrutiny and ultimately found the law unconstitutional. By contrast, because obscene speech is not protected by the First Amendment, the Court summarily upheld the part of the law regulating obscene phone calls:

> The District Court upheld § 223(b)'s prohibition of obscene telephone messages as constitutional. We agree with that judgment. In contrast to the prohibition on indecent communications, there is no constitutional barrier to the ban on obscene dial-a-porn recordings. We have repeatedly held that the protection of the First Amendment does not extend to obscene speech.

While the Supreme Court continues to acknowledge historically recognized categories of unprotected speech, it has been reluctant to identify any new categories and has expressly rejected the notion that it can declare new categories of unprotected speech based on a simple balancing of the speech's relative social costs and benefits. We will explore this topic further in Chapter 5 in the notes following the *Chaplinsky* case.

- **Exception #2: Speech in special settings.** The Supreme Court has also recognized that the government needs greater leeway to regulate speech in certain special settings than it has in generally regulating the public's speech. For example, teachers in public schools must be able to discipline disruptive students even though the students are being punished because of the content of their speech. Similarly, the government must make content-based decisions when deciding which artists to fund or which books to purchase for a public library. To allow the government more leeway in these specialized settings, the Supreme Court has created customized rules. For each setting, the rules strike a balance between the government's need to function effectively and an individual's desire to speak freely. We will examine these rules in Chapter 11, which discusses the government's ability to regulate speech when the government acts as a property owner, educator, employer, funder, and speaker.

- **Exception #3: The zoning of adult entertainment establishments and the "secondary effects doctrine."** The Supreme Court has developed a rule, known as the "secondary effects doctrine," that provides that a content-based law will be treated as content-neutral if the legislators enacted the law to address the secondary effects associated with the speech and not to address the speech's content. The landmark case establishing this doctrine was *Renton v. Playtime Theatres, Inc.*, 475 U.S. 41 (1986). In that case, a city had enacted a zoning ordinance that prohibited adult movie theaters from being located within 1,000 feet of any residential zone, single- or multiple-family dwelling, church, park, or school. Even though the application of the law depended upon the content of the movies being shown, the Court nevertheless treated the law as content-neutral because it was not aimed at the movies' content but rather at the secondary effects of adult movie theaters on surrounding neighborhoods, such as an increase in crime and declining property values. To date, the secondary effects doctrine has been applied only in the context of laws regulating adult entertainment establishments. You will learn more about this doctrine in Chapter 7 when you study laws that regulate sexual speech and in Chapter 14 when you study laws that regulate nude dancing.

2. The Rules for Evaluating Content-Neutral Regulations of Speech: The Elements of Intermediate Scrutiny

Content-neutral laws are the opposite of content-based laws. If content-based laws regulate speech because of its message, content-neutral laws regulate speech regardless of its message.

Imagine, for example, a law that prohibits rallies in a public park after 9 p.m. The purpose of this law is presumably to promote tranquility—to ensure that people are not disturbed by noise when they settle in for the night. Can you see how this law is content-neutral? Its application does not depend on the message being conveyed at a rally. The law would apply whether a rally promoted a workers' revolution, extolled the virtues of ice cream, or celebrated the local baseball team.

You may recall from the note about the *City of Austin* case that the majority of the Court concluded that Austin's on-premises/off-premises sign ordinance was content-neutral on its face. The Court then explained, as it prepared the case for remand, that this was only the first step in determining the law's constitutionality:

> This Court's determination that the City's ordinance is facially content neutral does not end the First Amendment inquiry. If there is evidence that an impermissible purpose or justification underpins a facially content-neutral restriction, for instance, that restriction may be content based. Moreover, to survive intermediate scrutiny, a restriction on speech or expression must be "narrowly tailored to serve a significant governmental interest."

There are three points worth considering here. First, the Court said that it found the Austin ordinance to be "facially" content-neutral. This meant that the words of the statute did not regulate speech based on its content.

Second, the Court noted that even a facially neutral law will be treated as content-based if there is an underlying "impermissible purpose." For example, recall how the Austin ordinance placed limits on signs that advertise "off-premises" activities. Now imagine that the Austin City Council was controlled by Democrats and council members knew that a Republican-owned company dominated the Austin billboard market and would sell advertising space to only Republican candidates for office. (Keep in mind that the First Amendment does not apply to private actors so the company could discriminate based on content and even viewpoint.) If there was evidence that the City Council limited off-premises advertising because it knew that these ads would benefit Republicans, a court would likely treat this otherwise facially content-neutral law as content-based because of the council's underlying discriminatory purpose.

The Supreme Court has sometimes refused to inquire into whether a facially content-neutral law had an underlying impermissible purpose. Most famously, in *United States v. O'Brien*, 391 U.S. 367, 383 (1968), a case we will study in Chapter 14, the Court said it would "not strike down an otherwise constitutional statute on the basis of an alleged illicit legislative motive." But *City of Austin* suggests that the Court is willing to do so, and this type of looking behind the curtain to find an illicit motive is common in other areas of constitutional law, such as in Equal Protection and Dormant Commerce Clause jurisprudence.

Finally, notice how the Court said that even if the Austin law were content-neutral, it would still have to pass "intermediate scrutiny," which the Court said would require the government to show that the regulation was "narrowly tailored to serve a significant governmental interest."

The takeaway from this last point is that content-neutral laws are not automatically constitutional but are subject to intermediate scrutiny. As noted previously, intermediate scrutiny is less demanding than strict scrutiny but more demanding than rational basis review.

In this section, we will parse through the elements of an intermediate scrutiny analysis and then let you read a classic case in which this scrutiny was applied. Let's begin with *City of Austin*'s description of intermediate scrutiny as requiring a government abridgment of speech to be "narrowly tailored to serve a significant governmental interest."

As is true with strict scrutiny, the government bears the burden of proof in intermediate scrutiny cases. Thus, it is up to the government to show both that the speech restriction furthers a "significant" governmental interest and that the regulatory means used are "narrowly tailored" to achieve that interest.

The requirements for passing intermediate scrutiny are more lenient than the requirements for strict scrutiny in two critical respects. First, the government need only prove that the government interest is "significant" as opposed to "compelling." The Court has never explained, and probably could not explain, what the quantitative difference is between a significant and compelling interest. But the Court has made it clear that the former is less demanding than the latter.

Second, the government need only show that the means used to further its interest are substantially related to serving the interest rather than the least restrictive means of doing so. Unfortunately, the Supreme Court often fails to make this distinction clear. In *City of Austin*, for example, the Court said intermediate scrutiny requires that a law be "narrowly tailored" to furthering the government's interest. But "narrowly tailored" is the exact language the Court sometimes uses for describing the means requirement for strict scrutiny. Notwithstanding the Court's imprecise terminology (fortunately for the justices, no one is grading their opinions), the Court has made it clear that the means requirement for intermediate scrutiny is less demanding that the means requirement for strict scrutiny. Strict scrutiny requires that the means used be the least restrictive means of furthering the government's purpose. In other words, there must be a nearly perfect fit between the ends and the means. By contrast, the Court has clarified that the fit between ends and means for intermediate scrutiny need only be reasonable.[9] The Court sometimes captures this notion by saying that the means used to satisfy intermediate scrutiny must be "substantially related" to furthering the government's purpose.

> FYI
>
> **A Word About Terminology**
>
> While the Supreme Court often describes the required governmental interest for passing intermediate scrutiny as "significant," it sometimes describes the interest as "important" or "substantial." The Court uses these terms interchangeably, suggesting that they have an equivalent meaning.

9 *Ward v. Rock Against Racism*, 491 U.S. 781, 798–99 (1989) ("Lest any confusion on the point remain, we reaffirm today that a regulation of the time, place, or manner of protected speech must be narrowly tailored to serve the government's legitimate, content-neutral interests but that it need not be the least restrictive or least intrusive means of doing so. Rather, the requirement of narrow tailoring is satisfied so long as the regulation promotes a substantial government interest that would be achieved less effectively absent the regulation.").

While the *City of Austin* summary captures the core requirements of intermediate scrutiny, it is important to note that the Court typically uses one of two tests for scrutinizing content-neutral laws. The tests have slightly different phrasings, and each has an element not found in the other. Nonetheless, the Court treats them as largely interchangeable and sometimes borrows an element from one when applying the other.[10] Here are the two tests:

- **Test for time, place, or manner regulations in a public forum.** You have already been introduced to the concept of public forums: government property that by tradition or choice has been open to the public for speech purposes. Classic examples are public streets, sidewalks, and parks. Content-neutral regulations of speech in these forums are referred to as "time, place, or manner" restrictions. The test the Court uses for these restrictions is typically stated as follows:

  > We have often noted that restrictions of this kind are valid provided that they are justified without reference to the content of the regulated speech, that they are narrowly tailored to serve a significant governmental interest, and that they leave open ample alternative channels for communication of the information.[11]

  The first part of the test—that the restriction be "justified without reference to the content of the regulated speech"—is another way of saying that the law must be content-neutral. If the government is justifying the restriction based on the content of the speech, it is content-based and should be analyzed under strict scrutiny. The second two elements—that the law be "narrowly tailored to serve a significant governmental interest"—match the ends and means requirements in *City of Austin*'s summary of intermediate scrutiny. The final element—that the law "leave open ample alternative channels for communication of the information"—helps ensure that content-neutral laws are not drafted so broadly as to preclude a speaker's ability to convey his or her message. To give an extreme example, imagine a law that prohibited people from speaking about anything. This law is content-neutral; its application does not depend upon the content of a speaker's message. But the law does not leave ample alternative channels for speakers to communicate their messages. In fact, it leaves no channels!

- ***O'Brien* test for conduct regulations that incidentally burden speech.** You learned in Chapter 3 that the First Amendment protects not only oral or written expression but also conduct that communicates

---

10 *Id.* at 798 ("we have held that the *O'Brien* test in the last analysis is little, if any, different from the standard applied to time, place, or manner restrictions").

11 *Clark v. Community for Creative Non-Violence*, 468 U.S. 288, 293 (1984).

a message. This means, however, that laws regulating conduct will sometimes interfere with a person's ability to engage in conduct for expressive purposes. In these situations, the Court uses a test from *United States v. O'Brien*, a case you will read in Chapter 14. Here is the test:

> A government regulation is sufficiently justified if it is within the constitutional power of the Government; if it furthers an important or substantial governmental interest; if the governmental interest is unrelated to the suppression of free expression; and if the incidental restriction on alleged First Amendment freedoms is no greater than is essential to the furtherance of that interest.

This version of the intermediate scrutiny test has the same two core "ends and means" elements as the time, place, and manner test. Instead of requiring the government to show that a law furthers a "significant" interest, the Court instead says that the government must show either an "important or substantial" governmental interest. But, as noted above, the Court treats the terms "significant," "important," and "substantial" as equivalents. Instead of saying the law must be "narrowly tailored" to further the government's interest, the *O'Brien* test says that the law must be "no greater than is essential" to the government's interest. Like the narrowly tailored requirement, the "no greater than is essential" requirement could be read as requiring the government to use the least restrictive means to further the government's end. But here, too, subsequent cases have indicated that this element of the *O'Brien* test requires only a substantial fit between the ends and means and not a perfect or nearly perfect fit.[12]

The first element—that a law is "within the constitutional power of the Government"—is especially relevant for federal laws. That's because the federal government is a government of limited and enumerated power. For Congress to enact a law, it must be able to point to a power in the Constitution that authorizes its action. Thus, the *O'Brien* test, which was announced in a case concerning a federal law, begins by asking whether the government had the power to enact the relevant law. But state and local governments do not need to point to a power in the Constitution to act. They have what is called "police power" to enact any law that they perceive to be within the public's interest. Consequently, *O'Brien*'s first element about whether a law was "within

[12] Rodney Smolla, Smolla & Nimmer on Freedom of Speech, § 9:16 (2023) (stating that "the most plausible interpretation of recent cases indicates that despite the surface resemblance of the phrases 'least restrictive' and 'no greater than is essential,' the Court if pressed would hold that prong four of *O'Brien* does not impose the rigorous precision contemplated by the least restrictive means test used for heightened scrutiny," and citing *Ward*, 491 U.S. 781, and *Clark*, 468 U.S. 288).

> the constitutional power of the Government" will rarely be a serious obstacle for state and local laws.
>
> Finally, note how the *O'Brien* test requires that a law be "unrelated to the suppression of free expression." This is equivalent to the requirement for time, place, or manner regulations that a law be "justified without reference to the content of the regulated speech." Both ensure that a law is not regulating speech because of its content. If it is, the law is content-based, and strict scrutiny should be applied.

The following case illustrates the application of intermediate scrutiny to a content-neutral regulation of speech. One could reasonably contend that the law at issue in the case was more like a time, place, or manner regulation of expression than a conduct regulation incidentally burdening expressive conduct and that the Supreme Court should have used the time, place, or manner test. Nevertheless, and as you'll see, the Court used the *O'Brien* test for its analysis. As noted above, however, the Court has treated these two tests as interchangeable. In addition, although the Court used the *O'Brien* test, it nevertheless considered whether the law at issue left open alternative channels for people to communicate their message, an element from the time, place, or manner test. This is an example of how the Court sometimes mixes elements from the two tests.

Members of City Council of Los Angeles v. Taxpayers for Vincent

Supreme Court of the United States, 1984
466 U.S. 789

JUSTICE STEVENS delivered the opinion of the Court.

Section 28.04 of the Los Angeles Municipal Code prohibits the posting of signs on public property. The question presented is whether that prohibition abridges appellees' freedom of speech within the meaning of the First Amendment.

In March 1979, Roland Vincent was a candidate for election to the Los Angeles City Council. A group of his supporters known as Taxpayers for Vincent (Taxpayers) entered into a contract with a political sign service company known as Candidates' Outdoor Graphics Service (COGS) to fabricate and post signs with Vincent's name on them. COGS produced 15- by 44-inch cardboard signs and attached them to utility poles at various locations by draping them over crosswires which support the poles and stapling the cardboard together at the bottom. The signs' message was: "Roland Vincent—City Council."

Acting under the authority of § 28.04 of the Municipal Code, employees of the city's Bureau of Street Maintenance routinely removed all posters attached to utility poles and similar objects covered by the ordinance, including the COGS signs. The weekly sign removal report covering the period March 1–March 7, 1979, indicated that among the 1,207 signs removed from public property during that week, 48 were identified as "Roland Vincent" signs. Most of the other signs identified in that report were apparently commercial in character.

On March 12, 1979, Taxpayers and COGS filed this action in the United States District Court for the Central District of California, naming the city, the Director of the Bureau of Street Maintenance, and members of the City Council as defendants. They sought an injunction against enforcement of the ordinance as well as compensatory and punitive damages. After engaging in discovery, the parties filed cross-motions for summary judgment on the issue of liability. The District Court entered findings of fact, concluded that the ordinance was constitutional, and granted the City's motion.

The Court of Appeals did not question any of the District Court's findings of fact, but it rejected some of its conclusions of law. The Court of Appeals reasoned that the ordinance was presumptively unconstitutional because significant First Amendment interests were involved. It noted that the City had advanced three separate justifications for the ordinance, but concluded that none of them was sufficient. The Court of Appeals held that the City had failed to make a sufficient showing that its asserted interests in esthetics and preventing visual clutter were substantial because it had not offered to demonstrate that the City was engaged in a comprehensive effort to remove other contributions to an unattractive environment in commercial and industrial areas. The City's interest in minimizing traffic hazards was rejected because it was readily apparent that no substantial traffic problems would result from permitting the posting of certain kinds of signs on many of the publicly owned objects covered by the ordinance. Finally, while acknowledging that a flat prohibition against signs on certain objects such as fire hydrants and traffic signals would be a permissible method of preventing interference with the intended use of public property, and that regulation of the size, design, and construction of posters, or of the method of removing them, might be reasonable, the Court of Appeals concluded that the City had not justified its total ban.

In its appeal to this Court the City challenges the Court of Appeals' holding that § 28.04 is unconstitutional on its face. Taxpayers and COGS defend that holding and also contend that the ordinance is unconstitutional as applied to their posting of political campaign signs on the crossarms of utility poles.

Taxpayers arguement

The ordinance prohibits appellees from communicating with the public in a certain manner, and presumably diminishes the total quantity of their communication in the City. The application of the ordinance to appellees' expressive activities surely raises the question whether the ordinance abridges their "freedom of speech" within the meaning of the First Amendment, and appellees certainly have standing to challenge the application of the ordinance to their own expressive activities. "But to say the ordinance presents a First Amendment issue is not necessarily to say that it constitutes a First Amendment violation." It has been clear since this Court's earliest decisions concerning the freedom of speech that the state may sometimes curtail speech when necessary to advance a significant and legitimate state interest.

There are some purported interests—such as a desire to suppress support for a minority party or an unpopular cause, or to exclude the expression of certain points of view from the marketplace of ideas—that are so plainly illegitimate that they would immediately invalidate the rule. The general principle that has emerged from this line of cases is that the First Amendment forbids the government to regulate speech in ways that favor some viewpoints or ideas at the expense of others.

That general rule has no application to this case. For there is not even a hint of bias or censorship in the City's enactment or enforcement of this ordinance. There is no claim that the ordinance was designed to suppress certain ideas that the City finds distasteful or that it has been applied to appellees because of the views that they express. The text of the ordinance is neutral—indeed it is silent—concerning any speaker's point of view, and the District Court's findings indicate that it has been applied to appellees and others in an evenhanded manner.

In *United States v. O'Brien*, 391 U.S. 367 (1968), the Court set forth the appropriate framework for reviewing a viewpoint-neutral regulation of this kind:

> A government regulation is sufficiently justified if it is within the constitutional power of the Government; if it furthers an important or substantial governmental interest; if the governmental interest is unrelated to the suppression of free expression; and if the incidental restriction on alleged First Amendment freedoms is no greater than is essential to the furtherance of that interest.

It is well settled that the state may legitimately exercise its police powers to advance esthetic values. In this case, taxpayers and COGS do not dispute that it is within the constitutional power of the City to attempt to improve its appearance, or that this interest is basically unrelated to the suppression of ideas. Therefore the critical inquiries are whether that interest is sufficiently substantial to justify the effect of the ordinance on appellees' expression, and whether that effect is no greater than necessary to accomplish the City's purpose.

Metromedia, Inc. v. San Diego, 453 U.S. 490 (1981), dealt with San Diego's prohibition of certain forms of outdoor billboards. There the Court considered the city's interest in avoiding visual clutter, and seven Justices explicitly concluded that this interest was sufficient to justify a prohibition of billboards. Justice White, writing for the plurality, expressly concluded that the city's esthetic interests were sufficiently substantial to provide an acceptable justification for a content-neutral prohibition against the use of billboards; San Diego's interest in its appearance was undoubtedly a substantial governmental goal.

We reaffirm the conclusion of the majority in *Metromedia.* The problem addressed by this ordinance—the visual assault on the citizens of Los Angeles presented by an accumulation of signs posted on public property—constitutes a significant substantive evil within the City's power to prohibit. "The city's interest in attempting to preserve or improve the quality of urban life is one that must be accorded high respect."

We turn to the question whether the scope of the restriction on appellees' expressive activity is substantially broader than necessary to protect the City's interest in eliminating visual clutter. The incidental restriction on expression which results from the City's attempt to accomplish such a purpose is considered justified as a reasonable regulation of the time, place, or manner of expression if it is narrowly tailored to serve that interest. The District Court found that the signs prohibited by the ordinance do constitute visual clutter and blight. By banning these signs, the City did no more than eliminate the exact source of the evil it sought to remedy.

- was it narrowly tailored

It is true that the esthetic interest in preventing the kind of litter that may result from the distribution of leaflets on the public streets and sidewalks cannot support a prophylactic prohibition against the citizen's exercise of that method of expressing his views. In *Schneider v. State,* 308 U.S. 147 (1939), the Court held that ordinances that absolutely prohibited handbilling on the streets were invalid. The Court explained that cities could adequately protect the esthetic interest in avoiding litter without abridging protected expression merely by penalizing those who actually litter.

schneider the ppl were talking? handing pamphlets to ppl directly

The rationale of *Schneider* is inapposite in the context of the instant case. There, individual citizens were actively exercising their right to communicate directly with potential recipients of their message. The conduct continued only while the speakers or distributors remained on the scene. In this case, appellees posted dozens of temporary signs throughout an area where they would remain unattended until removed.

With respect to signs posted by appellees, it is the tangible medium of expressing the message that has the adverse impact on the appearance of the landscape. In *Schneider,* an antilittering statute could have addressed the substantive evil without prohibiting expressive activity, whereas application of the prophylactic rule actually employed gratuitously infringed upon the right of an individual to communicate directly with a willing listener. Here, the substantive evil—visual blight—is not merely a possible by-product of the activity, but is created by the medium of expression itself. In contrast to *Schneider,* therefore, the application of the ordinance in this case responds precisely to the substantive problem which legitimately concerns the City. The ordinance curtails no more speech than is necessary to accomplish its purpose.

The Court of Appeals accepted the argument that a prohibition against the use of unattractive signs cannot be justified on esthetic grounds if it fails to apply to all equally unattractive signs wherever they might be located. But the validity of the esthetic interest in the elimination of signs on public property is not compromised by failing to extend the ban to private property. The private citizen's interest in controlling the use of his own property justifies the disparate treatment. Moreover, by not extending the ban to all locations, a significant opportunity to communicate by means of temporary signs is preserved, and private property owners' esthetic concerns will keep the posting of signs on their property within reasonable bounds. Even if some visual blight remains, a partial, content-neutral ban may nevertheless enhance the City's appearance.

they didn't ban private property from being able to have signs

While the First Amendment does not guarantee the right to employ every conceivable method of communication at all times and in all places, a restriction on expressive activity may be invalid if the remaining modes of communication are inadequate. The Los Angeles ordinance does not affect any individual's freedom to exercise the right to speak and to distribute literature in the same place where the posting of signs on public property is prohibited. To the extent that the posting of signs on public property has advantages over these forms of expression, there is no reason to believe that these same advantages cannot be obtained through other means. To the contrary, the findings of the District Court indicate that there are ample alternative modes of communication in Los Angeles.

Finally, Taxpayers and COGS argue that Los Angeles could have written an ordinance that would have had a less severe effect on expressive activity such as theirs, by permitting the posting of any kind of sign at any time on some types of public property, or by making a variety of other more specific exceptions to the ordinance: for signs carrying certain types of messages (such as political campaign signs), for signs posted during specific time periods (perhaps during political campaigns), for particular locations (perhaps for areas already cluttered by an excessive number of signs on adjacent private property), or for signs meeting design specifications (such as size or color). Plausible public policy arguments might well be made in support of any such exception, but it by no means follows that it is therefore constitutionally mandated, nor is it clear that some of the suggested exceptions would even be constitutionally permissible. For example, even though political speech is entitled to the fullest possible measure of constitutional protection, there are a host of other communications that command the same respect. An assertion that "Jesus Saves," that "Abortion is Murder," that every woman has the "Right to Choose," or that "Alcohol Kills," may have a claim to a constitutional exemption from the ordinance that is just as strong as "Roland Vincent—City Council." To create an exception for appellees' political speech and not these other types of speech might create a risk of engaging in constitutionally forbidden content discrimination. Moreover, the volume of permissible postings under such a mandated exemption might so limit the ordinance's effect as to defeat its aim of combating visual blight.

Any constitutionally mandated exception to the City's total prohibition against temporary signs on public property would necessarily rest on a judicial determination that the City's traffic control and safety interests had little or no applicability within the excepted category, and that the City's interests in esthetics are not sufficiently important to justify the prohibition in that category. But the findings of the District Court provide no basis for questioning the substantiality of the esthetic interest at stake, or for believing that a uniquely important form of communication has been abridged for the categories of expression engaged in by Taxpayers and COGS. Therefore, we accept the City's position that it may decide that the esthetic interest in avoiding "visual clutter" justifies a removal of signs creating or increasing that clutter. The findings of the District Court that COGS signs add to the problems addressed by the ordinance and, if permitted to remain, would encourage others to post additional signs, are sufficient to justify application of the ordinance to these appellees.

As recognized in Metromedia, if the city has a sufficient basis for believing that billboards are traffic hazards and are unattractive, "then obviously the most direct and perhaps the only effective approach to solving the problems they create is to prohibit them." As is true of billboards, the esthetic interests that are implicated by temporary signs are presumptively at work in all parts of the city, including those where appellees posted their signs, and there is no basis in the record in this case upon which to rebut that presumption. These interests are both psychological and economic. The character of the environment affects the quality of life and the value of property in both residential and commercial areas. We hold that on this record these interests are sufficiently substantial to justify this content-neutral, impartially administered prohibition against the posting of appellees' temporary signs on public property and that such an application of the ordinance does not create an unacceptable threat to the "profound national commitment to the principle that debate on public issues should be uninhibited, robust, and wide-open."

The judgment of the Court of Appeals is reversed, and the case is remanded to that Court.

Justice Brennan, with whom Justice Marshall and Justice Blackmun join, dissenting.

The Court finds that the City's "interest in eliminating visual clutter is sufficiently substantial to justify the effect of the ordinance on appellees' expression" and that the effect of the ordinance on speech is "no greater than necessary to accomplish the City's purpose." These are the right questions to consider when analyzing the constitutionality of the challenged ordinance, but the answers that the Court provides reflect a startling insensitivity to the principles embodied in the First Amendment. In my view, the City of Los Angeles has not shown that its interest in eliminating "visual clutter" justifies its restriction of appellees' ability to communicate with the local electorate.

In cases like this, where a total ban is imposed on a particularly valuable method of communication, a court should require the government to provide tangible proof of the legitimacy and substantiality of its aesthetic objective. Justifications for such restrictions articulated by the government should be critically examined to determine whether the government has committed itself to addressing the identified aesthetic problem.

In my view, such statements of aesthetic objectives should be accepted as substantial and unrelated to the suppression of speech only if the government demonstrates that it is pursuing an identified objective seriously and comprehensively and in ways that are unrelated to the restriction of speech. Without such a demonstration, I would invalidate the restriction as violative of the First Amendment.

Accordingly, in order for Los Angeles to succeed in defending its total ban on the posting of signs, the City would have to demonstrate that it is pursuing its goal of eliminating visual clutter in a serious and comprehensive manner. In this case, however, as the Court of Appeals found, there is no indication that the City has addressed its visual clutter problem in any way other than by prohibiting the posting of signs—throughout the City and without regard to the density of their presence. Therefore, I would hold that the prohibition violates appellees' First Amendment rights.

Points for Discussion

1. **Why did the Court think that the Los Angeles ordinance was content-neutral?** The ordinance prohibited the placement of signs on public property. Signs contain content. So why was the law content-neutral?

2. **Why did the Court uphold the Los Angeles ordinance?** Once the Court determined that the ordinance was content-neutral, it evaluated the ordinance under intermediate scrutiny. Can you articulate why the law satisfied the elements of intermediate scrutiny?

3. **Why not a political sign exception?** The plaintiffs in *Taxpayers for Vincent* contended that Los Angeles could have drafted a more narrowly tailored ordinance that would have allowed the posting of political signs on public property, but

not signs with other messages. That sounds like a reasonable compromise, especially given Chief Justice John Roberts' observation that "speech on public issues occupies the highest rung of the hierarchy of First Amendment values." *Snyder v. Phelps*, 562 U.S. 443, 452 (2011). Yet the *Taxpayers for Vincent* opinion suggests that an exception for political speech would create its own constitutional problem. Can you identify what that problem would be? *Compare City of Cincinnati v. Discovery Network, Inc.*, 507 U.S. 410 (1993) (striking down a city ordinance that permitted news racks on public property if they contained newspapers but not if they contained commercial handbills).

4. **What might cause a content-neutral law to fail intermediate scrutiny?** Content-neutral laws do not get a free pass but instead are subject to intermediate scrutiny, under which some laws will survive, and some laws will fail. That raises the conundrum of what factors might cause a content-neutral law to fail intermediate scrutiny. We will explore that topic in depth in Chapter 13, but the discussion in *Taxpayers for Vincent* gives you a hint of what lies ahead. The Court refers to a case in which a content-neutral ban on leafletting was struck down, *Schneider v. State*, 308 U.S. 147 (1939), but then explains why *Schneider*'s reasoning does not apply to the law at issue in *Taxpayers for Vincent*. What is the distinction the Court makes between the total ban on leafletting in *Schneider* and the total ban on signs on public property in *Taxpayers for Vincent*? You will read the *Schneider* opinion in Chapter 13.

5. **Regulating speech on private property.** The ordinance at issue in *Taxpayers for Vincent* concerned the placement of signs on public property, but don't let that mislead you into thinking that the government cannot regulate speech on private property. It can and does. For example, the law at issue in *Reed* regulated signage on both private and public property. The mere ownership of property does not give one the right to do whatever he wants on it (*e.g.*, run a prostitution ring, use cocaine, or host loud parties in the middle of the night). If you don't believe this, try putting a billboard on top of your suburban home (assuming you own one) and see what happens.

You Be the Judge!

Are these laws content-based or content-neutral?

Now that you're an expert on the content-based/content-neutral distinction, it's time to test your knowledge. Give your opinion on whether each of the following government actions is content-based or content-neutral. If you think there are good arguments either way, give both arguments.

1. A law prohibiting political signs that are larger than 10 square feet on people's lawns. CB

2. A law prohibiting signs that are larger than 10 square feet on people's lawns.

3. A law prohibiting signs advocating for the legalization of marijuana.

4. A law prohibiting expressive activities within 1,000 feet of a military base.

5. A law prohibiting expressive activities within 1,000 feet of a military base, except for expression concerning the rights of veterans, which may occur within 500 feet of a military base.

6. A law prohibiting expressive activities within 1,000 feet of a military base, except for expression by members of an organization that represents veterans, which may occur within 500 feet of a military base.

7. A law that makes it a crime to willfully disturb the peace as applied to a person who publicly wore a shirt that said, "What the Fuck?"

8. A law prohibiting expressive activities within 200 feet of an abortion clinic entrance.

9. A law requiring adult entertainment establishments to be concentrated in one area of a small city.

10. A law prohibiting fires on public sidewalks as applied to an anti-war protester who set fire to a military uniform on a public sidewalk.

B. How Is the Government Regulating Speech? Vagueness, Overbreadth, and Prior Restraints

In addition to considering *why* the government is regulating speech, judges consider *how* the government is regulating speech. Judges want to make sure that the government is using precisely drafted laws and not vague or overbroad laws that could chill speech. Judges are also concerned when the government prohibits people from speaking as opposed to punishing them after they have spoken. This section explores these topics.

1. Vagueness: When Speakers Are Unsure of What Speech Is Prohibited

Imagine a law that prohibits bookstores from selling books to anyone under 18 years of age if the books are "harmful to minors." Violators can be sentenced to jail for up to one year and subjected to a fine of up to $50,000.

Now imagine that you own a bookstore. Would it be clear to you which books you could or could not sell to minors? To avoid criminal liability, would you refuse to sell minors any book other than the most bland and innocuous? Would you be willing to sell minors *Catcher in the Rye, Huckleberry Finn, The Bluest Eye, To Kill a Mockingbird, Harry Potter and the Sorcerer's Stone, Beyond Magenta: Transgender Teens Speak Out*, or even *Captain Underpants*? Is it possible that a prosecutor might think that some or all these books could be "harmful to minors"?

The problem with this law is that it is vague. A vague law is a law that fails to give a reasonable person adequate notice as to what actions are prohibited. Any criminal law can be invalidated for vagueness on due process grounds, but the Supreme Court finds vague speech regulations especially problematic. That is because vague speech laws can chill protected speech.

The bookstore hypothetical is illustrative. If you are unsure of what books are harmful to minors and do not fancy spending a year in jail, you will be reluctant to sell any book to minors that has even the slightest chance of being considered harmful. Consequently, minors will be denied access to a wide range of books that they have a First Amendment right to read. This spillover effect on protected speech is how vague laws chill speech. As Justice Samuel Alito explained, "Vague laws force potential speakers to steer far wider of the unlawful zone than if the boundaries of the forbidden areas were clearly marked."[13]

Vague laws also endanger free speech interests because they create the risk of selective or arbitrary enforcement. Here, too, the bookstore example is instructive. Because an extremely wide range of books could potentially be considered harmful to minors, the law gives government officials broad discretion over which books to target for enforcement. Officials could exercise this discretion arbitrarily, such as by targeting books that they personally find offensive. As Justice Sandra Day O'Connor observed, a law that fails to provide "minimal guidelines to govern law enforcement allows policemen, prosecutors, and juries to pursue their personal predilections."[14]

The following case illustrates the Supreme Court's jurisprudence on vague speech regulations.

---

13 *Brown v. Entertainment Merchants Ass'n*, 564 U.S. 786, 807 (2011) (Alito, J., concurring).

14 *Kolender v. Lawson*, 461 U.S. 352, 358 (1983).

Coates v. City of Cincinnati

Supreme Court of the United States, 1971
402 U.S. 611

MR. JUSTICE STEWART delivered the opinion of the Court.

A Cincinnati, Ohio, ordinance makes it a criminal offense for "three or more persons to assemble on any of the sidewalks and there conduct themselves in a manner annoying to persons passing by." The issue before us is whether this ordinance is unconstitutional on its face.

The appellants were convicted of violating the ordinance, and the convictions were ultimately affirmed by a closely divided vote in the Supreme Court of Ohio, upholding the constitutional validity of the ordinance. An appeal from that judgment was brought and we noted probable jurisdiction. The record brought before the reviewing courts tells us no more than that the appellant Coates was a student involved in a demonstration and the other appellants were pickets involved in a labor dispute. For throughout this litigation it has been the appellants' position that the ordinance on its face violates the First and Fourteenth Amendments of the Constitution.

In rejecting this claim and affirming the convictions the Ohio Supreme Court did not give the ordinance any construction at variance with the apparent plain import of its language. The court simply stated:

> The ordinance prohibits, inter alia, "conduct annoying to persons passing by." The word "annoying" is a widely used and well understood word; it is not necessary to guess its meaning. "Annoying" is the present participle of the transitive verb "annoy" which means to trouble, to vex, to impede, to incommode, to provoke, to harass or to irritate.
>
> We conclude, as did the Supreme Court of the United States in *Cameron v. Johnson*, 390 U.S. 611, 616 in which the issue of the vagueness of a statute was presented, that the ordinance "clearly and precisely delineates its reach in words of common understanding. It is a precise and narrowly drawn regulatory statute evincing a legislative judgment that certain specific conduct be proscribed."

Beyond this, the only construction put upon the ordinance by the state court was its unexplained conclusion that "the standard of conduct which it specifies is not dependent upon each complainant's sensitivity." But the court did not indicate upon whose sensitivity a violation does depend—the sensitivity of the judge or jury, the sensitivity of the arresting officer, or the sensitivity of a hypothetical reasonable man.

We are thus relegated, at best, to the words of the ordinance itself. If three or more people meet together on a sidewalk or street corner, they must conduct themselves so as not to annoy any police officer or other person who should happen to pass by. In our opinion this ordinance is unconstitutionally vague because it subjects the exercise of the right of assembly to an unascertainable standard, and unconstitutionally broad because it authorizes the punishment of constitutionally protected conduct.

Conduct that annoys some people does not annoy others. Thus, the ordinance is vague, not in the sense that it requires a person to conform his conduct to an imprecise but comprehensible normative standard, but rather in the sense that no standard of conduct is specified at all. As a result, "men of common intelligence must necessarily guess at its meaning."

people have to guess what annoyance would be

It is said that the ordinance is broad enough to encompass many types of conduct clearly within the city's constitutional power to prohibit. And so, indeed, it is. The city is free to prevent people from blocking sidewalks, obstructing traffic, littering streets, committing assaults, or engaging in countless other forms of antisocial conduct. It can do so through the enactment and enforcement of ordinances directed with reasonable specificity toward the conduct to be prohibited. It cannot constitutionally do so through the enactment and enforcement of an ordinance whose violation may entirely depend upon whether or not a policeman is annoyed.

But the vice of the ordinance lies not alone in its violation of the due process standard of vagueness. The ordinance also violates the constitutional right of free assembly and association. Our decisions establish that mere public intolerance or animosity cannot be the basis for abridgment of these constitutional freedoms. The First and Fourteenth Amendments do not permit a State to make criminal the exercise of the right of assembly simply because its exercise may be "annoying" to some people. If this were not the rule, the right of the people to gather in public places for social or political purposes would be continually subject to summary suspension through the good-faith enforcement of a prohibition against annoying conduct. And such a prohibition, in addition, contains an obvious invitation to discriminatory enforcement against those whose association together is "annoying" because their ideas, their lifestyle, or their physical appearance is resented by the majority of their fellow citizens.

also violates free assembly

The ordinance before us makes a crime out of what under the Constitution cannot be a crime. It is aimed directly at activity protected by the Constitution. We need not lament that we do not have before us the details of the conduct found to be annoying. It is the ordinance on its face that sets the standard of conduct and warns against transgression. The details of the offense could no more serve to validate this ordinance than could the details of an offense charged under an ordinance suspending unconditionally the right of assembly and free speech.

The judgment is reversed.

[Justice Black's separate opinion is omitted, as is Justice White's dissenting opinion, which was joined by Chief Justice Burger and Justice Blackmun.]

Points for Discussion

1. **Why did the Court think that the Cincinnati ordinance was unconstitutionally vague?** The Court said the statute was broad enough to encompass conduct that was clearly within the city's constitutional power to prohibit. So why was the law unconstitutional?

2. **Can judges fix an overly vague law?** The Supreme Court observed that "the Ohio Supreme Court did not give the ordinance any construction at variance with the apparent plain import of its language." Consequently, the justices were "relegated, at best, to the words of the ordinance itself." But what if the Ohio court had construed the Cincinnati law in a manner that corrected its vagueness? The implication of the Supreme Court's opinion is that a lower court's narrowing interpretation of a facially vague law can save the law from being pronounced unconstitutional. That is correct. The Court also uses this principle to decide whether an overly broad speech regulation, a topic we turn to in the next section, has been repaired by a narrowing judicial construction.

3. **What is the difference between a "facial" and an "as applied" challenge?** Justice Potter Stewart began the *Coates* opinion by stating that "the issue before us is whether this ordinance is unconstitutional on its face." What did he mean by a law being unconstitutional "on its face"? As will become clearer in the next section on overbreadth, if a court finds a law to be unconstitutional on its face, or "facially unconstitutional," it means that the law is so problematic that it may not be enforced against anyone. The Court effectively strikes the law from the books even if it is not actually repealed and removed.

   If a law is not facially unconstitutional, parties can still claim that the law "as applied" to them is unconstitutional. If a party succeeds in bringing an "as applied" challenge, the law remains on the books, but the government may not use the law to punish the party's specific speech.

2. Overbreadth: When Laws Regulate Too Much Speech

Let's return to your imaginary bookstore. Now imagine that a state enacts a criminal law that prohibits the sale of material containing images of a naked body. The legislative history indicates that the law was intended to prevent the sale of obscene materials.

You learned earlier in this chapter that obscene speech is not protected by the First Amendment and that the government may constitutionally prohibit its distribution. As you will learn in Chapter 7, however, the Supreme Court has narrowly defined obscenity so that it includes only graphic sexual materials, such as depictions of ultimate sexual acts or lewd exhibitions of the genitals.

Now return to the state law criminalizing the sale of material containing images of a naked body. Could this law be used to punish the sale of obscene materials? Yes—obscene material invariably includes images of naked bodies. But could this law also be used to punish the sale of non-obscene materials? Yes, again. Indeed, this law potentially criminalizes the sale of vast amounts of protected speech, such as anatomy textbooks, books about breast cancer, sex education books, or art books reproducing Botticelli's *Birth of Venus* or Michelangelo's sculpture of David.

The problem with this law is its overbreadth. It regulates not only unprotected speech but also protected speech. Like vague laws, overly broad laws suffer from imprecision. With vagueness, this imprecision produces laws that are unclear about which speech is prohibited. With overbreadth, the imprecision leads to laws that sweep protected speech into a net aimed at unprotected speech.

Overbroad laws, like vague laws, can chill speech. As Justice William Brennan explained, the danger from overbroad laws is that "persons whose expression is constitutionally protected may well refrain from exercising their rights for fear of criminal sanctions."[15]

The Supreme Court is sufficiently concerned about overly broad speech restrictions that it allows parties whose speech is unprotected to challenge laws because of their impact on parties whose speech is protected. This is an exception to the usual standing rule that bars a party from asserting the rights of third parties. The Supreme Court created this exception to help ensure that overbroad laws will be stricken from the books:

> We have consistently allowed attacks on overly broad statutes with no requirement that the person making the attack demonstrate that his own conduct could not be regulated by a statute drawn with the requisite narrow specificity. We have fashioned this exception to the usual rules governing standing because of the danger of tolerating, in the area of First Amendment freedoms, the existence of a penal statute susceptible of sweeping and improper application.[16]

15 *Gooding v. Wilson*, 405 U.S. 518, 521 (1972).

16 *Dombrowski v. Pfister*, 380 U.S. 479, 486–87 (1965).

To appreciate this exception, let's return to the bookstore hypothetical. Assume that you are being prosecuted under the law that bans the sale of material with naked body images. Let's further assume that your bookstore is an adult bookstore and that most of the material you sell is obscene.

The fact that you are selling obscene materials means that the government could prosecute you under a more precisely drafted law. But here you are being prosecuted under a wildly overbroad law. And that, it turns out, is your good fortune.

The Supreme Court's expansive standing rule means that you can bring a facial challenge to this law even though the material you are selling is not protected by the First Amendment. In effect, you, the obscenity purveyor, get to argue that the law is unconstitutional because of its impact on innocent purveyors of anatomy texts and art books. If you succeed, you will not only get the law stricken from the books but also escape liability yourself because the government may not prosecute you under an unconstitutional statute. Of course, the legislature could adopt a more precisely drafted statute that could be used to prosecute you in the future. For now, however, you are off the hook.

Recognizing that the remedy of striking a law from the books is "strong medicine,"[17] the Supreme Court has taken action to limit its availability. After all, language is inherently imprecise, so some degree of overbreadth is inevitable in almost any speech regulation. To ensure that all speech regulations are not vulnerable to an overbreadth challenge, the Court has held that a facial overbreadth challenge will succeed only if a law's overbreadth is "substantial."[18]

But what happens if a law is somewhat, but not substantially, overbroad and is being applied to someone whose speech is protected? The law would not be struck down as facially unconstitutional because its overbreadth is not substantial. But the defendant could still claim that the law "as applied" to her is unconstitutional. If she succeeds, the law will not be stricken from the books, but the government will be barred from prosecuting her under the law.

Point for Discussion

1. **Overbreadth and vagueness are not the same.** It is not uncommon for laws to have problems with both vagueness and overbreadth, but it is important to keep in mind that the two concepts are different. A law that prohibits the distribution of any photographic image that displays a woman's breasts or a person's genitals is probably not vague. It gives people clear notice of what images may not be

---

17 *Broadrick v. Oklahoma*, 413 U.S. 601, 613 (1973).

18 *Id.* at 615.

distributed. But the law is overbroad because it applies to images that are both obscene and not obscene. By contrast, a law that makes it illegal to distribute "obscene material" but does not define the term "obscene" is unconstitutionally vague. People would have to guess what material would be considered obscene. At the same time, the law is not overbroad because it applies to only obscene material, which is not protected by the First Amendment.

3. Prior Restraints: When Government Prohibits People from Speaking

You were introduced to the concept of prior restraints in Chapter 2 when we learned about the English licensing system that required books to be approved by the government before they could be published. Parliament allowed this system to lapse in the late 17th century. Nevertheless, hostility to prior restraints became ingrained in the law. William Blackstone's treatise on English common law captured this hostility when it said that liberty of the press consists "of laying no previous restraints upon publications."[19]

The English aversion to prior restraints found its way across the Atlantic into American jurisprudence. This culminated in the Supreme Court's famous proclamation that "any system of prior restraints of expression comes to this Court bearing a heavy presumption against its constitutional validity."[20] This proclamation suggests that prior restraints are virtually never tolerated. In truth, the rules are more nuanced.

Prior restraints typically occur in two contexts: administrative licensing regimes, such as laws requiring a permit before holding a rally or parade, and court orders enjoining speech. This section briefly explores each topic. We will return to these topics at various points in subsequent chapters.

Before jumping into the material, it is worth pondering why prior restraints are so reviled. Probably the most salient concern is that prior restraints suppress speech before it enters the marketplace of ideas. Consequently, the public is deprived of the opportunity to hear the speaker's message. By contrast, the public is not denied this opportunity if a speaker is punished *after* he has spoken. As Professor Alexander Bickel pithily put it, "A criminal statute chills, prior restraint freezes."[21]

Some commentators contend that this critique exaggerates the chilling effect of prior restraints and understates the chilling effect of criminal sanctions. Consider two examples. In the first, a court, after a thorough hearing, concludes that a party's speech constitutes unprotected defamation and therefore enjoins the speech's publication. In

---

19 4 William Blackstone, Commentaries on the Laws of England 151 (1765).

20 *New York Times Co. v. United States*, 403 U.S. 713, 714 (1971)).

21 Alexander Bickel, The Morality of Consent 61 (1975).

the second, a law makes it a crime to criticize the president and provides a 20-year prison term for violations. The first is a prior restraint. The second is not. Yet the latter seems much more likely to chill speech than the former.

The notion that prior restraints prevent ideas from entering the marketplace of ideas is also misleading. Unless a court enjoining speech places the prospective speaker in jail, the court order will not physically stop the speaker from communicating her message. And, if the speaker violates the order, any punishment (such as contempt of court) would come only *after* the speaker's ideas had entered the marketplace.

Perhaps the strongest argument for why court orders enjoining speech are problematic is based on the implications of the "collateral bar" rule. This rule provides that a person may not defend against a contempt charge for violating a court order on the basis that the underlying order was invalid or even unconstitutional.[22] The idea is that people should respect court orders and not ignore them. If they believe an order is unconstitutional, they should appeal it to a higher court and get the issue resolved through the judicial process.

The collateral bar rule arguably makes court injunctions against speech especially troublesome because a person will be reluctant to speak even if she believes a court order is unconstitutional (and even if the order is unconstitutional). The Supreme Court has somewhat mitigated the rule's chilling effect by suggesting that people may challenge a contempt charge if the underlying order was "transparently invalid or had only a frivolous pretense to validity."[23] Nevertheless, the wisest course of action is to seek an expedited appeal to get the order vacated.

The danger of prior restraints is perhaps more evident in the context of administrative licensing. As Professor Thomas Emerson observed, prior restraints allow a government official to censor speech "by a simple stroke of the pen."[24] Emerson expressed concern that government bureaucrats, influenced by their personal "attitudes, drives, emotions, and impulses," will err on the side of over-censoring.[25] After all, Emerson noted, the "function of the censor is to censor."[26]

These are all valid concerns. But should they preclude the government from having any administrative licensing regimes? Read on to find out.

a. Administrative Licensing: Permits for Rallies and Parades

It is easy to appreciate why a law, such as the old English law requiring government permission to publish a book, is abhorrent to the First Amendment. The law

22 *Walker v. City of Birmingham*, 388 U.S. 307 (1967). *See* Stephen Barnett, *The Puzzle of Prior Restraint*, 29 Stan. L. Rev. 539, 552 (1977).

23 *Id.* at 315.

24 Thomas Emerson, *The Doctrine of Prior Restraint*, 20 Law & Contemp. Probs. 648, 657 (1955).

25 *Id.* at 658.

26 *Id.* at 659.

allows the government to decide which ideas the public may hear and raises the specter that the government will suppress speech that threatens its power or agenda.

But what about a New York City ordinance requiring a permit before holding a rally in Central Park? Here, too, a party is required to receive government permission before engaging in speech. Should that be enough to condemn the ordinance as an unconstitutional prior restraint? Or is it perfectly reasonable for a city to control when and where people hold large rallies?

As you might have guessed, cities are allowed to have permit requirements for large events like rallies and parades. Yet how does that square with the notion that prior restraints bear a "heavy presumption" of unconstitutionality?

Much of the answer lies in this chapter's earlier discussion of the content-based/content-neutral distinction. Administrative licensing regimes that award permits based on a speaker's message are virtually per se unconstitutional. One rare exception is a regime requiring movies to be cleared as non-obscene by a censorship board. The Supreme Court has said that such a regime can be constitutional if it contains rigorous procedural safeguards, including placing the burden of proof on the censor and requiring a prompt judicial determination to confirm a censor's decision that a work is obscene.[27]

By contrast, licensing regimes that issue permits based on content-neutral justifications, such as safety and security, traffic control, or tranquility, are much more likely to pass constitutional muster. We will study the legality of these regimes in Chapter 13 when we examine content-neutral regulations of speech.

b. Court Orders Enjoining Speech: Stop the Presses!

The other common type of prior restraint is a court order enjoining a party from speaking. Perhaps the most dramatic version of this would be a court injunction ordering a newspaper to "STOP THE PRESSES!" before publishing a story that the government wants suppressed. We will read a case involving such a scenario in Chapter 5 when we consider the legality of enjoining the press from publishing stories that the government claims will endanger national security. Similarly, in Chapter 16, we will consider whether courts can enjoin news reporting about a crime to ensure that a defendant receives a fair trial.

As noted above, court orders enjoining speech pose special First Amendment concerns because of the collateral bar rule. Perhaps for that reason, these orders bear a heavy presumption against their constitutionality.

Nevertheless, a blanket assertion about the unconstitutionality of court orders enjoining speech is misleading. For years, courts have routinely issued injunctions

[27] *Freedman v. Maryland*, 380 U.S. 51 (1965).

in intellectual property cases as remedies for copyright, trademark, and trade secret infringements, even though these orders enjoined speech. The tension between these perfunctorily issued remedies and the Supreme Court's condemnation of prior restraints went unnoticed for many years. More recently, scholars have called out this tension, and courts have begun wrestling with it.[28]

C. Where Do We Go from Here? A Quick Look Back and a Glance Forward

You now have the big picture of how free speech jurisprudence works. First, a court needs to determine if a claim implicates the First Amendment. This will depend on whether a person has successfully pleaded that the government has abridged her speech. If a court determines that the First Amendment has been implicated, it will then turn to the larger question of whether the abridgment of speech is constitutional. To answer that question, the court will consider both why the government is regulating speech (because of its message or regardless of its message) and how the government is regulating the speech (with vague or overbroad laws or a prior restraint). This will, in turn, inform the court's choice of which framework of analysis to use in determining the law's constitutionality.

Of course, as previously noted, the Supreme Court's framework for evaluating free speech claims is a work in progress that continues to evolve. As an example, the Court recently clarified that there is a fourth level of scrutiny, called "exacting scrutiny," that it uses in cases concerning compelled disclosure and campaign finance laws. The precise contours of this level of scrutiny are not fully fleshed out, but the Court did indicate that the standard is less demanding than strict scrutiny but more demanding than intermediate scrutiny.[29] The Court described the standard as requiring a "substantial relation" between a disclosure requirement and a "sufficiently important governmental interest," and that the disclosure requirement be "narrowly tailored to the interest it promotes."[30]

To help you get a handle on the various levels of scrutiny, we have provided a chart setting forth the rules for each level of scrutiny at the end of this chapter.

So where do we go from here?

---

[28] *See* Mark A. Lemley & Eugene Volokh, *Freedom of Speech and Injunctions in Intellectual Property Cases*, 48 Duke L.J. 147 (1998); *Garcia v. Google, Inc.*, 786 F.3d 733, 747 (9th Cir. 2015).

[29] For an early attempt to explore the meaning of "exacting scrutiny" and a general critique of how the Supreme Court applies the levels of scrutiny, *see* Alex Chemerinsky, *Tears of Scrutiny*, 57 Tulsa L. Rev. 341 (2022).

[30] *Americans for Prosperity Found. v. Bonta*, 141 S. Ct. 2373, 2383–84 (2021).

All levels of scrutiny focus on whether a purported governmental interest (whether it be compelling, sufficiently important, significant, or legitimate) is adequate to justify a government abridgment of speech. The remaining chapters on freedom of speech build on that framework by organizing the cases around the purported governmental justification for regulating speech. These interests range widely, from ensuring people's safety and security to fostering equality to eliminating visual clutter.

We begin in the next chapter with the most challenging issue of all: When may the government regulate speech that incites or provokes lawbreaking or threatens individuals with violence?

LEVELS OF SCRUTINY

Level of Scrutiny	Triggers	Burden of Proof	Government Interest	Tailoring (nexus between government interest and regulatory means used to achieve it)	Likely Outcome
Strict Scrutiny	Content-based laws and speaker-based laws Most prior restraints (court orders enjoining speech and licensing regimes that are content-based or give unfettered discretion to licensors) **Other areas of constitutional law:** Used for "suspect classifications" (such as race) in equal protection jurisprudence or for laws that burden "fundamental rights" in substantive due process jurisprudence	On government	"Compelling"	"Precisely tailored" or "least restrictive means" (Sometimes decisions use the phrase "narrowly tailored." But that phrase is more rigorous when used for strict scrutiny than for exacting scrutiny.)	Government almost always loses

Exacting Scrutiny	A rarely used level of scrutiny slightly less demanding than strict scrutiny but more demanding than intermediate scrutiny The principal use is for campaign finance and compelled disclosure laws	On government	Sufficiently important	"Narrowly tailored" Less demanding than the tailoring for strict scrutiny but more demanding than for intermediate scrutiny	Government usually loses
Intermediate Scrutiny	Content-neutral conduct regulations that incidentally burden expressive conduct (*O'Brien* test) Content-neutral restrictions on expression in the public forum (time, place, or manner test) Regulations of commercial speech (the *Central Hudson* test) **Other areas of constitutional law:** Used in equal protection jurisprudence for "quasi suspect" classifications such as gender and nonmarital children	On government	"Important" or "substantial" or "significant"	"Substantially related" (Sometimes decisions use phrases like "narrowly tailored" or "no greater than is essential," which might suggest the precise tailoring required for strict scrutiny, but intermediate scrutiny requires only a reasonable fit and not a nearly perfect fit. The requirement is better captured by the words "substantially related.")	50/50 While in theory this test is "even odds," in certain arenas the results tend to favor challengers, and in others the government. In current commercial speech cases, speakers tend to often win. By contrast, the government often prevails in "time, place, or manner" public forum cases. **Other areas of constitutional law:** In gender discrimination cases, the challengers almost always win

Rational Basis	Default level of review in constitutional law; not frequently used in First Amendment cases **Other areas of constitutional law:** Used in substantive due process and equal protection jurisprudence when no fundamental rights or suspect or quasi-suspect classifications are implicated The normal rule for review of most economic and social legislation	On challenger	"Legitimate" This means almost any conceivable interest, including an interest not mentioned when the law is enacted but later posited by the government's lawyers	"Rationally rated" Extremely deferential—almost any conceivable relation will do	Government almost always wins

Test Your Knowledge

To assess your understanding of the material in this chapter, click here to take a quiz.

Content-Based Regulations of Speech: When Speech Is Regulated Because of a Speaker's Message

Chapter Five

May Government Regulate Speech to Promote Safety and Security?

Incitement, Fighting Words, Hostile Audience, and True Threats

The most difficult issue confronting an open society is when the government may restrict the content of speech in the interest of safety and security. This chapter explores that topic by examining the rules the Supreme Court has developed for when the government may regulate speech that encourages lawbreaking, threatens others with violence, or provokes a violent reaction against the speaker. The final section of the chapter will consider the related question of when the government may use a prior restraint to prevent the publication of allegedly dangerous information.

The challenge posed by this speech is readily apparent. On the one hand, there is society's interest in its members' safety. Our constitutional rights are precious, but they can seem like a luxury if people lack basic security. Tragic events like 9/11 or the all-too-common mass shootings remind us that our most precious gift is to be safe.

On the other hand, there is our constitutional commitment to freedom of speech. In an open society, people must be free to criticize laws and the officials who enforce them. After all, laws can be unjust. Just think of the Rev. Martin Luther King, Jr. condemning Jim Crow laws.

What should happen when these two interests collide? People must be free to criticize laws without fear of retribution, but speech that criticizes laws can encourage others to disrespect or even break those laws. Speech that condemns the government as corrupt or oppressive can inspire others to pursue extra-legal means to effect political change. The question is how to balance our commitment to free speech against our competing interests in safety and security.

This chapter will examine how the Supreme Court has balanced these interests in four specific areas:

- ***Incitement:*** When may the government regulate speech that advocates, encourages, or incites unlawful action?
- ***Fighting words and hostile audience:*** When may the government regulate speech that provokes a violent reaction against the speaker?
- ***True threats:*** When may the government regulate speech that threatens violence against others?
- ***Prior restraints:*** When may courts enjoin publication of information that the government claims would endanger national security?

In each of these instances, the government would be regulating speech because of its message. As you know from the previous chapter, such content-based regulations of speech ordinarily trigger strict scrutiny and are usually struck down. If the Supreme Court were to uphold these regulations, it would be either because the regulations could survive strict scrutiny or, alternatively, because the speech had been declared categorically unprotected by the First Amendment. As you will discover, the Court does a bit of both in this area. On the one hand, the Court treats incitement, fighting words, and true threats as categories of unprotected speech. On the other hand, the Court's method for defining these categories has largely been driven, as it is with a strict scrutiny analysis, by a balancing of the government's interest in regulating the speech against the impact of any regulation on freedom of speech.

A. Incitement: Speech That Encourages, Advocates, or Incites Lawbreaking

The government may punish those who engage in violence, vandalize property, or violate other types of conduct regulations. In this section, we wrestle with a different issue: May the government punish those who merely encourage others to break the law? This issue arises even if the people encouraged by the speaker never break the law.

1. Introductory Hypothetical: What Should Be the Limits on Strident Anti-Abortion Speech?

To understand the incitement issue, it is helpful to begin with a hypothetical. Imagine that there is a deeply religious man named John who is stridently opposed to abortion. John's religion has taught him that a human life begins as soon as a woman's egg is fertilized and that the deliberate destruction of a fertilized egg is equivalent to murder. Given this perspective, John believes that abortion doctors are mass murderers and that the widespread use of abortions is an ongoing genocide of innocent children.

John feels a moral imperative to do everything he can to stop this genocide. But John is a law-abiding citizen. He would never engage in violence against an abortion doctor. He would never vandalize an abortion clinic. However, he does believe that the First Amendment gives him the right to speak openly and forcefully about what he perceives as mass murder.

John certainly does have a right to express his opposition to abortion. Politicians, pundits, and citizens have been vociferously exercising that right for decades. But how far can John legally go in voicing his opposition?

To answer that question, review the following list of possible statements John might make. In each case, indicate whether you *personally* think that John's statement should or should not be protected by the First Amendment. If you think that John's statement should be protected, it means that the government may not punish John for expressing his message. If you think that John's message should not be protected, it means that the government may punish John for his message.

For now, focus only on whether the government may punish John because his speech encourages others to break the law. That is the incitement issue. It is important to note, however, that even when the government may not regulate speech under one theory, it may be able to regulate it under another. So, even if you think that the government may not regulate one of John's messages because it encourages lawbreaking, it may be possible that the government could regulate the same message under a different theory, such as because the speech threatens violence or is integral to the commission of a crime. We will consider these other theories later in this chapter. As we cover each new theory, you can return to this chart and determine whether any of John's messages could be regulated under that theory.

John's Message	Government should not be able to punish speech	Government should be able to punish speech
"Abortion is murder."		
"Abortion doctors are murderers."		
"Abortion doctors are mass murderers."		
"We need to stop abortion doctors from committing the genocide of children."		
"We need to stop abortion doctors by any means necessary."		
"We must kill abortion doctors before they kill any more innocent children."		
"Dr. A is an abortion doctor/mass murderer who lives at 123 Elm Street and leaves for work at 7:30 a.m. each morning."		
(Passionately speaking at a conference of anti-abortion advocates) "Abortion doctors are mass murderers! We must stop these murderers before more innocent children are killed!"		
(Passionately speaking to a group of angry anti-abortion protesters gathered in front of an abortion clinic) "Abortion doctors are killing children every day. (Pointing) There is one of those mass murderers walking toward the clinic door!"		
Publishing an article in an anti-abortion magazine that includes detailed instructions for how to make pipe bombs.		

Let's consider the various ways in which you could have answered these survey questions and some factors that might have influenced your choices.

One End of the Spectrum: Speech Is Not Protected If It Has Any Tendency to Encourage Lawbreaking (the "Bad Tendency" Test)

At one extreme, you might have concluded that the government should be free to punish all of John's statements. This could reflect your belief that the government should be able to punish any speech that has a tendency, no matter how remote, to encourage lawbreaking. In other words, you believe that our societal interests in safety and security override an individual's right to encourage others to break the law.

In the early 20th century, lower courts adopted a test that resembled this extreme position. They used what scholars refer to as the "bad tendency" test, which held that speech lost its protection if it had any tendency to lead to lawbreaking.[1]

Like any test, this one has a logic behind it. If our society's highest priority is to ensure its members' safety, the bad tendency test is an ideal option. We would punish not only those who violate the law, but also those who encourage people to violate the law.

Nevertheless, and as you will soon learn, the Supreme Court has rejected the bad tendency test. The justices have recognized that the test gives too much weight to safety and security and not enough to freedom of speech. As noted above, in an open society, people must have the freedom to criticize laws. After all, laws might be racially discriminatory, favor the rich over the poor, or create needless red tape.

To ensure that people feel free to criticize laws and government policies, the Supreme Court protects speech even if it tends to encourage lawbreaking. In his famous concurring opinion in *Whitney v. California*, 274 U.S. 357 (1927), part of which you read in Chapter 2, Justice Louis Brandeis stressed that the government may not suppress speech merely because it could lead to disorder:

> Those who won our independence by revolution were not cowards. They did not fear political change. They did not exalt order at the cost of liberty.

Justice Oliver Wendell Holmes, who initially used but then rejected the bad tendency test, made Justice Brandeis' point even more powerfully in a dissenting opinion in *Gitlow v. New York*, 268 U.S. 652, 673 (1925), in which Justice Holmes objected to a defendant's conviction for circulating literature that advocated a proletarian (or workers) revolution:

> If in the long run the beliefs expressed in proletarian dictatorship are destined to be accepted by the dominant forces of the community, the only meaning of free speech is that they should be given their chance and have their way.

---

[1] Geoffrey R. Stone, Perilous Times: Free Speech in Wartime 159, 170–73 (2004). Stone suggests that judges at the time assumed that the First Amendment embodied the rules articulated in William Blackstone's Commentaries on the Laws of England, discussed in Chapter 2, that freedom of speech barred only prior restraints and not speech that was "adjudged of a pernicious tendency" and was "destructive of the ends of society."

Food for Thought

Do you agree with Justice Holmes that people should have a right to advocate overthrowing the government? One could argue that denying people this right would be inconsistent with the Declaration of Independence, which presumed "the Right of the People to alter or to abolish" any government that failed to protect their rights? But does it make sense to give people the right to advocate overthrowing the government and abolishing the very Constitution that protects their civil liberties, including freedom of speech?

The Other End of the Spectrum: Speech Is Always Protected No Matter How Likely It Is to Encourage Lawbreaking

If, in the survey of John's statements, you indicated that all of them should be protected by the First Amendment, then your position falls on the opposite end of the spectrum: that speech can never be punished no matter how likely it is to encourage lawbreaking.

This is not an unreasonable position. You would most likely be thinking that, if anyone should be punished, it is the people who act on John's words by attacking abortion doctors, but not John, who merely engaged in speech.

Despite the elegant simplicity of this absolutist approach, the Supreme Court has never adopted it. In rejecting this position, the Court has implicitly assumed that at some point speech advocating unlawful action becomes so dangerous that society should be able to punish it.

One reason for rejecting the absolutist approach is that it immunizes a speaker from legal recourse no matter how deliberately he tries to incite lawbreaking. Should the First Amendment protect a speaker who riles up an angry anti-abortion crowd in front of an abortion clinic, points out an abortion doctor walking past, and implores the crowd to attack the doctor? President Abraham Lincoln captured the illogic of such an absolutist position when he defended his government's decision to prosecute a Civil War opponent who encouraged soldiers to desert the Union Army: "Must I shoot a simple-minded soldier boy who deserts, while I must not touch a hair of a wily agitator who induces him to desert?"[2]

Another reason for rejecting the absolutist approach is that it ignores the reality that words can lead to actions. As Justice Holmes explained in *Gitlow*: "Every idea is an incitement. It offers itself for belief and if believed it is acted on unless some other belief outweighs it, or some failure of energy stifles the movement at its birth."

---

2 Abraham Lincoln, Letter to Erastus Corning and Others (June 12, 1863), in 6 The Collected Works of Abraham Lincoln 266 (Roy P. Basler, ed., 1953).

"Eloquence," he continued, "may set fire to reason."

One final note. You might be thinking that even a person who physically attacked an abortion doctor could raise a First Amendment defense because he intended to express a message—that he opposes abortions—through his conduct. As you learned in Chapter 3, conduct will be considered speech under the *Spence* test if the actor intended to communicate a message through this conduct and others are likely to understand the message. Isn't that true here?

That is a fair observation and arguably correct. But, as you will learn in Chapter 14, the argument will provide little solace for the attacker. Even if his conduct were considered expressive, the First Amendment would still not be an obstacle to his prosecution because the criminal law for which he would be prosecuted (whether it be assault, battery, or murder) would not be punishing him because of his message but because of the physical harm he caused. It would be the equivalent of punishing a flag burner for arson as opposed to flag desecration. The Supreme Court also made it clear in *Wisconsin v. Mitchell*, 508 U.S. 476, 484 (1993), a case you will read in Chapter 6, that "a physical assault is not by any stretch of the imagination expressive conduct protected by the First Amendment."

Food for Thought

In the previous section, we considered whether people should have the right to advocate overthrowing the government. Justice Holmes suggested in *Gitlow* that they should. But in a chilling dissent written in 1949, in *Terminiello v. Chicago*, 337 U.S. 1 (1949), Justice Robert Jackson warned that favoring civil liberties too heavily over safety and security comes with its own risk. Justice Jackson was dissenting from a majority opinion that struck down the breach-of-peace conviction of a speaker whom Justice Jackson thought resembled the recently defeated fascist leaders of Europe and who had been deliberately stoking the flames of anger and prejudice in a highly volatile environment:

> This Court has gone far toward accepting the doctrine that civil liberty means the removal of all restraints and that all local attempts to maintain order are impairments of the liberty of the citizen. The choice is not between order and liberty. It is between liberty with order and anarchy without either. There is danger that, if the Court does not temper its doctrinaire logic with a little practical wisdom, it will convert the constitutional Bill of Rights into a suicide pact.

Do you think that the "little practical wisdom" Justice Jackson referred to provides adequate guidance to judges who are deciding when civil liberties need tempering for the sake of security?

The Murky Middle: Which Factors Should Cause Speech That Encourages Lawbreaking to Lose Its Protection?

If, in answering the survey, you concluded that some of John's messages were protected and some were not, then your view is somewhere between the two poles discussed above. You did not think that speech advocating lawbreaking is *never* protected, but you also did not think that the speech is *always* protected.

The good news is that your position accords with that of the Supreme Court justices. The bad news is that you need to figure out when speech advocating lawbreaking crosses the line from being protected to unprotected. What factors should cause this speech to lose its First Amendment protection?

There is no right answer to this question. You will soon learn which factors the justices have focused on. For now, it is helpful to survey some of the possible factors and examine their relative benefits and detriments.

- ***Factor #1: Did the speaker expressly tell listeners to break the law?***

This factor focuses on the difference between "direct" and "indirect" incitement. Direct incitement occurs when a speaker expressly tells listeners to break the law. A speaker engages in indirect incitement when he implies that listeners should break the law but never explicitly says so. In our hypothetical examples, John was engaging in direct incitement when he said, "We must kill abortion doctors before they kill any more innocent children." He was engaging in indirect incitement when he said, "Dr. A is an abortion doctor/mass murderer who lives at 123 Elm Street and leaves for work at 7:30 a.m. each morning."

The benefit of prosecuting only speakers who engage in direct incitement, a position advocated by the late Learned Hand, a prominent federal judge, is that it gives speakers clear guidance as to when their speech will be unprotected and helps protect these speakers from juror bias. *See Masses Publ'g Co. v. Patten*, 244 F. 535 (S.D.N.Y. 1917). Jurors are often unsympathetic to defendants in incitement cases because the defendants tend to be advocating for unpopular causes. A direct-incitement standard limits jurors' ability to convict defendants out of animus because there must be proof that the defendants expressly told others to break the law.

The downside of this approach is that it ignores the reality that speakers can incite others to act without expressly telling them to do so. When John told an angry crowd in front of an abortion clinic that "abortion doctors are killing children every day" and then, pointing at an abortion doctor, said, "There is one of those mass murderers walking toward the clinic door," he never expressly told the crowd to attack the doctor, but that message was strongly implied.

Scholars make this point by alluding to the famous funeral oration of Mark Antony in the Shakespeare play *Julius Caesar*, a classic example of indirect incitement. Brutus and his fellow conspirators had killed Caesar. Antony, speaking to the public at Caesar's funeral, never says outright that Caesar's death was wrongful and should be avenged. To the contrary, he continuously repeats the refrain that "Brutus is an honourable man." Yet everything Antony says suggests that Caesar was a good leader who cared for his people and was wrongfully slain. Antony never said "avenge Caesar's death." But by the end of his oration, the crowd knew what to do.

Hear It

Click here to listen to Charlton Heston's rendition of Mark Antony's oration over the body of Caesar.

- ***Factor #2: Was the speaker's message "likely" to lead to lawbreaking?***

Under this rule, a person's speech is unprotected only if it is "likely" to lead to lawbreaking. This is a fact question that would depend on the context in which the words were spoken. If a strident speaker tells a riled-up crowd in front of an abortion clinic that abortion doctors must be stopped by any means necessary, the speech might be likely to lead to unlawful action. But if a 90-year-old man gave the exact same speech to his wheelchair-bound friends in an assisted living facility, the speech is unlikely to lead to action.

Like the requirement of direct incitement, this factor has its pros and cons. On the pro side, if the goal is to balance speech interests against safety and security concerns, it makes sense to punish speech only when it is likely to lead to lawbreaking. Society has a weak interest in suppressing speech that is unlikely to do so.

On the con side, protection for a speaker's message turns on a subjective decision about the facts: Was the speaker's message likely to lead to lawbreaking? This gives considerable discretion to factfinders to conclude that a message was likely to lead to lawbreaking, especially if they dislike the message or the person who delivered it.

- ***Factor #3: Was the speech likely to lead to "imminent" unlawful action?***

This factor focuses on the timing between the speech and any likely unlawful action. If John said to an angry crowd in front of an abortion clinic entrance that "abortion doctors are murderers who must be stopped by any means necessary," this statement might lead to imminent unlawful action. But if John made the same statement at an anti-abortion group's annual barbeque, the message is not likely to lead to imminent action, even though it could potentially encourage unlawful action in the future.

As you will soon learn, the Supreme Court has long thought that the proximity between inciting speech and any likely unlawful action is a relevant factor for determining whether the speech should lose its First Amendment protection. Justice Holmes famously injected this element into the Court's analysis when he said in a seminal 1919 decision that incitement is unprotected only if it creates a "clear and present danger." *Schenck v. United States*, 249 U.S. 47, 52 (1919).

Like the other factors, the imminence test has its pros and cons. The benefit of this factor is that it can be extremely protective of speech. If speech encouraging unlawful action is protected unless it is likely to lead to imminent unlawful action, then in many instances it will be difficult to find the speech unprotected. That is almost certainly true for entertainment like violent films, video games, books, or music. Rapper Ice-T's song "Cop Killer" arguably incites violence against police officers ("I'm 'bout to kill me somethin', a pig stopped me for nuthin' "!), but it is unlikely that playing the song will incite *immediate* violence.

The downside of this approach is that it may inadequately protect our societal interests in safety and security. If we wait to punish incitement until lawbreaking is imminent, it might be too late to stop the lawbreaking from occurring. In addition, this factor, like the "likelihood" factor, turns on a subjective fact determination: Was the speech likely to lead to *imminent* lawbreaking? Here, too, factfinders, whether they are judges or jurors, might abuse their discretion to convict defendants with unpopular messages. Judge Hand, who favored the more objective "direct" incitement test, expressed his concern about this discretionary aspect of the imminence test: "Once you admit that the matter is one of degree, you give [judges] so much latitude that the jig is at once up."[3]

- ***Factor #4: How dangerous was the unlawful action being encouraged?***

This factor focuses on the gravity of the harm being encouraged. If the unlawful action being advocated is especially grave (such as murdering an abortion doctor), the speech should not be protected. But if the unlawful action being encouraged is not especially serious (such as jaywalking across a residential street), the speech should be protected even if it is likely to lead to imminent lawbreaking.

Justice Brandeis advocated for this factor in his concurrence in *Whitney v. California*. He said a clear and present danger exists only when there is a "reasonable ground to believe that the evil to be prevented is a serious one." For example, Justice Brandeis said that the government could not constitutionally punish a society that advocated trespassing on "unenclosed, unposted, waste lands even if there was imminent danger that the advocacy would lead to a trespass."

---

[3] Gerald Gunter, *Learned Hand and the Origins of Modern First Amendment Doctrine: Some Fragments of History*, 27 Stan. L. Rev. 719, 749 (1975).

The benefit of this factor is that it gives speech full protection when the speech poses little danger. The downside is that, like other fact-dependent factors, it could be manipulated by factfinders predisposed against an unpopular defendant. For example, in *Dennis v. United States*, 341 U.S. 494 (1951), the majority of the Supreme Court thought that teaching from books that advocated a Communist revolution posed a grave danger to society. In a dissent, Justice William Douglas chastised the majority for vastly inflating the risk from Communism: "Communism has been so thoroughly exposed in this country that it has been crippled as a political force."

- ***Factor #5: Did the speaker intend to incite unlawful action?***

This factor focuses on the speaker's intent by asking whether he subjectively intended to incite unlawful action. Criminal laws usually require the government to prove that a defendant committed a crime with a culpable state of mind (what the law calls "*mens rea,*" which is Latin for "guilty mind"). The question here is whether this culpability requirement should be imposed as a matter of First Amendment law. Should speakers be shielded from criminal liability if they did not intend their speech to incite lawbreaking?

Like other factors, this factor also has its pros and cons. The pro is that it reserves punishment for those speakers with a culpable intent. The con is that speech can be dangerous even if a speaker lacks a culpable intent.

Consider an instructional manual on how to be a hitman. Yes, there is such a book, and it was successfully used by a hitman to kill three people in the 1990s. The book succeeded in helping the murderer execute his crime but not from being caught. The victims' families subsequently sued the publisher of the book for damages, claiming that the publisher had aided and abetted the hitman's crime.

If the publisher could be liable only if it subjectively intended to incite killing, the plaintiff family members would probably face an insurmountable hurdle. More likely than not, the publisher intended to make a profit, not to incite murder. The publisher could also try to immunize itself from liability by beginning the book with a disclaimer saying, "Murder is immoral and illegal and the publisher in no manner intends to encourage it." Should that be enough to shelter the publisher from liability? Would it make a difference if the first line on the following page said, "This chapter discusses 50 ways to kill someone with a knife"?

This hypothetical raises two additional questions. First, even if the First Amendment requires subjective intent for criminal liability, should the same standard be used for civil liability? Second, in either the criminal or civil context, should the required mental state be intentional (or what is sometimes phrased as "purposefully" or "knowingly"), or should it be enough that a speaker acted recklessly or even negligently?

2. The Road to *Brandenburg v. Ohio*: from the "Bad Tendency" Test to the "Clear and Present Danger" Test

The time has come to focus on which factors the Supreme Court believes are decisive in determining whether speech that encourages unlawful action is not protected under the First Amendment. As you will learn, the current test for determining whether such speech is unprotected is found in the Supreme Court's opinion in *Brandenburg v. Ohio*, 395 U.S. 444 (1969). You will soon be reading that opinion, and the notes following it will dissect the ruling.

Before getting to *Brandenburg*, we will first survey the Supreme Court's jurisprudence leading up to the decision. This historical recap is worthwhile for several reasons.

First, the Court's early incitement cases were the initial cases in which the justices seriously wrestled with the meaning of the First Amendment. This might surprise you, since the earliest of these cases was decided in 1919, more than a century after the First Amendment was ratified. The relative dearth of earlier cases is likely because the Free Speech Clause was not incorporated into the Fourteenth Amendment, and thereby made applicable to state and local governments, until 1925. In the early years of our country, the federal government played a less prominent role in people's lives so that the average person's encounters with the law were mostly with state and local laws. Before 1925, those laws would not have implicated the First Amendment even if they abridged speech.

A second reason to learn about the cases prior to *Brandenburg* is that, as the justices began grappling with First Amendment issues in earnest, they were forced to address the foundational question of why the Constitution protects speech. This led some justices to eloquently philosophize about the importance of free speech. The most notable of these opinions are Justice Holmes' dissent in *Abrams v. United States* and Justice Brandeis' concurrence in *Whitney v. California*. We examined passages from those opinions in Chapter 2 when we studied the theories for why the Constitution protects speech. You will read fuller excerpts of those opinions in this chapter.

A third reason for studying this history is that the justices, in various cases spanning decades, discussed many of the factors described in the prior section for determining whether speech inciting lawbreaking should be protected. The *Brandenburg* opinion states the current test for when incitement is not protected by the First Amendment, but *Brandenburg* did not address all the factors mentioned in earlier opinions. The earlier cases' discussions of those factors, such as the gravity of the danger posed by the speech, may continue to be relevant in future incitement cases.

A final reason for studying this history is that it provides a cautionary tale about the justices' willingness to protect unpopular speech when doing so would run counter to public sentiment. The Supreme Court's early incitement decisions were written during stressful times: World War I, the Red Scare following the Russian Revolution, and the Cold War in the 1950s. The justices must have felt considerable pressure to uphold the convictions of defendants whose speech allegedly interfered with military recruitment during World War I or whose speech in the 1950s espoused the virtues of communism while American soldiers were actively fighting communists in Korea. Perhaps not surprisingly, the Court upheld the convictions in most of these cases. The stirring paeans to freedom of speech in these cases, which have become lodestars of First Amendment jurisprudence, are typically found in the dissenting and concurring opinions—not the majority opinions.

The Evolution of the "Clear and Present Danger" Test

The Court's earliest incitement cases concerned events that occurred during and after World War I. This was a tumultuous period in U.S. history. Harsh criticism of American intervention in the war threatened to undermine the war effort by encouraging conscripts to dodge the draft (over 350,000 did). At the same time, American factory workers, many of whom were earning substandard wages in oppressive working conditions, found inspiration in the 1917 Bolshevik workers' revolution in Russia.

The Supreme Court's first leading incitement case was *Schenck v. United States* in 1919. The defendant was charged with violating the federal Espionage Act by obstructing military recruitment. The defendant had circulated a two-sided circular to men who had been conscripted into military service. One side reproduced the Thirteenth Amendment of the Constitution, which bans slavery, and claimed that conscription violated this amendment (see below). It said that a conscript was little better than a convict.

LONG LIVE THE CONSTITUTION OF THE UNITED STATES

Wake Up, America! Your Liberties Are in Danger!

The 13th Amendment, Section 1, of the Constitution of the United States says: "Neither slavery nor involuntary servitude, except as a punishment for crime whereof the party shall have been duly convicted, shall exist within the United States, or any place subject to their jurisdiction.

The Constitution of the United States is one of the greatest bulwarks of political liberty. It was born after a long, stubborn battle between king-rule and democracy. (We see little or no difference between arbitrary power under the name of a king and under a few misnamed "representatives.") In this battle the people of the United States established the principle that freedom of the individual and personal liberty are the most sacred things in life. Without them we become slaves.

See It

See one of the original Socialist Party pamphlets discussed in *Schenck* here.

Justice Holmes wrote an opinion that, at first blush, seemed to greatly increase First Amendment protection for speech that advocated or encouraged unlawful action. Rather than using the bad tendency test that lower courts had used in incitement cases, which held that speech was unprotected if it had any tendency to lead to lawbreaking, Justice Holmes instead insisted that speech encouraging lawbreaking was protected as long as it did not create a "clear and present danger" of producing harm.

The clear and present danger test appeared to ratchet up protection for speech that encouraged lawbreaking. The test's language suggested that speech would be protected unless it was *likely* to lead to *imminent* lawbreaking. That seemed to be the meaning of the words "clear" and "present." This perception was reinforced in *Schenck* by Justice Holmes' famous response to the argument that the First Amendment immunized all speech from punishment: "The most stringent protection of free speech would not protect a man in falsely shouting fire in a theatre and causing a panic." This hypothetical exemplified a situation where speech immediately leads to harm.

But any notion that the clear and present danger test dramatically increased protection for speech was dispelled when the time came for Justice Holmes to apply the test. In *Schenck* and two subsequent opinions in the same year, *Frohwerk v. United States*, 249 U.S. 204 (1919), and *Debs v. United States*, 249 U.S. 211 (1919), Justice Holmes applied the clear and present danger test as if it were little different from the bad tendency test. Notwithstanding the words "clear" and "present," Justice Holmes upheld convictions even when there was no evidence that the defendant's speech was likely to lead to imminent lawbreaking. This included upholding the conviction of Eugene Debs, a prominent leader of the Socialist Party of America, for a speech that expressed support for draft dodgers.

Running for President from Jail: *United States v. Debs*

Eugene Debs was a prominent Socialist Party leader who ran for president in five elections. In 1918, he delivered a speech in Canton, Ohio, in which he praised "comrades" who had been convicted of aiding and abetting others in dodging the World War I draft. He was subsequently convicted under the Espionage Act for obstructing the recruitment of soldiers and sentenced to 10 years in prison. Debs famously delivered these memorable lines at his sentencing hearing:

> Your Honor, years ago I recognized my kinship with all living beings, and I made up my mind that I was not one bit better than the meanest

> on earth. I said then, and I say now, that while there is a lower class, I am in it, and while there is a criminal element, I am of it, and while there is a soul in prison, I am not free.

Debs' appeal reached the Supreme Court, which upheld his conviction. Debs asserted the First Amendment as a defense, but Justice Holmes rejected this argument based on his earlier ruling in *Schenck*. Justice Holmes found that the jury had an adequate basis for convicting Debs because the "natural and intended effect" of his speech was to obstruct recruiting.

Debs' fifth and final run for president occurred while he was serving time for this conviction. He won 913,693 votes, or 3.4% of the total votes cast.

Eugene Debs

Later in the same year that *Schenck*, *Debs*, and *Frohwerk* were decided, Justice Holmes suddenly changed course. In his landmark dissent in *Abrams v. United States*, he reinterpreted his clear and present danger test to make it highly speech protective. Scholars believe Justice Holmes might have been influenced by criticism of his earlier decisions. Whatever the reason, his revised version of the clear and present danger test gave the test a ferocious bite.

The *Abrams* defendants were Russian immigrants who supported the recent Bolshevik revolution in Russia. They did not oppose America's war with Germany. Their publication said: "It is absurd to call us pro-German. We hate and despise German militarism more than do you hypocritical tyrants." The immigrants were instead concerned that armaments produced in American factories would be used against the proletarian revolutionaries in Russia: "Workers in the ammunition factories, you are producing bullets, bayonets, cannon, to murder not only the Germans, but also your dearest, best, who are in Russia and are fighting for freedom."

The immigrants, who printed their publication in English and Yiddish and tossed copies out of a building window in New York's Lower East Side, were convicted of violating the Espionage Act by advocating curtailment of armament production. Some were sentenced to 20 years in jail.

A majority of the justices upheld the convictions using the watered-down clear and present danger test that Justice Holmes himself had used in earlier cases. But Justice Holmes was now advocating for a much more rigorous version of this test. To bolster his conclusion, Justice Holmes first made the theoretical argument for a robust marketplace of ideas. You will recognize some of these passages from Chapter 2, when we discussed the theories for protecting speech. Fortunately, the passages are worth a second read.

Abrams v. United States

Supreme Court of the United States, 1919
250 U.S. 616

MR. JUSTICE CLARKE delivered the opinion of the Court.

On the record thus described it is argued, somewhat faintly, that the acts charged against the defendants were not unlawful because within the protection of that freedom of speech and of the press which is guaranteed by the First Amendment to the Constitution of the United States, and that the entire Espionage Act is unconstitutional because in conflict with that amendment. This contention is sufficiently discussed and is definitely negatived in *Schenck* and *Frohwerk*.

The claim chiefly elaborated upon by the defendants in the oral argument and in their brief is that there is no substantial evidence in the record to support the judgment upon the verdict of guilty and that the motion of the defendants for an instructed verdict in their favor was erroneously denied.

The language of these circulars was obviously intended to provoke and to encourage resistance to the United States in the war, as the third count runs, and, the defendants, in terms, plainly urged and advocated a resort to a general strike of workers in ammunition factories for the purpose of curtailing the production of ordnance and munitions necessary and essential to the prosecution of the war as is charged in the fourth count. Thus it is clear not only that some evidence but that much persuasive evidence was before the jury tending to prove that the defendants were guilty as charged in both the third and fourth counts of the indictment and under the long established rule of law hereinbefore stated the judgment of the District Court must be

Affirmed.

MR. JUSTICE HOLMES, dissenting.

I never have seen any reason to doubt that the questions of law that alone were before this Court in the cases of *Schenck*, *Frohwerk*, and *Debs* were rightly decided. I do not doubt for a moment that by the same reasoning that would justify punishing persuasion to murder, the United States constitutionally may punish speech that produces or is intended to produce a clear and imminent danger that it will bring about forthwith certain substantive evils that the United States constitutionally may seek to prevent. The power undoubtedly is greater in time of war than in time of peace because war opens dangers that do not exist at other times.

But as against dangers peculiar to war, as against others, the principle of the right to free speech is always the same. It is only the present danger of immediate evil or an intent to bring it about that warrants Congress in setting a limit to the expression of opinion where private rights are not concerned. Congress certainly cannot forbid all effort to change the mind of the country.

In this case sentences of twenty years imprisonment have been imposed for the publishing of two leaflets that I believe the defendants had as much right to publish as the Government has to publish the Constitution of the United States now vainly invoked by them. Even if I am technically wrong and enough can be squeezed from these poor and puny anonymities to turn the color of legal litmus paper; I will add, even if what I think the necessary intent were shown; the most nominal punishment seems to me all that possibly could be inflicted, unless the defendants are to be made to suffer not for what the indictment alleges but for the creed that they avow—a creed that I believe to be the creed of ignorance and immaturity when honestly held, as I see no reason to doubt that it was held here but which, although made the subject of examination at the trial, no one has a right even to consider in dealing with the charges before the Court.

Persecution for the expression of opinions seems to me perfectly logical. If you have no doubt of your premises or your power and want a certain result with all your heart you naturally express your wishes in law and sweep away all opposition. To allow opposition by speech seems to indicate that you think the speech impotent, as when a man says that he has squared the circle, or that you do not care whole heartedly for the result, or that you doubt either your power or your premises. But when men have realized that time has upset many fighting faiths, they may come to believe even more than they believe the very foundations of their own conduct that the ultimate good desired is better reached by free trade in ideas—that the best test of truth is the power of the thought to get itself accepted in the competition of the market, and that truth is the only ground upon which their wishes safely can be carried out. That at any rate is the theory of our Constitution. It is an experiment, as all life is an experiment. Every year if not every day we have to wager our salvation upon some prophecy based upon imperfect knowledge. While that experiment is part of our system I think that we should be eternally vigilant against attempts to check the expression of opinions that we loathe and believe to be fraught with death, unless they so imminently threaten immediate interference with the lawful and pressing purposes of the law that an immediate check is required to save the country. Only the emergency that makes it immediately dangerous to leave the correction of evil counsels to time warrants making any exception to the sweeping command, "Congress shall make no law abridging the freedom of speech." Of course I am speaking only of expressions of opinion and exhortations, which were all that were uttered here, but I regret that I cannot put into more impressive words my belief that in their conviction upon this indictment the defendants were deprived of their rights under the Constitution of the United States.

MR. JUSTICE BRANDEIS concurs with the foregoing opinion.

Points for Discussion

1. **Putting bite into the clear and present danger test.** The clear and present danger test Justice Holmes describes in his *Abrams* dissent appears to be much more speech-protective than his earlier interpretation of the test in *Schenck*. Can you identify how Justice Holmes reinterpreted the test to make it more speech-protective?

2. **The connection between theory and practice.** To bolster his argument for a more speech-protective clear and present danger test, Justice Holmes famously describes the "marketplace of ideas" theory for protecting speech. Can you explain how this theory relates to his decision to make the test more speech-protective?

The next major incitement case after *Abrams* was *Gitlow v. New York*, 268 U.S. 652 (1925). The earlier incitement cases had all involved federal laws restricting speech. But the *Gitlow* defendant had been convicted under a New York law that made it a crime to advocate the use of force or violence to overthrow the government. Before getting to the merits of the case, the *Gitlow* majority declared for the first time that the First Amendment's protections for freedom of speech and the press were incorporated into the Fourteenth Amendment's Due Process Clause and therefore also restrained state and local governments.

The *Gitlow* majority upheld the defendant's conviction. But rather than using even the toothless version of the clear and present danger test from *Schenck*, the majority instead introduced an even more deferential test for upholding the government's power to regulate incitement. The majority indicated that when a legislature declared speech to be dangerous, the Court should defer to the legislature's judgment rather than make an independent determination as to whether the speech created a clear and present danger:

> By enacting the present statute the State has determined, through its legislative body, that utterances advocating the overthrow of organized government by force, violence and unlawful means, are so inimical to the general welfare and involve such danger of substantive evil that they may be penalized in the exercise of its police power. That determination must be given great weight. Every presumption is to be indulged in favor of the validity of the statute.

Two years later, the Court followed this new deferential approach in *Whitney v. California*, which upheld the conviction of a woman for being a member of the Communist Labor Party, which advocated political change through violence. Justice Brandeis wrote a famous concurring opinion in *Whitney*. Although he voted to uphold the defendant's conviction based on the specific facts of the case, he built upon Justice Holmes' dissent in *Abrams* to argue for a highly speech-protective clear and present danger test. Like Justice Holmes, he laid out a theoretical foundation for his conclusions, so you will once again be seeing some familiar passages from the chapter on the theories for protecting speech.

Whitney v. California

Supreme Court of the United States, 1927
274 U.S. 357

MR. JUSTICE SANFORD delivered the opinion of the Court.

By a criminal information filed in the Superior Court of Alameda County, California, the plaintiff in error was charged, in five counts, with violations of the Criminal Syndicalism Act of that State. The pertinent provisions of the Criminal Syndicalism Act are:

> Section 1. The term "criminal syndicalism" as used in this act is hereby defined as any doctrine or precept advocating, teaching or aiding and abetting the commission of crime, sabotage, or unlawful acts of force and violence or unlawful methods of terrorism as a means of accomplishing a change in industrial ownership or control, or effecting any political change.
>
> Sec. 2. Any person who organizes or assists in organizing, or is or knowingly becomes a member of, any organization, society, group or assemblage of

persons organized or assembled to advocate, teach or aid and abet criminal syndicalism is guilty of a felony and punishable by imprisonment.

The first count of the information, on which the conviction was had, charged that on or about November 28, 1919, in Alameda County, the defendant, in violation of the Criminal Syndicalism Act, "did then and there unlawfully, willfully, wrongfully, deliberately and feloniously organize and assist in organizing, and was, is, and knowingly became a member of an organization, society, group and assemblage of persons organized and assembled to advocate, teach, aid and abet criminal syndicalism."

That the freedom of speech which is secured by the Constitution does not confer an absolute right to speak, without responsibility, whatever one may choose, or an unrestricted and unbridled license giving immunity for every possible use of language and preventing the punishment of those who abuse this freedom; and that a State in the exercise of its police power may punish those who abuse this freedom by utterances inimical to the public welfare, tending to incite to crime, disturb the public peace, or endanger the foundations of organized government and threaten its overthrow by unlawful means, is not open to question. *Gitlow*.

By enacting the provisions of the Syndicalism Act the State has declared, through its legislative body, that to knowingly be or become a member of or assist in organizing an association to advocate, teach or aid and abet the commission of crimes or unlawful acts of force, violence or terrorism as a means of accomplishing industrial or political changes, involves such danger to the public peace and the security of the State, that these acts should be penalized in the exercise of its police power. That determination must be given great weight. Every presumption is to be indulged in favor of the validity of the statute, and it may not be declared unconstitutional unless it is an arbitrary or unreasonable attempt to exercise the authority vested in the State in the public interest.

The essence of the offense denounced by the Act is the combining with others in an association for the accomplishment of the desired ends through the advocacy and use of criminal and unlawful methods. It partakes of the nature of a criminal conspiracy. That such united and joint action involves even greater danger to the public peace and security than the isolated utterances and acts of individuals is clear. We cannot hold that, as here applied, the Act is an unreasonable or arbitrary exercise of the police power of the State, unwarrantably infringing any right of free speech, assembly or association, or that those persons are protected from punishment by the due process clause who abuse such rights by joining and furthering an organization thus menacing the peace and welfare of the State.

The order dismissing the writ of error will be vacated and set aside, and the judgment of the Court of Appeal Affirmed.

MR. JUSTICE BRANDEIS, concurring.

It is said to be the function of the Legislature to determine whether at a particular time and under the particular circumstances the formation of, or assembly with, a society organized to advocate criminal syndicalism constitutes a clear and present danger of substantive evil; and that by enacting the law here in question the Legislature of California determined that question in the affirmative. Compare *Gitlow*. The Legislature must obviously decide, in the first instance, whether a danger exists which calls for a particular protective measure. But where a statute is valid only in case certain conditions exist, the enactment of the statute cannot alone establish the facts which are essential to its validity. Prohibitory legislation has repeatedly been held invalid, because unnecessary, where the denial of liberty involved was that of engaging in a particular business. The powers of the courts to strike down an offending law are no less when the interests involved are not property rights, but the fundamental personal rights of free speech and assembly.

This court has not yet fixed the standard by which to determine when a danger shall be deemed clear; how remote the danger may be and yet be deemed present; and what degree of evil shall be deemed sufficiently substantial to justify resort to abridgment of free speech and assembly as the means of protection. To reach sound conclusions on these matters, we must bear in mind why a State is, ordinarily, denied the power to prohibit dissemination of social, economic and political doctrine which a vast majority of its citizens believes to be false and fraught with evil consequence.

Those who won our independence believed that the final end of the State was to make men free to develop their faculties, and that in its government the deliberative forces should prevail over the arbitrary. They valued liberty both as an end and as a means. They believed liberty to be the secret of happiness and courage to be the secret of liberty. They believed that freedom to think as you will and to speak as you think are means indispensable to the discovery and spread of political truth; that without free speech and assembly discussion would be futile; that with them, discussion affords ordinarily adequate protection against the dissemination of noxious doctrine; that the greatest menace to freedom is an inert people; that public discussion is a political duty; and that this should be a fundamental principle of the American government. They recognized the risks to which all human institutions are subject. But they knew that order cannot be secured merely through fear of punishment for its infraction; that it is hazardous to discourage thought, hope and imagination; that fear breeds repression; that repression breeds hate; that hate menaces stable government; that the path of safety lies in the opportunity to discuss freely supposed grievances and proposed remedies; and that the fitting remedy for evil counsels is good ones. Believing in the power of reason as applied through public discussion, they eschewed silence coerced by law-the argument of force in its worst form. Recognizing the occasional tyrannies of governing majorities, they amended the Constitution so that free speech and assembly should be guaranteed.

Fear of serious injury cannot alone justify suppression of free speech and assembly. Men feared witches and burnt women. It is the function of speech to free men from the bondage of irrational fears. To justify suppression of free speech there must be reasonable ground to fear that serious evil will result if free speech is practiced. There must be reasonable ground to believe that the danger apprehended is imminent. There must be reasonable ground to believe that the evil to be prevented is a serious one. Every denunciation of existing law tends in some measure to increase the probability that there will be violation of it. Condonation of a breach enhances the probability. Expressions of approval add to the probability. Propagation of the criminal state of mind by teaching syndicalism increases it. Advocacy of lawbreaking heightens it still further. But even advocacy of violation, however reprehensible morally, is not a justification for denying free speech where the advocacy falls short of incitement and there is nothing to indicate that the advocacy would be immediately acted on. The wide difference between advocacy and incitement, between preparation and attempt, between assembling and conspiracy, must be borne in mind. In order to support a finding of clear and present danger it must be shown either that immediate serious violence was to be expected or was advocated, or that the past conduct furnished reason to believe that such advocacy was then contemplated.

Those who won our independence by revolution were not cowards. They did not fear political change. They did not exalt order at the cost of liberty. To courageous, self-reliant men, with confidence in the power of free and fearless reasoning applied through the processes of popular government, no danger flowing from speech can be deemed clear and present, unless the incidence of the evil apprehended is so imminent that it may befall before there is opportunity for full discussion. If there be time to expose through discussion the falsehood and fallacies, to avert the evil by the processes of education, the remedy to be applied is more speech, not enforced silence. Only an emergency can justify repression. Such must be the rule if authority is to be reconciled with freedom. Such, in my opinion, is the command of the Constitution. It is therefore always open to Americans to challenge a law abridging free speech and assembly by showing that there was no emergency justifying it.

Moreover, even imminent danger cannot justify resort to prohibition of these functions essential to effective democracy, unless the evil apprehended is relatively serious. Prohibition of free speech and assembly is a measure so stringent that it would be inappropriate as the means for averting a relatively trivial harm to society. A police measure may be unconstitutional merely because the remedy, although effective as means of protection, is unduly harsh or oppressive. Thus, a State might, in the exercise of its police power, make any trespass upon the land of another a crime, regardless of the results or of the intent or purpose of the trespasser. It might, also, punish an attempt, a conspiracy, or an incitement to commit the trespass. But it is hardly conceivable that this court would hold constitutional a statute which punished as a felony the mere voluntary assembly with a society formed to teach that pedestrians had the moral right to cross unenclosed, unposted, waste lands and to advocate their doing so, even if there was imminent danger that advocacy would lead to a trespass. The fact that speech is likely to result in some violence or in destruction of property is not enough to justify its suppression. There must be the probability of serious injury to the State. Among free men, the deterrents ordinarily to be applied to prevent crime are education and punishment for violations of the law, not abridgment of the rights of free speech and assembly.

Whether in 1919, when Miss Whitney did the things complained of, there was in California such clear and present danger of serious evil, might have been made the important issue in the case. She might have required that the issue be determined either by the court or the jury. She claimed below that the statute as applied to her violated the federal Constitution; but she did not claim that it was void because there was no clear and present danger of serious evil, nor did she request that the existence of these conditions of a valid measure thus restricting the rights of free speech and assembly be passed upon by the court of a jury. On the other hand, there was evidence on which the court or jury might have found that such danger existed. I am unable to assent to the suggestion in the opinion of the court that assembling with a political party, formed to advocate the desirability of a proletarian revolution by mass action at some date necessarily far in the future, is not a right within the protection of the Fourteenth Amendment. In the present case, however, there was other testimony which tended to establish the existence of a conspiracy, on the part of members of the International Workers of the World, to commit present serious crimes, and likewise to show that such a conspiracy would be furthered by the activity of the society of which Miss Whitney was a member. Under these circumstances the judgment of the state court cannot be disturbed.

MR. JUSTICE HOLMES joins in this opinion.

Points for Discussion

1. **Did Justice Brandeis accept *Gitlow*'s premise that judges should defer to legislators?** Recall how *Gitlow* said that judges should defer to legislative judgments about which speech was sufficiently dangerous that it could be regulated. Did Justice Brandeis agree with this premise, or did he think that judges should independently determine whether speech should be unprotected by the First Amendment?

2. **Did Justice Brandeis add any additional "bite" to the clear and present danger test articulated by Justice Holmes in *Abrams*?** Justice Holmes had already reinterpreted the clear and present danger test in *Abrams* to make it more robustly speech-protective. Did Justice Brandeis add any elements to the analysis to give the test even more bite?

3. **The safety valve theory for protecting speech.** In *Whitney*, Justice Brandeis articulated what some have called the "safety valve" theory for protection of speech:

> Those who won our independence knew that order cannot be secured merely through fear of punishment for its infraction; that it is hazardous to discourage thought, hope and imagination; that fear breeds repression; that repression breeds hate; that hate menaces stable government; that the path of safety lies in the opportunity to discuss freely supposed grievances and proposed remedies.

Can you articulate the logic of this safety-valve theory? Do you find the theory persuasive? Do you believe that allowing dangerous groups to vent their anger makes them less likely to resort to lawbreaking? Or has the rising number of hate crimes and acts of domestic terrorism, often spurred on by incendiary social media posts, proven the opposite to be true?

The clear and present danger test articulated by Justice Holmes in his *Abrams* dissent and by Justice Brandeis in his *Whitney* concurrence was fiercely speech-protective. The combination of this robust speech protection and the justices' eloquent articulations of the theories for why speech needs protection earned these opinions a place in the pantheon of free speech jurisprudence.

But keep in mind that these opinions were a dissent and concurrence. The majority of the Court was still using either Justice Holmes' watered-down clear and present danger test from *Schenck* or *Gitlow*'s deference to legislatures to uphold the convictions issued by the lower courts.

Justices Oliver Wendell Holmes (L) and Louis Brandeis (R)
Courtesy of Harvard Law School Library Historical
and Special Collections (L.C. Handy Studios)

The Cold War Era: Reinterpreting the Clear and Present Danger Test to Weaken Its Force

The next great test for how the Supreme Court would balance society's conflicting interests in free speech and security arose in the early 1950s when America was deeply fearful about the spread of Communism, including the presence of Communist sympathizers in the country. The issue came to the fore in *Dennis v. United States*, 341 U.S. 494 (1951), in which the Court reviewed the conviction of individuals for studying and teaching the foundational works of Communism. The defendants had been convicted for violating the federal Smith Act, which made it a crime to advocate the overthrow of the government by force or violence. The Supreme Court upheld their sentences.

Chief Justice Fred Vinson, writing for three other justices, refused to use the deferential approach used by the majorities in *Gitlow* and *Whitney*. Instead, Chief Justice Vinson said the Court's "subsequent opinions have inclined toward the Holmes-Brandeis rationale."

As you recall, the Holmes-Brandeis interpretation of the clear and present danger test was highly speech-protective. Most notably, it required that speech advocating unlawful action could be punished only if it was likely to lead to *imminent* lawbreaking. That was unlikely to be the case in *Dennis* if the defendants were merely teaching the classic works of Communist literature, and, at most, advocating for a government overthrow at some uncertain future time. Nevertheless, the Court voted to uphold the defendants' convictions. To accomplish this, Chief Justice Vinson's plurality opinion, as well as a concurrence by Justice Robert Jackson, recharacterized the Holmes-Brandeis test as intended for situations involving only mildly dangerous speech, such as the rants of a hotheaded soapbox speaker in a public park. The plurality opinion then adopted a different interpretation of the clear and present danger test for speech encouraging more serious harms, such as the violent overthrow of the government.

Justice Jackson, for example, wrote a concurrence in which he said he would save the Holmes-Brandeis analysis "as a rule of reason in the kind of case for which it was devised":

> When the issue is criminality of a hot-headed speech on a street corner, or circulation of a few incendiary pamphlets, or parading by some zealots behind a red flag, or refusal of a handful of school children to salute our flag, it is not beyond the capacity of the judicial process to gather, comprehend, and weigh the necessary materials for decision whether it is a clear and present danger of substantive evil or a harmless letting off of steam.

But Justice Jackson thought that courts were entirely unequipped to apply the Holmes-Brandeis test to something as dangerous and complex as a worldwide Communist conspiracy. Doing so, he said, would force the justices to "appraise imponderables, including international and national phenomena which baffle the best informed foreign offices and our most experienced politicians." For this kind of threat, Justice Jackson thought, an application of the clear and present danger test that required speech to be protected unless it was likely to lead to imminent harm was wholly inappropriate:

> The authors of the clear and present danger test never applied it to a case like this, nor would I. If applied as it is proposed here, it means that the Communist plotting is protected during its period of incubation; its preliminary stages of organization and preparation are immune from the law; the Government can move only after imminent action is manifest, when it would, of course, be too late.

Chief Justice Vinson echoed this concern: "Obviously, the words [clear and present danger] cannot mean that before the Government may act, it must wait until the putsch is about to be executed, the plans have been laid and the signal is awaited."

His solution was to adopt a revised interpretation of the clear and present danger test that had been developed by federal Court of Appeals Judge Learned Hand. This was not Hand's "direct" incitement test from *Masses Publishing Co.*, which the Supreme Court has not adopted. It was Hand's attempt to flesh out the meaning of Justice Holmes' clear and present danger test.

Hand suggested that courts apply the following formula to determine when speech created a clear and present danger: "In each case they must ask whether the gravity of the 'evil,' discounted by its improbability, justifies such invasion of free speech as is necessary to avoid the danger." If this test sounds familiar to you, that is because it resembles a similar test Hand proposed in *United States v. Carroll Towing Co.* for determining whether a defendant's conduct was unreasonable for purposes of tort liability in negligence.[4]

Under Hand's clear and present danger test, the probability that speech would lead to harm was inversely related to the gravity of the harm. If the evil to be averted were minor, the probability of it occurring had to be great. But if the evil were great, then the speech could be suppressed even if there were little likelihood it would lead to the harm.

Applying this formula to the facts in *Dennis*, it was easy for Chief Justice Vinson to uphold the defendants' convictions. The evil to be averted was a Communist overthrow of the American government. That was about as serious an evil as one could find. Given that, it did not matter that there was little likelihood that the defendants' speech would imminently lead to this harm. By using Hand's recharacterization of the clear and present danger test, Chief Justice Vinson was able to eliminate the immi-

[4] "If the probability be called P; the injury, L; and the burden, B; liability depends upon whether B is less than L multiplied by P: i.e., whether B less than PL." *United States v. Carroll Towing Co.*, 159 F.2d 169, 173 (2d Cir. 1947).

nence and likelihood requirements in cases where the threatened evil was sufficiently grave.

In a country gripped by the fear of Communism, the Court's decision probably seemed eminently reasonable. Knowing what we know now—that the fear of Communist infiltration into the United States was vastly overblown—the decision seems unsettling. Like the Court's earlier World War I opinions, the *Dennis* opinion was another example of the justices' upholding criminal convictions for speech that posed little or no danger.

The only two dissenters in *Dennis* were Justices Hugo Black and William Douglas, both of whom were famous for staking out powerful civil libertarian arguments in free speech cases. Their courage may have been attributable to the fact that they did not believe Communist infiltration was a serious threat. That certainly seems to have been Justice Douglas' attitude:

> Communism in the world scene is no bogeyman; but Communism as a political faction or party in this country plainly is. Communism has been so thoroughly exposed in this country that it has been crippled as a political force. Free speech has destroyed it as an effective political party. How it can be said that there is a clear and present danger that this advocacy will succeed is, therefore, a mystery. In America [Communists] are miserable merchants of unwanted ideas; their wares remain unsold.

One might admire the dissenting justices' courage to defend the defendants' civil liberties when so much of the nation was fearful of Communism. But it is worth acknowledging that even these justices were not always immune from the fears and anxieties that affected the rest of society. As you will learn in a different constitutional law class, the Supreme Court in *Korematsu v. United States* upheld the exclusion of Japanese Americans from the West Coast during World War II out of fear that there might be a tiny group among them who were sympathetic to our Japanese enemies.[5] The *Korematsu* decision has not stood the test of time. In 2018, Chief Justice John Roberts wrote, "*Korematsu* was gravely wrong the day it was decided, has been overruled in the court of history, and—to be clear—has no place in law under the Constitution."[6]

But at the time the *Korematsu* decision was written in 1944, the nation was at war—a war the country had joined only after Japan had bombed the U.S. naval base at Pearl Harbor. Justice Hugo Black, the great civil libertarian, wrote the majority opinion in *Korematsu*, joined by Justice Douglas and four other colleagues.

---

5 *Korematsu v. United States*, 323 U.S. 214 (1944).

6 *Trump v. Hawaii*, 585 U.S. 667 (2018).

Years later, Justice Douglas expressed regret for joining the majority opinion. He candidly admitted that the justices are subject to the same fears as the rest of us: "The Court is not isolated from life. Its members are very much a part of the community and know the fears, anxieties, cravings and wishes of their neighbors."[7]

3. The Current Test for When Incitement Is Unprotected: The "*Brandenburg* Test"

The Supreme Court's current rule for when speech encouraging unlawful action is unprotected was announced in *Brandenburg v. Ohio*.

Brandenburg v. Ohio

Supreme Court of the United States, 1969
395 U.S. 444

PER CURIAM.

The appellant, a leader of a Ku Klux Klan group, was convicted under the Ohio Criminal Syndicalism statute for "advocating the duty, necessity, or propriety of crime, sabotage, violence, or unlawful methods of terrorism as a means of accomplishing industrial or political reform" and for "voluntarily assembling with any society, group, or assemblage of persons formed to teach or advocate the doctrines of criminal syndicalism." He was fined $1,000 and sentenced to one to 10 years' imprisonment. The appellant challenged the constitutionality of the criminal syndicalism statute under the First and Fourteenth Amendments to the United States Constitution, but the intermediate appellate court of Ohio affirmed his conviction without opinion. The Supreme Court of Ohio dismissed his appeal, *sua sponte*, "for the reason that no substantial constitutional question exists herein." It did not file an opinion or explain its conclusions. Appeal was taken to this Court, and we noted probable jurisdiction. We reverse.

The record shows that a man, identified at trial as the appellant, telephoned an announcer-reporter on the staff of a Cincinnati television station and invited him to come to a Ku Klux Klan "rally" to be held at a farm in Hamilton County. With the cooperation of the organizers, the reporter and a cameraman attended the meeting and filmed the events. Portions of the films were later broadcast on the local station and on a national network.

---

7 William O. Douglas, The Autobiography of William O. Douglas: The Court Years 1939–1975 38 (1980). *See also* Christina E. Wells, *Fear and Loathing in Constitutional Decision-Making*, 2005 Wis. L. Rev. 115 (2005).

The prosecution's case rested on the films and on testimony identifying the appellant as the person who communicated with the reporter and who spoke at the rally. The State also introduced into evidence several articles appearing in the film, including a pistol, a rifle, a shotgun, ammunition, a Bible, and a red hood worn by the speaker in the films.

One film showed 12 hooded figures, some of whom carried firearms. They were gathered around a large wooden cross, which they burned. No one was present other than the participants and the newsmen who made the film. Most of the words uttered during the scene were incomprehensible when the film was projected, but scattered phrases could be understood that were derogatory of Negroes and, in one instance, of Jews. Another scene on the same film showed the appellant, in Klan regalia, making a speech. The speech, in full, was as follows:

> This is an organizers' meeting. We have had quite a few members here today which are—we have hundreds, hundreds of members throughout the State of Ohio. I can quote from a newspaper clipping from the Columbus, Ohio Dispatch, five weeks ago Sunday morning. The Klan has more members in the State of Ohio than does any other organization. We're not a revengent organization, but if our President, our Congress, our Supreme Court, continues to suppress the white, Caucasian race, it's possible that there might have to be some revengeance taken.
>
> We are marching on Congress July the Fourth, four hundred thousand strong. From there we are dividing into two groups, one group to march on St. Augustine, Florida, the other group to march into Mississippi. Thank you.

The second film showed six hooded figures one of whom, later identified as the appellant, repeated a speech very similar to that recorded on the first film. The reference to the possibility of "revengeance" was omitted, and one sentence was added: "Personally, I believe the nigger should be returned to Africa, the Jew returned to Israel." Though some of the figures in the films carried weapons, the speaker did not.

The Ohio Criminal Syndicalism Statute was enacted in 1919. From 1917 to 1920, identical or quite similar laws were adopted by 20 States and two territories. In 1927, this Court sustained the constitutionality of California's Criminal Syndicalism Act, the text of which is quite similar to that of the laws of Ohio. *Whitney.* The Court upheld the statute on the ground that, without more, "advocating" violent means to effect political and economic change involves such danger to the security of the State that the State may outlaw it. But *Whitney* has been thoroughly discredited by later decisions. *See Dennis.* These later decisions have fashioned the principle that the constitutional guarantees of free speech and free press do not permit a State to forbid or proscribe advocacy of the use of force or of law violation except where such advocacy is directed to inciting or producing imminent lawless action and is likely to incite or produce such action. As we said in *Noto v. United States*, 367 U.S. 290, 297–298 (1961), "the mere abstract teaching of the moral propriety or even moral necessity for a resort to force and violence, is not the same as preparing a group for violent action and steeling it to such action." A statute which fails to draw this distinction impermissibly intrudes upon the freedoms guaranteed by the First and Fourteenth Amendments. It sweeps within its condemnation speech which our Constitution has immunized from governmental control.

when statute does not draw the distinction the statute is not valid

Measured by this test, Ohio's Criminal Syndicalism Act cannot be sustained. The Act punishes persons who "advocate or teach the duty, necessity, or propriety" of violence "as a means of accomplishing industrial or political reform"; or who publish or circulate or display any book or paper containing such advocacy; or who "justify" the commission of violent acts "with intent to exemplify, spread or advocate the propriety of the doctrines of criminal syndicalism"; or who "voluntarily assemble" with a group formed "to teach or advocate the doctrines of criminal syndicalism." Neither the indictment nor the trial judge's instructions to the jury in any way refined the statute's bald definition of the crime in terms of mere advocacy not distinguished from incitement to imminent lawless action.

Accordingly, we are here confronted with a statute which, by its own words and as applied, purports to punish mere advocacy and to forbid, on pain of criminal punishment, assembly with others merely to advocate the described type of action. Such a statute falls within the condemnation of the First and Fourteenth Amendments. The contrary teaching of *Whitney* cannot be supported, and that decision is therefore overruled.

MR. JUSTICE DOUGLAS, concurring.

While I join the opinion of the Court, I desire to enter a caveat.

I see no place in the regime of the First Amendment for any "clear and present danger" test, whether strict and tight as some would make it, or free-wheeling as the Court in *Dennis* rephrased it.

When one reads the opinions closely and sees when and how the "clear and present danger" test has been applied, great misgivings are aroused. First, the threats were often loud but always puny and made serious only by judges so wedded to the status quo that critical analysis made them nervous. Second, the test was so twisted and perverted in *Dennis* as to make the trial of those teachers of Marxism an all-out political trial which was part and parcel of the cold war that has eroded substantial parts of the First Amendment.

[Justice Black's concurring opinion is omitted.]

Points for Discussion

1. **Parsing the elements of the *Brandenburg* test.** *Brandenburg* states that the government may not punish speech that advocates "the use of force or of law violation except where such advocacy is directed to inciting or producing imminent lawless action and is likely to incite or produce such action." This is the "*Brandenburg* test." Can you identify which of the previously mentioned factors the test uses for determining when speech advocating unlawful action is unprotected?

   Scholars believe that the *Brandenburg* test incorporates at least three of these factors: intent, likelihood, and imminence. In other words, the government may punish speech advocating unlawful action only if it can show that (1) the speaker *intended* to incite unlawful action, (2) the speech was *likely* to incite the unlawful action, and (3) the unlawful action was likely to occur *imminently*. Some scholars believe that the *Brandenburg* test also requires the government to show that the defendant's speech amounted to "direct" incitement—that the defendant expressly told listeners to break the law. There is no consensus on this last point. One argument in favor of this position is that the *Brandenburg* test refers to speech that is "directed" to inciting unlawful action. The Court also quoted language from *Noto v. United States*, which emphasized that "the mere abstract teaching of the moral propriety or even moral necessity for a resort to force and violence, is not the same as preparing a group for violent action and steeling it to such action."

2. **Did *Brandenburg* strike the right balance between speech and security?** The *Brandenburg* test is thought to be highly speech-protective, especially because of its requirements that speech be likely to lead to imminent lawless action. If imminence truly means immediately, then speech advocating unlawful action will only rarely be unprotected. An instruction manual for making bombs, an activist denouncing abortion doctors, and a speaker glorifying the 9/11 terrorist attacks are all conveying dangerous ideas, but their speech is not likely to lead to imminent lawbreaking.

   One case that lends support to the notion that the imminence requirement in *Brandenburg* does mean immediately is *Hess v. Indiana*, 414 U.S. 105 (1973), where the Court summarily reversed a conviction of an anti-war protester, who, after the police moved a group of protesters from the street to the sidewalk, said, "We'll take the fucking street later." The Court said there was no evidence that the defendant's words were "intended to produce, and likely to produce, *imminent* disorder." If anything, the "statement could be taken as counsel for present moderation."

Future cases will have to resolve just how much immediacy is required by the imminence factor. Does the unlawful action have to occur within minutes or even seconds? Is it enough that it is likely to happen later that day, that week, that month? Whether you think *Brandenburg* struck the right balance between free speech and security might depend on whether you think that the *Brandenburg* test leaves enough time for the government to respond to dangerous speech. If you believe that an overly stringent immediacy requirement fails to give the government adequate time, you might prefer a different test.

3. **Issues unresolved by *Brandenburg*.** *Brandenburg* is the Supreme Court's leading pronouncement on when speech inciting unlawful action is unprotected. It is also a half-century old. Absent more guidance from the justices, lower courts and commentators have had to grapple with a host of issues left open by *Brandenburg*. Here are some examples:

   a. **Speech facilitating crimes.** Should the *Brandenburg* test apply to speech that facilitates criminal behavior, such as books on how to grow anthrax or how to be a hitman? Recall John's article in an anti-abortion magazine about how to make pipe bombs.

   If the *Brandenburg* test controls these situations, then these how-to books are likely protected by the First Amendment. The books are not likely to lead to imminent unlawful action. People need to read and study the books before taking any action. But should these works be protected?

   A lower court wrestled with this issue in *Rice v. Palladin Enterprises, Inc.*, 128 F.3d 233 (4th Cir. 1997), a case concerning the previously mentioned hitman handbook. A man, relying on the book, killed three people. The book was later found in his apartment. The victims' families subsequently sued the publisher of the book for aiding and abetting the murderer. A lower court dismissed the lawsuit by using the *Brandenburg* test, holding that the book did not advocate that the reader go out and commit murder "now," thus failing the imminency requirement. The Court of Appeals reversed. In applying *Brandenburg*, the court held that the principal purpose of *Brandenburg* was to distinguish "abstract advocacy" from authentic incitement. The hitman book, the court concluded, was not "abstract advocacy" within the meaning of *Brandenburg*. A large part of the court's opinion, however, did not apply the formal *Brandenburg* "incitement" test at all, but instead treated the book as "aiding and abetting crime." This placed the book within a category of speech not deemed sheltered by the First Amendment that courts often describe as a criminal "speech act" or as speech "integral to crime," discussed in Point 4(d) below.

Do you like this result? For an account of the case by the lawyer who litigated it on behalf of the families, *see* Rod Smolla, *Deliberate Intent: A Lawyer Tells the True Story of Murder by the Book* (1999). For an attempt to articulate a rule for when crime-facilitating speech should be denied First Amendment protection, *see* Eugene Volokh, *Crime-Facilitating Speech*, 57 Stan. L. Rev. 1095 (2005).

b. **The line between incitement and threats.** Consider a case involving a pro-life group that published "Unwanted" posters with images of abortion doctors. For example, an "Unwanted" poster of Dr. David Gunn had his name, photograph, and address and stated that to "defenseless unborn babies" Gunn was "heavily armed and very dangerous." A group of abortion doctors brought a lawsuit seeking to enjoin the publication of these posters.

Should these posters be protected by the First Amendment? If they are characterized as speech that encourages unlawful action, and the *Brandenburg* test applies, it seems likely that the posters would be protected. The posters are not likely to lead to imminent lawbreaking. Alternatively, the posters could be characterized as "true threats," which, as you will learn later in this chapter, are a separate category of speech that is not protected by the First Amendment.

Where is the line between incitement and threats? Should speech be characterized as a threat only when the speaker is saying that he, or people under his control, will inflict violence on another? Is speech that encourages unrelated third parties to engage in unlawful action incitement governed by *Brandenburg*?

The Ninth Circuit concluded that the posters were unprotected threats. But there were several powerful dissents that contended that the posters should be analyzed as incitement and not threats. Here is passage from Judge Alex Kozinski's dissent capturing this argument:

> The majority cites not a scintilla of evidence—other than the posters themselves—that [defendants] or someone associated with them would carry out the threatened harm.
>
> Given this lack of evidence, the posters can be viewed, at most, as a call to arms for *other* abortion protesters to harm plaintiffs. However, the Supreme Court made it clear that under *Brandenburg*, encouragement or even advocacy of violence is protected by the First Amendment: "Mere *advocacy* of the use of force or violence does not remove speech from the protection of the First Amendment."

Planned Parenthood of the Columbia/Willamette, Inc. v. American Coal. of Life Activists, 290 F.3d 1058, 1092 (9th Cir. 2002) (*en banc*) (Kozinski, J., dissenting).

One final note to capture the seriousness of the current topic. After the "Unwanted" poster of Dr. Gunn was published, he was killed as he entered an abortion clinic in Pensacola, Florida.

c. **The line between advocacy and actions.** After the Unite the Right rally in Charlottesville, Virginia, in 2017, city residents brought a civil action against the League of the South, a "whites only" organization, and some of its leadership for injuries to the plaintiffs caused by members of the group. The defendants claimed that their "derogatory comments and political rhetoric" were protected by the First Amendment and consisted of nothing more than "abstract political rhetoric." The District Court refused to grant the defendants' summary judgment motion because the plaintiffs alleged that the defendants had not only spoken about but also engaged in acts of violence, and the latter are not entitled to First Amendment protection:

> The First Amendment does not protect violence. And so, if Defendants have formed or are engaged in a conspiracy against the public peace and order and thereby transcend the bounds of the freedom of speech which the Constitution protects, any law holding them liable for such conspiracy does not violate the First Amendment. As a result, the First Amendment does not prohibit tort liability for losses that are caused by violence and by threats of violence.

Sines v. Kessler, 558 F. Supp. 3d 250, 285–86 (W.D. Va. 2021).

d. **Does the *Brandenburg* test apply to speech integral to crime?** All the cases in the Supreme Court's incitement jurisprudence involved defendants engaged in "political speech," that is, speech about matters of public discussion and debate. They involved speech about the draft during World War I or the desirability of a socialist or communist system of government. Even the speech in *Brandenburg* had to do with government policies, albeit the rather repugnant message that government policies should favor white supremacy.

The Supreme Court in *Brandenburg* did not clarify whether the test announced in that case was intended to apply to only political speech or if it was meant to apply to all speech encouraging lawbreaking, including non-political speech about ordinary crimes like solicitation of murder. Reporters for the Model Penal Code recommended that the test be limited to political speech:

> Apparently, the Supreme Court does believe that even direct incitement of specific illegal acts enjoys some constitutional protection, perhaps because such incitement expresses most eloquently the intensity of opposition to hated laws or policies, and because speakers should not have to fear that whenever they slip from general advocacy to advocacy of specific illegal acts, they will be subject to criminal punishment. It would be difficult to make similar arguments about private solicitations to commit ordinary crimes made on wholly nonpolitical grounds and it seems unlikely that the Supreme Court meant to afford protection in such cases. But the precise bounds of application of the *Brandenburg* test are still uncertain.

Model Penal Code, § 5.02 cmt. 3(b) (1985).

In recent years, the Supreme Court has revived a long-dormant First Amendment doctrine that might, as it evolves over time, help elucidate the line between speech advocating lawbreaking for political purposes and speech integral to the commission of a crime. The doctrine derives from *Giboney v. Empire Storage & Ice Co.*, 336 U.S. 490 (1949), in which the Court stated, "It rarely has been suggested that the constitutional freedom for speech and press extends its immunity to speech or writing used as an integral part of conduct in violation of a valid criminal statute." In *United States v. Hansen*, 599 U.S. 762 (2023), a case involving a federal law that prohibits "encouraging or inducing" illegal immigration ("clause iv"), the Court quoted *Giboney* and emphatically affirmed the principle that speech integral to crime is not protected by the First Amendment:

> To the extent that clause (iv) reaches *any* speech, it stretches no further than speech integral to unlawful conduct. "It has never been deemed an abridgement of freedom of speech or press to make a course of conduct illegal merely because the conduct was in part initiated, evidenced, or carried out by means of language, either spoken, written, or printed." Speech intended to bring about a particular unlawful act has no social value; therefore, it is unprotected. We have applied this principle many times, including to the promotion of a particular piece of contraband, solicitation of unlawful employment, and picketing with the "sole, unlawful and immediate objective" of "inducing" a target to violate the law. It applies to clause (iv) too.

There is a strong intuitive appeal for categorically exempting speech integral to crime from First Amendment protection. There are, after all, many crimes in which speech is the vehicle through which the crime is committed. Think of bribery ("I will give you $1,000 if you give me a zoning variance"), extortion ("I will beat you up if you do not give me $1,000"), or agreements in restraint of trade ("I agree that I will not sell my product for less than $1,000"). But the line between protected advocacy and unprotected speech integral to crime can be more elusive when criminal laws target speech that advocates, induces, or encourages criminal activity. As Professor Eugene Volokh, a leader in examining this issue, has noted, "Given that speech sometimes both constitutes advocacy of social change and helps cause illegal conduct, the question is where the rule of law calls for the line to be drawn." Eugene Volokh, *The Speech Integral to Criminal Conduct Exception*, 101 Cornell L. Rev. 981, 986 (2016). Where the line is drawn matters. For example, did Donald Trump's speech questioning the validity of the 2020 election lose its First Amendment protection because it was integrally tied to a criminal plot to overturn the election? *See* Burt Neuborne, *There's a Good Chance Trump Will Be Found 'Willfully Blind,'* N.Y. Times, Aug. 28, 2023.

In the *Hansen* case, the Court upheld the provision criminalizing "encouraging or inducing" illegal immigration because it said that the terms, as properly construed, applied only when a defendant intended to solicit or facilitate a specific act of unlawful immigration. The Court said that the terms "encourage" and "induce" were terms of art in criminal law and that Congress intended for the terms to limit the law's reach to the well-established crimes of criminal solicitation or facilitation (also referred to as "aiding and abetting"), both of which "require an intent to bring about a particular lawful act." The Court thought that this narrow interpretation ensured that the law could not be applied to acts such as an op-ed criticizing federal immigration policy or a minister telling undocumented aliens that they had the community's "love and support," which might "encourage" or "induce" illegal immigration in a conventional sense but not in the legal sense of the narrowly construed statute. Justice Ketanji Brown Jackson, joined by Justice Sonia Sotomayor, dissented, finding the majority's narrow interpretation of the law to be inconsistent with both the statute's plain language and its legislative history.

e. **Is the *Dennis* test still available for speech endangering national security?** Recall that, in *Dennis v. United States*, Chief Justice Vinson relied on a formula developed by Judge Learned Hand for determining whether speech created a clear and present danger. Under Hand's formula, if the harm threatened by speech was sufficiently grave, the government did not need to show that the speech was likely to lead to imminent lawbreaking. This

Hand test is starkly different from the *Brandenburg* test. Unlike the Hand test, the *Brandenburg* test requires that speech be likely to lead to imminent lawbreaking even if the threatened harm is grave. The *Brandenburg* test also requires that a speaker intend to incite imminent lawbreaking. Nevertheless, the *Brandenburg* case favorably cited the *Dennis* opinion. Does that mean that the justices intended for the Hand test to still be a viable option, at least in fact patterns like the one in *Dennis,* where speech posed a threat to national security?

f. **The unknown impact of *Holder v. Humanitarian Law Project.*** Federal law prohibits the provision of "material support or resources" to foreign terrorist organizations. In *Holder v. Humanitarian Law Project*, 561 U.S. 1 (2010), the Court considered a challenge to this law by groups that wanted to provide advice to two foreign terrorist organizations: the Kurdistan Workers Party and the Liberation Tigers of Tamil Eelam. The plaintiffs contended that they wanted to advise these groups about *lawful* means to advance their interests, such as how to use international law or to petition the United Nations. Given their intentions, the plaintiffs claimed that it would be an unconstitutional infringement on their freedom of speech to treat their advice as unlawful material support to terrorist groups.

The Supreme Court rejected the plaintiffs' argument. Chief Justice Roberts said that the government had a compelling interest in fighting terrorism and that, even if the plaintiffs only advised the terrorist organizations about lawful activities, their support would free up resources that the organizations could use for unlawful actions.

Chief Justice Roberts nowhere cited *Brandenburg* in his opinion. But should he have used the *Brandenburg* test? If he had, would the plaintiffs' speech have been protected because the plaintiffs were advocating lawful actions, not unlawful actions? Justice Stephen Breyer raised this argument in a dissent, and he did cite *Brandenburg*:

> "Coordination" with a group that engages in unlawful activity does not deprive the plaintiffs of the First Amendment's protection under any traditional "categorical" exception to its protection. The plaintiffs do not propose to solicit a crime. They will not engage in fraud or defamation or circulate obscenity. And the First Amendment protects advocacy even of *unlawful* action so long as that advocacy is not "directed to inciting or producing *imminent lawless action* and *likely to incite or produce* such action." Here the plaintiffs seek to advocate peaceful, *lawful* action to secure *political* ends; and they seek to teach others how to do the same. No one

contends that the plaintiffs' speech to these organizations can be prohibited as incitement under *Brandenburg*.

Who has the better argument here, Chief Justice Roberts or Justice Breyer? Does the *Humanitarian Law Project* opinion create an end run around *Brandenburg*, or is *Brandenburg* not applicable to these facts? *See* David Cole, *The First Amendment Borders: The Place of* Holder v. Humanitarian Law Project *in First Amendment Doctrine*, 6 Harv. L. & Pol'y Rev. 147 (2012) (warning that *Humanitarian Law Project* could dramatically expand "government authority to suppress political expression and association in the name of national security" but advocating for a narrow reading of the opinion that "would do the least damage to First Amendment freedoms").

g. **Is the *Brandenburg* test obsolete in an interconnected world?** We live in a world in which a Florida man's posting a video of himself burning a Koran can lead to riots and killings in Afghanistan. Should the *Brandenburg* test be used to decide if this video is protected speech, or does the First Amendment calculus change because of the video's global impact? Justice Breyer, commenting extemporaneously about this topic during a television interview, suggested that a different standard might be appropriate and that the video might not be protected. After noting Justice Holmes' famous observation that free speech "doesn't mean you can shout 'fire' in a crowded theater," he asked: "And what is the crowded theater today? What is being trampled to death?" Alexander Tsesis, *Terrorist Speech on Social Media*, 70 Vand. L. Rev. 651, 655 (2017) (noting how "technically adept terrorist organizations and their devotees exploit social networking sites to spread ideologies, disseminate instructional videos, consolidate power, and threaten enemies").

4. **A comparative perspective: What can we learn from other countries?** The United States is often more speech-protective than other countries, including other liberal democracies. One example is our treatment of incitement. After terrorist bombings in London in 2005, Parliament adopted the British Terrorism Act, which prohibited publishing a statement that is "likely to be understood" by the audience as "direct or indirect encouragement" to commit acts of terrorism. The ban on indirect encouragement includes statements that glorify acts of terrorism. The British law does not require proof that the statements are likely to lead to imminent lawbreaking.

Would you have voted in favor of such a law? Has Britain struck a better balance between speech and security than the United States? *See* Michael C. Shaughnessy, *Praising the Enemy: Could the United States Criminalize the Glorification of Terror Under an Act Similar to the United Kingdom's Terrorism Act of 2006?*, 113 Dick. L. Rev. 923 (2009). *See also* Tsesis, *supra*, at 675–84 (surveying foreign laws regulating terrorist speech and noting how the international community, "unlike the United States," is "less tolerant of terrorist propaganda and less hesitant about criminalizing its dissemination").

Would your answer depend on how much you trusted the government enforcing the law? Consider, for example, China's recently enacted Hong Kong national security law. A law protecting a country from national security threats seems eminently reasonable. But China has used this measure to vigorously suppress anyone who has dared to challenge China's imposition of authoritarian rule in Hong Kong.

Do you feel confident that the U.S. government would exercise its power responsibly? Do the early incitement cases give you cause for concern?

5. **What about hate speech?** Wasn't the defendant's speech in *Brandenburg* hate speech? The defendant made disparaging remarks about African Americans and Jews. The participants burned a cross. The group had gathered for a Klan rally. What else do you need?

   Given all of this, did it surprise you that the Supreme Court did not resolve the case by saying that the defendant's speech was unprotected hate speech? To the contrary, the Court held that the defendant's speech was protected as long as it did not rise to level of unprotected incitement.

   What does the *Brandenburg* opinion imply about whether hate speech is protected by the First Amendment? We will explore that topic in detail in the next chapter.

You Be the Lawyer!
Did Donald Trump's January 6, 2021, speech constitute incitement under Brandenburg?

On January 6, 2021, President Donald Trump spoke to a crowd of agitated supporters who had gathered in front of the White House on the day that Congress was to certify the Electoral College vote and declare Joe Biden the winner of the presidential election. The crowd had come to Washington at Trump's behest. He had summoned them with a Tweet saying, "Be there, will be wild!"

During his speech Trump told the crowd that he had won the election "in a landslide" and that "if you don't fight like hell, you're not going to have a country anymore." He then directed the crowd to march to the Capitol: "And after this, we're going to walk down, and I'll be there with you. We're going to walk down to the Capitol." In the same speech Trump said, "I know that everyone here will soon be marching over to the Capitol building to peacefully and patriotically make your voices heard." You can read the full speech here.

Did Trump's speech amount to unprotected incitement under *Brandenburg*? If you were litigating this issue, either for or against finding the speech unprotected, what would your arguments be? After you've completed this exercise, check out how two courts analyzed this issue. *Thompson v. Trump*, 590 F. Supp. 3d 46, 108–18 (D.D.C. 2002); *Anderson v. Griswold*, 543 P.3d 283 (Colo. 2023) *rev'd sub nom. Trump v. Anderson*, 144 S. Ct. 662 (2024).

B. Fighting Words and Hostile Audience: Speech That Provokes Violence Against the Speaker

Incitement concerns speech that encourages others to engage in lawbreaking. The fear is that a speaker's message will be favorably received by listeners, who will then act on the speaker's message.

The current topic is the reverse dynamic. In this instance, the targeted audience dislikes the speaker's message. The fear is that the audience will express their displeasure by attacking the speaker.

The Supreme Court's jurisprudence breaks this topic into two categories: fighting words and hostile audience. The former concerns one-on-one personal insults that would provoke a reasonable person to attack the speaker. The latter concerns speech that is not directed at an individual, but rather to a broader audience. The concern in hostile audience cases is that a speaker's message will so upset an audience (imagine a neo-Nazi speaking to a Jewish audience) that the audience will rise up and attack the speaker.

The question in both instances is whether the government may try to avert a violent reaction by punishing the individual whose speech is provoking the reaction.

1. Fighting Words: One-on-One Insults Likely to Provoke a Violent Reaction

The foundational case declaring fighting words to be unprotected by the First Amendment is *Chaplinsky v. New Hampshire*. It is worth reading *Chaplinsky* because some of its language has become canonical in First Amendment jurisprudence. At the same time, and as the notes will explain, much of what *Chaplinsky* says is no longer accurate.

Chaplinsky v. New Hampshire

Supreme Court of the United States, 1942
315 U.S. 568

MR. JUSTICE MURPHY delivered the opinion of the Court.

Appellant, a member of the sect known as Jehovah's Witnesses, was convicted in the municipal court of Rochester, New Hampshire, for violation of Chapter 378, Section 2, of the Public Laws of New Hampshire: "No person shall address any offensive, derisive or annoying word to any other person who is lawfully in any street or other public place."

state law

The complaint charged that appellant did unlawfully repeat, the words following, addressed to the complainant, that is to say, "You are a God damned racketeer" and "a damned Fascist and the whole government of Rochester are Fascists or agents of Fascists," the same being offensive, derisive and annoying words and names.

There is no substantial dispute over the facts. Chaplinsky was distributing the literature of his sect on the streets of Rochester on a busy Saturday afternoon. Members of the local citizenry complained to the City Marshal, Bowering, that Chaplinsky was denouncing all religion as a "racket." Bowering told them that Chaplinsky was lawfully engaged, and then warned Chaplinsky that the crowd was getting restless. Some time later a disturbance occurred and the traffic officer on duty at the busy intersection started with Chaplinsky for the police station, but did not inform him that he was under arrest or that he was going to be arrested. On the way they encountered Marshal Bowering who had been advised that a riot was under way and was therefore hurrying to the scene. Bowering repeated his earlier warning to Chaplinsky who then addressed to Bowering the words set forth in the complaint.

It is now clear that "Freedom of speech and freedom of the press, which are protected by the First Amendment from infringement by Congress, are among the fundamental personal rights and liberties which are protected by the Fourteenth Amendment from invasion by state action." Allowing the broadest scope to the language and purpose of the Fourteenth Amendment, it is well understood that the right of free speech is not absolute at all times and under all circumstances. There are certain well-defined and narrowly limited classes of speech, the prevention and punishment of which have never been thought to raise any Constitutional problem. These include the lewd and obscene, the profane, the libelous, and the insulting or "fighting" words—those which by their very utterance inflict injury or tend to incite an immediate breach of the peace. It has been well observed that such utterances are no essential part of any exposition of ideas, and are of such slight social value as a step to truth that any benefit that may be derived from them is clearly outweighed by the social interest in order and morality. "Resort to epithets or personal abuse is not in any proper sense communication of information or opinion safeguarded by the Constitution, and its punishment as a criminal act would raise no question under that instrument."

The state court declared that the statute's purpose was to preserve the public peace, no words being "forbidden except such as have a direct tendency to cause acts of violence by the person to whom, individually, the remark is addressed." It was further said: "The word 'offensive' is not to be defined in terms of what a particular addressee thinks. The test is what men of common intelligence would understand would be words likely to cause an average addressee to fight. The statute, as construed, does no more than prohibit the face-to-face words plainly likely to cause a breach of the peace by the addressee."

We are unable to say that the limited scope of the statute as thus construed contravenes the constitutional right of free expression.

Nor can we say that the application of the statute to the facts disclosed by the record substantially or unreasonably impinges upon the privilege of free speech. Argument is unnecessary to demonstrate that the appellations "damn racketeer" and "damn Fascist" are epithets likely to provoke the average person to retaliation, and thereby cause a breach of the peace.

Affirmed.

Points for Discussion

1. **The categorical approach for identifying unprotected speech.** *Chaplinsky* is famous for its statement that there are certain categories of speech that are not protected by First Amendment:

   > There are certain well-defined and narrowly limited classes of speech, the prevention and punishment of which have never been thought to raise any Constitutional problem. These include the lewd and obscene, the profane, the libelous, and the insulting or "fighting" words—those which by their very utterance inflict injury or tend to incite an immediate breach of the peace. It has been well observed that such utterances are no essential part of any exposition of ideas, and are of such slight social value as a step to truth that any benefit that may be derived from them is clearly outweighed by the social interest in order and morality.

   Chaplinsky succinctly captures what has become known as the "categorical" approach to freedom of speech—the notion that, while most speech is protected by the First Amendment, there are certain categories of speech that are not. This categorical approach has become a core principle in First Amendment jurisprudence that continues to have traction. For example, here is a passage from a 2023 Supreme Court opinion reciting the standard litany about unprotected categories of speech:

> "From 1791 to the present," the First Amendment has "permitted restrictions upon the content of speech in a few limited areas." These "historic and traditional categories" are "long familiar to the bar" and perhaps, too, the general public. One is incitement—statements "directed at producing imminent lawless action," and likely to do so. Another is defamation—false statements of fact harming another's reputation. Still a third is obscenity—valueless material "appealing to the prurient interest" and describing "sexual conduct" in "a patently offensive way." This Court has "often described those historically unprotected categories of speech as being of such slight social value as a step to truth that any benefit that may be derived from them is clearly outweighed by the social interest" in their proscription.

Counterman v. Colorado, 600 U.S. 66, 73–74 (2023). While the categorical approach is firmly entrenched in First Amendment jurisprudence, it is not without its faults. The most salient problem is the conflict between the categorical approach and the neutrality principle that bars the government from deciding which ideas merit First Amendment protection. If public officials are precluded from evaluating the relative worth of ideas, how can judges declare that some ideas are unworthy of protection because they have such "slight social value"?

The Supreme Court is keenly aware of this tension. In *United States v. Stevens*, 559 U.S. 460 (2010), Chief Justice Roberts described the notion of judges' declaring speech unprotected based on a cost/benefit analysis as "startling and dangerous." As he explained, "The First Amendment's guarantee of free speech does not extend only to categories of speech that survive an ad hoc balancing of relative social costs and benefits."

Chief Justice Roberts sought to resolve this tension by stating that a category of speech will be unprotected only if there is a longstanding tradition of the category's being unprotected. He conceded that there might "some categories of speech that have been historically unprotected, but have not yet been specifically identified," but he implied that these would be few and far between. We will consider the merits of this historical approach when we analyze *Stevens* in Chapter 7.

The categorical approach also tends to exaggerate the difference between protected and unprotected speech. In many instances, an unprotected category of speech may be regulated only if the regulation satisfies a demanding standard that could easily be recharacterized as a form of strict scrutiny. For example, one could argue that the *Brandenburg* test is merely a more precise way of asking whether a regulation of inciteful speech is "necessary" to further a "compelling government interest." (Answer: It is when the speech is intended and likely to lead to imminent lawbreaking.) In this sense, incitement is no different than protected speech; it may be regulated based on its content, but only if the regulation passes strict scrutiny.

The Supreme Court's hostility to declaring new categories of unprotected speech has left the Court in an awkward truce with *Chaplinsky*. On the one hand, the Court continues to recite and apply the *Chaplinsky* mantra that there are categories of unprotected speech. On the other hand, the Court is reluctant to find new categories of unprotected speech and has disavowed *Chaplinsky*'s suggestion that judges may do so through a simple cost/benefit analysis.

2. **Is *Chaplinsky*'s list of unprotected categories of speech accurate?** *Chaplinsky* conveniently provided a list of the unprotected categories of speech: "the lewd and obscene, the profane, the libelous, and the insulting or fighting words." As you will learn, this list is no longer accurate. Lewd and profane language is often protected by the First Amendment, and while obscenity, libel, and fighting words are still considered to be unprotected categories of speech, that is only true if the speech satisfies the strict rules the Supreme Court has developed to ensure that these exceptions do not unduly encroach on free speech interests. The Court has also added other categories to the list of unprotected speech, including incitement, true threats, and child pornography, and justices sometimes mention other categories, such as fraud or speech integral to criminal conduct, even in the absence of a full-fledged opinion pronouncing these categories unprotected. *See, e.g., Stevens*, 559 U.S. at 468. Finally, the Court treats commercial speech as a unique category of speech that is protected, but less protected, than other forms of speech.

3. **When does speech rise to the level of unprotected "fighting words"?** *Chaplinsky* gives a twofold definition of fighting words: "those which by their very utterance inflict injury or tend to incite an immediate breach of the peace." The first definition—words that "by their very utterance inflict injury"—is potentially expansive. Under this definition, hate speech could be treated as unprotected fighting words because it inflicts psychic injury on the disparaged groups. But subsequent Supreme Court cases have indicated that *Chaplinsky*'s first definition of fighting words is no longer operable. Instead, only the second definition—words that "tend to incite an immediate breach of the peace"—is still viable. The Court has construed this to include only one-on-one personal insults that are likely to provoke a reasonable person to react with violence against the speaker.

In anticipation of future cases, you might want to ask yourself whether walking around in public with a jacket that says "Fuck the Draft" or burning the national flag at a public rally would constitute fighting words under this definition. *See Cohen v. California*, 403 U.S. 15 (1971); *Texas v. Johnson*, 491 U.S. 397 (1989).

4. **Fighting words directed at police officers.** People often have not-so-nice things to say to police officers who are arresting them or a family member or friend. These words might be exactly the type of insults that would provoke a reasonable person to respond with violence. But should a court treat them as unprotected speech when they are directed at a law enforcement officer? Lower courts have generally said no. In *Wood v. Eubanks*, 25 F. 4th 414 (6th Cir. 2022), for example, the police escorted Michael Wood from a county fairground because he was wearing a shirt that said "Fuck the Police." (You'll learn in Chapter 7 that a person can wear a shirt that says "Fuck.") Wood expressed his displeasure with the officers by hurling insults at them. The police then arrested him for disorderly conduct. The Sixth Circuit first emphasized that the fighting words exception is "very limited." It then added that this is particularly true when the words are directed at a police officer:

> Both the Supreme Court and this court have made clear that police officers are expected to exercise greater restraint in their response than the average citizen. Police officers are held to a higher standard than average citizens, because the First Amendment requires that they tolerate coarse criticism.

5. **Even if fighting words are unprotected, it can still be difficult to draft a law that passes constitutional muster.** As you learned in Chapter 4, the Supreme Court is leery of speech regulations that lack adequate precision. The Court will find laws facially unconstitutional if they are substantially overbroad, meaning that they regulate not only unprotected speech but also substantial amounts of protected speech. The Court will also strike down laws that are unconstitutionally vague, meaning that they fail to provide adequate notice of what speech is being regulated.

   Although the Supreme Court continues to say that fighting words are not protected by the First Amendment, in the years since *Chaplinsky* the Court has repeatedly struck down regulations of fighting words because the laws were overbroad or vague or both.

   Gooding v. Wilson, 405 U.S. 518 (1972), is a classic example. In that case, the Court considered the constitutionality of a Georgia statute, Section 26–6303, that stated, "Any person who shall, without provocation, use to or of another, and in his presence opprobrious words or abusive language, tending to cause a breach of the peace shall be guilty of a misdemeanor." In finding the statute unconstitutionally vague and overbroad, the Court stated:

> Georgia appellate decisions have not construed § 26–6303 to be limited in application, as in *Chaplinsky*, to words that "have a direct tendency to cause acts of violence by the person to whom, individually, the remark is addressed." The dictionary definitions of "opprobrious" and "abusive" give them greater reach than "fighting" words. Georgia appellate decisions have construed § 26–6303 to apply to utterances that, although within these definitions, are not "fighting" words as *Chaplinsky* defines them.

Even if a fighting words law is not overbroad or vague, it can still be found unconstitutional if it violates the rule established in *R.A.V. v. City of St. Paul*, which you'll read about in the next section.

The *R.A.V.* Trap: Even Regulations of Unprotected Speech Can Be Unconstitutional

We know that laws regulating fighting words can be unconstitutional if they are vague or overbroad. But assume that legislators enact a statute that passes both of those hurdles. In that instance, you would expect the law to be constitutional. After all, the law regulates only fighting words, and fighting words are unprotected.

You might think that, but the Court's decision in *R.A.V. v. City of St. Paul*, 505 U.S. 377 (1992), indicates that you need to be on the lookout for another constitutional defect. Justice Antonin Scalia wrote the majority opinion in *R.A.V.*, a notoriously complicated decision. We have included extensive notes following the case to help you process it.

The facts are horrid. The defendant and some of his teenage friends made a crude cross that they burned inside the fenced yard of an African American family in St. Paul, Minnesota. For the family, this act was almost certainly terrifying.

Justice Scalia readily acknowledged that the defendant could be prosecuted for his action. For example, he could have been prosecuted for arson, trespassing, or threatening the family. The issue in *R.A.V.*, however, was whether the defendant could be prosecuted under a specific St. Paul city ordinance called the "Bias-Motivated Crime Ordinance." Here is the text of the ordinance:

> Whoever places on public or private property a symbol, object, appellation, characterization or graffiti, including, but not limited to, a burning cross or Nazi swastika, which one knows or has reasonable grounds to know

> arouses anger, alarm or resentment in others on the basis of race, color, creed, religion or gender commits disorderly conduct and shall be guilty of a misdemeanor.

The language of the statute does not obviously limit its scope to fighting words. There is language about the speech arousing anger, alarm, or resentment, but there is nothing about the speech provoking a violent reaction against the speaker. Nevertheless, St. Paul argued that Minnesota courts had narrowly construed the statute to limit its application to fighting words. As you learned in Chapter 4, judges can fix overbroad laws by construing them in a manner that corrects their infirmity.

Four Supreme Court justices did not buy the argument that Minnesota courts had fixed the ordinance's overbreadth. They wanted to invalidate the law on that ground alone. Justice Byron White made this point in his concurring opinion:

> This case could easily be decided within the contours of established First Amendment law by holding, as petitioner argues, that the St. Paul ordinance is fatally overbroad because it criminalizes not only unprotected expression but expression protected by the First Amendment.

Justice Scalia declined to go down this path. Instead, he assumed for the sake of argument ("*arguendo*") that the law was not overbroad and applied to only unprotected fighting words. Here is how he put it: "We accept the Minnesota Supreme Court's authoritative statement that the ordinance reaches only those expressions that constitute 'fighting words' within the meaning of *Chaplinsky*."

This is where things get tricky. If the ordinance applied to only unprotected fighting words, then one would have expected Justice Scalia to find the ordinance constitutional. He did not. The question for you is why.

Following are the key passages from Justice Scalia's opinion. Try to identify the rule he is articulating, as well as the two exceptions he creates to the rule.

R.A.V. v. City of St. Paul

Supreme Court of the United States, 1992
505 U.S. 377

JUSTICE SCALIA delivered the opinion of the Court.

We accept the Minnesota Supreme Court's authoritative statement that the ordinance reaches only those expressions that constitute "fighting words" within the meaning of *Chaplinsky*. Petitioner and his *amici* urge us to modify the scope of the *Chaplinsky* formulation, thereby invalidating the ordinance as "substantially overbroad." We find it unnecessary to consider this issue. Assuming, *arguendo,* that all of the expression reached by the ordinance is proscribable under the "fighting words" doctrine, we nonetheless conclude that the ordinance is facially unconstitutional in that it prohibits otherwise permitted speech solely on the basis of the subjects the speech addresses.

The First Amendment generally prevents government from proscribing speech, or even expressive conduct, because of disapproval of the ideas expressed. Content-based regulations are presumptively invalid. From 1791 to the present, however, our society, like other free but civilized societies, has permitted restrictions upon the content of speech in a few limited areas, which are "of such slight social value as a step to truth that any benefit that may be derived from them is clearly outweighed by the social interest in order and morality."

We have sometimes said that these categories of expression are "not within the area of constitutionally protected speech," or that the "protection of the First Amendment does not extend" to them. Such statements must be taken in context, however, and are no more literally true than is the occasionally repeated shorthand characterizing obscenity "as not being speech at all." What they mean is that these areas of speech can, consistently with the First Amendment, be regulated *because of their constitutionally proscribable content* (obscenity, defamation, etc.)—not that they are categories of speech entirely invisible to the Constitution, so that they may be made the vehicles for content discrimination unrelated to their distinctively proscribable content. Thus, the government may proscribe libel; but it may not make the further content discrimination of proscribing *only* libel critical of the government.

Our cases surely do not establish the proposition that the First Amendment imposes no obstacle whatsoever to regulation of particular instances of such proscribable expression, so that the government "may regulate them freely." That would mean that a city council could enact an ordinance prohibiting only those legally obscene works that contain criticism of the city government or, indeed, that do not include endorsement of the city government. Such a simplistic, all-or-nothing-at-all approach to First Amendment protection is at odds with common sense and with our jurisprudence as well.

The proposition that a particular instance of speech can be proscribable on the basis of one feature (*e.g.,* obscenity) but not on the basis of another (*e.g.,* opposition to the city government) is commonplace and has found application in many contexts. We have long held, for example, that nonverbal expressive activity can be banned because of the action it entails, but not because of the ideas it expresses—so that burning a flag in violation of an ordinance against outdoor fires could be punishable, whereas burning a flag in violation of an ordinance against dishonoring the flag is not.

Similarly, we have upheld reasonable "time, place, or manner" restrictions, but only if they are "justified without reference to the content of the regulated speech." And just as the power to proscribe particular speech on the basis of a noncontent element (*e.g.,* noise) does not entail the power to proscribe the same speech on the basis of a content element; so also, the power to proscribe it on the basis of *one* content element (*e.g.,* obscenity) does not entail the power to proscribe it on the basis of *other* content elements.

In other words, the exclusion of "fighting words" from the scope of the First Amendment simply means that, for purposes of that Amendment, the unprotected features of the words are, despite their verbal character, essentially a "nonspeech" element of communication. Fighting words are thus analogous to a noisy sound truck: Each is, as Justice Frankfurter recognized, a "mode of speech;" both can be used to convey an idea; but neither has, in and of itself, a claim upon the First Amendment. As with the sound truck, however, so also with fighting words: The government may not regulate use based on hostility—or favoritism—towards the underlying message expressed.

The concurrences describe us as setting forth a new First Amendment principle that prohibition of constitutionally proscribable speech cannot be "underinclusive"—a First Amendment "absolutism" whereby "within a particular 'proscribable' category of expression, a government must either proscribe *all* speech or no speech at all." That easy target is of the concurrences' own invention. In our view, the First Amendment imposes not an "underinclusiveness" limitation but a "content discrimination" limitation upon a State's prohibition of proscribable speech. There is no problem whatever, for example, with a State's prohibiting obscenity (and other forms of proscribable expression) only in certain media or markets, for although that prohibition would be "underinclusive," it would not discriminate on the basis of content.

Even the prohibition against content discrimination that we assert the First Amendment requires is not absolute. It applies differently in the context of proscribable speech than in the area of fully protected speech. The rationale of the general prohibition, after all, is that content discrimination "raises the specter that the Government may effectively drive certain ideas or viewpoints from the marketplace." But content discrimination among various instances of a class of proscribable speech often does not pose this threat.

When the basis for the content discrimination consists entirely of the very reason the entire class of speech at issue is proscribable, no significant danger of idea or viewpoint discrimination exists. Such a reason, having been adjudged neutral enough to support exclusion of the entire class of speech from First Amendment protection, is also neutral enough to form the basis of distinction within the class. To illustrate: A State might choose to prohibit only that obscenity which is the most patently offensive *in its prurience—i.e.,* that which involves the most lascivious displays of sexual activity. But it may not prohibit, for example, only that obscenity which includes offensive *political* messages. And the Federal Government can criminalize only those threats of violence that are directed against the President—since the reasons why threats of violence are outside the First Amendment (protecting individuals from the fear of violence, from the disruption that fear engenders, and from the possibility that the threatened violence will occur) have special force when applied to the person of the President. But the Federal Government may not criminalize only those threats against the President that mention his policy on aid to inner cities. And to take a final example, a State may choose to regulate price advertising in one industry but not in others, because the risk of fraud (one of the characteristics of commercial speech that justifies depriving it of full First Amendment protection) is in its view greater there. But a State may not prohibit only that commercial advertising that depicts men in a demeaning fashion.

Another valid basis for according differential treatment to even a content-defined subclass of proscribable speech is that the subclass happens to be associated with particular "secondary effects" of the speech, so that the regulation is "*justified* without reference to the content of the speech." A State could, for example, permit all obscene live performances except those involving minors. Moreover, since words can in some circumstances violate laws directed not against speech but against conduct, a particular content-based subcategory of a proscribable class of speech can be swept up incidentally within the reach of a statute directed at conduct rather than speech. Thus, for example, sexually derogatory "fighting words," among other words, may produce a violation of Title VII's general prohibition against sexual discrimination in employment practices. Where the government does not target conduct on the basis of its expressive content, acts are not shielded from regulation merely because they express a discriminatory idea or philosophy.

These bases for distinction refute the proposition that the selectivity of the restriction is "even arguably conditioned upon the sovereign's agreement with what a speaker may intend to say." There may be other such bases as well. Indeed, to validate such selectivity (where totally proscribable speech is at issue) it may not even be necessary to identify any particular "neutral" basis, so long as the nature of the content discrimination is such that there is no realistic possibility that official suppression of ideas is afoot. (We cannot think of any First Amendment interest that would stand in the way of a State's prohibiting only those obscene motion pictures with blue-eyed actresses.) Save for that limitation, the regulation of "fighting words," like the regulation of noisy speech, may address some offensive instances and leave other, equally offensive, instances alone.

Applying these principles to the St. Paul ordinance, we conclude that, even as narrowly construed by the Minnesota Supreme Court, the ordinance is facially unconstitutional. Although the phrase in the ordinance, "arouses anger, alarm or resentment in others," has been limited by the Minnesota Supreme Court's construction to reach only those symbols or displays that amount to "fighting words," the remaining, unmodified terms make clear that the ordinance applies only to "fighting words" that insult, or provoke violence, "on the basis of race, color, creed, religion or gender." Displays containing abusive invective, no matter how vicious or severe, are permissible unless they are addressed to one of the specified disfavored topics. Those who wish to use "fighting words" in connection with other ideas—to express hostility, for example, on the basis of political affiliation, union membership, or homosexuality—are not covered. The First Amendment does not permit St. Paul to impose special prohibitions on those speakers who express views on disfavored subjects.

In its practical operation, moreover, the ordinance goes even beyond mere content discrimination, to actual viewpoint discrimination. Displays containing some words—odious racial epithets, for example—would be prohibited to proponents of all views. But "fighting words" that do not themselves invoke race, color, creed, religion, or gender—aspersions upon a person's mother, for example—would seemingly be usable *ad libitum* in the placards of those arguing *in favor* of racial, color, etc., tolerance and equality, but could not be used by those speakers' opponents. One could hold up a sign saying, for example, that all "anti-Catholic bigots" are misbegotten; but not that all "papists" are, for that would insult and provoke violence "on the basis of religion." St. Paul has no such authority to license one side of a debate to fight freestyle, while requiring the other to follow Marquis of Queensberry rules.

The content-based discrimination reflected in the St. Paul ordinance comes within neither any of the specific exceptions to the First Amendment prohibition we discussed earlier nor a more general exception for content discrimination that does not threaten censorship of ideas. It assuredly does not fall within the exception for content discrimination based on the very reasons why the particular class of speech at issue (here, fighting words) is proscribable. As explained earlier, the reason why fighting words are categorically excluded from the protection of the First Amendment is not that their content communicates any particular idea, but that their content embodies a particularly intolerable (and socially unnecessary) *mode* of expressing *whatever* idea the speaker wishes to convey. St. Paul has not singled out an especially offensive mode of expression—it has not, for example, selected for prohibition only those fighting words that communicate ideas in a threatening (as opposed to a merely obnoxious) manner. Rather, it has proscribed fighting words of whatever manner that communicate messages of racial, gender, or religious intolerance. Selectivity of this sort creates the possibility that the city is seeking to handicap the expression of particular ideas. That possibility would alone be enough to render the ordinance presumptively invalid, but St. Paul's comments and concessions in this case elevate the possibility to a certainty.

St. Paul argues that the ordinance comes within another of the specific exceptions we mentioned, the one that allows content discrimination aimed only at the "secondary effects" of the speech. According to St. Paul, the ordinance is intended, "not to impact on the right of free expression of the accused," but rather to "protect against the victimization of a person or persons who are particularly vulnerable because of their membership in a group that historically has been discriminated against." Even assuming that an ordinance that completely proscribes, rather than merely regulates, a specified category of speech can ever be considered to be directed only to the secondary effects of such speech, it is clear that the St. Paul ordinance is not directed to secondary effects within the meaning of *Renton.* As we said in *Boos v. Barry*, 485 U.S. 312 (1988), "Listeners' reactions to speech are not the type of 'secondary effects' we referred to in *Renton.*" "The emotive impact of speech on its audience is not a 'secondary effect.' "

It hardly needs discussion that the ordinance does not fall within some more general exception permitting *all* selectivity that for any reason is beyond the suspicion of official suppression of ideas. The statements of St. Paul in this very case afford ample basis for, if not full confirmation of, that suspicion.

Finally, St. Paul and its *amici* defend the conclusion of the Minnesota Supreme Court that, even if the ordinance regulates expression based on hostility towards its protected ideological content, this discrimination is nonetheless justified because it is narrowly tailored to serve compelling state interests. Specifically, they assert that the ordinance helps to ensure the basic human rights of members of groups that have historically been subjected to discrimination, including the right of such group members to live in peace where they wish. We do not doubt that these interests are compelling, and that the ordinance can be said to promote them. But the "danger of censorship" presented by a facially content-based statute, requires that that weapon be employed only where it is "*necessary* to serve the asserted compelling interest." The existence of adequate content-neutral alternatives thus "undercuts significantly" any defense of such a statute, casting considerable doubt on the government's protestations that "the asserted justification is in fact an accurate description of the purpose and effect of the law." The dispositive question in this case, therefore, is whether content discrimination is reasonably necessary to achieve St. Paul's compelling interests; it plainly is not. An ordinance not limited to the favored topics, for example, would have precisely the same beneficial effect. In fact the only interest distinctively served by the content limitation is that of displaying the city council's special hostility towards the particular biases thus singled out. That is precisely what the First Amendment forbids. The politicians of St. Paul are entitled to express that hostility—but not through the means of imposing unique limitations upon speakers who (however benightedly) disagree.

Let there be no mistake about our belief that burning a cross in someone's front yard is reprehensible. But St. Paul has sufficient means at its disposal to prevent such behavior without adding the First Amendment to the fire.

The judgment of the Minnesota Supreme Court is reversed, and the case is remanded for proceedings not inconsistent with this opinion.

JUSTICE WHITE, with whom JUSTICE BLACKMUN and JUSTICE O'CONNOR join, and with whom JUSTICE STEVENS joins except as to Part I-A, concurring in the judgment.

I agree with the majority that the judgment of the Minnesota Supreme Court should be reversed. However, our agreement ends there.

This case could easily be decided within the contours of established First Amendment law by holding, as petitioner argues, that the St. Paul ordinance is fatally overbroad because it criminalizes not only unprotected expression but expression protected by the First Amendment.

This Court's decisions have plainly stated that expression falling within certain limited categories so lacks the values the First Amendment was designed to protect that the Constitution affords no protection to that expression.

The majority holds that the First Amendment protects those narrow categories of expression long held to be undeserving of First Amendment protection—at least to the extent that lawmakers may not regulate some fighting words more strictly than others because of their content. The Court announces that such content-based distinctions violate the First Amendment because "the government may not regulate use based on hostility—or favoritism—towards the underlying message expressed." Should the government want to criminalize certain fighting words, the Court now requires it to criminalize all fighting words.

To borrow a phrase: "Such a simplistic, all-or-nothing-at-all approach to First Amendment protection is at odds with common sense and with our jurisprudence as well." It is inconsistent to hold that the government may proscribe an entire category of speech because the content of that speech is evil, but that the government may not treat a subset of that category differently without violating the First Amendment; the content of the subset is by definition worthless and undeserving of constitutional protection.

[Justice Blackmun's opinion concurring in the judgment is omitted, as is Justice Stevens' opinion concurring in the judgment, which Justice White and Justice Blackmun joined in part.]

Points for Discussion

1. **Headache relief! Deconstructing Justice Scalia's opinion.** If you have a headache after reading Justice Scalia's opinion, you're not alone. The opinion is a mental workout.

   The key conundrum of the *R.A.V.* case is why the St. Paul ordinance was unconstitutional if it was regulating only unprotected fighting words. After all, the whole point of a category of speech being unprotected is that the government is free to regulate it. As *Chaplinsky* observed, the punishment of these categories has "never been thought to raise any constitutional problems."

   Justice Scalia's answer is that a regulation of unprotected speech can violate the First Amendment if it regulates a subset of an unprotected category in a manner that constitutes unlawful content-based discrimination. That's easier said than comprehended, but a simple example can make Justice Scalia's abstract point more concrete. Earlier in this chapter, you learned that speech encouraging unlawful action ("incitement") is not protected by the First Amendment if it meets the *Brandenburg* test. Now ask yourself this: Does this mean that the government could enact an incitement regulation that prohibited incitement only when it was targeted at anti-abortion advocates and not abortion rights advocates? If your answer is no, you are grasping Justice Scalia's point. As in *R.A.V.*, the government in this example is only regulating unprotected speech (incitement), but it is doing so in a manner that permits some content (incitement toward abortion-rights advocates) but not other content (incitement toward anti-abortion advocates). Indeed, the law is not only content-based but also viewpoint discriminatory.

   Justice Scalia's problem with the St. Paul ordinance was that it regulated only fighting words aimed at certain ideas. Fighting words that expressed the idea of hostility toward a person's race, creed, religion, or gender were punishable under the ordinance. By contrast, as Justice Scalia explained, "those who wish to use 'fighting words' in connection with other ideas—to express hostility, for example, on the basis of political affiliation, union membership, or homosexuality—are not covered."

   If the problem with the St. Paul ordinance was that it regulated fighting words based on their content, then the real issue should have been whether the law's content-based regulation of speech could be constitutionally justified. In other words, was the ordinance necessary to further a compelling governmental interest? Justice Scalia addressed this issue toward the end of his opinion when he considered St. Paul's argument that the ordinance was necessary to "ensure the basic human rights of members of groups that have historically been subjected to discrimination." Justice Scalia accepted that this interest could be compelling but said it was not necessary for St. Paul to use a law that discriminated based on content to further this interest. "An ordinance not limited to the favored topics," he observed, "would have precisely the same beneficial effect."

2. **Exceptions to the *R.A.V.* rule.** Justice White concurred in the judgment of *R.A.V.* but not with Justice Scalia's reasoning. He preferred to declare the St. Paul ordinance unconstitutional based on overbreadth.

   Justice White contended that Justice Scalia's reasoning had the perverse effect of forcing the government to regulate more speech rather than less. If the government regulates only *some* fighting words, as in *R.A.V.*, the law is likely to be struck down as unlawful content-based discrimination. But if the government regulates *all* fighting words, the law is likely to be constitutional. "Such a simplistic, all-or-nothing-at-all approach to First Amendment protection," Justice White said, "is at odds with common sense and with our jurisprudence as well."

   Justice Scalia responded by denying that that his rule precluded the government from regulating a subset of an unprotected category. He announced two exceptions to prove his point.

   The first exception was this: "When the basis for the content discrimination consists entirely of the very reason the entire class of speech at issue is proscribable, no significant danger of idea or viewpoint discrimination exists."

   Is your headache coming back? Let's see if we can relieve your pain.

   To understand this exception, you must first recognize that each category of unprotected speech is unprotected for a reason. For example, you will soon learn that threats to commit violence against another person (referred to as "true threats") are not protected by the First Amendment because of the fear and disruption they generate in the targeted individual. Relying on this reasoning, Justice Scalia illustrated his first exception by saying the government could constitutionally enact a law that punished only threats directed at the president (*i.e.,* a subset of true threats) because such threats are especially likely to generate fear and disruption, which is the reason why true threats are unprotected. As Justice Scalia put it, "the basis for the content discrimination consists entirely of the very reason the entire class of speech at issue is proscribable." In these instances, Justice Scalia said, there is no danger of the government's engaging in idea or viewpoint discrimination.

   Does this reasoning make sense to you? If it does, do you also agree with the reasoning of Justice John Paul Stevens who, in a concurrence in *R.A.V.*, chided

Justice Scalia for not holding the St. Paul ordinance constitutional under this exception:

> Just as Congress may determine that threats against the President entail more severe consequences than other threats, so St. Paul's City Council may determine that threats based on the target's race, religion, or gender cause more severe harm to both the target and to society than other threats.

Justice Scalia's second exception relied on the secondary effects rule discussed in Chapter 4. The rule, which derives from *Renton v. Playtime Theatres, Inc.*, treats a content-based law as content-neutral if the regulation is aimed at speech's secondary effects (such as the impact of adult movie theaters on surrounding communities), not at its message. Justice Scalia offered as an example conduct regulations that incidentally burden speech, such as, Title VII of the federal Civil Rights Act, which prohibits discrimination in employment based on race, color, religion, sex, or national origin, and can be violated by speech that creates a hostile workplace environment (such as office speech that demeans women). On the surface, the application of Title VII to speech sounds a lot like the St. Paul ordinance that Justice Scalia invalidated in *R.A.V.* because Title VII is punishing speech only when it is targeted at some groups (race, sex, and religion) and not others. But Justice Scalia distinguished Title VII from the St. Paul ordinance by saying that the ordinance was aimed at *speech* (messages that aroused anger and resentment), whereas Title VII is aimed at *conduct* (employment discrimination) and only incidentally affects speech. The *R.A.V.* rule, he explained, does not apply to such conduct regulations. Do you find this distinction convincing?

3. **Fun with viewpoint discrimination.** Justice Scalia claimed that the St. Paul ordinance not only regulated speech based on its content but also engaged in viewpoint discrimination. For example, he said, "One could hold up a sign saying that all 'anti-Catholic bigots' are misbegotten; but not that all 'papists' are, for that would insult and provoke violence 'on the basis of religion.' " As Justice Scalia explained in his inimitable style, "St. Paul has no such authority to license one side of a debate to fight freestyle, while requiring the other to follow Marquis of Queensberry rules."

Justice Stevens contended that it was Justice Scalia's analysis that was misbegotten:

> Contrary to the suggestion of the majority, the St. Paul ordinance does *not* regulate expression based on viewpoint. Just as the ordinance would prohibit a Muslim from hoisting a sign claiming that all Catholics were misbegotten, so the ordinance would bar a Catholic from hoisting a similar sign attacking Muslims. The St. Paul ordinance is evenhanded.

Which argument, Justice Stevens' or Justice Scalia's, is misbegotten?

2. Hostile Audience: When an Audience Threatens to Attack a Speaker Because of the Speaker's Message

The second category of speech that has the potential of provoking a violent reaction against the speaker is called "hostile audience." Unlike fighting words, which are one-on-one personal insults, the hostile audience rule applies to speech delivered to a group. The problem here is that the speaker is delivering a message that the audience abhors, and the concern is that the audience might respond by attacking the speaker. The question is whether the government may restrict the speaker as a means of averting violence.

For starters, it is important to note that speech does not lose its protection merely because it stirs people to anger. Justice William Douglas famously made this point in *Terminiello v. Chicago*, 337 U.S. 1 (1949). In that case, a man known for being anti-Semitic spoke at an auditorium in a largely Jewish neighborhood of Chicago. Not surprisingly, a hostile crowd assembled outside the auditorium. The speaker deliberately threw fuel onto this fire. He "condemned the conduct of the crowd outside and vigorously, if not viciously, criticized various political and racial groups whose activities he denounced as inimical to the nation's welfare."

The speaker was later charged with breach of the peace. In construing the relevant statute, the trial judge instructed the jury that "misbehavior may constitute a breach of the peace if it stirs the public to anger, invites dispute, brings about a condition of unrest, or creates a disturbance, or if it molests the inhabitants in the enjoyment of peace and quiet by arousing alarm."

Justice Douglas never reached the issue of whether the defendant's speech was unprotected. He reversed the conviction solely on the ground that the trial judge's instruction to the jury violated the First Amendment. As Justice Douglas explained, speech does not lose its protection merely because it angers people or provokes dispute:

> A function of free speech under our system of government is to invite dispute. It may indeed best serve its high purpose when it induces a condition of unrest, creates dissatisfaction with conditions as they are, or even stirs people to anger.

The leading case concerning the hostile audience exception is *Feiner v. New York*. A young Army veteran, Irving Feiner, who was a university student in Syracuse, gave a speech to a mixed audience of blacks and whites. The purpose of the speech was to publicize a meeting of the Young Progressives of America to be held that evening. During his speech, Feiner called President Harry Truman and the Syracuse mayor bums and the American Legion a Nazi Gestapo.

Feiner v. New York

Supreme Court of the United States, 1951
340 U.S. 315

MR. CHIEF JUSTICE VINSON delivered the opinion of the Court.

The police officers made no effort to interfere with petitioner's speech, but were first concerned with the effect of the crowd on both pedestrian and vehicular traffic. They observed the situation from the opposite side of the street, noting that some pedestrians were forced to walk in the street to avoid the crowd. Since traffic was passing at the time, the officers attempted to get the people listening to petitioner back on the sidewalk. The crowd was restless and there was some pushing, shoving and milling around. One of the officers telephoned the police station from a nearby store, and then both policemen crossed the street and mingled with the crowd without any intention of arresting the speaker.

At this time, petitioner was speaking in a "loud, high-pitched voice." He gave the impression that he was endeavoring to arouse the Negro people against the whites, urging that they rise up in arms and fight for equal rights. The statements before such a mixed audience "stirred up a little excitement." Some of the onlookers made remarks to the police about their inability to handle the crowd and at least one threatened violence if the police did not act. There were others who appeared to be favoring petitioner's arguments. Because of the feeling that existed in the crowd both for and against the speaker, the officers finally "stepped in to prevent it from resulting in a fight." One of the officers approached the petitioner, not for the purpose of arresting him, but to get him to break up the crowd. He asked petitioner to get down off the box, but the latter refused to accede to his request and continued talking. The officer waited for a minute and then demanded that he cease talking. Although the officer had thus twice requested petitioner to stop over the course of several minutes, petitioner not only ignored him but continued talking. During all this time, the crowd was pressing closer around petitioner and the officer. Finally, the officer told petitioner he was under arrest and ordered him to get down from the box, reaching up to grab him. Petitioner stepped down, announcing over the microphone that "the law has arrived, and I suppose they will take over now." In all, the officer had asked petitioner to get down off the box three times over a space of four or five minutes. Petitioner had been speaking for over a half hour.

The language of *Cantwell v. State of Connecticut*, 310 U.S. 296 (1940), is appropriate here. "When clear and present danger of riot, disorder, interference with traffic upon the public streets, or other immediate threat to public safety, peace, or order, appears, the power of the State to prevent or punish is obvious." The findings of the New York courts as to the condition of the crowd and the refusal of petitioner to obey the police requests, supported as they are by the record of this case, are persuasive that the conviction of petitioner for violation of public peace, order and authority does not exceed the bounds of proper state police action. This Court respects, as it must, the interest of the community in maintaining peace and order on its streets. We cannot say that the preservation of that interest here encroaches on the constitutional rights of this petitioner.

dissent

MR. JUSTICE BLACK, dissenting.

The record before us convinces me that petitioner, a young college student, has been sentenced to the penitentiary for the unpopular views he expressed on matters of public interest while lawfully making a street-corner speech in Syracuse, New York. Even accepting every "finding of fact" below, I think this conviction makes a mockery of the free speech guarantees of the First and Fourteenth Amendments. The end result of the affirmance here is to approve a simple and readily available technique by which cities and states can with impunity subject all speeches, political or otherwise, on streets or elsewhere, to the supervision and censorship of the local police. I will have no part or parcel in this holding which I view as a long step toward totalitarian authority.

The Court's opinion apparently rests on this reasoning: The policeman, under the circumstances detailed, could reasonably conclude that serious fighting or even riot was imminent; therefore he could stop petitioner's speech to prevent a breach of peace; accordingly, it was "disorderly conduct" for petitioner to continue speaking in disobedience of the officer's request. As to the existence of a dangerous situation on the street corner, it seems farfetched to suggest that the "facts" show any imminent threat of riot or uncontrollable disorder. It is neither unusual nor unexpected that some people at public street meetings mutter, mill about, push, shove, or disagree, even violently, with the speaker. Indeed, it is rare where controversial topics are discussed that an outdoor crowd does not do some or all of these things. Nor does one isolated threat to assault the speaker forebode disorder. Especially should the danger be discounted where, as here, the person threatening was a man whose wife and two small children accompanied him and who, so far as the record shows, was never close enough to petitioner to carry out the threat.

Moreover, assuming that the "facts" did indicate a critical situation, I reject the implication of the Court's opinion that the police had no obligation to protect petitioner's constitutional right to talk. The police of course have power to prevent breaches of the peace. But if, in the name of preserving order, they ever can interfere with a lawful public speaker, they first must make all reasonable efforts to protect him. Here the policemen did not even pretend to try to protect petitioner. According to the officers' testimony, the crowd was restless but there is no showing of any attempt to quiet it; pedestrians were forced to walk into the street, but there was no effort to clear a path on the sidewalk; one person threatened to assault petitioner but the officers did nothing to discourage this when even a word might have sufficed. Their duty was to protect petitioner's right to talk, even to the extent of arresting the man who threatened to interfere. Instead, they shirked that duty and acted only to suppress the right to speak.

Finally, I cannot agree with the Court's statement that petitioner's disregard of the policeman's unexplained request amounted to such "deliberate defiance" as would justify an arrest or conviction for disorderly conduct. On the contrary, I think that the policeman's action was a "deliberate defiance" of ordinary official duty as well as of the constitutional right of free speech. For at least where time allows, courtesy and explanation of commands are basic elements of good official conduct in a democratic society. Here petitioner was "asked" then "told" then "commanded" to stop speaking, but a man making a lawful address is certainly not required to be silent merely because an officer directs it. Petitioner was entitled to know why he should cease doing a lawful act. Not once was he told. I understand that people in authoritarian countries must obey arbitrary orders. I had hoped that there was no such duty in the United States.

MR. JUSTICE DOUGLAS, with whom MR. JUSTICE MINTON concurs, dissenting.

another dissent

A speaker may not, of course, incite a riot any more than he may incite a breach of the peace by the use of 'fighting words.' But this record shows no such extremes. It shows an unsympathetic audience and the threat of one man to haul the speaker from the stage. It is against that kind of threat that speakers need police protection. If they do not receive it and instead the police throw their weight on the side of those who would break up the meetings, the police become the new censors of speech. Police censorship has all the vices of the censorship from city halls which we have repeatedly struck down.

[Justice Frankfurter's opinion concurring in the result is omitted.]

Points for Discussion

1. ***Feiner* and the problem of the heckler's veto.** *Feiner* has been understood to mean that a police officer can arrest a speaker if the speaker's message has angered an audience to the point that there is a clear and present danger of violence erupting against the speaker. Critics of *Feiner* say that its rule gives hostile audiences a heckler's veto. Can you explain why this is so?

   Justice Black addressed the problem of the heckler's veto in his dissent by suggesting a modification to the rule announced in the majority opinion:

> The police of course have power to prevent breaches of the peace. But if, in the name of preserving order, they ever can interfere with a lawful public speaker, they first must make all reasonable efforts to protect him.

Can you explain how Justice Black modified the majority's rule?

The Supreme Court has never overruled *Feiner*, but subsequent decisions concerning civil rights protests in the 1960s suggest that the Court has adopted Justice Black's gloss on *Feiner*. In one case after another, the Court reversed the convictions of black civil rights protesters who were arrested for breach of the peace, allegedly because of the danger posed by white counter-protesters. *Edwards v. South Carolina*, 372 U.S. 229 (1963); *Cox v. Louisiana*, 379 U.S. 536 (1965); *Gregory v. City of Chicago*, 394 U.S. 111 (1969). These decisions imply that the police must first protect a speaker from a hostile audience and may arrest a speaker only if these efforts fail.

You should be aware that the heckler's veto problem can arise in unexpected ways. For example, imagine a city ordinance that allowed the government to increase permit fees for parades if the parades were likely to draw a hostile audience and require an increased police presence. While this might seem like a reasonable measure to ensure that the city's costs are covered, it could also allow a hostile audience to drive up the cost of a permit by threatening to react violently to a parade. For example, angry white supremacists could make the permit for a civil rights march so prohibitively expensive that the parade organizers could not afford to pay the fee. The Supreme Court found such a sliding fee scale unconstitutional in *Forsyth County v. Nationalist Movement*, 505 U.S. 123 (1992). Here is a snippet of Justice Harry Blackmun's reasoning:

> The county envisions that the administrator, in appropriate instances, will assess a fee to cover the cost of necessary and reasonable protection of persons participating in or observing said activity. The fee assessed will depend on the administrator's measure of the amount of hostility likely to be created by the speech based on its content. Those wishing to express views unpopular with bottle throwers, for example, may have to pay more for their permit.
>
> The costs to which petitioner refers are those associated with the public's reaction to the speech. Listeners' reaction to speech is not a content-neutral basis for regulation. Speech cannot be financially burdened, any more than it can be punished or banned, simply because it might offend a hostile mob.

2. **Can you ignore a police order?** In *Feiner*, Chief Justice Vinson noted that "the officer had asked petitioner to get down off the box three times over a space of four or five minutes." Should the fact that Feiner ignored these requests be reason enough to justify his arrest, or does the First Amendment sometimes permit a speaker to ignore a police officer's order to stop speaking? In answering this question, you might consult Justice Black's dissent.

C. True Threats: Speech Threatening to Commit Violence Against an Individual or Group

Threats of violence are another category of speech that implicates societal concerns about safety and security. As you are about to learn, these threats, when they rise to the level of what the Supreme Court calls "true threats," are not protected by the First Amendment. Consequently, the government is free to regulate true threats without its regulations being subjected to strict scrutiny as long as the regulations do not violate *R.A.V.*'s prohibition on content-based discrimination (*e.g.*, a law may not regulate threats directed at only Republicans and not Democrats).

Surprisingly, the case cited for creating the category of unprotected true threats, *Watts v. United States*, 394 U.S. 705 (1969), did not involve a true threat but a fake one. The defendant had said the following at an anti-war rally during the Vietnam War: "Now I have already received my draft classification as 1-A and I have got to report for my physical this Monday coming. I am not going. If they ever make me carry a rifle the first man I want to get in my sights is L.B.J. They are not going to make me kill my black brothers."

The defendant was convicted of violating a federal law that makes it a crime to threaten the president. ("L.B.J." referred to President Lyndon Baines Johnson.)

In reversing the conviction, the Supreme Court made a distinction between a "threat" and "constitutionally protected speech." The Court said the First Amendment protected the defendant's speech because it was not an actual threat. Instead, it was merely "political hyperbole." His "only offense," the Court explained, "was a kind of very crude offensive method of stating a political opposition to the President." Nevertheless, the opinion implied that a true threat would not be protected by the First Amendment.

The Supreme Court elaborated on the true threats doctrine in the following case.

Virginia v. Black

Supreme Court of the United States, 2003
538 U.S. 343

Justice O'Connor announced the judgment of the Court and delivered the opinion of the Court with respect to Parts I, II, and III, and an opinion with respect to Parts IV and V, in which The Chief Justice, Justice Stevens, and Justice Breyer join.

In this case we consider whether the Commonwealth of Virginia's statute banning cross burning with "an intent to intimidate a person or group of persons" violates the First Amendment. Va. Code Ann. § 18.2–423 (1996). We conclude that while a State, consistent with the First Amendment, may ban cross burning carried out with the intent to intimidate, the provision in the Virginia statute treating any cross burning as prima facie evidence of intent to intimidate renders the statute unconstitutional in its current form.

I

Respondents Barry Black, Richard Elliott, and Jonathan O'Mara were convicted separately of violating Virginia's cross-burning statute. That statute provides:

statute

> It shall be unlawful for any person or persons, with the intent of intimidating any person or group of persons, to burn, or cause to be burned, a cross on the property of another, a highway or other public place. Any person who shall violate any provision of this section shall be guilty of a Class 6 felony.
>
> Any such burning of a cross shall be prima facie evidence of an intent to intimidate a person or group of persons.

On August 22, 1998, Barry Black led a Ku Klux Klan rally in Carroll County, Virginia. Twenty-five to thirty people attended this gathering, which occurred on private property with the permission of the owner, who was in attendance. The property was located on an open field just off Brushy Fork Road (State Highway 690) in Cana, Virginia.

When the sheriff of Carroll County learned that a Klan rally was occurring in his county, he went to observe it from the side of the road. During the approximately one hour that the sheriff was present, about 40 to 50 cars passed the site, a "few" of which stopped to ask the sheriff what was happening on the property. Eight to ten houses were located in the vicinity of the rally. Rebecca Sechrist, who was related to the owner of the property where the rally took place, "sat and watched to see what was going on" from the lawn of her in-laws' house. She looked on as the Klan prepared for the gathering and subsequently conducted the rally itself.

During the rally, Sechrist heard Klan members speak about "what they were" and "what they believed in." The speakers "talked real bad about the blacks and the Mexicans." At the conclusion of the rally, the crowd circled around a 25- to 30-foot cross. The cross was between 300 and 350 yards away from the road. According to the sheriff, the cross "then all of a sudden went up in a flame." As the cross burned, the Klan played Amazing Grace over the loudspeakers. Sechrist stated that the cross burning made her feel "awful" and "terrible."

When the sheriff observed the cross burning, he informed his deputy that they needed to "find out who's responsible and explain to them that they cannot do this in the State of Virginia." The sheriff then went down the driveway, entered the rally, and asked "who was responsible for burning the cross." Black responded, "I guess I am because I'm the head of the rally." The sheriff then told Black, "There's a law in the State of Virginia that you cannot burn a cross and I'll have to place you under arrest for this."

Black was charged with burning a cross with the intent of intimidating a person or group of persons, in violation of § 18.2–423. At his trial, the jury was instructed that "intent to intimidate means the motivation to intentionally put a person or a group of persons in fear of bodily harm. Such fear must arise from the willful conduct of the accused rather than from some mere temperamental timidity of the victim." The trial court also instructed the jury that "the burning of a cross by itself is sufficient evidence from which you may infer the required intent." The jury found Black guilty, and fined him $2,500. The Court of Appeals of Virginia affirmed Black's conviction.

On May 2, 1998, respondents Richard Elliott and Jonathan O'Mara, as well as a third individual, attempted to burn a cross on the yard of James Jubilee. Jubilee, an African-American, was Elliott's next-door neighbor in Virginia Beach, Virginia. Four months prior to the incident, Jubilee and his family had moved from California to Virginia Beach. Before the cross burning, Jubilee spoke to Elliott's mother to inquire about shots being fired from behind the Elliott home. Elliott's mother explained to Jubilee that her son shot firearms as a hobby, and that he used the backyard as a firing range.

On the night of May 2, respondents drove a truck onto Jubilee's property, planted a cross, and set it on fire. Their apparent motive was to "get back" at Jubilee for complaining about the shooting in the backyard. Respondents were not affiliated with the Klan. The next morning, as Jubilee was pulling his car out of the driveway, he noticed the partially burned cross approximately 20 feet from his house. After seeing the cross, Jubilee was "very nervous" because he "didn't know what would be the next phase," and because "a cross burned in your yard tells you that it's just the first round."

Elliott and O'Mara were charged with attempted cross burning and conspiracy to commit cross burning. O'Mara pleaded guilty to both counts, reserving the right to challenge the constitutionality of the cross-burning statute. A jury found Elliott guilty of attempted cross burning and acquitted him of conspiracy to commit cross burning.

Each respondent appealed to the Supreme Court of Virginia, arguing that § 18.2–423 is facially unconstitutional. The Supreme Court of Virginia consolidated all three cases, and held that the statute is unconstitutional on its face. It held that the Virginia cross-burning statute "is analytically indistinguishable from the ordinance found unconstitutional in *R.A.V. v. St. Paul*." The Virginia statute, the court held, discriminates on the basis of content since it "selectively chooses only cross burning because of its distinctive message." The court also held that the prima facie evidence provision renders the statute overbroad because "the enhanced probability of prosecution under the statute chills the expression of protected speech."

We granted certiorari.

II

Cross burning originated in the 14th century as a means for Scottish tribes to signal each other. Cross burning in this country, however, long ago became unmoored from its Scottish ancestry. Burning a cross in the United States is inextricably intertwined with the history of the Ku Klux Klan.

The first Ku Klux Klan began in Pulaski, Tennessee, in the spring of 1866. Although the Ku Klux Klan started as a social club, it soon changed into something far different. The Klan fought Reconstruction and the corresponding drive to allow freed blacks to participate in the political process. Soon the Klan imposed "a veritable reign of terror" throughout the South. The Klan employed tactics such as whipping, threatening to burn people at the stake, and murder. The Klan's victims included blacks, southern whites who disagreed with the Klan, and "carpetbagger" northern whites.

The activities of the Ku Klux Klan prompted legislative action at the national level. In 1871, "President Grant sent a message to Congress indicating that the Klan's reign of terror in the Southern States had rendered life and property insecure." In response, Congress passed what is now known as the Ku Klux Klan Act. President Grant used these new powers to suppress the Klan in South Carolina, the effect of which severely curtailed the Klan in other States as well. By the end of Reconstruction in 1877, the first Klan no longer existed.

The genesis of the second Klan began in 1905, with the publication of Thomas Dixon's The Clansmen: An Historical Romance of the Ku Klux Klan. Dixon's book was a sympathetic portrait of the first Klan, depicting the Klan as a group of heroes "saving" the South from blacks and the "horrors" of Reconstruction. Although the first Klan never actually practiced cross burning, Dixon's book depicted the Klan burning crosses to celebrate the execution of former slaves. Cross burning thereby became associated with the first Ku Klux Klan. When D.W. Griffith turned Dixon's book into the movie The Birth of a Nation in 1915, the association between cross burning and the Klan became indelible. In addition to the cross burnings in the movie, a poster advertising the film displayed a hooded Klansman riding a hooded horse, with his left hand holding the reins of the horse and his right hand holding a burning cross above his head. Soon thereafter, in November 1915, the second Klan began.

From the inception of the second Klan, cross burnings have been used to communicate both threats of violence and messages of shared ideology. Violence was also an elemental part of this new Klan. By September 1921, the New York World newspaper documented 152 acts of Klan violence, including 4 murders, 41 floggings, and 27 tar-and-featherings.

To this day, regardless of whether the message is a political one or whether the message is also meant to intimidate, the burning of a cross is a "symbol of hate." And while cross burning sometimes carries no intimidating message, at other times the intimidating message is the *only* message conveyed.

In sum, while a burning cross does not inevitably convey a message of intimidation, often the cross burner intends that the recipients of the message fear for their lives. And when a cross burning is used to intimidate, few if any messages are more powerful.

III

A

The First Amendment, applicable to the States through the Fourteenth Amendment, provides that "Congress shall make no law abridging the freedom of speech." The hallmark of the protection of free speech is to allow "free trade in ideas"—even ideas that the overwhelming majority of people might find distasteful or discomforting. Thus, the First Amendment "ordinarily" denies a State "the power to prohibit dissemination of social, economic and political doctrine which a vast majority of its citizens believes to be false and fraught with evil consequence." The First Amendment affords protection to symbolic or expressive conduct as well as to actual speech.

The protections afforded by the First Amendment, however, are not absolute, and we have long recognized that the government may regulate certain categories of expression consistent with the Constitution. The First Amendment permits "restrictions upon the content of speech in a few limited areas, which are of such slight social value as a step to truth that any benefit that may be derived from them is clearly outweighed by the social interest in order and morality."

Thus, for example, a State may punish those words "which by their very utterance inflict injury or tend to incite an immediate breach of the peace." We have consequently held that fighting words—"those personally abusive epithets which, when addressed to the ordinary citizen, are, as a matter of common knowledge, inherently likely to provoke violent reaction"—are generally proscribable under the First Amendment. Furthermore, "the constitutional guarantees of free speech and free press do not permit a State to forbid or proscribe advocacy of the use of force or of law violation except where such advocacy is directed to inciting or producing imminent lawless action and is likely to incite or produce such action." And the First Amendment also permits a State to ban a "true threat."

"True threats" encompass those statements where the speaker means to communicate a serious expression of an intent to commit an act of unlawful violence to a particular individual or group of individuals. See *Watts v. United States* ("political hyberbole" is not a true threat). The speaker need not actually intend to carry out the threat. Rather, a prohibition on true threats "protects individuals from the fear of violence" and "from the disruption that fear engenders," in addition to protecting people "from the possibility that the threatened violence will occur." Intimidation in the constitutionally proscribable sense of the word is a type of true threat, where a speaker directs a threat to a person or group of persons with the intent of placing the victim in fear of bodily harm or death. Respondents do not contest that some cross burnings fit within this meaning of intimidating speech, and rightly so. As noted in Part II, *supra,* the history of cross burning in this country shows that cross burning is often intimidating, intended to create a pervasive fear in victims that they are a target of violence.

B

The Supreme Court of Virginia ruled that in light of *R.A.V.,* even if it is constitutional to ban cross burning in a content-neutral manner, the Virginia cross-burning statute is unconstitutional because it discriminates on the basis of content and viewpoint. It is true, as the Supreme Court of Virginia held, that the burning of a cross is symbolic expression. The reason why the Klan burns a cross at its rallies, or individuals place a burning cross on someone else's lawn, is that the burning cross represents the message that the speaker wishes to communicate. Individuals burn crosses as opposed to other means of communication because cross burning carries a message in an effective and dramatic manner.

The fact that cross burning is symbolic expression, however, does not resolve the constitutional question. The Supreme Court of Virginia relied upon *R.A.V.* to conclude that once a statute discriminates on the basis of this type of content, the law is unconstitutional. We disagree.

In *R.A.V.*, we held that a local ordinance that banned certain symbolic conduct, including cross burning, when done with the knowledge that such conduct would "arouse anger, alarm or resentment in others on the basis of race, color, creed, religion or gender" was unconstitutional. We held that the ordinance did not pass constitutional muster because it discriminated on the basis of content by targeting only those individuals who "provoke violence" on a basis specified in the law.

Virginia's statute does not run afoul of the First Amendment insofar as it bans cross burning with intent to intimidate. Unlike the statute at issue in *R.A.V.*, the Virginia statute does not single out for opprobrium only that speech directed toward "one of the specified disfavored topics." It does not matter whether an individual burns a cross with intent to intimidate because of the victim's race, gender, or religion, or because of the victim's "political affiliation, union membership, or homosexuality." Moreover, as a factual matter it is not true that cross burners direct their intimidating conduct solely to racial or religious minorities.

The First Amendment permits Virginia to outlaw cross burnings done with the intent to intimidate because burning a cross is a particularly virulent form of intimidation. Instead of prohibiting all intimidating messages, Virginia may choose to regulate this subset of intimidating messages in light of cross burning's long and pernicious history as a signal of impending violence. Thus, just as a State may regulate only that obscenity which is the most obscene due to its prurient content, so too may a State choose to prohibit only those forms of intimidation that are most likely to inspire fear of bodily harm. A ban on cross burning carried out with the intent to intimidate is fully consistent with our holding in *R.A.V.* and is proscribable under the First Amendment.

IV

The Supreme Court of Virginia ruled in the alternative that Virginia's cross-burning statute was unconstitutionally overbroad due to its provision stating that "any such burning of a cross shall be prima facie evidence of an intent to intimidate a person or group of persons." The Commonwealth added the prima facie provision to the statute in 1968. The court below did not reach whether this provision is severable from the rest of the cross-burning statute under Virginia law. In this Court, as in the Supreme Court of Virginia, respondents do not argue that the prima facie evidence provision is unconstitutional as applied to any one of them. Rather, they contend that the provision is unconstitutional on its face.

The Supreme Court of Virginia has not ruled on the meaning of the prima facie evidence provision. It has, however, stated that "the act of burning a cross alone, with no evidence of intent to intimidate, will nonetheless suffice for arrest and prosecution and will insulate the Commonwealth from a motion to strike the evidence at the end of its case-in-chief." The jury in the case of Richard Elliott did not receive any instruction on the prima facie evidence provision, and the provision was not an issue in the case of Jonathan O'Mara because he pleaded guilty. The court in Barry Black's case, however, instructed the jury that the provision means: "The burning of a cross, by itself, is sufficient evidence from which you may infer the required intent." This jury instruction is the same as the Model Jury Instruction in the Commonwealth of Virginia.

prima facie evidence provision is what violates constitution

The prima facie evidence provision, as interpreted by the jury instruction, renders the statute unconstitutional. The prima facie evidence provision permits a jury to convict in every cross-burning case in which defendants exercise their constitutional right not to put on a defense. And even where a defendant like Black presents a defense, the prima facie evidence provision makes it more likely that the jury will find an intent to intimidate regardless of the particular facts of the case. The provision permits the Commonwealth to arrest, prosecute, and convict a person based solely on the fact of cross burning itself.

It is apparent that the provision as so interpreted "would create an unacceptable risk of the suppression of ideas." The act of burning a cross may mean that a person is engaging in constitutionally proscribable intimidation. But that same act may mean only that the person is engaged in core political speech. The prima facie evidence provision in this statute blurs the line between these two meanings of a burning cross.

As the history of cross burning indicates, a burning cross is not always intended to intimidate. Rather, sometimes the cross burning is a statement of ideology, a symbol of group solidarity. The prima facie provision makes no effort to distinguish among these different types of cross burnings. It does not distinguish between a cross burning at a public rally or a cross burning on a neighbor's lawn.

It may be true that a cross burning, even at a political rally, arouses a sense of anger or hatred among the vast majority of citizens who see a burning cross. But this sense of anger or hatred is not sufficient to ban all cross burnings. As Gerald Gunther has stated, "The lesson I have drawn from my childhood in Nazi Germany and my happier adult life in this country is the need to walk the sometimes difficult path of denouncing the bigot's hateful ideas with all my power, yet at the same time challenging any community's attempt to suppress hateful ideas by force of law." The prima facie evidence provision in this case ignores all of the contextual factors that are necessary to decide whether a particular cross burning is intended to intimidate. The First Amendment does not permit such a shortcut.

For these reasons, the prima facie evidence provision, as interpreted through the jury instruction and as applied in Barry Black's case, is unconstitutional on its face.

V

With respect to Barry Black, we agree with the Supreme Court of Virginia that his conviction cannot stand, and we affirm the judgment of the Supreme Court of Virginia. With respect to Elliott and O'Mara, we vacate the judgment of the Supreme Court of Virginia, and remand the case for further proceedings.

[Justice Stevens wrote a concurring opinion; Justice Scalia dissented in part because he believed that the *prima facie* provision in the Virginia statute was constitutional; Justice Souter, joined by Justice Kennedy and Justice Ginsburg, dissented in part because he believed the Virginia statute violated *R.A.V.*; Justice Thomas dissented because he believed that the Virginia statute regulated only conduct and not speech and did not implicate the First Amendment.]

Points for Discussion

1. **What are "true threats"?** *Virginia v. Black* holds that true threats are unprotected by the First Amendment? But what are true threats? Can you find where the Court defines the term?

2. **Did the statute in *Virginia v. Black* violate the *R.A.V.* rule?** The Virginia Supreme Court thought that the Virginia cross burning statute violated the rule set forth *R.A.V.* Did the U.S. Supreme Court agree? If not, why not? If the Court did not think that the Virginia law violated *R.A.V.*, why did it find the statute unconstitutional?

3. **Could you fix the statute in *Virginia v. Black*?** Based on the Court's reasoning, could you think of a way to amend the Virginia statute to make it constitutional? Why do you think your suggested amendment would work?

4. **Was the Virginia law regulating expressive conduct or just conduct?** Justice Sandra Day O'Connor readily accepted that cross burning is a form of expressive conduct and therefore its regulation implicates the First Amendment:

   > It is true, as the Supreme Court of Virginia held, that the burning of a cross is symbolic expression. The reason why the Klan burns a cross at its rallies, or individuals place a burning cross on someone else's lawn, is that the burning cross represents the message that the speaker wishes to communicate.

Justice Clarence Thomas argued in dissent that cross burning is not expressive and that the Virginia law regulating cross burning did not implicate the First Amendment:

> This statute prohibits only conduct, not expression. And, just as one cannot burn down someone's house to make a political point and then seek refuge in the First Amendment, those who hate cannot terrorize and intimidate to make their point. In light of my conclusion that the statute here addresses only conduct, there is no need to analyze it under any of our First Amendment tests.

Do you agree with Justice O'Connor or Justice Thomas?

5. **Gerald Gunther's lesson.** The Court's opinion includes this quote from former Stanford law professor Gerald Gunther: "The lesson I have drawn from my childhood in Nazi Germany and my happier adult life in this country is the need to walk the sometimes difficult path of denouncing the bigot's hateful ideas with all my power, yet at the same time challenging any community's attempt to suppress hateful ideas by force of law." Can you articulate what Gunther is saying in your own words? Do you agree with the lesson he learned from his life's experiences?

Does the Exclusion of True Threats from First Amendment Protection Depend on the Speaker's Mental State?

Virginia v. Black firmly established that true threats are not protected by the First Amendment. The opinion did not, however, clarify whether the exclusion of true threats from First Amendment protection depended on the state of mind of the person making the threat. The Supreme Court addressed that issue in *Counterman v. Colorado.*

Of course, the mental state, or *mens rea*, of an actor is a familiar concept in criminal law, which defines crimes based on a combination of an actor's mental state and the act committed ("*actus reus*"). The Model Penal Code speaks of four different mental states of decreasing culpability from purposefully to knowingly to recklessly to negligently.

As a matter of criminal law, the *mens rea* element for any given crime reflects a societal judgment about the level of culpability required for the imposition of criminal liability. But, as you will see in the *Counterman* case, the justices' discussions about the appropriate *mens rea* level for true threats are largely driven by the justices' efforts to balance free speech interests with the competing societal interests in regulating threats.

As you read the various opinions in *Counterman*, note how Justices Elena Kagan, Sonia Sotomayor, and Amy Coney Barrett strike different balances and, consequently, reach different conclusions. Ask yourself who has the better argument, but keep in mind that Justice Kagan's majority opinion is the binding precedent.

You should also note how the justices make analogies to the mental state requirements for other categories of unprotected speech, in particular incitement and defamation. You are familiar with the intent requirement for incitement, but you have not yet been introduced to the defamation jurisprudence. For now, it will be helpful for you to know that the Supreme Court held in *New York Times v. Sullivan*, 376 U.S. 254 (1964), that a public official who brings a defamation action may prevail only if he can prove that the defendant knew that his statement was false or recklessly disregarded whether the statement was true or false.

Counterman v. Colorado

Supreme Court of the United States, 2023
600 U.S. 66

JUSTICE KAGAN delivered the opinion of the Court.

True threats of violence are outside the bounds of First Amendment protection and punishable as crimes. Today we consider a criminal conviction for communications falling within that historically unprotected category. The question presented is whether the First Amendment still requires proof that the defendant had some subjective understanding of the threatening nature of his statements. We hold that it does, but that a mental state of recklessness is sufficient. The State must show that the defendant consciously disregarded a substantial risk that his communications would be viewed as threatening violence. The State need not prove any more demanding form of subjective intent to threaten another.

From 2014 to 2016, petitioner Billy Counterman sent hundreds of Facebook messages to C.W., a local singer and musician. The two had never met, and C.W. never responded. In fact, she repeatedly blocked Counterman. But each time, he created a new Facebook account and resumed his contacts. Some of his messages were utterly prosaic ("Good morning sweetheart"; "I am going to the store would you like anything?")—except that they were coming from a total stranger. Others suggested that Counterman might be surveilling C.W. He asked "was that you in the white Jeep?"; referenced "a fine display with your partner"; and noted "a couple of physical sightings." And most critically, a number expressed anger at C.W. and envisaged harm befalling her: "Fuck off permanently." "Staying in cyber life is going to kill you." "You're not being good for human relations. Die."

The messages put C.W. in fear and upended her daily existence. She believed that Counterman was "threatening her life"; "was very fearful that he was following" her; and was "afraid she would get hurt." As a result, she had "a lot of trouble sleeping" and suffered from severe anxiety. She stopped walking alone, declined social engagements, and canceled some of her performances, though doing so caused her financial strain. Eventually, C.W. decided that she had to contact the authorities.

Colorado charged Counterman under a statute making it unlawful to "repeatedly make any form of communication with another person" in "a manner that would cause a reasonable person to suffer serious emotional distress and does cause that person to suffer serious emotional distress." The only evidence the State proposed to introduce at trial were his Facebook messages.

Counterman moved to dismiss the charge on First Amendment grounds, arguing that his messages were not "true threats" and therefore could not form the basis of a criminal prosecution. In line with Colorado law, the trial court assessed the true-threat issue using an "objective 'reasonable person' standard." Under that standard, the State had to show that a reasonable person would have viewed the Facebook messages as threatening. By contrast, the State had no need to prove that Counterman had any kind of "subjective intent to threaten" C.W. The court decided, after "considering the totality of the circumstances," that Counterman's statements "rose to the level of a true threat." Because that was so, the court ruled, the First Amendment posed no bar to prosecution. The court accordingly sent the case to the jury, which found Counterman guilty as charged.

The Colorado Court of Appeals affirmed. Counterman had urged the court to hold that the First Amendment required the State to show that he was aware of the threatening nature of his statements. Relying on its precedent, the court turned the request down: It "declined today to say that a speaker's subjective intent to threaten is necessary" under the First Amendment to procure a conviction for threatening communications. Using the established objective standard, the court then approved the trial court's ruling that Counterman's messages were "true threats" and so were not protected by the First Amendment. The Colorado Supreme Court denied review.

Courts are divided about (1) whether the First Amendment requires proof of a defendant's subjective mindset in true-threats cases, and (2) if so, what *mens rea* standard is sufficient. We therefore granted certiorari.

True threats of violence, everyone agrees, lie outside the bounds of the First Amendment's protection. And a statement can count as such a threat based solely on its objective content. The first dispute here is about whether the First Amendment nonetheless demands that the State in a true-threats case prove that the defendant was aware in some way of the threatening nature of his communications. Colorado argues that there is no such requirement. Counterman contends that there is one, based mainly on the likelihood that the absence of such a *mens rea* requirement will chill protected, non-threatening speech. Counterman's view, we decide today, is the more consistent with our precedent. To combat the kind of chill he references, our decisions have often insisted on protecting even some historically unprotected speech through the adoption of a subjective mental-state element. We follow the same path today, holding that the State must prove in true-threats cases that the defendant had some understanding of his statements' threatening character. The second issue here concerns what precise *mens rea* standard suffices for the First Amendment purpose at issue. Again guided by our precedent, we hold that a recklessness standard is enough. Given that a subjective standard here shields speech not independently entitled to protection—and indeed posing real dangers—we do not require that the State prove the defendant had any more specific intent to threaten the victim.

"From 1791 to the present," the First Amendment has "permitted restrictions upon the content of speech in a few limited areas." These "historic and traditional categories" are "long familiar to the bar" and perhaps, too, the general public. One is incitement—statements "directed at producing imminent lawless action," and likely to do so. Another is defamation—false statements of fact harming another's reputation. Still a third is obscenity—valueless material "appealing to the prurient interest" and describing "sexual conduct" in "a patently offensive way." This Court has "often described those historically unprotected categories of speech as being of such slight social value as a step to truth that any benefit that may be derived from them is clearly outweighed by the social interest" in their proscription.

"True threats" of violence is another historically unprotected category of communications. The "true" in that term distinguishes what is at issue from jests, "hyperbole," or other statements that when taken in context do not convey a real possibility that violence will follow (say, "I am going to kill you for showing up late"). True threats are "serious expressions" conveying that a speaker means to "commit an act of unlawful violence." Whether the speaker is aware of, and intends to convey, the threatening aspect of the message is not part of what makes a statement a threat, as this Court recently explained. The existence of a threat depends not on "the mental state of the author," but on "what the statement conveys" to the person on the other end. When the statement is understood as a true threat, all the harms that have long made threats unprotected naturally follow. True threats subject individuals to "fear of violence" and to the many kinds of "disruption that fear engenders." The facts of this case well illustrate how.

Yet the First Amendment may still demand a subjective mental-state requirement shielding some true threats from liability. The reason relates to what is often called a chilling effect. Prohibitions on speech have the potential to chill, or deter, speech outside their boundaries. A speaker may be unsure about the side of a line on which his speech falls. Or he may worry that the legal system will err, and count speech that is permissible as instead not. Or he may simply be concerned about the expense of becoming entangled in the legal system. The result is "self-censorship" of speech that could not be proscribed—a "cautious and restrictive exercise" of First Amendment freedoms. And an important tool to prevent that outcome—to stop people from steering "wide of the unlawful zone"—is to condition liability on the State's showing of a culpable mental state. Such a requirement comes at a cost: It will shield some otherwise proscribable (here, threatening) speech because the State cannot prove what the defendant thought. But the added element reduces the prospect of chilling fully protected expression. As this Court has noted, the requirement lessens "the hazard of self-censorship" by "compensating" for the law's uncertainties. Or said a bit differently: "By reducing an honest speaker's fear that he may accidentally or erroneously incur liability," a *mens rea* requirement "provides 'breathing room' for more valuable speech."

That kind of "strategic protection" features in our precedent concerning the most prominent categories of historically unprotected speech. Defamation is the best known and best theorized example. False and defamatory statements of fact, we have held, have "no constitutional value." Yet a public figure cannot recover for the injury such a statement causes unless the speaker acted with "knowledge that it was false or with reckless disregard of whether it was false or not." *New York Times v. Sullivan.* That rule is based on fear of "self-censorship"—the worry that without such a subjective mental-state requirement, the uncertainties and expense of litigation will deter speakers from making even truthful statements. The same reasoning counsels in favor of requiring a subjective element in a true-threats case.

The next question concerns the type of subjective standard the First Amendment requires. The law of *mens rea* offers three basic choices. Purpose is the most culpable level in the standard mental-state hierarchy, and the hardest to prove. A person acts purposefully when he "consciously desires" a result—so here, when he wants his words to be received as threats. Next down, though not often distinguished from purpose, is knowledge. A person acts knowingly when "he is aware that a result is practically certain to follow"—so here, when he knows to a practical certainty that others will take his words as threats. A greater gap separates those two from recklessness. A person acts recklessly, in the most common formulation, when he "consciously disregards a substantial and unjustifiable risk that the conduct will cause harm to another." That standard involves insufficient concern with risk, rather than awareness of impending harm. But still, recklessness is morally culpable conduct, involving a "deliberate decision to endanger another." In the threats context, it means that a speaker is aware "that others could regard his statements as" threatening violence and "delivers them anyway."

Among those standards, recklessness offers the right path forward. We have so far mostly focused on the constitutional interest in free expression, and on the correlative need to take into account threat prosecutions' chilling effects. But the precedent we have relied on has always recognized—and insisted on "accommodating"—the "competing value" in regulating historically unprotected expression. Here, as we have noted, that value lies in protecting against the profound harms, to both individuals and society, that attend true threats of violence—as evidenced in this case. The injury associated with those statements caused history long ago to place them outside the First Amendment's bounds. When despite that judgment we require use of a subjective mental-state standard, we necessarily impede some true-threat prosecutions. And as we go up the subjective *mens rea* ladder, that imposition on States' capacity to counter true threats becomes still greater—and, presumably, with diminishing returns for protected expression. In advancing past recklessness, we make it harder for a State to substantiate the needed inferences about *mens rea* (absent, as is usual, direct evidence). And of particular importance, we prevent States from convicting morally culpable defendants. For reckless defendants have done more than make a bad mistake. They have consciously accepted a substantial risk of inflicting serious harm.

Using a recklessness standard also fits with the analysis in our defamation decisions. As noted earlier, the Court there adopted a recklessness rule, applicable in both civil and criminal contexts, as a way of accommodating competing interests. In the more than half-century in which that standard has governed, few have suggested that it needs to be higher—in other words, that still more First Amendment "breathing space" is required. And we see no reason to offer greater insulation to threats than to defamation. The societal interests in countering the former are at least as high. And the protected speech near the borderline of true threats is, if anything, further from the First Amendment's central concerns than the chilled speech in *Sullivan*-type cases (*i.e.*, truthful reputation-damaging statements about public officials and figures).

It is true that our incitement decisions demand more—but the reason for that demand is not present here. When incitement is at issue, we have spoken in terms of specific intent, presumably equivalent to purpose or knowledge. In doing so, we recognized that incitement to disorder is commonly a hair's-breadth away from political "advocacy"—and particularly from strong protests against the government and prevailing social order. Such protests gave rise to all the cases in which the Court demanded a showing of intent. And the Court decided those cases against a resonant historical backdrop: the Court's failure, in an earlier era, to protect mere advocacy of force or lawbreaking from legal sanction. A strong intent requirement was, and remains, one way to guarantee history was not repeated. It was a way to ensure that efforts to prosecute incitement would not bleed over, either directly or through a chilling effect, to dissenting political speech at the First Amendment's core. But the potency of that protection is not needed here. For the most part, the speech on the other side of the true-threats boundary line—as compared with the advocacy addressed in our incitement decisions—is neither so central to the theory of the First Amendment nor so vulnerable to government prosecutions. It is not just that our incitement decisions are distinguishable; it is more that they compel the use of a distinct standard here.

That standard, again, is recklessness. It offers "enough 'breathing space' for protected speech," without sacrificing too many of the benefits of enforcing laws against true threats. As with any balance, something is lost on both sides: The rule we adopt today is neither the most speech-protective nor the most sensitive to the dangers of true threats. But in declining one of those two alternative paths, something more important is gained: Not "having it all"—because that is impossible—but having much of what is important on both sides of the scale.

It is time to return to Counterman's case, though only a few remarks are necessary. Counterman, as described above, was prosecuted in accordance with an objective standard. The State had to show only that a reasonable person would understand his statements as threats. It did not have to show any awareness on his part that the statements could be understood that way. For the reasons stated, that is a violation of the First Amendment.

We accordingly vacate the judgment of the Colorado Court of Appeals and remand the case for further proceedings not inconsistent with this opinion.

JUSTICE SOTOMAYOR, with whom JUSTICE GORSUCH joins as to Parts I, II, III-A, and III-B, concurring in part and concurring in the judgment.

"From 1791 to the present, the First Amendment has permitted restrictions upon the content of speech in a few limited areas." "True threats" are one such category, and there is a tradition of criminalizing threats stretching back centuries. This includes punishing single utterances based on the message conveyed. One paradigmatic example of this would be writing and mailing a letter threatening to assassinate the President. Such laws are plainly important. There is no longstanding tradition, however, of punishing speech merely because it is unintentionally threatening. Instead, this Court's precedent, along with historical statutes and cases, reflect a commonsense understanding that threatening someone is an intentional act. As to what intent is needed, "traditionally, one intends certain consequences when he desires that his acts cause those consequences or knows that those consequences are substantially certain to result from his acts." This does not require showing that an individual intends to carry through with the threat. But it does require showing that an individual desires to threaten or is substantially certain that her statements will be understood as threatening. Today, unfortunately, the Court unnecessarily departs from this traditional understanding.

I

As an initial matter, I do not believe that this Court should reach the question whether recklessness is sufficient for true-threats prosecutions. Because petitioner was prosecuted for stalking involving threatening speech, this case does not require resort to the true-threats exemption to the First Amendment.

True-threats doctrine covers content-based prosecutions for single utterances of "pure speech," which need not even be communicated to the subject of the threat. The First Amendment would normally place strict limits on such prosecutions. So there is typically a need to determine whether the speech in question falls within the traditionally unprotected category of true threats.

This is not such a case, however. Petitioner was convicted for "stalking causing serious emotional distress" for a combination of threatening statements and repeated, unwanted, direct contact with C.W. This kind of prosecution raises fewer First Amendment concerns for a variety of reasons. While there is considerable risk with a single intemperate utterance that a speaker will "accidentally or erroneously incur liability," that risk is far reduced with a course of repeated unwanted contact. Take, for example, petitioner continuously contacting C.W. despite her blocking him.

Given this, prosecuting threatening statements made as part of a course of stalking does not squarely present the hardest questions about the *mens rea* required to prosecute isolated utterances based solely on their content. True-threats doctrine came up below only because of the lower courts' doubtful assumption that petitioner could be prosecuted only if his actions fell under the true-threats exception. I do not think that is accurate, given the lessened First Amendment concerns at issue. In such cases, recklessness is amply sufficient. And I would stop there. There is simply no need to reach out in this stalking case to determine whether anything more than recklessness is needed for punishing true threats generally.

II

Lest there be any doubt, the First Amendment stakes around the definition of "true threats" are high indeed. The First Amendment's mantle covers speech that is "vituperative, abusive and inexact." "It might be tempting to dismiss" seemingly low-value speech "as unworthy of robust First Amendment protections." Yet "most of what we say to one another lacks religious, political, scientific, educational, journalistic, historical, or artistic value (let alone serious value), but it is still sheltered from Government regulation." First Amendment vigilance is especially important when speech is disturbing, frightening, or painful, because the undesirability of such speech will place a heavy thumb in favor of silencing it.

The risk of overcriminalizing upsetting or frightening speech has only been increased by the internet. Our society's discourse occurs more and more in "the vast democratic forums of the Internet in general, and social media in particular." "Rapid changes in the dynamics of communication and information transmission" have led to equally rapid and ever-evolving changes "in what society accepts as proper behavior." Different corners of the internet have considerably different norms around appropriate speech. Online communication can also lack many normal contextual clues, such as who is speaking, tone of voice, and expression. Moreover, it is easy for speech made in a one context to inadvertently reach a larger audience.

Without sufficient protection for unintentionally threatening speech, a high school student who is still learning norms around appropriate language could easily go to prison for sending another student violent music lyrics, or for unreflectingly using language he read in an online forum. "A drunken joke" in bad taste can lead to criminal prosecution. In the heat of the moment, someone may post an enraged comment under a news story about a controversial topic. Another person might reply equally heatedly. In a Nation that has never been timid about its opinions, political or otherwise, this is commonplace.

Many of this Court's true-threats cases involve such charged political speech. Much of this speech exists in a gray area where it will be quite hard to predict whether a jury would find it threatening. And the ubiquity of such speech raises the possibility of highly discretionary enforcement.

On the other hand, the internet has also made stalking and harassment even easier. Stalking can be devastating and dangerous. Lives can be ruined, and in the most tragic instances, lives are lost. Harassers can hide behind online anonymity while tormenting others. This happens in the context of intimate relationships and it happens with strangers. Overly constraining our society's ability to respond to stalking would come at a real cost. For the reasons given, however, a *mens rea* standard for true threats would not hinder stalking prosecutions.

III

Speech inciting harm is the closest cousin to speech threatening harm. Both incitement and threats put other people at risk, and both "spring from [Justice] Holmes's 'clear and present danger' test." Like true threats, incitement's scope is defined in terms of both intention and effect, covering speech "intended to produce, and likely to produce, *imminent* disorder."

Despite their similar nature and source, the Court today draws a hard line between the two. Incitement requires "intent." While for threats, the speaker need only be "aware that others could regard his statements as threatening violence and deliver them anyway." The Court justifies this asymmetry by the idea "that incitement to disorder is commonly a hair's-breadth away from political advocacy," and the lead dissent says much the same. These opinions offer little basis for distinguishing threats on this ground, as this Court's own cases show time and again how true-threats prosecutions sweep in political speech. Not only that, but incitement itself is often only a hair's-breadth away from threats.

Speech inciting imminent and dangerous unlawful activity will reasonably be threatening to those who would be harmed by that illegality. In all such cases, whether seminal decisions by this Court or guilty pleas that barely see the inside of a courtroom, the Court's decision effectively downgrades to recklessness the *mens rea* required for incitement of unlawful force; prosecutors could now simply charge such offenses as true threats. That is a troubling standard for juries in a polarized nation to apply in cases involving heated political speech. This collateral damage can be avoided, however, if intent to threaten is understood as part of a true threat, just like intent to incite is part of incitement.

JUSTICE BARRETT, with whom JUSTICE THOMAS joins, dissenting. dissent

The nature of a true threat points to an objective test for determining the scope of First Amendment protection: Neither its "social value" nor its potential for "injury" depends on the speaker's subjective intent. They can relate, of course—a speaker who does not intend to threaten is less likely to utter a statement that could be taken that way. But the Constitution ultimately declines to protect true threats for objective reasons, not subjective ones. So an objective test "complements the explanation for excluding threats of violence from First Amendment protection in the first place."

The Court agrees that "the existence of a threat depends not on the mental state of the author, but on what the statement conveys to the person on the other end." And it acknowledges that "when the statement is understood as a true threat, all the harms that have long made threats unprotected naturally follow." Nonetheless, the Court holds Colorado's statute unconstitutional. Why? Because the Court installs a prophylactic buffer zone to avoid chilling protected speech—a buffer zone that protects true threats unless the speaker "consciously disregarded a substantial risk that his communications would be viewed as threatening violence." That reasoning is flawed.

The Court's first error is awarding true threats "pride of place among unprotected speech." We have held that nearly every category of unprotected speech may be regulated using an objective test. In concluding otherwise, the Court neglects certain cases and misreads others.

Start with fighting words—a category of unprotected speech that the Court skips past. Fighting words are "personally abusive epithets" that are "inherently likely to provoke violent reaction." Under our precedent, legislatures may regulate fighting words even when the speaker does not intend to provoke the listener (or does not recklessly disregard that possibility). Instead, we ask only whether "the ordinary citizen," using her "common knowledge," would reasonably understand the statement as a "direct personal insult."

Or take obscenity, which we have long held is "not protected by the freedoms of speech and press." Speech qualifies as obscene if the "average person, applying contemporary community standards," would conclude that "the work, taken as a whole, appeals to the prurient interest." The jury must also make an objective judgment about whether the speech "depicts or describes" sexual conduct "in a patently offensive way," and whether it "lacks serious literary, artistic, political, or scientific value." The speaker's "belief as to the obscenity or non-obscenity of the material is irrelevant." So long as the defendant has "knowledge of the contents of the materials," her speech may be constitutionally regulated. An objective, reasonable-person standard applies.

I will give the Court this much: Speakers must specifically intend to incite violence before they lose First Amendment protection. *Brandenburg.* A specific intent requirement helps draw the line between incitement and "political rhetoric lying at the core of the First Amendment." The Court does not contend that targeted threats and political commentary share a similarly close relationship.

In sum, our First Amendment precedent does not set a "baseline ban on an objective standard." Precedent does more than allow an objective test for true threats; on balance, it affirmatively supports one.

The Court's analysis gives short shrift to how an objective test works in practice. Two key features of true threats already guard against the risk of silencing protected speech. Thus, there is no need to go further and adopt the Court's heightened standard.

First, only a very narrow class of statements satisfies the definition of a true threat. To make a true threat, the speaker must express "an intent to commit *an act of unlawful violence*." Speech that is merely "offensive," "poorly chosen," or "unpopular" does not qualify. The statement must also threaten violence "to a particular individual or group of individuals"—not just in general. These tight guardrails distinguish true threats from public-figure defamation, the model for the Court's rule.

Second, the statement must be deemed threatening by a reasonable listener who is familiar with the "entire factual context" in which the statement occurs. This inquiry captures (among other things) the speaker's tone, the audience, the medium for the communication, and the broader exchange in which the statement occurs. Each consideration helps weed out protected speech from true threats.

The Court's holding affects the *civil* consequences for true threats just as much as it restricts criminal liability. And the civil context underscores the danger of adopting a *Sullivan*-style buffer zone for true threats.

Consider, for example, threat victims who seek restraining orders to protect themselves from their harassers. Civil orders can also keep individuals away from particular geographic areas. Imagine someone who threatens to bomb an airport, or "shoot up a courthouse." The speaker might well end up barred from the location in question—for good reason. Yet after today, such orders cannot be obtained without proof—not necessarily easy to secure—that the person who issued the threat anticipated that it would elicit fear.

In addition, employers and school administrators often discipline individuals who make true threats. Consider the student who was expelled after "drafting two violent, misogynic, and obscenity-laden rants expressing a desire to molest, rape, and murder" his ex-girlfriend. Or the one who was suspended after "talking about taking a gun to school to shoot everyone he hates." True threats can also be expressed by a parent, a teacher, or an employee in another context altogether.

Barring some reason why the speech receives lesser constitutional protection, the Court's new rule applies to all of these situations. That can make all the difference in some cases. A delusional speaker may lack awareness of the threatening nature of her speech; a devious speaker may strategically disclaim such awareness; and a lucky speaker may leave behind no evidence of mental state for the government to use against her. The Court's decision thus sweeps much further than it lets on.

The bottom line is this: Counterman communicated true threats, which, "everyone agrees, lie outside the bounds of the First Amendment's protection." He knew what the words meant. Those threats caused the victim to fear for her life, and they "upended her daily existence." Nonetheless, the Court concludes that Counterman can prevail on a First Amendment defense. Nothing in the Constitution compels that result. I respectfully dissent.

[Justice Thomas' dissenting opinion is omitted.]

Points for Discussion

1. **Three opinions advocating three different rules.** Can you articulate the rule that each justice (Kagan, Sotomayor, and Barrett) proposed in her opinion and the justice's reasoning for her position? Which opinion did you find the most convincing?

2. **Criminal vs. civil contexts.** Justice Barrett assumes that the recklessness requirement created by the majority opinion will also apply in civil contexts. She claims that this will complicate judges' ability to issue protective orders to restrain harassers or bar people who have made threatening statements from vulnerable areas like airports or schools. Does she have a point? Should the culpability standard be the same for both criminal and civil liability, or is a lesser standard appropriate in civil cases? When you study defamation cases in Chapter 9, look for what the Court says in that context about whether civil liability can chill speech as much as criminal liability. For a thoughtful argument advocating for First Amendment rules that vary depending on the type of sanction being imposed on a speaker, *see* Michael Coenen, *Of Speech and Sanctions: Toward a Penalty-Sensitive Approach to the First Amendment*, 112 Colum. L. Rev. 991 (2012).

D. Prior Restraints and Hazardous Information: May Judges Enjoin Publications Endangering National Security?

Imagine that you are a federal judge and lawyers from the Justice Department come to your court seeking an emergency order to enjoin *The New York Times* from publishing a story that the government claims will endanger national security. What would you do?

We previously learned about the First Amendment's strong aversion to prior restraints. Yet that is exactly what the government is seeking from you: a court order to STOP THE PRESSES!

Perhaps you welcome this opportunity to rule on this weighty matter. But you might also be intimidated. After all, you are trained in the law, not national security. Who are you to second-guess Executive Branch officials about what will endanger the country?

Justice Robert Jackson, who sat on the Supreme Court during World War II, understood your dilemma. Here is how he described the challenges a court faces when it is asked to balance national security interests against civil liberties:

> Measures violative of constitutional rights are claimed to be necessary to security, in the judgment of officials who are best in a position to know, but the necessity is not provable by ordinary evidence and the court is in no position to determine the necessity for itself. What does it do then?[8]

---

[8] Robert H. Jackson, *Wartime Security and Liberty under Law*, 1 Buff. L. Rev. 103, 115 (1951).

The easiest way out of this dilemma would be to defer to the elected officials. That is what Justice Felix Frankfurter chose to do in *United States v. Dennis*, the case we previously discussed about the government's prosecution of Communist sympathizers during the Cold War era:

> It is not for us to decide. Congress has determined that the danger created by advocacy of overthrow justifies the ensuing restriction on freedom of speech. To make validity of legislation depend on judicial reading of events still in the womb of time is to charge the judiciary with duties beyond its equipment.

Justice Frankfurter offers you an easy way out. You could grant the government's motion and be home in time for dinner. But would that be fulfilling your role as a judge? Is it your job, as the guardian of the Constitution, to ensure that the government's requested relief is justified? Of course, the request may be perfectly reasonable, yet it is also possible that the government is merely trying to suppress information about its own misfeasance or incompetence.

Fortunately, there is a landmark Supreme Court decision with almost identical facts that you can consult when weighing what to do. It is the opinion you about to read, *New York Times Co. v. United States*, which is often referred to as the Pentagon Papers case.

The case has its origins during the Vietnam War. While not a party to this litigation, the leading protagonist was Daniel Ellsberg, a Harvard graduate and longtime military analyst. As part of his work for the government, Ellsberg assisted in the preparation of a massive study, colloquially known as the Pentagon Papers, about the history of United States' involvement in Southeast Asia. The secretary of defense, Robert McNamara, commissioned the study so future generations could learn from this history.

Ellsberg had initially supported the Vietnam War but later came to believe it was a mistake. He thought that prolonging the war was causing needless deaths of both Americans and Vietnamese. He knew from his work that the Pentagon Papers contained proof that the government had lied to the American public about its actions in Vietnam. He believed that disclosing the report would help mobilize opposition to the war.

Ellsberg first reached out to U.S. senators to encourage them to release the papers. When those efforts failed, he took matters into his own hands. In March 1971, he delivered a copy of the Pentagon Papers to *The New York Times*. After a thorough review of the papers and an internal debate over whether to report on them, the *Times* began publishing a nine-part series on June 13, 1971. The Nixon administration promptly sought a temporary restraining order to prevent further publication. In the meantime, Ellsberg leaked a second copy to *The Washington Post*, which itself began publishing articles on June 18, prompting a second lawsuit. Both district courts denied the administration's request for a temporary injunction. The appellate courts reached mixed results, and the Supreme Court agreed to hear the case immediately.

To give you a sense of how seriously judges take prior restraints, the case moved through the lower courts to the Supreme Court within two weeks.[9]

Daniel Ellsberg (L) with his wife, Patricia (C), outside a Los Angeles courthouse on April 12, 1973. (AP Photo) Creative Commons (CY BY 2.0)

New York Times Co. v. United States

Supreme Court of the United States, 1971
403 U.S. 713

PER CURIAM.

We granted certiorari in these cases in which the United States seeks to enjoin the New York Times and the Washington Post from publishing the contents of a classified study entitled "History of U.S. Decision-Making Process on Viet Nam Policy."

---

9 For a detailed account of the Pentagon Papers saga, *see* Sanford J. Ungar, The Papers & The Papers: An Account of the Legal and Political Battles over the Pentagon Papers (1972). For an inside account of the case from *The New York Times*' chief legal counsel at the time, *see* James C. Goodale, Fighting for the Press: The Inside Story of the Pentagon Papers and Other Battles (2013). For Ellsberg's account, *see* Daniel Ellsberg, Secrets: A Memoir of Vietnam and the Pentagon Papers (2002).

"Any system of prior restraints of expression comes to this Court bearing a heavy presumption against its constitutional validity." The Government "thus carries a heavy burden of showing justification for the imposition of such a restraint." The District Court for the Southern District of New York in the *New York Times* case, and the District Court for the District of Columbia and the Court of Appeals for the District of Columbia Circuit in the *Washington Post* case held that the Government had not met that burden. We agree.

The judgment of the Court of Appeals for the District of Columbia Circuit is therefore affirmed. The order of the Court of Appeals for the Second Circuit is reversed, and the case is remanded with directions to enter a judgment affirming the judgment of the District Court for the Southern District of New York. The stays entered June 25, 1971, by the Court are vacated. The judgments shall issue forthwith.

Mr. Justice Black, with whom Mr. Justice Douglas joins, concurring.

I adhere to the view that the Government's case against the Washington Post should have been dismissed and that the injunction against the New York Times should have been vacated without oral argument when the cases were first presented to this Court. I believe that every moment's continuance of the injunctions against these newspapers amounts to a flagrant, indefensible, and continuing violation of the First Amendment. In my view it is unfortunate that some of my Brethren are apparently willing to hold that the publication of news may sometimes be enjoined. Such a holding would make a shambles of the First Amendment.

To find that the President has "inherent power" to halt the publication of news by resort to the courts would wipe out the First Amendment and destroy the fundamental liberty and security of the very people the Government hopes to make "secure." The word "security" is a broad, vague generality whose contours should not be invoked to abrogate the fundamental law embodied in the First Amendment. The guarding of military and diplomatic secrets at the expense of informed representative government provides no real security for our Republic. The Framers of the First Amendment, fully aware of both the need to defend a new nation and the abuses of the English and Colonial Governments, sought to give this new society strength and security by providing that freedom of speech, press, religion, and assembly should not be abridged.

Mr. Justice Douglas, with whom Mr. Justice Black joins, concurring.

The dominant purpose of the First Amendment was to prohibit the widespread practice of governmental suppression of embarrassing information. It is common knowledge that the First Amendment was adopted against the widespread use of the common law of seditious libel to punish the dissemination of material that is embarrassing to the powers-that-be. The present cases will, I think, go down in history as the most dramatic illustration of that principle. A debate of large proportions goes on in the Nation over our posture in Vietnam. That debate antedated the disclosure of the contents of the present documents. The latter are highly relevant to the debate in progress.

Secrecy in government is fundamentally anti-democratic, perpetuating bureaucratic errors. Open debate and discussion of public issues are vital to our national health. On public questions there should be "uninhibited, robust, and wide-open" debate.

MR. JUSTICE BRENNAN, concurring.

The First Amendment tolerates absolutely no prior judicial restraints of the press predicated upon surmise or conjecture that untoward consequences may result. Our cases, it is true, have indicated that there is a single, extremely narrow class of cases in which the First Amendment's ban on prior judicial restraint may be overridden. Our cases have thus far indicated that such cases may arise only when the Nation "is at war," during which times "no one would question but that a government might prevent actual obstruction to its recruiting service or the publication of the sailing dates of transports or the number and location of troops." *Near v. Minnesota ex rel. Olson*, 283 U.S. 697, 716 (1931). Even if the present world situation were assumed to be tantamount to a time of war, or if the power of presently available armaments would justify even in peacetime the suppression of information that would set in motion a nuclear holocaust, in neither of these actions has the Government presented or even alleged that publication of items from or based upon the material at issue would cause the happening of an event of that nature. "The chief purpose of the First Amendment's guaranty is to prevent previous restraints upon publication." Thus, only governmental allegation and proof that publication must inevitably, directly, and immediately cause the occurrence of an event kindred to imperiling the safety of a transport already at sea can support even the issuance of an interim restraining order.

MR. JUSTICE STEWART, with whom MR. JUSTICE WHITE joins, concurring.

It is clear to me that it is the constitutional duty of the Executive to protect the confidentiality necessary to carry out its responsibilities in the fields of international relations and national defense. This is not to say that Congress and the courts have no role to play. Undoubtedly Congress has the power to enact specific and appropriate criminal laws to protect government property and preserve government secrets. And if a criminal prosecution is instituted, it will be the responsibility of the courts to decide the applicability of the criminal law under which the charge is brought.

But in the cases before us we are asked neither to construe specific regulations nor to apply specific laws. We are asked, quite simply, to prevent the publication by two newspapers of material that the Executive Branch insists should not, in the national interest, be published. I am convinced that the Executive is correct with respect to some of the documents involved. But I cannot say that disclosure of any of them will surely result in direct, immediate, and irreparable damage to our Nation or its people. That being so, there can under the First Amendment be but one judicial resolution of the issues before us. I join the judgments of the Court.

MR. JUSTICE WHITE, with whom MR. JUSTICE STEWART joins, concurring.

I concur in today's judgments, but only because of the concededly extraordinary protection against prior restraints enjoyed by the press under our constitutional system. I do not say that in no circumstances would the First Amendment permit an injunction against publishing information about government plans or operations. Nor, after examining the materials the Government characterizes as the most sensitive and destructive, can I deny that revelation of these documents will do substantial damage to public interests. Indeed, I am confident that their disclosure will have that result. But I nevertheless agree that the United States has not satisfied the very heavy burden that it must meet to warrant an injunction against publication in these cases, at least in the absence of express and appropriately limited congressional authorization for prior restraints in circumstances such as these.

MR. JUSTICE MARSHALL, concurring.

The problem here is whether in these particular cases the Executive Branch has authority to invoke the equity jurisdiction of the courts to protect what it believes to be the national interest. It would, however, be utterly inconsistent with the concept of separation of powers for this Court to use its power of contempt to prevent behavior that Congress has specifically declined to prohibit. The Constitution provides that Congress shall make laws, the President execute laws, and courts interpret laws. It did not provide for government by injunction in which the courts and the Executive Branch can "make law" without regard to the action of Congress.

MR. CHIEF JUSTICE BURGER, dissenting.

We are in this posture because these cases have been conducted in unseemly haste. An issue of this importance should be tried and heard in a judicial atmosphere conducive to thoughtful, reflective deliberation, especially when haste, in terms of hours, is unwarranted in light of the long period the Times, by its own choice, deferred publication. We all crave speedier judicial processes but when judges are pressured as in these cases the result is a parody of the judicial function.

MR. JUSTICE HARLAN, with whom THE CHIEF JUSTICE and MR. JUSTICE BLACKMUN join, dissenting.

I agree that, in performance of its duty to protect the values of the First Amendment against political pressures, the judiciary must review the initial Executive determination to the point of satisfying itself that the subject matter of the dispute does lie within the proper compass of the President's foreign relations power. Constitutional considerations forbid "a complete abandonment of judicial control." Moreover, the judiciary may properly insist that the determination that disclosure of the subject matter would irreparably impair the national security be made by the head of the Executive Department concerned—here the Secretary of State or the Secretary of Defense—after actual personal consideration by that officer. This safeguard is required in the analogous area of executive claims of privilege for secrets of state.

But in my judgment the judiciary may not properly go beyond these two inquiries and redetermine for itself the probable impact of disclosure on the national security. "The very nature of executive decisions as to foreign policy is political, not judicial. Such decisions are wholly confided by our Constitution to the political departments of the government, Executive and Legislative. They are delicate, complex, and involve large elements of prophecy. They are and should be undertaken only by those directly responsible to the people whose welfare they advance or imperil. They are decisions of a kind for which the Judiciary has neither aptitude, facilities nor responsibility and have long been held to belong in the domain of political power not subject to judicial intrusion or inquiry."

MR. JUSTICE BLACKMUN, dissenting.

I would remand these cases to be developed expeditiously, of course, but on a schedule permitting the orderly presentation of evidence from both sides, with the use of discovery, if necessary, as authorized by the rules, and with the preparation of briefs, oral argument, and court opinions of a quality better than has been seen to this point. In making this last statement, I criticize no lawyer or judge. I know from past personal experience the agony of time pressure in the preparation of litigation. But these cases and the issues involved and the courts, including this one, deserve better than has been produced thus far.

The Court, however, decides the cases today the other way. I therefore add one final comment. I strongly urge, and sincerely hope, that these two newspapers will be fully aware of their ultimate responsibilities to the United States of America. If, with the Court's action today, these newspapers proceed to publish the critical documents and there results therefrom "the death of soldiers, the destruction of alliances, the greatly increased difficulty of negotiation with our enemies, the inability of our diplomats to negotiate," to which list I might add the factors of prolongation of the war and of further delay in the freeing of United States prisoners, then the Nation's people will know where the responsibility for these sad consequences rests.

Points for Discussion

1. **What is the rule of the Pentagon Papers case?** Did you notice that the nine justices who heard the Pentagon Papers case each wrote a separate opinion? Is it possible to derive legal principles from this morass? The one thing we do know is that the Supreme Court, notwithstanding the extraordinary circumstances, refused to enjoin *The New York Times* and *The Washington Post* from publishing information from the purloined Pentagon Papers. That bare fact sent a powerful signal about how difficult it will be to obtain a prior restraint in future cases. Beyond that, however, the justices left us with a potpourri of rules for when, if ever, a prior restraint should be permitted in future cases. Can you articulate the rules proposed by each opinion?

2. **What if a federal law had authorized an injunction in these circumstances?** Some of the justices focused on the fact that there was no federal law authorizing the Executive Branch to obtain an injunction in the circumstances of this case. But what if Congress had enacted such a law? Should that be enough to justify upholding a prior restraint? Should the justices' concerns with prior restraints evaporate merely because Congress authorized the restraints? Does such deference to Congress make sense, especially since Congress is the one branch of government that the First Amendment expressly restrains?

3. **Would a prior restraint in the interests of national security ever be permissible?** Justices Brennan and Stewart suggested that they would have been willing to uphold a prior restraint if the government had demonstrated that publication of the information would lead to immediate, irreparable, and grave harm. Justice Brennan used as his touchstone a famous line from *Near v. Minnesota*, 283 U.S. 697 (1931), the Supreme Court's leading case on prior restraints before the Pentagon Papers case:

   > No one would question but that a government might prevent actual obstruction to its recruiting service or the publication of the sailing dates of transports or the number and location of troops.

   Can you imagine a fact pattern that would satisfy this test? How about *United States v. The Progressive, Inc.*, 467 F. Supp. 990 (W.D. Wis. 1979), in which a district court judge enjoined *The Progressive* magazine from publishing an article with instructions on how to make a hydrogen bomb. Here is a sampling of the judge's reasoning:

   > A mistake in ruling against *The Progressive* will seriously infringe cherished First Amendment rights. If a preliminary injunction is issued, it

> will constitute the first instance of prior restraint against a publication in this fashion in the history of this country, to this Court's knowledge. Such notoriety is not to be sought. It will curtail defendants' First Amendment rights in a drastic and substantial fashion. It will infringe upon our right to know and to be informed as well.
>
> A mistake in ruling against the United States could pave the way for thermonuclear annihilation for us all. In that event, our right to life is extinguished and the right to publish becomes moot.
>
> In the *Near* case, the Supreme Court recognized that publication of troop movements in time of war would threaten national security and could therefore be restrained. Times have changed significantly since 1931 when *Near* was decided. Now war by foot soldiers has been replaced in large part by war by machines and bombs. No longer need there be any advance warning or any preparation time before a nuclear war could be commenced.
>
> In light of these factors, this Court concludes that publication of the technical information on the hydrogen bomb contained in the article is analogous to publication of troop movements or locations in time of war and falls within the extremely narrow exception to the rule against prior restraint.

4. **Will there be another Pentagon Papers case?** In recent years, there have been massive leaks of government information that the government claimed endangered national security, but there has not been another Pentagon Papers-like opinion from the Supreme Court. Why not? Has the internet made it physically impossible to stop a determined leaker from disseminating information? See Patricia L. Bellia, *WikiLeaks and the Institutional Framework for National Security Disclosures*, 121 Yale L.J. 1448 (2012).

5. **Can the government prosecute the leaker?** The Court's Pentagon Papers opinion addressed only the prior restraint issue. There is a separate question about whether the government could still prosecute the leaker, or the newspaper publishers, even if the government could not stop publication of the leaked information. The government did in fact criminally prosecute Daniel Ellsberg for leaking the Pentagon Papers. Fortunately for Ellsberg, the judge dismissed the case after learning that the government had illegally tapped Ellsberg's phone and burglarized his psychiatrist's office searching for compromising information about him. For a comprehensive discussion about leaks of national security information, *see* Mary-Rose Papandrea, *Leaker Traitor Whistleblower Spy: National Security Leaks and the First Amendment*, 94 B.U. L. Rev. 449 (2014).

6. **Can the government prosecute publishers of leaked information?** *The New York Times* and *Washington Post* were not involved in Ellsberg's initial decision to leak confidential government information. Their actions came only later when they decided to publish the information. Should that fact have immunized the newspapers from any liability, or is the government, notwithstanding the First Amendment, allowed to punish both the leaker and the publisher? We will explore this topic later in the chapters on privacy rights and freedom of the press. For a collection of essays on these and other related issues, *see* National Security, Leaks and Freedom of the Press: The Pentagon Papers Fifty Years On (Geoffrey R. Stone and Lee C. Bollinger, eds.) (2021).

Test Your Knowledge

To assess your understanding of the material in this chapter, click here to take a quiz.

Chapter Six

May Government Regulate Speech to Promote Equality?

Hate Speech and Sexist Speech

The images of white supremacists and neo-Nazis marching in the 2017 Unite the Right rally in Charlottesville, Virginia, are seared into the minds of many Americans: the angry faces of the young white men lit up by torchlight, marchers caught mid-scream while chanting "White Lives Matter" and "Jews will not replace us," and the post-march image of James Alex Fields' Dodge Charger plowing into counter-protesters.

Why did Charlottesville, a progressive Southern city best known as the home of the University of Virginia, allow this march to occur in the first place? The city even granted a permit for the rally to take place in the organizer's preferred location: a park containing a Robert E. Lee statue that had been designated for removal. A week before the rally, the city did try to revoke the permit if the rally was not moved to a different location, but the organizer, represented by the American Civil Liberties Union, obtained an injunction for the rally to proceed as originally planned.

Why did Charlottesville give this group of white supremacists a permit when the city knew that their message would deeply offend members of the local community? Why did the ACLU represent the organizer given the civil liberties group's commitment to racial justice? Indeed, 50 years earlier, the ACLU had represented Mildred and Richard Loving in their successful challenge to Virginia's ban on interracial marriage.

These are the types of questions we will wrestle with as we explore the topic of hate speech. The issue is challenging because it falls at the intersection of two cherished American values: free speech and equality. On the one hand, there is our country's "profound national commitment," as Justice William Brennan put it, to "uninhibited, robust, and wide-open" public debate. On the other hand, there is our comparably profound commitment to equality, a value that is similarly enshrined in the Constitution, most prominently in the Fourteenth Amendment's prohibition on denying people "the equal protection of the laws."

What should happen when these values collide? Should equality interests prevail and permit us to suppress speech that fosters prejudice and encourages discrimination? Or should free speech interests prevail and require us to tolerate hate speech if it does not rise to the level of incitement, fighting words, or threats?

Historically, free speech has been the ally of equality. Activists have used speeches, protest marches, rallies, leaflets, and door-to-door solicitations to advance causes such as abolition, women's suffrage, civil rights, gender equality, and gay and lesbian rights. The Rev. Martin Luther King, Jr.'s famous "I Have a Dream" speech during the 1963 March on Washington epitomizes the power of speech to further the goal of equality.

But speech can also be the enemy of equality. Hate speech can poison relations between groups of people, perpetuate false stereotypes, scapegoat groups for problems they did not create, and foster fear that the "other" is somehow dangerous or malevolent. Joseph Goebbels' virulent anti-Semitic diatribes as the Third Reich's propaganda minister exemplify the perniciousness of hate speech.

By the end of this chapter, you will learn whether communities like Charlottesville may prohibit public demonstrations that disparage people because of their race, national origin, religion, gender, or sexual orientation. May these communities declare their commitment to diversity and inclusion and ban speakers who oppose those values? Or must the communities grit their teeth and permit these speakers to voice their hateful ideas?

Read It

To read the district court judge's preliminary injunction ordering Charlottesville to permit the Unite the Right rally to be held at the originally designated location, click here.

To read a CBS News interview with ACLU Executive Director Anthony Romero in which he explained why the ACLU represented the organizers of the Unite the Right rally, click here.

A. Defining "Hate Speech": When Speech and Equality Interests Collide

Before we explore hate speech, we need to define the term. Hatred, after all, is a protean emotion that manifests itself in an infinite variety of forms. Some of these manifestations may be regulated by the government with little or no First Amendment constraints. Others may not. This section separates the two.

1. Distinguishing Hateful Ideas from Hateful Conduct: Sticks and Stones Versus Words

You know the saying: "Sticks and stones may break my bones, but words will never hurt me." There is a fundamental truth to this adage—sticks and stones can break bones, words cannot. But the adage oversimplifies. Words can and often do hurt. Perjury, false advertising, and defamation are a few examples. Similarly, hate speech can be emotionally scarring to those targeted by the speech.

For the moment, let us home in on instances when hateful *ideas* manifest themselves in hateful *conduct*. For example, consider a hypothetical in which Joe beats up Bill because of Bill's race.

Does the First Amendment create any obstacle to prosecuting Joe for this crime? Could Joe contend that his conduct was communicative under the *Spence* test because he intended to communicate a message through his violent act and others would understand the message?

A related question is whether the First Amendment places any limits on hate crime laws, which make it a crime to attack someone because of the person's race, religion, gender, or other protected characteristic. The same question goes for laws that enhance sentences for crimes motivated by hatred for specific groups.

Hate crime laws raise two First Amendment issues. The first is whether they constitute unlawful viewpoint discrimination in violation of the principle announced in *R.A.V. v. City of St. Paul.* Recall how the Supreme Court in *R.A.V.* struck down a St. Paul ordinance because the ordinance punished fighting words based on some characteristics (race, religion, and gender) and not others (political affiliation, union membership, and homosexuality). As Justice Antonin Scalia explained, "The First Amendment does not permit St. Paul to impose special prohibitions on those speakers who express views on disfavored subjects." Do hate crime laws suffer from this same defect because they apply only when a crime is targeted at some groups (*e.g.*, based on race, religion, or gender) and not others (*e.g.*, union membership)?

The second issue concerns the evidence that may be introduced to prove that a defendant committed a crime based on animus. May a prosecutor prove this animus by introducing the defendant's speech, such as his hateful rants on social media, or would that violate the defendant's First Amendment rights?

R.A.V. also potentially calls into question the constitutionality of laws that punish discrimination when it is directed at certain groups. A classic example is Title VII of the Civil Rights Act of 1964, which bars employment discrimination based on race, color, religion, sex, or national origin. Does this law, like the law in *R.A.V.*, reflect government bias against some ideas and not others? Should it matter if a Title VII discrimination claim is based entirely on a defendant's speech (such as decorating an office with photographs of naked women) as opposed to his conduct (such as unwanted touching)?

The following case wrestles with these questions.

Wisconsin v. Mitchell

Supreme Court of the United States, 1993
508 U.S. 476

CHIEF JUSTICE REHNQUIST delivered the opinion of the Court.

Respondent Todd Mitchell's sentence for aggravated battery was enhanced because he intentionally selected his victim on account of the victim's race. The question presented in this case is whether this penalty enhancement is prohibited by the First and Fourteenth Amendments. We hold that it is not.

On the evening of October 7, 1989, a group of young black men and boys, including Mitchell, gathered at an apartment complex in Kenosha, Wisconsin. Several members of the group discussed a scene from the motion picture "Mississippi Burning," in which a white man beat a young black boy who was praying. The group moved outside and Mitchell asked them: "Do you all feel hyped up to move on some white people?" Shortly thereafter, a young white boy approached the group on the opposite side of the street where they were standing. As the boy walked by, Mitchell said: "You all want to fuck somebody up? There goes a white boy; go get him." Mitchell counted to three and pointed in the boy's direction. The group ran toward the boy, beat him severely, and stole his tennis shoes. The boy was rendered unconscious and remained in a coma for four days.

After a jury trial in the Circuit Court for Kenosha County, Mitchell was convicted of aggravated battery. That offense ordinarily carries a maximum sentence of two years' imprisonment. But because the jury found that Mitchell had intentionally selected his victim because of the boy's race, the maximum sentence for Mitchell's offense was increased to seven years under § 939.645. That provision enhances the maximum penalty for an offense whenever the defendant "intentionally selects the person against whom the crime is committed because of the race, religion, color, disability, sexual orientation, national origin or ancestry of that person." The Circuit Court sentenced Mitchell to four years' imprisonment for the aggravated battery.

Mitchell unsuccessfully sought postconviction relief in the Circuit Court. Then he appealed his conviction and sentence, challenging the constitutionality of Wisconsin's penalty-enhancement provision on First Amendment grounds. The Wisconsin

Court of Appeals rejected Mitchell's challenge, but the Wisconsin Supreme Court reversed. The Supreme Court held that the statute "violates the First Amendment directly by punishing what the legislature has deemed to be offensive thought." It rejected the State's contention "that the statute punishes only the 'conduct' of intentional selection of a victim." According to the court, "the statute punishes the 'because of' aspect of the defendant's selection, the *reason* the defendant selected the victim, the *motive* behind the selection." And under *R.A.V. v. St. Paul,* "the Wisconsin legislature cannot criminalize bigoted thought with which it disagrees."

The Supreme Court also held that the penalty-enhancement statute was unconstitutionally overbroad. It reasoned that, in order to prove that a defendant intentionally selected his victim because of the victim's protected status, the State would often have to introduce evidence of the defendant's prior speech, such as racial epithets he may have uttered before the commission of the offense. This evidentiary use of protected speech, the court thought, would have a "chilling effect" on those who feared the possibility of prosecution for offenses subject to penalty enhancement. Finally, the court distinguished antidiscrimination laws, which have long been held constitutional, on the ground that the Wisconsin statute punishes the "subjective mental process" of selecting a victim because of his protected status, whereas antidiscrimination laws prohibit "objective acts of discrimination."

We granted certiorari because of the importance of the question presented and the existence of a conflict of authority among state high courts on the constitutionality of statutes similar to Wisconsin's penalty-enhancement provision. We reverse.

The State argues that the statute does not punish bigoted thought, as the Supreme Court of Wisconsin said, but instead punishes only conduct. While this argument is literally correct, it does not dispose of Mitchell's First Amendment challenge. To be sure, our cases reject the "view that an apparently limitless variety of conduct can be labeled 'speech' whenever the person engaging in the conduct intends thereby to express an idea." Thus, a physical assault is not by any stretch of the imagination expressive conduct protected by the First Amendment.

state arguement the statate punishes conduct

But the fact remains that under the Wisconsin statute the same criminal conduct may be more heavily punished if the victim is selected because of his race or other protected status than if no such motive obtained. Thus, although the statute punishes criminal conduct, it enhances the maximum penalty for conduct motivated by a discriminatory point of view more severely than the same conduct engaged in for some other reason or for no reason at all. Because the only reason for the enhancement is the defendant's discriminatory motive for selecting his victim, Mitchell argues (and the Wisconsin Supreme Court held) that the statute violates the First Amendment by punishing offenders' bigoted beliefs.

Traditionally, sentencing judges have considered a wide variety of factors in addition to evidence bearing on guilt in determining what sentence to impose on a convicted defendant. The defendant's motive for committing the offense is one important factor. Thus, in many States the commission of a murder, or other capital offense, for pecuniary gain is a separate aggravating circumstance under the capital sentencing statute.

But it is equally true that a defendant's abstract beliefs, however obnoxious to most people, may not be taken into consideration by a sentencing judge. *Dawson v. Delaware,* 503 U.S. 159 (1992). In *Dawson,* the State introduced evidence at a capital sentencing hearing that the defendant was a member of a white supremacist prison gang. Because "the evidence proved nothing more than the defendant's abstract beliefs," we held that its admission violated the defendant's First Amendment rights. In so holding, however, we emphasized that "the Constitution does not erect a *per se* barrier to the admission of evidence concerning one's beliefs and associations at sentencing simply because those beliefs and associations are protected by the First Amendment." Thus, in *Barclay v. Florida,* 463 U.S. 939 (1983) (plurality opinion), we allowed the sentencing judge to take into account the defendant's racial animus towards his victim. The evidence in that case showed that the defendant's membership in the Black Liberation Army and desire to provoke a "race war" were related to the murder of a white man for which he was convicted. Because "the elements of racial hatred in the murder" were relevant to several aggravating factors, we held that the trial judge permissibly took this evidence into account in sentencing the defendant to death.

Mitchell suggests that *Dawson* and *Barclay* are inapposite because they did not involve application of a penalty-enhancement provision. But in *Barclay* we held that it was permissible for the sentencing court to consider the defendant's racial animus in determining whether he should be sentenced to death, surely the most severe "enhancement" of all.

Mitchell argues that the Wisconsin penalty-enhancement statute is invalid because it punishes the defendant's discriminatory motive, or reason, for acting. But motive plays the same role under the Wisconsin statute as it does under federal and state antidiscrimination laws, which we have previously upheld against constitutional challenge. Title VII of the Civil Rights Act of 1964, for example, makes it unlawful for an employer to discriminate against an employee "*because of* such individual's race, color, religion, sex, or national origin." In *Hishon v. King & Spalding,* 467 U.S. 69 (1984), we rejected the argument that Title VII infringed employers' First Amendment rights. And more recently, in *R.A.V.,* we cited Title VII as an example of a permissible content-neutral regulation of conduct.

Nothing in our decision last Term in *R.A.V.* compels a different result here. That case involved a First Amendment challenge to a municipal ordinance prohibiting the use of "fighting words that insult, or provoke violence, on the basis of race, color, creed, religion or gender." Because the ordinance only proscribed a class of "fighting words" deemed particularly offensive by the city—*i.e.,* those "that contain messages of bias-motivated hatred," we held that it violated the rule against content-based discrimination. But whereas the ordinance struck down in *R.A.V.* was explicitly directed at expression (*i.e.,* "speech" or "messages"), the statute in this case is aimed at conduct unprotected by the First Amendment.

Moreover, the Wisconsin statute singles out for enhancement bias-inspired conduct because this conduct is thought to inflict greater individual and societal harm. For example, according to the State and its *amici,* bias-motivated crimes are more likely to provoke retaliatory crimes, inflict distinct emotional harms on their victims, and incite community unrest. The State's desire to redress these perceived harms provides an adequate explanation for its penalty-enhancement provision over and above mere disagreement with offenders' beliefs or biases. As Blackstone said long ago, "it is but reasonable that among crimes of different natures those should be most severely punished, which are the most destructive of the public safety and happiness."

Finally, there remains to be considered Mitchell's argument that the Wisconsin statute is unconstitutionally overbroad because of its "chilling effect" on free speech. Mitchell argues (and the Wisconsin Supreme Court agreed) that the statute is "overbroad" because evidence of the defendant's prior speech or associations may be used to prove that the defendant intentionally selected his victim on account of the victim's protected status. Consequently, the argument goes, the statute impermissibly chills free expression with respect to such matters by those concerned about the possibility of enhanced sentences if they should in the future commit a criminal offense covered by the statute. We find no merit in this contention.

The sort of chill envisioned here is far more attenuated and unlikely than that contemplated in traditional "overbreadth" cases. We must conjure up a vision of a Wisconsin citizen suppressing his unpopular bigoted opinions for fear that if he later commits an offense covered by the statute, these opinions will be offered at trial to establish that he selected his victim on account of the victim's protected status, thus qualifying him for penalty enhancement. To stay within the realm of rationality, we must surely put to one side minor misdemeanor offenses covered by the statute, such as negligent operation of a motor vehicle; for it is difficult, if not impossible, to conceive of a situation where such offenses would be racially motivated. We are left, then, with the prospect of a citizen suppressing his bigoted beliefs for fear that evidence of such beliefs will be introduced against him at trial if he commits a more serious offense against person or property. This is simply too speculative a hypothesis to support Mitchell's overbreadth claim.

The First Amendment, moreover, does not prohibit the evidentiary use of speech to establish the elements of a crime or to prove motive or intent. Evidence of a defendant's previous declarations or statements is commonly admitted in criminal trials subject to evidentiary rules dealing with relevancy, reliability, and the like.

For the foregoing reasons, we hold that Mitchell's First Amendment rights were not violated by the application of the Wisconsin penalty-enhancement provision in sentencing him. The judgment of the Supreme Court of Wisconsin is therefore reversed, and the case is remanded for further proceedings not inconsistent with this opinion.

Points for Discussion

1. **Should violent conduct be treated as speech if it communicates a message?** The Court categorically dismissed the argument that violent conduct will be considered speech: "a physical assault is not by any stretch of the imagination expressive conduct protected by the First Amendment." This might be a welcome conclusion, but the Court did not explain why violent conduct should not be considered speech if it meets the requirements of the *Spence* test. Indeed, it is quite possible that a defendant who commits a hate crime intends to communicate a message and that others are likely to understand the message.

   It should be emphasized, however, that even if a court were to treat violent conduct as expressive speech, that would only begin the First Amendment analysis. As we learned in Chapter 4, the Supreme Court uses the *O'Brien* test to determine whether a conduct regulation that incidentally burdens speech is unconstitutional. Under that test, a law will receive intermediate scrutiny as long it is not aimed at the communicative aspect of the conduct. Since criminal laws against assault, battery, and murder are not targeted at the violent conduct's message, these laws would only need to further an important governmental interest, a test they would easily pass.

2. **Do laws that enhance sentences for hate crimes violate the *R.A.V.* prohibition on viewpoint discrimination?** How did the Court respond to the defendant's claim that the Wisconsin law violated *R.A.V.*? What was the key factor that distinguished the law in *R.A.V.* from the Wisconsin sentence-enhancement law?

3. **Does it violate the First Amendment to use a defendant's speech to prove his criminal motive?** To enhance a defendant's sentence under the Wisconsin hate-crime law, the government must prove that the defendant's conduct was motivated by hatred toward a protected class. May the government use the defendant's speech for this purpose? What did the Court conclude and why?

4. **The constitutionality of antidiscrimination laws.** The Supreme Court brusquely dismissed the argument that Title VII, the federal employment discrimination law, violates an employer's First Amendment rights:

> In *Hishon v. King & Spalding*, we rejected the argument that Title VII infringed employers' First Amendment rights. And more recently, in *R.A.V.*, we cited Title VII as an example of a permissible content-neutral regulation of conduct.

Is it appropriate for the Court to treat Title VII as a content-neutral regulation of conduct if a Title VII claim is based on an employer's speech? Does the Court too easily dismiss the First Amendment issues raised by antidiscrimination laws? *See, e.g.,* Eugene Volokh, *How Harassment Law Restricts Free Speech*, 47 Rutgers L. Rev. 563 (1995).

5. **Brainteaser! Can you reconcile *Mitchell* and *Dawson*?** In *Dawson v. Delaware*, 503 U.S. 159 (1992), a cased decided the year before *Mitchell*, a white defendant was convicted of murdering a white victim. When the jury was deciding whether to sentence the defendant to death, it considered mitigating and aggravating factors about the defendant, David Dawson. During this "penalty phase" the prosecution introduced evidence that Dawson was a member of a white supremacist gang, the Aryan Brotherhood. The question was whether consideration of this evidence violated the First Amendment. The Supreme Court held that it did violate the First Amendment because there was no evidence that Dawson's membership in the racist gang had any bearing on his commission of the murder. The key passage in *Dawson* stated:

> Before the penalty hearing, the prosecution claimed that its expert witness would show that the Aryan Brotherhood is a white racist prison gang that is associated with drugs and violent escape attempts at prisons, and that advocates the murder of fellow inmates. If credible and otherwise admissible evidence to that effect had been presented, we would have a much different case. But, after reaching an agreement with Dawson, the prosecution limited its proof regarding the Aryan Brotherhood to the stipulation. The brief stipulation proved only that an Aryan Brotherhood prison gang originated in California in the 1960's, that it entertains white racist beliefs, and that a separate gang in the Delaware prison system calls itself the Aryan Brotherhood. We conclude that the narrowness of the stipulation left the Aryan Brotherhood evidence totally without relevance to Dawson's sentencing proceeding.

Can you reconcile or harmonize *Mitchell* and *Dawson*? Consider this argument: In *Mitchell* the racist intent was effectively an element of the crime itself, in that violence animated by racist intent triggered greater criminal liability. In *Dawson*, in contrast, the defendant was merely prosecuted for murder, not for "murder with racist intent," and his membership in a racist group had not been introduced as evidence of his intent in any sense. If a state increased the punishment for murders committed with racist intent, could a defendant's membership in a racist group be admitted in evidence for the purpose of establishing his intent? In such a case, would *Mitchell*, not *Dawson*, control?

2. Distinguishing Hate Speech from Other Categories of Speech: When Hate Speech Amounts to Incitement, Fighting Words, or True Threats or Occurs in a Special Setting

Even if hate speech is merely words, it will not be protected by the First Amendment if it fits into any of the unprotected categories of speech we studied in Chapter 5. If hate speech is directed and likely to lead to imminent lawbreaking, it will be unprotected as incitement. If hate speech is a one-on-one personal insult that would prompt a reasonable person to react violently, it will be unprotected fighting words. If hate speech expresses an intent to commit violence against a particular individual or group, it will be an unprotected true threat.

In addition to these established categories of unprotected speech, courts have indicated that speech that harasses people based on race, religion, sex, or other characteristics can constitute discrimination in violation of civil rights laws. For example, the Supreme Court has said that sexual harassment can create an actionable claim for employment discrimination under Title VII if it creates "a hostile or abusive work environment," and this environment can be created by speech such as "discriminatory intimidation, ridicule, and insult."[1] To be actionable, the harassment must be "sufficiently severe or pervasive to alter the conditions of the victim's employment and create an abusive working environment."[2] Similarly, lower courts have held that speech may be regulated if it creates a hostile learning environment at schools and universities.[3] Where the line should be drawn between unprotected harassment and protected speech is controversial and still a work in progress.[4]

---

1 *Meritor Sav. Bank v. Vinson*, 477 U.S. 57, 65, 66 (1986).

2 *Id.* at 67.

3 *Doe v. Valencia Coll.*, 903 F.3d 1220 (11th Cir. 2018). *See generally* Todd E. Pettys, *Hostile Learning Environments, the First Amendment, and Public Higher Education*, 54 Conn. L. Rev. 1 (2022); Erwin Chemerinsky & Howard Gillman, Free Speech on Campus (2017).

4 Rodney A. Smolla, Smolla & Nimmer on Freedom of Speech, §§ 13:1–13:42 (2023). *See generally* Jack M. Balkin, *Free Speech and Hostile Environments*, 99 Colum. L. Rev. 2295 (1999); Kingsley R. Browne, *Title VII as Censorship: Hostile Environment Harassment and the First Amendment*, 52 Ohio St. L.J. 481 (1991); Eugene Volokh, *Freedom of Speech and Workplace Harassment*, 39 UCLA L. Rev. 1791 (1992).

B. Should the First Amendment Protect Hate Speech? Arguments for Denying Protection to Hateful Ideas

We are now face to face with the core question of whether hate speech should be protected by the First Amendment. Even if hate speech does not rise to the level of incitement, fighting words, or true threats, should the government nevertheless be permitted to regulate and punish it?

If Supreme Court justices were inclined to permit hate speech regulation, they could reach this result by one of two well-trodden paths in First Amendment jurisprudence. First, they could build on the categorical approach developed in *Chaplinsky* and declare hate speech to be an unprotected category of speech. Alternatively, they could treat hate speech as protected speech, but still allow for its regulation under the fact-specific balancing approach of strict scrutiny. Under this approach, a content-based regulation of hate speech would be constitutional if it were narrowly tailored to serve a compelling state interest.

The next two sections explore each of these options.

1. Categorical Exclusion: Should Hate Speech Be a New Category of Unprotected Speech?

In the previous chapter, we discussed *Chaplinsky*'s "categorical approach" to First Amendment jurisprudence. Under this approach, the Supreme Court has declared certain categories of speech to be unprotected. As a result, the government may regulate the content of these categories without having to pass strict scrutiny.

In the notes following *Chaplinsky*, we discussed the Supreme Court's schizophrenic attitude toward the categorical approach. On the one hand, the Court continues to subscribe to the notion that there are categories of unprotected speech. On the other hand, the Court has been extremely reluctant to find new categories of unprotected speech.

Nevertheless, it is worth pondering whether hate speech should be categorized as unprotected. The argument would be that speech that denigrates and demeans groups of people is unworthy of First Amendment protection. In the words of *Chaplinsky*, such speech could be said to play "no essential part of any exposition of ideas," and any benefit from it is "clearly outweighed by the social interest in order and morality."

This argument is not fanciful. In fact, the Supreme Court opinion most directly addressing hate speech found it to be categorically unprotected. The opinion, *Beauharnais v. Illinois*, is reproduced below. The opinion does not use the contemporary term "hate speech," but hate speech is at the heart of the opinion. Note how the Court found the speech at issue in the case unprotected by relying on one of the existing categories of unprotected speech from *Chaplinsky*'s original list. See if you can identify which category the Court relies on.

Beauharnais v. Illinois

Supreme Court of the United States, 1952
343 U.S. 250

MR. JUSTICE FRANKFURTER delivered the opinion of the Court.

The petitioner was convicted upon information in the Municipal Court of Chicago of violating § 224a of the Illinois Criminal Code, Ill. Rev. Stat., 1949, c. 38, Div. 1, § 471. He was fined $200. The section provides:

> It shall be unlawful for any person, firm or corporation to manufacture, sell, or offer for sale, advertise or publish, present or exhibit in any public place in this state any lithograph, moving picture, play, drama or sketch, which publication or exhibition portrays depravity, criminality, unchastity, or lack of virtue of a class of citizens, of any race, color, creed or religion which said publication or exhibition exposes the citizens of any race, color, creed or religion to contempt, derision, or obloquy or which is productive of breach of the peace or riots.

Beauharnais challenged the statute as violating the liberty of speech and of the press guaranteed as against the States by the Due Process Clause of the Fourteenth Amendment, and as too vague, under the restrictions implicit in the same Clause, to support conviction for crime. The Illinois courts rejected these contentions and sustained defendant's conviction. We granted certiorari in view of the serious questions raised concerning the limitations imposed by the Fourteenth Amendment on the power of a State to punish utterances promoting friction among racial and religious groups.

The information, cast generally in the terms of the statute, charged that Beauharnais "did unlawfully exhibit in public places lithographs, which publications portray depravity, criminality, unchastity or lack of virtue of citizens of Negro race and color and which exposes citizens of Illinois of the Negro race and color to contempt, derision, or obloquy."

The Illinois Supreme Court tells us that § 224a "is a form of criminal libel law." Libel of an individual was a common-law crime, and thus criminal in the colonies. Indeed, at common law, truth or good motives was no defense. In the first decades after the adoption of the Constitution, this was changed by judicial decision, statute or constitution in most States, but nowhere was there any suggestion that the crime of libel be abolished. Today, every American jurisdiction—the forty-eight States, the District of Columbia, Alaska, Hawaii and Puerto Rico—punish libels directed at individuals. [*Authors' note:* The opinion then quotes *Chaplinsky*, which includes "libelous" speech in its list of unprotected categories whose regulation has "never been thought to raise any constitutional problem."]

No one will gainsay that it is libelous falsely to charge another with being a rapist, robber, carrier of knives and guns, and user of marijuana. The precise question before us, then, is whether the protection of "liberty" in the Due Process Clause of the Fourteenth Amendment prevents a State from punishing such libels directed at designated collectivities and flagrantly disseminated. If an utterance directed at an individual may be the object of criminal sanctions, we cannot deny to a State power to punish the same utterance directed at a defined group, unless we can say that this [is] a wilful and purposeless restriction unrelated to the peace and well-being of the State.

Illinois did not have to look beyond her own borders or await the tragic experience of the last three decades to conclude that wilful purveyors of falsehood concerning racial and religious groups promote strife and tend powerfully to obstruct the manifold adjustments required for free, ordered life in a metropolitan, polyglot community. From the murder of the abolitionist Love-joy in 1837 to the Cicero riots of 1951, Illinois has been the scene of exacerbated tension between races, often flaring into violence and destruction. In many of these outbreaks, utterances of the character here in question, so the Illinois legislature could conclude, played a significant part.

In the face of this history, we would deny experience to say that the Illinois legislature was without reason in seeking ways to curb false or malicious defamation of racial and religious groups, made in public places and by means calculated to have a powerful emotional impact on those to whom it was presented. "There are limits to the exercise of these liberties (of speech and of the press). The danger in these times from the coercive activities of those who in the delusion of racial or religious conceit would incite violence and breaches of the peace in order to deprive others of their equal right to the exercise of their liberties, is emphasized by events familiar to all. These and other transgressions of those limits the states appropriately may punish."

It may be argued, and weightily, that this legislation will not help matters; that tension and on occasion violence between racial and religious groups must be traced to causes more deeply embedded in our society than the rantings of modern Know-Nothings. Only those lacking responsible humility will have a confident solution for problems as intractable as the frictions attributable to differences of race, color or religion. This being so, it would be out of bounds for the judiciary to deny the legislature a choice of policy, provided it is not unrelated to the problem and not forbidden by some explicit limitation on the State's power.

We are warned that the choice open to the Illinois legislature here may be abused, that the law may be discriminatorily enforced; prohibiting libel of a creed or of a racial group, we are told, is but a step from prohibiting libel of a political party.

Every power may be abused, but the possibility of abuse is a poor reason for denying Illinois the power to adopt measures against criminal libels sanctioned by centuries of Anglo-American law. "While this Court sits" it retains and exercises authority to nullify action which encroaches on freedom of utterance under the guise of punishing libel. Of course discussion cannot be denied and the right, as well as the duty, of criticism must not be stifled.

Libelous utterances not being within the area of constitutionally protected speech, it is unnecessary, either for us or for the State courts, to consider the issues behind the phrase "clear and present danger." Certainly no one would contend that obscene speech, for example, may be punished only upon a showing of such circumstances. Libel, as we have seen, is in the same class.

We find no warrant in the Constitution for denying to Illinois the power to pass the law here under attack. But it bears repeating—although it should not—that our finding that the law is not constitutionally objectionable carries no implication of approval of the wisdom of the legislation or of its efficacy. These questions may raise doubts in our minds as well as in others. It is not for us, however, to make the legislative judgment. We are not at liberty to erect those doubts into fundamental law.

Affirmed.

MR. JUSTICE BLACK, with whom MR. JUSTICE DOUGLAS concurs, dissenting.

This Act sets up a system of state censorship which is at war with the kind of free government envisioned by those who forced adoption of our Bill of Rights. The motives behind the state law may have been to do good. But the same can be said about most laws making opinions punishable as crimes. History indicates that urges to do good have led to the burning of books and even to the burning of "witches."

We are told that freedom of petition and discussion are in no danger "while this Court sits." This case raises considerable doubt. I do not agree that the Constitution leaves freedom of petition, assembly, speech, press or worship at the mercy of a case-by-case, day-by-day majority of this Court. I had supposed that our people could rely for their freedom on the Constitution's commands, rather than on the grace of this Court on an individual case basis. Whatever the danger, if any, in such public discussions, it is a danger the Founders deemed outweighed by the danger incident to the stifling of thought and speech. The Court does not act on this view of the Founders. It calculates what it deems to be the danger of public discussion, holds the scales are tipped on the side of state suppression, and upholds state censorship. This method of decision offers little protection to First Amendment liberties "while this Court sits."

If there be minority groups who hail this holding as their victory, they might consider the possible relevancy of this ancient remark:

"Another such victory and I am undone."

MR. JUSTICE REED, with whom MR. JUSTICE DOUGLAS joins, dissenting.

These words—"virtue," "derision," and "obloquy"—have neither general nor special meanings well enough known to apprise those within their reach as to limitations on speech. Does the Bill of Rights permit Illinois to forbid any reflection on the virtue of racial or religious classes which a jury or a judge may think exposes them to derision or obloquy, words themselves of quite uncertain meaning as used in the statute? I think not. A general and equal enforcement of this law would restrain the mildest expressions of opinion in all those areas where "virtue" may be thought to have a role. Since this judgment may rest upon these vague and undefined words, which permit within their scope the punishment of incidents secured by the guarantee of free speech, the conviction should be reversed.

MR. JUSTICE DOUGLAS, dissenting.

Hitler and his Nazis showed how evil a conspiracy could be which was aimed at destroying a race by exposing it to contempt, derision, and obloquy. I would be willing to concede that such conduct directed at a race or group in this country could be made an indictable offense. For such a project would be more than the exercise of free speech. Like picketing, it would be free speech plus.

I would also be willing to concede that even without the element of conspiracy there might be times and occasions when the legislative or executive branch might call a halt to inflammatory talk, such as the shouting of "fire" in a school or a theatre.

My view is that if in any case other public interests are to override the plain command of the First Amendment, the peril of speech must be clear and present, leaving no room for argument, raising no doubts as to the necessity of curbing speech in order to prevent disaster.

[Justice Jackson's dissenting opinion is omitted.]

Points for Discussion

1. **Should hate speech be categorically unprotected by the First Amendment?** Justice Felix Frankfurter characterized hate speech as a form of group libel. With this characterization in mind, it was a short leap for him to conclude that if individual libel is not protected by the First Amendment, the same must be true of group libel.

   Regardless of how Justice Frankfurter reached his conclusion, is there anything wrong with it? Why shouldn't a state be able to suppress hate speech? Didn't Illinois correctly conclude, as Justice Frankfurter said, that "wilful purveyors of falsehood concerning racial and religious groups promote strife and tend powerfully to obstruct the manifold adjustments required for free, ordered life in a metropolitan, polyglot community"?

2. **The slippery slope problem.** A common argument against finding new categories of unprotected speech is the slippery slope dilemma. If the Supreme Court can declare hate speech an unprotected category, why not other speech? Unless there is a neutral principle that distinguishes hate speech from other speech, the creation of a hate speech exception could merely reflect the arbitrary judgment of nine justices, who would also be at liberty to define the contours of this exception. In his dissent, Justice Hugo Black made it clear that he was not comfortable relying on the "grace of this Court" to protect freedom of speech. He cautioned minority groups who might hail their victory in *Beauharnais* to ponder the immortal words of King Pyrrhus: "Another such victory and I am undone."

   Professor Mari Matsuda has offered a way out of this dilemma by contending that hate speech, or at least racist speech, is in fact unique. Mari J. Matsuda, *Public Response to Racist Speech: Considering the Victim's Story*, 87 Mich. L. Rev. 2320 (1989). She contends that it is possible, using neutral principles, to carve out an exception for racist speech without jeopardizing our society's robust commitment to an open marketplace of ideas.

   Matsuda illustrates her point by showing how a line can be drawn between racist speech, which she believes should not be protected by the First Amendment, and Marxist speech, which she believes should be protected:

   > One way to explain this is to consider the difference between racist hate messages and Marxist speech. Marxist speech is the kind of unpopular political expression the First Amendment is intended to protect. Marxist speech is, according to a once prevalent view, the advocacy of overthrow of existing governments, inevitably leading to dictator-

> ships and persecution of dissidents and capitalists. It is thus, it was argued, dangerous speech, properly censored. The legacy of this view was McCarthyism and the shattered lives of hundreds of decent citizens.
>
> How can one argue for censorship of racist hate messages without encouraging a revival of McCarthyism? There is an important difference that comes from human experience, our only source of collective knowledge. We know, from our collective historical knowledge, that slavery was wrong. We know the unspeakable horror of the holocaust was wrong. We know white minority rule in South Africa is wrong. This knowledge is reflected in the universal acceptance of the wrongness of the doctrine of racial supremacy. There is no nation left on this planet that submits as its national self-expression the view that Hitler was right. South Africa is alone in its official policy of apartheid, and even South Africa, in making its case to the world community, is careful to avoid an explicit ideology of racial supremacy, preferring instead the rhetoric of one-step-at-a-time. At the universities, at the centers of knowledge of the international community, the doctrines of racial supremacy and racial hatred are again uniformly rejected. At the United Nations the same is true. We have fought wars and spilled blood to establish the universal acceptance of this principle. The universality of the principle, in a world bereft of agreement on many things, is a mark of collective human progress. The victim's perspective, one mindful of the lessons of history, thus accepts racist speech as *sui generis* and universally condemned.
>
> Marxist speech, on the other hand, is not universally condemned. Marxism presents a philosophy for political organization, distribution of wealth and power, ordering of values, and promotion of social change. By its very content it is political speech going to the core of ongoing political debate. Many nations adhere to Marxist ideology, and it is impossible to achieve world consensus either for or against this view. Marxists teach in universities. While Marxist ideas are rejected and abhorred by many, Marxist thought, like liberal thought, neoconservative economic theory, and other conflicting structures for understanding life and politics, is part of the ongoing efforts of human beings to understand their world and improve life in it.

Do you find Matsuda's distinction convincing?

3. **Is *Beauharnais* still good law?** If, after reading *Beauharnais*, you wrote in your notes that the First Amendment does not protect hate speech, get out your eraser. While the Supreme Court has never expressly overruled *Beauharnais*, the

conventional wisdom is that the case has been implicitly overruled. You don't have to look far to understand why. Just think of three of the cases we studied in Chapter 5: *Brandenburg v. Ohio*, *R.A.V. v. St. Paul*, and *Virginia v. Black*. All three cases involved speech that could easily be classified as hate speech. *Brandenburg* and *Black* involved Klan rallies, and all three cases involved cross burnings. If hate speech were an unprotected category of speech, you would have expected the Court to have resolved these cases on that basis. But in each case the Court did the opposite. It assumed that hate speech was protected unless it fit into a preexisting category of unprotected speech (incitement in *Brandenburg*, fighting words in *R.A.V.*, and true threats in *Black*). Indeed, the *Black* opinion suggested that burning of a cross is sometimes "core political speech."

Beauharnais was also based on *Chaplinsky*'s statement that "libelous" speech is not protected by the First Amendment. But, as you will learn in Chapter 9, libel lawsuits are now subject to a multitude of First Amendment limitations.

Finally, and as you are about to discover, more recent cases have made it clear that hate speech is protected by the First Amendment.

2. Should Hate Speech Regulations Survive Strict Scrutiny? Compelling Interests for Justifying Hate Speech Regulation

Even if hate speech is not categorically unprotected by the First Amendment, the government could still regulate its content if a regulation were narrowly tailored to serve a compelling state interest. That, of course, is the default standard for all content-based regulations of speech.

The key question is whether there is any compelling governmental interest to justify this suppression. Advocates of hate speech regulation typically point to two interests. The first is that hate speech fosters prejudice, discrimination, and even violence toward members of disparaged groups. The second is that hate speech causes emotional distress to members of the targeted groups.

Should either of these interests justify the content-based suppression of hate speech?

a. May Government Suppress Hate Speech Because It Encourages Hateful Conduct? The Difficulty of Distinguishing Hate Speech from Other Speech That Encourages Unlawful Action

One argument for allowing hate speech regulation is that hate speech is likely to motivate people to engage in hateful behavior, whether it be discrimination in employment or housing, or, worse yet, violence toward members of disparaged groups. Should that be a reason for permitting the government to regulate hate speech?

Hate speech's power to shape people's perceptions was the theme of a song composed by Richard Rodgers and Oscar Hammerstein for their musical "South Pacific." The play premiered on Broadway in 1949, eight years after Pearl Harbor and five years before the Supreme Court decided *Brown v. Board of Education*. A character in the play, a lieutenant stationed in the Pacific during World War II, falls in love with a native woman and sings about the likely prejudice the couple would encounter if he married her. He sings a song, "You've Got to Be Carefully Taught," to explain how children are not innately hateful but are taught to be so:

> You've got to be taught to hate and fear,
> You've got to be taught from year to year,
> It's got to be drummed in your dear little ear—
> You've got to be carefully taught!
>
> You've got to be taught to be afraid
> Of people whose eyes are oddly made,
> And people whose skin is a different shade—
> You've got to be carefully taught.
>
> You've got to be taught before it's too late,
> Before you are six or seven or eight,
> To hate all the people your relatives hate—
> You've got to be carefully taught!
> You've got to be carefully taught!

If hateful ideas lead to hateful attitudes, and hateful attitudes lead to hateful actions, why not break the cycle by suppressing the ideas before they circulate?

Hear It

Click here to listen to the rendition of "You've Got to Be Carefully Taught" from the 1958 movie version of "South Pacific."

This argument has a tantalizing appeal. But it runs counter to the "marketplace of ideas" notion that the government should not control which ideas the public may express or hear. Indeed, the argument is at loggerheads with the jurisprudence we studied in Chapter 5. There, we learned that speech that encourages unlawful action can be suppressed only if it is directed and likely to lead to imminent lawbreaking (the *Brandenburg* test). The question is whether hate speech should be an exception to this rule.

Consider that question as you read the next case. Please note that this is a federal court of appeals opinion and not a Supreme Court opinion. The Supreme Court has not addressed the hate speech issue as directly as some lower courts. Consequently, this section and the next reproduce two prominent lower court opinions. The first case offers a powerful response to the argument that hate speech can be regulated because it encourages hateful actions. The hate speech at issue is speech that denigrates women.

American Booksellers Association v. Hudnut

United States Court of Appeals, Third Circuit, 1985
771 F.2d 323, aff'd mem., 475 U.S. 1001 (1986)

EASTERBROOK, CIRCUIT JUDGE.

Indianapolis enacted an ordinance defining "pornography" as a practice that discriminates against women. "Pornography" is to be redressed through the administrative and judicial methods used for other discrimination. The City's definition of "pornography" is considerably different from "obscenity," which the Supreme Court has held is not protected by the First Amendment.

"Pornography" under the ordinance is "the graphic sexually explicit subordination of women, whether in pictures or in words, that also includes one or more of the following:

(1) Women are presented as sexual objects who enjoy pain or humiliation; or

(2) Women are presented as sexual objects who experience sexual pleasure in being raped; or

(3) Women are presented as sexual objects tied up or cut up or mutilated or bruised or physically hurt, or as dismembered or truncated or fragmented or severed into body parts; or

(4) Women are presented as being penetrated by objects or animals; or

(5) Women are presented in scenarios of degradation, injury, abasement, torture, shown as filthy or inferior, bleeding, bruised, or hurt in a context that makes these conditions sexual; or

(6) Women are presented as sexual objects for domination, conquest, violation, exploitation, possession, or use, or through postures or positions of servility or submission or display.

Civil rights groups and feminists have entered this case as amici on both sides. Those supporting the ordinance say that it will play an important role in reducing the tendency of men to view women as sexual objects, a tendency that leads to both unacceptable attitudes and discrimination in the workplace and violence away from it. Those opposing the ordinance point out that much radical feminist literature is explicit and depicts women in ways forbidden by the ordinance and that the ordinance would reopen old battles. It is unclear how Indianapolis would treat works from James Joyce's *Ulysses* to Homer's *Iliad;* both depict women as submissive objects for conquest and domination.

We do not try to balance the arguments for and against an ordinance such as this. The ordinance discriminates on the ground of the content of the speech. Speech treating women in the approved way—in sexual encounters "premised on equality"—is lawful no matter how sexually explicit. Speech treating women in the disapproved way—as submissive in matters sexual or as enjoying humiliation—is unlawful no matter how significant the literary, artistic, or political qualities of the work taken as a whole. The state may not ordain preferred viewpoints in this way. The Constitution forbids the state to declare one perspective right and silence opponents.

The ordinance contains four prohibitions. People may not "traffic" in pornography, "coerce" others into performing in pornographic works, or "force" pornography on anyone. Anyone injured by someone who has seen or read pornography has a right of action against the maker or seller. Trafficking is defined in § 16–3(g)(4) as the "production, sale, exhibition, or distribution of pornography."

The district court held the ordinance unconstitutional. The court concluded that the ordinance regulates speech rather than the conduct involved in making pornography. The regulation of speech could be justified, the court thought, only by a compelling interest in reducing sex discrimination, an interest Indianapolis had not established. The ordinance is also vague and overbroad, the court believed, and establishes a prior restraint of speech.

The plaintiffs are a congeries of distributors and readers of books, magazines, and films. Collectively the plaintiffs (or their members, whose interests they represent) make, sell, or read just about every kind of material that could be affected by the ordinance, from hard-core films to W.B. Yeats's poem "Leda and the Swan" (from the myth of Zeus in the form of a swan impregnating an apparently subordinate Leda), to the collected works of James Joyce, D.H. Lawrence, and John Cleland.

"If there is any fixed star in our constitutional constellation, it is that no official, high or petty, can prescribe what shall be orthodox in politics, nationalism, religion, or other matters of opinion or force citizens to confess by word or act their faith therein." Under the First Amendment the government must leave to the people the evaluation of ideas. Bald or subtle, an idea is as powerful as the audience allows it to be. A belief may be pernicious—the beliefs of Nazis led to the death of millions, those of the Klan to the repression of millions. A pernicious belief may prevail. Totalitarian governments today rule much of the planet, practicing suppression of billions and spreading dogma that may enslave others. One of the things that separates our society from theirs is our absolute right to propagate opinions that the government finds wrong or even hateful.

The ideas of the Klan may be propagated. Communists may speak freely and run for office. The Nazi Party may march through a city with a large Jewish population. People may criticize the President by misrepresenting his positions, and they have a right to post their misrepresentations on public property. People may teach religions that others despise. People may seek to repeal laws guaranteeing equal opportunity in employment or to revoke the constitutional amendments granting the vote to blacks and women. They may do this because "above all else, the First Amendment means that government has no power to restrict expression because of its message or its ideas."

Under the ordinance graphic sexually explicit speech is "pornography" or not depending on the perspective the author adopts. Speech that "subordinates" women and also, for example, presents women as enjoying pain, humiliation, or rape, or even simply presents women in "positions of servility or submission or display" is forbidden, no matter how great the literary or political value of the work taken as a whole. Speech that portrays women in positions of equality is lawful, no matter how graphic the sexual content. This is thought control. It establishes an "approved" view of women, of how they may react to sexual encounters, of how the sexes may relate to each other. Those who espouse the approved view may use sexual images; those who do not, may not.

Indianapolis justifies the ordinance on the ground that pornography affects thoughts. Men who see women depicted as subordinate are more likely to treat them so. Pornography is an aspect of dominance. It does not persuade people so much as change them. It works by socializing, by establishing the expected and the permissible. In this view pornography is not an idea; pornography is the injury.

There is much to this perspective. Beliefs are also facts. People often act in accordance with the images and patterns they find around them. People raised in a religion tend to accept the tenets of that religion, often without independent examination. People taught from birth that black people are fit only for slavery rarely rebelled against that creed; beliefs coupled with the self-interest of the masters established a social structure that inflicted great harm while enduring for centuries. Words and images act at the level of the subconscious before they persuade at the level of the conscious. Even the truth has little chance unless a statement fits within the framework of beliefs that may never have been subjected to rational study.

Therefore we accept the premises of this legislation. Depictions of subordination tend to perpetuate subordination. The subordinate status of women in turn leads to affront and lower pay at work, insult and injury at home, battery and rape on the streets. In the language of the legislature, "pornography is central in creating and maintaining sex as a basis of discrimination. Pornography is a systematic practice of exploitation and subordination based on sex which differentially harms women. The bigotry and contempt it produces, with the acts of aggression it fosters, harm women's opportunities for equality and rights of all kinds."

Yet this simply demonstrates the power of pornography as speech. All of these unhappy effects depend on mental intermediation. Pornography affects how people see the world, their fellows, and social relations. If pornography is what pornography does, so is other speech. Hitler's orations affected how some Germans saw Jews. Communism is a world view, not simply a *Manifesto* by Marx and Engels or a set of speeches. Efforts to suppress communist speech in the United States were based on the belief that the public acceptability of such ideas would increase the likelihood of totalitarian government. Many people believe that the existence of television, apart from the content of specific programs, leads to intellectual laziness, to a penchant for violence, to many other ills. The Alien and Sedition Acts passed during the administration of John Adams rested on a sincerely held belief that disrespect for the government leads to social collapse and revolution—a belief with support in the history of many nations. Most governments of the world act on this empirical regularity, suppressing critical speech. In the United States, however, the strength of the support for this belief is irrelevant. Seditious libel is protected speech unless the danger is not only grave but also imminent.

Racial bigotry, anti-semitism, violence on television, reporters' biases—these and many more influence the culture and shape our socialization. None is directly answerable by more speech, unless that speech too finds its place in the popular culture. Yet all is protected as speech, however insidious. Any other answer leaves the government in control of all of the institutions of culture, the great censor and director of which thoughts are good for us.

anything else helps govt determine whats good for us

Sexual responses often are unthinking responses, and the association of sexual arousal with the subordination of women therefore may have a substantial effect. But almost all cultural stimuli provoke unconscious responses. Religious ceremonies condition their participants. Teachers convey messages by selecting what not to cover; the implicit message about what is off limits or unthinkable may be more powerful than the messages for which they present rational argument. Television scripts contain unarticulated assumptions. People may be conditioned in subtle ways. If the fact that speech plays a role in a process of conditioning were enough to permit governmental regulation, that would be the end of freedom of speech.

It is possible to interpret the claim that the pornography is the harm in a different way. Indianapolis emphasizes the injury that models in pornographic films and pictures may suffer. The record contains materials depicting sexual torture, penetration of women by red-hot irons and the like. These concerns have nothing to do with written materials subject to the statute, and physical injury can occur with or without the "subordination" of women. As we discuss [later], a state may make injury in the course of producing a film unlawful independent of the viewpoint expressed in the film.

Much of Indianapolis's argument rests on the belief that when speech is "unanswerable," and the metaphor that there is a "marketplace of ideas" does not apply, the First Amendment does not apply either. The metaphor is honored; Milton's *Areopagitica* and John Stuart Mill's *On Liberty* defend freedom of speech on the ground that the truth will prevail, and many of the most important cases under the First Amendment recite this position. The Framers undoubtedly believed it. As a general matter it is true. But the Constitution does not make the dominance of truth a necessary condition of freedom of speech. To say that it does would be to confuse an outcome of free speech with a necessary condition for the application of the amendment.

A power to limit speech on the ground that truth has not yet prevailed and is not likely to prevail implies the power to declare truth. At some point the government must be able to say (as Indianapolis has said): "We know what the truth is, yet a free exchange of speech has not driven out falsity, so that we must now prohibit falsity." If the government may declare the truth, why wait for the failure of speech? Under the First Amendment, however, there is no such thing as a false idea, so the government may not restrict speech on the ground that in a free exchange truth is not yet dominant.

Much speech is dangerous. Chemists whose work might help someone build a bomb, political theorists whose papers might start political movements that lead to riots, speakers whose ideas attract violent protesters, all these and more leave loss in their wake.

No amount of struggle with particular words and phrases in this ordinance can leave anything in effect. The district court came to the same conclusion. Its judgment is therefore

AFFIRMED.

[Judge Swygert's concurring opinion is omitted.]

Points for Discussion

1. **I accept your argument, but you still lose.** Indianapolis justified its regulation by contending that speech portraying women as subordinate leads to the

mistreatment of women. The Court readily agreed: "we accept the premises of this legislation." So why did the Court then declare the law unconstitutional? Can you articulate the Court's reasoning? Do you agree with it?

2. **What if truth fails to prevail in the marketplace of ideas?** Under the marketplace of ideas theory, the appropriate response to bad ideas is not censorship but good ideas. But Indianapolis contended that counter-speech had failed to eliminate misogynistic speech. Since truth had not prevailed, the city argued, it was appropriate for the government to intervene to suppress the speech.

   The Court rejected this argument. Why did it do so? Do you think that the marketplace of ideas can suffer from market failures just as economic markets do? If so, do you think that the government should be permitted to intervene to correct for these "failures"?

b. May Government Suppress Hate Speech Because It Causes Emotional Distress? Or Is the Response to Hate Speech Counter-Speech?

Should the government be able to regulate hate speech because of the emotional distress it causes the targeted groups?

Arguably no case better captures this issue than a case from the 1970s concerning a demand by neo-Nazis to march in Skokie, Illinois, a Chicago suburb with a large Jewish population, including thousands of Holocaust survivors. One can only imagine the trauma these residents would suffer when seeing men in Swastika-adorned uniforms marching through their neighborhood.

The Skokie city council tried to stop the march through a series of ordinances, including a ban on disseminating literature promoting or inciting hatred and a prohibition on parading in military-style uniforms. The neo-Nazis challenged the Skokie ordinances as unconstitutional.

The challenges worked their way through the state courts, a federal district court, and a federal appellate court. The Supreme Court made a brief appearance in the case to remind the Illinois state courts that prior restraints had to be afforded prompt judicial review.

The following opinion from the Seventh Circuit held the Skokie ordinances unconstitutional. The court readily acknowledged that a neo-Nazi march would "seriously disturb, emotionally and mentally, at least some, and probably many of the residents." Nevertheless, it ruled in favor of the neo-Nazis. What was its rationale for doing so?

Collin v. Smith

United States Court of Appeals, Seventh Circuit, 1978
578 F.2d 1197

PELL, CIRCUIT JUDGE.

Plaintiff-appellee, the National Socialist Party of America (NSPA) is a political group described by its leader, plaintiff-appellee Frank Collin, as a Nazi party. Among NSPA's more controversial and generally unacceptable beliefs are that black persons are biologically inferior to white persons and should be expatriated to Africa as soon as possible and that American Jews have "inordinate political and financial power" in the world and are "in the forefront of the international Communist revolution." NSPA members affect a uniform reminiscent of those worn by members of the German Nazi Party during the Third Reich, and display a swastika thereon and on a red, white, and black flag they frequently carry.

The Village of Skokie, Illinois, a defendant-appellant, is a suburb north of Chicago. It has a large Jewish population, including as many as several thousand survivors of the Nazi holocaust in Europe before and during World War II. Other defendants-appellants are Village officials.

When Collin and NSPA announced plans to march in front of the Village Hall in Skokie on May 1, 1977, Village officials responded by obtaining in state court a preliminary injunction against the demonstration. After state courts refused to stay the injunction pending appeal, the United States Supreme Court ordered a stay. The injunction was subsequently reversed first in part, and then in its entirety. On May 2, 1977, the Village enacted three ordinances to prohibit demonstrations such as the one Collin and NSPA had threatened. This lawsuit seeks declaratory and injunctive relief against enforcement of the ordinances.

Village Ordinance No. 994 is a comprehensive permit system for all parades or public assemblies of more than 50 persons. It requires permit applicants to obtain \$300,000 in public liability insurance and \$50,000 in property damage insurance. One of the prerequisites for a permit is a finding by the appropriate officials that the assembly will not portray criminality, depravity or lack of virtue in, or incite violence, hatred, abuse or hostility toward a person or group of persons by reason of reference to religious, racial, ethnic, national or regional affiliation. Another is a finding that the permit activity will not be conducted "for an unlawful purpose." To parade or assemble without a permit is a crime, punishable by fines from \$5 to \$500.

Village Ordinance No. 995 prohibits the dissemination of any materials within the Village of Skokie which promotes and incites hatred against persons by reason of their race, national origin, or religion, and is intended to do so. "Dissemination of materials" includes publication or display or distribution of posters, signs, handbills, or writings and public display of markings and clothing of symbolic significance. Violation is a crime punishable by fine of up to $500, or imprisonment of up to six months. Village Ordinance No. 996 prohibits public demonstrations by members of political parties while wearing "military-style" uniforms, and violation is punishable as in 995.

Collin and NSPA applied for a permit to march on July 4, 1977, which was denied on the ground the application disclosed an intention to violate 996. The Village apparently applies 994 so that an intention to violate 995 or 996 establishes an "unlawful purpose" for the march or assembly. The permit application stated that the march would last about a half hour, and would involve 30 to 50 demonstrators wearing uniforms including swastikas and carrying a party banner with a swastika and placards with statements thereon such as "White Free Speech," "Free Speech for the White Man," and "Free Speech for White America." A single file sidewalk march that would not disrupt traffic was proposed, without speeches or the distribution of handbills or literature. Counsel for the Village advises us that the Village does not maintain that Collin and NSPA will behave other than as described in the permit applications.

The district court, after considering memoranda, exhibits, depositions, and live testimony, issued a comprehensive and thorough opinion granting relief to Collin and NSPA. On its appeal, the Village concedes the invalidity of the insurance requirements as applied to these plaintiffs and of the uniform prohibition of 996.

The conflict underlying this litigation has commanded substantial public attention, and engendered considerable and understandable emotion. We would hopefully surprise no one by confessing personal views that NSPA's beliefs and goals are repugnant to the core values held generally by residents of this country, and, indeed, to much of what we cherish in civilization. As judges sworn to defend the Constitution, however, we cannot decide this or any case on that basis. Ideological tyranny, no matter how worthy its motivation, is forbidden as much to appointed judges as to elected legislators.

We cannot be unmindful of the horrors associated with the Nazi regime of the Third Reich, with which to some real and apparently intentional degree appellees associate themselves. Nor does the record allow us to ignore the certainty that appellees know full well that, in light of their views and the historical associations they would bring with them to Skokie, many people would find their demonstration extremely mentally and emotionally disturbing, or the suspicion that such a result may be relished by appellees.

But our task here is to decide whether the First Amendment protects the activity in which appellees wish to engage, not to render moral judgment on their views or tactics. No authorities need be cited to establish the proposition, which the Village does not dispute, that First Amendment rights are truly precious and fundamental to our national life. Nor is this truth without relevance to the saddening historical images this case inevitably arouses. It is, after all, in part the fact that our constitutional system protects minorities unpopular at a particular time or place from governmental harassment and intimidation, that distinguishes life in this country from life under the Third Reich.

Before undertaking specific analysis of the clash between the Village ordinances and appellees' desires to demonstrate in Skokie, it will be helpful to establish some general principles of pertinence to the decision required of us. Putting to one side for the moment the question of whether the content of appellees' views and symbols makes a constitutional difference here, we find we are unable to deny that the activities in which the appellees wish to engage are within the ambit of the First Amendment.

These activities involve the "cognate rights" of free speech and free assembly. "The wearing of an armband for the purpose of expressing certain views is the type of symbolic act that is within the Free Speech Clause of the First Amendment." Standing alone, at least, it is "closely akin to 'pure speech' which, we have repeatedly held, is entitled to comprehensive protection under the First Amendment." The same thing can be said of NSPA's intended display of a party flag, and of the messages intended for the placards party members would carry. Likewise, although marching, parading, and picketing, because they involve conduct implicating significant interests in maintaining public order, are less protected than pure speech, they are nonetheless subject to significant First Amendment protection. Indeed, an orderly and peaceful demonstration, with placards, in the vicinity of a seat of government, is "an exercise of the basic constitutional rights of speech, assembly, and petition in their most pristine and classic form."

No doubt, the Nazi demonstration could be subjected to reasonable regulation of its time, place, and manner. Because the ordinances turn on the content of the demonstration, they are necessarily not time, place, or manner regulations. Legislating against the content of First Amendment activity, however, launches the government on a slippery and precarious path.

We first consider ordinance 995, prohibiting the dissemination of materials which would promote hatred towards persons on the basis of their heritage. The Village would apparently apply this provision to NSPA's display of swastikas, their uniforms, and, perhaps, to the content of their placards.

The ordinance cannot be sustained on the basis of some of the more obvious exceptions to the rule against content control. While some would no doubt be willing to label appellees' views and symbols obscene, the constitutional rule that obscenity is unprotected applies only to material with erotic content. Furthermore, although the

Village introduced evidence in the district court tending to prove that some individuals, at least, might have difficulty restraining their reactions to the Nazi demonstration, the Village tells us that it does not rely on a fear of responsive violence to justify the ordinance, and does not even suggest that there will be any physical violence if the march is held. This confession takes this case out of the scope of *Brandenburg* and *Feiner*. The Village does not argue otherwise. The concession also eliminates any argument based on the fighting words doctrine of *Chaplinsky*.

Four basic arguments are advanced by the Village to justify the content restrictions of 995. First, it is said that the content criminalized by 995 is "totally lacking in social content," and that it consists of "false statements of fact" in which there is "no constitutional value." We disagree that, if applied to the proposed demonstration, the ordinance can be said to be limited to "statements of fact," false or otherwise. No handbills are to be distributed; no speeches are planned. To the degree that the symbols in question can be said to assert anything specific, it must be the Nazi ideology, which cannot be treated as a mere false "fact."

We may agree with the district court that if any philosophy should be regarded as completely unacceptable to civilized society, that of plaintiffs, who, while disavowing on the witness stand any advocacy of genocide, have nevertheless deliberately identified themselves with a regime whose record of brutality and barbarism is unmatched in modern history, would be a good place to start. But there can be no legitimate start down such a road.

Under the First Amendment there is no such thing as a false idea. However pernicious an opinion may seem, we depend for its correction not on the conscience of judges and juries but on the competition of other ideas. In the words of Justice Jackson, "every person must be his own watchman for truth, because the forefathers did not trust any government to separate the true from the false for us." The asserted falseness of Nazi dogma, and, indeed, its general repudiation, simply do not justify its suppression.

The Village's second argument, and the one on which principal reliance is placed, centers on *Beauharnais*. There a conviction was upheld under a statute prohibiting, in language substantially (and perhaps not unintentionally) similar to that used in the ordinance here, the dissemination of materials promoting racial or religious hatred.

In our opinion Beauharnais does not support ordinance 995, for two independent reasons. First, the rationale of that decision turns quite plainly on the strong tendency of the prohibited utterances to cause violence and disorder. It may be questioned, after cases such as *Gooding v. Wilson* and *Brandenburg*, whether the tendency to induce violence approach sanctioned implicitly in *Beauharnais* would pass constitutional muster today. Assuming that it would, however, it does not support ordinance 995, because the Village does not assert appellees' possible violence, an audience's possible responsive violence, or possible violence against third parties by those incited by appellees, as justifications for 995.

The Village asserts that *Beauharnais* implicitly sanctions prohibiting the use of First Amendment rights to invoke racial or religious hatred even without reference to fears of violence. We agree with the district court that decisions in the quarter-century since *Beauharnais* have abrogated the *Chaplinsky* dictum, made one of the premises of *Beauharnais*, that the punishment of libel "has never been thought to raise any Constitutional problem." [Subsequent cases provide] indisputable evidence that libel does indeed now raise serious and knotty First Amendment problems.

3rd argument.

The Village's third argument is that it has a policy of fair housing, which the dissemination of racially defamatory material could undercut. We reject this argument without extended discussion. That the effective exercise of First Amendment rights may undercut a given government's policy on some issue is, indeed, one of the purposes of those rights. No distinction is constitutionally admissible that turns on the intrinsic justice of the particular policy in issue.

4th argument

The Village's fourth argument is that the Nazi march, involving as it does the display of uniforms and swastikas, will create a substantive evil that it has a right to prohibit: the infliction of psychic trauma on resident holocaust survivors and other Jewish residents. The Village points out that Illinois recognizes the "new tort" of intentional infliction of severe emotional distress, the coverage of which may well include personally directed racial slurs. Assuming that specific individuals could proceed in tort under this theory to recover damages provably occasioned by the proposed march, and that a First Amendment defense would not bar the action, it is nonetheless quite a different matter to criminalize protected First Amendment conduct in anticipation of such results.

It would be grossly insensitive to deny, as we do not, that the proposed demonstration would seriously disturb, emotionally and mentally, at least some, and probably many of the Village's residents. The problem with engrafting an exception on the First Amendment for such situations is that they are indistinguishable in principle from speech that "invites dispute, induces a condition of unrest, creates dissatisfaction with conditions as they are, or even stirs people to anger." Yet these are among the "high purposes" of the First Amendment. It is perfectly clear that a state [may] not "make criminal the peaceful expression of unpopular views." Likewise, "mere public intolerance or animosity cannot be the basis for abridgement of these constitutional freedoms."

It is said that the proposed march is not speech, or even "speech plus," but rather an invasion, intensely menacing no matter how peacefully conducted. The Village's expert psychiatric witness, in fact, testified that the effect of the march would be much the same regardless of whether uniforms and swastikas were displayed, due to the intrusion of self-proclaimed Nazis into what he characterized as predominately Jewish "turf." There is room under the First Amendment for the government to protect targeted listeners from offensive speech, but only when the speaker intrudes on the privacy of the home, or a captive audience cannot practically avoid exposure. The Supreme Court has consistently stressed that "we are often 'captives' outside the sanctuary of the home and subject to objectionable speech." The ability of government, consonant with the Constitution, to shut off discourse solely to protect others from hearing it is, in other words, dependent upon a showing that substantial privacy interests are being invaded in an essentially intolerable manner. Any broader view of this authority would effectively empower a majority to silence dissidents simply as a matter of personal predilections.

This case does not involve intrusion into people's homes. There need be no captive audience, as Village residents may, if they wish, simply avoid the Village Hall for thirty minutes on a Sunday afternoon, which no doubt would be their normal course of conduct on a day when the Village Hall was not open in the regular course of business. Absent such intrusion or captivity, there is no justifiable substantial privacy interest to save 995 from constitutional infirmity, when it attempts, by fiat, to declare the entire Village, at all times, a privacy zone that may be sanitized from the offensiveness of Nazi ideology and symbols.

We conclude that 995 may not be applied to criminalize the conduct of the proposed demonstration. Because it is susceptible to such an application, we also conclude that it suffers from substantial overbreadth, even if some of the purposes 995 is said to serve might constitutionally be protectible by an appropriate and narrower ordinance. The latter conclusion is also supported by the fact that the ordinance could conceivably be applied to criminalize dissemination of The Merchant of Venice or a vigorous discussion of the merits of reverse racial discrimination in Skokie. Although there is reason to think, as the district court concluded, that the ordinance is fatally vague as well, because it turns in part on subjective reactions to prohibited conduct, we do not deem it necessary to rest our decision on that ground.

Our decision that 995 cannot constitutionally be applied to the proposed march necessarily means that a permit for the march may not be denied on the basis of anticipated violations thereof. We turn to the question of whether the similar provision built into 994 can be the basis of a permit denial.

The answer really follows with even greater strength from our conclusion on 995. Because 994 gives to Village "officials the power to deny use of a forum in advance of actual expression," it is a prior restraint, which thus "comes to this Court with a heavy presumption against its constitutional validity."

The presumption against prior restraints is heavier and the degree of protection broader than that against limits on expression imposed by criminal penalties. Behind the distinction is a theory deeply etched in our law: a free society prefers to punish the few who abuse rights of speech after they break the law than to throttle them and all others beforehand.

The preparation and issuance of this opinion has not been an easy task, or one which we have relished. Recognizing the implication that often seems to follow over-protestation, we nevertheless feel compelled once again to express our repugnance at the doctrines which the appellees desire to profess publicly. Indeed, it is a source of extreme regret that after several thousand years of attempting to strengthen the often thin coating of civilization with which humankind has attempted to hide brutal animal-like instincts, there would still be those who would resort to hatred and vilification of fellow human beings because of their racial background or their religious beliefs, or for that matter, because of any reason at all.

Retaining meaning in civil rights, particularly those many of the founding fathers believed sufficiently important as to delay the approval of the Constitution until they could be included in the Bill of Rights, seldom seems to be accomplished by the easy cases, however, and it was not so here.

Although we would have thought it unnecessary to say so, it apparently deserves emphasis in the light of the dissent's reference to this court apologizing as to the result, that our regret at the use appellees plan to make of their rights is not in any sense an apology for upholding the First Amendment. The result we have reached is dictated by the fundamental proposition that if these civil rights are to remain vital for all, they must protect not only those society deems acceptable, but also those whose ideas it quite justifiably rejects and despises.

The judgment of the district court is AFFIRMED.

[Judge Wood, Jr.'s concurring opinion and Judge Sprecher's concurrence in part and dissent in part are omitted.]

Points for Discussion

1. **Could Skokie stop the rally because it would cause the city's residents severe emotional distress?** The Seventh Circuit readily acknowledged the severe emotional distress a neo-Nazi march would cause to Skokie residents, who included many Holocaust survivors. Yet the court ruled in favor of the neo-Nazis. Why did the court hold that a community cannot prohibit hateful speech that will cause its residents great distress? Did you find the court's reasoning persuasive?

2. **The continued viability of *Beauharnais*.** The Skokie government cited the *Beauharnais* opinion to justify the city's regulation of hate speech. Why didn't the court find this argument convincing?

3. **Offensive speech and the captive audience doctrine.** The Seventh Circuit's opinion rejected the argument that the government can suppress speech to protect people from being offended. Why is that so? Why shouldn't the government have the power to protect people from offensive speech?

   The court did recognize two limited exceptions to its rule: "There is room under the First Amendment for the government to protect targeted listeners from offensive speech, but only when the speaker intrudes on the privacy of the home, or a captive audience cannot practically avoid exposure." The first exception recognizes that speech can sometimes be regulated to protect people in the privacy of their homes. In subsequent chapters, we will learn that the Supreme Court agrees that this interest can, in some instances, justify content-based regulation of speech. The second exception is the "captive audience" doctrine. This is the notion that content-based regulation of speech can occasionally be justified when speech is being foisted on an audience who "cannot practically avoid the exposure." The Supreme Court also recognizes this exception, but the Court has emphasized that this doctrine rarely, if ever, applies when people are outside their homes. The Seventh Circuit acknowledged this qualification in its opinion: "The Supreme Court has consistently stressed that we are often 'captives' outside the sanctuary of the home and subject to objectionable speech."

4. **Practice makes perfect.** John Wooden, the legendary college basketball coach who led the UCLA Bruins to 10 NCAA championships in a 12-year period, emphasized the importance of repetition in learning: "The eight laws of learning are explanation, demonstration, imitation, repetition, repetition, repetition, repetition, repetition."

   The *Collin* case provides an excellent opportunity for you to review material you studied in Chapters 3–5. See if you can answer these questions: (1) Why did the court treat the Skokie ordinances as content-based and not content-neutral? (2) Why did the court reject arguments that the neo-Nazi speech could be regulated because it constituted obscenity, incitement, fighting words, or speech that would provoke a hostile audience? (3) Why did the court reject Skokie's argument that ordinance 995 was necessary to protect the city's residents from emotional distress? and (4) What did the court say about overbreadth problems with ordinance 995 and prior restraint problems with ordinance 994?

You Be the Lawyer!

Would you represent this person?

Congratulations! You have become one of the nation's leading First Amendment litigators.

One day the leader of a white supremacist group comes to your office. He wants his group to hold a rally in a city with a large African American population. The leader said he applied to the city for a permit, but the city denied the permit on the grounds that the city's official policy supports diversity, equity, and inclusion and that the group's message would conflict with this policy.

The group's leader would like you to represent him in bringing a First Amendment challenge to the city's denial of the group's permit application. Would you agree to represent him?

Would it make a difference to you if the city is in a state that permits the open carrying of weapons and the group leader told you that many of the rally participants would be bringing weapons with them?

To help guide you in your decision, you might want to read Aryeh Neier's *Defending My Enemy: American Nazis, the Skokie Case, and the Risks of Freedom* (1979). Neier was the executive director of the ACLU when the organization agreed to represent the neo-Nazis seeking to march in Skokie. Neier was Jewish, he was born in Berlin, and his family narrowly escaped Nazi Germany. Almost all of his extended relatives in Germany and Poland were killed by the Nazis.

In the introduction to his book, Neier explained:

> I supported free speech for Nazis when they wanted to march in Skokie in order to defeat Nazis. Defending my enemy is the only way to protect a free society against the enemies of freedom. If that seems to be a paradox, I hope it will not be when you finish reading this book.

One final note. After representing Unite the Right in its effort to hold a rally in Charlottesville, the ACLU announced that it would no longer represent hate groups whose members plan to bring weapons to their rallies. You can read about the ACLU's decision here.

C. The Current Rule: The First Amendment Protects Hate Speech

When you pull the prior cases together, it becomes apparent that the First Amendment protects hate speech. Notwithstanding *Beauharnais*, courts do not treat hate speech as an unprotected category of speech. And courts have rejected arguments that the government may regulate hate speech because it encourages people to engage in wrongful behavior or because the speech causes its targets emotional distress. Unless hate speech fits into an established category of unprotected speech, such as incitement, fighting words, true threats, or harassment in special settings, it is protected by the First Amendment.

There is no Supreme Court opinion after *Beauharnais* that tackles the hate speech issue head-on. The facts of *Brandenburg*, *R.A.V.*, and *Black* all involved hate speech, but the Court implicitly assumed in those cases that hate speech was protected unless it rose to the level of incitement, fighting words, or true threats. The closest the Court has come to addressing hate speech directly is *Matal v. Tam*, 582 U.S. 218 (2017). *Matal* was an atypical hate speech case. The party wishing to use a racially derogatory term was a member of the group that the term disparaged. An Asian-American rock band called itself The Slants, even though this term is considered derogatory toward people of Asian descent. The band wanted to "reclaim" the term and defuse it of its racist connotation.

The group tried to trademark its name, but the U.S. Patent and Trademark Office refused because trademark law prohibited the registration of marks that disparaged people. In *Matal*, the Supreme Court held this prohibition unconstitutional.

In its argument defending the bar on derogatory trademarks, the government contended that the prohibition was necessary to protect "underrepresented groups from being bombarded with demeaning messages in commercial advertising." Here is how Justice Samuel Alito responded to the government's argument in a plurality opinion joined by Chief Justice Roberts, Justice Thomas, and Justice Breyer:

> No matter how the point is phrased, its unmistakable thrust is this: The Government has an interest in preventing speech expressing ideas that offend. And, as we have explained, that idea strikes at the heart of the First Amendment. Speech that demeans on the basis of race, ethnicity, gender, religion, age, disability, or any other similar ground is hateful; but the proudest boast of our free speech jurisprudence is that we protect the freedom to express "the thought that we hate."

Justice Kennedy wrote a concurring opinion, joined by Justices Ginsburg, Sotomayor, and Kagan, that did not join in the above passage from Justice Alito's opinion but did include the following statement:

> A law that can be directed against speech found offensive to some portion of the public can be turned against minority and dissenting views to the detriment of all. The First Amendment does not entrust that power to the government's benevolence. Instead, our reliance must be on the substantial safeguards of free and open discussion in a democratic society.

Points for Discussion

1. **Are there some things you don't boast about?** Justice Alito acknowledged that speech that demeans groups of people is hateful, but he nevertheless said that "the proudest boast of our free speech jurisprudence is that we protect the freedom to express the thought that we hate." Are you comfortable with how he described the protection of hate speech as the "proudest boast" of our free speech jurisprudence? Would you prefer it if he had described it as a regrettable, but necessary, side effect of our commitment to free speech? For example, in *Cohen v. California*, 403 U.S. 15 (1971), the Court described free expression as "powerful medicine" and the resultant offensive speech as a "necessary side effect." Which description do you favor: proud boast or regrettable side effect?

2. **The challenge of defining hate speech**. In deciding to invalidate the non-disparagement provision, Justice Alito pointed out that the provision was unconstitutionally overbroad. As he noted, the provision barred the registration of any mark that "disparages any person, group, or institution," which he said would include marks like "Down with racists" or "Down with sexists." As Justice Alito put it, the non-disparagement provision was a "happy-talk clause."

   Justice Alito's observation goes to a problem that arises any time the Court is asked to declare a category of speech unprotected. Even if the Court were inclined to do so, it would then face the challenge of defining the category with enough precision to avoid sweeping in protected speech.

   For example, try to come up with a definition of hate speech that would deny protection to only "bad" speech but not "good" speech. Can it be done? Or is it possible that your statute could someday be used by government officials in ways that you never intended? Could "Black Lives Matter" be characterized as hate speech toward whites because it does not acknowledge that white lives matter? Could Karl Marx's observation that "religion is the opium of the people" be characterized as hate speech toward religious adherents? Could opposition to same-sex marriage be characterized as hate speech toward gays and lesbians?

This "be careful what you wish for" problem was eloquently captured by Robert Bolt in his play about the life of Sir Thomas More, "A Man for All Seasons." In a famous exchange between More and his future son-in-law, William Roper, More explains why he would give even the devil the benefit of the law:

> **Roper:** So, now you give the Devil the benefit of law!
>
> **More:** Yes! What would you do? Cut a great road through the law to get after the Devil?

Watch It

Rather than read this exchange, why not watch actors perform it? You can do so here.

> **Roper:** Yes, I'd cut down every law in England to do that!
>
> **More:** Oh? And when the last law was down, and the Devil turned 'round on you, where would you hide, Roper, the laws all being flat? This country is planted thick with laws, from coast to coast, Man's laws, not God's! And if you cut them down, and you're just the man to do it, do you really think you could stand upright in the winds that would blow then? Yes, I'd give the Devil the benefit of law, for my own safety's sake!

3. **Do hate speech laws help or hurt minority groups?** Justice Kennedy's concurring opinion in *Matal v. Tam* warns that punishing speech because it offends a segment of the population "can be turned against minority and dissenting views." He suggests that it is safer for all to rely on "free and open discussion." This is a common refrain for those who question the wisdom of hate speech regulations. Nadine Strossen, *Hate: Why We Should Resist It with Free Speech, Not Censorship* 81 (2018) ("laws censoring 'hate speech' have predictably been enforced against those who lack political power, including government critics and members of the very minority groups these laws are intended to protect"); Erica Goldberg, *Free Speech Consequentialism*, 116 Colum. L. Rev. 687, 736–37 (2016) ("The U.S. approach of tolerating the intolerant may actually make society overall more tolerant and more welcoming to marginalized groups"). By contrast, supporters of hate speech regulation contend that societal toleration of hate speech disproportionately harms minority groups and perpetuates their subjugation. Mari J. Matsuda, *Public Response to Racist Speech: Considering the Victim's Story*, 87 Mich. L. Rev. 2320, 2323 (1989) (contending that "an absolutist First Amendment response to hate speech has the effect of perpetuating racism" and that tolerance of hate speech is "not borne by the community at large" but rather is "a psychic

tax imposed on those least able to pay"); Richard Delgado, *Words that Wound: A Tort Action for Racial Insults, Epithets, and Name-Calling*, 17 Harv. Civ. Rts.-Civ. Lib. L. Rev. 133, 173 (1982) (advocating for an independent tort action for racial insults and contending that racial insults further the "tradition of racism").

4. **Hate speech in special settings.** Even if the Supreme Court's decision to protect hate speech is wise, does the government still need greater power to regulate hate speech in special settings such as public schools and universities? Or would giving the government greater power in these contexts be an invitation for government abuse? We will return to this topic in Chapter 11 when we study government regulation of speech in special settings.

A Comparative Perspective

Many other countries, including many European nations, have laws that criminalize hate speech. Does their approach sound better than our approach of protecting hate speech? Have they built a better mousetrap?

The answer might depend on the effectiveness of these hate speech laws. Have they helped reduce racial and religious tensions, or have they had little or no effect? Have the laws unintentionally exacerbated tensions by denying people the opportunity to expel their hatred through speech rather than through conduct? (Recall Justice Louis Brandeis' "safety valve" theory discussed in Chapter 5.)

The answer might also depend on how these hate speech laws are enforced. Are they being applied to speakers whose words are truly hateful and dangerous, or are they being applied to speakers whose words are merely controversial or unpopular?

It is difficult to produce empirical data to answer these questions. Consequently, proponents and opponents of hate speech regulations typically offer anecdotal evidence to support their positions. For example, in her book *HATE: Why We Should Resist It with Free Speech, Not Censorship* 27–29 (2018), former ACLU President Nadine Strossen gives these and other examples in an effort to demonstrate that hate speech laws in Europe have been misused:

- A Danish historian and journalist was convicted for saying there was a high crime rate in areas with large Muslim populations.
- Two British street preachers were convicted for preaching biblical passages that were insulting to LBGTQ persons and Muslims.

- A French court upheld the conviction of pro-Palestinian activists for wearing T-shirts that said "Long Live Palestine, boycott Israel" and handing out flyers saying "buying Israeli products means legitimizing crimes in Gaza."
- A 15-year-old British boy was charged and investigated for displaying a sign that said "Scientology is not a religion, it is a dangerous cult."

Are these examples of hate speech laws run amok, or are they appropriate attempts to curb hateful speech? Is it your sense that hate speech laws have spared European countries from racial and religious tensions?

Test Your Knowledge

To assess your understanding of the material in this chapter, click here to take a quiz.

Chapter Seven

May Government Regulate Speech to Promote Morality?

Obscenity, Child Pornography, Indecency, Profanity, and Depictions of Violence

Should the government be able to regulate speech that is considered immoral?

From the start, this question seems riddled with problems. First and foremost, the question presupposes a societal consensus about what is immoral. Yet such a consensus does not exist. We might certainly hope that there is a societal consensus that murder is immoral, but it is doubtful there is a consensus about the propriety of using profane language on the radio or whether people should have a right to access graphic sexual materials.

Morality is a contested concept toward which people have varying attitudes. As Justice John Harlan famously observed, "one man's vulgarity is another's lyric."

But, for argument's sake, let's assume that there was a societal consensus about which speech was immoral. What then? Should that be enough to justify suppression of this speech?

That leads to the second problem. Wouldn't government censorship of immoral speech violate the "marketplace of ideas" principle that the government, including Supreme Court justices, should not be deciding which ideas Americans may hear? In the previous chapter, we observed how an unflinching commitment to this principle led courts to protect hate speech. In this chapter, we ponder whether there should be an exception to this principle for sexual imagery, profane language, and depictions of violence.

Our study covers the following topics:

- ***Obscenity:*** May the government regulate the distribution, display, or possession of graphically sexual speech?

- ***Child pornography:*** May the government regulate the distribution, display, or possession of child pornography?
- ***Indecent and profane speech:*** May the government regulate speech that is not obscene but is still sexual or profane?
- ***Depictions of violence:*** May the government regulate speech that depicts violence?

Keep in mind that we are concentrating on obscene, indecent, and violent speech that does not rise to the level of incitement, fighting words, or a true threat. If speech fits into one of those categories, the government could regulate it on that basis. Our focus is on whether speech may be regulated solely because of its sexual, profane, or violent content.

A. Obscenity: Speech Appealing to the Prurient Interest

Societal attitudes about sexual material have varied by time and place. Professor Geoffrey Stone has noted that people in ancient Greece and Rome viewed sex "as a natural and positive part of human experience" untethered to concerns of "sin, shame, or religion."[1] Stone says that literature from this era "depicted sex quite explicitly and in all of its various forms."[2]

Even the rise of Christianity, with its more negative perception of sex, did not translate into widespread censorship:

> Although the attitude towards sex in Western culture changed radically with the advent of Christianity, for most of Western history neither the Church nor the state censored sexual expression because it was thought to be obscene. Indeed, through the Middle Ages, the Renaissance, and the era of the Enlightenment, sexual expression and imagery were common, widespread, legal, and quite explicit, and this was true in the American colonies, as well as in England.[3]

Stone found no laws in the American colonies regulating obscene materials. Instead, bookstores offered "an extraordinary array of erotica."[4] The sale and pos-

---

[1] Geoffrey R. Stone, *Sex and the First Amendment: The Long and Winding History of Obscenity Law*, 17 First Amend. L. Rev. 134 (2022). For a comprehensive treatment of the subject, see Geoffrey R. Strone, Sex and the Constitution: Sex, Religion and Law from America's Origins to the Twenty-First Century (2017).

[2] Stone, *supra*, *Sex and the First Amendment*, at 134.

[3] *Id.* at 134–35.

[4] *Id.* at 135.

session of this material, Stone observed, was "not thought to be any of the state's business."[5]

1. The Rise of Obscenity Regulation and the Supreme Court's Response: The Path to *United States v. Roth*

The country's lax treatment of obscenity came under challenge in the early 19th century. The Second Great Awakening revived public interest in religious morality and prompted a movement to harmonize American law with evangelical Christian values. It was during this period that the country had its first obscenity prosecution. In 1815, the Pennsylvania Supreme Court upheld the conviction of a tavern owner for displaying an image that corrupted young people by "inflaming their passions."[6]

The pendulum swung back toward greater liberality in the mid-1880s. During this period, one could find New York City pushcart vendors selling photographs of women "in various stages of undress" and "concert saloons" with naked entertainers.[7]

Then, in the late 19th century, the pendulum swung back. This occurred in response to the mass migration of young men from rural to urban areas. As Professor Margaret Blanchard has explained, religious groups were concerned that "these inexperienced youths, if left to their own devices after work, might fall prey to the temptations of billiard parlors, bars, theaters, gambling tables, and houses of prostitution."[8] A campaign was thus launched to help prevent these youths from slipping into debauchery:

> This campaign appealed to individuals who believed that the national moral atmosphere needed to be purified in order to preserve a stable social structure. The era spawned the Young Men's Christian Association (YMCA), the Sunday school movement, the Salvation Army, and the Moody and Sankey revivals. The campaign also gave rise to the first great crusader for cleaning up American literature and artwork, Anthony Comstock.[9]

Anthony Comstock's name became synonymous with this era of heightened censorship. Working with the YMCA as the head of its Committee for the Suppression of Vice, Comstock persuaded New York to enact an obscenity law. More significantly, in 1873, he succeeded in getting Congress to adopt a law prohibiting the mailing of

---

5 *Id.*

6 *Commonwealth v. Sharpless*, 2 Serg. & Rawle 91, 102 (Pa. 1815).

7 *Stone, supra* note 1, *Sex and the First Amendment* at 136.

8 Margaret A. Blanchard, *The American Urge to Censor: Freedom of Expression versus the Desire to Sanitize—From Anthony Comstock to 2 Live Crew*, 23 Wm. & Mary L. Rev. 741, 744–45 (1992).

9 *Id.* at 745.

obscene materials. The law, colloquially referred to as the Comstock Act, threatened violators with fines and prison sentences of up to 10 years.[10]

Courts called upon to adjudicate obscenity cases needed a definition of obscenity. Many turned to an 1868 English precedent, *Regina v. Hicklin*, L.R. 3 Q.B. 360, in which Lord Chief Justice Cockburn articulated what would become a canonical test: "whether the tendency of the matter charged is to deprave and corrupt those whose minds are open to such immoral influences." Cockburn's test favored censorship because it focused on the reaction of the most vulnerable people to the most obscene aspects of a work. Justice William Brennan would later characterize *Hicklin* as judging obscenity "by the effect of isolated passages upon the most susceptible persons."[11]

Professor Stephen Gillers found American courts' reliance on *Hicklin* "muddled" and "inconsistent."[12] Judges eager to uphold censorship embraced the opinion. Judges disinclined to censor found ways to "escape the *Hicklin* straitjacket."[13] *Hicklin* nonetheless had a substantial censorial impact in the late 19th and early 20th centuries. During this period, books that would later be hailed as classic works of literature, such as D.H. Lawrence's *Lady Chatterley's Lover*, Edmund Wilson's *Memoirs of Hecate County*, and Theodore Dreiser's *An American Tragedy*, were found to be obscene under the *Hicklin* test.[14]

One important victory for censorship opponents was delivered by John W. Woolsey, a federal district judge in New York who refused to permit the confiscation and destruction of copies of James Joyce's *Ulysses*.[15] Woolsey focused on the book's impact on the average reader, not the most prudish. As Woolsey explained, "It is only with the normal person that the law is concerned." To apply this test, Woolsey read the book himself. He also sought the opinions of "two friends of mine." Here is a sampling of Judge Woolsey's evaluation:

> "Ulysses" is not an easy book to read. It is brilliant and dull, intelligible and obscure, by turns. In many places it seems to me to be disgusting, but although it contains many words usually considered dirty, I have not found anything that I consider to be dirt for dirt's sake. Each word of the book contributes like a bit of mosaic to the detail of the picture which Joyce is seeking to construct for his readers.

---

10 *Id.* at 747–48.

11 *Roth v. United States*, 354 U.S. 476, 489 (1957).

12 Stephen Gillers, *A Tendency to Deprave and Corrupt: The Transformation of American Obscenity Law from Hicklin to Ulysses II*, 85 Wash. U. L. Rev. 215, 219 (2007).

13 *Id.*

14 Rodney A. Smolla, Smolla & Nimmer on Freedom of Speech § 14:5 (2023).

15 *United States v. One Book Called "Ulysses,"* 5 F. Supp. 182 (S.D.N.Y. 1933).

Woolsey's friends agreed, and Woolsey denied the government's motion for forfeiture and destruction of Joyce's book.

James Joyce

The Supreme Court did not squarely address the obscenity issue until 1957, when it issued its opinion in *Roth v. United States*, 354 U.S. 476 (1957). Justice Brennan, who had joined the Supreme Court a year earlier, wrote the majority opinion. It was an opinion he would later regret.

Justice Brennan's core holding was unequivocal: "We hold that obscenity is not within the area of constitutionally protected speech or press." To reach this conclusion, he built upon the categorical approach the Court had articulated in *Chaplinsky*. Indeed, *Chaplinsky* had included obscene speech in its list of unprotected categories. As Justice Brennan explained:

> The protection given speech and press was fashioned to assure unfettered interchange of ideas for the bringing about of political and social changes desired by the people. All ideas having even the slightest redeeming social importance—unorthodox ideas, controversial ideas, even ideas hateful to the prevailing climate of opinion—have the full protection of the guaranties, unless excludable because they encroach upon the limited area of more important interests. But implicit in the history of the First Amendment is the rejection of obscenity as utterly without redeeming social importance.

> This rejection for that reason is mirrored in the universal judgment that obscenity should be restrained, reflected in the international agreement of over 50 nations, in the obscenity laws of all of the 48 States, and in the 20 obscenity laws enacted by the Congress from 1842 to 1956. This is the same judgment expressed by this Court in *Chaplinsky v. New Hampshire.*

While Justice Brennan declared obscene speech unprotected, he also emphasized that "sex and obscenity are not synonymous":

> Obscene material is material which deals with sex in a manner appealing to prurient interest. The portrayal of sex, *e.g.*, in art, literature and scientific works, is not itself sufficient reason to deny material the constitutional protection of freedom of speech and press. Sex, a great and mysterious motive force in human life, has indisputably been a subject of absorbing interest to mankind through the ages; it is one of the vital problems of human interest and public concern.

As this passage suggests, a critical aspect factoring into obscenity's unprotected status is its appeal to the "prurient" interest. That's not a term one encounters in everyday conversation. In a footnote of his opinion, Justice Brennan defined prurient as "material having a tendency to excite lustful thoughts." In the same footnote, he also included a seemingly more rigorous definition from the Model Penal Code: "A thing is obscene if, considered as a whole, its predominant appeal is to prurient interest, *i.e.*, a shameful or morbid interest in nudity, sex, or excretion, and if it goes substantially beyond customary limits of candor in description or representation of such matters."

Points for Discussion

1. **Distinguishing sex from obscenity.** Justice Brennan drew a distinction between speech about sex, which is protected by the First Amendment, and obscene speech, which is not. Do you think the line between these two is clear? Do you think that lower courts would know how to apply this distinction?

2. **Distinguishing between immoral ideas and obscenity.** In *Kingsley International Pictures Corp. v. Regents of New York*, 360 U.S. 684 (1959), the Court clarified that the obscenity exception does not give the government the power to suppress immoral ideas. The case concerned a New York movie licensing law that prohibited the exhibition of movies that were "immoral," which was defined to include portrayals of "sexual immorality" as being desirable or acceptable. Based on this law, a licensing board had refused to issue a license for the movie "Lady Chatterley's Lover" because it conveyed the idea that adultery is sometimes desirable. The Supreme Court found the New York law unconstitutional. The Court

described the statute as giving a meaning to sexual immorality that was "entirely different" from the meaning of obscenity. The Court said New York was trying to suppress the "idea" that sexual immorality may be desirable, but this idea was fully protected by the First Amendment. The First Amendment, the Court observed, "protected advocacy of the opinion that adultery may sometimes be proper, no less than advocacy of socialism or the single tax."

3. **Why no requirement of a clear and present danger?** In Chapter 5, we learned that the government cannot punish speech that encourages or advocates unlawful action unless the speech is likely to lead to imminent lawbreaking. Those challenging the obscenity laws at issue in *Roth* contended that obscene speech should similarly be protected absent evidence of a connection between obscene speech and antisocial conduct. But Justice Brennan rejected this argument outright. He said that obscenity's unprotected status obviated any need to show a likelihood that the speech would lead to unlawful action.

   If you weave together the rules we learned in Chapter 5 about incitement, fighting words, and threats, in Chapter 6 about hate speech, and in this chapter about obscene speech, you end up with a legal regime that protects neo-Nazi and Klan speech absent evidence that it is likely to lead to imminent harm, but denies protection to graphic sexual speech absent any evidence of imminent harm. Do these rules make sense to you, or do they seem topsy-turvy?

2. The Challenge of Defining "Obscenity": From "I Know It When I See It" to the *Miller* Test

Justice Brennan's holding in *Roth*, that obscene speech is not protected by the First Amendment, remains true to this day. But Justice Brennan also recognized that obscenity must be carefully defined to ensure that it did not become a gaping exception to the First Amendment's general ban on government censorship. As Justice Brennan put it in *Roth*, "The door barring federal and state intrusion into this area cannot be left ajar; it must be kept tightly closed and opened only the slightest crack necessary to prevent encroachment upon more important interests."

In the years following *Roth*, the justices struggled mightily to come up with a definition of obscenity that was acceptable to a majority of the Court. Two justices, Hugo Black and William Douglas, thought that *Roth* was wrongly decided and that adults had a right to access obscene speech. Of the remaining seven justices, some thought that obscene speech meant "hardcore pornography." Justice Potter Stewart acknowledged that he could not easily define hardcore pornography but felt confident in saying, "I know it when I see it." *Jacobellis v. Ohio*, 378 U.S. 184, 197 (1964) (Stewart, J., concurring).

The closest the Court came to a majority was in *Memoirs v. Massachusetts*, 383 U.S. 413 (1966), when three justices agreed to a definition that, among other things, provided that sexual material would be considered obscene only if it was "utterly without redeeming social value."

When convictions for exhibiting obscene films came to the Court during this period, the justices had no choice but to watch the films and then determine whether a majority of the justices, each using his own standard, thought the film was obscene. If less than a majority found the movie obscene, the conviction would be reversed. This practice came to be known as "Redrupping" after the case of *Redrup v. New York*, 386 U.S. 767 (1967). Justices Douglas and Black, who rejected the premise of an obscenity exception, didn't bother attending the screenings. "If I want to go see that film," Justice Black later said, "I should pay my money."[16]

Finally, in 1973, a majority of the justices settled on a definition of obscenity in *Miller v. California*. On the same day, the Court decided the accompanying case *Paris Adult Theatre I v. Slaton*. Chief Justice Warren Burger wrote the majority opinions in both cases.

Miller v. California

Supreme Court of the United States, 1973
413 U.S. 15

MR. CHIEF JUSTICE BURGER delivered the opinion of the Court.

This is one of a group of "obscenity-pornography" cases being reviewed by the Court in a re-examination of standards enunciated in earlier cases involving what Mr. Justice Harlan called "the intractable obscenity problem."

Appellant conducted a mass mailing campaign to advertise the sale of illustrated books, euphemistically called "adult" material. After a jury trial, he was convicted of violating California Penal Code § 311.2(a), a misdemeanor, by knowingly distributing obscene matter, and the Appellate Department, Superior Court of California, County of Orange, summarily affirmed the judgment without opinion. The brochures advertise four books entitled "Intercourse," "Man-Woman," "Sex Orgies Illustrated," and "An Illustrated History of Pornography," and a film entitled "Marital Intercourse." While the brochures contain some descriptive printed material, primarily they consist of pictures and drawings very explicitly depicting men and women in groups of two or more engaging in a variety of sexual activities, with genitals often prominently displayed.

---

16 Bob Woodward & Scott Armstrong, The Brethren: Inside the Supreme Court 198 (1979).

This case involves the application of a State's criminal obscenity statute to a situation in which sexually explicit materials have been thrust by aggressive sales action upon unwilling recipients who had in no way indicated any desire to receive such materials. This Court has recognized that the States have a legitimate interest in prohibiting dissemination or exhibition of obscene material when the mode of dissemination carries with it a significant danger of offending the sensibilities of unwilling recipients or of exposure to juveniles. It is in this context that we are called on to define the standards which must be used to identify obscene material that a State may regulate without infringing on the First Amendment as applicable to the States through the Fourteenth Amendment.

This much has been categorically settled by the Court, that obscene material is unprotected by the First Amendment. We acknowledge, however, the inherent dangers of undertaking to regulate any form of expression. State statutes designed to regulate obscene materials must be carefully limited. As a result, we now confine the permissible scope of such regulation to works which depict or describe sexual conduct. That conduct must be specifically defined by the applicable state law, as written or authoritatively construed. A state offense must also be limited to works which, taken as a whole, appeal to the prurient interest in sex, which portray sexual conduct in a patently offensive way, and which, taken as a whole, do not have serious literary, artistic, political, or scientific value.

The basic guidelines for the trier of fact must be: (a) whether "the average person, applying contemporary community standards" would find that the work, taken as a whole, appeals to the prurient interest; (b) whether the work depicts or describes, in a patently offensive way, sexual conduct specifically defined by the applicable state law; and (c) whether the work, taken as a whole, lacks serious literary, artistic, political, or scientific value. We do not adopt as a constitutional standard the "utterly without redeeming social value" test of *Memoirs v. Massachusetts*; that concept has never commanded the adherence of more than three Justices at one time. If a state law that regulates obscene material is thus limited, as written or construed, the First Amendment values applicable to the States through the Fourteenth Amendment are adequately protected by the ultimate power of appellate courts to conduct an independent review of constitutional claims when necessary.

We emphasize that it is not our function to propose regulatory schemes for the States. That must await their concrete legislative efforts. It is possible, however, to give a few plain examples of what a state statute could define for regulation under part (b) of the standard announced in this opinion, supra:

(a) Patently offensive representations or descriptions of ultimate sexual acts, normal or perverted, actual or simulated.

(b) Patently offensive representation or descriptions of masturbation, excretory functions, and lewd exhibition of the genitals.

Sex and nudity may not be exploited without limit by films or pictures exhibited or sold in places of public accommodation any more than live sex and nudity can be exhibited or sold without limit in such public places. At a minimum, prurient, patently offensive depiction or description of sexual conduct must have serious literary, artistic, political, or scientific value to merit First Amendment protection. For example, medical books for the education of physicians and related personnel necessarily use graphic illustrations and descriptions of human anatomy. In resolving the inevitably sensitive questions of fact and law, we must continue to rely on the jury system, accompanied by the safeguards that judges, rules of evidence, presumption of innocence, and other protective features provide, as we do with rape, murder, and a host of other offenses against society and its individual members.

Mr. Justice Brennan, author of the opinions of the Court, or the plurality opinions, in *Roth v. United States* and *Memoirs v. Massachusetts*, has abandoned his former position and now maintains that no formulation of this Court, the Congress, or the States can adequately distinguish obscene material unprotected by the First Amendment from protected expression. *Paris Adult Theatre I v. Slaton*, 413 U.S. 49, 73 (Brennan, J., dissenting). Paradoxically, Mr. Justice Brennan indicates that suppression of unprotected obscene material is permissible to avoid exposure to unconsenting adults, as in this case, and to juveniles, although he gives no indication of how the division between protected and nonprotected materials may be drawn with greater precision for these purposes than for regulation of commercial exposure to consenting adults only. Nor does he indicate where in the Constitution he finds the authority to distinguish between a willing "adult" one month past the state law age of majority and a willing "juvenile" one month younger.

Under the holdings announced today, no one will be subject to prosecution for the sale or exposure of obscene materials unless these materials depict or describe patently offensive "hard core" sexual conduct specifically defined by the regulating state law, as written or construed. We are satisfied that these specific prerequisites will provide fair notice to a dealer in such materials that his public and commercial activities may bring prosecution. If the inability to define regulated materials with ultimate, god-like precision altogether removes the power of the States or the Congress to regulate, then "hard core" pornography may be exposed without limit to the juvenile, the passerby, and the consenting adult alike, as, indeed, Mr. Justice Douglas contends. In this belief, however, Mr. Justice Douglas now stands alone.

Under a National Constitution, fundamental First Amendment limitations on the powers of the States do not vary from community to community, but this does not mean that there are, or should or can be, fixed, uniform national standards of precisely what appeals to the "prurient interest" or is "patently offensive." These are essentially questions of fact, and our Nation is simply too big and too diverse for this Court to reasonably expect that such standards could be articulated for all 50 States in a single formulation, even assuming the prerequisite consensus exists. When triers of fact are asked to decide whether "the average person, applying contemporary community standards" would consider certain materials "prurient," it would be unrealistic to require that the answer be based on some abstract formulation. The adversary system, with lay jurors as the usual ultimate factfinders in criminal prosecutions, has historically permitted triers of fact to draw on the standards of their community, guided always by limiting instructions on the law. To require a State to structure obscenity proceedings around evidence of a national "community standard" would be an exercise in futility.

It is neither realistic nor constitutionally sound to read the First Amendment as requiring that the people of Maine or Mississippi accept public depiction of conduct found tolerable in Las Vegas, or New York City. People in different States vary in their tastes and attitudes, and this diversity is not to be strangled by the absolutism of imposed uniformity. We hold that the requirement that the jury evaluate the materials with reference to "contemporary standards of the State of California" serves this protective purpose and is constitutionally adequate.

The dissenting Justices sound the alarm of repression. But, in our view, to equate the free and robust exchange of ideas and political debate with commercial exploitation of obscene material demeans the grand conception of the First Amendment and its high purposes in the historic struggle for freedom. It is a "misuse of the great guarantees of free speech and free press." The First Amendment protects works which, taken as a whole, have serious literary, artistic, political, or scientific value, regardless of whether the government or a majority of the people approve of the ideas these works represent. "The protection given speech and press was fashioned to assure unfettered interchange of *ideas* for the bringing about of political and social changes desired by the people." But the public portrayal of hard-core sexual conduct for its own sake, and for the ensuing commercial gain, is a different matter.

In sum, we (a) reaffirm the *Roth* holding that obscene material is not protected by the First Amendment; (b) hold that such material can be regulated by the States, subject to the specific safeguards enunciated above, without a showing that the material is "utterly without redeeming social value"; and (c) hold that obscenity is to be determined by applying "contemporary community standards," not "national standards." The judgment of the Appellate Department of the Superior Court, Orange County, California, is vacated and the case remanded to that court for further proceedings not inconsistent with the First Amendment standards established by this opinion.

MR. JUSTICE DOUGLAS, dissenting.

Today we leave open the way for California to send a man to prison for distributing brochures that advertise books and a movie under freshly written standards defining obscenity which until today's decision were never the part of any law.

The Court retreats from the earlier formulations of the constitutional test and undertakes to make new definitions. This effort, like the earlier ones, is earnest and well intentioned. The difficulty is that we do not deal with constitutional terms, since "obscenity" is not mentioned in the Constitution or Bill of Rights. And the First Amendment makes no such exception from "the press" which it undertakes to protect nor, as I have said on other occasions, is an exception necessarily implied, for there was no recognized exception to the free press at the time the Bill of Rights was adopted which treated "obscene" publications differently from other types of papers, magazines, and books. So there are no constitutional guidelines for deciding what is and what is not "obscene." The Court is at large because we deal with tastes and standards of literature. What shocks me may be sustenance for my neighbor. What causes one person to boil up in rage over one pamphlet or movie may reflect only his neurosis, not shared by others. We deal here with a regime of censorship which, if adopted, should be done by constitutional amendment after full debate by the people.

We deal with highly emotional, not rational, questions. To many the Song of Solomon is obscene. I do not think we, the judges, were ever given the constitutional power to make definitions of obscenity. If it is to be defined, let the people debate and decide by a constitutional amendment what they want to ban as obscene and what standards they want the legislatures and the courts to apply. Perhaps the people will decide that the path towards a mature, integrated society requires that all ideas competing for acceptance must have no censor. Perhaps they will decide otherwise. Whatever the choice, the courts will have some guidelines. Now we have none except our own predilections.

[Justice Brennan's dissenting opinion, which was joined by Justice Stewart and Justice Marshall, is omitted.]

Paris Adult Theatre I v. Slaton

Supreme Court of the United States, 1973
413 U.S. 49

[*Authors' note:* A local district attorney and court solicitor brought a civil complaint against two Atlanta movie theaters and their owners and managers to enjoin the exhibition of allegedly obscene films. The theaters had signs indicating that they were exhibiting "Atlanta's Finest Mature Feature Films," and the door to the theaters had a sign saying "Adult Theatre—You Must be 21 and able to prove it. If viewing the nude body offends you, Please Do Not Enter." The trial judge assumed that the movies were obscene, but dismissed the complaint on the ground that the Constitution protected the right to exhibit the films in a commercial theater if there was "requisite notice to the public of their nature" and there was "reasonable protection against the exposure of these films to minors." The Georgia Supreme Court reversed, holding that "the sale and delivery of obscene material to willing adults is not protected under the First Amendment."]

dimissed based on state law

MR. CHIEF JUSTICE BURGER delivered the opinion of the Court.

We categorically disapprove the theory, apparently adopted by the trial judge, that obscene, pornographic films acquire constitutional immunity from state regulation simply because they are exhibited for consenting adults only. This holding was properly rejected by the Georgia Supreme Court. Although we have often pointedly recognized the high importance of the state interest in regulating the exposure of obscene materials to juveniles and unconsenting adults, this Court has never declared these to be the only legitimate state interests permitting regulation of obscene material. The States have a long-recognized legitimate interest in regulating the use of obscene material in local commerce and in all places of public accommodation, as long as these regulations do not run afoul of specific constitutional prohibitions. "In an unbroken series of cases extending over a long stretch of this Court's history it has been accepted as a postulate that the primary requirements of decency may be enforced against obscene publications."

In particular, we hold that there are legitimate state interests at stake in stemming the tide of commercialized obscenity, even assuming it is feasible to enforce effective safeguards against exposure to juveniles and to passersby. Rights and interests "other than those of the advocates are involved." These include the interest of the public in the quality of life and the total community environment, the tone of commerce in the great city centers, and, possibly, the public safety itself. The Hill-Link Minority Report of the Commission on Obscenity and Pornography indicates that there is at least an arguable correlation between obscene material and crime. Quite apart from sex crimes, however, there remains one problem of large proportions aptly described by Professor Bickel:

> It concerns the tone of the society, the mode, or to use terms that have perhaps greater currency, the style and quality of life, now and in the future. A man may be entitled to read an obscene book in his room, or expose himself indecently there. We should protect his privacy. But if he demands a right to obtain the books and pictures he wants in the market, and to foregather in public places—discreet, if you will, but accessible to all—with others who share his tastes, then to grant him his right is to affect the world about the rest of us, and to impinge on other privacies. Even supposing that each of us

b/c its in a public place

> can, if he wishes, effectively avert the eye and stop the ear (which, in truth, we cannot), what is commonly read and seen and heard and done intrudes upon us all, want it or not.

As Mr. Chief Justice Warren stated, there is a "right of the Nation and of the States to maintain a decent society."

But, it is argued, there are no scientific data which conclusively demonstrate that exposure to obscene material adversely affects men and women or their society. It is urged on behalf of the petitioners that, absent such a demonstration, any kind of state regulation is "impermissible." We reject this argument. It is not for us to resolve empirical uncertainties underlying state legislation, save in the exceptional case where that legislation plainly impinges upon rights protected by the Constitution itself. Mr. Justice Brennan, speaking for the Court in *Ginsberg v. New York*, 390 U.S. 629, 642–643 (1968), said: "We do not demand of legislatures scientifically certain criteria of legislation. Although there is no conclusive proof of a connection between antisocial behavior and obscene material, the legislature of Georgia could quite reasonably determine that such a connection does or might exist. In deciding *Roth*, this Court implicitly accepted that a legislature could legitimately act on such a conclusion to protect the social interest in order and morality."

If we accept the unprovable assumption that a complete education requires the reading of certain books, and the well-nigh universal belief that good books, plays, and art lift the spirit, improve the mind, enrich the human personality, and develop character, can we then say that a state legislature may not act on the corollary assumption that commerce in obscene books, or public exhibitions focused on obscene conduct, have a tendency to exert a corrupting and debasing impact leading to antisocial behavior?

In this case we hold that the States have a legitimate interest in regulating commerce in obscene material and in regulating exhibition of obscene material in places of public accommodation, including so-called "adult" theaters from which minors are excluded. In light of these holdings, nothing precludes the State of Georgia from the regulation of the allegedly obscene material exhibited in Paris Adult Theatre I or II, provided that the applicable Georgia law, as written or authoritatively interpreted by the Georgia courts, meets the First Amendment standards set forth in *Miller v. California*. The judgment is vacated and the case remanded to the Georgia Supreme Court for further proceedings not inconsistent with this opinion and *Miller v. California*.

MR. JUSTICE BRENNAN, with whom MR. JUSTICE STEWART and MR. JUSTICE MARSHALL join, dissenting.

This case requires the Court to confront once again the vexing problem of reconciling state efforts to suppress sexually oriented expression with the protections of the First Amendment, as applied to the States through the Fourteenth Amendment. I am convinced that the approach initiated 16 years ago in *Roth v. United States*, and culminating in the Court's decision today, cannot bring stability to this area of the law without jeopardizing fundamental First Amendment values, and I have concluded that the time has come to make a significant departure from that approach.

Our experience with the *Roth* approach has certainly taught us that the outright suppression of obscenity cannot be reconciled with the fundamental principles of the First and Fourteenth Amendments. For we have failed to formulate a standard that sharply distinguishes protected from unprotected speech, and out of necessity, we have resorted to the *Redrup* approach, which resolves cases as between the parties, but offers only the most obscure guidance to legislation, adjudication by other courts, and primary conduct. After 16 years of experimentation and debate I am reluctantly forced to the conclusion that none of the available formulas, including the one announced today, can reduce the vagueness to a tolerable level while at the same time striking an acceptable balance between the protections of the First and Fourteenth Amendments, on the one hand, and on the other the asserted state interest in regulating the dissemination of certain sexually oriented materials. Any effort to draw a constitutionally acceptable boundary on state power must resort to such indefinite concepts as "prurient interest," "patent offensiveness," "serious literary value," and the like. The meaning of these concepts necessarily varies with the experience, outlook, and even idiosyncrasies of the person defining them. Although we have assumed that obscenity does exist and that we "know it when we see it," we are manifestly unable to describe it in advance except by reference to concepts so elusive that they fail to distinguish clearly between protected and unprotected speech.

[Justice Douglas' dissenting opinion is omitted.]

Points for Discussion

1. **Parsing the elements of the *Miller* test.** Sixteen years after *Roth*, a majority of justices finally settled on a definition of obscenity. The definition, referred to as the *Miller* test, has three prongs. A work will be considered obscene only if it satisfies all three prongs. If a work fails any prong, it is not obscene, and the First Amendment protects it.

   a. **The "prurient interest" requirement.** The first requirement focuses on "whether the average person, applying contemporary community standards, would find that the work, taken as a whole, appeals to the prurient interest." But what is a prurient interest?

i. **Where is the line between a normal and shameful interest in sex?** As previously noted, in a footnote of his *Roth* opinion, Justice Brennan defined prurient as "material having a tendency to excite lustful thoughts." In the same footnote, he also included a Model Penal Code definition that described prurient as "a shameful or morbid interest in nudity, sex, or excretion" that "goes substantially beyond customary limits of candor."

Of course, if a prurient interest merely means a "tendency to excite lustful thoughts," then much of contemporary media would fit the bill. (The adage "sex sells" didn't come from nowhere.) But in *Brockett v. Spokane Arcades, Inc.*, 472 U.S. 491 (1985), the Court clarified that prurient means more than a "normal" sexual desire:

> We are quite sure that by using the words "lustful thoughts" in footnote 20, the Court was referring to sexual responses over and beyond those that would be characterized as normal. At the end of that footnote, the *Roth* opinion referred to the Model Penal Code definition of obscenity—material whose predominate appeal is to "a shameful or morbid interest in nudity, sex, or excretion" and indicated that it perceived no significant difference between that definition and the meaning of obscenity developed in the case law. This effectively negated any inference that "lustful thoughts" as used earlier in the footnote was limited to or included normal sexual responses.

Do you feel confident the courts will be able to identify the line between a "normal" lustful interest in sex and a "shameful and morbid" one?

ii. **The "average person" considering the work "taken as a whole."** These factors derive from *Roth*'s rejection of the *Hicklin* test. Recall that *Hicklin* judged obscenity based on the effect of isolated passages upon the most susceptible person. The *Miller* test requires factfinders to consider the reaction of an average person to the work as a whole.

iii. **Applying "contemporary community standards."** *Miller* says that the determination of whether a work appeals to the prurient interest should be based on a community standard and not a national standard. As the Court explained, it would be "neither realistic nor constitutionally sound" to require people in Maine and Mississippi to abide by the same standards as people in Las Vegas and New York.

In *Hamling v. United States*, 418 U.S. 87 (1974), the Court clarified that "community standards" meant local community standards and not national or state standards. Indeed, in *Smith v. United States*, 431 U.S. 291 (1977), the Court held that a jury in a federal obscenity prosecution could find that a work appealed to the prurient interest in a local community even though the state where the community was located did not forbid the work's distribution.

Miller's community standard prong poses obvious difficulties for material posted on the internet, where it may be technologically impossible to geographically limit the distribution of the material. Nevertheless, in *Ashcroft v. American Civil Liberties Union*, 535 U.S. 164 (2002), the Court refused to declare a community standard facially unconstitutional when it was incorporated into in a federal law limiting minors' access to indecent sexual materials on the internet. While many of the justices expressed concern that this standard would force speakers to abide by the standards of the most puritanical community in the United States, a majority concluded that the statute's challengers had failed to show that the law was substantially overbroad and therefore facially unconstitutional. In a subsequent opinion, discussed later in this chapter, the Court upheld a lower court order enjoining the enforcement of the federal law on other grounds. *Ashcroft v. American Civil Liberties Union*, 542 U.S. 656 (2004).

b. **The "patently offensive" requirement.** The second element of the *Miller* test asks "whether the work depicts or describes, in a patently offensive way, sexual conduct specifically defined by the applicable state law." This section requires state obscenity laws, and by implication federal obscenity laws, to specifically describe the patently offensive material being regulated. While stressing that it is not the judiciary's role to tell states how to draft their laws, the Court nevertheless offered examples of what a law could provide: "(a) patently offensive representations or descriptions of ultimate sexual acts, normal or perverted, actual or simulated; (b) patently offensive representations or descriptions of masturbation, excretory functions, and lewd exhibition of the genitals."

Imagine that you are counsel to a state legislature and have been asked to draft a state obscenity law that would pass constitutional muster. Can you think of a way of drafting the "patently offensive" section of the law that would ensure its constitutionality? If you are unsure of what to do, read Delaware's obscenity law here.

In *Pope v. Illinois*, 481 U.S. 497 (1987), the Court confirmed that *Miller's* "patently offensive" requirement, like the prurient interest requirement, is to be evaluated by local community standards.

c. **The "lacking serious value" requirement.** The last prong of the *Miller* test asks "whether the work, taken as a whole, lacks serious literary, artistic, political, or scientific value." In *Pope v. Illinois*, the Court clarified that this standard, unlike the first two elements of the *Miller* test, is to be evaluated using a national reasonable person standard and not a local standard. This national standard can provide a crucial First Amendment check on obscenity prosecutions in particularly prudish communities.

In announcing the serious value standard, the *Miller* Court expressly rejected the "utterly without redeeming social value" test proposed by a plurality of justices in *Memoirs v. Massachusetts*.

2. **Did Justice Brennan have the better argument?** Justice Brennan authored *Roth*, the landmark opinion that held that obscene speech was not protected by the First Amendment. By the time of the *Miller* and *Paris Adult Theatre* opinions, however, Justice Brennan no longer believed that an obscenity exception was constitutionally viable. His primary concern was that the Court had failed to develop "sensitive tools" to separate unprotected obscene speech from protected speech.

   Now that you have waded through the elements of the *Miller* test, do you think that it succeeds in separating the wheat of protected speech from the chaff of unprotected speech? Would you have signed on to the majority opinions in *Miller* and *Paris Adult Theatre* or to Justice Brennan's dissents, or would you have written your own opinion?

3. **Obscene speech is unprotected even if the only audience is consenting adults.** In *Paris Adult Theatre*, the Court categorically disapproved of the notion that "obscene, pornographic films acquire constitutional immunity from state regulation simply because they are exhibited for consenting adults only." This means that the government may regulate and punish distributors and exhibitors of obscene material even if the only people receiving or viewing the material are willing adults. How does the Court justify this rule? Do you find the Court's reasoning persuasive?

4. **Why is obscene material so ubiquitous if it is not protected?** Having learned that obscene material is not protected by the First Amendment, you might be wondering why this material seems to be everywhere. A combination of factors likely contributes to this counterintuitive result. First, keep in mind that the *Miller* test is a demanding standard. Soft pornography, like that found in a Playboy magazine, is not going to be considered obscene. For example, in *Jenkins v.*

Georgia, 418 U.S. 153 (1974), the Court indicated that mainstream Hollywood movies (in that case, the Oscar-nominated film "Carnal Knowledge") are unlikely to be considered obscene. Second, the application of the *Miller* test depends on local community standards. In some locales, perhaps Las Vegas and New York, few works might be considered obscene. Third, in many parts of the country, law enforcement officials might focus their limited resources on more serious crimes than obscenity violations. Finally, it is difficult to stop the distribution of obscenity on the internet because servers can be located outside the country, and the ease of entry means that new sites can quickly replace sites that are shut down.

5. **Obscene speech and prior restraints.** Despite its strong aversion to content-based prior restraints, the Court permits the government to require a license before a movie is exhibited to give the government an opportunity to determine whether the movie is obscene. However, to ensure that this process does not unduly impinge on First Amendment rights, the Court insists on rigorous procedural safeguards, including a right to prompt judicial review and placing the burden on the government to establish that a film is obscene. *Freedman v. Maryland*, 380 U.S. 51 (1965). As you will learn in Chapter 13, the Court does not require the same rigorous procedural protections for content-neutral prior restraints, such as a permit requirement to hold a rally in a public park. *See Thomas v. Chicago Park Dist.*, 534 U.S. 316 (2002).

6. **The zoning of adult entertainment establishments and the "secondary effects" doctrine.** Many cities wishing to marginalize strip clubs and other sexually oriented establishments (such as adult bookstores or theaters) use zoning laws to require such establishments either to be placed outside of residential or mainstream commercial areas or to be concentrated all in one area (such as a "red light" district). Because these zoning laws are triggered even if the material in these establishments does not rise to the level of obscenity, one would expect that these laws would be subjected to strict scrutiny. After all, whether these laws apply to a specific establishment depends on the content of the speech being exhibited or sold by the establishment.

   Nevertheless, the Court treats these zoning laws as content-neutral regulations of speech and subjects them to the more forgiving intermediate scrutiny (making it much more likely these laws will be upheld). The logic for doing this was articulated in *Renton v. Playtime Theatres, Inc.*, 475 U.S. 41 (1986), in which the Court held that the more lenient scrutiny was appropriate because these zoning laws are not prompted by the content of the speech in these establishments but rather by the "secondary effects" these establishments have on surrounding communities, such as higher crime and lower property values.

Critics of the secondary effects doctrine have pointed out that it could be the exception that eats up the rule that content-based regulations of speech are subject to strict scrutiny. After all, virtually all content-based regulations of speech are ultimately aimed at the secondary effect of the speech. Laws regulating advocacy of illegal action are aimed at preventing speech from leading to lawbreaking. Laws regulating hate speech are aimed at preventing speech from leading to violence or discrimination against the disparaged groups. But the Court has never allowed the secondary effects doctrine to be used to transform these regulations into content-neutral regulations subject to intermediate scrutiny. In fact, the Court has thus far allowed the secondary effects doctrine to be used in only two contexts—the zoning of adult entertainment establishments and the regulation of nude dancing—and has been very leery of government attempts to extend the doctrine to other areas. For example, in *Reno v. American Civil Liberties Union*, 521 U.S. 844, 868 (1997), the Court rejected the argument that regulating indecent speech on the internet to protect children was a form of "cyberzoning" equivalent to the zoning upheld in *Renton* because the law was protecting children from the "primary" effect of the speech and not the "secondary" effect. Similarly, in *Boos v. Barry*, 485 U.S. 312, 321 (1988), the Court rejected the argument that a law prohibiting signs disparaging a foreign government within 500 feet of the government's embassy was a content-neutral law aimed at the secondary effect of the signs on international relations. Justice Sandra Day O'Connor, writing for the plurality, observed that this law was directed at the speech's impact on listeners and explained that "the emotive impact of speech on its audience is not a 'secondary effect.' " Justice Brennan wrote separately to register his broader objection to the secondary effects doctrine, but he began by acknowledging that the law in *Boos* was not even aimed at the speech's secondary effect: "Whatever 'secondary effects' means, I agree that it cannot include listeners' reactions to speech."

3. May Government Punish the Private Possession of Obscene Material? What a Man Reads in His Own Home

In *Paris Adult Theatre*, the Court held that the government may prohibit the showing of obscene films even if the only people in the audience are consenting adults. By that same logic, could the government also punish adults for reading or watching obscene material at home?

The following case answers that question.

Stanley v. Georgia

Supreme Court of the United States, 1969
394 U.S. 557

MR. JUSTICE MARSHALL delivered the opinion of the Court.

An investigation of appellant's alleged bookmaking activities led to the issuance of a search warrant for appellant's home. Under authority of this warrant, federal and state agents secured entrance. They found very little evidence of bookmaking activity, but while looking through a desk drawer in an upstairs bedroom, one of the federal agents, accompanied by a state officer, found three reels of eight-millimeter film. Using a projector and screen found in an upstairs living room, they viewed the films. The state officer concluded that they were obscene and seized them. Since a further examination of the bedroom indicated that appellant occupied it, he was charged with possession of obscene matter and placed under arrest. He was later indicted for "knowingly having possession of obscene matter" in violation of Georgia law. Appellant was tried before a jury and convicted. The Supreme Court of Georgia affirmed.

Appellant raises several challenges to the validity of his conviction. We find it necessary to consider only one. Appellant argues here, and argued below, that the Georgia obscenity statute, insofar as it punishes mere private possession of obscene matter, violates the First Amendment, as made applicable to the States by the Fourteenth Amendment. For reasons set forth below, we agree that the mere private possession of obscene matter cannot constitutionally be made a crime.

It is true that *Roth* does declare, seemingly without qualification, that obscenity is not protected by the First Amendment. However, neither *Roth* nor any subsequent decision of this Court dealt with the precise problem involved in the present case. None of the statements cited by the Court in *Roth* for the proposition that "this Court has always assumed that obscenity is not protected by the freedoms of speech and press" were made in the context of a statute punishing mere private possession of obscene material; the cases cited deal for the most part with use of the mails to distribute objectionable material or with some form of public distribution or dissemination. In this context, we do not believe that this case can be decided simply by citing *Roth*.

It is now well established that the Constitution protects the right to receive information and ideas. "This freedom (of speech and press) necessarily protects the right to receive." This right to receive information and ideas, regardless of their social worth, is fundamental to our free society. Moreover, in the context of this case—a prosecution for mere possession of printed or filmed matter in the privacy of a person's own home—that right takes on an added dimension. For also fundamental is the right to be free, except in very limited circumstances, from unwanted governmental intrusions into one's privacy.

"The makers of our Constitution undertook to secure conditions favorable to the pursuit of happiness. They recognized the significance of man's spiritual nature, of his feelings and of his intellect. They knew that only a part of the pain, pleasure and satisfactions of life are to be found in material things. They sought to protect Americans in their beliefs, their thoughts, their emotions and their sensations. They conferred, as against the government, the right to be let alone—the most comprehensive of rights and the right most valued by civilized man."

These are the rights that appellant is asserting in the case before us. He is asserting the right to read or observe what he pleases—the right to satisfy his intellectual and emotional needs in the privacy of his own home. He is asserting the right to be free from state inquiry into the contents of his library. Georgia contends that appellant does not have these rights, that there are certain types of materials that the individual may not read or even possess. Georgia justifies this assertion by arguing that the films in the present case are obscene. But we think that mere categorization of these films as "obscene" is insufficient justification for such a drastic invasion of personal liberties guaranteed by the First and Fourteenth Amendments. Whatever may be the justifications for other statutes regulating obscenity, we do not think they reach into the privacy of one's own home. If the First Amendment means anything, it means that a State has no business telling a man, sitting alone in his own house, what books he may read or what films he may watch. Our whole constitutional heritage rebels at the thought of giving government the power to control men's minds.

It is true that in *Roth* this Court rejected the necessity of proving that exposure to obscene material would create a clear and present danger of antisocial conduct or would probably induce its recipients to such conduct. But that case dealt with public distribution of obscene materials and such distribution is subject to different objections. For example, there is always the danger that obscene material might fall into the hands of children or that it might intrude upon the sensibilities or privacy of the general public. No such dangers are present in this case.

We hold that the First and Fourteenth Amendments prohibit making mere private possession of obscene material a crime. *Roth* and the cases following that decision are not impaired by today's holding. As we have said, the States retain broad power to regulate obscenity; that power simply does not extend to mere possession by the individual in the privacy of his own home. Accordingly, the judgment of the court below is reversed and the case is remanded for proceedings not inconsistent with this opinion.

[Justice Black's concurring opinion is omitted, as is Justice Stewart's opinion concurring in the result, which was joined by Justice Brennan and Justice White.]

Points for Discussion

1. **Reconciling *Stanley* and *Paris Adult Theatre*.** *Stanley* was decided after *Roth* but before *Paris Adult Theatre*. How can the Court's holding in *Paris Adult Theatre*—that the government may regulate the exhibition of obscene material to consenting adults—be reconciled with its holding in *Stanley*—that the government may not regulate what a man watches in his home?

2. **You can possess it, but how do you get it?** *Stanley* noted that the First Amendment gives people not only a right to speak but also a right to receive speech. This rule is now well established in First Amendment jurisprudence. At the same time, *Stanley* seemed to reaffirm the core holding of *Roth*, that the government may prohibit the distribution of obscene material. Combining these two rules creates a conundrum. A person may have a right to possess obscene material in his home, but how is he supposed to get it?

   In *United States v. Reidel*, 402 U.S. 351 (1971), a distributor of obscene material used this logic to contend that *Stanley* implicitly protected the right to distribute obscene material to consenting adults. The trial judge agreed: "If a person has the right to receive and possess this material, then someone must have the right to deliver it to him." The Supreme Court disagreed: "*Roth* has squarely placed obscenity and its distribution outside the reach of the First Amendment and they remain there today. *Stanley* did not overrule *Roth* and we decline to do so now."

   In *Smith v. California*, 361 U.S. 147 (1959), the Court did hold that a bookseller could not be strictly liable for possessing an obscene work in his store if the seller had no knowledge of its contents. In *Hamling v. United States*, 418 U.S. 87 (1974), the Court clarified that it was constitutionally sufficient to show that "a defendant had knowledge of the contents of the materials he distributed, and that he knew the character of the materials." The Court said the government did not need to show that a defendant knew the material satisfied the legal definition of obscenity. Otherwise, the Court observed, a defendant could "avoid prosecution by simply claiming he had not brushed up on the law."

   The Court added another gloss to its obscenity jurisprudence in *Ginzburg v. United States*, 383 U.S. 463 (1966), in which it held that a defendant could be liable for the distribution of material that might not otherwise be considered obscene if the defendant marketed the material based on its prurient or salacious appeal. As the Court explained, "We perceive no threat to First Amendment guarantees in thus holding that, in close cases, evidence of pandering may be probative with respect to the nature of the material in question, and thus satisfy the *Roth* test."

B. Child Pornography: Protecting Children from Abuse

The Supreme Court treats child pornography as a distinct category of speech that has its own set of First Amendment rules that differ from those for obscene speech.

1. A Categorical Exception for Child Pornography: *New York v. Ferber*

In *New York v. Ferber*, 458 U.S. 747 (1982), the Court held that child pornography was not protected by the First Amendment even if the material did not meet the requirements of the *Miller* obscenity test. In reaching this conclusion, Justice Byron White emphasized the exploitation of children that occurs in the making of such pornography. As he explained, the "prevention of sexual exploitation and abuse of children constitutes a government objective of surpassing importance." He noted that child pornography creates a "permanent record" of a child's exploitation and that the pornography's circulation exacerbates this harm. Given these concerns, the elements in the *Miller* test were inapposite:

> The *Miller* standard does not reflect the State's particular and more compelling interest in prosecuting those who promote the sexual exploitation of children. Thus, the question under the *Miller* test of whether a work, taken as a whole, appeals to the prurient interest of the average person bears no connection to the issue of whether a child has been physically or psychologically harmed in the production of the work. Similarly, a sexually explicit depiction need not be "patently offensive" in order to have required the sexual exploitation of a child for its production. In addition, a work which, taken on the whole, contains serious literary, artistic, political, or scientific value may nevertheless embody the hardest core of child pornography. "It is irrelevant to the child (who has been abused) whether or not the material has a literary, artistic, political or social value."

Justice White was convinced that the most effective way to address the exploitation of children was to shut down the network for distributing child pornography. Targeting the production of the pornography was challenging, he said, because those producing the material were part of a "low-profile, clandestine industry." Consequently, according to Justice White, "the most expeditious if not the only practical method of law enforcement may be to dry up the market for this material by imposing severe criminal penalties on persons selling, advertising, or otherwise promoting the product."

While Justice White declared child pornography to be categorically unprotected by the First Amendment, he was less clear about how to define the category. He did specify that any regulation must be limited to works that "visually depict" children engaged in "sexual conduct." Perhaps the most revealing guidance came from Justice White's decision to uphold the New York statute at issue in *Ferber*. That statute defined "sexual conduct" as "actual or simulated sexual intercourse, deviate sexual intercourse, sexual bestiality, masturbation, sado-masochistic abuse, or lewd exhibition of the genitals."

The federal Child Protection Act of 1984, enacted two years after *Ferber* was decided, was largely based on the New York law upheld in *Ferber*. However, the part of the New York law that referred to the "lewd" exhibition of the genitals was changed to the "lascivious" exhibition of the genitals. Professor Amy Adler has noted that it is this last element of child pornography's definition that raises the greatest risk of government overreach:

lascivious

> It is this latter term, "lewd" or "lascivious exhibition of the genitals," that launched the most problematic aspect of defining child pornography. Determining whether a photo depicts a child engaged in intercourse or masturbation, for example, would appear to be a relatively straightforward task. But what exactly is "lascivious exhibition of the genitals"? How does it differ from an "innocuous" photograph of a naked child—a family photograph of a child taking a bath, or an artistic masterpiece portraying a naked child model? It is at this margin of child pornography law, where its prohibitions bump up against "innocent" speech, that, ironically, the definition of child pornography has grown.[17]

Points for Discussion

1. **The line between art and exploitation.** Professor Adler expressed concern that prohibitions on pornography could potentially sweep in "an artistic masterpiece portraying a naked child model." But where is the line between art and exploitation? Might a 10-year-old model photographed naked for an artistic masterpiece later come to believe that she had been exploited? Would it help, or hurt, to know that her parents consented to her being photographed?

2. **What about virtual child pornography?** The federal Child Pornography Protection Act of 1996 (CPPA) expanded the prohibition on child pornography to include not only depictions of actual children engaged in sexual conduct but also depictions that appear to be of minors engaged in sexual conduct. This extension encompassed both computer-generated images of children engaged in sex ("virtual child pornography") and images of adult actors who portrayed minors engaged in sex.

17 Amy Adler, *The Perverse Law of Child Pornography*, 101 Colum. L. Rev. 209, 238–39 (2001).

In *Ashcroft v. Free Speech Coalition*, 535 U.S. 234 (2002), the Court, in an opinion written by Justice Anthony Kennedy, struck down this expanded definition because the reasoning of *Ferber* could not support it:

> *Ferber* upheld a prohibition on the distribution and sale of child pornography, as well as its production, because these acts were "intrinsically related" to the sexual abuse of children in two ways. First, as a permanent record of a child's abuse, the continued circulation itself would harm the child who had participated. Second, because the traffic in child pornography was an economic motive for its production, the State had an interest in closing the distribution network.
>
> In contrast to the speech in *Ferber*, the CPPA prohibits speech that records no crime and creates no victims by its production. Virtual child pornography is not "intrinsically related" to the sexual abuse of children, as were the materials in *Ferber*. While the Government asserts that the images can lead to actual instances of child abuse, the causal link is contingent and indirect. The harm does not necessarily follow from the speech, but depends upon some unquantified potential for subsequent criminal acts.
>
> The Government says these indirect harms are sufficient because, as *Ferber* acknowledged, child pornography rarely can be valuable speech. This argument, however, suffers from two flaws. First, *Ferber*'s judgment about child pornography was based upon how it was made, not on what it communicated. The case reaffirmed that where the speech is neither obscene nor the product of sexual abuse, it does not fall outside the protection of the First Amendment.
>
> The second flaw in the Government's position is that *Ferber* did not hold that child pornography is by definition without value. On the contrary, the Court recognized some works in this category might have significant value, but relied on virtual images—the very images prohibited by the CPPA—as an alternative and permissible means of expression: "If it were necessary for literary or artistic value, a person over the statutory age who perhaps looked younger could be utilized. Simulation outside of the prohibition of the statute could provide another alternative." *Ferber*, then, not only referred to the distinction between actual and virtual child pornography, it relied on it as a reason supporting its holding. *Ferber* provides no support for a statute that eliminates the distinction and makes the alternative mode criminal as well.

Justice Kennedy said that works portraying minors engaged in sexual conduct might have "significant value." Did that surprise you? In another part of his opinion, he explained that themes of teenage sexual activity, as well as teenage sexual abuse, have "inspired countless literary works," ranging from Shakespeare's *Romeo and Juliet* to the Academy Award-winning movie "American Beauty."

3. **What if prosecutors cannot distinguish between real and virtual child pornography?** The government in *Free Speech Coalition* contended that it was necessary to outlaw virtual child pornography because it can be difficult for prosecutors to prove that a work used real children and not computer-generated images of children. Justice Clarence Thomas picked up on this point in his concurrence:

> In my view, the Government's most persuasive asserted interest in support of the Child Pornography Prevention Act is the prosecution rationale—that persons who possess and disseminate pornographic images of real children may escape conviction by claiming that the images are computer-generated, thereby raising a reasonable doubt as to their guilt. At this time, however, the Government asserts only that defendants *raise* such defenses, not that they have done so successfully. In fact, the Government points to no case in which a defendant has been acquitted based on a "computer-generated images" defense. While this speculative interest cannot support the broad reach of the CPPA, technology may evolve to the point where it becomes impossible to enforce actual child pornography laws because the Government cannot prove that certain pornographic images are of real children. In the event this occurs, the Government should not be foreclosed from enacting a regulation of virtual child pornography that contains an appropriate affirmative defense or some other narrowly drawn restriction.

In his opinion for the Court, Justice Kennedy noted that producers of child pornography would likely stop using children if computer-generated images were functionally equivalent: "Few pornographers would risk prosecution by abusing real children if fictional, computerized images would suffice."

In *United States v. Williams*, 553 U.S. 285 (2008), the Court upheld a federal law, enacted in response to *Free Speech Coalition*, that made it a crime to advertise, promote, present, distribute, or solicit material that a party believed was child pornography involving actual children or caused another to believe was unprotected child pornography. Under the law, a defendant could be successfully prosecuted even if prosecutors could not prove that the material being offered or solicited included images of actual children and not computer-generated images. The Court noted that Congress feared that the emergence of new technologies and the repeated retransmission of files over the internet would make it impossible to prove that an image involved actual children.

In upholding the law, the Court noted that "offers to engage in illegal transactions are categorically excluded from First Amendment protection." The Court further noted that "offers to deal in illegal products or otherwise engage in illegal activity do not acquire First Amendment protection when the offeror is mistaken about the factual predicate of his offer." As we observed in a Point for Discussion following the *Stanley* case, the Court has similarly held that a person can be prosecuted for "pandering" or offering to sell obscene material even if the material was not in fact obscene. *Ginzburg v. United States*.

4. **The problem of "morphed" child pornography.** Morphed child pornography occurs when the face of an actual child is superimposed on the body of either a digitally generated body or the body of an adult to make it appear as if the child was engaged in sex. Unlike the child pornography in *Ferber*, morphed pornography does not involve the sexual exploitation of a child. But it does involve the exploitation of a child's image. Should the First Amendment protect this speech? In *United States v. Mecham*, 950 F.3d 257 (5th Cir. 2020), *cert. denied*, 141 S. Ct. 139 (2020), the Fifth Circuit said no. The court noted that one reason for denying child pornography protection was to shield children from reputational and emotional harm and that morphed child pornography can cause similar harms.

5. **"Sexting" and the First Amendment.** What if the photographer taking those lascivious images of a minor's genitalia is the minor? That is the issue raised by the ubiquitous practice of sexting, which one study found is practiced by 20% of American teenagers. *See* National Campaign to Prevent Teen and Unplanned Pregnancy, Sex and Tech: Results from a Survey of Teens and Young Adults 1 (2008). What these amateur photographers may not realize is that taking images of even oneself can violate state and federal child pornography laws. Professor John Humbach asks whether criminalizing this behavior is consistent with the spirit of *Ferber*:

> The broad categorical exclusion established for child pornography in 1982 seems, in its verbal formulation at least, to easily include teen sexting and other autopornography. That categorical exclusion was, however, motivated by a pressing need to address a particular set of serious harms: Adults' sexual exploitation and abuse of children used in the production of sexually explicit materials. It is a serious question, therefore, whether the categorical exclusion should be understood to include materials produced under entirely different circumstances, where the originally motivating harms are absent and the brunt of the suppression can savage the lives and future prospects of the very people whom the laws are supposed to protect.

John Humbach, *"Sexting" and the First Amendment*, 37 Hastings Const'l L.Q. 433, 439 (2010). Sexting can also lead to the problem of "revenge porn." This can occur when a woman voluntarily sends nude images of herself to her boyfriend, who, after the relationship ends, vengefully circulates the images. Should the boyfriend's actions be protected by the First Amendment? We will discuss that issue in Chapter 9 when we discuss First Amendment limits on the private-facts tort.

2. May Government Punish the Private Possession of Child Pornography? The Limits of *Stanley v. Georgia*

In *Stanley v. Georgia*, the Supreme Court held that the government could not punish an individual for the private possession of obscenity. Should the same rule apply to child pornography? The following case answers that question.

Osborne v. Ohio

Supreme Court of the United States, 1990
495 U.S. 103

[*Authors' note:* Ohio law made it a crime to "possess or view any material or performance that shows a minor who is not the person's child or ward in a state of nudity."]

JUSTICE WHITE delivered the opinion of the Court.

Petitioner, Clyde Osborne, was convicted of violating this statute and sentenced to six months in prison, after the Columbus, Ohio, police, pursuant to a valid search, found four photographs in Osborne's home. Each photograph depicts a nude male adolescent posed in a sexually explicit position. The Ohio Supreme Court affirmed Osborne's conviction, after an intermediate appellate court did the same. Relying on one of its earlier decisions, the court first rejected Osborne's contention that the First Amendment prohibits the States from proscribing the private possession of child pornography.

The threshold question in this case is whether Ohio may constitutionally proscribe the possession and viewing of child pornography or whether, as Osborne argues, our decision in *Stanley v. Georgia* compels the contrary result. We find this case distinct from *Stanley* because the interests underlying child pornography prohibitions far exceed the interests justifying the Georgia law at issue in *Stanley.* In *Stanley,* Georgia primarily sought to proscribe the private possession of obscenity because it was concerned that obscenity would poison the minds of its viewers. We responded that "whatever the power of the state to control public dissemination of ideas inimical to the public morality, it cannot constitutionally premise legislation on the desirability of controlling a person's private thoughts." The difference here is obvious: The State does not rely on a paternalistic interest in regulating Osborne's mind. Rather, Ohio has enacted [its law] in order to protect the victims of child pornography; it hopes to destroy a market for the exploitative use of children.

"It is evident beyond the need for elaboration that a State's interest in safeguarding the physical and psychological well-being of a minor is compelling. The legislative judgment, as well as the judgment found in relevant literature, is that the use of children as subjects of pornographic materials is harmful to the physiological, emotional, and mental health of the child. That judgment, we think, easily passes muster under the First Amendment." It is also surely reasonable for the State to conclude that it will decrease the production of child pornography if it penalizes those who possess and view the product, thereby decreasing demand.

Given the importance of the State's interest in protecting the victims of child pornography, we cannot fault Ohio for attempting to stamp out this vice at all levels in the distribution chain. According to the State, since the time of our decision in *Ferber*, much of the child pornography market has been driven underground; as a result, it is now difficult, if not impossible, to solve the child pornography problem by only attacking production and distribution. Indeed, 19 States have found it necessary to proscribe the possession of this material.

Other interests also support the Ohio law. First, as *Ferber* recognized, the materials produced by child pornographers permanently record the victim's abuse. The pornography's continued existence causes the child victims continuing harm by haunting the children in years to come. The State's ban on possession and viewing encourages the possessors of these materials to destroy them. Second, encouraging the destruction of these materials is also desirable because evidence suggests that pedophiles use child pornography to seduce other children into sexual activity.

Given the gravity of the State's interests in this context, we find that Ohio may constitutionally proscribe the possession and viewing of child pornography.

Justice Brennan, with whom Justice Marshall and Justice Stevens join, dissenting.

The Court today finds *Stanley* inapposite on the ground that "the interests underlying child pornography prohibitions far exceed the interests justifying the Georgia law at issue in *Stanley*." The majority's analysis does not withstand scrutiny. While the sexual exploitation of children is undoubtedly a serious problem, Ohio may employ other weapons to combat it. Indeed, the State already has enacted a panoply of laws prohibiting the creation, sale, and distribution of child pornography and obscenity involving minors. Ohio has not demonstrated why these laws are inadequate and why the State must forbid mere possession as well.

[Justice Blackmun's concurring opinion is omitted.]

Points for Discussion

1. **Why a different result from *Stanley*?** *Stanley* said the government could not punish someone for the personal possession of obscenity. *Osborne* reached the opposite conclusion for child pornography. How did the Supreme Court justify the differing results?

2. **Prosecutions for possession of child pornography can and do occur.** The U.S. Sentencing Commission reported that 43.5% of the child pornography offenders sentenced in 2021 were sentenced for possession. Read the report here.

C. Indecent Speech: Non-Obscene Sexual Speech

Governments sometimes regulate sexual speech that does not rise to the level of obscenity. This is particularly true of laws regulating minors' access to sexual speech. Governments also sometimes regulate profane speech. These two categories are often referred to as "indecent" speech.

What should the First Amendment rules be for laws regulating indecent speech? The most important distinction between regulations of indecent speech and regulations of obscenity and child pornography is that indecent speech is protected speech and obscenity and child pornography are not. Consequently, content-based regulations of indecent speech must pass the demanding requirements of strict scrutiny. As you learned in Chapter 4, this requires a law to further a compelling governmental interest, and the means used must be narrowly tailored to achieve that end.

Strict scrutiny is a demanding standard that usually results in a law's invalidation. Nevertheless, and as you are about to learn, the Supreme Court has occasionally upheld regulations of indecent speech. Governments typically offer one of two justifications for regulating indecent speech: to protect minors from speech that is considered harmful for them and to protect adults who do not want to be exposed to the speech. The Court has accepted that both these interests can sometimes be compelling.

We will consider how the Court has treated each of these interests separately even though governments sometimes claim that indecency regulations further both interests.

1. Regulating Indecent Speech to Protect Children: Don't Burn the House to Roast the Pig

The foundational case supporting the government's power to regulate minors' access to indecent speech is *Ginsberg v. New York*, 390 U.S. 629 (1968). The case concerned a New York law that prohibited the sale of non-obscene sexual speech to minors. The defendants in the case had sold what the Court referred to as "girlie" magazines to a 16-year-old boy. Today, people might refer to these magazines, such as a Playboy magazine, as soft porn. The Court acknowledged that the magazines were not obscene and could be sold to adults. The issue was whether the government could prohibit their sale to minors.

The Supreme Court found two governmental interests sufficient to uphold the New York law: the government's interest in protecting the "well-being of its youth" and the government's interest in supporting parents in their ability to "direct the rearing of their children."

We saw an example of the *Ginsberg* principle at work in our discussion of *Sable Communications v. FCC* in Chapter 4. *Sable* concerned a federal law that prohibited both obscene and indecent phone sex communications. The Court upheld the obscenity ban because obscene speech is not protected by the First Amendment. But the indecency ban required a more elaborate analysis because indecent speech is protected by the First Amendment and adults have a right to access it. The government sought to justify the indecency ban as necessary to protect minors. The Court in *Sable Communications* accepted that this could be a sufficiently compelling interest to pass strict scrutiny:

> Sexual expression which is indecent but not obscene is protected by the First Amendment; and the federal parties do not submit that the sale of such materials to adults could be criminalized solely because they are indecent. The Government may, however, regulate the content of constitutionally protected speech in order to promote a compelling interest if it chooses the least restrictive means to further the articulated interest. We have recognized that there is a compelling interest in protecting the physical and psychological well-being of minors. This interest extends to shielding minors from the influence of literature that is not obscene by adult standards.

Despite this acknowledgment that protecting minors from indecent speech can be a compelling interest, the Court nevertheless struck down the indecency ban because the ban was not the least restrictive means of furthering this interest. The Court pointed to evidence that technological measures could block minors from accessing indecent phone calls without also denying adult access. A total ban was thus unnecessary. Using a frequently invoked metaphor in these cases, the Court said the law was "another case of burning the house to roast the pig." In other cases, the justices make this same point by saying that adult discourse "cannot be limited to that which would be suitable for a sandbox." *Bolger v. Youngs Drug Prods. Corp.*, 463 U.S. 60, 74 (1983).

The government's power to protect minors from purportedly harmful sexual speech is not unlimited. For example, in *Erznoznik v. City of Jacksonville*, 422 U.S. 205 (1975), a city ordinance prohibited drive-in movie theaters from showing films with naked body images if those images could be seen from public streets. In response to the city's argument that the law was necessary to protect minors, the Court noted that the law's prohibition was so expansive as to potentially include "a picture of a baby's buttocks, the nude body of a war victim, or scenes from a culture in which nudity is indigenous." This led the Court to reject the government's child-protection justification:

> Clearly all nudity cannot be deemed obscene even as to minors. Nor can such a broad restriction be justified by any other governmental interest pertaining to minors. Speech that is neither obscene as to youths nor subject to some other legitimate proscription cannot be suppressed solely to protect the young from ideas or images that a legislative body thinks unsuitable for them.

The Court's unwillingness to give the government carte blanche power to regulate speech in the name of protecting minors means that indecency regulations, like all speech regulations, must be carefully drafted to avoid problems of overbreadth and vagueness. Legislators often find that the safest course of action is to take the *Miller* obscenity test and modify it so that each prong of the test focuses on the impact on minors: (*i.e.*, whether the speech appeals to the prurient interest "of minors," is patently offensive "as to minors," and lacks serious value "for minors").[1]

2. Regulating Indecent Speech to Protect Non-Consenting Adults: The Difference Between Being at Home and in Public

We learned in Chapter 5 that the Supreme Court has sometimes justified speech regulations as being necessary to protect a captive audience from speech that the audience is incapable of avoiding. At the same time, we also learned that the Court will almost never find this to be true when people are out in public. In that context, the Court puts the burden on people to either endure the exposure or avert their eyes.

1 See, e.g., *Ashcroft v. American Civil Liberties Union*, 542 U.S. 656, 661–62 (2004) (Child Online Protection Act defined speech that is "harmful to minors" by using the *Miller* test and adjusting it for minors).

Here is how the Court summarized this rule in *United States v. Playboy Entertainment Group,* 529 U.S. 803 (2000):

> Our precedents teach these principles. Where the designed benefit of a content-based speech restriction is to shield the sensibilities of listeners, the general rule is that the right of expression prevails, even where no less restrictive alternative exists. We are expected to protect our own sensibilities "simply by averting our eyes."

By contrast, the Court is more tolerant of government regulations to protect the sensibilities of listeners when they are at home. In that context, the listeners' privacy interests can sometimes override a speaker's expressive interests. You will see an example of this later in the chapter when you read *FCC v. Pacifica Foundation*, 438 U.S. 726 (1978), a case about indecent radio broadcasts coming into a home.

On the other hand, if the intrusion into people's privacy interests is minimal, the Court will often rule in favor of the speaker and place the burden on listeners to protect themselves. For example, in *Bolger*, the Court considered a challenge to a federal law that barred the mailing of unsolicited advertisements for contraceptives. One of the government's justifications for the law was to protect "recipients of mail from materials that they are likely to find offensive."

The Court began by noting that "offensiveness" is almost never an adequate justification for suppressing speech. The government tried to counter by noting that this speech was being delivered to people's homes. But the Court found this intrusion minimal because recipients could easily shield themselves from the unwanted speech:

> Recipients of objectionable mailings may "effectively avoid further bombardment of their sensibilities simply by averting their eyes." Consequently, the "short, though regular, journey from mail box to trash can is an acceptable burden, at least so far as the Constitution is concerned."

Note how the regulation in *Bolger* blanketly barred the mailing of contraceptive advertisements to all people regardless of whether some individuals might want to receive this information. The Court is very skeptical of such top-down "government knows best" censorship. It is much more willing to uphold laws that empower people to make their own censorship decisions. So, for example, in *Rowan v. U.S. Post Office Department*, 397 U.S. 728 (1970), the Court upheld a federal law that allowed individuals to notify the Postal Service that they do not want to receive "pandering advertisements."

D. Profane Speech: May Government Regulate Foul Language?

Chaplinsky included "profane" speech in its list of unprotected categories of speech. But, as the following two cases illustrate, the Court regards profane speech, or foul language, as protected speech. Since the First Amendment protects profane speech, the question in any given case is whether there is a compelling justification for regulating it.

Although not the focus of this section, it is worth noting that "profane" speech can also mean blasphemous speech or speech that is irreverent toward religion. The Court has held that this type of speech is also protected by the First Amendment, even while acknowledging that this speech can easily veer into "excesses and abuses." *Cantwell v. Connecticut*, 310 U.S. 296, 310 (1940). The issue in *Cantwell* arose in the context of Jehovah's Witnesses who had conveyed messages that were highly offensive to Catholics. In explaining why this speech was protected, the Court noted:

> In the realm of religious faith, and in that of political belief, sharp differences arise. In both fields the tenets of one man may seem the rankest error to his neighbor. To persuade others to his own point of view, the pleader, as we know, at times, resorts to exaggeration, to vilification of men who have been, or are, prominent in church or state, and even to false statement. But the people of this nation have ordained in the light of history, that, in spite of the probability of excesses and abuses, these liberties are, in the long view, essential to enlightened opinion and right conduct on the part of the citizens of a democracy.

For now, let us focus on the other connotation of profane speech: foul language. We begin with a man who used a particularly provocative word to communicate his opposition to the draft during the Vietnam War.

Cohen v. California

Supreme Court of the United States, 1971
403 U.S. 15

MR. JUSTICE HARLAN delivered the opinion of the Court.

This case may seem at first blush too inconsequential to find its way into our books, but the issue it presents is of no small constitutional significance.

Appellant Paul Robert Cohen was convicted in the Los Angeles Municipal Court of violating that part of California Penal Code § 415 which prohibits "maliciously and willfully disturbing the peace or quiet of any neighborhood or person by offensive conduct." He was given 30 days' imprisonment. The facts upon which his conviction rests are detailed in the opinion of the Court of Appeal of California, Second Appellate District, as follows:

> On April 26, 1968, the defendant was observed in the Los Angeles County Courthouse in the corridor outside of division 20 of the municipal court wearing a jacket bearing the words "Fuck the Draft" which were plainly visible. There were women and children present in the corridor. The defendant was arrested. The defendant testified that he wore the jacket knowing that the words were on the jacket as a means of informing the public of the depth of his feelings against the Vietnam War and the draft.
>
> The defendant did not engage in, nor threaten to engage in, nor did anyone as the result of his conduct in fact commit or threaten to commit any act of violence. The defendant did not make any loud or unusual noise, nor was there any evidence that he uttered any sound prior to his arrest.

In affirming the conviction, the Court of Appeal held that "offensive conduct" means "behavior which has a tendency to provoke others to acts of violence or to in turn disturb the peace," and that the State had proved this element because, on the facts of this case, "it was certainly reasonably foreseeable that such conduct might cause others to rise up to commit a violent act against the person of the defendant or attempt to forceably remove his jacket." The California Supreme Court declined review by a divided vote. We now reverse.

In order to lay hands on the precise issue which this case involves, it is useful first to canvass various matters which this record does not present.

The conviction quite clearly rests upon the asserted offensiveness of the words Cohen used to convey his message to the public. The only "conduct" which the State sought to punish is the fact of communication. Thus, we deal here with a conviction resting solely upon "speech," not upon any separately identifiable conduct which allegedly was intended by Cohen to be perceived by others as expressive. Further, the State certainly lacks power to punish Cohen for the underlying content of the message the inscription conveyed. At least so long as there is no showing of an intent to incite disobedience to or disruption of the draft, Cohen could not, consistently with the First and Fourteenth Amendments, be punished for asserting the evident position on the inutility or immorality of the draft his jacket reflected.

We think it important to note that several issues typically associated with such problems are not presented here. In the first place, Cohen was tried under a statute applicable throughout the entire State. Any attempt to support this conviction on the ground that the statute seeks to preserve an appropriately decorous atmosphere in the courthouse where Cohen was arrested must fail in the absence of any language in the statute that would have put appellant on notice that certain kinds of otherwise permissible speech or conduct would nevertheless, under California law, not be tolerated in certain places. No fair reading of the phrase "offensive conduct" can be said sufficiently to inform the ordinary person that distinctions between certain locations are thereby created.

In the second place, as it comes to us, this case cannot be said to fall within those relatively few categories of instances where prior decisions have established the power of government to deal more comprehensively with certain forms of individual expression simply upon a showing that such a form was employed. This is not, for example, an obscenity case. Whatever else may be necessary to give rise to the States' broader power to prohibit obscene expression, such expression must be, in some significant way, erotic. It cannot plausibly be maintained that this vulgar allusion to the Selective Service System would conjure up such psychic stimulation in anyone likely to be confronted with Cohen's crudely defaced jacket.

This Court has also held that the States are free to ban the simple use of so-called "fighting words," those personally abusive epithets which, when addressed to the ordinary citizen, are, as a matter of common knowledge, inherently likely to provoke violent reaction. While the four-letter word displayed by Cohen in relation to the draft is not uncommonly employed in a personally provocative fashion, in this instance it was clearly not "directed to the person of the hearer." No individual actually or likely to be present could reasonably have regarded the words on appellant's jacket as a direct personal insult. Nor do we have here an instance of the exercise of the State's police power to prevent a speaker from intentionally provoking a given group to hostile reaction. There is, as noted above, no showing that anyone who saw Cohen was in fact violently aroused or that appellant intended such a result.

Finally, in arguments before this Court much has been made of the claim that Cohen's distasteful mode of expression was thrust upon unwilling or unsuspecting viewers, and that the State might therefore legitimately act as it did in order to protect the sensitive from otherwise unavoidable exposure to appellant's crude form of protest. Of course, the mere presumed presence of unwitting listeners or viewers does not serve automatically to justify curtailing all speech capable of giving offense. While this Court has recognized that government may properly act in many situations to prohibit intrusion into the privacy of the home of unwelcome views and ideas which cannot be totally banned from the public dialogue, we have at the same time consistently stressed that "we are often captives outside the sanctuary of the home and subject to objectionable speech." The ability of government, consonant with the Constitution, to shut off discourse solely to protect others from hearing it is, in other words, dependent upon a showing that substantial privacy interests are being invaded in an essentially intolerable manner. Any broader view of this authority would effectively empower a majority to silence dissidents simply as a matter of personal predilections.

In this regard, persons confronted with Cohen's jacket were in a quite different posture than, say, those subjected to the raucous emissions of sound trucks blaring outside their residences. Those in the Los Angeles courthouse could effectively avoid further bombardment of their sensibilities simply by averting their eyes. And, while it may be that one has a more substantial claim to a recognizable privacy interest when walking through a courthouse corridor than, for example, strolling through Central Park, surely it is nothing like the interest in being free from unwanted expression in the confines of one's own home. Given the subtlety and complexity of the factors involved, if Cohen's "speech" was otherwise entitled to constitutional protection, we do not think the fact that some unwilling "listeners" in a public building may have been briefly exposed to it can serve to justify this breach of the peace conviction where, as here, there was no evidence that persons powerless to avoid appellant's conduct did in fact object to it, and where that portion of the statute upon which Cohen's conviction rests evinces no concern, either on its face or as construed by the California courts, with the special plight of the captive auditor, but, instead, indiscriminately sweeps within its prohibitions all "offensive conduct" that disturbs "any neighborhood or person."

Against this background, the issue flushed by this case stands out in bold relief. It is whether California can excise, as "offensive conduct," one particular scurrilous epithet from the public discourse, either upon the theory of the court below that its use is inherently likely to cause violent reaction or upon a more general assertion that the States, acting as guardians of public morality, may properly remove this offensive word from the public vocabulary.

The rationale of the California court is plainly untenable. At most it reflects an "undifferentiated fear or apprehension of disturbance which is not enough to overcome the right to freedom of expression." We have been shown no evidence that substantial numbers of citizens are standing ready to strike out physically at whoever may assault their sensibilities with execrations like that uttered by Cohen. There may be some persons about with such lawless and violent proclivities, but that is an insufficient base upon which to erect, consistently with constitutional values, a governmental power to force persons who wish to ventilate their dissident views into avoiding particular forms of expression. The argument amounts to little more than the self-defeating proposition that to avoid physical censorship of one who has not sought to provoke such a response by a hypothetical coterie of the violent and lawless, the States may more appropriately effectuate that censorship themselves.

Admittedly, it is not so obvious that the First and Fourteenth Amendments must be taken to disable the States from punishing public utterance of this unseemly expletive in order to maintain what they regard as a suitable level of discourse within the body politic. We think, however, that examination and reflection will reveal the shortcomings of a contrary viewpoint.

At the outset, we cannot overemphasize that, in our judgment, most situations where the State has a justifiable interest in regulating speech will fall within one or more of the various established exceptions, discussed above but not applicable here, to the usual rule that governmental bodies may not prescribe the form or content of individual expression. Equally important to our conclusion is the constitutional backdrop against which our decision must be made. The constitutional right of free expression is powerful medicine in a society as diverse and populous as ours. It is designed and intended to remove governmental restraints from the arena of public discussion, putting the decision as to what views shall be voiced largely into the hands of each of us, in the hope that use of such freedom will ultimately produce a more capable citizenry and more perfect polity and in the belief that no other approach would comport with the premise of individual dignity and choice upon which our political system rests.

To many, the immediate consequence of this freedom may often appear to be only verbal tumult, discord, and even offensive utterance. These are, however, within established limits, in truth necessary side effects of the broader enduring values which the process of open debate permits us to achieve. That the air may at times seem filled with verbal cacophony is, in this sense not a sign of weakness but of strength. We cannot lose sight of the fact that, in what otherwise might seem a trifling and annoying instance of individual distasteful abuse of a privilege, these fundamental societal values are truly implicated.

Against this perception of the constitutional policies involved, we discern certain more particularized considerations that peculiarly call for reversal of this conviction. First, the principle contended for by the State seems inherently boundless. How is one to distinguish this from any other offensive word? Surely the State has no right to cleanse public debate to the point where it is grammatically palatable to the most squeamish among us. Yet no readily ascertainable general principle exists for stopping short of that result were we to affirm the judgment below. For, while the particular four-letter word being litigated here is perhaps more distasteful than most others of its genre, it is nevertheless often true that one man's vulgarity is another's lyric. Indeed, we think it is largely because governmental officials cannot make principled distinctions in this area that the Constitution leaves matters of taste and style so largely to the individual.

Additionally, we cannot overlook the fact, because it is well illustrated by the episode involved here, that much linguistic expression serves a dual communicative function: it conveys not only ideas capable of relatively precise, detached explication, but otherwise inexpressible emotions as well. In fact, words are often chosen as much for their emotive as their cognitive force. We cannot sanction the view that the Constitution, while solicitous of the cognitive content of individual speech has little or no regard for that emotive function which practically speaking, may often be the more important element of the overall message sought to be communicated. Indeed, as Mr. Justice Frankfurter has said, "one of the prerogatives of American citizenship is the right to criticize public men and measures—and that means not only informed and responsible criticism but the freedom to speak foolishly and without moderation."

Finally, and in the same vein, we cannot indulge the facile assumption that one can forbid particular words without also running a substantial risk of suppressing ideas in the process. Indeed, governments might soon seize upon the censorship of particular words as a convenient guise for banning the expression of unpopular views. We have been able, as noted above, to discern little social benefit that might result from running the risk of opening the door to such grave results.

It is, in sum, our judgment that, absent a more particularized and compelling reason for its actions, the State may not, consistently with the First and Fourteenth Amendments, make the simple public display here involved of this single four-letter expletive a criminal offense. Because that is the only arguably sustainable rationale for the conviction here at issue, the judgment below must be reversed.

MR. JUSTICE BLACKMUN, with whom THE CHIEF JUSTICE and MR. JUSTICE BLACK join.

I dissent. Cohen's absurd and immature antic, in my view, was mainly conduct and little speech. The California Court of Appeal appears so to have described it, and I cannot characterize it otherwise. Further, the case appears to me to be well within the sphere of *Chaplinsky v. New Hampshire*, where Mr. Justice Murphy, a known champion of First Amendment freedoms, wrote for a unanimous bench. As a consequence, this Court's agonizing over First Amendment values seem misplaced and unnecessary.

Points for Discussion

1. **Is this a content-based or content-neutral regulation of speech?** On its face, the California breach-of-the-peace law is not obviously content-based or even a speech regulation. The law could apply to non-expressive conduct that breaches the peace, such as patting passersby on their rear ends. The law also does not single out any particular message for regulation, other than it would apply to only speech that amounted to "offensive conduct" and caused a breach of the peace. Does this mean that the regulation of speech in *Cohen* should have been classified as either a conduct regulation that incidentally burdened speech or a content-neutral regulation of expression? In the case of a generally applicable law like this, the best way to answer that question is to ask whether the application of the law was triggered by the content of the defendant's speech. If so, then the government is regulating the speech because of its message, and its application should be

treated as a content-based regulation of speech. Professor Eugene Volokh refers to this as "content-based application" and says that laws applied in this fashion "should be presumptively unconstitutional, just as facially content-based laws are presumptively unconstitutional." Eugene Volokh, *Speech as Conduct: Generally Applicable Laws, Illegal Courses of Conduct, "Situation-Altering Utterances," and the Uncharted Zones*, 90 Cornell L. Rev. 1277, 1286–87 (2005).

2. **Do you agree with Justice Harlan's opinion?** We might all agree that the government should not be able to punish someone for using a foul word in conversation even if the conversation occurs in a public place. But why should the Court protect a person's right to walk in public with profane words plastered on his clothing? Why isn't there a compelling interest in preserving a level of decorum in the public sphere? Why isn't there a compelling interest in shielding children from these profane displays? Has *Cohen* led to the coarsening of our public spaces? In anticipation of these complaints, Justice Harlan offered this consolation: "That the air may at times seem filled with verbal cacophony is not a sign of weakness but of strength." Do you agree?

3. **Fuck Pepsi!** Does the *Cohen* decision mean that Coca-Cola Co. could purchase a billboard that said "Fuck Pepsi! Buy Coke"? If not, how would you distinguish the billboard from Cohen's jacket? Might this be an instance when the captive audience doctrine could be applied outside the home? Are there non-legal reasons why Coca-Cola is unlikely to purchase such a billboard?

4. **The dual functions of speech.** Justice Harlan said speech "serves a dual communicative function." What are the two functions he is referring to? Does the First Amendment protect both functions? Is there a difference between a jacket that says "I Hate the Draft" and one that says "Fuck the Draft"?

5. **Trademarks with foul language.** Recall the *Matal v. Tam* opinion in which the Court struck down a provision in the federal trademark law that banned the registration of marks that disparaged individuals or groups of people. Two years after that decision, the Court struck down a separate provision in the trademark law that banned the registration of "immoral" or "scandalous" marks. *Iancu v. Brunetti*, 139 S. Ct. 2294 (2019). The party challenging this provision had a clothing line that used the trademark "FUCT." Even if the government may not forbid the use of this mark, should it be required to support it by registering the mark with the Patent and Trademark Office and providing it with the legal benefits that come from registration? Do you think that the Copyright Office could deny copyright protection to books that the government found objectionable?

You Be the Lawyer!

Would have you dropped the F-bomb during oral argument?

Imagine that you were the lawyer who had represented Cohen during the oral argument in *Cohen v. California*. You would have known that no one had ever dropped the F-bomb during oral argument at the Supreme Court and that some of the justices, particularly Chief Justice Warren Burger, would have been very displeased if foul language was used. Would you have done it anyway? What arguments can be made both for and against using the F-word?

To find out what Cohen's lawyer, Professor Melville Nimmer, did, you can listen to the first few minutes of the oral argument here. As you listen, imagine yourself in Nimmer's shoes and take note of how Chief Justice Burger reminded Nimmer that the Court is "thoroughly familiar with the factual setting of this case and it will not be necessary for you I'm sure to dwell on the facts." Does that sound like the chief justice was laying out the welcome mat for Nimmer to drop the bomb? *See generally* Alan E. Garfield, *To Swear or Not to Swear: Using Foul Language During a Supreme Court Oral Argument*, 90 Wash. U. L. Rev. 279 (2012).

Our second foul language case concerns a radio broadcast of George Carlin's "Filthy Words" routine, a comedy monologue in which Carlin discusses what he claims are the seven words you can never say on the public airwaves. According to Carlin, these words "will curve your spine" and "grow hair on your hands." If you are curious what they are, you can find them in this footnote.[2] But don't blame us if you need a chiropractor.

Hear It

You can listen to one version of George Carlin's "Filthy Words" routine here.

George Carlin performing in 2008
Photographer: Bonnie/image cropped/Creative Commons (CC BY-SA 2.0)

[2] Shit, piss, fuck, cunt, cocksucker, motherfucker, and tits.

FCC v. Pacifica Foundation

Supreme Court of the United States, 1978
438 U.S. 726

[*Authors' note*: This case concerns the constitutionality of the Federal Communications Commission's power to regulate indecent speech on broadcast radio and television. Broadcast radio and television is "free" (usually advertisement-supported) programming that is broadcast over the airwaves. In the radio context, it is FM and AM radio stations. It does not include satellite or cable radio services such as SiriusXM. In the television context, it is television programming that is broadcast over the airwaves. (That's right! You can cancel your cable or satellite television subscriptions, connect your television to a digital antenna, and receive some stations for free. Typically, you would pick up stations broadcasting programming from the major networks (ABC, CBS, NBC, Fox, and PBS), as well as some other stations.) Broadcast radio and television programs are disseminated via radio waves transmitted through the electromagnetic spectrum. The spectrum has a limited capacity so that only stations licensed by the FCC may broadcast. In cases predating *FCC v. Pacifica Foundation*, the Supreme Court seized on the fact that the electromagnetic spectrum is a scarce resource and that only some people receive a broadcast license as a justification for giving the government greater power to regulate speech in broadcast media than in other media like printed books and newspapers. *See, e.g.*, *Red Lion Broad. Co. v. FCC*, 395 U.S. 367 (1969).]

MR. JUSTICE STEVENS delivered the opinion of the Court (Parts I, II, III and IV-C) and an opinion in which THE CHIEF JUSTICE and MR. JUSTICE REHNQUIST joined (Parts IV-A and IV-B).

This case requires that we decide whether the Federal Communications Commission has any power to regulate a radio broadcast that is indecent but not obscene.

A satiric humorist named George Carlin recorded a 12-minute monologue entitled "Filthy Words" before a live audience in a California theater. He began by referring to his thoughts about "the words you couldn't say on the public, ah, airwaves, um, the ones you definitely wouldn't say, ever." He proceeded to list those words and repeat them over and over again in a variety of colloquialisms. The transcript of the recording, which is appended to this opinion, indicates frequent laughter from the audience.

At about 2 o'clock in the afternoon on Tuesday, October 30, 1973, a New York radio station, owned by respondent Pacifica Foundation, broadcast the "Filthy Words" monologue. A few weeks later a man, who stated that he had heard the broadcast while driving with his young son, wrote a letter complaining to the Commission. He stated that, although he could perhaps understand the "record's being sold for private use, I certainly cannot understand the broadcast of same over the air that, supposedly, you control."

The complaint was forwarded to the station for comment. In its response, Pacifica explained that the monologue had been played during a program about contemporary society's attitude toward language and that, immediately before its broadcast, listeners had been advised that it included "sensitive language which might be regarded as offensive to some." Pacifica characterized George Carlin as "a significant social satirist" who "like Twain and Sahl before him, examines the language of ordinary people. Carlin is not mouthing obscenities, he is merely using words to satirize as harmless and essentially silly our attitudes towards those words." Pacifica stated that it was not aware of any other complaints about the broadcast.

On February 21, 1975, the Commission issued a declaratory order granting the complaint and holding that Pacifica "could have been the subject of administrative sanctions." The Commission did not impose formal sanctions, but it did state that the order would be "associated with the station's license file, and in the event that subsequent complaints are received, the Commission will then decide whether it should utilize any of the available sanctions it has been granted by Congress."

Where FCC say gave them the power

The Commission found a power to regulate indecent broadcasting in two statutes: 18 U.S.C. § 1464 (1976 ed.), which forbids the use of "any obscene, indecent, or profane language by means of radio communications," and 47 U.S.C. § 303(g), which requires the Commission to "encourage the larger and more effective use of radio in the public interest."

The Commission characterized the language used in the Carlin monologue as "patently offensive," though not necessarily obscene, and expressed the opinion that it should be regulated by principles analogous to those found in the law of nuisance where the "law generally speaks to *channeling* behavior more than actually prohibiting it. The concept of 'indecent' is intimately connected with the exposure of children to language that describes, in terms patently offensive as measured by contemporary community standards for the broadcast medium, sexual or excretory activities and organs at times of the day when there is a reasonable risk that children may be in the audience."

Applying these considerations to the language used in the monologue as broadcast by respondent, the Commission concluded that certain words depicted sexual and excretory activities in a patently offensive manner, noted that they "were broadcast at a time when children were undoubtedly in the audience (i.e., in the early afternoon)," and that the prerecorded language, with these offensive words "repeated over and over," was "deliberately broadcast." In summary, the Commission stated: "We therefore hold that the language as broadcast was indecent and prohibited by 18 U.S.C. § 1464."

[Parts I, II, III, and IV-A are omitted.]

IV-B

When the issue is narrowed to the facts of this case, the question is whether the First Amendment denies government any power to restrict the public broadcast of indecent language in any circumstances. For if the government has any such power, this was an appropriate occasion for its exercise.

The words of the Carlin monologue are unquestionably "speech" within the meaning of the First Amendment. It is equally clear that the Commission's objections to the broadcast were based in part on its content. The order must therefore fall if, as Pacifica argues, the First Amendment prohibits all governmental regulation that depends on the content of speech. Our past cases demonstrate, however, that no such absolute rule is mandated by the Constitution.

The question in this case is whether a broadcast of patently offensive words dealing with sex and excretion may be regulated because of its content. Obscene materials have been denied the protection of the First Amendment because their content is so offensive to contemporary moral standards. But the fact that society may find speech offensive is not a sufficient reason for suppressing it. Indeed, if it is the speaker's opinion that gives offense, that consequence is a reason for according it constitutional protection. For it is a central tenet of the First Amendment that the government must remain neutral in the marketplace of ideas. If there were any reason to believe that the Commission's characterization of the Carlin monologue as offensive could be traced to its political content—or even to the fact that it satirized contemporary attitudes about four-letter words—First Amendment protection might be required. But that is simply not this case. These words offend for the same reasons that obscenity offends. Their place in the hierarchy of First Amendment values was aptly sketched by Mr. Justice Murphy when he said: "Such utterances are no essential part of any exposition of ideas, and are of such slight social value as a step to truth that any benefit that may be derived from them is clearly outweighed by the social interest in order and morality."

the narrowed issue

Although these words ordinarily lack literary, political, or scientific value, they are not entirely outside the protection of the First Amendment. Some uses of even the most offensive words are unquestionably protected. Indeed, we may assume, *arguendo*, that this monologue would be protected in other contexts. Nonetheless, the constitutional protection accorded to a communication containing such patently offensive sexual and excretory language need not be the same in every context. It is a characteristic of speech such as this that both its capacity to offend and its "social value," to use Mr. Justice Murphy's term, vary with the circumstances. Words that are commonplace in one setting are shocking in another. To paraphrase Mr. Justice Harlan, one occasion's lyric is another's vulgarity.

In this case it is undisputed that the content of Pacifica's broadcast was "vulgar," "offensive," and "shocking." Because content of that character is not entitled to absolute constitutional protection under all circumstances, we must consider its context in order to determine whether the Commission's action was constitutionally permissible.

IV-C

We have long recognized that each medium of expression presents special First Amendment problems. And of all forms of communication, it is broadcasting that has received the most limited First Amendment protection. Thus, although other speakers cannot be licensed except under laws that carefully define and narrow official discretion, a broadcaster may be deprived of his license and his forum if the Commission decides that such an action would serve "the public interest, convenience, and necessity."

The reasons for these distinctions are complex, but two have relevance to the present case. First, the broadcast media have established a uniquely pervasive presence in the lives of all Americans. Patently offensive, indecent material presented over the airwaves confronts the citizen, not only in public, but also in the privacy of the home, where the individual's right to be left alone plainly outweighs the First Amendment rights of an intruder. Because the broadcast audience is constantly tuning in and out, prior warnings cannot completely protect the listener or viewer from unexpected program content. To say that one may avoid further offense by turning off the radio when he hears indecent language is like saying that the remedy for an assault is to run away after the first blow. One may hang up on an indecent phone call, but that option does not give the caller a constitutional immunity or avoid a harm that has already taken place.

Second, broadcasting is uniquely accessible to children, even those too young to read. Although Cohen's written message might have been incomprehensible to a first grader, Pacifica's broadcast could have enlarged a child's vocabulary in an instant. Other forms of offensive expression may be withheld from the young without restricting the expression at its source. Bookstores and motion picture theaters, for example, may be prohibited from making indecent material available to children. We held in *Ginsberg v. New York*, 390 U.S. 629 that the government's interest in the "well-being of its youth" and in supporting "parents' claim to authority in their own household" justified the regulation of otherwise protected expression. The ease with which children may obtain access to broadcast material, coupled with the concerns recognized in *Ginsberg*, amply justify special treatment of indecent broadcasting.

It is appropriate, in conclusion, to emphasize the narrowness of our holding. This case does not involve a two-way radio conversation between a cab driver and a dispatcher, or a telecast of an Elizabethan comedy. We have not decided that an occasional expletive in either setting would justify any sanction or, indeed, that this broadcast would justify a criminal prosecution. The Commission's decision rested entirely on a nuisance rationale under which context is all-important. The concept requires consideration of a host of variables. The time of day was emphasized by the Commission. The content of the program in which the language is used will also affect the composition of the audience, and differences between radio, television, and perhaps closed-circuit transmissions, may also be relevant. As Mr. Justice Sutherland wrote a "nuisance may be merely a right thing in the wrong place—like a pig in the parlor instead of the barnyard." We simply hold that when the Commission finds that a pig has entered the parlor, the exercise of its regulatory power does not depend on proof that the pig is obscene.

The judgment of the Court of Appeals is reversed.

MR. JUSTICE POWELL, with whom MR. JUSTICE BLACKMUN joins, concurring in part and concurring in the judgment.

As the foregoing demonstrates, my views are generally in accord with what is said in Part IV-C of Mr. Justice Stevens' opinion. I therefore join that portion of his opinion. I do not join Part IV-B, however, because I do not subscribe to the theory that the Justices of this Court are free generally to decide on the basis of its content which speech protected by the First Amendment is most "valuable" and hence deserving of the most protection, and which is less "valuable" and hence deserving of less protection. In my view, the result in this case does not turn on whether Carlin's monologue, viewed as a whole, or the words that constitute it, have more or less "value" than a candidate's campaign speech. This is a judgment for each person to make, not one for the judges to impose upon him.

The result turns instead on the unique characteristics of the broadcast media, combined with society's right to protect its children from speech generally agreed to be inappropriate for their years, and with the interest of unwilling adults in not being assaulted by such offensive speech in their homes. Moreover, I doubt whether today's decision will prevent any adult who wishes to receive Carlin's message in Carlin's own words from doing so, and from making for himself a value judgment as to the merit of the message and words. These are the grounds upon which I join the judgment of the Court as to Part IV.

MR. JUSTICE BRENNAN, with whom MR. JUSTICE MARSHALL joins, dissenting.

For the second time in two years, the Court refuses to embrace the notion, completely antithetical to basic First Amendment values, that the degree of protection the First Amendment affords protected speech varies with the social value ascribed to that speech by five Members of this Court. Moreover, all Members of the Court agree that the Carlin monologue aired by Station WBAI does not fall within one of the categories of speech, such as "fighting words," or obscenity, that is totally without

First Amendment protection. Yet, a majority of the Court nevertheless finds that, on the facts of this case, the FCC is not constitutionally barred from imposing sanctions on Pacifica for its airing of the Carlin monologue.

Both the opinion of my Brother Stevens and the opinion of my Brother Powell rely principally on two factors in reaching this conclusion: (1) the capacity of a radio broadcast to intrude into the unwilling listener's home, and (2) the presence of children in the listening audience. Dispassionate analysis starkly reveals that these justifications simply do not support even the professedly moderate degree of governmental homogenization of radio that the Court today permits.

I am in wholehearted agreement with my Brethren that an individual's right "to be let alone" when engaged in private activity within the confines of his own home is encompassed within the "substantial privacy interests" to which Mr. Justice Harlan referred in *Cohen*, and is entitled to the greatest solicitude. However, I believe that an individual's actions in switching on and listening to communications transmitted over the public airways and directed to the public at large do not implicate fundamental privacy interests, even when engaged in within the home. Instead, because the radio is undeniably a public medium, these actions are more properly viewed as a decision to take part, if only as a listener, in an ongoing public discourse.

Even if an individual who voluntarily opens his home to radio communications retains privacy interests of sufficient moment to justify a ban on protected speech if those interests are "invaded in an essentially intolerable manner," the very fact that those interests are threatened only by a radio broadcast precludes any intolerable invasion of privacy; for unlike other intrusive modes of communication, such as sound trucks, "the radio can be turned off"—and with a minimum of effort.

The Court's balance, of necessity, fails to accord proper weight to the interests of listeners who wish to hear broadcasts the FCC deems offensive. It permits majoritarian tastes completely to preclude a protected message from entering the homes of a receptive, unoffended minority. No decision of this Court supports such a result.

The opinion of my Brother Powell acknowledges that there lurks in today's decision a potential for "reducing the adult population to hearing only what is fit for children," but expresses faith that the FCC will vigilantly prevent this potential from ever becoming a reality. I am far less certain than my Brother Powell that such faith in the Commission is warranted, and even if I shared it, I could not so easily shirk the responsibility assumed by each Member of this Court jealously to guard against encroachments on First Amendment freedoms.

In concluding that the presence of children in the listening audience provides an adequate basis for the FCC to impose sanctions for Pacifica's broadcast of the Carlin monologue, the opinions of my Brother Powell and my Brother Stevens, both stress the time-honored right of a parent to raise his child as he sees fit—a right this Court has consistently been vigilant to protect. As surprising as it may be to individual Members of this Court, some parents may actually find Mr. Carlin's unabashed attitude towards the seven "dirty words" healthy, and deem it desirable to expose their children to the manner in which Mr. Carlin defuses the taboo surrounding the words. Such parents may constitute a minority of the American public, but the absence of great numbers willing to exercise the right to raise their children in this fashion does not alter the right's nature or its existence. Only the Court's regrettable decision does that.

[Justice Stewart's dissenting opinion, which was joined by Justice Brennan, Justice White, and Justice Marshall, is omitted.]

Points for Discussion

1. **The majority's rejection of Justice Stevens' hierarchy of speech.** In *Pacifica* and *Young v. American Mini Theatres, Inc.*, 427 U.S. 50 (1976), which involved the zoning of adult entertainment establishments, Justice John Paul Stevens contended that the government's ability to regulate speech should vary based on the relative value of the speech's content. The government should be virtually barred from regulating the content of high-value speech, such as political speech, but it should have a freer hand to regulate low-value speech such as sexual or profane speech, even if this speech is not obscene. In both cases, however, Justice Stevens failed to win majority support for this hierarchical approach. Justice Brennan highlighted this fact in his *Pacifica* dissent: "For the second time in two years, the Court refuses to embrace the notion, completely antithetical to basic First Amendment values, that the degree of protection the First Amendment affords protected speech varies with the social value ascribed to that speech by five Members of this Court."

   While Justice Stevens lost the battle in these cases, he arguably won the war. In both cases, the majority upheld the speech regulations at issue. To this day, the government has considerable leeway to regulate the zoning of adult entertainment establishments. Can you recall the theory the Court uses to justify this? Likewise, the FCC continues to have power to regulate indecency on the public airwaves. Which of Justice Stevens' arguments for justifying the FCC's power won the majority's support?

2. **Why do I hear dirty words when I watch "Succession"?** Don't forget that the FCC indecency regime at issue in *Pacifica* is limited to broadcast radio and television. It does not apply to cable channels like HBO or streaming services like Netflix. It also does not apply to subscription radio, which is one of the reasons why Howard Stern moved his show from FM radio to SiriusXM.

3. **Why do I sometimes hear those words on broadcast stations?** The application of the FCC's indecency regime is highly contextual. There are times and circumstances when the use of otherwise prohibited words is permissible. As Justice Stevens colorfully put it, the problem in *Pacifica* was not that the foul language pig had gotten out of the barn but that the pig had entered the parlor. If the program had been aired at a different time or if its content had included only a single fleeting expletive, the case might have come out differently. For example, some network broadcasts of the January 6 investigation hearings included the profane language used by some of the witnesses. Given the newsworthy context of this broadcast, it would almost certainly be exempted under the FCC's indecency regime.

4. **Fleeting expletives (or what Bono, Cher, and Nicole Richie have in common).** The rigor with which the FCC has policed the use of fleeting expletives on broadcast radio and television has varied over time. For a period, agency policy suggested that a mere fleeting expletive (*i.e.*, one "fuck" or "shit") would not trigger agency action, but after U2 frontman Bono and singer-actress Cher used profane words during broadcasted awards ceremonies, the FCC changed its policy to clarify that even a single expletive could trigger agency action. In a case that reached the Supreme Court, the FCC brought an action against Fox Television for a broadcast of the Billboard Music Awards in which Nicole Richie said: "Have you ever tried to get cow shit out of a Prada purse? It's not so fucking simple." The Court never reached the question of whether the FCC's revised fleeting expletive policy violated the First Amendment. Instead, the Court found that the FCC's action violated Fox's due process rights because the program was aired before the new policy was adopted. *FCC v. Fox Television Stations, Inc.*, 567 U.S. 239 (2012).

5. **Is the FCC indecency regime an anachronistic holdout or a salutary compromise?** The FCC indecency policy is still in force even though the way in which people consume media has radically changed since the 1970s. People still cannot hear George Carlin's "Filthy Words" routine on broadcast radio or television, but they can hear it on satellite radio, cable television stations, and the internet. Does this sea change in how people consume media make the FCC indecency rule a quaint, but nonsensical, relic? Justice Thomas has suggested this might be the case:

> Traditional broadcast television and radio are no longer the "uniquely pervasive" media forms they once were. For most consumers, traditional broadcast media programming is now bundled with cable or satellite services. Broadcast and other video programming is also widely available over the Internet. And like radio and television broadcasts, Internet access is now often freely available over the airwaves and can be

> accessed by portable computer, cell phones, and other wireless devices. The extant facts that drove this Court to subject broadcasters to unique disfavor under the First Amendment simply do not exist today.

FCC v. Fox Television Stations, Inc., 556 U.S. 502, 533–34 (2009) (Thomas, J., concurring).

Justice Thomas' points are indisputable. But could there still be a benefit to retaining the FCC indecency regime even in this transformed landscape? Does it create an oasis for audiences who prefer tamer fare for themselves or their children? As Professor Adam Smaha observed, "FCC oversight adds a modest guarantee that one segment of mass media will stay faithful to ordinary or conservative sensibilities." Adam M. Smaha, *The Story of FCC v. Pacifica Foundation (and Its Second Life)*, in First Amendment Stories 375, 399 (Richard W. Garnett & Andrew Koppelman, eds., 2012).

Review the Rules for Indecent and Profane Speech by Making Arguments for and Against the Constitutionality of the Communications Decency Act

Between this chapter and the previous chapters, you are now armed with enough knowledge to be a shrewd First Amendment litigator. To test your skills, we are giving you the facts and relevant statutory provisions from a complex case concerning the legality of a federal law regulating sexual speech on the internet. The Court's opinion in the case, *Reno v. American Civil Liberties Union*, is reproduced afterward. Before you read the case (and no peeking!), make a serious effort to outline the potential arguments that the lawyers, both supporting and challenging this law, would likely have made. You will be paid at the going rate for students ($0 per hour).

Reno v. ACLU concerned a challenge to two provisions in the Communications Decency Act of 1996 (CDA). The government tried to justify these provisions as necessary to protect minors from harmful materials.

The first "indecent transmission" provision, Section 223(a), prohibited the knowing transmission of obscene or indecent messages to a recipient under 18 years of age. It also prohibited knowingly allowing the use of one's "telecommunications facility" for the purpose of transmitting obscene or indecent messages to a minor. The provision did not define the word "indecent." Violators could be subject to fines and up to two years' imprisonment. The plaintiffs challenged only the prohibition on "indecent" messages and not the prohibition on "obscene" messages. Can you explain why the plaintiffs would have made this distinction?

The second "patently offensive display" provision, Section 223(d), prohibited knowingly sending or displaying patently offensive messages in a manner that is available to a person under 18 years and also prohibited knowingly allowing the use of one's communications facilities for such purpose. The provision described the forbidden messages as "any comment, request, suggestion, proposal, image, or other communication that, in context, depicts or describes, in terms patently offensive as measured by contemporary community standards, sexual or excretory activities or organs." Violation of this provision could also subject a person to fines and potentially two years in prison.

The CDA provided two affirmative defenses to avoid liability. The first was if the defendant took "good faith, reasonable, effective, and appropriate actions" to restrict minors' access to the prohibited communications. The second protected those who restricted minors' access to the prohibited material "by requiring certain designated forms of age proof, such as a verified credit card or an adult identification number or code."

Here are a few clues to help you with your analysis. First, in arguing for the constitutionality of the above provisions, the government relied on *Ginsberg v. New York*, *FCC v. Pacifica*, and *Renton v. Playtime Theatres*. What arguments would the government have made based on each of these cases? Do you think that the Court would have found these arguments convincing?

Second, in challenging the constitutionality of the provisions, the plaintiffs brought in evidence about the effectiveness of filtering software to screen out indecent material on the internet. Where would this evidence fit into a constitutional analysis? There was also evidence that nonprofit entities, such as museums or organizations promoting breast cancer or AIDS awareness, often did not have the resources to pay for the credit card or age verification checks that would have sheltered them from liability under the law.

Finally, because this was the first case in which the Supreme Court considered the application of the First Amendment to the internet, questions were raised about whether the internet should be treated similarly to broadcast radio and television. How do you think that played out?

Your job is to identify the arguments both for and against the constitutionality of the indecent transmission provision and the patently offensive display provision and predict how the Court ruled on each issue. When you have finished, you can see how your arguments compare to those that were made in this complicated case.

Reno v. American Civil Liberties Union

Supreme Court of the United States, 1997
521 U.S. 844

JUSTICE STEVENS delivered the opinion of the Court.

At issue is the constitutionality of two statutory provisions enacted to protect minors from "indecent" and "patently offensive" communications on the Internet. Notwithstanding the legitimacy and importance of the congressional goal of protecting children from harmful materials, we agree with the three-judge District Court that the statute abridges "the freedom of speech" protected by the First Amendment.

In arguing for reversal, the Government contends that the CDA is plainly constitutional under three of our prior decisions: (1) *Ginsberg v. New York;* (2) *FCC v. Pacifica Foundation*; and (3) *Renton v. Playtime Theatres, Inc.* A close look at these cases, however, raises—rather than relieves—doubts concerning the constitutionality of the CDA.

In *Ginsberg,* we upheld the constitutionality of a New York statute that prohibited selling to minors under 17 years of age material that was considered obscene as to them even if not obscene as to adults. We relied not only on the State's independent interest in the well-being of its youth, but also on our consistent recognition of the principle that "the parents' claim to authority in their own household to direct the rearing of their children is basic in the structure of our society."

In four important respects, the statute upheld in *Ginsberg* was narrower than the CDA. First, we noted in *Ginsberg* that "the prohibition against sales to minors does not bar parents who so desire from purchasing the magazines for their children." Under the CDA, by contrast, neither the parents' consent—nor even their participation—in the communication would avoid the application of the statute. Second, the New York statute applied only to commercial transactions, whereas the CDA contains no such limitation. Third, the New York statute cabined its definition of material that is harmful to minors with the requirement that it be "utterly without redeeming social importance for minors." The CDA fails to provide us with any definition of the term "indecent" as used in § 223(a)(1) and, importantly, omits any requirement that the "patently offensive" material covered by § 223(d) lack serious literary, artistic, political, or scientific value. Fourth, the New York statute defined a minor as a person under the age of 17, whereas the CDA, in applying to all those under 18 years, includes an additional year of those nearest majority.

In *Pacifica,* we upheld a declaratory order of the Federal Communications Commission, holding that the broadcast of a recording of a 12-minute monologue entitled "Filthy Words" that had previously been delivered to a live audience "could have been the subject of administrative sanctions." As with the New York statute at issue in *Ginsberg,* there are significant differences between the order upheld in *Pacifica* and the CDA. First, the order in *Pacifica,* issued by an agency that had been regulating radio stations for decades, targeted a specific broadcast that represented a rather dramatic departure from traditional program content in order to designate when—rather than whether—it would be permissible to air such a program in that particular medium. The CDA's broad categorical prohibitions are not limited to particular times and are not dependent on any evaluation by an agency familiar with the unique characteristics of the Internet. Second, unlike the CDA, the Commission's declaratory order was not punitive; we expressly refused to decide whether the indecent broadcast "would justify a criminal prosecution." Finally, the Commission's order applied to a medium which as a matter of history had "received the most limited First Amendment protection," in large part because warnings could not adequately protect the listener from unexpected program content. The Internet, however, has no comparable history. Moreover, the District Court found that the risk of encountering indecent material by accident is remote because a series of affirmative steps is required to access specific material.

In *Renton,* we upheld a zoning ordinance that kept adult movie theaters out of residential neighborhoods. The ordinance was aimed, not at the content of the films shown in the theaters, but rather at the "secondary effects"—such as crime and deteriorating property values—that these theaters fostered: "It is the secondary effect which these zoning ordinances attempt to avoid, not the dissemination of 'offensive' speech." According to the Government, the CDA is constitutional because it constitutes a sort of "cyberzoning" on the Internet. But the CDA applies broadly to the entire universe of cyberspace. And the purpose of the CDA is to protect children from the primary effects of "indecent" and "patently offensive" speech, rather than any "secondary" effect of such speech. Thus, the CDA is a content-based blanket restriction on speech, and, as such, cannot be "properly analyzed as a form of time, place, and manner regulation."

These precedents, then, surely do not require us to uphold the CDA and are fully consistent with the application of the most stringent review of its provisions.

Some of our cases have recognized special justifications for regulation of the broadcast media that are not applicable to other speakers. In these cases, the Court relied on the history of extensive Government regulation of the broadcast medium; the scarcity of available frequencies at its inception; and its "invasive" nature.

Those factors are not present in cyberspace. Neither before nor after the enactment of the CDA have the vast democratic forums of the Internet been subject to the type of government supervision and regulation that has attended the broadcast industry. Moreover, the Internet is not as "invasive" as radio or television. The District Court specifically found that "communications over the Internet do not 'invade' an individual's home or appear on one's computer screen unbidden. Users seldom encounter content by accident." It also found that "almost all sexually explicit images are preceded by warnings as to the content," and cited testimony that "odds are slim that a user would come across a sexually explicit sight by accident."

Finally, unlike the conditions that prevailed when Congress first authorized regulation of the broadcast spectrum, the Internet can hardly be considered a "scarce" expressive commodity. It provides relatively unlimited, low-cost capacity for communication of all kinds. As the District Court found, "the content on the Internet is as diverse as human thought." We agree with its conclusion that our cases provide no basis for qualifying the level of First Amendment scrutiny that should be applied to this medium.

Regardless of whether the CDA is so vague that it violates the Fifth Amendment, the many ambiguities concerning the scope of its coverage render it problematic for purposes of the First Amendment. For instance, each of the two parts of the CDA uses a different linguistic form. The first uses the word "indecent," while the second speaks of material that "in context, depicts or describes, in terms patently offensive as measured by contemporary community standards, sexual or excretory activities or organs." Given the absence of a definition of either term, this difference in language will provoke uncertainty among speakers about how the two standards relate to each other and just what they mean. This uncertainty undermines the likelihood that the CDA has been carefully tailored to the congressional goal of protecting minors from potentially harmful materials.

The vagueness of the CDA is a matter of special concern for two reasons. First, the CDA is a content-based regulation of speech. The vagueness of such a regulation raises special First Amendment concerns because of its obvious chilling effect on free speech. Second, the CDA is a criminal statute. In addition to the opprobrium and stigma of a criminal conviction, the CDA threatens violators with penalties including up to two years in prison for each act of violation. The severity of criminal sanctions may well cause speakers to remain silent rather than communicate even arguably unlawful words, ideas, and images.

We are persuaded that the CDA lacks the precision that the First Amendment requires when a statute regulates the content of speech. In order to deny minors access to potentially harmful speech, the CDA effectively suppresses a large amount of speech that adults have a constitutional right to receive and to address to one another. That burden on adult speech is unacceptable if less restrictive alternatives would be at least as effective in achieving the legitimate purpose that the statute was enacted to serve.

It is true that we have repeatedly recognized the governmental interest in protecting children from harmful materials. But that interest does not justify an unnecessarily broad suppression of speech addressed to adults. As we have explained, the Government may not "reduce the adult population to only what is fit for children."

In arguing that the CDA does not so diminish adult communication, the Government relies on the incorrect factual premise that prohibiting a transmission whenever it is known that one of its recipients is a minor would not interfere with adult-to-adult communication. The findings of the District Court make clear that this premise is untenable. Given the size of the potential audience for most messages, in the absence of a viable age verification process, the sender must be charged with knowing that one or more minors will likely view it. Knowledge that, for instance, one or more members of a 100-person chat group will be a minor—and therefore that it would be a crime to send the group an indecent message—would surely burden communication among adults.

The District Court found that at the time of trial existing technology did not include any effective method for a sender to prevent minors from obtaining access to its communications on the Internet without also denying access to adults. The Court found no effective way to determine the age of a user who is accessing material through e-mail, mail exploders, newsgroups, or chat rooms. As a practical matter, the Court also found that it would be prohibitively expensive for noncommercial—as well as some commercial—speakers who have Web sites to verify that their users are adults. These limitations must inevitably curtail a significant amount of adult communication on the Internet. By contrast, the District Court found that "despite its limitations, currently available *user-based* software suggests that a reasonably effective method by which *parents* can prevent their children from accessing sexually explicit and other material which *parents* may believe is inappropriate for their children will soon be widely available."

The breadth of the CDA's coverage is wholly unprecedented. Unlike the regulations upheld in *Ginsberg* and *Pacifica*, the scope of the CDA is not limited to commercial speech or commercial entities. Its open-ended prohibitions embrace all nonprofit entities and individuals posting indecent messages or displaying them on their own computers in the presence of minors. The general, undefined terms "indecent" and "patently offensive" cover large amounts of nonpornographic material with serious educational or other value. Under the CDA, a parent allowing her 17-year-old to use the family computer to obtain information on the Internet that she, in her parental judgment, deems appropriate could face a lengthy prison term. Similarly, a parent who sent his 17-year-old college freshman information on birth control via e-mail could be incarcerated even though neither he, his child, nor anyone in their home community found the material "indecent" or "patently offensive," if the college town's community thought otherwise.

The breadth of this content-based restriction of speech imposes an especially heavy burden on the Government to explain why a less restrictive provision would not be as effective as the CDA. It has not done so. The arguments in this Court have referred to possible alternatives such as requiring that indecent material be "tagged" in a way that facilitates parental control of material coming into their homes, making exceptions for messages with artistic or educational value, providing some tolerance for parental choice, and regulating some portions of the Internet—such as commercial Web sites—differently from others, such as chat rooms. Particularly in the light of the absence of any detailed findings by the Congress, or even hearings addressing the special problems of the CDA, we are persuaded that the CDA is not narrowly tailored if that requirement has any meaning at all.

We agree with the District Court's conclusion that the CDA places an unacceptably heavy burden on protected speech, and that the defenses do not constitute the sort of "narrow tailoring" that will save an otherwise patently invalid unconstitutional provision. In *Sable Communications v. FCC,* we remarked that the speech restriction at issue there amounted to "burning the house to roast the pig." The CDA, casting a far darker shadow over free speech, threatens to torch a large segment of the Internet community.

For the foregoing reasons, the judgment of the District Court is affirmed.

[Justice O'Connor's opinion concurring in the judgment in part and dissenting in part, which was joined by Chief Justice Rehnquist, is omitted.]

Point for Discussion

1. **Congress' second attempt to protect children on the internet.** Congress responded to the Court's invalidation of the Communications Decency Act in *Reno* with a new law, the Child Online Protection Act (COPA), that tried to remedy the CDA's defects. In response to the concern that the CDA applied to noncommercial speakers, Congress restricted COPA's scope to communications for "commercial purposes." In response to the concern about the CDA's vagueness, Congress included a definition for material "harmful to minors" that paralleled the *Miller* obscenity test with qualifications of "as to minors" for each prong.

   Notwithstanding these efforts, the Supreme Court upheld a lower court order enjoining COPA's enforcement on the ground that the law was likely unconstitutional. *Ashcroft v. American Civil Liberties Union*, 542 U.S. 656 (2004). While acknowledging that there can be a compelling interest in protecting minors from indecent speech, the Court nevertheless found that COPA did not use the least restrictive means for furthering this interest. Specifically, the Court noted that filtering software could be as effective as COPA in protecting children, would not have the chilling effect of COPA's criminal sanctions, and would not deny adults access to the regulated speech.

E. Depictions of Violence: Films of Animal Abuse and Violent Video Games

Should the government be allowed to regulate depictions of violence? The two leading cases implicate very different concerns. In the first case, the violence depicted is real. It consists of images of animals being abused. This case raises issues similar to those raised by child pornography, where the government is concerned about the welfare of the children abused in the making of the images.

The second case concerns imaginary violence: specifically, the violence found in some video games. The Court acknowledged that the First Amendment protects this speech. The question was whether the government could limit minors' access to these games. This case raises issues similar to those raised in cases concerning limits on minors' access to sexual but non-obscene material.

Both cases were decided on narrow grounds of overbreadth and vagueness so that the broader issues did not get fully resolved.

1. Regulating Images of Animal Abuse: Is There a Difference Between Child Pornography and Images of Cruelty to Animals?

The law at issue in the next case was prompted by a concern over "crush videos," which you'll learn about in the opinion. Was the law's application limited to crush videos or did it encompass other images of animal abuse? Did that matter?

United States v. Stevens

Supreme Court of the United States, 2010
559 U.S. 460

CHIEF JUSTICE ROBERTS delivered the opinion of the Court.

Congress enacted 18 U.S.C. § 48 to criminalize the commercial creation, sale, or possession of certain depictions of animal cruelty. The statute does not address underlying acts harmful to animals, but only portrayals of such conduct. The question presented is whether the prohibition in the statute is consistent with the freedom of speech guaranteed by the First Amendment.

Section 48 establishes a criminal penalty of up to five years in prison for anyone who knowingly "creates, sells, or possesses a depiction of animal cruelty," if done "for commercial gain" in interstate or foreign commerce. A depiction of "animal cruelty" is defined as one "in which a living animal is intentionally maimed, mutilated, tortured, wounded, or killed," if that conduct violates federal or state law where "the creation, sale, or possession takes place." In what is referred to as the "exceptions clause," the law exempts from prohibition any depiction "that has serious religious, political, scientific, educational, journalistic, historical, or artistic value."

The legislative background of § 48 focused primarily on the interstate market for "crush videos." According to the House Committee Report on the bill, such videos feature the intentional torture and killing of helpless animals, including cats, dogs, monkeys, mice, and hamsters. Crush videos often depict women slowly crushing animals to death "with their bare feet or while wearing high heeled shoes," sometimes while "talking to the animals in a kind of dominatrix patter" over "the cries and squeals of the animals, obviously in great pain." Apparently these depictions "appeal to persons with a very specific sexual fetish who find them sexually arousing or otherwise exciting." The acts depicted in crush videos are typically prohibited by the animal cruelty laws enacted by all 50 States and the District of Columbia. But crush videos rarely disclose the participants' identities, inhibiting prosecution of the underlying conduct.

This case, however, involves an application of § 48 to depictions of animal fighting. Dogfighting, for example, is unlawful in all 50 States and the District of Columbia, and has been restricted by federal law since 1976. Respondent Robert J. Stevens ran a business, "Dogs of Velvet and Steel," and an associated Web site, through which he sold videos of pit bulls engaging in dogfights and attacking other animals. Among these videos were Japan Pit Fights and Pick-A-Winna: A Pit Bull Documentary, which include contemporary footage of dogfights in Japan (where such conduct is allegedly legal) as well as footage of American dogfights from the 1960's and 1970's. A third video, Catch Dogs and Country Living, depicts the use of pit bulls to hunt wild boar, as well as a "gruesome" scene of a pit bull attacking a domestic farm pig. On the basis of these videos, Stevens was indicted on three counts of violating § 48.

Stevens moved to dismiss the indictment, arguing that § 48 is facially invalid under the First Amendment. The District Court denied the motion. It held that the depictions subject to § 48, like obscenity or child pornography, are categorically unprotected by the First Amendment. It went on to hold that § 48 is not substantially overbroad, because the exceptions clause sufficiently narrows the statute to constitutional applications. The jury convicted Stevens on all counts, and the District Court sentenced him to three concurrent sentences of 37 months' imprisonment, followed by three years of supervised release.

The en banc Third Circuit, over a three-judge dissent, declared § 48 facially unconstitutional and vacated Stevens's conviction. The Court of Appeals first held that § 48 regulates speech that is protected by the First Amendment. The Court declined to recognize a new category of unprotected speech for depictions of animal cruelty, and rejected the Government's analogy between animal cruelty depictions and child pornography.

The Court of Appeals then held that § 48 could not survive strict scrutiny as a content-based regulation of protected speech. It found that the statute lacked a compelling government interest and was neither narrowly tailored to preventing animal cruelty nor the least restrictive means of doing so. It therefore held § 48 facially invalid.

We granted certiorari.

The Government's primary submission is that § 48 necessarily complies with the Constitution because the banned depictions of animal cruelty, as a class, are categorically unprotected by the First Amendment. We disagree.

The First Amendment provides that "Congress shall make no law abridging the freedom of speech." "As a general matter, the First Amendment means that government has no power to restrict expression because of its message, its ideas, its subject matter, or its content." Section 48 explicitly regulates expression based on content: The statute restricts "visual and auditory depictions," such as photographs, videos, or sound recordings, depending on whether they depict conduct in which a living animal is intentionally harmed. As such, § 48 is "presumptively invalid, and the Government bears the burden to rebut that presumption."

"From 1791 to the present," however, the First Amendment has "permitted restrictions upon the content of speech in a few limited areas," and has never "included a freedom to disregard these traditional limitations." These "historic and traditional categories long familiar to the bar"—including obscenity, defamation, fraud, incitement, and speech integral to criminal conduct—are "well-defined and narrowly limited classes of speech, the prevention and punishment of which have never been thought to raise any Constitutional problem."

The Government argues that "depictions of animal cruelty" should be added to the list. It contends that depictions of "illegal acts of animal cruelty" that are "made, sold, or possessed for commercial gain" necessarily "lack expressive value," and may accordingly "be regulated as *unprotected* speech." The claim is not just that Congress may regulate depictions of animal cruelty subject to the First Amendment, but that these depictions are outside the reach of that Amendment altogether—that they fall into a "First Amendment Free Zone."

As the Government notes, the prohibition of animal cruelty itself has a long history in American law, starting with the early settlement of the Colonies. But we are unaware of any similar tradition excluding *depictions* of animal cruelty from "the freedom of speech" codified in the First Amendment, and the Government points us to none.

The Government contends that "historical evidence" about the reach of the First Amendment is not "a necessary prerequisite for regulation today," and that categories of speech may be exempted from the First Amendment's protection without any long-settled tradition of subjecting that speech to regulation. Instead, the Government points to Congress's "legislative judgment that depictions of animals being intentionally tortured and killed are of such minimal redeeming value as to render them unworthy of First Amendment protection," and asks the Court to uphold the ban on the same basis. The Government thus proposes that a claim of categorical exclusion should be considered under a simple balancing test: "Whether a given category of speech enjoys First Amendment protection depends upon a categorical balancing of the value of the speech against its societal costs."

As a free-floating test for First Amendment coverage, that sentence is startling and dangerous. The First Amendment's guarantee of free speech does not extend only to categories of speech that survive an ad hoc balancing of relative social costs and benefits. The First Amendment itself reflects a judgment by the American people that the benefits of its restrictions on the Government outweigh the costs. Our Constitution forecloses any attempt to revise that judgment simply on the basis that some speech is not worth it. The Constitution is not a document "prescribing limits, and declaring that those limits may be passed at pleasure."

To be fair to the Government, its view did not emerge from a vacuum. As the Government correctly notes, this Court has often *described* historically unprotected categories of speech as being "of such slight social value as a step to truth that any benefit that may be derived from them is clearly outweighed by the social interest in order and morality." In *New York v. Ferber,* we noted that within these categories of unprotected speech, "the evil to be restricted so overwhelmingly outweighs the expressive interests, if any, at stake, that no process of case-by-case adjudication is required," because "the balance of competing interests is clearly struck." The Government derives its proposed test from these descriptions in our precedents.

But such descriptions are just that—descriptive. They do not set forth a test that may be applied as a general matter to permit the Government to imprison any speaker so long as his speech is deemed valueless or unnecessary, or so long as an ad hoc calculus of costs and benefits tilts in a statute's favor.

When we have identified categories of speech as fully outside the protection of the First Amendment, it has not been on the basis of a simple cost-benefit analysis. In *Ferber*, for example, we classified child pornography as such a category. We noted that the State of New York had a compelling interest in protecting children from abuse, and that the value of using children in these works (as opposed to simulated conduct or adult actors) was *de minimis*. But our decision did not rest on this "balance of competing interests" alone. We made clear that *Ferber* presented a special case: The market for child pornography was "intrinsically related" to the underlying abuse, and was therefore "an integral part of the production of such materials, an activity illegal throughout the Nation." As we noted, "it rarely has been suggested that the constitutional freedom for speech and press extends its immunity to speech or writing used as an integral part of conduct in violation of a valid criminal statute." *Ferber* thus grounded its analysis in a previously recognized, long-established category of unprotected speech, and our subsequent decisions have shared this understanding.

Our decisions in *Ferber* and other cases cannot be taken as establishing a free-wheeling authority to declare new categories of speech outside the scope of the First Amendment. Maybe there are some categories of speech that have been historically unprotected, but have not yet been specifically identified or discussed as such in our case law. But if so, there is no evidence that "depictions of animal cruelty" is among them. We need not foreclose the future recognition of such additional categories to reject the Government's highly manipulable balancing test as a means of identifying them.

Because we decline to carve out from the First Amendment any novel exception for § 48, we review Stevens's First Amendment challenge under our existing doctrine.

Stevens challenged § 48 on its face, arguing that any conviction secured under the statute would be unconstitutional. The court below decided the case on that basis, and we granted the Solicitor General's petition for certiorari to determine "whether 18 U.S.C. 48 is facially invalid under the Free Speech Clause of the First Amendment."

In the First Amendment context, this Court recognizes "a second type of facial challenge," whereby a law may be invalidated as overbroad if "a substantial number of its applications are unconstitutional, judged in relation to the statute's plainly legitimate sweep." Stevens argues that § 48 applies to common depictions of ordinary and lawful activities, and that these depictions constitute the vast majority of materials subject to the statute. The Government makes no effort to defend such a broad ban as constitutional. Instead, the Government's entire defense of § 48 rests on interpreting the statute as narrowly limited to specific types of "extreme" material. As the parties have presented the issue, therefore, the constitutionality of § 48 hinges on how broadly it is construed. It is to that question that we now turn.

We read § 48 to create a criminal prohibition of alarming breadth. To begin with, the text of the statute's ban on a "depiction of animal cruelty" nowhere requires that the depicted conduct be cruel. That text applies to "any depiction" in which "a living animal is intentionally maimed, mutilated, tortured, wounded, or killed." § 48(c)(1). "Maimed, mutilated, and tortured" convey cruelty, but "wounded" or "killed" do not suggest any such limitation.

The Government contends that the terms in the definition should be read to require the additional element of "accompanying acts of cruelty." But the phrase "wounded or killed" at issue here contains little ambiguity. The Government's opening brief properly applies the ordinary meaning of these words, stating for example that to " 'kill' is 'to deprive of life.' " We agree that "wounded" and "killed" should be read according to their ordinary meaning. Nothing about that meaning requires cruelty.

While not requiring cruelty, § 48 does require that the depicted conduct be "illegal." But this requirement does not limit § 48 along the lines the Government suggests. There are myriad federal and state laws concerning the proper treatment of animals, but many of them are not designed to guard against animal cruelty. Protections of endangered species, for example, restrict even the humane "wounding or killing" of "living animals." § 48(c)(1). Livestock regulations are often designed to protect the health of human beings, and hunting and fishing rules (seasons, licensure, bag limits, weight requirements) can be designed to raise revenue, preserve animal populations, or prevent accidents. The text of § 48(c) draws no distinction based on the reason the intentional killing of an animal is made illegal, and includes, for example, the humane slaughter of a stolen cow.

What is more, the application of § 48 to depictions of illegal conduct extends to conduct that is illegal in only a single jurisdiction. Under subsection (c)(1), the depicted conduct need only be illegal in "the State in which the creation, sale, or possession takes place, regardless of whether the wounding or killing took place in that State." A depiction of entirely lawful conduct runs afoul of the ban if that depiction later finds its way into another State where the same conduct is unlawful. This provision greatly expands the scope of § 48, because although there may be "a broad societal consensus" against cruelty to animals, there is substantial disagreement on what types of conduct are properly regarded as cruel. Both views about cruelty to animals and regulations having no connection to cruelty vary widely from place to place.

In the District of Columbia, for example, all hunting is unlawful. Other jurisdictions permit or encourage hunting, and there is an enormous national market for hunting-related depictions in which a living animal is intentionally killed. Hunting periodicals have circulations in the hundreds of thousands or millions, and hunting television programs, videos, and Web sites are equally popular. The demand for hunting depictions exceeds the estimated demand for crush videos or animal fighting depictions by several orders of magnitude. Nonetheless, because the statute allows each jurisdiction to export its laws to the rest of the country, § 48(a) extends to *any* magazine or video depicting lawful hunting, so long as that depiction is sold within the Nation's Capital.

However "growing" and "lucrative" the markets for crush videos and dogfighting depictions might be, they are dwarfed by the market for other depictions, such as hunting magazines and videos, that we have determined to be within the scope of § 48. We therefore need not and do not decide whether a statute limited to crush videos or other depictions of extreme animal cruelty would be constitutional. We hold only that § 48 is not so limited but is instead substantially overbroad, and therefore invalid under the First Amendment.

The judgment of the United States Court of Appeals for the Third Circuit is affirmed.

JUSTICE ALITO, dissenting.

The Court strikes down in its entirety a valuable statute, 18 U.S.C. § 48, that was enacted not to suppress speech, but to prevent horrific acts of animal cruelty—in particular, the creation and commercial exploitation of "crush videos," a form of depraved entertainment that has no social value. The Court's approach, which has the practical effect of legalizing the sale of such videos and is thus likely to spur a resumption of their production, is unwarranted.

Instead of applying the doctrine of overbreadth, I would vacate the decision below and instruct the Court of Appeals on remand to decide whether the videos that respondent sold are constitutionally protected. If the question of overbreadth is to be decided, however, I do not think the present record supports the Court's conclusion that § 48 bans a substantial quantity of protected speech.

The First Amendment protects freedom of speech, but it most certainly does not protect violent criminal conduct, even if engaged in for expressive purposes. Crush videos present a highly unusual free speech issue because they are so closely linked with violent criminal conduct. The videos record the commission of violent criminal acts, and it appears that these crimes are committed for the sole purpose of creating the videos. In addition, as noted above, Congress was presented with compelling evidence that the only way of preventing these crimes was to target the sale of the videos. Under these circumstances, I cannot believe that the First Amendment commands Congress to step aside and allow the underlying crimes to continue.

The most relevant of our prior decisions is *Feber,* which concerned child pornography. The Court there held that child pornography is not protected speech, and I believe that Ferber's reasoning dictates a similar conclusion here.

In *Ferber*, an important factor—I would say the most important factor—was that child pornography involves the commission of a crime that inflicts severe personal injury to the "children who are made to engage in sexual conduct for commercial purposes." The *Ferber* Court repeatedly described the production of child pornography as child "abuse," "molestation," or "exploitation." Second, *Ferber* emphasized the fact that these underlying crimes could not be effectively combated without targeting the distribution of child pornography. Third, the *Ferber* Court noted that the value of child pornography "is exceedingly modest, if not *de minimis*," and that any such value was "overwhelmingly outweighed" by "the evil to be restricted."

All three of these characteristics are shared by § 48, as applied to crush videos. First, the conduct depicted in crush videos is criminal in every State and the District of Columbia. Thus, any crush video made in this country records the actual commission of a criminal act that inflicts severe physical injury and excruciating pain and ultimately results in death. Those who record the underlying criminal acts are likely to be criminally culpable, either as aiders and abettors or conspirators.

Second, the criminal acts shown in crush videos cannot be prevented without targeting the conduct prohibited by § 48—the creation, sale, and possession for sale of depictions of animal torture with the intention of realizing a commercial profit. The evidence presented to Congress posed a stark choice: Either ban the commercial exploitation of crush videos or tolerate a continuation of the criminal acts that they record. Faced with this evidence, Congress reasonably chose to target the lucrative crush video market.

Finally, the harm caused by the underlying crimes vastly outweighs any minimal value that the depictions might conceivably be thought to possess. Section 48 reaches only the actual recording of acts of animal torture; the statute does not apply to verbal descriptions or to simulations. And, unlike the child pornography statute in *Ferber* or its federal counterpart, 18 U.S.C. § 2252, § 48(b) provides an exception for depictions having any "serious religious, political, scientific, educational, journalistic, historical, or artistic value."

It must be acknowledged that § 48 differs from a child pornography law in an important respect: preventing the abuse of children is certainly much more important than preventing the torture of the animals used in crush videos. It was largely for this reason that the Court of Appeals concluded that *Ferber* did not support the constitutionality of § 48. But while protecting children is unquestionably *more* important than protecting animals, the Government also has a compelling interest in preventing the torture depicted in crush videos.

Points for Discussion

1. **Why didn't *Ferber* resolve this case?** In his dissent, Justice Samuel Alito contended that the reasoning in *Ferber* for categorically excluding child pornography from First Amendment protection should similarly justify denying protection to images of animal abuse. Do you agree? Why was Chief Justice Roberts reluctant to carve out a new category of unprotected speech for images of animal cruelty? Would there be a problem with the Court's doing so? Can child abuse and animal abuse be equated? Would it be helpful to ponder that question over a meal of veal cutlets and foie gras?

2. **Would a more narrowly tailored statute be constitutional?** Even if images of animal abuse are not categorically unprotected, the government could still regulate these images if it had a compelling justification for doing so. Does Chief Justice Roberts deny that such an interest might exist for extreme depictions of animal cruelty such as crush videos? After *Stevens* was decided, Congress amended the statute to limit its application to only crush videos. Should that have been enough to eliminate any constitutional concerns?

3. **Limiting unprotected categories to historic categories.** Chief Justice Roberts forcefully rejected the government's suggestion that judges can declare new categories of speech unprotected through a simple weighing of the speech's costs and benefits. He characterized the very notion of judges doing this as "startling and dangerous." Instead, he said that unprotected categories are limited to "historic and traditional categories" that have "never been thought to raise any constitutional problem." Do you think that this historical approach makes sense? Professor Genevieve Lakier contends that the Court's historical approach is neither good history nor good policy. She says that the historical record fails to reveal well-defined categories of unprotected speech and that relying on this "false view of history" merely allows judges' "value judgments" to "remain silent and hidden." Genevieve Lakier, *The Invention of Low-Value Speech*, 128 Harv. L Rev. 2166 (2015).

2. Regulating Minors' Access to Violent Video Games: If Minors Can Be Denied Access to Indecent Sexual Material, Why Not Graphic Violent Material?

We have seen that the government is permitted to deny minors access to sexual speech even if that speech does not rise to the level of obscenity under the *Miller* test. Should the government also be permitted to deny minors access to violent speech even if adults have a right to access this speech? The issue came up in *Brown v. Entertain-*

ment Merchants Association, a case concerning a California law that prohibited the rental or sale of violent video games to minors. In a concurring opinion, Justice Alito described some of the games as being horrifically violent:

> In some of these games, the violence is astounding. Victims by the dozens are killed with every imaginable implement, including machineguns, shotguns, clubs, hammers, axes, swords, and chainsaws. Victims are dismembered, decapitated, disemboweled, set on fire, and chopped into little pieces. They cry out in agony and beg for mercy. Blood gushes, splatters, and pools. Severed body parts and gobs of human remains are graphically shown. In some games, points are awarded based, not only on the number of victims killed, but on the killing technique employed.
>
> It also appears that there is no antisocial theme too base for some in the video-game industry to exploit. There are games in which a player can take on the identity and reenact the killings carried out by the perpetrators of the murders at Columbine High School and Virginia Tech. The objective of one game is to rape a mother and her daughters; in another, the goal is to rape Native American women. There is a game in which players engage in "ethnic cleansing" and can choose to gun down African-Americans, Latinos, or Jews. In still another game, players attempt to fire a rifle shot into the head of President Kennedy as his motorcade passes by the Texas School Book Depository.

Brown v. Entertainment Merchants Association

Supreme Court of the United States, 2011
564 U.S. 786

JUSTICE SCALIA delivered the opinion of the Court.

We consider whether a California law imposing restrictions on violent video games comports with the First Amendment.

California Assembly Bill 1179 (2005) prohibits the sale or rental of "violent video games" to minors, and requires their packaging to be labeled "18." The Act covers games "in which the range of options available to a player includes killing, maiming, dismembering, or sexually assaulting an image of a human being, if those acts are depicted" in a manner that "a reasonable person, considering the game as a whole, would find appeals to a deviant or morbid interest of minors," that is "patently offensive to prevailing standards in the community as to what is suitable for minors," and that "causes the game, as a whole, to lack serious literary, artistic, political, or scientific value for minors." Violation of the Act is punishable by a civil fine of up to $1,000.

Respondents, representing the video-game and software industries, brought a preenforcement challenge to the Act in the United States District Court for the Northern District of California. That court concluded that the Act violated the First Amendment and permanently enjoined its enforcement. The Court of Appeals affirmed, and we granted certiorari.

California correctly acknowledges that video games qualify for First Amendment protection. The Free Speech Clause exists principally to protect discourse on public matters, but we have long recognized that it is difficult to distinguish politics from entertainment, and dangerous to try. "Everyone is familiar with instances of propaganda through fiction. What is one man's amusement, teaches another's doctrine." Like the protected books, plays, and movies that preceded them, video games communicate ideas—and even social messages—through many familiar literary devices (such as characters, dialogue, plot, and music) and through features distinctive to the medium (such as the player's interaction with the virtual world). That suffices to confer First Amendment protection. Under our Constitution, "esthetic and moral judgments about art and literature are for the individual to make, not for the Government to decree, even with the mandate or approval of a majority." And whatever the challenges of applying the Constitution to ever-advancing technology, "the basic principles of freedom of speech and the press, like the First Amendment's command, do not vary" when a new and different medium for communication appears.

The most basic of those principles is this: "As a general matter, government has no power to restrict expression because of its message, its ideas, its subject matter, or its content." There are of course exceptions. "From 1791 to the present, the First Amendment has permitted restrictions upon the content of speech in a few limited areas, and has never included a freedom to disregard these traditional limitations."

Last Term, in *Stevens,* we held that new categories of unprotected speech may not be added to the list by a legislature that concludes certain speech is too harmful to be tolerated. That holding controls this case. As in *Stevens,* California has tried to make violent-speech regulation look like obscenity regulation by appending a saving clause required for the latter. That does not suffice. Our cases have been clear that the obscenity exception to the First Amendment does not cover whatever a legislature finds shocking, but only depictions of "sexual conduct." Because speech about violence is not obscene, it is of no consequence that California's statute mimics the New York statute regulating obscenity for minors that we upheld in *Ginsberg*.

The California Act is something else entirely. It does not adjust the boundaries of an existing category of unprotected speech to ensure that a definition designed for adults is not uncritically applied to children. California does not argue that it is empowered to prohibit selling offensively violent works *to adults*—and it is wise not to, since that is but a hair's breadth from the argument rejected in *Stevens*. Instead, it wishes to create a wholly new category of content-based regulation that is permissible only for speech directed at children.

That is unprecedented and mistaken. "Minors are entitled to a significant measure of First Amendment protection, and only in relatively narrow and well-defined circumstances may government bar public dissemination of protected materials to them." No doubt a State possesses legitimate power to protect children from harm, but that does not include a free-floating power to restrict the ideas to which children may be exposed. "Speech that is neither obscene as to youths nor subject to some other legitimate proscription cannot be suppressed solely to protect the young from ideas or images that a legislative body thinks unsuitable for them."

California's argument would fare better if there were a longstanding tradition in this country of specially restricting children's access to depictions of violence, but there is none. Certainly the *books* we give children to read—or read to them when they are younger—contain no shortage of gore. Grimm's Fairy Tales, for example, are grim indeed. As her just deserts for trying to poison Snow White, the wicked queen is made to dance in red hot slippers "till she fell dead on the floor, a sad example of envy and jealousy." Cinderella's evil stepsisters have their eyes pecked out by doves. And Hansel and Gretel (children!) kill their captor by baking her in an oven.

High-school reading lists are full of similar fare. Homer's Odysseus blinds Polyphemus the Cyclops by grinding out his eye with a heated stake. In the Inferno, Dante and Virgil watch corrupt politicians struggle to stay submerged beneath a lake of boiling pitch, lest they be skewered by devils above the surface. And Golding's Lord of the Flies recounts how a schoolboy called Piggy is savagely murdered *by other children* while marooned on an island.

California claims that video games present special problems because they are "interactive," in that the player participates in the violent action on screen and determines its outcome. The latter feature is nothing new: Since at least the publication of The Adventures of You: Sugarcane Island in 1969, young readers of choose-your-own-adventure stories have been able to make decisions that determine the plot by following instructions about which page to turn to. As for the argument that video games enable participation in the violent action, that seems to us more a matter of degree than of kind. As Judge Posner has observed, all literature is interactive. "The better it is, the more interactive. Literature when it is successful draws the reader into the story, makes him identify with the characters, invites him to judge them and quarrel with them, to experience their joys and sufferings as the reader's own."

Because the Act imposes a restriction on the content of protected speech, it is invalid unless California can demonstrate that it passes strict scrutiny—that is, unless it is justified by a compelling government interest and is narrowly drawn to serve that interest. The State must specifically identify an "actual problem" in need of solving, and the curtailment of free speech must be actually necessary to the solution. That is a demanding standard. "It is rare that a regulation restricting speech because of its content will ever be permissible."

California cannot meet that standard. The State's evidence is not compelling. California relies primarily on the research of Dr. Craig Anderson and a few other research psychologists whose studies purport to show a connection between exposure to violent video games and harmful effects on children. These studies have been rejected by every court to consider them, and with good reason: They do not prove that violent video games *cause* minors to *act* aggressively (which would at least be a beginning). Instead, "nearly all of the research is based on correlation, not evidence of causation, and most of the studies suffer from significant, admitted flaws in methodology." They show at best some correlation between exposure to violent entertainment and minuscule real-world effects, such as children's feeling more aggressive or making louder noises in the few minutes after playing a violent game than after playing a nonviolent game.

Even taking for granted Dr. Anderson's conclusions that violent video games produce some effect on children's feelings of aggression, those effects are both small and indistinguishable from effects produced by other media. In his testimony in a similar lawsuit, Dr. Anderson admitted that the "effect sizes" of children's exposure to violent video games are "about the same" as that produced by their exposure to violence on television. And he admits that the *same* effects have been found when children watch cartoons starring Bugs Bunny or the Road Runner, or when they play video games like Sonic the Hedgehog that are rated "E" (appropriate for all ages), or even when they "view a picture of a gun."

Of course, California has (wisely) declined to restrict Saturday morning cartoons, the sale of games rated for young children, or the distribution of pictures of guns. The consequence is that its regulation is wildly underinclusive when judged against its asserted justification, which in our view is alone enough to defeat it. Underinclusiveness raises serious doubts about whether the government is in fact pursuing the interest it invokes, rather than disfavoring a particular speaker or viewpoint. Here, California has singled out the purveyors of video games for disfavored treatment—at least when compared to booksellers, cartoonists, and movie producers—and has given no persuasive reason why.

The Act is also seriously underinclusive in another respect—and a respect that renders irrelevant the contentions of the concurrence and the dissents that video games are qualitatively different from other portrayals of violence. The California Legislature is perfectly willing to leave this dangerous, mind-altering material in the hands of children so long as one parent (or even an aunt or uncle) says it's OK. And there are not even any requirements as to how this parental or avuncular relationship is to be verified; apparently the child's or putative parent's, aunt's, or uncle's say-so suffices. That is not how one addresses a serious social problem.

California claims that the Act is justified in aid of parental authority: By requiring that the purchase of violent video games can be made only by adults, the Act ensures that parents can decide what games are appropriate. At the outset, we note our doubts that punishing third parties for conveying protected speech to children *just in case* their parents disapprove of that speech is a proper governmental means of aiding parental authority. Accepting that position would largely vitiate the rule that "only in relatively narrow and well-defined circumstances may government bar public dissemination of protected materials to minors."

But leaving that aside, California cannot show that the Act's restrictions meet a substantial need of parents who wish to restrict their children's access to violent video games but cannot do so. The video-game industry has in place a voluntary rating system designed to inform consumers about the content of games. In 2009, the Federal Trade Commission (FTC) found that, as a result of this system, "the video game industry outpaces the movie and music industries" in "(1) restricting target-marketing of mature-rated products to children; (2) clearly and prominently disclosing rating information; and (3) restricting children's access to mature-rated products at retail." This system does much to ensure that minors cannot purchase seriously violent games on their own, and that parents who care about the matter can readily evaluate the games their children bring home. Filling the remaining modest gap in concerned parents' control can hardly be a compelling state interest.

And finally, the Act's purported aid to parental authority is vastly overinclusive. Not all of the children who are forbidden to purchase violent video games on their own have parents who *care* whether they purchase violent video games.

California's legislation straddles the fence between (1) addressing a serious social problem and (2) helping concerned parents control their children. Both ends are legitimate, but when they affect First Amendment rights they must be pursued by means that are neither seriously underinclusive nor seriously overinclusive. As a means of protecting children from portrayals of violence, the legislation is seriously underinclusive, not only because it excludes portrayals other than video games, but also because it permits a parental or avuncular veto. And as a means of assisting concerned parents it is seriously overinclusive because it abridges the First Amendment rights of young people whose parents (and aunts and uncles) think violent video games are a harmless pastime. And the overbreadth in achieving one goal is not cured by the underbreadth in achieving the other. Legislation such as this, which is neither fish nor fowl, cannot survive strict scrutiny.

We affirm the judgment below.

JUSTICE ALITO, with whom THE CHIEF JUSTICE joins, concurring in the judgment.

The California statute that is before us in this case represents a pioneering effort to address what the state legislature and others regard as a potentially serious social problem: the effect of exceptionally violent video games on impressionable minors, who often spend countless hours immersed in the alternative worlds that these games create. Although the California statute is well intentioned, its terms are not framed with the precision that the Constitution demands, and I therefore agree with the Court that this particular law cannot be sustained.

I disagree, however, with the approach taken in the Court's opinion. In considering the application of unchanging constitutional principles to new and rapidly evolving technology, this Court should proceed with caution. We should not jump to the conclusion that new technology is fundamentally the same as some older thing with which we are familiar. And we should not hastily dismiss the judgment of legislators, who may be in a better position than we are to assess the implications of new technology. The opinion of the Court exhibits none of this caution.

In the view of the Court, all those concerned about the effects of violent video games—federal and state legislators, educators, social scientists, and parents—are unduly fearful, for violent video games really present no serious problem. Spending hour upon hour controlling the actions of a character who guns down scores of innocent victims is not different in "kind" from reading a description of violence in a work of literature.

The Court is sure of this; I am not. There are reasons to suspect that the experience of playing violent video games just might be very different from reading a book, listening to the radio, or watching a movie or a television show.

JUSTICE THOMAS, dissenting.

The Court's decision today does not comport with the original public understanding of the First Amendment. The practices and beliefs of the founding generation establish that "the freedom of speech," as originally understood, does not include a right to speak to minors (or a right of minors to access speech) without going through the minors' parents or guardians. I would hold that the law at issue is not facially unconstitutional under the First Amendment, and reverse and remand for further proceedings.

JUSTICE BREYER, dissenting.

Applying traditional First Amendment analysis, I would uphold the statute as constitutional on its face and would consequently reject the industries' facial challenge. In my view, California's statute provides "fair notice of what is prohibited," and consequently it is not impermissibly vague. Like the majority, I believe that the California law must be "narrowly tailored" to further a "compelling interest," without there being a "less restrictive" alternative that would be "at least as effective."

The interest that California advances in support of the statute is compelling. As this Court has previously described that interest, it consists of both (1) the "basic" parental claim "to authority in their own household to direct the rearing of their children," which makes it proper to enact "laws designed to aid discharge of [parental] responsibility," and (2) the State's "independent interest in the well-being of its youth." Both interests are present here.

There are many scientific studies that support California's views. Social scientists, for example, have found *causal* evidence that playing these games results in harm. Longitudinal studies, which measure changes over time, have found that increased exposure to violent video games causes an increase in aggression over the same period. Experimental studies in laboratories have found that subjects randomly assigned to play a violent video game subsequently displayed more characteristics of aggression than those who played nonviolent games. Surveys of eighth and ninth grade students have found a correlation between playing violent video games and aggression.

Cutting-edge neuroscience has shown that "virtual violence in video game playing results in those neural patterns that are considered characteristic for aggressive cognition and behavior." And "meta-analyses," *i.e.*, studies of all the studies, have concluded that exposure to violent video games "was positively associated with aggressive behavior, aggressive cognition, and aggressive affect," and that "playing violent video games is a *causal* risk factor for long-term harmful outcomes." Some of these studies take care to explain in a commonsense way why video games are potentially more harmful than, say, films or books or television. In essence, they say that the closer a child's behavior comes, not to watching, but to *acting* out horrific violence, the greater the potential psychological harm.

Experts debate the conclusions of all these studies. I, like most judges, lack the social science expertise to say definitively who is right. But associations of public health professionals who do possess that expertise have reviewed many of these studies and found a significant risk that violent video games, when compared with more passive media, are particularly likely to cause children harm. Eleven years ago, for example, the American Academy of Pediatrics, the American Academy of Child & Adolescent Psychiatry, the American Psychological Association, the American Medical Association, the American Academy of Family Physicians, and the American Psychiatric Association released a joint statement, which said: "Over 1000 studies point overwhelmingly to a causal connection between media violence and aggressive behavior in some children." Five years later, after more research had been done, the American Psychological Association adopted a resolution that said:

> Comprehensive analysis of violent interactive video game research suggests such exposure increases aggressive behavior, increases aggressive thoughts, increases angry feelings, decreases helpful behavior, and increases physiological arousal.

Unlike the majority, I would find sufficient grounds in these studies and expert opinions for this Court to defer to an elected legislature's conclusion that the video games in question are particularly likely to harm children. This Court has always thought it owed an elected legislature some degree of deference in respect to legislative facts of this kind, particularly when they involve technical matters that are beyond our competence, and even in First Amendment cases.

I can find no "less restrictive" alternative to California's law that would be "at least as effective." The majority points to a voluntary alternative: The industry tries to prevent those under 17 from buying extremely violent games by labeling those games with an "M" (Mature) and encouraging retailers to restrict their sales to those 17 and older. But as of the FTC's most recent update to Congress, 20% of those under 17 are still able to buy M-rated video games, and, breaking down sales by store, one finds that this number rises to nearly 50% in the case of one large national chain.

The upshot is that California's statute, as applied to its heartland of applications (*i.e.,* buyers under 17; extremely violent, realistic video games), imposes a restriction on speech that is modest at most. That restriction is justified by a compelling interest. And there is no equally effective, less restrictive alternative. California's statute is consequently constitutional on its face—though litigants remain free to challenge the statute as applied in particular instances.

I add that the majority's different conclusion creates a serious anomaly in First Amendment law. *Ginsberg* makes clear that a State can prohibit the sale to minors of depictions of nudity; today the Court makes clear that a State cannot prohibit the sale to minors of the most violent interactive video games. But what sense does it make to forbid selling to a 13-year-old boy a magazine with an image of a nude woman, while protecting a sale to that 13-year-old of an interactive video game in which he actively, but virtually, binds and gags the woman, then tortures and kills her? What kind of First Amendment would permit the government to protect children by restricting sales of that extremely violent video game *only* when the woman—bound, gagged, tortured, and killed—is also topless?

Points for Discussion

1. **Did the Court categorically bar regulation of violent speech to protect children?** Justice Scalia was not enamored with the California statute, but did he rule

out the possibility that a more carefully drafted statute could pass constitutional muster?

2. **Are "Grand Theft Auto" and "Hansel and Gretel" comparable?** The government sought to extend the principle of *Ginsberg*, which allows the government to deny minors access to non-obscene sexual speech, to also allow the government to deny minors access to violent speech. Justice Scalia rejected this extension, in large part because he said there was no longstanding tradition of parents' denying their children access to violent material. To the contrary, he said, it is common for parents to read children stories that are replete with violence, such as Hansel and Gretel ("children!") pushing the witch into the oven? Do you think that it is fair to analogize parents' reading "Hansel and Gretel" to their children to teenagers' playing first-person-shooter video games alone in their bedrooms?

3. **You be the judge!** Would you be inclined to uphold a law that prohibited the sale or rental of violent video games to minors? Would it make a difference to you if there was evidence that teenagers who have committed mass shootings have been avid players of violent video games? Would it make a difference that the military uses video games to help soldiers overcome their resistance to shooting people? *See* Alan E. Garfield, *Protecting Children from Speech*, 57 Fla. L. Rev. 565 (2005).

4. **What should the government have to prove?** Justice Scalia said that California had failed to meet its burden under strict scrutiny because "it cannot show a direct causal link between violent video games and harm to minors." How easy do you think it is to prove such a causal link? Should it matter if social scientists are prohibited from showing the most violent video games to minors because doing so would be unethical? Do you think that the government should be required to meet this heavy empirical burden or that legislators should be able to rely on their common-sense perception that these games are harmful to minors?

   The Supreme Court did not insist on such empirical proof of harm when it upheld the regulation of obscene speech. In response to the argument that there was no scientific evidence of obscenity's harmfulness, the Court in *Paris Adult Theatre* said:

   > We do not demand of legislatures "scientifically certain criteria of legislation." Although there is no conclusive proof of a connection between antisocial behavior and obscene material, the legislature of Georgia could quite reasonably determine that such a connection does or might exist. In deciding *Roth*, this Court implicitly accepted that a legislature could legitimately act on such a conclusion to protect "the social interest in order and morality."

5. **Industry efforts to ward off government regulation.** Sometimes media industries will adopt their own standards to control minor access to sexual or violent material in the hope of warding off government regulation. For example, the video game industry established the Entertainment Software Ratings Board (ESRB) to create ratings for video games, and the Motion Picture Association sets ratings for movies. Why didn't Justice Breyer think that the ESRB ratings were sufficient to address the government's concerns with minors' access to violent video games?

6. **Was Justice Breyer right to be exasperated?** Toward the end of his dissent, Justice Breyer plaintively poses this question: "What kind of First Amendment would permit the government to protect children by restricting sales of [an] extremely violent video game *only* when the woman—bound, gagged, tortured, and killed—is also topless?" What was his point? Do you agree with him?

7. **Justice Thomas' originalist approach.** Justice Thomas sought to resolve this case using an originalist interpretation of the First Amendment. Does his analysis strike as you a good vehicle for resolving this or other First Amendment cases? Why or why not?

A Comparative Perspective

Other countries, including Canada, the United Kingdom, Australia, and Germany, have been more willing to permit restrictions on minors' access to violent video games. Have they struck a better balance between free speech and the protection of minors, or are they wrongfully denying minors access to expression? *See, e.g.*, Kevin W. Saunders, *A Comparative Look at Children and Free Expression*, 21 Transnat'l L. & Contemp. Probs. 455 (2013).

Test Your Knowledge

To assess your understanding of the material in this chapter, click here to take a quiz.

Chapter Eight

May Government Regulate Speech to Promote National Unity?

Pledge Protests and Flag Burnings

In this chapter, we examine whether the government may regulate speech to promote patriotism and a sense of national unity. We will explore whether the government may cultivate this loyalty by requiring public school students to recite the Pledge of Allegiance. We will also examine whether the government may punish those who desecrate symbols of national unity, such as protesters who burn the national flag.

Before diving into this material, you might want to ask yourself whether it is important for Americans to have a strong sense of national unity. What benefits arise when citizens have this sense? What problems arise when they do not? If it is desirable for citizens to have a strong sense of national unity, what measures may the government take to foster this unity? May it use only carrots to achieve this end, or may it also use sticks?

A. Mandatory Pledge Ceremonies: May Children Be Required to Say the Pledge of Allegiance?

Conventional wisdom attributes authorship of the Pledge of Allegiance to Francis Bellamy, a Baptist minister and Christian socialist.[1] Bellamy wrote the pledge in 1892 for *Youth Companion* magazine as part of a program to celebrate the quadricentennial of Columbus' voyage to the Americas.[2]

---

1 Recently discovered evidence suggests that the Pledge may have been written by a 13-year-old Kansas boy with a remarkably similar name, Frank Bellamy. Sam Roberts, *We Know the Pledge. It's Author, Maybe Not*, N.Y. Times, Apr. 2, 2022.

2 Vincent Blasi & Seana V. Shiffrin, *The Story of West Virginia State Board of Education v. Barnette: The Pledge of Allegiance and the Freedom of Thought*, in First Amendment Stories 99, 100 (Richard W. Garnett & Andrew Koppelman, eds., 2012).

The original pledge varied from the current version. It did not include the words "one nation under God." Those words were added during the Cold War to distinguish the United States from atheist Communist countries.[3] During the original recitation of the pledge, people extended their arms outright toward the flag. This was discontinued in the 1940s because of its resemblance to a Nazi salute.[4]

In 1898, New York became the first state to require public schools to have a flag salute ceremony. By 1940, nine states required such ceremonies.[5]

The next two cases concern Jehovah's Witnesses who refused to participate in these ceremonies. The children's families claimed that participation in these ceremonies amounted to worshiping a graven image, in violation of their faith. They argued that this violated both their First Amendment religious liberty rights and their freedom of speech.

The Court decided the first case in 1940 while war was raging in Europe but before the United States had entered the war. Justice Felix Frankfurter, the author of the opinion, had immigrated to the United States from Austria when he was 11 years old and did not know English. He rose to become a Harvard Law professor, one of the founders of the American Civil Liberties Union, and a close confidant of President Franklin Delano Roosevelt. He joined the Supreme Court in 1939.

Justice Felix Frankfurter
Harris & Ewing, Collection of the Supreme Court of the United States

3 Steven G. Gey, *Under God, The Pledge of Allegiance, and Other Constitutional Trivia*, 81 N.C. L. Rev. 1865, 1877–78 (2003).

4 Blasi & Shiffrin, *supra* note 2 at 102 n.14.

5 *Id.* at 100–101.

Minersville School District v. Gobitis

Supreme Court of the United States, 1940
310 U.S. 586

MR. JUSTICE FRANKFURTER delivered the opinion of the Court.

A grave responsibility confronts this Court whenever in course of litigation it must reconcile the conflicting claims of liberty and authority. But when the liberty invoked is liberty of conscience, and the authority is authority to safeguard the nation's fellowship, judicial conscience is put to its severest test. Of such a nature is the present controversy.

Lillian Gobitis, aged twelve, and her brother William, aged ten, were expelled from the public schools of Minersville, Pennsylvania, for refusing to salute the national flag as part of a daily school exercise. The local Board of Education required both teachers and pupils to participate in this ceremony. The ceremony is a familiar one. The right hand is placed on the breast and the following pledge recited in unison: "I pledge allegiance to my flag, and to the Republic for which it stands; one nation indivisible, with liberty and justice for all." While the words are spoken, teachers and pupils extend their right hands in salute to the flag. The Gobitis family are affiliated with "Jehovah's Witnesses," for whom the Bible as the Word of God is the supreme authority. The children had been brought up conscientiously to believe that such a gesture of respect for the flag was forbidden by command of scripture.

The Gobitis children were of an age for which Pennsylvania makes school attendance compulsory. Thus they were denied a free education and their parents had to put them into private schools. To be relieved of the financial burden thereby entailed, their father, on behalf of the children and in his own behalf, brought this suit. He sought to enjoin the authorities from continuing to exact participation in the flag-salute ceremony as a condition of his children's attendance at the Minersville school.

We must decide whether the requirement of participation in such a ceremony, exacted from a child who refuses upon sincere religious grounds, infringes without due process of law the liberty guaranteed by the Fourteenth Amendment.

Conscientious scruples have not, in the course of the long struggle for religious toleration, relieved the individual from obedience to a general law not aimed at the promotion or restriction of religious beliefs. Nor does the freedom of speech assured by Due Process move in a more absolute circle of immunity than that enjoyed by religious freedom. Even if it were assumed that freedom of speech goes beyond the historic concept of full opportunity to utter and to disseminate views, the question remains whether school children, like the Gobitis children, must be excused from conduct required of all the other children in the promotion of national cohesion. We are dealing with an interest inferior to none in the hierarchy of legal values. National unity is the basis of national security.

Situations like the present are phases of the profoundest problem confronting a democracy-the problem which Lincoln cast in memorable dilemma: "Must a government of necessity be too strong for the liberties of its people, or too weak to maintain its own existence?" No mere textual reading or logical talisman can solve the dilemma. And when the issue demands judicial determination, it is not the personal notion of judges of what wise adjustment requires which must prevail.

The ultimate foundation of a free society is the binding tie of cohesive sentiment. Such a sentiment is fostered by all those agencies of the mind and spirit which may serve to gather up the traditions of a people, transmit them from generation to generation, and thereby create that continuity of a treasured common life which constitutes a civilization. We live by symbols. The flag is the symbol of our national unity, transcending all internal differences, however large, within the framework of the Constitution.

The wisdom of training children in patriotic impulses by those compulsions which necessarily pervade so much of the educational process is not for our independent judgment. Even were we convinced of the folly of such a measure, such belief would be no proof of its unconstitutionality. For ourselves, we might be tempted to say that the deepest patriotism is best engendered by giving unfettered scope to the most crotchety beliefs. Perhaps it is best to give to the least popular sect leave from conformities like those here in issue. But the courtroom is not the arena for debating issues of educational policy. It is not our province to choose among competing considerations in the subtle process of securing effective loyalty to the traditional ideals of democracy, while respecting at the same time individual idiosyncracies among a people so diversified in racial origins and religious allegiances. So to hold would in effect make us the school board for the country. That authority has not been given to this Court, nor should we assume it.

What the school authorities are really asserting is the right to awaken in the child's mind considerations as to the significance of the flag contrary to those implanted by the parent. In such an attempt the state is normally at a disadvantage in competing with the parent's authority, so long—and this is the vital aspect of religious toleration—as parents are unmolested in their right to counteract by their own persuasiveness the wisdom and rightness of those loyalties which the state's educational system is seeking to promote.

The preciousness of the family relation, the authority and independence which give dignity to parenthood, indeed the enjoyment of all freedom, presuppose the kind of ordered society which is summarized by our flag. A society which is dedicated to the preservation of these ultimate values of civilization may in self-protection utilize the educational process for inculcating those almost unconscious feelings which bind men together in a comprehending loyalty, whatever may be their lesser differences and difficulties. That is to say, the process may be utilized so long as men's right to believe as they please, to win others to their way of belief, and their right to assemble in their chosen places of worship for the devotional ceremonies of their faith, are all fully respected.

[Justice Stone's dissent is omitted.]

Points for Discussion

1. **Where was the abridgment of speech?** The Minersville School District did not forbid the Gobitis parents or children from saying whatever they wanted to say about the flag, including that they considered the flag to be a graven image. What, then, was the basis for the children's claim that the mandatory pledge ceremony violated their freedom of speech?

2. **Why did the Court uphold the school district's mandatory pledge policy**? Even if the Minersville School District was abridging the students' free speech rights, the district's policy could still be upheld if there were a sufficiently compelling interest to justify it. In upholding the policy, what governmental interest did Justice Frankfurter allude to? Why did he think this interest was compelling?

3. **Judicial review and judicial restraint.** Justice Frankfurter was a strong proponent of judicial restraint. He believed that judges should use their power of judicial review sparingly by largely deferring to the decisions of the political branches. His penchant for judicial restraint was reflected in the *Gobitis* opinion when he emphasized that "the courtroom is not the arena for debating issues of educational policy" and warned that judicial meddling in this area would make the Court "the school board for the country."

   Yet Justice Frankfurter, one of the founders of the ACLU, was also keenly aware of the importance of protecting minority rights. This strain of thought is likewise reflected in the *Gobitis* opinion when he acknowledged that he and the other justices "might be tempted to say that the deepest patriotism is best engendered by giving unfettered scope to the most crotchety beliefs" and that it might be preferable "to give to the least popular sect leave from conformities like those here in issue."

Justice Frankfurter ultimately chose deference to the school district over the rights of the children and their parents. Do you think he made the right decision, or do you think he should have ruled in favor of the Gobitis family?

4. **The aftermath of *Gobitis*.** The Court's decision was issued on June 3, 1940. Professors Vincent Blasi and Seana Shiffrin note that the decision's timing coincided with the frantic evacuation of British and French troops from Dunkirk, France, to avoid a devastating defeat by the Germans.

The Jehovah's Witnesses' unwillingness to recite the Pledge of Allegiance did not sit well with the American public. As Blasi and Shiffrin explain, "many Americans regarded the Witnesses' refusal to recite the pledge as evidence of their disloyalty and of their sympathy and even collaboration with the Nazi regime." The Court's ruling against the Witnesses added fuel to the fire because some misinterpreted it as confirmation of their disloyalty. Blasi and Shiffrin describe the ensuing violence:

> In the weeks following the Supreme Court's decision, there were hundreds of violent attacks against Witnesses and their property, some abetted by local law enforcement officials. In Richwood, West Virginia, a group of American Legion vigilantes, led by a sheriff's deputy, forced several Witnesses to drink large quantities of castor oil, roped them together, then paraded them through the town. Over five hundred taunting citizens followed the procession, which at one point was halted for an impromptu flag salute ceremony and a reading of the American Legion constitution. Finally, the Witnesses were marched to the edge of town, where they found their automobiles painted with swastikas and graffiti accusing them of being "Hitler's spies" and a "Fifth Column." A Rawlins, Wyoming mob beat up five Witnesses, three men and two women, and burned their cars; in another Wyoming community, a member of the sect was literally tarred and feathered.

Vincent Blasi & Seana V. Shiffrin, *The Story of West Virginia State Board of Education v. Barnette; The Pledge of Allegiance and the Freedom of Thought*, in First Amendment Stories 99, 109–10 (Richard W. Garnett & Andrew Koppelman, eds., 2012). While people in the United States were attacking Jehovah's Witnesses for being Nazi sympathizers, the Nazis in Europe were persecuting Jehovah's Witnesses, including sending about 10,000 of them to concentration camps.

Three years after *Gobitis* was decided, the Court revisited mandatory pledge ceremonies. In the interim, two of the justices in the *Gobitis* majority had retired. Three other justices from the majority had signaled a willingness to overturn the decision. The resulting opinion in *West Virginia State Board of Education v. Barnette* follows. The opinion was written by Justice Robert Jackson, who had recently joined the Court. He is regarded as one of the Court's most eloquent writers. You are about to find out why.

Justice Robert Jackson
Harris & Ewing, Collection of the Supreme Court of the United States

West Virginia State Board of Education v. Barnette

Supreme Court of the United States, 1943
319 U.S. 624

MR. JUSTICE JACKSON delivered the opinion of the Court.

Following the decision by this Court on June 3, 1940, in *Minersville School District v. Gobitis,* the West Virginia legislature amended its statutes to require all schools therein to conduct courses of instruction in history, civics, and in the Constitutions of the United States and of the State "for the purpose of teaching, fostering and perpetuating the ideals, principles and spirit of Americanism, and increasing the knowledge of the organization and machinery of the government." Appellant Board of Education was directed, with advice of the State Superintendent of Schools, to "prescribe the courses of study covering these subjects" for public schools. The Act made it the duty of private, parochial and denominational schools to prescribe courses of study "similar to those required for the public schools."

The Board of Education on January 9, 1942, adopted a resolution containing recitals taken largely from the Court's *Gobitis* opinion and ordering that the salute to the flag become "a regular part of the program of activities in the public schools," that all teachers and pupils "shall be required to participate in the salute honoring the Nation represented by the Flag; provided, however, that refusal to salute the Flag be regarded as an Act of insubordination, and shall be dealt with accordingly."

Minerville case

Failure to conform is "insubordination" dealt with by expulsion. Readmission is denied by statute until compliance. Meanwhile the expelled child is "unlawfully absent" and may be proceeded against as a delinquent. His parents or guardians are liable to prosecution, and if convicted are subject to fine not exceeding $50 and jail term not exceeding thirty days.

Appellees, citizens of the United States and of West Virginia, brought suit in the United States District Court for themselves and others similarly situated asking its injunction to restrain enforcement of these laws and regulations against Jehovah's Witnesses. The Witnesses are an unincorporated body teaching that the obligation imposed by law of God is superior to that of laws enacted by temporal government. Their religious beliefs include a literal version of Exodus, Chapter 20, verses 4 and 5, which says: "Thou shalt not make unto thee any graven image, or any likeness of anything that is in heaven above, or that is in the earth beneath, or that is in the water under the earth; thou shalt not bow down thyself to them nor serve them." They consider that the flag is an "image" within this command. For this reason they refuse to salute it.

Children of this faith have been expelled from school and are threatened with exclusion for no other cause. Officials threaten to send them to reformatories maintained for criminally inclined juveniles. Parents of such children have been prosecuted and are threatened with prosecutions for causing delinquency.

This case calls upon us to reconsider a precedent decision, as the Court throughout its history often has been required to do. Before turning to the *Gobitis* case, however, it is desirable to notice certain characteristics by which this controversy is distinguished.

The freedom asserted by these appellees does not bring them into collision with rights asserted by any other individual. It is such conflicts which most frequently require intervention of the State to determine where the rights of one end and those of another begin. But the refusal of these persons to participate in the ceremony does not interfere with or deny rights of others to do so. Nor is there any question in this case that their behavior is peaceable and orderly. The sole conflict is between authority and rights of the individual. The State asserts power to condition access to public education on making a prescribed sign and profession and at the same time to coerce attendance by punishing both parent and child. The latter stand on a right of self-determination in matters that touch individual opinion and personal attitude.

As the present Chief Justice said in dissent in the *Gobitis* case, the State may "require teaching by instruction and study of all in our history and in the structure and organization of our government, including the guaranties of civil liberty which tend to inspire patriotism and love of country." Here, however, we are dealing with a compulsion of students to declare a belief. They are not merely made acquainted with the flag salute so that they may be informed as to what it is or even what it means. The issue here is whether this slow and easily neglected route to aroused loyalties constitutionally may be short-cut by substituting a compulsory salute and slogan.

To sustain the compulsory flag salute we are required to say that a Bill of Rights which guards the individual's right to speak his own mind, left it open to public authorities to compel him to utter what is not in his mind. The *Gobitis* decision *assumed* that power exists in the State to impose the flag salute discipline upon school children in general. We examine rather than assume existence of this power and re-examine specific grounds assigned for the *Gobitis* decision.

1. It was said that the flag-salute controversy confronted the Court with "the problem which Lincoln cast in memorable dilemma: Must a government of necessity be too strong for the liberties of its people, or too weak to maintain its own existence?" and that the answer must be in favor of strength. We think these issues may be examined free of pressure or restraint growing out of such considerations.

It may be doubted whether Mr. Lincoln would have thought that the strength of government to maintain itself would be impressively vindicated by our confirming power of the state to expel a handful of children from school. Such oversimplification, so handy in political debate, often lacks the precision necessary to postulates of judicial reasoning. If validly applied to this problem, the utterance cited would resolve every issue of power in favor of those in authority and would require us to override every liberty thought to weaken or delay execution of their policies.

2. It was also considered in the *Gobitis* case that functions of educational officers in states, counties and school districts were such that to interfere with their authority "would in effect make us the school board for the country."

14th protects citizens against the State

The Fourteenth Amendment, as now applied to the States, protects the citizen against the State itself and all of its creatures—Boards of Education not excepted. These have, of course, important, delicate, and highly discretionary functions, but none that they may not perform within the limits of the Bill of Rights. That they are educating the young for citizenship is reason for scrupulous protection of Constitutional freedoms of the individual, if we are not to strangle the free mind at its source and teach youth to discount important principles of our government as mere platitudes.

3. The *Gobitis* opinion reasoned that this is a field "where courts possess no marked and certainly no controlling competence," that it is committed to the legislatures as well as the courts to guard cherished liberties and that it is constitutionally appropriate to "fight out the wise use of legislative authority in the forum of public opinion and before legislative assemblies rather than to transfer such a contest to the judicial arena," since all the "effective means of inducing political changes are left free."

The very purpose of a Bill of Rights was to withdraw certain subjects from the vicissitudes of political controversy, to place them beyond the reach of majorities and officials and to establish them as legal principles to be applied by the courts. One's right to life, liberty, and property, to free speech, a free press, freedom of worship and assembly, and other fundamental rights may not be submitted to vote; they depend on the outcome of no elections.

4. Lastly, and this is the very heart of the *Gobitis* opinion, it reasons that "National unity is the basis of national security," that the authorities have "the right to select appropriate means for its attainment," and hence reaches the conclusion that such compulsory measures toward 'national unity' are constitutional. Upon the verity of this assumption depends our answer in this case.

National unity as an end which officials may foster by persuasion and example is not in question. The problem is whether under our Constitution compulsion as here employed is a permissible means for its achievement.

Struggles to coerce uniformity of sentiment in support of some end thought essential to their time and country have been waged by many good as well as by evil men. Nationalism is a relatively recent phenomenon but at other times and places the ends have been racial or territorial security, support of a dynasty or regime, and particular plans for saving souls. As first and moderate methods to attain unity have failed, those bent on its accomplishment must resort to an ever-increasing severity. As governmental pressure toward unity becomes greater, so strife becomes more bitter as to whose unity it shall be. Ultimate futility of such attempts to compel coherence is the lesson of every such effort from the Roman drive to stamp out Christianity as a disturber of its pagan unity, the Inquisition, as a means to religious and dynastic unity, the Siberian exiles as a means to Russian unity, down to the fast failing efforts of our present totalitarian enemies. Those who begin coercive elimination of dissent soon find themselves exterminating dissenters. Compulsory unification of opinion achieves only the unanimity of the graveyard.

It seems trite but necessary to say that the First Amendment to our Constitution was designed to avoid these ends by avoiding these beginnings. There is no mysticism in the American concept of the State or of the nature or origin of its authority. We set up government by consent of the governed, and the Bill of Rights denies those in power any legal opportunity to coerce that consent. Authority here is to be controlled by public opinion, not public opinion by authority.

The case is made difficult not because the principles of its decision are obscure but because the flag involved is our own. Nevertheless, we apply the limitations of the Constitution with no fear that freedom to be intellectually and spiritually diverse or even contrary will disintegrate the social organization. To believe that patriotism will not flourish if patriotic ceremonies are voluntary and spontaneous instead of a compulsory routine is to make an unflattering estimate of the appeal of our institutions to free minds. We can have intellectual individualism and the rich cultural diversities that we owe to exceptional minds only at the price of occasional eccentricity and abnormal attitudes. When they are so harmless to others or to the State as those we deal with here, the price is not too great. But freedom to differ is not limited to things that do not matter much. That would be a mere shadow of freedom. The test of its substance is the right to differ as to things that touch the heart of the existing order.

If there is any fixed star in our constitutional constellation, it is that no official, high or petty, can prescribe what shall be orthodox in politics, nationalism, religion, or other matters of opinion or force citizens to confess by word or act their faith therein. If there are any circumstances which permit an exception, they do not now occur to us.

We think the action of the local authorities in compelling the flag salute and pledge transcends constitutional limitations on their power and invades the sphere of intellect and spirit which it is the purpose of the First Amendment to our Constitution to reserve from all official control.

The decision of this Court in *Gobitis* and the holdings of those few *per curiam* decisions which preceded and foreshadowed it are overruled, and the judgment enjoining enforcement of the West Virginia Regulation is affirmed.

MR. JUSTICE FRANKFURTER, dissenting.

One who belongs to the most vilified and persecuted minority in history is not likely to be insensible to the freedoms guaranteed by our Constitution. Were my purely personal attitude relevant I should whole-heartedly associate myself with the general libertarian views in the Court's opinion, representing as they do the thought and action of a lifetime. But as judges we are neither Jew nor Gentile, neither Catholic nor agnostic. We owe equal attachment to the Constitution and are equally bound by our judicial obligations whether we derive our citizenship from the earliest or the latest immigrants to these shores. In the light of all the circumstances, including the history of this question in this Court, it would require more daring than I possess to deny that reasonable legislators could have taken the action which is before us for review. I cannot bring my mind to believe that the "liberty" secured by the Due Process Clause gives this Court authority to deny to the State of West Virginia the attainment of that which we all recognize as a legitimate legislative end, namely, the promotion of good citizenship, by employment of the means here chosen.

[Justice Black's concurring opinion, which was joined by Justice Douglas, is omitted, as is Justice Murphy's concurring opinion. Justice Roberts and Justice Reed dissented, indicating that they "adhere to the views expressed by the Court" in *Gobitis.*]

Points for Discussion

1. **Why did Justice Jackson reject Justice Frankfurter's reasoning?** Justice Jackson noted that "at the very heart" of the *Gobitis* opinion was Justice Frankfurter's belief that "national unity is the basis of national security." Justice Jackson did not deny the importance of national unity. But he rejected Justice Frankfurter's conclusion that government compulsion could be used to promote this unity. Why? What did he mean by this chilling line near the end of his opinion: "Compulsory unification of opinion achieves only the unanimity of the graveyard"?

2. **Using carrots and not sticks.** The West Virginia policy was a stick that compelled students to participate in the pledge ceremony or be expelled from school. The pressure was compounded by the fact that parents of expelled students could be criminally prosecuted for not sending their children to school.

   Barnette held this compulsion unconstitutional. But the fact that the government may not compel people to pledge their allegiance to the nation does not mean that the government is prohibited from using its resources to encourage this allegiance. The government is free to fly flags, hold parades, build monuments, and distribute information about the virtues of the country. Indeed, as you will learn in Chapter 11, when the government itself is speaking, as opposed to regulating what private parties may say, the First Amendment does not apply. The government is free to express a viewpoint on one side of an issue (that the United States is a great country) without expressing the opposite viewpoint (that the United States is a terrible country).

   But keep in mind what you learned about abridgements of speech in Chapter 3. What the government cannot do is distribute government benefits on the condition that people relinquish their constitutional rights. Doing so would constitute an unconstitutional condition. So, for example, public schools may not tell students that they can attend for free but only on the condition that they agree to say the Pledge of Allegiance. The government cannot so easily end-run the ruling in *Barnette.*

3. **May government require its employees to take loyalty oaths?** If public schools cannot compel students to recite the Pledge of Allegiance, may government employers compel employees to take loyalty oaths? The short answer is that it depends. On the one hand, the Court has said that "neither federal nor state government may condition employment on taking oaths that impinge on rights guaranteed by the First and Fourteenth Amendments." *Cole v. Richardson*, 405 U.S. 676, 680 (1972). This precludes conditioning government employment on "an oath that one has not engaged, or will not engage, in protected speech

activities such as the following: criticizing institutions of government; discussing political doctrine that approves the overthrow of certain forms of government; and supporting candidates for political office."

On the other hand, the Court allows governments to require employees to take oaths to protect and defend the Constitution. That is hardly surprising since the Constitution itself proscribes such oaths. Article II, Section 1, clause 8 provides that the president shall swear that he will "to best of [his] ability preserve, protect and defend the Constitution of the United States." Article IV, clause 3 provides that all state and federal officials are also bound by oath "to support this Constitution." The Court said in *Cole* that such oaths merely entail a commitment to perform one's public duties lawfully by abiding by "constitutional processes of government."

4. **May government insist that teachers portray the country in a positive light?** The *Barnette* decision begins by noting that:

> The West Virginia legislature amended its statutes to require all schools therein to conduct courses of instruction in history, civics, and in the Constitutions of the United States and of the State "for the purpose of teaching, fostering and perpetuating the ideals, principles and spirit of Americanism, and increasing the knowledge of the organization and machinery of the government."

The government certainly can require schools to teach students about American history and civics. As you will learn in Chapter 11, public schools have broad discretion to make content-based decisions about which subjects to teach and which books to purchase for a school library.

The West Virginia statute seems to assume that teaching American history and civics will enhance students' appreciation for the country. Justice Jackson made a similar assumption when he said that such lessons "tend to inspire patriotism and love of country."

But what if this assumption is wrong? What if lessons in American history will instead demonstrate the country's abject failure to live up to its ideals?

To ensure that students are left with a positive impression of the country, may the government insist that teachers emphasize the positive aspects of American history over the negative? This issue has been at the heart of a roiling political debate concerning the propriety of teaching students about the country's history of systemic racism. Those supporting candid discussions of this topic believe that the nation's ability to address racism depends on its acknowledgment and grappling with its troubling past. Those opposing such discussions believe that they would undermine student appreciation for and loyalty to the nation. In 2022, Florida Governor Ron DeSantis signed a law, the Stop WOKE Act, that restricts how race is discussed in schools, colleges, and universities. "We won't allow Florida tax dollars to be spent teaching kids to hate our country and to hate each other," he said.

Where do you fall in this debate? More importantly, do you think that the First Amendment limits the government's ability to dictate what teachers can teach? We will explore this topic further in Chapter 11 when we discuss freedom of speech in public schools. You can track federal, state, and local laws restricting the teaching of critical race theory at this website developed by the UCLA School of Law.

Jehovah's Witnesses and the First Amendment

Jehovah's Witnesses believe that the world is coming to an end. They are commanded to spread the word about their faith to give others an opportunity for salvation.

To fulfill this command, Witnesses engage in a wide range of activities, including delivering "soapbox" speeches in public forums, handing out literature, and going door to door to spread their message.

When laws have prevented Jehovah's Witnesses from fulfilling their mission, they have often gone to court to challenge the laws. An astonishing number of these cases reached the Supreme Court. Between just 1938 and 1946, the Court heard 23 First Amendment cases concerning Jehovah's Witnesses. A 1942 law review article described the Witnesses' outsized impact on First Amendment law:

> Seldom, if ever, in the past, has one individual or group been able to shape the course, over a period of time, of any phase of our vast body of constitutional law. But it can happen, and it has happened here. The group is Jehovah's Witnesses.

John E. Mulder & Marvin Comisky, *Jehovah's Witnesses Mold Constitutional Law*, 2 Bill Rts. Rev. 262 (1942).

B. Flag Burning: May Government Punish Flag Desecration?

Even if the government cannot compel professed allegiance to the flag, can the government at least punish those who desecrate the flag? After all, the flag is the most widely recognized symbol of national unity, and, as Justice Frankfurter recognized in *Gobitis*, "we live by symbols."

Texas v. Johnson

Supreme Court of the United States, 1989
491 U.S. 397

[*Authors' note:* The defendant in this case was prosecuted for violating Texas Penal Code § 42.09, Desecration of Venerated Object, which stated: "(a) A person commits an offense if he intentionally or knowingly desecrates: (1) a public monument; (2) a place of worship or burial; or (3) a state or national flag. (b) For purposes of this section, 'desecrate' means deface, damage, or otherwise physically mistreat in a way that the actor knows will seriously offend one or more persons likely to observe or discover his action." An offense under this law was a misdemeanor.]

JUSTICE BRENNAN delivered the opinion of the Court.

After publicly burning an American flag as a means of political protest, Gregory Lee Johnson was convicted of desecrating a flag in violation of Texas law. This case presents the question whether his conviction is consistent with the First Amendment. We hold that it is not.

While the Republican National Convention was taking place in Dallas in 1984, respondent Johnson participated in a political demonstration dubbed the "Republican War Chest Tour." As explained in literature distributed by the demonstrators and in speeches made by them, the purpose of this event was to protest the policies of the Reagan administration and of certain Dallas-based corporations. The demonstrators marched through the Dallas streets, chanting political slogans and stopping at several corporate locations to stage "die-ins" intended to dramatize the consequences of nuclear war. On several occasions they spray-painted the walls of buildings and overturned potted plants, but Johnson himself took no part in such activities. He did, however, accept an American flag handed to him by a fellow protestor who had taken it from a flagpole outside one of the targeted buildings.

The demonstration ended in front of Dallas City Hall, where Johnson unfurled the American flag, doused it with kerosene, and set it on fire. While the flag burned, the protestors chanted: "America, the red, white, and blue, we spit on you." After the demonstrators dispersed, a witness to the flag burning collected the flag's remains and buried them in his backyard. No one was physically injured or threatened with injury, though several witnesses testified that they had been seriously offended by the flag burning.

Gregory Lee Johnson (R) with his attorney, William Kunstler (L)
Photographer: Joel Seidenstein/Creative Commons (CC BY-SA 3.0)

Of the approximately 100 demonstrators, Johnson alone was charged with a crime. The only criminal offense with which he was charged was the desecration of a venerated object in violation of Tex. Penal Code Ann. § 42.09(a)(3). After a trial, he was convicted, sentenced to one year in prison, and fined $2,000. The Court of Appeals for the Fifth District of Texas at Dallas affirmed Johnson's conviction, but the Texas Court of Criminal Appeals reversed, holding that the State could not, consistent with the First Amendment, punish Johnson for burning the flag in these circumstances.

Because it reversed Johnson's conviction on the ground that § 42.09 was unconstitutional as applied to him, the state court did not address Johnson's argument that the statute was, on its face, unconstitutionally vague and overbroad. We granted certiorari and now affirm.

Johnson was convicted of flag desecration for burning the flag rather than for uttering insulting words. This fact somewhat complicates our consideration of his conviction under the First Amendment. We must first determine whether Johnson's burning of the flag constituted expressive conduct, permitting him to invoke the First Amendment in challenging his conviction. See, *e.g.*, *Spence v. Washington*. If his conduct was expressive, we next decide whether the State's regulation is related to the suppression of free expression. See, *e.g.*, *United States v. O'Brien*. If the State's regulation is not related to expression, then the less stringent standard we announced in *United States v. O'Brien* for regulations of noncommunicative conduct controls. If it is, then we are outside of *O'Brien*'s test, and we must ask whether this interest justifies Johnson's conviction under a more demanding standard. A third possibility is that the State's asserted interest is simply not implicated on these facts, and in that event the interest drops out of the picture.

The First Amendment literally forbids the abridgment only of "speech," but we have long recognized that its protection does not end at the spoken or written word. While we have rejected "the view that an apparently limitless variety of conduct can be labeled 'speech' whenever the person engaging in the conduct intends thereby to express an idea," we have acknowledged that conduct may be "sufficiently imbued with elements of communication to fall within the scope of the First and Fourteenth Amendments."

In deciding whether particular conduct possesses sufficient communicative elements to bring the First Amendment into play, we have asked whether "an intent to convey a particularized message was present, and whether the likelihood was great that the message would be understood by those who viewed it." *Spence*.

Especially pertinent to this case are our decisions recognizing the communicative nature of conduct relating to flags. Attaching a peace sign to the flag, refusing to salute the flag, and displaying a red flag, we have held, all may find shelter under the First Amendment. That we have had little difficulty identifying an expressive element in conduct relating to flags should not be surprising. The very purpose of a national flag is to serve as a symbol of our country; it is, one might say, "the one visible manifestation of two hundred years of nationhood." Pregnant with expressive content, the flag as readily signifies this Nation as does the combination of letters found in "America."

We have not automatically concluded, however, that any action taken with respect to our flag is expressive. Instead, in characterizing such action for First Amendment purposes, we have considered the context in which it occurred.

The State of Texas conceded for purposes of its oral argument in this case that Johnson's conduct was expressive conduct, and this concession seems to us as prudent. Johnson burned an American flag as part—indeed, as the culmination—of a political demonstration that coincided with the convening of the Republican Party and its renomination of Ronald Reagan for President. The expressive, overtly political nature of this conduct was both intentional and overwhelmingly apparent. In these circumstances, Johnson's burning of the flag was conduct "sufficiently imbued with elements of communication" to implicate the First Amendment.

The government generally has a freer hand in restricting expressive conduct than it has in restricting the written or spoken word. It may not, however, proscribe particular conduct *because* it has expressive elements. "What might be termed the more generalized guarantee of freedom of expression makes the communicative nature of conduct an inadequate *basis* for singling out that conduct for proscription. A law *directed at* the communicative nature of conduct must, like a law directed at speech itself, be justified by the substantial showing of need that the First Amendment requires." It is, in short, not simply the verbal or nonverbal nature of the expression, but the governmental interest at stake, that helps to determine whether a restriction on that expression is valid.

Thus, although we have recognized that where " 'speech' and 'nonspeech' elements are combined in the same course of conduct, a sufficiently important governmental interest in regulating the nonspeech element can justify incidental limitations on First Amendment freedoms," we have limited the applicability of *O'Brien*'s relatively lenient standard to those cases in which "the governmental interest is unrelated to the suppression of free expression." In stating, moreover, that *O'Brien*'s test "in the last analysis is little, if any, different from the standard applied to time, place, or manner restrictions," we have highlighted the requirement that the governmental interest in question be unconnected to expression in order to come under *O'Brien*'s less demanding rule.

In order to decide whether *O'Brien*'s test applies here, therefore, we must decide whether Texas has asserted an interest in support of Johnson's conviction that is unrelated to the suppression of expression. If we find that an interest asserted by the State is simply not implicated on the facts before us, we need not ask whether *O'Brien*'s test applies. The State offers two separate interests to justify this conviction: preventing breaches of the peace and preserving the flag as a symbol of nationhood and national unity. We hold that the first interest is not implicated on this record and that the second is related to the suppression of expression.

Texas claims that its interest in preventing breaches of the peace justifies Johnson's conviction for flag desecration. However, no disturbance of the peace actually occurred or threatened to occur because of Johnson's burning of the flag. Although the State stresses the disruptive behavior of the protestors during their march toward City Hall, it admits that "no actual breach of the peace occurred at the time of the flagburning or in response to the flagburning." The State's emphasis on the protestors' disorderly actions prior to arriving at City Hall is not only somewhat surprising given that no charges were brought on the basis of this conduct, but it also fails to show that a disturbance of the peace was a likely reaction to *Johnson's* conduct. The only evidence offered by the State at trial to show the reaction to Johnson's actions was the testimony of several persons who had been seriously offended by the flag burning.

The State's position, therefore, amounts to a claim that an audience that takes serious offense at particular expression is necessarily likely to disturb the peace and that the expression may be prohibited on this basis. Our precedents do not countenance such a presumption. On the contrary, they recognize that a principal "function of free speech under our system of government is to invite dispute. It may indeed best serve its high purpose when it induces a condition of unrest, creates dissatisfaction with conditions as they are, or even stirs people to anger." *Terminiello.* It would be odd indeed to conclude *both* that "if it is the speaker's opinion that gives offense, that consequence is a reason for according it constitutional protection," *and* that the government may ban the expression of certain disagreeable ideas on the unsupported presumption that their very disagreeableness will provoke violence.

Thus, we have not permitted the government to assume that every expression of a provocative idea will incite a riot, but have instead required careful consideration of the actual circumstances surrounding such expression, asking whether the expression "is directed to inciting or producing imminent lawless action and is likely to incite or produce such action." *Brandenburg.* To accept Texas' arguments that it need only demonstrate "the potential for a breach of the peace," and that every flag burning necessarily possesses that potential, would be to eviscerate our holding in *Brandenburg.* This we decline to do.

when looking @ breach of peace

Nor does Johnson's expressive conduct fall within that small class of "fighting words" that are "likely to provoke the average person to retaliation, and thereby cause a breach of the peace." *Chaplinsky.* No reasonable onlooker would have regarded Johnson's generalized expression of dissatisfaction with the policies of the Federal Government as a direct personal insult or an invitation to exchange fisticuffs.

We thus conclude that the State's interest in maintaining order is not implicated on these facts. The State need not worry that our holding will disable it from preserving the peace. We do not suggest that the First Amendment forbids a State to prevent "imminent lawless action." And, in fact, Texas already has a statute specifically prohibiting breaches of the peace, which tends to confirm that Texas need not punish this flag desecration in order to keep the peace.

The State also asserts an interest in preserving the flag as a symbol of nationhood and national unity. In *Spence,* we acknowledged that the government's interest in preserving the flag's special symbolic value "is directly related to expression in the context of activity" such as affixing a peace symbol to a flag. We are equally persuaded that this interest is related to expression in the case of Johnson's burning of the flag. The State, apparently, is concerned that such conduct will lead people to believe either that the flag does not stand for nationhood and national unity, but instead reflects other, less positive concepts, or that the concepts reflected in the flag do not in fact exist, that is, that we do not enjoy unity as a Nation. These concerns blossom only when a person's treatment of the flag communicates some message, and thus are related "to the suppression of free expression" within the meaning of *O'Brien.* We are thus outside of *O'Brien*'s test altogether.

It remains to consider whether the State's interest in preserving the flag as a symbol of nationhood and national unity justifies Johnson's conviction.

As in *Spence,* "we are confronted with a case of prosecution for the expression of an idea through activity," and "accordingly, we must examine with particular care the interests advanced by [petitioner] to support its prosecution." Johnson was not, we add, prosecuted for the expression of just any idea; he was prosecuted for his expression of dissatisfaction with the policies of this country, expression situated at the core of our First Amendment values.

Moreover, Johnson was prosecuted because he knew that his politically charged expression would cause "serious offense." If he had burned the flag as a means of disposing of it because it was dirty or torn, he would not have been convicted of flag desecration under this Texas law: federal law designates burning as the preferred means of disposing of a flag "when it is in such condition that it is no longer a fitting emblem for display," and Texas has no quarrel with this means of disposal. The Texas law is thus not aimed at protecting the physical integrity of the flag in all circumstances, but is designed instead to protect it only against impairments that would cause serious offense to others. Texas concedes as much: "Section 42.09(b) reaches only those severe acts of physical abuse of the flag carried out in a way likely to be offensive. The statute mandates intentional or knowing abuse, that is, the kind of mistreatment that is not innocent, but rather is intentionally designed to seriously offend other individuals."

Whether Johnson's treatment of the flag violated Texas law thus depended on the likely communicative impact of his expressive conduct. Our decision in *Boos v. Barry,* tells us that this restriction on Johnson's expression is content based. In *Boos,* we considered the constitutionality of a law prohibiting "the display of any sign within 500 feet of a foreign embassy if that sign tends to bring that foreign government into 'public odium' or 'public disrepute.' " Rejecting the argument that the law was content neutral because it was justified by "our international law obligation to shield diplomats from speech that offends their dignity," we held that "the emotive impact of speech on its audience is not a 'secondary effect' " unrelated to the content of the expression itself.

According to the principles announced in *Boos,* Johnson's political expression was restricted because of the content of the message he conveyed. We must therefore subject the State's asserted interest in preserving the special symbolic character of the flag to "the most exacting scrutiny."

Texas argues that its interest in preserving the flag as a symbol of nationhood and national unity survives this close analysis. Quoting extensively from the writings of this Court chronicling the flag's historic and symbolic role in our society, the State emphasizes the "special place" reserved for the flag in our Nation. The State's argument is not that it has an interest simply in maintaining the flag as a symbol of *something,* no matter what it symbolizes; indeed, if that were the State's position, it would be difficult to see how that interest is endangered by highly symbolic conduct such as Johnson's. Rather, the State's claim is that it has an interest in preserving the flag as a symbol of *nationhood* and *national unity,* a symbol with a determinate range of meanings. According to Texas, if one physically treats the flag in a way that would tend to cast doubt on either the idea that nationhood and national unity are the flag's referents or that national unity actually exists, the message conveyed thereby is a harmful one and therefore may be prohibited.

If there is a bedrock principle underlying the First Amendment, it is that the government may not prohibit the expression of an idea simply because society finds the idea itself offensive or disagreeable. We have not recognized an exception to this principle even where our flag has been involved.

Texas' focus on the precise nature of Johnson's expression misses the point of our prior decisions: their enduring lesson, that the government may not prohibit expression simply because it disagrees with its message, is not dependent on the particular mode in which one chooses to express an idea. If we were to hold that a State may forbid flag burning wherever it is likely to endanger the flag's symbolic role, but allow it wherever burning a flag promotes that role—as where, for example, a person ceremoniously burns a dirty flag—we would be saying that when it comes to impairing the flag's physical integrity, the flag itself may be used as a symbol—as a substitute for the written or spoken word or a "short cut from mind to mind"—only in one direction. We would be permitting a State to "prescribe what shall be orthodox" by saying that one may burn the flag to convey one's attitude toward it and its referents only if one does not endanger the flag's representation of nationhood and national unity.

We never before have held that the Government may ensure that a symbol be used to express only one view of that symbol or its referents. Indeed, in *Schacht v. United States,* [398 U.S. 58 (1970),] we invalidated a federal statute permitting an actor portraying a member of one of our Armed Forces to "wear the uniform of that armed force if the portrayal does not tend to discredit that armed force." This proviso, we held, "which leaves Americans free to praise the war in Vietnam but can send persons like Schacht to prison for opposing it, cannot survive in a country which has the First Amendment."

We perceive no basis on which to hold that the principle underlying our decision in *Schacht* does not apply to this case. To conclude that the government may permit designated symbols to be used to communicate only a limited set of messages would be to enter territory having no discernible or defensible boundaries. Could the government, on this theory, prohibit the burning of state flags? Of copies of the Presidential seal? Of the Constitution? In evaluating these choices under the First Amendment, how would we decide which symbols were sufficiently special to warrant this unique status? To do so, we would be forced to consult our own political preferences, and impose them on the citizenry, in the very way that the First Amendment forbids us to do.

There is, moreover, no indication—either in the text of the Constitution or in our cases interpreting it—that a separate juridical category exists for the American flag alone. Indeed, we would not be surprised to learn that the persons who framed our Constitution and wrote the Amendment that we now construe were not known for their reverence for the Union Jack. The First Amendment does not guarantee that other concepts virtually sacred to our Nation as a whole—such as the principle that discrimination on the basis of race is odious and destructive—will go unquestioned in the marketplace of ideas. We decline, therefore, to create for the flag an exception to the joust of principles protected by the First Amendment.

It is not the State's ends, but its means, to which we object. It cannot be gainsaid that there is a special place reserved for the flag in this Nation, and thus we do not doubt that the government has a legitimate interest in making efforts to "preserve the national flag as an unalloyed symbol of our country." We reject the suggestion, urged at oral argument by counsel for Johnson, that the government lacks "any state interest whatsoever" in regulating the manner in which the flag may be displayed. Congress has, for example, enacted precatory regulations describing the proper treatment of the flag, and we cast no doubt on the legitimacy of its interest in making such recommendations. To say that the government has an interest in encouraging proper treatment of the flag, however, is not to say that it may criminally punish a person for burning a flag as a means of political protest. "National unity as an end which officials may foster by persuasion and example is not in question. The problem is whether under our Constitution compulsion as here employed is a permissible means for its achievement."

We are fortified in today's conclusion by our conviction that forbidding criminal punishment for conduct such as Johnson's will not endanger the special role played by our flag or the feelings it inspires. To paraphrase Justice Holmes, we submit that nobody can suppose that this one gesture of an unknown man will change our

Nation's attitude towards its flag. Indeed, Texas' argument that the burning of an American flag "is an act having a high likelihood to cause a breach of the peace," and its statute's implicit assumption that physical mistreatment of the flag will lead to "serious offense," tend to confirm that the flag's special role is not in danger; if it were, no one would riot or take offense because a flag had been burned.

We are tempted to say, in fact, that the flag's deservedly cherished place in our community will be strengthened, not weakened, by our holding today. Our decision is a reaffirmation of the principles of freedom and inclusiveness that the flag best reflects, and of the conviction that our toleration of criticism such as Johnson's is a sign and source of our strength. Indeed, one of the proudest images of our flag, the one immortalized in our own national anthem, is of the bombardment it survived at Fort McHenry. It is the Nation's resilience, not its rigidity, that Texas sees reflected in the flag—and it is that resilience that we reassert today.

The way to preserve the flag's special role is not to punish those who feel differently about these matters. It is to persuade them that they are wrong. "To courageous, self-reliant men, with confidence in the power of free and fearless reasoning applied through the processes of popular government, no danger flowing from speech can be deemed clear and present, unless the incidence of the evil apprehended is so imminent that it may befall before there is opportunity for full discussion. If there be time to expose through discussion the falsehood and fallacies, to avert the evil by the processes of education, the remedy to be applied is more speech, not enforced silence." *Whitney v. California* (Brandeis, J., concurring). And, precisely because it is our flag that is involved, one's response to the flag burner may exploit the uniquely persuasive power of the flag itself. We can imagine no more appropriate response to burning a flag than waving one's own, no better way to counter a flag burner's message than by saluting the flag that burns, no surer means of preserving the dignity even of the flag that burned than by—as one witness here did—according its remains a respectful burial. We do not consecrate the flag by punishing its desecration, for in doing so we dilute the freedom that this cherished emblem represents.

Johnson was convicted for engaging in expressive conduct. The State's interest in preventing breaches of the peace does not support his conviction because Johnson's conduct did not threaten to disturb the peace. Nor does the State's interest in preserving the flag as a symbol of nationhood and national unity justify his criminal conviction for engaging in political expression. The judgment of the Texas Court of Criminal Appeals is therefore

Affirmed.

JUSTICE KENNEDY, concurring.

The hard fact is that sometimes we must make decisions we do not like. We make them because they are right, right in the sense that the law and the Constitution, as we see them, compel the result. And so great is our commitment to the process that, except in the rare case, we do not pause to express distaste for the result, perhaps for fear of undermining a valued principle that dictates the decision. This is one of those rare cases.

CHIEF JUSTICE REHNQUIST, with whom JUSTICE WHITE and JUSTICE O'CONNOR join, dissenting.

In holding this Texas statute unconstitutional, the Court ignores Justice Holmes' familiar aphorism that "a page of history is worth a volume of logic." For more than 200 years, the American flag has occupied a unique position as the symbol of our Nation, a uniqueness that justifies a governmental prohibition against flag burning in the way respondent Johnson did here.

The American flag does not represent the views of any particular political party, and it does not represent any particular political philosophy. The flag is not simply another "idea" or "point of view" competing for recognition in the marketplace of ideas. Millions and millions of Americans regard it with an almost mystical reverence regardless of what sort of social, political, or philosophical beliefs they may have. I cannot agree that the First Amendment invalidates the Act of Congress, and the laws of 48 of the 50 States, which make criminal the public burning of the flag.

Johnson was free to make any verbal denunciation of the flag that he wished; indeed, he was free to burn the flag in private. He could publicly burn other symbols of the Government or effigies of political leaders. He did lead a march through the streets of Dallas, and conducted a rally in front of the Dallas City Hall. He engaged in a "die-in" to protest nuclear weapons. He shouted out various slogans during the march, including: "Reagan, Mondale which will it be? Either one means World War III"; "Ronald Reagan, killer of the hour, Perfect example of U.S. power"; and "red, white and blue, we spit on you, you stand for plunder, you will go under." For none of these acts was he arrested or prosecuted; it was only when he proceeded to burn publicly an American flag stolen from its rightful owner that he violated the Texas statute.

[Johnson's] act, like Chaplinsky's provocative words, conveyed nothing that could not have been conveyed and was not conveyed just as forcefully in a dozen different ways. As with "fighting words," so with flag burning, for purposes of the First Amendment: It is "no essential part of any exposition of ideas, and is of such slight social value as a step to truth that any benefit that may be derived from it is clearly outweighed" by the public interest in avoiding a probable breach of the peace.

JUSTICE STEVENS, dissenting.

A country's flag is a symbol of more than "nationhood and national unity." It also signifies the ideas that characterize the society that has chosen that emblem as well as the special history that has animated the growth and power of those ideas. The fleurs-de-lis and the tricolor both symbolized "nationhood and national unity," but they had vastly different meanings. The message conveyed by some flags—the swastika, for example—may survive long after it has outlived its usefulness as a symbol of regimented unity in a particular nation.

So it is with the American flag. It is more than a proud symbol of the courage, the determination, and the gifts of nature that transformed 13 fledgling Colonies into a world power. It is a symbol of freedom, of equal opportunity, of religious tolerance, and of good will for other peoples who share our aspirations. The symbol carries its message to dissidents both at home and abroad who may have no interest at all in our national unity or survival.

The value of the flag as a symbol cannot be measured. Even so, I have no doubt that the interest in preserving that value for the future is both significant and legitimate. Conceivably that value will be enhanced by the Court's conclusion that our national commitment to free expression is so strong that even the United States as ultimate guarantor of that freedom is without power to prohibit the desecration of its unique symbol. But I am unpersuaded.

Points for Discussion

1. **Why did the Court consider flag burning speech?** The defendant was being prosecuted for burning the national flag, and not for the disparaging words he said about the flag. So why did this implicate the First Amendment? Can you recall the test the Court uses for determining whether conduct should be considered speech?

2. **Why did the Court evaluate the Texas law under strict scrutiny?** As you learned in Chapter 4, the default rule for conduct regulations that interfere with someone's ability to use conduct for expressive purposes is the *O'Brien* test, which is usually thought of as a form of intermediate scrutiny. What prompted the Court to switch from intermediate to strict scrutiny in its analysis of the Texas law?

3. **Would you have joined Justice Brennan's majority opinion?** Justice William Brennan ruled that the government may not punish people for desecrating the flag. Would you have signed on to his opinion? The state of Texas did not claim

that it could punish Johnson for saying "red, white and blue, we spit on you, you stand for plunder, you will go under." If Johnson could so vividly express his displeasure with the flag in words, why should the First Amendment also protect his right to express his displeasure by burning the flag?

4. **Are slippery slopes as slippery as some claim?** A common refrain for why the Court should not create exceptions to First Amendment protection is that carving out one exception will eventually lead to others. This is the slippery slope problem. If the Court carves out an exception for flag desecration, what will stop the Court from carving out exceptions for other national symbols? Justice Brennan made this point when he said that a flag desecration exception would have "no discernible or defensible boundaries." He queried: "Could the government, on this theory, prohibit the burning of state flags? Of copies of the Presidential seal? Of the Constitution?"

   But are slippery slopes really so slippery? Do you think that carving out an exception for flag desecration would inevitably lead to more exceptions? The dissenting justices suggested that the flag is unique among national symbols. Chief Justice William Rehnquist observed that it has "an almost mystical reverence" for Americans "regardless of what sort of social, political, or philosophical beliefs they may have." Could this be a limiting principle that would prevent a flag desecration exception from bleeding into more exceptions? For a deep dive (or should we say "slide") into slippery slope theory, see Eugene Volokh, *The Mechanisms of the Slippery Slope*, 116 Harv. L. Rev. 1026 (2003).

5. **Can too much speech protection undermine freedom of speech?** Is it possible that the Court's unflinching protection of free speech rights in cases like *Texas v. Johnson* will erode public support for free speech? Does that matter? Does our society's commitment to freedom of speech depend on public support?

6. **The price of authoring a controversial opinion:** Biographers of Justice Brennan describe how he was unprepared for the backlash to his opinion in *Texas v. Johnson*:

   > At the urging of a conservative radio talk-show host, listeners inundated Brennan's chambers with flags of all shapes and sizes. The Senate passed a resolution condemning the Court's ruling, 97–3. President George H. W. Bush called for a constitutional amendment to protect the flag, the first time in the nation's history that altering the Bill of Rights was seriously contemplated. Closer to home, one of Brennan's condominium neighbors draped an American flag over his door and

kept it there for several days, so Brennan would see it whenever he stepped off the elevator on their floor.

Seth Stern & Stephen Wermiel, *Justice Brennan: Liberal Champion* 527 (2010).

Justice William Brennan, Jr.
Robert S. Oakes, National Geographic
Courtesy of the Supreme Court of the United States

You Be the Senator!

***Would you have supported a constitutional amendment to override* Texas v. Johnson?**

The Court's decision in *Texas v. Johnson* did not sit well with many members of Congress. Some members advocated for a constitutional amendment to override the decision and permit punishment of flag desecration.

If you had been a U.S. senator at that time, would you have voted in favor of such an amendment? Why or why not?

Congress ultimately did not pass a proposed amendment, but it did enact a statute to punish flag desecration. The Flag Protection Act provided for fines and possible imprisonment for anyone who "knowingly mutilates, defaces, physically defiles, burns, maintains on the floor or ground, or tramples upon any flag of the United States." Can you find any differences between this federal law and the Texas law in *Texas v. Johnson* that might make enforcement of the federal law more likely to pass constitutional muster?

The federal law was challenged as violative of the First Amendment, and the case reached the Supreme Court. How do you think the Court should have ruled? To find out how it did rule, see *United States v. Eichman*, 496 U.S. 310 (1990).

Test Your Knowledge

To assess your understanding of the material in this chapter, click here to take a quiz.

Chapter Nine

May Government Regulate Speech to Protect Reputational, Privacy, Property, and Other Interests?

Defamation, Privacy, Appropriation, and Intentional Infliction of Emotional Distress

In this chapter, we explore whether the government may impose civil liability on speakers when their speech harms individuals or businesses. The umbrella term the law uses to refer to wrongs that harm another is "torts," which derives from the Latin word for "twisted." The central question addressed in this chapter is whether the First Amendment limits the imposition of tort liability when this liability is based on a defendant's speech. Our focus will be on tort causes of action that are always or often triggered by speech: defamation, privacy, appropriation, intentional infliction of emotional distress, and tortious interference with contract or economic advantage.

A. Defamation: May Government Regulate Speech to Protect People's Reputations?

The tort of defamation is intended to protect people from the dissemination of false statements that injure their reputations. For example, imagine that someone falsely stated that you collected and sold child pornography. If this rumor were disseminated to others, it could have dire consequences for your career and future earning capacity. It could also cause irreparable harm to your relationships with family members and friends, whose perceptions of you might permanently be altered if they believe the rumor to be true. The person who made the false statement merely engaged in speech. But the harm caused by this speech—economically, socially, and emotionally—could be devastating.

Shakespeare captured the preciousness of a person's reputation in a famous passage in Othello:

> Good name in man and woman, dear my lord,
> Is the immediate jewel of their souls:
> Who steals my purse steals trash; tis something, nothing,
> 'Twas mine, 'tis his, and has been slave to thousands;
> But he that filches from me my good name
> Robs me of that which not enriches him,
> And makes me poor indeed.

For centuries, people, as well as businesses, have turned to the common law tort of defamation to defend their reputations. That remains true today. Indeed, defamation lawsuits are a growth industry, and some of these cases touch on the most salient issues of our time. Consider just two examples:

- **Defamation and the "Big Lie."** Former President Donald Trump's claims that the November 2020 election was rigged and riddled by fraud gave rise to the so-called "Big Lie" that the election was stolen from him. This, in turn, led to the violent insurrection at the U.S. Capitol on January 6, 2021, that sought to prevent, for the first time in American history, the peaceful transition of power. In the aftermath of these events, many defamation suits were filed against those who advanced and amplified the false claims of election fraud. The most prominent of these cases pitted Dominion Voting Systems, one of the voting machine manufacturers falsely accused of complicity in the election fraud, against the conservative media giant Fox News. The lawsuit settled after Fox agreed to pay Dominion $787 million.[1]

- **Defamation and the #MeToo movement:** On the cultural level, many defamation suits have arisen from the #MeToo movement, which aims to raise awareness of sexual violence. Among the most dramatic was the defamation case actor Johnny Depp filed against his ex-wife Amber Heard. After their divorce, Heard wrote an op-ed in *The Washington Post* in 2018. The headline was "I spoke up against sexual violence—and faced our culture's wrath. That has to change." Heard never mentioned Depp by name, instead referring to him as "a public figure representing domestic abuse." Nevertheless, Depp and his legal team claimed that Heard clearly implied that Depp had abused her over the course of their year-long marriage. The trial in Fairfax, Virginia, lasted for six weeks in the spring of 2022 and was televised. The trial transfixed the nation as Depp and Heard traded charges and countercharges, each accusing the

---

1 Co-author Rodney A. Smolla was one of the lawyers who represented Dominion.

> other of abuse, and each marshalling witnesses supporting their version of the events that plagued the couple's marriage. The case took on the backdrop of the #MeToo movement, with Depp's cultural supporters seeing it as a form of correction or pushback against allegedly false or exaggerated charges of abuse, while supporters of Heard saw it as an exemplar of the obstacles facing alleged abuse victims who go public with their accusations.

These lawsuits, like all defamation actions, were based on a defendant's speech. If they had been brought before 1964, their success would have depended solely on the elements of state tort law. But, in 1964, with its decision in *New York Times v. Sullivan*, the Supreme Court dramatically altered the defamation landscape by imposing First Amendment limits on defamation actions.

1. Defamation Law Before *New York Times v. Sullivan*: The Common Law "Super Tort"

Prior to 1964, the American law of defamation was entirely a creature of state law. American states inherited the English common law rules for libel (written defamation) and slander (oral defamation). Plaintiffs bringing defamation actions could recover if they could prove that a defendant made (1) a defamatory statement (2) about the plaintiff (3) that was "published" (meaning communicated to third parties).

Common law defamation was a "supertort" that heavily favored plaintiffs over defendants. As Justice Oliver Wendell Holmes said, "Whatever a man publishes he publishes at his peril." *Peck v. Tribune Co.*, 214 U.S. 185, 189 (1909). If the statement was defamatory, the law presumed it to be false, on the logic that people are inherently good, and thus negative statements about them should be deemed false. The burden was therefore on the defendant to prove the negative statement was true. Defamation was also a strict liability tort—the plaintiff was under no obligation to prove negligence, or any level of fault, to recover. All the plaintiff needed to show was that the defendant "published," or communicated, the statement to third parties. Finally, damages at common law were "presumed," allowing a plaintiff to recover with no evidence of actual harm.[2] These common law principles, with some minor variations, set the rules governing defamation lawsuits under the tort laws of all 50 states.

2. The Landmark Decision in *Sullivan*: The Imposition of First Amendment Limits on Defamation Actions

In 1964, the Supreme Court upended centuries of defamation law in a case that arose out of the struggle for racial equality in the South. On Feb. 29, 1960, the Rev.

[2] Rodney A. Smolla, Law of Defamation §§ 1:6–1:8 (2023 ed.).

Martin Luther King, Jr., was arrested on trumped-up charges involving two counts of perjury in connection with the filing of his Alabama state income tax return. On March 19, 1960, three weeks after King's arrest, *The New York Times* ran an editorial in support of King's efforts. The *Times* praised the efforts of blacks in the South to resist racism and admonished Congress to "heed their rising voices, for they will be heard." The editorial phrase would later be picked up by the newly formed Committee to Defend Martin Luther King and the Struggle for Freedom in the South, which on March 29, 1960, published a full-page advertisement titled "Heed Their Rising Voices." At the bottom of the ad were the names of a number of prominent Americans who comprised the committee.

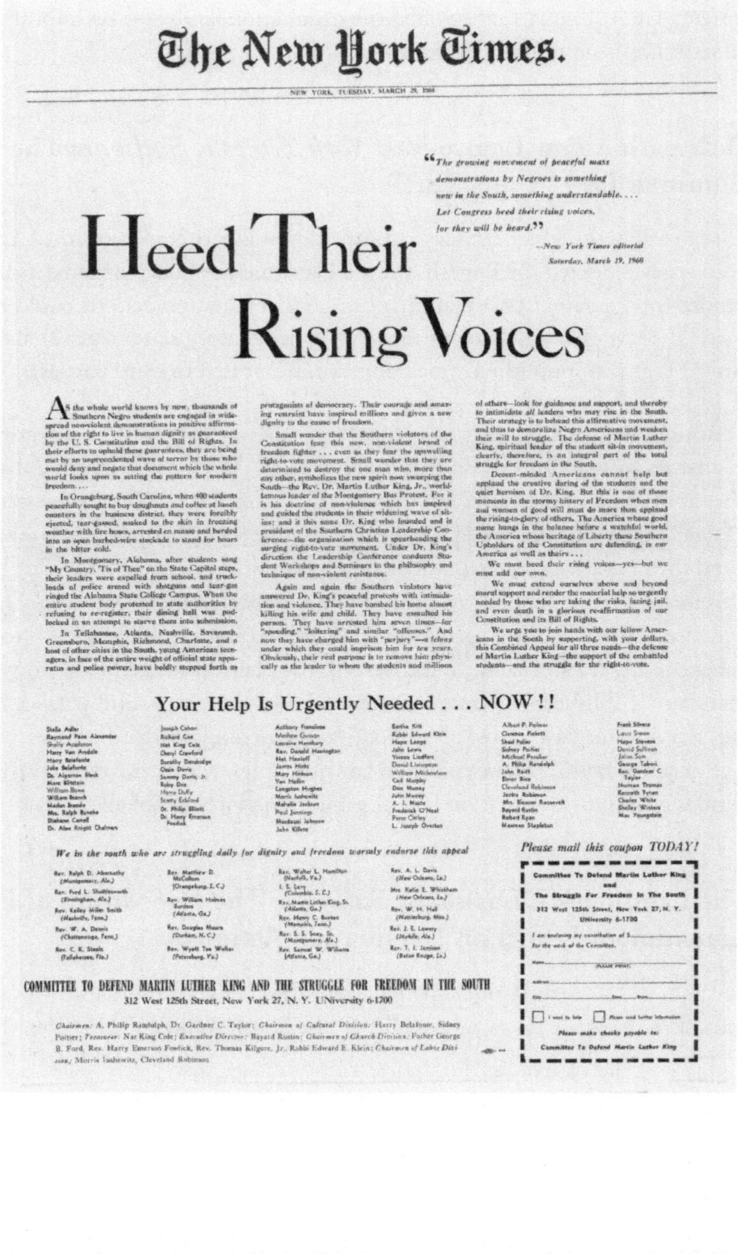

The New York Times.

NEW YORK, TUESDAY, MARCH 29, 1960

"The growing movement of peaceful mass demonstrations by Negroes is something new in the South, something understandable.... Let Congress heed their rising voices, for they will be heard."

—New York Times editorial Saturday, March 19, 1960

Heed Their Rising Voices

As the whole world knows by now, thousands of Southern Negro students are engaged in widespread non-violent demonstrations in positive affirmation of the right to live in human dignity as guaranteed by the U. S. Constitution and the Bill of Rights. In their efforts to uphold these guarantees, they are being met by an unprecedented wave of terror by those who would deny and negate that document which the whole world looks upon as setting the pattern for modern freedom....

In Orangeburg, South Carolina, when 400 students peacefully sought to buy doughnuts and coffee at lunch counters in the business district, they were forcibly ejected, tear-gassed, soaked to the skin in freezing weather with fire hoses, arrested en masse and herded into an open barbed-wire stockade to stand for hours in the bitter cold.

In Montgomery, Alabama, after students sang "My Country, 'Tis of Thee" on the State Capitol steps, their leaders were expelled from school, and truck-loads of police armed with shotguns and tear-gas ringed the Alabama State College Campus. When the entire student body protested to state authorities by refusing to re-register, their dining hall was padlocked in an attempt to starve them into submission.

In Tallahassee, Atlanta, Nashville, Savannah, Greensboro, Memphis, Richmond, Charlotte, and a host of other cities in the South, young American teenagers, in face of the entire weight of official state apparatus and police power, have boldly stepped forth as protagonists of democracy. Their courage and amazing restraint have inspired millions and given a new dignity to the cause of freedom.

Small wonder that the Southern violators of the Constitution fear this new, non-violent brand of freedom fighter . . . even as they fear the upswelling right-to-vote movement. Small wonder that they are determined to destroy the one man who, more than any other, symbolizes the new spirit now sweeping the South—the Rev. Dr. Martin Luther King, Jr., world-famous leader of the Montgomery Bus Protest. For it is his doctrine of non-violence which has inspired and guided the students in their widening wave of sit-ins; and it this same Dr. King who founded and is president of the Southern Christian Leadership Conference—the organization which is spearheading the surging right-to-vote movement. Under Dr. King's direction the Leadership Conference conducts Student Workshops and Seminars in the philosophy and technique of non-violent resistance.

Again and again the Southern violators have answered Dr. King's peaceful protests with intimidation and violence. They have bombed his home almost killing his wife and child. They have assaulted his person. They have arrested him seven times—for "speeding," "loitering" and similar "offenses." And now they have charged him with "perjury"—*a felony* under which they could imprison him *for ten years*. Obviously, their real purpose is to remove him physically as the leader to whom the students and millions of others—look for guidance and support, and thereby to intimidate *all* leaders who may rise in the South. Their strategy is to behead this affirmative movement, and thus to demoralize Negro Americans and weaken their will to struggle. The defense of Martin Luther King, spiritual leader of the student sit-in movement, clearly, therefore, is an integral part of the total struggle for freedom in the South.

Decent-minded Americans cannot help but applaud the creative daring of the students and the quiet heroism of Dr. King. But this is one of those moments in the stormy history of Freedom when men and women of good will must do more than applaud the rising-to-glory of others. The America whose good name hangs in the balance before a watchful world, the America whose heritage of Liberty these Southern Upholders of the Constitution are defending, is *our* America as well as theirs . . .

We must heed their rising voices—yes—but we must add our own.

We must extend ourselves above and beyond moral support and render the material help so urgently needed by those who are taking the risks, facing jail, and even death in a glorious re-affirmation of our Constitution and its Bill of Rights.

We urge you to join hands with our fellow Americans in the South by supporting, with your dollars, this Combined Appeal for all three needs—the defense of Martin Luther King—the support of the embattled students—and the struggle for the right-to-vote.

Your Help Is Urgently Needed . . . NOW!!

Stella Adler
Raymond Pace Alexander
Shelly Appleton
Harry Van Arsdale
Harry Belafonte
Julie Belafonte
Dr. Algernon Black
Marc Blitzstein
William Branch
Marlon Brando
Mrs. Ralph Bunche
Diahann Carroll
Dr. Alan Knight Chalmers
Joseph Cohen
Richard Coe
Nat King Cole
Cheryl Crawford
Dorothy Dandridge
Ossie Davis
Sammy Davis, Jr.
Ruby Dee
Henry Duffy
Scotty Eckford
Dr. Philip Elliott
Dr. Harry Emerson Fosdick
Anthony Franciosa
Matthew Gurnon
Lorraine Hansbury
Rev. Donald Harrington
Nat Hentoff
James Hicks
Mary Hinkson
Van Heflin
Langston Hughes
Morris Iushewitz
Mahalia Jackson
Paul Jennings
Mordecai Johnson
John Killens
Eartha Kitt
Rabbi Edward Klein
Hope Lange
John Lewis
Viveca Lindfors
David Livingston
William Michelson
Carl Murphy
Don Murray
John Murray
A. J. Muste
Frederick O'Neal
Peter Ottley
L. Joseph Overton
Albert P. Palmer
Clarence Pickett
Shad Polier
Sidney Poitier
Michael Potcher
A. Philip Randolph
John Raitt
Elmer Rice
Cleveland Robinson
Jackie Robinson
Mrs. Eleanor Roosevelt
Bayard Rustin
Robert Ryan
Maureen Stapleton
Frank Silvera
Louis Simon
Hope Stevens
David Sullivan
Julius Sum
George Tabori
Rev. Gardner C. Taylor
Norman Thomas
Kenneth Tynan
Charles White
Shelley Winters
Max Youngstein

We in the south who are struggling daily for dignity and freedom warmly endorse this appeal

Rev. Ralph D. Abernathy (Montgomery, Ala.)
Rev. Fred L. Shuttlesworth (Birmingham, Ala.)
Rev. Kelley Miller Smith (Nashville, Tenn.)
Rev. W. A. Dennis (Chattanooga, Tenn.)
Rev. C. K. Steele (Tallahassee, Fla.)
Rev. Matthew D. McCollom (Orangeburg, S. C.)
Rev. William Holmes Borders (Atlanta, Ga.)
Rev. Douglas Moore (Durham, N. C.)
Rev. Wyatt Tee Walker (Petersburg, Va.)
Rev. Walter L. Hamilton (Norfolk, Va.)
I. S. Levy (Columbia, S. C.)
Rev. Martin Luther King, Sr. (Atlanta, Ga.)
Rev. Henry C. Bunton (Memphis, Tenn.)
Rev. S. S. Seay, Sr. (Montgomery, Ala.)
Rev. Samuel W. Williams (Atlanta, Ga.)
Rev. A. L. Davis (New Orleans, La.)
Mrs. Katie E. Whickham (New Orleans, La.)
Rev. W. H. Hall (Hattiesburg, Miss.)
Rev. J. E. Lowery (Mobile, Ala.)
Rev. T. J. Jemison (Baton Rouge, La.)

Please mail this coupon TODAY!

Committee To Defend Martin Luther King
and
The Struggle For Freedom In The South
312 West 125th Street, New York 27, N. Y.
UNiversity 6-1700

I am enclosing my contribution of $ ________ for the work of the Committee.

Name ________ (PLEASE PRINT)

Address ________

City ________ Zone ____ State ________

☐ I want to help ☐ Please send further information

Please make checks payable to:
Committee To Defend Martin Luther King

COMMITTEE TO DEFEND MARTIN LUTHER KING AND THE STRUGGLE FOR FREEDOM IN THE SOUTH
312 West 125th Street, New York 27, N. Y. UNiversity 6-1700

Chairmen: A. Philip Randolph, Dr. Gardner C. Taylor; *Chairmen of Cultural Division:* Harry Belafonte, Sidney Poitier; *Treasurer:* Nat King Cole; *Executive Director:* Bayard Rustin; *Chairmen of Church Division:* Father George B. Ford, Rev. Harry Emerson Fosdick, Rev. Thomas Kilgore, Jr., Rabbi Edward E. Klein; *Chairman of Labor Division:* Morris Iushewitz, Cleveland Robinson

The *Times* ad stirred a whirlwind of bitter reaction in Alabama, and soon after its publication a number of Alabama politicians filed libel suits against the paper. One of the suits was brought by L.B. Sullivan, the Montgomery commissioner of public affairs and supervisor of the Montgomery departments of scales, cemeteries, fire, and police. The ad did not actually mention Sullivan by name, and much of it referred to events entirely outside Alabama. But Sullivan claimed that the ad's allegedly defamatory statements about the Montgomery police implicitly referred to him as the commissioner who supervised the police department. Some of the statements in the ad were false, but as described in the Court's opinion, those errors were largely technical and insubstantial, such as incorrectly reporting that civil rights protestors sang "My Country, 'Tis of Thee" when in fact they sang the National Anthem.

The case was tried in an Alabama court during a period of fierce Southern resistance to the civil right movement. As Professor Mary-Rose Papandrea has observed, the ubiquitous racism that existed outside the courthouse found its way inside the courtroom:

> The case proceeded to a jury trial and the atmosphere in the courtroom reflected the segregation and prejudice of the State. The courtroom was itself racially segregated. When one of Sullivan's lawyers Calvin Whitesell read the text of the advertisement to the jury, he repeatedly substituted the word "nigger" for "Negro." When the lawyer for the ministers protested, Whitesell explained that he was simply using the pronunciation of the word "Negro" that he had used "all his life." In the transcript, the stenographer referred to the white lawyers as "Mr. Nachman" and "Mr. Embry," but referred to black lawyers as "Lawyer Gray" and "Lawyer Crawford." From the bench, Judge Jones also refused to use the honorific "Mr." to refer to the black lawyers. In addition, the trial continued during a Centennial Celebration commemorating the 100th anniversary of the Confederacy. Incredibly, Judge Jones allowed some jurors to sit in the jury box wearing their Confederate uniforms, which included pistols and holsters, and a Confederate flag was placed behind the bench.[3]

The jury held the *Times* liable to Sullivan for $500,000. But the threat to the *Times* went well beyond the $500,000 verdict. A string of other libel suits against the paper had been filed in Alabama in connection with its reporting on racial matters; in one of those cases, a $500,000 verdict had already been returned, and the total potential liability from the various suits was $5.6 million.

More broadly, the verdict posed a threat to all media reporting on the civil rights movement. Martin Luther King's strategy of passive resistance and civil disobedience

---

[3] Mary-Rose Papandrea, *The Story of New York Times v. Sullivan, in* First Amendment Stories 229, 241 (Richard W. Garnett & Andrew Koppelman, eds., 2012).

followed a strategy similar to Mahatma Gandhi's efforts to gain independence for India from Great Britain. In exposing the oppression and violence suffered by people of color in the South, including the violence visited upon civil rights protesters, King, like Gandhi, believed that outside pressures from national and international observers would lead to reform and justice. If news organizations could not present those accounts and images to the outside world, however, the success of the movement would be threatened.

With the hindsight of history, as the case reached the Supreme Court, it seemed that somehow the Court would be forced to intervene and overturn the verdict, lest public discourse over the civil rights movement be imperiled. What was entirely uncertain, however, was the constitutional path the Court would take to reverse the Alabama decision. The path the Court chose, the adoption of the "actual malice" standard for defamation suits brought by public officials, may or may not have been the best path, and it remains controversial.

New York Times Co. v. Sullivan

Supreme Court of the United States, 1964
376 U.S. 254

MR. JUSTICE BRENNAN delivered the opinion of the Court.

We are required in this case to determine for the first time the extent to which the constitutional protections for speech and press limit a State's power to award damages in a libel action brought by a public official against critics of his official conduct.

The text appeared over the names of 64 persons, many widely known for their activities in public affairs, religion, trade unions, and the performing arts. Below these names, and under a line reading "We in the south who are struggling daily for dignity and freedom warmly endorse this appeal," appeared the names of the four individual petitioners and of 16 other persons, all but two of whom were identified as clergymen in various Southern cities. The advertisement was signed at the bottom of the page by the "Committee to Defend Martin Luther King and the Struggle for Freedom in the South," and the officers of the Committee were listed.

Although neither of these statements mentions respondent by name, he contended that the word "police" in the third paragraph referred to him as the Montgomery Commissioner who supervised the Police Department.

It is uncontroverted that some of the statements contained in the two paragraphs were not accurate descriptions of events which occurred in Montgomery. Although Negro students staged a demonstration on the State Capital steps, they sang the

National Anthem and not "My Country, 'Tis of Thee." Although nine students were expelled by the State Board of Education, this was not for leading the demonstration at the Capitol, but for demanding service at a lunch counter in the Montgomery County Courthouse on another day. Not the entire student body, but most of it, had protested the expulsion, not by refusing to register, but by boycotting classes on a single day; virtually all the students did register for the ensuing semester. The campus dining hall was not padlocked on any occasion, and the only students who may have been barred from eating there were the few who had neither signed a preregistration application nor requested temporary meal tickets. Although the police were deployed near the campus in large numbers on three occasions, they did not at any time "ring" the campus, and they were not called to the campus in connection with the demonstration on the State Capitol steps, as the third paragraph implied. Dr. King had not been arrested seven times, but only four; and although he claimed to have been assaulted some years earlier in connection with his arrest for loitering outside a courtroom, one of the officers who made the arrest denied that there was such an assault.

On the premise that the charges in the sixth paragraph could be read as referring to him, respondent was allowed to prove that he had not participated in the events described. Although Dr. King's home had in fact been bombed twice when his wife and child were there, both of these occasions antedated respondent's tenure as Commissioner, and the police were not only not implicated in the bombings, but had made every effort to apprehend those who were. Three of Dr. King's four arrests took place before respondent became Commissioner. Although Dr. King had in fact been indicted (he was subsequently acquitted) on two counts of perjury, each of which carried a possible five-year sentence, respondent had nothing to do with procuring the indictment.

We consider this case against the background of a profound national commitment to the principle that debate on public issues should be uninhibited, robust, and wide-open, and that it may well include vehement, caustic, and sometimes unpleasantly sharp attacks on government and public officials. The present advertisement, as an expression of grievance and protest on one of the major public issues of our time, would seem clearly to qualify for the constitutional protection. The question is whether it forfeits that protection by the falsity of some of its factual statements and by its alleged defamation of respondent.

Authoritative interpretations of the First Amendment guarantees have consistently refused to recognize an exception for any test of truth—whether administered by judges, juries, or administrative officials—and especially one that puts the burden of proving truth on the speaker. The constitutional protection does not turn upon "the truth, popularity, or social utility of the ideas and beliefs which are offered." Erroneous statement is inevitable in free debate, and it must be protected if the freedoms of expression are to have the "breathing space" that they "need to survive."

Injury to official reputation error affords no more warrant for repressing speech that would otherwise be free than does factual error. Where judicial officers are involved, this Court has held that concern for the dignity and reputation of the courts does not justify the punishment as criminal contempt of criticism of the judge or his decision. If judges are to be treated as "men of fortitude, able to thrive in a hardy climate," surely the same must be true of other government officials, such as elected city commissioners. Criticism of their official conduct does not lose its constitutional protection merely because it is effective criticism and hence diminishes their official reputations.

If neither factual error nor defamatory content suffices to remove the constitutional shield from criticism of official conduct, the combination of the two elements is no less inadequate. This is the lesson to be drawn from the great controversy over the Sedition Act of 1798, which first crystallized a national awareness of the central meaning of the First Amendment. That statute made it a crime, punishable by a $5,000 fine and five years in prison, "if any person shall write, print, utter or publish any false, scandalous and malicious writing or writings against the government of the United States, or either house of the Congress or the President with intent to defame or to bring them, or either of them, into contempt or disrepute; or to excite against them, or either or any of them, the hatred of the good people of the United States." The Act allowed the defendant the defense of truth, and provided that the jury were to be judges both of the law and the facts. Despite these qualifications, the Act was vigorously condemned as unconstitutional in an attack joined in by Jefferson and Madison.

Although the Sedition Act was never tested in this Court, the attack upon its validity has carried the day in the court of history. Fines levied in its prosecution were repaid by Act of Congress on the ground that it was unconstitutional. These views reflect a broad consensus that the Act, because of the restraint it imposed upon criticism of government and public officials, was inconsistent with the First Amendment.

A rule compelling the critic of official conduct to guarantee the truth of all his factual assertions—and to do so on pain of libel judgments virtually unlimited in amount—leads to a comparable "self-censorship." Allowance of the defense of truth, with the burden of proving it on the defendant, does not mean that only false speech will be deterred.

The constitutional guarantees require, we think, a federal rule that prohibits a public official from recovering damages for a defamatory falsehood relating to his official conduct unless he proves that the statement was made with "actual malice"—that is, with knowledge that it was false or with reckless disregard of whether it was false or not.

Applying these standards, we consider that the proof presented to show actual malice lacks the convincing clarity which the constitutional standard demands, and hence that it would not constitutionally sustain the judgment for respondent under the proper rule of law.

there was no showing of malice

[Justice Black's concurring opinion, which was joined by Justice Douglas, is omitted, as is Justice Goldberg's opinion concurring in the result, which Justice Douglas also joined.]

Points for Discussion

1. **What was the "state action" triggering the application of the First Amendment?** We now know that behind the scenes, the justices in *Sullivan* were initially perplexed by whether a simple tort suit between private parties even constituted "state action" of the sort required to implicate the First Amendment. The Court ultimately concluded that state action did exist because Alabama courts were applying rules of decision derived from and enforced under state law:

   > Although this is a civil lawsuit between private parties, the Alabama courts have applied a state rule of law which petitioners claim to impose invalid restrictions on their constitutional freedoms of speech and press. It matters not that that law has been applied in a civil action and that it is common law only, though supplemented by statute. The test is not the form in which state power has been applied but, whatever the form, whether such power has in fact been exercised.

   In "constitutionalizing" state tort law imposing civil liability for expressive activity, the Court set the stage for future cases that would apply the First Amendment to many other torts where liability was based on a defendant's speech, including false light invasion of privacy, publication of private facts, tortious interference with economic interests, appropriation of name or likeness, aiding and abetting violence, and intentional infliction of emotional distress.

   In reaching its conclusion, the Court noted that civil libel actions can have a greater chilling effect on speech than criminal libel laws:

   > What a State may not constitutionally bring about by means of a criminal statute is likewise beyond the reach of its civil law of libel. The fear of damage awards under a rule such as that invoked by the Alabama courts here may be markedly more inhibiting than the fear of prosecution under a criminal statute. Alabama, for example, has a criminal libel law which allows as punishment upon conviction a fine

not exceeding $500 and a prison sentence of six months. The judgment awarded in this case—without the need for any proof of actual pecuniary loss—was one thousand times greater than the maximum fine provided by the Alabama criminal statute, and one hundred times greater than that provided by the Sedition Act. And since there is no double-jeopardy limitation applicable to civil lawsuits, this is not the only judgment that may be awarded against petitioners for the same publication. Plainly the Alabama law of civil libel is "a form of regulation that creates hazards to protected freedoms markedly greater than those that attend reliance upon the criminal law."

2. **What is the purpose of the "actual malice" requirement?** The Court held that a public official cannot recover in a defamation action unless he can prove with "convincing clarity" that the defendant made the defamatory statement with "actual malice." What does the actual malice standard require a plaintiff to prove? What was the Court's reasoning for creating such a high hurdle to a public official's ability to recover?

3. **Who is a "public official"?** *Sullivan* imposes limits on defamation actions brought by public officials. But what makes someone a public official? Do *Sullivan*'s rules apply to anyone who works for the government? Do they apply to only high-level government officials? *See Rosenblatt v. Baer*, 383 U.S. 75, 85 (1966) (stating that the "public official" designation applies "at the very least" to government employees "who have, or appear to the public to have, substantial responsibility for or control over the conduct of governmental affairs"). Do the actual malice rules apply to candidates running for public office? *See Monitor Patriot Co. v. Roy*, 401 U.S. 265, 271 (1971) (stating that *Sullivan*'s rules were "intended to apply to candidates, in spite of the use of the more restricted 'public official' terminology").

4. **Can impersonal attacks on government operations be converted into personal attacks on those in charge?** Recall that the allegedly defamatory advertisement in *Sullivan* never mentioned Sullivan by name. Instead, Sullivan's defamation claim relied on the argument that defamatory statements about Montgomery police officers implicitly defamed him because he was the commissioner charged with supervising the police department. Justice William Brennan thought this proposition—of "transmuting criticism of government, however impersonal it may seem on its face, into personal criticism, and hence potential libel, of the officials of whom the government is composed"—had "disquieting implications for criticism of governmental conduct." He held that "such a proposition may not constitutionally be utilized to establish that an otherwise impersonal attack on governmental operations was a libel of an official responsible for those operations."

5. **Did the Court not go far enough in protecting free speech?** The Court's decision was unanimous. But three justices—Hugo Black, William Douglas, and Arthur Goldberg—thought that the Court did not go far enough to protect freedom of speech. In their concurring opinions they argued that the First Amendment should be understood to provide absolute immunity from liability for defamation arising from critiques of the public actions of public officials. Here is a sampling from Justice Black's concurrence:

   > The requirement that malice be proved provides at best an evanescent protection for the right critically to discuss public affairs and certainly does not measure up to the sturdy safeguard embodied in the First Amendment. Unlike the Court, therefore, I vote to reverse exclusively on the ground that the Times and the individual defendants had an absolute, unconditional constitutional right to publish in the Times advertisement their criticisms of the Montgomery agencies and officials.

   Do you agree with Justice Black that the Court did not go far enough in protecting free speech rights? Should speakers have an absolute right to criticize public officials, even if the speakers know that their statements are false?

6. **Did the Court go too far in protecting free speech (and, consequently, failing to adequately protect reputational interests)?** Media outlets and stalwart free speech advocates treated *Sullivan* as an occasion for dancing in the streets, and it has long been regarded by many as one of the canonical foundations of modern First Amendment law. *See* Anthony Lewis, *Make No Law: The Sullivan Case and the First Amendment* (1991). Yet not everyone has been convinced of its wisdom. Professor Richard Epstein, for example, has argued that the Court could have decided the case on much narrower grounds, by merely holding that the First Amendment precluded liability for what was essentially a critique of the *government* and not a critique personal to Sullivan, who, after all, was never referred to by name. Richard Epstein, *Was New York Times v. Sullivan Wrong?*, 53 U. Chi. L. Rev. 782, 799–800 (1986). Similarly, Justice Elena Kagan, before she joined the Court, expressed concern about the Court's extension of *Sullivan*'s rules to other contexts: "The adverse consequences of the actual malice rule do not prove *Sullivan* itself wrong, but they do force consideration of the question whether the Court, in subsequent decisions, has extended the *Sullivan* principle too far." Elena Kagan, *A Libel Story: Sullivan Then and Now*, 18 L. & Soc. Inquiry 197, 205 (1993).

   To get a sense of why some think that *Sullivan* overprotected free speech interests at the expense of reputational interests, consider the example of a public official whose reputation was damaged by a defendant's defamatory remark. Even if the public official could prove that the defendant's statement was false and injured his reputation, the official would still lose if he could not also prove that the defendant made the statement with actual malice. If he was unable to do this, the next day's newspaper headline might well read, "Public Official Loses Defamation Action." Does that seem like a fair result if the defendant's statement was indisputably false and irreparably harmed the official's reputation? Would the justices have struck a better balance of free speech and reputational interests if the Court, as Justice Bryon White later suggested, had not escalated "the plaintiff's burden of proof to an almost impossible level" and instead had limited "the recoverable damages to a level that would not unduly threaten the press"? *Dun & Bradstreet, Inc. v. Greenmoss Builders, Inc.*, 472 U.S. 749, 771 (1985) (White, J., concurring).

7. **A comparative perspective and the quandary of "libel tourism."** *Sullivan* has not fared well in the international arena. In the aftermath of the decision, other common law countries considered whether to alter their defamation rules and adopt the actual malice standard. The United Kingdom, Canada, and Australia all rejected it.

   The failure of other countries to adopt the same free speech safeguards in their defamation law has raised the problem of "libel tourism." Given the global nature of so much media, what should happen when a person brings a defamation action in a country with less speech-protective defamation laws than the United States, succeeds in the lawsuit, and then seeks to enforce the judgment in the United States? For a description of this problem and how American courts have responded, *see* Lili Levi, *The Problem of Trans-National Libel*, 60 Am. J. Comp. L. 507 (2012); Rodney A. Smolla, *Smolla & Nimmer on Freedom of Speech, Enforcement of Foreign Libel Judgments* § 23.14 (2022).

3. The Extension of *Sullivan* to Other Defamation Plaintiffs: Public Figures, Private Figures, and Speech About Matters of Public Concern

New York Times v. Sullivan established limits on defamation actions brought by public officials. In the years following the decision, the Court extended First Amendment limits to defamation actions brought by other types of plaintiffs. The result is a complex framework of rules that depend on both the status of a plaintiff and the substance of a defendant's defamatory statement.

The process of extending First Amendment limits to other defamation plaintiffs began three years after *Sullivan* when the Court applied the actual malice standard it had created for public *officials* to public *figures*. The clearest explanation of the Court's reasoning was found in a concurring opinion written by Chief Justice Earl Warren:

> It is plain that although they are not subject to the restraints of the political process, "public figures," like "public officials," often play an influential role in ordering society. And surely as a class these "public figures" have as ready access as "public officials" to mass media of communication, both to influence policy and to counter criticism of their views and activities. Our citizenry has a legitimate and substantial interest in the conduct of such persons, and freedom of the press to engage in uninhibited debate about their involvement in public issues and events is as crucial as it is in the case of "public officials." The fact that they are not amenable to the restraints of the political process only underscores the legitimate and substantial nature of the interest, since it means that public opinion may be the only instrument by which society can attempt to influence their conduct.

Curtis Publ'g Co. v. Butts; Associated Press v. Walker, 388 U.S. 130, 164 (1967) (Warren, C.J., concurring).

The result of this decision was that public figures who bring defamation actions are required, like public officials, to prove by clear and convincing evidence that a defendant's defamatory statement was made with actual malice.

The looming questions after the *Butts/Walker* opinion were how courts were supposed to determine whether a defamation plaintiff was a "public figure" as opposed to a "private figure" and whether the First Amendment placed any limits on defamation actions brought by private figures. The following case is the leading authority addressing both questions.

Gertz v. Robert Welch, Inc.

Supreme Court of the United States, 1974
418 U.S. 323

MR. JUSTICE POWELL delivered the opinion of the Court.

This Court has struggled for nearly a decade to define the proper accommodation between the law of defamation and the freedoms of speech and press protected by the First Amendment.

The principal issue in this case is whether a newspaper or broadcaster that publishes defamatory falsehoods about an individual who is neither a public official nor a public figure may claim a constitutional privilege against liability for the injury inflicted by those statements.

Three years after *New York Times*, a majority of the Court agreed to extend the constitutional privilege to defamatory criticism of "public figures." This extension was announced in *Curtis Publishing Co. v. Butts* and its companion, *Associated Press v. Walker*. The first case involved the Saturday Evening Post's charge that Coach Wally Butts of the University of Georgia had conspired with Coach "Bear" Bryant of the University of Alabama to fix a football game between their respective schools. *Walker* involved an erroneous Associated Press account of former Major General Edwin Walker's participation in a University of Mississippi campus riot. Because Butts was paid by a private alumni association and Walker had resigned from the Army, neither could be classified as a "public official" under *New York Times*. Although Mr. Justice Harlan announced the result in both cases, a majority of the Court agreed with Mr. Chief Justice Warren's conclusion that the *New York Times* test should apply to criticism of "public figures" as well as "public officials."

In his opinion for the plurality in *Rosenbloom v. Metromedia, Inc.*, 403 U.S. 29 (1971), Mr. Justice Brennan took the *New York Times* privilege one step further. He concluded that its protection should extend to defamatory falsehoods relating to private persons if the statements concerned matters of general or public interest.

We begin with the common ground. Under the First Amendment there is no such thing as a false idea. However pernicious an opinion may seem, we depend for its correction not on the conscience of judges and juries but on the competition of other ideas. But there is no constitutional value in false statements of fact. Neither the intentional lie nor the careless error materially advances society's interest in " 'uninhibited, robust, and wide-open" debate on public issues. They belong to that category of utterances which "are no essential part of any exposition of ideas, and are of such slight social value as a step to truth that any benefit that may be derived from them is clearly outweighed by the social interest in order and morality." *Chaplinsky v. New Hampshire*.

Although the erroneous statement of fact is not worthy of constitutional protection, it is nevertheless inevitable in free debate. Punishment of error runs the risk of inducing a cautious and restrictive exercise of the constitutionally guaranteed freedoms of speech and press. Our decisions recognize that a rule of strict liability that compels a publisher or broadcaster to guarantee the accuracy of his factual assertions may lead to intolerable self-censorship. The First Amendment requires that we protect some falsehood in order to protect speech that matters.

The need to avoid self-censorship by the news media is, however, not the only societal value at issue. If it were, this Court would have embraced long ago the view that publishers and broadcasters enjoy an unconditional and indefeasible immunity from liability for defamation. Such a rule would, indeed, obviate the fear that the prospect of civil liability for injurious falsehood might dissuade a timorous press from the effective exercise of First Amendment freedoms. Yet absolute protection for the communications media requires a total sacrifice of the competing value served by the law of defamation.

The legitimate state interest underlying the law of libel is the compensation of individuals for the harm inflicted on them by defamatory falsehood. We would not lightly require the State to abandon this purpose, for, as Mr. Justice Stewart has reminded us, the individual's right to the protection of his own good name

> reflects no more than our basic concept of the essential dignity and worth of every human being—a concept at the root of any decent system of ordered liberty. The protection of private personality, like the protection of life itself, is left primarily to the individual States under the Ninth and Tenth Amendments. But this does not mean that the right is entitled to any less recognition by this Court as a basic of our constitutional system. *Rosenblatt v. Baer*, 383 U.S. 75 (1966) (concurring opinion).

The *New York Times* standard defines the level of constitutional protection appropriate to the context of defamation of a public person. Those who, by reason of the notoriety of their achievements or the vigor and success with which they seek the public's attention, are properly classed as public figures and those who hold governmental office may recover for injury to reputation only on clear and convincing proof that the defamatory falsehood was made with knowledge of its falsity or with reckless disregard for the truth. This standard administers an extremely powerful antidote to the inducement to media self-censorship of the common law rule of strict liability for libel and slander. And it exacts a correspondingly high price from the victims of defamatory falsehood. Plainly many deserving plaintiffs, including some intentionally subjected to injury, will be unable to surmount the barrier of the *New York Times* test. Despite this substantial abridgment of the state law right to compensation for wrongful hurt to one's reputation, the Court has concluded that the protection of the *New York Times* privilege should be available to publishers and broadcasters of defamatory falsehood concerning public officials and public figures.

With that caveat we have no difficulty in distinguishing among defamation plaintiffs. The first remedy of any victim of defamation is self-help—using available opportunities to contradict the lie or correct the error and thereby to minimize its adverse impact on reputation. Public officials and public figures usually enjoy significantly greater access to the channels of effective communication and hence have a more realistic opportunity to counteract false statements than private individuals normally enjoy. Private individuals are therefore more vulnerable to injury, and the state interest in protecting them is correspondingly greater.

More important than the likelihood that private individuals will lack effective opportunities for rebuttal, there is a compelling normative consideration underlying the distinction between public and private defamation plaintiffs. An individual who decides to seek governmental office must accept certain necessary consequences of that involvement in public affairs. He runs the risk of closer public scrutiny than might otherwise be the case. And society's interest in the officers of government is not strictly limited to the formal discharge of official duties. As the Court pointed out in *Garrison v. Louisiana*, 379 U.S. 64, 77 (1964), the public's interest extends to "anything which might touch on an official's fitness for office. Few personal attributes are more germane to fitness for office than dishonesty, malfeasance, or improper motivation, even though these characteristics may also affect the official's private character."

Those classed as public figures stand in a similar position. Hypothetically, it may be possible for someone to become a public figure through no purposeful action of his own, but the instances of truly involuntary public figures must be exceedingly rare. For the most part those who attain this status have assumed roles of especial prominence in the affairs of society. Some occupy positions of such persuasive power and influence that they are deemed public figures for all purposes. More commonly, those classed as public figures have thrust themselves to the forefront of particular public controversies in order to influence the resolution of the issues involved. In either event, they invite attention and comment.

Even if the foregoing generalities do not obtain in every instance, the communications media are entitled to act on the assumption that public officials and public figures have voluntarily exposed themselves to increased risk of injury from defamatory falsehood concerning them. No such assumption is justified with respect to a private individual. He has not accepted public office or assumed an "influential role in ordering society." He has relinquished no part of his interest in the protection of his own good name, and consequently he has a more compelling call on the courts for redress of injury inflicted by defamatory falsehood. Thus, private individuals are not only more vulnerable to injury than public officials and public figures; they are also more deserving of recovery.

For these reasons we conclude that the States should retain substantial latitude in their efforts to enforce a legal remedy for defamatory falsehood injurious to the reputation of a private individual. The extension of the *New York Times* test proposed by the *Rosenbloom* plurality would abridge this legitimate state interest to a degree that we find unacceptable.

We hold that, so long as they do not impose liability without fault, the States may define for themselves the appropriate standard of liability for a publisher or broadcaster of defamatory falsehood injurious to a private individual.

The common law of defamation is an oddity of tort law, for it allows recovery of purportedly compensatory damages without evidence of actual loss. Under the traditional rules pertaining to actions for libel, the existence of injury is presumed from the fact of publication. Juries may award substantial sums as compensation for supposed damage to reputation without any proof that such harm actually occurred. The largely uncontrolled discretion of juries to award damages where there is no loss unnecessarily compounds the potential of any system of liability for defamatory falsehood to inhibit the vigorous exercise of First Amendment freedoms. Additionally, the doctrine of presumed damages invites juries to punish unpopular opinion rather than to compensate individuals for injury sustained by the publication of a false fact. More to the point, the States have no substantial interest in securing for plaintiffs such as this petitioner gratuitous awards of money damages far in excess of any actual injury.

We would not, of course, invalidate state law simply because we doubt its wisdom, but here we are attempting to reconcile state law with a competing interest grounded in the constitutional command of the First Amendment. It is therefore appropriate to require that state remedies for defamatory falsehood reach no farther than is necessary to protect the legitimate interest involved. It is necessary to restrict defamation plaintiffs who do not prove knowledge of falsity or reckless disregard for the truth to compensation for actual injury. We need not define "actual injury," as trial courts have wide experience in framing appropriate jury instructions in tort actions. Suffice it to say that actual injury is not limited to out-of-pocket loss. Indeed, the more customary types of actual harm inflicted by defamatory falsehood include impairment of reputation and standing in the community, personal humiliation, and mental anguish and suffering. Of course, juries must be limited by appropriate instructions, and all awards must be supported by competent evidence concerning the injury, although there need be no evidence which assigns an actual dollar value to the injury.

We also find no justification for allowing awards of punitive damages against publishers and broadcasters held liable under state-defined standards of liability for defamation. In most jurisdictions jury discretion over the amounts awarded is limited only by the gentle rule that they not be excessive. Consequently, juries assess punitive damages in wholly unpredictable amounts bearing no necessary relation to the actual harm caused. And they remain free to use their discretion selectively to punish expressions of unpopular views. Like the doctrine of presumed damages, jury discretion to award punitive damages unnecessarily exacerbates the danger of media self-censorship, but, unlike the former rule, punitive damages are wholly irrelevant to the state interest that justifies a negligence standard for private defamation actions. They are not compensation for injury. Instead, they are private fines levied by civil juries to punish reprehensible conduct and to deter its future occurrence. In short, the private defamation plaintiff who establishes liability under a less demanding standard than that stated by *New York Times* may recover only such damages as are sufficient to compensate him for actual injury.

[Justice Blackmun's concurring opinion is omitted, as are separate dissents written by Chief Justice Burger, Justice Douglas, Justice Brennan, and Justice White.]

Points for Discussion

1. **Was the extension of the actual malice standard to public figures justified?** The original decision creating the actual malice standard for defamation of public officials was buttressed principally by the constitutional interest in providing breathing space for critique of government and government officials. That rationale, however, applies with diminished force, and perhaps not all, to the extension of the actual malice standard to public figures who are not involved in matters relating to government. Did the Court err in extending the actual malice standard to public figures?

2. **What is the reality on the street?** How important is the divide the Court created between public and private defamation plaintiffs? While the Court left it to states to define the level of liability required for private-figure plaintiffs, all but a handful of states chose the more pro-plaintiff negligence standard for private figure cases. This in turn placed great pressure on the classification of the plaintiff as either a public official or public figure on the one hand, or a private plaintiff on the other. Public plaintiffs saddled with the actual malice standard do occasionally win, but the odds are heavily stacked against them. Courts applying the actual malice standard hold that a mere failure to act reasonably, such as a mere failure to investigate a story, is not sufficient to establish actual malice. Rather, the plaintiff must prove through clear and convincing evidence that the defendant either *knew* the story to be false or harbored *subjective doubt* that the story was true but published anyway. Private-figure plaintiffs who must prove only negligence, on the other hand, have a much higher success rate.

   Gertz recognized two classes of public figures. The "all purpose" public figure, typically a mega-celebrity, is deemed a public figure for defamation on any topic. Courts very rarely classify a plaintiff as such an all-purpose public figure. Far more common are "limited purpose" public figures. While tests for determining limited-purpose public figures differ somewhat among lower courts, the most popular approaches typically apply a multi-factor test. One of the most widespread approaches, adopted by many courts across the country, is a three-part test emanating from *Waldbaum v. Fairchild Publications, Inc.*, 627 F.2d 1287 (D.C. Cir. 1980). Under this approach, the first task is to isolate the public controversy, a dispute that in fact has received public attention because its ramifications will be felt by people who are not direct participants. Second, the court must analyze the plaintiff's role in the controversy. Trivial or tangential participation is not enough. To be a limited-purpose public figure, a plaintiff must have achieved a "special prominence" in the debate. The court can look to the plaintiff's past conduct, the extent of press coverage, and the public reaction to his conduct or statements. And third, the court must determine whether the alleged defamation was germane to the plaintiff's participation in the controversy.

3. **Who has the burden of proving falsity?** In cases of both public officials and public figures, the burden of proving falsity is on the plaintiff. What about private-figure cases? In *Philadelphia Newspapers, Inc. v. Hepps*, 475 U.S. 767 (1986), the Court held that held that the plaintiff bears the burden of establishing falsity in private-figure cases, at least when the speech involves issues of public concern and a media defendant.

4. **Separating false statements of fact from non-actionable opinions, rhetorical hyperbole, name-calling, or insults.** Under both common law and constitutional law principles, there can be no liability for statements of opinion, rhetorical hyperbole, or name-calling. These phrases are all variations of the same theme, separating insult and critique from palpable false statements of fact. In *Letter Carriers v. Austin*, 418 U.S. 264, 284 (1974), for example, the Court held that the use of the word "traitor" in reference to a union "scab" was not actionable because the word was used "in a loose, figurative sense" and was "merely rhetorical hyperbole, a lusty and imaginative expression of the contempt felt by union members towards those who refuse to join." Similarly, in *Greenbelt Cooperative Publishing Association v. Bresler*, 398 U.S. 6 (1970), the Court held that accusations of "blackmail" were protected under the First Amendment because the word, taken in context, was not used as a literal accusation of a crime, but as a figurative pejorative critiquing the plaintiff's business tactics. And as we will see later in this chapter in the context of infliction of emotional distress, the Court held in *Hustler Magazine v. Falwell* that statements that a famous television evangelist had sex with his mother in an outhouse were not actionable as defamation because no reasonable reader would have believed the statements, which were part of a comedic parody, were to be understood literally. The leading Supreme Court opinion on the issue is *Milkovich v. Lorain Journal Co.*, 497 U.S. 1 (1990), in which a high school wrestling coach, Michael Milkovich, brought a defamation action against a newspaper over an article implying that he had lied under oath in a judicial proceeding arising from an altercation at a wrestling match. The Court held that the statements communicated to readers that Milkovich had lied under oath. The Court rejected the argument that the statements were protected by the First Amendment just because they may have been superficially couched as opinion, noting that even a statement articulated in the form of an "opinion" may imply the existence of false defamatory facts. The Court famously stated that the First Amendment does not "create a wholesale defamation exemption for anything that might be labeled 'opinion.' " The key to *Milkovich* rests in the phrase "that might be labeled opinion." It is not the label that matters. What matters is what is communicated. Most importantly, *Milkovich* did not disturb the pre-existing First Amendment precedents on which it both relied and reinforced, requiring

that only false statements of fact are actionable. In the real world of defamation litigation, many cases turn on the distinction between fact and opinion. The distinction is often difficult to apply because many statements fall on the cusp.

5. **Do First Amendment protections apply at all in private-figure defamation actions that do not involve issues of public concern?** A critical "gatekeeper" for the triggering of any heightened First Amendment protections for defamation is the threshold requirement that the subject matter of the defamation involve issues of public concern. Some defamation cases involve entirely private matters that do not implicate any issues of concern to the public. In *Dun & Bradstreet*, the Court held that the *Gertz* rule restricting awards of presumed and punitive damages to cases in which actual malice is shown does not apply to defamatory statements that "do not involve matters of public concern." While *Dun & Bradstreet* did not discuss First Amendment fault rules, it is at least possible that in a case not involving any issue of public concern, state courts would be free to revert to the original common law strict liability standard. How does a court determine whether the issue is a matter of public concern? In *Dun & Bradstreet*, the Court held that a false credit report concerning the creditworthiness of a business was not a matter of public concern. The Court did not elaborate at length on the meaning of the phrase "public concern," merely stating broadly whether speech addresses a matter of public concern must be determined by its "content, form, and context." The Court emphasized that a credit report concerned only the interests of the specific business audience to whom it was addressed.

6. **Prior restraints and defamation actions.** As a matter of common law and First Amendment prior restraint doctrine, it has generally been thought that courts could not enjoin defamatory statements. Thus, the common law maxim evolved that "equity will not enjoin defamation." Some courts have begun to question this blanket prohibition, particularly when the statement being enjoined has been fully adjudicated and found to be defamatory. As the California Supreme Court observed in *Balboa Island Village Inn, Inc. v. Lemen*, 156 P.3d 339, 344 (Cal. 2007), there is a fundamental difference between enjoining a speaker from making a statement that would be defamatory if made and issuing "a posttrial injunction *after* a statement that already has been uttered has been found to constitute defamation." *See generally* Eugene Volokh, *Anti-Libel Injunctions*, 168 U. Pa. L. Rev. 73 (2019); Doug Rendleman, *The Defamation Injunction Meets the Prior Restraint Doctrine*, 56 San Diego L. Rev. 615 (2019).

7. **Can contracts be used to end-run First Amendment restraints on defamation actions?** Private companies, celebrities, and occasionally government entities sometimes require parties with whom they contract to agree to nondisparagement clauses. For example, the Trump campaign required its employees to promise not

to "demean or disparage publicly" Trump, his family, or their companies. *Denson v. Donald J. Trump for President, Inc.*, 530 F. Supp. 3d 412 (S.D.N.Y. 2021).

Absent a nondisparagement clause, the recourse for a disparaged party like Trump would presumably be a defamation lawsuit. But this would require the plaintiff to surmount the many hurdles the Supreme Court has created to ensure that defamation actions do not chill freedom of speech. Can a person end-run these hurdles by simply suing a party for breaching a contractual nondisparagement clause? Should it matter whether the contract was carefully negotiated or was a form adhesion contract imposed on a party with no bargaining power? Should it matter that a person was waiving his First Amendment rights? Should it matter if the party that insisted upon the nondisparagement clause was the government? *See, e.g.*, *Overbey v. Mayor of Balt.*, 930 F.3d 215 (4th Cir. 2019). In answering these questions, consider the broader implications of contractual provisions suppressing speech. For example, confidentiality and nondisparagement clauses have often been used to deny the public access to information about sexual predators, dangerously defective products, and compromising information about candidates for public office. *See generally* Burt Neuborne, *Limiting the Right to Buy Silence: A Hearer-Centered Approach*, 90 U. Colo. L. Rev. 411 (2019); David A. Hoffman & Erik Lampmann, *Hushing Contracts*, 97 Wash. U. L. Rev. 165 (2019); Clay Calvert, *Gag Clauses and the Right to Gripe: The Consumer Review Fairness Act of 2016 & State Efforts to Protect Online Reviews from Contractual Censorship*, 24 Widener L. Rev. 203 (2018); Alan E. Garfield, *Contract Law and Freedom of Speech*, 83 Cornell L. Rev. 261 (1998).

FIRST AMENDMENT LIMITS ON DEFAMATION ACTIONS

Who is the plaintiff?	What is the burden of proof?
Public Official	• The plaintiff must prove by clear and convincing evidence that the defendant made the statement with actual malice. • The plaintiff must prove that the defendant's statement was false.
Public Figure	• The plaintiff must prove by clear and convincing evidence that the defendant made the statement with actual malice. • The plaintiff must prove that the defendant's statement was false.

Private Figure/Public Concern (when the allegedly defamatory statement was a matter of public concern)	• To recover compensatory damages, the plaintiff must at least prove that the defendant acted with negligence. • The plaintiff must prove that the defendant's statement was false (at least for media defendants). • To recover presumed and/or punitive damages, the plaintiff must prove that the defendant made the statement with actual malice.
Private Figure/Private Concern (when the allegedly defamatory statement was not a matter of public concern)	The First Amendment limits on these actions are uncertain, and it is possible that there are no First Amendment limits. The Supreme Court has only indicated that these plaintiffs do not have to show actual malice to recover presumed or punitive damages.
Supplemental Rules	**Modification of quotes:** Alteration of a plaintiff's words does not equate to knowledge of falsity under *Sullivan* unless the alteration materially changed the meaning of the plaintiff's words. *Masson v. New Yorker Magazine*, 501 U.S. 496 (1991). **Independent judgment by appellate courts:** Appellate courts should use independent judgment when reviewing lower court determinations of actual malice (*i.e.*, de novo review as opposed to a deferential "clearly erroneous" standard). *Bose Corp. v. Consumers Union*, 466 U.S. 485 (1984).

4. Should *Sullivan* and Its Progeny Be Abandoned? A Shot Across the Bow from Justice Clarence Thomas

The rules established in *Sullivan* have always been controversial. That has not stopped the opinion and subsequent opinions expanding upon it from becoming an entrenched part of the First Amendment canon.

Nevertheless, some Supreme Court justices, particularly Justices Clarence Thomas and Neil Gorsuch, have openly questioned whether *Sullivan* should be reconsidered.

The following concurrence to a denial of *certiorari*, written by Justice Thomas, is an example.

McKee v. Cosby

Supreme Court of the United States, 2019
139 S. Ct. 675

JUSTICE THOMAS, concurring in the denial of *certiorari*.

In December 2014, petitioner Kathrine McKee publicly accused actor and comedian Bill Cosby of forcibly raping her some 40 years earlier. McKee contends that Cosby's attorney responded on his behalf by writing and leaking a defamatory letter. According to McKee, the letter deliberately distorts her personal background to "damage her reputation for truthfulness and honesty, and further to embarrass, harass, humiliate, intimidate, and shame" her. She alleges that excerpts of the letter were disseminated via the Internet and published by news outlets around the world.

McKee filed suit in federal court for defamation under state law, but her case was dismissed. Applying *New York Times Co. v. Sullivan*, and its progeny, the Court of Appeals concluded that, by disclosing her accusation to a reporter, McKee had "thrust herself to the forefront" of the public controversy over "sexual assault allegations implicating Cosby" and was therefore a "limited-purpose public figure." Under this Court's First Amendment precedents, public figures are barred from recovering damages for defamation unless they can show that the statement at issue was made with "actual malice—that is, with knowledge that it was false or with reckless disregard of whether it was false or not." Like many plaintiffs subject to this "almost impossible" standard, McKee was unable to make that showing.

New York Times and the Court's decisions extending it were policy-driven decisions masquerading as constitutional law. Instead of simply applying the First Amendment as it was understood by the people who ratified it, the Court fashioned its own federal rules by balancing the "competing values at stake in defamation suits."

We should not continue to reflexively apply this policy-driven approach to the Constitution. Instead, we should carefully examine the original meaning of the First and Fourteenth Amendments. If the Constitution does not require public figures to satisfy an actual-malice standard in state-law defamation suits, then neither should we.

None of these decisions made a sustained effort to ground their holdings in the Constitution's original meaning. As the Court itself acknowledged, "the rule enunciated in the *New York Times* case" is "largely a judge-made rule of law," the "content" of which is "given meaning through the evolutionary process of common-law adjudication."

The constitutional libel rules adopted by this Court in *New York Times* and its progeny broke sharply from the common law of libel, and there are sound reasons to question whether the First and Fourteenth Amendments displaced this body of common law.

common law public figures it was more serious

The common law of libel at the time the First and Fourteenth Amendments were ratified did not require public figures to satisfy any kind of heightened liability standard as a condition of recovering damages.

Far from increasing a public figure's burden in a defamation action, the common law deemed libels against public figures to be, if anything, more serious and injurious than ordinary libels.

These common-law protections for the "core private right" of a person's "uninterrupted enjoyment of his reputation" formed the backdrop against which the First and Fourteenth Amendments were ratified. Before our decision in *New York Times*, we consistently recognized that the First Amendment did not displace the common law of libel. As Justice Story explained,

> The liberty of speech, or of the press, has nothing to do with this subject. They are not endangered by the punishment of libelous publications. The liberty of speech and the liberty of the press do not authorize malicious and injurious defamation.

There are sound reasons to question whether either the First or Fourteenth Amendment, as originally understood, encompasses an actual-malice standard for public figures or otherwise displaces vast swaths of state defamation law.

Historical practice further suggests that protections for free speech and a free press—whether embodied in state constitutions, the First Amendment, or the Fourteenth Amendment—did not abrogate the common law of libel.

As against this body of historical evidence, *New York Times* pointed only to opposition surrounding the Sedition Act of 1798. After discussing other opposition to the Act, the Court concluded that "the attack upon its validity has carried the day in the court of history."

The Court gleaned from this evidence a "broad consensus" that the First Amendment protects "criticism of government and public officials." And the Court further inferred that because the Act allowed truth to be offered as a defense and applied to defamatory statements, a libel law prohibiting only false defamation could still fail First Amendment scrutiny. But constitutional opposition to the Sedition Act—a federal law directly criminalizing criticism of the Government—does not necessarily support a constitutional actual-malice rule in all civil libel actions brought by public figures. Madison did not contend that the Constitution abrogated the common law applicable to these private actions. Instead, he seemed to contemplate that "those who administer [the Federal Government]" retain "a remedy, for their injured reputations, under the same laws, and in the same tribunals, which protect their lives, their liberties, and their properties." Moreover, a central assumption of Madison's view was the historical absence of a national common law "pervading and operating through" each colony "as one society." Yet the Court elevated just such a rule to constitutional status in *New York Times*.

It is certainly true that defamation law did not remain static after the founding. For example, many States acted "by judicial decision, statute or constitution" during the early 19th century to allow truth or good motives to serve as a defense to a libel prosecution. But these changes appear to have reflected changing policy judgments, not a sense that existing law violated the original meaning of the First or Fourteenth Amendment.

In short, there appears to be little historical evidence suggesting that the *New York Times* actual-malice rule flows from the original understanding of the First or Fourteenth Amendment.

Like Justice White, I assume that *New York Times* and our other constitutional decisions displacing state defamation law have been popular in some circles, "but this is not the road to salvation for a court of law." We did not begin meddling in this area until 1964, nearly 175 years after the First Amendment was ratified. The States are perfectly capable of striking an acceptable balance between encouraging robust public discourse and providing a meaningful remedy for reputational harm. We should reconsider our jurisprudence in this area.

Points for Discussion

1. **What is the proper role of history?** In Chapter 2, we discussed the historic antecedents to the adoption of the First Amendment. If Justice Thomas is correct that the Framers had no intention of displacing the common law of defamation with a standard such as actual malice, does that mean that *Sullivan* was wrongly decided? In this casebook we encounter dozens of tests and standards applicable to various discrete arenas of modern free speech law. Most of these standards are, like the actual malice standard, judge-made law. Would the emphasis on history advocated by Justice Thomas make many of these judicial elaborations on the meaning of the First Amendment suspect and vulnerable to overruling?

2. **Do changes in society and technology warrant reconsidering *Sullivan*?** Justice Gorsuch joined forces with Justice Thomas in calling for reconsideration of *Sullivan* in *Berisha v. Lawson*, 141 S. Ct. 2424 (2021) (Gorsuch, J., dissenting from denial of *certiorari*). Justice Gorsuch pointed out that the media landscape has changed dramatically since 1964. He argued that modern public discourse is battered by a perfect storm of technological and social changes, including the specter that social media can make a person a public figure overnight.

You Be the Judge!
Defamation with all the toppings

A restaurateur owns and operates a highly successful pizza restaurant. His name and picture appear on billboards and other media advertising for the restaurant, touting its traditional family recipes. A waitress who works at the restaurant posts a message on Facebook claiming that the restaurateur is a "sexist pig" and a "sexual predator" and that "he sexually assaulted me at work, groping me from behind the bar while I was bending down to place drinks on a serving platter." The restaurateur, who is married, denies the allegations, claiming that the waitress was a disgruntled employee angry at him because she was passed over for a management position at the restaurant. Issues relating to sexual assault are prominent in the restaurant business, but the restaurateur has never participated in debates or discussions regarding those issues and has never before been accused of any sexual misconduct. The waitress sends her Facebook post to a local newspaper journalist. That journalist believes the waitress, and the newspaper publishes a story repeating her allegations. The reporter does not investigate the allegations. Had the reporter done so, she would have found several other workers at the restaurant who would have cast doubt on the waitress's story, repeating a rumor among the staff that the incident never happened and that the waitress was indeed retaliating against the boss for not promoting her. The restaurateur sues both the waitress and the newspaper for defamation. It later comes out that the waitress fabricated the allegations. In a conversation recorded by a co-worker, she is overheard stating that she made up the entire episode because she was so angry at not being selected as a manager. As the judge assigned to preside over the defamation case, consider the following questions:

1. The restaurateur argues that this was a run-of-the-mill private employment dispute involving a disgruntled employee and the employee's boss and thus was not a matter of public concern at all, meaning that no heightened First Amendment protections of any kind should apply to the case. How would you rule on this point?

2. The waitress and newspaper argue that the restaurateur should be deemed a public figure because he voluntarily entered a business in

which a public controversy exists over allegations of sexual assault, particularly since the beginning of the #MeToo movement. The restaurateur claims that he is simply an ordinary restaurant owner who works hard to promote his business but is not a public figure for purposes of an allegation involving sexual assault. How would you rule?

3. If you find that the restaurateur is a public figure, is the newspaper entitled to summary judgment on the issue of actual malice?

4. If you find that the restaurateur is a private figure, is the newspaper entitled to summary judgment on the issue of negligence?

5. The defendants claim that while the groping allegation is admittedly an assertion of fact, the statements that the restaurateur is a "sexist pig" and a "sexual predator" are non-actionable opinion, rhetorical hyperbole, or mere insult or name-calling. How would you rule on those statements?

6. Focusing only on the waitress, is the restaurateur entitled to summary judgment (or alternatively a directed verdict) against her on the issue of liability, leaving the only issue for the jury the assessment of damages? Could a jury award presumed and/or punitive damages against the waitress?

B. Privacy: May Government Regulate Speech to Protect People's Privacy?

The origins of modern privacy law are traced to an 1890 law review article written by Louis Brandeis, long before he became a Supreme Court justice, and lawyer Samuel Warren.[4] The authors sought to address abuses by the paparazzi of their age:

> Recent inventions and business methods call attention to the next step which must be taken for the protection of the person, and for securing to the individual what Judge [Thomas] Cooley calls the right "to be let alone." Instantaneous photographs and newspaper enterprise have invaded the sacred precincts of private and domestic life; and numerous mechanical devices threaten to make good the prediction that "what is whispered in the closet shall be proclaimed from the house-tops."

---

4 Samuel D. Warren & Louis B. Brandeis, *The Right to Privacy*, 4 Harv. L. Rev. 193 (1890).

The preeminent tort law scholar Dean William Prosser categorized invasions of privacy into four separate torts, which were codified in the *Restatement (Second) of Torts*: false light privacy, public disclosure of private facts, intrusion upon seclusion, and appropriation of a person's name or likeness.

Each of these torts is designed to protect specific societal interests in privacy. Some directly collide with free speech interests while others do so only indirectly. The following subsections survey each tort's interaction with the First Amendment.

1. False Light Privacy: When Speech Casts a Person in a False Light

The tort of false light privacy is a close cousin to the tort of defamation. Both concern a false statement about the plaintiff. But the single distinguishing characteristic of the false light tort is that the statement need not be defamatory. A false light claim may involve statements that say something *good* about the plaintiff, statements that enhance the plaintiff's reputation yet are nonetheless "false." False light swaps the element of "defamatory meaning" for the requirement that the statement would be "highly offensive to a reasonable person." So how could a statement that expresses something positive or neutral about a person still be deemed highly offensive?

The answer is that there may be instances in which even a positive lie is offensive—the lie alone causes injury, even if the lie is laudatory. Imagine, for example, a war veteran who experienced many episodes of violent combat during the war, saw many comrades die, and witnessed many acts of valor on the part of others. The soldier did his duty and served his country well, yet was neither uncommonly brave nor cowardly. Now imagine that on the anniversary of the veteran's return from the war, a local newspaper published an article about him, and to embellish the story invented acts of valor by the veteran, making him out as a hero, when in fact he was just a good soldier. These exaggerated acts of courage might well have enhanced the veteran's reputation, but he would still have a valid action for false light invasion of privacy. To the reasonable person in the veteran's circumstances, these manufactured stories would likely be deeply offensive and embarrassing because the person had been made out as something he was not.

Two false light cases have reached the Supreme Court. In *Time, Inc. v. Hill*, 385 U.S. 374 (1967), the Hill family had been held hostage for 19 hours by three escaped convicts. The abductors treated the Hills civilly. A novel was written about the event, followed by a Broadway play. *Life* magazine did a pictorial article on the play, which it said was inspired by the Hill family episode. The article and the accompanying pictures (from the play) portrayed the convicts as violent and abusive toward the Hills and the Hills courageously defying them.

The Court held that the plaintiff, James Hill, could recover for false light privacy only if he could prove that the magazine's false reports were made with actual malice. In other words, the Court imported the actual malice standard from defamation cases into the false light privacy context.

The *Hill* decision was issued prior to *Gertz* and its dichotomy between public- and private-figure plaintiffs. This led to a debate over whether *Hill* should be deemed modified by *Gertz*, so that in private-figure false light cases, liability could attach on a showing of mere negligence, thus tracking the fault standards for defamation.

The Supreme Court did not settle this debate in its second false light case, *Cantrell v. Forest City Publishing Co.*, 419 U.S. 245 (1974), which concerned a newspaper's false characterization of a woman as stoically bearing her grief after her husband's death in a bridge collapse. The case was decided after *Gertz*, but the issues were framed in a manner that made it unnecessary to address the implications of *Gertz*. As the Court explained, "this case presents no occasion to consider whether a State may constitutionally apply a more relaxed standard of liability for a publisher or broadcaster of false statements injurious to a private individual under a false-light theory of invasion of privacy."

Since *Hill* has never been overruled and was not discussed in *Gertz*, many courts have held that the actual malice standard applies to *all* false light claims involving issues of public concern, without regard to the public or private status of the plaintiff. The *Restatement (Second) of Torts* takes this position.

2. Publication of Private Facts: When Speech Reveals Intimate Personal Information

Whereas defamation and false light invasion of privacy are both triggered by the publication of false statements, the privacy tort known as "publication of private facts" involves publication of *true* facts that the common law regards as private. Not all states recognize the existence of this tort. Those that do generally require that the disclosure be public, the fact disclosed be private, and the disclosure be highly offensive to a reasonable person. The most significant defense to the publication of private facts tort is the "newsworthiness privilege," a defense that is now usually articulated as an outgrowth of First Amendment doctrine but that actually has antecedents in the common law.

A colorful example of a jury delivering a major award for the publication of private facts is *Gawker Media, LLC v. Bollea*, 170 So. 3d 125 (Fla. 2d Dist. Ct. App. 2015). The plaintiff was Terry Bollea, a former professional wrestler known publicly as Hulk Hogan. Bollea had sex with Heather Clem, then married to Bollea's friend Todd Clem, a "shock jock" radio personality known as "Bubba the Love Sponge." The encounter between Clem and Bollea was videotaped, with audio. Bollea claimed he did not know he was being filmed. A copy of the video was leaked to the celebrity news and gossip website Gawker.com. Gawker wrote a story describing the incident and posted an excerpt of the video on its website. After a two-week trial, a jury awarded Bollea $115 million in compensatory damages and $25 million in punitive damages. Gawker then filed for bankruptcy protection, effectively ending the lawsuit. Gawker ultimately settled with Bollea for $31 million. The bankruptcy settlement prevented any additional appellate litigation over whether the First Amendment protected Gawker's story and video. One plausible argument in the matter was that the *fact* of Bollea's affair with his friend's wife was perhaps newsworthy, but not the playing of the actual video and audio of the two having sex.

The Supreme Court has not clearly articulated the contours of the First Amendment newsworthiness privilege. Even so, there are decisions that bear on the inquiry.

Two of leading cases concerned the disclosure of a rape victim's identity. In *Cox Broadcasting Corp. v. Cohn*, 420 U.S. 469 (1975), the Court held that no civil liability could be imposed for a television station's news report that mentioned the name of a woman who had been raped and murdered. The reporter had learned of the victim's name by reading copies of the indictments, which had been made available for inspection in the courtroom. The Court held that the First Amendment at least prohibits the creation of tort liability for the publication of facts "obtained from public records—more specifically, from judicial records which are maintained in connection with a public prosecution and which themselves are open to public inspection."

In *Florida Star v. B.J.F.*, 491 U.S. 524 (1989), the Court similarly held that a newspaper could not be liable for publishing a rape victim's name in violation of a Florida statute that made it unlawful to print, publish, or broadcast in any instrument of mass communication the name, address, or other identifying fact of a victim of a sexual offense. As in *Cox*, the Court emphasized the fact that the press had lawfully obtained the victim's name from public records—in this instance, from a posting in the police department pressroom. At the same time, the Court emphasized the narrowness of its holding:

> We do not hold that truthful publication is automatically constitutionally protected, or that there is no zone of personal privacy within which the State may protect the individual from intrusion by the press, or even that a State may never punish publication of the name of a victim of a sexual offense.

In *Bartnicki v. Vopper*, 532 U.S. 514 (2001), a third case concerning the balancing of privacy and speech interests, the Court held that no liability could be imposed on a media outlet that published or broadcast illegally intercepted phone conversations in which the participants appeared to be discussing potential violent criminal activity. The news organizations did not themselves participate in the illegal phone interceptions but were merely passive recipients of the private and illegally intercepted material. The "newsworthiness" of the discussion of potential criminal violence was the factor that tipped the balance in favor of the defendants for the two concurring justices whose votes helped form the majority.

The decisions in *Cox*, *Florida Star*, and *Bartnicki* are discussed at greater length in Chapter 16, which deals with regulation of the press and explores the circumstances in which media outlets are or are not constitutionally protected from liability for publication of truthful material.

Points for Discussion

1. **Should the publication of a rape victim's name always be protected?** Neither *Cox* nor *Florida Star* reached the issue of whether the press could ever be punished for the truthful publication of a rape victim's name. The press could argue that information about criminal activity, including a victim's name, is newsworthy and deserves First Amendment protection. Privacy advocates could counter that the public will be adequately informed even if a victim's name is withheld. Where do you come out in this debate? Would it matter if the victim was a public official or figure?

2. **Can the publication of a sex tape ever be newsworthy?** Could there be a situation in which the publication of even a sex tape should be protected by the First Amendment? Imagine a prominent "family values" politician who had vehemently denied having an affair. If a tape of the politician *in flagrante delicto* was dropped off at a newspaper's office, should the paper's editors feel confident that the First Amendment would protect them if they posted the tape on the paper's website?

3. **Does the First Amendment protect revenge porn?** The term "revenge porn" refers to the circulation of nude images or sexually explicit material without the person's consent. A typical situation involves a couple who took videos of themselves naked or engaged in sexual activity. The original video may or may not have been consensual, depending on whether it was surreptitiously or openly recorded. But in either case, there was never any consent to transmit the images to others. Then, typically following the couple's breakup, one party posts the video on social media as revenge against the other. Responding to revenge porn, states around the country began to enact laws creating criminal or civil liability for trafficking in such nonconsensual images. The Vermont Supreme Court was

the first court to entertain a challenge to such laws under the First Amendment, upholding the Vermont law. *State v. VanBuren*, 214 A.3d 791 (Vt. 2018). Other states have similarly upheld such laws. *See People v. Austin*, 155 N.E.3d 439 (Ill. 2019); *State v. Katz*, 179 N.E.3d 431 (Ind. 2022). In upholding these laws, the approach has not been to treat revenge porn as a newly unprotected category of speech. Nor has it been to treat the material as obscene under *Miller v. California*. A simple picture of a former lover nude, for example, would not meet the three-part *Miller* test. Rather, the approach has been to apply routine strict scrutiny analysis and uphold the law. In applying strict scrutiny, courts have recognized as compelling the victim's interest in personal privacy. Because the laws typically have very clearly defined intent requirements, courts have found the laws also satisfy the precise tailoring required by strict scrutiny.

3. Intrusion upon Seclusion: When a Person Invades Another's Personal Space

The *Restatement (Second) of Torts* sets out the elements of the tort of intrusion upon seclusion: "One who intentionally intrudes, physically or otherwise, upon the solitude or seclusion of another or his private affairs or concerns, is subject to liability to the other for invasion of his privacy, if the intrusion would be highly offensive to a reasonable person." Restatement (Second) of Torts § 652B (1977). One may think of intrusion as a form of "psychic trespass." Eavesdropping, peeping through windows, or surreptitiously opening another's mail are classic examples. Broadly speaking, exactly what constitutes a reasonable expectation of privacy is an ever-moving target, influenced by changes in technology and cultural mores.

Because the gravamen of the tort of intrusion is *invasion*, physical or otherwise, and not *publication*, it is generally treated as not constrained directly by the First Amendment. The actions giving rise to intrusion may occur *before* the exercise of First Amendment rights, but the actions themselves are not typically regarded as expressive.

Intrusion may precede expressive activity when a person invades a private space to gather information that will later be published or broadcast in an effort to expose alleged wrongdoing inside the private space.

For example, animal rights activists may engage in undercover operations to expose incidents of animal cruelty at a slaughterhouse. Or a news organization may use secret cameras and deception to gain access to a business where misconduct of some kind is suspected. Or "paparazzi" may engage in intrusion to capture intimate photographs or videos of a celebrity.

Sometimes the intrusion may also include a physical invasion of property and thus also constitute criminal or tortious trespass. The intrusion may also be accomplished through deception or fraud, like when a journalist gains access to a factory by showing fake credentials and posing as an employee.

The common law cause of action for intrusion has often been bolstered by legislative enactments, including statutes that prohibit surreptitious gathering of information in particular industries, such as agricultural production facilities.

As you will read in Chapter 16, dealing with regulation of the institutional press, the Supreme Court has held that the First Amendment generally does not provide the press with any special dispensation from generally applicable laws. In *Cohen v. Cowles Media Co.*, 501 U.S. 663 (1991), for example, the Court held that a news organization was not exempted from liability arising from general contract or promissory estoppel principles when the organization breached a promise of confidentiality made to a source.

Applying this principle, journalists or activists do not enjoy any First Amendment immunity for acts that would otherwise constitute fraud, trespass, or intrusion. A journalist or activist seeking to uncover wrongdoing has no First Amendment privilege to break into a company's office and rifle through locked filing cabinets.

When a journalist or activist engages in fraud, trespass, or intrusion to enter a private space, the damages that may be recovered in a civil action must be limited to the harm caused by the "invasion." They may not include damage caused by the later publication of what was *revealed* in the invasion unless that publication is otherwise actionable. Imagine, for example, that a journalist engages in fraud, trespass, and intrusion to secretly record video footage inside a hospital room where a celebrity patient is being treated. If the footage is edited to create a false impression that a doctor committed malpractice on the patient, when in fact the doctor treated the patient properly, the doctor might have a valid suit for intrusion, as well as a claim for defamation, and she could recover damages for both. If the journalist recorded some intimate private fact concerning the patient, such as images of the patient's naked body, the patient might have a valid suit for both intrusion and publication of private facts and could recover for both. If the patient's name or likeness is used for a commercial purpose to sell a medical device without the patient's permission, the patient might have a valid cause of action for both intrusion and appropriation of name or likeness and could recover for both.

But what if the publication of what was surreptitiously recorded did *not* constitute an independent tort? What if, for example, it could not qualify as defamation, because what was revealed was true, and it also could not qualify as revelation of a private fact or an appropriation, because the revelation was newsworthy? Now, the only damages recoverable would be for the intrusion, fraud, or trespass itself.

A famous example is *Food Lion, Inc. v. Capital Cities/ABC, Inc.*, 194 F.3d 505 (4th Cir. 1999), in which two ABC News reporters, after using false resumes to get jobs at Food Lion supermarkets, secretly videotaped what appeared to be unsanitary food-handling practices. Food Lion could not recover for defamation, because the secretly recorded practices did in fact occur. The company suffered substantial economic harm from the ABC broadcasts, but it could not recover damages for that harm, the Court held, because what was revealed was in fact true and newsworthy. Food Lion was permitted to recover for the harm caused by the fraud, trespass, and intrusion—it got $2.

Point for Discussion

1. **Statutory restrictions on collecting information—the conundrum of "ag-gag" laws.** Several states have enacted "ag-gag" laws to prevent animal rights activists from using misrepresentations, trespass, or other means to gain access to agricultural facilities, such as so-called factory farms, in an effort to expose animal abuse. For example, an Idaho law made it a crime to use force, threat, misrepresentation, or trespass to gain access to an agricultural production facility or the facility's records. How should a court analyze the constitutionality of this law if it were challenged as violating the First Amendment? Is the law regulating speech or conduct? If speech, is the law content-based or content-neutral? To the extent that the law punishes misrepresentations, what should be the relevance of the Supreme Court's decision in *United States v. Alvarez*, which we discussed in Chapter 2? Recall that the Court held in *Alvarez* that the defendant could not be punished for falsely stating that he had received military honors in the absence of any evidence that his misrepresentations caused harm, such as inducing someone to give him a benefit. Given *Alvarez*, is there any reason why a court, in evaluating the constitutionality of the Idaho law, might distinguish between using a misrepresentation to gain entry to an agricultural facility and using a misrepresentation to gain access to the facility's business records? As you ponder these issues, ask yourself whether the First Amendment should protect the rights of journalists or activists to go "undercover" (presumably by using misrepresentations) to expose illegal actions occurring behind closed doors. Keep in mind Upton Sinclair's famous undercover work in the early 1900s that allowed him to expose harsh working conditions and health hazards in the meatpacking industry. To find out how the Ninth Circuit ruled on the Idaho law, *see Animal Legal Defense Fund v. Wasden*, 878 F.3d 1184 (9th Cir. 2018). For a case wrestling with a Kansas ag-gag law, *see Animal Legal Defense Fund v. Kelly*, 9 F.4th 1219 (10th Cir. 2021), *cert. denied*, 142 S. Ct. 2647 (2022). The Fourth Circuit struck down a North Carolina ag-gag statute in *People for the Ethical Treatment of Animals v. North Carolina Farm Bureau Federation*, 60 F.4th 815 (4th Cir. 2023), *cert. denied*, 144 S. Ct. 325 (2023).

4. Appropriation or the Right of Publicity: When Speech Exploits Another's Name or Likeness for Commercial Advantage

Many states, through either common law development or statute, protect people against the unauthorized exploitation of their names or likenesses for commercial purposes. Known variously as invasion of the "right of publicity" or "appropriation," these causes of action are not actually about protecting privacy interests, but instead are about vindicating what is essentially a form of intellectual property in an individual's name or likeness. In this sense, the actions are more akin to a copyright or trademark claim.

Enforcement of this tort is subject to First Amendment limitations when the person's name or likeness is used in connection with newsworthy expression. In this respect, the First Amendment newsworthiness exception operates in a manner similar to the fair use doctrine in copyright law. To use a simple example, it is obvious that no company selling stereo speakers could appropriate the name or image of Lady Gaga to sell its equipment without her permission, which would likely be conditioned on payment. So too, no sporting goods company could appropriate the name or likeness of LeBron James to sell basketball shoes. *Rolling Stone* magazine, however, would be free to put a picture of Lady Gaga on its cover in connection with a story about her latest music release or movie, and *Sports Illustrated* would be free to put LeBron James on its cover in connection with a story on the NBA. While the images of Lady Gaga or LeBron James on the covers might help sell magazines, the First Amendment protects such use of names and likenesses of real people in conjunction with news or entertainment stories. The Supreme Court has decided one famous right-of-publicity case, holding that a news broadcast was not protected by the First Amendment.

Zacchini v. Scripps-Howard Broadcasting Co.

Supreme Court of the United States, 1977
433 U.S. 562

MR. JUSTICE WHITE delivered the opinion of the Court.

Petitioner, Hugo Zacchini, is an entertainer. He performs a "human cannonball" act in which he is shot from a cannon into a net some 200 feet away. Each performance occupies some 15 seconds. In August and September 1972, petitioner was engaged to perform his act on a regular basis at the Geauga County Fair in Burton, Ohio. He performed in a fenced area, surrounded by grandstands, at the fair grounds. Members of the public attending the fair were not charged a separate admission fee to observe his act.

On August 30, a freelance reporter for Scripps-Howard Broadcasting Co., the operator of a television broadcasting station and respondent in this case, attended the fair. He carried a small movie camera. Petitioner noticed the reporter and asked him not to film the performance. The reporter did not do so on that day; but on the instructions of the producer of respondent's daily newscast, he returned the following day and videotaped the entire act. This film clip, approximately 15 seconds in length, was shown on the 11 o'clock news program that night, together with favorable commentary.

Petitioner then brought this action for damages.

The Ohio Supreme Court held that respondent is constitutionally privileged to include in its newscasts matters of public interest that would otherwise be protected by the right of publicity, absent an intent to injure or to appropriate for some nonprivileged purpose. If under this standard respondent had merely reported that petitioner was performing at the fair and described or commented on his act, with or without showing his picture on television, we would have a very different case. But petitioner is not contending that his appearance at the fair and his performance could not be reported by the press as newsworthy items. His complaint is that respondent filmed his entire act and displayed that film on television for the public to see and enjoy. This, he claimed, was an appropriation of his professional property.

The broadcast of a film of petitioner's entire act poses a substantial threat to the economic value of that performance. As the Ohio court recognized, this act is the product of petitioner's own talents and energy, the end result of much time, effort, and expense. Much of its economic value lies in the "right of exclusive control over the publicity given to his performance"; if the public can see the act free on television, it will be less willing to pay to see it at the fair. The effect of a public broadcast of the performance is similar to preventing petitioner from charging an admission fee.

There is no doubt that entertainment, as well as news, enjoys First Amendment protection. It is also true that entertainment itself can be important news. But it is important to note that neither the public nor respondent will be deprived of the benefit of petitioner's performance as long as his commercial stake in his act is appropriately recognized. Petitioner does not seek to enjoin the broadcast of his performance; he simply wants to be paid for it. Nor do we think that a state-law damages remedy against respondent would represent a species of liability without fault contrary to the letter or spirit of *Gertz v. Robert Welch, Inc.* Respondent knew that petitioner objected to televising his act, but nevertheless displayed the entire film.

We conclude that although the State of Ohio may as a matter of its own law privilege the press in the circumstances of this case, the First and Fourteenth Amendments do not require it to do so.

[Justice Powell's dissenting opinion, which was joined by Justice Brennan and Justice Marshall, is omitted, as is Justice Stevens' dissenting opinion.]

Points for Discussion

1. **Copyright and the First Amendment.** Federal copyright law prohibits third parties from reproducing, adapting, distributing, performing, or displaying a work of authorship without the copyright owner's permission. This limited monopoly provides an incentive for authors to create works and businesses to disseminate them.

   Copyright law both complements and exists in tension with the First Amendment. On the one hand, copyright advances free speech interests by providing an incentive for authors to create expression. In this sense, copyright law, as Justice Sandra Day O'Connor famously observed, is an "engine of free expression." *Harper & Row, Publishers, Inc. v. Nation Enters.*, 471 U.S. 539, 558 (1985). On the other hand, copyright law abridges speech by limiting other parties' ability to use and disseminate expressive works.

   The Supreme Court is aware of the tension between copyright law and the First Amendment, but it has generally assumed that this tension is resolved by two free speech safeguards built into copyright law: that copyright protects only the expression of ideas and not the ideas themselves and that copyright allows, through the fair use doctrine, the unauthorized use of expression when the benefits of the use outweigh the harm to the copyright owner. *Eldred v. Ashcroft*, 537 U.S. 186, 219–20 (2003).

   Is the Court justified in assuming that these safeguards adequately protect free speech rights? Recall how Justice John Harlan, in *Cohen v. California*, the "Fuck the Draft" case, suggested that suppressing expression can also suppress ideas: "we cannot indulge the facile assumption that one can forbid particular words without also running a substantial risk of suppressing ideas in the process." Interestingly, the copyright scholar who had the most influence in convincing courts that copyright law's built-in safeguards should immunize it from First Amendment scrutiny, Melville Nimmer, was also a First Amendment scholar who represented the defendant in *Cohen*. A seminal article Nimmer published in 1970 helped persuade courts that the copyright safeguards noted above, as well as the limited duration given to copyrighted works, largely resolved the tension between copyright and the First Amendment. Melville B. Nimmer, *Does Copyright Abridge the First Amendment Guarantees of Free Speech and Press?*, 17 UCLA L. Rev. 1180 (1970). Professor Neil Weinstock Netanel has argued that copyright's internal safeguards no longer adequately protect free speech rights and consequently, that "contemporary First Amendment doctrine demands a considerably more searching examination of copyright's free speech burden than it did when Professor Nimmer authored his seminal article." Neil Weinstock Netanel, *Locating Copyright within the First Amendment Skein*, 54 Stan. L. Rev. 1, 12 (2001).

2. **Trademark law and the First Amendment.** Trademarks are names, symbols, or even the overall appearance of an article of commerce that are used to identify the source of a good or service. "In other words, a mark tells the public who is responsible for a product." *Jack Daniel's Props., Inc. v. VIP Prods. LLC*, 143 S. Ct. 1578, 1583 (2023). Trademark law protects consumers by assuring them that a product comes from a specific source, and it protects producers by ensuring that other companies do not profit from a producer's goodwill by selling products with confusingly similar marks. First Amendment issues can arise in trademark cases when someone uses another's trademark for expressive purposes such as parody or commentary. For example, the Ninth Circuit permitted a band to use the name "Barbie Girl" for a song that mocked the doll, even though "Barbie" is a registered trademark. *See Mattel, Inc. v. MCA Records, Inc.*, 296 F.3d 894 (9th Cir. 2002). Lower courts often use a test derived from a Second Circuit opinion, *Rogers v. Grimaldi*, 875 F.2d 994 (2d Cir. 1989), to determine whether free speech interests should override trademark rights. The *Rogers* test instructs courts to ask whether a second party's trademark use has "artistic relevance" and, if it does, to permit the use unless it "explicitly misleads as to the source or the content of the work."

In *Jack Daniel's Properties*, a company sold a squeaky dog toy that was shaped like a bottle of Jack Daniel's whiskey and was called "Bad Spaniels."

The Ninth Circuit held that the liquor company's infringement claim was subject to the threshold *Rogers* test because the dog toy was an "expressive work." The Supreme Court reversed because the dog toy maker, VIP Products, was using the "Bad Spaniels" name and the shape of the toy as trademarks to identify itself as the source of the toys. The Court declined to take a position on the use of the *Rogers* test in cases where a defendant uses another's mark in a "non-source-identifying way," but it did hold that the test does not apply when, as in this case, a defendant used a mark to identify its own goods and services. In that instance, the Court said, the case should be decided solely based on the standard trademark infringement question of whether a defendant's use is likely to create consumer confusion about the source of a product:

> VIP's conduct is its own admission that it is using the Bad Spaniels (née Jack Daniel's) trademarks as trademarks, to identify product source. Because that is so, the only question in this suit going forward is whether the Bad Spaniels marks are likely to cause confusion. There is no threshold test working to kick out all cases involving "expressive works." But a trademark's expressive message—particularly a parodic one, as VIP asserts—may properly figure in assessing the likelihood of confusion.

The Court said the First Amendment did not require an application of the *Rogers* test any time an allegedly infringing use had an expressive element. Indeed, it said that if the test did apply, few trademark cases would ever get to the likelihood-of-confusion inquiry because virtually all marks have some expressive element beyond just acting as a source identifier.

C. Intentional Infliction of Emotional Distress: May Government Regulate Speech That Causes Emotional Distress?

Society is rife with expression that inflicts severe emotional distress on victims. When that distress is incident to other palpable invasions of legally protected interests, as in defamation, publication of private facts, or appropriation, the emotional distress component may take the form of damages for which the plaintiff is compensated. Recall that "actual injury" for defamation as defined in *Gertz* includes a plaintiff's internal distress or anguish. But what if the only harm to the victim is distress, caused by a virulent attack targeting the victim? In the two important cases in this section, the Court held that when that distress is caused by expression on matters of public concern and is not otherwise tortious, the First Amendment bars recovery.

In the first of the two cases, pornographer Larry Flynt, publisher of *Hustler* magazine, published a parody attacking Jerry Falwell, a famous conservative televangelist. The ad parody published in *Hustler* played on a popular real ad campaign for Campari, a bitter-tasting Italian liqueur popular in Europe but not the United States. Campari sought to come up with advertising that would encourage Americans to keep trying the liqueur. It came up with a clever ad campaign in which celebrities would muse whimsically about their "first time." The first time was never that great, but it got better with repetition. While ostensibly they were recalling their "first time" tasting Campari, the double entendre was that Campari, like sex, gets better with practice.

Playing on these real ads, and sparing no cruelty, the *Hustler* parody depicted Falwell remembering his "first time" as having sex with his own mother in an outhouse.

Hustler Magazine v. Falwell

Supreme Court of the United States, 1988
485 U.S. 46

CHIEF JUSTICE REHNQUIST delivered the opinion of the Court.

Generally speaking the law does not regard the intent to inflict emotional distress as one which should receive much solicitude, and it is quite understandable that most if not all jurisdictions have chosen to make it civilly culpable where the conduct in question is sufficiently "outrageous." But in the world of debate about public affairs, many things done with motives that are less than admirable are protected by the First Amendment.

In *Garrison v. Louisiana*, 379 U.S. 64 (1964), we held that even when a speaker or writer is motivated by hatred or ill will his expression was protected by the First Amendment:

> Debate on public issues will not be uninhibited if the speaker must run the risk that it will be proved in court that he spoke out of hatred; even if he did speak out of hatred, utterances honestly believed contribute to the free interchange of ideas and the ascertainment of truth.

Thus while such a bad motive may be deemed controlling for purposes of tort liability in other areas of the law, we think the First Amendment prohibits such a result in the area of public debate about public figures.

Were we to hold otherwise, there can be little doubt that political cartoonists and satirists would be subjected to damages awards without any showing that their work falsely defamed its subject. The appeal of the political cartoon or caricature is often based on exploitation of unfortunate physical traits or politically embarrassing events—an exploitation often calculated to injure the feelings of the subject of the portrayal. The art of the cartoonist is often not reasoned or evenhanded, but slashing and one-sided.

Despite their sometimes caustic nature, from the early cartoon portraying George Washington as an ass down to the present day, graphic depictions and satirical cartoons have played a prominent role in public and political debate. Nast's castigation of the Tweed Ring, Walt McDougall's characterization of Presidential candidate James G. Blaine's banquet with the millionaires at Delmonico's as "The Royal Feast of Belshazzar," and numerous other efforts have undoubtedly had an effect on the course and outcome of contemporaneous debate. Lincoln's tall, gangling posture, Teddy Roosevelt's glasses and teeth, and Franklin D. Roosevelt's jutting jaw and cigarette holder have been memorialized by political cartoons with an effect that could not have been obtained by the photographer or the portrait artist. From the viewpoint of history it is clear that our political discourse would have been considerably poorer without them.

Respondent contends, however, that the caricature in question here was so "outrageous" as to distinguish it from more traditional political cartoons. There is no doubt that the caricature of respondent and his mother published in Hustler is at best a distant cousin of the political cartoons described above, and a rather poor relation at that. If it were possible by laying down a principled standard to separate the one from the other, public discourse would probably suffer little or no harm. But we doubt that there is any such standard, and we are quite sure that the pejorative description "outrageous" does not supply one. "Outrageousness" in the area of political and social discourse has an inherent subjectiveness about it which would allow a jury to impose liability on the basis of the jurors' tastes or views, or perhaps on the basis of their dislike of a particular expression. An "outrageousness" standard thus runs afoul of our longstanding refusal to allow damages to be awarded because the speech in question may have an adverse emotional impact on the audience.

Admittedly, these oft-repeated First Amendment principles, like other principles, are subject to limitations. But the sort of expression involved in this case does not seem to us to be governed by any exception.

We conclude that public figures and public officials may not recover for the tort of intentional infliction of emotional distress by reason of publications such as the one here at issue without showing in addition that the publication contains a false statement of fact which was made with "actual malice," i.e., with knowledge that the statement was false or with reckless disregard as to whether or not it was true.

Here it is clear that respondent Falwell is a "public figure" for purposes of First Amendment law. The jury found against respondent on his libel claim when it decided that the *Hustler* ad parody could not "reasonably be understood as describing actual facts about respondent or actual events in which he participated." Respondent is thus relegated to his claim for damages awarded by the jury for the intentional infliction of emotional distress by "outrageous" conduct. But for reasons heretofore stated this claim cannot, consistently with the First Amendment, form a basis for the award of damages when the conduct in question is the publication of a caricature such as the ad parody involved here.

[Justice White's opinion concurring in the judgment is omitted.]

The second emotional distress case, *Snyder v. Phelps*, involved utterly outrageous and reprehensible expression targeted at a fallen soldier's funeral. The decision is arguably among the most poignant and difficult-to-accept holdings of modern First Amendment law.

Snyder v. Phelps

Supreme Court of the United States, 2011
562 U.S. 443

CHIEF JUSTICE ROBERTS delivered the opinion of the Court.

A jury held members of the Westboro Baptist Church liable for millions of dollars in damages for picketing near a soldier's funeral service. The picket signs reflected the church's view that the United States is overly tolerant of sin and that God kills American soldiers as punishment. The question presented is whether the First Amendment shields the church members from tort liability for their speech in this case.

Fred Phelps founded the Westboro Baptist Church in Topeka, Kansas, in 1955. The church's congregation believes that God hates and punishes the United States for its tolerance of homosexuality, particularly in America's military. The church frequently communicates its views by picketing, often at military funerals. In the more than 20 years that the members of Westboro Baptist have publicized their message, they have picketed nearly 600 funerals.

Marine Lance Corporal Matthew Snyder was killed in Iraq in the line of duty. Lance Corporal Snyder's father selected the Catholic church in the Snyders' hometown of Westminster, Maryland, as the site for his son's funeral. Local newspapers provided notice of the time and location of the service.

Phelps became aware of Matthew Snyder's funeral and decided to travel to Maryland with six other Westboro Baptist parishioners (two of his daughters and four of his grandchildren) to picket. On the day of the memorial service, the Westboro congregation members picketed on public land adjacent to public streets near the Maryland State House, the United States Naval Academy, and Matthew Snyder's funeral. The Westboro picketers carried signs that were largely the same at all three locations. They stated, for instance: "God Hates the USA/Thank God for 9/11," "America is Doomed," "Don't Pray for the USA," "Thank God for IEDs," "Thank God for Dead Soldiers," "Pope in Hell," "Priests Rape Boys," "God Hates Fags," "You're Going to Hell," and "God Hates You."

The Westboro picketers displayed their signs for about 30 minutes before the funeral began and sang hymns and recited Bible verses. None of the picketers entered church property or went to the cemetery. They did not yell or use profanity, and there was no violence associated with the picketing.

The funeral procession passed within 200 to 300 feet of the picket site. Although Snyder testified that he could see the tops of the picket signs as he drove to the funeral, he did not see what was written on the signs until later that night, while watching a news broadcast covering the event.

A jury found for Snyder on the intentional infliction of emotional distress, intrusion upon seclusion, and civil conspiracy claims, and held Westboro liable for $2.9 million in compensatory damages and $8 million in punitive damages.

Whether the First Amendment prohibits holding Westboro liable for its speech in this case turns largely on whether that speech is of public or private concern, as determined by all the circumstances of the case. "Speech on 'matters of public concern' is at the heart of the First Amendment's protection." The First Amendment reflects "a profound national commitment to the principle that debate on public issues should be uninhibited, robust, and wide-open." That is because "speech concerning public affairs is more than self-expression; it is the essence of self-government." Accordingly, "speech on public issues occupies the highest rung of the hierarchy of First Amendment values, and is entitled to special protection."

"Not all speech is of equal First Amendment importance," however, and where matters of purely private significance are at issue, First Amendment protections are often less rigorous. That is because restricting speech on purely private matters does not implicate the same constitutional concerns as limiting speech on matters of public interest.

We noted a short time ago, in considering whether public employee speech addressed a matter of public concern, that "the boundaries of the public concern test are not well defined." Although that remains true today, we have articulated some guiding principles, principles that accord broad protection to speech to ensure that courts themselves do not become inadvertent censors.

Speech deals with matters of public concern when it can "be fairly considered as relating to any matter of political, social, or other concern to the community," or when it "is a subject of legitimate news interest; that is, a subject of general interest and of value and concern to the public." The arguably "inappropriate or controversial character of a statement is irrelevant to the question whether it deals with a matter of public concern."

Deciding whether speech is of public or private concern requires us to examine the "content, form, and context" of that speech, "as revealed by the whole record." As in other First Amendment cases, the court is obligated "to make an independent examination of the whole record in order to make sure that the judgment does not constitute a forbidden intrusion on the field of free expression." In considering content, form, and context, no factor is dispositive, and it is necessary to evaluate all the circumstances of the speech, including what was said, where it was said, and how it was said.

The "content" of Westboro's signs plainly relates to broad issues of interest to society at large, rather than matters of "purely private concern." The placards read "God Hates the USA/Thank God for 9/11," "America is Doomed," "Don't Pray for the USA," "Thank God for IEDs," "Fag Troops," "Semper Fi Fags," "God Hates Fags," "Maryland Taliban," "Fags Doom Nations," "Not Blessed Just Cursed," "Thank God for Dead Soldiers," "Pope in Hell," "Priests Rape Boys," "You're Going to Hell," and "God Hates You." While these messages may fall short of refined social or political commentary, the issues they highlight—the political and moral conduct of the United States and its citizens, the fate of our Nation, homosexuality in the military, and scandals involving the Catholic clergy—are matters of public import.

Apart from the content of Westboro's signs, Snyder contends that the "context" of the speech—its connection with his son's funeral—makes the speech a matter of private rather than public concern. The fact that Westboro spoke in connection with a funeral, however, cannot by itself transform the nature of Westboro's speech. Westboro's signs, displayed on public land next to a public street, reflect the fact that the church finds much to condemn in modern society.

Snyder argues that the church members in fact mounted a personal attack on Snyder and his family, and then attempted to "immunize their conduct by claiming that they were actually protesting the United States' tolerance of homosexuality or the supposed evils of the Catholic Church."

Snyder goes on to argue that Westboro's speech should be afforded less than full First Amendment protection "not only because of the words" but also because the church members exploited the funeral "as a platform to bring their message to a broader audience." There is no doubt that Westboro chose to stage its picketing at the Naval Academy, the Maryland State House, and Matthew Snyder's funeral to increase publicity for its views and because of the relation between those sites and its views—in the case of the military funeral, because Westboro believes that God is killing American soldiers as punishment for the Nation's sinful policies.

Westboro's choice to convey its views in conjunction with Matthew Snyder's funeral made the expression of those views particularly hurtful to many, especially to Matthew's father. The record makes clear that the applicable legal term—"emotional distress"—fails to capture fully the anguish Westboro's choice added to Mr. Snyder's already incalculable grief. But Westboro conducted its picketing peacefully on matters of public concern at a public place adjacent to a public street.

Simply put, the church members had the right to be where they were. Westboro alerted local authorities to its funeral protest and fully complied with police guidance on where the picketing could be staged. The picketing was conducted under police supervision some 1,000 feet from the church, out of the sight of those at the church. The protest was not unruly; there was no shouting, profanity, or violence.

Given that Westboro's speech was at a public place on a matter of public concern, that speech is entitled to "special protection" under the First Amendment. Such speech cannot be restricted simply because it is upsetting or arouses contempt. "If there is a bedrock principle underlying the First Amendment, it is that the government may not prohibit the expression of an idea simply because society finds the idea itself offensive or disagreeable."

The jury here was instructed that it could hold Westboro liable for intentional infliction of emotional distress based on a finding that Westboro's picketing was "outrageous." "Outrageousness," however, is a highly malleable standard with "an inherent subjectiveness about it which would allow a jury to impose liability on the basis of the jurors' tastes or views, or perhaps on the basis of their dislike of a particular expression." *Hustler Magazine v. Falwell.* In a case such as this, a jury is "unlikely to be neutral with respect to the content of the speech," posing "a real danger of becoming an instrument for the suppression of vehement, caustic, and sometimes unpleasant" expression. Such a risk is unacceptable; "in public debate we must tolerate insulting, and even outrageous, speech in order to provide adequate 'breathing space' to the freedoms protected by the First Amendment." What Westboro said, in the whole context of how and where it chose to say it, is entitled to "special protection" under the First Amendment, and that protection cannot be overcome by a jury finding that the picketing was outrageous.

For all these reasons, the jury verdict imposing tort liability on Westboro for intentional infliction of emotional distress must be set aside.

Snyder argues that even assuming Westboro's speech is entitled to First Amendment protection generally, the church is not immunized from liability for intrusion upon seclusion because Snyder was a member of a captive audience at his son's funeral. We do not agree. In most circumstances, "the Constitution does not permit the government to decide which types of otherwise protected speech are sufficiently offensive to require protection for the unwilling listener or viewer. Rather, the burden normally falls upon the viewer to avoid further bombardment of his sensibilities simply by averting his eyes." As a result, "the ability of government, consonant with the Constitution, to shut off discourse solely to protect others from hearing it is dependent upon a showing that substantial privacy interests are being invaded in an essentially intolerable manner." *Cohen v. California.*

As a general matter, we have applied the captive audience doctrine only sparingly to protect unwilling listeners from protected speech. For example, we have upheld a statute allowing a homeowner to restrict the delivery of offensive mail to his home, *Rowan v. Post Office Dept.*, 397 U.S. 728, 736–738 (1970), and an ordinance prohibiting picketing "before or about" any individual's residence, *Frisby v. Schultz*, 487 U.S. 474 (1988).

Here, Westboro stayed well away from the memorial service. Snyder could see no more than the tops of the signs when driving to the funeral. And there is no indication that the picketing in any way interfered with the funeral service itself. We decline to expand the captive audience doctrine to the circumstances presented here.

Because we find that the First Amendment bars Snyder from recovery for intentional infliction of emotional distress or intrusion upon seclusion—the alleged unlawful activity Westboro conspired to accomplish—we must likewise hold that Snyder cannot recover for civil conspiracy based on those torts.

Our holding today is narrow. We are required in First Amendment cases to carefully review the record, and the reach of our opinion here is limited by the particular facts before us. As we have noted, "the sensitivity and significance of the interests presented in clashes between First Amendment and [state law] rights counsel relying on limited principles that sweep no more broadly than the appropriate context of the instant case." *Florida Star v. B.J.F.*

Westboro believes that America is morally flawed; many Americans might feel the same about Westboro. Westboro's funeral picketing is certainly hurtful and its contribution to public discourse may be negligible. But Westboro addressed matters of public import on public property, in a peaceful manner, in full compliance with the guidance of local officials. The speech was indeed planned to coincide with Matthew Snyder's funeral, but did not itself disrupt that funeral, and Westboro's choice to conduct its picketing at that time and place did not alter the nature of its speech.

Speech is powerful. It can stir people to action, move them to tears of both joy and sorrow, and—as it did here—inflict great pain. On the facts before us, we cannot react to that pain by punishing the speaker. As a Nation we have chosen a different course—to protect even hurtful speech on public issues to ensure that we do not stifle public debate. That choice requires that we shield Westboro from tort liability for its picketing in this case.

JUSTICE BREYER, concurring.

The dissent requires us to ask whether our holding unreasonably limits liability for intentional infliction of emotional distress—to the point where A (in order to draw attention to his views on a public matter) might launch a verbal assault upon B, a private person, publicly revealing the most intimate details of B's private life, while knowing that the revelation will cause B severe emotional harm. Does our decision leave the State powerless to protect the individual against invasions of, e.g., personal privacy, even in the most horrendous of such circumstances?

As I understand the Court's opinion, it does not hold or imply that the State is always powerless to provide private individuals with necessary protection. Rather, the Court has reviewed the underlying facts in detail, as will sometimes prove necessary where First Amendment values and state-protected (say, privacy-related) interests seriously conflict.

JUSTICE ALITO, dissenting.

Our profound national commitment to free and open debate is not a license for the vicious verbal assault that occurred in this case.

Petitioner Albert Snyder is not a public figure. He is simply a parent whose son, Marine Lance Corporal Matthew Snyder, was killed in Iraq. Mr. Snyder wanted what is surely the right of any parent who experiences such an incalculable loss: to bury his son in peace. But respondents, members of the Westboro Baptist Church, deprived him of that elementary right. They first issued a press release and thus turned Matthew's funeral into a tumultuous media event. They then appeared at the church, approached as closely as they could without trespassing, and launched a malevolent verbal attack on Matthew and his family at a time of acute emotional vulnerability. As a result, Albert Snyder suffered severe and lasting emotional injury. The Court now holds that the First Amendment protected respondents' right to brutalize Mr. Snyder. I cannot agree.

This Court has recognized that words may "by their very utterance inflict injury" and that the First Amendment does not shield utterances that form "no essential part of any exposition of ideas, and are of such slight social value as a step to truth that any benefit that may be derived from them is clearly outweighed by the social interest in order and morality." *Chaplinsky v. New Hampshire*. See also *Cantwell v. Connecticut*, 310 U.S. 296, 310 (1940) ("Personal abuse is not in any proper sense communication of information or opinion safeguarded by the Constitution"). When grave injury is intentionally inflicted by means of an attack like the one at issue here, the First Amendment should not interfere with recovery.

On the morning of Matthew Snyder's funeral, respondents could have chosen to stage their protest at countless locations. They could have picketed the United States Capitol, the White House, the Supreme Court, the Pentagon, or any of the more than 5,600 military recruiting stations in this country. They could have returned to the Maryland State House or the United States Naval Academy, where they had been the day before. They could have selected any public road where pedestrians are allowed. (There are more than 4,000,000 miles of public roads in the United States.) They could have staged their protest in a public park. (There are more than 20,000 public parks in this country.) They could have chosen any Catholic church where no funeral was taking place. (There are nearly 19,000 Catholic churches in the United States.) But of course, a small group picketing at any of these locations would have probably gone unnoticed.

The Westboro Baptist Church, however, has devised a strategy that remedies this problem. As the Court notes, church members have protested at nearly 600 military funerals. They have also picketed the funerals of police officers, firefighters, and the victims of natural disasters, accidents, and shocking crimes. And in advance of these protests, they issue press releases to ensure that their protests will attract public attention.

This strategy works because it is expected that respondents' verbal assaults will wound the family and friends of the deceased and because the media is irresistibly drawn to the sight of persons who are visibly in grief. The more outrageous the funeral protest, the more publicity the Westboro Baptist Church is able to obtain. Thus, when the church recently announced its intention to picket the funeral of a 9-year-old girl killed in the shooting spree in Tucson—proclaiming that she was "better off dead"—their announcement was national news, and the church was able to obtain free air time on the radio in exchange for canceling its protest. Similarly, in 2006, the church got air time on a talk radio show in exchange for canceling its threatened protest at the funeral of five Amish girls killed by a crazed gunman.

In this case, respondents implemented the Westboro Baptist Church's publicity-seeking strategy. Their press release stated that they were going "to picket the funeral of Lance Cpl. Matthew A. Snyder" because "God Almighty killed Lance Cpl. Snyder. He died in shame, not honor—for a fag nation cursed by God. Now in Hell—sine die." This announcement guaranteed that Matthew's funeral would be transformed into a raucous media event and began the wounding process. It is well known that anticipation may heighten the effect of a painful event.

On the day of the funeral, respondents, true to their word, displayed placards that conveyed the message promised in their press release. Signs stating "God Hates You" and "Thank God for Dead Soldiers" reiterated the message that God had caused Matthew's death in retribution for his sins. Others, stating "You're Going to Hell" and "Not Blessed Just Cursed," conveyed the message that Matthew was "in Hell—sine die."

After the funeral, the Westboro picketers reaffirmed the meaning of their protest. They posted an online account entitled "The Burden of Marine Lance Cpl. Matthew A. Snyder. The Visit of Westboro Baptist Church to Help the Inhabitants of Maryland Connect the Dots!" Belying any suggestion that they had simply made general comments about homosexuality, the Catholic Church, and the United States military, the "epic" addressed the Snyder family directly:

> God blessed you, Mr. and Mrs. Snyder, with a resource and his name was Matthew. He was an arrow in your quiver! In thanks to God for the comfort the child could bring you, you had a DUTY to prepare that child to serve the LORD his GOD—PERIOD! You did JUST THE OPPOSITE—you raised him for the devil.
>
> Albert and Julie RIPPED that body apart and taught Matthew to defy his Creator, to divorce, and to commit adultery. They taught him how to support the largest pedophile machine in the history of the entire world, the Roman Catholic monstrosity. Every dime they gave the Roman Catholic monster they condemned their own souls. They also, in supporting satanic Catholicism, taught Matthew to be an idolater.
>
> Then after all that they sent him to fight for the United States of Sodom, a filthy country that is in lock step with his evil, wicked, and sinful manner of life, putting him in the cross hairs of a God that is so mad He has smoke coming from his nostrils and fire from his mouth! How dumb was that?

In light of this evidence, it is abundantly clear that respondents, going far beyond commentary on matters of public concern, specifically attacked Matthew Snyder because (1) he was a Catholic and (2) he was a member of the United States military. Both Matthew and petitioner were private figures, and this attack was not speech on a matter of public concern. While commentary on the Catholic Church or the United States military constitutes speech on matters of public concern, speech regarding Matthew Snyder's purely private conduct does not.

The Court of Appeals appears to have concluded that the First Amendment does not permit an IIED [intentional infliction of emotional distress] plaintiff to recover for speech that cannot reasonably be interpreted as stating actual facts about an individual. In reaching this conclusion, the Court of Appeals relied on two of our cases—*Milkovich v. Lorain Journal Co.* and *Hustler*—but neither supports the broad proposition that the Court of Appeals adopted.

Milkovich was a defamation case, and falsity is an element of defamation. Nothing in *Milkovich* even hints that the First Amendment requires that this defamation element be engrafted onto the IIED tort.

Hustler did involve an IIED claim, but the plaintiff there was a public figure, and the Court did not suggest that its holding would also apply in a case involving a private figure. Nor did the Court suggest that its holding applied across the board to all types of IIED claims. Instead, the holding was limited to "publications such as the one here at issue," namely, a caricature in a magazine. Unless a caricature of a public figure can reasonably be interpreted as stating facts that may be proved to be wrong, the caricature does not have the same potential to wound as a personal verbal assault on a vulnerable private figure.

Respondents' outrageous conduct caused petitioner great injury, and the Court now compounds that injury by depriving petitioner of a judgment that acknowledges the wrong he suffered.

In order to have a society in which public issues can be openly and vigorously debated, it is not necessary to allow the brutalization of innocent victims like petitioner. I therefore respectfully dissent.

Points for Discussion

1. **Was the holding in *Snyder* required by the holding in *Hustler*?** The *Hustler* case involved a pointed attack on a prominent public figure. *Snyder* targeted a private family burying a fallen soldier. Do you agree with Justice Samuel Alito that the outcome in *Snyder* was not required by *Hustler*? If you had been on the Court, would you have joined the majority opinion or Justice Alito's dissent?

2. **Were Chief Justice John Roberts and Justice Alito writing about the same case?** The opinions by Chief Justice Roberts and Justice Alito present starkly different characterizations of the facts. In the Chief Justice's version, Fred Phelps' speech was primarily targeted at a general audience and was focused on "matters of public import," such as gays in the military or sexual abuse by Catholic clergy. This more anodyne characterization of the speech made it easier for Chief Justice Roberts to find the words protected. By contrast, Justice Alito characterized the Phelps' speech as being specifically targeted at Matthew Snyder and his family: "it is abundantly clear that [Phelps], going far beyond commentary on matters of public concern, specifically attacked Matthew Snyder because (1) he was a Catholic and (2) he was a member of the United States military." To support this characterization, Justice Alito quoted several passages from an internet posting that Phelps uploaded after the funeral protest. This so-called "epic," Justice Alito said, "addressed the Snyder family directly." The difficulty in comparing Chief Justice Roberts' and Justice Alito's opinions is that the Chief Justice, in the first footnote of his opinion, said the contents of the epic were not properly before the Court and would not be considered in deciding the case. Given that, were the two justices ruling on two very different cases?

3. **Would content-neutral laws adequately address the concerns raised by funeral protests?** In another part of his opinion, Chief Justice Roberts suggests that content-neutral regulations could adequately address the concern raised by funeral protests:

> Westboro's choice of where and when to conduct its picketing is not beyond the Government's regulatory reach—it is "subject to reasonable time, place, or manner restrictions" that are consistent with the standards announced in this Court's precedents. Maryland now has a law imposing restrictions on funeral picketing, as do 43 other States and the Federal Government. To the extent these laws are content neutral, they raise very different questions from the tort verdict at issue in this case.

In his dissent, Justice Alito says that such content-neutral regulations are "no substitute for the protection provided by the established IIED tort." Who do you think is right?

4. **Should there be different rules for speech that harms individuals and speech that harms groups?** The plaintiffs in both *Hustler* and *Snyder* found their claims of intentional infliction of emotional distress barred by the First Amendment, but the two opinions do not suggest that the First Amendment bars all IIED claims brought by individuals. That stands in stark contrast to the hate speech cases we studied in Chapter 6, which suggest that hate speech is fully protected by the First Amendment even if the speech causes severe emotional distress to a whole category of people, such as a racial or religious group.

   We encountered similar rules in the defamation context. Although the 1952 *Beauharnais* decision held that group libel, like individual libel, is not protected by the First Amendment, subsequent Supreme Court opinions have implicitly overruled *Beauharnais*. The result is that the First Amendment permits defamation actions brought by individuals, even if the individuals must sometimes overcome high hurdles to recover. By contrast, the implicit overruling of *Beauharnais* suggests an absolute bar to defamation claims by racial, religious, or other groups.

   Does it make sense to have different First Amendment rules for speech that targets individuals and speech that targets groups?

5. **Does the Court's focus on whether speech is a matter of public concern violate the neutrality principle?** Time and again, the Court has proclaimed its allegiance to the neutrality principle: the concept that all ideas are welcome into the marketplace of ideas and that government officials, including judges, should not be deciding which ideas are worthy of First Amendment protection. But in two instances in this chapter, in the *Dun & Bradstreet* defamation case and the *Snyder* emotional distress case, the Court constructed different First Amendment rules depending on whether the speech involved a matter of public or private concern. In *Snyder*, Chief Justice Roberts explicitly proclaimed that "not all speech is of equal First Amendment importance," that "speech on public issues occupies

the highest rung of the hierarchy of First Amendment values," and that "speech on purely private matters does not implicate the same constitutional concerns as limiting speech on matters of public interest." In Chapter 11, we will again see the Court relying on the public concern/private concern distinction in cases involving speech by government employees.

Chief Justice Roberts' observations about the relative importance of speech on matters of public or private concern might have a strong intuitive appeal. But do they create a back door through which justices can weigh the relative value of ideas in violation of the neutrality principle? Consider this criticism of the public concern test by Professor Cynthia Estlund:

> The public concern test will generate, by the inexorable operation of stare decisis, a judicially approved catalogue of legitimate subjects of public discussion. That prospect alone should condemn the entire undertaking, for the Constitution empowers the people, not any branch of the government, to define the public agenda.
>
> Yet even if we were to accept the idea of judges defining the appropriate topics of public debate the public concern test looms as a significant threat to freedom of speech. That is because many of the countless decisions-judicial or otherwise-that will become part of the evolving definition of matters of public concern will inevitably be wrong. Judges and other decisionmakers will inevitably exclude from this category, and thus from constitutional protection, speech that others would consider to be relevant to public debate. These "mistakes," whether or not they can be identified with any precision, will do real damage to the system of freedom of speech. . . . Much that is important, or could become important, to public debate will assuredly be left unprotected, vulnerable to suppression and often simply unspoken.

Cynthia L. Estlund, *Speech on Matters of Public Concern: The Perils of an Emerging First Amendment Category*, 59 Geo. Wash. L. Rev. 1, 3–4 (1990).

D. Tortious Interference with Contract or Economic Advantage: May Government Regulate Speech That Interferes with Business Interests?

In yet another example of the intersection of tort law with the civil rights movement, in 1966, a branch of the NAACP boycotted white merchants in Claiborne County, Mississippi. Charles Evers was the field secretary of the NAACP in Mississippi and a principal organizer of the boycott. The purpose of the boycott was to coerce civic and business leaders to accede to a lengthy list of demands for equality and racial justice. At meetings organizing and encouraging black citizens to participate in the boycott, Evers engaged in vitriolic rhetoric. The white merchants sued, seeking injunctive relief and civil damages for what was allegedly a tortious interference with their business interests.

NAACP v. Claiborne Hardware Co.

Supreme Court of the United States, 1982
458 U.S. 886

JUSTICE STEVENS delivered the opinion of the Court.

The term "concerted action" encompasses unlawful conspiracies and constitutionally protected assemblies. The "looseness and pliability" of legal doctrine applicable to concerted action led Justice Jackson to note that certain joint activities have a "chameleon-like" character. The boycott of white merchants in Claiborne County, Miss., that gave rise to this litigation had such a character; it included elements of criminality and elements of majesty. Evidence that fear of reprisals caused some black citizens to withhold their patronage from respondents' businesses convinced the Supreme Court of Mississippi that the entire boycott was unlawful and that each of the 92 petitioners was liable for all of its economic consequences. Evidence that persuasive rhetoric, determination to remedy past injustices, and a host of voluntary decisions by free citizens were the critical factors in the boycott's success presents us with the question whether the state court's judgment is consistent with the Constitution of the United States.

business is saying they were economically damaged b/c of the boycott

Each of these elements of the boycott is a form of speech or conduct that is ordinarily entitled to protection under the First and Fourteenth Amendments. The black citizens named as defendants in this action banded together and collectively expressed their dissatisfaction with a social structure that had denied them rights to equal treatment and respect.

The right to associate does not lose all constitutional protection merely because some members of the group may have participated in conduct or advocated doctrine that itself is not protected.

Speech itself also was used to further the aims of the boycott. Nonparticipants repeatedly were urged to join the common cause, both through public address and through personal solicitation. These elements of the boycott involve speech in its most direct form. In addition, names of boycott violators were read aloud at meetings at the First Baptist Church and published in a local black newspaper. Petitioners admittedly sought to persuade others to join the boycott through social pressure and the "threat" of social ostracism. Speech does not lose its protected character, however, simply because it may embarrass others or coerce them into action.

While States have broad power to regulate economic activity, we do not find a comparable right to prohibit peaceful political activity such as that found in the boycott in this case.

The First Amendment does not protect violence. "Certainly violence has no sanctuary in the First Amendment, and the use of weapons, gunpowder, and gasoline may not constitutionally masquerade under the guise of 'advocacy.' " *Samuels v. Mackell*, 401 U.S. 66, 75 (Douglas, J., concurring). Although the extent and significance of the violence in this case are vigorously disputed by the parties, there is no question that acts of violence occurred. No federal rule of law restricts a State from imposing tort liability for business losses that are caused by violence and by threats of violence. When such conduct occurs in the context of constitutionally protected activity, however, "precision of regulation" is demanded. Specifically, the presence of activity protected by the First Amendment imposes restraints on the grounds that may give rise to damages liability and on the persons who may be held accountable for those damages.

Civil liability may not be imposed merely because an individual belonged to a group, some members of which committed acts of violence. For liability to be imposed by reason of association alone, it is necessary to establish that the group itself possessed unlawful goals and that the individual held a specific intent to further those illegal aims.

For the reasons set forth above, liability may not be imposed on Evers for his presence at NAACP meetings or his active participation in the boycott itself. To the extent that Evers caused respondents to suffer business losses through his organization of the boycott, his emotional and persuasive appeals for unity in the joint effort, or his "threats" of vilification or social ostracism, Evers' conduct is constitutionally protected and beyond the reach of a damages award.

Strong and effective extemporaneous rhetoric cannot be nicely channeled in purely dulcet phrases. An advocate must be free to stimulate his audience with spontaneous and emotional appeals for unity and action in a common cause. When such appeals do not incite lawless action, they must be regarded as protected speech. To rule otherwise would ignore the "profound national commitment" that "debate on public issues should be uninhibited, robust, and wide-open." *New York Times Co. v. Sullivan.*

The taint of violence colored the conduct of some of the petitioners. They, of course, may be held liable for the consequences of their violent deeds. The burden of demonstrating that it colored the entire collective effort, however, is not satisfied by evidence that violence occurred or even that violence contributed to the success of the boycott. A massive and prolonged effort to change the social, political, and economic structure of a local environment cannot be characterized as a violent conspiracy simply by reference to the ephemeral consequences of relatively few violent acts. Such a characterization must be supported by findings that adequately disclose the evidentiary basis for concluding that specific parties agreed to use unlawful means, that carefully identify the impact of such unlawful conduct, and that recognize the importance of avoiding the imposition of punishment for constitutionally protected activity. The burden of demonstrating that fear rather than protected conduct was the dominant force in the movement is heavy. A court must be wary of a claim that the true color of a forest is better revealed by reptiles hidden in the weeds than by the foliage of countless freestanding trees. The findings of the chancellor, framed largely in the light of two legal theories rejected by the Mississippi Supreme Court, are constitutionally insufficient to support the judgment that all petitioners are liable for all losses resulting from the boycott.

[Justice Rehnquist's opinion concurring in the result is omitted.]

Point for Discussion

1. **Can the press be liable for speaking to a party who is bound by a nondisclosure agreement?** Jeffrey Wigand, a former executive with Brown & Williamson Tobacco Co., entered into a settlement agreement with the company in which he promised not to disclose any information he learned during his employment or to make any disparaging comments about the company or its products. The producers of "60 Minutes," a CBS news magazine show, wanted to broadcast an interview with Wigand in which he made negative accusations about the company in connection with its sale and marketing of tobacco products. Brown & Williamson threatened to sue CBS for tortious interference with Wigand's confidentiality agreement. Should the First Amendment protect CBS in this instance?

You Be the Judge!

Analyze the many torts of an anti-abortion activist

Fred Smith is the leader of an anti-abortion activist group that has targeted the Reproductive Services Center, a nonprofit clinic that performs abortions, in a state in which abortion services are legal prior to fetal viability.

Smith posts on social media an attack on a Dr. Mary Jones, a physician who works at the clinic, stating that "Jones, an abortion provider, is a murderer of children." Smith organizes a boycott of the Reproductive Services Center, urging companies that provide services or goods to the clinic, such as office supplies and medical equipment, to stop doing business with the Center. Smith tells the companies that in providing services and products to the clinic, they are aiding and abetting murder, and he threatens to organize boycotts of the companies that service the Center if they continue to do business with the facility.

Posing as an electrician, Smith gains entry to the clinic under false pretenses and hacks into a computer database, finding the names of patients who have had abortions. Smith posts an article on social media disclosing the fact that Kate Higgens, a member of the U.S. Congress who is a liberal supporter of abortion rights, once had an abortion at the clinic. Higgens had never told anyone other than her doctor about the abortion. Smith also posts a statement that the Rev. Alice B. Arthur, a Baptist minister opposed to abortion, had an abortion as a teenager. In fact, this was false. Although the clinic's computer database did correctly identify a woman named "Alice Arthur" as having received an abortion, that patient was actually "Alice C. Arthur," a different person from Rev. Alice B. Arthur. The database, however, did not include the patient's middle initial. Smith sincerely but mistakenly believed that Rev. Alice B. Arthur was the patient who had received the abortion. He negligently failed to verify that Rev. Alice B. Arthur was the patient. Indeed, he never even attempted to reach Rev. Alice B. Arthur to confront her with his allegation.

These events triggered multiple civil liability claims. You are clerking for a judge before whom the following claims are pending. The judge asks you for a brief memorandum setting forth your analysis of the First Amendment issues implicated by the following claims:

1. A defamation action brought by Dr. Jones against Smith for the statement "Jones, an abortion provider, is a murderer of children."

2. An action for tortious interference with contract and economic advantage brought by the clinic against Smith for organizing the boycott.

3. An action for intrusion, fraud, and trespass brought by the clinic against Smith for his entry into the facility and hacking into the clinic's database.

4. An action by Higgens against Smith for publication of private facts.

5. An action for false light invasion of privacy by Rev. Alice B. Arthur arising from the claim that she had an abortion at the clinic.

Test Your Knowledge

To assess your understanding of the material in this chapter, click here to take a quiz.

Chapter Ten

May Government Regulate Speech to Protect Consumers and Ensure Professionalism?

Commercial Speech

In a marketplace economy, an enormous amount of speech has one primary purpose: to sell something. Advertising is the lifeblood of commerce. It generates demand for products and services and provides consumers with essential information about what's for sale and how much it costs.

Money spent on advertising also plays a critical role in subsidizing other forms of speech. Advertising dollars fund free over-the-air radio and television. Advertising also helps subsidize news reporting. Indeed, some of the current woes plaguing local newspapers are attributable to the migration of advertising dollars from print media to the internet. The public also enjoys free access to a broad array of online applications because these applications mine people's personal data and then use this information to send targeted advertising.

In this chapter, we consider whether speech that advertises products or services—what the Supreme Court refers to as "commercial speech"—should be protected by the First Amendment. Is an advertisement for a smartphone, shampoo, or legal services worthy of First Amendment protection? If it is, should it nevertheless receive reduced protection because it is less critical than other speech to furthering the First Amendment interests of discovering the truth, promoting effective self-governance, and fostering human autonomy? Or would reducing protection for commercial speech violate the core neutrality principle that judges should avoid evaluating the relative worth of ideas?

A. What Is Commercial Speech? Condom Ads and Tupperware Parties

Before discussing how the First Amendment addresses commercial speech, we need to define the term. That is not hard to do in a general sense. But, as you will discover later in this chapter, the precise scope of what commercial speech encompasses is still a work in progress.

For starters, it is important to note that "commercial speech" does not mean speech done for profit. Much of what we consider high-value speech—books, magazines, newspapers, movies, and radio and television programming—is created for profit. That does not convert these works into commercial speech.

Likewise, paid-for political advertisements, like the ad in *New York Times v. Sullivan* or the barrage of campaign ads before an election, are not commercial speech. These ads are not selling goods and services. Solicitations for money from religious institutions and other nonprofit groups are similarly not commercial speech.

If these ads are not "commercial speech," what is? The Supreme Court has proffered several definitions. Its most instructive defines commercial speech as speech that does "no more than propose a commercial transaction." *Virginia State Bd. of Pharmacy v. Virginia Citizens Consumer Council*, 425 U.S. 748, 762 (1976). This definition has come to encompass the vast array of commercial advertising that is ubiquitous in everyday life. It covers everything from a Super Bowl commercial to a "For Sale" sign in a car window to the solicitations of an ambulance-chasing lawyer.

The Court has also clarified that advertising is commercial speech even if public service information is bundled with the sales information. For example, in *Bolger v. Youngs Drug Products Corp.*, 463 U.S. 60 (1983), the Court held that advertisements for contraceptives were commercial speech even though they included information about unintended pregnancies and sexually transmitted infections. As Justice Thurgood Marshall explained:

> The mailings constitute commercial speech notwithstanding the fact that they contain discussions of important public issues such as venereal disease and family planning. A company has the full panoply of protections available for its direct comments on public issues, so there is no reason for providing similar constitutional protection when such statements are made in the context of commercial transactions.

Similarly, in *Board of Trustees, State University of New York v. Fox*, 492 U.S. 469 (1989), the Court concluded that "Tupperware parties" on college campuses were commercial speech even though the promoters of these plastic storage containers were also educating students about "how to be financially responsible and how to run an efficient home."

The vast range of commercial speech explains why the jurisprudence on this topic is so rich and complex. But before this jurisprudence could begin to evolve, the Supreme Court first had to address the foundational question of whether commercial speech was even protected by the First Amendment.

B. Does Commercial Speech Merit First Amendment Protection? Of Keener Interest than the Day's Most Urgent Political Debate

In its earliest encounters with commercial speech, the Supreme Court held that the speech was not entitled to First Amendment protection. The leading case, *Valentine v. Chrestensen*, 316 U.S. 52 (1942), concerned a businessman who wanted to distribute leaflets advertising tours of a former Navy submarine moored to a New York City pier. Police restrained the man from distributing the literature because a sanitary ordinance forbid the distribution of commercial literature in public streets. In rejecting the businessman's First Amendment challenge, the Court stated that "the Constitution imposes no such restraint on government as respects purely commercial advertising."

Valentine's blanket exclusion of commercial speech from First Amendment protection was not enduring. In the 1970s, the Court overruled the decision. The seminal opinion marking this transition was *Virginia State Board of Pharmacy v. Virginia Citizens Consumer Council.*

Virginia State Board of Pharmacy v. Virginia Citizens Consumer Council, Inc.

Supreme Court of the United States, 1976
425 U.S. 748

MR. JUSTICE BLACKMUN delivered the opinion of the Court.

The plaintiff-appellees in this case attack, as violative of the First and Fourteenth Amendments, that portion of s 54–524.35 of Va.Code Ann. (1974), which provides that a pharmacist licensed in Virginia is guilty of unprofessional conduct if he "publishes, advertises or promotes, directly or indirectly, in any manner whatsoever, any amount, price, fee, premium, discount, rebate or credit terms for any drugs which may be dispensed only by prescription."

The present attack on the statute is one made not by one directly subject to its prohibition, that is, a pharmacist, but by prescription drug consumers who claim that they would greatly benefit if the prohibition were lifted and advertising freely allowed. The question first arises whether, even assuming that First Amendment protection attaches to the flow of drug price information, it is a protection enjoyed by the appellees as recipients of the information, and not solely, if at all, by the advertisers themselves who seek to disseminate that information.

Freedom of speech presupposes a willing speaker. But where a speaker exists, as is the case here, the protection afforded is to the communication, to its source and to its recipients both. This is clear from the decided cases. In *Lamont v. Postmaster General*, 381 U.S. 301 (1965), the Court upheld the First Amendment rights of citizens to receive political publications sent from abroad. More recently, in *Kleindienst v. Mandel*, 408 U.S. 753, 762–763 (1972), we acknowledged that this Court has referred to a First Amendment right to "receive information and ideas," and that freedom of speech "necessarily protects the right to receive." If there is a right to advertise, there is a reciprocal right to receive the advertising, and it may be asserted by these appellees.

The appellants contend that the advertisement of prescription drug prices is outside the protection of the First Amendment because it is "commercial speech." There can be no question that in past decisions the Court has given some indication that commercial speech is unprotected.

Here the question whether there is a First Amendment exception for "commercial speech" is squarely before us. Our pharmacist does not wish to editorialize on any subject, cultural, philosophical, or political. He does not wish to report any particularly newsworthy fact, or to make generalized observations even about commercial matters. The "idea" he wishes to communicate is simply this: "I will sell you the X prescription drug at the Y price." Our question, then, is whether this communication is wholly outside the protection of the First Amendment.

We begin with several propositions that already are settled or beyond serious dispute. It is clear, for example, that speech does not lose its First Amendment protection because money is spent to project it, as in a paid advertisement of one form or another. Speech likewise is protected even though it is carried in a form that is "sold" for profit, and even though it may involve a solicitation to purchase or otherwise pay or contribute money.

If there is a kind of commercial speech that lacks all First Amendment protection, therefore, it must be distinguished by its content. Yet the speech whose content deprives it of protection cannot simply be speech on a commercial subject. No one would contend that our pharmacist may be prevented from being heard on the subject of whether, in general, pharmaceutical prices should be regulated, or their advertisement forbidden. Nor can it be dispositive that a commercial advertisement is noneditorial, and merely reports a fact. Purely factual matter of public interest may claim protection.

Our question is whether speech which does "no more than propose a commercial transaction" is so removed from any "exposition of ideas," and from "truth, science, morality, and arts in general, in its diffusion of liberal sentiments on the administration of Government," that it lacks all protection. Our answer is that it is not.

Focusing first on the individual parties to the transaction that is proposed in the commercial advertisement, we may assume that the advertiser's interest is a purely economic one. That hardly disqualifies him from protection under the First Amendment. The interests of the contestants in a labor dispute are primarily economic, but it has long been settled that both the employee and the employer are protected by the First Amendment when they express themselves on the merits of the dispute in order to influence its outcome.

As to the particular consumer's interest in the free flow of commercial information, that interest may be as keen, if not keener by far, than his interest in the day's most urgent political debate. Appellees' case in this respect is a convincing one. Those whom the suppression of prescription drug price information hits the hardest are the poor, the sick, and particularly the aged. A disproportionate amount of their income tends to be spent on prescription drugs; yet they are the least able to learn, by shopping from pharmacist to pharmacist, where their scarce dollars are best spent. When drug prices vary as strikingly as they do, information as to who is charging what becomes more than a convenience. It could mean the alleviation of physical pain or the enjoyment of basic necessities.

Generalizing, society also may have a strong interest in the free flow of commercial information. Even an individual advertisement, though entirely "commercial," may be of general public interest. The facts of decided cases furnish illustrations: advertisements stating that referral services for legal abortions are available; that a manufacturer of artificial furs promotes his product as an alternative to the extinction by his competitors of fur-bearing mammals; and that a domestic producer advertises his product as an alternative to imports that tend to deprive American residents of their jobs. Obviously, not all commercial messages contain the same or even a very great public interest element. There are few to which such an element, however, could not be added. Our pharmacist, for example, could cast himself as a commentator on store-to-store disparities in drug prices, giving his own and those of a competitor as proof. We see little point in requiring him to do so, and little difference if he does not.

Moreover, there is another consideration that suggests that no line between publicly "interesting" or "important" commercial advertising and the opposite kind could ever be drawn. Advertising, however tasteless and excessive it sometimes may seem, is nonetheless dissemination of information as to who is producing and selling what product, for what reason, and at what price. So long as we preserve a predominantly free enterprise economy, the allocation of our resources in large measure will be made through numerous private economic decisions. It is a matter of public interest that those decisions, in the aggregate, be intelligent and well informed. To this end, the free flow of commercial information is indispensable. And if it is indispensable to the proper allocation of resources in a free enterprise system, it is also indispensable to the formation of intelligent opinions as to how that system ought to be regulated or altered. Therefore, even if the First Amendment were thought to be primarily an instrument to enlighten public decisionmaking in a democracy, we could not say that the free flow of information does not serve that goal.

Arrayed against these substantial individual and societal interests are a number of justifications for the advertising ban. These have to do principally with maintaining a high degree of professionalism on the part of licensed pharmacists. Indisputably, the State has a strong interest in maintaining that professionalism. A pharmacist who has a continuous relationship with his customer is in the best position, of course, to exert professional skill for the customer's protection.

Price advertising, it is argued, will place in jeopardy the pharmacist's expertise and, with it, the customer's health. It is claimed that the aggressive price competition that will result from unlimited advertising will make it impossible for the pharmacist to supply professional services in the compounding, handling, and dispensing of prescription drugs. Such services are time consuming and expensive; if competitors who economize by eliminating them are permitted to advertise their resulting lower prices, the more painstaking and conscientious pharmacist will be forced either to follow suit or to go out of business. It is also claimed that prices might not necessarily fall as a result of advertising. If one pharmacist advertises, others must, and the resulting expense will inflate the cost of drugs. It is further claimed that advertising will lead people to shop for their prescription drugs among the various pharmacists who offer the lowest prices, and the loss of stable pharmacist-customer relationships will make individual attention and certainly the practice of monitoring impossible. Finally, it is argued that damage will be done to the professional image of the pharmacist. This image, that of a skilled and specialized craftsman, attracts talent to the profession and reinforces the better habits of those who are in it. Price advertising, it is said, will reduce the pharmacist's status to that of a mere retailer.

The strength of these proffered justifications is greatly undermined by the fact that high professional standards, to a substantial extent, are guaranteed by the close regulation to which pharmacists in Virginia are subject. And this case concerns the retail sale by the pharmacist more than it does his professional standards. Surely, any pharmacist guilty of professional dereliction that actually endangers his customer will promptly lose his license. At the same time, we cannot discount the Board's justifications entirely. The Court regarded justifications of this type sufficient to sustain the advertising bans challenged on due process and equal protection grounds.

The challenge now made, however, is based on the First Amendment. This casts the Board's justifications in a different light, for on close inspection it is seen that the State's protectiveness of its citizens rests in large measure on the advantages of their being kept in ignorance. The advertising ban does not directly affect professional standards one way or the other. It affects them only through the reactions it is assumed people will have to the free flow of drug price information.

It appears to be feared that if the pharmacist who wishes to provide low cost, and assertedly low quality, services is permitted to advertise, he will be taken up on his offer by too many unwitting customers. They will choose the low-cost, low-quality service and drive the "professional" pharmacist out of business. They will respond only to costly and excessive advertising, and end up paying the price. They will go from one pharmacist to another, following the discount, and destroy the pharmacist-customer relationship. They will lose respect for the profession because it advertises. All this is not in their best interests, and all this can be avoided if they are not permitted to know who is charging what.

There is, of course, an alternative to this highly paternalistic approach. That alternative is to assume that this information is not in itself harmful, that people will perceive their own best interests if only they are well enough informed, and that the best means to that end is to open the channels of communication rather than to close them. If they are truly open, nothing prevents the "professional" pharmacist from marketing his own assertedly superior product, and contrasting it with that of the low-cost, high-volume prescription drug retailer. But the choice among these alternative approaches is not ours to make or the Virginia General Assembly's. It is precisely this kind of choice, between the dangers of suppressing information, and the dangers of its misuse if it is freely available, that the First Amendment makes for us. Virginia is free to require whatever professional standards it wishes of its pharmacists; it may subsidize them or protect them from competition in other ways. But it may not do so by keeping the public in ignorance of the entirely lawful terms that competing pharmacists are offering. In this sense, the justifications Virginia has offered for suppressing the flow of prescription drug price information, far from persuading us that the flow is not protected by the First Amendment, have reinforced our view that it is. We so hold.

In concluding that commercial speech, like other varieties, is protected, we of course do not hold that it can never be regulated in any way. Some forms of commercial speech regulation are surely permissible. We mention a few only to make clear that they are not before us and therefore are not foreclosed by this case.

There is no claim, for example, that the prohibition on prescription drug price advertising is a mere time, place, and manner restriction. We have often approved restrictions of that kind provided that they are justified without reference to the content of the regulated speech, that they serve a significant governmental interest, and that in so doing they leave open ample alternative channels for communication of the information. Whatever may be the proper bounds of time, place, and manner restrictions on commercial speech, they are plainly exceeded by this Virginia statute, which singles out speech of a particular content and seeks to prevent its dissemination completely.

Nor is there any claim that prescription drug price advertisements are forbidden because they are false or misleading in any way. Untruthful speech, commercial or otherwise, has never been protected for its own sake. Obviously, much commercial speech is not provably false, or even wholly false, but only deceptive or misleading. We foresee no obstacle to a State's dealing effectively with this problem. The First Amendment, as we construe it today does not prohibit the State from insuring that the stream of commercial information flows cleanly as well as freely.

Also, there is no claim that the transactions proposed in the forbidden advertisements are themselves illegal in any way. Finally, the special problems of the electronic broadcast media are likewise not in this case.

What is at issue is whether a State may completely suppress the dissemination of concededly truthful information about entirely lawful activity, fearful of that information's effect upon its disseminators and its recipients. Reserving other questions, we conclude that the answer to this one is in the negative.

dissent

MR. JUSTICE REHNQUIST, dissenting.

The logical consequences of the Court's decision in this case, a decision which elevates commercial intercourse between a seller hawking his wares and a buyer seeking to strike a bargain to the same plane as has been previously reserved for the free marketplace of ideas, are far reaching indeed. Under the Court's opinion the way will be open not only for dissemination of price information but for active promotion of prescription drugs, liquor, cigarettes, and other products the use of which it has previously been thought desirable to discourage. Now, however, such promotion is protected by the First Amendment so long as it is not misleading or does not promote an illegal product or enterprise.

In the final footnote the opinion tosses a bone to the traditionalists in the legal and medical professions by suggesting that because they sell services rather than drugs the holding of this case is not automatically applicable to advertising in those professions. But if the sole limitation on permissible state proscription of advertising is that it may not be false or misleading, surely the difference between pharmacists' advertising and lawyers' and doctors' advertising can be only one of degree and not of kind. I cannot distinguish between the public's right to know the price of drugs and its right to know the price of title searches or physical examinations or other professional services for which standardized fees are charged.

In the case of "our" hypothetical pharmacist, he may now presumably advertise not only the prices of prescription drugs but may attempt to energetically promote their sale so long as he does so truthfully. Quite consistently with Virginia law requiring prescription drugs to be available only through a physician, "our" pharmacist might run any of the following representative advertisements in a local newspaper:

> "Pain getting you down? Insist that your physician prescribe Demerol. You pay a little more than for aspirin, but you get a lot more relief."
>
> "Can't shake the flu? Get a prescription for Tetracycline from your doctor today."
>
> "Don't spend another sleepless night. Ask your doctor to prescribe Seconal without delay."

Unless the State can show that these advertisements are either actually untruthful or misleading, it presumably is not free to restrict in any way commercial efforts on the part of those who profit from the sale of prescription drugs to put them in the widest possible circulation. But such a line simply makes no allowance whatever for what appears to have been a considered legislative judgment in most States that while prescription drugs are a necessary and vital part of medical care and treatment, there are sufficient dangers attending their widespread use that they simply may not be promoted in the same manner as hair creams, deodorants, and toothpaste.

[The concurring opinions of Chief Justice Burger and Justice Stewart are omitted.]

Points for Discussion

1. **Is there a right to receive information?** The parties challenging the Virginia law were not the pharmacists who were subject to the law's restrictions but consumers of pharmaceutical products. Why did these consumers have standing to challenge the law if the law did not apply to them?

2. **What was the Court's reasoning for providing protection to commercial speech?** The Court acknowledged that the case was merely about whether a pharmacist could convey the message "I will sell you the X prescription drug at

the Y price." Why did the Court think that such a pedestrian message was worthy of First Amendment protection? Did you find the Court's reasoning persuasive?

3. **Did the Court find Virginia's justifications for regulating pharmacist advertising persuasive?** After concluding that the First Amendment protected drug price advertising by pharmacists, the Court turned to whether Virginia had adequate justifications for suppressing this speech. What were Virginia's reasons for restricting price advertising by pharmacists? Did the Court find these justifications persuasive?

4. **The limits of commercial speech protection.** *Virginia Pharmacy* established that the First Amendment applied to commercial speech, but the decision also ended with a series of qualifications on this protection. For starters, the opinion made the uncontroversial observation that commercial speech, like other forms of speech, may be subject to reasonable time, place, and manner regulations. So, while a company might have a First Amendment right to advertise its products, it does not have a right to blast advertisements from a sound truck in the middle of the night or glue advertisements to the walls of government buildings.

   The Court also added two more significant qualifications:

   a. **No protection for false or misleading commercial speech.** Justice Harry Blackmun clarified that the government was free to regulate false or misleading commercial speech. This was true even if the speech was not provably false but merely deceptive. As Justice Blackmun explained, the First Amendment "does not prohibit the State from insuring that the stream of commercial information flow cleanly as well as freely."

      It is important to recognize the potential breadth of this exception. There is a multitude of federal, state, and local laws designed to protect consumers in the commercial bargaining context. These can range from prohibitions on false advertising, bait-and-switch laws, and statutes banning unfair and deceptive trade practices. *Virginia Pharmacy* suggests that these laws are constitutional, at least when applied to garden-variety acts of consumer deception. Justice Blackmun also dropped a footnote that indicated that laws requiring advertisements to include warnings or disclaimers or requiring advertisements to appear in a specific form are likely constitutional. So, for example, the requirements in Article II of the Uniform Commercial Code about disclaimers of the implied warranty of merchantability being conspicuous or mentioning the word merchantability are almost certainly constitutional.

   b. **No protection for speech advertising unlawful goods or services.** *Virginia Pharmacy* also noted that there was no claim in the case that the proposed transactions were "illegal in any way." This has been understood to mean that ads for illegal goods or services are not protected by the First Amendment. That might explain why you do not see advertisements by hitmen.

5. **Was Chief Justice William Rehnquist clairvoyant?** In his dissent, Chief Justice Rehnquist predicted that pharmacists in the future would not only advertise the price of pharmaceuticals but also "energetically promote their sale." He foresaw pharmacists and drug manufacturers running ads like: "Pain getting you down? Insist that your physician prescribe Demerol." Did Chief Justice Rehnquist's prediction come true? He also predicted that *Virginia Pharmacy* would lead to robust advertising by lawyers and other professionals. Did that prediction come true?

C. The Standard for Evaluating Regulations of Commercial Speech: The *Central Hudson* Test and Its Refinements

While *Virginia Pharmacy* established that the First Amendment protected commercial speech, it did not identify the level of scrutiny to be used in evaluating regulations of this speech. That occurred four years later in *Central Hudson Gas & Electric Corp. v. Public Service Commission of New York,* 447 U.S. 557 (1980).

1. The Standard for Scrutinizing Commercial Speech Regulations: *Central Hudson*'s Intermediate Scrutiny Test

In 1980, the Supreme Court settled on a formal test for evaluating regulations of commercial speech: a four-prong version of "intermediate scrutiny" articulated in *Central Hudson*. The *Central Hudson* test remains the governing standard in commercial speech jurisprudence. Here are the test's four prongs:

(1) The speech must concern lawful activity and not be misleading;

(2) The government must have a substantial interest in restricting the speech;

(3) The regulation must directly and materially advance the asserted governmental interest; and

(4) The regulation must be narrowly tailored to serve the governmental purpose.

The first prong operates as a "gatekeeper." Speech that fails this prong is not protected by the First Amendment and may be freely regulated. The prong has two parts. Failing either renders the speech unprotected.

The first part requires advertisements to be for a "lawful activity." Consequently, and quite expectedly, there is no First Amendment protection for a drug dealer to advertise the sale of heroin or for a prostitute to advertise illegal sex for sale. The second part requires that advertising not be "misleading." This codifies *Virginia Pharmacy*'s observation that the government may ensure that commercial information "flows cleanly." This exception gives the government broad leeway to prohibit false advertising.

When the advertising at issue involves a legal activity and is not misleading, prong one of *Central Hudson* is satisfied. The burden then shifts to the government to satisfy prongs two, three, and four. The language of these prongs generally resembles the language of "intermediate scrutiny" in constitutional law.

In the years since *Central Hudson*, the Supreme Court has entertained scores of commercial speech cases, rendering the regulation of commercial speech one of the most active arenas of all constitutional law. In the early days of the commercial speech doctrine, advertisers sometimes won and sometimes lost, reflecting the "intermediate scrutiny" qualities of the test. However, as commercial speech jurisprudence has evolved, the Supreme Court has been increasingly protective of commercial speech, so that while the "official language" of *Central Hudson* continues to adhere to the nomenclature of "intermediate scrutiny," the actual outcomes come closer to the application of "strict scrutiny." Or, to put it bluntly, once commercial speakers get past prong one, they now almost always win. Indeed, a number of Supreme Court justices have openly suggested that the existing distinction between the First Amendment tests applicable to content-based regulation of noncommercial speech and the *Central Hudson* test used for commercial speech should be abandoned, which would result in applying "strict scrutiny"—the Court's default standard for content-based regulations of speech—to commercial speech regulation.

Refinements of *Central Hudson*

The steady roll of advertisers successfully challenging commercial speech regulations is largely attributable to refinements the Court has made to the *Central Hudson* test. As a result of these refinements, the application of the test has more and more come to resemble the unforgiving nature of strict scrutiny. Here are the most important principles:

- **Narrowing the scope of government interests that qualify as substantial.** In the years following *Central Hudson*, the Court permitted the government to satisfy the second prong of the test, that a regulation further a "substantial" government interest, by claiming that a regulation furthered a paternalistic interest in suppressing demand for a product that the government had deemed harmful. The high point of this jurisprudence was *Posadas de Puerto Rico Associates v. Tourism Company of Puerto Rico*, 478 U.S. 328 (1986), which upheld a Puerto Rico law that barred casinos from advertising to island residents. Puerto Rico claimed that the law furthered the government's substantial interest in curbing excessive gambling by its residents. Chief Justice Rehnquist, writing for the majority, readily agreed: "We have no difficulty in concluding that the Puerto Rico Legislature's interest in the health, safety, and welfare of its citizens constitutes a 'substantial' governmental interest." Later in his opinion, Chief Justice Rehnquist took this argument a step further by reasoning that Puerto Rico's power to ban gambling implicitly included the power to regulate the advertising of gambling. As he explained, "the greater power to completely ban casino gambling necessarily includes the lesser power to ban advertising of casino gambling."

However, in subsequent decisions, perhaps seen most vividly in the *44 Liquormart, Inc. v. Rhode Island* opinion reproduced below, the Court rejected *Posadas*' reasoning and strongly signaled that paternalistically regulating commercial speech to suppress consumer demand will almost never qualify as a substantial interest. This anti-paternalism principle is one of the most powerful drivers of the expanding protection for commercial speech. *44 Liquormart* also rejected *Posadas*' reasoning that the greater power to regulate an activity includes the lesser power to regulate advertising for the activity. As you read *44 Liquormart*, try to discern why the justices found *Posadas*' reasoning flawed.

Even when the Court acknowledges that a law is furthering a substantial government interest, the Court will still invalidate the law if the harm the law is addressing is unrelated to the commercial nature of the speech and is instead caused equally by both commercial and noncommercial speech. The classic case demonstrating this point is *City of Cincinnati v. Discovery Network, Inc.*, 507 U.S. 410 (1993). There, Cincinnati sought to reduce congestion and improve the attractiveness of its streets and sidewalks by banning the distribution of commercial publications in freestanding kiosks and news racks. The ban did not apply, however, to identical kiosks and news racks used to sell newspapers, such as the *Cincinnati Enquirer* or *The Wall Street Journal*. Because the clutter caused by commercial and noncommercial news racks was identical, the Court struck down the regulation, emphasizing that "the distinction bears no relationship *whatsoever* to the particular interests that the city has asserted. It is therefore an impermissible means of responding to the city's admittedly legitimate interests."

- **Insisting that a law truly advance the government's interest.** In applying prong three of the *Central Hudson* test, which requires that a regulation "directly and materially" advance the government's asserted substantial interest, the Supreme Court and lower courts have become increasingly rigorous. When a law has "loopholes" that allow some speech to continue even though other speech is banned, the so-called "Swiss cheese" problem, courts often find that the law fails prong three because the loopholes undermine the statute's effectiveness. Courts are also troubled by laws that accomplish their desired results only indirectly. Decisions in favor of advertisers and against government regulators often turn on prong three.

- **Striking down laws when there are readily available alternatives for furthering the government's interest.** Following the *Central Hudson* decision, the Supreme Court clarified that prong four, which requires that a law be narrowly tailored to serve the government's purpose, does not require the government to use the "least restrictive means" to further its interest. Unlike strict scrutiny, which requires a nearly perfect fit between a law's end and the means used to achieve it, *Central Hudson*'s prong four requires only that there be a "reasonable" fit between means and ends. Thus, the Court instructed:

  > What our decisions require is a "fit between the legislature's ends and the means chosen to accomplish those ends"—a fit that is not necessarily perfect, but reasonable; that represents not necessarily the single best disposition but one whose scope is "in proportion to the interest served," that employs not necessarily the least restrictive means but, as we have put it in the other contexts discussed above, a means narrowly tailored to achieve the desired objective.

  Board of Trustees, State Univ. of N.Y. v. Fox, 492 U.S. 469, 480 (1989). While this elaboration appeared to relax the tailoring requirement, thus favoring the government, many courts have nonetheless relied on prong four to strike down commercial speech regulations. This has been especially true for paternalistic regulations that aim to suppress consumer demand for purportedly harmful products by suppressing the advertising for the products. As noted above, these laws were already vulnerable to attack under prong two as not furthering a substantial government interest. They are vulnerable under prong four because the Supreme Court almost invariably finds that there are readily available means of achieving the government's end of reduced consumer demand that do not entail any speech regulation, such as taxing the products or limiting the quantity that may be purchased. You will see how Justice Sandra Day O'Connor, joined by three other justices, used this approach in *44 Liquormart.*

In the following subsections, we will explore three significant areas of commercial speech jurisprudence. The first concerns challenges to paternalistic speech regulations. The second concerns the question of whether information used by companies to inform their marketing strategies is protected by the First Amendment. The final section concerns regulations of advertising by professionals, particularly lawyers.

2. May Government Regulate Commercial Speech to Influence Consumer Behavior? Suppressing Speech to Suppress Demand

Legislators could justifiably conclude that some advertised goods and services are harmful for consumers. Topping the list might be ads involving "vice" activities such as drinking alcohol, smoking cigarettes, and gambling, but one could easily add to this list such commonly advertised items as processed foods and sugary drinks. Not surprisingly, legislators have sometimes sought to decrease consumer demand for these products by restricting advertising for them. The question is whether this paternalistic regulation of commercial speech is permissible.

Before jumping into the cases, it is important to keep in mind that the issue is not whether the government can enact laws to protect consumers. Governments can and do enact such laws all the time. There are laws regulating which foods and drugs may be sold, laws requiring cars to have seat belts and air bags, and laws banning outright the sale of dangerous products such as heroin or plutonium.

During the "*Lochner* Era" in the late 19th century and early 20th century, the Supreme Court did review paternalistic consumer protection laws to determine if they were adequately justified by health and safety concerns. But this jurisprudence was repudiated in the late 1930s and has not been revived.[1]

The question addressed in this section is not whether the government may enact consumer protection laws, but whether it may achieve its paternalistic objectives by controlling consumer access to speech. It is the attempt to influence consumer behavior by regulating what consumers may hear that triggers the First Amendment.

---

1 *Compare Weaver v. Palmer Bros. Co.*, 270 U.S. 402 (1926), *with United States v. Carolene Prods. Co.*, 304 U.S. 144 (1938).

44 Liquormart, Inc. v. Rhode Island

Supreme Court of the United States, 1996
517 U.S. 484

Justice Stevens announced the judgment of the Court and delivered the opinion of the Court with respect to Parts I, II, VII, and VIII, an opinion with respect to Parts III and V, in which Justice Kennedy, Justice Souter, and Justice Ginsburg join, an opinion with respect to Part VI, in which Justice Kennedy, Justice Thomas, and Justice Ginsburg join, and an opinion with respect to Part IV, in which Justice Kennedy and Justice Ginsburg join.

Last Term we held that a federal law abridging a brewer's right to provide the public with accurate information about the alcoholic content of malt beverages is unconstitutional. *Rubin v. Coors Brewing Co.*, 514 U.S. 476, 491 (1995). We now hold that Rhode Island's statutory prohibition against advertisements that provide the public with accurate information about retail prices of alcoholic beverages is also invalid. Our holding rests on the conclusion that such an advertising ban is an abridgment of speech protected by the First Amendment.

I

In 1956, the Rhode Island Legislature enacted two separate prohibitions against advertising the retail price of alcoholic beverages. The first applies to vendors licensed in Rhode Island as well as to out-of-state manufacturers, wholesalers, and shippers. It prohibits them from "advertising in any manner whatsoever" the price of any alcoholic beverage offered for sale in the State; the only exception is for price tags or signs displayed with the merchandise within licensed premises and not visible from the street. The second statute applies to the Rhode Island news media. It contains a categorical prohibition against the publication or broadcast of any advertisements—even those referring to sales in other States—that "make reference to the price of any alcoholic beverages."

II

Petitioners 44 Liquormart, Inc. and Peoples Super Liquor Stores, Inc. are licensed retailers of alcoholic beverages. Petitioner 44 Liquormart operates a store in Rhode Island and petitioner Peoples operates several stores in Massachusetts that are patronized by Rhode Island residents. Peoples uses alcohol price advertising extensively in Massachusetts, where such advertising is permitted, but Rhode Island newspapers and other media outlets have refused to accept such ads.

III

Advertising has been a part of our culture throughout our history. Even in colonial days, the public relied on "commercial speech" for vital information about the market. Early newspapers displayed advertisements for goods and services on their front pages, and town criers called out prices in public squares.

IV

When a State regulates commercial messages to protect consumers from misleading, deceptive, or aggressive sales practices, or requires the disclosure of beneficial consumer information, the purpose of its regulation is consistent with the reasons for according constitutional protection to commercial speech and therefore justifies less than strict review. However, when a State entirely prohibits the dissemination of truthful, nonmisleading commercial messages for reasons unrelated to the preservation of a fair bargaining process, there is far less reason to depart from the rigorous review that the First Amendment generally demands.

Our commercial speech cases have recognized the dangers that attend governmental attempts to single out certain messages for suppression.

The special dangers that attend complete bans on truthful, nonmisleading commercial speech cannot be explained away by appeals to the "commonsense distinctions" that exist between commercial and noncommercial speech. Regulations that suppress the truth are no less troubling because they target objectively verifiable information, nor are they less effective because they aim at durable messages. As a result, neither the "greater objectivity" nor the "greater hardiness" of truthful, nonmisleading commercial speech justifies reviewing its complete suppression with added deference.

It is the State's interest in protecting consumers from "commercial harms" that provides "the typical reason why commercial speech can be subject to greater governmental regulation than noncommercial speech." Yet bans that target truthful, nonmisleading commercial messages rarely protect consumers from such harms. Instead, such bans often serve only to obscure an "underlying governmental policy" that could be implemented without regulating speech. In this way, these commercial speech bans not only hinder consumer choice, but also impede debate over central issues of public policy.

Precisely because bans against truthful, nonmisleading commercial speech rarely seek to protect consumers from either deception or overreaching, they usually rest solely on the offensive assumption that the public will respond "irrationally" to the truth. The First Amendment directs us to be especially skeptical of regulations that seek to keep people in the dark for what the government perceives to be their own good. That teaching applies equally to state attempts to deprive consumers of accurate information about their chosen products:

> The commercial marketplace, like other spheres of our social and cultural life, provides a forum where ideas and information flourish. Some of the ideas and information are vital, some of slight worth. But the general rule is that the speaker and the audience, not the government, assess the value of the information presented. Thus, even a communication that does no more than propose a commercial transaction is entitled to the coverage of the First Amendment.

V

In this case, there is no question that Rhode Island's price advertising ban constitutes a blanket prohibition against truthful, nonmisleading speech about a lawful product. There is also no question that the ban serves an end unrelated to consumer protection. Accordingly, we must review the price advertising ban with "special care" mindful that speech prohibitions of this type rarely survive constitutional review.

The State argues that the price advertising prohibition should nevertheless be upheld because it directly advances the State's substantial interest in promoting temperance, and because it is no more extensive than necessary. Although there is some confusion as to what Rhode Island means by temperance, we assume that the State asserts an interest in reducing alcohol consumption.

In evaluating the ban's effectiveness in advancing the State's interest, we note that a commercial speech regulation "may not be sustained if it provides only ineffective or remote support for the government's purpose." For that reason, the State bears the burden of showing not merely that its regulation will advance its interest, but also that it will do so "to a material degree." The need for the State to make such a showing is particularly great given the drastic nature of its chosen means—the wholesale suppression of truthful, nonmisleading information. Accordingly, we must determine whether the State has shown that the price advertising ban will significantly reduce alcohol consumption.

We can agree that common sense supports the conclusion that a prohibition against price advertising, like a collusive agreement among competitors to refrain from such advertising, will tend to mitigate competition and maintain prices at a higher level than would prevail in a completely free market. Despite the absence of proof on the point, we can even agree with the State's contention that it is reasonable to assume that demand, and hence consumption throughout the market, is somewhat lower whenever a higher, noncompetitive price level prevails. However, without any findings of fact, or indeed any evidentiary support whatsoever, we cannot agree with the assertion that the price advertising ban will significantly advance the State's interest in promoting temperance.

Although the record suggests that the price advertising ban may have some impact on the purchasing patterns of temperate drinkers of modest means, the State has presented no evidence to suggest that its speech prohibition will significantly reduce marketwide consumption. Indeed, the District Court's considered and uncontradicted finding on this point is directly to the contrary. Moreover, the evidence suggests that the abusive drinker will probably not be deterred by a marginal price increase, and that the true alcoholic may simply reduce his purchases of other necessities.

In addition, as the District Court noted, the State has not identified what price level would lead to a significant reduction in alcohol consumption, nor has it identified the amount that it believes prices would decrease without the ban. Thus, the State's own showing reveals that any connection between the ban and a significant change in alcohol consumption would be purely fortuitous.

As is evident, any conclusion that elimination of the ban would significantly increase alcohol consumption would require us to engage in the sort of "speculation or conjecture" that is an unacceptable means of demonstrating that a restriction on commercial speech directly advances the State's asserted interest. Such speculation certainly does not suffice when the State takes aim at accurate commercial information for paternalistic ends.

The State also cannot satisfy the requirement that its restriction on speech be no more extensive than necessary. It is perfectly obvious that alternative forms of regulation that would not involve any restriction on speech would be more likely to achieve the State's goal of promoting temperance. As the State's own expert conceded, higher prices can be maintained either by direct regulation or by increased taxation. Per capita purchases could be limited as is the case with prescription drugs. Even educational campaigns focused on the problems of excessive, or even moderate, drinking might prove to be more effective.

As a result, even under the less than strict standard that generally applies in commercial speech cases, the State has failed to establish a "reasonable fit" between its abridgment of speech and its temperance goal.

VI

The State responds by arguing that it merely exercised appropriate "legislative judgment" in determining that a price advertising ban would best promote temperance. Relying on the *Central Hudson* analysis set forth in *Posadas de Puerto Rico Associates v. Tourism Co. of P.R.* and *United States v. Edge Broadcasting Co.*, 509 U.S. 418 (1993), Rhode Island first argues that, because expert opinions as to the effectiveness of the price advertising ban "go both ways," the Court of Appeals correctly concluded that the ban constituted a "reasonable choice" by the legislature.

In *Edge*, we upheld a federal statute that permitted only those broadcasters located in States that had legalized lotteries to air lottery advertising. The statute was designed to regulate advertising about an activity that had been deemed illegal in the jurisdiction in which the broadcaster was located. Here, by contrast, the commercial speech ban targets information about entirely lawful behavior.

Posadas is more directly relevant. There, a five-Member majority held that, under the Central Hudson test, it was "up to the legislature" to choose to reduce gambling by suppressing in-state casino advertising rather than engaging in educational speech. Rhode Island argues that this logic demonstrates the constitutionality of its own decision to ban price advertising in lieu of raising taxes or employing some other less speech-restrictive means of promoting temperance.

The reasoning in *Posadas* does support the State's argument, but, on reflection, we are now persuaded that *Posadas* erroneously performed the First Amendment analysis. The casino advertising ban was designed to keep truthful, nonmisleading speech from members of the public for fear that they would be more likely to gamble if they received it. As a result, the advertising ban served to shield the State's antigambling policy from the public scrutiny that more direct, nonspeech regulation would draw.

Given our longstanding hostility to commercial speech regulation of this type, Posadas clearly erred in concluding that it was "up to the legislature" to choose suppression over a less speech-restrictive policy. The *Posadas* majority's conclusion on that point cannot be reconciled with the unbroken line of prior cases striking down similarly broad regulations on truthful, nonmisleading advertising when non-speech-related alternatives were available.

Because the 5-to-4 decision in *Posadas* marked such a sharp break from our prior precedent, and because it concerned a constitutional question about which this Court is the final arbiter, we decline to give force to its highly deferential approach.

Instead, in keeping with our prior holdings, we conclude that a state legislature does not have the broad discretion to suppress truthful, nonmisleading information for paternalistic purposes that the *Posadas* majority was willing to tolerate.

We also cannot accept the State's second contention, which is premised entirely on the "greater-includes-the-lesser" reasoning endorsed toward the end of the majority's opinion in *Posadas*. There, the majority stated that "the greater power to completely ban casino gambling necessarily includes the lesser power to ban advertising of casino gambling."

As a matter of First Amendment doctrine, the *Posadas* syllogism is even less defensible. The text of the First Amendment makes clear that the Constitution presumes that attempts to regulate speech are more dangerous than attempts to regulate conduct. That presumption accords with the essential role that the free flow of information plays in a democratic society. As a result, the First Amendment directs that government may not suppress speech as easily as it may suppress conduct, and that speech restrictions cannot be treated as simply another means that the government may use to achieve its ends.

Finally, we find unpersuasive the State's contention that, under *Posadas* and *Edge*, the price advertising ban should be upheld because it targets commercial speech that pertains to a "vice" activity. Respondents premise their request for a so-called "vice" exception to our commercial speech doctrine on language in *Edge* which characterized gambling as a "vice." Respondents misread our precedent. Our decision last Term striking down an alcohol-related advertising restriction effectively rejected the very contention respondents now make. See *Rubin v. Coors Brewing Co.*

Moreover, the scope of any "vice" exception to the protection afforded by the First Amendment would be difficult, if not impossible, to define. Almost any product that poses some threat to public health or public morals might reasonably be characterized by a state legislature as relating to "vice activity." Such characterization, however, is anomalous when applied to products such as alcoholic beverages, lottery tickets, or playing cards, that may be lawfully purchased on the open market. The recognition of such an exception would also have the unfortunate consequence of either allowing state legislatures to justify censorship by the simple expedient of placing the "vice" label on selected lawful activities, or requiring the federal courts to establish a federal common law of vice. For these reasons, a "vice" label that is unaccompanied by a corresponding prohibition against the commercial behavior at issue fails to provide a principled justification for the regulation of commercial speech about that activity.

VII

From 1919 until 1933, the Eighteenth Amendment to the Constitution totally prohibited "the manufacture, sale, or transportation of intoxicating liquors" in the United States and its territories. Section 1 of the Twenty-first Amendment repealed that prohibition, and § 2 delegated to the several States the power to prohibit commerce in, or the use of, alcoholic beverages.

Although the Twenty-first Amendment limits the effect of the dormant Commerce Clause on a State's regulatory power over the delivery or use of intoxicating beverages within its borders, "the Amendment does not license the States to ignore their obligations under other provisions of the Constitution."

just b/c 21st amend allows ~~prohibition~~ regulation of alcoholic beverages states still can't ignore other amendments to the constitution

VIII

Because Rhode Island has failed to carry its heavy burden of justifying its complete ban on price advertising, we conclude that R.I. Gen. Laws §§ 3–8–7 and 3–8–8.1 (1989), as well as Regulation 32 of the Rhode Island Liquor Control Administration, abridge speech in violation of the First Amendment as made applicable to the States by the Due Process Clause of the Fourteenth Amendment. The judgment of the Court of Appeals is therefore reversed.

JUSTICE SCALIA, concurring in part and concurring in the judgment.

I share Justice Thomas's discomfort with the *Central Hudson* test, which seems to me to have nothing more than policy intuition to support it. I also share Justice Stevens's aversion towards paternalistic governmental policies that prevent men and women from hearing facts that might not be good for them. On the other hand, it would also be paternalism for us to prevent the people of the States from enacting laws that we consider paternalistic, unless we have good reason to believe that the Constitution itself forbids them.

Since I do not believe we have before us the wherewithal to declare *Central Hudson* wrong—or at least the wherewithal to say what ought to replace it—I must resolve this case in accord with our existing jurisprudence, which all except Justice Thomas agree would prohibit the challenged regulation. I am not disposed to develop new law, or reinforce old, on this issue, and accordingly I merely concur in the judgment of the Court.

JUSTICE THOMAS, concurring in Parts I, II, VI, and VII, and concurring in the judgment.

In cases such as this, in which the government's asserted interest is to keep legal users of a product or service ignorant in order to manipulate their choices in the marketplace, the balancing test adopted in *Central Hudson* should not be applied, in my view. Rather, such an "interest" is *per se* illegitimate and can no more justify regulation of "commercial" speech than it can justify regulation of "noncommercial" speech.

In *Virginia Board of Pharmacy v. Virginia Citizens Consumer Council, Inc.*, this Court held that speech that does "no more than propose a commercial transaction" was protected by the First Amendment, and struck down a ban on price advertising regarding prescription drugs. The Court sharply rebuffed the State's argument that consumers would make irresponsible choices if they were able to choose between higher priced but higher quality pharmaceuticals accompanied by high quality prescription monitoring services resulting from a "stable pharmacist-customer relationship," on the one hand, and cheaper but lower quality pharmaceuticals unaccompanied by such services, on the other.

In case after case following *Virginia Board of Pharmacy*, the Court, and individual Members of the Court, have continued to stress the importance of free dissemination of information about commercial choices in a market economy; the antipaternalistic premises of the First Amendment; the impropriety of manipulating consumer choices or public opinion through the suppression of accurate "commercial" information; the near impossibility of severing "commercial" speech from speech necessary to democratic decisionmaking; and the dangers of permitting the government to do covertly what it might not have been able to muster the political support to do openly.

In other decisions, however, the Court has appeared to accept the legitimacy of laws that suppress information in order to manipulate the choices of consumers—so long as the government could show that the manipulation was in fact successful. *Central Hudson* was the first decision to clearly embrace this position, although the Court applied a very strict overbreadth analysis to strike down the advertising ban at issue. In two other decisions, *Posadas* and *Edge*, the Court simply presumed that advertising of a product or service leads to increased consumption; since, as in *Central Hudson*, the Court saw nothing impermissible in the government's suppressing information in order to discourage consumption, it upheld the advertising restrictions in those cases.

I do not join the principal opinion's application of the *Central Hudson* balancing test because I do not believe that such a test should be applied to a restriction of "commercial" speech, at least when, as here, the asserted interest is one that is to be achieved through keeping would-be recipients of the speech in the dark.

Both Justice Stevens and Justice O'Connor appear to adopt a stricter, more categorical interpretation of the fourth prong of *Central Hudson* than that suggested in some of our other opinions, one that could, as a practical matter, go a long way toward the position I take. The opinions would appear to commit the courts to striking down restrictions on speech whenever a direct regulation (*i.e.*, a regulation involving no restriction on speech regarding lawful activity at all) would be an equally effective method of dampening demand by legal users.

In my view, the *Central Hudson* test asks the courts to weigh incommensurables—the value of knowledge versus the value of ignorance—and to apply contradictory premises—that informed adults are the best judges of their own interests, and that they are not. Rather than continuing to apply a test that makes no sense to me when the asserted state interest is of the type involved here, I would return to the reasoning and holding of *Virginia Board of Pharmacy*. Under that decision, these restrictions fall.

JUSTICE O'CONNOR, with whom THE CHIEF JUSTICE, JUSTICE SOUTER, and JUSTICE BREYER join, concurring in the judgment.

I agree with the Court that Rhode Island's price-advertising ban is invalid. I would resolve this case more narrowly, however, by applying our established *Central*

Hudson test to determine whether this commercial speech regulation survives First Amendment scrutiny.

Both parties agree that the first two prongs of the *Central Hudson* test are met. Even if we assume, *arguendo*, that Rhode Island's regulation also satisfies the requirement that it directly advance the governmental interest, Rhode Island's regulation fails the final prong; that is, its ban is more extensive than necessary to serve the States interest.

Rhode Island offers one, and only one, justification for its ban on price advertising. Rhode Island says that the ban is intended to keep alcohol prices high as a way to keep consumption low.

The fit between Rhode Island's method and this particular goal is not reasonable. If the target is simply higher prices generally to discourage consumption, the regulation imposes too great, and unnecessary, a prohibition on speech in order to achieve it. The State has other methods at its disposal—methods that would more directly accomplish this stated goal without intruding on sellers' ability to provide truthful, nonmisleading information to customers.

It is true that *Posadas* accepted as reasonable, without further inquiry, Puerto Rico's assertions that the regulations furthered the government's interest and were no more extensive than necessary to serve that interest. Since *Posadas*, however, this Court has examined more searchingly the State's professed goal, and the speech restriction put into place to further it, before accepting a State's claim that the speech restriction satisfies First Amendment scrutiny.

Points for Discussion

1. **What is the holding in *44 Liquormart*? How would you conduct a *Marks* analysis?** For brevity's sake, this casebook often removes Roman numerals that identify different segments of a Supreme Court opinion and omits concurring opinions. But none of these was omitted in the *44 Liquormart* opinion reproduced above. This was necessary because of the splintered aspects of the Court's disposition. The principal opinion, written by Justice John Paul Stevens, only counted as the majority opinion as to Parts I, II, VII, and VIII. Four justices (Justice Stevens himself, joined by Justices Anthony Kennedy, David Souter, and Ruth Bader Ginsburg) joined in Parts III and V of the opinion. A different lineup of four justices (again, Justice Stevens himself, joined by Justices Kennedy, Clarence Thomas, and Ginsburg) joined Part VI of the opinion. Three justices (Justice Stevens himself, and Justices Kennedy and Ginsburg) joined Part IV of the opinion. On top of all this confusing math, Justices Antonin Scalia and

Thomas each wrote his own individual concurring opinion, and Justice Sandra Day O'Connor wrote an opinion joined by Chief Justice Rehnquist and Justices Souter and Stephen Breyer.

In situations such as this, the binding precedential impact on lower courts requires a so-called "*Marks* analysis," named for *Marks v. United States*, 430 U.S. 188 (1977). A *Marks* analysis is used to determine the precedential impact of a Supreme Court decision in which a fragmented Court decides a case and no single rationale explaining the result enjoys the assent of five justices. In such instances the holding of the case is deemed to be based on the position taken by those justices who concurred in the judgment on the narrowest grounds. But if the plurality and concurring opinions take distinct approaches, and there is no narrowest opinion representing the common denominator of the Court's reasoning, a *Marks* analysis becomes problematic. Consider the following propositions: (1) Justice Thomas stood alone in his express willingness to scrap *Central Hudson*; (2) all the justices appear to reject the reasoning in *Posadas*, which *44 Liquormart* effectively overruled; and (3) all the justices expressed hostility toward paternalistic efforts to manipulate consumer choices by restricting advertising, though they expressed that skepticism through slightly different verbal formulations. Consider how these themes resurface in the *Sorrell v. IMS Health* case discussed below, involving another form of attempted manipulation of the marketplace through regulation of commercial speech.

2. **Did Justices Stevens and O'Connor apply the *Central Hudson* test in a manner that resembled strict scrutiny?** As the previous Point for Discussion indicated, *44 Liquormart* produced a multitude of opinions that relied on differing reasons for striking down the Rhode Island laws. Some justices, like Justice Thomas, advocated abandoning the *Central Hudson* test and instead applying strict scrutiny to regulations of truthful, non-misleading commercial speech. Other justices, such as Justices Stevens and O'Connor, resolved the case using the *Central Hudson* test. Can you articulate which prongs of the *Central Hudson* test they relied on to find the Rhode Island laws unconstitutional? Can you explain why Justice Thomas thought that Justice Stevens' and Justice O'Connor's application of fourth prong went "a long way toward the position" he was advocating?

3. **Why shouldn't the government have greater power to regulate advertising involving "vice" activities?** Justice Stevens acknowledged that some of the Court's earlier commercial speech opinions, such as *Posadas*, seemed to imply that the government had greater power to regulate advertisements for "vice" activities such as smoking, drinking, and gambling. What was his reasoning for rejecting a vice exception?

4. **Are paternalistic regulations ever permissible?** The majority of justices in *44 Liquormart* expressed hostility toward paternalistic commercial speech regulations that try to manipulate consumer behavior by keeping people in the dark. But there is one context in which the justices appear to accept paternalistic speech regulation: to protect children from harmful products. For example, in *Lorillard Tobacco Co. v. Reilly*, 533 U.S. 525 (2001), the Court reviewed a Massachusetts regulation that prohibited the outdoor advertising of cigars and smokeless tobacco products within 1,000 feet of a school or playground. The Court readily accepted that the "State's interest in preventing underage tobacco use is substantial, and even compelling," but concluded that the regulation was not narrowly tailored because it effectively banned all outdoor advertising of the products in metropolitan areas. The Court said the manufacturers and retailers of these tobacco products have a legitimate interest in "conveying truthful information about their products to adults, and adults have a corresponding interest in receiving truthful information." In other words, paternalistic regulation of commercial speech to protect children may be constitutional but it must be narrowly tailored. This parallels the Court's jurisprudence that permits laws denying minors access to indecent sexual speech, but not if the laws have the effect of reducing public discourse to that which "would be suitable for a sandbox."

5. **Where did all the cigarette ads go?** The authors of this casebook are old enough to remember a time when it was common to see ads for cigarettes in a wide variety of media. There were slogans like "Winston tastes good like a cigarette should" and "You've come a long way, baby," the latter designed to appeal to women emboldened by the burgeoning women's liberation movement in the 1970s. In 1988, R.J. Reynolds launched its "Old Joe Camel" ads to market its Camel cigarettes. The ads have been described as a "transparent effort" to increase the company's market share of young smokers. You can read a critique of the advertising campaign and see a collection of Joe Camel ads here.

   The dramatic decrease in tobacco advertising is attributable to a combination of factors, including laws regulating the advertising and a major litigation settlement between states and the tobacco companies in which the companies agreed to limit their marketing efforts. Nevertheless, tobacco companies have at times asserted their First Amendment rights to challenge new regulations, most notably a Food and Drug Administration regulation that required the use of graphic images on cigarette packages. The images showed the health effects of smoking, including diseased lungs and a man with a breathing tube. A federal court in Texas found the regulation unconstitutional. *R.J. Reynolds Tobacco Co. v. U.S. Food & Drug Admin.*, No. 20-cv-176, 2022 WL 17489170 (E.D. Tex. Dec. 7, 2022). *See generally* Bianca Nunes, *The Future of Government-Mandated Health Warnings after R.J. Reynolds and American Meat Institute*, 163 U. Pa. L. Rev. Online 177 (2015);

Ellen P. Goodman, *Visual Gut Punch: Persuasion, Emotion, and the Constitutional Meaning of Graphic Disclosure*, 99 Cornell L. Rev. 513 (2014).

Recall how the *Central Hudson* test's first prong provides that commercial speech is not protected by the First Amendment if it advertises illegal products or services or is false or misleading. Based on this prong alone, can you make an argument that Joe Camel ads would not be entitled to First Amendment protection? Can you similarly make an argument that Marlboro ads featuring a strong, healthy cowboy enjoying cigarettes out in the fresh country air would also not be protected?

6. **How should the First Amendment be applied to corporate public relations campaigns?** In the earlier discussion about the definition of commercial speech, you learned that the Supreme Court treats advertisements as commercial speech even if the ads include public service information, such as a contraceptive ad that included a discussion about sexually transmitted infections. How should the Court treat corporate public relations materials that are designed to win or preserve customer loyalty but not advertise the sale of goods or services? This issue was raised in the late 1990s when Nike, in response to complaints that foreign workers producing its merchandise were mistreated, issued press releases, wrote letters to editors, and circulated a commissioned report to counter these claims. Should this literature be treated as fully protected speech because it never proposes a commercial transaction, or should it be treated as commercial speech

because its goal is to persuade consumers to keep buying the company's products? The Supreme Court was poised to consider this issue at the start of the new millennium, but then dismissed the initial *certiorari* order as improvidently granted. *Nike, Inc. v. Kasky*, 539 U.S. 654 (2003). Similar issues have arisen as companies have engaged in PR campaigns to extol their commitment to combating climate change. Commentators dubious of this literature refer to it as "greenwashing." Amanda Shanor & Sarah E. Light, *Greenwashing and the First Amendment*, 122 Colum. L. Rev. 2033 (2022).

3. Does Commercial Speech Encompass Information Companies Use for Marketing? The Collision of Big Data and Commercial Speech

In the era of big data, consumers' internet searches and purchases, both online and off, are recorded, sorted, and analyzed for clues about how to best target the customers with future advertisements. Should the commercial speech doctrine apply to this marketing information or only to the resultant advertising?

The following case concerns restrictions on the commercial use of data about doctors' prescribing practices. One of the questions the justices wrestle with is how to characterize this information. Is it fully protected speech, commercial speech, or something else altogether?

Sorrell v. IMS Health Inc.

Supreme Court of the United States, 2011
564 U.S. 552

Justice Kennedy delivered the opinion of the Court.

Vermont law restricts the sale, disclosure, and use of pharmacy records that reveal the prescribing practices of individual doctors. Vt. Stat. Ann., Tit. 18, § 4631. Subject to certain exceptions, the information may not be sold, disclosed by pharmacies for marketing purposes, or used for marketing by pharmaceutical manufacturers. Vermont argues that its prohibitions safeguard medical privacy and diminish the likelihood that marketing will lead to prescription decisions not in the best interests of patients or the State. It can be assumed that these interests are significant. Speech in aid of pharmaceutical marketing, however, is a form of expression protected by the Free Speech Clause of the First Amendment. As a consequence, Vermont's statute must be subjected to heightened judicial scrutiny. The law cannot satisfy that standard.

Pharmaceutical manufacturers promote their drugs to doctors through a process called "detailing." This often involves a scheduled visit to a doctor's office to persuade the doctor to prescribe a particular pharmaceutical. Detailers bring drug samples as well as medical studies that explain the "details" and potential advantages of various prescription drugs. Interested physicians listen, ask questions, and receive followup data. Salespersons can be more effective when they know the background and purchasing preferences of their clientele, and pharmaceutical salespersons are no exception. Knowledge of a physician's prescription practices—called "prescriber-identifying information"—enables a detailer better to ascertain which doctors are likely to be interested in a particular drug and how best to present a particular sales message. Detailing is an expensive undertaking, so pharmaceutical companies most often use it to promote high-profit brand-name drugs protected by patent. Once a brand-name drug's patent expires, less expensive bioequivalent generic alternatives are manufactured and sold.

In 2007, Vermont enacted the Prescription Confidentiality Law. The measure is also referred to as Act 80.

The provision begins by prohibiting pharmacies, health insurers, and similar entities from selling prescriber-identifying information, absent the prescriber's consent. The parties here dispute whether this clause applies to all sales or only to sales for marketing. The provision then goes on to prohibit pharmacies, health insurers, and similar entities from allowing prescriber-identifying information to be used for marketing, unless the prescriber consents. This prohibition in effect bars pharmacies from disclosing the information for marketing purposes. Finally, the provision's second sentence bars pharmaceutical manufacturers and pharmaceutical marketers from using prescriber-identifying information for marketing, again absent the prescriber's consent. The Vermont attorney general may pursue civil remedies against violators.

The present case involves two consolidated suits. One was brought by three Vermont data miners, the other by an association of pharmaceutical manufacturers that produce brand-name drugs.

On its face, Vermont's law enacts content-and speaker-based restrictions on the sale, disclosure, and use of prescriber-identifying information. The provision first forbids sale subject to exceptions based in large part on the content of a purchaser's speech. For example, those who wish to engage in certain "educational communications," § 4631(e)(4), may purchase the information. The measure then bars any disclosure when recipient speakers will use the information for marketing. Finally, the provision's second sentence prohibits pharmaceutical manufacturers from using the information for marketing. The statute thus disfavors marketing, that is, speech with a particular content. More than that, the statute disfavors specific speakers, namely pharmaceutical manufacturers. As a result of these content- and speaker-based rules, detailers cannot obtain prescriber-identifying information, even though the information may be purchased or acquired by other speakers with diverse purposes and viewpoints. Detailers are likewise barred from using the information for marketing, even though the information may be used by a wide range of other speakers. For example, it appears that Vermont could supply academic organizations with prescriber-identifying information to use in countering the messages of brand-name pharmaceutical manufacturers and in promoting the prescription of generic drugs. But § 4631(d) leaves detailers no means of purchasing, acquiring, or using prescriber-identifying information. The law on its face burdens disfavored speech by disfavored speakers.

Act 80 is designed to impose a specific, content-based burden on protected expression. It follows that heightened judicial scrutiny is warranted.

The State argues that heightened judicial scrutiny is unwarranted because its law is a mere commercial regulation. It is true that restrictions on protected expression are distinct from restrictions on economic activity or, more generally, on nonexpressive conduct. It is also true that the First Amendment does not prevent restrictions directed at commerce or conduct from imposing incidental burdens on speech. That is why a ban on race-based hiring may require employers to remove "White Applicants Only" signs, why "an ordinance against outdoor fires" might forbid "burning a flag," and why antitrust laws can prohibit "agreements in restraint of trade."

But § 4631(d) imposes more than an incidental burden on protected expression. Both on its face and in its practical operation, Vermont's law imposes a burden based on the content of speech and the identity of the speaker. While the burdened speech results from an economic motive, so too does a great deal of vital expression. Vermont's law does not simply have an effect on speech, but is directed at certain content and is aimed at particular speakers. The Constitution "does not enact Mr. Herbert Spencer's Social Statics." *Lochner v. New York*, 198 U.S. 45, 75 (1905) (Holmes, J., dissenting). It does enact the First Amendment.

The State also contends that heightened judicial scrutiny is unwarranted in this case because sales, transfer, and use of prescriber-identifying information are conduct, not speech. Consistent with that submission, the United States Court of Appeals for the First Circuit has characterized prescriber-identifying information as a mere "commodity" with no greater entitlement to First Amendment protection than "beef jerky."

This Court has held that the creation and dissemination of information are speech within the meaning of the First Amendment. Facts, after all, are the beginning point for much of the speech that is most essential to advance human knowledge and to conduct human affairs. There is thus a strong argument that prescriber-identifying information is speech for First Amendment purposes.

The State asks for an exception to the rule that information is speech, but there is no need to consider that request in this case. The State has imposed content- and speaker-based restrictions on the availability and use of prescriber-identifying information. So long as they do not engage in marketing, many speakers can obtain and use the information. But detailers cannot. Vermont's statute could be compared with a law prohibiting trade magazines from purchasing or using ink.

In the ordinary case it is all but dispositive to conclude that a law is content based and, in practice, viewpoint discriminatory. *See R.A.V.* ("Content-based regulations are presumptively invalid"). The State argues that a different analysis applies here because, assuming § 4631(d) burdens speech at all, it at most burdens only commercial speech. As in previous cases, however, the outcome is the same whether a special commercial speech inquiry or a stricter form of judicial scrutiny is applied.

Under a commercial speech inquiry, it is the State's burden to justify its content-based law as consistent with the First Amendment. The State's asserted justifications for § 4631(d) come under two general headings. First, the State contends that its law is necessary to protect medical privacy, including physician confidentiality, avoidance of harassment, and the integrity of the doctor-patient relationship. Second, the State argues that § 4631(d) is integral to the achievement of policy objectives—namely, improved public health and reduced healthcare costs. Neither justification withstands scrutiny.

Perhaps the State could have addressed physician confidentiality through "a more coherent policy." For instance, the State might have advanced its asserted privacy interest by allowing the information's sale or disclosure in only a few narrow and well-justified circumstances. A statute of that type would present quite a different case from the one presented here. But the State did not enact a statute with that purpose or design. Instead, Vermont made prescriber-identifying information available to an almost limitless audience. The explicit structure of the statute allows the information to be studied and used by all but a narrow class of disfavored speakers. Given the information's widespread availability and many permissible uses, the State's asserted interest in physician confidentiality does not justify the burden that § 4631(d) places on protected expression.

The State contends that § 4631(d) advances important public policy goals by lowering the costs of medical services and promoting public health. If prescriber-identifying information were available for use by detailers, the State contends, then detailing would be effective in promoting brand-name drugs that are more expensive and less safe than generic alternatives. This logic is set out at length in the legislative findings accompanying § 4631(d). Yet at oral argument here, the State declined to acknowledge that § 4631(d)'s objective purpose and practical effect were to inhibit detailing and alter doctors' prescription decisions. The State's reluctance to embrace its own legislature's rationale reflects the vulnerability of its position.

While Vermont's stated policy goals may be proper, § 4631(d) does not advance them in a permissible way. As the Court of Appeals noted, the "state's own explanation of how" § 4631(d) "advances its interests cannot be said to be direct." The State seeks to achieve its policy objectives through the indirect means of restraining certain speech by certain speakers—that is, by diminishing detailers' ability to influence prescription decisions. Those who seek to censor or burden free expression often assert that disfavored speech has adverse effects. But the "fear that people would make bad decisions if given truthful information" cannot justify content-based burdens on speech. "The First Amendment directs us to be especially skeptical of regulations that seek to keep people in the dark for what the government perceives to be their own good." *44 Liquormart* (opinion of Stevens, J.). These precepts apply with full force when the audience, in this case prescribing physicians, consists of "sophisticated and experienced" consumers.

As Vermont's legislative findings acknowledge, the premise of § 4631(d) is that the force of speech can justify the government's attempts to stifle it. Indeed the State defends the law by insisting that "pharmaceutical marketing has a strong influence on doctors' prescribing practices." This reasoning is incompatible with the First Amendment. In an attempt to reverse a disfavored trend in public opinion, a State could not ban campaigning with slogans, picketing with signs, or marching during the daytime. Likewise the State may not seek to remove a popular but disfavored product from the marketplace by prohibiting truthful, nonmisleading advertisements that contain impressive endorsements or catchy jingles. That the State finds expression too persuasive does not permit it to quiet the speech or to burden its messengers.

The defect in Vermont's law is made clear by the fact that many listeners find detailing instructive. Indeed the record demonstrates that some Vermont doctors view targeted detailing based on prescriber-identifying information as "very helpful" because it allows detailers to shape their messages to each doctor's practice. Even the United States, which appeared here in support of Vermont, took care to dispute the State's "unwarranted view that the dangers of new drugs outweigh their benefits to patients." There are divergent views regarding detailing and the prescription of brand-name drugs. Under the Constitution, resolution of that debate must result from free and uninhibited speech. As one Vermont physician put it: "We have a saying in medicine, information is power. And the more you know, or anyone knows, the better decisions can be made." There are similar sayings in law, including that "information is not in itself harmful, that people will perceive their own best interests if only they are well enough informed, and that the best means to that end is to open the channels of communication rather than to close them." *Virginia Bd. of Pharmacy*. The choice, "between the dangers of suppressing information, and the dangers of its misuse if it is freely available," is one that "the First Amendment makes for us."

Vermont may be displeased that detailers who use prescriber-identifying information are effective in promoting brand-name drugs. The State can express that view through its own speech. But a State's failure to persuade does not allow it to hamstring the opposition. The State may not burden the speech of others in order to tilt public debate in a preferred direction. "The commercial marketplace, like other spheres of our social and cultural life, provides a forum where ideas and information flourish. Some of the ideas and information are vital, some of slight worth. But the general rule is that the speaker and the audience, not the government, assess the value of the information presented."

The capacity of technology to find and publish personal information, including records required by the government, presents serious and unresolved issues with respect to personal privacy and the dignity it seeks to secure. In considering how to protect those interests, however, the State cannot engage in content-based discrimination to advance its own side of a debate.

If Vermont's statute provided that prescriber-identifying information could not be sold or disclosed except in narrow circumstances then the State might have a stronger position. Here, however, the State gives possessors of the information broad discretion and wide latitude in disclosing the information, while at the same time restricting the information's use by some speakers and for some purposes, even while the State itself can use the information to counter the speech it seeks to suppress. Privacy is a concept too integral to the person and a right too essential to freedom to allow its manipulation to support just those ideas the government prefers.

When it enacted § 4631(d), the Vermont Legislature found that the "marketplace for ideas on medicine safety and effectiveness is frequently one-sided in that brand-name companies invest in expensive pharmaceutical marketing campaigns to doctors." "The goals of marketing programs," the legislature said, "are often in conflict with the goals of the state." The text of § 4631(d), associated legislative findings, and the record developed in the District Court establish that Vermont enacted its law for this end. The State has burdened a form of protected expression that it found too persuasive. At the same time, the State has left unburdened those speakers whose messages are in accord with its own views. This the State cannot do.

JUSTICE BREYER, with whom JUSTICE GINSBURG and JUSTICE KAGAN join, dissenting. dissent

The Vermont statute before us adversely affects expression in one, and only one, way. It deprives pharmaceutical and data-mining companies of data, collected pursuant to the government's regulatory mandate, that could help pharmaceutical companies create better sales messages. In my view, this effect on expression is inextricably related to a lawful governmental effort to regulate a commercial enterprise. The First Amendment does not require courts to apply a special "heightened" standard of review when reviewing such an effort. And, in any event, the statute meets the First

Amendment standard this Court has previously applied when the government seeks to regulate commercial speech. For any or all of these reasons, the Court should uphold the statute as constitutional.

Because many, perhaps most, activities of human beings living together in communities take place through speech, and because speech-related risks and offsetting justifications differ depending upon context, this Court has distinguished for First Amendment purposes among different contexts in which speech takes place. Thus, the First Amendment imposes tight constraints upon government efforts to restrict, e.g., "core" political speech, while imposing looser constraints when the government seeks to restrict, e.g., commercial speech, the speech of its own employees, or the regulation-related speech of a firm subject to a traditional regulatory program.

These test-related distinctions reflect the constitutional importance of maintaining a free marketplace of ideas, a marketplace that provides access to "social, political, esthetic, moral, and other ideas and experiences." Without such a marketplace, the public could not freely choose a government pledged to implement policies that reflect the people's informed will.

At the same time, our cases make clear that the First Amendment offers considerably less protection to the maintenance of a free marketplace for goods and services. The Court has also normally applied a yet more lenient approach to ordinary commercial or regulatory legislation that affects speech in less direct ways.

To apply a strict First Amendment standard virtually as a matter of course when a court reviews ordinary economic regulatory programs (even if that program has a modest impact upon a firm's ability to shape a commercial message) would work at cross-purposes with this more basic constitutional approach. Since ordinary regulatory programs can affect speech, particularly commercial speech, in myriad ways, to apply a "heightened" First Amendment standard of review whenever such a program burdens speech would transfer from legislatures to judges the primary power to weigh ends and to choose means, threatening to distort or undermine legitimate legislative objectives. To apply a "heightened" standard of review in such cases as a matter of course would risk what then-Justice Rehnquist, dissenting in *Central Hudson,* described as a "return to the bygone era of *Lochner*, in which it was common practice for this Court to strike down economic regulations adopted by a State based on the Court's own notions of the most appropriate means for the State to implement its considered policies."

The Court (suggesting a standard yet stricter than *Central Hudson*) says that we must give content-based restrictions that burden speech "heightened" scrutiny. It adds that "commercial speech is no exception." And the Court then emphasizes that this is a case involving both "content-based" and "speaker-based" restrictions.

But neither of these categories—"content-based" nor "speaker-based"—has ever before justified greater scrutiny when regulatory activity affects commercial speech.

Turning to the constitutional merits, I believe Vermont's statute survives application of *Central Hudson*'s "intermediate" commercial speech standard as well as any more limited "economic regulation" test.

Vermont has thus developed a record that sufficiently shows that its statute meaningfully furthers substantial state interests. Neither the majority nor respondents suggests any equally effective "more limited" restriction. And the First Amendment harm that Vermont's statute works is, at most, modest. I consequently conclude that, even if we apply an "intermediate" test such as that in *Central Hudson*, this statute is constitutional.

Points for Discussion

1. **How do courts determine whether speech is commercial or noncommercial?** When the government regulates traditional advertising, as in *44 Liquormart*, determining whether the speech is or is not "commercial speech" and thus falling within the domain of *Central Hudson* and its progeny is not difficult. Advertising the price of vodka is obviously commercial speech, falling within the often-repeated statement in Supreme Court cases defining commercial speech as "speech that does no more than propose a commercial transaction." Yet as *Sorrell* illustrates, in many other contexts the correct classification is not so obvious. Much of our public discourse is *about* commercial transactions, but certainly we would not treat an article in *The Wall Street Journal* discussing a proposed corporate merger as commercial speech. Information about the prescribing habits of doctors at issue in *Sorrell* certainly had commercial implications and was integral to pharmaceutical companies' enormous financial interests, but it was also public health and economic information *about* health and commercial "transactions," though not speech that literally "proposed" a commercial transaction. This is a vexing First Amendment conundrum.

2. **How should we classify speech that on its face is purely "informational," perhaps even "political," yet plainly engaged in to assist in commercial marketing?** An intriguing example of the problem is *Hunter v. Virginia State Bar*, 744 S.E.2d 611 (Va. 2013), *cert. denied*, 570 U.S. 919 (2013), in which lawyer Horace Hunter wrote a blog titled "This Week in Richmond Criminal Defense." The blog was accessible to the general public through a link on the website for Hunter's law firm and directly through a routine internet search. Hunter's blog contained a variety of content relating to legal affairs and court decisions. Some

of the posts contained Hunter's commentary on national legal events, such as the controversy surrounding the dismissal of U.S. attorneys while Alberto Gonzales was serving as attorney general. Others described legal decisions by state or federal courts in which Hunter was not a participating lawyer. The majority of entries, however, described the facts and outcomes of cases in which Hunter served as counsel for a criminal defendant and which resulted in a favorable outcome for the defendant. A divided Virginia Supreme Court ruled that Hunter's blog was commercial speech, because one of his motives in writing the blog was to attract clients. Two justices dissented, arguing that Hunter's blog was political speech and ought not be deemed "lawyer advertising" just because one of his motives was to attract clients. Rodney Smolla, co-author of this casebook, represented Hunter in the case.

Do you see the similarities between this Point for Discussion and the one about corporate PR campaigns and greenwashing in the previous section?

3. **How and why do courts sometimes avoid the classification issue?** Whether speech is classified as commercial or noncommercial will affect whether a content-based regulation of the speech receives strict or intermediate scrutiny. But, as you've just learned, it is sometimes difficult to know how speech should be classified. When confronted with this dilemma, courts sometimes dodge the issue by finding it unnecessary to resolve because the regulation at issue would fail even the lower level of scrutiny. That is precisely what the Supreme Court did in *Sorrell.* In the opening part of his opinion, Justice Kennedy uses language suggesting that the Vermont law is regulating fully protected speech and should be subject to strict scrutiny. But he then shifts to doing a commercial speech analysis and resolves the case using *Central Hudson*'s intermediate scrutiny. As Justice Kennedy explained, he could do this because "the outcome is the same whether a special commercial speech inquiry or a stricter form of judicial scrutiny is applied."

   As Justice Kennedy's resolution suggests, the decision concerning which level of scrutiny to apply only matters if a regulation would be upheld under a lower level of scrutiny, such as intermediate scrutiny, but would be struck down under a more rigorous standard, such as strict scrutiny. If a law fails even the lower standard, a court need not reach the question of whether a higher level of scrutiny is required by the facts. Judge J. Harvie Wilkinson of the Fourth Circuit analogized the technique used in *Sorrell* to ski slopes. "The Supreme Court in *Sorrell* could rightly say that a law failing intermediate scrutiny would also fail strict scrutiny. After all, if you can't ski a blue run successfully, you obviously can't tackle a double black diamond. Yet failing to navigate a treacherous course does not imply an inability to handle a gentler slope. Likewise, that a statute fails strict scrutiny means little for how it would fare under a more lenient intermediate standard." *Recht v. Morrisey*, 32 F.4th 398, 410 (4th Cir. 2022) (Wilkinson, J.).

4. **Is the Supreme Court wrong to treat commercial speech as protected by the First Amendment?** Scholars and jurists have long debated the level of constitutional protection that commercial speech should receive. Many prominent constitutional scholars have argued that the Supreme Court is wrong in extending First Amendment protection to commercial speech. Professor Edwin Baker, for example, thought that commercial speech deserves zero constitutional protection because "it lacks the crucial connections with individual liberty and self-realization that are central to the justifications for the constitutional protection of speech." C. Edwin Baker, *Human Liberty and Freedom of Speech* 196 (1989). *See also* Thomas H. Jackson & John Calvin Jeffries, Jr., *Commercial Speech: Economic Due Process and the First Amendment*, 65 Va. L. Rev. 1, 5–6 (1979) ("The First Amendment guarantee of freedom of speech and press protects only certain identifiable values. Chief among them is effective self-government. Additionally, the First Amendment may protect the opportunity for individual self-fulfillment through free expression. Neither value is implicated by governmental regulation of commercial speech."); Lillian R. BeVier, *The First Amendment and Political Speech: An Inquiry into the Substance and Limits of Principle*, 30 Stan. L. Rev. 299 (1978) (arguing against protection for commercial speech because it bears no relation to processes of politics and public decision-making); Ronald K.L. Collins & David Skover, *Commerce and Communication*, 71 Tex. L. Rev. 697, 29–32 (1993) (critiquing protection of commercial speech); Steven H. Shiffrin, *The First Amendment and Economic Regulation: Away From a General Theory of the First Amendment*, 78 Nw. U. L. Rev. 1212, 122–51 (1983) (arguing against protection for commercial speech). Other scholars believe the opposite, that commercial speech should receive the same protection as noncommercial speech. Rodney A. Smolla, *Information, Imagery, and the First Amendment: A Case for Expansive Protection of Commercial Speech*, 71 Tex. L. Rev. 777 (1993); Martin H. Redish, *The First Amendment in the Marketplace: Commercial Speech and the Values of Free Expression*, 39 Geo. Wash. L. Rev. 429 (1971).

5. ***Lochner* by another name? Is the Court indirectly bringing back economic substantive due process?** In a different constitutional law class, you will study an often criticized and much debated decision called *Lochner v. New York*, 198 U.S. 45 (1905), in which the Court struck down a New York law regulating the number of hours bakers could work. To reach this result, the Court implied into the Due Process Clause of the Fourteenth Amendment a substantive "liberty of contract" right and held that the New York law infringed on this right. The Court in later years repudiated this jurisprudence and instead applies highly deferential rational basis review to garden-variety economic regulations. As Justice William Douglas famously explained, "The day is gone when this Court uses the Due Process Clause of the Fourteenth Amendment to strike down state laws, regulatory of business and industrial conditions, because they may be unwise, improvident, or out of harmony with a particular school of thought." *Williamson*

v. Lee Optical of Okla., Inc., 348 U.S. 483, 488 (1955). In his dissent in *Sorrell*, Justice Breyer warned, as Chief Justice Rehnquist had in earlier opinions, that the Court's commercial speech jurisprudence threatens to revive the *Lochner*-like judicial second-guessing of economic regulations. Is he right? *See* Robert Post & Amanda Shanor, *Adam Smith's First Amendment*, 128 Harv. L. Rev. 165 (2015); Amanda Shanor, *The New Lochner*, 2016 Wis. L. Rev. 133 (2016).

You Be the Law Clerk!
What speech matters?

Imagine you are clerking for a newly appointed Supreme Court justice, who has told you that she is not a particularly strong adherent to *stare decisis* and is willing to reexamine precedents. A commercial speech case is pending before the Court, scheduled for oral argument a few weeks after the Super Bowl. The justice calls you into her chamber immediately after Super Bowl weekend, several weeks before the scheduled oral argument. She says that she has been mulling over the level of constitutional protection that commercial speech should receive and that her mind is open to every possible standard from "zero protection" to the current intermediate protection of *Central Hudson* to the full level of protection that noncommercial speech receives. She wants you to write a memorandum discussing the pros and cons of the various approaches. Somewhat impishly, she brings up the Super Bowl. "You know, I spent the day with our family and friends watching the entire ritual. The broadcasts included all kinds of patriotic and political speech, including recitations from the Preamble to the Constitution, images of armed forces overseas, the National Anthem and God Bless America, and even a short address by the president. It also included the concert at halftime, and of course the game itself. Then, of course, all the commercials. I noticed that some people at the party were really zoned in on the game, but a lot of folks were not. Many were most moved by the political messages. Others seemed to pay attention only to the commercials. It made me think about what speech really matters—politics, sports, entertainment, advertising—and why?" How would you craft the memorandum for the justice?

4. Regulations of Professional Advertising: Should Government Have Greater Leeway to Regulate Lawyer Advertising?

In *Virginia Board of Pharmacy*, you learned that regulations of professional advertising, in that case by pharmacists, trigger the First Amendment and will sometimes be struck down. In this section, we further explore this topic by focusing on the constitutionality of laws regulating lawyer advertising, a subject that should be of keen interest to students preparing to enter the legal profession.

While the commercial speech doctrine was still in its infancy in the 1970s, the Supreme Court decided its first major lawyer advertising case, *Bates v. State Bar of Arizona*, holding that the legal profession's long-standing ban on lawyer advertising violated the First Amendment. This, in turn, spurred a series of cases, constituting a special subset of the commercial speech doctrine, dealing with advertising by professionals. Many of those cases focused on advertising by lawyers.

Lawyers in the 19th century often advertised. Among them was Abraham Lincoln.

LINCOLN & HERNDON,
ATTORNEYS AND COUNSELLORS AT LAW, will practice in the courts of Law and Chancery in this State.—Springfield, Ill. aug5

But as regulation of the practice of law gathered steam at the turn of the century, state bar associations and state supreme courts became aggressively hostile to all forms of lawyer advertising and marketing. The practice of law, it was argued, was supposed to be a learned profession, not a business. At times, the state bars enforced the clampdown with extraordinary fervor. A lawyer could be censured even for allowing a journalist to do a story profiling his firm's practice, for hiring a public relations expert, for soliciting a speaking engagement, or for holding a press conference. Even sending a Christmas card to a client could get a lawyer in ethical difficulty, unless the client was also a personal friend. *See* Rodney A. Smolla, *Law of Lawyer Advertising* § 1:4 (2022 ed.)

This all suddenly changed with *Bates*. Two Arizona lawyers, John Bates and Van O'Steen, left their jobs at a legal aid society to start a private practice, aimed at providing legal services at modest fees to people of moderate income who did not qualify for governmental legal aid. They took on only routine matters, such as uncontested divorces, uncontested adoptions, simple personal bankruptcies, and name changes. After two years, they realized that they could only remain viable if they advertised. And so they took out an ad in *The Arizona Republic*, a Phoenix newspaper.

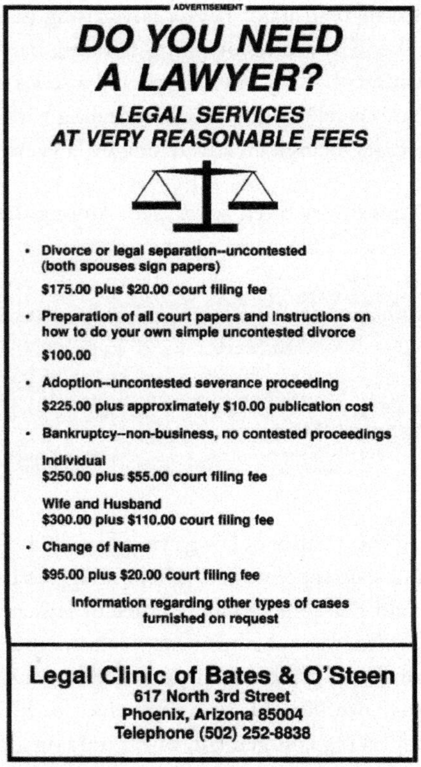

Bates v. State Bar of Arizona

Supreme Court of the United States, 1977
433 U.S. 350

MR. JUSTICE BLACKMUN delivered the opinion of the Court.

As part of its regulation of the Arizona Bar, the Supreme Court of that State has imposed and enforces a disciplinary rule that restricts advertising by attorneys.

Last Term, in *Virginia Bd. of Pharmacy*, the Court considered the validity under the First Amendment of a Virginia statute declaring that a pharmacist was guilty of "unprofessional conduct" if he advertised prescription drug prices. Although acknowledging that the State had a strong interest in maintaining professionalism among pharmacists, this Court concluded that the proffered justifications were inadequate to support the advertising ban. High professional standards were assured in large part by the close regulation to which pharmacists in Virginia were subject. And we observed that "on close inspection it is seen that the State's protectiveness of its citizens rests in large measure on the advantages of their being kept in ignorance." But we noted the presence of a potent alternative to this "highly paternalistic" approach: "That alternative is to assume that this information is not in itself harmful, that people will perceive their own best interests if only they are well enough informed, and that the best means to that end is to open the channels of communication rather than to close them." The choice between the dangers of suppressing information and the dangers arising from its free flow was seen as precisely the choice "that the First Amendment makes for us."

We have set out this detailed summary of the *Pharmacy* opinion because the conclusion that Arizona's disciplinary rule is violative of the First Amendment might be said to flow a fortiori from it. Like the Virginia statutes, the disciplinary rule serves to inhibit the free flow of commercial information and to keep the public in ignorance. Because of the possibility, however, that the differences among professions might bring different constitutional considerations into play, we specifically reserved judgment as to other professions.

The issue presently before us is a narrow one. First, we need not address the peculiar problems associated with advertising claims relating to the quality of legal services. Such claims probably are not susceptible of precise measurement or verification and, under some circumstances, might well be deceptive or misleading to the public, or even false. Appellee does not suggest, nor do we perceive, that appellants' advertisement contained claims, extravagant or otherwise, as to the quality of services. Accordingly, we leave that issue for another day. Second, we also need not resolve the problems associated with in-person solicitation of clients at the hospital room or the accident site, or in any other situation that breeds undue influence by attorneys or their agents or "runners." Activity of that kind might well pose dangers of overreaching and misrepresentation not encountered in newspaper announcement advertising. Hence, this issue also is not before us. Third, we note that appellee's criticism of advertising by attorneys does not apply with much force to some of the basic factual content of advertising: information as to the attorney's name, address, and telephone number, office hours, and the like.

The heart of the dispute before us today is whether lawyers also may constitutionally advertise the prices at which certain routine services will be performed. Numerous justifications are proffered for the restriction of such price advertising. We consider each in turn:

1. The Adverse Effect on Professionalism. Appellee places particular emphasis on the adverse effects that it feels price advertising will have on the legal profession. The key to professionalism, it is argued, is the sense of pride that involvement in the discipline generates. It is claimed that price advertising will bring about commercialization, which will undermine the attorney's sense of dignity and self-worth. The hustle of the marketplace will adversely affect the profession's service orientation, and irreparably

damage the delicate balance between the lawyer's need to earn and his obligation selflessly to serve. Advertising is also said to erode the client's trust in his attorney: Once the client perceives that the lawyer is motivated by profit, his confidence that the attorney is acting out of a commitment to the client's welfare is jeopardized. And advertising is said to tarnish the dignified public image of the profession.

We recognize, of course, and commend the spirit of public service with which the profession of law is practiced and to which it is dedicated. The present Members of this Court, licensed attorneys all, could not feel otherwise. And we would have reason to pause if we felt that our decision today would undercut that spirit. But we find the postulated connection between advertising and the erosion of true professionalism to be severely strained. At its core, the argument presumes that attorneys must conceal from themselves and from their clients the real-life fact that lawyers earn their livelihood at the bar. We suspect that few attorneys engage in such self-deception. And rare is the client, moreover, even one of the modest means, who enlists the aid of an attorney with the expectation that his services will be rendered free of charge. In fact, the American Bar Association advises that an attorney should reach "a clear agreement with his client as to the basis of the fee charges to be made," and that this is to be done "as soon as feasible after a lawyer has been employed." If the commercial basis of the relationship is to be promptly disclosed on ethical grounds, once the client is in the office, it seems inconsistent to condemn the candid revelation of the same information before he arrives at that office.

Moreover, the assertion that advertising will diminish the attorney's reputation in the community is open to question. Bankers and engineers advertise, and yet these professions are not regarded as undignified. In fact, it has been suggested that the failure of lawyers to advertise creates public disillusionment with the profession. The absence of advertising may be seen to reflect the profession's failure to reach out and serve the community: Studies reveal that many persons do not obtain counsel even when they perceive a need because of the feared price of services or because of an inability to locate a competent attorney. Indeed, cynicism with regard to the profession may be created by the fact that it long has publicly eschewed advertising, while condoning the actions of the attorney who structures his social or civic associations so as to provide contacts with potential clients.

It appears that the ban on advertising originated as a rule of etiquette and not as a rule of ethics. Early lawyers in Great Britain viewed the law as a form of public service, rather than as a means of earning a living, and they looked down on "trade" as unseemly. Eventually, the attitude toward advertising fostered by this view evolved into an aspect of the ethics of the profession. But habit and tradition are not in themselves an adequate answer to a constitutional challenge. In this day, we do not belittle the person who earns his living by the strength of his arm or the force of his mind.

Since the belief that lawyers are somehow "above" trade has become an anachronism, the historical foundation for the advertising restraint has crumbled.

2. The Inherently Misleading Nature of Attorney Advertising. It is argued that advertising of legal services inevitably will be misleading (a) because such services are so individualized with regard to content and quality as to prevent informed comparison on the basis of an advertisement, (b) because the consumer of legal services is unable to determine in advance just what services he needs, and (c) because advertising by attorneys will highlight irrelevant factors and fail to show the relevant factor of skill.

We are not persuaded that restrained professional advertising by lawyers inevitably will be misleading. Although many services performed by attorneys are indeed unique, it is doubtful that any attorney would or could advertise fixed prices for services of that type. The only services that lend themselves to advertising are the routine ones: the uncontested divorce, the simple adoption, the uncontested personal bankruptcy, the change of name, and the like, the very services advertised by appellants. Although the precise service demanded in each task may vary slightly, and although legal services are not fungible, these facts do not make advertising misleading so long as the attorney does the necessary work at the advertised price. The argument that legal services are so unique that fixed rates cannot meaningfully be established is refuted by the record in this case: The appellee, State Bar itself sponsors a Legal Services Program in which the participating attorneys agree to perform services like those advertised by the appellants at standardized rates. Indeed, until the decision of this Court in *Goldfarb v. Virginia State Bar*, 421 U.S. 773 (1975), the Maricopa County Bar Association apparently had a schedule of suggested minimum fees for standard legal tasks. We thus find of little force the assertion that advertising is misleading because of an inherent lack of standardization in legal services.

The second component of the argument that advertising ignores the diagnostic role fares little better. It is unlikely that many people go to an attorney merely to ascertain if they have a clean bill of legal health. Rather, attorneys are likely to be employed to perform specific tasks. Although the client may not know the detail involved in performing the task, he no doubt is able to identify the service he desires at the level of generality to which advertising lends itself.

The third component is not without merit: Advertising does not provide a complete foundation on which to select an attorney. But it seems peculiar to deny the consumer, on the ground that the information is incomplete, at least some of the relevant information needed to reach an informed decision. The alternative, the prohibition of advertising, serves only to restrict the information that flows to consumers. Moreover, the argument assumes that the public is not sophisticated enough to realize the limitations of advertising, and that the public is better kept in ignorance than trusted with correct but incomplete information. We suspect the argument rests on an underestimation of the public. In any event, we view as dubious any justification that is based on the benefits of public ignorance. *See Virginia Bd. of Pharmacy*. Although, of course, the bar retains the power to correct omissions that have the effect of presenting an inaccurate picture, the preferred remedy is more disclosure, rather than less. If the naivete of the public will cause advertising by attorneys to be misleading, then it is the bar's role to assure that the populace is sufficiently informed as to enable it to place advertising in its proper perspective.

3. The Adverse Effect on the Administration of Justice. Advertising is said to have the undesirable effect of stirring up litigation. The judicial machinery is designed to serve those who feel sufficiently aggrieved to bring forward their claims. Advertising, it is argued, serves to encourage the assertion of legal rights in the courts, thereby undesirably unsettling societal repose. There is even a suggestion of barratry.

But advertising by attorneys is not an unmitigated source of harm to the administration of justice. It may offer great benefits. Although advertising might increase the use of the judicial machinery, we cannot accept the notion that it is always better for a person to suffer a wrong silently than to redress it by legal action. As the bar acknowledges, "the middle 70% of our population is not being reached or served adequately by the legal profession." Among the reasons for this underutilization is fear of the cost, and an inability to locate a suitable lawyer. Advertising can help to solve this acknowledged problem: Advertising is the traditional mechanism in a free-market economy for a supplier to inform a potential purchaser of the availability and terms of exchange. The disciplinary rule at issue likely has served to burden access to legal services, particularly for the not-quite-poor and the unknowledgeable. A rule allowing restrained advertising would be in accord with the bar's obligation to "facilitate the process of intelligent selection of lawyers, and to assist in making legal services fully available."

4. The Undesirable Economic Effects of Advertising. It is claimed that advertising will increase the overhead costs of the profession, and that these costs then will be passed along to consumers in the form of increased fees. Moreover, it is claimed that the additional cost of practice will create a substantial entry barrier, deterring or preventing young attorneys from penetrating the market and entrenching the position of the bar's established members.

These two arguments seem dubious at best. Neither distinguishes lawyers from others, and neither appears relevant to the First Amendment. The ban on advertising serves to increase the difficulty of discovering the lowest cost seller of acceptable ability. As a result, to this extent attorneys are isolated from competition, and the incentive to price competitively is reduced. Although it is true that the effect of advertising on the price of services has not been demonstrated, there is revealing evidence with regard to products; where consumers have the benefit of price advertising, retail prices often are dramatically lower than they would be without advertising. It is entirely possible that advertising will serve to reduce, not advance, the cost of legal services to the consumer.

The entry-barrier argument is equally unpersuasive. In the absence of advertising, an attorney must rely on his contacts with the community to generate a flow of business. In view of the time necessary to develop such contacts, the ban in fact serves to perpetuate the market position of established attorneys. Consideration of entry-barrier problems would urge that advertising be allowed so as to aid the new competitor in penetrating the market.

5. The Adverse Effect of Advertising on the Quality of Service. It is argued that the attorney may advertise a given "package" of service at a set price, and will be inclined to provide, by indiscriminate use, the standard package regardless of whether it fits the client's needs.

Restraints on advertising, however, are an ineffective way of deterring shoddy work. An attorney who is inclined to cut quality will do so regardless of the rule on advertising. And the advertisement of a standardized fee does not necessarily mean that the services offered are undesirably standardized. Indeed, the assertion that an attorney who advertises a standard fee will cut quality is substantially undermined by the fixed-fee schedule of appellee's own prepaid Legal Services Program. Even if advertising leads to the creation of "legal clinics" like that of appellants' clinics that emphasize standardized procedures for routine problems, it is possible that such clinics will improve service by reducing the likelihood of error.

restraing advertising not a good way to deter bad work

6. The Difficulties of Enforcement. Finally, it is argued that the wholesale restriction is justified by the problems of enforcement if any other course is taken. Because the public lacks sophistication in legal matters, it may be particularly susceptible to misleading or deceptive advertising by lawyers. After-the-fact action by the consumer lured by such advertising may not provide a realistic restraint because of the inability of the layman to assess whether the service he has received meets professional standards. Thus, the vigilance of a regulatory agency will be required. But because of the numerous purveyors of services, the overseeing of advertising will be burdensome.

It is at least somewhat incongruous for the opponents of advertising to extol the virtues and altruism of the legal profession at one point, and, at another, to assert that its members will seize the opportunity to mislead and distort. We suspect that, with advertising, most lawyers will behave as they always have: They will abide by their solemn oaths to uphold the integrity and honor of their profession and of the legal system. For every attorney who overreaches through advertising, there will be thousands of others who will be candid and honest and straightforward. And, of course, it will be in the latter's interest, as in other cases of misconduct at the bar, to assist in weeding out those few who abuse their trust.

In sum, we are not persuaded that any of the proffered justifications rise to the level of an acceptable reason for the suppression of all advertising by attorneys.

The constitutional issue in this case is only whether the State may prevent the publication in a newspaper of appellants' truthful advertisement concerning the availability and terms of routine legal services. We rule simply that the flow of such information may not be restrained, and we therefore hold the present application of the disciplinary rule against appellants to be violative of the First Amendment.

[Chief Justice Burger's opinion concurring in part and dissenting in part is omitted, as is Justice Powell's opinion concurring in part and dissenting in part, which was joined by Justice Stewart. Justice Rehnquist's dissent is also omitted.]

Points for Discussion

1. **What happened after *Bates*?** The Court's decision in *Bates* commanded a full majority of five justices. The concurring and dissenting opinions were omitted because the issues they raise have been largely addressed in the Court's many post-*Bates* opinions on the regulation of professional advertising, many of which, like *Bates*, involve advertising by lawyers. Following *Bates*, the Court issued a long series of lawyer advertising decisions:

   - *Ohralik v. Ohio State Bar Association*, 436 U.S. 447 (1978), held that the First Amendment did not bar rules prohibiting in-person solicitation of clients.

   - *In re Primus*, 436 U.S. 412 (1978), decided the same day as *Ohralik*, held that the First Amendment did protect solicitation by public interest lawyers acting on behalf of political and ideological causes.

   - *In re R.M.J.*, 455 U.S. 191 (1982), upheld lawyers' right to advertise their areas of practice and the courts to which they are admitted.

   - *Zauderer v. Office of Disciplinary Counsel*, 471 U.S. 626 (1985), struck down many limitations on lawyer advertising imposed in Ohio, including prohibitions on self-recommendation and the use of illustrations in advertising. The Court emphasized that the burden of justifying restrictions was on the state. The Court, however, upheld certain disclosure requirements, including one that lawyers taking cases on a contingency-fee basis must explain to clients that clients might still be liable for litigation costs, as opposed to fees, even if their lawsuits were unsuccessful.

- *Shapero v. Kentucky Bar Association*, 486 U.S. 466 (1988), struck down a Kentucky restriction categorically prohibiting lawyers from soliciting business for pecuniary gain by sending truthful and non-deceptive letters to potential clients known to face particular legal problems.

- *Peel v. Attorney Registration and Disciplinary Commission*, 496 U.S. 91 (1990), held that Illinois violated an attorney's rights by prohibiting him from including on his letterhead the fact that he was a "Certified Civil Trial Specialist" by the National Board of Trial Advocacy.

- *Ibanez v. Florida Department of Business and Professional Regulation*, 512 U.S. 136 (1994), upheld the First Amendment right of a member of the Florida Bar to advertise that she was also a certified public accountant and certified financial planner.

- *Florida Bar v. Went For It, Inc.*, 515 U.S. 618 (1995), upheld a Florida rule prohibiting personal injury lawyers from sending targeted direct-mail solicitations to victims and their relatives for 30 days after an accident or disaster. The Florida Bar submitted a 106-page summary of its two-year study of lawyer advertising and solicitation to support its rule. That summary, the Court emphasized, contained data—both statistical and anecdotal—supporting the Bar's contentions that the Florida public viewed direct-mail solicitations in the immediate wake of accidents "as an intrusion on privacy that reflects poorly upon the profession." Justice Kennedy wrote a pointed dissent that was joined by three other justices. He noted that when a serious accident occurs, "it is often urgent at once to investigate the occurrence, identify witnesses, and preserve evidence," so that vital interests are at stake "when by law an attorney cannot direct a letter to the victim or the family explaining this simple fact and offering competent legal assistance." Justice Kennedy dismissed the privacy argument by noting that the recipients of mail are "not a captive audience" and that all they need do is "take the short, though regular, journey from mail box to trash can."

- *Edenfield v. Fane*, 507 U.S. 761 (1993), while not a lawyer advertising case, is nonetheless important as a foil for the Court's lawyer advertising opinions. The Court in *Edenfield* held that a prophylactic ban on in-person solicitation of new clients by certified public accountants violated the First Amendment, ruling that the dangers of overreaching attendant to in-person solicitation by lawyers, particularly of accident victims, simply did not apply to solicitation by accountants.

2. **Does the First Amendment provide less protection for lawyer advertising than other forms of advertising?** First Amendment protection of commercial speech has steadily expanded since the 1980s. Notwithstanding that expansion, First Amendment law remains unclear as to whether lawyer advertising is entitled to the same robust protection as other forms of advertising. Rodney Smolla, co-author of this casebook, captured the dilemma facing legal professionals:

> Professionalism abhors self-promotion, but the general marketplace adores it. American judges and lawyers, at once Americans and lawyers, are caught betwixt and between. What are they to do? When judges run for office, may they engage in self-promotion? What if that self-promotion includes articulation of their views or judicial persona—such as portraying themselves as tough on crime? When lawyers advertise, do they get the benefit of the same relatively high levels of protection for commercial speech enjoyed by other advertisers in the general marketplace? Or is lawyer advertising better understood as a poor relation that receives a second-class level of commercial speech protection that only applies to plain-vanilla *informational* advertising?

Rodney A. Smolla, *Regulating the Speech of Judges and Lawyers: The First Amendment and the Soul of the Profession*, 66 Fla. L. Rev. 961, 980–81 (2014). Advertising in the general marketplace is all about being self-promoting and self-laudatory, often with a healthy dose of hyperbole and puffery. Advertising often involves music, humor, imagery, emotion, and many other visual and auditory effects that have nothing much to do with the actual product or service. It is unclear, however, whether lawyers are permitted to use similar advertising devices or may instead be required to exercise restraint, limiting advertising only to what is "dignified" and conveys objectively simple "plain vanilla" information about legal services. States around the country differ significantly as to whether they permit lawyer advertising that uses music, humor, or appeals to emotion. Many states, for example, prohibit forms of self-promotion and comparison to one's competitors in the legal profession that would be common fare and outside the pale of regulation in the general marketplace. The Supreme Court has yet to confront whether the First Amendment permits regulation limiting lawyers to advertising that is simple and dignified. On the judicial front, the Court has indicated that a state may not prohibit candidates for judicial office from announcing their views on disputed legal and political issues but may prohibit the candidates from personally soliciting funds for their campaigns. *Republican Party of Minn. v. White*, 536 U.S. 765 (2002); *Williams-Yulee v. Florida Bar*, 575 U.S. 433 (2015).

3. **Are there special First Amendment rules permitting heavy regulation of "professional speech"?** A number of federal appeals courts have adopted a rule that gives the government greater leeway to regulate professional speech even outside of the narrow context of advertising. This rule has come to be known as the "professional speech doctrine." The courts defined "professionals" as individuals who provide personalized services to clients and who are subject to a generally applicable licensing and regulatory regime. The courts, in turn, treated "professional speech" as any speech by those individuals that is based on their expert knowledge and judgment. Government regulation of such professional speech, the courts reasoned, should not be judged by the strict scrutiny test normally applicable to content-based regulation of speech, but instead should be judged under some lower standard, such as rational basis or intermediate scrutiny review. In *National Institute of Family and Life Advocates v. Becerra*, 585 U.S. 755 (2018), the Supreme Court appeared to reject the professional speech doctrine, holding that no such exception to normal First Amendment principles exists. The Court recognized the vast reach of the professional speech doctrine as a governmental device for exercising leverage over the expressive freedom of citizens engaging in a seemingly limitless array of occupations. "As defined by the courts of appeals," the Court said, "the professional-speech doctrine would cover a wide array of individuals—doctors, lawyers, nurses, physical therapists, truck drivers, bartenders, barbers, and many others."

You Be the Judge!
Call 1-800-PIT-BULL

John R. Pape and Marc A. Chandler were personal injury attorneys in Fort Lauderdale, Florida, practicing as the firm Pape & Chandler. They adopted the image of a pit bull dog as an advertising device. Two images of the faces of pit bulls, each about the size of a quarter, appeared on the top of their firm letterhead. The firm's toll-free telephone number was 1-800-PIT-BULL. The firm's website was similar: www.800pitbull.com. The pit bull logo and pit bull phone number appeared in the firm's television ads. For these actions Pape and Chandler were disciplined by the Florida Supreme Court. The court agreed with the State Bar that the pit bull advertising violated two provisions of the legal ethics rules. To the extent that using the pit bull imagery connoted that the lawyers were more aggressive in fighting for clients than other lawyers, the court reasoned, the advertising was unethical. "This Court would not condone an advertisement that stated that a lawyer will get results through combative and vicious tactics that will maim, scar, or harm the opposing party, conduct that would violate our Rules of Professional Conduct. We construe the prohibitions on advertising statements that characterize the quality of lawyer services and depictions that are false or misleading to prohibit a lawyer from advertising his or her services by suggesting behavior, conduct, or tactics that are contrary to our Rules of Professional Conduct." The court also held that the pit bull advertising devices could be banned because they "demean all lawyers and thereby harm both the legal profession and the public's trust and confidence in our system of justice." The U.S. Supreme Court refused to hear the case. *Florida Bar v. Pape*, 918 So. 2d 240 (Fla. 2005), *cert. denied*, 547 U.S. 1041 (2006). (Co-author Rodney Smolla represented Pape and Chandler in their effort to have the U.S. Supreme Court review the case.)

Imagine that the same pit bull advertising were to be used by lawyers in another state, with identical facts, and that the high court of that state, following the lead of Florida, also held that the lawyers had violated the state's disciplinary rules. This time around, however, the U.S. Supreme Court does agree to review the matter. If you were a justice on the Court, how would you rule, and why?

Test Your Knowledge

To assess your understanding of the material in this chapter, click here to take a quiz.

CHAPTER ELEVEN

May Government Regulate Speech to Promote Effective Government Operations?

Government as Landlord, Educator, Employer, Funder, and Speaker

In the preceding chapters, we examined various ways in which governments regulate people's speech and the rules for determining whether these regulations are constitutional. But governments—federal, state, and local—do much more than regulate speech. Governments perform a vast range of functions from defending the country to collecting trash to educating children. To fulfill their many responsibilities, governments hire and manage employees, oversee government properties, operate public institutions such as prisons, libraries, and schools, and spend vast sums of money to purchase goods and services and incentivize private behavior.

Governments could not perform these functions if they could not regulate speech. Public school teachers could not teach if they could not control disruptive student speech. Judges could not conduct trials if the public could hold rallies in their courtrooms. Government employers could not evaluate the quality of their employees' work if they could not consider the content of the employees' speech. And government funders could not decide which artists to fund if they could not consider the content of the artists' grant proposals.

In this chapter, we explore the rules for when the government may regulate speech to further the government's interests as a property owner, educator, employer, and funder. As in other areas of First Amendment jurisprudence, the topic requires judges to balance competing interests. In this instance, there is our societal commitment to free speech on one side of the scale versus our interest in effective governmental operations on the other.

Added to this mix is the government's own need to speak. Governments often advance their policy agendas by using the bully pulpit. For example, the Centers for Disease Control and Prevention put out public service announcements during the Covid epidemic that encouraged people to get vaccinated. How should the First Amendment apply in these instances? Is the government free to express one viewpoint on an issue and not another? Does the government have a right not to speak just as private individuals do?

Before the Supreme Court could address these issues, it first had to decide whether the First Amendment applied in these special settings.

A. Does the First Amendment Apply in Special Settings? The Right/Privilege Distinction and the Doctrine of Unconstitutional Conditions

It is not immediately apparent that the First Amendment is implicated when the government regulates speech in special settings. For example, consider the case of a government employee who was fired because of her speech. There is no doubt that the employee as an individual has a constitutional right to speak. But the employee does not have a constitutional right to her job. The conundrum is how this latter fact affects the former. If the employee does not have a constitutional right to her job, why should it violate the Constitution if she lost her job, even if she was fired because of her speech? The government has not stopped her from speaking. It has merely stopped her from receiving a paycheck.

A similar conundrum arises when an artist applies for a government grant but is denied. The applicant has a right to express herself through art, but she does not have a right to a government subsidy. So why would there be any First Amendment problem if the government denied her application, even if the administrators rejected her proposal because they disliked the content of her artwork?

As the following sections indicate, the answers to these questions have evolved over time.

1. Justice Holmes and the Right/Privilege Distinction: A Right to Talk Politics but Not to Be a Police Officer

When judges first encountered this dilemma of speech in special settings, they often concluded that parties lacked a constitutional claim. Their reasoning relied on one of the oldest concepts in constitutional law: the "right/privilege distinction." It is a doctrine often attributed to Justice Oliver Wendell Holmes, particularly in his early years as a jurist when he sat on the Massachusetts Supreme Judicial Court before his elevation to the U.S. Supreme Court. We learned in Chapter 5 that Justice Holmes had a mixed relationship with freedom of speech. When he first encountered speech advocating illegal action, he announced a seemingly speech-protective "clear and present danger" test but then applied it in a manner that rendered it toothless. But we also know that Justice Holmes underwent a conversion by the time he wrote his famous dissent in *Abrams v. United States*, which advocated for making the clear and present danger test highly speech-protective. His sweeping assertion in *Abrams* that we should be "eternally vigilant" against attempts to suppress even speech we loathe or believe "fraught with death" ensured Justice Holmes a spot in legal culture as one of the greatest champions of free speech.

It was the earlier speech-antagonistic Holmes, however, who wrote about the right/privilege distinction. His opinions drew an austere hard-headed line between a citizen's "right" to freedom of speech and the "privilege" of entering government property or holding a government job. Two famous decisions by Holmes illustrate his tough-minded approach.

In *Commonwealth v. Davis*, 39 N.E. 113 (Mass. 1895), Holmes upheld the fine imposed on William Davis for engaging in public speaking without a permit in Boston Common, the famous park in Boston's center. In summarily rejecting Davis' argument that the fine violated his First Amendment rights, Holmes reasoned that because the city owned the park, it could establish whatever rules it wanted for the park's use, just as a private property owner could. If Boston wanted to, Holmes reasoned, it could exclude access to the Common altogether. "For the legislature absolutely or conditionally to forbid public speaking in a highway or public park," Holmes wrote, "is no more an infringement of the rights of a member of the public than for the owner of a private house to forbid it in his house." Holmes did not think of this as a restriction on Davis' freedom of speech, for he was free to speak all he wanted. The First Amendment, however, guaranteed him only a right to speak, not a right of entry to property that was not his. The iron-clad simplicity of this logic was most appealing, and when the U.S. Supreme Court reviewed the decision Holmes had written for the Massachusetts high court, it entirely embraced his theory. "The right to absolutely exclude all right to use, necessarily includes the authority to determine under what circumstances such use may be availed of," the Court stated, "as the greater power contains the lesser." *Davis v. Massachusetts*, 167 U.S. 43, 48 (1897).

Holmes used the same right/privilege reasoning to squelch the free speech rights of government employees. In *McAuliffe v. Mayor of New Bedford*, 29 N.E. 517 (Mass. 1892), police officer John McAuliffe was fired by the city of New Bedford for talking politics while walking the beat. McAuliffe challenged his dismissal as a violation of the First Amendment. Holmes dismissed his claim as if it bordered on the frivolous, bluntly stating, "The petitioner may have a constitutional right to talk politics, but he has no constitutional right to be a policeman." McAuliffe was free to talk politics to his heart's content, but once he signed his contract of employment with the city, he was bound by its terms, which included a ban on discussing politics while on the job.

In contracts, people often surrender rights that they would otherwise enjoy as part of the inducement to the other side to join the bargain. As Holmes put it, there are "few employments for hire in which the servant does not agree to suspend his constitutional right of free speech, as well as of idleness, by the implied terms of his contract."

The right/privilege distinction, if followed with undiminished force, would severely diminish the exercise of free speech in American society. Citizens would have a right to freedom of speech, but since entry to government property is a privilege, the government could, if it wanted to, severely restrict or even entirely ban speech in public spaces. These spaces are ones in which expressive activity is most important: parks, plazas, streets, or sidewalks, from the Washington Mall to the Boston Common to Chicago's Grant Park. Students would have a right to free speech, but not on public school grounds or a state college campus. The students would check their rights at the schoolhouse gate. Citizens would have a right to free speech, but not a right to speak when exercising the privilege of working for the government. Artists or researchers would have a right to free speech, but not a right to speak anything they wish if their speech is government funded.

2. The Doctrine of Unconstitutional Conditions: A Privilege May Not Be Conditioned on Giving up a Constitutional Right

As constitutional law evolved, an antidote to the harshness of the right/privilege distinction emerged called the "doctrine of unconstitutional conditions." In a variety of contexts, the Supreme Court began to declare that the government could not place "unconstitutional conditions" on receipt of government benefits or the exercise of a government-granted privilege, from entry to government property, to attendance at a public school or university, to holding a government job, to receipt of public funding. In *Perry v. Sindermann*, 408 U.S. 593, 597 (1972), the Court provided one of the most famous articulations of the unconstitutional conditions doctrine:

> For at least a quarter-century, this Court has made clear that, even though a person has no "right" to a valuable governmental benefit, and even though the government may deny him the benefit for any number of reasons, there are some reasons upon which the government may not rely. It may not deny a benefit to a person on a basis that infringes his constitutionally protected interest, especially his interest in freedom of speech. For if the government could deny a benefit to a person because of his constitutionally protected speech or associations, his exercise of those freedoms would in effect be penalized and inhibited.

Does this mean that the doctrine of constitutional conditions overruled the right/privilege distinction, completely obliterating the Holmes view, as paper covers rock in a game of rock, paper, scissors? Not exactly.

What the unconstitutional conditions doctrine does to the right/privilege distinction is not so much a cry of "you're out of here!" as a cry of "not so fast." Many of the values that animate the right/privilege distinction continue to exert a gravitational pull on the arc of constitutional law policy and doctrine. Yes, citizens must have some right to speak on government property, but is the right the same for all government property, and are there limits that may be imposed, such as restrictions on the time of day or the loudness of amplifiers? Yes, government employees must have some retained right to free speech, but does that mean that the government is entirely powerless to discipline or fire an employee for engaging in expressive activity? Yes, students and faculty at public schools and universities retain free speech rights and do not check those rights at the schoolhouse gate, but does that mean that anything goes in the school building or the campus classroom? Yes, the recipient of government funding subsidizing speech may retain free speech rights, but does that mean that the government lacks any power whatsoever to place conditions on what sorts of expressive activity it chooses to underwrite?

3. The Great Free Speech Compromise: Intricate Rules for Balancing Freedom of Speech and Government's Interest in Operating Effectively

As you will see throughout this chapter, to a large degree constitutional law has evolved to accept what might be coined the "great free speech compromise." A series of stylized, intricate, and often difficult to apply set of doctrines has emerged, setting forth the principles that govern free speech in specialized contexts. These include speech on government properties, speech of public school and university students and faculty, speech of government employees, and speech subsidized through government funding.

These doctrines differ in their formulations, but all are of a piece. In every instance the doctrines reflect a compromise between recognition of the government's legitimate claims to some power to regulate speech when acting as a property owner, educator, employer, or funder, on the one hand, and the importance of retaining a healthy measure of protection for citizens' free speech rights in these settings, on the other. In effect, all the doctrines in this area reflect a compromise mediating between the right/privilege distinction, which retains a significant degree of common sense to commend it, and the doctrine of unconstitutional conditions, which also has powerful intuitive appeal.

As is common in constitutional law arenas in which the tests that evolve are attempts to strike a compromise balancing competing interests, the doctrines that have emerged in this area are often quite complicated, difficult to comprehend, uneven, and inconsistent in their outcomes. *See generally* William W. Van Alstyne, *The Demise of the Right-Privilege Distinction in Constitutional Law*, 81 Harv. L. Rev. 1439 (1968); Rodney A. Smolla, *The Reemergence of the Right-Privilege Distinction in Constitutional Law: The Price of Protesting Too Much*, 35 Stan. L. Rev. 69 (1982); Kathleen Sullivan, *Unconstitutional Conditions*, 102 Harv. L. Rev. 1413 (1989); Richard Epstein, *Unconstitutional Conditions, State Power, and the Limits of Consent*, 102 Harv. L. Rev. 4 (1988); Seth Kreimer, *Allocational Sanctions: The Problem of Negative Rights in a Positive State*, 132 U. Pa. L. Rev. 1293 (1984).

B. Government as Property Owner: The Public Forum Doctrine

Federal, state, and local governments collectively own vast amounts of property ranging from Yellowstone National Park to local schools, libraries, courthouses, and parks. The properties range not only in size but use. There are military bases, office buildings, highways, sidewalks, jailhouses, post offices, elementary schools, and dog parks.

The vast array of government properties has made it difficult to have a one-size-fits-all free speech regime for all properties. While some government properties, such as parks and sidewalks, can easily accommodate speakers, other government properties, such as the interior of the Pentagon or a federal prison, cannot.

The Supreme Court's solution has been to create a complex set of First Amendment rules that vary depending on the type of government property at issue. Collectively, these rules are known as the "public forum doctrine." This doctrine has emerged from dozens of Supreme Court opinions that have dealt with speech occurring on or in government property, facilities, and programs. In lieu of reading any one of those opinions, it is more efficient to provide a narrative summary of the rules. In subsequent sections of this chapter, you will see the Court apply public forum concepts, either directly or by analogy, to frame the issues before it. You should note that disputes over the proper application of public forum laws are among the most often litigated First Amendment issues in lower courts, with hundreds of cases adjudicated in state and federal courts each year.

1. The Four Types of Public Forums: From Streets and Parks to Military Bases

Four categories of public forums are now recognized. Here are the categories of public forums and the doctrinal rules that apply to them.

Traditional public forums. Traditional public forums are places that "have immemorially been held in trust for the use of the public and, time out of mind, have been used for purposes of assembly, communicating thoughts between citizens, and discussing public questions." *Perry Educ. Ass'n v. Perry Local Educators' Ass'n*, 460 U.S. 37, 45 (1983). Parks, streets, and sidewalks are classic examples.

The key to understanding traditional public forums is that these spaces must be open to expressive activity. The government has no choice in the matter. The First Amendment, of its own force, requires that government permit expressive activity in these spaces. The traditional public forum concept rejects the right/privilege reasoning used by Holmes in *Commonwealth v. Davis*, reasoning instead that these spaces are "held in trust" for the public to engage in free expression. Thus, the Holmes notion that the government controls such spaces just as any private landlord is rejoined by the notion that there is an "easement" of sorts imposed by the First Amendment reserving these spaces for the public to engage in expressive activity.

Content-based regulation of speech in traditional public forums is subject to strict scrutiny. Government attempts to regulate the content of expression in a traditional public forum will almost always be struck down.

The government is, however, permitted to regulate speech in a traditional public forum under the rules governing content-neutral reasonable "time, place, or manner" regulations. The "time, place, or manner" test, a variant of intermediate scrutiny, is described in the next section.

Designated public forums. Designated public forums are spaces, places, or programs that are not automatically public forums, in that they do not fall within the list of parks, plazas, streets, and sidewalks that must be open to expressive activity because they are traditional public forums. Designated public forums are spaces, places, or programs that the government voluntarily chooses to treat as public forums, by intentionally opening the locations or programs to indiscriminate use by the public for expressive activity. In a somewhat jocular sense, it might be said that traditional public forums are often open-air venues—parks, plazas, streets, or sidewalks—while designated public forums often have roofs—public auditoriums, or the large lobbies inside major public buildings, such as city halls or county courthouses.

The First Amendment rules governing designated and traditional public forums are identical, which makes matters easy. Thus, in both traditional and designated public forums, content-based regulation is subject to strict scrutiny, and content-neutral regulation must satisfy the "time, place, or manner" rules. The key distinction between designated and traditional public forums is that the government can stop making property available as a designated public forum, but it may not stop making a traditional public forum available for speech.

Limited forums. In a limited public forum, the government creates a channel for a specific or limited type of expression where one did not previously exist. In such a limited forum, the government may be justified in reserving its forum for certain groups or for the discussion of certain topics, subject only to the limitation that its actions must be viewpoint neutral and reasonable. A classic example would be the conference rooms or classrooms of a public university or law school, which are available to be reserved for meetings by members of the school community for issues germane to the school's mission. A public university law school, for example, might make its classrooms available outside of scheduled classes for use by student organizations or faculty members for meetings and events related to law. This would be a "limited forum" designated for specific users (members of the school community) and certain topics (issues related to law). Such speaker-based and content-based "discrimination" might ordinarily trigger strict scrutiny, but in the case of the creation of a limited public forum, such speaker-based or content-based regulation used to define the boundaries of the limited forum is not subject to strict scrutiny but need only be "reasonable." What is not permitted within the limited forum, however, is viewpoint-based discrimination. If the public law school's moot courtroom is made available to student organizations, for example, it would violate the First Amendment if the school were to permit access to a group advocating abortion rights but were to refuse access to an anti-abortion group.

Nonforums. Nonforums are publicly owned facilities that do not fall within any of the other forum categories, but rather are used to carry on the business of government. A nonforum is thus a space, place, or program that is not a traditional forum, such as a park, plaza, street, or sidewalk; not a designated forum, such as a public auditorium; and not a limited forum, a space reserved for expression for certain users or topics. A nonforum is, essentially, "everything else." Expression often takes place within a nonforum—government workers talk to each other or to the public to conduct public business—but the space, place, or program does not exist as a forum for expression, but as a place in which the government carries out its business. The government may entirely exclude general access for expressive activity in such spaces, places, and programs. Most government offices, for example, are nonforums. Even much larger spaces or places may be nonforums. The Supreme Court has held that military bases and post offices, for example, are nonforums. The formal doctrinal rules governing nonforums are similar to limited forums. The government regulation must be reasonable, and viewpoint discrimination is forbidden.

2. The Rule for "Time, Place, or Manner" Regulations: A Variant of Intermediate Scrutiny

We noted above that content-based regulations of speech in traditional and designated public forums are subject to the same strict scrutiny review applied to content-based regulations of speech generally. We also noted that content-neutral regulations of speech in these forums are subject to a specialized test for "time, place, or manner" regulations. This test is a variant of intermediate scrutiny. You were introduced to the test in Chapter 4. Now is the time to flesh out its elements.

Most importantly, the time, place, or manner test applies only to content-neutral regulations of speech. If the application of a regulation depends on the message being conveyed, the regulation is content-based and will be subject to strict scrutiny. By contrast, content-neutral time, place, or manner regulations do not focus on what a speaker is saying but how he is saying it. A "time" regulation, for example, might restrict expressive activity in a city park to certain hours of the day, such as requiring that the park be quiet after midnight so that local residents may sleep. A "place" regulation may restrict the particular area within which expression may occur in a public forum. People passing out leaflets or circulating petitions have a constitutional right to engage in activity in a traditional public forum such as a sidewalk, street, park, or plaza, for example. But the government might require that the expression not block traffic in the middle of a busy intersection, or impede the flow of people on a sidewalk, or trample a flower garden in a park. "Manner" regulations often involve restrictions on amplification of the loudness of expression, such as limiting the use of loudspeakers to certain decibel levels. Manner regulations may also restrict physical structures in public forums, such as forbidding overnight camping in sit-in demonstrations or the erection of "shanty town" structures in public parks.

Here is the formal three-part "time, place, or manner" test: A content-neutral regulation of expression in a public forum is permissible if the regulation (1) is justified by a significant government interest, (2) is narrowly tailored to achieve that interest, and (3) leaves open ample alternative channels for communication of the information.

The intermediate scrutiny nature of the time, place, or manner test is exemplified by its "significant" governmental interest requirement and its "narrow tailoring" requirement. As with other invocations of intermediate scrutiny, the governmental interest cannot be tied to the content of a speaker's message. If it is, the regulation is content-based and will be judged under strict scrutiny.

Finally, the time, place, or manner test includes the additional requirement that the government leave open ample alternative channels for communication. This final requirement can be important. For example, if the government were to restrict protests on the Washington Mall to one small corner, away from the sight and mind of most government officials and members of the public, a court would find that the restriction does not leave open an ample adequate channel.

In applying the time, place, or manner test, one enormously important bright-line rule is that government may not restrict passing out pamphlets, leaflets, or other written materials in a public forum to address concerns that such paper will result in clutter, as people toss an unwanted leaflet on the ground. Passing out literature is deemed to be a core form of expression in traditional public forums, and government must deal with clutter through other means, such as policing rules against discarding material in parks, sidewalks, or streets. In Chapter 13, you will read the foundational cases establishing this principle when we study content-neutral regulations of expression.

3. The Public Forum Doctrine in Action: The Example of Religious Speech on Government Property

One heavily litigated area of public forum law concerns the expression of religious speech on or in government property, facilities, or programs. In a typical case, the government has prohibited religious speech in a public forum even though it is permitting speech on other topics. This exclusion of religious speakers is not usually borne of animus; instead, it emanates from a concern that permitting religious speech on government property would violate the Establishment Clause.

When these cases are litigated, the would-be speakers claim that the exclusion of religious speech constitutes unlawful content-based discrimination. The government responds that the exclusion was necessary to comply with the Establishment Clause.

A good example is *Capitol Square Review & Advisory Board v. Pinette*, 515 U.S. 753 (1995), which concerned a 10-acre square that surrounds the Ohio statehouse. For over a century, the public had used the square for speech purposes. Ohio also allowed people to post signs in the square. But when the Ohio Ku Klux Klan sought a permit to put up a Latin cross in the square, the request was denied. The board overseeing the square claimed that a cross displayed near the statehouse would imply that the government endorsed the cross' religious message, in violation of the Establishment Clause.

The Supreme Court produced a fractured decision, but the majority ruled in favor of the Klan. Ohio acknowledged that the denial of the Klan's permit was content-based so that the denial could not be treated as a content-neutral time, place, or manner restriction. The justices acknowledged that the Free Speech Clause protected religious speech. Justice Antonin Scalia, in his characteristically lively prose, noted that government suppression of religious speech has been so common in Anglo-American history that "a free-speech clause without religion would be Hamlet without the prince."

Since the First Amendment protects religious speech, and the Klan's permit was denied because of the group's proposed message, the denial had to be justified by a compelling government interest. As noted above, the board overseeing the square claimed that the compelling interest was avoiding an Establishment Clause violation. It was over the assessment of this latter claim that the justices disagreed.

Justice Scalia favored a per se rule that religious expression in a traditional or designated public forum never violates the Establishment Clause if the forum is equally open to all. Justice Sandra Day O'Connor favored a more nuanced, fact-specific analysis to determine whether members of the public would perceive the cross as bearing the government's imprimatur. In this instance, she found the board's Establishment Clause argument lacking because there was "no realistic danger that the community would think that the [State] was endorsing religion or any particular creed."[1]

The Court reached similar conclusions in a series of cases involving public schools and universities that opened their facilities for use by students or public groups. In each case, the government refused to allow the facilities to be used for religious purposes. As in *Capitol Square*, the Court in all these cases found that the bar on religious speech violated the speakers' First Amendment rights and was not necessary to avoid an Establishment Clause violation.

For example, in *Lamb's Chapel v. Center Moriches Union Free School District*, 508 U.S. 384 (1993), a New York school district permitted community groups to use school property after hours for social, civic, and recreational events but did not permit the premises to by "used by any group for religious purposes." Under these rules, the school district refused to allow an evangelical church to use school facilities to show films addressing child-rearing from a Christian perspective.

The church argued that the school district had created a designated forum when it opened its property for public use. The Court acknowledged that this argument had "considerable force" but said it was unnecessary to decide the issue because the exclusion of the church's speech was unconstitutional even if the school property were a non-public forum because it constituted unlawful viewpoint discrimination. The Court also found that the discrimination was not required by the Establishment Clause:

> The showing of this film series would not have been during school hours, would not have been sponsored by the school, and would have been open to the public, not just to church members. Under these circumstances, there would have been no realistic danger that the community would think that the District was endorsing religion or any particular creed, and any benefit to religion or to the Church would have been no more than incidental.

1 Justices John Paul Stevens and Ruth Bader Ginsburg wrote dissenting opinions supporting the board's claim that permitting the display of the cross would violate the Establishment Clause.

In perhaps the most dramatic application of this principle, the Court held in *Good News Club v. Milford Central School,* 533 U.S. 98 (2001), that a school that had opened its facilities for public use could not exclude a private Christian organization from meeting at the school even though students attending the group's programs would be hearing Bible lessons and memorizing scripture.

The following opinion is from another case involving religious speech in a public forum.

Rosenberger v. Rector & Visitors of University of Virginia

Supreme Court of the United States, 1995
515 U.S. 819

JUSTICE KENNEDY delivered the opinion of the Court.

The University of Virginia, an instrumentality of the Commonwealth for which it is named and thus bound by the First and Fourteenth Amendments, authorizes the payment of outside contractors for the printing costs of a variety of student publications. It withheld any authorization for payments on behalf of petitioners for the sole reason that their student paper "primarily promotes or manifests a particular belief in or about a deity or an ultimate reality."

Before a student group is eligible to submit bills from its outside contractors for payment by the fund described below, it must become a "Contracted Independent Organization" (CIO). CIO status is available to any group the majority of whose members are students, whose managing officers are fulltime students, and that complies with certain procedural requirements.

Wide Awake Productions (WAP), qualified as a CIO. Formed by petitioner Ronald Rosenberger and other undergraduates in 1990, WAP was established "to publish a magazine of philosophical and religious expression," "to facilitate discussion which fosters an atmosphere of sensitivity to and tolerance of Christian viewpoints," and "to provide a unifying focus for Christians of multicultural backgrounds." WAP publishes Wide Awake: A Christian Perspective at the University of Virginia.

A few months after being given CIO status, WAP requested the Student Activities Fund (SAF) to pay its printer $5,862 for the costs of printing its newspaper. The Appropriations Committee of the Student Council denied WAP's request on the ground that Wide Awake was a "religious activity" within the meaning of the Guidelines, *i.e.,* that the newspaper "promoted or manifested a particular belief in or about a deity or an ultimate reality."

It is axiomatic that the government may not regulate speech based on its substantive content or the message it conveys. Other principles follow from this precept. In the realm of private speech or expression, government regulation may not favor one speaker over another. Discrimination against speech because of its message is presumed to be unconstitutional. These rules informed our determination that the government offends the First Amendment when it imposes financial burdens on certain speakers based on the content of their expression. When the government targets not subject matter, but particular views taken by speakers on a subject, the violation of the First Amendment is all the more blatant. Viewpoint discrimination is thus an egregious form of content discrimination. The government must abstain from regulating speech when the specific motivating ideology or the opinion or perspective of the speaker is the rationale for the restriction.

These principles provide the framework forbidding the State to exercise viewpoint discrimination, even when the limited public forum is one of its own creation.

The necessities of confining a forum to the limited and legitimate purposes for which it was created may justify the State in reserving it for certain groups or for the discussion of certain topics. Once it has opened a limited forum, however, the State must respect the lawful boundaries it has itself set. The State may not exclude speech where its distinction is not "reasonable in light of the purpose served by the forum," nor may it discriminate against speech on the basis of its viewpoint. Thus, in determining whether the State is acting to preserve the limits of the forum it has created so that the exclusion of a class of speech is legitimate, we have observed a distinction between, on the one hand, content discrimination, which may be permissible if it preserves the purposes of that limited forum, and, on the other hand, viewpoint discrimination, which is presumed impermissible when directed against speech otherwise within the forum's limitations.

The SAF is a forum more in a metaphysical than in a spatial or geographic sense, but the same principles are applicable.

The University does acknowledge (as it must in light of our precedents) that "ideologically driven attempts to suppress a particular point of view are presumptively unconstitutional in funding, as in other contexts," but insists that this case does not present that issue because the Guidelines draw lines based on content, not viewpoint. As we have noted, discrimination against one set of views or ideas is but a subset or particular instance of the more general phenomenon of content discrimination. And, it must be acknowledged, the distinction is not a precise one. It is, in a sense, something of an understatement to speak of religious thought and discussion as just a viewpoint, as distinct from a comprehensive body of thought. The nature of our origins and destiny and their dependence upon the existence of a divine being have been subjects of philosophic inquiry throughout human history. We conclude, nonetheless, that here, as in *Lamb's Chapel*, viewpoint discrimination is the proper way to interpret the University's objections to Wide Awake.

The University tries to escape the consequences of our holding in *Lamb's Chapel* by urging that this case involves the provision of funds rather than access to facilities. The University begins with the unremarkable proposition that the State must have substantial discretion in determining how to allocate scarce resources to accomplish its educational mission. It does not follow, however, that viewpoint-based restrictions are proper when the University does not itself speak or subsidize transmittal of a message it favors but instead expends funds to encourage a diversity of views from private speakers. A holding that the University may not discriminate based on the viewpoint of private persons whose speech it facilitates does not restrict the University's own speech, which is controlled by different principles.

The University urges that, from a constitutional standpoint, funding of speech differs from provision of access to facilities because money is scarce and physical facilities are not. Beyond the fact that in any given case this proposition might not be true as an empirical matter, the underlying premise that the University could discriminate based on viewpoint if demand for space exceeded its availability is wrong as well. The government cannot justify viewpoint discrimination among private speakers on the economic fact of scarcity. Had the meeting rooms in *Lamb's Chapel* been scarce, had the demand been greater than the supply, our decision would have been no different. It would have been incumbent on the State, of course, to ration or allocate the scarce resources on some acceptable neutral principle; but nothing in our decision indicated that scarcity would give the State the right to exercise viewpoint discrimination that is otherwise impermissible.

Vital First Amendment speech principles are at stake here. The first danger to liberty lies in granting the State the power to examine publications to determine whether or not they are based on some ultimate idea and, if so, for the State to classify them. The second, and corollary, danger is to speech from the chilling of individual thought and expression. That danger is especially real in the University setting, where the State acts against a background and tradition of thought and experiment that is at the center of our intellectual and philosophic tradition. In ancient Athens, and, as Europe entered into a new period of intellectual awakening, in places like Bologna, Oxford, and Paris, universities began as voluntary and spontaneous assemblages or concourses for students to speak and to write and to learn. The quality and creative power of student intellectual life to this day remains a vital measure of a school's influence and attainment. For the University, by regulation, to cast disapproval on particular viewpoints of its students risks the suppression of free speech and creative inquiry in one of the vital centers for the Nation's intellectual life, its college and university campuses.

The Guideline invoked by the University to deny third-party contractor payments on behalf of WAP effects a sweeping restriction on student thought and student inquiry in the context of University sponsored publications. The prohibition on funding on behalf of publications that "primarily promote or manifest a particular belief in or about a deity or an ultimate reality," in its ordinary and commonsense meaning, has a vast potential reach. The term "promotes" as used here would comprehend any writing advocating a philosophic position that rests upon a belief in a deity or ultimate reality. And the term "manifests" would bring within the scope of the prohibition any writing that is explicable as resting upon a premise that presupposes the existence of a deity or ultimate reality. Were the prohibition applied with much vigor at all, it would bar funding of essays by hypothetical student contributors named Plato, Spinoza, and Descartes. And if the regulation covers, as the University says it does, those student journalistic efforts that primarily manifest or promote a belief that there is no deity and no ultimate reality, then under-graduates named Karl Marx, Bertrand Russell, and Jean-Paul Sartre would likewise have some of their major essays excluded from student publications. If any manifestation of beliefs in first principles disqualifies the writing, as seems to be the case, it is indeed difficult to name renowned thinkers whose writings would be accepted, save perhaps for articles disclaiming all connection to their ultimate philosophy. Plato could contrive perhaps to submit an acceptable essay on making pasta or peanut butter cookies, provided he did not point out their (necessary) imperfections.

Based on the principles we have discussed, we hold that the regulation invoked to deny SAF support, both in its terms and in its application to these petitioners, is a denial of their right of free speech guaranteed by the First Amendment. It remains to be considered whether the violation following from the University's action is excused by the necessity of complying with the Constitution's prohibition against state establishment of religion. We turn to that question.

It does not violate the Establishment Clause for a public university to grant access to its facilities on a religion-neutral basis to a wide spectrum of student groups, including groups that use meeting rooms for sectarian activities, accompanied by some devotional exercises.

To obey the Establishment Clause, it was not necessary for the University to deny eligibility to student publications because of their viewpoint. The neutrality commanded of the State by the separate Clauses of the First Amendment was compromised by the University's course of action. The viewpoint discrimination inherent in the University's regulation required public officials to scan and interpret student publications to discern their underlying philosophic assumptions respecting religious theory and belief. That course of action was a denial of the right of free speech and would risk fostering a pervasive bias or hostility to religion, which could undermine the very neutrality the Establishment Clause requires. There is no Establishment Clause violation in the University's honoring its duties under the Free Speech Clause.

[Justice O'Connor's and Justice Thomas' concurring opinions are omitted, as is Justice Souter's dissenting opinion, which was joined by Justice Stevens, Justice Ginsburg, and Justice Breyer.]

Points for Discussion

1. **What was the public forum in *Rosenberger*?** Our previous discussion of the public forum doctrine largely concerned speech occurring on real property owned by the government. But the *Rosenberger* case is not about the use of real property. What, then, was the alleged public forum in *Rosenberger*?

2. **What type of forum was at issue in *Rosenberger*?** We learned above that the Court has identified four types of public forums. How did the Court classify the public forum in *Rosenberger*? What are the legal rules applicable to that type of forum? Did the Court conclude that the University of Virginia had violated these rules? If so, how?

3. **A peek at upcoming Establishment Clause jurisprudence.** The University of Virginia was founded by Thomas Jefferson, who coined the phrase "wall of separation" between church and state. The university defended its refusal to fund the religious message of Wide Awake by arguing that funding the magazine would violate the Establishment Clause, prohibiting any law "respecting an establishment of religion." The concurring and dissenting opinions in *Rosenberger* are omitted. Among the dissenters was Justice David Souter, who said the university was correct in its Establishment Clause concerns. As we will see in Chapter 19, dealing with the Establishment Clause, Justice Souter's view has not prevailed, and *Rosenberger* remains influential precedent in religious matters, standing for the proposition that the Establishment Clause is not violated by government funding that includes religious groups among the recipients of a wider program.

4. **When analytical frameworks collide.** *Rosenberger* is a classic example of how a First Amendment conflict may often be analyzed through many different doctrinal prisms. Indeed, the case could have been placed in several different sections of this casebook, treated as an "education law" case, a "public forum law" case, a "government funding" case, or an "establishment of religion" case. This is not uncommon in First Amendment cases, and savvy lawyers will use whichever analytical framework furthers their clients' interests.

You Be the Lawyer!

What types of forums exist on a university campus?

You have just taken a job as a lawyer in the general counsel's office of a large state university. The university president, who is not a lawyer, has asked for guidance on the rules governing freedom of expression in various settings at the university. Your supervisor, the general counsel, says: "I am not a First Amendment expert. But I remember from my constitutional law class that the extent to which regulation of expression on government property is or is not permitted often turns on the 'public forum' status of the particular place." She asks you to write a memorandum on the likely public forum status of the following spaces on campus and the rules that apply to them:

- A huge open grassy space about the size of six city blocks, surrounded by various academic buildings at the center of campus.
- The main central campus auditorium, where the university has permitted lectures and presentations by outside speakers on virtually all topics imaginable over the years.
- Classrooms, at times in which classes are scheduled.
- Meeting rooms in the library and across many campus facilities, which are available to be reserved by members of the campus community for expressive activities of any kind.
- The inside of faculty offices.
- The president's office.
- The waiting room outside the president's office.
- The student dining hall.
- Athletic recreation fields and facilities.
- Individual student dormitory rooms.
- Student lounges in dormitories.
- The spacious main indoor lobby of the student union building.

C. Government as Educator: The Free Speech Rights of Public School Students

Public schools could not function if the government could not regulate speech. School administrators necessarily make content-based decisions about which subjects to include in a school's curriculum and which books to buy for the school's library. Teachers regulate speech to maintain discipline in their classrooms and award grades based on the content of students' work.

The fact that speech needs to be regulated in the school context, however, does not mean that students lack any free speech rights while at school. Indeed, in the first landmark case on the subject, the Supreme Court held that students do not shed their free speech rights at the schoolhouse gate. The case concerned students who wore black armbands to school to protest the Vietnam War.

Mary Beth (L) and John Tinker (R)

Tinker v. Des Moines Independent Community School District

Supreme Court of the United States, 1969
393 U.S. 503

MR. JUSTICE FORTAS delivered the opinion of the Court.

Petitioner John F. Tinker, 15 years old, and petitioner Christopher Eckhardt, 16 years old, attended high schools in Des Moines, Iowa. Petitioner Mary Beth Tinker, John's sister, was a 13-year-old student in junior high school.

In December 1965, a group of adults and students in Des Moines held a meeting at the Eckhardt home. The group determined to publicize their objections to the hostilities in Vietnam and their support for a truce by wearing black armbands during the holiday season and by fasting on December 16 and New Year's Eve. Petitioners and their parents had previously engaged in similar activities, and they decided to participate in the program.

The principals of the Des Moines schools became aware of the plan to wear armbands. On December 14, 1965, they met and adopted a policy that any student wearing an armband to school would be asked to remove it, and if he refused he would be suspended until he returned without the armband. Petitioners were aware of the regulation that the school authorities adopted.

On December 16, Mary Beth and Christopher wore black armbands to their schools. John Tinker wore his armband the next day. They were all sent home and suspended from school until they would come back without their armbands. They did not return to school until after the planned period for wearing armbands had expired—that is, until after New Year's Day.

This complaint was filed in the United States District Court by petitioners, through their fathers, under § 1983 of Title 42 of the United States Code. [*Authors' note:* Section 1983 allows individuals to bring civil causes of action against state or local officials for violations of constitutional rights.]

First Amendment rights, applied in light of the special characteristics of the school environment, are available to teachers and students. It can hardly be argued that either students or teachers shed their constitutional rights to freedom of speech or expression at the schoolhouse gate. This has been the unmistakable holding of this Court for almost 50 years.

On the other hand, the Court has repeatedly emphasized the need for affirming the comprehensive authority of the States and of school officials, consistent with fundamental constitutional safeguards, to prescribe and control conduct in the schools. Our problem lies in the area where students in the exercise of First Amendment rights collide with the rules of the school authorities.

The problem posed by the present case does not relate to regulation of the length of skirts or the type of clothing, to hair style, or deportment. It does not concern aggressive, disruptive action or even group demonstrations. Our problem involves direct, primary First Amendment rights akin to "pure speech."

The school officials banned and sought to punish petitioners for a silent, passive expression of opinion, unaccompanied by any disorder or disturbance on the part of petitioners. There is here no evidence whatever of petitioners' interference, actual or nascent, with the schools' work or of collision with the rights of other students to be secure and to be let alone. Accordingly, this case does not concern speech or action that intrudes upon the work of the schools or the rights of other students.

Only a few of the 18,000 students in the school system wore the black armbands. Only five students were suspended for wearing them. There is no indication that the work of the schools or any class was disrupted. Outside the classrooms, a few students made hostile remarks to the children wearing armbands, but there were no threats or acts of violence on school premises.

The District Court concluded that the action of the school authorities was reasonable because it was based upon their fear of a disturbance from the wearing of the armbands. But, in our system, undifferentiated fear or apprehension of disturbance is not enough to overcome the right to freedom of expression. Any departure from absolute regimentation may cause trouble. Any variation from the majority's opinion may inspire fear. Any word spoken, in class, in the lunchroom, or on the campus, that deviates from the views of another person may start an argument or cause a disturbance. But our Constitution says we must take this risk, and our history says that it is this sort of hazardous freedom—this kind of openness—that is the basis of our national strength and of the independence and vigor of Americans who grow up and live in this relatively permissive, often disputatious, society.

In order for the State in the person of school officials to justify prohibition of a particular expression of opinion, it must be able to show that its action was caused by something more than a mere desire to avoid the discomfort and unpleasantness that always accompany an unpopular viewpoint. Certainly where there is no finding and no showing that engaging in the forbidden conduct would "materially and substantially interfere with the requirements of appropriate discipline in the operation of the school," the prohibition cannot be sustained.

In the present case, the District Court made no such finding, and our independent examination of the record fails to yield evidence that the school authorities had reason to anticipate that the wearing of the armbands would substantially interfere with the work of the school or impinge upon the rights of other students. Even an official memorandum prepared after the suspension that listed the reasons for the ban on wearing the armbands made no reference to the anticipation of such disruption.

On the contrary, the action of the school authorities appears to have been based upon an urgent wish to avoid the controversy which might result from the expression, even by the silent symbol of armbands, of opposition to this Nation's part in the conflagration in Vietnam. It is revealing, in this respect, that the meeting at which the school principals decided to issue the contested regulation was called in response to a student's statement to the journalism teacher in one of the schools that he wanted to write an article on Vietnam and have it published in the school paper. (The student was dissuaded.)

It is also relevant that the school authorities did not purport to prohibit the wearing of all symbols of political or controversial significance. The record shows that students in some of the schools wore buttons relating to national political campaigns, and some even wore the Iron Cross, traditionally a symbol of Nazism. The order prohibiting the wearing of armbands did not extend to these. Instead, a particular symbol—black armbands worn to exhibit opposition to this Nation's involvement in Vietnam—was singled out for prohibition. Clearly, the prohibition of expression of one particular opinion, at least without evidence that it is necessary to avoid material and substantial interference with schoolwork or discipline, is not constitutionally permissible.

In our system, state-operated schools may not be enclaves of totalitarianism. School officials do not possess absolute authority over their students. Students in school as well as out of school are "persons" under our Constitution. They are possessed of fundamental rights which the State must respect, just as they themselves must respect their obligations to the State. In our system, students may not be regarded as closed-circuit recipients of only that which the State chooses to communicate. They may not be confined to the expression of those sentiments that are officially approved. In the absence of a specific showing of constitutionally valid reasons to regulate their speech, students are entitled to freedom of expression of their views.

This principle has been repeated by this Court on numerous occasions during the intervening years. The principle of these cases is not confined to the supervised and ordained discussion which takes place in the classroom. The principal use to which the schools are dedicated is to accommodate students during prescribed hours for the purpose of certain types of activities. Among those activities is personal intercommunication among the students. This is not only an inevitable part of the process of attending school; it is also an important part of the educational process. A student's rights, therefore, do not embrace merely the classroom hours. When he is in the cafeteria, or on the playing field, or on the campus during the authorized hours, he may express his opinions, even on controversial subjects like the conflict in Vietnam, if he does so without "materially and substantially interfering with the requirements of appropriate discipline in the operation of the school" and without colliding with the rights of others. But conduct by the student, in class or out of it, which for any reason—whether it stems from time, place, or type of behavior—materially disrupts classwork or involves substantial disorder or invasion of the rights of others is, of course, not immunized by the constitutional guarantee of freedom of speech. If a regulation were adopted by school officials forbidding discussion of the Vietnam conflict, or the expression by any student of opposition to it anywhere on school property except as part of a prescribed classroom exercise, it would be obvious that the regulation would violate the constitutional rights of students, at least if it could not be justified by a showing that the students' activities would materially and substantially disrupt the work and discipline of the school. In the circumstances of the present case, the prohibition of the silent, passive "witness of the armbands," as one of the children called it, is no less offensive to the constitution's guarantees.

As we have discussed, the record does not demonstrate any facts which might reasonably have led school authorities to forecast substantial disruption of or material interference with school activities, and no disturbances or disorders on the school premises in fact occurred. These petitioners merely went about their ordained rounds in school. Their deviation consisted only in wearing on their sleeve a band of black cloth, not more than two inches wide. They wore it to exhibit their disapproval of the Vietnam hostilities and their advocacy of a truce, to make their views known, and, by their example, to influence others to adopt them. They neither interrupted school activities nor sought to intrude in the school affairs or the lives of others. They caused discussion outside of the classrooms, but no interference with work and no disorder. In the circumstances, our Constitution does not permit officials of the State to deny their form of expression.

MR. JUSTICE BLACK, dissenting.

In my view, teachers in state-controlled public schools are hired to teach there. Although Mr. Justice McReynolds may have intimated to the contrary in *Meyer v. Nebraska*, 262 U.S. 390 (1923), certainly a teacher is not paid to go into school and teach subjects the State does not hire him to teach as a part of its selected curriculum. Nor are public school students sent to the schools at public expense to broadcast political or any other views to educate and inform the public. The original idea of schools, which I do not believe is yet abandoned as worthless or not of date, was that children had not yet reached the point of experience and wisdom which enabled them to teach all of their elders. It may be that the Nation has outworn the old-fashioned slogan that "children are to be seen not heard," but one may, I hope, be permitted to harbor the thought that taxpayers send children to school on the premise that at their age they need to learn, not teach.

[Justice Stewart's and Justice White's concurring opinions are omitted, as is Justice Harlan's dissenting opinion.]

Points for Discussion

1. **Striking a balance between student rights and administrative concerns.** Justice Abe Fortas declared in *Tinker* that students do not shed their First Amendment rights at the schoolhouse gate. At the same time, he affirmed the "comprehensive

authority" of school officials "to proscribe and control conduct in the schools." The upshot is the "great compromise" in the public school context: students have First Amendment rights at school, but they must be "applied in light of the special characteristics of the school environment." What test does the Court use to strike this balance? Do you think that the test tips more in favor of students' speech rights or more in favor of school authority to regulate student speech?

2. **Schools are not enclaves of totalitarianism.** Justice Fortas proclaimed that schools "may not be enclaves of totalitarianism" and students "may not be confined to the expression of those sentiments that are officially approved." But he also said that schools may regulate student speech that would "substantially interfere with the work of the school or impinge upon the rights of other students." It is not always easy to know which of these principles should control the outcome of a case. Imagine a school committed to diversity, equity, and inclusion. One of the school's educational goals is to teach students to tolerate and accept those who are different from them. If one day a student wore a shirt to school that said, "Marriage is between a man and woman," may the school order the student to put on a different shirt? Would that be an instance of a school's properly ensuring that student speech did not interfere with the school's work or collide with the rights of other students, or would that be an instance of a school's acting as an "enclave of totalitarianism" in which students are allowed to convey only officially approved messages?

3. **Student speech cases following *Tinker*.** The *Tinker* case is often thought of as the highwater mark of free speech protection for public school students. In the Court's next three cases on student speech, the students all lost.

   a. **Regulating lewd and vulgar speech: *Bethel School District No. 403 v. Fraser*, 478 U.S. 675 (1986).** A student at a school-sponsored assembly gave a nominating speech for a fellow student that was laced with sexual innuendo. In upholding the school's disciplinary action against the student, the Supreme Court noted the "marked distinction between the political 'message' of the armbands in *Tinker* and the sexual content of respondent's speech." The Court stressed the school's role in teaching students about the boundaries of civil discourse and said that "the essential lessons of civil, mature conduct cannot be conveyed in a school that tolerates lewd, indecent, and offensive speech." *Fraser* has been understood to give schools broad leeway to regulate vulgar and lewd speech. But what are the boundaries of this rule? Do you think that the school could have disciplined the student if he gave the exact same speech to friends on the playground during recess?

   b. **Speech in the context of curricular programming: *Hazelwood School District v. Kuhlmeier*, 484 U.S. 260 (1988).** The Court upheld a high school principal's decision to block the publication of two articles in a school newspaper. One article concerned the experiences of pregnant students and the other the effect of parental divorce on students. The Court drew a distinction between personal student speech occurring on campus, to which the *Tinker* "substantial disruption" test applied, and student speech occurring in school-sponsored activities, to which the Court applied a much more deferential standard: that the school's action be "reasonably related to legitimate pedagogical concerns." Here is a key passage from the opinion:

> The question whether the First Amendment requires a school to tolerate particular student speech—the question that we addressed in *Tinker*—is different from the question whether the First Amendment requires a school affirmatively to promote particular student speech. The former question addresses educators' ability to silence a student's personal expression that happens to occur on the school premises. The latter question concerns educators' authority over school-sponsored publications, theatrical productions, and other expressive activities that students, parents, and members of the public might reasonably perceive to bear the imprimatur of the school. These activities may fairly be characterized as part of the school curriculum, whether or not they occur in a traditional classroom setting, so long as they are supervised by faculty members and designed to impart particular knowledge or skills to student participants and audiences.
>
> Educators are entitled to exercise greater control over this second form of student expression to assure that participants learn whatever lessons the activity is designed to teach, that readers or listeners are not exposed to material that may be inappropriate for their level of maturity, and that the views of the individual speaker are not erroneously attributed to the school.
>
> Accordingly, we conclude that the standard articulated in *Tinker* for determining when a school may punish student expression need not also be the standard for determining when a school may refuse to lend its name and resources to the dissemination of student expression. Instead, we hold that educators do not offend the First Amendment by exercising editorial control over the style and content of student speech in school-sponsored expressive activities so long as their actions are reasonably related to legitimate pedagogical concerns.

c. **Student speech encouraging drug use: *Morse v. Frederick*, 551 U.S. 393 (2007).** In perhaps the most colorful of the cases, the Court found no First Amendment violation in a high school's disciplinary action against a student for unfurling a banner at a school event that said, "BONG HiTs 4 JESUS." The banner was unfurled as students were standing in front of the school to watch an Olympic torchbearer pass by. The Court reasoned that school officials reasonably interpreted the message as advocating illegal drug use and that the government has a compelling interest in deterring drug use by children.

d. **School regulation of off-campus student speech:** What these earlier cases did not address was the ability of schools to regulate student speech occurring off-campus. In *Morse v. Frederick*, the disciplined student argued that his speech was not student speech because it occurred outside the school and across the street. Chief Justice John Roberts was unconvinced, especially because the school had authorized the students to gather outside to watch the Olympic torch relay. As Chief Justice Roberts explained, the disciplined student "cannot stand in the midst of his fellow students, during school hours, at a school-sanctioned activity and claim he is not at school." The Supreme Court finally addressed the question of school authority to regulate off-campus student speech in the following case.

Mahanoy Area School District v. B.L.

Supreme Court of the United States, 2021
141 S. Ct. 2038

JUSTICE BREYER delivered the opinion of the Court.

A public high school student used, and transmitted to her Snapchat friends, vulgar language and gestures criticizing both the school and the school's cheerleading team. The student's speech took place outside of school hours and away from the school's campus. In response, the school suspended the student for a year from the cheerleading team. We must decide whether the Court of Appeals for the Third Circuit correctly held that the school's decision violated the First Amendment. Although we do not agree with the reasoning of the Third Circuit panel's majority, we do agree with its conclusion that the school's disciplinary action violated the First Amendment.

B.L. (who, together with her parents, is a respondent in this case) was a student at Mahanoy Area High School, a public school in Mahanoy City, Pennsylvania. At the end of her freshman year, B.L. tried out for a position on the school's varsity cheerleading squad and for right fielder on a private softball team.

She did not make the varsity cheerleading team or get her preferred softball position, but she was offered a spot on the cheerleading squad's junior varsity team. B.L. did not accept the coach's decision with good grace, particularly because the squad coaches had placed an entering freshman on the varsity team.

That weekend, B.L. and a friend visited the Cocoa Hut, a local convenience store. There, B.L. used her smartphone to post two photos on Snapchat, a social media application that allows users to post photos and videos that disappear after a set period of time. B.L. posted the images to her Snapchat "story," a feature of the application that allows any person in the user's "friend" group (B.L. had about 250 "friends") to view the images for a 24 hour period.

The first image B.L. posted showed B.L. and a friend with middle fingers raised; it bore the caption: "Fuck school fuck softball fuck cheer fuck everything." The second image was blank but for a caption, which read: "Love how me and [another student] get told we need a year of jv before we make varsity but that doesn't matter to anyone else?" The caption also contained an upside-down smiley-face emoji.

B.L.'s Snapchat "friends" included other Mahanoy Area High School students, some of whom also belonged to the cheerleading squad. At least one of them, using a separate cellphone, took pictures of B.L.'s posts and shared them with other members of the cheerleading squad. One of the students who received these photos showed them to her mother (who was a cheerleading squad coach), and the images spread.

That week, several cheerleaders and other students approached the cheerleading coaches "visibly upset" about B.L.'s posts. Questions about the posts persisted during an Algebra class taught by one of the two coaches.

After discussing the matter with the school principal, the coaches decided that because the posts used profanity in connection with a school extracurricular activity, they violated team and school rules. As a result, the coaches suspended B.L. from the junior varsity cheerleading squad for the upcoming year. B.L.'s subsequent apologies did not move school officials. The school's athletic director, principal, superintendent, and school board, all affirmed B. L.'s suspension from the team. In response, B.L., together with her parents, filed this lawsuit in Federal District Court.

The District Court found in B.L.'s favor. It first granted a temporary restraining order and a preliminary injunction ordering the school to reinstate B.L. to the cheerleading team. In granting B.L.'s subsequent motion for summary judgment, the District Court found that B. L.'s Snapchats had not caused substantial disruption at the school. *Cf. Tinker.*

We have made clear that students do not "shed their constitutional rights to freedom of speech or expression," even "at the schoolhouse gate." But we have also made clear that courts must apply the First Amendment "in light of the special characteristics of the school environment." One such characteristic, which we have stressed, is the fact that schools at times stand *in loco parentis, i.e.*, in the place of parents.

This Court has previously outlined three specific categories of student speech that schools may regulate in certain circumstances: (1) "indecent," "lewd," or "vulgar" speech uttered during a school assembly on school grounds; *see Fraser;* (2) speech, uttered during a class trip, that promotes "illegal drug use," *see Morse*; and (3) speech that others may reasonably perceive as "bearing the imprimatur of the school," such as that appearing in a school-sponsored newspaper, *see Kuhlmeier.*

Finally, in *Tinker*, we said schools have a special interest in regulating speech that "materially disrupts classwork or involves substantial disorder or invasion of the rights of others." These special characteristics call for special leeway when schools regulate speech that occurs under its supervision.

Unlike the Third Circuit, we do not believe the special characteristics that give schools additional license to regulate student speech always disappear when a school regulates speech that takes place off campus. The school's regulatory interests remain significant in some off-campus circumstances. The parties' briefs, and those of amici, list several types of off-campus behavior that may call for school regulation. These include serious or severe bullying or harassment targeting particular individuals; threats aimed at teachers or other students; the failure to follow rules concerning lessons, the writing of papers, the use of computers, or participation in other online school activities; and breaches of school security devices, including material maintained within school computers.

Even B.L. herself and the amici supporting her would redefine the Third Circuit's off-campus/on-campus distinction, treating as on campus: all times when the school is responsible for the student; the school's immediate surroundings; travel en route to and from the school; all speech taking place over school laptops or on a school's website; speech taking place during remote learning; activities taken for school credit; and communications to school e-mail accounts or phones. And it may be that speech related to extracurricular activities, such as team sports, would also receive special treatment under B.L.'s proposed rule.

We are uncertain as to the length or content of any such list of appropriate exceptions or carveouts to the Third Circuit majority's rule. That rule, basically, if not entirely, would deny the off-campus applicability of *Tinker*'s highly general statement about the nature of a school's special interests. Particularly given the advent of computer-based learning, we hesitate to determine precisely which of many school-related off-campus activities belong on such a list. Neither do we now know how such a list might vary, depending upon a student's age, the nature of the school's off-campus activity, or the impact upon the school itself. Thus, we do not now set forth a broad, highly general First Amendment rule stating just what counts as "off campus" speech and whether or how ordinary First Amendment standards must give way off campus to a school's special need to prevent, *e.g.*, substantial disruption of learning-related activities or the protection of those who make up a school community.

We can, however, mention three features of off-campus speech that often, even if not always, distinguish schools' efforts to regulate that speech from their efforts to regulate on-campus speech. Those features diminish the strength of the unique educational characteristics that might call for special First Amendment leeway.

First, a school, in relation to off-campus speech, will rarely stand *in loco parentis*. The doctrine of *in loco parentis* treats school administrators as standing in the place of students' parents under circumstances where the children's actual parents cannot protect, guide, and discipline them. Geographically speaking, off-campus speech will normally fall within the zone of parental, rather than school-related, responsibility.

Second, from the student speaker's perspective, regulations of off-campus speech, when coupled with regulations of on-campus speech, include all the speech a student utters during the full 24-hour day. That means courts must be more skeptical of a school's efforts to regulate off-campus speech, for doing so may mean the student cannot engage in that kind of speech at all. When it comes to political or religious speech that occurs outside school or a school program or activity, the school will have a heavy burden to justify intervention.

Third, the school itself has an interest in protecting a student's unpopular expression, especially when the expression takes place off campus. America's public schools are the nurseries of democracy. Our representative democracy only works if we protect the "marketplace of ideas." This free exchange facilitates an informed public opinion, which, when transmitted to lawmakers, helps produce laws that reflect the People's will. That protection must include the protection of unpopular ideas, for popular ideas have less need for protection. Thus, schools have a strong interest in ensuring that future generations understand the workings in practice of the well-known aphorism, "I disapprove of what you say, but I will defend to the death your right to say it." (Although this quote is often attributed to Voltaire, it was likely coined by an English writer, Evelyn Beatrice Hall.)

Given the many different kinds of off-campus speech, the different potential school-related and circumstance-specific justifications, and the differing extent to which those justifications may call for First Amendment leeway, we can, as a general matter, say little more than this: Taken together, these three features of much off-campus speech mean that the leeway the First Amendment grants to schools in light of their special characteristics is diminished. We leave for future cases to decide where, when, and how these features mean the speaker's off-campus location will make the critical difference. This case can, however, provide one example.

Consider B.L.'s speech. Putting aside the vulgar language, the listener would hear criticism, of the team, the team's coaches, and the school—in a word or two, criticism of the rules of a community of which B.L. forms a part. This criticism did not involve features that would place it outside the First Amendment's ordinary protection. B.L.'s posts, while crude, did not amount to fighting words. And while B.L. used vulgarity, her speech was not obscene as this Court has understood that term. To the contrary, B.L. uttered the kind of pure speech to which, were she an adult, the First Amendment would provide strong protection.

Consider too when, where, and how B.L. spoke. Her posts appeared outside of school hours from a location outside the school. She did not identify the school in her posts or target any member of the school community with vulgar or abusive language. B.L. also transmitted her speech through a personal cellphone, to an audience consisting of her private circle of Snapchat friends. These features of her speech, while risking transmission to the school itself, nonetheless (for reasons we have just explained) diminish the school's interest in punishing B.L.'s utterance.

But what about the school's interest, here primarily an interest in prohibiting students from using vulgar language to criticize a school team or its coaches—at least when that criticism might well be transmitted to other students, team members, coaches, and faculty? We can break that general interest into three parts.

First, we consider the school's interest in teaching good manners and consequently in punishing the use of vulgar language aimed at part of the school community. The strength of this anti-vulgarity interest is weakened considerably by the fact that B.L. spoke outside the school on her own time.

B.L. spoke under circumstances where the school did not stand *in loco parentis*. And there is no reason to believe B.L.'s parents had delegated to school officials their own control of B.L.'s behavior at the Cocoa Hut. Moreover, the vulgarity in B.L.'s posts encompassed a message, an expression of B.L.'s irritation with, and criticism of, the school and cheerleading communities. Further, the school has presented no evidence of any general effort to prevent students from using vulgarity outside the classroom. Together, these facts convince us that the school's interest in teaching good manners is not sufficient, in this case, to overcome B.L.'s interest in free expression.

Second, the school argues that it was trying to prevent disruption, if not within the classroom, then within the bounds of a school-sponsored extracurricular activity. But we can find no evidence in the record of the sort of "substantial disruption" of a school activity or a threatened harm to the rights of others that might justify the school's action. Rather, the record shows that discussion of the matter took, at most, 5 to 10 minutes of an Algebra class "for just a couple of days" and that some members of the cheerleading team were "upset" about the content of B.L.'s Snapchats. But when one of B.L.'s coaches was asked directly if she had "any reason to think that this particular incident would disrupt class or school activities other than the fact that kids kept asking about it," she responded simply, "No." As we said in *Tinker*, "for the State in the person of school officials to justify prohibition of a particular expression of opinion, it must be able to show that its action was caused by something more than a mere desire to avoid the discomfort and unpleasantness that always accompany an unpopular viewpoint."

The alleged disturbance here does not meet *Tinker*'s demanding standard.

Third, the school presented some evidence that expresses (at least indirectly) a concern for team morale. One of the coaches testified that the school decided to suspend B.L., not because of any specific negative impact upon a particular member of the school community, but "based on the fact that there was negativity put out there that could impact students in the school." There is little else, however, that suggests any serious decline in team morale—to the point where it could create a substantial interference in, or disruption of, the school's efforts to maintain team cohesion. As we have previously said, simple "undifferentiated fear or apprehension is not enough to overcome the right to freedom of expression." *Tinker.*

It might be tempting to dismiss B.L.'s words as unworthy of the robust First Amendment protections discussed herein. But sometimes it is necessary to protect the superfluous in order to preserve the necessary. "We cannot lose sight of the fact that, in what otherwise might seem a trifling and annoying instance of individual distasteful abuse of a privilege, these fundamental societal values are truly implicated." *Cohen v. California*.

Although we do not agree with the reasoning of the Third Circuit's panel majority, for the reasons expressed above, resembling those of the panel's concurring opinion, we nonetheless agree that the school violated B.L.'s First Amendment rights. The judgment of the Third Circuit is therefore affirmed.

JUSTICE ALITO, with whom JUSTICE GORSUCH joins, concurring.

I start with this threshold question: Why does the First Amendment ever allow the free-speech rights of public school students to be restricted to a greater extent than the rights of other juveniles who do not attend a public school? As the Court recognized in *Tinker*, when a public school regulates student speech, it acts as an arm of the State in which it is located. Suppose that B.L. had been enrolled in a private school and did exactly what she did in this case—send out vulgar and derogatory messages that focused on her school's cheerleading squad. The Commonwealth of Pennsylvania would have had no legal basis to punish her and almost certainly would not have even tried. So why should her status as a public school student give the Commonwealth any greater authority to punish her speech?

Our cases involving the regulation of student speech have not directly addressed this question. All those cases involved either in-school speech or speech that was tantamount to in-school speech. And in those cases, the Court appeared to take it for granted that "the special characteristics of the school environment" justified special rules.

Why the Court took this for granted is not hard to imagine. As a practical matter, it is impossible to see how a school could function if administrators and teachers could not regulate on-premises student speech, including by imposing content-based restrictions in the classroom. In a math class, for example, the teacher can insist that students talk about math, not some other subject. In addition, when a teacher asks a question, the teacher must have the authority to insist that the student respond to that question and not some other question, and a teacher must also have the authority to speak without interruption and to demand that students refrain from interrupting one another. Practical necessity likewise dictates that teachers and school administrators have related authority with respect to other in-school activities like auditorium programs attended by a large audience.

Because no school could operate effectively if teachers and administrators lacked the authority to regulate in-school speech in these ways, the Court may have felt no need to specify the source of this authority or to explain how the special rules applicable to in-school student speech fit into our broader framework of free-speech case law. But when a public school regulates what students say or write when they are not on school grounds and are not participating in a school program, the school has the obligation to answer the question with which I began: Why should enrollment in a public school result in the diminution of a student's free-speech rights?

The only plausible answer that comes readily to mind is consent, either express or implied. The theory must be that by enrolling a child in a public school, parents consent on behalf of the child to the relinquishment of some of the child's free-speech rights.

This understanding is consistent with the conditions to which an adult would implicitly consent by enrolling in an adult education class run by a unit of state or local government. If an adult signs up for, say, a French class, the adult may be required to speak French, to answer the teacher's questions, and to comply with other rules that are imposed for the sake of orderly instruction.

When it comes to children, courts in this country have analyzed the issue of consent by adapting the common-law doctrine of *in loco parentis*. Under the common law, as Blackstone explained, "[a father could] delegate part of his parental authority . . . to the tutor or schoolmaster of his child; who is then *in loco parentis*, and has such a portion of the power of the parent committed to his charge, [namely,] that of restraint and correction, as may be necessary to answer the purposes for which he is employed." 1 W. Blackstone, Commentaries on the Laws of England 441 (1765).

Blackstone's explanation of the doctrine seems to treat it primarily as an implied term in a private employment agreement between a father and those with whom he contracted for the provision of educational services for his child, and therefore the scope of the delegation that could be inferred depended on "the purposes for which [the tutor or schoolmaster was] employed." If a child was sent to a boarding school, the parents would not have been in a position to monitor or control the child's behavior or to attend to the child's welfare on a daily basis, and the schoolmaster would be regarded as having implicitly received the authority to perform those functions around the clock while the child was in residence. On the other hand, if parents hired a tutor to instruct a child in the home on certain subjects during certain hours, the scope of the delegation would be different. The tutor would be in charge during lessons, but the parents would retain most of their authority. In short, the scope of the delegation depended on the scope of the agreed-upon undertaking.

Today, of course, the educational picture is quite different. The education of children within a specified age range is compulsory, and States specify the minimum number of hours per day and the minimum number of days per year that a student must attend classes, as well as many aspects of the school curriculum. Parents are not required to enroll their children in a public school. They can select a private school if a suitable one is available and they can afford the tuition, and they may also be able to educate their children at home if they have the time and ability and can meet the standards that their State imposes. But by choice or necessity, nearly 90% of the students in this country attend public schools, and parents and public schools do not enter into a contractual relationship.

If *in loco parentis* is transplanted from Blackstone's England to the 21st century United States, what it amounts to is simply a doctrine of inferred parental consent to a public school's exercise of a degree of authority that is commensurate with the task that the parents ask the school to perform. Because public school students attend school for only part of the day and continue to live at home, the degree of authority conferred is obviously less than that delegated to the head of a late-18th century boarding school, but because public school students are taught outside the home, the authority conferred may be greater in at least some respects than that enjoyed by a tutor of Blackstone's time.

So how much authority to regulate speech do parents implicitly delegate when they enroll a child at a public school? The answer must be that parents are treated as having relinquished the measure of authority that the schools must be able to exercise in order to carry out their state-mandated educational mission, as well as the authority to perform any other functions to which parents expressly or implicitly agree—for example, by giving permission for a child to participate in an extracurricular activity or to go on a school trip.

The degree to which enrollment in a public school can be regarded as a delegation of authority over off-campus speech depends on the nature of the speech and the circumstances under which it occurs. I will not attempt to provide a complete taxonomy of off-premises speech, but relevant lower court cases tend to fall into a few basic groups. And with respect to speech in each of these groups, the question that courts must ask is whether parents who enroll their children in a public school can reasonably be understood to have delegated to the school the authority to regulate the speech in question.

One category of off-premises student speech falls easily within the scope of the authority that parents implicitly or explicitly provide. This category includes speech that takes place during or as part of what amounts to a temporal or spatial extension of the regular school program, *e.g.*, online instruction at home, assigned essays or other homework, and transportation to and from school. Also included are statements made during other school activities in which students participate with their parents' consent, such as school trips, school sports and other extracurricular activities that may take place after regular school hours or off school premises, and after-school programs for students who would otherwise be without adult supervision during that time. Abusive speech that occurs while students are walking to and from school may also fall into this category on the theory that it is school attendance that puts students on that route and in the company of the fellow students who engage in the abuse. The imperatives that justify the regulation of student speech while in school—the need for orderly and effective instruction and student protection—apply more or less equally to these off-premises activities.

At the other end of the spectrum, there is a category of speech that is almost always beyond the regulatory authority of a public school. This is student speech that is not expressly and specifically directed at the school, school administrators, teachers, or fellow students and that addresses matters of public concern, including sensitive subjects like politics, religion, and social relations.

If a school tried to regulate such speech, the most that it could claim is that offensive off-premises speech on important matters may cause controversy and recriminations among students and may thus disrupt instruction and good order on school premises. But it is a "bedrock principle" that speech may not be suppressed simply because it expresses ideas that are "offensive or disagreeable." *Texas v. Johnson.*

This is true even if the student's off-premises speech on a matter of public concern is intemperate and crude. When a student engages in oral or written communication of this nature, the student is subject to whatever restraints the student's parents impose, but the student enjoys the same First Amendment protection against government regulation as all other members of the public.

Between these two extremes (*i.e.*, off-premises speech that is tantamount to on-campus speech and general statements made off premises on matters of public concern) lie the categories of off-premises student speech that appear to have given rise to the most litigation. A survey of lower court cases reveals several prominent categories. I will mention some of those categories, but like the Court, I do not attempt to set out the test to be used in judging the constitutionality of a public school's efforts to regulate such speech.

One group of cases involves perceived threats to school administrators, teachers, other staff members, or students. Laws that apply to everyone prohibit defined categories of threats, but schools have claimed that their duties demand broader authority.

Another common category involves speech that criticizes or derides school administrators, teachers, or other staff members. Schools may assert that parents who send their children to a public school implicitly authorize the school to demand that the child exhibit the respect that is required for orderly and effective instruction, but parents surely do not relinquish their children's ability to complain in an appropriate manner about wrongdoing, dereliction, or even plain incompetence.

Perhaps the most difficult category involves criticism or hurtful remarks about other students. Bullying and severe harassment are serious (and age-old) problems, but these concepts are not easy to define with the precision required for a regulation of speech.

The present case does not fall into any of these categories. Instead, it simply involves criticism (albeit in a crude manner) of the school and an extracurricular activity. Unflattering speech about a school or one of its programs is different from speech that criticizes or derides particular individuals, and for the reasons detailed by the Court and by Judge Ambro in his separate opinion below, the school's justifications for punishing B.L.'s speech were weak.

There are more than 90,000 public school principals in this country and more than 13,000 separate school districts. The overwhelming majority of school administrators, teachers, and coaches are men and women who are deeply dedicated to the best interests of their students, but it is predictable that there will be occasions when some will get carried away, as did the school officials in the case at hand. If today's decision teaches any lesson, it must be that the regulation of many types of off-premises student speech raises serious First Amendment concerns, and school officials should proceed cautiously before venturing into this territory.

JUSTICE THOMAS, dissenting.

While the majority entirely ignores the relevant history, I would begin the assessment of the scope of free-speech rights incorporated against the States by looking to "what 'ordinary citizens' at the time of the Fourteenth Amendment's ratification would have understood" the right to encompass. Cases and treatises from that era reveal that public schools retained substantial authority to discipline students. As I have previously explained, that authority was near plenary while students were at school.

Authority also extended to when students were traveling to or from school. And, although schools had less authority after a student returned home, it was well settled that they still could discipline students for off-campus speech or conduct that had a proximate tendency to harm the school environment.

Perhaps the most familiar example applying this rule is a case where a student, after returning home from school, used "disrespectful language" against a teacher—he called the teacher "old"—"in presence of the teacher and of some of his fellow pupils." The Vermont Supreme Court held that the teacher could discipline a student for this speech because the speech had "a direct and immediate tendency to injure the school, to subvert the master's authority, and to beget disorder and insubordination."

The majority declines to consider any of this history, instead favoring a few pragmatic guideposts. This is not the first time the Court has chosen intuition over history when it comes to student speech. The larger problem facing us today is that our student-speech cases are untethered from any textual or historical foundation.

The Court's failure to explain itself in *Tinker* needlessly makes this case more difficult.

Perhaps there are good constitutional reasons to depart from the historical rule, and perhaps this Court and lower courts will identify and explain these reasons in the future. But because the Court does not do so today, and because it reaches the wrong result under the appropriate historical test, I respectfully dissent.

Points for Discussion

1. **A bright-line rule for school authority to regulate off-campus speech?** Until *Mahanoy*, there was little clarity in the jurisprudence about the extent of a school's authority to regulate off-campus student speech. When the Third Circuit heard the *Mahanoy* case, it opted for an easily administered bright-line rule: that schools lack authority to regulate off-campus speech. Did the Supreme Court adopt the Third Circuit's rule? If not, why? What examples does the Court give of off-campus speech that schools should have authority to regulate? Do you prefer the Third Circuit's bright-line rule or the Supreme Court's approach?

2. **If not a bright-line rule, then what?** Justice Stephen Breyer, the author of the majority opinion, eschewed a crisp doctrinal test for off-campus speech. Instead, he described a series of animating principles for determining when a school should have authority to regulate off-campus student speech. Does *Mahanoy* provide sufficient guidance to school officials and lower courts to determine when off-campus speech may be regulated? What questions did it appear to answer, and what questions did it appear to leave unsettled?

3. **Should the Court have used an originalist approach?** In his dissent, Justice Clarence Thomas laments the fact that the majority had "chosen intuition over history" to answer the question posed by the case. He would have preferred to focus on what rights students had at the time the Fourteenth Amendment was adopted, presumably because the First Amendment applies to the Mahanoy Area School District through its incorporation into the Fourteenth Amendment. Do you think this "originalist" approach is a better way of resolving the question of whether the school's disciplinary action violated the student's First Amendment rights? If yes, why do you prefer this approach? If not, why would you reject the approach? Even if Justice Thomas makes a convincing case for using an original-

ist approach, is it obvious to you why, in interpreting the First Amendment, it makes sense to focus on when the Fourteenth Amendment was ratified (1868) as opposed to when the First Amendment was ratified (1791) or when the Supreme Court first announced that the First Amendment was incorporated into the Fourteenth Amendment (1925)?

You Be the Principal!

Which students can be punished for their speech?

If you think that being a lawyer sounds challenging, try being a high school principal. Imagine that you are the principal of a large public high school. The students in your school like to express themselves and use a wide variety of means for doing so, ranging from T-shirts emblazoned with messages to the color of their hair.

For each of the following, determine whether you may constitutionally regulate the student speech. As you consider these scenarios, ask yourself whether it would be helpful to have additional information and what that information would be.

- A student comes to school wearing a shirt with a gang symbol. While not common, there has occasionally been gang-related violence at the school. Can you tell the student that he must change into a different shirt?

- A student comes to school wearing a shirt that displays a Confederate flag. The school has an official policy committing the school to the goals of diversity, equity, and inclusion. Can you tell the student that he must change into a different shirt?

- A student comes to school wearing a shirt with this line from Karl Marx: "Religion is the opium of the people." The school has a substantial number of students who are fundamentalist Christians. Can you tell the student that he must change into a different shirt?

- A student comes to school wearing a shirt that says "Legalize Marijuana" and has a picture of a leaf from a cannabis plant. Recreational marijuana use is not legal in the state where your school is located. Can you tell the student that he must change into a different shirt?

- A student comes to school wearing a shirt with a drawing of an assault weapon and this question: "What part of 'shall not be infringed' do you not understand?" (The words "shall not be infringed" are taken from the Second Amendment.) The school has a policy that prohibits students from wearing clothing about products that minors are not permitted to purchase (such as beer, cigarettes, and, yes, assault weapons). Can you tell the student that he must change into a different shirt?

- A girl comes to school with pink hair in violation of a school rule that requires hair to be a natural color. Would disciplining the girl violate her First Amendment rights?

- The student leaders in the school's drama program are complaining that they selected the Broadway show "Hair" for the school's annual musical, but the drama teacher vetoed their decision because the show has too many references to sex and drug use. Was the teacher allowed to override the students' preference?

- A student, using a computer in his house, makes disparaging comments about a teacher on his social media account. The remark is only accessible to the student's "friends," but almost 100 students at the school have befriended the student. Can the student be disciplined for posting her comments?

- A student goes to a public park on a Sunday wearing a shirt that says, "Fuck [insert name of high school]." Can the student be disciplined for wearing this shirt?

If you find making these decisions stressful, could you make your life easier by changing the school dress code to require all students to wear uniforms to school? Would this uniform requirement violate the students' First Amendment rights? Are clothing choices expressive? *See* Deborah M. Ahrens & Andrew M. Siegel, *Of Dress and Redress: Student Dress Restrictions in Constitutional Law and Culture*, 54 Harv. C.R.-C.L. L. Rev. 49 (2019).

Book Bans at Public School Libraries

What are the First Amendment rules when a school board votes to ban books from a school library? The reasons for such a ban can vary widely, from concerns that a book has racist language (such as *The Adventures of Huckleberry Finn* and *To Kill a Mockingbird*) or that a book discusses homosexuality or transsexuality (such as *This Book is Gay* and *Beyond Magenta: Transgender Teens Speak Out*). According to the

American Library Association, the 100 most banned and challenged books during the years 2010–2019 included the *Captain Underpants* series by Dav Pilkey, *The Bluest Eye* by Toni Morrison, and *The Hunger Games* by Suzanne Collins. The list for 2000–2009 includes the *Harry Potter* series by J.K. Rowling.

© American Library Association
To find out the names of these books and the reasons they were banned, go to the American Library Association's banned-books webpage here.

Supreme Court jurisprudence on the legality of book bans is lean. The most important case is *Board of Education v. Pico*, 457 U.S. 853 (1982). In that case, a school board voted to remove books from school libraries that a conservative group had identified as objectionable. Among the books were Kurt Vonnegut's *Slaughter-house Five*, Desmond Morris' *The Naked Ape*, and *Best Short Stories by Negro Writers*, edited by Langston Hughes.

A plurality of the Court indicated that the removal of books from a school library could violate the First Amendment if the underlying motive was to suppress viewpoints that the school administrators disliked. Here is the key passage from the opinion:

> Petitioners rightly possess significant discretion to determine the content of their school libraries. But that discretion may not be exercised in a narrowly partisan or political manner. If a Democratic school board, motivated by party affiliation, ordered the removal of all books written by or in favor of Republicans, few would doubt that the order violated the constitutional rights of the students denied access to those books. The same conclusion would surely apply if an all-white school board, motivated by racial animus, decided to remove all books authored by blacks or advocating racial equal-

> ity and integration. Our Constitution does not permit the official suppression of *ideas.* Thus whether petitioners' removal of books from their school libraries denied respondents their First Amendment rights depends upon the motivation behind petitioners' actions. If petitioners *intended* by their removal decision to deny respondents access to ideas with which petitioners disagreed, and if this intent was the decisive factor in petitioners' decision, then petitioners have exercised their discretion in violation of the Constitution. To permit such intentions to control official actions would be to encourage the precise sort of officially prescribed orthodoxy unequivocally condemned in *Barnette.*

The plurality emphasized that its rule applied only to decisions to remove books from a school library, not to add them. The case was remanded to the lower courts to resolve the factual question of whether the school board's decision to remove the books was improperly motivated.

Does the *Pico* rule seem like an easy standard to administer? Does it set too high a bar for those challenging book bans?

Whether *Pico* remains good law is questionable. It was only a plurality decision. And it was a decision that preceded the emergence of the "government speech" doctrine, discussed later in this chapter. As you will learn, when expression is treated as the speech of the government, no First Amendment challenge may be brought. For example, decisions as to what monuments to include in a public park are deemed government speech immune from First Amendment challenge. While the books that appear in a public school library are undoubtedly the private speech of the authors, the decisions as to which books to include or not include arguably are decisions in which the "government," such as a school board, is engaging in its own expression. How would you decide this issue?

D. Government as Employer: The Free Speech Rights of Government Employees

The First Amendment rights of government employees arise in two distinct contexts. The first is when the government retaliates against an employee because of his or her speech. The second is when a government employee is fired or denied employment opportunities because of her association with a disfavored political party.

1. Punishing Employees Because of Their Speech: Retaliation and the *Pickering/Connick/Garcetti* Test

Millions of people work for federal, state, and local governments. Does the First Amendment afford these workers any protection if their employers dismiss them or deny them benefits because of their speech?

This short answer is yes. The days of governments' having unfettered discretion to dismiss employees because of their speech are gone. Courts no longer brusquely dismiss employee free speech complaints by saying, as Justice Holmes did of the garrulous police officer in *McAuliffe v. Mayor of New Bedford*, that "petitioner may have a constitutional right to talk politics, but he has no constitutional right to be a policeman." You saw evidence of this in *Tinker* when Justice Fortas observed that public school teachers, like their students, do not shed their First Amendment rights at the schoolhouse gate.

But just as public schools have greater leeway to regulate student speech that disrupts school operations, so, too, do government employers have greater leeway to regulate employee speech that undermine the effectiveness of government operations. Like any employer, government office managers need the ability to address employee speech that foments office insurrections or antagonizes fellow employees. Government employers must also be able to evaluate the quality of the speech that employees produce as part of their jobs.

As it has done in other special settings, the Supreme Court has had to strike a balance in the government employee context. In this instance, the balance is between the government employees' legitimate free speech rights and the government's need to regulate speech for its offices to function effectively. The seminal case that initiated this balancing process was *Pickering v. Board of Education*, 391 U.S. 563 (1968). The case concerned an Illinois high school teacher who wrote a letter to the editor of a local newspaper that criticized the board of education over several issues, including the board's allocation of money between athletic and academic programs. "To sod football fields on borrowed money and then not be able to pay teachers' salaries," the letter stated, "is getting the cart before the horse."

The school board fired the teacher for writing the letter. The board claimed that the letter contained falsehoods, impugned the integrity of the board and the school administration, and would foment conflict among teachers and administrators, although the board failed to introduce evidence to substantiate these claims.

In a critical passage, Justice Thurgood Marshall, the author of the majority opinion, articulated the need to strike a balance between a government employee's right to speak and a government employer's right to manage its operations:

> To the extent that the Illinois Supreme Court's opinion may be read to suggest that teachers may constitutionally be compelled to relinquish the First Amendment rights they would otherwise enjoy as citizens to comment on matters of public interest in connection with the operation of the public schools in which they work, it proceeds on a premise that has been unequivocally rejected in numerous prior decisions of this Court. "The theory that public employment which may be denied altogether may be subjected to any conditions, regardless of how unreasonable, has been uniformly rejected." At the same time it cannot be gainsaid that the State has interests as an employer in regulating the speech of its employees that differ significantly from those it possesses in connection with regulation of the speech of the citizenry in general. The problem in any case is to arrive at a balance between the interests of the teacher, as a citizen, in commenting upon matters of public concern and the interest of the State, as an employer, in promoting the efficiency of the public services it performs through its employees.

After analyzing the facts, the Court ruled in favor of the teacher. It acknowledged that the teacher did erroneously report on the amount of funds the school district allocated for athletics, but it noted that these numbers were public records and that the board could have easily rebutted the teacher's claim through its own letter to the editor. The Court continued:

> What we do have before us is a case in which a teacher has made erroneous public statements upon issues then currently the subject of public attention, which are critical of his ultimate employer but which are neither shown nor can be presumed to have in any way either impeded the teacher's proper performance of his daily duties in the classroom or to have interfered with the regular operation of the schools generally. In these circumstances we conclude that the interest of the school administration in limiting teachers' opportunities to contribute to public debate is not significantly greater than its interest in limiting a similar contribution by any member of the general public.

In summarizing its holding, the Court said that, in the absence of proof that the teacher made his false statements either knowingly or with reckless disregard for the truth, the "teacher's exercise of his right to speak on issues of public importance may not furnish the basis for his dismissal from public employment."

The Court's next major opinion on the topic, *Connick v. Myers*, 461 U.S. 138 (1983), illustrated how *Pickering*'s balancing test can also tip in favor of an employer. In *Connick*, an assistant district attorney, Sheila Myers, was upset about a decision to transfer her to a different section of the criminal court. In response, she prepared and circulated a questionnaire among fellow employees that asked about office morale and the level of confidence the employees had in their supervisors. The district attorney's first assistant characterized Myers' action as causing a "mini-insurrection." As a result of her actions, Myers was fired.

In upholding Myers' termination, the Court emphasized that her speech was less about a matter of public concern and more about an employee's grievance with her unwelcome transfer:

> This is not a case where an employee, out of purely academic interest, circulated a questionnaire so as to obtain useful research. Myers acknowledges that it is no coincidence that the questionnaire followed upon the heels of the transfer notice. When employee speech concerning office policy arises from an employment dispute concerning the very application of that policy to the speaker, additional weight must be given to the supervisor's view that the employee has threatened the authority of the employer to run the office.

The following case added an important gloss to the *Pickering/Connick* test for analyzing employee speech issues.

Garcetti v. Ceballos

Supreme Court of the United States, 2006
547 U.S. 410

JUSTICE KENNEDY delivered the opinion of the Court.

It is well settled that "a State cannot condition public employment on a basis that infringes the employee's constitutionally protected interest in freedom of expression." The question presented by the instant case is whether the First Amendment protects a government employee from discipline based on speech made pursuant to the employee's official duties.

Respondent Richard Ceballos has been employed since 1989 as a deputy district attorney for the Los Angeles County District Attorney's Office. During the period relevant to this case, Ceballos was a calendar deputy in the office's Pomona branch, and in this capacity he exercised certain supervisory responsibilities over other lawyers. In February 2000, a defense attorney contacted Ceballos about a pending criminal case. The defense attorney said there were inaccuracies in an affidavit used to obtain a critical search warrant. The attorney informed Ceballos that he had filed a motion to traverse, or challenge, the warrant, but he also wanted Ceballos to review the case. According to Ceballos, it was not unusual for defense attorneys to ask calendar deputies to investigate aspects of pending cases.

After examining the affidavit and visiting the location it described, Ceballos determined the affidavit contained serious misrepresentations.

Ceballos spoke on the telephone to the warrant affiant, a deputy sheriff from the Los Angeles County Sheriff's Department, but he did not receive a satisfactory explanation for the perceived inaccuracies. He relayed his findings to his supervisors, petitioners Carol Najera and Frank Sundstedt, and followed up by preparing a disposition memorandum. The memo explained Ceballos' concerns and recommended dismissal of the case. On March 2, 2000, Ceballos submitted the memo to Sundstedt for his review. A few days later, Ceballos presented Sundstedt with another memo, this one describing a second telephone conversation between Ceballos and the warrant affiant.

Based on Ceballos' statements, a meeting was held to discuss the affidavit. Attendees included Ceballos, Sundstedt, and Najera, as well as the warrant affiant and other employees from the sheriff's department. The meeting allegedly became heated, with one lieutenant sharply criticizing Ceballos for his handling of the case.

Despite Ceballos' concerns, Sundstedt decided to proceed with the prosecution, pending disposition of the defense motion to traverse. The trial court held a hearing on the motion. Ceballos was called by the defense and recounted his observations about the affidavit, but the trial court rejected the challenge to the warrant.

Ceballos claims that in the aftermath of these events he was subjected to a series of retaliatory employment actions.

Petitioners responded that no retaliatory actions were taken against Ceballos and that all the actions of which he complained were explained by legitimate reasons such as staffing needs. They further contended that, in any event, Ceballos' memo was not protected speech under the First Amendment. Petitioners moved for summary judgment, and the District Court granted their motion.

The Court of Appeals for the Ninth Circuit reversed, holding that "Ceballos's allegations of wrongdoing in the memorandum constitute protected speech under the First Amendment. In reaching its conclusion the court looked to the First Amendment analysis set forth in *Pickering* and *Connick*. *Connick* instructs courts to begin by considering whether the expressions in question were made by the speaker "as a citizen upon matters of public concern." The Court of Appeals determined that Ceballos' memo, which recited what he thought to be governmental misconduct, was "inherently a matter of public concern." The court did not, however, consider whether the speech was made in Ceballos' capacity as a citizen. Rather, it relied on Circuit precedent rejecting the idea that "a public employee's speech is deprived of First Amendment protection whenever those views are expressed, to government workers or others, pursuant to an employment responsibility."

Having concluded that Ceballos' memo satisfied the public-concern requirement, the Court of Appeals proceeded to balance Ceballos' interest in his speech against his supervisors' interest in responding to it. The court struck the balance in Ceballos' favor, noting that petitioners "failed even to suggest disruption or inefficiency in the workings of the District Attorney's Office" as a result of the memo. The court further concluded that Ceballos' First Amendment rights were clearly established and that petitioners' actions were not objectively reasonable.

As [this] Court's decisions have noted, for many years "the unchallenged dogma was that a public employee had no right to object to conditions placed upon the terms of employment—including those which restricted the exercise of constitutional rights." That dogma has been qualified in important respects. The Court has made clear that public employees do not surrender all their First Amendment rights by reason of their employment. Rather, the First Amendment protects a public employee's right, in certain circumstances, to speak as a citizen addressing matters of public concern.

Pickering provides a useful starting point in explaining the Court's doctrine. There the relevant speech was a teacher's letter to a local newspaper addressing issues including the funding policies of his school board. "The problem in any case," the Court stated, "is to arrive at a balance between the interests of the teacher, as a citizen, in commenting upon matters of public concern and the interest of the State, as an employer, in promoting the efficiency of the public services it performs through its employees." The Court found the teacher's speech "neither was shown nor can be presumed to have in any way either impeded the teacher's proper performance of his daily duties in the classroom or to have interfered with the regular operation of the schools generally." Thus, the Court concluded that "the interest of the school administration in limiting teachers' opportunities to contribute to public debate is not significantly greater than its interest in limiting a similar contribution by any member of the general public."

Pickering and the cases decided in its wake identify two inquiries to guide interpretation of the constitutional protections accorded to public employee speech. The first requires determining whether the employee spoke as a citizen on a matter of public concern. If the answer is no, the employee has no First Amendment cause of action based on his or her employer's reaction to the speech. If the answer is yes, then the possibility of a First Amendment claim arises. The question becomes whether the relevant government entity had an adequate justification for treating the employee differently from any other member of the general public. This consideration reflects the importance of the relationship between the speaker's expressions and employment. A government entity has broader discretion to restrict speech when it acts in its role as employer, but the restrictions it imposes must be directed at speech that has some potential to affect the entity's operations.

To be sure, conducting these inquiries sometimes has proved difficult. This is the necessary product of "the enormous variety of fact situations in which critical statements by teachers and other public employees may be thought by their superiors to furnish grounds for dismissal." The Court's overarching objectives, though, are evident.

When a citizen enters government service, the citizen by necessity must accept certain limitations on his or her freedom. Government employers, like private employers, need a significant degree of control over their employees' words and actions; without it, there would be little chance for the efficient provision of public services. *Connick* ("Government offices could not function if every employment decision became a constitutional matter"). Public employees, moreover, often occupy trusted positions in society. When they speak out, they can express views that contravene governmental policies or impair the proper performance of governmental functions.

At the same time, the Court has recognized that a citizen who works for the government is nonetheless a citizen. The First Amendment limits the ability of a public employer to leverage the employment relationship to restrict, incidentally or intentionally, the liberties employees enjoy in their capacities as private citizens. So long as employees are speaking as citizens about matters of public concern, they must face only those speech restrictions that are necessary for their employers to operate efficiently and effectively.

The Court's employee-speech jurisprudence protects, of course, the constitutional rights of public employees. Yet the First Amendment interests at stake extend beyond the individual speaker. The Court has acknowledged the importance of promoting the public's interest in receiving the well-informed views of government employees engaging in civic discussion.

The Court's decisions, then, have sought both to promote the individual and societal interests that are served when employees speak as citizens on matters of public concern and to respect the needs of government employers attempting to perform their important public functions.

The controlling factor in Ceballos' case is that his expressions were made pursuant to his duties as a calendar deputy. That consideration—the fact that Ceballos spoke as a prosecutor fulfilling a responsibility to advise his supervisor about how best to proceed with a pending case—distinguishes Ceballos' case from those in which the First Amendment provides protection against discipline. We hold that when public employees make statements pursuant to their official duties, the employees are not speaking as citizens for First Amendment purposes, and the Constitution does not insulate their communications from employer discipline.

Ceballos wrote his disposition memo because that is part of what he, as a calendar deputy, was employed to do. It is immaterial whether he experienced some personal gratification from writing the memo; his First Amendment rights do not depend on his job satisfaction. The significant point is that the memo was written pursuant to Ceballos' official duties. Restricting speech that owes its existence to a public employee's professional responsibilities does not infringe any liberties the employee might have enjoyed as a private citizen. It simply reflects the exercise of employer control over what the employer itself has commissioned or created. *Cf. Rosenberger* ("When the government appropriates public funds to promote a particular policy of its own it is entitled to say what it wishes"). Contrast, for example, the expressions made by the speaker in *Pickering*, whose letter to the newspaper had no official significance and bore similarities to letters submitted by numerous citizens every day.

Ceballos did not act as a citizen when he went about conducting his daily professional activities, such as supervising attorneys, investigating charges, and preparing filings. In the same way he did not speak as a citizen by writing a memo that addressed the proper disposition of a pending criminal case. When he went to work and performed the tasks he was paid to perform, Ceballos acted as a government employee. The fact that his duties sometimes required him to speak or write does not mean his supervisors were prohibited from evaluating his performance.

This result is consistent with our precedents' attention to the potential societal value of employee speech. Refusing to recognize First Amendment claims based on government employees' work product does not prevent them from participating in public debate. The employees retain the prospect of constitutional protection for their contributions to the civic discourse. This prospect of protection, however, does not invest them with a right to perform their jobs however they see fit.

Our holding likewise is supported by the emphasis of our precedents on affording government employers sufficient discretion to manage their operations. Employers have heightened interests in controlling speech made by an employee in his or her professional capacity. Official communications have official consequences, creating a need for substantive consistency and clarity. Supervisors must ensure that their employees' official communications are accurate, demonstrate sound judgment, and promote the employer's mission. Ceballos' memo is illustrative. It demanded the attention of his supervisors and led to a heated meeting with employees from the sheriff's department. If Ceballos' superiors thought his memo was inflammatory or misguided, they had the authority to take proper corrective action.

Two final points warrant mentioning. First, as indicated above, the parties in this case do not dispute that Ceballos wrote his disposition memo pursuant to his employment duties. We thus have no occasion to articulate a comprehensive framework for defining the scope of an employee's duties in cases where there is room for serious debate. We reject, however, the suggestion that employers can restrict employees' rights by creating excessively broad job descriptions. The proper inquiry is a practical one. Formal job descriptions often bear little resemblance to the duties an employee actually is expected to perform, and the listing of a given task in an employee's written job description is neither necessary nor sufficient to demonstrate that conducting the task is within the scope of the employee's professional duties for First Amendment purposes.

Second, Justice Souter suggests today's decision may have important ramifications for academic freedom, at least as a constitutional value. There is some argument that expression related to academic scholarship or classroom instruction implicates additional constitutional interests that are not fully accounted for by this Court's customary employee-speech jurisprudence. We need not, and for that reason do not, decide whether the analysis we conduct today would apply in the same manner to a case involving speech related to scholarship or teaching.

Exposing governmental inefficiency and misconduct is a matter of considerable significance. As the Court noted in *Connick*, public employers should, "as a matter of good judgment," be "receptive to constructive criticism offered by their employees." The dictates of sound judgment are reinforced by the powerful network of legislative enactments—such as whistle-blower protection laws and labor codes—available to those who seek to expose wrongdoing. Cases involving government attorneys implicate additional safeguards in the form of, for example, rules of conduct and constitutional obligations apart from the First Amendment. These imperatives, as well as obligations arising from any other applicable constitutional provisions and mandates of the criminal and civil laws, protect employees and provide checks on supervisors who would order unlawful or otherwise inappropriate actions.

We reject, however, the notion that the First Amendment shields from discipline the expressions employees make pursuant to their professional duties. Our precedents do not support the existence of a constitutional cause of action behind every statement a public employee makes in the course of doing his or her job.

JUSTICE STEVENS, dissenting.

The proper answer to the question "whether the First Amendment protects a government employee from discipline based on speech made pursuant to the employee's official duties," is "Sometimes," not "Never."

JUSTICE SOUTER, with whom JUSTICE STEVENS and JUSTICE GINSBURG join, dissenting.

Open speech by a private citizen on a matter of public importance lies at the heart of expression subject to protection by the First Amendment. At the other extreme, a statement by a government employee complaining about nothing beyond treatment under personnel rules raises no greater claim to constitutional protection against retaliatory response than the remarks of a private employee. In between these points lies a public employee's speech unwelcome to the government but on a significant public issue. Such an employee speaking as a citizen, that is, with a citizen's interest, is protected from reprisal unless the statements are too damaging to the government's capacity to conduct public business to be justified by any individual or public benefit thought to flow from the statements. Entitlement to protection is thus not absolute.

This significant, albeit qualified, protection of public employees who irritate the government is understood to flow from the First Amendment, in part, because a government paycheck does nothing to eliminate the value to an individual of speaking on public matters, and there is no good reason for categorically discounting a speaker's interest in commenting on a matter of public concern just because the government employs him. Still, the First Amendment safeguard rests on something more, being the value to the public of receiving the opinions and information that a public employee may disclose.

The majority accepts the fallacy propounded by the county petitioners and the Federal Government as amicus that any statement made within the scope of public employment is (or should be treated as) the government's own speech, and should thus be differentiated as a matter of law from the personal statements the First Amendment protects. The majority invokes the interpretation set out in *Rosenberger* of *Rust v. Sullivan*, 500 U.S. 173 (1991), which held there was no infringement of the speech rights of Title X funds recipients and their staffs when the Government forbade any on-the-job counseling in favor of abortion as a method of family planning. We have read *Rust* to mean that "when the government appropriates public funds to promote a particular policy of its own it is entitled to say what it wishes." *Rosenberger*.

The key to understanding the difference between this case and *Rust* lies in the terms of the respective employees' jobs and, in particular, the extent to which those terms require espousal of a substantive position prescribed by the government in advance. Some public employees are hired to "promote a particular policy" by broadcasting a particular message set by the government, but not everyone working for the government, after all, is hired to speak from a government manifesto.

The fallacy of the majority's reliance on *Rosenberger*'s understanding of *Rust* doctrine, moreover, portends a bloated notion of controllable government speech going well beyond the circumstances of this case. Consider the breadth of the new formulation:

> Restricting speech that owes its existence to a public employee's professional responsibilities does not infringe any liberties the employee might have enjoyed as a private citizen. It simply reflects the exercise of employer control over what the employer itself has commissioned or created.

This ostensible domain beyond the pale of the First Amendment is spacious enough to include even the teaching of a public university professor, and I have to hope that today's majority does not mean to imperil First Amendment protection of academic freedom in public colleges and universities, whose teachers necessarily speak and write "pursuant to official duties." *See Grutter v. Bollinger*, 539 U.S. 306, 329 (2003) ("We have long recognized that, given the important purpose of public education and the expansive freedoms of speech and thought associated with the university environment, universities occupy a special niche in our constitutional tradition"); *Keyishian v. Board of Regents of Univ. of State of N. Y.*, 385 U.S. 589, 603 (1967) ("Our Nation is deeply committed to safeguarding academic freedom, which is of transcendent value to all of us and not merely to the teachers concerned. That freedom is therefore a special concern of the First Amendment, which does not tolerate laws that cast a pall of orthodoxy over the classroom. The vigilant protection of constitutional freedoms is nowhere more vital than in the community of American schools" (*quoting Shelton v. Tucker*, 364 U.S. 479, 487 (1960)); *Sweezy v. New Hampshire*, 354 U.S. 234, 250 (1957) (a governmental enquiry into the contents of a scholar's lectures at a state university "unquestionably was an invasion of his liberties in the areas of academic freedom and political expression—areas in which government should be extremely reticent to tread").

JUSTICE BREYER, dissenting.

This case asks whether the First Amendment protects public employees when they engage in speech that both (1) involves matters of public concern and (2) takes place in the ordinary course of performing the duties of a government job. I write separately to explain why I cannot fully accept either the Court's or Justice Souter's answer to the question presented.

I conclude that the First Amendment sometimes does authorize judicial actions based upon a government employee's speech that both (1) involves a matter of public concern and also (2) takes place in the course of ordinary job-related duties. But it does so only in the presence of augmented need for constitutional protection and diminished risk of undue judicial interference with governmental management of the public's affairs. In my view, these conditions are met in this case and *Pickering* balancing is consequently appropriate.

Points for Discussion

1. **What are the limits on the *Garcetti* exception?** *Garcetti* indicated that the First Amendment does not protect a government employee's speech when the employee is speaking pursuant to his official duties. Left open after *Garcetti* were

the precise parameters of when an employee is speaking pursuant to his official duties. In *Lane v. Franks*, 573 U.S. 228 (2014), the Court added an important limitation on *Garcetti*. In that case, Edward Lane had been the director of a youth training program that was run under the auspices of a community college. In his capacity as director, Lane discovered that an Alabama state representative, Suzanne Schmitz, had been on the program's payroll but had not actually performed any work. Lane fired her. Schmitz's termination came to the attention of the FBI, which initiated an investigation. This led to Lane's testifying before a federal grand jury about his reasons for firing Schmitz. The grand jury later indicted Schmitz. The community college then fired Lane, and he sued, claiming that he was terminated because of the testimony he gave to the grand jury.

The Eleventh Circuit, following the logic of *Garcetti*, held that the First Amendment did not protect Lane's testimony because he was testifying about information he had acquired while performing his job responsibilities. The Supreme Court rejected this expansive interpretation of *Garcetti*:

> In rejecting Lane's argument that his testimony was speech as a citizen, the Eleventh Circuit gave short shrift to the nature of sworn judicial statements and ignored the obligation borne by all witnesses testifying under oath. Sworn testimony in judicial proceedings is a quintessential example of speech as a citizen for a simple reason: Anyone who testifies in court bears an obligation, to the court and society at large, to tell the truth.
>
> In holding that Lane did not speak as a citizen when he testified, the Eleventh Circuit read *Garcetti* far too broadly. It reasoned that, because Lane learned of the subject matter of his testimony in the course of his employment with [the youth training program], *Garcetti* requires that his testimony be treated as the speech of an employee rather than that of a citizen. It does not.
>
> *Garcetti* said nothing about speech that simply relates to public employment or concerns information learned in the course of public employment. The *Garcetti* Court made explicit that its holding did not turn on the fact that the memo at issue "concerned the subject matter of [the prosecutor's] employment," because "the First Amendment protects some expressions related to the speaker's job." In other words, the mere fact that a citizen's speech concerns information acquired by virtue of his public employment does not transform that speech into employee—rather than citizen—speech. The critical question under *Garcetti* is whether the speech at issue is itself ordinarily within the scope of an employee's duties, not whether it merely concerns those duties.

Contrary to the Eleventh Circuit, the Supreme Court held that when Lane testified before the grand jury he was speaking as a citizen and not as an employee. Consequently, his speech was protected by the First Amendment.

2. **May a public employee be disciplined or fired for engaging in expressive activity if the government proves that it had other legitimate grounds for its actions?** The answer is yes. Under the "*Mt. Healthy* rule," once an employee demonstrates that he or she has been penalized for constitutionally protected expression, the state may still prevail if it is able to demonstrate that it would have taken the disciplinary action notwithstanding the protected expression. Once the employee demonstrates that he or she engaged in constitutionally protected speech, and that such protected speech was a "substantial" or "motivating" factor in the disciplinary action taken, the burden shifts to the government to prove by a preponderance of the evidence that it would have taken the disciplinary action even in the absence of the protected expression. *Mt. Healthy City Sch. Dist. Bd. of Educ. v. Doyle*, 429 U.S. 274 (1977).

3. **Do government employees ever win?** Government employees who are fired or disciplined do often bring lawsuits challenging the government's action, and free speech "retaliation claims" governed by the *Pickering/Connick/Garcetti* test are often elements of those lawsuits. Do government employees ever win such cases? They do, but particularly in light of *Garcetti* and the *Mt. Healthy* rule, the obstacles are daunting. Here is a summary of the gauntlet that must be run:

    - First, the employee must pass "prong one" of the test, demonstrating that the speech for which the employee was fired or disciplined was speech made by the employee "as a citizen on a matter of public concern." *Garcetti* made it much harder for employees to get past prong one, by establishing a bright-line rule that if the employee was speaking pursuant to the employee's "official duties," it follows automatically that the employee was not speaking as a "citizen" for First Amendment purposes. If the employee does not get past prong one, the employee's case is over—no free speech claim may be brought.

    - Second, even if the employee manages to survive prong one, the government employer may still win. Under prong two, courts engage in a balancing test, asking whether the employee's interest in expression is outweighed by any injury the speech could cause to the interest of the government, as an employer, in promoting the efficiency of the public services it performs through its employees. In applying prong two, courts typically weigh a multitude of factors, such as whether the speech would create problems in maintaining discipline or harmony among co-workers; whether the employment relationship is one in which personal loyalty and confidence are necessary; whether the speech impeded the employee's ability to perform his or her responsibilities; the time, place, and manner of the speech; and the context within which the underlying dispute arose. Courts are particularly apt to strike the balance in favor of the government in employment contexts in which strict discipline, following orders, and *esprit de corps* are highly valued. Police and fire departments are prime examples. So too, may be prosecutors' offices. It is perhaps no accident that in two of the famous cases, *Connick* and *Garcetti*, the "bosses" were prosecutors. In *Connick* the boss was New Orleans District Attorney Harry Connick, the father of the famous entertainer Harry Connick, Jr. In *Garcetti* the bosses were senior prosecutors in the Los Angeles District Attorney's Office.

- Third, under the *Mt. Healthy* rule, even if the government employee manages to jump successfully through hoops one and two, the employee may still lose if the government establishes that it had legitimate grounds for firing or disciplining the employee anyway.

You Be the Judge!

Denying tenure to a controversial professor

Jane Smith, a tenure-track professor at a state university law school is denied tenure and fired. At her law school, a recommendation on whether to grant or deny tenure is made in the first instance by an elected committee of five tenured professors. That recommendation then goes to the law school dean, who makes the final determination. Smith had "mixed reviews" from students with regard to her teaching. Some students really liked her classes, others strongly disliked them. Her scholarship, consisting of four law review articles, also received mixed reviews, with some reviewers praising the scholarship, and others strongly criticizing the articles. Smith also has a reputation for making provocative statements in faculty meetings that often disturb or upset many colleagues. In a law review article, she strongly supported the jurisprudence of conservative Supreme Court justices, including those who favor the death penalty and are against abortion rights, same-sex marriage, and affirmative action. In the article she wrote, "Left-wing progressive critics of the conservative wing of the Court are contemporary fascists, determined to impose their progressive policy agenda upon the American people through judicial fiat, destabilizing democracy and subverting the very idea that constitutional interpretation should be an exercise of law, not politics." Smith made the same comment while teaching a constitutional law class, which caused many students to become upset and complain to the dean. When the dean, in a faculty meeting, brought up the statement, chastising professors "not to use their classrooms as a bully pulpit for expressing their private views," Smith responded by saying, "I was not expressing my 'private views,' but telling students the truth about constitutional interpretation, and exposing persons exactly like you, Dean, for the politically correct subverters of democracy that you are."

The faculty tenure committee voted 3–2 to recommend tenure. The majority expressed disapproval of Smith's statements in the law review article, the classroom, and the faculty meeting as "intemperate." Even so, the majority reasoned, Smith should have the "academic freedom" to express herself in all three settings. The majority noted that Smith had received "mixed reviews," as a teacher, scholar, and colleague, but concluded that "the mixed reviews the professor has received have nothing to do, really, with the quality of the professor's teaching, scholarship, or participation in faculty governance, but with the views the professor expresses in those settings, which are often expressed in passionate and intemperate rhetoric that offends many people." Two faculty members on the committee dissented, finding Smith's statements in all three settings to be "disruptive and unprofessional." The dean denied Smith tenure, agreeing with the two dissenting committee members. The dean's report denying tenure said that the statements made in the three settings were "unprofessional and disruptive of the law school's educational mission." The report further recited that "even setting those statements aside, the mixed reviews the professor has received regarding her scholarship, teaching, and collegial interactions warrant denial of tenure."

The professor sued, claiming that the tenure denial violated the First Amendment. If you were the judge, how would you rule, and why?

2. Punishing Employees Because of Party Affiliation: Political Patronage and the Spoils System

Imagine that you are an employee in a county sheriff's office. The sheriff had been a Republican, but in the most recent election he was replaced by a Democrat. In the time-honored tradition of political patronage, the new sheriff decided to fire any employees who were affiliated with the Republican Party and replace them with employees affiliated with the Democratic Party. Because you are a Republican, you lost your job.

You obviously didn't appreciate being fired, but do you have any basis for objecting to your termination? In some instances, there are statutory schemes protecting government employees from patronage dismissals, but you are not covered by such a law. Could you bring a First Amendment claim?

The *Pickering* line of cases would not be applicable in this instance because you were not terminated because of your speech. Rather, you were terminated because of your affiliation with the "wrong" political party. Nevertheless, and as you are about to learn, this can also implicate the First Amendment. It concerns a right—freedom of association—that is not expressly mentioned in the First Amendment but has been implied into the amendment by the Supreme Court. We will fully explore the right of association in Chapter 15, but the general idea is that the right to speak is unlikely to be effective unless speakers also have a corollary right to associate with others to communicate their messages. The right of association protects people's right to associate with organizations that engage in expressive activities, such as the NAACP, the Sierra Club, and the National Rifle Association. The right similarly protects the right of people to associate with political parties. It is this right that is implicated when a government employee is fired because of his or her party affiliation.

The Court first recognized that patronage dismissals can violate an employee's First Amendment freedom of association in *Elrod v. Burns*, 427 U.S. 347 (1976), which had facts similar to those mentioned in the above scenario. Justice William Brennan explained in a plurality opinion why patronage dismissals can undermine First Amendment values:

> The cost of the practice of patronage is the restraint it places on freedoms of belief and association. In order to maintain their jobs, respondents were required to pledge their political allegiance to the Democratic Party, work for the election of other candidates of the Democratic Party, contribute a portion of their wages to the Party, or obtain the sponsorship of a member of the Party, usually at the price of one of the first three alternatives. Regardless of the incumbent party's identity, Democratic or otherwise, the consequences for association and belief are the same. An individual who is a member of the out-party maintains affiliation with his own party at the risk of losing his job.

Justice Brennan rejected the blanket assertion that patronage dismissals were necessary for effective government operations. He doubted whether firing qualified and experienced employees because of their party affiliation would enhance government efficiency. He also noted that the First Amendment did not prevent government employers from terminating employees for good cause, including poor work or insubordination.

At the same time, Justice Brennan acknowledged that party affiliation is sometimes a relevant criterion for a government position. For example, a Democratic president may want his cabinet members to be Democrats and thus committed to same political agenda. Justice Brennan thought this legitimate interest could be accommodated by an exception that permitted patronage dismissals for "policymaking positions." Justice Potter Stewart, in a concurring opinion, said this exception should also include employees with access to confidential information.

The Supreme Court's next major case on the topic follows.

Branti v. Finkel

Supreme Court of the United States, 1980
445 U.S. 507

MR. JUSTICE STEVENS delivered the opinion of the Court.

The question presented is whether the First and Fourteenth Amendments to the Constitution protect an assistant public defender who is satisfactorily performing his job from discharge solely because of his political beliefs.

Respondents, Aaron Finkel and Alan Tabakman, commenced this action in the United States District Court for the Southern District of New York in order to preserve their positions as assistant public defenders in Rockland County, New York.

The critical facts can be summarized briefly. The Rockland County Public Defender is appointed by the County Legislature for a term of six years. He in turn appoints nine assistants who serve at his pleasure. The two respondents have served as assistants since their respective appointments in March 1971 and September 1975; they are both Republicans.

Petitioner Branti's predecessor, a Republican, was appointed in 1972 by a Republican-dominated County Legislature. By 1977, control of the legislature had shifted to the Democrats and petitioner, also a Democrat, was appointed to replace the incumbent when his term expired. As soon as petitioner was formally appointed on January 3, 1978, he began executing termination notices for six of the nine assistants then in office. Respondents were among those who were to be terminated. With one possible exception, the nine who were to be appointed or retained were all Democrats and were all selected by Democratic legislators or Democratic town chairmen on a basis that had been determined by the Democratic caucus.

The District Court found that Finkel and Tabakman had been selected for termination solely because they were Republicans and thus did not have the necessary Democratic sponsors.

In *Elrod v. Burns*, the Court held that the newly elected Democratic Sheriff of Cook County, Ill., had violated the constitutional rights of certain non-civil-service employees by discharging them "because they did not support and were not members of the Democratic Party and had failed to obtain the sponsorship of one of its leaders."

That holding was supported by two separate opinions.

Writing for the plurality, Mr. Justice Brennan identified two separate but interrelated reasons supporting the conclusion that the discharges were prohibited by the First and Fourteenth Amendments. First, he analyzed the impact of a political patronage system on freedom of belief and association. Noting that in order to retain their jobs, the Sheriff's employees were required to pledge their allegiance to the Democratic Party, work for or contribute to the party's candidates, or obtain a Democratic sponsor, he concluded that the inevitable tendency of such a system was to coerce employees into compromising their true beliefs. That conclusion, in his opinion, brought the practice within the rule of cases like *Board of Education v. Barnette*, condemning the use of governmental power to prescribe what the citizenry must accept as orthodox opinion.

Second, apart from the potential impact of patronage dismissals on the formation and expression of opinion, Mr. Justice Brennan also stated that the practice had the effect of imposing an unconstitutional condition on the receipt of a public benefit and therefore came within the rule of cases like *Perry v. Sindermann*.

If the First Amendment protects a public employee from discharge based on what he has said, it must also protect him from discharge based on what he believes. Under this line of analysis, unless the government can demonstrate "an overriding interest," "of vital importance," requiring that a person's private beliefs conform to those of the hiring authority, his beliefs cannot be the sole basis for depriving him of continued public employment.

Mr. Justice Stewart's opinion concurring in the judgment avoided comment on the first branch of Mr. Justice Brennan's analysis, but expressly relied on the same passage from *Perry v. Sindermann*.

In sum, there is no requirement that dismissed employees prove that they, or other employees, have been coerced into changing, either actually or ostensibly, their political allegiance. To prevail in this type of an action, it was sufficient, as *Elrod* holds, for respondents to prove that they were discharged "solely for the reason that they were not affiliated with or sponsored by the Democratic Party."

Both opinions in *Elrod* recognize that party affiliation may be an acceptable requirement for some types of government employment. Thus, if an employee's private political beliefs would interfere with the discharge of his public duties, his First

Amendment rights may be required to yield to the State's vital interest in maintaining governmental effectiveness and efficiency. In *Elrod*, it was clear that the duties of the employees—the chief deputy of the process division of the sheriff's office, a process server and another employee in that office, and a bailiff and security guard at the Juvenile Court of Cook County—were not of that character, for they were, as Mr. Justice Stewart stated, "nonpolicymaking, nonconfidential" employees.

As Mr. Justice Brennan noted in *Elrod*, it is not always easy to determine whether a position is one in which political affiliation is a legitimate factor to be considered. Under some circumstances, a position may be appropriately considered political even though it is neither confidential nor policymaking in character. As one obvious example, if a State's election laws require that precincts be supervised by two election judges of different parties, a Republican judge could be legitimately discharged solely for changing his party registration. That conclusion would not depend on any finding that the job involved participation in policy decisions or access to confidential information. Rather, it would simply rest on the fact that party membership was essential to the discharge of the employee's governmental responsibilities.

It is equally clear that party affiliation is not necessarily relevant to every policymaking or confidential position. The coach of a state university's football team formulates policy, but no one could seriously claim that Republicans make better coaches than Democrats, or vice versa, no matter which party is in control of the state government. On the other hand, it is equally clear that the Governor of a State may appropriately believe that the official duties of various assistants who help him write speeches, explain his views to the press, or communicate with the legislature cannot be performed effectively unless those persons share his political beliefs and party commitments. In sum, the ultimate inquiry is not whether the label "policymaker" or "confidential" fits a particular position; rather, the question is whether the hiring authority can demonstrate that party affiliation is an appropriate requirement for the effective performance of the public office involved.

Having thus framed the issue, it is manifest that the continued employment of an assistant public defender cannot properly be conditioned upon his allegiance to the political party in control of the county government. The primary, if not the only, responsibility of an assistant public defender is to represent individual citizens in controversy with the State.

MR. JUSTICE STEWART, dissenting.

I joined the judgment of the Court in *Elrod v. Burns*, because it is my view that, under the First and Fourteenth Amendments, "a nonpolicymaking, nonconfidential government employee cannot be discharged from a job that he is satisfactorily performing upon the sole ground of his political beliefs." That judgment in my opinion does not control the present case for the simple reason that the respondents here clearly are not "nonconfidential" employees.

MR. JUSTICE POWELL, with whom MR. JUSTICE REHNQUIST joins, and with whom MR. JUSTICE STEWART joins as to Part I, dissenting.

The Court today continues the evisceration of patronage practices begun in *Elrod v. Burns*. With scarcely a glance at almost 200 years of American political tradition, the Court further limits the relevance of political affiliation to the selection and retention of public employees. Many public positions previously filled on the basis of membership in national political parties now must be staffed in accordance with a constitutionalized civil service standard that will affect the employment practices of federal, state, and local governments. Governmental hiring practices long thought to be a matter of legislative and executive discretion now will be subjected to judicial oversight. Today's decision is an exercise of judicial lawmaking that, as the Chief Justice wrote in his *Elrod* dissent, "represents a significant intrusion into the area of legislative and policy concerns."

Patronage appointments help build stable political parties by offering rewards to persons who assume the tasks necessary to the continued functioning of political organizations.

Strong political parties also aid effective governance after election campaigns end. Elected officials depend upon appointees who hold similar views to carry out their policies and administer their programs. Patronage—the right to select key personnel and to reward the party "faithful"—serves the public interest by facilitating the implementation of policies endorsed by the electorate.

The breakdown of party discipline that handicaps elected officials also limits the ability of the electorate to choose wisely among candidates. Voters with little information about individuals seeking office traditionally have relied upon party affiliation as a guide to choosing among candidates. With the decline in party stability, voters are less able to blame or credit a party for the performance of its elected officials. Our national party system is predicated upon the assumption that political parties sponsor, and are responsible for, the performance of the persons they nominate for office.

The benefits of political patronage and the freedom of voters to structure their representative government are substantial governmental interests that justify the selection of the assistant public defenders of Rockland County on the basis of political affiliation. The decision to place certain governmental positions within a civil service system is a sensitive political judgment that should be left to the voters and to elected representatives of the people. But the Court's constitutional holding today displaces political responsibility with judicial fiat. In my view, the First Amendment does not incorporate a national civil service system.

Points for Discussion

1. **Does the *Elrod/Branti* line of cases apply to employment decisions besides terminations?** In *Rutan v. Republican Party of Illinois*, 497 U.S. 62 (1990), the Court clarified that the *Elrod/Branti* rules also apply to employment decisions short of termination, such party favoritism in hiring, promotions, transfers, and recalls after layoffs.

2. **What about independent contractors working for the government?** The *Pickering/Connick/Garcetti* line of cases and the *Elrod/Branti* cases concerned actions taken against government employees. Should similar First Amendment protections apply to independent contractors who work for the government? While these contractors are not employees of the government, they, too, may be heavily dependent on the government for their livelihoods and thus vulnerable to threats to terminate their contracts if they express opinions that government leaders dislike or fail to support the leaders' political parties.

   In two separate decisions, the Court concluded that public contractors are covered by the *Pickering* line of cases (*Board of County Commissioners v. Umbehr*, 518 U.S. 668 (1996)) and the *Elrod/Branti* line of cases (*O'Hare Truck Service, Inc. v. City of Northlake*, 518 U.S. 712 (1996)).

3. **Statutory limits on government employees' political activities.** Section 9 of the federal Hatch Act, 5 U.S.C. § 7323(a), prohibits federal employees from taking "an active part in political management or in political campaigns." The statute directly restricts government employees' political speech, but the Supreme Court nevertheless upheld it in *U.S. Civil Service Commission v. National Association of Letter Carriers, AFL-CIO*, 413 U.S. 548 (1973). The Court said the Hatch Act was intended to ensure that government execution of the laws is impartial. To further that end, the Court said, it was "essential that federal employees not take formal positions in political parties, not undertake to play substantial roles in partisan political campaigns, and not run for office on partisan political tickets." The Court also said the Hatch Act ensured that employment and advancement in government jobs did "not depend on political performance."

You Be the Judge!

Delaware's political balance requirements

Delaware is unique among American states in the way judges are appointed to its courts. The Delaware Constitution requires political balance on the state judiciary. Delaware created this system to ensure that the judiciary would be bipartisan. Ironically, Delaware was using politics as a tool to limit politics in its judicial system. For its courts to be bipartisan, they needed to be politically balanced, and to maintain balance, governors nominating persons to fill vacancies were often limited to considering candidates from only one party.

One provision of the Delaware Constitution, known as the bare majority provision, applies to all five of the state's principal courts and provides that no more than a "bare majority" of judges on those courts may be members of any one party. A second constitutional provision, known as the "major party" provision, applies to the state's three most influential courts: the Supreme Court, Chancery Court, and Superior Court. The provision restricts membership on these courts to judges who belong to one of the state's two major parties, which in modern times means Republicans or Democrats.

To illustrate these rules, consider the Delaware Supreme Court, which has five justices. The "bare majority" provision ensures that no more than three justices can be from the same political party. If three of the justices are Democrats, then the "major party" provision requires that the other two be Republicans because all members on the court must belong to one of the state's two major political parties.

A Delaware lawyer who was registered as an Independent challenged this regime. He argued that the Delaware system violated the First Amendment by limiting eligibility for the bench to either Democrats or Republicans, excluding Independents or members of other parties. The government responded by arguing that its system was designed to reduce the influence of politics on the state judiciary, and that in any event, party affiliation was an appropriate consideration for selection of persons to the judiciary.

Delaware has since modified its system for selecting judges.[2] But how would you have ruled on the "bare majority" and "major party" provisions if it had not done so?

[2] The challenge to the "bare majority" and "major party" provisions in the Delaware Constitution made its way to the U.S. Supreme Court, which dismissed the case after concluding that the plaintiff lacked standing to bring the action. *Carney v. Adams*, 141 S. Ct. 493 (2020). The same plaintiff filed a new lawsuit with more details to bolster his standing claim. The case settled when Delaware agreed to eliminate the "major party" provision. The "bare majority" provision remains in force. Do you think that this remaining provision passes constitutional muster? *See* Randall Chase, *Carney agrees restriction on judgeships is unconstitutional*, Associated Press, Jan. 30, 2023.

E. Government as Funder: Distinguishing Non-Subsidies from Leveraging Funding to Regulate Speech

When the government funds speech, to what extent may it attach conditions to the receipt of those funds that regulate the expression of the recipient? The question has proven to be one of the most confusing and vexing problems of First Amendment law. Perhaps more than any other topic within this chapter, the funding question exposes the inherent tensions between the right/privilege distinction and the unconstitutional conditions doctrine. The cases decided by the Supreme Court often appear to be contradictory, and the "rules" articulating what conditions are permitted and what conditions are not remain opaque.

On the one hand, there is the appeal of the commonsense notion that it is the government's money, so the government should be able to decide for itself what speech it chooses to subsidize, and what speech it does not. The refusal to fund speech does not in a literal sense "censor" the speaker, but merely requires the speaker to finance the speech without government assistance. The speaker who objects to the conditions may simply decline the money. A powerful articulation of this position was penned by Justice William Rehnquist, writing in dissent in *Federal Communications Commission v. League of Women Voters of California*, 468 U.S. 364 (1984), a case in which the majority held that a federal law that banned the recipients of public broadcasting funds from editorializing or endorsing political candidates violated the First Amendment. As Justice Rehnquist saw it, using the imagery of the Big Bad Wolf and Little Red Riding Hood, the holding could not be more wrong:

> All but three paragraphs of the Court's lengthy opinion in this case are devoted to the development of a scenario in which the Government appears as the "Big Bad Wolf," and appellee Pacifica as "Little Red Riding Hood." In the Court's scenario the Big Bad Wolf cruelly forbids Little Red Riding Hood to take to her grandmother some of the food that she is carrying in her basket. Only three paragraphs are used to delineate a truer picture of the litigants, wherein it appears that some of the food in the basket was given to Little Red Riding Hood by the Big Bad Wolf himself, and that the Big Bad Wolf had told Little Red Riding Hood in advance that if she accepted his food she would have to abide by his conditions. Congress in enacting § 399 of the Public Broadcasting Act, has simply determined that public funds shall not be used to subsidize noncommercial, educational broadcasting stations which engage in "editorializing" or which support or oppose any political candidate. I do not believe that anything in the First Amendment to the United States Constitution prevents Congress from choosing to spend public moneys in that manner. Perhaps a more appropriate analogy than that of Little Red Riding Hood and the Big Bad Wolf is that of Faust

> and Mephistopheles; Pacifica, well aware of § 399's condition on its receipt of public money, nonetheless accepted the public money and now seeks to avoid the conditions which Congress legitimately has attached to receipt of that funding.

Existing in tension with this view is the contemporary unconstitutional conditions doctrine, particularly the often quoted passage from *Perry v. Sindermann*, reciting that the conditions attached to government benefits may violate the Constitution when they abridge First Amendment rights.

Recognizing the uneasy tension between the two positions, Chief Justice Roberts sought to harmonize the cases by reciting a rule that draws a distinction between conditions that define the boundaries of a spending program, which are permissible under the First Amendment, and conditions that reach outside the program and attempt to leverage the grant of money to regulate speech, which are not. In the majority opinion in *Agency for International Development v. Alliance for Open Society International, Inc.*, 570 U.S. 205 (2013), Chief Justice Roberts wrote:

> As a general matter, if a party objects to a condition on the receipt of federal funding, its recourse is to decline the funds. This remains true when the objection is that a condition may affect the recipient's exercise of its First Amendment rights.
>
> At the same time, however, we have held that the Government "may not deny a benefit to a person on a basis that infringes his constitutionally protected freedom of speech even if he has no entitlement to that benefit." In some cases, a funding condition can result in an unconstitutional burden on First Amendment rights.
>
> In the present context, the relevant distinction that has emerged from our cases is between conditions that define the limits of the government spending program—those that specify the activities Congress wants to subsidize—and conditions that seek to leverage funding to regulate speech outside the contours of the program itself. The line is hardly clear, in part because the definition of a particular program can always be manipulated to subsume the challenged condition. We have held, however, that "Congress cannot recast a condition on funding as a mere definition of its program in every case, lest the First Amendment be reduced to a simple semantic exercise." *Legal Services Corporation v. Velazquez*, 531 U.S. 533, 547 (2001).

The passage above candidly recognizes that application of this distinction is not always easy. The two famous cases that follow, which appear to reach opposite results, well illustrate the point.

Rust v. Sullivan

Supreme Court of the United States, 1991
500 U.S. 173

CHIEF JUSTICE REHNQUIST delivered the opinion of the Court.

In 1970, Congress enacted Title X of the Public Health Service Act, which provides federal funding for family-planning services. Section 1008 of the Act, however, provides that "none of the funds appropriated under this subchapter shall be used in programs where abortion is a method of family planning." Regulations require that Title X projects be organized so that they are "physically and financially separate" from prohibited abortion activities.

Petitioners contend that the regulations violate the First Amendment by impermissibly discriminating based on viewpoint because they prohibit "all discussion about abortion as a lawful option—including counseling, referral, and the provision of neutral and accurate information about ending a pregnancy—while compelling the clinic or counselor to provide information that promotes continuing a pregnancy to term."

There is no question but that the statutory prohibition contained in § 1008 is constitutional. In *Maher v. Roe*, 432 U.S. 464 (1977), we upheld a state welfare regulation under which Medicaid recipients received payments for services related to childbirth, but not for nontherapeutic abortions. The Court rejected the claim that this unequal subsidization worked a violation of the Constitution. We held that the government may "make a value judgment favoring childbirth over abortion, and implement that judgment by the allocation of public funds."

The challenged regulations implement the statutory prohibition by prohibiting counseling, referral, and the provision of information regarding abortion as a method of family planning. They are designed to ensure that the limits of the federal program are observed.

To hold that the Government unconstitutionally discriminates on the basis of viewpoint when it chooses to fund a program dedicated to advance certain permissible goals, because the program in advancing those goals necessarily discourages alternative goals, would render numerous Government programs constitutionally suspect. When Congress established a National Endowment for Democracy to encourage other countries to adopt democratic principles, it was not constitutionally required to fund a program to encourage competing lines of political philosophy such as communism and fascism. Petitioners' assertions ultimately boil down to the position that if the government chooses to subsidize one protected right, it must subsidize analogous counterpart rights. But the Court has soundly rejected that proposition.

Petitioners also contend that the restrictions on the subsidization of abortion-related speech contained in the regulations are impermissible because they condition the receipt of a benefit, in these cases Title X funding, on the relinquishment of a constitutional right, the right to engage in abortion advocacy and counseling. Relying on *Perry v. Sindermann*, and *FCC v. League of Women Voters*, petitioners argue that "even though the government may deny a benefit for any number of reasons, there are some reasons upon which the government may not rely. It may not deny a benefit to a person on a basis that infringes his constitutionally protected interests—especially, his interest in freedom of speech."

Petitioners' reliance on these cases is unavailing, however, because here the Government is not denying a benefit to anyone, but is instead simply insisting that public funds be spent for the purposes for which they were authorized. The Secretary's regulations do not force the Title X grantee to give up abortion-related speech; they merely require that the grantee keep such activities separate and distinct from Title X activities.

In contrast, our "unconstitutional conditions" cases involve situations in which the Government has placed a condition on the recipient of the subsidy rather than on a particular program or service, thus effectively prohibiting the recipient from engaging in the protected conduct outside the scope of the federally funded program.

The doctor is always free to make clear that advice regarding abortion is simply beyond the scope of the program. In these circumstances, the general rule that the Government may choose not to subsidize speech applies with full force.

JUSTICE BLACKMUN, with whom JUSTICE MARSHALL joins, with whom JUSTICE STEVENS joins as to Parts II and III, and with whom JUSTICE O'CONNOR joins as to Part I, dissenting.

Until today, the Court never has upheld viewpoint-based suppression of speech simply because that suppression was a condition upon the acceptance of public funds. Whatever may be the Government's power to condition the receipt of its largess upon the relinquishment of constitutional rights, it surely does not extend to a condition that suppresses the recipient's cherished freedom of speech based solely upon the content or viewpoint of that speech.

The regulations are also clearly viewpoint based. While suppressing speech favorable to abortion with one hand, the Secretary compels antiabortion speech with the other.

[Justice Stevens' and Justice O'Connor's dissenting opinions are omitted.]

Legal Services Corp. v. Velazquez

Supreme Court of the United States, 2001
531 U.S. 533

JUSTICE KENNEDY delivered the opinion of the Court.

In 1974, Congress enacted the Legal Services Corporation Act. The Act establishes the Legal Services Corporation (LSC) as a District of Columbia nonprofit corporation. LSC's mission is to distribute funds appropriated by Congress to eligible local grantee organizations "for the purpose of providing financial support for legal assistance in noncriminal proceedings or matters to persons financially unable to afford legal assistance."

This suit requires us to decide whether one of the conditions imposed by Congress on the use of LSC funds violates the First Amendment rights of LSC grantees and their clients. For purposes of our decision, the restriction, to be quoted in further detail, prohibits legal representation funded by recipients of LSC moneys if the representation involves an effort to amend or otherwise challenge existing welfare law. As interpreted by the LSC and by the Government, the restriction prevents an attorney from arguing to a court that a state statute conflicts with a federal statute or that either a state or federal statute by its terms or in its application is violative of the United States Constitution.

The United States and LSC rely on *Rust v. Sullivan* as support for the LSC program restrictions. The Court in *Rust* did not place explicit reliance on the rationale that the counseling activities of the doctors under Title X amounted to governmental speech; when interpreting the holding in later cases, however, we have explained *Rust* on this understanding. We have said that viewpoint-based funding decisions can be sustained in instances in which the government is itself the speaker, or instances, like *Rust*, in which the government "used private speakers to transmit specific information pertaining to its own program."

Although the LSC program differs from the program at issue in *Rosenberger* in that its purpose is not to "encourage a diversity of views," the salient point is that, like the program in *Rosenberger*, the LSC program was designed to facilitate private speech, not to promote a governmental message. Congress funded LSC grantees to provide attorneys to represent the interests of indigent clients. In the specific context of suits for benefits, an LSC-funded attorney speaks on the behalf of the client in a claim against the government for welfare benefits. The lawyer is not the government's speaker. The attorney defending the decision to deny benefits will deliver the government's message in the litigation. The LSC lawyer, however, speaks on the behalf of his or her private, indigent client.

The Government has designed this program to use the legal profession and the established Judiciary of the States and the Federal Government to accomplish its end of assisting welfare claimants in determination or receipt of their benefits. The advice from the attorney to the client and the advocacy by the attorney to the courts cannot be classified as governmental speech even under a generous understanding of the concept. In this vital respect this suit is distinguishable from *Rust.*

The private nature of the speech involved here, and the extent of LSC's regulation of private expression, are indicated further by the circumstance that the Government seeks to use an existing medium of expression and to control it, in a class of cases, in ways which distort its usual functioning. Where the government uses or attempts to regulate a particular medium, we have been informed by its accepted usage in determining whether a particular restriction on speech is necessary for the program's purposes and limitations.

When the government creates a limited forum for speech, certain restrictions may be necessary to define the limits and purposes of the program. The same is true when the government establishes a subsidy for specified ends. *Rust.* As this suit involves a subsidy, limited forum cases such as *Perry*, *Lamb's Chapel*, and *Rosenberger* may not be controlling in a strict sense, yet they do provide some instruction.

By providing subsidies to LSC, the Government seeks to facilitate suits for benefits by using the state and federal courts and the independent bar on which those courts depend for the proper performance of their duties and responsibilities. Restricting LSC attorneys in advising their clients and in presenting arguments and analyses to the courts distorts the legal system by altering the traditional role of the attorneys in much the same way broadcast systems or student publication networks were changed in the limited forum cases we have cited. Just as government in those cases could not elect to use a broadcasting network or a college publication structure in a regime which prohibits speech necessary to the proper functioning of those systems, it may not design a subsidy to effect this serious and fundamental restriction on advocacy of attorneys and the functioning of the judiciary.

The effect of the restriction, however, is to prohibit advice or argumentation that existing welfare laws are unconstitutional or unlawful. Congress cannot recast a condition on funding as a mere definition of its program in every case, lest the First Amendment be reduced to a simple semantic exercise. Here, notwithstanding Congress' purpose to confine and limit its program, the restriction operates to insulate current welfare laws from constitutional scrutiny and certain other legal challenges, a condition implicating central First Amendment concerns. In no lawsuit funded by the Government can the LSC attorney, speaking on behalf of a private client, challenge existing welfare laws. As a result, arguments by indigent clients that a welfare statute is unlawful or unconstitutional cannot be expressed in this Government-funded program for petitioning the courts, even though the program was created for litigation involving welfare benefits, and even though the ordinary course of litigation involves the expression of theories and postulates on both, or multiple, sides of an issue.

Congress was not required to fund an LSC attorney to represent indigent clients; and when it did so, it was not required to fund the whole range of legal representations or relationships. The LSC and the United States, however, in effect ask us to permit Congress to define the scope of the litigation it funds to exclude certain vital theories and ideas.

JUSTICE SCALIA, with whom THE CHIEF JUSTICE, JUSTICE O'CONNOR, and JUSTICE THOMAS join, dissenting.

Regulations directly restrict speech; subsidies do not. Subsidies, it is true, may *indirectly* abridge speech, but only if the funding scheme is "manipulated to have a coercive effect" on those who do not hold the subsidized position.

In *Rust*, the Court applied these principles to a statutory scheme that is in all relevant respects indistinguishable from § 504(a)(16). This was not, we said, the type of "discrimination on the basis of viewpoint" that triggers strict scrutiny, because the "decision not to subsidize the exercise of a fundamental right does not infringe the right."

The same is true here. The LSC Act, like the scheme in *Rust*, does not create a public forum. Far from encouraging a diversity of views, it has always, as the Court accurately states, "placed restrictions on its use of funds." Nor does § 504(a)(16) discriminate on the basis of viewpoint, since it funds neither challenges to nor defenses of existing welfare law. The provision simply declines to subsidize a certain class of litigation, and under *Rust* that decision "does not infringe the right" to bring such litigation.

The Court contends that *Rust* is different because the program at issue subsidized government speech, while the LSC funds private speech. This is so unpersuasive it hardly needs response. If the private doctors' confidential advice to their patients at issue in *Rust* constituted "government speech," it is hard to imagine what subsidized speech would not be government speech. Moreover, the majority's contention that the subsidized speech in these cases is not government speech because the lawyers have a professional obligation to represent the interests of their clients founders on the reality that the doctors in *Rust* had a professional obligation to serve the interests of their patients—which at the time of *Rust* we had held to be highly relevant to the permissible scope of federal regulation. Even respondents agree that "the true speaker in *Rust* was not the government, but a doctor."

This has been a very long discussion to make a point that is embarrassingly simple: The LSC subsidy neither prevents anyone from speaking nor coerces anyone to change speech, and is indistinguishable in all relevant respects from the subsidy upheld in *Rust*. There is no legitimate basis for declaring § 504(a)(16) facially unconstitutional.

Points for Discussion

1. **If you find Justice Scalia's dissent in *Velazquez* is right in arguing that *Rust* and *Velazquez* cannot be distinguished, does it follow that *Velazquez* was wrongly decided?** Do you agree with Justice Scalia's argument that there is no appreciable difference between *Rust* and *Velazquez*? If you do, does that require you to also agree with him that the majority opinion in *Velazquez* is wrong? Not necessarily. Even if you accept that *Velazquez* and *Rust* are irreconcilable, you might still decide that the *Velazquez* approach, not the *Rust* approach, is more faithful to the unconstitutional conditions doctrine and the better approach. In short, you might decide that the fault is with *Rust*, not *Velazquez*. Note that the majority in *Velazquez* sought to avoid an outright overruling of *Rust*, instead choosing to "recast" *Rust* as derivative of the "government speech" doctrine. While the doctors in *Rust* may not have been literally "the government speaking," *Velazquez* suggests that they were in effect government contractors delivering the government's message. It is to this "government speech doctrine," a relatively new concept in First Amendment law, that we will shortly turn.

2. **When the government makes content-based decisions in awarding grants.** The *Rust* and *Velazquez* cases considered whether the First Amendment was violated when the government placed conditions on a grant that limited a grantee's speech. But what about situations where the government simply declines to give a grant based on the content of an applicant's speech? For example, is there a First Amendment issue when the National Endowment for the Arts (NEA) chooses to award a grant to one artist and not another based on the content of each applicant's proposal?

   In this situation, it is inevitable that the government will be making content-based decisions, just as school administrators must do when deciding which subjects to cover in a school curriculum and as librarians must do when deciding which books to purchase for their libraries.

   In *National Endowment for the Arts v. Finley*, 524 U.S. 569 (1998), the Supreme Court readily acknowledged that the NEA must make content-based decisions when awarding grants:

> Any content-based considerations that may be taken into account in the grant-making process are a consequence of the nature of arts funding. The NEA has limited resources and it must deny the majority of the grant applications that it receives, including many that propose "artistically excellent" projects. The "very assumption" of the NEA is that grants will be awarded according to the "artistic worth of competing applications," and absolute neutrality is simply "inconceivable."

At the same time, the Court clarified that the NEA would violate the First Amendment if it used its discretion to engage in viewpoint discrimination:

> If the NEA were to leverage its power to award subsidies on the basis of subjective criteria into a penalty on disfavored viewpoints, then we would confront a different case. We have stated that, even in the provision of subsidies, the Government may not "aim at the suppression of dangerous ideas."

Do you see the resemblance between this test and the test articulated by a plurality of the Court in *Board of Education v. Pico* for when the removal of books from a school library would violate the Constitution? Could the government escape this restriction on viewpoint discrimination by arguing that the artists funded by the government are engaging in government speech, which is not restrained by the First Amendment? You might want to return to that question after reading the material on government speech in the next section.

F. Government as Speaker: Distinguishing Government Speech from the Suppression of Private Speech

The normal First Amendment principles prohibiting content and viewpoint discrimination do not apply when the government itself is speaking. This rule, which the Court now applies quite firmly, is a relatively new development in First Amendment law.

While the rule itself is easy to recite, it is not always easy to apply. Sometimes it is difficult to determine whether the expression at issue is government speech or private speech in a public forum. The *Walker* case below poses such a conundrum. The question was whether a "specialty" license plate program run by Texas was a public forum of some kind, in which case the First Amendment would likely prohibit the state from discriminating against speech it found offensive, or if the program was instead the speech of Texas itself, in which case First Amendment strictures would not apply. Here is an image of the specialty plate that fueled the controversy:

Walker v. Texas Division, Sons of Confederate Veterans, Inc.

Supreme Court of the United States, 2015
576 U.S. 200

JUSTICE BREYER delivered the opinion of the Court.

Texas offers automobile owners a choice between ordinary and specialty license plates. Those who want the State to issue a particular specialty plate may propose a plate design, comprising a slogan, a graphic, or (most commonly) both. If the Texas Department of Motor Vehicles Board approves the design, the State will make it available for display on vehicles registered in Texas.

In this case, the Texas Division of the Sons of Confederate Veterans proposed a specialty license plate design featuring a Confederate battle flag. The Board rejected the proposal. We must decide whether that rejection violated the Constitution's free speech guarantees. We conclude that it did not.

When government speaks, it is not barred by the Free Speech Clause from determining the content of what it says. *Pleasant Grove City v. Summum*, 555 U.S. 460 (2009). That freedom in part reflects the fact that it is the democratic electoral process that first and foremost provides a check on government speech. Thus, government statements (and government actions and programs that take the form of speech) do not normally trigger the First Amendment rules designed to protect the marketplace of ideas. Instead, the Free Speech Clause helps produce informed opinions among members of the public, who are then able to influence the choices of a government that, through words and deeds, will reflect its electoral mandate.

Were the Free Speech Clause interpreted otherwise, government would not work. How could a city government create a successful recycling program if officials, when writing householders asking them to recycle cans and bottles, had to include in the letter a long plea from the local trash disposal enterprise demanding the contrary? How could a state government effectively develop programs designed to encourage and provide vaccinations, if officials also had to voice the perspective of those who oppose this type of immunization? "It is not easy to imagine how government could function if it lacked the freedom" to select the messages it wishes to convey.

We have therefore refused "to hold that the Government unconstitutionally discriminates on the basis of viewpoint when it chooses to fund a program dedicated to advance certain permissible goals, because the program in advancing those goals necessarily discourages alternative goals." *Rust v. Sullivan.* We have pointed out that a contrary holding "would render numerous Government programs constitutionally suspect."

That is not to say that a government's ability to express itself is without restriction. Constitutional and statutory provisions outside of the Free Speech Clause may limit government speech. And the Free Speech Clause itself may constrain the government's speech if, for example, the government seeks to compel private persons to convey the government's speech. But, as a general matter, when the government speaks it is entitled to promote a program, to espouse a policy, or to take a position. In doing so, it represents its citizens and it carries out its duties on their behalf.

In our view, specialty license plates issued pursuant to Texas's statutory scheme convey government speech. Our reasoning rests primarily on our analysis in *Summum*, a recent case that presented a similar problem. We conclude here, as we did there, that our precedents regarding government speech (and not our precedents regarding forums for private speech) provide the appropriate framework through which to approach the case.

In *Summum*, we considered a religious organization's request to erect in a 2.5-acre city park a monument setting forth the organization's religious tenets. In the park were 15 other permanent displays. At least 11 of these—including a wishing well, a September 11 monument, a historic granary, the city's first fire station, and a Ten Commandments monument—had been donated to the city by private entities. The religious organization argued that the Free Speech Clause required the city to display the organization's proposed monument because, by accepting a broad range of permanent exhibitions at the park, the city had created a forum for private speech in the form of monuments.

This Court rejected the organization's argument. We held that the city had not "provided a forum for private speech" with respect to monuments. Rather, the city, even when "accepting a privately donated monument and placing it on city property," had "engaged in expressive conduct." The speech at issue, this Court decided, was "best viewed as a form of government speech" and "therefore was not subject to scrutiny under the Free Speech Clause."

We based our conclusion on several factors. First, history shows that "governments have long used monuments to speak to the public." Thus, we observed that "when a government entity arranges for the construction of a monument, it does so because it wishes to convey some thought or instill some feeling in those who see the structure."

Second, we noted that it "is not common for property owners to open up their property for the installation of permanent monuments that convey a message with which they do not wish to be associated." As a result, "persons who observe donated monuments routinely—and reasonably—interpret them as conveying some message on the property owner's behalf." And "observers" of such monuments, as a consequence, ordinarily "appreciate the identity of the speaker."

Third, we found relevant the fact that the city maintained control over the selection of monuments. We thought it "fair to say that throughout our Nation's history, the general government practice with respect to donated monuments has been one of selective receptivity." And we observed that the city government in *Summum* "effectively controlled the messages sent by the monuments in the park by exercising final approval authority over their selection."

In light of these and a few other relevant considerations, the Court concluded that the expression at issue was government speech. And, in reaching that conclusion, the Court rejected the premise that the involvement of private parties in designing the monuments was sufficient to prevent the government from controlling which monuments it placed in its own public park.

Our analysis in *Summum* leads us to the conclusion that here, too, government speech is at issue. First, the history of license plates shows that, insofar as license plates have conveyed more than state names and vehicle identification numbers, they long have communicated messages from the States.

Second, Texas license plate designs "are often closely identified in the public mind with the State." Each Texas license plate is a government article serving the governmental purposes of vehicle registration and identification. The governmental nature of the plates is clear from their faces: The State places the name "TEXAS" in large letters at the top of every plate. Moreover, the State requires Texas vehicle owners to display license plates, and every Texas license plate is issued by the State. Texas also owns the designs on its license plates, including the designs that Texas adopts on the basis of proposals made by private individuals and organizations. And Texas dictates the manner in which drivers may dispose of unused plates.

Texas license plates are, essentially, government IDs. And issuers of ID "typically do not permit" the placement on their IDs of "messages with which they do not wish to be associated." Consequently, "persons who observe" designs on IDs "routinely—and reasonably—interpret them as conveying some message on the issuer's behalf."

Indeed, a person who displays a message on a Texas license plate likely intends to convey to the public that the State has endorsed that message. If not, the individual could simply display the message in question in larger letters on a bumper sticker right next to the plate. But the individual prefers a license plate design to the purely private speech expressed through bumper stickers. That may well be because Texas's license plate designs convey government agreement with the message displayed.

Third, Texas maintains direct control over the messages conveyed on its specialty plates. Texas law provides that the State "has sole control over the design, typeface, color, and alphanumeric pattern for all license plates."

These considerations, taken together, convince us that the specialty plates here in question are similar enough to the monuments in *Summum* to call for the same result.

We have previously used what we have called "forum analysis" to evaluate government restrictions on purely private speech that occurs on government property. But forum analysis is misplaced here. Because the State is speaking on its own behalf, the First Amendment strictures that attend the various types of government-established forums do not apply.

The parties agree that Texas's specialty license plates are not a "traditional public forum," such as a street or a park.

It is equally clear that Texas's specialty plates are neither a "designated public forum," which exists where "government property that has not traditionally been regarded as a public forum is intentionally opened up for that purpose," nor a "limited public forum," which exists where a government has "reserved a forum for certain groups or for the discussion of certain topics." A government "does not create a public forum by inaction or by permitting limited discourse, but only by intentionally opening a nontraditional forum for public discourse."

For similar reasons, we conclude that Texas's specialty license plates are not a "nonpublic forum," which exists "where the government is acting as a proprietor, managing its internal operations." With respect to specialty license plate designs, Texas is not simply managing government property, but instead is engaging in expressive conduct.

For the reasons stated, we hold that Texas's specialty license plate designs constitute government speech and that Texas was consequently entitled to refuse to issue plates featuring SCV's proposed design.

JUSTICE ALITO, with whom THE CHIEF JUSTICE, JUSTICE SCALIA, and JUSTICE KENNEDY join, dissenting.

The Court's decision passes off private speech as government speech and, in doing so, establishes a precedent that threatens private speech that government finds displeasing. Under our First Amendment cases, the distinction between government speech and private speech is critical.

Unfortunately, the Court's decision categorizes private speech as government speech and thus strips it of all First Amendment protection. The Court holds that all the privately created messages on the many specialty plates issued by the State of Texas convey a government message rather than the message of the motorist displaying the plate. Can this possibly be correct?

Here is a test. Suppose you sat by the side of a Texas highway and studied the license plates on the vehicles passing by. You would see, in addition to the standard Texas plates, an impressive array of specialty plates. (There are now more than 350 varieties.) You would likely observe plates that honor numerous colleges and universities. You might see plates bearing the name of a high school, a fraternity or sorority, the Masons, the Knights of Columbus, the Daughters of the American Revolution, a realty company, a favorite soft drink, a favorite burger restaurant, and a favorite NASCAR driver.

As you sat there watching these plates speed by, would you really think that the sentiments reflected in these specialty plates are the views of the State of Texas and not those of the owners of the cars? If a car with a plate that says "Rather Be Golfing" passed by at 8:30 am on a Monday morning, would you think: "This is the official policy of the State—better to golf than to work?" If you did your viewing at the start of the college football season and you saw Texas plates with the names of the University of Texas's out-of-state competitors in upcoming games—Notre Dame, Oklahoma State, the University of Oklahoma, Kansas State, Iowa State—would you assume that the State of Texas was officially (and perhaps treasonously) rooting for the Longhorns' opponents? And when a car zipped by with a plate that reads "NASCAR—24 Jeff Gordon," would you think that Gordon (born in California, raised in Indiana, resides in North Carolina) is the official favorite of the State government?

The Court says that all of these messages are government speech. It is essential that government be able to express its own viewpoint, the Court reminds us, because otherwise, how would it promote its programs, like recycling and vaccinations? So when Texas issues a "Rather Be Golfing" plate, but not a "Rather Be Playing Tennis" or "Rather Be Bowling" plate, it is furthering a state policy to promote golf but not tennis or bowling. And when Texas allows motorists to obtain a Notre Dame license plate but not a University of Southern California plate, it is taking sides in that long-time rivalry.

This capacious understanding of government speech takes a large and painful bite out of the First Amendment. Specialty plates may seem innocuous. They make motorists happy, and they put money in a State's coffers. But the precedent this case sets is dangerous. While all license plates unquestionably contain some government speech (*e.g.*, the name of the State and the numbers and/or letters identifying the vehicle), the State of Texas has converted the remaining space on its specialty plates into little mobile billboards on which motorists can display their own messages. And what Texas did here was to reject one of the messages that members of a private group wanted to post on some of these little billboards because the State thought that many of its citizens would find the message offensive. That is blatant viewpoint discrimination.

If the State can do this with its little mobile billboards, could it do the same with big, stationary billboards? Suppose that a State erected electronic billboards along its highways. Suppose that the State posted some government messages on these billboards and then, to raise money, allowed private entities and individuals to purchase the right to post their own messages. And suppose that the State allowed only those messages that it liked or found not too controversial. Would that be constitutional?

What if a state college or university did the same thing with a similar billboard or a campus bulletin board or dorm list serve? What if it allowed private messages that are consistent with prevailing views on campus but banned those that disturbed some students or faculty? Can there be any doubt that these examples of viewpoint discrimination would violate the First Amendment? I hope not, but the future uses of today's precedent remain to be seen.

A final factor that was important in *Summum* was space. A park can accommodate only so many permanent monuments. Often large and made of stone, monuments can last for centuries and are difficult to move. License plates, on the other hand, are small, light, mobile, and designed to last for only a relatively brief time. The only absolute limit on the number of specialty plates that a State could issue is the number of registered vehicles. The variety of available plates is limitless, too. Today Texas offers more than 350 varieties. In 10 years, might it be 3,500?

In sum, the Texas specialty plate program has none of the factors that were critical in *Summum*, and the Texas program exhibits a very important characteristic that was missing in that case: Individuals who want to display a Texas specialty plate, instead of the standard plate, must pay an increased annual registration fee. How many groups or individuals would clamor to pay $8,000 (the cost of the deposit required to create a new plate) in order to broadcast the government's message as opposed to their own? And if Texas really wants to speak out in support of, say, Iowa State University (but not the University of Iowa) or "Young Lawyers" (but not old ones), why must it be paid to say things that it really wants to say? The fees Texas collects pay for much more than merely the administration of the program.

Messages that are proposed by private parties and placed on Texas specialty plates are private speech, not government speech. Texas cannot forbid private speech based on its viewpoint. That is what it did here. Because the Court approves this violation of the First Amendment, I respectfully dissent.

Points for Discussion

1. **What is the interplay between the government speech doctrine and public forum law?** *Walker* illustrates how the government speech doctrine and public forum law principles may both claim ascendancy in the same fact pattern. Choosing which of the two doctrines is most appropriate to apply will often dictate the outcome. If the license plate program in *Walker* were deemed a public forum, then the censorship of the confederate organization and confederate iconography would plainly be impermissible viewpoint discrimination. Treating the program as government speech, however, took the normal First Amendment prohibition on viewpoint discrimination out of the picture.

   By contrast, in *Shurtleff v. City of Boston*, 142 S. Ct. 1583 (2022), the Court concluded that public forum principles, not the government speech doctrine, controlled the case. *Shurtleff* concerned a program in which Boston allowed private groups to temporarily fly a flag of their choosing on a flagpole outside City Hall, alongside the U.S. flag and the Massachusetts state flag. The city had not denied a single request until 2017 when it rejected Harold Shurtleff's request to fly a Christian flag that portrayed a Latin cross. In its defense, the city claimed that these temporary flags constituted government speech so that the city was free to discriminate based on viewpoint. The Supreme Court rejected this characterization after noting that Boston's policy had been to approve all flag requests and that the city had no written policy about which requests to grant. This led the Court to conclude that the temporary flags were private speech and that the city's refusal to fly Shurtleff's flag constituted unlawful viewpoint discrimination.

2. **Like the result, dislike the reasoning?** Is *Walker* an example of a hard case making bad law? Did it seem like Justice Breyer artificially stretched the government speech doctrine so he could justify Texas's rejection of the proposed specialty plate? While this may have served Justice Breyer's interest in this case, could it

come back to haunt him? After all, if specialty plates are government speech, why couldn't Texas decide in the future to authorize anti-abortion rights specialty plates and not pro-abortion rights plates? Maybe a state should be allowed to do that, but does it seem problematic to you?

On the other hand, one might sympathize with Justice Breyer's conclusion that a state should not be obliged to place a racist symbol on a government-issued license plate. The question is whether there is a way to get that result without having to characterize the private messages on specialty plates as government speech. If the First Amendment did not protect hate speech, the problem would be solved. Texas could reject the proposed specialty plate on that basis alone. But the First Amendment does protect hate speech. Nonetheless, is there a difference between the government's regulating what is clearly private hate speech, such as forbidding the placement of Confederate flag bumper stickers on cars, and the government's declining to permit hate speech on something that includes both government and private speech, especially when this juxtaposition could imply, as Justice Breyer suggested, government endorsement of the private speech? Similar issues arose in *Matal v. Tam*, which we discussed in Chapter 6, where the Court wrestled with whether the Patent and Trademark Office was required to register and provide legal protection for marks that disparaged groups of people. How do you think these cases should be resolved?

3. **May a place both be a public forum and contain government speech?** It is worth noting that the same geographic location may both contain government speech and be a public forum for other purposes. The monuments in the park in *Summum* were government speech and outside the reach of the First Amendment. But imagine that the group that sought to donate the monument in *Summum* staged a march through the park to protest the city's decision not to accept the monument. The expression of the marchers, along with any placards or pictures displaying the rejected monument, would plainly be the private expression of the marchers and not government speech. Consequently, any attempt by the city to ban the protest because of disagreement with the protesters' message would violate the First Amendment.

4. **The Establishment Clause is still a check on government speech.** While the Free Speech Clause does not restrict government speech, another First Amendment clause, the Establishment Clause, does. As you will learn when we study the Establishment Clause in Chapter 19, concern about maintaining adequate separation of church and state has prompted the Supreme Court to invalidate government speech when it appears to endorse one religion over others or religion over secularism.

5. **Can you compare and contrast?** In this chapter we have studied public forum law and the government as educator, employer, funder, and speaker. Yet as you have seen within the cases themselves, these categories are not hermetically sealed off from one another. In all of them, you will often see the tugs and pulls of the right/privilege distinction and the doctrine of unconstitutional conditions. Note particularly how public forum law principles are often invoked, almost interchangeably, in government funding cases. The Court in both *Rosenberger* and *Velazquez* borrowed from public forum law concepts in dealing with restrictions on how government funds subsidizing speech were restricted. Note as well that while the government speech doctrine does not apply directly in cases involving government funding, the Court in *Velazquez* heavily borrowed from government speech concepts in its recasting and narrowing of the holding in *Rust*, treating *Rust* as if it were "almost" a government speech case.

You Be the Judge!

The constitutionality of the Stop WOKE Act

Ready for a problem that involves speech by government employees in an educational setting and raises government speech issues?

The Florida legislature passed the Stop WOKE Act, alternatively known as the Individual Freedom Act, which prohibits professors in Florida state universities from expressing certain viewpoints while teaching. The law prohibits training or instruction that espouses, promotes, advances, inculcates, or compels students or employees to believe any of one eight specific concepts. To take one example, Concept #6 provides:

> A person, by virtue of his or her race, color, national origin, or sex should be discriminated against or receive adverse treatment to achieve diversity, equity, or inclusion.

The Stop WOKE Act required the Florida Board of Governors of the State University System to enact regulations to implement the law. A group of college professors and students sued the board, seeking to enjoin the provisions restricting expression on the eight specific concepts.

At oral argument, the attorney for the board conceded that Concept #6 was referring to affirmative action and that the law prohibited instructors during class time from expressing approval of affirmative action as an idea worthy of merit. The board's lawyer also asserted that the prohibition applied to guest speakers invited to participate in a class.

According to the federal district court judge who heard the challenge to the law, the defendants grounded their argument in "the notion that anything professors utter in a state university classroom during 'in-class instruction' is government speech, and thus, the government can both determine the content of that speech and prohibit the expression of certain viewpoints."

What arguments can be made both for and against the constitutionality of the Florida law? Do you think that the plaintiffs or defendants should prevail in this litigation?

If you're curious how the judge ruled in the case, read *Pernell v. Florida Board of Governors of the State University System*, 641 F. Supp. 3d 1218 (N.D. Fla. 2022).

Test Your Knowledge

To assess your understanding of the material in this chapter, click here to take a quiz.

CHAPTER TWELVE

May Government Regulate Speech to Promote a Vibrant Marketplace of Ideas?

Media Regulations to Promote Diverse Viewpoints and Limits on Campaign Financing

The metaphor of the marketplace of ideas has been an enduring and foundational concept in First Amendment jurisprudence. Justice Oliver Wendell Holmes famously introduced the metaphor into First Amendment jurisprudence in his *Abrams v. United States* dissent, where he observed that "the best test of truth is the power of the thought to get itself accepted in the competition of the market."

The core premise of the marketplace theory is that it is better to give people access to ideas than to let the government decide which ideas people may hear. Any other system, Judge Easterbrook observed in *American Booksellers Association v. Hudnut*, would make the government "the great censor and director of which thoughts are good for us."[1] The marketplace theory explains the Supreme Court's rigorous scrutiny of content-based regulations because these regulations raise that specter that "official suppression of ideas is afoot."[2] Time and again we have seen this principle in action as the Court invalidated laws regulating hateful, offensive, and even dangerous speech.

The Court's close scrutiny of content-based laws helps ensure that the government does not distort the marketplace of ideas. But what if private parties have the ability to distort the market? That might occur, for instance, if one party has a monopoly or close to monopoly power over the means of communication. Imagine, for example, a private company that owned all the major media outlets in a community. The market can also be distorted by wealthy parties saturating the market with their preferred ideas while drowning out the ideas they dislike. Some observers believe that individuals and corporations have been doing this through their large expenditures on political campaigns.

---

1 771 F.2d 323, 330 (3d Cir. 1985).

2 *R.A.V. v. City of St. Paul*, 505 U.S. 377, 390 (1992).

The government has long intervened in economic markets to combat monopolies and to level the playing field when there is unequal bargaining power. Should the government similarly intervene in the marketplace of ideas to correct for market distortions? Should it combat media concentration by requiring outlets to host speakers with diverse viewpoints? Should it limit campaign expenditures to curb the influence of wealthy donors?

These are the issues we will wrestle with as we consider whether the government may regulate speech to promote a vibrant marketplace of ideas.

A. Media Regulations to Promote Diverse Viewpoints: An Outdated Concern or a Contemporary Issue?

There was a time in American history in which policymakers seriously worried that the concentration of power within a small, limited number of media voices threatened diversity of thought in the marketplace of ideas, particularly in the presentation of news in the "mainstream media." The concern was genuine and well-grounded. When people thought of "print media" in the context of "news," they tended to think of newspapers and news magazines. In many major American cities and in almost all smaller cities and rural areas, only one or two newspapers were in general circulation. A few national magazines, such as *Time*, *Newsweek*, and *U.S. News and World Report*, published weekly compendiums of news. Television news was dominated by three major commercial networks, ABC, CBS, and NBC, and their local affiliates. Again, for most American television viewers, there were only a handful of local television stations that could be received through over-the-air broadcasts. While there were more radio stations available to most listeners, many of the stations primarily played music, often with a defined genre (rock, country, classical, etc.), and it was not uncommon for there to be only a one or two stations that reported the news.

This led to a push to have the government intervene to force media outlets to carry diverse viewpoints. In the print media context, the proposed solution was the enactment of "right of reply" or "right of access" laws that would entitle a person or business attacked in a newspaper article to "equal space" to write a "reply" to the attack that the newspaper was forced to publish. In the broadcast context, the Federal Communications Commission promulgated rules based on similar notions, requiring that broadcasters provide equal time to opposing views on issues, or permitting persons attacked to have free airtime to respond.

The Supreme Court responded to these efforts by striking down the "right of reply" laws as applied to print media but upholding comparable laws as applied to broadcasters. In the *Miami Herald* case below, the Court reasoned that newspapers were private journalistic companies that had the right under the First Amendment to decide for themselves what to print. In contrast, in the *Red Lion* case below, the Court upheld the FCC's equal-time regulation, on the theory that because the broadcast spectrum (the electronic airwaves over which broadcast signals travel) was "scarce," broadcasters granted "spectrum space" (a broadcast channel) held that space as a public trust and could be forced to dedicate part of that space to presenting diverse points of view.

All of this is now essentially obsolete, to the point at which it may seem frivolous to even include *Miami Herald* and *Red Lion* in a contemporary casebook. Modern technology has essentially ended scarcity. Through the internet, cable, or satellite, most Americans have an essentially infinite variety of content choices. Indeed, very few people now receive their news through a physical newspaper or an over-the-air television broadcast. Almost everyone receives their news via the internet, cable, or satellite, on a computer screen, a smartphone, or a flat-screen TV. There are hundreds, if not tens of thousands, of choices for virtually everyone.

Even so, it is worth briefly examining *Miami Herald* and *Red Lion* for one purpose, which is for the light they may shed on the one arena of modern First Amendment law in which the issue still does matter: the government's attempts to control alleged censorship by major social media providers such as Meta, which owns Facebook and Instagram. The concern is that these social media giants tend to have a left-wing progressive bias and are more likely to censure (by taking down or otherwise frustrating) conservative viewpoints.

1. Broadcast Media: Upholding the Fairness Doctrine

In *Red Lion Broadcasting Co. v. FCC*, the Court upheld an FCC regulation that required licensed broadcasters to offer a diversity of viewpoints and provide a right of reply to people who had been attacked on the air.

Red Lion Broadcasting Co. v. FCC

Supreme Court of the United States, 1969
395 U.S. 367

MR. JUSTICE WHITE delivered the opinion of the Court.

The Federal Communications Commission has for many years imposed on radio and television broadcasters the requirement that discussion of public issues be presented on broadcast stations, and that each side of those issues must be given fair coverage. This is known as the fairness doctrine, which originated very early in the history of broadcasting and has maintained its present outlines for some time. It is an obligation whose content has been defined in a long series of FCC rulings in particular cases, and which is distinct from the statutory requirement of § 315 of the Communications Act that equal time be allotted all qualified candidates for public office. Two aspects of the fairness doctrine, relating to personal attacks in the context of controversial public issues and to political editorializing, were codified more precisely in the form of FCC regulations in 1967.

The broadcasters challenge the fairness doctrine and its specific manifestations in the personal attack and political editorial rules on conventional First Amendment grounds, alleging that the rules abridge their freedom of speech and press. Their contention is that the First Amendment protects their desire to use their allotted frequencies continuously to broadcast whatever they choose, and to exclude whomever they choose from ever using that frequency. No man may be prevented from saying or publishing what he thinks, or from refusing in his speech or other utterances to give equal weight to the views of his opponents. This right, they say, applies equally to broadcasters.

Although broadcasting is clearly a medium affected by a First Amendment interest, differences in the characteristics of new media justify differences in the First Amendment standards applied to them. Only a tiny fraction of those with resources and intelligence can hope to communicate by radio at the same time if intelligible communication is to be had, even if the entire radio spectrum is utilized in the present state of commercially acceptable technology.

It was this fact, and the chaos which ensued from permitting anyone to use any frequency at whatever power level he wished, which made necessary the enactment of the Radio Act of 1927 and the Communications Act of 1934, as the Court has noted at length before. *National Broadcasting Co. v. United States*, 319 U.S. 190 (1943). It was this reality which at the very least necessitated first the division of the radio spectrum into portions reserved respectively for public broadcasting and for other important radio uses such as amateur operation, aircraft, police, defense, and navigation; and then the subdivision of each portion, and assignment of specific frequencies to individual users or groups of users. Beyond this, however, because the frequencies reserved for public broadcasting were limited in number, it was essential for the Government to tell some applicants that they could not broadcast at all because there was room for only a few.

Where there are substantially more individuals who want to broadcast than there are frequencies to allocate, it is idle to posit an unabridgeable First Amendment right to broadcast comparable to the right of every individual to speak, write, or publish. If 100 persons want broadcast licenses but there are only 10 frequencies to allocate, all of them may have the same "right" to a license; but if there is to be any effective communication by radio, only a few can be licensed and the rest must be barred from the airwaves. It would be strange if the First Amendment, aimed at protecting and furthering communications, prevented the Government from making radio communication possible by requiring licenses to broadcast and by limiting the number of licenses so as not to overcrowd the spectrum.

By the same token, as far as the First Amendment is concerned those who are licensed stand no better than those to whom licenses are refused. A license permits broadcasting, but the license has no constitutional right to be the one who holds the license or to monopolize a radio frequency to the exclusion of his fellow citizens. There is nothing in the First Amendment which prevents the Government from requiring a licensee to share his frequency with others and to conduct himself as a proxy or fiduciary with obligations to present those views and voices which are representative of his community and which would otherwise, by necessity, be barred from the airwaves.

2. Print Media: Striking Down a Right of Reply Law

Five years after *Red Lion* was decided, the Court considered whether a newspaper could be required to provide a right of reply for political candidates who were criticized in the publication. The Court's opinion never mentioned *Red Lion*.

Miami Herald Publishing Co. v. Tornillo

Supreme Court of the United States, 1974
418 U.S. 241

MR. CHIEF JUSTICE BURGER delivered the opinion of the Court.

The issue in this case is whether a state statute granting a political candidate a right to equal space to reply to criticism and attacks on his record by a newspaper violates the guarantees of a free press.

The appellee and supporting advocates of an enforceable right of access to the press vigorously argue that government has an obligation to ensure that a wide variety of views reach the public. The contentions of access proponents will be set out in some detail. It is urged that at the time the First Amendment to the Constitution was ratified in 1791 as part of our Bill of Rights the press was broadly representative of the people it was serving. While many of the newspapers were intensely partisan and narrow in their views, the press collectively presented a broad range of opinions to readers. Entry into publishing was inexpensive; pamphlets and books provided meaningful alternatives to the organized press for the expression of unpopular ideas and often treated events and expressed views not covered by conventional newspapers. A true marketplace of ideas existed in which there was relatively easy access to the channels of communication.

Newspapers have become big business and there are far fewer of them to serve a larger literate population. Chains of newspapers, national newspapers, national wire and news services, and one-newspaper towns, are the dominant features of a press that has become noncompetitive and enormously powerful and influential in its capacity to manipulate popular opinion and change the course of events. Major metropolitan newspapers have collaborated to establish news services national in scope. Such national news organizations provide syndicated 'interpretive reporting' as well as syndicated features and commentary, all of which can serve as part of the new school of "advocacy journalism."

The elimination of competing newspapers in most of our large cities, and the concentration of control of media that results from the only newspaper's being owned by the same interests which own a television station and a radio station, are important components of this trend toward concentration of control of outlets to inform the public.

However, much validity may be found in these arguments, at each point the implementation of a remedy such as an enforceable right of access necessarily calls for some mechanism, either governmental or consensual. If it is governmental coercion, this at once brings about a confrontation with the express provisions of the First Amendment and the judicial gloss on that Amendment developed over the years.

Appellee's argument that the Florida statute does not amount to a restriction of appellant's right to speak because "the statute in question here has not prevented the Miami Herald from saying anything it wished" begs the core question. Compelling editors or publishers to publish that which "reason tells them should not be published" is what is at issue in this case. The Florida statute operates as a command in the same sense as a statute or regulation forbidding appellant to publish specified matter. Governmental restraint on publishing need not fall into familiar or traditional patterns to be subject to constitutional limitations on governmental powers.

Even if a newspaper would face no additional costs to comply with a compulsory access law and would not be forced to forgo publication of news or opinion by the inclusion of a reply, the Florida statute fails to clear the barriers of the First Amendment because of its intrusion into the function of editors. A newspaper is more than a passive receptacle or conduit for news, comment, and advertising. The choice of material to go into a newspaper, and the decisions made as to limitations on the size and content of the paper, and treatment of public issues and public officials—whether fair or unfair—constitute the exercise of editorial control and judgment. It has yet to be demonstrated how governmental regulation of this crucial process can be exercised consistent with First Amendment guarantees of a free press as they have evolved to this time.

[Justice Brennan's concurring opinion, which was joined by Justice Rehnquist, is omitted, as is Justice White's concurring opinion.]

3. Social Media: Speakers, Editors, or Common Carriers?

Some legislators have been persuaded that powerful social media platforms such as Facebook operate as censors, favoring progressive liberal speakers over conservative voices. Laws passed to prevent social media platforms from engaging in such perceived censorship place the contrast between *Miami Herald* and *Red Lion* in a new context. Efforts to control the speech of social media outlets implicate the state action doctrine, discussed in Chapter 3, because social media companies are private entities, not governmental entities. Such efforts also implicate fundamental First Amendment questions about the government's power to regulate the marketplace to attempt to ensure that the public has access to competing ideas. (As noted in the following section, much the same "distortion" issue is in play when it comes to political campaign finance regulation.)

social media-comp are private entities

Two federal courts of appeal addressed the constitutionality of laws limiting censorship by social media companies. They reached opposite conclusions. You can try to resolve this conflict yourself when you do the following exercise.

You Be the Judge!

May government dictate how social media companies regulate speech on their platforms?

In *NetChoice, LLC v. Paxton*, 49 F.4th 439 (5th Cir. 2022), the Fifth Circuit upheld a Texas law prohibiting social media platforms from censoring private users' speech based on viewpoint. The law defined censorship as "to block, ban, remove, deplatform, demonetize, de-boost, restrict, deny equal access or visibility to, or otherwise discriminate against expression." The court held that the law did not violate the First Amendment rights of social media platforms, rejecting the analogy to *Miami Herald*. "The Platforms are nothing like the newspaper in *Miami Herald*. Unlike newspapers, the Platforms exercise virtually no editorial control or judgment. The Platforms use algorithms to screen out certain obscene and spam-related content. And then virtually everything else is just posted to the Platform with zero editorial control or judgment."

In contrast, in *NetChoice, LLC v. Attorney General*, 34 F.4th 1196 (11th Cir. 2022), the Eleventh Circuit invoked *Miami Herald* to reach the opposite result, holding that a Florida law restricting censorship by social media platforms did violate the First Amendment. The court reasoned that social media companies are private enterprises, not governmental entities. While social media platforms do not create most of the content on their sites, relying instead on users' posts, they "do engage in some speech of their own: A platform, for example, might publish terms of service or community standards specifying the type of content that it will (and won't) allow on its site, add addenda or disclaimers to certain posts (say, warning of misinformation or mature content), or publish its own posts." The Eleventh Circuit concluded: "Whether we assess social-media platforms' content-moderation activities against the *Miami Herald* line of cases or against our own decisions explaining what constitutes expressive conduct, the result is the same: Social-media platforms exercise editorial judgment that is inherently expressive. When platforms choose to remove users or posts, deprioritize content in viewers' feeds or search results, or sanction breaches of their community standards, they engage in First-Amendment-protected activity."

Assume this conflict reaches the Supreme Court. If you were on the Court, how would you rule, and why?

(Update: The Supreme Court decided to hear the two *NetChoice* cases so you'll be able to compare your analysis with the Court's.)

Points for Discussion

1. **What later happened to *Miami Herald* and *Red Lion*?** The decisions in *Miami Herald* and *Red Lion* are striking by today's sensibilities in that both were unanimous opinions. (The three short concurring opinions in *Miami Herald* were omitted above). *Miami Herald* has fared well. It remains good law and is highly influential, as seen in the Eleventh Circuit's *NetChoice* decision striking down Florida's efforts to fight perceived bias at social media platforms, and even in the Fifth Circuit's perceived obligation to distinguish *Miami Herald* in its own contrary *NetChoice* ruling. *Red Lion*, however, has not fared so well. To begin, the FCC of its own volition ultimately repealed the fairness doctrine, as well as the personal attack and editorial provisions discussed in *Red Lion*, deciding that they operated to chill free speech. More than that, however, many believe that the core underlying theory of *Red Lion*, the notion of broadcast spectrum scarcity, is no longer persuasive. The broadcast spectrum itself remains scarce, in that there are only so many "spaces" on the electromagnetic broadcast spectrum. That scarcity is dictated by laws of science. But that spectrum scarcity, while still sound as scientific law, may now be irrelevant as constitutional law, for the simple reason that so little content uses the broadcast spectrum anymore. Advances such as broadband internet may render *Red Lion* a "double dinosaur," extinct as law

(since the FCC has repealed its rules) and extinct as constitutional theory. Judge Kenneth Starr was among the first to question the continued viability of the scarcity rationale in *Red Lion*, even before the internet revolution. *See Syracuse Peace Council v. FCC*, 867 F.2d 654, 685 (D.C. Cir. 1989) (Starr, J., concurring).

2. **Are digital platforms really "speakers," or are they more akin to "common carriers"?** Note that the debate over whether government may regulate the content of social media sites is influenced in part by the fact that such enterprises are indisputably private companies, not government agencies, and thus outside the First Amendment prohibitions on content and viewpoint discrimination. Yet that social media platforms are indisputably "private enterprises" does not determine whether they are "private speakers" engaged in "speech" in the First Amendment sense. Note that this was a core divide between the Eleventh Circuit and Fifth Circuit in their opposing *NetChoice* decisions. Justice Clarence Thomas has suggested that the First Amendment would permit laws that treat private media platforms as "common carriers" and use the "common carrier" model in turn to prevent those digital platforms from blocking users on the basis of content. "In many ways, digital platforms that hold themselves out to the public resemble traditional common carriers. Though digital instead of physical, they are at bottom communications networks, and they 'carry' information from one user to another. A traditional telephone company laid physical wires to create a network connecting people. Digital platforms lay information infrastructure that can be controlled in much the same way. And unlike newspapers, digital platforms hold themselves out as organizations that focus on distributing the speech of the broader public. Federal law dictates that companies cannot 'be treated as the publisher or speaker' of information that they merely distribute." *Biden v. Knight First Amendment Inst.*, 141 S. Ct. 1220, 1224 (2021) (Thomas, J., concurring in denial of *certiorari*).

B. Constitutional Limits on Campaign Finance Regulations: Is Money Speech, and, if so, When Can It Be Restricted?

Few areas of First Amendment jurisprudence have generated more controversy than the Supreme Court's opinions on campaign finance regulations. Critics complain that the decisions have unleashed a tsunami of money that is undermining our democracy and making politicians beholden to wealthy donors. Defenders contend that the decisions protect core political speech and ensure that incumbents do not structure campaign finance laws to advance their personal interest in remaining in office.

1. Setting the Ground Rules for Limits on Campaign Financing: The Difference Between Contributions and Independent Expenditures

Buckley v. Valeo is the seminal decision that established the framework for analyzing campaign finance regulations.

Buckley v. Valeo

Supreme Court of the United States, 1976
424 U.S. 1

PER CURIAM.

These appeals present constitutional challenges to the key provisions of the Federal Election Campaign Act of 1971 and related provisions of the Internal Revenue Code of 1954, all as amended in 1974.

I. CONTRIBUTION AND EXPENDITURE LIMITATIONS

The intricate statutory scheme adopted by Congress to regulate federal election campaigns includes restrictions on political contributions and expenditures that apply broadly to all phases of and all participants in the election process. The major contribution and expenditure limitations in the Act prohibit individuals from contributing more than $25,000 in a single year or more than $1,000 to any single candidate for an election campaign and from spending more than $1,000 a year "relative to a clearly identified candidate." Other provisions restrict a candidate's use of personal and family resources in his campaign and limit the overall amount that can be spent by a candidate in campaigning for federal office.

A. General Principles

The Act's contribution and expenditure limitations operate in an area of the most fundamental First Amendment activities. Discussion of public issues and debate on the qualifications of candidates are integral to the operation of the system of government established by our Constitution. The First Amendment affords the broadest protection to such political expression in order "to assure the unfettered interchange of ideas for the bringing about of political and social changes desired by the people." Although First Amendment protections are not confined to "the exposition of ideas," "there is practically universal agreement that a major purpose of that Amendment was to protect the free discussion of governmental affairs, of course including discussions of candidates." This no more than reflects our "profound national commitment to the principle that debate on public issues should be uninhibited, robust, and wide-open." In a republic where the people are sovereign, the ability of the citizenry to make informed choices among candidates for office is essential, for the identities of those who are elected will inevitably shape the course that we follow as a nation. As the Court observed in *Monitor Patriot Co. v. Roy*, 401 U.S. 265, 272 (1971), "it can hardly be doubted that the constitutional guarantee has its fullest and most urgent application precisely to the conduct of campaigns for political office."

The First Amendment protects political association as well as political expression. The constitutional right of association explicated in *NAACP v. Alabama*, 357 U.S. 449, 460 (1958), stemmed from the Court's recognition that "effective advocacy of both public and private points of view, particularly controversial ones, is undeniably enhanced by group association." Subsequent decisions have made clear that the First and Fourteenth Amendments guarantee "freedom to associate with others for the common advancement of political beliefs and ideas," a freedom that encompasses "the right to associate with the political party of one's choice."

It is with these principles in mind that we consider the primary contentions of the parties with respect to the Act's limitations upon the giving and spending of money in political campaigns. Those conflicting contentions could not more sharply define the basic issues before us. Appellees contend that what the Act regulates is conduct, and that its effect on speech and association is incidental at most. Appellants respond that contributions and expenditures are at the very core of political speech, and that the Act's limitations thus constitute restraints on First Amendment liberty that are both gross and direct.

A restriction on the amount of money a person or group can spend on political communication during a campaign necessarily reduces the quantity of expression by restricting the number of issues discussed, the depth of their exploration, and the size of the audience reached. This is because virtually every means of communicating ideas in today's mass society requires the expenditure of money. The distribution of the humblest handbill or leaflet entails printing, paper, and circulation costs. Speeches and rallies generally necessitate hiring a hall and publicizing the event. The electorate's increasing dependence on television, radio, and other mass media for news and information has made these expensive modes of communication indispensable instruments of effective political speech.

The expenditure limitations contained in the Act represent substantial rather than merely theoretical restraints on the quantity and diversity of political speech.

By contrast with a limitation upon expenditures for political expression, a limitation upon the amount that any one person or group may contribute to a candidate or political committee entails only a marginal restriction upon the contributor's ability to engage in free communication. A contribution serves as a general expression of support for the candidate and his views, but does not communicate the underlying basis for the support. The quantity of communication by the contributor does not increase perceptibly with the size of his contribution, since the expression rests solely on the undifferentiated, symbolic act of contributing. At most, the size of the contribution provides a very rough index of the intensity of the contributor's support for the candidate. A limitation on the amount of money a person may give to a candidate or campaign organization thus involves little direct restraint on his political communication, for it permits the symbolic expression of support evidenced by a contribution but does not in any way infringe the contributor's freedom to discuss candidates and issues. While contributions may result in political expression if spent by a candidate or an association to present views to the voters, the transformation of contributions into political debate involves speech by someone other than the contributor.

Given the important role of contributions in financing political campaigns, contribution restrictions could have a severe impact on political dialogue if the limitations prevented candidates and political committees from amassing the resources necessary for effective advocacy. There is no indication, however, that the contribution limitations imposed by the Act would have any dramatic adverse effect on the funding of campaigns and political associations. The overall effect of the Act's contribution ceilings is merely to require candidates and political committees to raise funds from a greater number of persons and to compel people who would otherwise contribute amounts greater than the statutory limits to expend such funds on direct political expression, rather than to reduce the total amount of money potentially available to promote political expression.

The Act's contribution and expenditure limitations also impinge on protected associational freedoms. Making a contribution, like joining a political party, serves to affiliate a person with a candidate. In addition, it enables like-minded persons to pool their resources in furtherance of common political goals. The Act's contribution ceilings thus limit one important means of associating with a candidate or committee, but leave the contributor free to become a member of any political association and to assist personally in the association's efforts on behalf of candidates. And the Act's contribution limitations permit associations and candidates to aggregate large sums of money to promote effective advocacy. By contrast, the Act's $1,000 limitation on independent expenditures "relative to a clearly identified candidate" precludes most associations from effectively amplifying the voice of their adherents, the original basis for the recognition of First Amendment protection of the freedom of association.

In sum, although the Act's contribution and expenditure limitations both implicate fundamental First Amendment interests, its expenditure ceilings impose significantly more severe restrictions on protected freedoms of political expression and association than do its limitations on financial contributions.

B. Contribution Limitations

Appellees argue that the Act's restrictions on large campaign contributions are justified by three governmental interests. According to the parties and amici, the primary interest served by the limitations and, indeed, by the Act as a whole, is the prevention of corruption and the appearance of corruption spawned by the real or imagined coercive influence of large financial contributions on candidates' positions and on their actions if elected to office. Two "ancillary" interests underlying the Act are also allegedly furthered by the $1,000 limits on contributions. First, the limits serve to mute the voices of affluent persons and groups in the election process and thereby to equalize the relative ability of all citizens to affect the outcome of elections. Second, it is argued, the ceilings may to some extent act as a brake on the skyrocketing cost of political campaigns and thereby serve to open the political system more widely to candidates without access to sources of large amounts of money.

It is unnecessary to look beyond the Act's primary purpose to limit the actuality and appearance of corruption resulting from large individual financial contributions in order to find a constitutionally sufficient justification for the $1,000 contribution limitation.

Of almost equal concern as the danger of actual quid pro quo arrangements is the impact of the appearance of corruption stemming from public awareness of the opportunities for abuse inherent in a regime of large individual financial contributions.

Appellants contend that the contribution limitations must be invalidated because bribery laws and narrowly drawn disclosure requirements constitute a less restrictive means of dealing with "proven and suspected quid pro quo arrangements." But laws making criminal the giving and taking of bribes deal with only the most blatant and specific attempts of those with money to influence governmental action. And while disclosure requirements serve the many salutary purposes discussed elsewhere in this opinion, Congress was surely entitled to conclude that disclosure was only a partial measure, and that contribution ceilings were a necessary legislative concomitant to deal with the reality or appearance of corruption inherent in a system permitting unlimited financial contributions, even when the identities of the contributors and the amounts of their contributions are fully disclosed.

We find that, under the rigorous standard of review established by our prior decisions, the weighty interests served by restricting the size of financial contributions to political candidates are sufficient to justify the limited effect upon First Amendment freedoms caused by the $1,000 contribution ceiling.

C. Expenditure Limitations

The Act's expenditure ceilings impose direct and substantial restraints on the quantity of political speech.

We find that the governmental interest in preventing corruption and the appearance of corruption is inadequate to justify § 608(e)(1)'s ceiling on independent expenditures. The parties defending § 608(e)(1) contend that it is necessary to prevent would-be contributors from avoiding the contribution limitations by the simple expedient of paying directly for media advertisements or for other portions of the candidate's campaign activities. They argue that expenditures controlled by or coordinated with the candidate and his campaign might well have virtually the same value to the candidate as a contribution and would pose similar dangers of abuse. Yet such controlled or coordinated expenditures are treated as contributions rather than expenditures under the Act. By contrast, § 608(e)(1) limits expenditures for express advocacy of candidates made totally independently of the candidate and his campaign. Unlike contributions, such independent expenditures may well provide little assistance to the candidate's campaign and indeed may prove counterproductive. The absence of prearrangement and coordination of an expenditure with the candidate or his agent not only undermines the value of the expenditure to the candidate, but also alleviates the danger that expenditures will be given as a quid pro quo for improper commitments from the candidate.

While the independent expenditure ceiling thus fails to serve any substantial governmental interest in stemming the reality or appearance of corruption in the electoral process, it heavily burdens core First Amendment expression.

It is argued, however, that the ancillary governmental interest in equalizing the relative ability of individuals and groups to influence the outcome of elections serves to justify the limitation on express advocacy of the election or defeat of candidates imposed by § 608(e)(1)'s expenditure ceiling. But the concept that government may restrict the speech of some elements of our society in order to enhance the relative voice of others is wholly foreign to the First Amendment, which was designed "to secure the widest possible dissemination of information from diverse and antagonistic sources," and "to assure unfettered interchange of ideas for the bringing about of political and social changes desired by the people." The First Amendment's protection against governmental abridgment of free expression cannot properly be made to depend on a person's financial ability to engage in public discussion.

The Court's decisions in *Mills v. Alabama*, 384 U.S. 214 (1966), and *Miami Herald* held that legislative restrictions on advocacy of the election or defeat of political candidates are wholly at odds with the guarantees of the First Amendment. In *Mills*, the Court addressed the question whether "a State, consistently with the United States

Constitution, can make it a crime for the editor of a daily newspaper to write and publish an editorial on election day urging people to vote a certain way on issues submitted to them." We held that "no test of reasonableness can save such a state law from invalidation as a violation of the First Amendment." Yet the prohibition of election-day editorials invalidated in *Mills* is clearly a lesser intrusion on constitutional freedom than a $1,000 limitation on the amount of money any person or association can spend during an entire election year in advocating the election or defeat of a candidate for public office. More recently in *Tornillo*, the Court held that Florida could not constitutionally require a newspaper to make space available for a political candidate to reply to its criticism. Yet under the Florida statute, every newspaper was free to criticize any candidate as much as it pleased so long as it undertook the modest burden of printing his reply.

For the reasons stated, we conclude that § 608(e)(1)'s independent expenditure limitation is unconstitutional under the First Amendment.

It is unconstitutional under 1st

The Act also sets limits on expenditures by a candidate "from his personal funds, or the personal funds of his immediate family, in connection with his campaigns during any calendar year." These ceilings vary from $50,000 for Presidential or Vice Presidential candidates to $35,000 for senatorial candidates, and $25,000 for most candidates for the House of Representatives.

The ceiling on personal expenditures by candidates on their own behalf, like the limitations on independent expenditures contained in § 608(e)(1), imposes a substantial restraint on the ability of persons to engage in protected First Amendment expression. The candidate, no less than any other person, has a First Amendment right to engage in the discussion of public issues and vigorously and tirelessly to advocate his own election and the election of other candidates. Indeed, it is of particular importance that candidates have the unfettered opportunity to make their views known so that the electorate may intelligently evaluate the candidates' personal qualities and their positions on vital public issues before choosing among them on election day.

the candidate still has 1st amend right

The ancillary interest in equalizing the relative financial resources of candidates competing for elective office, therefore, provides the sole relevant rationale for § 608(a)'s expenditure ceiling. That interest is clearly not sufficient to justify the provision's infringement of fundamental First Amendment rights. First, the limitation may fail to promote financial equality among candidates. A candidate who spends less of his personal resources on his campaign may nonetheless outspend his rival as a result of more successful fundraising efforts. Indeed, a candidate's personal wealth may impede his efforts to persuade others that he needs their financial contributions or volunteer efforts to conduct an effective campaign. Second, and more fundamentally, the First Amendment simply cannot tolerate § 608(a)'s restriction upon the freedom of a candidate to speak without legislative limit on behalf of his own candidacy. We therefore hold that § 608(a)'s restriction on a candidate's personal expenditures is unconstitutional.

Section 608(c) places limitations on overall campaign expenditures by candidates seeking nomination for election and election to federal office. Presidential candidates may spend $10,000,000 in seeking nomination for office and an additional $20,000,000 in the general election campaign. The ceiling on senatorial campaigns is pegged to the size of the voting-age population of the State with minimum dollar amounts applicable to campaigns in States with small populations.

No governmental interest that has been suggested is sufficient to justify the restriction on the quantity of political expression imposed by § 608(c)'s campaign expenditure limitations.

The interest in equalizing the financial resources of candidates competing for federal office is no more convincing a justification for restricting the scope of federal election campaigns.

The campaign expenditure ceilings appear to be designed primarily to serve the governmental interests in reducing the allegedly skyrocketing costs of political campaigns. [But] the mere growth in the cost of federal election campaigns in and of itself provides no basis for governmental restrictions on the quantity of campaign spending and the resulting limitation on the scope of federal campaigns. The First Amendment denies government the power to determine that spending to promote one's political views is wasteful, excessive, or unwise. In the free society ordained by our Constitution it is not the government, but the people individually as citizens and candidates and collectively as associations and political committees who must retain control over the quantity and range of debate on public issues in a political campaign.

For these reasons we hold that § 608(c) is constitutionally invalid.

II. REPORTING AND DISCLOSURE REQUIREMENT

[The Act's] primary disclosure provisions impose reporting obligations on "political committees" and candidates. Each political committee is required to register with the Commission, and to keep detailed records of both contributions and expenditures. These records must include the name and address of everyone making a contribution in excess of $10, along with the date and amount of the contribution. If a person's contributions aggregate more than $100, his occupation and principal place of business are also to be included. These files are subject to periodic audits and field investigations by the Commission.

Each committee and each candidate also is required to file quarterly reports. The reports are to contain detailed financial information, including the full name, mailing address, occupation, and principal place of business of each person who has contributed over $100 in a calendar year, as well as the amount and date of the contributions. They are to be made available by the Commission "for public inspection and copying." Every candidate for federal office is required to designate a "principal campaign committee," which is to receive reports of contributions and expenditures made on the candidate's behalf from other political committees and to compile and file these reports, together with its own statements, with the Commission.

Unlike the overall limitations on contributions and expenditures, the disclosure requirements impose no ceiling on campaign-related activities. But we have repeatedly found that compelled disclosure, in itself, can seriously infringe on privacy of association and belief guaranteed by the First Amendment.

The strict test established by *NAACP v. Alabama* is necessary because compelled disclosure has the potential for substantially infringing the exercise of First Amendment rights. But we have acknowledged that there are governmental interests sufficiently important to outweigh the possibility of infringement, particularly when the "free functioning of our national institutions" is involved.

The governmental interests sought to be vindicated by the disclosure requirements are of this magnitude. They fall into three categories. First, disclosure provides the electorate with information "as to where political campaign money comes from and how it is spent by the candidate" in order to aid the voters in evaluating those who seek federal office. It allows voters to place each candidate in the political spectrum more precisely than is often possible solely on the basis of party labels and campaign speeches. The sources of a candidate's financial support also alert the voter to the interests to which a candidate is most likely to be responsive and thus facilitate predictions of future performance in office.

Second, disclosure requirements deter actual corruption and avoid the appearance of corruption by exposing large contributions and expenditures to the light of publicity. This exposure may discourage those who would use money for improper purposes either before or after the election. A public armed with information about a candidate's most generous supporters is better able to detect any post-election special favors that may be given in return. Congress could reasonably conclude that full disclosure during an election campaign tends "to prevent the corrupt use of money to affect elections." In enacting these requirements it may have been mindful of Mr. Justice Brandeis' advice:

> Publicity is justly commended as a remedy for social and industrial diseases. Sunlight is said to be the best of disinfectants; electric light the most efficient policeman.

Third, and not least significant, recordkeeping, reporting, and disclosure requirements are an essential means of gathering the data necessary to detect violations of the contribution limitations described above.

We are not unmindful that the damage done by disclosure to the associational interests of the minor parties and their members and to supporters of independents could be significant. These movements are less likely to have a sound financial base and thus are more vulnerable to falloffs in contributions. In some instances fears of reprisal may deter contributions to the point where the movement cannot survive. The public interest also suffers if that result comes to pass, for there is a consequent reduction in the free circulation of ideas both within and without the political arena.

There could well be a case, similar to those before the Court in *NAACP v. Alabama* and *Bates v. Little Rock*, 361 U.S. 516 (1960), where the threat to the exercise of First Amendment rights is so serious and the state interest furthered by disclosure so insubstantial that the Act's requirements cannot be constitutionally applied. But no appellant in this case has tendered record evidence of the sort proffered in *NAACP v. Alabama.* Instead, appellants primarily rely on "the clearly articulated fears of individuals, well experienced in the political process."

Where it exists the type of chill and harassment identified in *NAACP v. Alabama* can be shown. We cannot assume that courts will be insensitive to similar showings when made in future cases.

III. PUBLIC FINANCING OF PRESIDENTIAL ELECTION CAMPAIGNS

It cannot be gainsaid that public financing as a means of eliminating the improper influence of large private contributions furthers a significant governmental interest.

We also reject as without merit appellants' argument that the matching formula favors wealthy voters and candidates. The thrust of the legislation is to reduce financial barriers and to enhance the importance of smaller contributions. Some candidates undoubtedly could raise large sums of money and thus have little need for public funds, but candidates with lesser fundraising capabilities will gain substantial benefits from matching funds. In addition, one eligibility requirement for matching funds is acceptance of an expenditure ceiling, and candidates with little fundraising ability will be able to increase their spending relative to candidates capable of raising large amounts in private funds.

For the reasons stated, we reject appellants' claims that Subtitle H is facially unconstitutional.

[Chief Justice Burger, Justice White, Justice Marshall, Justice Rehnquist, and Justice Blackmun each wrote a separate opinion that joined with the Court's opinion in part and dissented in part. These opinions have been omitted.]

Points for Discussion

1. **Is spending money speech?** Why did the Supreme Court think that spending money is a form of speech? Do you agree with the Court's reasoning? A footnote to the opinion in *Buckley* uses this metaphor to demonstrate the absurdity of protecting political speech but not the money required to communicate it:

   > Being free to engage in unlimited political expression subject to a ceiling on expenditures is like being free to drive an automobile as far and as often as one desires on a single tank of gasoline.

   Justice John Paul Stevens countered this metaphor in a subsequent campaign finance opinion:

   > While a car cannot run without fuel, a candidate can speak without spending money. And while a car can only travel so many miles per gallon, there is no limit on the number of speeches or interviews a candidate may give on a limited budget. Moreover, provided that this budget is above a certain threshold, a candidate can exercise due care to ensure that her message reaches all voters. Just as a driver need not use a Hummer to reach her destination, so a candidate need not flood the airways with ceaseless sound-bites of trivial information in order to provide voters with reasons to support her.

   Randall v. Sorrell, 548 U.S. 230, 277 (2006) (Stevens, J., dissenting)

   Which metaphor is a better characterization of the role of money in political speech?

2. **Why and how does the Court distinguish between campaign contributions and expenditures?** The Court makes a sharp distinction between campaign contributions and independent expenditures in terms of both the speech interests implicated by each and the extent to which each implicates the government's interest in combatting corruption. Can you articulate the Court's reasoning on these points?

3. **Can spending be limited to level the playing field?** The government contended that limits on expenditures furthered its interest in "equalizing the relative ability

of individuals and groups to influence the outcome of elections." Did the Court find the government's argument convincing? Do you agree with the Court's conclusion and reasoning?

4. **Why do disclosure laws implicate the First Amendment?** The Court said that compelled disclosure "can seriously infringe on privacy of association and belief guaranteed by the First Amendment." Can you explain why this is so? Given this observation, why did the Court nevertheless uphold the disclosure requirements? Can you think of a situation where compelled disclosure of contributions or expenditures would violate the First Amendment? We will return to this topic in Chapter 15 when we discuss the impact of compelled disclosures on First Amendment rights.

2. Extending *Buckley*'s Impact: Corporations (and Unions) Have a Right to Spend Too

Buckley provided robust First Amendment protection to independent expenditures. But, even after the case was decided, there remained an open question as to whether this robust protection applied to expenditures by corporations. The following case answered that question.

Citizens United v. Federal Election Commission

Supreme Court of the United States, 2010
558 U.S. 310

JUSTICE KENNEDY delivered the opinion of the Court.

Federal law prohibits corporations and unions from using their general treasury funds to make independent expenditures for speech defined as an "electioneering communication" or for speech expressly advocating the election or defeat of a candidate. Limits on electioneering communications were upheld in *McConnell v. Federal Election Comm'n*, 540 U.S. 93 (2003). The holding of *McConnell* rested to a large extent on an earlier case, *Austin v. Michigan Chamber of Commerce,* 494 U.S. 652 (1990). *Austin* had held that political speech may be banned based on the speaker's corporate identity.

In this case we are asked to reconsider *Austin* and, in effect, *McConnell.* It has been noted that "*Austin* was a significant departure from ancient First Amendment principles," *Federal Election Comm'n v. Wisconsin Right to Life, Inc.,* 551 U.S. 449, 490 (2007) (Scalia, J., concurring in part and concurring in judgment). We agree with that conclusion and hold that *stare decisis* does not compel the continued acceptance of

Austin. The Government may regulate corporate political speech through disclaimer and disclosure requirements, but it may not suppress that speech altogether. We turn to the case now before us.

Citizens United is a nonprofit corporation. It brought this action in the United States District Court for the District of Columbia. A three-judge court later convened to hear the cause. The resulting judgment gives rise to this appeal.

Citizens United has an annual budget of about $12 million. Most of its funds are from donations by individuals; but, in addition, it accepts a small portion of its funds from for-profit corporations.

In January 2008, Citizens United released a film entitled *Hillary: The Movie*. We refer to the film as *Hillary*. It is a 90-minute documentary about then-Senator Hillary Clinton, who was a candidate in the Democratic Party's 2008 Presidential primary elections. *Hillary* mentions Senator Clinton by name and depicts interviews with political commentators and other persons, most of them quite critical of Senator Clinton. *Hillary* was released in theaters and on DVD, but Citizens United wanted to increase distribution by making it available through video-on-demand.

See It

You can watch the trailer for *Hillary: The Movie* here.

Before the Bipartisan Campaign Reform Act of 2002 (BCRA), federal law prohibited—and still does prohibit—corporations and unions from using general treasury funds to make direct contributions to candidates or independent expenditures that expressly advocate the election or defeat of a candidate, through any form of media, in connection with certain qualified federal elections.

Under this test, *Hillary* is equivalent to express advocacy. The movie, in essence, is a feature-length negative advertisement that urges viewers to vote against Senator Clinton for President. In light of historical footage, interviews with persons critical of her, and voiceover narration, the film would be understood by most viewers as an extended criticism of Senator Clinton's character and her fitness for the office of the Presidency.

The law before us is an outright ban, backed by criminal sanctions. Section 441b makes it a felony for all corporations—including nonprofit advocacy corporations—either to expressly advocate the election or defeat of candidates or to broadcast electioneering communications within 30 days of a primary election and 60 days of a general election. Thus, the following acts would all be felonies under § 441b: The Sierra Club runs an ad, within the crucial phase of 60 days before the general election, that exhorts the public to disapprove of a Congressman who favors logging in national forests; the National Rifle Association publishes a book urging the public to vote for the challenger because the incumbent U.S. Senator supports a handgun ban; and the American Civil Liberties Union creates a Web site telling the public to vote for a Presidential candidate in light of that candidate's defense of free speech. These prohibitions are classic examples of censorship.

Speech is an essential mechanism of democracy, for it is the means to hold officials accountable to the people. The right of citizens to inquire, to hear, to speak, and to use information to reach consensus is a precondition to enlightened self-government and a necessary means to protect it. The First Amendment "has its fullest and most urgent application to speech uttered during a campaign for political office."

For these reasons, political speech must prevail against laws that would suppress it, whether by design or inadvertence. Laws that burden political speech are "subject to strict scrutiny," which requires the Government to prove that the restriction "furthers a compelling interest and is narrowly tailored to achieve that interest." We shall employ it here.

Premised on mistrust of governmental power, the First Amendment stands against attempts to disfavor certain subjects or viewpoints. Prohibited, too, are restrictions distinguishing among different speakers, allowing speech by some but not others. As instruments to censor, these categories are interrelated: Speech restrictions based on the identity of the speaker are all too often simply a means to control content.

Quite apart from the purpose or effect of regulating content, moreover, the Government may commit a constitutional wrong when by law it identifies certain preferred speakers. By taking the right to speak from some and giving it to others, the Government deprives the disadvantaged person or class of the right to use speech to strive to establish worth, standing, and respect for the speaker's voice. The Government may not by these means deprive the public of the right and privilege to determine for itself what speech and speakers are worthy of consideration. The First Amendment protects speech and speaker, and the ideas that flow from each.

We find no basis for the proposition that, in the context of political speech, the Government may impose restrictions on certain disfavored speakers. Both history and logic lead us to this conclusion.

The Court has recognized that First Amendment protection extends to corporations. This protection has been extended by explicit holdings to the context of political speech.

At least since the latter part of the 19th century, the laws of some States and of the United States imposed a ban on corporate direct contributions to candidates. Yet not until 1947 did Congress first prohibit independent expenditures by corporations and labor unions in § 304 of the Labor Management Relations Act 1947.

For almost three decades thereafter, the Court did not reach the question whether restrictions on corporate and union expenditures are constitutional.

In *Buckley*, the Court addressed various challenges to the Federal Election Campaign Act of 1971 (FECA) as amended in 1974.

The *Buckley* Court recognized a "sufficiently important" governmental interest in "the prevention of corruption and the appearance of corruption."

heightend scrutiny

The *Buckley* Court explained that the potential for *quid pro quo* corruption distinguished direct contributions to candidates from independent expenditures. The Court emphasized that "the independent expenditure ceiling fails to serve any substantial governmental interest in stemming the reality or appearance of corruption in the electoral process." *Buckley* invalidated § 608(e)'s restrictions on independent expenditures, with only one Justice dissenting.

direct contributions vs independent expenditures

Less than two years after *Buckley*, *First National Bank v. Bellotti*, 435 U.S. 765 (1978), reaffirmed the First Amendment principle that the Government cannot restrict political speech based on the speaker's corporate identity. *Bellotti* could not have been clearer when it struck down a state-law prohibition on corporate independent expenditures related to referenda issues:

> We thus find no support in the First Amendment, or in the decisions of this Court, for the proposition that speech that otherwise would be within the protection of the First Amendment loses that protection simply because its source is a corporation that cannot prove, to the satisfaction of a court, a material effect on its business or property. [That proposition] amounts to an impermissible legislative prohibition of speech based on the identity of the interests that spokesmen may represent in public debate over controversial issues and a requirement that the speaker have a sufficiently great interest in the subject to justify communication.

"In the realm of protected speech, the legislature is constitutionally disqualified from dictating the subjects about which persons may speak and the speakers who may address a public issue."

It is important to note that the reasoning and holding of *Bellotti* did not rest on the existence of a viewpoint-discriminatory statute. It rested on the principle that the Government lacks the power to ban corporations from speaking.

Bellotti did not address the constitutionality of the State's ban on corporate independent expenditures to support candidates. In our view, however, that restriction would have been unconstitutional under *Bellotti*'s central principle: that the First Amendment does not allow political speech restrictions based on a speaker's corporate identity.

Austin "upheld a direct restriction on the independent expenditure of funds for political speech for the first time in this Court's history." There, the Michigan Chamber of Commerce sought to use general treasury funds to run a newspaper ad supporting a specific candidate. Michigan law, however, prohibited corporate independent expenditures that supported or opposed any candidate for state office. A violation of the law was punishable as a felony. The Court sustained the speech prohibition.

To bypass *Buckley* and *Bellotti*, the *Austin* Court identified a new governmental interest in limiting political speech: an antidistortion interest. *Austin* found a compelling governmental interest in preventing "the corrosive and distorting effects of immense aggregations of wealth that are accumulated with the help of the corporate form and that have little or no correlation to the public's support for the corporation's political ideas."

The Court is thus confronted with conflicting lines of precedent: a pre-*Austin* line that forbids restrictions on political speech based on the speaker's corporate identity and a post-*Austin* line that permits them. No case before *Austin* had held that Congress could prohibit independent expenditures for political speech based on the speaker's corporate identity.

Austin's antidistortion rationale cannot support § 441b.

If the First Amendment has any force, it prohibits Congress from fining or jailing citizens, or associations of citizens, for simply engaging in political speech. If the antidistortion rationale were to be accepted, however, it would permit Government to ban political speech simply because the speaker is an association that has taken on the corporate form. The Government contends that *Austin* permits it to ban corporate expenditures for almost all forms of communication stemming from a corporation. If *Austin* were correct, the Government could prohibit a corporation from expressing political views in media beyond those presented here, such as by printing books. The Government responds "that the FEC has never applied this statute to a book," and if it did, "there would be quite a good as-applied challenge." This troubling assertion of brooding governmental power cannot be reconciled with the confidence and stability in civic discourse that the First Amendment must secure.

Austin's antidistortion rationale would produce the dangerous, and unacceptable, consequence that Congress could ban political speech of media corporations. Media corporations are now exempt from § 441b's ban on corporate expenditures. Yet media corporations accumulate wealth with the help of the corporate form, the largest media corporations have "immense aggregations of wealth," and the views expressed by media corporations often "have little or no correlation to the public's support" for those views. Thus, under the Government's reasoning, wealthy media corporations could have their voices diminished to put them on par with other media entities. There is no precedent for permitting this under the First Amendment.

The law's exception for media corporations is, on its own terms, all but an admission of the invalidity of the antidistortion rationale. And the exemption results in a further, separate reason for finding this law invalid: Again by its own terms, the law exempts some corporations but covers others, even though both have the need or the motive to communicate their views. The exemption applies to media corporations owned or controlled by corporations that have diverse and substantial investments and participate in endeavors other than news. So even assuming the most doubtful proposition that a news organization has a right to speak when others do not, the exemption would allow a conglomerate that owns both a media business and an unrelated business to influence or control the media in order to advance its overall business interest. At the same time, some other corporation, with an identical business interest but no media outlet in its ownership structure, would be forbidden to speak or inform the public about the same issue. This differential treatment cannot be squared with the First Amendment.

The censorship we now confront is vast in its reach. By suppressing the speech of manifold corporations, both for-profit and nonprofit, the Government prevents their voices and viewpoints from reaching the public and advising voters on which persons or entities are hostile to their interests. Factions will necessarily form in our Republic, but the remedy of "destroying the liberty" of some factions is "worse than the disease." The Federalist No. 10. Factions should be checked by permitting them all to speak and by entrusting the people to judge what is true and what is false.

The purpose and effect of this law is to prevent corporations, including small and nonprofit corporations, from presenting both facts and opinions to the public. This makes *Austin*'s antidistortion rationale all the more an aberration.

When Government seeks to use its full power, including the criminal law, to command where a person may get his or her information or what distrusted source he or she may not hear, it uses censorship to control thought. This is unlawful. The First Amendment confirms the freedom to think for ourselves.

What we have said also shows the invalidity of other arguments made by the Government. For the most part relinquishing the antidistortion rationale, the Government falls back on the argument that corporate political speech can be banned in order to prevent corruption or its appearance. In *Buckley*, the Court found this interest "sufficiently important" to allow limits on contributions but did not extend that reasoning to expenditure limits.

Limits on independent expenditures, such as § 441b, have a chilling effect extending well beyond the Government's interest in preventing *quid pro quo* corruption. The anticorruption interest is not sufficient to displace the speech here in question. Indeed, 26 States do not restrict independent expenditures by for-profit corporations. The Government does not claim that these expenditures have corrupted the political process in those States.

The appearance of influence or access, furthermore, will not cause the electorate to lose faith in our democracy. By definition, an independent expenditure is political speech presented to the electorate that is not coordinated with a candidate. The fact that a corporation, or any other speaker, is willing to spend money to try to persuade voters presupposes that the people have the ultimate influence over elected officials.

When Congress finds that a problem exists, we must give that finding due deference; but Congress may not choose an unconstitutional remedy. If elected officials succumb to improper influences from independent expenditures; if they surrender their best judgment; and if they put expediency before principle, then surely there is cause for concern. We must give weight to attempts by Congress to seek to dispel either the appearance or the reality of these influences. The remedies enacted by law, however, must comply with the First Amendment; and, it is our law and our tradition that more speech, not less, is the governing rule. An outright ban on corporate political speech during the critical preelection period is not a permissible remedy. Here Congress has created categorical bans on speech that are asymmetrical to preventing *quid pro quo* corruption.

The Government contends further that corporate independent expenditures can be limited because of its interest in protecting dissenting shareholders from being compelled to fund corporate political speech. This asserted interest, like *Austin*'s antidistortion rationale, would allow the Government to ban the political speech even of media corporations. The First Amendment does not allow that power. There is, furthermore, little evidence of abuse that cannot be corrected by shareholders "through the procedures of corporate democracy."

Those reasons are sufficient to reject this shareholder-protection interest; and, moreover, the statute is both underinclusive and overinclusive. As to the first, if Congress had been seeking to protect dissenting shareholders, it would not have banned corporate speech in only certain media within 30 or 60 days before an election. A dissenting shareholder's interests would be implicated by speech in any media at any time. As to the second, the statute is overinclusive because it covers all corporations, including nonprofit corporations and for-profit corporations with only single shareholders. As to other corporations, the remedy is not to restrict speech but to consider and explore other regulatory mechanisms. The regulatory mechanism here, based on speech, contravenes the First Amendment.

Austin should be and now is overruled. We return to the principle established in *Buckley* and *Bellotti* that the Government may not suppress political speech on the basis of the speaker's corporate identity. No sufficient governmental interest justifies limits on the political speech of nonprofit or for-profit corporations.

Austin is overruled, so it provides no basis for allowing the Government to limit corporate independent expenditures.

Given our conclusion we are further required to overrule the part of *McConnell* that upheld BCRA § 203's extension of § 441b's restrictions on corporate independent expenditures. The *McConnell* Court relied on the antidistortion interest recognized in *Austin* to uphold a greater restriction on speech than the restriction upheld in *Austin*, and we have found this interest unconvincing and insufficient. This part of *McConnell* is now overruled.

Modern day movies, television comedies, or skits on Youtube.com might portray public officials or public policies in unflattering ways. Yet if a covered transmission during the blackout period creates the background for candidate endorsement or opposition, a felony occurs solely because a corporation, other than an exempt media corporation, has made the "purchase, payment, distribution, loan, advance, deposit, or gift of money or anything of value" in order to engage in political speech.

Some members of the public might consider *Hillary* to be insightful and instructive; some might find it to be neither high art nor a fair discussion on how to set the Nation's course; still others simply might suspend judgment on these points but decide to think more about issues and candidates. Those choices and assessments, however, are not for the Government to make. "The First Amendment underwrites the freedom to experiment and to create in the realm of thought and speech. Citizens must be free to use new forms, and new forums, for the expression of ideas. The civic discourse belongs to the people, and the Government may not prescribe the means used to conduct it."

JUSTICE STEVENS, with whom JUSTICE GINSBURG, JUSTICE BREYER, and JUSTICE SOTOMAYOR join, concurring in part and dissenting in part.

The basic premise underlying the Court's ruling is its iteration, and constant reiteration, of the proposition that the First Amendment bars regulatory distinctions based on a speaker's identity, including its "identity" as a corporation. While that glittering generality has rhetorical appeal, it is not a correct statement of the law. Nor does it tell us when a corporation may engage in electioneering that some of its shareholders oppose. It does not even resolve the specific question whether Citizens United may be required to finance some of its messages with the money in its PAC. The conceit that corporations must be treated identically to natural persons in the political sphere is not only inaccurate but also inadequate to justify the Court's disposition of this case.

In the context of election to public office, the distinction between corporate and human speakers is significant. Although they make enormous contributions to our society, corporations are not actually members of it. They cannot vote or run for office. Because they may be managed and controlled by nonresidents, their interests may conflict in fundamental respects with the interests of eligible voters. The financial resources, legal structure, and instrumental orientation of corporations raise legitimate concerns about their role in the electoral process. Our lawmakers have a compelling constitutional basis, if not also a democratic duty, to take measures designed to guard against the potentially deleterious effects of corporate spending in local and national races.

The majority's approach to corporate electioneering marks a dramatic break from our past.

Let us start from the beginning. The Court invokes "ancient First Amendment principles," and original understandings to defend today's ruling, yet it makes only a perfunctory attempt to ground its analysis in the principles or understandings of those who drafted and ratified the Amendment. Perhaps this is because there is not a scintilla of evidence to support the notion that anyone believed it would preclude regulatory distinctions based on the corporate form. To the extent that the Framers' views are discernible and relevant to the disposition of this case, they would appear to cut strongly against the majority's position.

It is an interesting question "who" is even speaking when a business corporation places an advertisement that endorses or attacks a particular candidate. Presumably it is not the customers or employees, who typically have no say in such matters. It cannot realistically be said to be the shareholders, who tend to be far removed from the day-to-day decisions of the firm and whose political preferences may be opaque to management. Perhaps the officers or directors of the corporation have the best claim to be the ones speaking, except their fiduciary duties generally prohibit them from using corporate funds for personal ends. Some individuals associated with the corporation must make the decision to place the ad, but the idea that these individuals are thereby fostering their self-expression or cultivating their critical faculties is fanciful. It is entirely possible that the corporation's electoral message will conflict with their personal convictions. Take away the ability to use general treasury funds for some of those ads, and no one's autonomy, dignity, or political equality has been impinged upon in the least.

Today's decision is backwards in many senses. It elevates the majority's agenda over the litigants' submissions, facial attacks over as-applied claims, broad constitutional theories over narrow statutory grounds, individual dissenting opinions over precedential holdings, assertion over tradition, absolutism over empiricism, rhetoric over reality. Our colleagues have arrived at the conclusion that *Austin* must be overruled and that § 203 is facially unconstitutional only after mischaracterizing both the reach and rationale of those authorities, and after bypassing or ignoring rules of judicial restraint used to cabin the Court's lawmaking power. Their conclusion that the societal interest in avoiding corruption and the appearance of corruption does not provide an adequate justification for regulating corporate expenditures on candidate elections relies on an incorrect description of that interest, along with a failure to acknowledge the relevance of established facts and the considered judgments of state and federal legislatures over many decades.

[Chief Justice Roberts' concurring opinion, which was joined by Justice Alito, is omitted, as is the concurring opinion by Justice Scalia, which was joined by Justice Alito and Justice Thomas. Also omitted is Justice Thomas' opinion concurring in part and dissenting in part.]

Points for Discussion

1. **Contributions vs. expenditures.** The core distinction at the heart of *Buckley* is the distinction between limits on contributions, which generally do not violate the First Amendment, and limits on independent expenditures, which do violate the First Amendment. This core holding of *Buckley* remains good law.

   The Court's reasoning for treating contributions differently from independent expenditures is that contributions create a risk of corruption whereas independent expenditures, which cannot be coordinated with the candidate, do not. The impact of this distinction was amplified two months after *Citizens United* when the D.C. Circuit, in *SpeechNow.org v. Federal Election Commission,* 599 F.3d 686 (D.C. Cir. 2010), held that contributions to political action committees, as opposed to a candidate's campaign, cannot be restricted because the PACs will use these contributions to make independent expenditures.

   The Court's disparate treatment of contributions and independent expenditures assumes that the government can effectively police the line between them. Some commentators, however, have questioned that assumption. Trevor Potter, a former member and chairman of the Federal Election Commission, the agency charged with protecting the integrity of the campaign finance process, has been outspoken about the lack of adequate enforcement:

> From that pair of decisions [*Citizens United* and *SpeechNow.org*] came the modern era of "independent expenditure-only" groups that raise and spend unlimited amounts from individuals, corporations, and unions: super PACs. Since 2010, super PACs and other purportedly independent outside groups have spent over $4.5 billion in federal elections, and super PACs that support only a single candidate have spent over $1 billion, according to the Center for Responsive Politics.
>
> A large and growing number of these groups regularly engage in close relationships with the campaigns they purport to be independent from: super PACs hire close aides and recent employees of the candidate; candidates appear as "special guests" at super PAC fundraisers; super PACs creatively synchronize media strategy with the campaign through vendors, aides, the internet, or other channels; candidates regularly signal to donors which super PAC to direct funds to after they reach the maximum legal limit to the campaign; and much more.
>
> By most reasonable observations, activities like this would appear to directly contravene the Court's rationale in *Citizens United*. And when it does, such non-independent spending, as Justice Kennedy did not dispute, can be extremely valuable to candidates, functions similarly as direct campaign contributions, and presents a host of dangers of corruption. The question, then, is: why has this non-independent spending flourished?
>
> Fundamentally, it is happening because actual independence turns out to be very difficult to ensure in practice. The Federal Election Commission has [also] woefully failed to perform the core tasks with which Congress entrusted it.

Trevor Potter, *The Failed Promise of Unlimited "Independent" Spending in Elections*, Human Rights Magazine (ABA), Vol. 45, No. 3 (June 25, 2020).

One final note. While the Court has generally upheld limits on campaign contributions, it struck down contribution limits in a Vermont law for being too restrictive. *Randall v. Sorrell*, 548 U.S. 230 (2006). In a plurality opinion, Justice Breyer explained that "contribution limits that are too low can also harm the electoral process by preventing challengers from mounting effective campaigns against incumbent officeholders, thereby reducing democratic accountability."

2. **Corporations and individuals face the same rules.** In urban lore it has been said that "what's good for General Motors is good for America." (There is some dispute as to whether this is an actual quote from a corporate leader or mythologized legend.) *Citizens United* might be mythologized as standing for the proposition

that "what's good for corporations is good for the First Amendment." Justice Stevens argued in dissent that the law often makes distinctions between corporations, which are artificial beings, and individuals, who are natural beings. Among other things, he argued that when corporations spend money on political causes, they typically are spending "other people's money," in that shareholders who buy stock normally are not thinking of themselves as buying stock to advance political causes, but simply as business investments. But Justice Stevens lost. And so, at present, the First Amendment rules applicable to individuals, such as the core distinction in *Buckley* between expenditures and contributions, apply with the same force to corporations.

In the *Citizens United* majority opinion, Justice Kennedy expressed concern that the same logic for applying different First Amendment rules to corporations—that corporations accumulate immense wealth and that shareholders should not be forced to fund corporate political speech—could be used to justify restrictions on the political speech of media companies. Indeed, First Amendment jurisprudence generally frowns upon exceptions in the law that treat some speakers more favorably than others. The challenge for those who support limits on corporate campaign spending is to find a principled basis for exempting media corporations. That, in turn, raises the knotty problem of defining which corporations are media corporations, a problem that parallels the difficulty the Court has confronted in defining the "press" for purposes of enforcing the First Amendment's Press Clause. For a suggested path out of this dilemma, *see* Sonja R. West, *The Media Exemption Puzzle of Campaign Finance Laws*, 164 U. Pa. L. Rev. Online 253 (2016).

Many expected *Citizens United* to unleash a tsunami of corporate money into American politics. That did not materialize. The Committee for Economic Development of the Conference Board examined independent expenditures in the 2014 and 2016 elections and found little evidence of increased spending by business organizations. Nevertheless, there was a dramatic increase in contributions to super PACs, mostly from wealthy individuals. The report found that "a relatively small number of individuals who made seven or eight figure contributions have been responsible for the dramatic growth of Super PACs." *See* Committee for Econ. Dev., The Landscape of Campaign Contributions: Campaign Finance after Citizens United (July 10, 2017).

3. **Disclosure and reporting.** *Buckley* upheld disclosure and reporting requirements, though it held out the possibility that in future cases, a minority party would be free to challenge these requirements, as specifically applied to it, if the disclosure of contributors would interfere with the party's right of free association. Such a challenge might succeed, for example, if a minority cause or candidate were so controversial that donors would be deterred from contributing for fear of reprisal.

This is an application of the distinction between a "facial" challenge to a law and an "as applied" challenge, as discussed in Chapter 3. We will study a related case in Chapter 15 concerning a California law that required the disclosure of the names, addresses, and donations of contributors to charities. *Americans for Prosperity Found. v. Bonta*, 141 S. Ct. 2373 (2021).

4. **Corruption vs. distortion.** One of the central philosophical divides in the campaign finance cases is a fundamental disagreement over what should or should not qualify as a "governmental interest" sufficient to justify regulation. It is settled, and not particularly controversial, that the prevention of corruption, particularly core quid pro quo corruption, does qualify. It is also settled, but very controversial, that combating "distortion" does not qualify. This is the key philosophical debate in *Citizens United*. "Distortion" is the phrase that has come to be used to describe efforts to level the playing field, by preventing large expenditures of money to "distort" the marketplace of ideas by giving money-backed positions more amplification than positions with less financial support. Those who support the anti-distortion rationale argue that the merits of ideas, or the merits of candidates, are what should matter, not how much money is behind them. *Buckley* focused on the corruption rationale. The law then wavered for a period, with decisions such as *Austin* seeming to embrace anti-distortion as a worthy justification for campaign finance restrictions. *Citizens United* overruled *Austin* and rejected the anti-distortion rationale, holding it antithetical to First Amendment values. Professor Kathleen Sullivan described the opinion as representing "a triumph of the libertarian over the egalitarian vision of free speech." Kathleen M. Sullivan, *Two Concepts of Freedom of Speech*, 124 Harv. L. Rev. 143, 145 (2010).

   Critics of the Court's jurisprudence claim that it is undermining our democracy by giving undue influence in the political process to wealthy actors, whether individual billionaires or large corporations. *See, e.g.*, Tim Lau, Brennan Ctr. for Justice, Citizens United Explained (Dec. 12, 2019). While this assumption—that greater spending leads to greater influence—is intuitively appealing, it is easier to assume than to empirically prove. Political scientist Martin Gilens set out to test the assumption by comparing decades of survey data indicating the policy preferences of lower-income and higher-income Americans with the policies government adopted. He concluded that the government is responsive to public policy preferences but that this responsiveness is "strongly tilted toward the most affluent citizens." Nevertheless, he cautioned that "popular impressions of a Congress for sale to the highest bidder, or an electoral system in which money is the singular key to victory, are grossly oversimplified." At the same time, he said that it would be "equally naïve" to think that money, the "mother's milk of politics," is "of little importance." Martin Gilens, *Affluence & Influence: Economic Inequality and Political Power in America* 1, 246 (2012).

5. **Is public financing of elections the answer?** In *Buckley*, the Court approved the use of public financing to combat the influence of large donors. The Court also said the government could constitutionally require recipients of public funding to limit private fundraising: "Just as a candidate may voluntarily limit the size of the contributions he chooses to accept, he may decide to forgo private fundraising and accept public funding."

   The Court, however, has since placed limits on public financing. Most notably, it has invalidated programs that boost public funding for candidates when spending by privately financed candidates passes certain thresholds. In *Arizona Free Enterprise Club's Freedom Club PAC v. Bennett*, 564 U.S. 721 (2011), a five-justice majority said that increasing public funding in response to privately financed candidates' spending penalizes the privately financed candidates for robustly exercising their First Amendment rights. Writing for the four dissenters, Justice Elena Kagan noted that public financing will be attractive only if candidates receive enough funding to fairly compete with privately financed candidates. She noted, however, that it is not financially sustainable for governments to immediately offer high subsidies. Consequently, programs that boost funding only as needed, as in the Arizona case, are the perfect "Goldilocks solution—not too large, not too small, but just right." Justice Kagan said the Arizona scheme did not burden political speech. If anything, it enhanced political speech by subsidizing the production of more speech. "Except in a world gone topsy-turvy," she lamented, "additional campaign speech and electoral competition is not a First Amendment injury."

6. **How does distortion in politics compare to distortion in social media?** There may be some irony in the observation that when it comes to efforts to regulate social media platforms, the animating concern is often expressed as the worry that the current regime distorts the marketplace of ideas by giving too much power to the progressive left, which purportedly tends to dominate the management of the platforms. When it comes to political campaign contributions, critics of *Citizens United* tend to fear that distortion favors the political right. (While in popular lore we might reflexively assume that Republicans are more likely to be happy with *Citizens United* and Democrats opposed to it, in fairness there have been famous Republican leaders, such as Senator John McCain, who ran for president as a Republican, who strongly favored campaign finance reform.) While the role of distortion as applied to both media regulation and political finance regulation remains a work in progress, it is fair to say that existing First Amendment doctrine appears generally skeptical of the anti-distortion justification in both settings.

A Comparative Perspective

The Supreme Court of Canada has taken a decidedly different approach to campaign spending limits than the approach taken by its sister court in the United States. The Canadian court expressly embraced an "egalitarian model of elections" in which wealth is perceived as "the main obstacle to equal participation." Not surprisingly, the court upheld limits on third-party spending during elections. "In the absence of spending limits," the court explained, "it is possible for the affluent or a number of persons or groups pooling their resources and acting in concert to dominate the political discourse." The court continued:

> Where those having access to the most resources monopolize the election discourse, their opponents will be deprived of a reasonable opportunity to speak and be heard. This unequal dissemination of points of view undermines the voter's ability to be adequately informed of all views. In this way, equality in the political discourse is necessary for meaningful participation in the electoral process and ultimately enhances the right to vote.

Harper v. Canada, 1 S.C.R. 827 (2004).

Test Your Knowledge

To assess your understanding of the material in this chapter, click here to take a quiz.

Content-Neutral Regulations of Speech: When Speech Is Regulated for Reasons Unrelated to a Speaker's Message

Chapter Thirteen

May Government Regulate Speech for Order, Tranquility, and Aesthetics?

Grassroots Communications, Picketing, and Permit Requirements

This chapter marks our transition from the discussion of content-based regulations of speech to content-neutral regulations. The laws discussed in this chapter and the next regulate speech for reasons unrelated to a speaker's message. This form of regulation arises in two contexts. The first is content-neutral regulations of expression, such as laws that regulate the time, place, or manner in which speech is expressed. This type of content-neutral regulation is the subject of this chapter. The second is conduct regulations that incidentally burden a person's ability to use conduct for expressive purposes. That type of regulation is the subject of the following chapter.

You learned in Chapter 4 that content-neutral regulations of speech are subject to intermediate scrutiny. This level of scrutiny requires the government to prove that a law is narrowly tailored (or "substantially related") to furthering an important (or "substantial" or "significant") governmental interest. In Chapter 11, you learned that the Supreme Court has developed a specialized version of intermediate scrutiny for laws that regulate the time, place, or manner of speech occurring in a public forum:

> We have often noted that restrictions of this kind are valid provided that they are justified without reference to the content of the regulated speech, that they are narrowly tailored to serve a significant governmental interest,

and that they leave open ample alternative channels for communication of the information.[1]

The first part of this test—that the restriction is "justified without reference to the content of the regulated speech"—is another way of saying that the law must be content-neutral. If the government is justifying the restriction based on the content of the speech, it is content-based and should be analyzed under strict scrutiny. The second two elements—that the law be "narrowly tailored to serve a significant governmental interest"—are the core requirements for a law to pass intermediate scrutiny. While the Court sometimes uses the words "narrowly tailored" to mean the least restrictive alternative, in the intermediate scrutiny context these words have a more forgiving connotation. There does not need to be a perfect fit between the end and means but only a reasonable fit.[2] The final element of the time, place, or manner test—that the law "leave open ample alternative channels for communication of the information"—helps ensure that content-neutral laws are not drafted so broadly as to preclude a speaker's ability to convey his or her message.

In earlier chapters, you learned that content-based regulations of speech are subject to strict scrutiny and are very likely to be struck down. As the *Burson* opinion observed, it is the "rare case" that survives strict scrutiny.

By contrast, content-neutral laws are often upheld. Unlike content-based regulations, these laws do not raise the specter that "official suppression of ideas is afoot." The Court has also recognized that governments have legitimate reasons for regulating the time, place, or manner of speech. These reasons include protecting the public's interests in tranquility (*e.g.*, laws prohibiting rallies late at night), aesthetics (*e.g.*, laws restricting the placement of billboards), and order (*e.g.*, laws requiring a permit to hold a parade).

While content-neutral laws are often upheld, that is not always the case. Intermediate scrutiny is still a form of heightened judicial scrutiny, and not all laws will survive its application. The Court's unwillingness to give content-neutral laws a "free pass" comes from a recognition that these laws can also undermine free speech interests. To take an extreme example, imagine a law that banned all leafleting, door-to-door solicitations, and rallies.

---

1 *Clark v. Community for Creative Non-Violence*, 468 U.S. 288, 293 (1984).

2 *Ward v. Rock Against Racism*, 491 U.S. 781, 798–99 (1989) ("Lest any confusion on the point remain, we reaffirm today that a regulation of the time, place, or manner of protected speech must be narrowly tailored to serve the government's legitimate, content-neutral interests but that it need not be the least restrictive or least intrusive means of doing so. Rather, the requirement of narrow tailoring is satisfied 'so long as the regulation promotes a substantial government interest that would be achieved less effectively absent the regulation.' ").

The challenge with content-neutral regulations is to figure out which ones will be upheld as constitutional and which ones will not. What factors cause a content-neutral law to cross the line from lawful to unlawful? We take up that challenge in this chapter.

Since content-neutral laws come in a wide variety of forms, we can give only a sampling of how the Court treats these laws. We have chosen to focus on three areas that have generated substantial and significant precedent:

- Laws regulating core grassroots means of communication.
- Laws regulating picketing.
- Licensing regimes that require permits for rallies, parades, and other expressive activities.

A. When Content-Neutral Laws Impinge on Grassroots Communication: Leafleting, Door-to-Door Solicitations, Loudspeakers, and Residential Signs

Professor Harry Kalven famously called traditional public forums the "poor man's printing press."[3] It is in public forums where people can hand out leaflets, give soapbox speeches, circulate petitions, and hold rallies. Most people don't own a newspaper or radio station. For these people, leaflets are their newspapers and loudspeakers their radio stations.

As the following cases illustrate, the Court has been leery of content-neutral regulations that unduly burden grassroots means of communication. The Court acknowledges the need for reasonable regulations of these activities—there is no right to circulate leaflets by throwing them out of windows and no right to use loudspeakers in the middle of the night. But laws that entirely ban or heavily burden people's rights to engage in cheap and easy means of grassroots communication have been viewed skeptically by the justices.

1. Leaflets: "Historic Weapons in the Defense of Liberty"

May the government require people to obtain a permit before circulating leaflets? May the government ban leafleting because it leads to littering?

---

[3] Harry Kalven, Jr., *The Concept of the Public Forum: Cox v. Louisiana*, 1965 Sup. Ct. Rev. 1, 30 (1965).

Lovell v. City of Griffin

Supreme Court of the United States, 1938
303 U.S. 444

MR. CHIEF JUSTICE HUGHES delivered the opinion of the Court.

Appellant, Alma Lovell, was convicted in the recorder's court of the City of Griffin, Ga., of the violation of a city ordinance and was sentenced to imprisonment for fifty days in default of the payment of a fine of $50.

The ordinance in question is as follows:

> Section 1. That the practice of distributing, either by hand or otherwise, circulars, handbooks, advertising, or literature of any kind, whether said articles are being delivered free, or whether same are being sold, within the limits of the City of Griffin, without first obtaining written permission from the City Manager of the City of Griffin, such practice shall be deemed a nuisance, and punishable as an offense against the City of Griffin.

The violation, which is not denied, consisted of the distribution without the required permission of a pamphlet and magazine in the nature of religious tracts, setting forth the gospel of the "Kingdom of Jehovah." Appellant did not apply for a permit, as she regarded herself as sent "by Jehovah to do His work" and that such an application would have been "an act of disobedience to His commandment."

The ordinance is comprehensive with respect to the method of distribution. It covers every sort of circulation "either by hand or otherwise." There is thus no restriction in its application with respect to time or place. It is not limited to ways which might be regarded as inconsistent with the maintenance of public order, or as involving disorderly conduct, the molestation of the inhabitants, or the misuse or littering of the streets. The ordinance prohibits the distribution of literature of any kind at any time, at any place, and in any manner without a permit from the city manager.

We think that the ordinance is invalid on its face. Whatever the motive which induced its adoption, its character is such that it strikes at the very foundation of the freedom of the press by subjecting it to license and censorship. The struggle for the freedom of the press was primarily directed against the power of the licensor. It was against that power that John Milton directed his assault by his "Appeal for the Liberty of Unlicensed Printing." And the liberty of the press became initially a right to publish "without a license what formerly could be published only with one." While this freedom from previous restraint upon publication cannot be regarded as exhausting the guaranty of liberty, the prevention of that restraint was a leading purpose in the adoption of the constitutional provision. Legislation of the type of the ordinance in question would restore the system of license and censorship in its baldest form.

The liberty of the press is not confined to newspapers and periodicals. It necessarily embraces pamphlets and leaflets. These indeed have been historic weapons in the defense of liberty, as the pamphlets of Thomas Paine and others in our own history abundantly attest. The press in its historic connotation comprehends every sort of publication which affords a vehicle of information and opinion. What we have had recent occasion to say with respect to the vital importance of protecting this essential liberty from every sort of infringement need not be repeated.

The ordinance cannot be saved because it relates to distribution and not to publication. "Liberty of circulating is as essential to that freedom as liberty of publishing; indeed, without the circulation, the publication would be of little value."

The judgment is reversed and the cause is remanded for further proceedings not inconsistent with this opinion.

Schneider v. New Jersey

Supreme Court of the United States, 1939
308 U.S. 147

[*Authors' note*: This case concerns four consolidated lawsuits that concerned limits on leafleting, including some that placed blanket bans on circulating leaflets. For example, a Los Angeles ordinance provided that "no person shall distribute any handbill to or among pedestrians along or upon any street, sidewalk or park, or to passengers on any street car, or throw, place or attach any hand-bill in, to, or upon any automobile or other vehicle."]

MR. JUSTICE ROBERTS delivered the opinion of the Court.

Although a municipality may enact regulations in the interest of the public safety, health, welfare or convenience, these may not abridge the individual liberties secured by the Constitution to those who wish to speak, write, print or circulate information or opinion.

Municipal authorities, as trustees for the public, have the duty to keep their communities' streets open and available for movement of people and property, the primary purpose to which the streets are dedicated. So long as legislation to this end does not abridge the constitutional liberty of one rightfully upon the street to impart information through speech or the distribution of literature, it may lawfully regulate the conduct of those using the streets. For example, a person could not exercise this liberty by taking his stand in the middle of a crowded street, contrary to traffic regulations, and maintain his position to the stoppage of all traffic; a group of distributors could not insist upon a constitutional right to form a cordon across the street and to allow no pedestrian to pass who did not accept a tendered leaflet; nor does the guarantee of freedom of speech or of the press deprive a municipality of power to enact regulations against throwing literature broadcast in the streets. Prohibition of such conduct would not abridge the constitutional liberty since such activity bears no necessary relationship to the freedom to speak, write, print or distribute information or opinion.

This court has characterized the freedom of speech and that of the press as fundamental personal rights and liberties. The phrase is not an empty one and was not lightly used. It reflects the belief of the framers of the Constitution that exercise of the rights lies at the foundation of free government by free men. It stresses, as do many opinions of this court, the importance of preventing the restriction of enjoyment of these liberties. In every case, therefore, where legislative abridgment of the rights is asserted, the courts should be astute to examine the effect of the challenged legislation.

In *Lovell v. City of Griffin*, this court held void an ordinance which forbade the distribution by hand or otherwise of literature of any kind without written permission from the city manager. The court said that the ordinance was bad because it imposed penalties for the distribution of pamphlets, which had become historical weapons in the defense of liberty, by subjecting such distribution to license and censorship; and that the ordinance was void on its face, because it abridged the freedom of the press.

The Los Angeles, the Milwaukee, and the Worcester ordinances under review do not purport to license distribution but all of them absolutely prohibit it in the streets and, one of them, in other public places as well.

The motive of the legislation under attack is held by the courts below to be the prevention of littering of the streets and, although the alleged offenders were not charged with themselves scattering paper in the streets, their convictions were sustained upon the theory that distribution by them encouraged or resulted in such littering. We are of opinion that the purpose to keep the streets clean and of good appearance is insufficient to justify an ordinance which prohibits a person rightfully on a public street from handing literature to one willing to receive it. Any burden imposed upon the city authorities in cleaning and caring for the streets as an indirect consequence of such distribution results from the constitutional protection of the freedom of speech and press. This constitutional protection does not deprive a city of all power to prevent street littering. There are obvious methods of preventing littering. Amongst these is the punishment of those who actually throw papers on the streets.

It is suggested that the Los Angeles and Worcester ordinances are valid because their operation is limited to streets and alleys and leaves persons free to distribute printed matter in other public places. But, as we have said, the streets are natural and proper places for the dissemination of information and opinion; and one is not to have the exercise of his liberty of expression in appropriate places abridged on the plea that it may be exercised in some other place.

The judgment in each case is reversed and the cases are remanded for further proceedings not inconsistent with this opinion.

Points for Discussion

1. **Why were the laws in *Lovell* and *Schneider* struck down?** The laws in both *Lovell* and *Schneider* were content-neutral, so why did they get struck down? Was the Court suggesting that the government can never regulate leafleting? If not, what was it about these laws that caused the Court to find them unconstitutional?

2. **When are leafleting regulations constitutional?** The *Schneider* opinion indicated that regulations of leafleting can be constitutional if they do not unduly impinge on free speech interests. For example, the Court noted that a municipality could enact an ordinance "against throwing literature broadcast in the streets." Similarly, in *Heffron v. International Society for Krishna Consciousness*, 452 U.S. 640 (1981), the Court upheld a limitation on the distribution of literature. In *Heffron*, adherents of the Krishna religion challenged a prohibition against distributing or selling literature at the Minnesota State Fair except from a licensed booth. Permits for the booths were issued on a first-come-first-served basis. The Krishna members contended that the prohibition interfered with their ability to communicate with fair visitors, but the Court upheld the prohibition as a valid content-neutral regulation of speech. The Court said that the regulation furthered the state's important interest in managing crowd control at the heavily attended event and that Krishna members had ample alternative channels to communicate their messages, including by renting a booth, orally interacting with people, or distributing their literature outside the fairgrounds.

2. Residential Solicitation: "Essential to the Poorly Financed Causes of Little People"

May the government require people to obtain a permit before making door-to-door solicitations? Should it matter whether the solicitations are for political or charitable causes or to sell merchandise?

Watchtower Bible & Tract Society of New York, Inc. v. Village of Stratton

Supreme Court of the United States, 2002
536 U.S. 150

JUSTICE STEVENS delivered the opinion of the Court.

Petitioners contend that a village ordinance making it a misdemeanor to engage in door-to-door advocacy without first registering with the mayor and receiving a permit violates the First Amendment. Through this facial challenge, we consider the door-to-door canvassing regulation not only as it applies to religious proselytizing, but also to anonymous political speech and the distribution of handbills.

For over 50 years, the Court has invalidated restrictions on door-to-door canvassing and pamphleteering. It is more than historical accident that most of these cases involved First Amendment challenges brought by Jehovah's Witnesses, because door-to-door canvassing is mandated by their religion. As we noted in *Murdock v. Pennsylvania*, 319 U.S. 105 (1943), the Jehovah's Witnesses "claim to follow the example of Paul, teaching 'publickly, and from house to house.' Acts 20:20. They take literally the mandate of the Scriptures, 'Go ye into all the world, and preach the gospel to every creature.' Mark 16:15. In doing so they believe that they are obeying a commandment of God." Moreover, because they lack significant financial resources, the ability of the Witnesses to proselytize is seriously diminished by regulations that burden their efforts to canvass door-to-door.

Although our past cases involving Jehovah's Witnesses, most of which were decided shortly before and during World War II, do not directly control the question we confront today, they provide both a historical and analytical backdrop for consideration of petitioners' First Amendment claim that the breadth of the Village's ordinance offends the First Amendment. Those cases involved petty offenses that raised constitutional questions of the most serious magnitude—questions that implicated the free exercise of religion, the freedom of speech, and the freedom of the press. From these decisions, several themes emerge that guide our consideration of the ordinance at issue here.

First, the cases emphasize the value of the speech involved. For example, in *Murdock v. Pennsylvania*, the Court noted that "hand distribution of religious tracts is an age-old form of missionary evangelism—as old as the history of printing presses. It has been a potent force in various religious movements down through the years. This form of religious activity occupies the same high estate under the First Amendment as do worship in the churches and preaching from the pulpits. It has the same claim to protection as the more orthodox and conventional exercises of religion. It also has the same claim as the others to the guarantees of freedom of speech and freedom of the press."

In addition, the cases discuss extensively the historical importance of door-to-door canvassing and pamphleteering as vehicles for the dissemination of ideas. In *Schneider,* the petitioner was a Jehovah's Witness who had been convicted of canvassing without a permit based on evidence that she had gone from house to house offering to leave books or booklets. Writing for the Court, Justice Roberts stated that "pamphlets have proved most effective instruments in the dissemination of opinion. And perhaps the most effective way of bringing them to the notice of individuals is their distribution at the homes of the people."

Despite the emphasis on the important role that door-to-door canvassing and pamphleteering has played in our constitutional tradition of free and open discussion, these early cases also recognized the interests a town may have in some form of regulation, particularly when the solicitation of money is involved. In *Cantwell v. Connecticut,* 310 U.S. 296 (1940), the Court held that an ordinance requiring Jehovah's Witnesses to obtain a license before soliciting door to door was invalid because the issuance of the license depended on the exercise of discretion by a city official. Our opinion recognized that "a State may protect its citizens from fraudulent solicitation by requiring a stranger in the community, before permitting him publicly to solicit funds for any purpose, to establish his identity and his authority to act for the cause which he purports to represent." Similarly, in *Martin v. City of Struthers,* 319 U.S. 141, 144 (1943), the Court recognized crime prevention as a legitimate interest served by these ordinances and noted that "burglars frequently pose as canvassers, either in order that they may have a pretense to discover whether a house is empty and hence ripe for burglary, or for the purpose of spying out the premises in order that they may return later." Despite recognition of these interests as legitimate, our precedent is clear that there must be a balance between these interests and the effect of the regulations on First Amendment rights. We "must be astute to examine the effect of the challenged legislation and must weigh the circumstances and appraise the substantiality of the reasons advanced in support of the regulation."

Finally, the cases demonstrate that efforts of the Jehovah's Witnesses to resist speech regulation have not been a struggle for their rights alone. In *Martin,* after cataloging the many groups that rely extensively upon this method of communication, the Court summarized that "door to door distribution of circulars is essential to the poorly financed causes of little people."

That the Jehovah's Witnesses are not the only "little people" who face the risk of silencing by regulations like the Village's is exemplified by our cases involving nonreligious speech. In *Thomas v. Collins,* 323 U.S. 516 (1945), the issue was whether a labor leader could be required to obtain a permit before delivering a speech to prospective union members. After reviewing the Jehovah's Witnesses cases discussed above, the Court observed:

> As a matter of principle a requirement of registration in order to make a public speech would seem generally incompatible with an exercise of the rights of free speech and free assembly. If the exercise of the rights of free speech and free assembly cannot be made a crime, we do not think this can be accomplished by the device of requiring previous registration as a condition for exercising them and making such a condition the foundation for restraining in advance their exercise and for imposing a penalty for violating such a restraining order. So long as no more is involved than exercise of the rights of free speech and free assembly, it is immune to such a restriction. If one who solicits support for the cause of labor may be required to register as a condition to the exercise of his right to make a public speech, so may he who seeks to rally support for any social, business, religious or political cause. We think a requirement that one must register before he undertakes to make a public speech to enlist support for a lawful movement is quite incompatible with the requirements of the First Amendment.

The mere fact that the ordinance covers so much speech raises constitutional concerns. It is offensive—not only to the values protected by the First Amendment, but to the very notion of a free society—that in the context of everyday public discourse a citizen must first inform the government of her desire to speak to her neighbors and then obtain a permit to do so. Even if the issuance of permits by the mayor's office is a ministerial task that is performed promptly and at no cost to the applicant, a law requiring a permit to engage in such speech constitutes a dramatic departure from our national heritage and constitutional tradition.

[Justice Breyer's concurring opinion, which was joined by Justice Souter and Justice Ginsburg, is omitted, as is Justice Scalia's opinion concurring in the judgment, which was joined by Justice Thomas. Chief Justice Rehnquist's dissenting opinion is also omitted.]

Points for Discussion

1. **Why did the Court strike down the law in *Watchtower*?** Given the potential privacy and safety issues raised by door-to-door solicitations, why did the Court strike down the law in *Watchtower*? Does the Court's reasoning give any clues as to when a regulation of door-to-door solicitations could be legal?

2. **Could a city make it an offense to knock on a door with a "No Solicitations" sign?** Could the government make it a crime for door-to-door solicitors to knock

on a door when the homeowner has posted a sign indicating that she does not want solicitations? If such a law is constitutional, can you explain why it would be constitutional but not the law in *Watchtower*? *See Martin v. City of Struthers*, 319 U.S. 141, 147–49 (1943). Do the cases involving the unsolicited mailing of indecent materials to homes, such as *Bolger v. Youngs Drug Products Corp.*, 463 U.S. 60 (1983), and *Rowan v. U.S. Post Office Department*, 397 U.S. 728 (1970), provide any guidance for answering these questions? You can find a discussion of those cases in Chapter 7.

3. Loudspeakers: "Annoyance at Ideas Can Be Cloaked in Annoyance at Sound"

Loudspeakers can be both an effective tool for communicating one's thoughts and an annoying irritant. Can the government ban the use of loudspeakers altogether? Can it require a person to get a permit before using a loudspeaker? Can it limit how high the volume can be turned up?

In *Saia v. New York*, 334 U.S. 558 (1948), the Court struck down a city ordinance that prohibited the use of sound amplification equipment without first getting permission from the police chief. Justice William Douglas declared the law an unlawful prior restraint, noting in particular that it placed no restraints on the police chief's discretion. Justice Douglas readily acknowledged that the government has power to regulate amplification systems through more narrowly drawn laws. But he said that the law in this case was an invitation for abuse:

> The present ordinance would be a dangerous weapon if it were allowed to get a hold on our public life. Noise can be regulated by regulating decibels. The hours and place of public discussion can be controlled. Any abuses which loud-speakers create can be controlled by narrowly drawn statutes. When a city allows an official to ban them in his uncontrolled discretion, it sanctions a device for suppression of free communication of ideas. Annoyance at ideas can be cloaked in annoyance at sound.

The following case illustrates how a more narrowly drawn regulation of amplification equipment may be upheld.

Ward v. Rock Against Racism

Supreme Court of the United States, 1989
491 U.S. 781

JUSTICE KENNEDY delivered the opinion of the Court.

In the southeast portion of New York City's Central Park, about 10 blocks upward from the park's beginning point at 59th Street, there is an amphitheater and stage structure known as the Naumberg Acoustic Bandshell. The bandshell faces west across the remaining width of the park. In close proximity to the bandshell, and lying within the directional path of its sound, is a grassy open area called the Sheep Meadow. The city has designated the Sheep Meadow as a quiet area for passive recreations like reclining, walking, and reading. Just beyond the park, and also within the potential sound range of the bandshell, are the apartments and residences of Central Park West.

Naumberg Acoustic Bandshell in Central Park
Photographer: Pablo Costa Tirado/Creative Commons (CC BY-SA 3.0)

This case arises from the city's attempt to regulate the volume of amplified music at the bandshell so the performances are satisfactory to the audience without intruding upon those who use the Sheep Meadow or live on Central Park West and in its vicinity.

Rock Against Racism, respondent in this case, is an unincorporated association which, in its own words, is "dedicated to the espousal and promotion of antiracist views."

Music is one of the oldest forms of human expression. From Plato's discourse in the Republic to the totalitarian state in our own times, rulers have known its capacity to appeal to the intellect and to the emotions, and have censored musical compositions to serve the needs of the state. The Constitution prohibits any like attempts in our own legal order. Music, as a form of expression and communication, is protected under the First Amendment. In the case before us the performances apparently consisted of remarks by speakers, as well as rock music, but the case has been presented as one in which the constitutional challenge is to the city's regulation of the musical aspects of the concert; and, based on the principle we have stated, the city's guideline must meet the demands of the First Amendment. The parties do not appear to dispute that proposition.

Though it did demonstrate its own interest in the effort to insure high quality performances by providing the equipment in question, the city justifies its guideline as a regulatory measure to limit and control noise. Here the bandshell was open, apparently, to all performers; and we decide the case as one in which the bandshell is a public forum for performances in which the government's right to regulate expression is subject to the protections of the First Amendment.

Our cases make clear, however, that even in a public forum the government may impose reasonable restrictions on the time, place, or manner of protected speech, provided the restrictions "are justified without reference to the content of the regulated speech, that they are narrowly tailored to serve a significant governmental interest, and that they leave open ample alternative channels for communication of the information."

The principal inquiry in determining content neutrality, in speech cases generally and in time, place, or manner cases in particular, is whether the government has adopted a regulation of speech because of disagreement with the message it conveys. The government's purpose is the controlling consideration. A regulation that serves purposes unrelated to the content of expression is deemed neutral, even if it has an incidental effect on some speakers or messages but not others. *See Renton v. Playtime Theatres, Inc.* Government regulation of expressive activity is content neutral so long as it is "justified without reference to the content of the regulated speech."

The principal justification for the sound-amplification guideline is the city's desire to control noise levels at bandshell events, in order to retain the character of the Sheep Meadow and its more sedate activities, and to avoid undue intrusion into residential areas and other areas of the park. This justification for the guideline "has nothing to do with content," and it satisfies the requirement that time, place, or manner regulations be content neutral.

The city's regulation is also "narrowly tailored to serve a significant governmental interest."

We think it also apparent that the city's interest in ensuring the sufficiency of sound amplification at bandshell events is a substantial one. The record indicates that inadequate sound amplification has had an adverse affect on the ability of some audiences to hear and enjoy performances at the bandshell. The city enjoys a substantial interest in ensuring the ability of its citizens to enjoy whatever benefits the city parks have to offer, from amplified music to silent meditation.

Lest any confusion on the point remain, we reaffirm today that a regulation of the time, place, or manner of protected speech must be narrowly tailored to serve the government's legitimate, content-neutral interests but that it need not be the least restrictive or least intrusive means of doing so. Rather, the requirement of narrow tailoring is satisfied "so long as the regulation promotes a substantial government interest that would be achieved less effectively absent the regulation."

The final requirement, that the guideline leave open ample alternative channels of communication, is easily met. Indeed, in this respect the guideline is far less restrictive than regulations we have upheld in other cases, for it does not attempt to ban any particular manner or type of expression at a given place or time. Rather, the guideline continues to permit expressive activity in the bandshell, and has no effect on the quantity or content of that expression beyond regulating the extent of amplification. That the city's limitations on volume may reduce to some degree the potential audience for respondent's speech is of no consequence, for there has been no showing that the remaining avenues of communication are inadequate.

The city's sound-amplification guideline is narrowly tailored to serve the substantial and content-neutral governmental interests of avoiding excessive sound volume and providing sufficient amplification within the bandshell concert ground, and the guideline leaves open ample channels of communication. Accordingly, it is valid under the First Amendment as a reasonable regulation of the place and manner of expression.

JUSTICE MARSHALL, with whom JUSTICE BRENNAN and JUSTICE STEVENS join, dissenting.

No one can doubt that government has a substantial interest in regulating the barrage of excessive sound that can plague urban life. Unfortunately, the majority plays to our shared impatience with loud noise to obscure the damage that it does to our First Amendment rights. Until today, a key safeguard of free speech has been government's obligation to adopt the least intrusive restriction necessary to achieve its goals. By abandoning the requirement that time, place, and manner regulations must be narrowly tailored, the majority replaces constitutional scrutiny with mandatory deference. The majority's willingness to give government officials a free hand in achieving their policy ends extends so far as to permit, in this case, government control of speech in advance of its dissemination. Because New York City's Use Guidelines are not narrowly tailored to serve its interest in regulating loud noise, and because they constitute an impermissible prior restraint, I dissent.

[Justice Blackmun's opinion concurring in the judgment is omitted.]

Points for Discussion

1. **Why the different results in *Saia* and *Ward*?** Can you explain why the Supreme Court struck down the regulation of amplification equipment in *Saia* but upheld the regulation in *Ward*?

2. **The law of honking?** Are you attending law school because you intend to specialize in the law of honking? If so, we recommend expanding your area of practice if you enjoy eating and having a roof over your head. But this is not to say that there are no First Amendment cases concerning honking.

   The first question might be whether honking a car horn is even speech. How would you analyze that? Consider three different scenarios: (1) a driver honks a horn in response to someone holding a sign that says "Honk if you believe in Jesus"; (2) a driver honks a horn to alert another driver whose car is getting dangerously close; and (3) a newly licensed teenage driver repeatedly honks a horn to practice using it. Even if honking is considered speech, how should a court analyze the constitutionality of a honking regulation? Consider a California statute that forbids honking a car horn except "when reasonably necessary to insure safe operation" of a vehicle. How would you analyze this law as applied to someone who honked her horn to show support for a group of protesters gathered outside a government building? For a robust discussion of this issue, *see Porter v. Martinez*, 68 F.4th 429 (9th Cir. 2023).

4. Residential Signs: "An Unusually Cheap and Convenient Form of Communication"

We have already encountered signage laws in earlier chapters. In Chapter 4, we read the *Reed* and *Taxpayers for Vincent* cases and read a description of the *City of Austin* decision. In Chapter 9, we encountered laws regulating signs with commercial speech.

The *Reed* and *City of Austin* cases are important reminders that the first crucial question in evaluating any signage regulation is whether the regulation is content-based or content-neutral. If the law is content-based, as the Court found in *Reed*, it will be subject to strict scrutiny. If the law is content-neutral, as the Court found in *City of Austin*, it will be reviewed under intermediate scrutiny. The commercial speech cases remind us that signage laws targeted at advertising are reviewed under the specialized version of intermediate scrutiny articulated in *Central Hudson*.

The following case concerns a signage law that regulates a simple and easy means of communication. Exceptions in the law arguably made it content-based, which is how the lower courts characterized the law. But the Supreme Court treated the law as a content-neutral regulation of speech yet still found it unconstitutional.

City of Ladue v. Gilleo

Supreme Court of the United States, 1994
512 U.S. 43

JUSTICE STEVENS delivered the opinion of the Court.

An ordinance of the City of Ladue prohibits homeowners from displaying any signs on their property except "residence identification" signs, "for sale" signs, and signs warning of safety hazards. The ordinance permits commercial establishments, churches, and nonprofit organizations to erect certain signs that are not allowed at residences. The question presented is whether the ordinance violates a Ladue resident's right to free speech.

Respondent Margaret P. Gilleo owns one of the 57 single-family homes in the Willow Hill subdivision of Ladue. On December 8, 1990, she placed on her front lawn a 24- by 36-inch sign printed with the words "Say No to War in the Persian Gulf, Call Congress Now." After that sign disappeared, Gilleo put up another but it was knocked to the ground. When Gilleo reported these incidents to the police, they advised her that such signs were prohibited in Ladue. The City Council denied her petition for a variance. Gilleo then filed this action under 42 U.S.C. § 1983 against the City, the Mayor, and members of the City Council, alleging that Ladue's sign ordinance violated her First Amendment right of free speech.

The District Court issued a preliminary injunction against enforcement of the ordinance. Gilleo then placed an 8.5- by 11-inch sign in the second story window of her home stating, "For Peace in the Gulf." The Ladue City Council responded to the injunction by repealing its ordinance and enacting a replacement. Like its predecessor, the new ordinance contains a general prohibition of "signs" and defines that term broadly.

The ordinance prohibits all signs except those that fall within one of ten exemptions. Thus, "residential identification signs" no larger than one square foot are allowed, as are signs advertising "that the property is for sale, lease or exchange" and identifying the owner or agent. Also exempted are signs "for churches, religious institutions, and schools," "commercial signs in commercially or industrial zoned districts," and on-site signs advertising "gasoline filling stations."

Unlike its predecessor, the new ordinance contains a lengthy "Declaration of Findings, Policies, Interests, and Purposes," part of which recites that the "proliferation of an unlimited number of signs in private, residential, commercial, industrial, and public areas of the City of Ladue would create ugliness, visual blight and clutter, tarnish the natural beauty of the landscape as well as the residential and commercial architecture, impair property values, substantially impinge upon the privacy and special ambience of the community, and may cause safety and traffic hazards to motorists, pedestrians, and children."

While signs are a form of expression protected by the Free Speech Clause, they pose distinctive problems that are subject to municipalities' police powers. Unlike oral speech, signs take up space and may obstruct views, distract motorists, displace alternative uses for land, and pose other problems that legitimately call for regulation. It is common ground that governments may regulate the physical characteristics of signs—just as they can, within reasonable bounds and absent censorial purpose, regulate audible expression in its capacity as noise. However, because regulation of a medium inevitably affects communication itself, it is not surprising that we have had occasion to review the constitutionality of municipal ordinances prohibiting the display of certain outdoor signs.

[Earlier] decisions identify two analytically distinct grounds for challenging the constitutionality of a municipal ordinance regulating the display of signs. One is that the measure in effect restricts too little speech because its exemptions discriminate on the basis of the signs' messages. Alternatively, such provisions are subject to attack on the ground that they simply prohibit too much protected speech. The City of Ladue contends, first, that the Court of Appeals' reliance on the former rationale was misplaced because the City's regulatory purposes are content-neutral, and, second, that those purposes justify the comprehensiveness of the sign prohibition. A comment on the former contention will help explain why we ultimately base our decision on a rejection of the latter.

While surprising at first glance, the notion that a regulation of speech may be impermissibly underinclusive is firmly grounded in basic First Amendment principles. Thus, an exemption from an otherwise permissible regulation of speech may represent a governmental "attempt to give one side of a debatable public question an advantage in expressing its views to the people." Alternatively, through the combined operation of a general speech restriction and its exemptions, the government might seek to select the "permissible subjects for public debate" and thereby to "control the search for political truth."

The City argues that its sign ordinance implicates neither of these concerns, and that the Court of Appeals therefore erred in demanding a "compelling" justification for the exemptions. The mix of prohibitions and exemptions in the ordinance, Ladue maintains, reflects legitimate differences among the side effects of various kinds of signs. These differences are only adventitiously connected with content, and supply a sufficient justification, unrelated to the City's approval or disapproval of specific messages, for carving out the specified categories from the general ban.

Exemptions from an otherwise legitimate regulation of a medium of speech may be noteworthy for a reason quite apart from the risks of viewpoint and content discrimination: they may diminish the credibility of the government's rationale for restricting speech in the first place. In this case, at the very least, the exemptions from Ladue's ordinance demonstrate that Ladue has concluded that the interest in allowing certain messages to be conveyed by means of residential signs outweighs the City's aesthetic interest in eliminating outdoor signs. Ladue has not imposed a flat ban on signs because it has determined that at least some of them are too vital to be banned.

Under the Court of Appeals' content discrimination rationale, the City might theoretically remove the defects in its ordinance by simply repealing all of the exemptions. If, however, the ordinance is also vulnerable because it prohibits too much speech, that solution would not save it. Moreover, if the prohibitions in Ladue's ordinance are impermissible, resting our decision on its exemptions would afford scant relief for respondent Gilleo. She is primarily concerned not with the scope of the exemptions available in other locations, such as commercial areas and on church property. She asserts a constitutional right to display an antiwar sign at her own home. Therefore, we first ask whether Ladue may properly prohibit Gilleo from displaying her sign, and then, only if necessary, consider the separate question whether it was improper for the City simultaneously to permit certain other signs. In examining the propriety of Ladue's near-total prohibition of residential signs, we will assume, arguendo, the validity of the City's submission that the various exemptions are free of impermissible content or viewpoint discrimination.

In *Linmark Associates, Inc. v. Willingboro*, 431 U.S. 85 (1981), we held that the City's interest in maintaining a stable, racially integrated neighborhood was not sufficient to support a prohibition of residential "For Sale" signs. We recognized that even such a narrow sign prohibition would have a deleterious effect on residents' ability to convey important information because alternatives were "far from satisfactory." Ladue's sign ordinance is supported principally by the City's interest in minimizing the visual clutter associated with signs, an interest that is concededly valid but certainly no more compelling than the interests at stake in *Linmark*. Moreover, whereas the ordinance in *Linmark* applied only to a form of commercial speech, Ladue's ordinance covers even such absolutely pivotal speech as a sign protesting an imminent governmental decision to go to war.

The impact on free communication of Ladue's broad sign prohibition, moreover, is manifestly greater than in *Linmark*. Gilleo and other residents of Ladue are forbidden to display virtually any "sign" on their property. The ordinance defines that term sweepingly. A prohibition is not always invalid merely because it applies to a sizeable category of speech; the sign ban we upheld in *Vincent*, for example, was quite broad. But in *Vincent* we specifically noted that the category of speech in question—signs placed on public property—was not a "uniquely valuable or important mode of communication," and that there was no evidence that "appellees' ability to communicate effectively is threatened by ever-increasing restrictions on expression."

Here, in contrast, Ladue has almost completely foreclosed a venerable means of communication that is both unique and important. It has totally foreclosed that medium to political, religious, or personal messages. Signs that react to a local happening or express a view on a controversial issue both reflect and animate change in the life of a community. Often placed on lawns or in windows, residential signs play an important part in political campaigns, during which they are displayed to signal the resident's support for particular candidates, parties, or causes. They may not afford the same opportunities for conveying complex ideas as do other media, but residential signs have long been an important and distinct medium of expression.

Our prior decisions have voiced particular concern with laws that foreclose an entire medium of expression. Thus, we have held invalid ordinances that completely banned the distribution of pamphlets within the municipality, handbills on the public streets, the door-to-door distribution of literature, and live entertainment. Although prohibitions foreclosing entire media may be completely free of content or viewpoint discrimination, the danger they pose to the freedom of speech is readily apparent—by eliminating a common means of speaking, such measures can suppress too much speech.

Ladue contends, however, that its ordinance is a mere regulation of the "time, place, or manner" of speech because residents remain free to convey their desired messages by other means, such as hand-held signs, "letters, handbills, flyers, telephone calls, newspaper advertisements, bumper stickers, speeches, and neighborhood or community meetings." However, even regulations that do not foreclose an entire medium of expression, but merely shift the time, place, or manner of its use, must "leave open ample alternative channels for communication." In this case, we are not persuaded that adequate substitutes exist for the important medium of speech that Ladue has closed off.

Displaying a sign from one's own residence often carries a message quite distinct from placing the same sign someplace else, or conveying the same text or picture by other means. Precisely because of their location, such signs provide information about the identity of the "speaker." As an early and eminent student of rhetoric observed, the identity of the speaker is an important component of many attempts to persuade. A sign advocating "Peace in the Gulf" in the front lawn of a retired general or decorated war veteran may provoke a different reaction than the same sign in a 10-year-old child's bedroom window or the same message on a bumper sticker of a passing automobile. An espousal of socialism may carry different implications when displayed on the grounds of a stately mansion than when pasted on a factory wall or an ambulatory sandwich board.

Residential signs are an unusually cheap and convenient form of communication. Especially for persons of modest means or limited mobility, a yard or window sign may have no practical substitute. Even for the affluent, the added costs in money or time of taking out a newspaper advertisement, handing out leaflets on the street, or standing in front of one's house with a hand-held sign may make the difference between participating and not participating in some public debate. Furthermore, a person who puts up a sign at her residence often intends to reach neighbors, an audience that could not be reached nearly as well by other means.

A special respect for individual liberty in the home has long been part of our culture and our law; that principle has special resonance when the government seeks to constrain a person's ability to speak there. Most Americans would be understandably dismayed, given that tradition, to learn that it was illegal to display from their window an 8- by 11-inch sign expressing their political views. Whereas the government's need to mediate among various competing uses, including expressive ones, for public streets and facilities is constant and unavoidable, its need to regulate temperate speech from the home is surely much less pressing.

Our decision that Ladue's ban on almost all residential signs violates the First Amendment by no means leaves the City powerless to address the ills that may be associated with residential signs. It bears mentioning that individual residents themselves have strong incentives to keep their own property values up and to prevent "visual clutter" in their own yards and neighborhoods—incentives markedly different from those of persons who erect signs on others' land, in others' neighborhoods, or on public property. Residents' self-interest diminishes the danger of the "unlimited" proliferation of residential signs that concerns the City of Ladue. We are confident that more temperate measures could in large part satisfy Ladue's stated regulatory needs without harm to the First Amendment rights of its citizens. As currently framed, however, the ordinance abridges those rights.

JUSTICE O'CONNOR, concurring.

It is unusual for us, when faced with a regulation that on its face draws content distinctions, to "assume, arguendo, the validity of the City's submission that the various exemptions are free of impermissible content or viewpoint discrimination." With rare exceptions, content discrimination in regulations of the speech of private citizens on private property or in a traditional public forum is presumptively impermissible, and this presumption is a very strong one. The normal inquiry that our doctrine dictates is, first, to determine whether a regulation is content-based or content-neutral, and then, based on the answer to that question, to apply the proper level of scrutiny.

Over the years, some cogent criticisms have been leveled at our approach. And it is quite true that regulations are occasionally struck down because of their content-based nature, even though common sense may suggest that they are entirely reasonable. The content distinctions present in this ordinance may, to some, be a good example of this.

But though our rule has flaws, it has substantial merit as well. It is a rule, in an area where fairly precise rules are better than more discretionary and more subjective balancing tests. On a theoretical level, it reflects important insights into the meaning of the free speech principle—for instance, that content-based speech restrictions are especially likely to be improper attempts to value some forms of speech over others, or are particularly susceptible to being used by the government to distort public debate. On a practical level, it has in application generally led to seemingly sensible results. And, perhaps most importantly, no better alternative has yet come to light.

I would have preferred to apply our normal analytical structure in this case, which may well have required us to examine this law with the scrutiny appropriate to content-based regulations. Perhaps this would have forced us to confront some of the difficulties with the existing doctrine; perhaps it would have shown weaknesses in the rule, and led us to modify it to take into account the special factors this case presents. But such reexamination is part of the process by which our rules evolve and improve.

Nonetheless, I join the Court's opinion, because I agree with its conclusion that even if the restriction were content-neutral, it would still be invalid.

Points for Discussion

1. **Why did the Court strike down Ladue's sign regulation?** The Court said it is "common ground that governments may regulate the physical characteristics of signs—just as they can, within reasonable bounds and absent censorial purpose, regulate audible expression in its capacity as noise." Given this concession that

sign regulations are often permissible, why did the Court strike down the Ladue sign regulation?

2. **Should this law have been analyzed as content-based or content-neutral?** The Court of Appeals analyzed the Ladue ordinance under strict scrutiny because it thought the exceptions in the law made the law content-based. The Supreme Court acknowledged that the law might be analyzed that way, but the Court preferred to analyze the law as a content-neutral regulation of speech. Why did it do so?

3. **The ongoing debate over how to apply the content-based/content-neutral distinction.** In her concurrence, Justice Sandra Day O'Connor said she would have preferred to analyze the Ladue ordinance as a content-based law that was subject to strict scrutiny. She acknowledged that the Court's rigid content-based/content-neutral framework has been criticized and can cause regulations to be struck down under strict scrutiny "even though common sense may suggest that they are entirely reasonable." Still, she said that the Court's use of the admittedly wooden distinction has "in application generally led to seemingly sensible results" and that "no better alternative has yet come to light."

   Two decades later, in cases such as *Reed* and *City of Austin*, the justices were still debating whether they should rigidly apply strict scrutiny to all laws that make content-based distinctions or whether, as Justice Elena Kagan suggested in *Reed*, the justices should "relax our guard" in evaluating content-based laws when there is no "realistic possibility that official suppression of ideas is afoot."

   The difference between the two sides reflects the classical debate between using clear, but rigid, rules versus vaguer, but more flexible, standards. Justice O'Connor, while acknowledging the potential downside of a rigid approach, nevertheless thought that the First Amendment is an area "where fairly precise rules are better than more discretionary and more subjective balancing tests."

4. **Do these "old school" cases still matter?** In this first section of this chapter, we read a series of dated opinions that endorsed the importance of "grassroots" expression in "old school" environments—the world of pamphlets on the street and door-to-door proselytizing. Does any of this matter anymore? In a world dominated by digital communication and social media interactions on the likes of Facebook, X (formerly Twitter), or Instagram, are these cases anything more than quaint nostalgia for an earlier, simpler life? Or is there something primal and quintessentially important about old-school grassroots physical expression that is worth preserving and enshrining in our constitutional law? In answering that question, how important is it that many of the "new school" modes of grassroots communication are privately owned?

5. **How should a court decide whether a content-neutral regulation is unconstitutional?** As you learned in Chapter 4, content-neutral regulations of speech are subject to intermediate scrutiny, which means that they have a relatively equal chance of being upheld or struck down. Of course, how a court rules in any given case will depend on the specific facts and law. Is it nevertheless possible to extract principles from the preceding cases for when a content-neutral law is likely to be unconstitutional? For example, in *City of Ladue*, the Court said content-neutral laws will be invalidated when they "prohibit too much protected speech." Did the opinion give you any clues as to what "too much" speech suppression means?

B. Content-Neutral Regulations of Picketing: From Residential Picketing to Protests at Abortion Clinics

Picketing is another classic form of grassroots communication. Depending on the context in which it occurs, picketing can sometimes raise unique concerns about safety or privacy. We will see an example of this in the following case.

As always, it is important to remember that laws regulating picketing will be subject to strict scrutiny if they are regulating the picketers' speech based on its message. The most famous example of this is a Chicago ordinance that was invalidated by the Supreme Court in *Police Department of Chicago v. Mosley*, 408 U.S. 92 (1972). The ordinance prohibited picketing or demonstrations within 150 feet of a school while the school was in session, but it made an exception for "the peaceful picketing of any school involved in a labor dispute." In a famous passage that you first encountered in Chapter 4, Justice Thurgood Marshall explained the law's fatal infirmity:

> The central problem with Chicago's ordinance is that it describes permissible picketing in terms of its subject matter. Peaceful picketing on the subject of a school's labor-management dispute is permitted, but all other peaceful picketing is prohibited. The operative distinction is the message on a picket sign. But, above all else, the First Amendment means that government has no power to restrict expression because of its message, its ideas, its subject matter, or its content.

While it is often easy to determine whether a regulation is content-based or content-neutral simply by looking at the face of the law, that is not always the case. Consider a law that forbids any expressive activities within 100 feet of an abortion clinic entrance. On its face, the law is content-neutral. It doesn't matter whether the expression occurring is anti-abortion rights, pro-abortion rights, or pro-chocolate. But the reality may be that the only people who protest in front of abortion clinics are pro-life activists, and the lawmakers who enacted the law may have specifically intended to curb the speech of these activists. Supreme Court justices have occasionally sparred over whether to characterize a regulation or injunction of speech near an abortion clinic as content-based or content-neutral. *See, e.g., Madsen v. Women's Health Ctr., Inc.*, 512 U.S. 753 (1994); *Hill v. Colorado*, 530 U.S. 703 (2000).

The following case considers the unique concerns raised by targeted picketing in a residential area.

Frisby v. Schultz

Supreme Court of the United States, 1988
487 U.S. 474

JUSTICE O'CONNOR delivered the opinion of the Court.

Brookfield, Wisconsin, has adopted an ordinance that completely bans picketing "before or about" any residence. This case presents a facial First Amendment challenge to that ordinance.

Brookfield, Wisconsin, is a residential suburb of Milwaukee with a population of approximately 4,300. The appellees, Sandra C. Schultz and Robert C. Braun, are individuals strongly opposed to abortion and wish to express their views on the subject by picketing on a public street outside the Brookfield residence of a doctor who apparently performs abortions at two clinics in neighboring towns. Appellees and others engaged in precisely that activity, assembling outside the doctor's home on at least six occasions between April 20, 1985, and May 20, 1985, for periods ranging from one to one and a half hours. The size of the group varied from 11 to more than 40. The picketing was generally orderly and peaceful; the town never had occasion to invoke any of its various ordinances prohibiting obstruction of the streets, loud and unnecessary noises, or disorderly conduct. Nonetheless, the picketing generated substantial controversy and numerous complaints.

The Town Board therefore resolved to enact an ordinance to restrict the picketing. On May 7, 1985, the town passed an ordinance that prohibited all picketing in residential neighborhoods except for labor picketing. But after reviewing this Court's decision in *Carey v. Brown*, 447 U.S. 455 (1980), which invalidated a similar ordinance as a violation of the Equal Protection Clause, the town attorney instructed the police not to enforce the new ordinance and advised the Town Board that the ordinance's labor picketing exception likely rendered it unconstitutional. This ordinance was repealed on May 15, 1985, and replaced with the following flat ban on all residential picketing:

> It is unlawful for any person to engage in picketing before or about the residence or dwelling of any individual in the Town of Brookfield.

The ordinance itself recites the primary purpose of this ban: "the protection and preservation of the home" through assurance "that members of the community enjoy in their homes and dwellings a feeling of well-being, tranquility, and privacy." The Town Board believed that a ban was necessary because it determined that "the practice of picketing before or about residences and dwellings causes emotional disturbance and distress to the occupants and has as its object the harassing of such occupants." The ordinance also evinces a concern for public safety, noting that picketing obstructs and interferes with "the free use of public sidewalks and public ways of travel."

The antipicketing ordinance operates at the core of the First Amendment by prohibiting appellees from engaging in picketing on an issue of public concern. Because of the importance of "uninhibited, robust, and wide-open" debate on public issues, we have traditionally subjected restrictions on public issue picketing to careful scrutiny. Of course, "even protected speech is not equally permissible in all places and at all times."

To ascertain what limits, if any, may be placed on protected speech, we have often focused on the "place" of that speech, considering the nature of the forum the speaker seeks to employ. Our cases have recognized that the standards by which limitations on speech must be evaluated "differ depending on the character of the property at issue." Specifically, we have identified three types of fora: "the traditional public forum, the public forum created by government designation, and the nonpublic forum."

The relevant forum here may be easily identified: appellees wish to picket on the public streets of Brookfield. Ordinarily, a determination of the nature of the forum would follow automatically from this identification; we have repeatedly referred to public streets as the archetype of a traditional public forum. "Time out of mind" public streets and sidewalks have been used for public assembly and debate, the hallmarks of a traditional public forum. Appellants, however, urge us to disregard these "cliches." They argue that the streets of Brookfield should be considered a nonpublic forum. Pointing to the physical narrowness of Brookfield's streets as well as to their residential character, appellants contend that such streets have not by tradition or designation been held open for public communication.

We reject this suggestion. Our prior holdings make clear that a public street does not lose its status as a traditional public forum simply because it runs through a residential neighborhood.

In short, our decisions identifying public streets and sidewalks as traditional public fora are not accidental invocations of a "cliche," but recognition that "wherever the title of streets and parks may rest, they have immemorially been held in trust for the use of the public." No particularized inquiry into the precise nature of a specific street is necessary; all public streets are held in the public trust and are properly considered traditional public fora. Accordingly, the streets of Brookfield are traditional public fora. The residential character of those streets may well inform the application of the relevant test, but it does not lead to a different test; the antipicketing ordinance must be judged against the stringent standards we have established for restrictions on speech in traditional public fora:

> In these quintessential public fora, the government may not prohibit all communicative activity. For the State to enforce a content-based exclusion it must show that its regulation is necessary to serve a compelling state interest and that it is narrowly drawn to achieve that end. The State may also enforce regulations of the time, place, and manner of expression which are content-neutral, are narrowly tailored to serve a significant government interest, and leave open ample alternative channels of communication.

The appropriate level of scrutiny is initially tied to whether the statute distinguishes between prohibited and permitted speech on the basis of content. We accept the lower courts' conclusion that the Brookfield ordinance is content-neutral. Accordingly, we turn to consider whether the ordinance is "narrowly tailored to serve a significant government interest" and whether it "leaves open ample alternative channels of communication."

Because the last question is so easily answered, we address it first. Of course, before we are able to assess the available alternatives, we must consider more carefully the reach of the ordinance. The precise scope of the ban is not further described within the text of the ordinance, but in our view the ordinance is readily subject to a narrowing construction that avoids constitutional difficulties. Specifically, the use of the singular form of the words "residence" and "dwelling" suggests that the ordinance is intended to prohibit only picketing focused on, and taking place in front of, a particular residence. As Justice White's concurring opinion recounts, the lower courts described the ordinance as banning "all picketing in residential areas." But these general descriptions do not address the exact scope of the ordinance and are in no way inconsistent with our reading of its text. "Picketing," after all, is defined as posting at a particular place, a characterization in line with viewing the ordinance as limited to activity focused on a single residence. Moreover, while we ordinarily defer to lower court constructions of state statutes, we do not invariably do so. We are particularly reluctant to defer when the lower courts have fallen into plain error, which is precisely the situation presented here. To the extent they endorsed a broad reading of the ordinance, the lower courts ran afoul of the well-established principle that statutes will be interpreted to avoid constitutional difficulties. We instead construe the ordinance more narrowly. This narrow reading is supported by the representations of counsel for the town at oral argument, which indicate that the town takes, and will enforce, a limited view of the "picketing" proscribed by the ordinance. Thus, generally speaking, "picketing would be having the picket proceed on a definite course or route in front of a home." The picket need not be carrying a sign, but in order to fall within the scope of the ordinance the picketing must be directed at a single residence. Generally marching through residential neighborhoods, or even walking a route in front of an entire block of houses, is not prohibited by this ordinance. Accordingly, we construe the ban to be a limited one; only focused picketing taking place solely in front of a particular residence is prohibited.

So narrowed, the ordinance permits the more general dissemination of a message. As appellants explain, the limited nature of the prohibition makes it virtually self-evident that ample alternatives remain:

> Protestors have not been barred from the residential neighborhoods. They may enter such neighborhoods, alone or in groups, even marching. They may go door-to-door to proselytize their views. They may distribute literature in this manner or through the mails. They may contact residents by telephone, short of harassment.

We readily agree that the ordinance preserves ample alternative channels of communication and thus move on to inquire whether the ordinance serves a significant government interest. We find that such an interest is identified within the text of the ordinance itself: the protection of residential privacy.

"The State's interest in protecting the well-being, tranquility, and privacy of the home is certainly of the highest order in a free and civilized society." Our prior decisions have often remarked on the unique nature of the home, "the last citadel of the tired, the weary, and the sick," and have recognized that "preserving the sanctity of the home, the one retreat to which men and women can repair to escape from the tribulations of their daily pursuits, is surely an important value."

One important aspect of residential privacy is protection of the unwilling listener. Although in many locations, we expect individuals simply to avoid speech they do not want to hear, the home is different. "That we are often 'captives' outside the sanctuary of the home and subject to objectionable speech does not mean we must be captives everywhere." Instead, a special benefit of the privacy all citizens enjoy within their own walls, which the State may legislate to protect, is an ability to avoid intrusions. Thus, we have repeatedly held that individuals are not required to welcome unwanted speech into their own homes and that the government may protect this freedom.

It remains to be considered, however, whether the Brookfield ordinance is narrowly tailored to protect only unwilling recipients of the communications. A statute is narrowly tailored if it targets and eliminates no more than the exact source of the "evil" it seeks to remedy. A complete ban can be narrowly tailored, but only if each activity within the proscription's scope is an appropriately targeted evil. For example, in *Taxpayers for Vincent*, we upheld an ordinance that banned all signs on public property because the interest supporting the regulation, an esthetic interest in avoiding visual clutter and blight, rendered each sign an evil. Complete prohibition was necessary because "the substantive evil—visual blight—was not merely a possible by-product of the activity, but was created by the medium of expression itself."

The same is true here. The type of focused picketing prohibited by the Brookfield ordinance is fundamentally different from more generally directed means of communication that may not be completely banned in residential areas. In such cases "the flow of information is not into households, but to the public." Here, in contrast, the picketing is narrowly directed at the household, not the public. The type of picketers banned by the Brookfield ordinance generally do not seek to disseminate a message to the general public, but to intrude upon the targeted resident, and to do so in an especially offensive way. Moreover, even if some such picketers have a broader communicative purpose, their activity nonetheless inherently and offensively intrudes on residential privacy.

In this case, for example, appellees subjected the doctor and his family to the presence of a relatively large group of protestors on their doorstep in an attempt to force the doctor to cease performing abortions. But the actual size of the group is irrelevant; even a solitary picket can invade residential privacy.

The First Amendment permits the government to prohibit offensive speech as intrusive when the "captive" audience cannot avoid the objectionable speech. The target of the focused picketing banned by the Brookfield ordinance is just such a "captive." The resident is figuratively, and perhaps literally, trapped within the home, and because of the unique and subtle impact of such picketing is left with no ready means of avoiding the unwanted speech. Accordingly, the Brookfield ordinance's complete ban of that particular medium of expression is narrowly tailored.

Of course, this case presents only a facial challenge to the ordinance. Particular hypothetical applications of the ordinance—to, for example, a particular resident's use of his or her home as place of business or public meeting, or to picketers present at a particular home by invitation of the resident—may present somewhat different questions. Because the picketing prohibited by the Brookfield ordinance is speech directed primarily at those who are presumptively unwilling to receive it, the State has a substantial and justifiable interest in banning it. The nature and scope of this interest make the ban narrowly tailored. The ordinance also leaves open ample alternative channels of communication and is content-neutral. Thus, largely because of its narrow scope, the facial challenge to the ordinance must fail.

JUSTICE BRENNAN, with whom JUSTICE MARSHALL joins, dissenting.

The Court today sets out the appropriate legal tests and standards governing the question presented, and proceeds to apply most of them correctly. Regrettably, though, the Court errs in the final step of its analysis, and approves an ordinance banning significantly more speech than is necessary to achieve the government's substantial and legitimate goal. Accordingly, I must dissent.

The ordinance before us absolutely prohibits picketing "before or about" any residence in the town of Brookfield, thereby restricting a manner of speech in a traditional public forum. Consequently, as the Court correctly states, the ordinance is subject to the well-settled time, place, and manner test: the restriction must be content and viewpoint neutral, leave open ample alternative channels of communication, and be narrowly tailored to further a substantial governmental interest.

Assuming one construes the ordinances as the Court does, I agree that the regulation reserves ample alternative channels of communication. I also agree with the Court that the town has a substantial interest in protecting its residents' right to be left alone in their homes. It is, however, critical to specify the precise scope of this interest. The mere fact that speech takes place in a residential neighborhood does not automatically implicate a residential privacy interest. It is the intrusion of speech into the home or the unduly coercive nature of a particular manner of speech around the home that is subject to more exacting regulation. Thus, the intrusion into the home of an unwelcome solicitor or unwanted mail may be forbidden. Similarly, the government may forbid the intrusion of excessive noise into the home or, in appropriate circumstances, perhaps even radio waves. Similarly, the government may prohibit unduly coercive conduct around the home, even though it involves expressive elements. A crowd of protesters need not be permitted virtually to imprison a person in his or her own house merely because they shout slogans or carry signs. But so long as the speech remains outside the home and does not unduly coerce the occupant, the government's heightened interest in protecting residential privacy is not implicated.

The foregoing distinction is crucial here because it directly affects that last prong of the time, place, and manner text: whether the ordinance is narrowly tailored to achieve the governmental interest. The application of this test requires that the government demonstrate that the offending aspects of the prohibited manner of speech cannot be separately, and less intrusively, controlled. Thus here, if the intrusive and unduly coercive elements of residential picketing can be eliminated without simultaneously eliminating residential picketing completely, the Brookfield ordinance fails the *Vincent* test.

Without question there are many aspects of residential picketing that, if unregulated, might easily become intrusive or unduly coercive. Indeed, some of these aspects are illustrated by this very case. As the District Court found, before the ordinance took effect up to 40 sign-carrying, slogan-shouting protesters regularly converged on Dr. Victoria's home and, in addition to protesting, warned young children not to go near the house because Dr. Victoria was a "baby killer." Further, the throng repeatedly trespassed onto the Victorias' property and at least once blocked the exits to their home. Surely it is within the government's power to enact regulations as necessary to prevent such intrusive and coercive abuses. Thus, for example, the government could constitutionally regulate the number of residential picketers, the hours during which a residential picket may take place, or the noise level of such a picket. In short, substantial regulation is permitted to neutralize the intrusive or unduly coercive aspects of picketing around the home. But to say that picketing may be substantially regulated is not to say that it may be prohibited in its entirety. Once size, time, volume, and the like have been controlled to ensure that the picket is no longer intrusive or coercive, only the speech itself remains, conveyed perhaps by a lone, silent individual, walking back and forth with a sign. Such speech, which no longer implicates the heightened governmental interest in residential privacy, is nevertheless banned by the Brookfield law. Therefore, the ordinance is not narrowly tailored.

JUSTICE STEVENS, dissenting.

"GET WELL CHARLIE—OUR TEAM NEEDS YOU."

In Brookfield, Wisconsin, it is unlawful for a fifth grader to carry such a sign in front of a residence for the period of time necessary to convey its friendly message to its intended audience.

The Court's analysis of the question whether Brookfield's ban on picketing is constitutional begins with an acknowledgment that the ordinance "operates at the core of the First Amendment," and that the streets of Brookfield are a "traditional public forum." It concludes, however, that the total ban on residential picketing is "narrowly tailored" to protect "only unwilling recipients of the communications." The plain language of the ordinance, however, applies to communications to willing and indifferent recipients as well as to the unwilling.

The picketing that gave rise to the ordinance enacted in this case was obviously intended to do more than convey a message of opposition to the character of the doctor's practice; it was intended to cause him and his family substantial psychological distress. As the record reveals, the picketers' message was repeatedly redelivered by a relatively large group—in essence, increasing the volume and intrusiveness of the same message with each repeated assertion. As is often the function of picketing, during the periods of protest the doctor's home was held under a virtual siege. I do not believe that picketing for the sole purpose of imposing psychological harm on a family in the shelter of their home is constitutionally protected. I do believe, however, that the picketers have a right to communicate their strong opposition to abortion to the doctor, but after they have had a fair opportunity to communicate that message, I see little justification for allowing them to remain in front of his home and repeat it over and over again simply to harm the doctor and his family. Thus, I agree that the ordinance may be constitutionally applied to the kind of picketing that gave rise to its enactment.

On the other hand, the ordinance is unquestionably "overbroad" in that it prohibits some communication that is protected by the First Amendment. The question, then, is whether to apply the overbreadth doctrine's "strong medicine," *see Broadrick v. Oklahoma*, 413 U.S. 601, 613 (1973), or to put that approach aside "and await further developments." In *Broadrick*, the Court framed the inquiry thusly:

> To put the matter another way, particularly where conduct and not merely speech is involved, we believe that the overbreadth of a statute must not only be real, but substantial as well, judged in relation to the statute's plainly legitimate sweep.

In this case the overbreadth is unquestionably "real." Whether or not it is "substantial" in relation to the "plainly legitimate sweep" of the ordinance is a more difficult question. My hunch is that the town will probably not enforce its ban against friendly, innocuous, or even brief unfriendly picketing, and that the Court may be right in concluding that its legitimate sweep makes its overbreadth insubstantial. But there are two countervailing considerations that are persuasive to me. The scope of the ordinance gives the town officials far too much discretion in making enforcement decisions; while we sit by and await further developments, potential picketers must act at their peril. Second, it is a simple matter for the town to amend its ordinance and to limit the ban to conduct that unreasonably interferes with the privacy of the home and does not serve a reasonable communicative purpose. Accordingly, I respectfully dissent.

[Justice White's opinion concurring in the judgment is omitted.]

Points for Discussion

1. **What was the public forum status in *Frisby*?** The Court in *Frisby* accepts that even residential streets qualify as traditional public forums. Yet it goes on to hold that focused picketing may be banned in such a traditional public forum as a content-neutral time, place, or manner regulation. Are you persuaded?

2. **What is the "captive audience" concept described in *Frisby*?** *Frisby* makes much of the notion of the "captive audience." The normal rule in First Amendment law is that the government may not censor offensive speech in a public forum. Instead, the burden is on offended viewers to avert their eyes (or ears). *Snyder v. Phelps* is a particularly poignant example. First Amendment doctrine recognizes an exception to this "avert the eyes" principle, however, when the viewer is part of a "captive audience." What does it mean to be a "captive"? Why did the Court conclude that the doctor and his family in *Frisby* were a captive audience?

You Be the Judge!

May protesters march in circles around a residential block?

You are a newly appointed state court judge in the Circuit Court of the town of Bloomingdale. A town ordinance provides:

> It is unlawful for any person to engage in picketing before or about the residence or dwelling of any individual in the Town of Bloomingdale. The Circuit Court shall have the power to enforce the provisions of this Ordinance through appropriate injunctive relief.

In the aftermath of a police shooting of an unarmed citizen, a protest is organized. Thousands of protesters from Bloomingdale and around the nation arrive in the town for a massive rally protesting what they regard as police brutality. The protesters are calling for the firing of the chief of police. They organize a march, in which thousands of people participate, to circle around one square block within a normally quiet residential neighborhood in Bloomingdale. The police chief's private residence is located in the middle of one street on the block. The marchers do not stop in front of his home, but rather keep moving in a continuing circling of the block, chanting and singing protest songs, and carrying signs calling for the chief's firing. Because the number of marchers is so large, the entire square block is constantly filled with protesters, going round and round the block. The protesters have obeyed police instructions to confine their walking to certain parts of the streets and sidewalks so as not to block traffic. Some of the protesters are using loudspeakers. The chanting and singing can be heard inside the residences on the block.

The police chief, joined by his neighbors on the block, files a suit in your court, seeking an injunction to order the demonstration stopped. How would you rule, and why? Would you entirely grant the relief sought, entirely deny the relief sought, or tailor your injunction in some manner?

C. Content-Neutral Permit Requirements: When Are Administrative Licensing Regimes Constitutional?

In Chapter 2, you learned about the much reviled licensing system in England in which works had to be approved by the government before they could be published. Justice Oliver Wendell Holmes would later write that the "main purpose" of the First Amendment was to "prevent all such previous restraints upon publication."

In Chapter 4, you learned that the Court's leeriness of prior restraints manifests itself in two contexts: court orders enjoining speech and administrative licensing regimes. In Chapter 5, you encountered the Court's extreme skepticism of judicial orders enjoining speech when you read the Pentagon Papers case. By contrast, in Chapter 4, you learned that the Court takes a more nuanced approach with administrative licensing. Most importantly, the Court has acknowledged that governments may have permit requirements for large expressive events such as parades or rallies. This section reviews the rules governing these types of permit regimes.

For starters, it is important to remember that permit requirements that discriminate against applicants based on the content of their speech will be evaluated under strict scrutiny and will almost certainly be struck down. The one exception could be an administrative regime that is allocating space in a limited public forum, where the government may lawfully make content-based decisions about which speech is appropriate for the forum as long as those decisions are viewpoint-neutral.

Even if a permit regime is facially content-neutral, it will nevertheless be treated like a content-based regulation if there are no standards limiting the discretion of the officials issuing the permits. The Court has recognized that standardless regimes create the risk that officials will abuse their discretion by issuing permits based on their like or dislike of an applicant's message. For example, in *Saia*, the Court observed that "when a city allows an official to ban [loudspeakers] in his uncontrolled discretion, it sanctions a device for suppression of free communication of ideas." Similarly, in a portion of the *Schneider* decision that was not reproduced above, the Court voiced a similar concern about an ordinance that required door-to-door solicitors to obtain a permit from the police chief:

> Conceding that fraudulent appeals may be made in the name of charity and religion, we hold a municipality cannot require all who wish to disseminate ideas to present them first to police authorities for their consideration and approval, with a discretion in the police to say some ideas may, while others may not, be carried to the homes of citizens.

The same concern was raised in *Forsyth County v. Nationalist Movement*, 505 U.S. 123 (1992), a case discussed in Chapter 5 when we studied the rules governing speech that provokes a hostile audience. In that chapter, you learned that the government may not increase permit fees because an event is likely to draw a hostile audience. The Court recognized that such a regime gives hostile audiences a heckler's veto because they can drive up a permit's cost by threatening to give a speaker an unruly reception. In another part of the opinion, the Court also condemned the fact that the determination of the fee amount was left to the unfettered discretion of the licensing authority:

> The decision how much to charge for police protection or administrative time—or even whether to charge at all—is left to the whim of the administrator. There are no articulated standards either in the ordinance or in the county's established practice. The administrator is not required to rely on any objective factors. He need not provide any explanation for his decision, and that decision is unreviewable. Nothing in the law or its application prevents the official from encouraging some views and discouraging others through the arbitrary application of fees. The First Amendment prohibits the vesting of such unbridled discretion in a government official.

By contrast, when content-neutral permit regimes do not give administrators unfettered discretion, the Court is likely to uphold them. A good example is found in *Cox v. New Hampshire*, 312 U.S. 569 (1941). In *Cox*, the Court upheld the conviction of Jehovah's Witnesses for violating a state law that required a license and the payment of a fee before holding a parade or procession on a public street. The Court began by acknowledging the practical need for regulating expressive gatherings on public streets:

> The authority of a municipality to impose regulations in order to assure the safety and convenience of the people in the use of public highways has never been regarded as inconsistent with civil liberties but rather as one of the means of safeguarding the good order upon which they ultimately depend. The control of travel on the streets of cities is the most familiar illustration of this recognition of social need. Where a restriction of the use of highways in that relation is designed to promote the public convenience in the interest of all, it cannot be disregarded by the attempted exercise of some civil right which in other circumstances would be entitled to protection.

The Court then upheld the permit statute because the New Hampshire Supreme Court had construed the law to ensure that it did not give the licensing authority unfettered discretion:

> It was with this view of the limited objective of the statute that the state court considered and defined the duty of the licensing authority and the rights of the appellants to a license for their parade, with regard only to considerations of time, place and manner so as to conserve the public convenience. The obvious advantage of requiring application for a permit was noted as giving the public authorities notice in advance so as to afford opportunity for proper policing. And the court further observed that, in fixing time and place, the license served "to prevent confusion by overlapping parades or processions, to secure convenient use of the streets by other travelers, and to minimize the risk of disorder." But the court held that the licensing board was not vested with arbitrary power or an unfettered discretion; that its discretion must be exercised with "uniformity of method of treatment upon the facts of each application, free from improper or inappropriate consid-

erations and from unfair discrimination"; that a "systematic, consistent and just order of treatment, with reference to the convenience of public use of the highways, is the statutory mandate."

What about fee requirements for permits? We know from *Forsyth County* that fees cannot be left to the unfettered discretion of a licensing authority or increased based on the likelihood of there being a hostile audience. But in the absence of such defects, the Court, in cases like *Cox*, has indicated that reasonable flat-fee charges to defray government expenses can be constitutional.

Two final notes. First, in Chapter 4, we discussed how the chilling effect of court orders enjoining speech was magnified by the collateral bar rule, which holds that a party can be held in contempt for violating a court order even if the order is ultimately found to be unconstitutional. The notion is that people should not unilaterally ignore court orders but should seek to have them overridden through the judicial process. The Supreme Court, in *Walker v. City of Birmingham*, 388 U.S. 307, 315 (1967), slightly mitigated this rule by suggesting that it did not apply if an injunction was "transparently invalid or had only a frivolous pretense to validity."

The Supreme Court has indicated that a similar collateral-bar-like rule applies to challenges to administrative licensing regimes. If a law creating a permit requirement is facially invalid, a party can violate the law without first seeking a permit and still preserve his right to challenge the law if charged for violating it. For example, in the *Lovell v. City of Griffin* case reproduced earlier in this chapter, the defendant successfully challenged an ordinance requiring a permit to distribute literature even though the defendant distributed her literature without ever seeking a permit. The Supreme Court ruled that "it was not necessary for [the defendant] to seek a permit" because the ordinance was "void on its face." By contrast, in *Poulos v. New Hampshire*, 345 U.S. 395 (1953), the Court held that a party could not unilaterally ignore a facially valid permit requirement but instead had to apply for a permit and challenge a denial through the appropriate administrative and judicial appeals. The Court rejected the defendant's argument that the delay caused by litigating the challenge was itself a First Amendment violation. The Court acknowledged that this delay was "unfortunate," but said that "the expense and annoyance of litigation is a price citizens must pay for life in an orderly society where the rights of the First Amendment have a real and abiding meaning."

Second, in Chapter 4 we also noted that licensing regimes based on the content of speech will be subject to strict scrutiny and are almost certain to be invalidated. An exception to this rule is a licensing regime that requires pre-approval of movies to ensure that they are not obscene. In *Freedman v. Maryland*, 380 U.S. 51 (1965), the Court held that such a regime is permissible but only if there are rigorous procedural safeguards in place that put the burden on the censor to prove that a film is obscene and allow for prompt judicial review of the licensing agency's determination.

In *Thomas v. Chicago Park District*, 534 U.S. 316, 322 (2002), the Court clarified that these rigorous procedural requirements apply only to licensing regimes based on the content of speech and not to content-neutral regimes: "We have never required that a content-neutral permit scheme regulating speech in a public forum adhere to the procedural requirements set forth in *Freedman*."

Test Your Knowledge

To assess your understanding of the material in this chapter, click here to take a quiz.

CHAPTER FOURTEEN

May Government Regulate Conduct When It Is Used for Expressive Purposes?

Burning Draft Cards, Sleeping in the Park, and Dancing Naked

In Chapter 3, you learned that the First Amendment protects not only words and images but also conduct that is used for expressive purposes. The Supreme Court refers to this conduct as "expressive conduct" or "symbolic speech." In subsequent chapters, you encountered numerous examples of expressive conduct being treated as speech. For example, in *Texas v. Johnson*, the Court recognized that the burning of the national flag at a political demonstration constituted speech:

> The expressive, overtly political nature of this conduct was both intentional and overwhelmingly apparent. In these circumstances Johnson's burning of the flag was conduct "sufficiently imbued with elements of communication" to implicate the First Amendment.

Similarly, in *Virginia v. Black*, the Court acknowledged that cross burning can be a form of speech, and in *Tinker*, the Court accepted that wearing an armband to protest the Vietnam War was expressive.

While the Court accepts that conduct can be expressive, it has also said that it "cannot accept the view that an apparently limitless variety of conduct can be labeled 'speech' whenever the person engaging in the conduct intends thereby to express an idea." *United States v. O'Brien*, 391 U.S. 367, 376 (1968). This raises the question of when conduct will be considered expressive and when it will not. That is the first topic we explore in this chapter.

Even if conduct is expressive, that doesn't mean the government is powerless to regulate it. One might have a right to burn a flag in protest, but that doesn't mean one has a right to burn a flag whenever, wherever, and however one wants. The second topic we explore addresses the framework judges use to determine whether a regulation burdening expressive conduct is unconstitutional.

A. When Is Conduct Expressive? The *Spence* Test and Its Nuances

You learned in Chapter 3 that the Supreme Court uses the *Spence* test to determine whether conduct will be considered speech. In *Spence*, a man taped a peace symbol to both sides of an American flag and hung it out his apartment window. He was charged with violating a Washington state law that prohibited the display of a modified flag. In explaining its reasoning for finding the defendant's conduct expressive, the Court articulated what would become known as the *Spence* test:

> An intent to convey a particularized message was present, and in the surrounding circumstances the likelihood was great that the message would be understood by those who viewed it.

While courts continue to use the *Spence* test to determine whether conduct will be considered speech, Justice David Souter added a gloss to the test in *Hurley v. Irish-American Gay, Lesbian and Bisexual Group of Boston*, 515 U.S. 557 (1995), which addressed whether the St. Patrick's Day parade in Boston was expressive. In doing so, Justice Souter clarified that the *Spence* test's requirement that conduct convey a "particularized message" was not hard and fast. Thus, a parade that consisted of a hodgepodge of messages could still be considered protected speech:

> The protected expression that inheres in a parade is not limited to its banners and songs, for the Constitution looks beyond written or spoken words as mediums of expression. Noting that "symbolism is a primitive but effective way of communicating ideas," our cases have recognized that the First Amendment shields such acts as saluting a flag (and refusing to do so), wearing an armband to protest a war, displaying a red flag, and even "marching, walking or parading" in uniforms displaying the swastika. As some of these examples show, a narrow, succinctly articulable message is not a condition of constitutional protection, which if confined to expressions conveying a "particularized message," would never reach the unquestionably shielded painting of Jackson Pollock, music of Arnold Schoenberg, or Jabberwocky verse of Lewis Carroll.

If conduct fails to pass the *Spence* test, it is not considered speech and its regulation does not implicate the First Amendment. If conduct passes the *Spence* test, that merely begins the First Amendment analysis. A court must next determine whether the regulation burdening the conduct constitutes an unlawful abridgment of speech. We will turn to that topic next.

Before doing so, however, it is important to recognize that the First Amendment is not implicated by every conduct regulation that negatively affects speech. For example, it would not trigger the First Amendment if the government shut down a bookstore because the store had failed to install fire sprinklers required by local safety regulations. Similarly, the First Amendment would not be implicated if a police officer pulled over a reporter for speeding even if the stop delayed the reporter's ability to cover an unfolding story. In both examples, the conduct that triggered the government's action (not installing fire sprinklers and driving too fast) was not inherently expressive and did not, under the circumstances, have a significantly expressive element.

Similarly, the First Amendment is not implicated when a generally applicable sales tax is applied to the sale of works containing speech, such as newspapers, magazines, or books. The sales tax increases the costs of these works and in that sense might diminish their dissemination. But, as long as the tax is generally applicable and not targeted at works containing speech (such as a tax on only newspapers), it is not considered an abridgment of speech. *But see Minneapolis Star & Tribune Co. v. Minnesota Comm'r of Revenue*, 460 U.S. 575 (1983) (invalidating a tax that singled out the press by taxing the use of ink and paper).

A case that summarizes these principles is *Arcara v. Cloud Books, Inc.*, 478 U.S. 697 (1986), in which the Court held that the First Amendment was not implicated by the closure of an adult bookstore that was deemed a public health nuisance because of sexual acts and solicitations of prostitution occurring on the premises. Here is how the Court explained why the closure of a bookstore did not implicate the First Amendment:

> It is true that the closure order in this case would require respondents to move their bookselling business to another location. Yet we have not traditionally subjected every criminal and civil sanction imposed through legal process to [heightened] scrutiny simply because each particular remedy will have some effect on the First Amendment activities of those subject to sanction. Rather, we have subjected such restrictions to scrutiny only where it was conduct with a significant expressive element that drew the legal remedy in the first place, as in *O'Brien*, or where a statute based on a nonexpressive activity has the inevitable effect of singling out those engaged in expressive activity, as in *Minneapolis Star*. This case involves neither situation, and we conclude the First Amendment is not implicated by the enforcement of a public health regulation of general application against the physical premises in which respondents happen to sell books.

B. When Do Conduct Regulations Violate the First Amendment? The *O'Brien* Test and Its Nuances

In Chapter 4, you learned that the Supreme Court uses the *O'Brien* test to determine whether a conduct regulation that burdens expressive conduct is constitutional. In Chapter 8, you saw this test in action when the Court applied it to the flag desecration law in *Texas v. Johnson*.

While you have been exposed to the *O'Brien* test, you have not yet read the opinion from which it derives. Until now.

United States v. O'Brien

Supreme Court of the United States, 1968
391 U.S. 367

MR. CHIEF JUSTICE WARREN delivered the opinion of the Court.

On the morning of March 31, 1966, David Paul O'Brien and three companions burned their Selective Service registration certificates on the steps of the South Boston Courthouse. A sizable crowd, including several agents of the Federal Bureau of Investigation, witnessed the event.

For this act, O'Brien was indicted, tried, convicted, and sentenced in the United States District Court for the District of Massachusetts. He did not contest the fact that he had burned the certificate. He stated in argument to the jury that he burned the certificate publicly to influence others to adopt his antiwar beliefs, as he put it, "so that other people would reevaluate their positions with Selective Service, with the armed forces, and reevaluate their place in the culture of today, to hopefully consider my position."

The indictment upon which he was tried charged that he "willfully and knowingly did mutilate, destroy, and change by burning his Registration Certificate in violation of 50 U.S.C. § 462(b)." Section 462(b) was amended by Congress in 1965 (adding the words italicized below), so that at the time O'Brien burned his certificate an offense was committed by any person,

> who forges, alters, *knowingly destroys*, *knowingly mutilates*, or in any manner changes any such certificate.

The Court of Appeals for the First Circuit held the 1965 Amendment unconstitutional as a law abridging freedom of speech. At the time the Amendment was enacted, a regulation of the Selective Service System required registrants to keep their registration certificates in their "personal possession at all times." Wilful violations of regulations were made criminal by statute. The Court of Appeals was of the opinion that conduct punishable under the 1965 Amendment was already punishable under the nonpossession regulation, and consequently that the Amendment served no valid purpose and must have been "directed at public as distinguished from private destruction." On this basis, the court concluded that the 1965 Amendment ran afoul of the First Amendment by singling out persons engaged in protests for special treatment.

We hold that the 1965 Amendment is constitutional both as enacted and as applied.

When a male reaches the age of 18, he is required to register with a local draft board. He is assigned a Selective Service number, and within five days he is issued a registration certificate. Subsequently, and based on a questionnaire completed by the registrant, he is assigned a classification denoting his eligibility for induction and issued a Notice of Classification.

Both the registration and classification certificates bear notices that the registrant must notify his local board in writing of every change in address, physical condition, and occupational, marital, family, dependency, and military status, and of any other fact which might change his classification. Both also contain a notice that the registrant's Selective Service number should appear on all communications to his local board.

By the 1965 Amendment, Congress added the provision subjecting to criminal liability not only one who "forges, alters, or in any manner changes" but also one who "knowingly destroys or knowingly mutilates" a certificate. We note at the outset that the 1965 Amendment plainly does not abridge free speech on its face. It prohibits the knowing destruction of certificates issued by the Selective Service System, and there is nothing necessarily expressive about such conduct. The Amendment does not distinguish between public and private destruction, and it does not punish only destruction engaged in for the purpose of expressing views.

O'Brien nonetheless argues that the 1965 Amendment is unconstitutional in its application to him, and is unconstitutional as enacted because what he calls the "purpose" of Congress was "to suppress freedom of speech." We consider these arguments separately.

O'Brien first argues that the 1965 Amendment is unconstitutional as applied to him because his act of burning his registration certificate was protected "symbolic speech" within the First Amendment. His argument is that the freedom of expression which the First Amendment guarantees includes all modes of "communication of ideas by conduct," and that his conduct is within this definition because he did it in "demonstration against the war and against the draft."

We cannot accept the view that an apparently limitless variety of conduct can be labeled "speech" whenever the person engaging in the conduct intends thereby to express an idea. However, even on the assumption that the alleged communicative element in O'Brien's conduct is sufficient to bring into play the First Amendment, it does not necessarily follow that the destruction of a registration certificate is constitutionally protected activity. This Court has held that when "speech" and "nonspeech" elements are combined in the same course of conduct, a sufficiently important governmental interest in regulating the nonspeech element can justify incidental limitations on First Amendment freedoms. We think it clear that a government regulation is sufficiently justified if it is within the constitutional power of the Government; if it furthers an important or substantial governmental interest; if the governmental interest is unrelated to the suppression of free expression; and if the incidental restriction on alleged First Amendment freedoms is no greater than is essential to the furtherance of that interest. We find that the 1965 Amendment meets all of these requirements, and consequently that O'Brien can be constitutionally convicted for violating it.

The constitutional power of Congress to raise and support armies and to make all laws necessary and proper to that end is broad and sweeping. Pursuant to this power, Congress may establish a system of registration for individuals liable for training and service. The issuance of certificates indicating the registration and eligibility classification of individuals is a legitimate and substantial administrative aid in the functioning of this system.

We think it apparent that the continuing availability to each registrant of his Selective Service certificates substantially furthers the smooth and proper functioning of the system that Congress has established to raise armies. It is equally clear that the 1965 Amendment specifically protects this substantial governmental interest. We perceive no alternative means that would more precisely and narrowly assure the continuing availability of issued Selective Service certificates than a law which prohibits their wilful mutilation or destruction. The 1965 Amendment prohibits such conduct and does nothing more. In other words, both the governmental interest and the operation of the 1965 Amendment are limited to the noncommunicative aspect of O'Brien's conduct. For this noncommunicative impact of his conduct, and for nothing else, he was convicted.

In conclusion, we find that because of the Government's substantial interest in assuring the continuing availability of issued Selective Service certificates, because amended § 462(b) is an appropriately narrow means of protecting this interest and condemns only the independent noncommunicative impact of conduct within its reach, and because the noncommunicative impact of O'Brien's act of burning his registration certificate frustrated the Government's interest, a sufficient governmental interest has been shown to justify O'Brien's conviction.

O'Brien finally argues that the 1965 Amendment is unconstitutional as enacted because what he calls the "purpose" of Congress was "to suppress freedom of speech." We reject this argument because under settled principles the purpose of Congress is not a basis for declaring this legislation unconstitutional. It is a familiar principle of constitutional law that this Court will not strike down an otherwise constitutional statute on the basis of an alleged illicit legislative motive.

Inquiries into congressional motives or purposes are a hazardous matter. When the issue is simply the interpretation of legislation, the Court will look to statements by legislators for guidance as to the purpose of the legislature, because the benefit to sound decision-making in this circumstance is thought sufficient to risk the possibility of misreading Congress' purpose. It is entirely a different matter when we are asked to void a statute that is, under well-settled criteria, constitutional on its face, on the basis of what fewer than a handful of Congressmen said about it. What motivates one legislator to make a speech about a statute is not necessarily what motivates scores of others to enact it, and the stakes are sufficiently high for us to eschew guesswork. We decline to void essentially on the ground that it is unwise legislation which Congress had the undoubted power to enact and which could be reenacted in its exact form if the same or another legislator made a "wiser" speech about it.

Since the 1965 Amendment is constitutional as enacted and as applied, the Court of Appeals should have affirmed the judgment of conviction entered by the District Court. Accordingly, we vacate the judgment of the Court of Appeals, and reinstate the judgment and sentence of the District Court.

[Justice Douglas' dissenting opinion is omitted.]

Points for Discussion

1. **Parsing the elements of the *O'Brien* test.** The test articulated in *O'Brien* has become the canonical test for evaluating the constitutionality of conduct regulations that burden expressive conduct. Here is the test:

> We think it clear that a government regulation is sufficiently justified if it is within the constitutional power of the Government; if it furthers an important or substantial governmental interest; if the governmental interest is unrelated to the suppression of free expression; and if the incidental restriction on alleged First Amendment freedoms is no greater than is essential to the furtherance of that interest.

The test is poorly worded and confusing. Here is a guide to what it means, and how it should be applied in action.

Overview. The first prong about the government's power to enact the law precedes the First Amendment analysis and is not a First Amendment issue. Prongs two and four set forth an intermediate scrutiny test, which is the default standard for conduct regulations that incidentally burden speech. But that standard applies *only* if a court determines, under prong three, that the government's interest in regulating the conduct is "unrelated to the suppression of free expression." If the government is regulating the conduct because of its message, the law is content-based and will be subject to strict scrutiny and not *O'Brien*'s less demanding intermediate scrutiny standard. Prong three, therefore, plays a critical "gatekeeper" function that determines which level of scrutiny will be applied to a conduct regulation.

Prong one. This requires that the law at issue be "within the constitutional power of the Government." This is not actually a First Amendment free speech condition, but rather a general requirement of constitutional law applicable to all federal statutes. That is because the federal government is a government of limited and enumerated powers. Consequently, when Congress enacts a law, it must be able to point to a power in the Constitution that authorizes its action. (In *O'Brien*, that was not a problem because the law was regulating draft cards, which Congress could regulate under its power to raise and support armies.) By contrast, state and local governments have "police power," which means that they can enact laws for the health, safety, and welfare of their people without having to point to a constitutional power authorizing their actions. The upshot is that prong one never matters in First Amendment free speech terms. If the law is federal, and a court decides that Congress lacked the power to pass it (such as holding that Congress exceeded its powers under the Commerce Clause), the law will be struck down on that basis and the court will never reach the First Amendment issue. If the law is a state law, and a court holds that the state legislature lacked the power to pass it (less common, because of state "police power," but still conceivably possible), again, the law will be struck down anyway, and the First Amendment issue need never be reached.

Prong three. This is the critical "gatekeeper" prong that will determine whether a conduct regulation will be evaluated under strict or intermediate scrutiny. By asking whether the government's interest in regulating the conduct is "unrelated to the suppression of free expression," courts zero in on the key question: Is the law at issue content-neutral or content-based? If the government is regulating the conduct because of its message, the law is "related" to the suppression of free expression and is content-based. The law will then be taken outside the *O'Brien* test and evaluated under strict scrutiny. Conversely, if the government is regulating the conduct regardless of its message, the law is "unrelated" to the suppression of free expression and is content-neutral. In that instance, the *O'Brien* test will continue to apply, and the law will be subject to the intermediate scrutiny analysis in prongs two and four. Not surprisingly, lawyers representing government agencies frequently contend that conduct regulations are content-neutral and that intermediate scrutiny should apply. Lawyers representing speakers typically counter that the regulations are in fact content-based and should be subject to strict scrutiny. Courts tend to be alert to government attempts to invoke *O'Brien* too often and inappropriately. A good example is the Supreme Court's discussion of the issue in *Holder v. Humanitarian Law Project*, which also discussed the Court's rulings in *Cohen v. California* and *Texas v. Johnson*:

> The Government argues that [the federal law prohibiting the provision of material support or resources to designated foreign terrorist organizations] should nonetheless receive intermediate scrutiny because it generally functions as a regulation of conduct. That argument runs headlong into a number of our precedents, most prominently *Cohen v. California. Cohen* also involved a generally applicable regulation of conduct, barring breaches of the peace. But when Cohen was convicted for wearing a jacket bearing an epithet, we did not apply *O'Brien*. Instead, we recognized that the generally applicable law was directed at Cohen because of what his speech communicated—he violated the breach of the peace statute because of the offensive content of his particular message. We accordingly applied more rigorous scrutiny and reversed his conviction.
>
> This suit falls into the same category. The law here may be described as directed at conduct, as the law in *Cohen* was directed at breaches of the peace, but as applied to plaintiffs the conduct triggering coverage under the statute consists of communicating a message. As we explained in *Texas v. Johnson*: "If the regulation is not related to expression, then the less stringent standard we announced in *United States v. O'Brien* for regulations of noncommunicative conduct controls. If it is, then we are outside of *O'Brien's* test, and we must apply a more demanding standard."

Prongs two and four. If the law is content-neutral and thus survives the "gatekeeper" prong, proceed to apply prongs two and four, which are simply restatements of the standard intermediate scrutiny test. This is comparable to the intermediate scrutiny test the Supreme Court uses for time, place, or manner regulations. The *O'Brien* test requires a conduct-based regulation to further an "important" or "substantial" governmental interest, which is the terminology the Court uses generally for intermediate scrutiny. The means part of the *O'Brien* test—that the restriction on speech must be "no greater than is essential"—seems to require the government to use the least speech-restrictive means to achieve its end, a requirement typically associated with strict scrutiny. But subsequent cases have indicated that the *O'Brien* test only requires the means to be "substantially related" to the government's purpose, or a "reasonable fit," the standard associated with intermediate scrutiny. Indeed, in *Clark v. Community for Creative Non-Violence*, the case we will be studying next, the justices treat the *O'Brien* test as equivalent to the intermediate scrutiny test used for time, place, or manner regulations.

2. ***Texas v. Johnson*** **redux.** This is a good time to review the *Texas v. Johnson* flag burning case you studied in Chapter 8. Recall that the defendant had burned the national flag at a protest march and was charged with violating a Texas law that made it a crime to desecrate the flag in a manner that "the actor knows will seriously offend one or more persons." Try to figure out how the Court would have analyzed this fact pattern using the lessons from this chapter. Then go back to the *Texas v. Johnson* case and compare notes.

   Once you're done, try changing the facts of *Texas v. Johnson* and assume that the defendant had been convicted under a different state law that made it illegal to start a fire on a public sidewalk. Assume that the law had been enacted to protect public safety. How would you analyze that fact pattern? Would it come out differently from *Texas v. Johnson*? If so, why?

3. **Should judges consider the motive underlying a content-neutral regulation?** The *O'Brien* opinion rejects the notion that judges should treat a facially content-neutral law as content-based if there is evidence of an underlying illicit motive to discriminate based on content. As Chief Justice Earl Warren explained, "It is a familiar principle of constitutional law that this Court will not strike down an otherwise constitutional statute on the basis of an alleged illicit legislative motive." He described efforts to ascertain the motive of a collective legislative body as a "hazardous matter" and cautioned that doing so raised the risk that the comments of a few legislators would be attributed to the whole.

   While judges continue to cite Chief Justice Warren's ban on inquiries into legislative motive, the Chief Justice's rule is at odds with other areas of constitutional law, such as Equal Protection and Dormant Commerce Clauses, where inquiries into legislative motive are common. Chief Justice Warren's ban is even at loggerheads with other First Amendment cases. For example, in *City of Austin v. Reagan National Advertising*, a 2022 case we studied in Chapter 4, the Court stated that a content-neutral law will be treated as content-based if "there is evidence [of] an impermissible purpose or justification."

1. The *O'Brien* Test in Action: May Government Stop Protesters from Sleeping in a Park?

Can sleeping in a park be expressive? If it can, would a law that barred people from doing so violate the First Amendment?

Clark v. Community for Creative Non-Violence

Supreme Court of the United States, 1984
468 U.S. 288

JUSTICE WHITE delivered the opinion of the Court.

The issue in this case is whether a National Park Service regulation prohibiting camping in certain parks violates the First Amendment when applied to prohibit demonstrators from sleeping in Lafayette Park and the Mall in connection with a demonstration intended to call attention to the plight of the homeless. We hold that it does not and reverse the contrary judgment of the Court of Appeals.

The Interior Department, through the National Park Service, is charged with responsibility for the management and maintenance of the National Parks and is authorized to promulgate rules and regulations for the use of the parks in accordance with the purposes for which they were established. The network of National Parks includes the National Memorial-core parks, Lafayette Park and the Mall, which are set in the heart of Washington, D.C., and which are unique resources that the Federal Government holds in trust for the American people. Lafayette Park is a roughly 7-acre square located across Pennsylvania Avenue from the White House. Although originally part of the White House grounds, President Jefferson set it aside as a park for the use of residents and visitors. The Mall is a stretch of land running westward from the Capitol to the Lincoln Memorial some two miles away. It includes the Washington Monument, a series of reflecting pools, trees, lawns, and other greenery. It is bordered by, inter alia, the Smithsonian Institution and the National Gallery of Art. Both the Park and the Mall were included in Major Pierre L'Enfant's original plan for the Capital. Both are visited by vast numbers of visitors from around the country, as well as by large numbers of residents of the Washington metropolitan area.

Under the regulations involved in this case, camping in National Parks is permitted only in campgrounds designated for that purpose. No such campgrounds have ever been designated in Lafayette Park or the Mall.

Demonstrations for the airing of views or grievances are permitted in the Memorial-core parks, but for the most part only by Park Service permits. Temporary structures may be erected for demonstration purposes but may not be used for camping.

In 1982, the Park Service issued a renewable permit to respondent Community for Creative Non-Violence (CCNV) to conduct a wintertime demonstration in Lafayette Park and the Mall for the purpose of demonstrating the plight of the homeless. The permit authorized the erection of two symbolic tent cities: 20 tents in Lafayette Park that would accommodate 50 people and 40 tents in the Mall with a capacity of up to 100. The Park Service, however, relying on the above regulations, specifically denied CCNV's request that demonstrators be permitted to sleep in the symbolic tents.

CCNV and several individuals then filed an action to prevent the application of the no-camping regulations to the proposed demonstration, which, it was claimed, was not covered by the regulation. It was also submitted that the regulations were unconstitutionally vague, had been discriminatorily applied, and could not be applied to prevent sleeping in the tents without violating the First Amendment. The District Court granted summary judgment in favor of the Park Service. The Court of Appeals, sitting *en banc*, reversed. The 11 judges produced 6 opinions. Six of the judges believed that application of the regulations so as to prevent sleeping in the tents would infringe the demonstrators' First Amendment right of free expression. The other five judges disagreed and would have sustained the regulations as applied to CCNV's proposed demonstration. We granted the Government's petition for certiorari, and now reverse.

We need not differ with the view of the Court of Appeals that overnight sleeping in connection with the demonstration is expressive conduct protected to some extent by the First Amendment. We assume for present purposes, but do not decide, that such is the case, but this assumption only begins the inquiry. Expression, whether oral or written or symbolized by conduct, is subject to reasonable time, place, or manner restrictions. We have often noted that restrictions of this kind are valid provided that they are justified without reference to the content of the regulated speech, that they are narrowly tailored to serve a significant governmental interest, and that they leave open ample alternative channels for communication of the information.

It is also true that a message may be delivered by conduct that is intended to be communicative and that, in context, would reasonably be understood by the viewer to be communicative. Symbolic expression of this kind may be forbidden or regulated if the conduct itself may constitutionally be regulated, if the regulation is narrowly drawn to further a substantial governmental interest, and if the interest is unrelated to the suppression of free speech. *O'Brien*.

Petitioners submit, as they did in the Court of Appeals, that the regulation forbidding sleeping is defensible either as a time, place, or manner restriction or as a regulation of symbolic conduct. We agree with that assessment. The permit that was issued authorized the demonstration but prohibits "camping" on park lands, that is, the use of park lands for living accommodations, such as sleeping, storing personal belongings, making fires, digging, or cooking. These provisions, including the ban on sleeping, are clearly limitations on the manner in which the demonstration could be carried out. That sleeping, like the symbolic tents themselves, may be expressive and part of the message delivered by the demonstration does not make the ban any less a limitation on the manner of demonstrating, for reasonable time, place, or manner regulations normally have the purpose and direct effect of limiting expression but are nevertheless valid. Neither does the fact that sleeping, arguendo, may be expressive conduct, rather than oral or written expression, render the sleeping prohibition any less a time, place, or manner regulation.

The requirement that the regulation be content-neutral is clearly satisfied. The courts below accepted that view, and it is not disputed here that the prohibition on camping, and on sleeping specifically, is content-neutral and is not being applied because of disagreement with the message presented. Neither was the regulation faulted, nor could it be, on the ground that without overnight sleeping the plight of the homeless could not be communicated in other ways. The regulation otherwise left the demonstration intact, with its symbolic city, signs, and the presence of those who were willing to take their turns in a day-and-night vigil. Respondents do not suggest that there was, or is, any barrier to delivering to the media, or to the public by other means, the intended message concerning the plight of the homeless.

It is also apparent to us that the regulation narrowly focuses on the Government's substantial interest in maintaining the parks in the heart of our Capital in an attractive and intact condition, readily available to the millions of people who wish to see and enjoy them by their presence. To permit camping—using these areas as living accommodations—would be totally inimical to these purposes, as would be readily understood by those who have frequented the National Parks across the country and observed the unfortunate consequences of the activities of those who refuse to confine their camping to designated areas.

It is urged by respondents, and the Court of Appeals was of this view, that if the symbolic city of tents was to be permitted and if the demonstrators did not intend to cook, dig, or engage in aspects of camping other than sleeping, the incremental benefit to the parks could not justify the ban on sleeping, which was here an expressive activity said to enhance the message concerning the plight of the poor and homeless. We cannot agree. In the first place, we seriously doubt that the First Amendment requires the Park Service to permit a demonstration in Lafayette Park and the Mall involving a 24-hour vigil and the erection of tents to accommodate 150 people. Furthermore, although we have assumed for present purposes that the sleeping banned in this case would have an expressive element, it is evident that its major value to this demonstration would be facilitative. Without a permit to sleep, it would be difficult to get the poor and homeless to participate or to be present at all. This much is apparent from the permit application filed by respondents: "Without the incentive of sleeping space or a hot meal, the homeless would not come to the site." The sleeping ban, if enforced, would thus effectively limit the nature, extent, and duration of the demonstration and to that extent ease the pressure on the parks.

Beyond this, however, it is evident from our cases that the validity of this regulation need not be judged solely by reference to the demonstration at hand. Absent the prohibition on sleeping, there would be other groups who would demand permission to deliver an asserted message by camping in Lafayette Park. Some of them would surely have as credible a claim in this regard as does CCNV, and the denial of permits to still others would present difficult problems for the Park Service. If the Government has a legitimate interest in ensuring that the National Parks are adequately protected, which we think it has, and if the parks would be more exposed to harm without the sleeping prohibition than with it, the ban is safe from invalidation under the First Amendment as a reasonable regulation of the manner in which a demonstration may be carried out. As in *City Council of Los Angeles v. Taxpayers for Vincent*, the regulation "responds precisely to the substantive problems which legitimately concern the Government." We have difficulty, therefore, in understanding why the prohibition against camping, with its ban on sleeping overnight, is not a reasonable time, place, or manner regulation that withstands constitutional scrutiny.

Contrary to the conclusion of the Court of Appeals, the foregoing analysis demonstrates that the Park Service regulation is sustainable under the four-factor standard of *United States v. O'Brien* for validating a regulation of expressive conduct, which, in the last analysis is little, if any, different from the standard applied to time, place, or manner restrictions. No one contends that aside from its impact on speech a rule against camping or overnight sleeping in public parks is beyond the constitutional power of the Government to enforce. And for the reasons we have discussed above, there is a substantial Government interest in conserving park property, an interest that is plainly served by, and requires for its implementation, measures such as the proscription of sleeping that are designed to limit the wear and tear on park properties. That interest is unrelated to suppression of expression.

We are unmoved by the Court of Appeals' view that the challenged regulation is unnecessary, and hence invalid, because there are less speech-restrictive alternatives that could have satisfied the Government interest in preserving park lands. There is no gainsaying that preventing overnight sleeping will avoid a measure of actual or threatened damage to Lafayette Park and the Mall. The Court of Appeals' suggestions that the Park Service minimize the possible injury by reducing the size, duration, or frequency of demonstrations would still curtail the total allowable expression in which demonstrators could engage, whether by sleeping or otherwise, and these suggestions represent no more than a disagreement with the Park Service over how much protection the core parks require or how an acceptable level of preservation is to be attained. We do not believe, however, that either *United States v. O'Brien* or the time, place, or manner decisions assign to the judiciary the authority to replace the Park Service as the manager of the Nation's parks or endow the judiciary with the competence to judge how much protection of park lands is wise and how that level of conservation is to be attained.

Accordingly, the judgment of the Court of Appeals is reversed.

JUSTICE MARSHALL, with whom JUSTICE BRENNAN joins, dissenting.

The primary purpose for making sleep an integral part of the demonstration was "to re-enact the central reality of homelessness," and to impress upon public consciousness, in as dramatic a way as possible, that homelessness is a widespread problem, often ignored, that confronts its victims with life-threatening deprivations. As one of the homeless men seeking to demonstrate explained: "Sleeping in Lafayette Park or on the Mall, for me, is to show people that conditions are so poor for the homeless and poor in this city that we would actually sleep outside in the winter to get the point across." By using sleep as an integral part of their mode of protest, respondents "can express with their bodies the poignancy of their plight. They can physically demonstrate the neglect from which they suffer with an articulateness even Dickens could not match."

It is true that we all go to sleep as part of our daily regimen and that, for the most part, sleep represents a physical necessity and not a vehicle for expression. But these characteristics need not prevent an activity that is normally devoid of expressive purpose from being used as a novel mode of communication. Sitting or standing in a library is a commonplace activity necessary to facilitate ends usually having nothing to do with making a statement. Moreover, sitting or standing is not conduct that an observer would normally construe as expressive conduct. However, for Negroes to stand or sit in a "whites only" library in Louisiana in 1965 was powerfully expressive; in that particular context, those acts became "monuments of protest" against segregation.

[Chief Justice Burger's concurring opinion is omitted.]

Points for Discussion

1. **The commonality of the *O'Brien* test and the time, place, or manner test.** The time, place, or manner test would seem to be the appropriate test to use when a content-neutral law is regulating expression, such as laws regulating the placement of signs or the volume of a speaker system. By contrast, the *O'Brien* test would seem to be the appropriate test to use when a conduct regulation interferes with expressive conduct. Yet the line between when one test is appropriate and

not the other is not always clear. For example, in *Clark*, the Court treated the prohibition on sleeping in Lafayette Park as both a time, place, or manner regulation (*i.e.*, it was regulating the "manner" in which the protesters could convey their message) as well as a conduct regulation burdening the expressive conduct of sleeping in the park. Fortunately, the Court said the two ways of analyzing the law were essentially the same so that the choice was ultimately inconsequential. The majority described the *O'Brien* test as "little, if any, different from the standard applied to time, place, or manner restrictions," and Justice Thurgood Marshall, in a footnote in his dissent, agreed.

2. **Did the Court underestimate the value of symbolic speech?** Denying the protesters the right to sleep in the park might seem like a trivial limitation on their rights, especially given that the Park Service allowed them to set up a symbolic tent city in the park. But would the dramatic act of sleeping in the park, in the dead of winter, have made it more likely that the protesters would attract news coverage and the public's attention? As Justice Marshall observed, sleeping in the park would have allowed the protesters to "express with their bodies the poignancy of their plight." Did the Court fail to appreciate how its ruling would weaken the power of the protesters' message? Could one argue that sleeping in the park was the symbolic speech equivalent of putting "Fuck the Draft" on one's jacket rather than "I Hate the Draft"? *Compare Cohen v. California.*

2. The Curious Case of Nude Dancing Regulations: May Government Require Pasties and G-Strings?

Is nude dancing speech? If it is, would a law requiring the use of pasties and G-strings be content-based or content-neutral? The Supreme Court has twice wrestled with these perplexing questions. The following case was the Court's first attempt.

Barnes v. Glen Theatre, Inc.

Supreme Court of the United States, 1991
501 U.S. 560

CHIEF JUSTICE REHNQUIST announced the judgment of the Court and delivered an opinion, in which JUSTICE O'CONNOR and JUSTICE KENNEDY join.

Respondents are two establishments in South Bend, Indiana, that wish to provide totally nude dancing as entertainment, and individual dancers who are employed at these establishments. They claim that the First Amendment's guarantee of freedom of expression prevents the State of Indiana from enforcing its public indecency law to prevent this form of dancing. We reject their claim.

The facts appear from the pleadings and findings of the District Court and are uncontested here. The Kitty Kat Lounge, Inc. (Kitty Kat), is located in the city of South Bend. It sells alcoholic beverages and presents "go-go dancing." Its proprietor desires to present "totally nude dancing," but an applicable Indiana statute regulating public nudity requires that the dancers wear "pasties" and "G-strings" when they dance.

Respondent Glen Theatre, Inc., is an Indiana corporation with a place of business in South Bend. Its primary business is supplying so-called adult entertainment through written and printed materials, movie showings, and live entertainment at an enclosed "bookstore." The live entertainment at the "bookstore" consists of nude and seminude performances and showings of the female body through glass panels.

Several of our cases contain language suggesting that nude dancing of the kind involved here is expressive conduct protected by the First Amendment. [This language supports] the conclusion of the Court of Appeals that nude dancing of the kind sought to be performed here is expressive conduct within the outer perimeters of the First Amendment, though we view it as only marginally so. This, of course, does not end our inquiry. We must determine the level of protection to be afforded to the expressive conduct at issue and must determine whether the Indiana statute is an impermissible infringement of that protected activity.

Indiana, of course, has not banned nude dancing as such, but has proscribed public nudity across the board. The Supreme Court of Indiana has construed the Indiana statute to preclude nudity in what are essentially places of public accommodation such as the Glen Theatre and the Kitty Kat Lounge. In such places, respondents point out, minors are excluded and there are no nonconsenting viewers. Respondents contend that while the State may license establishments such as the ones involved here and limit the geographical area in which they do business, it may not in any way limit the performance of the dances within them without violating the First Amendment.

Applying the four-part *O'Brien* test, we find that Indiana's public indecency statute is justified despite its incidental limitations on some expressive activity. The public indecency statute is clearly within the constitutional power of the State and furthers substantial governmental interests. It is impossible to discern, other than from the text of the statute, exactly what governmental interest the Indiana legislators had in mind when they enacted this statute, for Indiana does not record legislative history, and the State's highest court has not shed additional light on the statute's purpose. Nonetheless, the statute's purpose of protecting societal order and morality is clear from its text and history. Public indecency statutes of this sort are of ancient origin and presently exist in at least 47 States. Public indecency statutes such as the one before us reflect moral disapproval of people appearing in the nude among strangers in public places. The Indiana public indecency statute furthers a substantial government interest in protecting order and morality.

This interest is unrelated to the suppression of free expression. Some may view restricting nudity on moral grounds as necessarily related to expression. We disagree. It can be argued, of course, that almost limitless types of conduct—including appearing in the nude in public—are "expressive," and in one sense of the word this is true. People who go about in the nude in public may be expressing something about themselves by so doing. But the court rejected this expansive notion of "expressive conduct" in *O'Brien,* saying: "We cannot accept the view that an apparently limitless variety of conduct can be labeled 'speech' whenever the person engaging in the conduct intends thereby to express an idea."

Respondents contend that even though prohibiting nudity in public generally may not be related to suppressing expression, prohibiting the performance of nude dancing is related to expression because the State seeks to prevent its erotic message. Therefore, they reason that the application of the Indiana statute to the nude dancing in this case violates the First Amendment, because it fails the third part of the *O'Brien* test, viz: the governmental interest must be unrelated to the suppression of free expression.

But we do not think that when Indiana applies its statute to the nude dancing in these nightclubs it is proscribing nudity because of the erotic message conveyed by the dancers. Presumably numerous other erotic performances are presented at these establishments and similar clubs without any interference from the State, so long as the performers wear a scant amount of clothing. Likewise, the requirement that the dancers don pasties and G-strings does not deprive the dance of whatever erotic message it conveys; it simply makes the message slightly less graphic. The perceived evil that Indiana seeks to address is not erotic dancing, but public nudity. The appearance of people of all shapes, sizes and ages in the nude at a beach, for example, would convey little if any erotic message, yet the State still seeks to prevent it. Public nudity is the evil the State seeks to prevent, whether or not it is combined with expressive activity.

The fourth part of the *O'Brien* test requires that the incidental restriction on First Amendment freedom be no greater than is essential to the furtherance of the governmental interest. As indicated in the discussion above, the governmental interest served by the text of the prohibition is societal disapproval of nudity in public places and among strangers. The statutory prohibition is not a means to some greater end, but an end in itself. It is without cavil that the public indecency statute is "narrowly tailored"; Indiana's requirement that the dancers wear at least pasties and G-strings is modest, and the bare minimum necessary to achieve the State's purpose.

The judgment of the Court of Appeals accordingly is *Reversed.*

JUSTICE SCALIA, concurring in the judgment.

I agree that the judgment of the Court of Appeals must be reversed. In my view, however, the challenged regulation must be upheld, not because it survives some lower level of First Amendment scrutiny, but because, as a general law regulating conduct and not specifically directed at expression, it is not subject to First Amendment scrutiny at all.

On its face, this law is not directed at expression in particular. As Judge Easterbrook put it in his dissent below: "Indiana does not regulate dancing. It regulates public nudity. Almost the entire domain of Indiana's statute is unrelated to expression, unless we view nude beaches and topless hot dog vendors as speech." The intent to convey a "message of eroticism" (or any other message) is not a necessary element of the statutory offense of public indecency. Since the Indiana regulation is a general law not specifically targeted at expressive conduct, its application to such conduct does not in my view implicate the First Amendment.

We have explicitly adopted such a regime in another First Amendment context: that of free exercise. In *Employment Div., Dept. of Human Resources of Ore. v. Smith*, 494 U.S. 872 (1990), we held that general laws not specifically targeted at religious practices did not require heightened First Amendment scrutiny even though they diminished some people's ability to practice their religion. "The government's ability to enforce generally applicable prohibitions of socially harmful conduct, like its ability to carry out other aspects of public policy, cannot depend on measuring the effects of a governmental action on a religious objector's spiritual development." There is even greater reason to apply this approach to the regulation of expressive conduct. Relatively few can plausibly assert that their illegal conduct is being engaged in for religious reasons; but almost anyone can violate almost any law as a means of expression. In the one case, as in the other, if the law is not directed against the protected value (religion or expression) the law must be obeyed.

Indiana may constitutionally enforce its prohibition of public nudity even against those who choose to use public nudity as a means of communication. The State is regulating conduct, not expression, and those who choose to employ conduct as a means of expression must make sure that the conduct they select is not generally forbidden. For these reasons, I agree that the judgment should be reversed.

JUSTICE SOUTER, concurring in the judgment.

I agree with the plurality that the appropriate analysis to determine the actual protection required by the First Amendment is the four-part enquiry described in *United States v. O'Brien*, for judging the limits of appropriate state action burdening expressive acts as distinct from pure speech or representation. I nonetheless write separately to rest my concurrence in the judgment, not on the possible sufficiency of society's moral views to justify the limitations at issue, but on the State's substantial interest in combating the secondary effects of adult entertainment establishments of the sort typified by respondents' establishments.

It is, of course, true that this justification has not been articulated by Indiana's Legislature or by its courts. While it is certainly sound in such circumstances to infer general purposes "of protecting societal order and morality from [the statute's] text and history," I think that we need not so limit ourselves in identifying the justification for the legislation at issue here, and may legitimately consider petitioners' assertion that the statute is applied to nude dancing because such dancing "encourages prostitution, increases sexual assaults, and attracts other criminal activity."

In my view, the interest asserted by petitioners in preventing prostitution, sexual assault, and other criminal activity, although presumably not a justification for all applications of the statute, is sufficient under *O'Brien* to justify the State's enforcement of the statute against the type of adult entertainment at issue here.

JUSTICE WHITE, with whom JUSTICE MARSHALL, JUSTICE BLACKMUN, and JUSTICE STEVENS join, dissenting.

Legislators do not just randomly select certain conduct for proscription; they have reasons for doing so and those reasons illuminate the purpose of the law that is passed. Indeed, a law may have multiple purposes. The purpose of forbidding people to appear nude in parks, beaches, hot dog stands, and like public places is to protect others from offense. But that could not possibly be the purpose of preventing nude dancing in theaters and barrooms since the viewers are exclusively consenting adults who pay money to see these dances. The purpose of the proscription in these contexts is to protect the viewers from what the State believes is the harmful message that nude dancing communicates. This is why *Clark v. Community for Creative Non-Violence* is of no help to the State: "In *Clark* the damage to the parks was the same whether the sleepers were camping out for fun, were in fact homeless, or wished by sleeping in the park to make a symbolic statement on behalf of the homeless." That cannot be said in this case: The perceived damage to the public interest caused by appearing nude on the streets or in the parks, as I have said, is not what the State seeks to avoid in preventing nude dancing in theaters and taverns. There the perceived harm is the communicative aspect of the erotic dance.

The plurality nevertheless holds that the third requirement of the *O'Brien* test, that the governmental interest be unrelated to the suppression of free expression, is satisfied because in applying the statute to nude dancing, the State is not "proscribing nudity because of the erotic message conveyed by the dancers." The plurality suggests that this is so because the State does not ban dancing that sends an erotic message; it is only nude erotic dancing that is forbidden. The perceived evil is not erotic dancing but public nudity, which may be prohibited despite any incidental impact on expressive activity. This analysis is transparently erroneous.

In arriving at its conclusion, the plurality concedes that nude dancing conveys an erotic message and concedes that the message would be muted if the dancers wore pasties and G-strings. Indeed, the emotional or erotic impact of the dance is intensified by the nudity of the performers. The sight of a fully clothed, or even a partially clothed, dancer generally will have a far different impact on a spectator than that of a nude dancer, even if the same dance is performed. The nudity is itself an expressive component of the dance, not merely incidental "conduct."

This being the case, it cannot be that the statutory prohibition is unrelated to expressive conduct. Since the State permits the dancers to perform if they wear pasties and G-strings but forbids nude dancing, it is precisely because of the distinctive, expressive content of the nude dancing performances at issue in this case that the State seeks to apply the statutory prohibition. It is only because nude dancing performances may generate emotions and feelings of eroticism and sensuality among the spectators that the State seeks to regulate such expressive activity, apparently on the assumption that creating or emphasizing such thoughts and ideas in the minds of the spectators may lead to increased prostitution and the degradation of women. But generating thoughts, ideas, and emotions is the essence of communication. The nudity element of nude dancing performances cannot be neatly pigeonholed as mere "conduct" independent of any expressive component of the dance.

That fact dictates the level of First Amendment protection to be accorded the performances at issue here. In *Texas v. Johnson*, the Court observed: "Whether Johnson's treatment of the flag violated Texas law thus depended on the likely communicative impact of his expressive conduct. We must therefore subject the State's asserted interest in preserving the special symbolic character of the flag to the most exacting scrutiny." Content based restrictions "will be upheld only if narrowly drawn to accomplish a compelling governmental interest."

As I see it, our cases require us to affirm absent a compelling state interest supporting the statute. Neither the plurality nor the State suggest that the statute could withstand scrutiny under that standard.

Points for Discussion

1. **What was the basis for the Court's ruling?** The Court upheld the restrictions on nude dancing in *Barnes*, but a majority of justices could not agree on why. Can you articulate the differences between the reasoning in Chief Justice William Rehnquist's opinion, Justice Antonin Scalia's opinion, and Justice Souter's opin-

ion? Justice Scalia's reasoning gives you a preview of his reasoning in a landmark Free Exercise case, *Employment Division v. Smith*, which you will be reading in Chapter 18.

2. **How did the dissenting opinion differ from Chief Justice Rehnquist's plurality opinion?** What was the major difference between how Justice White's dissenting opinion characterized the law and how Chief Justice Rehnquist's plurality opinion characterized the law? What were the implications of this difference?

3. ***Barnes* redux: *City of Erie v. Pap's A.M.*** Less than a decade after the *Barnes* decision, the Court was again considering the constitutionality of a law that required nude dancers to wear pasties and G-strings. The law in this case was an ordinance enacted by the city of Erie, Pennsylvania. When the Pennsylvania Supreme Court considered the constitutionality of the law, it acknowledged that the law was "strikingly similar" to the law upheld in *Barnes.* Nevertheless, the court said it was not bound by *Barnes* because the fragmented opinion failed to produce a binding majority rule. Consequently, the Pennsylvania court felt at liberty to make its own determination of whether the Erie ordinance was constitutional. Applying the *O'Brien* test, the court concluded that the law was content-based and failed to pass strict scrutiny.

   The U.S. Supreme Court took the case and reversed. Justice Sandra Day O'Connor wrote a plurality opinion that was joined by Chief Justice Rehnquist and Justices Anthony Kennedy and Steven Breyer, which treated the Erie ordinance as a content-neutral regulation because the law was aimed at the secondary effects of nude dancing establishments. Justice Scalia wrote a concurring opinion, joined by Justice Clarence Thomas, that concurred in the judgment but not with Justice O'Connor's reasoning. Justice Scalia reiterated the principle he had announced in *Barnes*: that a generally applicable conduct regulation that does not target the conduct's message does not implicate the First Amendment. Justice Souter wrote separately to say that he concurred with Justice O'Connor's use of the secondary effects doctrine but thought that the city had failed to provide adequate evidence that nude dancing establishments produced negative secondary effects. Justice John Paul Stevens, joined by Justice Ruth Bader Ginsburg, wrote a dissent that objected to Justice O'Connor's extension of the secondary effects doctrine, which had been previously used to justify only the zoning of adult entertainment establishments, to justify the regulation of speech occurring inside these establishments. *City of Erie v. Pap's A.M.*, 529 U.S. 277 (2000).

You Be the Judge!

Equality, speech, and sunscreen

A state prohibits public nudity on state beaches. Women who believe they have a constitutional right to sunbathe and swim topless stage a topless protest at a state beach, arguing among other things that to permit men to bathe topless but not women is a violation of their equal protection rights and impermissible speaker-based discrimination under the First Amendment. How should the case be decided?

Test Your Knowledge

To assess your understanding of the material in this chapter, click here to take a quiz.

Chapter Fifteen

When Government Compels Speech or Interferes with Expressive Association:

The Right Not to Speak and the Right to Associate

In this chapter and the next, we examine rights that complement and reinforce the free speech rights discussed in previous chapters. This chapter focuses on two of these rights: the right not to speak and the right to associate for expressive purposes. The next chapter focuses on freedom of the press.

We begin the chapter with the right not to speak. We will encounter a comparable right, the right not to associate, when we turn to the topic of freedom of association.

A. The Right Not to Speak: First Amendment Limits on Government-Compelled Speech

While the First Amendment is more commonly implicated when the government restricts speech, it is also implicated when the government compels speech. In Chapter 8, you read what is probably the "purest" of all "compelled speech" cases, *West Virginia State Board of Education v. Barnette,* 319 U.S. 624 (1943), in which the Supreme Court struck down a West Virginia law that required public school students to recite the Pledge of Allegiance. The case was brought by Jehovah's Witnesses who believed that engaging in the flag ceremony violated their religion. Justice Robert Jackson's opinion included one of the most famous sentences in First Amendment jurisprudence: "If there is any fixed star in our constitutional constellation, it is that no official, high or petty, can prescribe what shall be orthodox in politics, nationalism, religion, or other matters of opinion *or force citizens to confess by word or act their faith therein.*"

The compelled speech doctrine was extended in *Wooley v. Maynard*, 430 U.S. 705 (1966), another case involving Jehovah's Witnesses. George and Maxine Maynard, for religious reasons, objected to displaying the motto "Live Free or Die" on their New Hampshire license plates. Consequently, the couple covered the message with tape, in violation of a state law. The Supreme Court, after noting that the First Amendment protects "both the right to speak freely and the right to refrain from speaking at all," ruled in favor of the Maynards:

> New Hampshire's statute in effect requires that appellees use their private property as a "mobile billboard" for the State's ideological message—or suffer a penalty, as Maynard already has. As a condition to driving an automobile—a virtual necessity for most Americans—the Maynards must display "Live Free or Die" to hundreds of people each day. The fact that most individuals agree with the thrust of New Hampshire's motto is not the test; most Americans also find the flag salute acceptable. The First Amendment protects the right of individuals to hold a point of view different from the majority and to refuse to foster, in the way New Hampshire commands, an idea they find morally objectionable.

Barnette and *Wooley* were landmark decisions establishing the First Amendment's general prohibition on compelled speech. In both cases, the Court refused to permit private individuals to be conscripted into espousing government-prescribed orthodoxies.

But *Barnette* and *Wooley* should not be understood as creating an absolute bar on compelled speech. Indeed, there are many instances in which the government can and does compel speech. For example, the law requires food manufacturers to provide nutritional information on their products and requires pharmaceutical companies to disclose the possible side effects of their drugs. Similarly, the law requires attorneys to disclose conflicts of interest to clients and requires doctors to provide information about medical procedures so patients can give informed consent. As the next section indicates, the line between these lawful compulsions to speak and the unlawful compulsions in cases like *Barnette* and *Wooley* is sometimes difficult to discern.

Points for Discussion

1. **Are people really being forced to convey unwanted messages?** Just because people claim that the government is compelling them to speak does not mean a

fact finder will accept this characterization. For example, in Chapter 3, we discussed a case in which a private mall owner complained that California was forcing the owner to convey unwanted messages by requiring the owner to allow the distribution of literature in the mall. The Court rejected the owner's compelled speech argument because it said that the public would not associate the views expressed in the literature with those of the mall owner. *PruneYard Shopping Ctr. v. Robins*, 447 U.S. 74, 87 (1980). Similarly, in *Rumsfeld v. Forum for Academic & Institutional Rights, Inc.*, 547 U.S. 47 (2006), the Court refused to find that law schools were being compelled to speak because federal law required them to give military recruiters the same access to students as other recruiters. The Court noted that the schools were free to criticize military policy, and the simple act of allowing military recruiters on campus would not be perceived as endorsement of military policy.

The rulings in *PruneYard* and *Rumsfeld* could make one wonder whether the Court in *Wooley* properly characterized the "Live Free or Die" motto on a license plate as the compelled speech of a car owner. It seems unlikely that people would think that car owners endorse the messages on their state-issued license plates. Indeed, *Wooley* seems to be at loggerheads with the Court's treatment of specialized license plates in *Walker v. Texas Division*, a case we studied in Chapter 11. In that case, the Court concluded that license plates are government speech and not private speech, even though, ironically, the private party in *Walker* proposed part of the license plate's message.

2. **The right to speak anonymously.** A corollary to the right not to speak is the right to speak anonymously. The concern here is not that the government is forcing speakers to espouse the government's message, but that the government is forcing speakers to identify themselves. In several cases, the Court has recognized a right to speak anonymously. In *Talley v. California*, 362 U.S. 60 (1960), the Court struck down a city ordinance that required leaflets to identify the people who wrote, produced, or distributed them. Justice Hugo Black explained that speakers with controversial viewpoints might be reluctant to identify themselves because of fear of reprisals. He noted that "persecuted groups and sects from time to time throughout history have been able to criticize oppressive practices and laws either anonymously or not at all." Similarly, in *McIntyre v. Ohio Elections Commission*, 514 U.S. 334 (1995), the Court struck down an Ohio law that prohibited the distribution of anonymous campaign literature. "Under our Constitution," Justice John Paul Stevens explained, "anonymous pamphleteering is not a pernicious, fraudulent practice, but an honorable tradition of advocacy and of dissent. Anonymity is a shield from the tyranny of the majority."

   While the Court has recognized a right to speak anonymously, it has not found this right to be absolute. For example, in Chapter 12, you learned that the Court in *Buckley* upheld campaign finance laws that required the disclosure of donor names. Similarly, in *Doe v. Reed*, 561 U.S. 186 (2010), the Court rejected a facial challenge to a Washington state law that permitted public access to the names of signers on a referendum petition. In both cases, the Court left open the possibility that opponents of disclosure could bring an "as applied" challenge if there was a reasonable probability the disclosure would lead to harassment or threats.

While the right to speak anonymously can provide crucial protection for speakers who wish to criticize those in power or challenge existing conventions, it can also be a license for abusive speech, particularly in the Wild West of the internet. As Professors Lyrissa Barnett Lidsky and Thomas F. Cotter have observed, anonymous speech is a double-edged sword:

> Although speech emanating from unidentifiable sources contributes to the diversity, quantity, and quality of voices in the marketplace of ideas, anonymity can also shield speakers from liability for a variety of torts, including defamation, invasion of privacy, fraud, copyright infringement, and trade secret misappropriation.

Lyrissa Barnett Lidsky & Thomas F. Cotter, *Authorship, Audiences, and Anonymous Speech*, 82 Notre Dame L. Rev. 1537, 1538–39 (2007). *See also* Jason M. Shepard & Genelle Belmas, *Anonymity, Disclosure and First Amendment Balancing in the Internet Era: Developments in Libel, Copyright, and Election Speech*, 15 Yale J. L. & Tech. 92, 96 (2012) ("Anonymity can shield individuals from being accountable for their speech; it can hinder the investigation and prosecution of crimes and civil wrongs; it has the potential to undermine government authority and security; and it can undermine business interests and e-commerce"). The challenge for courts is to strike the right balance between anonymity and accountability.

1. Distinguishing Lawful from Unlawful Compulsions: Reasonable Disclosure Requirements Versus Conscripted Government Mouthpieces

The following case illustrates the difficult line-drawing problems that arise when compelled speech has both the ideological overtones of *Barnette* and *Wooley* and the non-ideological overtones of garden-variety consumer protection regulations.

National Institute of Family & Life Advocates v. Becerra

Supreme Court of the United States, 2018
585 U.S. 755

JUSTICE THOMAS delivered the opinion of the Court.

The California Reproductive Freedom, Accountability, Comprehensive Care, and Transparency Act (FACT Act) requires clinics that primarily serve pregnant women to provide certain notices. Licensed clinics must notify women that California provides free or low-cost services, including abortions, and give them a phone number to call. Unlicensed clinics must notify women that California has not licensed the clinics to provide medical services. The question in this case is whether these notice requirements violate the First Amendment.

The California State Legislature enacted the FACT Act to regulate crisis pregnancy centers. Crisis pregnancy centers—according to a report commissioned by the California State Assembly—are "pro-life (largely Christian belief-based) organizations that offer a limited range of free pregnancy options, counseling, and other services to individuals that visit a center." "Unfortunately," the author of the FACT Act stated, "there are nearly 200 licensed and unlicensed" crisis pregnancy centers in California. These centers "aim to discourage and prevent women from seeking abortions." The author of the FACT Act observed that crisis pregnancy centers "are commonly affiliated with or run by organizations whose stated goal" is to oppose abortion—including "the National Institute of Family and Life Advocates," one of the petitioners here. To address this perceived problem, the FACT Act imposes two notice requirements on facilities that provide pregnancy-related services—one for licensed facilities and one for unlicensed facilities.

We first address the licensed notice.

The licensed notice is a content-based regulation of speech. By compelling individuals to speak a particular message, such notices alter the content of their speech. Here, for example, licensed clinics must provide a government-drafted script about the availability of state-sponsored services, as well as contact information for how to obtain them. One of those services is abortion—the very practice that petitioners are devoted to opposing. By requiring petitioners to inform women how they can obtain state-subsidized abortions—at the same time petitioners try to dissuade women from choosing that option—the licensed notice plainly "alters the content" of petitioners' speech.

Although the licensed notice is content based, the Ninth Circuit did not apply strict scrutiny because it concluded that the notice regulates "professional speech."

But this Court has not recognized "professional speech" as a separate category of speech. Speech is not unprotected merely because it is uttered by "professionals." This Court has "been reluctant to mark off new categories of speech for diminished constitutional protection." And it has been especially reluctant to "exempt a category of speech from the normal prohibition on content-based restrictions." This Court's precedents do not permit governments to impose content-based restrictions on speech without persuasive evidence of a long (if heretofore unrecognized) tradition to that effect.

This Court's precedents do not recognize such a tradition for a category called "professional speech." This Court has afforded less protection for professional speech in two circumstances—neither of which turned on the fact that professionals were speaking. First, our precedents have applied more deferential review to some laws that require professionals to disclose factual, noncontroversial information in their "commercial speech." *See, e.g., Zauderer v. Office of Disciplinary Counsel of Supreme Court of Ohio*, 471 U.S. 626, 651 (1985). Second, under our precedents, States may regulate professional conduct, even though that conduct incidentally involves speech. But neither line of precedents is implicated here.

The dangers associated with content-based regulations of speech are also present in the context of professional speech. As with other kinds of speech, regulating the content of professionals' speech "poses the inherent risk that the Government seeks not to advance a legitimate regulatory goal, but to suppress unpopular ideas or information."

"Professional speech" is also a difficult category to define with precision. As defined by the courts of appeals, the professional-speech doctrine would cover a wide array of individuals—doctors, lawyers, nurses, physical therapists, truck drivers, bartenders, barbers, and many others. See Rodney Smolla, *Professional Speech and the First Amendment*, 119 W. Va. L. Rev. 67, 68 (2016). One court of appeals has even applied it to fortune tellers. All that is required to make something a "profession," according to these courts, is that it involves personalized services and requires a professional license from the State. But that gives the States unfettered power to reduce a group's First Amendment rights by simply imposing a licensing requirement. States cannot choose the protection that speech receives under the First Amendment, as that would give them a powerful tool to impose "invidious discrimination of disfavored subjects." State labels cannot be dispositive of the degree of First Amendment protection.

California could inform low-income women about its services "without burdening a speaker with unwanted speech." Most obviously, it could inform the women itself with a public-information campaign. California could even post the information on public property near crisis pregnancy centers. California argues that it has already tried an advertising campaign, and that many women who are eligible for publicly-funded healthcare have not enrolled. But California has identified no evidence to that effect. And regardless, a "tepid response" does not prove that an advertising campaign is not a sufficient alternative. Here, for example, individuals might not have enrolled in California's services because they do not want them, or because California spent insufficient resources on the advertising campaign. Either way, California cannot co-opt the licensed facilities to deliver its message for it.

We next address the unlicensed notice.

We need not decide what type of state interest is sufficient to sustain a disclosure requirement like the unlicensed notice. California has not demonstrated any justification for the unlicensed notice that is more than "purely hypothetical."

Even if California had presented a nonhypothetical justification for the unlicensed notice, the FACT Act unduly burdens protected speech. The unlicensed notice imposes a government-scripted, speaker-based disclosure requirement that is wholly disconnected from California's informational interest. It requires covered facilities to post California's precise notice, no matter what the facilities say on site or in their advertisements. And it covers a curiously narrow subset of speakers. While the licensed notice applies to facilities that provide "family planning" services and "contraception or contraceptive methods," the California Legislature dropped these triggering conditions for the unlicensed notice. The unlicensed notice applies only to facilities that primarily provide "pregnancy-related" services. Thus, a facility that advertises and provides pregnancy tests is covered by the unlicensed notice, but a facility across the street that advertises and provides nonprescription contraceptives is excluded—even though the latter is no less likely to make women think it is licensed. This Court's precedents are deeply skeptical of laws that "distinguish among different speakers, allowing speech by some but not others." Speaker-based laws run the risk that "the State has left unburdened those speakers whose messages are in accord with its own views."

The application of the unlicensed notice to advertisements demonstrates just how burdensome it is. The notice applies to all "print and digital advertising materials" by an unlicensed covered facility. These materials must include a government-drafted statement that "this facility is not licensed as a medical facility by the State of California and has no licensed medical provider who provides or directly supervises the provision of services." An unlicensed facility must call attention to the notice, instead of its own message, by some method such as larger text or contrasting type or color. This scripted language must be posted in English and as many other languages as California chooses to require. As California conceded at oral argument, a billboard for an unlicensed facility that says "Choose Life" would have to surround that two-word statement with a 29-word statement from the government, in as many as 13 different languages. In this way, the unlicensed notice drowns out the facility's own message.

More likely, the "detail required" by the unlicensed notice "effectively rules out" the possibility of having such a billboard in the first place.

For all these reasons, the unlicensed notice does not satisfy *Zauderer*, assuming that standard applies. California has offered no justification that the notice plausibly furthers. It targets speakers, not speech, and imposes an unduly burdensome disclosure requirement that will chill their protected speech. Taking all these circumstances together, we conclude that the unlicensed notice is unjustified and unduly burdensome under *Zauderer*. We express no view on the legality of a similar disclosure requirement that is better supported or less burdensome.

JUSTICE KENNEDY, with whom THE CHIEF JUSTICE, JUSTICE ALITO, and JUSTICE GORSUCH join, concurring.

I join the Court's opinion in all respects.

This separate writing seeks to underscore that the apparent viewpoint discrimination here is a matter of serious constitutional concern. The Court, in my view, is correct not to reach this question. It was not sufficiently developed, and the rationale for the Court's decision today suffices to resolve the case. And had the Court's analysis been confined to viewpoint discrimination some legislators might have inferred that if the law were reenacted with a broader base and broader coverage it then would be upheld.

It does appear that viewpoint discrimination is inherent in the design and structure of this Act. This law is a paradigmatic example of the serious threat presented when government seeks to impose its own message in the place of individual speech, thought, and expression. For here the State requires primarily pro-life pregnancy centers to promote the State's own preferred message advertising abortions. This compels individuals to contradict their most deeply held beliefs, beliefs grounded in basic philosophical, ethical, or religious precepts, or all of these. And the history of the Act's passage and its underinclusive application suggest a real possibility that these individuals were targeted because of their beliefs.

The California Legislature included in its official history the congratulatory statement that the Act was part of California's legacy of "forward thinking." But it is not forward thinking to force individuals to "be an instrument for fostering public adherence to an ideological point of view they find unacceptable." *Wooley v. Maynard.* It is forward thinking to begin by reading the First Amendment as ratified in 1791; to understand the history of authoritarian government as the Founders then knew it; to confirm that history since then shows how relentless authoritarian regimes are in their attempts to stifle free speech; and to carry those lessons onward as we seek to preserve and teach the necessity of freedom of speech for the generations to come. Governments must not be allowed to force persons to express a message contrary to their deepest convictions. Freedom of speech secures freedom of thought and belief. This law imperils those liberties.

JUSTICE BREYER, with whom JUSTICE GINSBURG, JUSTICE SOTOMAYOR, and JUSTICE KAGAN join, dissenting.

dissent

The petitioners ask us to consider whether two sections of a California statute violate the First Amendment. The first section requires licensed medical facilities (that provide women with assistance involving pregnancy or family planning) to tell those women where they might obtain help, including financial help, with comprehensive family planning services, prenatal care, and abortion. The second requires unlicensed facilities offering somewhat similar services to make clear that they are unlicensed. In my view both statutory sections are likely constitutional, and I dissent from the Court's contrary conclusions.

Before turning to the specific law before us, I focus upon the general interpretation of the First Amendment that the majority says it applies. It applies heightened scrutiny to the Act because the Act, in its view, is "content based." "By compelling individuals to speak a particular message," it adds, "such notices alter the content of their speech." "As a general matter," the majority concludes, such laws are "presumptively unconstitutional" and are subject to "stringent" review.

The majority recognizes exceptions to this general rule: It excepts laws that "require professionals to disclose factual, noncontroversial information in their 'commercial speech,' " provided that the disclosure "relates to the services that [the regulated entities] provide." It also excepts laws that "regulate professional conduct" and only "incidentally burden speech."

This constitutional approach threatens to create serious problems. Because much, perhaps most, human behavior takes place through speech and because much, perhaps most, law regulates that speech in terms of its content, the majority's approach at the least threatens considerable litigation over the constitutional validity of much, perhaps most, government regulation. Virtually every disclosure law could be considered "content based," for virtually every disclosure law requires individuals "to speak a particular message." See *Reed v. Town of Gilbert* (Breyer, J., concurring in judgment) (listing regulations that inevitably involve content discrimination, ranging from securities disclosures to signs at petting zoos). Thus, the majority's view, if taken literally, could radically change prior law, perhaps placing much securities law or consumer protection law at constitutional risk, depending on how broadly its exceptions are interpreted.

Many ordinary disclosure laws would fall outside the majority's exceptions for disclosures related to the professional's own services or conduct. These include numerous commonly found disclosure requirements relating to the medical profession. See, *e.g.*, Cal. Veh. Code Ann. § 27363.5 (West 2014) (requiring hospitals to tell parents about child seat belts); Cal. Health & Safety Code Ann. § 123222.2 (requiring hospitals to ask incoming patients if they would like the facility to give their family information about patients' rights and responsibilities); N.C. Gen. Stat. Ann. § 131E–79.2 (2017) (requiring hospitals to tell parents of newborns about pertussis disease and the available vaccine). These also include numerous disclosure requirements found in other areas. See, *e.g.*, N.Y.C. Rules & Regs., tit. 1, § 27–01 (2018) (requiring signs by elevators showing stair locations); San Francisco Dept. of Health, Director's Rules & Regs., Garbage and Refuse (July 8, 2010) (requiring property owners to inform tenants about garbage disposal procedures).

The majority, perhaps recognizing this problem, adds a general disclaimer. It says that it does not "question the legality of health and safety warnings long considered permissible, or purely factual and uncontroversial disclosures about commercial products." But this generally phrased disclaimer would seem more likely to invite litigation than to provide needed limitation and clarification. The majority, for example, does not explain why the Act here, which is justified in part by health and safety considerations, does not fall within its "health" category. See also *Planned Parenthood of Southeastern Pa. v. Casey*, 505 U.S. 833, 882–884 (1992) (joint opinion of O'Connor, Kennedy, and Souter, JJ.) (reasoning that disclosures related to fetal development and childbirth are related to the health of a woman seeking an abortion). Nor does the majority opinion offer any reasoned basis that might help apply its disclaimer for distinguishing lawful from unlawful disclosures. In the absence of a reasoned explanation of the disclaimer's meaning and rationale, the disclaimer is unlikely to withdraw the invitation to litigation that the majority's general broad "content-based" test issues. That test invites courts around the Nation to apply an unpredictable First Amendment to ordinary social and economic regulation, striking down disclosure laws that judges may disfavor, while upholding others, all without grounding their decisions in reasoned principle.

Notably, the majority says nothing about limiting its language to the kind of instance where the Court has traditionally found the First Amendment wary of content-based laws, namely, in cases of viewpoint discrimination. "Content-based laws merit this protection because they present, albeit sometimes in a subtler form, the same dangers as laws that regulate speech based on viewpoint." Accordingly, "limiting speech based on its 'topic' or 'subject' " can favor "those who do not want to disturb the status quo." But the mine run of disclosure requirements do nothing of that sort. They simply alert the public about child seat belt laws, the location of stairways, and the process to have their garbage collected, among other things.

Precedent does not require a test such as the majority's. Rather, in saying the Act is not a longstanding health and safety law, the Court substitutes its own approach—without a defining standard—for an approach that was reasonably clear. Historically, the Court has been wary of claims that regulation of business activity, particularly health-related activity, violates the Constitution. Ever since this Court departed from the approach it set forth in *Lochner v. New York*, 198 U.S. 45 (1905), ordinary economic and social legislation has been thought to raise little constitutional concern. As Justice Brandeis wrote, typically this Court's function in such cases "is only to determine the reasonableness of the Legislature's belief in the existence of evils and in the effectiveness of the remedy provided."

The Court has taken this same respectful approach to economic and social legislation when a First Amendment claim like the claim present here is at issue. See, *e.g.*, *Zauderer* (upholding reasonable disclosure requirements for attorneys); cf. *Central Hudson* (applying intermediate scrutiny to other restrictions on commercial speech); *In re R.M.J.*, 455 U.S. 191 (1982) (no First Amendment protection for misleading or deceptive commercial speech). But see *Sorrell v. IMS Health* (striking down regulation of pharmaceutical drug-related information).

Even during the *Lochner* era, when this Court struck down numerous economic regulations concerning industry, this Court was careful to defer to state legislative judgments concerning the medical profession. The Court took the view that a State may condition the practice of medicine on any number of requirements, and physicians, in exchange for following those reasonable requirements, could receive a license to practice medicine from the State. Medical professionals do not, generally speaking, have a right to use the Constitution as a weapon allowing them rigorously to control the content of those reasonable conditions. In the name of the First Amendment, the majority today treads into territory where the pre-New Deal, as well as the post-New Deal, Court refused to go.

The Court, in justification, refers to widely accepted First Amendment goals, such as the need to protect the Nation from laws that "suppress unpopular ideas or information" or inhibit the "marketplace of ideas in which truth will ultimately prevail." The concurrence highlights similar First Amendment interests. I, too, value this role that the First Amendment plays—in an appropriate case. But here, the majority enunciates a general test that reaches far beyond the area where this Court has examined laws closely in the service of those goals. And, in suggesting that heightened scrutiny applies to much economic and social legislation, the majority pays those First Amendment goals a serious disservice through dilution. Using the First Amendment to strike down economic and social laws that legislatures long would have thought themselves free to enact will, for the American public, obscure, not clarify, the true value of protecting freedom of speech.

The majority contends that the disclosure here is unrelated to a "medical procedure," unlike that in *Casey*, and so the State has no reason to inform a woman about alternatives to childbirth (or, presumably, the health risks of childbirth). Really? No one doubts that choosing an abortion is a medical procedure that involves certain health risks. But the same is true of carrying a child to term and giving birth. That is why prenatal care often involves testing for anemia, infections, measles, chicken pox, genetic disorders, diabetes, pneumonia, urinary tract infections, preeclampsia, and hosts of other medical conditions. Childbirth itself, directly or through pain management, risks harms of various kinds, some connected with caesarean or surgery-related deliveries, some related to more ordinary methods of delivery. Indeed, nationwide "childbirth is 14 times more likely than abortion to result in" the woman's death. Health considerations do not favor disclosure of alternatives and risks associated with the latter but not those associated with the former.

In any case, informed consent principles apply more broadly than only to discrete "medical procedures." Prescription drug labels warn patients of risks even though taking prescription drugs may not be considered a "medical procedure." In California, clinics that screen for breast cancer must post a sign in their offices notifying patients that, if they are diagnosed with breast cancer, their doctor must provide "a written summary of alternative efficacious methods of treatment," a notification that does not relate to the screening procedure at issue. If even these disclosures fall outside the majority's cramped view of *Casey* and informed consent, it undoubtedly would invalidate the many other disclosures that are routine in the medical context as well.

There is no basis for finding the State's interest "hypothetical." The legislature heard that information-related delays in qualified healthcare negatively affect women seeking to terminate their pregnancies as well as women carrying their pregnancies to term, with delays in qualified prenatal care causing life-long health problems for infants. Even without such testimony, it is "self-evident" that patients might think they are receiving qualified medical care when they enter facilities that collect health information, perform obstetric ultrasounds or sonograms, diagnose pregnancy, and provide counseling about pregnancy options or other prenatal care. The State's conclusion to that effect is certainly reasonable.

Points for Discussion

1. **Trampling free speech rights or garden-variety social and economic regulation?** Notice the wildly different views of the majority and the dissenters in this case, which is referred to as *NIFLA*. The majority saw the case through the prism of the First Amendment's compelled speech line of cases, treating California's law as a deep affront to the First Amendment. In contrast, the dissenters seemed to view the case as not implicating any significant First Amendment interests at all, treating it instead as the sort of routine social and economic legislation that modern constitutional law generally regards as subject to highly deferential review.

Justice Stephen Breyer, in his dissent, goes so far as to suggest that the majority is reviving the discredited interventionist approach associated most infamously with *Lochner v. New York*. The division reflects a fundamental divide in modern constitutional law. Following the New Deal, the Court essentially split judicial review into two tracks: a highly deferential rational basis standard of review for economic and social legislation—a standard under which the government almost always prevails—and a much more rigorous standard of review (often articulated as "strict scrutiny") when legislation is based on a suspect classification or regulates fundamental rights, such as freedom of speech. The majority treated California's law as landing on the regulation of the fundamental rights side of the spectrum. The dissenters saw it as ordinary economic and social legislation akin to consumer protection or professional regulation laws. Which view do you find more persuasive?

2. **Should "professional speech" receive less protection than other forms of speech?** Note how in *NIFLA* the compelled speech line of First Amendment law intersected with the nascent "professional speech" doctrine, which multiple federal courts of appeal had begun to recognize. Yet the Court in *NIFLA* repudiated the existence of the doctrine. Does *NIFLA* in turn suggest that the First Amendment may limit what sorts of activities the government may subject to licensure? No one doubts that the government may require a license to practice law or medicine or to do business as an electrician or plumber. Yet certainly the government could not require a license to work as an author, journalist, philosopher, or theologian. What about occupations "on the cusp"? The government could not require a license to write a diet book. It might be able to require a license to charge customers for individualized diet and nutrition advice. Yet imagine that a person maintains a blog providing free nutrition and diet information to the public at large and to individuals, using the platform to advertise products or sell diet books.

2. Compelling Financial Support for Someone Else's Message: Can People Be Forced to Pay for Messages They Oppose?

Congratulations! You have completed law school and passed a state's bar exam. Let's assume that you are living in California, which has an "integrated bar," meaning that the state's bar association is a creation of state law and that lawyers practicing in California must join the association and pay annual dues. You might not like paying the annual dues, but you acknowledge that the Bar Association plays an important role in regulating the legal profession and in facilitating public access to legal services. But you also discover that the Bar Association takes positions on controversial ideological and political issues and engages in lobbying efforts to advance the association's ideological agenda. You further learn that you disagree with much of the association's ideological agenda. Can you be forced, as a condition of practicing law, to pay dues to an organization that uses your money to finance political activities you disapprove of?

That was the issue raised in *Keller v. State Bar of California*, 496 U.S. 1 (1990), in which the Court held that the state bar could compel its members to pay for the association's ordinary work in regulating the legal profession but could not compel members to pay for the association's unrelated ideological and political activities. To reach this result, the Court recognized that there is not only a right not to speak but also a right not to subsidize the speech of others.

A similar issue has played out in the context of unions representing government employees. In some states, state or local laws provide that if one union acquires the support of the majority of employees, the union will be authorized to represent all the employees when it bargains with the employer. Employees are not required to join the union, even though they will enjoy the benefits of the union-negotiated contract. But while employees are not required to join the union, they are often required to pay an "agency fee" to the union.

In *Abood v. Detroit Board of Education*, 431 U.S. 209 (1977), government employees who did not join the union were required to pay agency fees that were equivalent to the union dues. In responding to the claims of non-union employees who objected to being compelled to pay the agency fees, the Court reached a "Solomonic" solution akin to the one struck by the Court a decade later in *Keller*. The Court held that the employees could be required to pay for the costs of the union's collective bargaining efforts because they were the beneficiaries of those efforts, but they could not be required to pay for the union's unrelated ideological activities.

Abood was the law of the land until the Court issued the following decision.

Janus v. American Federation of State, County & Municipal Employees, Council 31

Supreme Court of the United States, 2018
585 U.S. 878

JUSTICE ALITO delivered the opinion of the Court.

Under Illinois law, public employees are forced to subsidize a union, even if they choose not to join and strongly object to the positions the union takes in collective bargaining and related activities. We conclude that this arrangement violates the free speech rights of nonmembers by compelling them to subsidize private speech on matters of substantial public concern.

We upheld a similar law in *Abood*, and we recognize the importance of following precedent unless there are strong reasons for not doing so. But there are very strong reasons in this case. Fundamental free speech rights are at stake. *Abood* was poorly reasoned. It has led to practical problems and abuse. It is inconsistent with other First Amendment cases and has been undermined by more recent decisions. Developments since *Abood* was handed down have shed new light on the issue of agency fees, and no reliance interests on the part of public-sector unions are sufficient to justify the perpetuation of the free speech violations that *Abood* has countenanced for the past 41 years. *Abood* is therefore overruled.

As illustrated by the record in this case, unions charge nonmembers, not just for the cost of collective bargaining per se, but also for many other supposedly connected activities. Here, the nonmembers were told that they had to pay for lobbying, social and recreational activities, advertising, membership meetings and conventions, and litigation, as well as other unspecified services that "may ultimately inure to the benefit of the members of the local bargaining unit." The total chargeable amount for nonmembers was 78.06% of full union dues.

Petitioner Mark Janus is employed by the Illinois Department of Healthcare and Family Services as a child support specialist. The employees in his unit are among the 35,000 public employees in Illinois who are represented by respondent American Federation of State, County, and Municipal Employees, Council 31. Janus refused to join the Union because he opposes "many of the public policy positions that it advocates," including the positions it takes in collective bargaining. Janus believes that the Union's "behavior in bargaining does not appreciate the current fiscal crises in Illinois and does not reflect his best interests or the interests of Illinois citizens." Therefore, if he had the choice, he would not pay any fees or otherwise subsidize the Union. Under his unit's collective-bargaining agreement, however, he was required to pay an agency fee of $44.58 per month—which would amount to about $535 per year.

We first consider whether *Abood*'s holding is consistent with standard First Amendment principles.

The First Amendment, made applicable to the States by the Fourteenth Amendment, forbids abridgment of the freedom of speech. We have held time and again that freedom of speech "includes both the right to speak freely and the right to refrain from speaking at all." The right to eschew association for expressive purposes is likewise protected. As Justice Jackson memorably put it: "If there is any fixed star in our constitutional constellation, it is that no official, high or petty, can prescribe what shall be orthodox in politics, nationalism, religion, or other matters of opinion or *force citizens to confess by word or act their faith therein*." *West Virginia Bd. of Ed. v. Barnette* (emphasis added).

Compelling individuals to mouth support for views they find objectionable violates that cardinal constitutional command, and in most contexts, any such effort would be universally condemned. Suppose, for example, that the State of Illinois required all residents to sign a document expressing support for a particular set of positions on controversial public issues—say, the platform of one of the major political parties. No one, we trust, would seriously argue that the First Amendment permits this.

Perhaps because such compulsion so plainly violates the Constitution, most of our free speech cases have involved restrictions on what can be said, rather than laws compelling speech. But measures compelling speech are at least as threatening.

Free speech serves many ends. It is essential to our democratic form of government, and it furthers the search for truth, Whenever the Federal Government or a State prevents individuals from saying what they think on important matters or compels them to voice ideas with which they disagree, it undermines these ends.

When speech is compelled, however, additional damage is done. In that situation, individuals are coerced into betraying their convictions. Forcing free and independent individuals to endorse ideas they find objectionable is always demeaning, and for this reason, one of our landmark free speech cases said that a law commanding "involuntary affirmation" of objected-to beliefs would require "even more immediate and urgent grounds" than a law demanding silence.

Compelling a person to *subsidize* the speech of other private speakers raises similar First Amendment concerns. As Jefferson famously put it, "to compel a man to furnish contributions of money for the propagation of opinions which he disbelieves and abhors is sinful and tyrannical." We have therefore recognized that a "significant impingement on First Amendment rights" occurs when public employees are required to provide financial support for a union that "takes many positions during collective bargaining that have powerful political and civic consequences."

In *Abood*, the main defense of the agency-fee arrangement was that it served the State's interest in "labor peace." By "labor peace," the *Abood* Court meant avoidance of the conflict and disruption that it envisioned would occur if the employees in a unit were represented by more than one union. In such a situation, the Court predicted, "inter-union rivalries" would foster "dissension within the work force," and the employer could face "conflicting demands from different unions." Confusion would ensue if the employer entered into and attempted to "enforce two or more agreements specifying different terms and conditions of employment." And a settlement with one union would be "subject to attack from a rival labor organization."

We assume that "labor peace," in this sense of the term, is a compelling state interest, but *Abood* cited no evidence that the pandemonium it imagined would result if agency fees were not allowed, and it is now clear that *Abood*'s fears were unfounded. The *Abood* Court assumed that designation of a union as the exclusive representative of all the employees in a unit and the exaction of agency fees are inextricably linked, but that is simply not true.

In addition to the promotion of "labor peace," *Abood* cited "the risk of free riders" as justification for agency fees. Respondents and some of their *amici* endorse this reasoning, contending that agency fees are needed to prevent nonmembers from enjoying the benefits of union representation without shouldering the costs.

Petitioner strenuously objects to this free-rider label. He argues that he is not a free rider on a bus headed for a destination that he wishes to reach but is more like a person shanghaied for an unwanted voyage.

Whichever description fits the majority of public employees who would not subsidize a union if given the option, avoiding free riders is not a compelling interest. As we have noted, "free-rider arguments are generally insufficient to overcome First Amendment objections." To hold otherwise across the board would have startling consequences. Many private groups speak out with the objective of obtaining government action that will have the effect of benefiting nonmembers. May all those who are thought to benefit from such efforts be compelled to subsidize this speech?

Suppose that a particular group lobbies or speaks out on behalf of what it thinks are the needs of senior citizens or veterans or physicians, to take just a few examples. Could the government require that all seniors, veterans, or doctors pay for that service even if they object? It has never been thought that this is permissible. "Private speech often furthers the interests of nonspeakers," but "that does not alone empower the state to compel the speech to be paid for." In simple terms, the First Amendment does not permit the government to compel a person to pay for another party's speech just because the government thinks that the speech furthers the interests of the person who does not want to pay.

Those supporting agency fees contend that the situation here is different because unions are statutorily required to "represent the interests of all public employees in the unit," whether or not they are union members. Why might this matter?

We can think of two possible arguments. It might be argued that a State has a compelling interest in requiring the payment of agency fees because (1) unions would otherwise be unwilling to represent nonmembers or (2) it would be fundamentally unfair to require unions to provide fair representation for nonmembers if nonmembers were not required to pay. Neither of these arguments is sound.

First, it is simply not true that unions will refuse to serve as the exclusive representative of all employees in the unit if they are not given agency fees. As noted, unions represent millions of public employees in jurisdictions that do not permit agency fees. No union is ever compelled to seek that designation. On the contrary, designation as exclusive representative is avidly sought. Why is this so?

Even without agency fees, designation as the exclusive representative confers many benefits. As noted, that status gives the union a privileged place in negotiations over wages, benefits, and working conditions. Not only is the union given the exclusive right to speak for all the employees in collective bargaining, but the employer is required by state law to listen to and to bargain in good faith with only that union. Designation as exclusive representative thus "results in a tremendous increase in the power" of the union.

In addition, a union designated as exclusive representative is often granted special privileges, such as obtaining information about employees, and having dues and fees deducted directly from employee wages. The collective-bargaining agreement in this case guarantees a long list of additional privileges.

These benefits greatly outweigh any extra burden imposed by the duty of providing fair representation for nonmembers.

In any event, whatever unwanted burden is imposed by the representation of nonmembers in disciplinary matters can be eliminated "through means significantly less restrictive of associational freedoms" than the imposition of agency fees.

In sum, we do not see any reason to treat the free-rider interest any differently in the agency-fee context than in any other First Amendment context. We therefore hold that agency fees cannot be upheld on free-rider grounds.

The principal defense of *Abood* advanced by respondents and the dissent is based on our decision in *Pickering*, which held that a school district violated the First Amendment by firing a teacher for writing a letter critical of the school administration. Under *Pickering* and later cases in the same line, employee speech is largely unprotected if it is part of what the employee is paid to do, *see Garcetti v. Ceballos*, or if it involved a matter of only private concern, *see Connick*. On the other hand, when a public employee speaks as a citizen on a matter of public concern, the employee's speech is protected unless "the interest of the state, as an employer, in promoting the efficiency of the public services it performs through its employees outweighs the interests of the employee, as a citizen, in commenting upon matters of public concern."

We see no good reason, at this late date, to try to shoehorn *Abood* into the *Pickering* framework. Even if we were to apply some form of *Pickering*, Illinois' agency-fee arrangement would not survive.

Respondents begin by suggesting that union speech in collective-bargaining and grievance proceedings should be treated like the employee speech in *Garcetti*, *i.e.*, as speech "pursuant to an employee's official duties.

This argument distorts collective bargaining and grievance adjustment beyond recognition. When an employee engages in speech that is part of the employee's job duties, the employee's words are really the words of the employer. The employee is effectively the employer's spokesperson. But when a union negotiates with the employer or represents employees in disciplinary proceedings, the union speaks for the employees, not the employer. Otherwise, the employer would be negotiating with itself and disputing its own actions. That is not what anybody understands to be happening.

What is more, if the union's speech is really the employer's speech, then the employer could dictate what the union says. Unions, we trust, would be appalled by such a suggestion. For these reasons, *Garcetti* is totally inapposite here.

For the reasons given above, we conclude that public-sector agency-shop arrangements violate the First Amendment, and *Abood* erred in concluding otherwise.

Abood was wrongly decided and is now overruled.

JUSTICE SOTOMAYOR, dissenting.

I join Justice Kagan's dissent in full. Although I joined the majority in *Sorrell v. IMS Health*, I disagree with the way that this Court has since interpreted and applied that opinion. See, e.g., *NIFLA*. Having seen the troubling development in First Amendment jurisprudence over the years, both in this Court and in lower courts, I agree fully with Justice Kagan that *Sorrell*—in the way it has been read by this Court—has allowed courts to "wield the First Amendment in an aggressive way" just as the majority does today.

JUSTICE KAGAN, with whom JUSTICE GINSBURG, JUSTICE BREYER, and JUSTICE SOTOMAYOR join, dissenting.

For over 40 years, *Abood* struck a stable balance between public employees' First Amendment rights and government entities' interests in running their workforces as they thought proper. Under that decision, a government entity could require public employees to pay a fair share of the cost that a union incurs when negotiating on their behalf over terms of employment. But no part of that fair-share payment could go to any of the union's political or ideological activities.

That holding fit comfortably with this Court's general framework for evaluating claims that a condition of public employment violates the First Amendment. The

Court's decisions have long made plain that government entities have substantial latitude to regulate their employees' speech—especially about terms of employment—in the interest of operating their workplaces effectively. *Abood* allowed governments to do just that. While protecting public employees' expression about non-workplace matters, the decision enabled a government to advance important managerial interests—by ensuring the presence of an exclusive employee representative to bargain with. Far from an "anomaly," the *Abood* regime was a paradigmatic example of how the government can regulate speech in its capacity as an employer.

Not any longer. Today, the Court succeeds in its 6-year campaign to reverse *Abood.*

But basic economic theory shows why a government would think that agency fees are necessary for exclusive representation to work. What ties the two together, as *Abood* recognized, is the likelihood of free-riding when fees are absent. Remember that once a union achieves exclusive-representation status, the law compels it to fairly represent all workers in the bargaining unit, whether or not they join or contribute to the union. Because of that legal duty, the union cannot give special advantages to its own members. And that in turn creates a collective action problem of nightmarish proportions. Everyone—not just those who oppose the union, but also those who back it—has an economic incentive to withhold dues; only altruism or loyalty—as against financial self-interest—can explain why an employee would pay the union for its services. And so emerged *Abood*'s rule allowing fair-share agreements: That rule ensured that a union would receive sufficient funds, despite its legally imposed disability, to effectively carry out its duties as exclusive representative of the government's employees.

In many cases over many decades, this Court has addressed how the First Amendment applies when the government, acting not as sovereign but as employer, limits its workers' speech. Those decisions have granted substantial latitude to the government, in recognition of its significant interests in managing its workforce so as to best serve the public. *Abood* fit neatly with that caselaw, in both reasoning and result. Indeed, its reversal today creates a significant anomaly—an exception, applying to union fees alone, from the usual rules governing public employees' speech.

In striking the proper balance between employee speech rights and managerial interests, the Court has long applied a test originating in *Pickering*. That case arose out of an individual employment action: the firing of a public school teacher. As we later described the *Pickering* inquiry, the Court first asks whether the employee "spoke as a citizen on a matter of public concern." *Garcetti*. If she did not—but rather spoke as an employee on a workplace matter—she has no "possibility of a First Amendment claim": A public employer can curtail her speech just as a private one could. But if she did speak as a citizen on a public matter, the public employer must demonstrate "an adequate justification for treating the employee differently from any other member of the general public." The government, that is, needs to show that legitimate workplace interests lay behind the speech regulation.

Abood coheres with that framework.

Abood thus dovetailed with the Court's usual attitude in First Amendment cases toward the regulation of public employees' speech. That attitude is one of respect—even solicitude—for the government's prerogatives as an employer. So long as the government is acting as an employer—rather than exploiting the employment relationship for other ends—it has a wide berth, comparable to that of a private employer. And when the regulated expression concerns the terms and conditions of employment—the very stuff of the employment relationship—the government really cannot lose. There, managerial interests are obvious and strong. And so government employees are . . . just employees, even though they work for the government. Except that today the government does lose, in a first for the law. Now, the government can constitutionally adopt all policies regulating core workplace speech in pursuit of managerial goals—save this single one.

There is no sugarcoating today's opinion. The majority overthrows a decision entrenched in this Nation's law—and in its economic life—for over 40 years. As a result, it prevents the American people, acting through their state and local officials, from making important choices about workplace governance. And it does so by weaponizing the First Amendment, in a way that unleashes judges, now and in the future, to intervene in economic and regulatory policy.

The majority has overruled *Abood* for no exceptional or special reason, but because it never liked the decision. It has overruled *Abood* because it wanted to.

Because, that is, it wanted to pick the winning side in what should be—and until now, has been—an energetic policy debate. Some state and local governments (and the constituents they serve) think that stable unions promote healthy labor relations and thereby improve the provision of services to the public. Other state and local governments (and their constituents) think, to the contrary, that strong unions impose excessive costs and impair those services. Americans have debated the pros and cons for many decades—in large part, by deciding whether to use fair-share arrangements. Yesterday, 22 States were on one side, 28 on the other (ignoring a couple of in-betweeners). Today, that healthy—that democratic—debate ends. The majority has adjudged who should prevail. Indeed, the majority is bursting with pride over what it has accomplished: Now those 22 States, it crows, "can follow the model of the federal government and 28 other States."

And maybe most alarming, the majority has chosen the winners by turning the First Amendment into a sword, and using it against workaday economic and regulatory policy. Today is not the first time the Court has wielded the First Amendment in such an aggressive way. *See, e.g.*, *NIFLA* (invalidating a law requiring medical and counseling facilities to provide relevant information to users); *Sorrell v. IMS Health* (striking down a law that restricted pharmacies from selling various data). And it threatens not to be the last. Speech is everywhere—a part of every human activity (employment, health care, securities trading, you name it). For that reason, almost all economic and regulatory policy affects or touches speech. So the majority's road runs long. And at every stop are black-robed rulers overriding citizens' choices. The First Amendment was meant for better things. It was meant not to undermine but to protect democratic governance—including over the role of public-sector unions.

Points for Discussion

1. **How does the division among the justices in *Janus* parallel the division in *NIFLA*? To what extent is the division in *Janus* even deeper?** Note how the majority saw the forced support for the union as a serious affront to the First Amendment, while the dissenters saw it as ordinary economic legislation. Justice Elena Kagan's dissent has become famous in modern debates over the First Amendment for the colorful turn of phrase she used to criticize the majority, accusing it of "weaponizing the First Amendment." There was a time, in the 1960s and 1970s, when strong "pro-free speech" positions were commonly associated with liberal members of the Court, and positions favoring the government's power to regulate free speech were commonly associated with conservatives. Note how now the pattern often appears to have changed, with the conservatives adopting strong pro-free speech positions, and liberals favoring the government's power to regulate speech. *See generally* Louis Michael Seidman, *Can Free Speech Be Progressive?*, 118 Colum. L. Rev. 2219 (2018) (contending that free speech took a "sharp right turn" after the liberal Warren Court era and "became a sword used by people at the apex of the American power hierarchy," citing cases like *Citizens United*, *Janus*, *R.A.V.*, *Rumsfeld*, and *Boy Scouts of America*, a case you'll be reading later in this chapter).

2. **Does the reasoning in *Janus* square with the reasoning in the Court's Establishment Clause jurisprudence?** Justice Samuel Alito's majority opinion in *Janus* bolsters its argument against compelling people to subsidize speech they oppose with a quote from Thomas Jefferson: "To compel a man to furnish contributions of money for the propagation of opinions which he disbelieves and abhors is sinful and tyrannical." This quote is from a Bill for Establishing Religious Freedom, which was drafted by Jefferson and enacted by the Virginia General Assembly in 1786, five years before the First Amendment was ratified. The line quoted by Justice Alito was not discussing the compelled subsidization of speech in general, but rather the much more specific issue of compelling people to subsidize religion

against their will. For example, Section II of the bill states, "We the General Assembly of Virginia do enact that no man shall be compelled to frequent or support any religious worship, place, or ministry whatsoever."

In Chapter 19, we will study the Supreme Court's Establishment Clause jurisprudence, which wrestles with the question of how much separation between church and state is required by the Constitution. In that context, both Justice Alito and the other justices who joined his opinion in *Janus* have repeatedly held that, if the government offers a benefit to secular programs, it must also offer the same benefit to religious institutions. A dramatic example of that is *Espinoza v. Montana Department of Revenue*, 140 S. Ct. 2246 (2020), in which the Court held that Montana could not offer tuition assistance for private secular schools without also offering tuition assistance for private religious schools. Chief Justice John Roberts, who joined Justice Alito's majority opinion in *Janus*, wrote the majority opinion in *Espinoza*, which was joined by Justice Alito as well as by Justices Clarence Thomas and Neil Gorsuch, both of whom joined in Justice Alito's *Janus* opinion.

Justice Stephen Breyer, who joined Justice Kagan's vehement dissent in *Janus*, wrote his own vehement dissent in *Espinoza*. He quoted the exact same line from Jefferson's Bill for Establishing Religious Freedom that Justice Alito quoted in *Janus*, about how it is "sinful and tyrannical" to compel people to support opinions they disbelieve. Justice Breyer said there was "no meaningful difference" between the concerns raised by Jefferson in his bill and those raised by "taxpayer support for scholarships to religious schools." "In both cases," Justice Breyer said, this "would compel taxpayers to support the propagation of opinions on matters of religion with which they may disagree, by teachers whom they have not chosen."

Who has the better argument here? The justices who believe that it is unconstitutional to compel non-union employees to pay agency fees but constitutional to use taxpayer money to pay for religious education, or the justices who believe the opposite? How do you think Thomas Jefferson would have answered that question? You can return to this question when you study the cases concerning financial support for religion in Chapter 19.

3. **When is the exercise of judicial power appropriate, and when is it an abuse of power?** In Chapter 1, we discussed how the power of judicial review—the power of judges to declare laws unconstitutional—creates a conundrum: why, in a democracy, should unelected judges be able to overturn laws enacted by the people's elected representatives? The divisions one encounters in constitutional law, particularly the heated rhetoric in majority and dissenting opinions, are often driven by the justices' differing views over when it is appropriate for judges to override democratically enacted laws.

Justice Kagan's dissenting opinion in *Janus* is a prime example of one justice accusing others of abusing their power to override policies made by elected officials. The majority opinion, she says, "prevents the American people, acting through their state and local officials, from making important choices about workplace governance." Justice Kagan strongly sounds the theme that the majority has subverted the democratic process, describing the justices in the majority as "black-robed rulers overriding citizens' choices."

In other arenas of constitutional law, conservative justices have leveled the same critique against Supreme Court decisions adopting progressive liberal positions. Consider the Court's landmark decision in *Obergefell v. Hodges*, 576 U.S. 644 (2015), widely celebrated for recognizing a constitutional right for same-sex couples to marry. Chief Justice Roberts and three conservative members of the Court dissented. Note how the following excerpt from Chief Justice Roberts' dissenting opinion in *Obergefell* so closely tracks the structure and language of Justice Kagan's lament in *Janus*:

> Today, the Court takes the extraordinary step of ordering every State to license and recognize same-sex marriage. Many people will rejoice at this decision, and I begrudge none their celebration. But for those who believe in a government of laws, not of men, the majority's approach is deeply disheartening. Supporters of same-sex marriage have achieved considerable success persuading their fellow citizens—through the democratic process—to adopt their view. That ends today. Five lawyers have closed the debate and enacted their own vision of marriage as a matter of constitutional law. Stealing this issue from the people will for many cast a cloud over same-sex marriage, making a dramatic social change that much more difficult to accept.

You Be the Law Clerk!

Solve the riddle of judicial review in 200 words or fewer!

Imagine that you clerk for a newly appointed Supreme Court justice. A controversial free speech case is pending before the Court. The briefs of both parties, and amicus briefs filed by scores of others, make strong arguments for extending current First Amendment doctrine to invalidate laws adopted by Congress and about half the American states. All sides disagree on what to make of the colonial experience and whether such laws would or would not have been supported by the Constitution's Framers. The division is in part fueled by the fact that the laws involve the regulation of speech on the internet, which would have been entirely foreign to anything in the Framers' experience. The newly appointed justice is a person with impeccable legal credentials, but relatively little familiarity with modern constitutional law. (This is not unprecedented. Chief Justice Earl Warren was the governor of California before he was appointed to the Court, with little constitutional law experience. Justice Lewis Powell was a famous corporate lawyer in the private sector and president of the American Bar Association, but no constitutional law expert.) Your justice asks you to write a memorandum explaining to her when it is generally appropriate to intervene and overrule laws that are widely adopted through a democratic process, and when instead the Court should defer to the results of a democratic process. The justice asks this against the backdrop of the First Amendment case pending before her but invites you to borrow from other areas of constitutional law to the extent they may usefully inform your recommendations.

3. Compelled Speech Versus Civil Rights: Requiring a Speaker to Convey an Unwanted Message

One of the most controversial areas of the Supreme Court's compelled speech jurisprudence concerns the intersection of the First Amendment right not to speak and the enforcement of antidiscrimination laws. In the typical case, a person claims that the First Amendment shields her from having to comply with a civil rights law because doing so would force her to convey a message that she does not wish to convey.

You will encounter a similar issue when you study freedom of association later in this chapter. In that context, groups of people who associate for expressive purposes are typically claiming that a civil rights law is forcing their association to accept members who will undermine the association's message.

Hurley v. Irish-American Gay, Lesbian & Bisexual Group of Boston

Supreme Court of the United States, 1995
515 U.S. 557

JUSTICE SOUTER delivered the opinion of the Court.

The issue in this case is whether Massachusetts may require private citizens who organize a parade to include among the marchers a group imparting a message the organizers do not wish to convey. We hold that such a mandate violates the First Amendment.

March 17 is set aside for two celebrations in South Boston. As early as 1737, some people in Boston observed the feast of the apostle to Ireland, and since 1776 the day has marked the evacuation of royal troops and Loyalists from the city, prompted by the guns captured at Ticonderoga and set up on Dorchester Heights under General Washington's command. Washington himself reportedly drew on the earlier tradition in choosing "St. Patrick" as the response to "Boston," the password used in the colonial lines on evacuation day. Although the General Court of Massachusetts did not officially designate March 17 as Evacuation Day until 1938, the City Council of Boston had previously sponsored public celebrations of Evacuation Day, including notable commemorations on the centennial in 1876, and on the 125th anniversary in 1901, with its parade, salute, concert, and fireworks display.

The tradition of formal sponsorship by the city came to an end in 1947, however, when Mayor James Michael Curley himself granted authority to organize and conduct the St. Patrick's Day-Evacuation Day Parade to the petitioner South Boston Allied War Veterans Council, an unincorporated association of individuals elected from various South Boston veterans groups.

In 1992, a number of gay, lesbian, and bisexual descendants of the Irish immigrants joined together with other supporters to form the respondent organization, GLIB, to march in the parade as a way to express pride in their Irish heritage as openly gay, lesbian, and bisexual individuals, to demonstrate that there are such men and women among those so descended, and to express their solidarity with like individuals who sought to march in New York's St. Patrick's Day Parade.

In 1993, after the Council refused to admit GLIB to the upcoming parade, the organization and some of its members filed this suit against the Council, alleging violations of the state public accommodations law, which prohibits "any distinction, discrimination or restriction on account of sexual orientation relative to the admission of any person to, or treatment in any place of public accommodation, resort or amusement."

The trial court ruled that the parade fell within the statutory definition of a public accommodation. The court held that because the statute did not mandate inclusion of GLIB but only prohibited discrimination based on sexual orientation, any infringement on the Council's right to expressive association was only "incidental" and "no greater than necessary to accomplish the statute's legitimate purpose" of eradicating discrimination. The Supreme Judicial Court of Massachusetts affirmed.

We granted certiorari to determine whether the requirement to admit a parade contingent expressing a message not of the private organizers' own choosing violates the First Amendment. We hold that it does and reverse.

If there were no reason for a group of people to march from here to there except to reach a destination, they could make the trip without expressing any message beyond the fact of the march itself. Some people might call such a procession a parade, but it would not be much of one. Real "parades are public dramas of social relations, and in them performers define who can be a social actor and what subjects and ideas are available for communication and consideration."

The protected expression that inheres in a parade is not limited to its banners and songs, however, for the Constitution looks beyond written or spoken words as mediums of expression. Noting that "symbolism is a primitive but effective way of communicating ideas," our cases have recognized that the First Amendment shields such acts as saluting a flag (and refusing to do so), wearing an armband to protest a war, displaying a red flag, and even "marching, walking or parading" in uniforms displaying the swastika. As some of these examples show, a narrow, succinctly articulable message is not a condition of constitutional protection, which if confined to expressions conveying a "particularized message," would never reach the unquestionably shielded painting of Jackson Pollock, music of Arnold Schoenberg, or Jabberwocky verse of Lewis Carroll.

"Since all speech inherently involves choices of what to say and what to leave unsaid," one important manifestation of the principle of free speech is that one who chooses to speak may also decide "what not to say." Although the State may at times "prescribe what shall be orthodox in commercial advertising" by requiring the dissemination of "purely factual and uncontroversial information," *Zauderer*, outside that context it may not compel affirmance of a belief with which the speaker disagrees. Indeed this general rule, that the speaker has the right to tailor the speech, applies not only to expressions of value, opinion, or endorsement, but equally to statements of fact the speaker would rather avoid, subject, perhaps, to the permissive law of defamation. Nor is the rule's benefit restricted to the press, being enjoyed by business corporations generally and by ordinary people engaged in unsophisticated expression as well as by professional publishers. Its point is simply the point of all speech protection, which is to shield just those choices of content that in someone's eyes are misguided, or even hurtful.

Although GLIB's point (like the Council's) is not wholly articulate, a contingent marching behind the organization's banner would at least bear witness to the fact that some Irish are gay, lesbian, or bisexual, and the presence of the organized marchers would suggest their view that people of their sexual orientations have as much claim to unqualified social acceptance as heterosexuals and indeed as members of parade units organized around other identifying characteristics. The parade's organizers may not believe these facts about Irish sexuality to be so, or they may object to unqualified social acceptance of gays and lesbians or have some other reason for wishing to keep GLIB's message out of the parade. But whatever the reason, it boils down to the choice of a speaker not to propound a particular point of view, and that choice is presumed to lie beyond the government's power to control. While the law is free to promote all sorts of conduct in place of harmful behavior, it is not free to interfere with speech for no better reason than promoting an approved message or discouraging a disfavored one, however enlightened either purpose may strike the government.

Our holding today rests not on any particular view about the Council's message but on the Nation's commitment to protect freedom of speech. Disapproval of a private speaker's statement does not legitimize use of the Commonwealth's power to compel the speaker to alter the message by including one more acceptable to others. Accordingly, the judgment of the Supreme Judicial Court is reversed, and the case is remanded for proceedings not inconsistent with this opinion.

Points for Discussion

1. **Are all parades created equal?** For First Amendment purposes, likely not. Parades in the United States are typically held on public streets, which are temporarily closed for the event. The street itself is a traditional public forum. When the government itself sponsors the parade, the parade might be considered an exercise in "government speech," which would allow the government to decide which groups to include and exclude. A city conducting a Martin Luther King Day parade could thus exclude a Ku Klux Klan group from marching, on the theory that the parade is government speech. On the other hand, the parade could conceivably be deemed a limited public forum, which would prevent the government from discriminating on the basis of viewpoint. If that is how the parade is treated, a city's effort to exclude the Klan could be vulnerable to attack as unconstitutional viewpoint discrimination. When the government "sublets" the street to a private organization to run the parade, however, the parade is no longer government speech or a public forum, but private speech being conducted within the public forum. A private civil rights group that is granted a permit to use the street for a Martin Luther King Day parade could not, under the authority of *Hurley*, be forced to accept the Klan group as a participant in the parade.

2. **Can the government outsource to avoid constitutional restrictions?** The *Hurley* case noted that Boston's St. Patrick's Day festivities and parade had long been sponsored by the City Council. In 1947, however, the mayor ended the formal sponsorship by delegating this authority to the South Boston Allied War Veterans Council. It was that group that refused to include GLIB in the St. Patrick's Day Parade.

In the previous Point for Discussion, it was noted that a government-sponsored parade, unlike a privately sponsored parade, will sometimes be subject to First Amendment restraints. The presence of restraints depends on whether the parade is characterized as government speech or a limited public forum. In the latter case, the government may not discriminate based on viewpoint. Let us assume that a city-sponsored St. Patrick's Day parade would be considered a limited public forum and that excluding GLIB would constitute unlawful viewpoint discrimination. Could the city in that instance avoid this constitutional restraint by outsourcing responsibility for the parade to a private party? In thinking about this issue, you might want to recall the material we studied in Chapter 3, including the *Manhattan Community Access Corp. v. Halleck* case, which considered whether a private entity that had been delegated a responsibility by the government should be treated as a private actor or a state actor.

303 Creative LLC v. Elenis

Supreme Court of the United States, 2023
600 U.S. 570

JUSTICE GORSUCH delivered the opinion of the Court.

Like many States, Colorado has a law forbidding businesses from engaging in discrimination when they sell goods and services to the public. Laws along these lines have done much to secure the civil rights of all Americans. But in this particular case Colorado does not just seek to ensure the sale of goods or services on equal terms. It seeks to use its law to compel an individual to create speech she does not believe. The question we face is whether that course violates the Free Speech Clause of the First Amendment.

Through her business, 303 Creative LLC, Lorie Smith offers website and graphic design, marketing advice, and social media management services. Recently, she decided to expand her offerings to include services for couples seeking websites for their weddings.

While Ms. Smith has laid the groundwork for her new venture, she has yet to carry out her plans. She worries that, if she does so, Colorado will force her to express views with which she disagrees. Ms. Smith provides her website and graphic services to customers regardless of their race, creed, sex, or sexual orientation. But she has never created expressions that contradict her own views for anyone—whether that means generating works that encourage violence, demean another person, or defy her religious beliefs by, say, promoting atheism. Ms. Smith does not wish to do otherwise now, but she worries Colorado has different plans. Specifically, she worries that, if she enters the wedding website business, the State will force her to convey messages

She has not entered wedding website business yet

inconsistent with her belief that marriage should be reserved to unions between one man and one woman. Ms. Smith acknowledges that her views about marriage may not be popular in all quarters. But, she asserts, the First Amendment's Free Speech Clause protects her from being compelled to speak what she does not believe. The Constitution, she insists, protects her right to differ.

The framers designed the Free Speech Clause of the First Amendment to protect the "freedom to think as you will and to speak as you think." By allowing all views to flourish, the framers understood, we may test and improve our own thinking both as individuals and as a Nation. For all these reasons, "if there is any fixed star in our constitutional constellation," it is the principle that the government may not interfere with "an uninhibited marketplace of ideas."

From time to time, governments in this country have sought to test these foundational principles. In *Barnette*, for example, the Court faced an effort by the State of West Virginia to force schoolchildren to salute the Nation's flag and recite the Pledge of Allegiance. If the students refused, the State threatened to expel them and fine or jail their parents. Some families objected on the ground that the State sought to compel their children to express views at odds with their faith as Jehovah's Witnesses. When the dispute arrived here, this Court offered a firm response. In seeking to compel students to salute the flag and recite a pledge, the Court held, state authorities had "transcended constitutional limitations on their powers."

A similar story unfolded in *Hurley*. There, veterans organizing a St. Patrick's Day parade in Boston refused to include a group of gay, lesbian, and bisexual individuals in their event. The group argued that Massachusetts's public accommodations statute entitled it to participate in the parade as a matter of law. Whatever state law may demand, this Court explained, the parade was constitutionally protected speech and requiring the veterans to include voices they wished to exclude would impermissibly require them to "alter the expressive content of their parade." The veterans' choice of what to say (and not say) might have been unpopular, but they had a First Amendment right to present their message undiluted by views they did not share.

Then there is *Boy Scouts of America v. Dale*, 530 U.S. 640 (2000). In that case, the Boy Scouts excluded James Dale, an assistant scoutmaster, from membership after learning he was gay. Mr. Dale argued that New Jersey's public accommodations law required the Scouts to reinstate him. The New Jersey Supreme Court sided with Mr. Dale, but again this Court reversed. The decision to exclude Mr. Dale may not have implicated pure speech, but this Court held that the Boy Scouts "is an expressive association" entitled to First Amendment protection. And, the Court found, forcing the Scouts to include Mr. Dale would "interfere with its choice not to propound a point of view contrary to its beliefs."

The Tenth Circuit held that the wedding websites Ms. Smith seeks to create qualify as "pure speech" under this Court's precedents. We agree. It is a conclusion that flows directly from the parties' stipulations. They have stipulated that Ms. Smith's websites promise to contain "images, words, symbols, and other modes of expression."

A hundred years ago, Ms. Smith might have furnished her services using pen and paper. Those services are no less protected speech today because they are conveyed with a "voice that resonates farther than it could from any soapbox." All manner of speech—from "pictures, films, paintings, drawings, and engravings," to "oral utterance and the printed word"—qualify for the First Amendment's protections; no less can hold true when it comes to speech like Ms. Smith's conveyed over the Internet.

We part ways with the Tenth Circuit only when it comes to the legal conclusions that follow. While that court thought Colorado could compel speech from Ms. Smith consistent with the Constitution, our First Amendment precedents laid out above teach otherwise. In *Hurley,* the Court found that Massachusetts impermissibly compelled speech in violation of the First Amendment. In *Dale,* the Court held that New Jersey intruded on the Boy Scouts' First Amendment rights when it tried to require the group to "propound a point of view contrary to its beliefs" by directing its membership choices. And in *Barnette,* this Court found impermissible coercion when West Virginia required schoolchildren to recite a pledge that contravened their convictions on threat of punishment or expulsion. Here, Colorado seeks to put Ms. Smith to a similar choice: If she wishes to speak, she must either speak as the State demands or face sanctions for expressing her own beliefs, sanctions that may include compulsory participation in "remedial training," filing periodic compliance reports as officials deem necessary, and paying monetary fines. Under our precedents, that is enough, more than enough, to represent an impermissible abridgment of the First Amendments right to speak freely.

Consider what a contrary approach would mean. Under Colorado's logic, the government may compel anyone who speaks for pay on a given topic to accept all commissions on that same topic—no matter the underlying message—if the topic somehow implicates a customer's statutorily protected trait. Taken seriously, that principle would allow the government to force all manner of artists, speechwriters, and others whose services involve speech to speak what they do not believe on pain of penalty. The government could require "an unwilling Muslim movie director to make a film with a Zionist message," or "an atheist muralist to accept a commission celebrating Evangelical zeal," so long as they would make films or murals for other members of the public with different messages. Equally, the government could force a male website designer married to another man to design websites for an organization that advocates against same-sex marriage. Countless other creative professionals, too, could be forced to choose between remaining silent, producing speech that violates their beliefs, or speaking their minds and incurring sanctions for doing so.

JUSTICE SOTOMAYOR, with whom JUSTICE KAGAN and JUSTICE JACKSON join, dissenting.

Five years ago, this Court recognized the "general rule" that religious and philosophical objections to gay marriage "do not allow business owners and other actors in the economy and in society to deny protected persons equal access to goods and services under a neutral and generally applicable public accommodations law." *Masterpiece Cakeshop, Ltd. v. Colorado Civil Rights Comm'n,* 584 U.S. 617 (2018). The Court also recognized the "serious stigma" that would result if "purveyors of goods and services who object to gay marriages for moral and religious reasons" were "allowed to put up signs saying 'no goods or services will be sold if they will be used for gay marriages.' "

Today, the Court, for the first time in its history, grants a business open to the public a constitutional right to refuse to serve members of a protected class. Specifically, the Court holds that the First Amendment exempts a website-design company from a state law that prohibits the company from denying wedding websites to same-sex couples if the company chooses to sell those websites to the public.

"What a difference five years makes." And not just at the Court. Around the country, there has been a backlash to the movement for liberty and equality for gender and sexual minorities. New forms of inclusion have been met with reactionary exclusion. This is heartbreaking. Sadly, it is also familiar. When the civil rights and women's rights movements sought equality in public life, some public establishments refused. Some even claimed, based on sincere religious beliefs, constitutional rights to discriminate. The brave Justices who once sat on this Court decisively rejected those claims.

Now the Court faces a similar test. A business open to the public seeks to deny gay and lesbian customers the full and equal enjoyment of its services based on the owner's religious belief that same-sex marriages are "false." The business argues, and a majority of the Court agrees, that because the business offers services that are customized and expressive, the Free Speech Clause of the First Amendment shields the business from a generally applicable law that prohibits discrimination in the sale of publicly available goods and services. That is wrong. Profoundly wrong. As I will explain, the law in question targets conduct, not speech, for regulation, and the act of discrimination has never constituted protected expression under the First Amendment. Our Constitution contains no right to refuse service to a disfavored group. I dissent.

Not only have public accommodations laws expanded to recognize more forms of unjust discrimination, such as discrimination based on race, sex, and disability, such laws have also expanded to include more goods and services as "public accommodations." What began with common inns, carriers, and smiths has grown to include restaurants, bars, movie theaters, sports arenas, retail stores, salons, gyms, hospitals, funeral homes, and transportation networks.

This broader scope, though more inclusive than earlier state public accommodations laws, is in keeping with the fundamental principle—rooted in the common law, but alive and blossoming in statutory law—that the duty to serve without unjust discrimination is owed to everyone, and it extends to any business that holds itself out as ready to serve the public. If you have ever taken advantage of a public business without being denied service because of who you are, then you have come to enjoy the dignity and freedom that this principle protects.

Lesbian, gay, bisexual, and transgender (LGBT) people, no less than anyone else, deserve that dignity and freedom. The movement for LGBT rights, and the resulting expansion of state and local laws to secure gender and sexual minorities' full and equal enjoyment of publicly available goods and services, is the latest chapter of this great American story.

LGBT people have existed for all of human history. And as sure as they have existed, others have sought to deny their existence, and to exclude them from public life. Those who would subordinate LGBT people have often done so with the backing of law. For most of American history, there were laws criminalizing same-sex intimacy. "Gays and lesbians were also prohibited from most government employment, barred from military service, excluded under immigration laws, targeted by police, and burdened in their rights to associate." "These policies worked to create and reinforce the belief that gay men and lesbians" constituted "an inferior class."

One significant change has been the addition of sexual orientation and gender identity to public accommodations laws. Yet for as long as public accommodations laws have been around, businesses have sought exemptions from them. The civil rights and women's liberation eras are prominent examples of this. Backlashes to race and sex equality gave rise to legal claims of rights to discriminate, including claims based on First Amendment freedoms of expression and association. This Court was unwavering in its rejection of those claims, as invidious discrimination "has never been accorded affirmative constitutional protections." In particular, the refusal to deal with or to serve a class of people is not an expressive interest protected by the First Amendment.

Opponents of the Civil Rights Act of 1964 objected that the law would force business owners to defy their beliefs. They argued that the Act would deny them "any freedom to speak or to act on the basis of their religious convictions or their deep-rooted preferences for associating or not associating with certain classifications of people." Congress rejected those arguments.

✓ ppl during civil rights used this arguement

Having failed to persuade Congress, opponents of Title II turned to the federal courts. In *Heart of Atlanta Motel v. United States*, 379 U.S. 241 (1964), one of several arguments made by the plaintiff motel owner was that Title II violated his Fifth Amendment due process rights by "taking away the personal liberty of an individual to run his business as he sees fit with respect to the selection and service of his customers." This Court disagreed, based on "a long line of cases" holding that "prohibition of racial discrimination in public accommodations" did not "interfere with personal liberty."

This Court has long held that "the First Amendment does not prevent restrictions directed at commerce or conduct from imposing incidental burdens on speech." *Sorrell.* "Congress, for example, can prohibit employers from discriminating in hiring on the basis of race. The fact that this will require an employer to take down a sign reading 'White Applicants Only' hardly means that the law should be analyzed as one regulating the employer's speech rather than conduct." *Rumsfeld.* This principle explains "why an ordinance against outdoor fires might forbid burning a flag and why antitrust laws can prohibit agreements in restraint of trade." *Sorrell.*

Consider *United States v. O'Brien.* In that case, the Court upheld the application of a law against the destruction of draft cards to a defendant who had burned his draft card to protest the Vietnam War. The protester's conduct was indisputably expressive. Indeed, it was political expression, which lies at the heart of the First Amendment. Yet the *O'Brien* Court focused on whether the Government's interest in regulating the conduct was to burden expression. Because it was not, the regulation was subject to lesser constitutional scrutiny. The *O'Brien* standard is satisfied if a regulation is unrelated to the suppression of expression and "promotes a substantial government interest that would be achieved less effectively absent the regulation."

The Colorado Anti-Discrimination Act's [CADA's] Accommodation Clause and its application here are valid regulations of conduct. It is well settled that a public accommodations law like the Accommodation Clause does not "target speech or discriminate on the basis of its content." Rather, "the focal point of its prohibition" is "on the *act* of discriminating against individuals in the provision of publicly available goods, privileges, and services." The State confirms this reading of CADA. The law applies only to status-based refusals to provide the full and equal enjoyment of whatever services petitioners choose to sell to the public.

Although the consequences of today's decision might be most pressing for the LGBT community, the decision's logic cannot be limited to discrimination on the basis of sexual orientation or gender identity. The decision threatens to balkanize the market and to allow the exclusion of other groups from many services. A website designer could equally refuse to create a wedding website for an interracial couple, for example. How quickly we forget that opposition to interracial marriage was often because "Almighty God did not intend for the races to mix." *Loving v. Virginia*, 388 U.S. 1, 3 (1967). Yet the reason for discrimination need not even be religious, as this case arises under the Free Speech Clause. A stationer could refuse to sell a birth announcement for a disabled couple because she opposes their having a child. A large retail store could reserve its family portrait services for "traditional" families. And so on.

The unattractive lesson of the majority opinion is this: What's mine is mine, and what's yours is yours. The lesson of the history of public accommodations laws is altogether different. It is that in a free and democratic society, there can be no social castes. And for that to be true, it must be true in the public market. For the "promise of freedom" is an empty one if the Government is "powerless to assure that a dollar in the hands of one person will purchase the same thing as a dollar in the hands of another." *Jones v. Alfred H. Mayer Co.*, 392 U.S. 409, 443 (1968). Because the Court today retreats from that promise, I dissent.

Points for Discussion

1. **How should the Colorado public accommodations law be characterized?** For Justice Gorsuch, *303 Creative* was a straightforward compelled speech case. He readily acknowledged that public accommodations laws had "done much to secure the civil rights of all Americans," but he said the government in this case was not just seeking to "ensure the sale of goods or services on equal terms" but "to compel an individual to create speech she does not believe." By contrast, Justice Sotomayor said the Colorado law and its application were "valid regulations of conduct." Public accommodations laws, she explained, do not "target speech or discriminate on the basis of its content," but rather focus on the "*act* of discriminating against individuals in the provision of publicly available goods, privileges, and services." Who has the better argument? Have there been other cases in which the justices have disagreed over whether a law was regulating conduct or speech? Do you think that the distinction between the two is clear, or can the distinction be surprisingly elusive?

2. **Who had the more convincing parade of horribles?** Both Justice Gorsuch and Justice Sotomayor foresaw a parade of horribles if the Court failed to adopt their reasoning. According to Justice Gorsuch, if the Court did not rule the way it did, the government could force a Muslim movie director to make a film with a pro-Zionist message and could make an atheist muralist paint a mural celebrating "Evangelical zeal." According to Justice Sotomayor, because the Court ruled the way it did, a website designer could refuse to make a wedding website for an interracial couple and a printing company could refuse to make a birth announcement for a disabled couple. Which justice's doomsday prediction seems more convincing?

3. **What if the facts were changed?** What if Lorie Smith said her religion prohibited her from making wedding websites for African American couples, interracial couples, or Jewish couples? Do you think that the case would have come out differently? If yes, how could a court justify the differing result?

4. **The protean nature of "speech" and "religion."** Is part of the difficulty in cases like *303 Creative* the fact that both "speech" and "religion" are such malleable concepts? For example, Justice Gorsuch's reasoning in *303 Creative* could potentially be applied to forms of speech that are less obviously expressive than a wedding website. Imagine, for instance, a restaurant owner who claimed that his religion prohibits men and women from sitting together and that forcing him to allow mixed seating would compel him to communicate a message he does not wish to convey? In addition, and as you will learn in Chapter 17, judges are generally prohibited from second-guessing a religious adherent's sincerely held beliefs. Does this mean that a judge could not question a website designer's sincerely held belief that her religion forbids her from serving Hispanic Americans, mixed-race couples, Mormons, or people with disabilities?

B. Freedom of Association: An Implied Right to Associate with Others for Expressive Purposes

The First Amendment does not explicitly refer to "freedom of association." The closest the text comes to any such recognition is the guarantee of the "right of the people peaceably to assemble." Yet an expansive "freedom of association" has long been recognized as an implied First Amendment right.

Unlike other implied constitutional rights, freedom of association has never been particularly controversial, especially when articulated as "freedom of *expressive* association." On reflection, it is easy to see why. Many of the rights explicitly articulated in the First Amendment's text are rights commonly exercised by groups of persons acting collectively. Freedom of religion, speech, press, assembly, and petition are all commonly exercised by individuals or organizations acting in concert with others. The Supreme Court has recognized that these individual rights can be fully realized only if there is a concomitant right to exercise them collectively: "An individual's freedom to speak, to worship, and to petition the government for the redress of grievances could not be vigorously protected from interference by the State unless a correlative freedom to engage in group effort toward those ends were not also guaranteed."[1]

Freedom of association issues arise when government actions interfere with individuals' rights to associate for expressive purposes. We saw an example of this in

---

1 *Roberts v. United States Jaycees*, 468 U.S. 609, 622 (1984).

Chapter 11 when we studied the First Amendment rights of government employees. In that section, you learned that the First Amendment limits a government employer's ability to terminate or disadvantage employees because of their affiliation with a disfavored political party. The Supreme Court recognized that such actions impinge upon an employee's right to associate with an expressive organization.

The most extreme form of government interference with freedom of association would be outlawing an association or criminalizing membership in the association. While such extreme measures are rare, they do occur and are not necessarily unconstitutional. To the contrary, the Supreme Court evaluates such actions under a demanding standard that resembles the high bar the Court uses when evaluating regulations of speech advocating unlawful action. For example, the Court has said that the government may punish an individual for being a member of an organization only if the government can prove that the individual knew of the organization's illegal objectives and specifically intended to help the organization accomplish its illicit ends.[2]

The following material surveys some of the more salient issues in the jurisprudence on freedom of association. The first section considers the potentially chilling effect of forcing an expressive association to disclose its members. The second considers the tension between freedom of association and antidiscrimination laws. This tension arises when an expressive association is compelled by an antidiscrimination law to accept members whom the association claims will interfere with its message.

1. Compelling an Association to Disclose Its Members: When Disclosure Threatens to Chill Expressive Association

In Section A, you learned that the First Amendment protects a person's right to speak anonymously. The Supreme Court recognized that this right was particularly important in instances when speakers feared that their speech might provoke reprisals.

Comparable concerns arise in the context of freedom of association. People who associate with organizations that express unpopular views might fear retaliation if their membership in the organizations is made public. Similarly, people who donate money to controversial political candidates or divisive referenda might fear reprisals if their donations are disclosed.

In *Buckley*, the campaign finance case we studied in Chapter 12, the Supreme Court upheld laws requiring the disclosure of campaign donors. The Court found that the interests served by disclosure, including providing transparency in campaign financing and fighting corruption, outweighed any chilling effects the disclosures might have on political association. At the same time, the Court acknowledged that this chilling effect could be real, particularly for minor parties, and explicitly acknowl-

2 *Scales v. United States*, 367 U.S. 203, 229 (1961).

edged that there could be a case "where the threat to the exercise of First Amendment rights is so serious and the state interest furthered by disclosure so insubstantial that [disclosure] requirements cannot be constitutionally applied."

The following case is the leading authority to address the chilling effect of laws requiring the disclosure of an expressive association's membership.

NAACP v. Alabama

Supreme Court of the United States, 1958
357 U.S. 449

MR. JUSTICE HARLAN delivered the opinion of the Court.

The question presented is whether Alabama, consistently with the Due Process Clause of the Fourteenth Amendment, can compel petitioner to reveal to the State's Attorney General the names and addresses of all its Alabama members and agents, without regard to their positions or functions in the Association. The judgment of contempt was based upon petitioner's refusal to comply fully with a court order requiring in part the production of membership lists.

The National Association for the Advancement of Colored People is a nonprofit membership corporation organized under the laws of New York. Its purposes, fostered on a nationwide basis, are those indicated by its name, and it operates through chartered affiliates which are independent unincorporated associations, with membership therein equivalent to membership in petitioner. The first Alabama affiliates were chartered in 1918. Since that time the aims of the Association have been advanced through activities of its affiliates, and in 1951 the Association itself opened a regional office in Alabama, at which it employed two supervisory persons and one clerical worker.

Effective advocacy of both public and private points of view, particularly controversial ones, is undeniably enhanced by group association, as this Court has more than once recognized by remarking upon the close nexus between the freedoms of speech and assembly. It is beyond debate that freedom to engage in association for the advancement of beliefs and ideas is an inseparable aspect of the "liberty" assured by the Due Process Clause of the Fourteenth Amendment, which embraces freedom of speech. Of course, it is immaterial whether the beliefs sought to be advanced by association pertain to political, economic, religious or cultural matters, and state action which may have the effect of curtailing the freedom to associate is subject to the closest scrutiny.

It is hardly a novel perception that compelled disclosure of affiliation with groups engaged in advocacy may constitute [an] effective restraint on freedom of association.

This Court has recognized the vital relationship between freedom to associate and privacy in one's associations. When referring to the varied forms of governmental action which might interfere with freedom of assembly, it said in *American Communications Ass'n v. Douds*, 339 U.S. 382 (1950): "A requirement that adherents of particular religious faiths or political parties wear identifying arm-bands, for example, is obviously of this nature." Compelled disclosure of membership in an organization engaged in advocacy of particular beliefs is of the same order. Inviolability of privacy in group association may in many circumstances be indispensable to preservation of freedom of association, particularly where a group espouses dissident beliefs.

We think that the production order, in the respects here drawn in question, must be regarded as entailing the likelihood of a substantial restraint upon the exercise by petitioner's members of their right to freedom of association. Petitioner has made an uncontroverted showing that on past occasions revelation of the identity of its rank-and-file members has exposed these members to economic reprisal, loss of employment, threat of physical coercion, and other manifestations of public hostility. Under these circumstances, we think it apparent that compelled disclosure of petitioner's Alabama membership is likely to affect adversely the ability of petitioner and its members to pursue their collective effort to foster beliefs which they admittedly have the right to advocate, in that it may induce members to withdraw from the Association and dissuade others from joining it because of fear of exposure of their beliefs shown through their associations and of the consequences of this exposure.

It is not sufficient to answer, as the State does here, that whatever repressive effect compulsory disclosure of names of petitioner's members may have upon participation by Alabama citizens in petitioner's activities follows not from state action but from private community pressures. The crucial factor is the interplay of governmental and private action, for it is only after the initial exertion of state power represented by the production order that private action takes hold.

It is important to bear in mind that petitioner asserts no right to absolute immunity from state investigation, and no right to disregard Alabama's laws. As shown by its substantial compliance with the production order, petitioner does not deny Alabama's right to obtain from it such information as the State desires concerning the purposes of the Association and its activities within the State. Petitioner has not objected to divulging the identity of its members who are employed by or hold official positions with it. It has urged the rights solely of its ordinary rank-and-file members.

We conclude that Alabama has fallen short of showing a controlling justification for the deterrent effect on the free enjoyment of the right to associate which disclosure of membership lists is likely to have.

Points for Discussion

1. **When the risk of disclosing donors threatens freedom of association.** In *Americans for Prosperity Foundation v. Bonta*, 141 S. Ct. 2373 (2021), the Court reviewed a regulatory scheme developed by the California Attorney General's Office for charities operating in the state. California law requires charities to register with the Attorney General's Office, and California Department of Justice regulations require the charities to submit an Internal Revenue Service form (Form 990 Schedule B) that discloses the names of larger donors. The disclosure forms list the donors' names and addresses, as well as their total contributions. The policy of the Attorney General's Office was to keep the forms confidential, but in the past many of the forms ended up being publicly available on the office's website. After the suit was filed, the California legislature adopted a law prohibiting the disclosure of the forms.

   Two conservative charities challenged the disclosure obligation, claiming that it violated the First Amendment rights of both the organizations and their donors. The Supreme Court agreed. Chief Justice Roberts applied an "exacting scrutiny" standard, which requires that there be "a substantial relation between the disclosure requirement and a sufficiently important governmental interest." While acknowledging that California had an important interest in preventing wrongdoing by charities, Chief Justice Roberts nevertheless concluded that the disclosure rule was not narrowly tailored to furthering the state's interest and was fatally overbroad. He pointed to the trial court's finding that "there was not a single, concrete instance in which pre-investigation collection of a Schedule B did anything to advance the Attorney General's investigative, regulatory or enforcement efforts." At the same time, Chief Justice Roberts pointed to the disclosure regime's chilling effect on freedom of association:

   > The disclosure requirement "creates an unnecessary risk of chilling" [association] in violation of the First Amendment, indiscriminately sweeping up the information of *every* major donor with reason to remain anonymous. The petitioners here, for example, introduced evidence that they and their supporters have been subjected to bomb threats, protests, stalking, and physical violence. Such risks are heightened in the 21st century and seem to grow with each passing year, as "anyone with access to a computer can compile a wealth of information about" anyone else, including such sensitive details as a person's home address or the school attended by his children.

2. **The "exacting scrutiny" standard for evaluating disclosure requirements.** In his *Bonta* opinion, Chief Justice Roberts stated that disclosure requirements should be evaluated under "exacting scrutiny." Here is the key passage:

> *NAACP v. Alabama* did not phrase in precise terms the standard of review that applies to First Amendment challenges to compelled disclosure. We have since settled on a standard referred to as "exacting scrutiny." *Buckley v. Valeo*. Under that standard, there must be "a substantial relation between the disclosure requirement and a sufficiently important governmental interest." "To withstand this scrutiny, the strength of the governmental interest must reflect the seriousness of the actual burden on First Amendment rights." Such scrutiny, we have held, is appropriate given the "deterrent effect on the exercise of First Amendment rights" that arises as an "inevitable result of the government's conduct in requiring disclosure."

Chief Justice Roberts described exacting scrutiny as being less demanding than strict scrutiny but more demanding than intermediate scrutiny. Perhaps most notably, he said the means aspect of the test was less rigorous than the "least restrictive alternative" test used in strict scrutiny, but more demanding than the "substantial relation" test used in intermediate scrutiny.

2. Compelling Associations to Accept Members: When Forced Association Interferes with a Group's Message

The First Amendment freedom of expressive association includes a concomitant right not to associate with those who would interfere with an association's message. The tension between this latter right and government enforcement of antidiscrimination laws has produced some of the most perplexing jurisprudence in modern First Amendment law. The cases navigating this clash are in conflict and difficult to harmonize.

The three opinions selected below illustrate the intensity of this issue. You will notice strong parallels between these cases and the *Hurley* and *303 Creative* cases, which addressed a similar conflict between civil rights laws and the First Amendment right not to speak. Indeed, the *Hurley* case, which implicated both the right not to speak and the right not to associate, could have been included in this section.

Board of Directors of Rotary International v. Rotary Club of Duarte

Supreme Court of the United States, 1987
481 U.S. 537

JUSTICE POWELL delivered the opinion of the Court.

We must decide whether a California statute that requires California Rotary Clubs to admit women members violates the First Amendment.

In *Roberts v. United States Jaycees*, 468 U.S. 609 (1984), we upheld against First Amendment challenge a Minnesota statute that required the Jaycees to admit women as full voting members. *Roberts* provides the framework for analyzing appellants' constitutional claims. As we observed in *Roberts*, our cases have afforded constitutional protection to freedom of association in two distinct senses. First, the Court has held that the Constitution protects against unjustified government interference with an individual's choice to enter into and maintain certain intimate or private relationships. Second, the Court has upheld the freedom of individuals to associate for the purpose of engaging in protected speech or religious activities. In many cases, government interference with one form of protected association will also burden the other form of association. In *Roberts* we determined the nature and degree of constitutional protection by considering separately the effect of the challenged state action on individuals' freedom of private association and their freedom of expressive association. We follow the same course in this case.

The evidence in this case indicates that the relationship among Rotary Club members is not the kind of intimate or private relation that warrants constitutional protection. The size of local Rotary Clubs ranges from fewer than 20 to more than 900. There is no upper limit on the membership of any local Rotary Club. About 10 percent of the membership of a typical club moves away or drops out during a typical year. The clubs therefore are instructed to "keep a flow of prospects coming" to make up for the attrition and gradually to enlarge the membership. The purpose of Rotary "is to produce an inclusive, not exclusive, membership, making possible the recognition of all useful local occupations, and enabling the club to be a true cross section of the business and professional life of the community." The membership undertakes a variety of service projects designed to aid the community, to raise the standards of the members' businesses and professions, and to improve international relations. Such an inclusive "fellowship for service based on diversity of interest," however beneficial to the members and to those they serve, does not suggest the kind of private or personal relationship to which we have accorded protection under the First Amendment. To be sure, membership in Rotary Clubs is not open to the general public. But each club is instructed to include in its membership "all fully qualified prospective members located within its territory," to avoid "arbitrary limits on the number of members in the club," and to "establish and maintain a membership growth pattern."

The Court also has recognized that the right to engage in activities protected by the First Amendment implies "a corresponding right to associate with others in pursuit of a wide variety of political, social, economic, educational, religious, and cultural ends." In this case, however, the evidence fails to demonstrate that admitting women to Rotary Clubs will affect in any significant way the existing members' ability to carry out their various purposes.

As a matter of policy, Rotary Clubs do not take positions on "public questions," including political or international issues. To be sure, Rotary Clubs engage in a variety of commendable service activities that are protected by the First Amendment. But the Unruh Act [California's antidiscrimination law] does not require the clubs to abandon or alter any of these activities. It does not require them to abandon their basic goals of humanitarian service, high ethical standards in all vocations, good will, and peace. Nor does it require them to abandon their classification system or admit members who do not reflect a cross section of the community. Indeed, by opening membership to leading business and professional women in the community, Rotary Clubs are likely to obtain a more representative cross section of community leaders with a broadened capacity for service.

Even if the Act does work some slight infringement on Rotary members' right of expressive association, that infringement is justified because it serves the State's compelling interest in eliminating discrimination against women.

L States has compelling interest in limiting discrimination

Points for Discussion

1. **Cases where civil rights claims prevailed over freedom of association claims.** In the earliest cases addressing the tension between antidiscrimination laws and the right of expressive association, the civil rights claimants all prevailed. In *Roberts,* a case relied on in the *Rotary Club* case, the Court upheld a Minnesota civil rights law that required the United States Jaycees, a private group, to accept women as full voting members. The Court noted that the right of expressive association is not absolute and can be overridden when a law is necessary to further a compelling state interest. The Court held that the Minnesota law furthered a compelling interest in combatting discrimination and that its enforcement would not seriously impinge upon the group's expression, even though the organization was dedicated to advancing the interests of young men:

> There is, however, no basis in the record for concluding that admission of women as full voting members will impede the organization's ability

> to engage in these protected activities or to disseminate its preferred views. The Act requires no change in the Jaycees' creed of promoting the interests of young men, and it imposes no restrictions on the organization's ability to exclude individuals with ideologies or philosophies different from those of its existing members.

Similarly, in *New York State Club Association v. City of New York*, 487 U.S. 1 (1988), the Court upheld rejected a facial challenge to a New York public accommodations law that prohibited discrimination against minorities and women by private clubs. The challenge was brought by a consortium of 125 private clubs. The Court acknowledged that compelling some private clubs to accept new members could interfere with the clubs' messaging, but it said "many of the large clubs covered by the Law are not of this kind."

2. **Justice O'Connor's distinction between commercial associations and expressive associations.** Justice Sandra Day O'Connor concurred in the judgment in *Roberts*, but she parted company with the majority over how to reach that result. She thought that the Court should have focused on the difference between what she called "expressive associations" and "commercial associations." The former primarily engage in expressive activities and the latter primarily engage in commercial activities. She said expressive associations are entitled to full First Amendment protection, but commercial associations are entitled to only minimal protection. Justice O'Connor acknowledged that "many associations cannot readily be described as purely expressive or purely commercial," but she said that courts needed to make this distinction to prevent commercial associations from using the First Amendment to evade the application of antidiscrimination laws. She agreed with the result in *Roberts* because she thought that the Jaycees—otherwise known as the Junior Chamber of Commerce—was primarily a commercial association.

Do you find Justice O'Connor's distinction between expressive and commercial associations constructive? Does her analysis help prevent associations that are primarily business networks from using freedom of association to justify their continued exclusion of historically disadvantaged groups like women and minorities?

Joining Sandra Day on a Job Interview

Justice O'Connor had good reason for being suspicious of groups that excluded women from their ranks. Even though she graduated near the top of her class at Stanford Law School, she was unable to secure a position at a law firm because she was a woman. Here is how she described an interview she had with a partner of the prominent law firm Gibson, Dunn & Crutcher. A friend had connected her with the partner, and she had traveled to Los Angeles to meet him.

> "You have a fine resume, Miss Day," the partner explained. "Fine. But, Miss Day, this firm has never hired a woman lawyer. I don't see that it will. Our clients won't stand for it."
>
> Then, as Sandra liked to tell the story, the Gibson Dunn partner asked, "Well, how well do you type?" She answered, "So-so." He said, "Well, if you type well enough, we might be able to get you a job as a legal secretary."

Evan Thomas, First: Sandra Day O'Connor 43 (2019).

Sandra Day in 1950 Stanford yearbook photo

Boy Scouts of America v. Dale

Supreme Court of the United States, 2000
530 U.S. 640

CHIEF JUSTICE REHNQUIST delivered the opinion of the Court.

Petitioners are the Boy Scouts of America and the Monmouth Council, a division of the Boy Scouts of America. The Boy Scouts is a private, not-for-profit organization engaged in instilling its system of values in young people. The Boy Scouts asserts that homosexual conduct is inconsistent with the values it seeks to instill. Respondent is James Dale, a former Eagle Scout whose adult membership in the Boy Scouts was revoked when the Boy Scouts learned that he is an avowed homosexual and gay rights activist. The New Jersey Supreme Court held that New Jersey's public accommodations law requires that the Boy Scouts readmit Dale. This case presents the question whether applying New Jersey's public accommodations law in this way violates the Boy Scouts' First Amendment right of expressive association. We hold that it does.

The forced inclusion of an unwanted person in a group infringes the group's freedom of expressive association if the presence of that person affects in a significant way the group's ability to advocate public or private viewpoints. But the freedom of expressive association, like many freedoms, is not absolute. We have held that the freedom could be overridden "by regulations adopted to serve compelling state interests, unrelated to the suppression of ideas, that cannot be achieved through means significantly less restrictive of associational freedoms."

To determine whether a group is protected by the First Amendment's expressive associational right, we must determine whether the group engages in "expressive association." The First Amendment's protection of expressive association is not reserved for advocacy groups. But to come within its ambit, a group must engage in some form of expression, whether it be public or private.

The general mission of the Boy Scouts is clear: "To instill values in young people." The Boy Scouts seeks to instill these values by having its adult leaders spend time with the youth members, instructing and engaging them in activities like camping, archery, and fishing. During the time spent with the youth members, the scoutmasters and assistant scoutmasters inculcate them with the Boy Scouts' values—both expressly and by example. It seems indisputable that an association that seeks to transmit such a system of values engages in expressive activity.

Given that the Boy Scouts engages in expressive activity, we must determine whether the forced inclusion of Dale as an assistant scoutmaster would significantly affect the Boy Scouts' ability to advocate public or private viewpoints. This inquiry necessarily requires us first to explore, to a limited extent, the nature of the Boy Scouts' view of homosexuality.

James Dale

The values the Boy Scouts seeks to instill are "based on" those listed in the Scout Oath and Law. The Boy Scouts explains that the Scout Oath and Law provide "a positive moral code for living; they are a list of 'do's' rather than 'don'ts.' " The Boy Scouts asserts that homosexual conduct is inconsistent with the values embodied in the Scout Oath and Law, particularly with the values represented by the terms "morally straight" and "clean."

Obviously, the Scout Oath and Law do not expressly mention sexuality or sexual orientation. And the terms "morally straight" and "clean" are by no means self-defining. Different people would attribute to those terms very different meanings.

The New Jersey Supreme Court analyzed the Boy Scouts' beliefs and found that the "exclusion of members solely on the basis of their sexual orientation is inconsistent with Boy Scouts' commitment to a diverse and 'representative' membership and contradicts Boy Scouts' overarching objective to reach 'all eligible youth.' "

previous ct said it was inconsistent w/ boy scouts diverse view

The Boy Scouts asserts that it "teaches that homosexual conduct is not morally straight," and that it does "not want to promote homosexual conduct as a legitimate form of behavior." We accept the Boy Scouts' assertion. We need not inquire further to determine the nature of the Boy Scouts' expression with respect to homosexuality.

We must then determine whether Dale's presence as an assistant scoutmaster would significantly burden the Boy Scouts' desire to not "promote homosexual conduct as a legitimate form of behavior." As we give deference to an association's assertions regarding the nature of its expression, we must also give deference to an association's view of what would impair its expression. That is not to say that an expressive association can erect a shield against antidiscrimination laws simply by asserting that mere acceptance of a member from a particular group would impair its message. But here Dale, by his own admission, is one of a group of gay Scouts who have "become leaders in their community and are open and honest about their sexual orientation." Dale was the copresident of a gay and lesbian organization at college and remains a gay rights activist. Dale's presence in the Boy Scouts would, at the very least, force the organization to send a message, both to the youth members and the world, that the Boy Scouts accepts homosexual conduct as a legitimate form of behavior.

Having determined that the Boy Scouts is an expressive association and that the forced inclusion of Dale would significantly affect its expression, we inquire whether the application of New Jersey's public accommodations law to require that the Boy Scouts accept Dale as an assistant scoutmaster runs afoul of the Scouts' freedom of expressive association. We conclude that it does.

We recognized in cases such as *Roberts* and *Duarte* that States have a compelling interest in eliminating discrimination against women in public accommodations. But in each of these cases we went on to conclude that the enforcement of these statutes would not materially interfere with the ideas that the organization sought to express.

We have already concluded that a state requirement that the Boy Scouts retain Dale as an assistant scoutmaster would significantly burden the organization's right to oppose or disfavor homosexual conduct. The state interests embodied in New Jersey's public accommodations law do not justify such a severe intrusion on the Boy Scouts' rights to freedom of expressive association. That being the case, we hold that the First Amendment prohibits the State from imposing such a requirement through the application of its public accommodations law.

We are not, as we must not be, guided by our views of whether the Boy Scouts' teachings with respect to homosexual conduct are right or wrong; public or judicial disapproval of a tenet of an organization's expression does not justify the State's effort to compel the organization to accept members where such acceptance would derogate from the organization's expressive message. "While the law is free to promote all sorts of conduct in place of harmful behavior, it is not free to interfere with speech for no better reason than promoting an approved message or discouraging a disfavored one, however enlightened either purpose may strike the government."

dissent

JUSTICE STEVENS, with whom JUSTICE SOUTER, JUSTICE GINSBURG, and JUSTICE BREYER join, dissenting.

Several principles are made perfectly clear by *Jaycees* and *Rotary Club*. First, to prevail on a claim of expressive association in the face of a State's antidiscrimination law, it is not enough simply to engage in some kind of expressive activity. Both the Jaycees and the Rotary Club engaged in expressive activity protected by the First Amendment, yet that fact was not dispositive. Second, it is not enough to adopt an openly avowed exclusionary membership policy. Both the Jaycees and the Rotary Club did that as well. Third, it is not sufficient merely to articulate some connection between the group's expressive activities and its exclusionary policy.

The evidence before this Court makes it exceptionally clear that BSA has, at most, simply adopted an exclusionary membership policy and has no shared goal of disapproving of homosexuality.

As in *Jaycees*, there is "no basis in the record for concluding that admission of homosexuals will impede the Boy Scouts' ability to engage in its protected activities or to disseminate its preferred views" and New Jersey's law "requires no change in BSA's creed." And like *Rotary Club*, New Jersey's law "does not require BSA to abandon or alter any of" its activities.

Surely there are instances in which an organization that truly aims to foster a belief at odds with the purposes of a State's antidiscrimination laws will have a First Amendment right to association that precludes forced compliance with those laws. But that right is not a freedom to discriminate at will, nor is it a right to maintain an exclusionary membership policy simply out of fear of what the public reaction would be if the group's membership were opened up. It is an implicit right designed to protect the enumerated rights of the First Amendment, not a license to act on any discriminatory impulse. To prevail in asserting a right of expressive association as a defense to a charge of violating an antidiscrimination law, the organization must at least show it has adopted and advocated an unequivocal position inconsistent with a position advocated or epitomized by the person whom the organization seeks to exclude. If this Court were to defer to whatever position an organization is prepared to assert in its briefs, there would be no way to mark the proper boundary between genuine exercises of the right to associate, on the one hand, and sham claims that are simply attempts to insulate nonexpressive private discrimination, on the other hand. Shielding a litigant's claim from judicial scrutiny would, in turn, render civil rights legislation a nullity, and turn this important constitutional right into a farce.

Furthermore, it is not likely that BSA would be understood to send any message, either to Scouts or to the world, simply by admitting someone as a member. Over the years, BSA has generously welcomed over 87 million young Americans into its ranks. In 1992 over one million adults were active BSA members.

The State of New Jersey has decided that people who are open and frank about their sexual orientation are entitled to equal access to employment as schoolteachers, police officers, librarians, athletic coaches, and a host of other jobs filled by citizens who serve as role models for children and adults alike. Dozens of Scout units throughout the State are sponsored by public agencies, such as schools and fire departments, that employ such role models. BSA's affiliation with numerous public agencies that comply with New Jersey's law against discrimination cannot be understood to convey any particular message endorsing or condoning the activities of all these people.

That such prejudices are still prevalent and that they have caused serious and tangible harm to countless members of the class New Jersey seeks to protect are established matters of fact that neither the Boy Scouts nor the Court disputes. That harm can only be aggravated by the creation of a constitutional shield for a policy that is itself the product of a habitual way of thinking about strangers. As Justice Brandeis so wisely advised, "we must be ever on our guard, lest we erect our prejudices into legal principles."

If we would guide by the light of reason, we must let our minds be bold. I respectfully dissent.

[Justice Souter's dissenting opinion, which was joined by Justice Ginsburg and Justice Breyer, is omitted.]

Points for Discussion

1. **What is the difference between Chief Justice William Rehnquist's opinion and Justice Stevens' dissent?** Did the justices disagree about the applicable law or how the law should be applied to the specific facts of the case? Did the justices agree about how much deference should be given to an expressive association's assertion that including a new member would interfere with the association's message?

2. **Was Dale denied access to a valuable network?** The New Jersey Supreme Court pointed out that the Boy Scouts did not just provide boys with an opportunity to learn about camping. It also provided them with valuable training and networking opportunities:

   > We find that Boy Scout membership is both a "privilege" and "advantage." Boy Scout leaders are given the "advantage" of numerous training courses that teach valuable lessons in leadership and management. Scouting indirectly benefits its members through the "advantage" of a large influential network, including Air Force Academy, Annapolis

> and West Point graduates, Rhodes Scholars, astronauts, United States Presidents and Congressmen, as well as businessmen and community leaders. Indeed, Boy Scouts advertises the "privileges" and "advantages" of being a member in order to attract new members.

Dale v. Boy Scouts of Am., 734 A.2d 1196, 1218 (N.J. 1999).

Does the fact that the Boy Scouts offer these advantages suggest that the U.S. Supreme Court should have been more concerned, as Justice O'Connor was in *Roberts*, that the Boy Scouts were using the First Amendment to deny a disadvantaged group access to a commercially and politically valuable network of people?

3. **The evolution of Boy Scout membership policies.** In 2013, the Boy Scouts of America (BSA) voted to allow gays to become Scouts. In 2017, it voted to allow transgender boys to be members. One driver of the Boy Scouts' newfound inclusiveness was the precipitous drop in membership from a peak of 5 million in the 1970s down to 2.3 million in 2017. In 2019, the BSA even agreed to accept girls and rebranded itself as "Scouts BSA." The Boy Scouts still bar atheists from their ranks. *See* Jason Daley, *Five Things You Didn't Know About the Boy Scouts of America*, Smithsonian Magazine, Oct. 13, 2017.

Christian Legal Society Chapter of University of California, Hastings College of the Law v. Martinez

Supreme Court of the United States, 2010
561 U.S. 661

[*Authors' note*: Hastings College of Law, now known as UC Law San Francisco, is a public law school affiliated with the University of California. Hastings officially recognizes and gives special benefits to student organizations that qualify for its "registered student organization" (RSO) program. Qualifying organizations are eligible for financial assistance, may use official Hastings channels for communicating with students, may use the school's facilities for meetings and office space, and may use its name and logo. To qualify as an RSO, a student organization must abide by Hastings' nondiscrimination policy, which required groups to "allow any student to participate, become a member, or seek leadership positions in the organization, regardless of their status or beliefs." So, for example, the law school stipulated that "the Hastings Democratic Caucus cannot bar students holding Republican political beliefs from becoming members or seeking leadership positions in the organization." The Christian Legal Society at Hastings was denied RSO status because its bylaws precluded gays and lesbians from becoming members.]

JUSTICE GINSBURG delivered the opinion of the Court.

In a series of decisions, this Court has emphasized that the First Amendment generally precludes public universities from denying student organizations access to school-sponsored forums because of the groups' viewpoints. See *Rosenberger v. Rector and Visitors of University of Virginia*; *Widmar v. Vincent*; *Healy v. James*, 408 U.S. 169 (1972). This case concerns a novel question regarding student activities at public universities: May a public law school condition its official recognition of a student group—and the attendant use of school funds and facilities—on the organization's agreement to open eligibility for membership and leadership to all students?

CLS view ✓

In the view of petitioner Christian Legal Society (CLS), an accept-all-comers policy impairs its First Amendment rights to free speech, expressive association, and free exercise of religion by prompting it, on pain of relinquishing the advantages of recognition, to accept members who do not share the organization's core beliefs about religion and sexual orientation. From the perspective of respondent Hastings College of the Law (Hastings or the Law School), CLS seeks special dispensation from an across-the-board open-access requirement designed to further the reasonable educational purposes underpinning the school's student-organization program.

In support of the argument that Hastings' all-comers policy treads on its First Amendment rights to free speech and expressive association, CLS draws on two lines of decisions. First, in a progression of cases, this Court has employed forum analysis to determine when a governmental entity, in regulating property in its charge, may place limitations on speech. Recognizing a State's right "to preserve the property under its control for the use to which it is lawfully dedicated," the Court has permitted restrictions on access to a limited public forum, like the RSO program here, with this key caveat: Any access barrier must be reasonable and viewpoint neutral.

Second, as evidenced by another set of decisions, this Court has rigorously reviewed laws and regulations that constrain associational freedom. In the context of public accommodations, we have subjected restrictions on that freedom to close scrutiny; such restrictions are permitted only if they serve "compelling state interests" that are "unrelated to the suppression of ideas"—interests that cannot be advanced "through significantly less restrictive means." *Roberts*; *Boy Scouts of America v. Dale*. "Freedom of association," we have recognized, "plainly presupposes a freedom not to associate." Insisting that an organization embrace unwelcome members, we have therefore concluded, "directly and immediately affects associational rights."

CLS would have us engage each line of cases independently, but its expressive-association and free-speech arguments merge: Who speaks on its behalf, CLS reasons, colors what concept is conveyed.

This case fits comfortably within the limited-public-forum category, for CLS, in seeking what is effectively a state subsidy, faces only indirect pressure to modify its membership policies; CLS may exclude any person for any reason if it forgoes the benefits of official recognition. The expressive-association precedents on which CLS relies, in contrast, involved regulations that compelled a group to include unwanted members, with no choice to opt out.

In diverse contexts, our decisions have distinguished between policies that require action and those that withhold benefits. See, e.g., *Grove City College v. Bell*, 465 U.S. 555 (1984); *Bob Jones Univ. v. United States*, 461 U.S. 574 (1983). Application of the less restrictive limited-public-forum analysis better accounts for the fact that Hastings, through its RSO program, is dangling the carrot of subsidy, not wielding the stick of prohibition. Cf. *Norwood v. Harrison*, 413 U.S. 455 (1973) ("That the Constitution may compel toleration of private discrimination in some circumstances does not mean that it requires state support for such discrimination.").

With appropriate regard for school administrators' judgment, we review the justifications Hastings offers in defense of its all-comers requirement. First, the open-access policy "ensures that the leadership, educational, and social opportunities afforded by [RSOs] are available to all students."

Second, the all-comers requirement helps Hastings police the written terms of its Nondiscrimination Policy without inquiring into an RSO's motivation for membership restrictions. To bring the RSO program within CLS's view of the Constitution's limits, CLS proposes that Hastings permit exclusion because of belief but forbid discrimination due to status. But that proposal would impose on Hastings a daunting labor. How should the Law School go about determining whether a student organization cloaked prohibited status exclusion in belief-based garb? If a hypothetical Male-Superiority Club barred a female student from running for its presidency, for example, how could the Law School tell whether the group rejected her bid because of her sex or because, by seeking to lead the club, she manifested a lack of belief in its fundamental philosophy?

Third, the Law School reasonably adheres to the view that an all-comers policy, to the extent it brings together individuals with diverse backgrounds and beliefs, "encourages tolerance, cooperation, and learning among students." And if the policy sometimes produces discord, Hastings can rationally rank among RSO-program goals development of conflict-resolution skills, toleration, and readiness to find common ground.

Fourth, Hastings' policy, which incorporates—in fact, subsumes—state-law proscriptions on discrimination, conveys the Law School's decision "to decline to subsidize with public monies and benefits conduct of which the people of California disapprove." State law, of course, may not command that public universities take action impermissible under the First Amendment. But so long as a public university does not contravene constitutional limits, its choice to advance state-law goals through the school's educational endeavors stands on firm footing.

We next consider whether Hastings' all-comers policy is viewpoint neutral.

Although this aspect of limited-public-forum analysis has been the constitutional sticking point in our prior decisions, as earlier recounted, we need not dwell on it here. It is, after all, hard to imagine a more viewpoint-neutral policy than one requiring all student groups to accept all comers. In contrast to *Healy*, *Widmar*, and *Rosenberger*, in which universities singled out organizations for disfavored treatment because of their points of view, Hastings' all-comers requirement draws no distinction between groups based on their message or perspective. An all-comers condition on access to RSO status, in short, is textbook viewpoint neutral.

For the foregoing reasons, we affirm the Court of Appeals' ruling that the all-comers policy is constitutional and remand the case for further proceedings consistent with this opinion.

Justice Alito, with whom The Chief Justice, Justice Scalia, and Justice Thomas join, dissenting.

The proudest boast of our free speech jurisprudence is that we protect the freedom to express "the thought that we hate." *United States v. Schwimmer*, 279 U.S. 644 (1929) (Holmes, J., dissenting). Today's decision rests on a very different principle: no freedom for expression that offends prevailing standards of political correctness in our country's institutions of higher learning.

To appreciate how far the Court has strayed, it is instructive to compare this case with *Healy v. James*, our only First Amendment precedent involving a public college's refusal to recognize a student group. The group in *Healy* was a local chapter of the Students for a Democratic Society (SDS). When the students who applied for recognition of the chapter were asked by a college committee whether they would "respond to issues of violence as other S.D.S. chapters have," their answer was that their "action would have to be dependent upon each issue." They similarly refused to provide a definitive answer when asked whether they would be willing to "use any means possible" to achieve their aims. The president of the college refused to allow the group to be recognized, concluding that the philosophy of the SDS was "antithetical to the school's policies" and that it was doubtful that the local chapter was independent of the national organization, the "published aims and philosophy" of which included "disruption and violence."

The effects of nonrecognition in *Healy* were largely the same as those present here. The SDS was denied the use of campus facilities, as well as access to the customary means used for communication among the members of the college community. The lower federal courts held that the First Amendment rights of the SDS chapter had not been violated, and when the case reached this Court, the college, much like today's majority, sought to minimize the effects of nonrecognition, arguing that the SDS members "still may meet as a group off campus, that they still may distribute written material off campus, and that they still may meet together informally on campus as individuals."

This Court took a different view. The Court held that the denial of recognition substantially burdened the students' right to freedom of association.

In this case, the forum consists of the RSO program. Once a public university opens a limited public forum, it "must respect the lawful boundaries it has itself set." *Rosenberger*. The university "may not exclude speech where its distinction is not reasonable in light of the purpose served by the forum." And the university must maintain strict viewpoint neutrality.

This requirement of viewpoint neutrality extends to the expression of religious viewpoints. In an unbroken line of decisions analyzing private religious speech in limited public forums, we have made it perfectly clear that "religion is a viewpoint from which ideas are conveyed."

We have applied this analysis in cases in which student speech was restricted because of the speaker's religious viewpoint, and we have consistently concluded that such restrictions constitute viewpoint discrimination. We have also stressed that the rules applicable in a limited public forum are particularly important in the university setting, where "the State acts against a background of tradition of thought and experiment that is at the center of our intellectual and philosophic tradition." *Rosenberger*.

Analyzed under this framework, Hastings' refusal to register CLS pursuant to its Nondiscrimination Policy plainly fails.

The Court is also wrong in holding that the accept-all-comers policy is viewpoint neutral. The Court proclaims that it would be "hard to imagine a more viewpoint-neutral policy," but I would not be so quick to jump to this conclusion. Even if it is assumed that the policy is viewpoint neutral on its face, there is strong evidence in the record that the policy was announced as a pretext.

The adoption of a facially neutral policy for the purpose of suppressing the expression of a particular viewpoint is viewpoint discrimination. See *Crawford v. Board of Ed. of Los Angeles*, 458 U.S. 527 (1982) ("A law neutral on its face still may be unconstitutional if motivated by a discriminatory purpose"). A simple example illustrates this obvious point. Suppose that a hated student group at a state university has never been able to attract more than 10 members. Suppose that the university administration, for the purpose of preventing that group from using the school grounds for meetings, adopts a new rule under which the use of its facilities is restricted to groups with more than 25 members. Although this rule would be neutral on its face, its adoption for a discriminatory reason would be illegal.

Here, CLS has made a strong showing that Hastings' sudden adoption and selective application of its accept-all-comers policy was a pretext for the law school's unlawful denial of CLS's registration application under the Nondiscrimination Policy.

I do not think it is an exaggeration to say that today's decision is a serious setback for freedom of expression in this country. Our First Amendment reflects a "profound national commitment to the principle that debate on public issues should be uninhibited, robust, and wide-open." *New York Times Co. v. Sullivan.* Even if the United States is the only Nation that shares this commitment to the same extent, I would not change our law to conform to the international norm. I fear that the Court's decision marks a turn in that direction. Even those who find CLS's views objectionable should be concerned about the way the group has been treated—by Hastings, the Court of Appeals, and now this Court. I can only hope that this decision will turn out to be an aberration.

[Justice Stevens' and Justice Kennedy's concurring opinions are omitted.]

Points for Discussion

1. **Did Hastings engage in viewpoint discrimination in a limited public forum?** In his dissent, Justice Alito said this case was similar to a long line of cases in which the Court held that the exclusion of religious groups from a limited public forum constituted unlawful viewpoint discrimination. Recall the *Rosenberger*, *Lamb's Chapel*, and *Good News Club* cases we studied in Chapter 11. How does Justice Ruth Bader Ginsburg distinguish that line of cases?

2. **Is it possible to reconcile and harmonize *Roberts*, *Rotary Club*, *Hurley*, *Dale*, and *Martinez*?** Or are the cases in hopeless tension? The *Roberts* and *Rotary Club* cases held that the government could require these expressive associations to accept new members, but the *Hurley* and *Dale* cases reached the opposite results. What explains these different outcomes? Did the Court apply different rules of law in the cases, or were the cases merely factually distinct? And where does *Martinez* fit into the picture? Is *Martinez* best understood as a freedom of association case, a limited public forum case, a government funding case, or a bit of all three?

3. **Changing justices, changing law?** *Martinez* was a 5–4 decision, and the composition of the Court has changed considerably since it was decided in 2010. Given the lineup of justices in more recent decisions such as *303 Creative*, *NIFLA*, and *Janus*, do you think *Martinez* would come out the same way if the issue were to once again reach the Court?

Test Your Knowledge

To assess your understanding of the material in this chapter, click here to take a quiz.

CHAPTER SIXTEEN

When Government Interferes with Freedom of the Press:

Access to Government Information, Gag Orders, Newsgathering, and Confidential Sources

The First Amendment refers to both freedom of speech and freedom of the press. The constitutional conundrum, which we address in this chapter, is what, if anything, the latter adds to the former. Does freedom of the press mean that the Constitution treats the institutional press (*e.g.*, *The New York Times* or *The Wall Street Journal*) as a unique constitutional actor with enhanced rights beyond those guaranteed to the general public? Or is the reference to "press" merely clarifying that any speaker, whether a professional journalist or a layperson, has the right to use technology—from the printing press to the internet—to broadly disseminate his or her ideas? Professor Eugene Volokh described these dueling conceptions as "press as industry" versus "press as technology."[1]

The first section of this chapter examines how the Supreme Court has addressed this interpretative question. The remaining sections examine a series of First Amendment issues that have special relevance for the press.

A. Does the Press Have Greater Rights than the General Public? Is Freedom of the Press Distinct from Freedom of Speech?

The First Amendment expressly prohibits "abridging the freedom of speech, or of the press." The separate references to speech and press raise the question of whether the amendment should be understood as recognizing a "freedom of press" that is somehow different, and potentially more expansive, than "freedom of speech." That, in turn, raises two interpretative issues: first, whether there is a select group of

1 Eugene Volokh, *Freedom for the Press as an Industry, or for the Press as a Technology—From the Framing to Today*, 160 U. Pa. L. Rev. 459, 461–463 (2012).

institutions or people who constitute the "press" and, second, if there is such a group, whether the Press Clause provides this group with rights that go beyond the rights given to the public at large by the Free Speech Clause.

Consider, for example, whether judges should interpret the Press Clause as giving journalists greater rights than the public in the following contexts:

- Access to government institutions and information.
- Freedom from prior restraints.
- A right to use illegally obtained information.
- A right to broader immunity from tort liability when journalists commit torts in the course of newsgathering.
- A right to be exempted from providing court testimony, such as an exemption from revealing the identity of a confidential source.

Powerful arguments have been made both for and against giving the press enhanced protection. Proponents of enhanced protection emphasize the press' institutional role as a check on government. After all, if one purpose of the First Amendment is to ensure effective self-governance, and if the institutional press plays a crucial role in this process by investigating and reporting on government, then enhanced rights for the press might be warranted.

Justice Potter Stewart, the justice most strongly identified with the expansive view of the Press Clause, described the clause as a "*structural* provision of the Constitution" that was designed to "create a fourth institution outside the Government as an additional check on the three official branches."[2] He emphasized the critical role of the press in keeping the public informed. "When on assignment, a journalist does not tour a jail simply for his own edification," Justice Stewart wrote in a concurring opinion in *Houchins v. KQED, Inc.*, 438 U.S. 1, 17 (1978). "He is there to gather information to be passed on to others, and his mission is protected by the Constitution for very specific reasons." Justice Stewart believed that the First Amendment's separate references to speech and press were "no constitutional accident." To the contrary, he said, it was "an acknowledgment of the critical role played by the press in American society." Justice Stewart thought that "the Constitution requires sensitivity to that role, and to the special needs of the press in performing it effectively."

---

[2] Potter Stewart, *Or of the Press*, 26 Hastings L.J. 631, 633–34 (1975). Justice Stewart's reference to a "fourth institution" echoed an earlier observation by the English parliamentarian Edmund Burke, who reportedly said "there were Three Estates in Parliament; but, in the Reporters' Gallery yonder, there sat a Fourth Estate more important far than they all."

Those opposing enhanced protection note that treating the press as a unique constitutional actor would require the Court to answer the thorny, if not intractable, question of who qualifies for membership in this protected class.[3] That was always a difficult question, but it has become exponentially more difficult with the advent of the internet, where anyone with a computer or cellphone can widely disseminate information. Chief Justice Warren Burger contended that this definitional hurdle created a "fundamental difficulty with interpreting the Press Clause as conferring special status on a limited group."[4] "The First Amendment does not 'belong' to any definable category of persons or entities," he said, but rather "belongs to all who exercise its freedoms."[5]

Opponents have also expressed concern that giving enhanced protection to the press might be used to justify giving reduced First Amendment protection to non-press speakers.[6] Or, and perhaps counterintuitively, granting special status to the press could be used to justify greater regulation of the press because of its vital role in our society.[7]

If you were a Supreme Court justice, how would you decide which position to take in this debate? Would your decision be based on whether you thought the Framers intended for the Press Clause to provide enhanced protection for the press?[8] Or would your decision turn on whether you thought, as a functional matter in the 21st century, that it was important for the Constitution to provide special protection to the press to ensure that it could fulfill its role in informing the public and holding the government accountable?

As the remaining materials in this chapter indicate, the Supreme Court has been reluctant to treat the Press Clause as granting the institutional press more expansive rights than those enjoyed by the public under the Free Speech Clause. To the contrary, the Court has rendered the Press Clause largely superfluous by declining to give it substantive meaning. A district court judge encapsulated the Court's jurisprudence by posing and answering the key interpretive question: "Does the Press Clause today have jurisdictional significance distinct from the Speech Clause? For the most part, the answer appears to be 'no.' "[9]

---

3 Professor Sonja R. West notes that "the primary roadblock to recognizing independent meaning in the Press Clause is the definitional problem—who or what is the 'press'?" She believes that the Court should embrace this challenge and offers suggestions for how to develop a viable definition. Sonja R. West, *Awakening the Press Clause*, 58 U.C.L.A. L. Rev. 1025, 1029 (2011).

4 *First Nat'l Bank of Boston v. Bellotti*, 435 U.S. 765, 801 (1978) (Burger, C.J., concurring).

5 *Id.* at 802.

6 Anthony Lewis, *A Preferred Position for Journalism?*, 7 Hofstra L. Rev. 595, 609 (1979).

7 William W. Van Alstyne, *The First Amendment and the Free Press: A Comment on Some New Trends and Some Old Theories*, 9 Hofstra L. Rev. 1, 18–19 (1980).

8 Scholars have tried to discern the Framers' intent and have reached differing conclusions. *See, e.g.*, Sonja R. West, *The "Press," Then & Now*, 77 Ohio St. L.J. 49 (2016); Volokh, *supra* note 1; David A. Anderson, *The Origins of the Press Clause*, 30 U.C.L.A. L. Rev. 455 (1983).

9 *McConnell v. Federal Election Comm'n*, 251 F. Supp. 2d 176, 234 (D.D.C. 2003).

But the picture is not entirely clear. The Supreme Court does at times appear to focus with particular sensitivity on the rights of the press, and sometimes the Court seemingly relies exclusively on the Press Clause in articulating its decisions, as in the *Nebraska Press* case dealing with prior restraints, which you'll read about later in this chapter.

Perhaps most importantly, even if the press is not considered a unique constitutional actor with enhanced rights, it has nevertheless been at the vanguard in many of the most important battles for expansive First Amendment rights. We encountered examples of this in prior chapters. Recall, for instance, the landmark victories by the press in both *New York Times v. Sullivan*, which established the "actual malice" standard in defamation actions brought by public officials, and *New York Times v. United States*, which prompted the Supreme Court's pronouncement that any system of prior restraints "bears a heavy presumption against its constitutional validity."

In this chapter, we focus on First Amendment issues that are particularly relevant to members of the press. These include whether there is a First Amendment right to access government information, whether courts can issue "gag orders" barring the press from reporting on certain topics, whether newsgathering is entitled to special protection, and whether reporters have a constitutional right to keep their sources confidential. While the First Amendment principles articulated in this chapter often benefit the news media, these principles are generally understood to apply with equal force to the media and other citizens alike, though it may be that journalists and news organizations are often positioned to take greater advantage of them.

B. Is There a First Amendment Right to Access Government Information? Does the Right to Report About Government Include the Right to Information About What Government Is Doing?

If a function of freedom of speech and press is to serve as a check on government, then one might have expected the justices to facilitate this function by interpreting the First Amendment to provide a broad right of access to government information. In other words, the First Amendment would not merely be a shield that protected speakers from government interference, but would also be a sword that ensured public access to the workings of government.

One might have anticipated that, but it is not what the justices have done. They have not interpreted the First Amendment to create an expansive constitutional right to access government information. The one notable exception is public access to judicial proceedings.

1. Access to Judicial Proceedings: An Implied Right to Attend Criminal Trials

The following case is the foundational authority for the right of the people, not just the press, to view judicial proceedings.

Richmond Newspapers, Inc. v. Virginia

Supreme Court of the United States, 1980
448 U.S. 555

MR. CHIEF JUSTICE BURGER announced the judgment of the Court and delivered an opinion, in which MR. JUSTICE WHITE and MR. JUSTICE STEVENS joined.

The narrow question presented in this case is whether the right of the public and press to attend criminal trials is guaranteed under the United States Constitution.

The origins of the proceeding which has become the modern criminal trial in Anglo-American justice can be traced back beyond reliable historical records.

The historical evidence demonstrates conclusively that at the time when our organic laws were adopted, criminal trials both here and in England had long been presumptively open. This is no quirk of history; rather, it has long been recognized as an indispensible attribute of an Anglo-American trial. Both Hale in the 17th century and Blackstone in the 18th saw the importance of openness to the proper functioning of a trial; it gave assurance that the proceedings were conducted fairly to all concerned, and it discouraged perjury, the misconduct of participants, and decisions based on secret bias or partiality.

The early history of open trials in part reflects the widespread acknowledgment, long before there were behavioral scientists, that public trials had significant community therapeutic value. Even without such experts to frame the concept in words, people sensed from experience and observation that, especially in the administration of criminal justice, the means used to achieve justice must have the support derived from public acceptance of both the process and its results.

When a shocking crime occurs, a community reaction of outrage and public protest often follows. Thereafter the open processes of justice serve an important prophylactic purpose, providing an outlet for community concern, hostility, and emotion. Without an awareness that society's responses to criminal conduct are underway, natural human reactions of outrage and protest are frustrated and may manifest themselves in some form of vengeful "self-help," as indeed they did regularly in the activities of vigilante "committees" on our frontiers. "The accusation and conviction or acquittal, as much perhaps as the execution of punishment, operate to restore the imbalance which was created by the offense or public charge, to reaffirm the temporarily lost feeling of security and, perhaps, to satisfy that latent 'urge to punish.' "

Civilized societies withdraw both from the victim and the vigilante the enforcement of criminal laws, but they cannot erase from people's consciousness the fundamental, natural yearning to see justice done—or even the urge for retribution. The crucial prophylactic aspects of the administration of justice cannot function in the dark; no community catharsis can occur if justice is "done in a corner or in any covert manner." It is not enough to say that results alone will satiate the natural community desire for "satisfaction." A result considered untoward may undermine public confidence, and where the trial has been concealed from public view an unexpected outcome can cause a reaction that the system at best has failed and at worst has been corrupted. To work effectively, it is important that society's criminal process "satisfy the appearance of justice," and the appearance of justice can best be provided by allowing people to observe it.

People in an open society do not demand infallibility from their institutions, but it is difficult for them to accept what they are prohibited from observing. When a criminal trial is conducted in the open, there is at least an opportunity both for understanding the system in general and its workings in a particular case.

From this unbroken, uncontradicted history, supported by reasons as valid today as in centuries past, we are bound to conclude that a presumption of openness inheres in the very nature of a criminal trial under our system of justice.

Despite the history of criminal trials being presumptively open since long before the Constitution, the State presses its contention that neither the Constitution nor the Bill of Rights contains any provision which by its terms guarantees to the public the right to attend criminal trials. Standing alone, this is correct, but there remains the question whether, absent an explicit provision, the Constitution affords protection against exclusion of the public from criminal trials.

The First Amendment, in conjunction with the Fourteenth, prohibits governments from "abridging the freedom of speech, or of the press; or the right of the people peaceably to assemble, and to petition the Government for a redress of grievances." These expressly guaranteed freedoms share a common core purpose of assuring freedom of communication on matters relating to the functioning of government. Plainly it would be difficult to single out any aspect of government of higher concern and importance to the people than the manner in which criminal trials are conducted; as we have shown, recognition of this pervades the centuries-old history of open trials and the opinions of this Court.

In guaranteeing freedoms such as those of speech and press, the First Amendment can be read as protecting the right of everyone to attend trials so as to give meaning to those explicit guarantees. "The First Amendment goes beyond protection of the press and the self-expression of individuals to prohibit government from limiting the stock of information from which members of the public may draw." Free speech carries with it some freedom to listen. "In a variety of contexts this Court has referred to a First Amendment right to receive information and ideas." What this means in the context of trials is that the First Amendment guarantees of speech and press, standing alone, prohibit government from summarily closing courtroom doors which had long been open to the public at the time that Amendment was adopted.

It is not crucial whether we describe this right to attend criminal trials to hear, see, and communicate observations concerning them as a "right of access," or a "right to gather information," for we have recognized that "without some protection for seeking out the news, freedom of the press could be eviscerated." The explicit, guaranteed rights to speak and to publish concerning what takes place at trial would lose much meaning if access to observe the trial could, as it was here, be foreclosed arbitrarily.

The State argues that the Constitution nowhere spells out a guarantee for the right of the public to attend trials, and that accordingly no such right is protected. The possibility that such a contention could be made did not escape the notice of the Constitution's draftsmen; they were concerned that some important rights might be thought disparaged because not specifically guaranteed.

But arguments such as the State makes have not precluded recognition of important rights not enumerated. Notwithstanding the appropriate caution against reading into the Constitution rights not explicitly defined, the Court has acknowledged that certain unarticulated rights are implicit in enumerated guarantees. For example, the rights of association and of privacy, the right to be presumed innocent, and the right to be judged by a standard of proof beyond a reasonable doubt in a criminal trial, as well as the right to travel, appear nowhere in the Constitution or Bill of Rights. Yet these important but unarticulated rights have nonetheless been found to share constitutional protection in common with explicit guarantees. The concerns expressed by Madison and others have thus been resolved; fundamental rights, even though not expressly guaranteed, have been recognized by the Court as indispensable to the enjoyment of rights explicitly defined.

We hold that the right to attend criminal trials is implicit in the guarantees of the First Amendment; without the freedom to attend such trials, which people have exercised for centuries, important aspects of freedom of speech and "of the press could be eviscerated."

MR. JUSTICE REHNQUIST, dissenting.

In the Gilbert and Sullivan operetta "Iolanthe," the Lord Chancellor recites:

The Law is the true embodiment
of everything that's excellent,
It has no kind of fault or flaw,
And I, my Lords, embody the Law.

It is difficult not to derive more than a little of this flavor from the various opinions supporting the judgment in this case.

I do not believe that either the First or Sixth Amendment, as made applicable to the States by the Fourteenth, requires that a State's reasons for denying public access to a trial, where both the prosecuting attorney and the defendant have consented to an order of closure approved by the judge, are subject to any additional constitutional review at our hands. And I most certainly do not believe that the Ninth Amendment confers upon us any such power to review orders of state trial judges closing trials in such situations.

We have at present 50 state judicial systems and one federal judicial system in the United States, and our authority to reverse a decision by the highest court of the State is limited to only those occasions when the state decision violates some provision of the United States Constitution. And that authority should be exercised with a full sense that the judges whose decisions we review are making the same effort as we to uphold the Constitution. As said by Mr. Justice Jackson, concurring in the result in *Brown v. Allen*, 344 U.S. 443, 540 (1953), "We are not final because we are infallible, but we are infallible only because we are final."

The proper administration of justice in any nation is bound to be a matter of the highest concern to all thinking citizens. But to gradually rein in, as this Court has done over the past generation, all of the ultimate decisionmaking power over how justice shall be administered, not merely in the federal system but in each of the 50 States, is a task that no Court consisting of nine persons, however gifted, is equal to. Nor is it desirable that such authority be exercised by such a tiny numerical fragment of the 220 million people who compose the population of this country.

It is basically unhealthy to have so much authority concentrated in a small group of lawyers who have been appointed to the Supreme Court and enjoy virtual life tenure.

I dissent.

[Justice White's concurring opinion and Justice Stevens' concurring opinion are omitted, as are Justice Brennan's opinion concurring in the judgment, which was joined by Justice Marshall, Justice Stewart's opinion concurring in the judgment, and Justice Blackmun's opinion concurring in the judgment.]

Points for Discussion

1. **How should the *Richmond Newspapers* principle apply to criminal trials involving sexual abuse of minors?** In *Globe Newspaper Co. v. Superior Court*, 457 U.S. 596 (1982), the Court invalidated a Massachusetts law that excluded the press and general public from a sex-offense trial during the testimony of a minor victim. The state interests asserted to defend the statute were the protection of minor victims of sex crimes from further trauma and embarrassment and the need to encourage such victims to testify at trial. But the Court noted that the weight of these interests will vary from case to case depending on the victim's age and psychological maturity, the nature of the crime, and the desires of the victim and relatives. The Court held the law invalid under the First Amendment because it required press and public exclusion in every case, regardless of variables in the above factors. The Court was quite assertive in articulating the strength of the constitutional presumption against closure. "The circumstances under which the press and public can be barred from a criminal trial are limited; the State's justification in denying access must be a weighty one. Where the State attempts to deny the right of access in order to inhibit the disclosure of sensitive information, it must be shown that the denial is necessitated by a compelling governmental interest, and is narrowly tailored to serve that interest."

2. **Does the right of access to criminal trials extend to events and documents outside the actual trial itself?** In a series of opinions the Supreme Court and lower courts have steadily expanded the scope of the right of access to criminal proceedings. The Court has adopted a two-prong "experience and logic" test to evaluate access claims. Under the "experience" prong, a judicial proceeding or record must have historically been open to the press and general public, and under the "logic" prong, public access must play a significant positive role in the functioning of the particular process in question. This is often referred to as the "*Press-Enterprise* test," derived from *Press-Enterprise Co. v. Superior Court*, 478 U.S. 1 (1986). The right of access to criminal proceedings has been extended, for example, to criminal court documents and transcripts.

3. **Does the right of access apply to civil judicial proceedings?** The Supreme Court has not decided the question. Lower courts confronted with the issue have generally been inclined to extend the *Richmond Newspapers* rationale to

civil proceedings as well. *See Courthouse News Serv. v. Planet*, 947 F.3d 581, 590 (9th Cir. 2020) ("The Supreme Court has yet to explicitly rule on whether the First Amendment right of access to information reaches civil judicial proceedings and records, but the federal courts of appeals widely agree that it does."). In what respects are the rationales justifying access to criminal proceedings like or unlike claims of access to civil proceedings?

4. **Does the right of access apply to juvenile criminal proceedings?** Again, the Supreme Court has never definitively resolved the issue. Lower court opinions are split. The trend is toward recognition of a qualified right of access to juvenile criminal proceedings, to be applied on a case-by-case basis. *See Hartford Courant Co. v. Carroll*, 986 F.3d 211, 222 (2d Cir. 2021) ("While the Supreme Court's cases are not entirely on point, their holdings logically apply here. Connecticut's interest in protecting juveniles will be sufficiently served if there is a presumption of openness that can be reviewed on a case-by-case basis. Indeed, defendants have offered no explanation as to why this would not adequately serve the state's interest in protecting juveniles from the stigma of being criminally tried.").

5. **Does the right of access to judicial proceedings include a right of access to the discovery materials produced by parties in litigation?** The American litigation system, particularly the system governing civil litigation, provides for robust discovery. Through such devices as interrogatories, production of documents, and depositions, parties are required to produce information that may ultimately be introduced in court during a trial or prior to trial during motion practice, such as evidentiary exhibits accompanying a motion for summary judgment. Discovery is often subject to "protective orders" entered by the court, often through the parties' mutual consent, in which material exchanged in discovery is deemed confidential. Such protective orders typically restrict the party receiving the information from using it for purposes other than the litigation, and the orders also restrict access to the information by outsiders to the litigation, including the press and general public. As noted in Part C of this chapter, dealing with prior restraints, the First Amendment has been interpreted as allowing such protective orders, restricting access to information obtained in discovery but not yet introduced in court filings or open court proceedings.

2. Access to Other Governmental Institutions and Information: No General Right to Access Government Information

In contrast to its robust right of access to judicial proceedings, First Amendment doctrine does not provide a comparably expansive right to access other governmental institutions or information. A series of decisions in the 1970s, for example, refused to recognize any special right of access by journalists to jails and prisons. *See, e.g., Pell v. Procunier*, 417 U.S. 817 (1974) (refusing to recognize a right of press access to prisons and jails, over and above whatever rights of access to those institutions would be permitted for the general public); *Saxbe v. Washington Post Co.*, 417 U.S. 843 (1974) (same).

In *Houchins,* the Court rejected a television broadcasting company's claim that it should have a First Amendment right to inspect and take photographs of a portion of a county jail where a prisoner's suicide had reportedly occurred and where conditions were allegedly inhumane. The opinion is of somewhat limited precedential force because Justices Thurgood Marshall and Harry Blackmun did not participate, leaving the Court with only seven justices on the case. The plurality opinion, written by Chief Justice Burger and joined by Justices Byron White and William Rehnquist, contained these salient passages:

> We can agree with many of the respondents' generalized assertions; conditions in jails and prisons are clearly matters "of great public importance." Penal facilities are public institutions which require large amounts of public funds, and their mission is crucial in our criminal justice system. Each person placed in prison becomes, in effect, a ward of the state for whom society assumes broad responsibility. It is equally true that with greater information, the public can more intelligently form opinions about prison conditions. Beyond question, the role of the media is important; acting as the "eyes and ears" of the public, they can be a powerful and constructive force, contributing to remedial action in the conduct of public business. They have served that function since the beginning of the Republic, but like all other components of our society media representatives are subject to limits.
>
> The public importance of conditions in penal facilities and the media's role of providing information afford no basis for reading into the Constitution a right of the public or the media to enter these institutions, with camera equipment, and take moving and still pictures of inmates for broadcast purposes. This Court has never intimated a First Amendment guarantee of a right of access to all sources of information within government control.
>
> "There is no constitutional right to have access to particular government information, or to require openness from the bureaucracy. The public's interest in knowing about its government is protected by the guarantee of a Free Press, but the protection is indirect. The Constitution itself is neither a Freedom of Information Act nor an Official Secrets Act. The Constitution, in other words, establishes the contest, not its resolution. Congress may provide a resolution, at least in some instances, through carefully drawn legislation. For the rest, we must rely, as so often in our system we must, on the tug and pull of the political forces in American society."

Justice John Paul Stevens, joined by Justices William Brennan and Lewis Powell, dissented. They would have granted the television station access to the jail. Here is one of the key passages from Justice Stevens' opinion:

> In addition to safeguarding the right of one individual to receive what another elects to communicate, the First Amendment serves an essential societal function. Our system of self-government assumes the existence of an informed citizenry. As Madison wrote: "A popular Government, without popular information, or the means of acquiring it, is but a Prologue to a Farce or a tragedy; or, perhaps both. Knowledge will forever govern ignorance: And a people who mean to be their own Governors, must arm themselves with the power which knowledge gives."
>
> It is not sufficient, therefore, that the channels of communication be free of governmental restraints. Without some protection for the acquisition of information about the operation of public institutions such as prisons by the public at large, the process of self-governance contemplated by the Framers would be stripped of its substance.
>
> For that reason information gathering is entitled to some measure of constitutional protection.

The Court was thus divided 3–3, with the deciding vote left in the hands of Justice Stewart. His opinion appeared to adopt a middle ground, meaning *Houchins* concluded with a curious 3–1–3 vote. Here are the salient passages from Justice Stewart's opinion:

> I agree that the preliminary injunction issued against the petitioner was unwarranted, and therefore concur in the judgment. In my view, however, [television station] KQED was entitled to injunctive relief of more limited scope.
>
> The First and Fourteenth Amendments do not guarantee the public a right of access to information generated or controlled by government, nor do they guarantee the press any basic right of access superior to that of the public generally. The Constitution does no more than assure the public and the press equal access once government has opened its doors. Accordingly, I agree substantially with what the opinion of The Chief Justice has to say on that score.
>
> We part company, however, in applying these abstractions to the facts of this case. Whereas he appears to view "equal access" as meaning access that is identical in all respects, I believe that the concept of equal access must be

accorded more flexibility in order to accommodate the practical distinctions between the press and the general public.

When on assignment, a journalist does not tour a jail simply for his own edification. He is there to gather information to be passed on to others, and his mission is protected by the Constitution for very specific reasons. "Enlightened choice by an informed citizenry is the basic ideal upon which an open society is premised." Our society depends heavily on the press for that enlightenment. Though not without its lapses, the press "has been a mighty catalyst in awakening public interest in governmental affairs, exposing corruption among public officers and employees and generally informing the citizenry of public events and occurrences."

That the First Amendment speaks separately of freedom of speech and freedom of the press is no constitutional accident, but an acknowledgment of the critical role played by the press in American society. The Constitution requires sensitivity to that role, and to the special needs of the press in performing it effectively. A person touring Santa Rita jail can grasp its reality with his own eyes and ears. But if a television reporter is to convey the jail's sights and sounds to those who cannot personally visit the place, he must use cameras and sound equipment. In short, terms of access that are reasonably imposed on individual members of the public may, if they impede effective reporting without sufficient justification, be unreasonable as applied to journalists who are there to convey to the general public what the visitors see.

Under these principles, KQED was clearly entitled to some form of preliminary injunctive relief.

In two respects, however, the District Court's preliminary injunction was overbroad. It ordered the Sheriff to permit reporters into the [jail] and it required him to let them interview randomly encountered inmates. In both these respects, the injunction gave the press access to areas and sources of information from which persons on the public tours had been excluded, and thus enlarged the scope of what the Sheriff and Supervisors had opened to public view. The District Court erred in concluding that the First and Fourteenth Amendments compelled this broader access for the press.

Because the preliminary injunction exceeded the requirements of the Constitution in these respects. I agree that the judgment of the Court of Appeals affirming the District Court's order must be reversed. But I would not foreclose the possibility of further relief for KQED on remand. In my view, the availability and scope of future permanent injunctive relief must depend upon the extent of access then permitted the public, and the decree must be framed to accommodate equitably the constitutional role of the press and the institutional requirements of the jail.

Points for Discussion

1. **Should the First Amendment provide a right of access beyond judicial proceedings?** While under *Richmond Newspapers* and its progeny, the public and the institutional media share a constitutional right to access judicial proceedings, the decisions in cases such as *Pell*, *Saxbe*, and *Houchins* are at best ambivalent as to the existence of any such right to other government institutions or information. Nevertheless, and as Justice Stewart suggests in his *Houchins* opinion, the existing precedent does not necessarily slam the door with finality on the recognition of any more expanded constitutional right. The "You Be the Law Clerk" problem below invites contemplation on whether any such expansion would be sound.

2. **Statutory rights of access to government information.** As is often the case in our constitutional system, legislatures are free to establish rights greater than rights the Constitution creates of its own force. Access to government proceedings and access to government information have been granted more robust protection through enactments of "Sunshine Laws" that grant the public rights of access to certain government proceedings and "Freedom of Information Acts" that grant the public access to certain government information. These ubiquitous laws, which exist at both the federal and state levels, differ among various jurisdictions in their breadth and enforcement mechanisms. Generally, however, they operate as powerful tools for public access to government institutions and information, tools available to all citizens that are often of particular use and importance to media organizations and advocacy groups.

You Be the Law Clerk!

Is there a First Amendment right to watch a ballot recount?

Imagine that you clerk for a Supreme Court justice. Pending before the Court is a case in which it is claimed that the First Amendment grants members of "the press" a right of access to a facility in which public officials are examining paper ballots to conduct a legally required recount involving a contested political election. The state law governing such recounts permits any candidate on the ballot to designate an official representative to be in the room in which the recount is conducted to monitor the process on the candidate's behalf. However, other than state election officials and the official representatives of candidates, state law does not permit any other person to be in the room in which the recount is being conducted.

Television news outlets CNN, Fox News, and MSNBC, joined by National Public Radio, several podcast producers, a filmmaker who is doing a documentary about the political campaign, an independent freelance author who is writing a book about the campaign, and four citizens who curate websites containing personal political commentary and have taken strong positions supporting the two candidates, brought a lawsuit seeking an injunction permitting them to enter the room in which the recount is being conducted to observe the recount and report their impressions of the process.

The justice for whom you clerk asks you for a memorandum on the issues posed by the case. She asks you if in your view the Court should or should not recognize the Press Clause as providing a right of access, qualified or absolute, to the recount room. She further asks you to opine on this question: If the Press Clause were interpreted to grant such access, over and above any access that other private citizens would possess, how should courts determine who qualifies as the "press"? On this second question, consider whether you find the Third Circuit's following observation persuasive or not persuasive:

> More recently, membership in the Fourth Estate has been democratized. Access to blogs, smartphones, and an extensive network of social media sites (not the least of which are Twitter and Facebook) have transformed all of us into potential members of the media. While in almost any other situation this would be a boon to a free and democratic society, in the context of the voting process, the confusion and chaos that would result from a potentially limitless number of reporters in a polling place would work the opposite effect, potentially creating confusion, frustration, and delay. This is to say nothing of our earlier holding that the rights of access for the press and public are co-extensive. In this situation, anyone could record in the polling place if the First Amendment protected the right of access thereto.

PG Publ'g Co. v. Aichele, 705 F.3d 91, 112 n.24 (3d Cir. 2013).

C. May Government Enjoin the Press from Reporting? Prior Restraints in the Litigation Context

You learned in previous chapters that First Amendment jurisprudence has a special antipathy for prior restraints on expression, such as injunctions on publishing or broadcasting or licensing regimes that require expression to be submitted for advance approval by government officials. The jurisprudence's presumption against the constitutionality of prior restraints is not a special "freedom of the press" rule applicable to only the institutional media, but, like the other rules discussed in this chapter, a broader free speech principle protecting all members of the public. Even so, members of the institutional press will often be among the most likely targets of prior restraints, and often the most prominent litigators fighting against them in court. The famous Pentagon Papers case, *New York Times v. United States*, discussed in Chapter 5, is an exemplar. As the *Nebraska Press* and *Seattle Times* decisions below illustrate, issues involving prior restraints also play a significant role in the context of litigation.

Nebraska Press Association v. Stuart

Supreme Court of the United States, 1976
427 U.S. 539

MR. CHIEF JUSTICE BURGER delivered the opinion of the Court.

The respondent State District Judge entered an order restraining the petitioners from publishing or broadcasting accounts of confessions or admissions made by the accused or facts "strongly implicative" of the accused in a widely reported murder of six persons. We granted certiorari to decide whether the entry of such an order on the showing made before the state court violated the constitutional guarantee of freedom of the press.

The problems presented by this case are almost as old as the Republic. Neither in the Constitution nor in contemporaneous writings do we find that the conflict between these two important rights was anticipated, yet it is inconceivable that the authors of the Constitution were unaware of the potential conflicts between the right to an unbiased jury and the guarantee of freedom of the press. The unusually able lawyers who helped write the Constitution and later drafted the Bill of Rights were familiar with the historic episode in which John Adams defended British soldiers charged with homicide for firing into a crowd of Boston demonstrators; they were intimately familiar with the clash of the adversary system and the part that passions of the populace sometimes play in influencing potential jurors.

The trial of Aaron Burr in 1807 presented Mr. Chief Justice Marshall, presiding as a trial judge, with acute problems in selecting an unbiased jury. Few people in the area of Virginia from which jurors were drawn had not formed some opinions concerning Mr. Burr or the case, from newspaper accounts and heightened discussion both private and public. The Chief Justice conducted a searching voir dire of the two panels eventually called, and rendered a substantial opinion on the purposes of voir dire and the standards to be applied. Burr was acquitted, so there was no occasion for appellate review to examine the problem of prejudicial pretrial publicity. Mr. Chief Justice Marshall's careful voir dire inquiry into the matter of possible bias makes clear that the problem is not a new one.

The speed of communication and the pervasiveness of the modern news media have exacerbated these problems, however, as numerous appeals demonstrate. The trial of Bruno Hauptmann in a small New Jersey community for the abduction and murder of the Charles Lindberghs' infant child probably was the most widely covered trial up to that time, and the nature of the coverage produced widespread public reaction. The excesses of press and radio and lack of responsibility of those in authority in the Hauptmann case and others of that era led to efforts to develop voluntary guidelines for courts, lawyers, press, and broadcasters.

The state trial judge in the case before us acted responsibly, out of a legitimate concern, in an effort to protect the defendant's right to a fair trial.

The thread running through all these cases is that prior restraints on speech and publication are the most serious and the least tolerable infringement on First Amendment rights. A criminal penalty or a judgment in a defamation case is subject to the whole panoply of protections afforded by deferring the impact of the judgment until all avenues of appellate review have been exhausted. Only after judgment has become final, correct or otherwise, does the law's sanction become fully operative.

A prior restraint, by contrast and by definition, has an immediate and irreversible sanction. If it can be said that a threat of criminal or civil sanctions after publication "chills" speech, prior restraint "freezes" it at least for the time.

The extraordinary protections afforded by the First Amendment carry with them something in the nature of a fiduciary duty to exercise the protected rights responsibly, a duty widely acknowledged but not always observed by editors and publishers. It is not asking too much to suggest that those who exercise First Amendment rights in newspapers or broadcasting enterprises direct some effort to protect the rights of an accused to a fair trial by unbiased jurors.

Of course, the order at issue like the order requested in *New York Times* does not prohibit but only postpones publication. Some news can be delayed and most commentary can even more readily be delayed without serious injury, and there often is a self-imposed delay when responsible editors call for verification of information. But such delays are normally slight and they are self-imposed. Delays imposed by governmental authority are a different matter.

"We have learned, and continue to learn, from what we view as the unhappy experiences of other nations where government has been allowed to meddle in the internal editorial affairs of newspapers. Regardless of how beneficent-sounding the purposes of controlling the press might be, we remain intensely skeptical about those measures that would allow government to insinuate itself into the editorial rooms of this Nation's press." *Miami Herald Publishing Co. v. Tornillo* (White, J., concurring).

Most of the alternatives to prior restraint of publication in these circumstances were discussed with obvious approval in *Sheppard v. Maxwell*, 384 U.S. 333, 357–362 (1966): (a) change of trial venue to a place less exposed to the intense publicity that seemed imminent in Lincoln County; (b) postponement of the trial to allow public attention to subside; (c) searching questioning of prospective jurors, as Mr. Chief Justice Marshall used in the Burr Case, to screen out those with fixed opinions as to guilt or innocence; (d) the use of emphatic and clear instructions on the sworn duty of each juror to decide the issues only on evidence presented in open court. Sequestration of jurors is, of course, always available. Although that measure insulates jurors only after they are sworn, it also enhances the likelihood of dissipating the impact of pretrial publicity and emphasizes the elements of the jurors' oaths.

The record demonstrates, as the Nebraska courts held, that there was indeed a risk that pretrial news accounts, true or false, would have some adverse impact on the attitudes of those who might be called as jurors. But on the record now before us it is not clear that further publicity, unchecked, would so distort the views of potential jurors that 12 could not be found who would, under proper instructions, fulfill their sworn duty to render a just verdict exclusively on the evidence presented in open court. We cannot say on this record that alternatives to a prior restraint on petitioners would not have sufficiently mitigated the adverse effects of pretrial publicity so as to make prior restraint unnecessary. Nor can we conclude that the restraining order actually entered would serve its intended purpose. Reasonable minds can have few doubts about the gravity of the evil pretrial publicity can work, but the probability that it would do so here was not demonstrated with the degree of certainty our cases on prior restraint require.

Of necessity our holding is confined to the record before us. But our conclusion is not simply a result of assessing the adequacy of the showing made in this case; it results in part from the problems inherent in meeting the heavy burden of demonstrating, in advance of trial, that without prior restraint a fair trial will be denied. The practical problems of managing and enforcing restrictive orders will always be present. In this sense, the record now before us is illustrative rather than exceptional. It is significant that when this Court has reversed a state conviction, because of prejudicial publicity, it has carefully noted that some course of action short of prior restraint would have made a critical difference. However difficult it may be, we need not rule out the possibility of showing the kind of threat to fair trial rights that would possess the requisite degree of certainty to justify restraint. This Court has frequently denied that First Amendment rights are absolute and has consistently rejected the proposition that a prior restraint can never be employed.

Our analysis ends as it began, with a confrontation between prior restraint imposed to protect one vital constitutional guarantee and the explicit command of another that the freedom to speak and publish shall not be abridged. We reaffirm that the guarantees of freedom of expression are not an absolute prohibition under all circumstances, but the barriers to prior restraint remain high and the presumption against its use continues intact. We hold that, with respect to the order entered in this case prohibiting reporting or commentary on judicial proceedings held in public, the barriers have not been overcome; to the extent that this order restrained publication of such material, it is clearly invalid. To the extent that it prohibited publication based on information gained from other sources, we conclude that the heavy burden imposed as a condition to securing a prior restraint was not met and the judgment of the Nebraska Supreme Court is therefore

Reversed.

MR. JUSTICE WHITE, concurring.

Technically there is no need to go farther than the Court does to dispose of this case, and I join the Court's opinion. I should add, however, that for the reasons which the Court itself canvasses there is grave doubt in my mind whether orders with respect to the press such as were entered in this case would ever be justifiable.

MR. JUSTICE POWELL, concurring.

In my judgment a prior restraint properly may issue only when it is shown to be necessary to prevent the dissemination of prejudicial publicity that otherwise poses a high likelihood of preventing, directly and irreparably, the impaneling of a jury meeting the Sixth Amendment requirement of impartiality. This requires a showing that (i) there is a clear threat to the fairness of trial, (ii) such a threat is posed by the actual publicity to be restrained, and (iii) no less restrictive alternatives are available.

MR. JUSTICE BRENNAN, with whom MR. JUSTICE STEWART and MR. JUSTICE MARSHALL join, concurring in the judgment.

The right to a fair trial by a jury of one's peers is unquestionably one of the most precious and sacred safeguards enshrined in the Bill of Rights. I would hold, however, that resort to prior restraints on the freedom of the press is a constitutionally impermissible method for enforcing that right.

MR. JUSTICE STEVENS, concurring in the judgment.

For the reasons eloquently stated by Mr. Justice Brennan, I agree that the judiciary is capable of protecting the defendant's right to a fair trial without enjoining the press from publishing information in the public domain, and that it may not do so. Whether the same absolute protection would apply no matter how shabby or illegal the means by which the information is obtained, no matter how serious an intrusion on privacy might be involved, no matter how demonstrably false the information might be, no matter how prejudicial it might be to the interests of innocent persons, and no matter how perverse the motivation for publishing it, is a question I would not answer without further argument. I do, however, subscribe to most of what Mr. Justice Brennan says and, if ever required to face the issues squarely, may well accept his ultimate conclusion.

Points for Discussion

1. **Is it possible to control access to information in the internet age?** Today we are quite used to hearing every conceivable angle and seeing every piece of publicly available evidence in the press coverage leading up to trials concerning notorious crimes. Consider, for example, the common practice of examining in painstaking detail videos of police brutality released before the allegedly culpable officers are put on trial for murder. It is almost impossible to imagine how any court could, as a practical matter, restrain the proliferation of video footage that has gone viral on social media in such instances, even if such a restraint were ever constitutionally permissible.

2. **The practical impact of *Nebraska Press*.** While technically the unanimous decision striking down the gag order in *Nebraska Press* left open the possibility that such an order would be constitutionally justifiable in some future case, the Court's opinion has come to be understood as a virtually absolute prohibition on such prior restraints, as applied to members of the press and public. This "absolutist" gloss arises in part from the various opinions of the concurring justices.

   Justices Brennan, Stewart, and Marshall took the view that prior restraints are never permissible to deter coverage of criminal trials, recognizing a possible exception only for national security purposes. Justice Brennan's lengthy opinion is largely omitted above, save for his conclusion that prior restraints on coverage of criminal trials are essentially never allowed. Justice White came very close to the same position, stating that "there is grave doubt in my mind whether orders with respect to the press such as were entered in this case would ever be justifiable." Justice Stevens wrote an opinion very much like Justice White's, stating that he agreed with the reasons "eloquently stated" by Justice Brennan for an absolute rule, but was not willing to go quite that far without further debate on the point. Justice Powell's opinion did appear to allow for prior restraints in exceptional cases, though he held that such an order would not be permitted unless there is a "clear threat" to the fairness of the trial, the threat is posed by the "actual publicity" to be restrained, and "no less restrictive alternatives are available." Thus, the real vote in *Nebraska Press* was as close to an absolute bar on prior restraints as one can get without actually getting there, and that is how most lower courts have read the case in the years that followed.

3. **Are gag orders and other legal rules restricting what lawyers and other direct participants in litigation may say during the pendency of proceedings constitutional?** The ruling in *Nebraska Press* dealt with the robust First Amendment protection afforded to the publication or broadcast of material concerning pending litigation by outsiders to the litigation, such as the press and public. Are the rules of the game different for participants in the litigation, such as attorneys, parties, witnesses, jurors, or court personnel? The answer is yes. In most states, rules of professional responsibility governing the conduct of lawyers restrict what they may say publicly about pending cases. For example, Rule 3.6 of the American Bar Association Model Rules of Professional Conduct says, "A lawyer who is participating or has participated in the investigation or litigation of a matter shall not make an extrajudicial statement that the lawyer knows or reasonably should know will be disseminated by means of public communication and will have a substantial likelihood of materially prejudicing an adjudicative proceeding in the matter." The Supreme Court in *Gentile v. State Bar of Nevada*, 501 U.S. 1030 (1991), considered a case in which a prominent criminal defense attorney, Dominic Gentile, was held to have violated a state rule prohibiting a lawyer from making such extrajudicial statements. The result was somewhat confusing, because Chief Justice Rehnquist and Justice Anthony Kennedy combined through different opinions to deliver the holding of the Court. Chief Justice Rehnquist distinguished between parties to litigation and strangers to it, holding that lawyers are not protected by the First Amendment to the same extent as other professionals. He deemed the "substantial likelihood of material prejudice" standard a constitutionally permissible balance between the First Amendment rights of attorneys in pending cases and the government interest in fair trials. The specific Nevada rule was held void for vagueness, however, in a portion of the opinion authored by Justice Kennedy. Nevada allowed a lawyer a "safe harbor," stating that it was not a violation of the rule "to state without elaboration the general nature of the defense." The Court held this language was so vague that it required lawyers attempting to abide by the rule to make their own interpretations of it. Justice Kennedy pointed out that "general" and "elaboration" are both

terms of degree with no settled usage in the interpretation of law. Consequently, he concluded, "the lawyer has no principle for determining when his remarks pass from the safe harbor of the general to the forbidden sea of the elaborated."

4. **Should greater First Amendment protection attach to gag orders against other participants in judicial proceedings, such as parties or jurors?** The correct answer is yes, according to the Fourth Circuit in *In re Murphy-Brown, LLC*, 907 F.3d 788 (4th Cir. 2018). The appeals court overturned a gag order imposing stringent restrictions on participants and potential participants in a series of nuisance suits brought against the hog industry in North Carolina. Under the challenged gag order, the parties, their lawyers, and all potential witnesses were not allowed to "give or authorize any extrajudicial statement relating to the trial, the parties or issues in this case" if such statement could reasonably reach "public communications media" and could "interfere with a fair trial or prejudice any plaintiff, the defendant, or the administration of justice." Gag orders, the court noted, trigger rigorous First Amendment scrutiny for two independent reasons. As prior restraints, they implicate the presumption of invalidity attached to all prior restraints. And as content-based restrictions, they are presumptively unconstitutional, subject to strict scrutiny: "Gag orders inherently target speech relating to pending litigation, a topic right at the core of public and community life." Resting at the confluence of these twin presumptions, the court held, gag orders are invalid unless they survive strict scrutiny. "Gag orders," it concluded, "should be a last resort, not a first impulse."

Seattle Times Co. v. Rhinehart

Supreme Court of the United States, 1984
467 U.S. 20

JUSTICE POWELL delivered the opinion of the Court.

This case presents the issue whether parties to civil litigation have a First Amendment right to disseminate, in advance of trial, information gained through the pretrial discovery process.

Respondent Rhinehart is the spiritual leader of a religious group, the Aquarian Foundation. The Foundation has fewer than 1,000 members, most of whom live in the State of Washington. Aquarian beliefs include life after death and the ability to communicate with the dead through a medium. Rhinehart is the primary Aquarian medium.

In recent years, the Seattle Times and the Walla Walla Union-Bulletin have published stories about Rhinehart and the Foundation. Altogether 11 articles appeared in the newspapers during the years 1973, 1978, and 1979. The five articles that appeared in 1973 focused on Rhinehart and the manner in which he operated the Foundation. They described seances conducted by Rhinehart in which people paid him to put them in touch with deceased relatives and friends. The articles also stated that Rhinehart had sold magical "stones" that had been "expelled" from his body. One article referred to Rhinehart's conviction, later vacated, for sodomy. The four articles that appeared in 1978 concentrated on an "extravaganza" sponsored by Rhinehart at the Walla Walla State Penitentiary. The articles stated that he had treated 1,100 inmates to a 6-hour-long show, during which he gave away between $35,000 and $50,000 in cash and prizes. One article described a "chorus line of girls who shed their gowns and bikinis and sang." The two articles that appeared in 1979 referred to a purported connection between Rhinehart and Lou Ferrigno, star of the popular television program, "The Incredible Hulk."

Rhinehart brought this action in the Washington Superior Court on behalf of himself and the Foundation against the Seattle Times, the Walla Walla Union-Bulletin, the authors of the articles, and the spouses of the authors. Five female members of the Foundation who had participated in the presentation at the penitentiary joined the suit as plaintiffs. The complaint alleges that the articles contained statements that were "fictional and untrue," and that the defendants—petitioners here—knew, or should have known, they were false. According to the complaint, the articles "did and were calculated to hold Rhinehart up to public scorn, hatred and ridicule, and to impeach his honesty, integrity, virtue, religious philosophy, reputation as a person and in his profession as a spiritual leader."

Respondents filed a motion for a protective order. They submitted affidavits of several Foundation members to support their request. The affidavits detailed a series of letters and telephone calls defaming the Foundation, its members, and Rhinehart—including several that threatened physical harm to those associated with the Foundation. The affiants also described incidents at the Foundation's headquarters involving attacks, threats, and assaults directed at Foundation members by anonymous individuals and groups. In general, the affidavits averred that public release of the donor lists would adversely affect Foundation membership and income and would subject its members to additional harassment and reprisals.

Persuaded by these affidavits, the trial court issued a protective order covering all information obtained through the discovery process that pertained to "the financial affairs of the various plaintiffs, the names and addresses of Aquarian Foundation members, contributors, or clients, and the names and addresses of those who have been contributors, clients, or donors to any of the various plaintiffs." The order prohibited petitioners from publishing, disseminating, or using the information in any way except where necessary to prepare for and try the case. By its terms, the order did not apply to information gained by means other than the discovery process. In an accompanying opinion, the trial court recognized that the protective order would restrict petitioners' right to publish information obtained by discovery, but the court reasoned that the restriction was necessary to avoid the "chilling effect" that dissemination would have on "a party's willingness to bring his case to court."

Petitioners argue that the First Amendment imposes strict limits on the availability of any judicial order that has the effect of restricting expression. They contend that civil discovery is not different from other sources of information, and that therefore the information is "protected speech" for First Amendment purposes. Petitioners assert the right in this case to disseminate any information gained through discovery.

The critical question that this case presents is whether a litigant's freedom comprehends the right to disseminate information that he has obtained pursuant to a court order that both granted him access to that information and placed restraints on the way in which the information might be used. In addressing that question it is necessary to consider whether the "practice in question furthers an important or substantial governmental interest unrelated to the suppression of expression" and whether "the limitation of First Amendment freedoms is no greater than is necessary or essential to the protection of the particular governmental interest involved."

At the outset, it is important to recognize the extent of the impairment of First Amendment rights that a protective order, such as the one at issue here, may cause. As in all civil litigation, petitioners gained the information they wish to disseminate only by virtue of the trial court's discovery processes. As the Rules authorizing discovery were adopted by the state legislature, the processes thereunder are a matter of legislative grace. A litigant has no First Amendment right of access to information made available only for purposes of trying his suit.

Moreover, pretrial depositions and interrogatories are not public components of a civil trial. Such proceedings were not open to the public at common law, and, in general, they are conducted in private as a matter of modern practice. Much of the information that surfaces during pretrial discovery may be unrelated, or only tangentially related, to the underlying cause of action. Therefore, restraints placed on discovered, but not yet admitted, information are not a restriction on a traditionally public source of information.

Finally, it is significant to note that an order prohibiting dissemination of discovered information before trial is not the kind of classic prior restraint that requires exacting First Amendment scrutiny. As in this case, such a protective order prevents a party from disseminating only that information obtained through use of the discovery process. Thus, the party may disseminate the identical information covered by the protective order as long as the information is gained through means independent of the court's processes. In sum, judicial limitations on a party's ability to disseminate information discovered in advance of trial implicates the First Amendment rights of the restricted party to a far lesser extent than would restraints on dissemination of information in a different context. Therefore, our consideration of the provision for protective orders contained in the Washington Civil Rules takes into account the unique position that such orders occupy in relation to the First Amendment.

We therefore hold that where, as in this case, a protective order is entered on a showing of good cause as required by Rule 26(c), is limited to the context of pretrial civil discovery, and does not restrict the dissemination of the information if gained from other sources, it does not offend the First Amendment.

[Justice Brennan's concurring opinion, which was joined by Justice Marshall, is omitted.]

Point for Discussion

1. **Do judges in civil cases too often issue protective orders that permit documents to be filed under seal and thereby hide information from the public?** While the ruling in *Seattle Times* makes clear that protective orders prohibiting the dissemination of material obtained in discovery typically do not violate the First Amendment, the Court did not provide guidance on the extent to which discovery material filed later or introduced in court afterward may be sealed and hidden from public view. In the real world of litigation, opposing parties are often quite content to agree that much of what is filed in court should be filed under seal, and judges are often too busy with other matters to carefully scrutinize the practice, resulting in a great deal of cases in public courts effectively being tried in secret. Consider the following observations by Judge Colm Connolly of the U.S. District Court for the District of Delaware:

   > Unopposed motions to seal are filed regularly with this Court. Judge [Richard G.] Andrews noted recently that "in his experience, corporate parties in complex litigation generally prefer to litigate in secret." I similarly find that parties in my civil cases routinely ask to seal pleadings that cannot reasonably be characterized as disclosing confidential or proprietary information. And in my (albeit short) tenure on the bench, I cannot recall a party in a civil case opposing a request to seal or objecting to the scope of redactions in the public version of a pleading that was filed pursuant to an order that granted a motion to seal.
   >
   > The District Court is not a star chamber. We are a public institution in a democratic republic and the public has a right of access to our filings. That right is founded in the common law and "antedates the Constitu-

> tion." The public's right of access is not absolute; but it is strongly presumed, and it can be overcome only if a party demonstrates that public disclosure of a filing will result in "a clearly defined and serious injury."
>
> The problem I encounter with unopposed motions to seal pleadings is threefold. First, it falls solely on me to scrutinize the proffered justification for the motion without the benefit of the industry knowledge that is often necessary to determine if a clearly defined and serious injury would result if I denied the motion. Second, if I grant the motion—and I almost always do—it falls solely on me to scrutinize the redactions in the movant's subsequently filed public version of the pleading. Here again, I lack industry knowledge to guide me in assessing whether the proposed redactions are necessary to avoid a clearly defined and serious injury. Third, because of my caseload, I lack time. I currently have on my docket 582 civil cases (including 288 patent cases, of which 119 are Abbreviated New Drug Act cases), 22 criminal cases, 10 miscellaneous actions, and 342 pending motions. I have 32 trials and 25 patent claim construction hearings scheduled for the remainder of this year. I simply do not have the time to review parties' proposed redactions in a meaningful way to ensure that those redactions do not violate the public's right of access.

In re Application of Storag Etzel GmbH, 2020 WL 2949742 (D. Del. Jan. 23, 2020). Judge Connolly appointed Rodney Smolla, co-author of this casebook, as a special master to review the issues and determine what filings ought to be made public on the court's docket. In his report and recommendation, which resulted in the unsealing of much of the material that had been filed, Smolla articulated the governing legal standards:

> Three discrete bodies of law govern the principles pertaining to confidentiality, sealing, and redactions of documents in federal court litigation. They apply in ascending orders of scrutiny.
>
> First, there are principles governing the issuance of protective orders in federal litigation. These principles emanate from Rule 26(c) of the Federal Rules of Civil Procedure, and the attendant gloss courts have applied to the application of Rule 26(c).
>
> Second, federal courts recognize a common law right of access to judicial records. "The existence of a common law right of access to judicial proceedings and to inspect judicial records is beyond dispute." There is a "presumption in favor of access to public records and documents, including judicial records and documents."

> Third, "the public and the press have a First Amendment right of access to civil trials." "The First Amendment, independent of the common law, protects the public's right of access to the records of civil proceedings." "The First Amendment right of access requires a much higher showing than the common law right to access before a judicial proceeding can be sealed." Any restriction on the First Amendment right of public access is "evaluated under strict scrutiny."

In re Application of Storag Etzel GmbH (Smolla, Special Master), 2020 WL 2949742 (D. Del. Mar. 25, 2020), report and recommendation adopted in part, 2020 WL 2915781 (D. Del. June 3, 2020).

D. Trafficking in Intercepted or Leaked Information: May the Press Publish Illegally Obtained Information?

Recall the facts of the Pentagon Papers case we studied in Chapter 5. The Supreme Court's opinion focused on the prior restraint issue: Could courts enjoin *The New York Times* and *The Washington Post* from publishing the leaked documents? As Justice John Harlan noted in a dissent, the majority in its haste to resolve the prior restraint issue failed to fully address other underlying issues, including the newspaper's use of a knowingly purloined document:

> This frenzied train of events took place in the name of the presumption against prior restraints created by the First Amendment. Due regard for the extraordinarily important and difficult questions involved in these litigations should have led the Court to shun such a precipitate timetable. In order to decide the merits of these cases properly, some questions should have been faced [including whether] the newspapers are entitled to retain and use the documents notwithstanding the seemingly uncontested facts that the documents, or the originals of which they are duplicates, were purloined from the Government's possession and that the newspapers received them with knowledge that they had been feloniously acquired.

In the following case, the Court again confronted a fact pattern in which the press knowingly disseminated information that the journalists knew, or at least should have known, had been illegally obtained.

Bartnicki v. Vopper

Supreme Court of the United States, 2001
532 U.S. 514

JUSTICE STEVENS delivered the opinion of the Court.

These cases raise an important question concerning what degree of protection, if any, the First Amendment provides to speech that discloses the contents of an illegally intercepted communication. That question is both novel and narrow. Despite the fact that federal law has prohibited such disclosures since 1934, this is the first time that we have confronted such an issue.

During 1992 and most of 1993, the Pennsylvania State Education Association, a union representing the teachers at the Wyoming Valley West High School, engaged in collective-bargaining negotiations with the school board. Petitioner Kane, then the president of the local union, testified that the negotiations were "contentious" and received "a lot of media attention." In May 1993, petitioner Bartnicki, who was acting as the union's "chief negotiator," used the cellular phone in her car to call Kane and engage in a lengthy conversation about the status of the negotiations. An unidentified person intercepted and recorded that call.

In their conversation, Kane and Bartnicki discussed the timing of a proposed strike, difficulties created by public comment on the negotiations, and the need for a dramatic response to the board's intransigence. At one point, Kane said: "If they're not gonna move for three percent, we're gonna have to go to their, their homes. To blow off their front porches, we'll have to do some work on some of those guys. (PAUSES). Really, uh, really and truthfully because this is, you know, this is bad news. (UNDECIPHERABLE)."

In the early fall of 1993, the parties accepted a nonbinding arbitration proposal that was generally favorable to the teachers. In connection with news reports about the settlement, respondent Vopper, a radio commentator who had been critical of the union in the past, played a tape of the intercepted conversation on his public affairs talk show. Another station also broadcast the tape, and local newspapers published its contents. After filing suit against Vopper and other representatives of the media, Bartnicki and Kane learned through discovery that Vopper had obtained the tape from respondent Jack Yocum, the head of a local taxpayers' organization that had opposed the union's demands throughout the negotiations. Yocum, who was added as a defendant, testified that he had found the tape in his mailbox shortly after the interception and recognized the voices of Bartnicki and Kane. Yocum played the tape for some members of the school board, and later delivered the tape itself to Vopper.

In their amended complaint, petitioners alleged that their telephone conversation had been surreptitiously intercepted by an unknown person using an electronic device, that Yocum had obtained a tape of that conversation, and that he intentionally disclosed it to Vopper, as well as other individuals and media representatives.

Thereafter, Vopper and other members of the media repeatedly published the contents of that conversation. The amended complaint alleged that each of the defendants "knew or had reason to know" that the recording of the private telephone conversation had been obtained by means of an illegal interception. Relying on both federal and Pennsylvania statutory provisions, petitioners sought actual damages, statutory damages, punitive damages, and attorney's fees and costs.

"Congress undertook to draft comprehensive legislation both authorizing the use of evidence obtained by electronic surveillance on specified conditions, and prohibiting its use otherwise." The ultimate result of those efforts was Title III of the Omnibus Crime Control and Safe Streets Act of 1968.

One of the stated purposes of that title was "to protect effectively the privacy of wire and oral communications." Subsection (a) applied to any person who "willfully intercepts any wire or oral communication." Subsection (c), the original version of the provision most directly at issue in this suit, applied to any person who "willfully discloses, or endeavors to disclose, to any other person the contents of any wire or oral communication, knowing or having reason to know that the information was obtained through the interception of a wire or oral communication in violation of this subsection."

We agree with petitioners that § 2511(1)(c), as well as its Pennsylvania analog, is in fact a content-neutral law of general applicability.

The statute does not distinguish based on the content of the intercepted conversations, nor is it justified by reference to the content of those conversations. Rather, the communications at issue are singled out by virtue of the fact that they were illegally intercepted—by virtue of the source, rather than the subject matter.

On the other hand, the naked prohibition against disclosures is fairly characterized as a regulation of pure speech. Unlike the prohibition against the "use" of the contents of an illegal interception in § 2511(1)(d), subsection (c) is not a regulation of conduct. It is true that the delivery of a tape recording might be regarded as conduct, but given that the purpose of such a delivery is to provide the recipient with the text of recorded statements, it is like the delivery of a handbill or a pamphlet, and as such, it is the kind of "speech" that the First Amendment protects.

As a general matter, "state action to punish the publication of truthful information seldom can satisfy constitutional standards." *Smith v. Daily Mail Publishing* Co.,

443 U.S. 97, 102 (1979). More specifically, this Court has repeatedly held that "if a newspaper lawfully obtains truthful information about a matter of public significance then state officials may not constitutionally punish publication of the information, absent a need of the highest order." *Id.*; see also *Florida Star v. B.J.F.*, 491 U.S. 524 (1989); *Landmark Communications, Inc. v. Virginia*, 435 U.S. 829 (1978).

In *New York Times Co. v. United States*, the Court upheld the right of the press to publish information of great public concern obtained from documents stolen by a third party. In so doing, that decision resolved a conflict between the basic rule against prior restraints on publication and the interest in preserving the secrecy of information that, if disclosed, might seriously impair the security of the Nation. In resolving that conflict, the attention of every Member of this Court was focused on the character of the stolen documents' contents and the consequences of public disclosure. Although the undisputed fact that the newspaper intended to publish information obtained from stolen documents was noted in Justice Harlan's dissent, neither the majority nor the dissenters placed any weight on that fact.

However, *New York Times v. United States* raised, but did not resolve, the question "whether, in cases where information has been acquired unlawfully by a newspaper or by a source, government may ever punish not only the unlawful acquisition, but the ensuing publication as well." The question here, however, is a narrower version of that still-open question. Simply put, the issue here is this: "Where the punished publisher of information has obtained the information in question in a manner lawful in itself but from a source who has obtained it unlawfully, may the government punish the ensuing publication of that information based on the defect in a chain?"

The Government identifies two interests served by the statute—first, the interest in removing an incentive for parties to intercept private conversations, and second, the interest in minimizing the harm to persons whose conversations have been illegally intercepted. We assume that those interests adequately justify the prohibition in § 2511(1)(d) against the interceptor's own use of information that he or she acquired by violating § 2511(1)(a), but it by no means follows that punishing disclosures of lawfully obtained information of public interest by one not involved in the initial illegality is an acceptable means of serving those ends.

The normal method of deterring unlawful conduct is to impose an appropriate punishment on the person who engages in it.

Although this suit demonstrates that there may be an occasional situation in which an anonymous scanner will risk criminal prosecution by passing on information without any expectation of financial reward or public praise, surely this is the exceptional case. Moreover, there is no basis for assuming that imposing sanctions upon respondents will deter the unidentified scanner from continuing to engage in surreptitious interceptions.

The Government's second argument, however, is considerably stronger. Privacy of communication is an important interest, and Title III's restrictions are intended to protect that interest, thereby "encouraging the uninhibited exchange of ideas and information among private parties." Moreover, the fear of public disclosure of private conversations might well have a chilling effect on private speech.

We need not decide whether that interest is strong enough to justify the application of § 2511(c) to disclosures of trade secrets or domestic gossip or other information of purely private concern. In other words, the outcome of these cases does not turn on whether § 2511(1)(c) may be enforced with respect to most violations of the statute without offending the First Amendment. The enforcement of that provision in these cases, however, implicates the core purposes of the First Amendment because it imposes sanctions on the publication of truthful information of public concern.

In these cases, privacy concerns give way when balanced against the interest in publishing matters of public importance. As Warren and Brandeis stated in their classic law review article: "The right of privacy does not prohibit any publication of matter which is of public or general interest." The Right to Privacy, 4 Harv. L. Rev. 193, 214 (1890). One of the costs associated with participation in public affairs is an attendant loss of privacy.

We think it clear that parallel reasoning requires the conclusion that a stranger's illegal conduct does not suffice to remove the First Amendment shield from speech about a matter of public concern. The months of negotiations over the proper level of compensation for teachers at the Wyoming Valley West High School were unquestionably a matter of public concern, and respondents were clearly engaged in debate about that concern. That debate may be more mundane than the Communist rhetoric that inspired Justice Brandeis' classic opinion in *Whitney v. California,* but it is no less worthy of constitutional protection.

Justice Breyer, with whom Justice O'Connor joins, concurring.

I join the Court's opinion. I agree with its narrow holding limited to the special circumstances present here: (1) the radio broadcasters acted lawfully (up to the time of final public disclosure); and (2) the information publicized involved a matter of unusual public concern, namely, a threat of potential physical harm to others. I write separately to explain why, in my view, the Court's holding does not imply a significantly broader constitutional immunity for the media.

As a general matter, despite the statutes' direct restrictions on speech, the Federal Constitution must tolerate laws of this kind because of the importance of these privacy and speech-related objectives. Rather than broadly forbid this kind of legislative enactment, the Constitution demands legislative efforts to tailor the laws in order reasonably to reconcile media freedom with personal, speech-related privacy.

Nonetheless, looked at more specifically, the statutes, as applied in these circumstances, do not reasonably reconcile the competing constitutional objectives. Rather, they disproportionately interfere with media freedom. For one thing, the broadcasters here engaged in no unlawful activity other than the ultimate publication of the information another had previously obtained. They "neither encouraged nor participated directly or indirectly in the interception." No one claims that they ordered, counseled, encouraged, or otherwise aided or abetted the interception, the later delivery of the tape by the interceptor to an intermediary, or the tape's still later delivery by the intermediary to the media. And, as the Court points out, the statutes do not forbid the receipt of the tape itself. The Court adds that its holding "does not apply to punishing parties for obtaining the relevant information unlawfully."

For another thing, the speakers had little or no legitimate interest in maintaining the privacy of the particular conversation. That conversation involved a suggestion about "blow[ing] off front porches" and "do[ing] some work on some of those guys," thereby raising a significant concern for the safety of others. Where publication of private information constitutes a wrongful act, the law recognizes a privilege allowing the reporting of threats to public safety. See Restatement (Second) of Torts § 595, Comment g (1977) (general privilege to report that "another intends to kill or rob or commit some other serious crime against a third person"); *id.*, § 652G (privilege applies to invasion of privacy tort). Cf. Restatement (Third) of Unfair Competition § 40, Comment c (1995) (trade secret law permits disclosures relevant to public health or safety, commission of crime or tort, or other matters of substantial public concern); *Lachman v. Sperry-Sun Well Surveying Co.*, 457 F.2d 850, 853 (C.A.10 1972) (nondisclosure agreement not binding in respect to criminal activity); *Tarasoff v. Regents of Univ. of Cal.*, 17 Cal. 3d 425 (1976) (psychiatric privilege not binding in presence of danger to self or others). Even where the danger may have passed by the time of publication, that fact cannot legitimize the speaker's earlier privacy expectation. Nor should editors, who must make a publication decision quickly, have to determine present or continued danger before publishing this kind of threat.

CHIEF JUSTICE REHNQUIST, with whom JUSTICE SCALIA and JUSTICE THOMAS join, dissenting.

Technology now permits millions of important and confidential conversations to occur through a vast system of electronic networks. These advances, however, raise significant privacy concerns. We are placed in the uncomfortable position of not knowing who might have access to our personal and business e-mails, our medical and financial records, or our cordless and cellular telephone conversations. In an attempt to prevent some of the most egregious violations of privacy, the United States, the District of Columbia, and 40 States have enacted laws prohibiting the intentional interception and knowing disclosure of electronic communications. The Court holds that all of these statutes violate the First Amendment insofar as the illegally intercepted conversation touches upon a matter of "public concern," an amorphous concept that the Court does not even attempt to define. But the Court's decision diminishes, rather than enhances, the purposes of the First Amendment, thereby chilling the speech of the millions of Americans who rely upon electronic technology to communicate each day.

The Court correctly observes that these are "content-neutral laws of general applicability" which serve recognized interests of the "highest order": "the interest in individual privacy and in fostering private speech." It nonetheless subjects these laws to the strict scrutiny normally reserved for governmental attempts to censor different viewpoints or ideas. There is scant support, either in precedent or in reason, for the Court's tacit application of strict scrutiny.

The Court's attempt to avoid these precedents by reliance upon the *Daily Mail* string of newspaper cases is unpersuasive. In these cases, we held that statutes prohibiting the media from publishing certain truthful information—the name of a rape victim, *Florida Star*; *Cox Broadcasting Corp. v. Cohn*, 420 U.S. 469 (1975), the confidential proceedings before a state judicial review commission, *Landmark Communications,* and the name of a juvenile defendant, *Daily Mail*; *Oklahoma Publishing Co. v. District Court, Oklahoma Cty.*, 430 U.S. 308 (1977) (per curiam)—violated the First Amendment. In so doing, we stated that "if a newspaper lawfully obtains truthful information about a matter of public significance then state officials may not constitutionally punish publication of the information, absent a need to further a state interest of the highest order." *Daily Mail.* Neither this *Daily Mail* principle nor any other aspect of these cases, however, justifies the Court's imposition of strict scrutiny here.

Each of the laws at issue in the *Daily Mail* cases regulated the content or subject matter of speech. This fact alone was enough to trigger strict scrutiny, and suffices to distinguish these antidisclosure provisions. But, as our synthesis of these cases in *Florida Star* made clear, three other unique factors also informed the scope of the *Daily Mail* principle.

First, the information published by the newspapers had been lawfully obtained from the government itself. "Where information is entrusted to the government, a less drastic means than punishing truthful publication almost always exists for guarding against the dissemination of private facts." *Florida Star*. See, e.g., *Landmark Communications* (noting that the State could have taken steps to protect the confidentiality of its proceedings, such as holding in contempt commission members who breached their duty of confidentiality). Indeed, the State's ability to control the information undermined the claim that the restriction was necessary, for "by placing the information in the public domain on official court records, the State must be presumed to have concluded that the public interest was thereby being served." *Cox Broadcasting.*

This factor has no relevance in the present cases, where we deal with private conversations that have been intentionally kept out of the public domain.

Second, the information in each case was already "publicly available," and punishing further dissemination would not have advanced the purported government interests of confidentiality. Such is not the case here. These statutes only prohibit "disclosure," and one cannot "disclose" what is already in the public domain. These laws thus do not fall under the axiom that "the interests in privacy fade when the information involved already appears on the public record."

Third, these cases were concerned with "the timidity and self-censorship which may result from allowing the media to be punished for publishing certain truthful information." But fear of "timidity and self-censorship" is a basis for upholding, not striking down, these antidisclosure provisions: They allow private conversations to transpire without inhibition. And unlike the statute at issue in *Florida Star*, which had no scienter requirement, these statutes only address those who knowingly disclose an illegally intercepted conversation. They do not impose a duty to inquire into the source of the information and one could negligently disclose the contents of an illegally intercepted communication without liability.

In sum, it is obvious that the *Daily Mail* cases upon which the Court relies do not address the question presented here. Our decisions themselves made this clear: "The *Daily Mail* principle does not settle the issue whether, in cases where information has been acquired unlawfully by a newspaper or by a source, government may ever punish not only the unlawful acquisition, but the ensuing publication as well." *Florida Star*; *Landmark Communications* ("We are not here concerned with the possible applicability of the statute to one who secures the information by illegal means and thereafter divulges it").

Surely "the interest in individual privacy," at its narrowest, must embrace the right to be free from surreptitious eavesdropping on, and involuntary broadcast of, our cellular telephone conversations. The Court subordinates that right, not to the claims of those who themselves wish to speak, but to the claims of those who wish to publish the intercepted conversations of others. Congress' effort to balance the above claim to privacy against a marginal claim to speak freely is thereby set at naught.

Point for Discussion

1. **What exactly is the holding in *Bartnicki*?** Did the Court hold that the First Amendment protects anyone who has lawfully obtained truthful information from liability for public disclosure of that information? Or is the holding narrower? Some courts and commentators do not believe that *Bartnicki* stands for a

sweeping "no liability ever" proposition. *See Boehner v. McDermott*, 484 F.3d 573, 577–78 (D.C. Cir. 2007) ("Whatever the *Bartnicki* majority meant by 'lawfully obtain,' the decision does not stand for the proposition that anyone who has lawfully obtained truthful information of public importance has a First Amendment right to disclose that information. *Bartnicki* avoided laying down such a broad rule of law, and for good reason."). One argument for reading *Bartnicki* more narrowly is that two of the justices in the 6–3 majority, Justices Stephen Breyer and Sandra Day O'Connor, took positions that appeared to straddle the arguments of Justice Stevens and Chief Justice Rehnquist, resulting in a far more ambivalent holding. Consider this comparison of Justice Breyer's concurring opinion, which was joined by Justice O'Connor, and Justice Stevens' majority opinion:

> Whereas the opinion for the Court by Justice Stevens emphasized the *Daily Mail* line of cases and the presumptive unconstitutionality of laws that burden trafficking in truthful information, Justice Breyer's opinion adopted exactly the opposite baseline. Laws protecting private electronic conversations, like "laws that would award damages caused through publication of information obtained by theft from a private bedroom," must as "a general matter" be tolerated by the First Amendment, he argued, because of the importance of privacy, including its role in fostering private speech. In Justice Breyer's view, the question was merely one of balance and tailoring; the Constitution does not broadly forbid legislation against trafficking in privacy contraband, it merely "demands legislative efforts to tailor the laws in order reasonably to reconcile media freedom with personal, speech-related privacy."
>
> And therein was the crux of the concurring views of Justices Breyer and O'Connor. Their quarrel was not with the general principle of banning the disclosure of illegally intercepted communication, but with the specific balance struck by the statutes being reviewed, as applied to the specific factual circumstances in *Bartnicki*, circumstances the two concurring Justices viewed through a prism of factual assumptions that cast them in their most sinister possible light. The statutes, as applied, failed to "reasonably reconcile" the competing interests, interfering "disproportionately" with "media freedom."
>
> The broadcasters, Justice Breyer noted, did not "encourage" or "participate directly or indirectly in the interception." "No one claims that they ordered, counseled, encouraged, or otherwise aided or abetted the interception, the later delivery of the tape by the interceptor to an intermediary, or the tape's still later delivery by the intermediary to the media." This observation suggested that in Justice Breyer's view, any such involvement by the media would have disqualified it from the

protection the Court granted in *Bartnicki*, and rendered the media answerable under the statutes.

In a particularly intriguing discussion, Justice Breyer also emphasized that the laws at issue did "not forbid the receipt of the tape itself." Justice Breyer seemed to be signaling that if the law made it illegal to receive the actual tape recording, to obtain it (at least with knowledge that it contained illegally purloined conversations) would itself be unlawful conduct. In such a case, Justice Breyer appeared to be arguing, the media could no longer claim the safety-base of having acquired the information "lawfully," and would now be outside the ambit of the *Bartnicki* protection. If this is what Justice Breyer in fact meant, he had identified a sizable constitutional loophole, and all but invited legislatures to amend their statutes and drive through.

Justices Breyer and O'Connor seemed offended by the conversation between Gloria Bartnicki and Anthony Kane, treating it not as angry "union-talk" but as actual authentic discussion of the need to engage in violence against persons and property. Had Bartnicki and Kane been merely expressing their anger at the school board for its negotiating positions, Justices Breyer and O'Connor might not have gone along with Justices Stevens, Ginsburg and Kennedy, and instead defected to the camp of the Chief Justice, and Justices Thomas and Scalia. It was The Sopranos talk of blowing off porches and "doing some work on some of these guys" (or "dese guys") that appeared to overwhelm Justices Breyer and O'Connor, leading them to the view that "the speakers had little or no legitimate interest in maintaining the privacy of the particular conversation." Noting that in other contexts in which the law normally respects the confidentiality of private conversations, exemptions exist permitting or even requiring disclosure in the interest of public safety, Justices Breyer and O'Connor found that the threat of violence, even if it had grown somewhat stale with time, trumped the privacy interests of the parties to the conversation.

Rodney A. Smolla, *Information as Contraband: The First Amendment and Liability for Trafficking in Speech*, 96 Nw. U. L. Rev. 1099, 1143–44 (2002).

You Be the Judge!

Privacy, paparazzi, and publishers

A famous young actress is talking to her mother from her cellphone while in a car in Los Angeles. In the conversation the actress discloses that she is deeply depressed because she had an abortion, choosing to end a pregnancy caused by her having been raped by a famous director while filming a popular movie. The mother is supportive of and consoling to her distraught actress daughter. Unbeknownst to the actress, at the time she is having this conversation she is being closely followed in another vehicle by a freelance "paparazzi" journalist who specializes in stalking the rich and famous. The paparazzo, using an electronic interception device, illegally intercepts and records the conversation, in violation of California and federal laws. He sells the recording to a national tabloid for $50,000. The tabloid publishes a sensational article repeating verbatim everything said in the intercepted conversation and posts the actual audio recording on its website. The actress sues the tabloid for money damages for publishing the article, relying on state and federal laws that authorize such damages, as well as for the common-law tort of publication of private facts (see Chapter 9) for revealing her abortion, her depression, her internal mental state, and her status as a rape victim. The tabloid seeks dismissal, arguing that under *Bartnicki*, the tabloid's printed and audio publication of the intercepted conversation is insulated from liability as a matter of law. The tabloid asserts, and it is not controverted, that the tabloid itself did not know that the paparazzo was trailing the actress and did not in advance hire him to intercept the conversation. It is also not controverted, however, that the tabloid had previously paid paparazzi, including the paparazzo in this case, for photographs or videos of celebrities—though none of those prior acquisitions involved illegally obtained photographs or videos. Finally, it is not controverted that the tabloid knew that the recording it purchased was illegally intercepted in violation of state and federal laws. If you were the judge before whom the motion is pending, how would you rule and why?

this is a personal private concern

the press paid for the tape

E. Restraints on Newsgathering Imposed by Generally Applicable Law: Does the First Amendment Protect Journalists Who Commit Torts or Breach Contracts in Pursuit of a Story?

In Chapter 9, we noted how journalists sometimes engage in tortious behavior such as trespass or misrepresentation in their efforts to uncover information. Should the First Amendment afford these journalists any special immunity from civil liability because their actions were committed in furtherance of the First Amendment goal of informing the public? A similar issue was raised in the following case in which newspapers editors chose to "burn" a source, in violation of a nondisclosure agreement, because, in their determination, it was in the public's best interests to know the source's identity.

Cohen v. Cowles Media Co.

Supreme Court of the United States, 1991
501 U.S. 663

JUSTICE WHITE delivered the opinion of the Court.

The question before us is whether the First Amendment prohibits a plaintiff from recovering damages, under state promissory estoppel law, for a newspaper's breach of a promise of confidentiality given to the plaintiff in exchange for information. We hold that it does not.

During the closing days of the 1982 Minnesota gubernatorial race, Dan Cohen, an active Republican associated with Wheelock Whitney's Independent-Republican gubernatorial campaign, approached reporters from the St. Paul Pioneer Press Dispatch (Pioneer Press) and the Minneapolis Star and Tribune (Star Tribune) and offered to provide documents relating to a candidate in the upcoming election. Cohen made clear to the reporters that he would provide the information only if he was given a promise of confidentiality. Reporters from both papers promised to keep Cohen's identity anonymous and Cohen turned over copies of two public court records concerning Marlene Johnson, the Democratic-Farmer-Labor candidate for Lieutenant Governor. The first record indicated that Johnson had been charged in 1969 with three counts of unlawful assembly, and the second that she had been convicted in 1970 of petit theft. Both newspapers interviewed Johnson for her explanation and one reporter tracked down the person who had found the records for Cohen. As it turned out, the unlawful assembly charges arose out of Johnson's participation in a protest of an alleged failure to hire minority workers on municipal construction projects, and the charges were eventually dismissed. The petit theft conviction was for leaving a store without paying for $6 worth of sewing materials. The incident apparently occurred at a time during which Johnson was emotionally distraught, and the conviction was later vacated.

After consultation and debate, the editorial staffs of the two newspapers independently decided to publish Cohen's name as part of their stories concerning Johnson. In their stories, both papers identified Cohen as the source of the court records, indicated his connection to the Whitney campaign, and included denials by Whitney campaign officials of any role in the matter. The same day the stories appeared, Cohen was fired by his employer.

Cohen sued respondents, the publishers of the Pioneer Press and Star Tribune, in Minnesota state court, alleging fraudulent misrepresentation and breach of contract.

A divided Minnesota Supreme Court reversed the compensatory damages award.

In addressing the promissory estoppel question, the court decided that the most problematic element in establishing such a cause of action here was whether injustice could be avoided only by enforcing the promise of confidentiality made to Cohen. The court stated: "Under a promissory estoppel analysis there can be no neutrality towards the First Amendment. In deciding whether it would be unjust not to enforce the promise, the court must necessarily weigh the same considerations that are weighed for whether the First Amendment has been violated. The court must balance the constitutional rights of a free press against the common law interest in protecting a promise of anonymity." After a brief discussion, the court concluded that "in this case enforcement of the promise of confidentiality under a promissory estoppel theory would violate defendants' First Amendment rights."

We granted certiorari to consider the First Amendment implications of this case.

Respondents rely on the proposition that "if a newspaper lawfully obtains truthful information about a matter of public significance then state officials may not constitutionally punish publication of the information, absent a need to further a state interest of the highest order." *Smith v. Daily Mail Publishing Co.* That proposition is unexceptionable, and it has been applied in various cases that have found insufficient the asserted state interests in preventing publication of truthful, lawfully obtained information. *See, e.g., Florida Star v. B.J.F.*; *Smith v. Daily Mail*; *Landmark Communications, Inc. v. Virginia.*

This case, however, is not controlled by this line of cases but, rather, by the equally well-established line of decisions holding that generally applicable laws do not offend the First Amendment simply because their enforcement against the press has incidental effects on its ability to gather and report the news. As the cases relied on by respondents recognize, the truthful information sought to be published must have been lawfully acquired. The press may not with impunity break and enter an office or dwelling to gather news. Neither does the First Amendment relieve a newspaper reporter of the obligation shared by all citizens to respond to a grand jury subpoena and answer questions relevant to a criminal investigation, even though the reporter might be required to reveal a confidential source. *Branzburg v. Hayes*, 408 U.S. 665 (1972). The press, like others interested in publishing, may not publish copyrighted material without obeying the copyright laws. *See Zacchini v. Scripps-Howard Broadcasting Co.* Similarly, the media must obey the National Labor Relations Act, *Associated*

Press v. NLRB, 301 U.S. 103 (1937), and the Fair Labor Standards Act, *Oklahoma Press Publishing Co. v. Walling*, 327 U.S. 186 (1946); may not restrain trade in violation of the antitrust laws, *Associated Press v. United States*, 326 U.S. 1 (1945); *Citizen Publishing Co. v. United States*, 394 U.S. 131 (1969); and must pay non-discriminatory taxes, *Murdock v. Pennsylvania*, 319 U.S. 105, 112 (1943); *Minneapolis Star & Tribune Co. v. Minnesota Comm'r of Revenue*, 460 U.S. 575 (1983). Cf. *University of Pennsylvania v. EEOC*, 493 U.S. 182 (1990). It is, therefore, beyond dispute that "the publisher of a newspaper has no special immunity from the application of general laws. He has no special privilege to invade the rights and liberties of others." Accordingly, enforcement of such general laws against the press is not subject to stricter scrutiny than would be applied to enforcement against other persons or organizations.

There can be little doubt that the Minnesota doctrine of promissory estoppel is a law of general applicability. It does not target or single out the press. Rather, insofar as we are advised, the doctrine is generally applicable to the daily transactions of all the citizens of Minnesota. The First Amendment does not forbid its application to the press.

Justice Blackmun suggests that applying Minnesota promissory estoppel doctrine in this case will "punish" respondents for publishing truthful information that was lawfully obtained. This is not strictly accurate because compensatory damages are not a form of punishment, as were the criminal sanctions at issue in *Smith v. Daily Mail*. If the contract between the parties in this case had contained a liquidated damages provision, it would be perfectly clear that the payment to petitioner would represent a cost of acquiring newsworthy material to be published at a profit, rather than a punishment imposed by the State. The payment of compensatory damages in this case is constitutionally indistinguishable from a generous bonus paid to a confidential news source. In any event, as indicated above, the characterization of the payment makes no difference for First Amendment purposes when the law being applied is a general law and does not single out the press. Moreover, Justice Blackmun's reliance on cases like *Florida Star v. B.J.F.*, and *Smith v. Daily Mail* is misplaced. In those cases, the State itself defined the content of publications that would trigger liability. Here, by contrast, Minnesota law simply requires those making promises to keep them. The parties themselves, as in this case, determine the scope of their legal obligations, and any restrictions that may be placed on the publication of truthful information are self-imposed.

Also, it is not at all clear that respondents obtained Cohen's name "lawfully" in this case, at least for purposes of publishing it. Unlike the situation in *Florida Star*, where the rape victim's name was obtained through lawful access to a police report, respondents obtained Cohen's name only by making a promise that they did not honor. The dissenting opinions suggest that the press should not be subject to any law, including copyright law for example, which in any fashion or to any degree limits or restricts the press' right to report truthful information. The First Amendment does not grant the press such limitless protection.

Nor is Cohen attempting to use a promissory estoppel cause of action to avoid the strict requirements for establishing a libel or defamation claim. As the Minnesota Supreme Court observed here, "Cohen could not sue for defamation because the information disclosed [his name] was true." Cohen is not seeking damages for injury to his reputation or his state of mind. He sought damages in excess of $50,000 for breach of a promise that caused him to lose his job and lowered his earning capacity. Thus, this is not a case like *Hustler Magazine, Inc. v. Falwell,* where we held that the constitutional libel standards apply to a claim alleging that the publication of a parody was a state-law tort of intentional infliction of emotional distress.

Respondents and *amici* argue that permitting Cohen to maintain a cause of action for promissory estoppel will inhibit truthful reporting because news organizations will have legal incentives not to disclose a confidential source's identity even when that person's identity is itself newsworthy. Justice Souter makes a similar argument. But if this is the case, it is no more than the incidental, and constitutionally insignificant, consequence of applying to the press a generally applicable law that requires those who make certain kinds of promises to keep them.

JUSTICE BLACKMUN, with whom JUSTICE MARSHALL and JUSTICE SOUTER join, dissenting.

Contrary to the majority, I regard our decision in *Hustler Magazine, Inc. v. Falwell,* to be precisely on point. There, we found that the use of a claim of intentional infliction of emotional distress to impose liability for the publication of a satirical critique violated the First Amendment. There was no doubt that Virginia's tort of intentional infliction of emotional distress was "a law of general applicability" unrelated to the suppression of speech. Nonetheless, a unanimous Court found that, when used to penalize the expression of opinion, the law was subject to the strictures of the First Amendment. In applying that principle, we concluded that "public figures and public officials may not recover for the tort of intentional infliction of emotional distress by reason of publications such as the one here at issue without showing in addition that the publication contains a false statement of fact which was made with 'actual malice,' " as defined by *New York Times Co. v. Sullivan.* In so doing, we rejected the argument that Virginia's interest in protecting its citizens from emotional distress was sufficient to remove from First Amendment protection a "patently offensive" expression of opinion.

As in *Hustler,* the operation of Minnesota's doctrine of promissory estoppel in this case cannot be said to have a merely "incidental" burden on speech; the publication of important political speech is the claimed violation. Thus, as in *Hustler,* the law may not be enforced to punish the expression of truthful information or opinion. In the instant case, it is undisputed that the publication at issue was true.

To the extent that truthful speech may ever be sanctioned consistent with the First Amendment, it must be in furtherance of a state interest "of the highest order." *Smith v. Daily Mail.* Because the Minnesota Supreme Court's opinion makes clear that the State's interest in enforcing its promissory estoppel doctrine in this case was far from compelling, I would affirm that court's decision.

dissent

JUSTICE SOUTER, with whom JUSTICE MARSHALL, JUSTICE BLACKMUN, and JUSTICE O'CONNOR join, dissenting.

I agree with Justice Blackmun that this case does not fall within the line of authority holding the press to laws of general applicability where commercial activities and relationships, not the content of publication, are at issue. Even such general laws as do entail effects on the content of speech, like the one in question, may of course be found constitutional, but only, as Justice Harlan observed, "when [such effects] have been found justified by subordinating valid governmental interests, a prerequisite to constitutionality which has necessarily involved a weighing of the governmental interest involved. Whenever, in such a context, these constitutional protections are asserted against the exercise of valid governmental powers a reconciliation must be effected, and that perforce requires an appropriate weighing of the respective interests involved."

Thus, "there is nothing talismanic about neutral laws of general applicability," for such laws may restrict First Amendment rights just as effectively as those directed specifically at speech itself. Because I do not believe the fact of general applicability to be dispositive, I find it necessary to articulate, measure, and compare the competing interests involved in any given case to determine the legitimacy of burdening constitutional interests, and such has been the Court's recent practice in publication cases. See *Hustler; Zacchini.*

Nor can I accept the majority's position that we may dispense with balancing because the burden on publication is in a sense "self-imposed" by the newspaper's voluntary promise of confidentiality. This suggests both the possibility of waiver, the requirements for which have not been met here, as well as a conception of First Amendment rights as those of the speaker alone, with a value that may be measured without reference to the importance of the information to public discourse. But freedom of the press is ultimately founded on the value of enhancing such discourse for the sake of a citizenry better informed and thus more prudently self-governed.

The importance of this public interest is integral to the balance that should be struck in this case. There can be no doubt that the fact of Cohen's identity expanded the universe of information relevant to the choice faced by Minnesota voters in that

State's 1982 gubernatorial election, the publication of which was thus of the sort quintessentially subject to strict First Amendment protection. The propriety of his leak to respondents could be taken to reflect on his character, which in turn could be taken to reflect on the character of the candidate who had retained him as an adviser. An election could turn on just such a factor; if it should, I am ready to assume that it would be to the greater public good, at least over the long run.

This is not to say that the breach of such a promise of confidentiality could never give rise to liability. One can conceive of situations in which the injured party is a private individual, whose identity is of less public concern than that of petitioner; liability there might not be constitutionally prohibited. Nor do I mean to imply that the circumstances of acquisition are irrelevant to the balance, although they may go only to what balances against, and not to diminish, the First Amendment value of any particular piece of information.

Because I believe the State's interest in enforcing a newspaper's promise of confidentiality insufficient to outweigh the interest in unfettered publication of the information revealed in this case, I respectfully dissent.

Points for Discussion

1. **Does *Cohen* conflict with *Hustler*?** Note that the majority and dissents fundamentally disagree on whether imposing liability for breach of promise in *Cohen* is or is not consistent with the Court's refusal to allow the imposition of liability for intentional infliction of emotional distress in *Hustler* (discussed in Chapter 9). Who has the better argument? How critical is it that *Hustler* was a tort case, in which Virginia established the elements of liability through the standards of tort law, whereas *Cohen* was a contract/promissory estoppel case, in which, as Justice White's opinion for the majority contends, the media defendants themselves established the standards of liability by making a promise they later breached?

2. **Civil liability for tortious behavior in acquiring information.** As discussed at length in Chapter 9, the First Amendment generally does not shelter news organizations, advocacy groups, or private citizens from criminal or civil liability from generally applicable criminal and civil rules against trespass, fraud, and the like. In *Planned Parenthood Federation of America, Inc. v. Newman*, 51 F.4th 1125 (9th Cir. 2022), for example, the Ninth Circuit applied the principle that undercover investigations enjoy no First Amendment immunity from generally applicable laws, holding that infiltrators who invaded Planned Parenthood to procure negative information against the organization were not sheltered by the First Amendment from liability for violating such neutral laws. The infiltrators

were found liable for trespass, fraud, conspiracy, breach of contract, unlawful and fraudulent business practices, civil RICO violations, and unlawful wiretapping. Planned Parenthood was awarded statutory, compensatory, and punitive damages, as well as limited injunctive relief. The Ninth Circuit followed the learning of *Cohen v. Cowles Media* that "generally applicable laws do not offend the First Amendment simply because their enforcement against the press has incidental effects on its ability to gather and report the news."

F. Keeping Informants Confidential: Does the First Amendment Shield Journalists from Having to Reveal Their Sources?

In *Cohen v. Cowles Media*, the press insisted on its right to reveal a confidential source. But that case was an aberration. More typically, the press is insisting on its right to keep its sources confidential.

In the following case, the Court addressed the question of whether journalists have a First Amendment right to refuse to respond to subpoenas or questions seeking the names of their sources. As you will soon discover, the precise holding of the case has been a source of ongoing dispute.

Branzburg v. Hayes

Supreme Court of the United States, 1972
408 U.S. 665

Opinion of the Court by MR. JUSTICE WHITE, announced by THE CHIEF JUSTICE.

The issue in these cases is whether requiring newsmen to appear and testify before state or federal grand juries abridges the freedom of speech and press guaranteed by the First Amendment. We hold that it does not.

On November 15, 1969, the Courier-Journal carried a story under petitioner's by-line describing in detail his observations of two young residents of Jefferson County synthesizing hashish from marihuana, an activity which, they asserted, earned them about $5,000 in three weeks. Petitioner was shortly subpoenaed by the Jefferson County grand jury; he appeared, but refused to identify the individuals he had seen possessing marihuana or the persons he had seen making hashish from marihuana.

The second case involving petitioner Branzburg arose out of his later story published on January 10, 1971, which described in detail the use of drugs in Frankfort,

Kentucky. The article reported that in order to provide a comprehensive survey of the "drug scene" in Frankfort, petitioner had "spent two weeks interviewing several dozen drug users in the capital city" and had seen some of them smoking marihuana. A number of conversations with and observations of several unnamed drug users were recounted. Subpoenaed to appear before a Franklin County grand jury "to testify in the matter of violation of statutes concerning use and sale of drugs," petitioner Branzburg moved to quash the summons.

In re Pappas, originated when petitioner Pappas, a television newsman-photographer working out of the Providence, Rhode Island, office of a New Bedford, Massachusetts, television station, was called to New Bedford on July 30, 1970, to report on civil disorders there which involved fires and other turmoil. He intended to cover a Black Panther news conference at that group's headquarters in a boarded-up store. Petitioner found the streets around the store barricaded, but he ultimately gained entrance to the area and recorded and photographed a prepared statement read by one of the Black Panther leaders at about 3 p.m. He then asked for and received permission to re-enter the area. Returning at about 9 o'clock, he was allowed to enter and remain inside Panther headquarters. As a condition of entry, Pappas agreed not to disclose anything he saw or heard inside the store except an anticipated police raid, which Pappas, "on his own," was free to photograph and report as he wished. Pappas stayed inside the headquarters for about three hours, but there was no police raid, and petitioner wrote no story and did not otherwise reveal what had occurred in the store while he was there. Two months later, petitioner was summoned before the Bristol County Grand Jury and appeared, answered questions as to his name, address, employment, and what he had seen and heard outside Panther headquarters, but refused to answer any questions about what had taken place inside headquarters while he was there, claiming that the First Amendment afforded him a privilege to protect confidential informants and their information.

United States v. Caldwell arose from subpoenas issued by a federal grand jury in the Northern District of California to respondent Earl Caldwell, a reporter for the New York Times assigned to cover the Black Panther Party and other black militant groups. A subpoena duces tecum was served on respondent on February 2, 1970, ordering him to appear before the grand jury to testify and to bring with him notes and tape recordings of interviews given him for publication by officers and spokesmen of the Black Panther Party concerning the aims, purposes, and activities of that organization.

Petitioners Branzburg and Pappas and respondent Caldwell press First Amendment claims that may be simply put: that to gather news it is often necessary to agree either not to identify the source of information published or to publish only part of the facts revealed, or both; that if the reporter is nevertheless forced to reveal these confidences to a grand jury, the source so identified and other confidential sources of other reporters will be measurably deterred from furnishing publishable information, all to the detriment of the free flow of information protected by the First Amendment. Although the newsmen in these cases do not claim an absolute privilege against official interrogation in all circumstances, they assert that the reporter should not be forced either to appear or to testify before a grand jury or at trial until and unless sufficient grounds are shown for believing that the reporter possesses information relevant to a crime the grand jury is investigating, that the information the reporter has is unavailable from other sources, and that the need for the information is sufficiently compelling to override the claimed invasion of First Amendment interests occasioned by the disclosure. Principally relied upon are prior cases emphasizing the importance of the First Amendment guarantees to individual development and to our system of representative government, decisions requiring that official action with adverse impact on First Amendment rights be justified by a public interest that is "compelling" or "paramount," and those precedents establishing the principle that justifiable governmental goals may not be achieved by unduly broad means having an unnecessary impact on protected rights of speech, press, or association. The heart of the claim is that the burden on news gathering resulting from compelling reporters to disclose confidential information outweighs any public interest in obtaining the information.

We do not question the significance of free speech, press, or assembly to the country's welfare. Nor is it suggested that news gathering does not qualify for First Amendment protection; without some protection for seeking out the news, freedom of the press could be eviscerated. But these cases involve no intrusions upon speech or assembly, no prior restraint or restriction on what the press may publish, and no express or implied command that the press publish what it prefers to withhold. No exaction or tax for the privilege of publishing, and no penalty, civil or criminal, related to the content of published material is at issue here. The use of confidential sources by the press is not forbidden or restricted; reporters remain free to seek news from any source by means within the law. No attempt is made to require the press to publish its sources of information or indiscriminately to disclose them on request.

The sole issue before us is the obligation of reporters to respond to grand jury subpoenas as other citizens do and to answer questions relevant to an investigation into the commission of crime. Citizens generally are not constitutionally immune from grand jury subpoenas; and neither the First Amendment nor any other constitutional provision protects the average citizen from disclosing to a grand jury information that he has received in confidence. The claim is, however, that reporters are exempt from these obligations because if forced to respond to subpoenas and identify their sources or disclose other confidences, their informants will refuse or be reluctant to furnish newsworthy information in the future. This asserted burden on news gathering is said to make compelled testimony from newsmen constitutionally suspect and to require a privileged position for them.

It is clear that the First Amendment does not invalidate every incidental burdening of the press that may result from the enforcement of civil or criminal statutes of general applicability.

The prevailing view is that the press is not free to publish with impunity everything and anything it desires to publish. Although it may deter or regulate what is said or published, the press may not circulate knowing or reckless falsehoods damaging to private reputation without subjecting itself to liability for damages, including punitive damages, or even criminal prosecution. A newspaper or a journalist may also be punished for contempt of court, in appropriate circumstances. It has generally been held that the First Amendment does not guarantee the press a constitutional right of special access to information not available to the public generally.

Despite the fact that news gathering may be hampered, the press is regularly excluded from grand jury proceedings, our own conferences, the meetings of other official bodies gathered in executive session, and the meetings of private organizations. Newsmen have no constitutional right of access to the scenes of crime or disaster when the general public is excluded, and they may be prohibited from attending or publishing information about trials if such restrictions are necessary to assure a defendant a fair trial before an impartial tribunal.

It is thus not surprising that the great weight of authority is that newsmen are not exempt from the normal duty of appearing before a grand jury and answering questions relevant to a criminal investigation. At common law, courts consistently refused to recognize the existence of any privilege authorizing a newsman to refuse to reveal confidential information to a grand jury.

The prevailing constitutional view of the newsman's privilege is very much rooted in the ancient role of the grand jury that has the dual function of determining if there is probable cause to believe that a crime has been committed and of protecting citizens against unfounded criminal prosecutions.

A number of States have provided newsmen a statutory privilege of varying breadth, but the majority have not done so, and none has been provided by federal statute.

The preference for anonymity of those confidential informants involved in actual criminal conduct is presumably a product of their desire to escape criminal prosecution, and this preference, while understandable, is hardly deserving of constitutional protection. It would be frivolous to assert—and no one does in these cases—that the First Amendment, in the interest of securing news or otherwise, confers a license on either the reporter or his news sources to violate valid criminal laws. Although stealing documents or private wiretapping could provide newsworthy information, neither reporter nor source is immune from conviction for such conduct, whatever the impact on the flow of news. Neither is immune, on First Amendment grounds, from testifying against the other, before the grand jury or at a criminal trial. The Amendment does not reach so far as to override the interest of the public in ensuring that neither reporter nor source is invading the rights of other citizens through reprehensible conduct forbidden to all other persons.

Thus, we cannot seriously entertain the notion that the First Amendment protects a newsman's agreement to conceal the criminal conduct of his source, or evidence thereof, on the theory that it is better to write about crime than to do something about it.

There remain those situations where a source is not engaged in criminal conduct but has information suggesting illegal conduct by others. Newsmen frequently receive information from such sources pursuant to a tacit or express agreement to withhold the source's name and suppress any information that the source wishes not published. Such informants presumably desire anonymity in order to avoid being entangled as a witness in a criminal trial or grand jury investigation. They may fear that disclosure will threaten their job security or personal safety or that it will simply result in dishonor or embarrassment.

We note first that the privilege claimed is that of the reporter, not the informant, and that if the authorities independently identify the informant, neither his own reluctance to testify nor the objection of the newsman would shield him from grand jury inquiry, whatever the impact on the flow of news or on his future usefulness as a secret source of information. More important, it is obvious that agreements to conceal information relevant to commission of crime have very little to recommend them from the standpoint of public policy.

Of course, the press has the right to abide by its agreement not to publish all the information it has, but the right to withhold news is not equivalent to a First Amendment exemption from the ordinary duty of all other citizens to furnish relevant information to a grand jury performing an important public function.

We are admonished that refusal to provide a First Amendment reporter's privilege will undermine the freedom of the press to collect and disseminate news. But this is not the lesson history teaches us. From the beginning of our country the press has operated without constitutional protection for press informants, and the press has flourished. The existing constitutional rules have not been a serious obstacle to either the development or retention of confidential news sources by the press.

The privilege claimed here is conditional, not absolute; given the suggested preliminary showings and compelling need, the reporter would be required to testify. Presumably, such a rule would reduce the instances in which reporters could be required to appear, but predicting in advance when and in what circumstances they could be compelled to do so would be difficult. Such a rule would also have implications for the issuance of compulsory process to reporters at civil and criminal trials and at legislative hearings. If newsmen's confidential sources are as sensitive as they are claimed to be, the prospect of being unmasked whenever a judge determines the situation justifies it is hardly a satisfactory solution to the problem. For them, it would appear that only an absolute privilege would suffice.

We are unwilling to embark the judiciary on a long and difficult journey to such an uncertain destination. The administration of a constitutional newsman's privilege would present practical and conceptual difficulties of a high order. Sooner or later, it would be necessary to define those categories of newsmen who qualified for the privilege, a questionable procedure in light of the traditional doctrine that liberty of the press is the right of the lonely pamphleteer who uses carbon paper or a mimeograph just as much as of the large metropolitan publisher who utilizes the latest photocomposition methods.

So ordered.

MR. JUSTICE POWELL, concurring.

I add this brief statement to emphasize what seems to me to be the limited nature of the Court's holding. The Court does not hold that newsmen, subpoenaed to testify before a grand jury, are without constitutional rights with respect to the gathering of news or in safeguarding their sources. Certainly, we do not hold, as suggested in Mr. Justice Stewart's dissenting opinion, that state and federal authorities are free to "annex" the news media as "an investigative arm of government." The solicitude repeatedly shown by this Court for First Amendment freedoms should be sufficient assurance against any such effort, even if one seriously believed that the media—properly free and untrammeled in the fullest sense of these terms—were not able to protect themselves.

As indicated in the concluding portion of the opinion, the Court states that no harassment of newsmen will be tolerated. If a newsman believes that the grand jury investigation is not being conducted in good faith he is not without remedy. Indeed, if the newsman is called upon to give information bearing only a remote and tenuous relationship to the subject of the investigation, or if he has some other reason to believe that his testimony implicates a confidential source relationship without a legitimate need of law enforcement, he will have access to the court on a motion to quash and an appropriate protective order may be entered. The asserted claim to privilege should be judged on its facts by the striking of a proper balance between freedom of the press and the obligation of all citizens to give relevant testimony with respect to criminal conduct. The balance of these vital constitutional and societal interests on a case-by-case basis accords with the tried and traditional way of adjudicating such questions.

In short, the courts will be available to newsmen under circumstances where legitimate First Amendment interests require protection.

MR. JUSTICE STEWART, with whom MR. JUSTICE BRENNAN and MR. JUSTICE MARSHALL join, dissenting.

The Court's crabbed view of the First Amendment reflects a disturbing insensitivity to the critical role of an independent press in our society. The question whether a reporter has a constitutional right to a confidential relationship with his source is of first impression here, but the principles that should guide our decision are as basic as any to be found in the Constitution. While Mr. Justice Powell's enigmatic concurring opinion gives some hope of a more flexible view in the future, the Court in these cases holds that a newsman has no First Amendment right to protect his sources when called before a grand jury. The Court thus invites state and federal authorities to undermine the historic independence of the press by attempting to annex the journalistic profession as an investigative arm of government. Not only will this decision impair performance of the press' constitutionally protected functions, but it will, I am convinced, in the long run, harm rather than help the administration of justice.

The reporter's constitutional right to a confidential relationship with his source stems from the broad societal interest in a full and free flow of information to the public. It is this basic concern that underlies the Constitution's protection of a free press because the guarantee is "not for the benefit of the press so much as for the benefit of all of us."

Enlightened choice by an informed citizenry is the basic ideal upon which an open society is premised, and a free press is thus indispensable to a free society. Not only does the press enhance personal self-fulfillment by providing the people with the widest possible range of fact and opinion, but it also is an incontestable precondition of self-government. The press "has been a mighty catalyst in awakening public interest in governmental affairs, exposing corruption among public officers and employees and generally informing the citizenry of public events and occurrences." As private and public aggregations of power burgeon in size and the pressures for conformity necessarily mount, there is obviously a continuing need for an independent press to disseminate a robust variety of information and opinion through reportage, investigation, and criticism, if we are to preserve our constitutional tradition of maximizing freedom of choice by encouraging diversity of expression.

MR. JUSTICE DOUGLAS, dissenting.

It is my view that there is no "compelling need" that can be shown which qualifies the reporter's immunity from appearing or testifying before a grand jury, unless the reporter himself is implicated in a crime. His immunity in my view is therefore quite complete, for, absent his involvement in a crime, the First Amendment protects him against an appearance before a grand jury and if he is involved in a crime, the Fifth Amendment stands as a barrier. Since in my view there is no area of inquiry not protected by a privilege, the reporter need not appear for the futile purpose of invoking one to each question. And, since in my view a newsman has an absolute right not to appear before a grand jury, it follows for me that a journalist who voluntarily appears before that body may invoke his First Amendment privilege to specific questions.

Today's decision will impede the wide open and robust dissemination of ideas and counterthought which a free press both fosters and protects and which is essential to the success of intelligent self-government. Forcing a reporter before a grand jury will have two retarding effects upon the ear and the pen of the press. Fear of exposure will cause dissidents to communicate less openly to trusted reporters. And, fear of accountability will cause editors and critics to write with more restrained pens.

Points for Discussion

1. **What was the holding in *Branzburg*?** Most students who read the case assume that the Court rejected, by a 5–4 vote, the existence of any journalist's privilege. The majority opinion certainly reads that way, as a brusque and unequivocal statement that journalists, like everyone else in society, are bound by the rule of law and required to give evidence to grand juries. That is how one co-author of this casebook, Rodney Smolla, interprets the case. Notwithstanding what seemed on the surface to be a resounding pounding for the press in *Branzburg*, however, some lower courts, relying on Justice Powell's cryptic concurring opinion, held that the First Amendment did provide a conditional reporter's privilege of some kind. *See, e.g., United States v. Burke*, 700 F.2d 70, 76–77 (2d Cir. 1983), *cert. denied*, 464 U.S. 816 (1983) (allowing reporters a qualified privilege in criminal, as well as civil, cases, conditioned on a clear and specific showing that the information sought (1) is highly material and relevant, (2) is necessary or critical to the claim, and (3) is not obtainable from other available sources); *LaRouche v. National Broad. Co., Inc.*, 780 F.2d 1134, 1139 (4th Cir. 1986), *cert. denied*, 479 U.S. 818 (1986) (holding that whether the journalist's privilege will protect the source depends on whether the information sought is relevant, can be obtained by alternate means, and is the subject of a compelling interest); *Miller v. Transamerican Press, Inc.*, 621 F.2d 721, 725 (5th Cir. 1980), *cert. denied*, 450 U.S. 1041 (1981) (holding that a reporter has a First Amendment privilege that protects the refusal to disclose a confidential informant's identity, although privilege is not absolute).

   Many other courts have held the opposite, reasoning that the 5–4 rejection of the privilege in *Branzburg* was indeed a 5–4 rejection and that nothing in Justice

Powell's concurring opinion changed that. *See In re Grand Jury Proceedings, Storer Commc'ns, Inc. v. Giovan*, 810 F.2d 580, 585 (6th Cir. 1987) ("We decline to join some other circuit courts, to the extent that they have adopted the qualified privilege balancing process urged by the three *Branzburg* dissenters and rejected by the majority. That portion of Justice Powell's opinion certainly does not warrant the rewriting of the majority opinion to grant a First Amendment testimonial privilege to news reporters, especially when the quoted language is considered in the context of that language which precedes it."). The most influential of these opinions was *In re Grand Jury Subpoena (Miller)*, 397 F.3d 964 (D.C. Cir. 2005), *cert. denied*, 545 U.S. 1150 (2005), involving journalists' reports leaking the story that the wife of an American diplomat was an American spy working for the CIA. A grand jury subpoena was issued to reporters to determine who had leaked the story. The reporters claimed a First Amendment privilege emanating from *Branzburg*. The D.C. Circuit rejected the assertion that Justice Powell's opinion should be read to recognize a First Amendment reporter's privilege: "In any event, whatever Justice Powell specifically intended, he joined the majority. Not only did he join the majority in name, but because of his joinder with the rest of a majority, the Court reached a result that rejected a First Amendment privilege not to testify before the grand jury for reporters situated precisely like those in the present case."

2. **What did Justice Powell think his concurrence meant?** Rodney Smolla, co-author of this casebook, examined the papers of Justice Powell, which are held at the Washington & Lee Law School library. Justice Powell kept a "scorecard" in which he would note how each justice voted in every case, including his own vote, sometimes with a brief commentary. The scorecard for *Branzburg* showed Justice Powell self-recording his vote as joining the majority, with this handwritten note: "As I do not believe there is a Const. privilege." Thus, Justice Powell's own notes appear to stand against reading his concurring opinion as if it were intended to recognize any sort of constitutional privilege.

3. **Statutory protection for journalists.** In much the same manner as legislatures stepped in to enact sunshine laws and freedom of information laws to create some statutory rights of access to government information and institutions, many states have enacted "shield laws" that do provide some measure of protection for journalists' confidential sources. These laws vary as to whom they apply to—some apply specifically to journalists and news organizations, while others apply more broadly to anyone engaged in public dissemination of information—and they also vary widely in the strength of the protection provided, such as whether the privilege they create is conditional or absolute. The U.S. Congress, however, has never enacted a federal journalist's privilege of any kind. Thus, in the federal litigation system, no privilege exists in those federal circuits that read *Branzburg* as rejecting the existence of a privilege, but a qualified privilege does exist in those

circuits that have interpreted Justice Powell's opinion in *Branzburg* as creating a qualified privilege. For a review of the landscape, *see* Rodney A. Smolla, *The First Amendment, Journalists, and Sources: A Curious Study in "Reverse Federalism,"* 29 Cardozo L. Rev. 1423, 1424 (2008). *See also* Geoffrey R. Stone, *Why We Need a Federal Reporter's Privilege*, 34 Hofstra L. Rev. 39, 43 (2005) (noting how the absence of a federal shield law breeds uncertainty because a journalist's ability to invoke the reporter's privilege may vary depending on whether a case is in federal or state court and this "uncertainty breeds silence"); Mary-Rose Papandrea, *Citizen Journalism and the Reporter's Privilege*, 91 Minn. L. Rev. 515, 520 (2007) (contending that a reporter's privilege "should not be limited to those who are serving as traditional journalists; rather, it should extend to anyone who is contributing to the marketplace of ideas by disseminating information to the public").

Test Your Knowledge

To assess your understanding of the material in this chapter, click here to take a quiz.

Part III

Freedom of Religion

Chapter Seventeen

Introduction to the Religion Clauses:
Why Protect Religion, and What Is It?

This chapter marks our transition from the study of freedom of speech to the study of freedom of religion. But do not conclude from this shift in focus that these two fields are entirely separate. The practice of religion, after all, occurs through expressive activities, such as praying, delivering sermons, and proselytizing, and religious adherents exercise their right to assemble when they gather for services and other community programs. In the free speech section of this casebook, we read numerous cases brought by Jehovah's Witnesses who claimed that speech regulations hampered their ability to spread their faith. We also encountered numerous cases, such as *Lamb's Chapel* and *Rosenberger*, in which regulations were invalidated because they discriminated against religious speech.

Before immersing ourselves in the jurisprudence interpreting the First Amendment's religion clauses, it is worth pausing to consider why the Framers chose to protect religious liberty, as well as the preliminary question of what makes something a "religion."

A. Lessons from History: What Prompted the Framers to Protect Religious Liberty?

In *Everson v. Board of Education*, 330 U.S. 1 (1947), the Supreme Court described the history leading up the adoption of the Constitution's religion clauses:

> A large proportion of the early settlers of this country came here from Europe to escape the bondage of laws which compelled them to support and attend government-favored churches. The centuries immediately before and contemporaneous with the colonization of America had been filled with turmoil, civil strife, and persecutions, generated in large part by established sects determined to maintain their absolute political and religious supremacy. With the power of government supporting them, at various times and

places, Catholics had persecuted Protestants, Protestants had persecuted Catholics, Protestant sects had persecuted other Protestant sects, Catholics of one shade of belief had persecuted Catholics of another shade of belief, and all of these had from time to time persecuted Jews. In efforts to force loyalty to whatever religious group happened to be on top and in league with the government of a particular time and place, men and women had been fined, cast in jail, cruelly tortured, and killed. Among the offenses for which these punishments had been inflicted were such things as speaking disrespectfully of the views of ministers of government-established churches, non-attendance at those churches, expressions of non-belief in their doctrines, and failure to pay taxes and tithes to support them.

Engraving by J. Luyken depicting the execution of Dutch Anabaptists by Catholic authorities in Ghent in 1554. T.J.V. Bracht, The Bloody Theater or Martyr's Mirror (*Het Bloedig Tooneel De Martelaers Spiegel*) (1685). Rare Book and Special Collections Division of the Library of Congress.

These practices of the old world were transplanted to and began to thrive in the soil of the new America. The very charters granted by the English Crown to the individuals and companies designated to make the laws which would control the destinies of the colonials authorized these individuals and companies to erect religious establishments which all, whether believers or non-believers, would be required to support and attend. An exercise of this authority was accompanied by a repetition of many of the old-world practices and persecutions. Catholics found themselves hounded and proscribed because of their faith; Quakers who followed their conscience went to jail; Baptists were peculiarly obnoxious to certain dominant Protestant sects; men and women of varied faiths who happened to be in a minority in a particular locality were persecuted because they steadfastly persisted in worshipping God only as their own consciences dictated. And all of these dissenters were compelled to pay tithes and taxes to support government-sponsored churches whose ministers preached inflammatory sermons designed to strengthen and consolidate the established faith by generating a burning hatred against dissenters.

Points for Discussion

1. **What does this history teach about *why* we should protect religious liberty?** Based on this history, what lessons can you draw as to why the Framers might have wanted to protect religious liberty? Consider some of the following possibilities:

    a. **The danger of religious strife.** The *Everson* decision describes how the centuries before and contemporaneous with the colonization of America were "filled with turmoil, civil strife, and persecutions, generated in large part by established sects determined to maintain their absolute political and religious supremacy." Can you think of places in the world today that are plagued by religious strife? Do religious tensions still exist in the United States?

    b. **The problem of compelled support for established churches.** *Everson* says that "a large proportion of the early settlers of this country came here from Europe to escape the bondage of laws which compelled them to support and attend government-favored churches." While this compelled support for churches might sound problematic, it is worth noting that governments routinely spend taxpayer money on programs that some taxpayers might find objectionable. Tax payments might pay for a war that people oppose or for a regulatory regime people think is misguided. So why is it problematic for governments to use taxpayer money to pay for religious activities even if some taxpayers object? Does the government currently provide financial support to religious institutions?

    c. **The problem of compelled participation in religious activities.** *Everson* also referred to people leaving Europe to escape laws that compelled them to "attend government-favored churches." Why is it a problem to compel people to participate in religious activities? What types of government pressure rise to the level of compulsion? If a legislative body begins its sessions with a prayer, does that coerce individual legislators or visitors to engage in a religious ritual? If a high school football coach says a prayer after games, does that compel his players to participate?

d. **The danger when religious and political power are aligned.** *Everson* refers to the turmoil and strife caused by "established sects determined to maintain their absolute political and religious supremacy." Throughout much of history, and continuing to this day, many political regimes have been aligned with a specific religion, from the Roman Empire's embrace of Christianity to today's Islamic Republic of Iran. Are there problems with having religious and political power aligned, and if so, what are they?

e. **The problem of churches' being dependent on the state.** We have already mentioned the concern of compelling people to support religious institutions, but does government support for religion also lead to other problems? Could competition between religious groups for government funding fan the flames of religious strife? If churches are financially dependent on government, could that undermine their independence?

f. **The problem with favored insiders and second-class outsiders.** Why would it be bad to have an established national church? Most Americans are Christian, so why not declare the United States a Christian nation? Why not place a large cross on top of the Capitol building instead of the current Statue of Freedom? How would this make non-Christian Americans feel? Could this even lead to tensions among various Christian groups? Don't forget *Everson*'s description of how Catholics and Protestants persecuted each other for centuries.

A Comparative Perspective

Religious persecution, including government-led religious persecution, is neither a relic of history nor an isolated occurrence. It remains a widespread phenomenon in the world today. The Pew Research Center reported that government restrictions on religion rose to a record high in 2018. Samirah Majumdar, *Government restrictions on religion around the world reached new record in 2018*, Pew Research Ctr. (Nov. 10, 2020). You can find the report here.

B. Defining Religion: The Framers Provided Protection for Religion, but What Is It?

The Framers responded to the history described in *Everson* by adopting the two religion clauses of the First Amendment: "Congress shall make no law respecting an establishment of religion, or protecting the free exercise thereof." The first clause, the Establishment Clause, is typically implicated when government actions benefit religion, such as through funding, endorsement, or favoritism. We will explore the Establishment Clause in Chapter 19. The second clause, the Free Exercise Clause, is typically implicated when government actions burden religion. We will study this clause in Chapter 18.

In addition to the two religion clauses in the First Amendment, the Framers included in the original Constitution a prohibition on the use of religious tests for federal office holders: "no religious Test shall ever be required as a Qualification to any Office or public Trust under the United States." U.S. Const. Art. VI, cl. 3.

What the Framers did not do, however, was define the core term implicated by these clauses: "religion." In the absence of this guidance, one might have expected there to be a rich Supreme Court jurisprudence defining the term. Instead, the Court's jurisprudence on the topic is surprisingly sparse.

The Court's most significant exploration of the issue was in *Wisconsin v. Yoder*, 406 U.S. 205 (1972), a case you'll read in Chapter 18. The case involved a claim by Amish parents and children that they should be exempt from a compulsory education law that required children to attend school until age 16. A threshold question in the case was whether Amish people's rejection of mainstream secular values and their preference for isolation were "philosophical and personal," in which case they would not come within the coverage of the religion clauses, or were matters of religious conviction, in which case they would. As you will see when you read the opinion, the Court contrasted the isolation preferred by Henry David Thoreau at Walden Pond, which was not "religious," with the isolation preferred by the Amish, which the Court deemed to flow from "deep religious conviction."

As one might expect, the earliest discussions of religion in the Supreme Court seemed to contemplate traditional theistic religions centered on a belief in a supreme being. In *Davis v. Beason*, 133 U.S. 333, 342 (1890), for example, the Court held that "the term 'religion' has reference to one's views of his relations to his Creator, and to the obligations they impose of reverence for his being and character, and of obedience to his will."

More recent references have been more commodious, cautioning against linking "religion" to a belief in God. In *Torcaso v. Watkins*, 367 U.S. 488, 495 n.11 (1961), for example, the Court observed, "Among religions in this country which do not teach what would generally be considered a belief in the existence of God are Buddhism, Taoism, Ethical Culture, Secular Humanism and others." Indeed, the Court has made it clear that a person need not be a member of an organized religion to claim the protections of the Free Exercise Clause and may even be merely a "religion of one." In *Frazee v. Illinois Department of Employment Security*, 489 U.S. 829 (1989), for example, a unanimous Court rejected the argument that the protections of the Free Exercise Clause required adherence to "a tenet or dogma of an established religious sect."

The most comprehensive modern judicial attempt to define "religion" for constitutional purposes comes not from a Supreme Court opinion, but from the decision of a federal district judge in Wyoming finding the "First Church of Marijuana" was not a qualifying "religion." *United States v. Meyers*, 906 F. Supp. 1494, 1499–500 (D. Wyo. 1995), *aff'd*, 95 F.3d 1475 (10th Cir. 1996), *cert. denied*, 522 U.S. 1006 (1997).

Practice Pointer!

The *Meyers* case illustrates the importance of comprehensive research across multiple levels of the state and federal judiciary. If you were faced with a litigation matter that turned on the definition of "religion" and you limited your search to the Supreme Court, you would not discover *Meyers*, perhaps the most thoughtful judicial opinion ever rendered on the subject.

The judge in *Meyers* adopted a low threshold for inclusion as a religion, stating (simply by way of illustration and not intending to be exhaustive) that the following established religions and belief systems would all qualify as "religions" for constitutional purposes: Judaism, Christianity, Islam, Hinduism, Buddhism, Shintoism, Confucianism, Taoism, Mormonism, Scientology, the International Society of Krishna Consciousness (Hare Krishna), Bantu, the Seventh Day Adventist Church, Christian Science, Branch Davidian, the Unification Church, the Native American Church (including Shamanists and Ghost Dancers), Paganism, Zoroastrianism, Pantheism, Animism, Wicca, Druidism, Satanism, and Santeria, as well as ancient Greek, Norse, and Roman mythology. More important than this listing, however, was the court's intriguing methodology. It created a sort of "scorecard" of characteristics that are commonly associated with "religions." Not all the characteristics are required to qualify as a religion. The list was intended to be descriptive, or anthropological, not normative. The judge thus described the following characteristics as typical of constitutionally qualifying religions:

1. **Ultimate Ideas:** Religious beliefs often address fundamental questions about life, purpose, and death. As one court has put it, "a religion

addresses fundamental and ultimate questions having to do with deep and imponderable matters." These matters may include existential matters, such as man's perception of life; ontological matters, such as man's sense of being; teleological matters, such as man's purpose in life; and cosmological matters, such as man's place in the universe.

2. **Metaphysical Beliefs:** Religious beliefs often are "metaphysical," that is, they address a reality which transcends the physical and immediately apparent world. Adherents to many religions believe that there is another dimension, place, mode, or temporality, and they often believe that these places are inhabited by spirits, souls, forces, deities, and other sorts of inchoate or intangible entities.

3. **Moral or Ethical System:** Religious beliefs often prescribe a particular manner of acting, or way of life, that is "moral" or "ethical." In other words, these beliefs often describe certain acts in normative terms, such as "right and wrong," "good and evil," or "just and unjust." The beliefs then proscribe those acts that are "wrong," "evil," or "unjust." A moral or ethical belief structure also may create duties—duties often imposed by some higher power, force, or spirit—that require the believer to abnegate elemental self-interest.

4. **Comprehensiveness of Beliefs:** Another hallmark of "religious" ideas is that they are comprehensive. More often than not, such beliefs provide a telos, an overarching array of beliefs that coalesce to provide the believer with answers to many, if not most, of the problems and concerns that confront humans. In other words, religious beliefs generally are not confined to one question or a single teaching.

5. **Accoutrements of Religion:** By analogy to many of the established or recognized religions, the presence of the following external signs may indicate that a particular set of beliefs is "religious":

    a. **Founder, Prophet, or Teacher:** Many religions have been wholly founded or significantly influenced by a deity, teacher, seer, or prophet who is considered to be divine, enlightened, gifted, or blessed.

    b. **Important Writings:** Most religions embrace seminal, elemental, fundamental, or sacred writings. These writings often include creeds, tenets, precepts, parables, commandments, prayers, scriptures, catechisms, chants, rites, or mantras.

c. **Gathering Places:** Many religions designate particular structures or places as sacred, holy, or significant. These sites often serve as gathering places for believers. They include physical structures, such as churches, mosques, temples, pyramids, synagogues, or shrines; and natural places, such as springs, rivers, forests, plains, or mountains.

d. **Keepers of Knowledge:** Most religions have clergy, ministers, priests, reverends, monks, shamans, teachers, or sages. By virtue of their enlightenment, experience, education, or training, these people are keepers and purveyors of religious knowledge.

e. **Ceremonies and Rituals:** Most religions include some form of ceremony, ritual, liturgy, sacrament, or protocol. These acts, statements, and movements are prescribed by the religion and are imbued with transcendent significance.

f. **Structure or Organization:** Many religions have a congregation or group of believers who are led, supervised, or counseled by a hierarchy of teachers, clergy, sages, priests, etc.

g. **Holidays:** As is etymologically evident, many religions celebrate, observe, or mark "holy," sacred, or important days, weeks, or months.

h. **Diet or Fasting:** Religions often prescribe or prohibit the eating of certain foods and the drinking of certain liquids on particular days or during particular times.

i. **Appearance and Clothing:** Some religions prescribe the manner in which believers should maintain their physical appearance, and other religions prescribe the type of clothing that believers should wear.

j. **Propagation:** Most religious groups, thinking that they have something worthwhile or essential to offer non-believers, attempt to propagate their views and persuade others of their correctness. This is sometimes called "mission work," "witnessing," "converting," or proselytizing.

Applying these principles, the judge in *Meyers* rejected the argument that the First Church of Marijuana was a religion. The "Church" appeared to have only one attribute: a belief in the heavy use of marijuana. The judge was not impressed.

Points for Discussion

1. **Judges cannot rule on the veracity of a person's religious beliefs.** Imagine that a federal inmate contends that the prison is violating his Free Exercise rights because it is not giving him pasta to eat at every meal. He claims to believe in the Pasta God who commands him to eat pasta and nothing else.

   Should a judge be able to reject the inmate's claim solely on the basis that the inmate's alleged religion is not credible? The short answer is no. In *United States v. Ballard*, 322 U.S. 78 (1944), Justice William Douglas announced an absolute bar on judges' evaluating the veracity of an individual's faith:

   > Freedom of thought, which includes freedom of religious belief, is basic in a society of free men. It embraces the right to maintain theories of life and of death and of the hereafter which are rank heresy to followers of the orthodox faiths. Heresy trials are foreign to our Constitution. Men may believe what they cannot prove. If one could be sent to jail because a jury in a hostile environment found those teachings false, little indeed would be left of religious freedom.

   Consequently, secular courts are not permitted to judge the truth or falsity of religious dogma. Opinions on such questions as to whether it is true or false that God exists or that Moses parted the Red Sea are out of bounds.

2. **But judges can rule on whether a belief is sincerely held.** The Supreme Court has said that judges can evaluate whether a religious claimant's beliefs are sincerely held. But how is a judge supposed to do that? On rare occasions there may be clear evidence of a lack of sincerity. For example, imagine that witnesses had seen our pasta-loving inmate happily devouring all manner of foods even when pasta was readily available. Absent such evidence, proving that a religious claimant's beliefs are not sincere can be challenging. A judge might be tempted to conclude that the beliefs are insincere if he finds the beliefs themselves unbelievable (such as a belief in the Pasta God). But Justice Douglas' admonition in *Ballard* precludes the judge from doing so. That may be so, but Justice Robert Jackson rightfully pointed out in a dissent in *Ballard* that it is hard to separate one from the other: "As a matter of either practice or philosophy I do not see how we can separate an issue as to what is believed from considerations as to what is believable. If we try religious sincerity severed from religious verity, we isolate the dispute from the very considerations which in common experience provide its most reliable answer."

You Be the Lawyer!

Is fortune-telling a religion?

A metropolitan area consisting of three different municipalities, First City, Second City, and Third City, borders on a large collection of military bases, including Navy, Marine, Army, and Air Force facilities. Two of the cities, First City and Second City, heavily cater to the military personnel on the bases. These cities have many "family-oriented" and "less family-oriented" commercial activities. Among the "less family-oriented" establishments that proliferate in these two cities are bars, erotic dance clubs, massage parlors, tattoo shops, and fortune tellers. Third City, however, is not particularly hospitable to the members of the military and seeks to distance itself from these more "adult" establishments. It uses zoning regulations to severely hamper the ability of these establishments to operate. Rather than put up with the hassle of dealing with Third City's complex zoning regulations, many of these establishments simply chose to locate in First City and Second City. In addition to its severe zoning regulations, Third City has an ordinance that entirely bans certain establishments. One ordinance prohibits the charging of any fee for fortune-telling.

You are a lawyer practicing law in Third City. A potential client, who calls herself "Reverend Mary Worth," has scheduled an appointment with you. She states that she is an ordained spiritualist priest who writes books and uses tarot cards and a crystal ball to look into the future of her patrons, also providing those patrons with spiritual advice and counseling. When she writes a new book, she often goes on national tours to spiritualist and mystic bookstores and offers, for a fee of $100, a copy of her book, a reading using the tarot cards and crystal ball, and a counseling session. A spiritualist bookstore in Third City has advertised her visit for this purpose. Her appearance is scheduled in four weeks. Upon seeing the advertisement, a local prosecutor in Third City notified the bookstore that the city regards the scheduled event as commercial fortune-telling forbidden by the city ordinance.

Reverend Mary Worth wants to know her legal options. She tells you that she considers her book tour activities to be the exercise of her religion. She regards it as particularly important that any legal action she might take be grounded in what she claims is her constitutional right to religious liberty.

You are trying to determine whether Reverend Worth would have a viable case for enjoining enforcement of the ban on commercial fortune-telling. One avenue for seeking relief would be a claim based on an alleged violation of her free speech rights. But you are also keenly interested in thinking through whether she might also have a valid claim for a violation of her rights under the Free Exercise Clause. However, you are not sure whether what she does, in reading tarot cards and looking into a crystal ball, constitutes the exercise of "religion." You also wonder what her status as a "Reverend" means. Compile a list of questions to ask her that would help you determine whether the fortune-telling she does would be considered a religion.

Test Your Knowledge

To assess your understanding of the material in this chapter, click here to take a quiz.

Chapter Eighteen

When Does Government Unlawfully Burden Religion?

The Free Exercise Clause

The Free Exercise Clause provides that "Congress shall make no law . . . prohibiting the free exercise [of religion]." The clause acts as a restraint on all branches of the federal government and not merely Congress. It has been incorporated into the Fourteenth Amendment, so it also acts as a restraint on state and local governments.[1]

Free Exercise Clause issues arise when governments burden religion. At a minimum, the clause means that the government may not regulate what a person believes. As Justice Antonin Scalia explained in *Employment Division v. Smith*:

> The free exercise of religion means, first and foremost, the right to believe and profess whatever religious doctrine one desires. Thus, the First Amendment obviously excludes all "governmental regulation of religious *beliefs* as such."[2]

Since governments typically regulate conduct and not beliefs, the restraint on the government's ability to regulate beliefs is rarely an issue. One context in which it has arisen is religious tests for holding public office, such a requirement that an office holder take an oath espousing her belief in God. The Constitution has a clause, independent of the Free Exercise Clause, that specifically forbids such religious tests for federal office holders.[3] The Supreme Court has also indicated that the Free Exercise Clause, through its incorporation into the Fourteenth Amendment, prohibits similar tests for state and local government officials.

In *Torcaso v. Watkins*,[4] for example, the Court struck down a Maryland law that required office holders to declare a belief in God. The Court stated that "neither a State nor the Federal Government can constitutionally force a person to profess a

1 *Cantwell v. Connecticut*, 310 U.S. 296, 303 (1940).
2 *Employment Division, Dep't of Human Res. of Or. v. Smith*, 494 U.S. 872, 877 (1990).
3 U.S. Const. Art. VI, cl. 3.
4 *Torcaso v. Watkins*, 367 U.S. 488, 495 (1961).

belief or disbelief in any religion." The Court has similarly held that clergy members cannot be barred from serving in public office merely because they are clergy.[5]

The more typical free exercise case arises when a government regulates conduct in a manner that interferes with religious practice. A law might prohibit a religious adherent from engaging in conduct that his religion requires, or it might require an adherent to engage in conduct that his religion forbids. The issue then becomes whether the Constitution requires the government to exempt the adherent from the law's application or, as it is sometimes said, to provide the adherent with an "accommodation."

Section B of this chapter will focus on the question of when, if ever, a religious adherent should be exempted from a neutral law that does not target the adherent's religious practice but nevertheless burdens it. Before getting to that issue, we will explore the more serious concern of government regulations that discriminate against religious practice.

A. When Government Targets Religion: Government Actions That Reflect Hostility Toward Religion

Governments occasionally regulate in a manner that singles out religious conduct for less favorable treatment than other conduct. In these instances, the government is regulating religious practice because of its religious motivation. Such laws, often prompted by hostility toward a particular religious group, trigger strict scrutiny and are invariably struck down. The leading authority is *Church of the Lukumi Babalu Aye v. City of Hialeah.*

Church of the Lukumi Babalu Aye, Inc. v. City of Hialeah

Supreme Court of the United States, 1993
508 U.S. 520

JUSTICE KENNEDY delivered the opinion of the Court, except as to Part II-A-2[6]

The principle that government may not enact laws that suppress religious belief or practice is so well understood that few violations are recorded in our opinions.

5 *McDaniel v. Paty*, 435 U.S. 618 (1978).

6 The decision in *Lukumi* striking down Hialeah's enactments was unanimous. A number of justices wrote concurring opinions, which have been omitted here, in which they offered views on the issue taken up in Section B of this chapter, dealing with what the standards should be in analyzing

Our review confirms that the laws in question were enacted by officials who did not understand, failed to perceive, or chose to ignore the fact that their official actions violated the Nation's essential commitment to religious freedom. The challenged laws had an impermissible object; and in all events the principle of general applicability was violated because the secular ends asserted in defense of the laws were pursued only with respect to conduct motivated by religious beliefs.

This case involves practices of the Santeria religion, which originated in the 19th century. When hundreds of thousands of members of the Yoruba people were brought as slaves from western Africa to Cuba, their traditional African religion absorbed significant elements of Roman Catholicism. The resulting syncretion, or fusion, is Santeria, "the way of the saints." The Cuban Yoruba express their devotion to spirits, called orishas, through the iconography of Catholic saints, Catholic symbols are often present at Santeria rites, and Santeria devotees attend the Catholic sacraments.

The Santeria faith teaches that every individual has a destiny from God, a destiny fulfilled with the aid and energy of the orishas. The basis of the Santeria religion is the nurture of a personal relation with the orishas, and one of the principal forms of devotion is an animal sacrifice. The sacrifice of animals as part of religious rituals has ancient roots. Animal sacrifice is mentioned throughout the Old Testament, and it played an important role in the practice of Judaism before destruction of the second Temple in Jerusalem. In modern Islam, there is an annual sacrifice commemorating Abraham's sacrifice of a ram in the stead of his son.

According to Santeria teaching, the orishas are powerful but not immortal. They depend for survival on the sacrifice. Sacrifices are performed at birth, marriage, and death rites, for the cure of the sick, for the initiation of new members and priests, and during an annual celebration. Animals sacrificed in Santeria rituals include chickens, pigeons, doves, ducks, guinea pigs, goats, sheep, and turtles. The animals are killed by the cutting of the carotid arteries in the neck. The sacrificed animal is cooked and eaten, except after healing and death rituals.

Petitioner Church of the Lukumi Babalu Aye, Inc., is a not-for-profit corporation organized under Florida law in 1973. The Church and its congregants practice the Santeria religion. In April 1987, the Church leased land in the City of Hialeah, Florida, and announced plans to establish a house of worship as well as a school, cultural center, and museum.

The prospect of a Santeria church in their midst was distressing to many members of the Hialeah community, and the announcement of the plans to open a Santeria

---

"neutral" laws that incidentally burden religion. That is why Justice Kennedy's opinion for the Court included the exception "as to Part II-A-2," which you may ignore for present purposes.

church in Hialeah prompted the city council to hold an emergency public session on June 9, 1987.

The city council responded at first with a hortatory enactment, that noted its residents' "great concern regarding the possibility of public ritualistic animal sacrifices." The resolution declared the city policy "to oppose the ritual sacrifices of animals" within Hialeah and announced that any person or organization practicing animal sacrifice "will be prosecuted."

In September 1987, the city council adopted three substantive ordinances addressing the issue of religious animal sacrifice. Ordinance 87–52 defined "sacrifice" as "to unnecessarily kill, torment, torture, or mutilate an animal in a public or private ritual or ceremony not for the primary purpose of food consumption," and prohibited owning or possessing an animal "intending to use such animal for food purposes." It restricted application of this prohibition, however, to any individual or group that "kills, slaughters or sacrifices animals for any type of ritual, regardless of whether or not the flesh or blood of the animal is to be consumed." The ordinance contained an exemption for slaughtering by "licensed establishments" of animals "specifically raised for food purposes."

The Free Exercise Clause of the First Amendment, which has been applied to the States through the Fourteenth Amendment, provides that "Congress shall make no law respecting an establishment of religion, or *prohibiting the free exercise thereof*." The city does not argue that Santeria is not a "religion" within the meaning of the First Amendment. Nor could it. Although the practice of animal sacrifice may seem abhorrent to some, "religious beliefs need not be acceptable, logical, consistent, or comprehensible to others in order to merit First Amendment protection." Given the historical association between animal sacrifice and religious worship, petitioners' assertion that animal sacrifice is an integral part of their religion "cannot be deemed bizarre or incredible." Neither the city nor the courts below, moreover, have questioned the sincerity of petitioners' professed desire to conduct animal sacrifices for religious reasons.

At a minimum, the protections of the Free Exercise Clause pertain if the law at issue discriminates against some or all religious beliefs or regulates or prohibits conduct because it is undertaken for religious reasons.

Although a law targeting religious beliefs as such is never permissible, if the object of a law is to infringe upon or restrict practices because of their religious motivation, the law is not neutral, and it is invalid unless it is justified by a compelling interest and is narrowly tailored to advance that interest. To determine the object of a law, we must begin with its text, for the minimum requirement of neutrality is that a law not discriminate on its face. Petitioners contend that three of the ordinances fail this test of facial neutrality because they use the words "sacrifice" and "ritual," words with strong religious connotations. We agree that these words are consistent with the claim of facial discrimination, but the argument is not conclusive. The words "sacrifice" and "ritual" have a religious origin, but current use admits also of secular meanings.

We reject the contention advanced by the city, that our inquiry must end with the text of the laws at issue. Facial neutrality is not determinative. The Free Exercise Clause, like the Establishment Clause, extends beyond facial discrimination. The Clause "forbids subtle departures from neutrality," and "covert suppression of particular religious beliefs." Official action that targets religious conduct for distinctive treatment cannot be shielded by mere compliance with the requirement of facial neutrality. The Free Exercise Clause protects against governmental hostility which is masked, as well as overt.

The record in this case compels the conclusion that suppression of the central element of the Santeria worship service was the object of the ordinances. First, though use of the words "sacrifice" and "ritual" does not compel a finding of improper targeting of the Santeria religion, the choice of these words is support for our conclusion.

The ordinances had as their object the suppression of religion. The pattern we have recited discloses animosity to Santeria adherents and their religious practices; the ordinances by their own terms target this religious exercise; the texts of the ordinances were gerrymandered with care to proscribe religious killings of animals but to exclude almost all secular killings; and the ordinances suppress much more religious conduct than is necessary in order to achieve the legitimate ends asserted in their defense.

The city concedes that neither the State of Florida nor the City has enacted a generally applicable ban on the killing of animals. It asserts, however, that animal sacrifice is "different" from the animal killings that are permitted by law. According to the city, it is "self-evident" that killing animals for food is "important"; the eradication of insects and pests is "obviously justified"; and the euthanasia of excess animals "makes sense." These *ipse dixits* do not explain why religion alone must bear the burden of the ordinances, when many of these secular killings fall within the city's interest in preventing the cruel treatment of animals.

The principle that government, in pursuit of legitimate interests, cannot in a selective manner impose burdens only on conduct motivated by religious belief is essential to the protection of the rights guaranteed by the Free Exercise Clause.

A law that targets religious conduct for distinctive treatment or advances legitimate governmental interests only against conduct with a religious motivation will survive strict scrutiny only in rare cases. It follows from what we have already said that these ordinances cannot withstand this scrutiny.

not compelling

Respondent has not demonstrated, moreover, that, in the context of these ordinances, its governmental interests are compelling. Where government restricts only conduct protected by the First Amendment and fails to enact feasible measures to restrict other conduct producing substantial harm or alleged harm of the same sort, the interest given in justification of the restriction is not compelling.

The Free Exercise Clause commits government itself to religious tolerance, and upon even slight suspicion that proposals for state intervention stem from animosity to religion or distrust of its practices, all officials must pause to remember their own high duty to the Constitution and to the rights it secures. Those in office must be resolute in resisting importunate demands and must ensure that the sole reasons for imposing the burdens of law and regulation are secular. Legislators may not devise mechanisms, overt or disguised, designed to persecute or oppress a religion or its practices. The laws here in question were enacted contrary to these constitutional principles, and they are void.

Points for Discussion

1. **What constitutes "hostility" toward religion?** In *Lukumi*, it was relatively easy to establish that Hialeah had passed its ordinances out of hostility toward the Santeria religion. While the use of "code words" such as "ritual" and "sacrifice" did not definitively do the trick, when combined with the history of the city's "emergency" meetings and the exclusion of all other forms of animal slaughter, Hialeah's hostility toward Santeria was readily apparent. A harder problem is posed, however, when the law on its face does indeed appear neutral, but there are allegations of anti-religious animus purportedly tainting the law's application or underlying its enactment. The *Masterpiece Cakeshop* and *Trump v. Hawaii* cases discussed below illustrate those conundrums.

2. **When expressions of hostility toward religion are sufficient to taint governmental action and render it unconstitutional.** In *Masterpiece Cakeshop, Ltd. v. Colorado Civil Rights Commission*, 584 U.S. 617 (2018), a same-sex couple visited a Colorado bakery to inquire about ordering a cake for their wedding reception. The shop's owner, Jack Phillips, told the couple that he would not create a cake for their wedding because of his religious opposition to same-sex marriages. The couple filed a charge with the Colorado Civil Rights Commission, alleging discrimination based on sexual orientation in violation of the state's antidiscrimination law. Colorado argued that its civil rights law prohibiting discrimination based on sexual orientation was a neutral law of general applicability, thereby raising the problem discussed in Section B of this chapter. The Supreme Court, however, in a 7–2 decision written by Justice Anthony Kennedy (the author

of the *Lukumi* decision), held that certain statements by one of the Colorado officials charged with applying the law tainted the law's application, shifting it into the realm of action hostile to religion, triggering the analysis in *Lukumi.* Here is what the Colorado official said: "I would also like to reiterate what we said in the hearing or the last meeting. Freedom of religion and religion has been used to justify all kinds of discrimination throughout history, whether it be slavery, whether it be the holocaust, whether it be—I mean, we can list hundreds of situations where freedom of religion has been used to justify discrimination. And to me it is one of the most despicable pieces of rhetoric that people can use to—to use their religion to hurt others." The Court reacted very negatively to these comments, holding that they pushed the case into the *Lukumi* category. As Justice Kennedy's opinion for the Court phrased it: "To describe a man's faith as 'one of the most despicable pieces of rhetoric that people can use' is to disparage his religion in at least two distinct ways: by describing it as despicable, and also by characterizing it as merely rhetorical—something insubstantial and even insincere. The commissioner even went so far as to compare Phillips' invocation of his sincerely held religious beliefs to defenses of slavery and the Holocaust. This sentiment is inappropriate for a Commission charged with the solemn responsibility of fair and neutral enforcement of Colorado's antidiscrimination law—a law that protects against discrimination on the basis of religion as well as sexual orientation."

3. **When expressions of hostility toward religion are insufficient to taint governmental action and render it unconstitutional.** Only a few weeks after the decision in *Masterpiece Cakeshop*, the Court decided *Trump v. Hawaii*, 585 U.S. 667 (2018). When he was running for president in 2016, Donald Trump constantly stated that "Islam hates us" and called for "total and complete shutdown of Muslims entering the United States until our country's representatives can figure out what is going on." After getting elected, President Trump issued an executive order that was characterized as a "Muslim ban." It did not ban all Muslims from entering the United States, but rather banned entrants from Iran, Iraq, Libya, Somalia, Sudan, Syria, and Yemen, all countries with predominantly Muslim populations. Trump rescinded the first iteration of that executive order and substituted a second, and finally a third, version of the order. It was that third executive order that reached the Supreme Court. The third order did not mention religion and banned entrants from eight countries (Chad, Iran, Iraq, Libya, North Korea, Syria, Venezuela, and Yemen) on grounds that entrants from those nations posed a threat to U.S. national security. Two of those countries, Venezuela and North Korea, did not have significant Muslim populations. In this posture the Court, by a close 5–4 vote, rejected an Establishment Clause challenge to the executive order, finding that it did not discriminate based on religion and could not be held to have been tainted by Trump's apparent animus against Muslims. The majority opinion by Chief Justice John Roberts, joined by Justices

Kennedy, Clarence Thomas, Samuel Alito, and Neil Gorsuch, was unwilling to hold the third order invalid because of Trump's anti-Muslim statements. A key passage in the majority opinion sought to separate the statements of the particular president (Trump) from the deference the Court deemed appropriate toward the presidency as an institution in matters relating to international affairs: "Plaintiffs argue that this President's words strike at fundamental standards of respect and tolerance, in violation of our constitutional tradition. But the issue before us is not whether to denounce the statements. It is instead the significance of those statements in reviewing a Presidential directive, neutral on its face, addressing a matter within the core of executive responsibility. In doing so, we must consider not only the statements of a particular President, but also the authority of the Presidency itself." The four dissenters, Justices Stephen Breyer, Elena Kagan, Sonia Sotomayor, and Ruther Bader Ginsburg, saw the matter quite differently. Justice Sotomayor was particularly critical of Trump's motivation: "The United States of America is a Nation built upon the promise of religious liberty. Our Founders honored that core promise by embedding the principle of religious neutrality in the First Amendment. The Court's decision today fails to safeguard that fundamental principle. It leaves undisturbed a policy first advertised openly and unequivocally as a 'total and complete shutdown of Muslims entering the United States' because the policy now masquerades behind a facade of national-security concerns. But this repackaging does little to cleanse Presidential Proclamation No. 9645 of the appearance of discrimination that the President's words have created. Based on the evidence in the record, a reasonable observer would conclude that the Proclamation was motivated by anti-Muslim animus."

4. **Questioning sincerity must not veer into hostility.** In Chapter 17, you learned that judges may not evaluate the credibility of religious beliefs, but they may evaluate whether a religious adherent's beliefs are sincere. In this vein, note that for both government officials and reviewing courts, there is an important distinction between questioning a claimant's sincerity, which is permitted, and expressing disdain or hostility toward the claimant's religious views—the sort of hostility that is forbidden by *Lukumi* and *Masterpiece Cakeshop*—which is not permitted.

You Be the Judge!

What would you do in a* Trump v. Hawaii *redux?

Imagine that sometime in the future the facts posed by *Trump v. Hawaii* are repeated. A future president, while running for office, touts the necessity of a total ban on Muslims entering the country, but then after being elected promulgates an executive order identical to the one at issue in *Trump v. Hawaii*. The makeup of the Supreme Court has now changed significantly after the retirements of many justices, and once again the issue is before the Court, which is being invited to overturn *Trump v. Hawaii* and adopt the views of dissenting

Justice Sotomayor. If you were a newly appointed Justice, and the likely "swing vote" that would decide the outcome of the case, how would you vote, and why?

B. When Government Incidentally Burdens Religion: Neutral Laws of General Applicability

This section deals with the much more common situation of neutral laws of general applicability that incidentally burden religious practice. These laws are not targeted at religious practices but still negatively impact them. Imagine, for example, a city ordinance that prohibited keeping animals like sheep, goats, or chickens within city limits because of sanitation concerns. This law is neutral on its face, and we will assume that those who enacted it did not have an underlying illicit purpose to target religious practices. Nevertheless, this neutral law of general applicability could still burden a religious group, like the one in *Lukumi*, that wanted to keep sheep, goats, or chickens within city limits for animal sacrifices.

What should the constitutional rule be in these instances? Should the Free Exercise Clause require the government to exempt religious adherents from neutral laws that burden their religious practice? Or should religious adherents be required to obey these laws like everyone else?

This quandary over how much scrutiny to give to neutral laws of general applicability is common to many areas of constitutional law, and the rules vary from one area to another. Sometimes, as in jurisprudence involving the dormant commerce clause, neutral laws with a negative impact are subject to a variant of intermediate scrutiny and will occasionally be invalidated.[7] At other times, as in equal protection jurisprudence, these laws are subject to only deferential rational basis review and are almost never invalidated. So, for example, a law that has a negative impact on a racial group will receive only rational basis review if there is no evidence of an underlying discriminatory purpose.[8]

We have seen examples of the Court's disparate treatment of neutral laws of general applicability in previous chapters of this casebook. A line of cases involving the press appears to endorse the principle that the press enjoys no special First Amendment exemption from generally applicable laws. In *Cohen v. Cowles Media Co.*, for example, the Court refused to graft a First Amendment defense on a promissory estoppel claim brought against a newspaper that violated a promise of confidentiality it had granted to a source. The Court stated that "generally applicable laws do not offend the First Amendment simply because their enforcement against the press has incidental

---

7 *Pike v. Bruce Church, Inc.*, 397 U.S. 137, 142 (1970).

8 *Washington, D.C. v. Davis*, 426 U.S. 229, 239 (1976).

effects on its ability to gather and report the news." Similarly, cases involving taxes on the press generally appear to track Equal Protection Clause analysis, sustaining taxes that are generally applicable, but striking down taxes that single out the press, or any subset of it, for disadvantageous tax treatment.[9]

In contrast to these press cases, free speech law is governed largely by a different test, that imposed by *United States v. O'Brien*. In *O'Brien*, the Court applied an intermediate scrutiny standard when a law "unrelated to suppression of expression" caused an "incidental restriction" on free expression. *O'Brien* is a workhorse of contemporary First Amendment law, applied constantly by courts to subject neutral laws of general applicability that nevertheless adversely impact speech to intermediate scrutiny review.[10]

As you are about to discover, the Court's treatment of neutral laws of general applicability in the Free Exercise Clause context has been wildly inconsistent. At times, decisions have held that when neutral laws of general applicability substantially burden religion, no First Amendment issue is triggered at all, and the laws are upheld. The *Reynolds* and *Smith* cases, which you will read below, are famous exemplars. At other times, however, the Court has applied strict scrutiny to such laws and struck them down. Two other cases you'll read in this chapter, *Sherbert* and *Yoder*, are prime examples. The Court currently adheres to the rule that neutral laws do not trigger First Amendment scrutiny, but the Court appears increasingly hostile to this regime and more sympathetic to the notion that some level of significant judicial scrutiny should apply to such laws—though what that level should be (such as whether it should be strict scrutiny or intermediate scrutiny) remains opaque.

It is important to note that the issue in these cases is usually not whether a neutral law of general applicability should be struck down as unconstitutional. Instead, it is whether the Free Exercise Clause requires the government to exempt a religious adherent from the law's application.

1. Early Cases: No Scrutiny for Neutral Regulations Burdening Religion

The first case to deal with a neutral law incidentally burdening religious practice was *Reynolds v. United States*, decided in 1878, when Utah was a federal territory. The defendant, a Mormon, was prosecuted for the crime of polygamy, which was forbidden under the federal law governing the territory.

---

9 *Minneapolis Star & Tribune Co. v. Minnesota Comm'r of Revenue*, 460 U.S. 575 (1983).

10 For an overview of the Supreme Court's disparate treatment of neutral laws of general applicability, *see* Rodney A. Smolla, *The Free Exercise of Religion After the Fall: The Case for Intermediate Scrutiny*, 39 Wm. & Mary L. Rev. 925, 938–41 (1998).

Reynolds v. United States

Supreme Court of the United States, 1878
98 U.S. 145

MR. CHIEF JUSTICE WAITE delivered the opinion of the Court.

On the trial, the plaintiff in error, the accused, proved that at the time of his alleged second marriage he was, and for many years before had been, a member of the Church of Jesus Christ of Latter-Day Saints, commonly called the Mormon Church, and a believer in its doctrines; that it was an accepted doctrine of that church "that it was the duty of male members of said church, circumstances permitting, to practice polygamy; that this duty was enjoined by different books which the members of said church believed to be of divine origin, and among others the Holy Bible, and also that the members of the church believed that the practice of polygamy was directly enjoined upon the male members thereof by the Almighty God, in a revelation to Joseph Smith, the founder and prophet of said church; that the failing or refusing to practice polygamy by such male members of said church, when circumstances would admit, would be punished, and that the penalty for such failure and refusal would be damnation in the life to come."

The question is raised, whether religious belief can be accepted as a justification of an overt act made criminal by the law of the land. The inquiry is not as to the power of Congress to prescribe criminal laws for the Territories, but as to the guilt of one who knowingly violates a law which has been properly enacted, if he entertains a religious belief that the law is wrong.

The word "religion" is not defined in the Constitution. We must go elsewhere, therefore, to ascertain its meaning, and nowhere more appropriately, we think, than to the history of the times in the midst of which the provision was adopted. The precise point of the inquiry is, what is the religious freedom which has been guaranteed.

Polygamy has always been odious among the northern and western nations of Europe, and, until the establishment of the Mormon Church, was almost exclusively a feature of the life of Asiatic and of African people.

In our opinion, the statute immediately under consideration is within the legislative power of Congress. It is constitutional and valid as prescribing a rule of action for all those residing in the Territories, and in places over which the United States have exclusive control. This being so, the only question which remains is, whether those who make polygamy a part of their religion are excepted from the operation of the statute. If they are, then those who do not make polygamy a part of their religious belief may be found guilty and punished, while those who do, must be acquitted and go free. This would be introducing a new element into criminal law. Laws are made for the government of actions, and while they cannot interfere with mere religious belief and opinions, they may with practices. Suppose one believed that human sacrifices were a necessary part of religious worship, would it be seriously contended that the civil government under which he lived could not interfere to prevent a sacrifice? Or if a wife religiously believed it was her duty to burn herself upon the funeral pile of her dead husband, would it be beyond the power of the civil government to prevent her carrying her belief into practice?

Holding

So here, as a law of the organization of society under the exclusive dominion of the United States, it is provided that plural marriages shall not be allowed. Can a man excuse his practices to the contrary because of his religious belief? To permit this would be to make the professed doctrines of religious belief superior to the law of the land, and in effect to permit every citizen to become a law unto himself. Government could exist only in name under such circumstances.

[Justice Field's concurring opinion is omitted.]

2. The 1960s to 1990: Strict Scrutiny for Neutral Regulations Burdening Religion

In the 1960s, the Court switched to a regime that seemed to strongly favor religious adherents. Under the rule of *Sherbert v. Verner*, judges were instructed to apply strict scrutiny to neutral laws of general applicability that burdened a religious adherent's free exercise rights. If the government could not show that the law was necessary to further a compelling interest, the government was required to exempt the adherent from the law's application.

The Court's opinion in *Sherbert* is immediately below. It is followed by *Wisconsin v. Yoder*, which illustrates the application of *Sherbert*'s strict scrutiny test.

Sherbert v. Verner

Supreme Court of the United States, 1963
374 U.S. 398

MR. JUSTICE BRENNAN delivered the opinion of the Court.

Appellant, a member of the Seventh-day Adventist Church was discharged by her South Carolina employer because she would not work on Saturday, the Sabbath Day of her faith. When she was unable to obtain other employment because from conscientious scruples she would not take Saturday work, she filed a claim for unemployment compensation benefits under the South Carolina Unemployment

Compensation Act. That law provides that, to be eligible for benefits, a claimant must be able to work and is available for work; and, further, that a claimant is ineligible for benefits if he has failed, without good cause to accept available suitable work when offered him by the employment office or the employer. The appellee Employment Security Commission, in administrative proceedings under the statute, found that appellant's restriction upon her availability for Saturday work brought her within the provision disqualifying for benefits insured workers who fail, without good cause, to accept suitable work when offered by the employment office or the employer.

We turn first to the question whether the disqualification for benefits imposes any burden on the free exercise of appellant's religion. We think it is clear that it does. In a sense the consequences of such a disqualification to religious principles and practices may be only an indirect result of welfare legislation within the State's general competence to enact; it is true that no criminal sanctions directly compel appellant to work a six-day week. But this is only the beginning, not the end, of our inquiry. For if the purpose or effect of a law is to impede the observance of one or all religions or is to discriminate invidiously between religions, that law is constitutionally invalid even though the burden may be characterized as being only indirect. Here not only is it apparent that appellant's declared ineligibility for benefits derives solely from the practice of her religion, but the pressure upon her to forego that practice is unmistakable. The ruling forces her to choose between following the precepts of her religion and forfeiting benefits, on the one hand, and abandoning one of the precepts of her religion in order to accept work, on the other hand. Governmental imposition of such a choice puts the same kind of burden upon the free exercise of religion as would a fine imposed against appellant for her Saturday worship.

Nor may the South Carolina court's construction of the statute be saved from constitutional infirmity on the ground that unemployment compensation benefits are not appellant's "right" but merely a "privilege." It is too late in the day to doubt that the liberties of religion and expression may be infringed by the denial of or placing of conditions upon a benefit or privilege. To condition the availability of benefits upon this appellant's willingness to violate a cardinal principle of her religious faith effectively penalizes the free exercise of her constitutional liberties.

Significantly South Carolina expressly saves the Sunday worshipper from having to make the kind of choice which we here hold infringes the Sabbatarian's religious liberty. When in times of "national emergency" the textile plants are authorized by the State Commissioner of Labor to operate on Sunday, "no employee shall be required to work on Sunday who is conscientiously opposed to Sunday work; and if any employee should refuse to work on Sunday on account of conscientious objections he or she shall not jeopardize his or her seniority by such refusal or be discriminated against in any other manner."

We must next consider whether some compelling state interest enforced in the eligibility provisions of the South Carolina statute justifies the substantial infringement of appellant's First Amendment right. For even if the possibility of spurious claims did threaten to dilute the fund and disrupt the scheduling of work, it would plainly be incumbent upon the appellees to demonstrate that no alternative forms of regulation would combat such abuses without infringing First Amendment rights.

In holding as we do, plainly we are not fostering the "establishment" of the Seventh-day Adventist religion in South Carolina, for the extension of unemployment benefits to Sabbatarians in common with Sunday worshippers reflects nothing more than the governmental obligation of neutrality in the face of religious differences, and does not represent that involvement of religious with secular institutions which it is the object of the Establishment Clause to forestall.

Nor does the recognition of the appellant's right to unemployment benefits under the state statute serve to abridge any other person's religious liberties. Nor do we, by our decision today, declare the existence of a constitutional right to unemployment benefits on the part of all persons whose religious convictions are the cause of their unemployment. This is not a case in which an employee's religious convictions serve to make him a nonproductive member of society. Our holding today is only that South Carolina may not constitutionally apply the eligibility provisions so as to constrain a worker to abandon his religious convictions respecting the day of rest. This holding but reaffirms a principle that we announced a decade and a half ago, namely that no State may "exclude individual Catholics, Lutherans, Mohammedans, Baptists, Jews, Methodists, Non-believers, Presbyterians, or the members of any other faith, because of their faith, or lack of it, from receiving the benefits of public welfare legislation." *Everson v. Board of Education*.

It is so ordered.

MR. JUSTICE DOUGLAS, concurring.

Religious scruples of Moslems require them to attend a mosque on Friday and to pray five times daily. Religious scruples of a Sikh require him to carry a regular or a symbolic sword. Religious scruples of a Jehovah's Witness teach him to be a colporteur, going from door to door, from town to town, distributing his religious pamphlets. Religious scruples of a Quaker compel him to refrain from swearing and to affirm instead. Religious scruples of a Buddhist may require him to refrain from partaking of any flesh, even of fish.

The examples could be multiplied, including those of the Seventh-day Adventist whose Sabbath is Saturday and who is advised not to eat some meats.

These suffice, however, to show that many people hold beliefs alien to the majority of our society—beliefs that are protected by the First Amendment but which could easily be trod upon under the guise of "police" or "health" regulations reflecting the majority's views.

MR. JUSTICE HARLAN, whom MR. JUSTICE WHITE joins, dissenting.

The implications of the present decision are far more troublesome than its apparently narrow dimensions would indicate at first glance. The meaning of today's holding, as already noted, is that the State must furnish unemployment benefits to one who is unavailable for work if the unavailability stems from the exercise of religious convictions. The State, in other words, must single out for financial assistance those whose behavior is religiously motivated, even though it denies such assistance to others whose identical behavior (in this case, inability to work on Saturdays) is not religiously motivated.

For very much the same reasons, however, I cannot subscribe to the conclusion that the State is constitutionally compelled to carve out an exception to its general rule of eligibility in the present case. Those situations in which the Constitution may require special treatment on account of religion are, in my view, few and far between, and this view is amply supported by the course of constitutional litigation in this area.

[Justice Stewart's opinion concurring in the result is omitted.]

Wisconsin v. Yoder

Supreme Court of the United States, 1972
406 U.S. 205

MR. CHIEF JUSTICE BURGER delivered the opinion of the Court.

Respondents Jonas Yoder and Wallace Miller are members of the Old Order Amish religion, and respondent Adin Yutzy is a member of the Conservative Amish Mennonite Church. Wisconsin's compulsory school-attendance law required them to cause their children to attend public or private school until reaching age 16 but the respondents declined to send their children, ages 14 and 15, to public school after they complete the eighth grade.

A related feature of Old Order Amish communities is their devotion to a life in harmony with nature and the soil, as exemplified by the simple life of the early Christian era that continued in America during much of our early national life. Amish beliefs require members of the community to make their living by farming or closely related activities. Broadly speaking, the Old Order Amish religion pervades and determines the entire mode of life of its adherents. Their conduct is regulated in great detail by the Ordnung, or rules, of the church community. Adult baptism, which occurs in late adolescence, is the time at which Amish young people voluntarily undertake heavy obligations, not unlike the Bar Mitzvah of the Jews, to abide by the rules of the church community.

Amish objection to formal education beyond the eighth grade is firmly grounded in these central religious concepts. They object to the high school, and higher education generally, because the values they teach are in marked variance with Amish values and the Amish way of life; they view secondary school education as an impermissible exposure of their children to a "worldly" influence in conflict with their beliefs. The high school tends to emphasize intellectual and scientific accomplishments, self-distinction, competitiveness, worldly success, and social life with other students. Amish society emphasizes informal learning-through-doing; a life of "goodness," rather than a life of intellect; wisdom, rather than technical knowledge, community welfare, rather than competition; and separation from, rather than integration with, contemporary worldly society.

Formal high school education beyond the eighth grade is contrary to Amish beliefs, not only because it places Amish children in an environment hostile to Amish beliefs with increasing emphasis on competition in class work and sports and with pressure to conform to the styles, manners, and ways of the peer group, but also because it takes them away from their community, physically and emotionally, during the crucial and formative adolescent period of life. During this period, the children must acquire Amish attitudes favoring manual work and self-reliance and the specific skills needed to perform the adult role of an Amish farmer or housewife. They must learn to enjoy physical labor. Once a child has learned basic reading, writing, and elementary mathematics, these traits, skills, and attitudes admittedly fall within the category of those best learned through example and "doing" rather than in a classroom. And, at this time in life, the Amish child must also grow in his faith and his relationship to the Amish community if he is to be prepared to accept the heavy obligations imposed by adult baptism. In short, high school attendance with teachers who are not of the Amish faith—and may even be hostile to it—interposes a serious barrier to the integration of the Amish child into the Amish religious community. Dr. John Hostetler, one of the experts on Amish society, testified that the modern high school is not equipped, in curriculum or social environment, to impart the values promoted by Amish society.

The Amish do not object to elementary education through the first eight grades as a general proposition because they agree that their children must have basic skills in the "three R's" in order to read the Bible, to be good farmers and citizens, and to be able to deal with non-Amish people when necessary in the course of daily affairs. They view such a basic education as acceptable because it does not significantly expose their children to worldly values or interfere with their development in the Amish community during the crucial adolescent period. While Amish accept compulsory elementary education generally, wherever possible they have established their own elementary schools in many respects like the small local schools of the past. In the Amish belief higher learning tends to develop values they reject as influences that alienate man from God.

We come then to the quality of the claims of the respondents concerning the alleged encroachment of Wisconsin's compulsory school-attendance statute on their rights and the rights of their children to the free exercise of the religious beliefs they and their forbears have adhered to for almost three centuries. In evaluating those claims we must be careful to determine whether the Amish religious faith and their mode of life are, as they claim, inseparable and interdependent. A way of life, however virtuous and admirable, may not be interposed as a barrier to reasonable state regulation of education if it is based on purely secular considerations; to have the protection of the Religion Clauses, the claims must be rooted in religious belief. Although a determination of what is a "religious" belief or practice entitled to constitutional protection may present a most delicate question, the very concept of ordered liberty precludes allowing every person to make his own standards on matters of conduct in which society as a whole has important interests. Thus, if the Amish asserted their claims because of their subjective evaluation and rejection of the contemporary secular values accepted by the majority, much as Thoreau rejected the social values of his time and isolated himself at Walden Pond, their claims would not rest on a religious basis. Thoreau's choice was philosophical and personal rather than religious, and such belief does not rise to the demands of the Religion Clauses.

Giving no weight to such secular considerations, however, we see that the record in this case abundantly supports the claim that the traditional way of life of the Amish is not merely a matter of personal preference, but one of deep religious conviction, shared by an organized group, and intimately related to daily living.

Nor can this case be disposed of on the grounds that Wisconsin's requirement for school attendance to age 16 applies uniformly to all citizens of the State and does not, on its face, discriminate against religions or a particular religion, or that it is motivated by legitimate secular concerns. A regulation neutral on its face may, in its application, nonetheless offend the constitutional requirement for governmental neutrality if it unduly burdens the free exercise of religion. *Sherbert v. Verner.*

We turn, then, to the State's broader contention that its interest in its system of compulsory education is so compelling that even the established religious practices of the Amish must give way.

The State, however, supports its interest in providing an additional one or two years of compulsory high school education to Amish children because of the possibility that some such children will choose to leave the Amish community, and that if this occurs they will be ill-equipped for life. The State argues that if Amish children leave their church they should not be in the position of making their way in the world without the education available in the one or two additional years the State requires. However, on this record, that argument is highly speculative. There is no specific evidence of the loss of Amish adherents by attrition, nor is there any showing that upon leaving the Amish community Amish children, with their practical agricultural training and habits of industry and self-reliance, would become burdens on society because of educational shortcomings.

Insofar as the State's claim rests on the view that a brief additional period of formal education is imperative to enable the Amish to participate effectively and intelligently in our democratic process, it must fall. The Amish alternative to formal secondary school education has enabled them to function effectively in their day-to-day life under self-imposed limitations on relations with the world, and to survive and prosper in contemporary society as a separate, sharply identifiable and highly self-sufficient community for more than 200 years in this country. In itself this is strong evidence that they are capable of fulfilling the social and political responsibilities of citizenship without compelled attendance beyond the eighth grade at the price of jeopardizing their free exercise of religious belief.

Contrary to the suggestion of the dissenting opinion of Mr. Justice Douglas, our holding today in no degree depends on the assertion of the religious interest of the child as contrasted with that of the parents. It is the parents who are subject to prosecution here for failing to cause their children to attend school, and it is their right of free exercise, not that of their children, that must determine Wisconsin's power to impose criminal penalties on the parent. The dissent argues that a child who expresses a desire to attend public high school in conflict with the wishes of his parents should not be prevented from doing so. There is no reason for the Court to consider that point since it is not an issue in the case.

Our holding in no way determines the proper resolution of possible competing interests of parents, children, and the State in an appropriate state court proceeding in which the power of the State is asserted on the theory that Amish parents are preventing their minor children from attending high school despite their expressed desires to the contrary. Recognition of the claim of the State in such a proceeding would, of course, call into question traditional concepts of parental control over the religious upbringing and education of their minor children recognized in this Court's past decisions. It is clear that such an intrusion by a State into family decisions in the area of religious training would give rise to grave questions of religious freedom comparable to those raised here and those presented in *Pierce v. Society of Sisters*, 268 U.S. 510 (1925). On this record we neither reach nor decide those issues.

For the reasons stated we hold, with the Supreme Court of Wisconsin, that the First and Fourteenth Amendments prevent the State from compelling respondents to cause their children to attend formal high school to age 16.

MR. JUSTICE DOUGLAS, dissenting in part.

It is the future of the student, not the future of the parents, that is imperiled by today's decision. If a parent keeps his child out of school beyond the grade school, then the child will be forever barred from entry into the new and amazing world of diversity that we have today. The child may decide that that is the preferred course, or he may rebel. It is the student's judgment, not his parents', that is essential if we are to give full meaning to what we have said about the Bill of Rights and of the right of students to be masters of their own destiny. If he is harnessed to the Amish way of life by those in authority over him and if his education is truncated, his entire life may be stunted and deformed. The child, therefore, should be given an opportunity to be heard before the State gives the exemption which we honor today.

[Justice Stewart's concurring opinion, which was joined by Justice Brennan, is omitted, as is Justice White's concurring opinion, which was joined by Justice Brennan and Justice Stewart.]

Points for Discussion

1. **Are there grounds for reconciliation?** Can the decisions in *Sherbert* and *Yoder* be reconciled with the decision in *Reynolds*? In all three cases, the religious claimants were being forced to choose between obedience to the secular laws of the government and obedience to the dictates of their religions. In *Sherbert* and *Yoder* the Court required the government to justify the burden on religion with "compelling interests," the traditional parlance of strict scrutiny, and ruled that the states had not met their compelling interest burden. *Reynolds* was decided in the 19th century, long before phrases such as "strict scrutiny" or "compelling governmental interests" entered the lexicon of constitutional law. *Reynolds* was written in almost apocalyptic language, suggesting that the entire social compact required for civilization would fall if individuals were allowed to exempt themselves from criminal laws because those laws conflict with their religious beliefs. If we were to retroactively apply the strict scrutiny test to *Reynolds*, however, is it possible that the Morman claimant might still lose, because the government could in fact come forward with "compelling interests" to justify the ban on polygamy? To what extent might the strength of that claim be weakened today by recognition of a constitutional right to nontraditional marriage, such as the right to same-sex marriage recognized by the Court in *Obergefell v. Hodges*, 576 U.S. 644 (2015)?

2. **The elusive nature of neutrality.** Some scholars contend that the religion clauses require the government to act neutrally toward religion. These scholars believe that government should not treat religion more favorably than other interests, but it should also not treat religion less favorably than other interests. *See, e.g.*, Philip B. Kurland, *Of Church and State and the Supreme Court*, 29 U. Chi. L. Rev. 1 (1961); Douglas Laycock, *Formal, Substantive, and Disaggregated Neutrality Toward Religion*, 39 DePaul L. Rev. 993 (1990). This principle can shed valuable light on how to interpret the religion clauses, but it can be difficult to apply in practice. Consider, for example, the differing conceptions of neutrality in the *Sherbert* case. Justice William Brennan's majority opinion stated that "the extension of unemployment benefits to Sabbatarians in common with Sunday worshippers reflects nothing more than the governmental obligation of neutrality in the face of religious differences." Justice John Harlan, writing in dissent, found that granting unemployment benefits to those with religious objections to working on Saturdays, but not to other people, was anything but neutral: "The State must *single out* for financial assistance those whose behavior is religiously motivated, even though it denies such assistance to others whose identical behavior (in this case, inability to work on Saturdays) is not religiously motivated." If the federal government declares December 25 a holiday for its employees, has the government acted non-neutrally toward religion by favoring Christianity, or has it made a religiously neutral decision by basing its decision on which date was the most convenient for employees?

3. **Chief Justice Burger's favorite case.** Rodney Smolla, one of the co-authors of the casebook, once had the duty of periodically hosting Chief Justice Warren Burger, after his retirement from the Court, when he became chancellor of the College of William and Mary, where Smolla was a law professor. Smolla once asked the chief justice, over drinks, out of all the opinions he had written while on the Court, which one he was most proud of. He answered, "*Wisconsin v. Yoder*."

4. **Doctrinal tensions**. At the end of the day, citizens, lawyers, legislators, government officials, and jurists want some formal doctrinal test expressing the constitutional law standard to be applied when a neutral law of general applicability imposes a substantial burden on the exercise of religion. Two extremes have emerged. One is the tough-minded position that there is no viable Free Exercise Clause claim that may be brought when a neutral law of general applicability substantially burdens religious exercise. That absolutist position is sometimes identified as the holding in *Reynolds*. Alternatively, *Sherbert* and *Yoder* appear to stand for the doctrinal proposition that when a neutral law of general applicability does impose a substantial burden on the free exercise of religion, the law will be upheld as applied only if the government satisfies the rigors of strict scrutiny, carrying its burden of proving the law is narrowly tailored to address a compelling governmental interest. These two competing doctrines came to a showdown in the case that follows.

3. *Employment Division v. Smith*: A Return to No Scrutiny for Neutral Regulations Burdening Religion

The strict scrutiny test announced in *Sherbert* proved to be far less demanding than the label would suggest. In most areas of constitutional law, the government almost always fails to satisfy the demanding requirements of strict scrutiny. But, with the exceptions of *Yoder* and some other employment compensation cases that resembled *Sherbert*, religious objectors almost always failed to win an accommodation from neutral laws burdening their religion. For example, in *United States v. Lee*, 455 U.S. 252 (1982), an Amish employer failed to be relieved of his obligation to pay Social Security taxes for his employees, even though he claimed that doing so violated his faith, and in *Goldman v. Weinberger*, 475 U.S. 503 (1986), an Orthodox Jewish psychologist serving in the U.S. Air Force was denied an exemption from a military dress regulation that prohibited him from wearing a yarmulke.

In *Employment Division v. Smith*, the Court abandoned the *Sherbert* rule and even suggested that the Court had never applied strict scrutiny to neutral laws of general applicability. Justice Scalia explained that the favorable results for religious objectors in the employment benefits cases and *Yoder* were due to the unique circumstances of those cases.

Employment Division, Department of Human Resources of Oregon v. Smith

Supreme Court of the United States, 1990
494 U.S. 872

JUSTICE SCALIA delivered the opinion of the Court.

This case requires us to decide whether the Free Exercise Clause of the First Amendment permits the State of Oregon to include religiously inspired peyote use within the reach of its general criminal prohibition on use of that drug, and thus permits the State to deny unemployment benefits to persons dismissed from their jobs because of such religiously inspired use.

Respondents Alfred Smith and Galen Black (hereinafter respondents) were fired from their jobs with a private drug rehabilitation organization because they ingested peyote for sacramental purposes at a ceremony of the Native American Church, of which both are members. When respondents applied to petitioner Employment Division (hereinafter petitioner) for unemployment compensation, they were determined to be ineligible for benefits because they had been discharged for work-related "misconduct."

The free exercise of religion means, first and foremost, the right to believe and profess whatever religious doctrine one desires. Thus, the First Amendment obviously excludes all "governmental regulation of religious beliefs as such."

But the "exercise of religion" often involves not only belief and profession but the performance of (or abstention from) physical acts: assembling with others for a worship service, participating in sacramental use of bread and wine, proselytizing, abstaining from certain foods or certain modes of transportation. It would be true, we think (though no case of ours has involved the point), that a State would be "prohibiting the free exercise [of religion]" if it sought to ban such acts or abstentions only when they are engaged in for religious reasons, or only because of the religious belief that they display. It would doubtless be unconstitutional, for example, to ban the casting of "statues that are to be used for worship purposes," or to prohibit bowing down before a golden calf.

Respondents in the present case, however, seek to carry the meaning of "prohibiting the free exercise of religion" one large step further. They contend that their religious motivation for using peyote places them beyond the reach of a criminal law that is not specifically directed at their religious practice, and that is concededly constitutional as applied to those who use the drug for other reasons. They assert, in other words, that "prohibiting the free exercise [of religion]" includes requiring any individual to observe a generally applicable law that requires (or forbids) the performance of an act that his religious belief forbids (or requires).

We have never held that an individual's religious beliefs excuse him from compliance with an otherwise valid law prohibiting conduct that the State is free to regulate. On the contrary, the record of more than a century of our free exercise jurisprudence contradicts that proposition. We first had occasion to assert that principle in *Reynolds v. United States*, where we rejected the claim that criminal laws against polygamy could not be constitutionally applied to those whose religion commanded the practice. "Laws," we said, "are made for the government of actions, and while they cannot interfere with mere religious belief and opinions, they may with practices. Can a man excuse his practices to the contrary because of his religious belief? To permit this would be to make the professed doctrines of religious belief superior to the law of the land, and in effect to permit every citizen to become a law unto himself."

The only decisions in which we have held that the First Amendment bars application of a neutral, generally applicable law to religiously motivated action have involved not the Free Exercise Clause alone, but the Free Exercise Clause in conjunction with other constitutional protections, such as freedom of speech and of the press, *see Cantwell v. Connecticut*, 310 U.S. 296 (1940), or the right of parents, acknowledged in *Pierce v. Society of Sisters*, 268 U.S. 510 (1925), to direct the education of their children, *see Wisconsin v. Yoder*.

The present case does not present such a hybrid situation, but a free exercise claim unconnected with any communicative activity or parental right.

Respondents argue that even though exemption from generally applicable criminal laws need not automatically be extended to religiously motivated actors, at least the claim for a religious exemption must be evaluated under the balancing test set forth in *Sherbert v. Verner*. Under the *Sherbert* test, governmental actions that substantially burden a religious practice must be justified by a compelling governmental interest.

Even if we were inclined to breathe into *Sherbert* some life beyond the unemployment compensation field, we would not apply it to require exemptions from a generally applicable criminal law. The *Sherbert* test, it must be recalled, was developed in a context that lent itself to individualized governmental assessment of the reasons for the relevant conduct. Our decisions in the unemployment cases stand for the proposition that where the State has in place a system of individual exemptions, it may not refuse to extend that system to cases of "religious hardship" without compelling reason.

The "compelling government interest" requirement seems benign, because it is familiar from other fields. But using it as the standard that must be met before the government may accord different treatment on the basis of race, or before the government may regulate the content of speech, is not remotely comparable to using it for the purpose asserted here. What it produces in those other fields—equality of treatment and an unrestricted flow of contending speech—are constitutional norms; what it would produce here—a private right to ignore generally applicable laws—is a constitutional anomaly.

Nor is it possible to limit the impact of respondents' proposal by requiring a "compelling state interest" only when the conduct prohibited is "central" to the individual's religion. It is no more appropriate for judges to determine the "centrality" of religious beliefs before applying a "compelling interest" test in the free exercise field, than it would be for them to determine the "importance" of ideas before applying the "compelling interest" test in the free speech field. What principle of law or logic can be brought to bear to contradict a believer's assertion that a particular act is "central" to his personal faith?

If the "compelling interest" test is to be applied at all, then, it must be applied across the board, to all actions thought to be religiously commanded. Moreover, if "compelling interest" really means what it says (and watering it down here would subvert its rigor in the other fields where it is applied), many laws will not meet the test. Any society adopting such a system would be courting anarchy, but that danger increases in direct proportion to the society's diversity of religious beliefs, and its determination to coerce or suppress none of them. Precisely because "we are a cosmopolitan nation made up of people of almost every conceivable religious preference," and precisely because we value and protect that religious divergence, we cannot afford the luxury of deeming *presumptively invalid,* as applied to the religious objector, every regulation of conduct that does not protect an interest of the highest order. The rule respondents favor would open the prospect of constitutionally required religious exemptions from civic obligations of almost every conceivable kind—ranging from compulsory military service, to the payment of taxes, to health and safety regulation such as manslaughter and child neglect laws, compulsory vaccination laws, drug laws, and traffic laws; to social welfare legislation such as minimum wage laws, child labor laws, animal cruelty laws, environmental protection laws, and laws providing for equality of opportunity for the races. The First Amendment's protection of religious liberty does not require this.

Values that are protected against government interference through enshrinement in the Bill of Rights are not thereby banished from the political process. It is therefore not surprising that a number of States have made an exception to their drug laws for sacramental peyote use. But to say that a nondiscriminatory religious-practice exemption is permitted, or even that it is desirable, is not to say that it is constitutionally required, and that the appropriate occasions for its creation can be discerned by the courts. It may fairly be said that leaving accommodation to the political process will place at a relative disadvantage those religious practices that are not widely engaged in; but that unavoidable consequence of democratic government must be preferred to a system in which each conscience is a law unto itself or in which judges weigh the social importance of all laws against the centrality of all religious beliefs.

Because respondents' ingestion of peyote was prohibited under Oregon law, and because that prohibition is constitutional, Oregon may, consistent with the Free Exercise Clause, deny respondents unemployment compensation when their dismissal results from use of the drug.

It is so ordered.

JUSTICE O'CONNOR, with whom JUSTICE BRENNAN, JUSTICE MARSHALL, and JUSTICE BLACKMUN join as to Parts I and II, concurring in the judgment.

Although I agree with the result the Court reaches in this case, I cannot join its opinion. In my view, today's holding dramatically departs from well-settled First Amendment jurisprudence, appears unnecessary to resolve the question presented, and is incompatible with our Nation's fundamental commitment to individual religious liberty.

The Court today interprets the Free Exercise Clause to permit the government to prohibit, without justification, conduct mandated by an individual's religious beliefs, so long as that prohibition is generally applicable. But a law that prohibits certain conduct—conduct that happens to be an act of worship for someone—manifestly does prohibit that person's free exercise of his religion. A person who is barred from engaging in religiously motivated conduct is barred from freely exercising his religion. Moreover, that person is barred from freely exercising his religion regardless of whether the law prohibits the conduct only when engaged in for religious reasons, only by members of that religion, or by all persons. It is difficult to deny that a law that prohibits religiously motivated conduct, even if the law is generally applicable, does not at least implicate First Amendment concerns.

The Court endeavors to escape from our decisions in *Cantwell* and *Yoder* by labeling them "hybrid" decisions, but there is no denying that both cases expressly relied on the Free Exercise Clause, and that we have consistently regarded those cases as part of the mainstream of our free exercise jurisprudence.

The Court today gives no convincing reason to depart from settled First Amendment jurisprudence. There is nothing talismanic about neutral laws of general applicability or general criminal prohibitions, for laws neutral toward religion can coerce a person to violate his religious conscience or intrude upon his religious duties just as effectively as laws aimed at religion. Although the Court suggests that the compelling interest test, as applied to generally applicable laws, would result in a "constitutional anomaly," the First Amendment unequivocally makes freedom of religion, like freedom from race discrimination and freedom of speech, a "constitutional norm," not an "anomaly."

The Court today suggests that the disfavoring of minority religions is an "unavoidable consequence" under our system of government and that accommodation of such religions must be left to the political process. In my view, however, the First Amendment was enacted precisely to protect the rights of those whose religious practices are not shared by the majority and may be viewed with hostility. The history of our free exercise doctrine amply demonstrates the harsh impact majoritarian rule has had on unpopular or emerging religious groups such as the Jehovah's Witnesses and the Amish.

I would therefore adhere to our established free exercise jurisprudence and hold that the State in this case has a compelling interest in regulating peyote use by its citizens and that accommodating respondents' religiously motivated conduct "will unduly interfere with fulfillment of the governmental interest." Accordingly, I concur in the judgment of the Court.

JUSTICE BLACKMUN, with whom JUSTICE BRENNAN and JUSTICE MARSHALL join, dissenting.

This Court over the years painstakingly has developed a consistent and exacting standard to test the constitutionality of a state statute that burdens the free exercise of religion. Such a statute may stand only if the law in general, and the State's refusal to allow a religious exemption in particular, are justified by a compelling interest that cannot be served by less restrictive means.

Points for Discussion

1. **The political fallout of *Smith* and the passage of RFRA.** The decision in *Smith* was highly controversial from the beginning. Federal legislators reacted very negatively to the decision. In a rare example of bipartisan unanimity, Congress passed the Religious Freedom Restoration Act of 1993 (RFRA), 42 U.S.C. § 2000bb. RFRA was quite extraordinary in Congress' direct and blunt statement of its disagreement with *Smith* and its endorsement of *Sherbert* and *Yoder*. Here is the statute's opening section:

    (a) Findings. The Congress finds that—

    (1) the framers of the Constitution, recognizing free exercise of religion as an unalienable right, secured its protection in the First Amendment to the Constitution;

    (2) laws "neutral" toward religion may burden religious exercise as surely as laws intended to interfere with religious exercise;

    (3) governments should not substantially burden religious exercise without compelling justification;

    (4) in *Employment Division v. Smith*, 494 U.S. 872 (1990) the Supreme Court virtually eliminated the requirement that the government justify burdens on religious exercise imposed by laws neutral toward religion; and

    (5) the compelling interest test as set forth in prior Federal court rulings is a workable test for striking sensible balances between religious liberty and competing prior governmental interests.

    (b) Purposes. The purposes of this Act are—

    (1) to restore the compelling interest test as set forth in *Sherbert v. Verner*, 374 U.S. 398 (1963) and *Wisconsin v. Yoder*, 406 U.S. 205 (1972) and to guarantee its application in all cases where free exercise of religion is substantially burdened; and

    (2) to provide a claim or defense to persons whose religious exercise is substantially burdened by government.

You might be thinking that Congress overturned *Smith* through its enactment of RFRA, but it is important to recognize that *Smith* announced a rule of constitutional law, and the only way to overturn that rule is with a constitutional amendment. RFRA did not and could not change the constitutional rule. Thus, the *Smith* rule—that the Constitution does not require governments to exempt religious adherents from neutral laws of general applicability—is still good law.

But even if Congress cannot overturn a constitutional rule through ordinary legislation, it still can enact laws that create obligations regardless of whether those obligations are constitutionally mandated. For example, the Constitution does not require employers to pay a minimum wage, but federal law nevertheless requires them to do so. By enacting RFRA, Congress created a statutory obligation for governments to exempt religious adherents from neutral laws absent a compelling justification.

Of course, if legislation violates the Constitution, it is likely to be struck down. But, in *Smith*, Justice Scalia invited legislators to enact statutory exemptions for religious adherents. Nevertheless, after RFRA was enacted, the Supreme Court did invalidate RFRA but only to the extent it applied to state and local governments. Recall that Congress must point to a power in the Constitution to enact a law. In *City of Boerne v. Flores*, 521 U.S. 507 (1997), the Court concluded that Congress lacked the power under Section 5 of the Fourteenth Amendment to impose RFRA's obligations on states. Section 5 does give Congress the power to "enforce" the Fourteenth Amendment against states, but the Court reasoned that applying RFRA to the states did not enforce any Fourteenth Amendment right because *Smith* had declared that there was no constitutional right to be exempted from neutral laws. Consequently, even though the Free Exercise Clause is incorporated into the Fourteenth Amendment and therefore binds the states, there was still no Fourteenth Amendment right for Congress to "enforce."

After *Boerne*, many states enacted versions of RFRA, sometimes called "mini-RFRAs." (Recall that states, unlike Congress, have "police power" and do not need to point to a power in the Constitution to act.) Nevertheless, RFRA remains applicable to federal restrictions on religious liberty, and the Supreme Court has tended to interpret RFRA as applied to federal programs quite expansively—that is, with a great deal of deference to religious claimants. Perhaps the most striking example is the Court's decision in *Gonzales v. O Centro Espírita Beneficente União do Vegetal*, 546 U.S. 418 (2006). The case involved a Christian Spiritist sect based in Brazil with an American branch of about 130 individuals. Central to the group's faith was receiving communion through hoasca (pronounced "wass-ca"), a sacramental tea made from two plants unique to the Amazon region. The tea contains a hallucinogen regulated under the federal Controlled Substances Act. Applying RFRA, the Court ruled that the United States could not ban importation of the tea for religious sacramental use. *Gonzales* was in many respects identical to *Smith*, yet it reached the opposite result, relying on RFRA.

Also after the *Boerne* decision, Congress enacted the Religious Land Use and Institutionalized Persons Act of 2000 (RLUIPA), 42 U.S.C. § 2000cc, which is limited to government actions that burden religious practice through land use regulations, such as zoning laws, or through the regulation of prisoners. RLUIPA applies to both the federal government and state and local governments. Rather than relying on its Fourteenth Amendment enforcement power to enact RLUIPA, Congress relied on its spending power and its power to regulate interstate commerce. The Supreme Court has sustained RLUIPA's constitutionality. *See Holt v. Hobbs*, 574 U.S. 352 (2015) (holding that the Arkansas Department of Corrections violated RLUIPA by refusing to allow a Muslim inmate to grow a ½-inch beard).

2. **Judicial discontent with *Smith* at the time it was decided.** Justice Scalia's rejection of the *Sherbert* strict scrutiny test did not sit well with many of his colleagues. As you read above, Justice Sandra Day O'Connor wrote a harsh critique of Justice Scalia's reasoning in an opinion that was joined by three other justices. Who do you think made the more persuasive argument: Justice Scalia or Justice O'Connor? If you had been on the Court at the time, would you have joined either of their opinions? Would you have written a separate opinion with an entirely different analysis?

3. **Growing judicial discontent with *Smith* in subsequent years.** As the makeup of the Supreme Court has changed, the *Smith* decision has become increasingly unpopular among the justices, leading to the distinct possibility that it will be overruled. Indeed, it may not be a question of whether *Smith* will be rejected but when. To date, however, the Court has not overturned *Smith*. But the justices have acted to limit the decision's reach by narrowing the scope of laws that qualify as neutral laws of general applicability.

   Most notably, the Court has indicated that if a law has exemptions, it is not a neutral law of general applicability, and the government must offer exemptions to religious objectors absent a compelling justification. In *Fulton v. City of Philadelphia*, 141 S. Ct. 1868 (2021), for example, the Court confronted a provision in a contract that Philadelphia used with private foster care providers and agencies:

   > Provider shall not reject a child or family including, but not limited to, prospective foster or adoptive parents, for Services based upon their sexual orientation . . . unless an exception is granted by the Commissioner [of the Department of Human Services] or the Commissioner's designee, in his/her sole discretion.

The city relied on this provision to justify terminating its contract with Catholic Social Services because of the organization's refusal to place children with same-sex couples. Philadelphia contended that the contractual provision was a neutral law of general applicability and that *Smith* applied. The Supreme Court disagreed because it thought the provision's exemption clause made the provision non-neutral. The Court said the commissioner's discretion to exempt individual providers was analogous to the individualized determination process for awarding unemployment benefits in *Sherbert*. As the Court observed, even *Smith* acknowledged that such individualized processes do not constitute neutral laws of general applicability:

> *Smith* explained that the unemployment benefits law in *Sherbert* was not generally applicable because the "good cause" standard permitted the government to grant exemptions based on the circumstances underlying each application. *Smith* went on to hold that "where the State has in place a system of individual exemptions, it may not refuse to extend that system to cases of 'religious hardship' without compelling reason."

Because the contractual provision was not a neutral law of general applicability, it was subjected to strict scrutiny and found unconstitutional.

4. **If *Smith* is overturned, what will replace it?** The Court seems poised to overturn *Smith*, but it is not clear what rule would replace it. Consider, for example, the following observation from Justice Amy Coney Barrett in a concurring opinion in *Fulton*:

> Petitioners, their amici, scholars, and Justices of this Court have made serious arguments that *Smith* ought to be overruled. While history looms large in this debate, I find the historical record more silent than supportive on the question whether the founding generation understood the First Amendment to require religious exemptions from generally applicable laws in at least some circumstances. In my view, the textual and structural arguments against *Smith* are more compelling. As a matter of text and structure, it is difficult to see why the Free Exercise Clause—lone among the First Amendment freedoms—offers nothing more than protection from discrimination.
>
> Yet what should replace *Smith*? The prevailing assumption seems to be that strict scrutiny would apply whenever a neutral and generally applicable law burdens religious exercise. But I am skeptical about swapping *Smith*'s categorical antidiscrimination approach for an equally categorical strict scrutiny regime, particularly when this Court's resolution of

conflicts between generally applicable laws and other First Amendment rights—like speech and assembly—has been much more nuanced.

5. **Free exercise during Covid.** The Court issued a complex series of decisions dealing with restrictions on First Amendment liberties affecting religious practices imposed during the Covid-19 pandemic, which began in March 2020. The results of the cases were not consistent, and the outcomes appear to reflect personnel changes on the Court, including the confirmation of Justice Barrett. In the early days of the pandemic, a closely divided Court rejected challenges to restrictions on places of worship in California and Nevada. *See South Bay United Pentecostal Church v. Newsom,* 140 S. Ct. 1613 (2020); *Calvary Chapel Dayton Valley v. Sisolak,* 140 S. Ct. 2603 (2020). In *Roman Catholic Diocese of Brooklyn v. Cuomo,* 141 S. Ct. 63 (2020), however, the Court seemed to reverse course. The plaintiffs in that case, a Jewish synagogue and the Roman Catholic Diocese of Brooklyn, challenged the state's Covid-19 pandemic restrictions as applied to religious organizations. In particular, the suit challenged an executive order issued by the governor imposing severe restrictions on attendance at religious services in areas classified as "red" or "orange" zones. In red zones, no more than 10 people could attend each religious service, and in orange zones, attendance was capped at 25. The Court held that the religious organizations made the required strong showing that the challenged restrictions violate "the minimum requirement of neutrality" toward religion, reasoning that the executive order singled out religious services for more onerous treatment than other activities. The Court noted that in a red zone, a synagogue or church could not admit more than 10 people, but businesses categorized as "essential" could let in as many people as they wanted. Moreover, the list of "essential" businesses included acupuncture facilities, campgrounds, and garages, as well as all chemical and microelectronics plants and all transportation facilities. This disparate treatment, the Court observed, was even more striking in an orange zone. While attendance at houses of worship was limited to 25 people, the Court noted, even nonessential businesses in New York could decide for themselves how many people to admit.

6. **The complexity of free exercise jurisprudence.** The Supreme Court's waffling jurisprudence over whether religious adherents should be exempted from neutral laws of general applicability reflects the underlying complexity of this topic. In cases like *Gonzales* and *Smith,* where a neutral law seems to substantially burden a person's religious practice, and exempting the person would have little or no impact on third parties, it is easy to be sympathetic toward a constitutional rule that would compel governments to grant exemptions. That is especially true when the law burdens members of a minority faith who might not have the influence to secure a statutory exemption through the political process. But when granting an exemption is likely to have a negative impact on other people or on society at large, the balancing act between the interests of religious objectors and

the interests of society becomes more complicated. *See, e.g.*, *Thornton v. Caldor, Inc.*, 472 U.S. 703 (1985) (In *Thornton* the Court struck down a Connecticut law that gave employees an absolute right not to work on any day of the week that the employee observed as the employee's Sabbath, holding that the law violated the Establishment Clause. The Court noted that the law took "no account of the convenience or interests of the employer or those of other employees who do not observe a Sabbath."). Indeed, part of what drove the divisions in the Court's decisions issued during the Covid pandemic were the justices' varying views of the risks posed by people gathering for religious services.

The complexity of these free exercise issues was on full display in a pre-Covid case concerning whether religious employers had a right under RFRA to be exempted from federal regulations that required employers to purchase health insurance for their employees that covered all FDA-approved contraceptives. *Burwell v. Hobby Lobby Stores, Inc.*, 573 U.S. 682 (2014). The employers at issue in the case were two for-profit corporations. The religious objectors were the families (the Hahns and Greens) who owned a controlling interest in the corporations. The families objected to purchasing the insurance because their faith told them that life begins at conception, and some of the FDA-approved contraceptives can terminate a pregnancy after an egg has been fertilized. The Court concluded that the employers were entitled to an exemption. But the Court was divided 5–4 with fierce disagreements between the majority and the dissenters. Here is a sampling of two points of contention:

- **Does RFRA apply to for-profit corporations?** The law requiring the purchase of health insurance applied to the corporations, not to the corporation's shareholders. Since corporations do not have religious beliefs, should RFRA apply to them? For Justice Alito, who wrote the majority opinion, the answer was an unequivocal yes: "A corporation is simply a form of organization used by human beings to achieve desired ends. When rights, whether constitutional or statutory, are extended to corporations, the purpose is to protect the rights of these people." Justice Ginsburg, who wrote a dissenting opinion, reached the opposite conclusion: "Until this litigation, no decision of this Court recognized a for-profit corporation's qualification for a religious exemption from a generally applicable law, whether under the Free Exercise Clause or RFRA. Corporations, Justice Stevens recently reminded, 'have no consciences, no beliefs, no feelings, no thoughts, no desires.' " Do you think RFRA or the Free Exercise Clause should apply to for-profit corporations?

- **Did the law substantially burden religious practice?** In her dissent, Justice Ginsburg rejected the argument that the regulations substantially burdened the families' free exercise rights. She contended that "the connection between the families' religious objections and the contraceptive coverage requirement is too attenuated to rank as substantial." The law did not require the family members to buy or use contraceptives. It only required the corporations "to direct money into undifferentiated funds that finance a wide variety of benefits." The decision whether to purchase and use contraceptives would be made by individual employees. Justice Alito, however, said the justices were precluded from second-guessing the families' good-faith assertion that providing the insurance would burden their religious practice: "The Hahns and Greens and their companies sincerely believe that providing the insurance coverage demanded by the [federal] regulations lies on the forbidden side of the line, and it is not for us to say that their religious beliefs are mistaken or insubstantial. Instead, our 'narrow function in this context is to determine' whether the line drawn reflects 'an honest conviction,' and there is no dispute that it does." Which judge, Justice Ginsburg or Justice Alito, makes the better argument?

C. Excluding Religious Organizations from Government Benefit Programs: May Government Be "More Separationist" than the Establishment Clause Requires?

While this chapter is focused on the Free Exercise Clause, it is impossible to study this clause without also considering its interplay with the Establishment Clause. Both clauses help secure religious liberty, but while the clauses can complement each other, they can also conflict. The Supreme Court has even described the clauses as being "frequently in tension."

It is easy to understand why. As we discussed in Chapter 17, Free Exercise Clause issues arise when the government burdens religion, and Establishment Clause issues arise when the government benefits religion. But often addressing an issue under one clause raises concerns under the other.

Consider, for example, some of the free exercise cases we have studied in this chapter. In *Sherbert,* the Court remedied the free exercise violation by ordering the government to pay unemployment benefits to a claimant who refused to work on Saturdays for religious reasons. That fixed the free exercise problem, but it arguably created an Establishment Clause problem because the law now favored religious adherents over those who objected to Saturday work for non-religious reasons.

Similarly, while Justice Scalia in *Smith* did not provide a constitutional remedy to the church members who wanted to use peyote for ritual purposes, he invited them to seek relief through the political process. But if a legislature enacted a law that prohibited everyone but these church members from using peyote, it would arguably be favoring religion over secularism.

The Supreme Court acknowledges the tension between the two religion clauses and has said there needs to be "play in the joints" between them. In other words, the government must sometimes be able to make accommodations for free exercise rights without violating the Establishment Clause, and it must sometimes be able to exclude religious groups, to maintain separation of church and state, without violating the Free Exercise Clause.

This section explores the limits of this play in the joints. It discusses whether the government can exclude religions institutions from government benefits when these benefits are offered to non-religious institutions. Viewed through an Establishment Clause lens, this might be seen as not only permissible but even required to ensure that taxpayer money is not funding religion. Viewed through a Free Exercise Clause lens, this might be seen as discrimination against religion in violation of the rule announced in *Lukumi* and *Masterpiece Cakeshop*.

Adding to this complexity is the fact that the Court's Establishment Clause jurisprudence has radically shifted over the years. We will study this in more detail in the next chapter. Suffice it to say for now that the Court used to be very suspicious of government funds going to religious institutions. Recall the line from the 1947 *Everson* opinion in which the Court said that many of the nation's early settlers came here "to escape the bondage of laws which compelled them to support government favored churches." This led the Court to say later in its opinion that the Establishment Clause means, at the least, that "no tax in any amount, large and small, can be levied to support any religious activities or institutions."

In subsequent decades, the Court largely abandoned this rule, at least when government benefits are given out equally to religious and non-religious institutions alike. In that context, the Court has said there is no Establishment Clause violation because the government is not favoring religion but only treating it equally. Perhaps the most notable example is the Court's decision in *Zelman v. Simmons-Harris*, 536 U.S. 639 (2002), in which the Court held that the Establishment Clause did not preclude a state from providing education vouchers to families, even if the families used the vouchers to pay for tuition at private religious schools.

Still, there is a difference between the Court's saying that the government may allow religious institutions to participate in government programs and saying that the government must allow them to participate. To put the issue in doctrinal terms, the question is whether the government may choose to be "more separationist" than the Establishment Clause requires.

This issue has arisen frequently because many states have constitutional provisions that forbid them from providing financial support to religious institutions. Challenges are often brought when these states, pursuant to these provisions, exclude religious institutions from government benefits. Are these states acting benignly to preserve separation of church and state, or are they acting maliciously to discriminate against religion?

The first case we will study suggests that there is some "room within the play in the joints" for states to exclude religious institutions from government benefits. The second case suggests that this room has shrunken to the point of being almost nonexistent.

One final caveat. You need to be aware that both justices and scholars have widely varying views about the history underlying the state constitutional provisions. Some view these provisions as well-intentioned attempts to enshrine the value of separation of church and state into state constitutions. But others view these provisions as prejudicially motivated reactions to the large influx of Catholic immigrants in the mid-19th century and intended to ensure that government money would not be used to fund Catholic institutions.

Locke v. Davey

Supreme Court of the United States, 2004
540 U.S. 712

CHIEF JUSTICE REHNQUIST delivered the opinion of the Court.

The State of Washington established the Promise Scholarship Program to assist academically gifted students with postsecondary education expenses. In accordance with the State Constitution, students may not use the scholarship at an institution where they are pursuing a degree in devotional theology. We hold that such an exclusion from an otherwise inclusive aid program does not violate the Free Exercise Clause of the First Amendment.

To be eligible for the scholarship, a student must meet academic, income, and enrollment requirements. Finally, the student must enroll "at least half time in an eligible postsecondary institution in the state of Washington," and may not pursue a degree in theology at that institution while receiving the scholarship. A "degree in theology" is not defined in the statute, but, as both parties concede, the statute simply codifies the State's constitutional prohibition on providing funds to students to pursue degrees that are "devotional in nature or designed to induce religious faith."

Respondent, Joshua Davey, was awarded a Promise Scholarship, and chose to attend Northwest College. Northwest is a private, Christian college affiliated with the Assemblies of God denomination, and is an eligible institution under the Promise Scholarship Program. Davey had "planned for many years to attend a Bible college and to prepare himself through that college training for a lifetime of ministry, specifically as a church pastor." To that end, when he enrolled in Northwest College, he decided to pursue a double major in pastoral ministries and business management/administration. There is no dispute that the pastoral ministries degree is devotional and therefore excluded under the Promise Scholarship Program.

At the beginning of the 1999–2000 academic year, Davey met with Northwest's director of financial aid. He learned for the first time at this meeting that he could not use his scholarship to pursue a devotional theology degree. Davey then brought an action under 42 U.S.C. § 1983, against various state officials (hereinafter State) to enjoin the State from refusing to award the scholarship solely because a student is pursuing a devotional theology degree, and for damages.

The Religion Clauses of the First Amendment provide: "Congress shall make no law respecting an establishment of religion, or prohibiting the free exercise thereof." These two Clauses, the Establishment Clause and the Free Exercise Clause, are frequently in tension. Yet we have long said that "there is room for play in the joints" between them. In other words, there are some state actions permitted by the Establishment Clause but not required by the Free Exercise Clause.

This case involves that "play in the joints" described above. Under our Establishment Clause precedent, the link between government funds and religious training is broken by the independent and private choice of recipients. *See Zelman v. Simmons-Harris.* As such, there is no doubt that the State could, consistent with the Federal Constitution, permit Promise Scholars to pursue a degree in devotional theology, and the State does not contend otherwise. The question before us, however, is whether Washington, pursuant to its own constitution, which has been authoritatively interpreted as prohibiting even indirectly funding religious instruction that will prepare students for the ministry, can deny them such funding without violating the Free Exercise Clause.

Davey urges us to answer that question in the negative. He contends that under the rule we enunciated in *Church of Lukumi Babalu Aye, Inc. v. Hialeah,* the program is presumptively unconstitutional because it is not facially neutral with respect to religion. We reject his claim of presumptive unconstitutionality, however; to do otherwise would extend the *Lukumi* line of cases well beyond not only their facts but their reasoning. In *Lukumi,* the city of Hialeah made it a crime to engage in certain kinds of animal slaughter. We found that the law sought to suppress ritualistic animal sacrifices of the Santeria religion. In the present case, the State's disfavor of religion (if it can be called that) is of a far milder kind. It imposes neither criminal nor civil sanctions on any type of religious service or rite. It does not deny to ministers the right to participate in the political affairs of the community. And it does not require students to choose between their religious beliefs and receiving a government benefit. The State has merely chosen not to fund a distinct category of instruction.

Even though the differently worded Washington Constitution draws a more stringent line than that drawn by the United States Constitution, the interest it seeks to further is scarcely novel. In fact, we can think of few areas in which a State's antiestablishment interests come more into play. Since the founding of our country, there have been popular uprisings against procuring taxpayer funds to support church leaders, which was one of the hallmarks of an "established" religion.

Most States that sought to avoid an establishment of religion around the time of the founding placed in their constitutions formal prohibitions against using tax funds to support the ministry. The plain text of these constitutional provisions prohibited *any* tax dollars from supporting the clergy. That early state constitutions saw no problem in explicitly excluding *only* the ministry from receiving state dollars reinforces our conclusion that religious instruction is of a different ilk.

Far from evincing the hostility toward religion which was manifest in *Lukumi,* we believe that the entirety of the Promise Scholarship Program goes a long way toward including religion in its benefits. The program permits students to attend pervasively religious schools, so long as they are accredited. And under the Promise Scholarship Program's current guidelines, students are still eligible to take devotional theology courses.

In short, we find neither in the history or text of Article I, § 11, of the Washington Constitution, nor in the operation of the Promise Scholarship Program, anything that suggests animus toward religion. Given the historic and substantial state interest at issue, we therefore cannot conclude that the denial of funding for vocational religious instruction alone is inherently constitutionally suspect.

Without a presumption of unconstitutionality, Davey's claim must fail. The State's interest in not funding the pursuit of devotional degrees is substantial and the exclusion of such funding places a relatively minor burden on Promise Scholars. If any room exists between the two Religion Clauses, it must be here. We need not venture further into this difficult area in order to uphold the Promise Scholarship Program as currently operated by the State of Washington.

[Justice Scalia's dissenting opinion, which was joined by Justice Thomas, is omitted, as is Justice Thomas' dissenting opinion.]

Carson v. Makin

Supreme Court of the United States, 2022
596 U.S. 767

CHIEF JUSTICE ROBERTS delivered the opinion of the Court.

Maine has enacted a program of tuition assistance for parents who live in school districts that do not operate a secondary school of their own. Under the program, parents designate the secondary school they would like their child to attend—public or private—and the school district transmits payments to that school to help defray the costs of tuition. Most private schools are eligible to receive the payments, so long as they are "nonsectarian." The question presented is whether this restriction violates the Free Exercise Clause of the First Amendment.

Prior to 1981, parents could also direct the tuition assistance payments to religious schools. In 1981, however, Maine imposed a new requirement that any school receiving tuition assistance payments must be "a nonsectarian school in accordance with the First Amendment of the United States Constitution." The "nonsectarian" requirement for participation in Maine's tuition assistance program remains in effect today. The Department [of Education] has stated that, in administering this requirement, it "considers a sectarian school to be one that is associated with a particular faith or belief system and which, in addition to teaching academic subjects, promotes the faith or belief system with which it is associated and/or presents the material taught through the lens of this faith." "The Department's focus is on what the school teaches through its curriculum and related activities, and how the material is presented." "Affiliation or association with a church or religious institution is one potential indicator of a sectarian school," but "it is not dispositive." Absent the "nonsectarian" requirement, [petitioners] the Carsons and the Nelsons would have asked their respective [school districts] to pay the tuition to send their children to Bangor Christian Schools (BCS) and Temple Academy, respectively.

In 2018, petitioners brought suit against the commissioner of the Maine Department of Education. They alleged that the "nonsectarian" requirement of Maine's tuition assistance program violated the Free Exercise Clause and the Establishment Clause of the First Amendment, as well as the Equal Protection Clause of the Fourteenth Amendment.

The Free Exercise Clause of the First Amendment protects against "indirect coercion or penalties on the free exercise of religion, not just outright prohibitions." In particular, we have repeatedly held that a State violates the Free Exercise Clause when it excludes religious observers from otherwise available public benefits. A State may not withhold unemployment benefits, for instance, on the ground that an individual lost his job for refusing to abandon the dictates of his faith. *See Sherbert.*

We have recently applied these principles in the context of two state efforts to withhold otherwise available public benefits from religious organizations. In *Trinity Lutheran Church of Columbia, Inc.* v. *Comer*, 137 S. Ct. 2012 (2017), we considered a Missouri program that offered grants to qualifying nonprofit organizations that installed cushioning playground surfaces made from recycled rubber tires. The Missouri Department of Natural Resources maintained an express policy of denying such grants to any applicant owned or controlled by a church, sect, or other religious entity. The Trinity Lutheran Church Child Learning Center applied for a grant to resurface its gravel playground, but the Department denied funding on the ground that the Center was operated by the Church.

We deemed it "unremarkable in light of our prior decisions" to conclude that the Free Exercise Clause did not permit Missouri to "expressly discriminate against otherwise eligible recipients by disqualifying them from a public benefit solely because of their religious character." While it was true that Trinity Lutheran remained "free to continue operating as a church," it could enjoy that freedom only "at the cost of automatic and absolute exclusion from the benefits of a public program for which the Center was otherwise fully qualified." Such discrimination, we said, was "odious to our Constitution" and could not stand.

Two Terms ago, in *Espinoza v. Montana Department of Revenue*, 140 S. Ct. 2246 (2020), we reached the same conclusion as to a Montana program that provided tax credits to donors who sponsored scholarships for private school tuition. The Montana Supreme Court held that the program, to the extent it included religious schools, violated a provision of the Montana Constitution that barred government aid to any school controlled in whole or in part by a church, sect, or denomination. As a result of that holding, the State terminated the scholarship program, preventing the petitioners from accessing scholarship funds they otherwise would have used to fund their children's educations at religious schools.

We again held that the Free Exercise Clause forbade the State's action. The application of the Montana Constitution's no-aid provision, we explained, required strict scrutiny because it "barred religious schools from public benefits solely because of the religious character of the schools." "A State need not subsidize private education," we concluded, "but once a State decides to do so, it cannot disqualify some private schools solely because they are religious."

The "unremarkable" principles applied in *Trinity Lutheran* and *Espinoza* suffice to resolve this case. Maine offers its citizens a benefit: tuition assistance payments for any family whose school district does not provide a public secondary school. Just like the wide range of nonprofit organizations eligible to receive playground resurfacing grants in *Trinity Lutheran*, a wide range of private schools are eligible to receive Maine tuition assistance payments here. And like the daycare center in *Trinity Lutheran*,

BCS and Temple Academy are disqualified from this generally available benefit "solely because of their religious character." By "conditioning the availability of benefits" in that manner, Maine's tuition assistance program—like the program in *Trinity Lutheran*—"effectively penalizes the free exercise" of religion.

Our recent decision in *Espinoza* applied these basic principles in the context of religious education that we consider today. There, as here, we considered a state benefit program under which public funds flowed to support tuition payments at private schools. And there, as here, that program specifically carved out private religious schools from those eligible to receive such funds. While the wording of the Montana and Maine provisions is different, their effect is the same: to "disqualify some private schools" from funding "solely because they are religious." A law that operates in that manner, we held in *Espinoza*, must be subjected to "the strictest scrutiny."

To satisfy strict scrutiny, government action "must advance interests of the highest order and must be narrowly tailored in pursuit of those interests." *Lukumi*. "A law that targets religious conduct for distinctive treatment will survive strict scrutiny only in rare cases."

This is not one of them. As noted, a neutral benefit program in which public funds flow to religious organizations through the independent choices of private benefit recipients does not offend the Establishment Clause. Maine's decision to continue excluding religious schools from its tuition assistance program thus promotes stricter separation of church and state than the Federal Constitution requires.

But as we explained in both *Trinity Lutheran* and *Espinoza*, such an "interest in separating church and state more fiercely than the Federal Constitution cannot qualify as compelling in the face of the infringement of free exercise." Justice Breyer stresses the importance of "government neutrality" when it comes to religious matters, but there is nothing neutral about Maine's program. The State pays tuition for certain students at private schools—so long as the schools are not religious. That is discrimination against religion. A State's antiestablishment interest does not justify enactments that exclude some members of the community from an otherwise generally available public benefit because of their religious exercise.

The dissents are wrong to say that under our decision today Maine "*must*" fund religious education. Maine chose to allow some parents to direct state tuition payments to private schools; that decision was not "forced upon" it. The State retains a number of options: it could expand the reach of its public school system, increase the availability of transportation, provide some combination of tutoring, remote learning, and partial attendance, or even operate boarding schools of its own. As we held in *Espinoza*, a "State need not subsidize private education. But once a State decides to do so, it cannot disqualify some private schools solely because they are religious."

Maine and the dissents invoke *Locke v. Davey* in support of the argument that the State may preclude parents from designating a religious school to receive tuition assistance payments. Our opinions in *Trinity Lutheran* and *Espinoza*, however, have already explained why *Locke* can be of no help to Maine here. Both precedents emphasized, as did *Locke* itself, that the funding in *Locke* was intended to be used "to prepare for the ministry." Funds could be and were used for theology courses; only pursuing a "vocational religious" *degree* was excluded.

Locke's reasoning expressly turned on what it identified as the "historic and substantial state interest" against using "taxpayer funds to support church leaders." But as we explained at length in *Espinoza*, "it is clear that there is no 'historic and substantial' tradition against aiding private religious schools comparable to the tradition against state-supported clergy invoked by *Locke*." *Locke* cannot be read beyond its narrow focus on vocational religious degrees to generally authorize the State to exclude religious persons from the enjoyment of public benefits on the basis of their anticipated religious use of the benefits.

Maine's "nonsectarian" requirement for its otherwise generally available tuition assistance payments violates the Free Exercise Clause of the First Amendment. Regardless of how the benefit and restriction are described, the program operates to identify and exclude otherwise eligible schools on the basis of their religious exercise.

JUSTICE BREYER, with whom JUSTICE KAGAN joins, and with whom JUSTICE SOTOMAYOR joins except as to Part I-B, dissenting.

The First Amendment begins by forbidding the government from "mak[ing] [any] law respecting an establishment of religion." It next forbids them to make any law "prohibiting the free exercise thereof." The Court today pays almost no attention to the words in the first Clause while giving almost exclusive attention to the words in the second. The majority also fails to recognize the "play in the joints" between the two Clauses. That "play" gives States some degree of legislative leeway. It sometimes allows a State to further antiestablishment interests by withholding aid from religious institutions without violating the Constitution's protections for the free exercise of religion. In my view, Maine's nonsectarian requirement falls squarely within the scope of that constitutional leeway.

I have previously discussed my views of the relationship between the Religion Clauses and how I believe these Clauses should be interpreted to advance their goal of avoiding religious strife. Here I simply note the increased risk of religiously based social conflict when government promotes religion in its public school system. This potential for religious strife is still with us. We are today a Nation with well over 100 different religious groups, from Free Will Baptist to African Methodist, Buddhist to Humanist. People in our country adhere to a vast array of beliefs, ideals, and philosophies. And with greater religious diversity comes greater risk of religiously based strife, conflict, and social division.

We have previously found, as the majority points out, that "a neutral benefit program in which public funds flow to religious organizations through the independent choices of private benefit recipients does not offend the Establishment Clause." We have thus concluded that a State *may*, consistent with the Establishment Clause, provide funding to religious schools through a general public funding program if the "government aid reaches religious institutions only by way of the deliberate choices of individual aid recipients." But the key word is "may." We have never previously held what the Court holds today, namely, that a State *must* (not *may*) use state funds to pay for religious education as part of a tuition program designed to ensure the provision of free statewide public school education.

Maine wishes to provide children within the State with a secular, public education. This wish embodies, in significant part, the constitutional need to avoid spending public money to support what is essentially the teaching and practice of religion. That need is reinforced by the fact that we are today a Nation of more than 330 million people who ascribe to over 100 different religions. In that context, state neutrality with respect to religion is particularly important. The Religion Clauses give Maine the right to honor that neutrality by choosing not to fund religious schools as part of its public school tuition program. I believe the majority is wrong to hold the contrary.

JUSTICE SOTOMAYOR, dissenting.

This Court continues to dismantle the wall of separation between church and state that the Framers fought to build. This Court should not have started down this path five years ago. Before *Trinity Lutheran*, it was well established that "both the United States and state constitutions embody distinct views" on "the subject of religion"—"in favor of free exercise, but opposed to establishment"—"that find no counterpart" with respect to other constitutional rights. Because of this tension, the Court recognized "room for play in the joints between" the Religion Clauses, with "some state actions permitted by the Establishment Clause but not required by the Free Exercise Clause." Using this flexibility, and consistent with a rich historical tradition, States and the Federal Government could decline to fund religious institutions. Moreover, the Court for many decades understood the Establishment Clause to prohibit government from funding religious exercise.

Trinity Lutheran veered sharply away from that understanding. Two Terms ago, the Court reprised and extended *Trinity Lutheran*'s error to hold that a State could not limit a private-school voucher program to secular schools. *Espinoza*.

The consequences of the Court's rapid transformation of the Religion Clauses must not be understated. From a doctrinal perspective, the Court's failure to apply the play-in-the-joints principle here, leaves one to wonder what, if anything, is left of it. The Court's increasingly expansive view of the Free Exercise Clause risks swallowing the space between the Religion Clauses that once "permitted religious exercise to exist without sponsorship and without interference."

From a practical perspective, today's decision directs the State of Maine (and, by extension, its taxpaying citizens) to subsidize institutions that undisputedly engage in religious instruction. In addition, while purporting to protect against discrimination of one kind, the Court requires Maine to fund what many of its citizens believe to be discrimination of other kinds. *See ante* (Breyer, J., dissenting) (summarizing Bangor Christian Schools' and Temple Academy's policies denying enrollment to students based on gender identity, sexual orientation, and religion). The upshot is that Maine must choose between giving subsidies to its residents or refraining from financing religious teaching and practices.

Today, the Court leads us to a place where separation of church and state becomes a constitutional violation. If a State cannot offer subsidies to its citizens without being required to fund religious exercise, any State that values its historic antiestablishment interests more than this Court does will have to curtail the support it offers to its citizens. With growing concern for where this Court will lead us next, I respectfully dissent.

Points for Discussion

1. **What's left of the play in the joints?** In *Locke v. Davey*, Chief Justice William Rehnquist acknowledged the inherent tension between the Free Exercise Clause and the Establishment Clause and the need for some "play in the joints." This meant, the Chief Justice explained, that "there are some state actions permitted by the Establishment Clause but not required by the Free Exercise Clause." The Court has not overruled *Locke*, but after *Trinity Lutheran*, *Espinoza*, and *Carson*, how much room has the Court left for governments to take actions that are "more separationist" than the Establishment Clause requires?

2. **Is the Court furthering or undermining the values underlying the religion clauses?** Justice Sotomayor lamented in her *Carson* dissent that the practical effect of the Court's decision is that Maine will have to pay for education at religious schools. But is that a problem? Justice Breyer warned of "the increased risk of religiously based social conflict when government promotes religion in its public school system." Does he have a valid point? Does forcing the government to pay for sectarian religious education further, or undermine, the underlying values of the religion clauses?

Were State Constitutional Limits on Support to Religious Institutions Motivated by Prejudice?

In a concurrence in *Espinoza*, Justice Alito made a passionate argument that the Montana constitutional provision barring aid to religion was modeled after the failed "Blaine Amendment" to the U.S. Constitution in 1875, which Justice Alito said "was prompted by virulent prejudice against immigrants, particularly Catholic immigrants." Justice Alito said that, after the Blaine Amendment failed, most states adopted similar provisions in their constitutions, "often as a condition of entering the Union." Here is how Justice Alito described the basis of this prejudice:

> Catholics were considered by such groups not as citizens of the United States, but as "soldiers of the Church of Rome," who "would attempt to subvert representative government." Catholic education was a particular concern. As one series of newspaper articles argued, "Popery is the natural enemy of *general* education. If it is establishing schools, it is to make them *prisons* of the youthful intellect of the country." The feelings of the day are perhaps best encapsulated by this famous cartoon, published in Harper's Weekly in 1871, which depicts Catholic priests as crocodiles slithering hungrily toward American children as a public school crumbles in the background:

D. The Ecclesiastical Abstention Doctrine and the Ministerial Exception: Limits on Governmental Intrusion into Religious Affairs

Religious groups, no less than any other organizations in society, may become embroiled in legal disputes. Just as there may be divisions among shareholders and management of a secular for-profit corporation over corporate governance, ownership, and mergers and acquisitions, there may be similar battles for control within nonprofit organizations, including religious organizations. These may in turn devolve into battles over who is the lawful leader of a religious organization and thus the owner of its property. Sometimes these struggles are carried out internally, through the religious organization's own ruling bodies and tribunals. But sometimes the disputes spill over into the courts. The question then becomes whether the First Amendment allows a court to adjudicate the issue.

The body of law that has evolved to address this issue is sometimes referred to as the "ecclesiastical abstention doctrine," a kind of "spiritual federalism" reflecting the principle that secular courts in the United States should normally "abstain" from adjudicating issues involving theological or spiritual judgment or the internal governance of religious bodies and, instead, should leave these matters to appropriate religious tribunals. The birth of the doctrine is usually traced to the Court's decision in *Watson v. Jones*, 80 U.S. 679 (1871), involving a dispute over ownership and control of the Walnut Street Presbyterian Church in Louisville, Kentucky. The Court decided the dispute on common law grounds, yielding to the authority of the hierarchical structures of the Presbyterian Church.

Decades later, the Court elevated the deference first articulated in *Watson* to constitutional stature, invoking the First Amendment's Free Exercise Clause in *Kedroff v. St. Nicholas Cathedral of Russian Orthodox Church in North America*, 344 U.S. 94 (1952). That case involved an attempt to transfer control of New York churches of the Russian Orthodox religion from the central governing hierarchy of the Russian Orthodox Church, the Patriarch of Moscow and the Holy Synod, to governing authorities of the Russian Church in America. As in *Watson*, the Court in *Kedroff* required deference to the church's own ruling authorities: "There are occasions when civil courts must draw lines between the responsibilities of church and state for the disposition or use of property. Even in those cases when the property right follows as an incident from decisions of the church custom or law on ecclesiastical issues, the church rule controls. This under our Constitution necessarily follows in order that there may be free exercise of religion."

One specific offshoot of this body of law involves what has come to be known as the "ministerial exception" to civil rights laws. Various civil rights statutes prohibit discrimination in employment on grounds such as race, gender, sexual orientation, age, and disability. A religious organization is normally bound by such laws. Surely, for example, a religious organization could be held liable for gender discrimination in the hiring or firing of a maintenance worker. But when a religious organization dismisses or takes some other adverse employment action against someone exercising authority as "clergy"—a minister, priest, rabbi, or imam, for example—may that person seek legal redress by alleging that the action constituted discrimination in violation of civil rights laws? Consider, for example, the long-standing practice of the Roman Catholic Church prohibiting the ordination of women as priests. Could a woman who claimed to be qualified for the priesthood successfully sue the Catholic Church for gender discrimination? In the decisions below, the Supreme Court established the ministerial exception, exempting religious groups from the coverage of civil rights laws as applied to positions involving the propagation of religious faith.

Hosanna-Tabor Evangelical Lutheran Church & School v. EEOC

Supreme Court of the United States, 2012
565 U.S. 171

CHIEF JUSTICE ROBERTS delivered the opinion of the Court.

Certain employment discrimination laws authorize employees who have been wrongfully terminated to sue their employers for reinstatement and damages. The question presented is whether the Establishment and Free Exercise Clauses of the First Amendment bar such an action when the employer is a religious group and the employee is one of the group's ministers.

Hosanna-Tabor Evangelical Lutheran Church and School is a member congregation of the Lutheran Church-Missouri Synod, the second largest Lutheran denomination in America. Hosanna-Tabor operated a small school in Redford, Michigan, offering a "Christ-centered education" to students in kindergarten through eighth grade.

The Synod classifies teachers into two categories: "called" and "lay." "Called" teachers are regarded as having been called to their vocation by God through a congregation.

"Lay" or "contract" teachers, by contrast, are not required to be trained by the Synod or even to be Lutheran.

Cheryl Perich was first employed by Hosanna-Tabor as a lay teacher in 1999. After Perich completed her colloquy later that school year, Hosanna-Tabor asked her to become a called teacher.

Perich became ill in June 2004 with what was eventually diagnosed as narcolepsy. Symptoms included sudden and deep sleeps from which she could not be roused. Because of her illness, Perich began the 2004–2005 school year on disability leave. On January 27, 2005, however, Perich notified the school principal, Stacey Hoeft, that she would be able to report to work the following month. Hoeft responded that the school had already contracted with a lay teacher to fill Perich's position for the remainder of the school year. Hoeft also expressed concern that Perich was not yet ready to return to the classroom.

On the morning of February 22—the first day she was medically cleared to return to work—Perich presented herself at the school. Hoeft asked her to leave but she would not do so until she obtained written documentation that she had reported to work. Later that afternoon, Hoeft called Perich at home and told her that she would likely be fired. Perich responded that she had spoken with an attorney and intended to assert her legal rights.

Perich filed a charge with the Equal Employment Opportunity Commission, alleging that her employment had been terminated in violation of the Americans with Disabilities Act of 1990.

Hosanna-Tabor moved for summary judgment. Invoking what is known as the "ministerial exception," the Church argued that the suit was barred by the First Amendment because the claims at issue concerned the employment relationship between a religious institution and one of its ministers.

Controversy between church and state over religious offices is hardly new. In 1215, the issue was addressed in the very first clause of Magna Carta. There, King John agreed that "the English church shall be free, and shall have its rights undiminished and its liberties unimpaired." The King in particular accepted the "freedom of elections," a right "thought to be of the greatest necessity and importance to the English church."

That freedom in many cases may have been more theoretical than real. See, e.g., W. Warren, Henry II 312 (1973) (recounting the writ sent by Henry II to the electors of a bishopric in Winchester, stating: "I order you to hold a free election, but forbid you to elect anyone but Richard my clerk"). In any event, it did not survive the reign of Henry VIII, even in theory. The Act of Supremacy of 1534 made the English monarch the supreme head of the Church, and the Act in Restraint of Annates, passed that same year, gave him the authority to appoint the Church's high officials.

Seeking to escape the control of the national church, the Puritans fled to New England, where they hoped to elect their own ministers and establish their own modes of worship. Colonists in the South, in contrast, brought the Church of England with them. But even they sometimes chafed at the control exercised by the Crown and its representatives over religious offices.

It was against this background that the First Amendment was adopted. Familiar with life under the established Church of England, the founding generation sought to foreclose the possibility of a national church.

Given this understanding of the Religion Clauses—and the absence of government employment regulation generally—it was some time before questions about government interference with a church's ability to select its own ministers came before the courts. This Court touched upon the issue indirectly, however, in the context of disputes over church property. Our decisions in that area confirm that it is impermissible for the government to contradict a church's determination of who can act as its ministers.

Until today, we have not had occasion to consider whether this freedom of a religious organization to select its ministers is implicated by a suit alleging discrimination in employment.

We agree that there is such a ministerial exception. The members of a religious group put their faith in the hands of their ministers. Requiring a church to accept or retain an unwanted minister, or punishing a church for failing to do so, intrudes upon more than a mere employment decision. Such action interferes with the internal governance of the church, depriving the church of control over the selection of those who will personify its beliefs. By imposing an unwanted minister, the state infringes the Free Exercise Clause, which protects a religious group's right to shape its own faith and mission through its appointments. According the state the power to determine which individuals will minister to the faithful also violates the Establishment Clause, which prohibits government involvement in such ecclesiastical decisions.

The EEOC and Perich acknowledge that employment discrimination laws would be unconstitutional as applied to religious groups in certain circumstances. They grant, for example, that it would violate the First Amendment for courts to apply such laws to compel the ordination of women by the Catholic Church or by an Orthodox Jewish seminary. According to the EEOC and Perich, religious organizations could successfully defend against employment discrimination claims in those circumstances by invoking the constitutional right to freedom of association—a right "implicit" in the First Amendment. *Roberts v. United States Jaycees*. The EEOC and Perich thus see no need—and no basis—for a special rule for ministers grounded in the Religion Clauses themselves.

We find this position untenable. The right to freedom of association is a right enjoyed by religious and secular groups alike. It follows under the EEOC's and Perich's view that the First Amendment analysis should be the same, whether the association in question is the Lutheran Church, a labor union, or a social club. That result is hard to square with the text of the First Amendment itself, which gives special solicitude to the rights of religious organizations. We cannot accept the remarkable view that the Religion Clauses have nothing to say about a religious organization's freedom to select its own ministers.

The EEOC and Perich also contend that our decision in *Employment Division v. Smith* precludes recognition of a ministerial exception.

It is true that the ADA's prohibition on retaliation, like Oregon's prohibition on peyote use, is a valid and neutral law of general applicability. But a church's selection of its ministers is unlike an individual's ingestion of peyote. *Smith* involved government regulation of only outward physical acts. The present case, in contrast, concerns government interference with an internal church decision that affects the faith and mission of the church itself.

Having concluded that there is a ministerial exception grounded in the Religion Clauses of the First Amendment, we consider whether the exception applies in this case. We hold that it does.

To begin with, Hosanna-Tabor held Perich out as a minister, with a role distinct from that of most of its members. When Hosanna-Tabor extended her a call, it issued her a "diploma of vocation" according her the title "Minister of Religion, Commissioned."

Perich's job duties reflected a role in conveying the Church's message and carrying out its mission. As a source of religious instruction, Perich performed an important role in transmitting the Lutheran faith to the next generation.

In light of these considerations—the formal title given Perich by the Church, the substance reflected in that title, her own use of that title, and the important religious functions she performed for the Church—we conclude that Perich was a minister covered by the ministerial exception.

Because Perich was a minister within the meaning of the exception, the First Amendment requires dismissal of this employment discrimination suit against her religious employer.

JUSTICE THOMAS, concurring.

I join the Court's opinion. I write separately to note that, in my view, the Religion Clauses require civil courts to apply the ministerial exception and to defer to a religious organization's good-faith understanding of who qualifies as its minister.

JUSTICE ALITO, with whom JUSTICE KAGAN joins, concurring.

I join the Court's opinion, but I write separately to clarify my understanding of the significance of formal ordination and designation as a "minister" in determining whether an "employee" of a religious group falls within the so-called "ministerial" exception. The term "minister" is commonly used by many Protestant denominations to refer to members of their clergy, but the term is rarely if ever used in this way by Catholics, Jews, Muslims, Hindus, or Buddhists. In addition, the concept of ordination as understood by most Christian churches and by Judaism has no clear counterpart in some Christian denominations and some other religions. Because virtually every religion in the world is represented in the population of the United States, it would be a mistake if the term "minister" or the concept of ordination were viewed as central to the important issue of religious autonomy that is presented in cases like this one. Instead, courts should focus on the function performed by persons who work for religious bodies.

Point for Discussion

1. **How far does the ministerial exception extend?** If the ministerial exception extends to some but not all employee positions in a religious organization, where is the line to be drawn? The Court in *Our Lady of Guadalupe School v. Morrissey-Berru*, 140 S. Ct. 2049 (2020), elaborated on the reach of the principle established in *Hosanna-Tabor*. *Our Lady of Guadalupe* involved two elementary school teachers at Catholic schools who did not have the title of "minister." The Court concluded, however, that a title was not controlling for purposes of the ministerial exception. The Court explained that the "religious education and formation of students is the very reason for the existence of most private religious schools, and therefore the selection and supervision of the teachers upon whom the schools rely to do this work lie at the core of their mission." For courts to engage in judicial review of the way in which religious schools discharge those responsibilities, the Court concluded, "would undermine the independence of religious institutions in a way that the First Amendment does not tolerate." As the Court explained:

> When we apply this understanding of the Religion Clauses to the cases now before us, it is apparent that [the teachers] qualify for the exemption we recognized in *Hosanna-Tabor*. There is abundant record evidence that they both performed vital religious duties. Educating and forming students in the Catholic faith lay at the core of the mission of the schools where they taught, and their employment agreements and faculty handbooks specified in no uncertain terms that they were

> expected to help the schools carry out this mission and that their work would be evaluated to ensure that they were fulfilling that responsibility. As elementary school teachers responsible for providing instruction in all subjects, including religion, they were the members of the school staff who were entrusted most directly with the responsibility of educating their students in the faith. And not only were they obligated to provide instruction about the Catholic faith, but they were also expected to guide their students, by word and deed, toward the goal of living their lives in accordance with the faith. They prayed with their students, attended Mass with the students, and prepared the children for their participation in other religious activities. Their positions did not have all the attributes of [the plaintiff in *Hosanna-Tabor*]. Their titles did not include the term "minister," and they had less formal religious training, but their core responsibilities as teachers of religion were essentially the same. And both their schools expressly saw them as playing a vital part in carrying out the mission of the church, and the schools' definition and explanation of their roles is important. In a country with the religious diversity of the United States, judges cannot be expected to have a complete understanding and appreciation of the role played by every person who performs a particular role in every religious tradition. A religious institution's explanation of the role of such employees in the life of the religion in question is important.

The decision in *Our Lady of Guadalupe* thus articulated a sweeping immunity for religious schools from teachers' employment discrimination claims. Do you think the Court went too far in granting this immunity? Before answering that question, consider these passages from Justice Sotomayor's dissent in the case:

> Two employers fired their employees allegedly because one had breast cancer and the other was elderly. Purporting to rely on this Court's decision in *Hosanna-Tabor*, the majority shields those employers from disability and age-discrimination claims. In the Court's view, because the employees taught short religion modules at Catholic elementary schools, they were "ministers" of the Catholic faith and thus could be fired for any reason, whether religious or nonreligious, benign or bigoted, without legal recourse. The Court reaches this result even though the teachers taught primarily secular subjects, lacked substantial religious titles and training, and were not even required to be Catholic. In foreclosing the teachers' claims, the Court skews the facts, ignores the applicable standard of review, and collapses *Hosanna-Tabor*'s careful analysis into a single consideration: whether a church thinks its employees play an important religious role. Because that simplistic ap-

proach has no basis in law and strips thousands of schoolteachers of their legal protections, I respectfully dissent.

The Court's conclusion portends grave consequences. As the Government explained to the Ninth Circuit, "thousands of Catholic teachers" may lose employment-law protections because of today's outcome. In expanding the ministerial exception far beyond its historic narrowness, the Court overrides Congress' carefully tailored exceptions for religious employers. Little if nothing appears left of the statutory exemptions after today's constitutional broadside. So long as the employer determines that an employee's "duties" are "vital" to "carrying out the mission of the church," then today's laissez-faire analysis appears to allow that employer to make employment decisions because of a person's skin color, age, disability, sex, or any other protected trait for reasons having nothing to do with religion.

Test Your Knowledge

To assess your understanding of the material in this chapter, click here to take a quiz.

Chapter Nineteen

When Does Government Unlawfully Benefit Religion?

The Establishment Clause

In the previous chapter on the Free Exercise Clause, we explored constitutional limits on government actions that burden religion. In this chapter on the Establishment Clause, we consider constitutional limits on government actions that benefit religion. Establishment Clause issues are raised when the government provides financial support to religious institutions, such as giving books to parochial schools; engages in religious exercises, such as offering prayers before a legislative session; or uses religious symbols, such as having a Ten Commandments monument on government property.

While this burden/benefit distinction encapsulates the difference between Free Exercise and Establishment Clause jurisprudence, it is overly simplistic and obscures overlaps in the jurisprudence. For example, if a government action demonstrates a clear preference for one religion, it can potentially violate both the Free Exercise Clause and the Establishment Clause. It violates the former because it discriminates against the disfavored faiths and violates the latter by endorsing one faith to the exclusion of others. In *Larson v. Valente*, 456 U.S. 228 (1982), the Supreme Court roundly condemned such preferential treatment as an Establishment Clause violation: "The clearest command of the Establishment Clause is that one religious denomination cannot be officially preferred over another." Given potential overlaps between Free Exercise and Establishment Clause jurisprudence, it is not uncommon for religion-based challenges to invoke both clauses.

The Establishment Clause, like the Free Exercise Clause, restrains all branches of the federal government. The Establishment Clause has also been incorporated into the Fourteenth Amendment and therefore acts as a restraint on state and local governments. However, the incorporation of the Establishment Clause, unlike the incorporation of the Free Exercise Clause, has been a source of controversy among the justices.

The leading opponent of incorporation is Justice Clarence Thomas. He believes that the Establishment Clause was not intended to be an individual rights provision but rather a "federalism" provision that was intended to police the boundary between federal and state authority. Since he believes that the Establishment Clause does not protect individual rights, he thinks the clause should not have been incorporated into the Fourteenth Amendment's Due Process Clause. Here is sampling of Justice Thomas' reasoning from a concurring opinion in *Town of Greece v. Galloway*, a case you will be reading later in this chapter:

> I write separately to reiterate my view that the Establishment Clause is "best understood as a federalism provision." As an initial matter, the Clause probably prohibits Congress from establishing a national religion. The text of the Clause also suggests that Congress "could not interfere with state establishments, notwithstanding any argument that could be made based on Congress' power under the Necessary and Proper Clause." Construing the Establishment Clause as a federalism provision accords with the variety of church-state arrangements that existed at the Founding.
>
> The Federalist logic of the original Establishment Clause poses a special barrier to its mechanical incorporation against the States through the Fourteenth Amendment. Unlike the Free Exercise Clause, which "plainly protects individuals against congressional interference with the right to exercise their religion," the Establishment Clause "does not purport to protect individual rights." Instead, the States are the particular beneficiaries of the Clause. Incorporation therefore gives rise to a paradoxical result: Applying the Clause against the States eliminates their right to establish a religion free from federal interference, thereby "prohibiting exactly what the Establishment Clause protected."

While Justice Thomas continues to adhere to this position, he has not been successful in recruiting other justices. Consequently, the Establishment Clause remains safely incorporated into the Fourteenth Amendment and continues to place restraints on state and local governments. Nevertheless, it is worth pausing to consider if you agree with Justice Thomas, whether for historical, textual, or policy reasons. In answering that question, ask yourself whether it would be problematic to not have a federal constitutional check on state establishments of religion.

As we noted in the previous chapter, the two religion clauses work in tandem to foster religious liberty but also exist in tension. Providing an exemption to ease a burden on religious exercise creates a benefit for religious adherents that can trigger Establishment Clause concerns. Excluding religious groups from benefits to ensure separation of church and state creates a burden on these groups that can raise free exercise concerns. We witnessed justices wrestling with these tensions, including their differing views on the "play in the joints" between the two religion clauses, when we studied free exercise challenges to benefit programs that excluded religious groups.

If there is an overall theme to this chapter and the chapter on the Free Exercise Clause, it is the trend in the Supreme Court's jurisprudence toward increasingly welcoming religion into the public sphere and treating the exclusion of religion as unlawful discrimination. You have encountered examples of this trend in both the Court's free speech and free exercise jurisprudence. For example, when you studied freedom of speech, you read cases in which public schools opened classrooms for after-hours use but then barred religious groups from participating. Time and again, the Court ruled that excluding religious groups was unlawful viewpoint discrimination and was not required by the Establishment Clause. Similarly, you learned that excluding religious groups from government benefit programs is likely to violate the Free Exercise Clause and is not necessary to comply with the Establishment Clause.

A. The Big Picture: Three Degrees of Separation

When we introduced you to the Establishment Clause in Chapter 1, we said that the relevant jurisprudence is muddled and that you should expect a little cognitive dissonance as you read the cases. We know that the complexity in Free Exercise jurisprudence is driven by the tension between wanting to relieve burdens on religious practice but not wanting every conscience to become "a law unto itself." But what drives the complexity in Establishment Clause jurisprudence? A good place to start answering that question is *Everson v. Board of Education*, the Court's first major foray into Establishment Clause issues and the case in which the Court announced that the Establishment Clause was incorporated into the Fourteenth Amendment. As you are about to learn, the tension underlying Establishment Clause jurisprudence was baked into the jurisprudence from the very beginning.

In Chapter 17, you read an excerpt from *Everson* in which the Court described the history leading up to the adoption of the Establishment Clause. We repeat a shortened version of that history here to set the stage for the remainder of the opinion.

Everson v. Board of Education

Supreme Court of the United States, 1947
330 U.S. 1

MR. JUSTICE BLACK delivered the opinion of the Court.

A New Jersey statute authorizes its local school districts to make rules and contracts for the transportation of children to and from schools. The appellee, a township board of education, acting pursuant to this statute authorized reimbursement to parents of money expended by them for the bus transportation of their children on regular buses operated by the public transportation system. Part of this money was for the payment of transportation of some children in the community to Catholic parochial schools. These church schools give their students, in addition to secular education, regular religious instruction conforming to the religious tenets and modes of worship of the Catholic faith. The superintendent of these schools is a Catholic priest.

The New Jersey statute is challenged as a "law respecting an establishment of religion." Whether this New Jersey law is one respecting the "establishment of religion" requires an understanding of the meaning of that language, particularly with respect to the imposition of taxes. It is not inappropriate briefly to review the background and environment of the period in which that constitutional language was fashioned and adopted.

A large proportion of the early settlers of this country came here from Europe to escape the bondage of laws which compelled them to support and attend government favored churches. These practices of the old world were transplanted to and began to thrive in the soil of the new America. Catholics found themselves hounded and proscribed because of their faith; Quakers who followed their conscience went to jail; Baptists were peculiarly obnoxious to certain dominant Protestant sects; men and women of varied faiths who happened to be in a minority in a particular locality were persecuted because they steadfastly persisted in worshipping God only as their own consciences dictated. And all of these dissenters were compelled to pay tithes and taxes to support government-sponsored churches whose ministers preached inflammatory sermons designed to strengthen and consolidate the established faith by generating a burning hatred against dissenters.

These practices became so commonplace as to shock the freedom-loving colonials into a feeling of abhorrence. The imposition of taxes to pay ministers' salaries and to build and maintain churches and church property aroused their indignation. It was these feelings which found expression in the First Amendment. No one locality and no one group throughout the Colonies can rightly be given entire credit for having aroused the sentiment that culminated in adoption of the Bill of Rights' provisions embracing religious liberty. But Virginia, where the established church had achieved a dominant influence in political affairs and where many excesses attracted wide public attention, provided a great stimulus and able leadership for the movement. The people there, as elsewhere, reached the conviction that individual religious liberty could be achieved best under a government which was stripped of all power to tax, to support, or otherwise to assist any or all religions, or to interfere with the beliefs of any religious individual or groups.

The movement toward this end reached its dramatic climax in Virginia in 1785–87 when the Virginia legislative body was about to renew Virginia's tax levy for the support of the established church. Thomas Jefferson and James Madison led the fight against this tax. Madison wrote his great Memorial and Remonstrance against the law. In it, he eloquently argued that a true religion did not need the support of law; that no person, either believer or non-believer, should be taxed to support a religious institution of any kind; that the best interest of a society required that the minds of men always be wholly free; and that cruel persecutions were the inevitable result of government-established religions. Madison's Remonstrance received strong support throughout Virginia, and the Assembly postponed consideration of the proposed tax measure until its next session. When the proposal came up for consideration at that session, it not only died in committee, but the Assembly enacted the famous "Virginia Bill for Religious Liberty" originally written by Thomas Jefferson. The preamble to that Bill stated among other things that "to compel a man to furnish contributions of money for the propagation of opinions which he disbelieves, is sinful and tyrannical."

This Court has previously recognized that the provisions of the First Amendment, in the drafting and adoption of which Madison and Jefferson played such leading roles, had the same objective and were intended to provide the same protection against governmental intrusion on religious liberty as the Virginia statute.

The "establishment of religion" clause of the First Amendment means at least this: Neither a state nor the Federal Government can set up a church. Neither can pass laws which aid one religion, aid all religions, or prefer one religion over another. Neither can force nor influence a person to go to or to remain away from church against his will or force him to profess a belief or disbelief in any religion. No person can be punished for entertaining or professing religious beliefs or disbeliefs, for church attendance or non-attendance. No tax in any amount, large or small, can be levied to support any religious activities or institutions, whatever they may be called, or whatever form they may adopt to teach or practice religion. Neither a state nor the Federal Government can, openly or secretly, participate in the affairs of any religious organizations or groups and vice versa. In the words of Jefferson, the clause against establishment of religion by law was intended to erect "a wall of separation between Church and State."

We must consider the New Jersey statute in accordance with the foregoing limitations imposed by the First Amendment. But we must not strike that state statute down if it is within the state's constitutional power even though it approaches the verge of that power. New Jersey cannot consistently with the "establishment of religion" clause of the First Amendment contribute tax-raised funds to the support of an institution which teaches the tenets and faith of any church. On the other hand, other language of the Amendment commands that New Jersey cannot hamper its citizens in the free exercise of their own religion.

Measured by these standards, we cannot say that the First Amendment prohibits New Jersey from spending tax-raised funds to pay the bus fares of parochial school pupils as a part of a general program under which it pays the fares of pupils attending public and other schools. It is undoubtedly true that children are helped to get to church schools. There is even a possibility that some of the children might not be sent to the church schools if the parents were compelled to pay their children's bus fares out of their own pockets when transportation to a public school would have been paid for by the State. The same possibility exists where the state requires a local transit company to provide reduced fares to school children including those attending parochial schools, or where a municipally owned transportation system undertakes to carry all school children free of charge. Moreover, state-paid policemen, detailed to protect children going to and from church schools from the very real hazards of traffic, would serve much the same purpose and accomplish much the same result as state provisions intended to guarantee free transportation of a kind which the state deems to be best for the school children's welfare. And parents might refuse to risk their children to the serious danger of traffic accidents going to and from parochial schools, the approaches to which were not protected by policemen. Similarly, parents might be reluctant to permit their children to attend schools which the state had cut off from such general government services as ordinary police and fire protection, connections for sewage disposal, public highways and sidewalks. Of course, cutting off church schools from these services, so separate and so indisputably marked off from the religious function, would make it far more difficult for the schools to operate. But such is obviously not the purpose of the First Amendment. That Amendment requires the state to be a neutral in its relations with groups of religious believers and non-believers; it does not require the state to be their adversary. State power is no more to be used so as to handicap religions, than it is to favor them.

This Court has said that parents may, in the discharge of their duty under state compulsory education laws, send their children to a religious rather than a public school if the school meets the secular educational requirements which the state has power to impose. It appears that these parochial schools meet New Jersey's requirements. The State contributes no money to the schools. It does not support them. Its legislation, as applied, does no more than provide a general program to help parents get their children, regardless of their religion, safely and expeditiously to and from accredited schools.

The First Amendment has erected a wall between church and state. That wall must be kept high and impregnable. We could not approve the slightest breach. New Jersey has not breached it here.

MR. JUSTICE RUTLEDGE, with whom MR. JUSTICE FRANKFURTER, MR. JUSTICE JACKSON, and MR. JUSTICE BURTON agree, dissenting.

Not simply an established church, but any law respecting an establishment of religion is forbidden. The Amendment was broadly but not loosely phrased. It is the compact and exact summation of its author's views formed during his long struggle for religious freedom. In Madison's own words characterizing Jefferson's Bill for Establishing Religious Freedom, the guaranty he put in our national charter, like the bill he piloted through the Virginia Assembly, was "a Model of technical precision, and perspicuous brevity." Madison could not have confused "church" and "religion," or "an established church" and "an establishment of religion."

The Amendment's purpose was not to strike merely at the official establishment of a single sect, creed or religion, outlawing only a formal relation such as had prevailed in England and some of the colonies. Necessarily it was to uproot all such relationships. But the object was broader than separating church and state in this narrow sense. It was to create a complete and permanent separation of the spheres of religious activity and civil authority by comprehensively forbidding every form of public aid or support for religion. In proof the Amendment's wording and history unite with this Court's consistent utterances whenever attention has been fixed directly upon the question.

No provision of the Constitution is more closely tied to or given content by its generating history than the religious clause of the First Amendment. It is at once the refined product and the terse summation of that history. The history includes not only Madison's authorship and the proceedings before the First Congress, but also the long and intensive struggle for religious freedom in America, more especially in Virginia, of which the Amendment was the direct culmination. In the documents of the times, particularly of Madison, who was leader in the Virginia struggle before he became the Amendment's sponsor, but also in the writings of Jefferson and others and in the issues which engendered them is to be found irrefutable confirmation of the Amendment's sweeping content. In view of this history no further proof is needed that the Amendment forbids any appropriation, large or small, from public funds to aid or support any and all religious exercises.

Does New Jersey's action furnish support for religion by use of the taxing power? Certainly it does, if the test remains undiluted as Jefferson and Madison made it, that money taken by taxation from one is not to be used or given to support another's religious training or belief, or indeed one's own. Today as then the furnishing of "contributions of money for the propagation of opinions which he disbelieves" is the forbidden exaction; and the prohibition is absolute for whatever measure brings that consequence and whatever amount may be sought or given to that end.

The funds used here were raised by taxation. The Court does not dispute nor could it that their use does in fact give aid and encouragement to religious instruction. Here parents pay money to send their children to parochial schools and funds raised by taxation are used to reimburse them. This not only helps the children to get to school and the parents to send them. It aids them in a substantial way to get the very thing which they are sent to the particular school to secure, namely, religious training and teaching.

Believers of all faiths, and others who do not express their feeling toward ultimate issues of existence in any creedal form, pay the New Jersey tax. When the money so raised is used to pay for transportation to religious schools, the Catholic taxpayer to the extent of his proportionate share pays for the transportation of Lutheran, Jewish and otherwise religiously affiliated children to receive their non-Catholic religious instruction. Their parents likewise pay proportionately for the transportation of Catholic children to receive Catholic instruction. Each thus contributes to "the propagation of opinions which he disbelieves" in so far as their religions differ, as to others who accept no creed without regard to those differences.

No one conscious of religious values can be unsympathetic toward the burden which our constitutional separation puts on parents who desire religious instruction mixed with secular for their children. They pay taxes for others' children's education, at the same time the added cost of instruction for their own. Nor can one happily see benefits denied to children which others receive, because in conscience they or their parents for them desire a different kind of training others do not demand.

But if those feelings should prevail, there would be an end to our historic constitutional policy and command. No more unjust or discriminatory in fact is it to deny attendants at religious schools the cost of their transportation than it is to deny them tuitions, sustenance for their teachers, or any other educational expense which others receive at public cost. Hardship in fact there is which none can blink. But, for assuring to those who undergo it the greater, the most comprehensive freedom, it is one written by design and firm intent into our basic law.

Two great drives are constantly in motion to abridge, in the name of education, the complete division of religion and civil authority which our forefathers made. One is to introduce religious education and observances into the public schools. The other, to obtain public funds for the aid and support of various private religious schools. In my opinion both avenues were closed by the Constitution. Neither should be opened by this Court. The matter is not one of quantity, to be measured by the amount of money expended. Now as in Madison's day it is one of principle, to keep separate the separate spheres as the First Amendment drew them; to prevent the first experiment upon our liberties; and to keep the question from becoming entangled in corrosive precedents. We should not be less strict to keep strong and untarnished the one side of the shield of religious freedom than we have been of the other.

[Justice Jackson's dissenting opinion, which was joined by Justice Frankfurter, is omitted.]

Points for Discussion

1. **Is your cognitive dissonance kicking in?** Did you notice something peculiar about Justice Hugo Black's opinion? The earlier part of his opinion used soaring rhetoric about the history behind the Establishment Clause and the conclusions to be drawn from this history. This rhetoric pointed toward an interpretation of the Establishment Clause that required maximal separation between church and state. A passage near the end of the opinion matched this high-separationist rhetoric: "The First Amendment has erected a wall between church and state. That wall must be kept high and impregnable. We could not approve the slightest breach."

   Yet, in the middle of this same opinion, Justice Black concluded that New Jersey may use government funds to pay for transportation of students to religious schools. How did he pull that off? How in one breath could he simultaneously say that the Court could not "approve the slightest breach" in the wall separating church and state and then conclude that "New Jersey has not breached it here"?

2. **Justice Wiley Rutledge's dissenting opinion.** Justice Rutledge believed that using taxpayer money to cover children's transportation to religious schools was the type of compelled support for religion that Thomas Jefferson condemned as "sinful and tyrannical." In arguing that New Jersey did breach the wall separating church and state, Justice Rutledge embraced the "aid to the enterprise" theory. By covering these transportation expenses, New Jersey was providing aid to the enterprise of the religious schools, which would otherwise have to fund that transportation themselves by charging parents for the transportation or building it into the tuition structure.

   Justice Rutledge's dissenting opinion was quintessentially high separationist. Yet how would he respond to Justice Black's argument that government already provides support to religious schools through police and fire protection and connections to municipal sewage systems? How would Justice Rutledge counter Justice Black's argument that the Establishment Clause was meant to ensure government neutrality toward religion, not government hostility toward religion?

3. **Who do you think reached the better conclusion?** Do you think that Justice Black or Justice Rutledge reached the better conclusion? Can you explain why you think one of these justices' arguments is more persuasive? Do you think the government should be able to pay the bus fare of children traveling to private religious schools? If so, do you think the government can also provide books and maps to religious schools? How about computers? Do you think the government should be able to give vouchers to children and their parents that can be used to

pay the tuition at religious schools? We will explore these questions in the last section of this chapter.

Why Is Establishment Clause Jurisprudence so Confusing?

The competing opinions in *Everson* capture the tension that drives Establishment Clause jurisprudence. All justices recognize, and history strongly suggests, that the clause was intended to ensure at least some separation between church and state. Even Justice Thomas acknowledges that the clause likely prohibits Congress from establishing a national religion.

But once the Court ventures beyond the easy cases, the consensus among the justices breaks down. The confusion is driven by a disagreement over the extent to which American society, and the Constitution, should be deemed to embrace what Thomas Jefferson described as a "wall of separation" between church and state. The phrase derives from a letter Jefferson wrote to the Danbury, Connecticut, Baptist Association on January 1, 1802.

See It

Thomas Jefferson's letter to the Danbury, Connecticut, Baptist Association

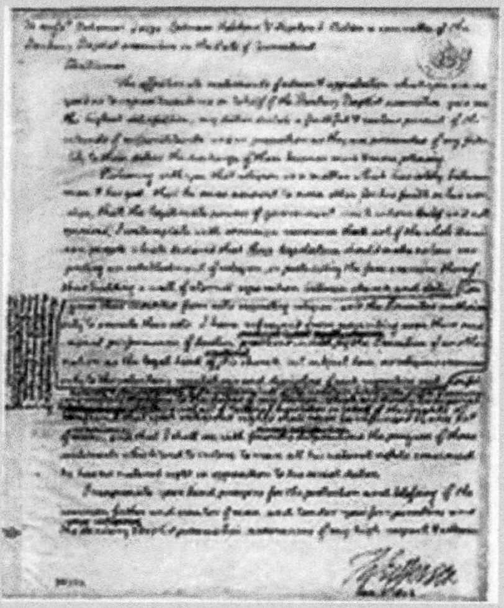

You can see Jefferson's letter and find a link to the letter's text here.

Whether the Establishment Clause was meant to erect a "wall of separation" between church and state, and how high that wall should be, have been matters of deep disputation ever since the founding of the Republic. American political, cultural, and legal thinkers on separation of church and state have tended to fall into one of three camps, which we might impishly label "high," "low," and "middle" separationists.

High separationists. High separationists are ardent in their insistence that the secular state be completely scrubbed of religious symbols, religious rituals, and government financial support for religious purposes. To high separationists, the wall separating church and state is high, thick, and impenetrable. High separationists would hold unconstitutional nearly all government financial assistance to religious enterprises and prohibit virtually all references to religion or God in governmental programs and symbols. High separationists might object to the inclusion of the phrase "one nation, under God" in the Pledge of Allegiance or the incantation "God Save the United States and this Honorable Court" at the commencement of a Supreme Court session. President Teddy Roosevelt, for example, opposed the phrase "In God We Trust" on currency. High separationists would also oppose monuments of the Ten Commandments on government property or placements of nativity scenes on government property during the Christmas season. There have been a number of high separationists on the Supreme Court, including Justices Ruth Bader Ginsburg, Elena Kagan, and Wiley Rutledge. High separationists have never, however, commanded a majority of the Court. As *Everson* and the upcoming *American Legion* and *Town of Greece* cases demonstrate, the high separationist views of Justices Ginsburg, Kagan, and Rutledge were all confined to dissenting opinions.

Low separationists. Low separationists bristle at the notion of a wall separating church and state. They prefer to invoke a famous statement from Justice William O. Douglas, writing for the Supreme Court in *Zorach v. Clauson*, 343 U.S. 306 (1952): "We are a religious people whose institutions presuppose a Supreme Being." Low separationists view religion as an integral part of our nation's history, tradition, and identity. They believe that religion should be treated as a welcome guest in the public arena, not as a baleful intruder. On the Supreme Court, Justices Thomas and Samuel Alito are prime exemplars of the low separationist position.

Middle separationists. Middle separationists are, as the name suggests, in the middle. They are unwilling to prohibit all financial aid to religion or strike down all rituals and symbols used by government that invoke religion, but they will draw lines at some point when activities appear too religious. Not surprisingly, middle separationists on the Supreme Court have often been justices regarded as more "centrist" in their views, such as Justices Sandra Day O'Connor, Anthony Kennedy, and Stephen Breyer. The tests adopted by middle separationists are often less precise than those used by the justices at the high and low extremes, leading to results that can be difficult to predict and reconcile.

The justices' varying attitudes toward separation of church and state have manifested themselves in battles over the appropriate test for identifying Establishment Clause violations. Three competing tests have loomed large in the Court's jurisprudence:

- **The *Lemon* test:** For many years, this test, which was originally articulated in *Lemon v. Kurtzman*, 403 U.S. 602 (1971), was the gold standard for determining whether a government action violated the Establishment Clause. There are three parts to the *Lemon* test. If a government action fails any part of the test, it will be declared unconstitutional:

    - **Purpose:** Government action must have a secular purpose.

    - **Effect:** The principal or primary effect of government action must neither advance nor inhibit religion.

    - **Entanglement:** Government action must not foster an excessive government entanglement with religion.

  The *Lemon* test tends to produce results that favor greater separation of church and state. Not surprisingly, the test is favored by justices with a high separationist orientation. Equally unsurprising, the test is disfavored by justices with a low separationist bent. One of those justices, Justice Scalia, long had knives out for the *Lemon* test, which he described as "a ghoul in a late-night horror movie that repeatedly sits up in its grave and shuffles abroad, after being repeatedly killed and buried." *Lamb's Chapel v. Center Moriches Union Free Sch. Dist.*, 508 U.S. 384, 398 (1993). The *Lemon* test outlasted Justice Scalia, but as you read more contemporary opinions, you might ask yourself whether the test has finally been laid to rest.

- **The endorsement test.** This test was announced by Justice O'Connor in a concurring opinion in *Lynch v. Donnelly*, 465 U.S. 668 (1984), where she declared that government endorsement of religion violates the Establishment Clause. She said the clause "prohibits government from making adherence to a religion relevant in any way to a person's standing in the political community." The problem with government endorsement of religion, she explained, was that it "sends a message to nonadherents that they are outsiders, not full members of the political community, and an accompanying message to adherents that they are insiders, favored members of the political community."

  Whether government action fails the endorsement test depends on whether it endorses one religion over others or, more controversially, whether it endorses religion over nonreligion. This determination is made from the perspective of a reasonable person witnessing the government action, although there are disagreements over how much background information this reasonable person should be assumed to know (such as whether the action is occurring in a traditional public forum).

The endorsement test is often used by middle separationists.

- **The coercion test.** In *Lee v. Weisman*, 505 U.S. 577, 587 (1992), Justice Anthony Kennedy succinctly captured the coercion test: "It is beyond dispute that, at a minimum, the Constitution guarantees that government may not coerce anyone to support or participate in religion or its exercise."

  All justices agree that coercing people to participate in a religious exercise can violate the Establishment Clause. Indeed, even without the Establishment Clause, such coercion would likely violate the Free Exercise Clause. The justices have disagreed over what constitutes unlawful coercion. For a low separationist like Justice Scalia, the only coercion that counts is coercion by force of law and threat of penalty. By contrast, Justice Kennedy concluded in *Weisman* that even psychological coercion, such as peer pressure from school classmates, could rise to the level of coercion. Justice Scalia, who dissented in *Weisman*, expressed his disagreement in characteristically trenchant terms: "I see no warrant for expanding the concept of coercion beyond acts backed by threat of penalty—a brand of coercion that, happily, is readily discernible to those of us who have made a career of reading the disciples of Blackstone rather than of Freud."

Lurking in the background of these tests is the ever-present question of how justices believe the Constitution should be interpreted. Justices with an originalist orientation are inclined to look at history and tradition to determine the Establishment Clause's meaning. As you will discover when you read more contemporary cases, this originalist approach is becoming increasingly dominant in the Court's jurisprudence. By contrast, non-originalists tend to focus on the broader values underlying the Establishment Clause, such as avoiding religious strife or ensuring equal treatment of religious minorities and nonbelievers. Non-originalists also tend to be concerned with the real-world impact of the Court's decisions.

These contests among high, low, and middle separationists, and between originalists and non-originalists, have played out at the Supreme Court in four principal arenas:

- **Symbols.** The Court has struggled with the extent to which government may display religious symbols on its property. These include displays such as Ten Commandments monuments, Christian crèches and Jewish menorahs during the holiday season, and a large Latin cross to honor fallen soldiers.

- **Rituals.** The Court has also wrestled with the extent to which prayers or other religious rituals are permitted at government events, such as opening state legislative sessions or town board meetings with the invocation of a prayer.

- **Schools.** Many Establishment Clause cases have arisen in the context of schools. The Court has tended to be more sensitive to concerns of endorsement and coercion in the school environment than in other contexts.

- **Support.** The Court has struggled with the extent to which government may provide financial support to religious institutions. These cases have largely involved funding for religious schools and universities.

We will explore each of these areas in the following sections.

B. Religious Symbols on Government Property: Crosses, Crèches, and Commandments

A recurring issue in Establishment Clause cases is the legality of religious displays on government property. These displays can range from overtly religious symbols, such as a crèche scene of baby Jesus in the manger, to symbols that arguably have a mixed religious/secular message, such as a Ten Commandments monument, to symbols that have morphed into secular seasonal holiday displays with little or no religious content, such as Rudolph the Red-Nosed Reindeer.

For decades, battles over religious displays were fought under the rubric of the *Lemon* test, which, as noted above, favored a high separationist approach. However, as Supreme Court personnel changed over time and more justices aligned with the middle or low separationist camps, the *Lemon* test gradually fell into disfavor. Many decisions ignored the test even though it remained official legal doctrine. With each passing Supreme Court term, the test increasingly resembled Justice Scalia's "ghoul in a late-night horror movie" hanging on by a thread.

The following cases bear witness to this shift in the Court's jurisprudence away from higher separationism toward lower separationism. By the last opinion, you might ask yourself whether the *Lemon* test has met its final demise or still haunts the halls of the Supreme Court.

1. Ten Commandments Monuments: Thou Shalt Not Reach the Same Conclusion

In two cases decided on the same day, the Court upheld a display of the Ten Commandments on the grounds of the Texas State Capitol but struck down a display of the Ten Commandments in Kentucky courthouses. How could that be?

These contrasting opinions are an ideal illustration of both the waning high separationist approach to the Establishment Clause and the waxing lower separationist approach. Justice David Souter's opinion in *McCreary County v. ACLU* represents the former. Chief Justice Rehnquist's opinion in *Van Orden v. Perry* represents the latter. Chief Justice Rehnquist's opinion set the stage for *American Legion v. American Humanist Association*, which broke even further from earlier precedent. You'll read that opinion later.

Before you dive into the opinions, we offer one piece of advice: Keep your eyes on Justice Breyer. How does he play a pivotal role in these decisions?

Justice Stephen Breyer
Steve Pettaway, Collection of the Supreme Court of the United States

McCreary County v. American Civil Liberties Union of Kentucky, Inc.

Supreme Court of the United States, 2005
545 U.S. 844

[*Authors' note*: This case arose after two counties in Kentucky posted a version of the Ten Commandments on the walls of their courthouses. After the American Civil Liberties Union challenged these displays, the counties revised them to include eight other framed documents, each of which highlighted the religious elements of other documents. For example, one frame had the passage "endowed by their Creator" from the Declaration of Independence and another had the national motto, "In God We Trust." After a court enjoined the second version of the displays, the counties installed a third version that incorporated more secular documents. Justice Souter's opinion for the Court began by describing the first two displays. The excerpted opinion picks up as he introduces the third display.]

JUSTICE SOUTER delivered the opinion of the Court.

The Counties filed a notice of appeal from the preliminary injunction but voluntarily dismissed it after hiring new lawyers. They then installed another display in each courthouse, the third within a year. The posting consists of nine framed documents of equal size, one of them setting out the Ten Commandments explicitly identified as the "King James Version" at Exodus 20:3-17.

Assembled with the Commandments are framed copies of the Magna Carta, the Declaration of Independence, the Bill of Rights, the lyrics of the Star Spangled Banner, the Mayflower Compact, the National Motto, the Preamble to the Kentucky Constitution, and a picture of Lady Justice. The collection is entitled "The Foundations of American Law and Government Display" and each document comes with a statement about its historical and legal significance. The comment on the Ten Commandments reads:

> The Ten Commandments have profoundly influenced the formation of Western legal thought and the formation of our country. That influence is clearly seen in the Declaration of Independence, which declared that "We hold these truths to be self-evident, that all men are created equal, that they are endowed by their Creator with certain unalienable Rights, that among these are Life, Liberty, and the pursuit of Happiness." The Ten Commandments provide the moral background of the Declaration of Independence and the foundation of our legal tradition.

Twenty-five years ago in a case prompted by posting the Ten Commandments in Kentucky's public schools, this Court recognized that the Commandments "are undeniably a sacred text in the Jewish and Christian faiths" and held that their display in public classrooms violated the First Amendment's bar against establishment of religion. *Stone v. Graham*, 449 U.S. 39 (1980). *Stone* found a predominantly religious purpose in the government's posting of the Commandments, given their prominence as "an instrument of religion." The Counties ask for a different approach here by arguing that official purpose is unknowable and the search for it inherently vain. In the alternative, the Counties would avoid the District Court's conclusion by having us limit the scope of the purpose enquiry so severely that any trivial rationalization would suffice, under a standard oblivious to the history of religious government action like the progression of exhibits in this case.

Ever since *Lemon v. Kurtzman* summarized the three familiar considerations for evaluating Establishment Clause claims, looking to whether government action has "a secular legislative purpose" has been a common, albeit seldom dispositive, element of our cases. The touchstone for our analysis is the principle that the "First Amendment mandates governmental neutrality between religion and religion, and between religion and nonreligion." When the government acts with the ostensible and predominant purpose of advancing religion, it violates that central Establishment Clause value of official religious neutrality, there being no neutrality when the government's ostensible object is to take sides. Manifesting a purpose to favor one faith over another, or adherence to religion generally, clashes with the "understanding, reached after decades of religious war, that liberty and social stability demand a religious tolerance that respects the religious views of all citizens." By showing a purpose to favor religion, the government "sends the message to nonadherents that they are outsiders, not full members of the political community, and an accompanying message to adherents that they are insiders, favored members."

After declining the invitation to abandon concern with purpose wholesale, we also have to avoid the Counties' alternative tack of trivializing the enquiry into it. The Counties would read the cases as if the purpose enquiry were so naive that any transparent claim to secularity would satisfy it, and they would cut context out of the enquiry, to the point of ignoring history, no matter what bearing it actually had on the significance of current circumstances. There is no precedent for the Counties' arguments, or reason supporting them.

This case comes to us on appeal from a preliminary injunction. We accordingly review the District Court's legal rulings *de novo,* and its ultimate conclusion for abuse of discretion. In holding the preliminary injunction adequately supported by evidence that the Counties' purpose had not changed at the third stage, we do not decide that the Counties' past actions forever taint any effort on their part to deal with the subject matter. We hold only that purpose needs to be taken seriously under the Establishment Clause and needs to be understood in light of context; an implausible claim that governmental purpose has changed should not carry the day in a court of law any more than in a head with common sense.

Nor do we have occasion here to hold that a sacred text can never be integrated constitutionally into a governmental display on the subject of law, or American history. We do not forget, and in this litigation have frequently been reminded, that our own courtroom frieze was deliberately designed in the exercise of governmental authority so as to include the figure of Moses holding tablets exhibiting a portion of the Hebrew text of the later, secularly phrased Commandments; in the company of 17 other lawgivers, most of them secular figures, there is no risk that Moses would strike an observer as evidence that the National Government was violating neutrality in religion.

The importance of neutrality as an interpretive guide is no less true now than it was when the Court broached the principle in *Everson*, and a word needs to be said about the different view taken in today's dissent. We all agree, of course, on the need for some interpretative help. The First Amendment contains no textual definition of "establishment," and the term is certainly not self-defining. No one contends that the prohibition of establishment stops at a designation of a national (or with Fourteenth Amendment incorporation, a state) church, but nothing in the text says just how much more it covers. There is no simple answer, for more than one reason.

The prohibition on establishment covers a variety of issues from prayer in widely varying government settings, to financial aid for religious individuals and institutions, to comment on religious questions. In these varied settings, issues of interpreting inexact Establishment Clause language, like difficult interpretative issues generally, arise from the tension of competing values, each constitutionally respectable, but none open to realization to the logical limit.

The fair inference is that there was no common understanding about the limits of the establishment prohibition, and the dissent's conclusion that its narrower view was the original understanding, stretches the evidence beyond tensile capacity. What the evidence does show is a group of statesmen, like others before and after them, who proposed a guarantee with contours not wholly worked out, leaving the Establishment Clause with edges still to be determined.

Historical evidence thus supports no solid argument for changing course (whatever force the argument might have when directed at the existing precedent), whereas public discourse at the present time certainly raises no doubt about the value of the interpretative approach invoked for 60 years now. We are centuries away from the St. Bartholomew's Day massacre and the treatment of heretics in early Massachusetts, but the divisiveness of religion in current public life is inescapable. This is no time to deny the prudence of understanding the Establishment Clause to require the Government to stay neutral on religious belief, which is reserved for the conscience of the individual.

JUSTICE SCALIA, with whom THE CHIEF JUSTICE and JUSTICE THOMAS join, and with whom JUSTICE KENNEDY joins as to Parts II and III, dissenting.

I would uphold [the] McCreary County and Pulaski County displays of the Ten Commandments. The Court's oft repeated assertion that the government cannot favor religious practice is false.

What distinguishes the rule of law from the dictatorship of a shifting Supreme Court majority is the absolutely indispensable requirement that judicial opinions be grounded in consistently applied principle. That is what prevents judges from ruling now this way, now that—thumbs up or thumbs down—as their personal preferences dictate. Today's opinion forthrightly (or actually, somewhat less than forthrightly) admits that it does not rest upon consistently applied principle.

If religion in the public forum had to be entirely nondenominational, there could be no religion in the public forum at all. One cannot say the word "God," or "the Almighty," one cannot offer public supplication or thanksgiving, without contradicting the beliefs of some people that there are many gods, or that God or the gods pay no attention to human affairs. With respect to public acknowledgment of religious belief, it is entirely clear from our Nation's historical practices that the Establishment Clause permits this disregard of polytheists and believers in unconcerned deities, just as it permits the disregard of devout atheists. The Thanksgiving Proclamation issued by George Washington at the instance of the First Congress was scrupulously nondenominational—but it was monotheistic. In *Marsh v. Chambers*, 463 U.S. 783 (1983), we said that the fact the particular prayers offered in the Nebraska Legislature were "in the Judeo-Christian tradition," posed no additional problem, because "there is no indication that the prayer opportunity has been exploited to proselytize or advance any one, or to disparage any other, faith or belief.

Historical practices thus demonstrate that there is a distance between the acknowledgment of a single Creator and the establishment of a religion. The former is, as *Marsh v. Chambers* put it, "a tolerable acknowledgment of beliefs widely held among the people of this country." The three most popular religions in the United States, Christianity, Judaism, and Islam—which combined account for 97.7% of all believers—are monotheistic. All of them, moreover (Islam included), believe that the Ten Commandments were given by God to Moses, and are divine prescriptions for a virtuous life. Publicly honoring the Ten Commandments is thus indistinguishable, insofar as discriminating against other religions is concerned, from publicly honoring God. Both practices are recognized across such a broad and diverse range of the population—from Christians to Muslims—that they cannot be reasonably understood as a government endorsement of a particular religious viewpoint.

[Justice O'Connor's concurring opinion is omitted.]

Van Orden v. Perry

Supreme Court of the United States, 2005
545 U.S. 677

CHIEF JUSTICE REHNQUIST announced the judgment of the Court and delivered an opinion, in which JUSTICE SCALIA, JUSTICE KENNEDY, and JUSTICE THOMAS join.

The question here is whether the Establishment Clause of the First Amendment allows the display of a monument inscribed with the Ten Commandments on the Texas State Capitol grounds. We hold that it does.

The 22 acres surrounding the Texas State Capitol contain 17 monuments and 21 historical markers commemorating the "people, ideals, and events that compose Texan identity." The monolith challenged here stands 6-feet high and 3½-feet wide. It is located to the north of the Capitol building, between the Capitol and the Supreme Court building. Its primary content is the text of the Ten Commandments. An eagle grasping the American flag, an eye inside of a pyramid, and two small tablets with what appears to be an ancient script are carved above the text of the Ten Commandments. Below the text are two Stars of David and the superimposed Greek letters Chi and Rho, which represent Christ. The bottom of the monument bears the inscription "PRESENTED TO THE PEOPLE AND YOUTH OF TEXAS BY THE FRATERNAL ORDER OF EAGLES OF TEXAS 1961."

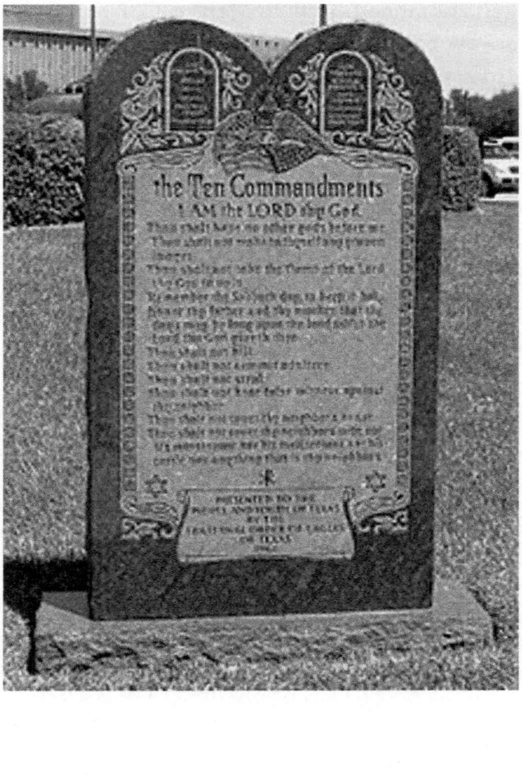

Forty years after the monument's erection and six years after [petitioner Thomas] Van Orden began to encounter the monument frequently, he sued numerous state officials, seeking both a declaration that the monument's placement violates the Establishment Clause and an injunction requiring its removal.

Whatever may be the fate of the *Lemon* test in the larger scheme of Establishment Clause jurisprudence, we think it not useful in dealing with the sort of passive monument that Texas has erected on its Capitol grounds. Instead, our analysis is driven both by the nature of the monument and by our Nation's history.

As we explained in *Lynch v. Donnelly*: "There is an unbroken history of official acknowledgment by all three branches of government of the role of religion in American life from at least 1789." For example, both Houses passed resolutions in 1789 asking President George Washington to issue a Thanksgiving Day Proclamation to "recommend to the people of the United States a day of public thanksgiving and prayer, to be observed, by acknowledging, with grateful hearts, the many and signal favors of Almighty God."

Recognition of the role of God in our Nation's heritage has also been reflected in our decisions. We have acknowledged, for example, that "religion has been closely identified with our history and government," and that "the history of man is inseparable from the history of religion," This recognition has led us to hold that the Establishment Clause permits a state legislature to open its daily sessions with a prayer by a chaplain paid by the State. Such a practice, we thought, was "deeply embedded in the history and tradition of this country."

In this case we are faced with a display of the Ten Commandments on government property outside the Texas State Capitol. Such acknowledgments of the role played by the Ten Commandments in our Nation's heritage are common throughout America. We need only look within our own Courtroom. Since 1935, Moses has stood, holding two tablets that reveal portions of the Ten Commandments written in Hebrew, among other lawgivers in the south frieze. Representations of the Ten Commandments adorn the metal gates lining the north and south sides of the Courtroom as well as the doors leading into the Courtroom. Moses also sits on the exterior east facade of the building holding the Ten Commandments tablets.

Of course, the Ten Commandments are religious—they were so viewed at their inception and so remain. The monument, therefore, has religious significance. According to Judeo-Christian belief, the Ten Commandments were given to Moses by God on Mt. Sinai. But Moses was a lawgiver as well as a religious leader. And the Ten Commandments have an undeniable historical meaning, as the foregoing examples demonstrate. Simply having religious content or promoting a message consistent with a religious doctrine does not run afoul of the Establishment Clause.

There are, of course, limits to the display of religious messages or symbols. For example, we held unconstitutional a Kentucky statute requiring the posting of the Ten Commandments in every public schoolroom. *Stone v. Graham*, 449 U.S. 39 (1980). In the classroom context, we found that the Kentucky statute had an improper and plainly religious purpose.

The placement of the Ten Commandments monument on the Texas State Capitol grounds is a far more passive use of those texts than was the case in *Stone*, where the text confronted elementary school students every day. Indeed, Van Orden, the petitioner here, apparently walked by the monument for a number of years before bringing this lawsuit. Texas has treated its Capitol grounds monuments as representing the several strands in the State's political and legal history. The inclusion of the Ten Commandments monument in this group has a dual significance, partaking of both religion and government. We cannot say that Texas' display of this monument violates the Establishment Clause of the First Amendment.

JUSTICE SCALIA, concurring.

I join the opinion of the Chief Justice because I think it accurately reflects our current Establishment Clause jurisprudence—or at least the Establishment Clause jurisprudence we currently apply some of the time. I would prefer to reach the same result by adopting an Establishment Clause jurisprudence that is in accord with our Nation's past and present practices, and that can be consistently applied—the central relevant feature of which is that there is nothing unconstitutional in a State's favoring religion generally, honoring God through public prayer and acknowledgment, or, in a nonproselytizing manner, venerating the Ten Commandments.

JUSTICE THOMAS, concurring.

There is no question that, based on the original meaning of the Establishment Clause, the Ten Commandments display at issue here is constitutional. In no sense does Texas compel petitioner Van Orden to do anything. The only injury to him is that he takes offense at seeing the monument as he passes it on his way to the Texas Supreme Court Library. He need not stop to read it or even to look at it, let alone to express support for it or adopt the Commandments as guides for his life. The mere presence of the monument along his path involves no coercion and thus does not violate the Establishment Clause.

JUSTICE BREYER, concurring in the judgment.

If the relation between government and religion is one of separation, but not of mutual hostility and suspicion, one will inevitably find difficult borderline cases. And in such cases, I see no test-related substitute for the exercise of legal judgment. That judgment is not a personal judgment. Rather, as in all constitutional cases, it must reflect and remain faithful to the underlying purposes of the Clauses, and it must take account of context and consequences measured in light of those purposes. While the Court's prior tests provide useful guideposts—and might well lead to the same result the Court reaches today, no exact formula can dictate a resolution to such fact-intensive cases.

The case before us is a borderline case. It concerns a large granite monument bearing the text of the Ten Commandments located on the grounds of the Texas State Capitol. On the one hand, the Commandments' text undeniably has a religious message, invoking, indeed emphasizing, the Deity. On the other hand, focusing on the text of the Commandments alone cannot conclusively resolve this case. Rather, to determine the message that the text here conveys, we must examine how the text is used. And that inquiry requires us to consider the context of the display.

In certain contexts, a display of the tablets of the Ten Commandments can convey not simply a religious message but also a secular moral message (about proper standards of social conduct). And in certain contexts, a display of the tablets can also convey a historical message (about a historic relation between those standards and the law)—a fact that helps to explain the display of those tablets in dozens of courthouses throughout the Nation, including the Supreme Court of the United States.

Here the tablets have been used as part of a display that communicates not simply a religious message, but a secular message as well. The circumstances surrounding the display's placement on the capitol grounds and its physical setting suggest that the State itself intended the latter, nonreligious aspects of the tablets' message to predominate. And the monument's 40-year history on the Texas state grounds indicates that that has been its effect.

If these factors provide a strong, but not conclusive, indication that the Commandments' text on this monument conveys a predominantly secular message, a further factor is determinative here. As far as I can tell, 40 years passed in which the presence of this monument, legally speaking, went unchallenged (until the single legal objection raised by petitioner). And I am not aware of any evidence suggesting that this was due to a climate of intimidation. Hence, those 40 years suggest more strongly than can any set of formulaic tests that few individuals, whatever their system of beliefs, are likely to have understood the monument as amounting, in any significantly detrimental way, to a government effort to favor a particular religious sect, primarily to promote religion over nonreligion, to engage in any religious practice, to compel any religious practice, or to work deterrence of any religious belief. Those 40 years suggest that the public visiting the capitol grounds has considered the religious aspect of the tablets' message as part of what is a broader moral and historical message reflective of a cultural heritage.

To reach a contrary conclusion here, based primarily on the religious nature of the tablets' text would, I fear, lead the law to exhibit a hostility toward religion that has no place in our Establishment Clause traditions. Such a holding might well encourage disputes concerning the removal of longstanding depictions of the Ten Commandments from public buildings across the Nation. And it could thereby create the very kind of religiously based divisiveness that the Establishment Clause seeks to avoid.

JUSTICE STEVENS, with whom JUSTICE GINSBURG joins, dissenting.

The sole function of the monument on the grounds of Texas' State Capitol is to display the full text of one version of the Ten Commandments. The monument is not a work of art and does not refer to any event in the history of the State. It is significant because, and only because, it communicates the following message:

I AM the LORD thy God.

Thou shalt have no other gods before me.
Thou shalt not make to thyself any graven images.
Thou shalt not take the Name of the Lord thy God in vain.
Remember the Sabbath day, to keep it holy.
Honor thy father and thy mother, that thy days may be long
upon the land which the Lord thy God giveth thee.
Thou shalt not kill.
Thou shalt not commit adultery.
Thou shalt not steal.
Thou shalt not bear false witness against thy neighbor.
Thou shalt not covet thy neighbor's house.
Thou shalt not covet thy neighbor's wife, nor his manservant, nor his
maidservant, nor his cattle, nor anything that is thy neighbor's.

Viewed on its face, Texas' display has no purported connection to God's role in the formation of Texas or the founding of our Nation; nor does it provide the reasonable observer with any basis to guess that it was erected to honor any individual or organization. The message transmitted by Texas' chosen display is quite plain: This State endorses the divine code of the "Judeo-Christian" God.

For those of us who learned to recite the King James version of the text long before we understood the meaning of some of its words, God's Commandments may seem like wise counsel. The question before this Court, however, is whether it is counsel that the State of Texas may proclaim without violating the Establishment Clause of the Constitution. If any fragment of Jefferson's metaphorical "wall of separation between church and State" is to be preserved—if there remains any meaning to the "wholesome 'neutrality' of which this Court's Establishment Clause cases speak"—a negative answer to that question is mandatory.

Even if, however, the message of the monument, despite the inscribed text, fairly could be said to represent the belief system of all Judeo-Christians, it would still run afoul of the Establishment Clause by prescribing a compelled code of conduct from one God, namely a Judeo-Christian God, that is rejected by prominent polytheistic sects, such as Hinduism, as well as nontheistic religions, such as Buddhism.

JUSTICE O'CONNOR, dissenting.

For essentially the reasons given by Justice Souter, as well as the reasons given in my concurrence in *McCreary County*, I respectfully dissent.

JUSTICE SOUTER, with whom JUSTICE STEVENS and JUSTICE GINSBURG join, dissenting.

Although the First Amendment's Religion Clauses have not been read to mandate absolute governmental neutrality toward religion, the Establishment Clause requires neutrality as a general rule, and thus expresses Madison's condemnation of "employing Religion as an engine of Civil policy," Memorial and Remonstrance Against Religious Assessments, 2 Writings of James Madison 183, 187 (G. Hunt ed.1901). A governmental display of an obviously religious text cannot be squared with neutrality, except in a setting that plausibly indicates that the statement is not placed in view with a predominant purpose on the part of government either to adopt the religious message or to urge its acceptance by others.

Until today, only one of our cases addressed the constitutionality of posting the Ten Commandments, *Stone v. Graham*. A Kentucky statute required posting the Commandments on the walls of public school classrooms, and the Court described the State's purpose as being at odds with the obligation of religious neutrality:

> The pre-eminent purpose for posting the Ten Commandments on schoolroom walls is plainly religious in nature. The Ten Commandments are undeniably a sacred text in the Jewish and Christian faiths, and no legislative recitation of a supposed secular purpose can blind us to that fact. The Commandments do not confine themselves to arguably secular matters, such as honoring one's parents, killing or murder, adultery, stealing, false witness, and covetousness. Rather, the first part of the Commandments concerns the religious duties of believers: worshipping the Lord God alone, avoiding idolatry, not using the Lord's name in vain, and observing the Sabbath Day.

What these observations underscore are the simple realities that the Ten Commandments constitute a religious statement, that their message is inherently religious, and that the purpose of singling them out in a display is clearly the same.

Thus, a pedestrian happening upon the monument at issue here needs no training in religious doctrine to realize that the statement of the Commandments, quoting

God himself, proclaims that the will of the divine being is the source of obligation to obey the rules, including the facially secular ones. In this case, moreover, the text is presented to give particular prominence to the Commandments' first sectarian reference, "I am the Lord thy God." That proclamation is centered on the stone and written in slightly larger letters than the subsequent recitation. To ensure that the religious nature of the monument is clear to even the most casual passerby, the word "Lord" appears in all capital letters (as does the word "am"), so that the most eye-catching segment of the quotation is the declaration "I AM the LORD thy God." What follows, of course, are the rules against other gods, graven images, vain swearing, and Sabbath breaking. And the full text of the fifth Commandment puts forward filial respect as a condition of long life in the land "which the Lord thy God giveth thee." These "words make the religious meaning unmistakably clear."

Points for Discussion

1. **Can you spot the differing approaches to the Establishment Clause?** Two decisions issued on the same day, both about Ten Commandments displays, yet somehow worlds apart. Can you identify the differences in the justices' reasoning?

   a. Compare Chief Justice Rehnquist's treatment of the *Lemon* test with Justice Souter's treatment of the *Lemon* test.

   b. Compare Chief Justice Rehnquist's use of history with Justice Souter's use of history.

   c. Justices across the spectrum agree that the Establishment Clause prohibits government from favoring one religion over others (what is sometimes called "non-preferentialism"). Divisions arise, however, over whether the Establishment Clause also requires the government to be neutral as between religion and nonreligion. Compare what Chief Justice Rehnquist and Justice Scalia said about this latter type of neutrality with what Justice Souter said.

2. **Did you keep your eyes on Justice Breyer?** Justice Breyer voted to uphold the Texas Ten Commandments display but to invalidate the Kentucky courthouse displays. How did he manage to thread that needle? Did he agree with the reasoning of Chief Justice Rehnquist's opinion in *Van Orden*? Did he agree with the reasoning of Justice Souter's opinion in *McCreary County*? Can you explain why Justice Breyer ruled the way he did in each case?

3. **Can a Ten Commandments display ever be neutral?** In his dissent in *McCreary County*, Justice Scalia stressed that the vast bulk of believers in the United States, whether Christian, Jewish, or Muslim, accept the Ten Commandments. Does

that make a Ten Commandments display neutral? Professor Paul Finkelman has suggested that it is impossible to have a neutral Ten Commandments display. To begin with, there are religions such as Hinduism and Buddhism that do not have the Ten Commandments as part of their traditions. But even among Judeo-Christian religions, there is no consensus on the precise wording and content of the commandments:

> Jews, Catholics, Lutherans, and most Protestants differ in the way they number and organize the Commandments. These religions, and denominations within them, also differ in how they translate the Commandments from the original Hebrew into English. Thus, any display of the Commandments is inherently sectarian, because it must choose a translation, ordering, and numbering system that will favor, or endorse one or more religions, and therefore disfavor other religions.

Paul Finkelman, *The Ten Commandments on the Courthouse Lawn and Elsewhere*, 73 Fordham L. Rev. 1477, 1478–79 (2005).

2. Crosses: Can a Latin Cross Have a Secular Meaning?

Fourteen years after it issued the two Ten Commandments opinions, the Court decided a case about the constitutionality of a large cross on government property. During the intervening period, Justice O'Connor was replaced by Justice Alito; Justice Scalia, who passed away, was replaced by Justice Neil Gorsuch; and Justice Kennedy was replaced by Justice Brett Kavanaugh. Some of these transitions might have been an "even trade" for Establishment Clause purposes in the sense that the new and departing justices may have had comparable views about separation of church and state. But, in some instances, that was not the case. Most notably, the middle separationist Justice O'Connor was replaced by the low separationist Justice Alito. In the two Ten Commandments cases, Justice O'Connor voted to invalidate both displays. Justice Alito wrote the lead opinion in the cross case.

The Bladensburg Peace Cross

American Legion v. American Humanist Association

Supreme Court of the United States, 2019
139 S. Ct. 2067

JUSTICE ALITO announced the judgment of the Court and delivered the opinion of the Court with respect to Parts I, II-B, II-C, III, and IV, and an opinion with respect to Parts II-A and II-D, in which THE CHIEF JUSTICE, JUSTICE BREYER, and JUSTICE KAVANAUGH join.

Since 1925, the Bladensburg Peace Cross (Cross) has stood as a tribute to 49 area soldiers who gave their lives in the First World War. Eighty-nine years after the dedication of the Cross, respondents filed this lawsuit, claiming that they are offended by the sight of the memorial on public land and that its presence there and the expenditure of public funds to maintain it violate the Establishment Clause of the First Amendment.

Although the cross has long been a preeminent Christian symbol, its use in the Bladensburg memorial has a special significance. After the First World War, the picture of row after row of plain white crosses marking the overseas graves of soldiers who had lost their lives in that horrible conflict was emblazoned on the minds of Americans at home, and the adoption of the cross as the Bladensburg memorial must be viewed in that historical context. For nearly a century, the Bladensburg Cross has expressed the community's grief at the loss of the young men who perished, its thanks for their sacrifice, and its dedication to the ideals for which they fought. It has become a prominent community landmark, and its removal or radical alteration at this date would be seen by many not as a neutral act but as the manifestation of "a hostility toward religion that has no place in our Establishment Clause traditions." *Van Orden v. Perry* (Breyer, J., concurring in judgment). And contrary to respondents' intimations, there is no evidence of discriminatory intent in the selection of the design of the memorial or the decision of a Maryland commission to maintain it. The Religion Clauses of the Constitution aim to foster a society in which people of all beliefs can live together harmoniously, and the presence of the Bladensburg Cross on the land where it has stood for so many years is fully consistent with that aim.

I

A

The cross came into widespread use as a symbol of Christianity by the fourth century, and it retains that meaning today. But there are many contexts in which the symbol has also taken on a secular meaning. Indeed, there are instances in which its message is now almost entirely secular.

A cross appears as part of many registered trademarks held by businesses and secular organizations, including Blue Cross Blue Shield, the Bayer Group, and some Johnson & Johnson products. Many of these marks relate to health care, and it is likely that the association of the cross with healing had a religious origin. But the current use of these marks is indisputably secular.

The image used in the Bladensburg memorial—a plain Latin cross—also took on new meaning after World War I. "During and immediately after the war, the army marked soldiers' graves with temporary wooden crosses or Stars of David"—a departure from the prior practice of marking graves in American military cemeteries with uniform rectangular slabs. The vast majority of these grave markers consisted of crosses, and thus when Americans saw photographs of these cemeteries, what struck them were rows and rows of plain white crosses. As a result, the image of a simple white cross "developed into a central symbol" of the conflict. Contemporary literature, poetry, and art reflected this powerful imagery.

After the 1918 armistice, the War Department announced plans to replace the wooden crosses and Stars of David with uniform marble slabs like those previously used in American military cemeteries. But the public outcry against that proposal was swift and fierce. Many organizations, including the American War Mothers, a nonsectarian group founded in 1917, urged the Department to retain the design of the temporary markers. When the American Battle Monuments Commission took over the project of designing the headstones, it responded to this public sentiment by opting to replace the wooden crosses and Stars of David with marble versions of those symbols. A Member of Congress likewise introduced a resolution noting that "these wooden symbols have, during and since the World War, been regarded as emblematic of the great sacrifices which that war entailed, have been so treated by poets and artists and have become peculiarly and inseparably associated in the thought of surviving relatives and comrades and of the Nation with these World War graves." This national debate and its outcome confirmed the cross's widespread resonance as a symbol of sacrifice in the war.

B

Recognition of the cross's symbolism extended to local communities across the country. In late 1918, residents of Prince George's County, Maryland, formed a committee for the purpose of erecting a memorial for the county's fallen soldiers. Among the committee's members were the mothers of 10 deceased soldiers. The committee decided that the memorial should be a cross and hired sculptor and architect John Joseph Earley to design it. Although we do not know precisely why the committee chose the cross, it is unsurprising that the committee—and many others commemorating World War I—adopted a symbol so widely associated with that wrenching event.

The completed monument is a 32-foot tall Latin cross that sits on a large pedestal. The American Legion's emblem is displayed at its center, and the words "Valor," "Endurance," "Courage," and "Devotion" are inscribed at its base, one on each of the four faces. The pedestal also features a 9- by 2.5-foot bronze plaque explaining that the monument is "Dedicated to the heroes of Prince George's County, Maryland who lost their lives in the Great War for the liberty of the world." The plaque lists the names of 49 local men, both Black and White, who died in the war. It identifies the dates of American involvement, and quotes President Woodrow Wilson's request for a declaration of war: "The right is more precious than peace. We shall fight for the things we have always carried nearest our hearts. To such a task we dedicate our lives."

As the area around the Cross developed, the monument came to be at the center of a busy intersection. In 1961, the Maryland-National Capital Park and Planning Commission (Commission) acquired the Cross and the land on which it sits in order to preserve the monument and address traffic-safety concerns.

C

In 2012, nearly 90 years after the Cross was dedicated and more than 50 years after the Commission acquired it, the American Humanist Association lodged a complaint with the Commission. The complaint alleged that the Cross's presence on public land and the Commission's maintenance of the memorial violate the Establishment Clause of the First Amendment.

II

A

The Establishment Clause of the First Amendment provides that "Congress shall make no law respecting an establishment of religion." While the concept of a formally established church is straightforward, pinning down the meaning of a "law respecting an establishment of religion" has proved to be a vexing problem. Prior to the Court's decision in *Everson*, the Establishment Clause was applied only to the Federal Government, and few cases involving this provision came before the Court. After *Everson* recognized the incorporation of the Clause, however, the Court faced a steady stream of difficult and controversial Establishment Clause issues, ranging from Bible reading and prayer in the public schools, to Sunday closing laws, to state subsidies for church-related schools or the parents of students attending those schools. After grappling with such cases for more than 20 years, *Lemon v. Kurtzman* ambitiously attempted to distill from the Court's existing case law a test that would bring order and predictability to Establishment Clause decisionmaking.

If the *Lemon* Court thought that its test would provide a framework for all future Establishment Clause decisions, its expectation has not been met. In many cases, this Court has either expressly declined to apply the test or has simply ignored it. This pattern is a testament to the *Lemon* test's shortcomings. As Establishment Clause cases involving a great array of laws and practices came to the Court, it became more and more apparent that the *Lemon* test could not resolve them.

For at least four reasons, the *Lemon* test presents particularly daunting problems in cases, including the one now before us, that involve the use, for ceremonial, celebratory, or commemorative purposes, of words or symbols with religious associations. Together, these considerations counsel against efforts to evaluate such cases under *Lemon* and toward application of a presumption of constitutionality for longstanding monuments, symbols, and practices.

B

First, these cases often concern monuments, symbols, or practices that were first established long ago, and in such cases, identifying their original purpose or purposes may be especially difficult.

The truth is that 70 years after the fact, there was no way to be certain about the motivations of the men who were responsible for the creation of the monument. And this is often the case with old monuments, symbols, and practices. Yet it would be inappropriate for courts to compel their removal or termination based on supposition.

Second, as time goes by, the purposes associated with an established monument, symbol, or practice often multiply. Take the example of Ten Commandments monuments, the subject we addressed in *Van Orden* and *McCreary County*.

For believing Jews and Christians, the Ten Commandments are the word of God handed down to Moses on Mount Sinai, but the image of the Ten Commandments has also been used to convey other meanings. They have historical significance as one of the foundations of our legal system, and for largely that reason, they are depicted in the marble frieze in our courtroom and in other prominent public buildings in our Nation's capital.

The existence of multiple purposes is not exclusive to longstanding monuments, symbols, or practices, but this phenomenon is more likely to occur in such cases. Even if the original purpose of a monument was infused with religion, the passage of time may obscure that sentiment. As our society becomes more and more religiously diverse, a community may preserve such monuments, symbols, and practices for the sake of their historical significance or their place in a common cultural heritage.

Third, just as the purpose for maintaining a monument, symbol, or practice may evolve, "the message conveyed may change over time." Consider, for example, the message of the Statue of Liberty, which began as a monument to the solidarity and friendship between France and the United States and only decades later came to be seen "as a beacon welcoming immigrants to a land of freedom."

With sufficient time, religiously expressive monuments, symbols, and practices can become embedded features of a community's landscape and identity. The community may come to value them without necessarily embracing their religious roots. The recent tragic fire at Notre Dame in Paris provides a striking example. Although the French Republic rigorously enforces a secular public square, the cathedral remains a symbol of national importance to the religious and nonreligious alike. Notre Dame is fundamentally a place of worship and retains great religious importance, but its meaning has broadened. For many, it is inextricably linked with the very idea of Paris and France. Speaking to the nation shortly after the fire, President Macron said that Notre Dame "is our history, our literature, our imagination. The place where we survived epidemics, wars, liberation. It has been the epicenter of our lives."

In the same way, consider the many cities and towns across the United States that bear religious names. Religion undoubtedly motivated those who named Bethlehem, Pennsylvania; Las Cruces, New Mexico; Providence, Rhode Island; Corpus Christi, Texas; Nephi, Utah, and the countless other places in our country with names that are rooted in religion. Yet few would argue that this history requires that these names be erased from the map. Or take a motto like Arizona's, "Ditat Deus" ("God enriches"), which was adopted in 1864, or a flag like Maryland's, which has included two crosses since 1904. Familiarity itself can become a reason for preservation.

Fourth, when time's passage imbues a religiously expressive monument, symbol, or practice with this kind of familiarity and historical significance, removing it may no longer appear neutral, especially to the local community for which it has taken on particular meaning. A government that roams the land, tearing down monuments with religious symbolism and scrubbing away any reference to the divine will strike many as aggressively hostile to religion. Militantly secular regimes have carried out such projects in the past, and for those with a knowledge of history, the image of monuments being taken down will be evocative, disturbing, and divisive.

These four considerations show that retaining established, religiously expressive monuments, symbols, and practices is quite different from erecting or adopting new ones. The passage of time gives rise to a strong presumption of constitutionality.

C

The role of the cross in World War I memorials is illustrative of each of the four preceding considerations. Immediately following the war, "communities across America built memorials to commemorate those who had served the nation in the struggle to make the world safe for democracy." Although not all of these communities included a cross in their memorials, the cross had become a symbol closely linked to the war. "The First World War witnessed a dramatic change in the symbols used to commemorate the service" of the fallen soldiers. In the wake of the war, the United States adopted the cross as part of its military honors, establishing the Distinguished Service Cross and the Navy Cross in 1918 and 1919, respectively. And as already noted, the fallen soldiers' final resting places abroad were marked by white crosses or Stars of David. The solemn image of endless rows of white crosses became inextricably linked with and symbolic of the ultimate price paid by 116,000 soldiers. And this relationship between the cross and the war undoubtedly influenced the design of the many war memorials that sprang up across the Nation.

This is not to say that the cross's association with the war was the sole or dominant motivation for the inclusion of the symbol in every World War I memorial that features it. But today, it is all but impossible to tell whether that was so. The passage of time means that testimony from those actually involved in the decisionmaking process is generally unavailable, and attempting to uncover their motivations invites rampant speculation. And no matter what the original purposes for the erection of a monument, a community may wish to preserve it for very different reasons, such as the historic preservation and traffic-safety concerns the Commission has pressed here.

As World War I monuments have endured through the years and become a familiar part of the physical and cultural landscape, requiring their removal would not be viewed by many as a neutral act. Thus, a campaign to obliterate items with religious associations may evidence hostility to religion even if those religious associations are no longer in the forefront.

For example, few would say that the State of California is attempting to convey a religious message by retaining the names given to many of the State's cities by their original Spanish settlers—San Diego, Los Angeles, Santa Barbara, San Jose, San Francisco, etc. But it would be something else entirely if the State undertook to change all those names. Much the same is true about monuments to soldiers who sacrificed their lives for this country more than a century ago.

D

While the *Lemon* Court ambitiously attempted to find a grand unified theory of the Establishment Clause, in later cases, we have taken a more modest approach that focuses on the particular issue at hand and looks to history for guidance. Our cases involving prayer before a legislative session are an example.

III

Applying these principles, we conclude that the Bladensburg Cross does not violate the Establishment Clause.

As we have explained, the Bladensburg Cross carries special significance in commemorating World War I. Due in large part to the image of the simple wooden crosses that originally marked the graves of American soldiers killed in the war, the cross became a symbol of their sacrifice, and the design of the Bladensburg Cross must be understood in light of that background. That the cross originated as a Christian symbol and retains that meaning in many contexts does not change the fact that the symbol took on an added secular meaning when used in World War I memorials.

Not only did the Bladensburg Cross begin with this meaning, but with the passage of time, it has acquired historical importance. It reminds the people of Bladensburg and surrounding areas of the deeds of their predecessors and of the sacrifices they made in a war fought in the name of democracy. As long as it is retained in its original place and form, it speaks as well of the community that erected the monument nearly a century ago and has maintained it ever since. The memorial represents what the relatives, friends, and neighbors of the fallen soldiers felt at the time and how they chose to express their sentiments. And the monument has acquired additional layers of historical meaning in subsequent years. The Cross now stands among memorials to veterans of later wars. It has become part of the community.

The monument would not serve that role if its design had deliberately disrespected area soldiers who perished in World War I. More than 3,500 Jewish soldiers gave their lives for the United States in that conflict, and some have wondered whether the names of any Jewish soldiers from the area were deliberately left off the list on the memorial or whether the names of any Jewish soldiers were included on the Cross against the wishes of their families. There is no evidence that either thing was done, and we do know that one of the local American Legion leaders responsible for the Cross's construction was a Jewish veteran.

JUSTICE BREYER, with whom JUSTICE KAGAN joins, concurring.

I have long maintained that there is no single formula for resolving Establishment Clause challenges. The Court must instead consider each case in light of the basic purposes that the Religion Clauses were meant to serve: assuring religious liberty and tolerance for all, avoiding religiously based social conflict, and maintaining that separation of church and state that allows each to flourish in its "separate sphere."

I agree with the Court that allowing the State of Maryland to display and maintain the Peace Cross poses no threat to those ends. The Court's opinion eloquently explains why that is so: The Latin cross is uniquely associated with the fallen soldiers of World War I; the organizers of the Peace Cross acted with the undeniably secular motive of commemorating local soldiers; no evidence suggests that they sought to disparage or exclude any religious group; the secular values inscribed on the Cross and its place among other memorials strengthen its message of patriotism and commemoration; and, finally, the Cross has stood on the same land for 94 years, generating no controversy in the community until this lawsuit was filed. In light of all these circumstances, the Peace Cross cannot reasonably be understood as "a government effort to favor a particular religious sect" or to "promote religion over nonreligion." And, as the Court explains, ordering its removal or alteration at this late date would signal "a hostility toward religion that has no place in our Establishment Clause traditions."

The case would be different, in my view, if there were evidence that the organizers had "deliberately disrespected" members of minority faiths or if the Cross had been erected only recently, rather than in the aftermath of World War I. Nor do I understand the Court's opinion today to adopt a "history and tradition test" that would permit any newly constructed religious memorial on public land. The Court appropriately "looks to history for guidance," but it upholds the constitutionality of the Peace Cross only after considering its particular historical context and its long-held place in the community. A newer memorial, erected under different circumstances, would not necessarily be permissible under this approach.

JUSTICE KAVANAUGH, concurring.

Consistent with the Court's case law, the Court today applies a history and tradition test in examining and upholding the constitutionality of the Bladensburg Cross. As this case again demonstrates, this Court no longer applies the old test articulated in *Lemon*. If *Lemon* guided this Court's understanding of the Establishment Clause, then many of the Court's Establishment Clause cases over the last 48 years would have been decided differently.

JUSTICE GINSBURG, with whom JUSTICE SOTOMAYOR joins, dissenting.

An immense Latin cross stands on a traffic island at the center of a busy three-way intersection in Bladensburg, Maryland. "Monumental, clear, and bold" by day, the cross looms even larger illuminated against the night-time sky. Both the Peace Cross and the traffic island are owned and maintained by the Maryland-National Capital Park and Planning Commission (Commission), an agency of the State of Maryland.

Decades ago, this Court recognized that the Establishment Clause of the First Amendment to the Constitution demands governmental neutrality among religious faiths, and between religion and nonreligion. See *Everson*. Numerous times since, the Court has reaffirmed the Constitution's commitment to neutrality. Today the Court erodes that neutrality commitment, diminishing precedent designed to preserve individual liberty and civic harmony in favor of a "presumption of constitutionality for longstanding monuments, symbols, and practices."

The Latin cross is the foremost symbol of the Christian faith, embodying the "central theological claim of Christianity: that the son of God died on the cross, that he rose from the dead, and that his death and resurrection offer the possibility of eternal life." Just as a Star of David is not suitable to honor Christians who died serving their country, so a cross is not suitable to honor those of other faiths who died defending their nation. Soldiers of all faiths "are united by their love of country, but they are not united by the cross."

By maintaining the Peace Cross on a public highway, the Commission elevates Christianity over other faiths, and religion over nonreligion. Memorializing the service of American soldiers is an "admirable and unquestionably secular" objective. But the Commission does not serve that objective by displaying a symbol that bears "a starkly sectarian message."

[Justice Kagan's opinion concurring in part is omitted, as is Justice Thomas' opinion concurring in the judgment. Justice Gorsuch's opinion concurring in the judgment, which was joined by Justice Thomas, is also omitted.]

Points for Discussion

1. **Does anyone have a scorecard?** In Part II-A of his opinion Justice Alito strongly suggests that the *Lemon* test was ill-conceived from the start, and in Part II-D he contends that the Court has moved away from using the *Lemon* test as the "grand unified theory of the Establishment Clause." Clearly, Justice Alito is not a fan of the *Lemon* test. But how many justices joined those parts of his opinion? Was it a majority of the Court?

2. **Older versus newer religious displays.** A majority of the justices did join Part II-B of Justice Alito's opinion, which explained why the *Lemon* test is not particularly helpful when the Court is examining long-standing religious displays. Should there be a difference between how the Court analyzes long-standing religious displays versus recently installed displays? Does this difference explain the varying outcomes in the two Ten Commandments cases? What does Justice Breyer, who voted to uphold both the long-standing Texas Ten Commandments monument and the Bladensburg Peace Cross, think about how the Court should treat newly installed religious displays?

3. **Should history and tradition be the guide?** Justice Alito said the Court, as it has turned away from the *Lemon* test, has shifted to "a more modest approach that focuses on the particular issue at hand and looks to history for guidance." You will shortly encounter another example of the Court's looking to history as its guide when you read *Town of Greece v. Galloway*. Do you think that examining historical practices is a good method for resolving Establishment Clause issues? Why or why not?

4. **The Breyer/Scalia show.** For many years Justices Breyer and Scalia toured together to make joint presentations at colleges, laws schools, bar conferences, and other forums to debate their opposing approaches to constitutional interpretation. During his many years on the Court, Justice Breyer often eschewed the adoption of formal legal tests and doctrines, opting instead for a case-by-case balancing of competing interests. Justice Scalia, in his many years on the Court, was one of its most ardent textualists and originalists. These contrasting approaches appear in vivid relief in their opinions in the Ten Commandments cases. Justice Breyer's concurring opinion in *Van Orden* may be his most famous abdication of any effort to articulate a formal legal basis for his decision. Note his statement: "In such cases, I see no test-related substitute for the exercise of legal judgment." Perhaps anticipating how his real-life friend and on-the-job nemesis Justice Scalia might scoff at this sentence, Justice Breyer followed by insisting, "That judgment is not a personal judgment." Justice Scalia, in contrast, had no use for such "judgments" at all. While he did not attack his colleague by name, Justice Scalia surely had Justice Breyer in mind for his biting attack on the flip-flops so visible in Establishment Clause cases, as exemplified by the two Ten Commandments cases reaching opposite results on the same day. Consider Justice Scalia's sarcastic critique in his *McCreary County* dissent: "What distinguishes the rule of law from the dictatorship of a shifting Supreme Court majority is the absolutely indispensable requirement that judicial opinions be grounded in consistently applied principle. That is what prevents judges from ruling now this way, now that—thumbs up or thumbs down—as their personal preferences dictate."

3. Crèches, Menorahs, and Other Holiday Displays: Best Diluted with Santa and Candy Canes

Establishment Clause cases concerning holiday displays on government property have proven particularly perplexing.

In *Lynch v. Donnelly*, 465 U.S. 668 (1984), the Court held that a crèche in an annual Christmas display erected by the city of Pawtucket, Rhode Island, did not violate the Establishment Clause. The crèche included figures such as the infant Jesus, Mary and Joseph, angels, shepherds, kings, and animals. In addition, the Christmas display included secular Christmas figures and decorations, including a Santa Claus house, reindeer pulling Santa's sleigh, candy-striped poles, a Christmas tree, carolers, cutout figures representing an elephant and a teddy bear, hundreds of colored lights, and a large banner wishing "Seasons Greetings." The Court stated: "To forbid the use of this one passive symbol—the crèche—at the very time people are taking note of the season with Christmas hymns and carols in public schools and other public places, and while the Congress and legislatures open sessions with prayers by paid chaplains, would be a stilted overreaction contrary to our history and to our holdings. If the presence of the crèche in this display violates the Establishment Clause, a host of other forms of taking official note of Christmas, and of our religious heritage, are equally offensive to the Constitution."

The Court reached a different result in *County of Allegheny v. American Civil Liberties Union*, 492 U.S. 573 (1989), which involved two holiday displays on public property in downtown Pittsburgh. The first was a crèche placed on the main staircase in the county courthouse. The second was a menorah placed outside a city/county office building, next to a Christmas tree and a sign saluting liberty. A splintered Court held that the crèche display was unconstitutional, reasoning that "unlike in *Lynch*, nothing in the context of the display detracts from the crèche's religious message." But the Court upheld the menorah in the second display. The Court reasoned that the menorah had both a religious and secular message and that the combined display of a menorah next to a Christmas tree and a salute to liberty made the overall display a secular, not religious, message.

You might be scratching your head as to why the *Lynch* majority was not troubled by the Christmas tree and the reindeer pulling Santa's sleigh. After all, those are symbols of Christmas, a Christian holiday. One could argue that the government display of these symbols amounts to endorsement of Christianity. The Court, however, seems to treat these less overtly religious symbols—Christmas trees, Santa, and Rudolph—as secular symbols of the holiday season.

To get a sense of how this distinction has played out in the real world, consider this summary of the General Services Administration's former policy regarding seasonal decorations on federal properties:

> The current policy prohibits the purchase or display of any "religiously significant" seasonal decoration in the public spaces of such properties. The policy identifies certain "religiously significant" items, such as a cross, menorah, or crèche, and identifies other items that are not "religiously significant," such as a Christmas tree or Santa Claus.

Memorandum Opinion for the General Counsel General Services Administration, Religious Seasonal Decorations in Federal Government Buildings, Slip Opinion (January 15, 2021). In response to the *American Legion* decision, the General Services Administration modified its rule to sometimes permit religiously significant displays in federal buildings. Here is how the memorandum opinion reframed the issue in light of *American Legion*:

> The correct question is not whether the displays themselves are religiously significant, or whether they satisfy the *Lemon* framework, but rather whether they are the kind of displays that are consistent with the "history and tradition" of this country. *Am. Legion*, 139 S. Ct. at 2092 (Kavanaugh, J., concurring).

C. Prayers and Religious Rituals at Government Functions: History and Tradition as a Guide

You should not infer from the Supreme Court's recent use of history and tradition to resolve Establishment Clause cases that the justices did not make historical arguments in the past. To the contrary, debates over the historical record were common in earlier decisions. You saw an example of this in *Everson*. The primary difference is that there were fewer justices in earlier years who thought that history and tradition should be decisive, so that other tests, whether the *Lemon*, endorsement, or coercion test, loomed larger. Perhaps not coincidentally, the Court during those earlier years also had more justices who aligned with the middle or high separationist camps.

Nevertheless, there are older precedents in which history and tradition were decisive. That was especially true in the Court's leading case about the constitutionality of prayers at the opening of legislative sessions, *Marsh v. Chambers*, 463 U.S. 783 (1983). Justice Alito cited *Marsh* in *American Legion* as a prime example of the Court's historical approach.

Marsh concerned the constitutionality of the Nebraska legislature's long-standing practice of beginning its sessions with a clergy-led prayer. Chief Justice Warren Burger, who wrote the opinion for the Court, jumped immediately to history and tradition at the start of his legal analysis: "The opening of sessions of legislative and other deliberative public bodies with prayer is deeply embedded in the history and tradition of this country." In examining this history, Chief Justice Burger found it especially noteworthy that the same Congress that proposed the First Amendment also hired a chaplain to open its sessions:

> On September 25, 1789, three days after Congress authorized the appointment of paid chaplains, final agreement was reached on the language of the Bill of Rights. Clearly the men who wrote the First Amendment Religion Clauses did not view paid legislative chaplains and opening prayers as a violation of that Amendment, for the practice of opening sessions with prayer has continued without interruption ever since that early session of Congress.

Should this historic tradition of opening sessions in federal and state legislatures with prayers also justify the use of prayers in more intimate settings, such as town council or school board meetings?

Town of Greece v. Galloway

Supreme Court of the United States, 2014
572 U.S. 565

JUSTICE KENNEDY delivered the opinion of the Court, except as to Part II-B.

The Court must decide whether the town of Greece, New York, imposes an impermissible establishment of religion by opening its monthly board meetings with a prayer. It must be concluded, consistent with the Court's opinion in *Marsh v. Chambers* that no violation of the Constitution has been shown.

I.

Greece, a town with a population of 94,000, is in upstate New York. For some years, it began its monthly town board meetings with a moment of silence. In 1999, the newly elected town supervisor, John Auberger, decided to replicate the prayer practice he had found meaningful while serving in the county legislature. Following the roll call and recitation of the Pledge of Allegiance, Auberger would invite a local clergyman to the front of the room to deliver an invocation. After the prayer, Auberger would thank the minister for serving as the board's "chaplain for the month" and present him with a commemorative plaque. The prayer was intended to place town board members in a solemn and deliberative frame of mind, invoke divine guidance in town affairs, and follow a tradition practiced by Congress and dozens of state legislatures.

The town followed an informal method for selecting prayer givers, all of whom were unpaid volunteers. A town employee would call the congregations listed in a local directory until she found a minister available for that month's meeting. The town eventually compiled a list of willing "board chaplains" who had accepted invitations and agreed to return in the future. The town at no point excluded or denied an opportunity to a would-be prayer giver. Its leaders maintained that a minister or layperson of any persuasion, including an atheist, could give the invocation. But nearly all of the congregations in town were Christian; and from 1999 to 2007, all of the participating ministers were too.

Greece neither reviewed the prayers in advance of the meetings nor provided guidance as to their tone or content, in the belief that exercising any degree of control over the prayers would infringe both the free exercise and speech rights of the ministers. The town instead left the guest clergy free to compose their own devotions. The resulting prayers often sounded both civic and religious themes. Typical were invocations that asked the divinity to abide at the meeting and bestow blessings on the community:

> Lord we ask you to send your spirit of servanthood upon all of us gathered here this evening to do your work for the benefit of all in our community. We ask you to bless our elected and appointed officials so they may deliberate with wisdom and act with courage. Bless the members of our community who come here to speak before the board so they may state their cause with honesty and humility. Lord we ask you to bless us all, that everything we do here tonight will move you to welcome us one day into your kingdom as good and faithful servants. We ask this in the name of our brother Jesus. Amen.

Some of the ministers spoke in a distinctly Christian idiom; and a minority invoked religious holidays, scripture, or doctrine, as in the following prayer:

> Lord, God of all creation, we give you thanks and praise for your presence and action in the world. We look with anticipation to the celebration of Holy Week and Easter. It is in the solemn events of next week that we find the very heart and center of our Christian faith. We acknowledge the saving sacrifice of Jesus Christ on the cross. We draw strength, vitality, and confidence from his resurrection at Easter. We pray for peace in the world, an end to terrorism, violence, conflict, and war. We pray for stability, democracy, and good government in those countries in which our armed forces are now serving, especially in Iraq and Afghanistan. Praise and glory be yours, O Lord, now and forever more. Amen.

Respondents Susan Galloway and Linda Stephens attended town board meetings to speak about issues of local concern, and they objected that the prayers violated their religious or philosophical views. At one meeting, Galloway admonished board members that she found the prayers "offensive," "intolerable," and an affront to a "diverse community." After respondents complained that Christian themes pervaded the prayers, to the exclusion of citizens who did not share those beliefs, the town invited a Jewish layman and the chairman of the local Baha'i temple to deliver prayers. A Wiccan priestess who had read press reports about the prayer controversy requested, and was granted, an opportunity to give the invocation.

Galloway and Stephens brought suit in the United States District Court for the Western District of New York. They alleged that the town violated the First Amendment's Establishment Clause by preferring Christians over other prayer givers and by sponsoring sectarian prayers, such as those given "in Jesus' name." They did not seek an end to the prayer practice, but rather requested an injunction that would limit the town to "inclusive and ecumenical" prayers that referred only to a "generic God" and would not associate the government with any one faith or belief.

II.

In *Marsh v. Chambers*, the Court found no First Amendment violation in the Nebraska Legislature's practice of opening its sessions with a prayer delivered by a chaplain paid from state funds. The decision concluded that legislative prayer, while religious in nature, has long been understood as compatible with the Establishment Clause. As practiced by Congress since the framing of the Constitution, legislative prayer lends gravity to public business, reminds lawmakers to transcend petty differences in pursuit of a higher purpose, and expresses a common aspiration to a just and peaceful society. The Court has considered this symbolic expression to be a "tolerable acknowledgement of beliefs widely held," rather than a first, treacherous step towards establishment of a state church.

Marsh is sometimes described as "carving out an exception" to the Court's Establishment Clause jurisprudence, because it sustained legislative prayer without subjecting the practice to "any of the formal 'tests' that have traditionally structured" this inquiry. The Court in *Marsh* found those tests unnecessary because history supported the conclusion that legislative invocations are compatible with the Establishment Clause. The First Congress made it an early item of business to appoint and pay official chaplains, and both the House and Senate have maintained the office virtually uninterrupted since that time. When *Marsh* was decided, in 1983, legislative prayer had persisted in the Nebraska Legislature for more than a century, and the majority of the other States also had the same, consistent practice. Although no information has been cited by the parties to indicate how many local legislative bodies open their meetings with prayer, this practice too has historical precedent.

The Court's inquiry, then, must be to determine whether the prayer practice in the town of Greece fits within the tradition long followed in Congress and the state legislatures. Respondents assert that the town's prayer exercise falls outside that tradition and transgresses the Establishment Clause for two independent but mutually reinforcing reasons. First, they argue that *Marsh* did not approve prayers containing sectarian language or themes, such as the prayers offered in Greece that referred to the "death, resurrection, and ascension of the Savior Jesus Christ," and the "saving sacrifice of Jesus Christ on the cross." Second, they argue that the setting and conduct of the town board meetings create social pressures that force nonadherents to remain in the room or even feign participation in order to avoid offending the representatives who sponsor the prayer and will vote on matters citizens bring before the board. The sectarian content of the prayers compounds the subtle coercive pressures, they argue, because the nonbeliever who might tolerate ecumenical prayer is forced to do the same for prayer that might be inimical to his or her beliefs.

A.

An insistence on nonsectarian or ecumenical prayer as a single, fixed standard is not consistent with the tradition of legislative prayer outlined in the Court's cases. The Court found the prayers in *Marsh* consistent with the First Amendment not because they espoused only a generic theism but because our history and tradition have shown that prayer in this limited context could "coexist with the principles of disestablishment and religious freedom." The Congress that drafted the First Amendment would have been accustomed to invocations containing explicitly religious themes of the sort respondents find objectionable.

To hold that invocations must be nonsectarian would force the legislatures that sponsor prayers and the courts that are asked to decide these cases to act as supervisors and censors of religious speech, a rule that would involve government in religious matters to a far greater degree than is the case under the town's current practice of neither editing or approving prayers in advance nor criticizing their content after the fact.

In rejecting the suggestion that legislative prayer must be nonsectarian, the Court does not imply that no constraints remain on its content. The relevant constraint derives from its place at the opening of legislative sessions, where it is meant to lend gravity to the occasion and reflect values long part of the Nation's heritage. Prayer that is solemn and respectful in tone, that invites lawmakers to reflect upon shared ideals and common ends before they embark on the fractious business of governing, serves that legitimate function. If the course and practice over time shows that the invocations denigrate nonbelievers or religious minorities, threaten damnation, or preach conversion, many present may consider the prayer to fall short of the desire to elevate the purpose of the occasion and to unite lawmakers in their common effort. That circumstance would present a different case than the one presently before the Court.

B

The prayer opportunity in this case must be evaluated against the backdrop of historical practice. As a practice that has long endured, legislative prayer has become part of our heritage and tradition, part of our expressive idiom, similar to the Pledge of Allegiance, inaugural prayer, or the recitation of "God save the United States and this honorable Court" at the opening of this Court's sessions. It is presumed that the reasonable observer is acquainted with this tradition and understands that its purposes are to lend gravity to public proceedings and to acknowledge the place religion holds in the lives of many private citizens, not to afford government an opportunity to proselytize or force truant constituents into the pews. That many appreciate these acknowledgments of the divine in our public institutions does not suggest that those who disagree are compelled to join the expression or approve its content. *West Virginia Bd. of Educ. v. Barnette.*

Ceremonial prayer is but a recognition that, since this Nation was founded and until the present day, many Americans deem that their own existence must be understood by precepts far beyond the authority of government to alter or define and that willing participation in civic affairs can be consistent with a brief acknowledgment of their belief in a higher power, always with due respect for those who adhere to other beliefs. The prayer in this case has a permissible ceremonial purpose. It is not an unconstitutional establishment of religion.

The town of Greece does not violate the First Amendment by opening its meetings with prayer that comports with our tradition and does not coerce participation by nonadherents.

JUSTICE ALITO, with whom JUSTICE SCALIA joins, concurring.

There can be little doubt that the decision in *Marsh* reflected the original understanding of the First Amendment. It is virtually inconceivable that the First Congress, having appointed chaplains whose responsibilities prominently included the delivery of prayers at the beginning of each daily session, thought that this practice was inconsistent with the Establishment Clause. And since this practice was well established and undoubtedly well known, it seems equally clear that the state legislatures that ratified the First Amendment had the same understanding. In the case before us, the Court of Appeals appeared to base its decision on one of the Establishment Clause "tests" set out in the opinions of this Court, but if there is any inconsistency between any of those tests and the historic practice of legislative prayer, the inconsistency calls into question the validity of the test, not the historic practice.

JUSTICE KAGAN, with whom JUSTICE GINSBURG, JUSTICE BREYER, and JUSTICE SOTOMAYOR join, dissenting.

For centuries now, people have come to this country from every corner of the world to share in the blessing of religious freedom. Our Constitution promises that they may worship in their own way, without fear of penalty or danger, and that in itself is a momentous offering. Yet our Constitution makes a commitment still more remarkable—that however those individuals worship, they will count as full and equal American citizens. A Christian, a Jew, a Muslim (and so forth)—each stands in the same relationship with her country, with her state and local communities, and with every level and body of government. So that when each person performs the duties or seeks the benefits of citizenship, she does so not as an adherent to one or another religion, but simply as an American.

I respectfully dissent from the Court's opinion because I think the Town of Greece's prayer practices violate that norm of religious equality—the breathtakingly generous constitutional idea that our public institutions belong no less to the Buddhist or Hindu than to the Methodist or Episcopalian. I do not contend that principle translates here into a bright separationist line. To the contrary, I agree with the Court's decision in *Marsh v. Chambers,* upholding the Nebraska Legislature's tradition of beginning each session with a chaplain's prayer. And I believe that pluralism and inclusion in a town hall can satisfy the constitutional requirement of neutrality; such a forum need not become a religion-free zone. But still, the Town of Greece should lose this case. The practice at issue here differs from the one sustained in *Marsh* because Greece's town meetings involve participation by ordinary citizens, and the invocations given—directly to those citizens—were predominantly sectarian in content. Still more, Greece's Board did nothing to recognize religious diversity: In arranging for clergy members to open each meeting, the Town never sought (except briefly when this suit was filed) to involve, accommodate, or in any way reach out to adherents of non-Christian religions. So month in and month out for over a decade, prayers steeped in only one faith, addressed toward members of the public, commenced meetings to discuss local affairs and distribute government benefits. In my view, that practice does not square with the First Amendment's promise that every citizen, irrespective of her religion, owns an equal share in her government.

To begin to see what has gone wrong in the Town of Greece, consider several hypothetical scenarios in which sectarian prayer—taken straight from this case's record—infuses governmental activities. None involves, as this case does, a proceeding that could be characterized as a legislative session, but they are useful to elaborate some general principles. In each instance, assume (as was true in Greece) that the invocation is given pursuant to government policy and is representative of the prayers generally offered in the designated setting:

- You are a party in a case going to trial; let's say you have filed suit against the government for violating one of your legal rights. The judge bangs his gavel to call the court to order, asks a minister to come to the front of the room, and instructs the 10 or so individuals present to rise for an opening prayer. The clergyman faces those in attendance and says: "Lord, God of all creation, we acknowledge the saving sacrifice of Jesus Christ on the cross. We draw strength from his resurrection at Easter. Jesus Christ, who took away the sins of the world, destroyed our death, through his dying and in his rising, he has restored our life. Blessed are you, who has raised up the Lord Jesus, you who will raise us, in our turn, and put us by His side. Amen." The judge then asks your lawyer to begin the trial.

- It's election day, and you head over to your local polling place to vote. As you and others wait to give your names and receive your ballots, an election official asks everyone there to join him in prayer. He says: "We pray this day for the guidance of the Holy Spirit as we vote. Let's just say the Our Father together. Our Father, who art in Heaven, hallowed be thy name; thy Kingdom come, thy will be done, on earth as it is in Heaven." And after he concludes, he makes the sign of the cross, and appears to wait expectantly for you and the other prospective voters to do so too.

- You are an immigrant attending a naturalization ceremony to finally become a citizen. The presiding official tells you and your fellow applicants that before administering the oath of allegiance, he would like a minister to pray for you and with you. The pastor steps to the front of the room, asks everyone to bow their heads, and recites: "Father, son, and Holy Spirit—it is with a due sense of reverence and awe that we come before you today seeking your blessing. You are a wise God, oh Lord, as evidenced even in the plan of redemption that is fulfilled in Jesus Christ. We ask that you would give freely and abundantly wisdom to one and to all in the name of the Lord and Savior Jesus Christ, who lives with you and the Holy Spirit, one God for ever and ever. Amen."

I would hold that the government officials responsible for the above practices—that is, for prayer repeatedly invoking a single religion's beliefs in these settings—crossed a constitutional line. I have every confidence the Court would agree. And even Greece's attorney conceded that something like the first hypothetical (he was not asked about the others) would violate the First Amendment. Why?

One glaring problem is that the government in all these hypotheticals has aligned itself with, and placed its imprimatur on, a particular religious creed. "The clearest command of the Establishment Clause," this Court has held, "is that one religious denomination cannot be officially preferred over another." *Larson v. Valente*. Justices have often differed about a further issue: whether and how the Clause applies to governmental policies favoring religion (of all kinds) over non-religion. But no one has disagreed with this much: "Our constitutional tradition, from the Declaration of Independence and the first inaugural address of Washington down to the present day, has ruled out of order government-sponsored endorsement of religion where the endorsement is sectarian." *Lee v. Weisman* (Scalia, J., dissenting).

And making matters still worse: They have done so in a place where individuals come to interact with, and participate in, the institutions and processes of their government. A person goes to court, to the polls, to a naturalization ceremony—and a government official or his hand-picked minister asks her, as the first order of official business, to stand and pray with others in a way conflicting with her own religious beliefs. Perhaps she feels sufficient pressure to go along—to rise, bow her head, and join in whatever others are saying: After all, she wants, very badly, what the judge or poll worker or immigration official has to offer. Or perhaps she is made of stronger mettle, and she opts not to participate in what she does not believe—indeed, what would, for her, be something like blasphemy. She then must make known her dissent from the common religious view, and place herself apart from other citizens, as well as from the officials responsible for the invocations. And so a civic function of some kind brings religious differences to the fore: That public proceeding becomes (whether intentionally or not) an instrument for dividing her from adherents to the community's majority religion, and for altering the very nature of her relationship with her government.

That is not the country we are, because that is not what our Constitution permits. Here, when a citizen stands before her government, whether to perform a service or request a benefit, her religious beliefs do not enter into the picture.

Relying on that "unbroken" national tradition, *Marsh* upheld (I think correctly) the Nebraska Legislature's practice of opening each day with a chaplain's prayer as "a tolerable acknowledgment of beliefs widely held among the people of this country." And so I agree with the majority that the issue here is "whether the prayer practice in the Town of Greece fits within the tradition long followed in Congress and the state legislatures."

Where I depart from the majority is in my reply to that question. The town hall here is a kind of hybrid. Greece's Board indeed has legislative functions, as Congress and state assemblies do—and that means some opening prayers are allowed there. But much as in my hypotheticals, the Board's meetings are also occasions for ordinary citizens to engage with and petition their government, often on highly individualized matters. That feature calls for Board members to exercise special care to ensure that the prayers offered are inclusive—that they respect each and every member of the community as an equal citizen. But the Board, and the clergy members it selected, made no such effort. Instead, the prayers given in Greece, addressed directly to the Town's citizenry, were *more* sectarian, and *less* inclusive, than anything this Court sustained in *Marsh*. For those reasons, the prayer in Greece departs from the legislative tradition that the majority takes as its benchmark.

In 1790, George Washington traveled to Newport, Rhode Island, a longtime bastion of religious liberty and the home of the first community of American Jews. Among the citizens he met there was Moses Seixas, one of that congregation's lay officials. The ensuing exchange between the two conveys, as well as anything I know, the promise this country makes to members of every religion.

Seixas wrote first, welcoming Washington to Newport. He spoke of "a deep sense of gratitude" for the new American Government—"a Government, which to bigotry gives no sanction, to persecution no assistance—but generously affording to All liberty of conscience, and immunities of Citizenship: deeming every one, of whatever Nation, tongue, or language, equal parts of the great governmental Machine." Washington responded the very next day. Like any successful politician, he appreciated a great line when he saw one—and knew to borrow it too. And so he repeated, word for word, Seixas's phrase about neither sanctioning bigotry nor assisting persecution. But he no less embraced the point Seixas had made about equality of citizenship. "It is now no more," Washington said, "that toleration is spoken of, as if it was by the indulgence of one class of people" to another, lesser one. For "all possess alike immunities of citizenship." That is America's promise in the First Amendment: full and equal membership in the polity for members of every religious group, assuming only that they, like anyone "who lives under the Government's protection, should demean themselves as good citizens."

For me, that remarkable guarantee means at least this much: When the citizens of this country approach their government, they do so only as Americans, not as members of one faith or another. And that means that even in a partly legislative body, they should not confront government-sponsored worship that divides them along religious lines. I believe, for all the reasons I have given, that the Town of Greece betrayed that promise. I therefore respectfully dissent from the Court's decision.

[Justice Thomas' opinion concurring in part and concurring in the judgment, which was joined by Justice Scalia in part, is omitted, as is Justice Breyer's dissenting opinion.]

Points for Discussion

1. **Is the majority opinion insensitive to the concerns of religious minorities?** Justice O'Connor famously noted that government endorsement of religion "sends a message to nonadherents that they are outsiders, not full members of the political community, and an accompanying message to adherents that they are insiders, favored members of the political community." Do you think that the *Town of Greece* prayer practice violated this principle by making religious minorities or nonbelievers feel like "outsiders"? Was Justice Kagan correct when she argued in her dissent that American citizens who approach the government "should not confront government-sponsored worship that divides them along religious lines"?

2. **When legislative prayers cross the line.** Justic Kennedy held that legislative prayers are not unconstitutional simply because they are sectarian. But he did suggest that legislative prayers could sometimes violate the Establishment Clause. Can you identify the factors Justice Kennedy identified that could make a legislative prayer unconstitutional?

3. **When Satanists come calling.** In upholding the town's prayer practice, Justice Kennedy emphasized the town's representation that "it would welcome a prayer by any minister or layman who wished to give one." If a Satanist priest approached the town board, would the board be required to allow him to give a prayer? Could a legislature exclude nontheists (those who do not espouse a belief in a god or gods) from offering prayers? *See Fields v. Speaker of the Pa. House of Representatives*, 936 F.3d 142 (3d Cir. 2019) (upholding a ban on nontheistic prayers in the Pennsylvania House of Representatives "because only theistic prayer can satisfy the historical purpose of appealing for divine guidance in lawmaking").

D. Prayers and Other Religious Content in Public Schools: Football, Faith, and the First Amendment

The Supreme Court has decided scores of Establishment Clause cases dealing with religious symbols and rituals in public schools—enough to fill an entire casebook. In this section, we present two principal cases, both of which involve prayer and football.

The two cases were decided against a backdrop of earlier decisions about prayer in public schools. In *Engel v. Vitale*, 370 U.S. 421 (1962), the Court's initial foray into the area, the majority held that New York could not require public schools to begin each school day with the recitation of this state-composed prayer: "Almighty God, we acknowledge our dependence upon Thee, and we beg Thy blessings upon us, our parents, our teachers and our Country." The Court found the practice unconstitutional even though the prayer was nondenominational and students could not be required to recite it: "We think that the constitutional prohibition against laws respecting an establishment of religion must at least mean that in this country it is no part of the business of government to compose official prayers for any group of the American people to recite as a part of a religious program carried on by government." The next year, in *School District of Abington Township v. Schempp*, 374 U.S. 203 (1963), the Court held unconstitutional the practice of reading verses from the Bible and saying the Lord's Prayer in Pennsylvania public schools.

Three decades later, in *Lee v. Weisman*, the Court issued what might be its most expansive decision on school prayer. In an opinion written by Justice Kennedy, the Court held that it was unlawful to have even nonsectarian prayers at a public school graduation ceremony. This is the opinion referred to earlier in which Justice Kennedy articulated the coercion test and concluded that even peer pressure can constitute unlawful coercion. In the same case, Justice Scalia, in dissent, contended that coercion should be limited to "acts backed by threat of penalty."

Santa Fe Independent School District v. Doe

Supreme Court of the United States, 2000
530 U.S. 290

[*Authors' note*: This case concerned the following policy of the Santa Fe Independent School District: "The board has chosen to permit students to deliver a brief invocation and/or message to be delivered during the pre-game ceremonies of home varsity football games to solemnize the event, to promote good sportsmanship and student safety, and to establish the appropriate environment for the competition. Upon advice and direction of the high school principal, each spring, the high school student council shall conduct an election, by the high school student body, by secret ballot, to determine whether such a message or invocation will be a part of the pre-game ceremonies and if so, shall elect a student, from a list of student volunteers, to deliver the statement or invocation. The student volunteer who is selected by his or her classmates may decide what statement or invocation to deliver, consistent with the goals and purposes of this policy. Any message and/or invocation delivered by a student must be nonsectarian and nonproselytizing."]

JUSTICE STEVENS delivered the opinion of the Court.

Prior to 1995, the Santa Fe High School student who occupied the school's elective office of student council chaplain delivered a prayer over the public address system before each varsity football game for the entire season. This practice, along with others, was challenged in District Court as a violation of the Establishment Clause of the First Amendment. While these proceedings were pending in the District Court, the school district adopted a different policy that permits, but does not require, prayer initiated and led by a student at all home games.

In this case the District first argues that messages are private student speech, not public speech. It reminds us that "there is a crucial difference between government speech endorsing religion, which the Establishment Clause forbids, and private speech endorsing religion, which the Free Speech and Free Exercise Clauses protect."

These invocations are authorized by a government policy and take place on government property at government-sponsored school-related events. Of course, not every message delivered under such circumstances is the government's own. We have held, for example, that an individual's contribution to a government-created forum was not government speech. See *Rosenberger v. Rector and Visitors of University of Virginia.* Although the District relies heavily on *Rosenberger* and similar cases involving such forums, it is clear that the pregame ceremony is not the type of forum discussed in those cases.

In *Lee v. Weisman*, the school district made the related argument that its policy of endorsing only "civic or nonsectarian" prayer was acceptable because it minimized the intrusion on the audience as a whole. We rejected that claim by explaining that such a majoritarian policy "does not lessen the offense or isolation to the objectors. At best it narrows their number, at worst increases their sense of isolation and affront." Similarly, while Santa Fe's majoritarian election might ensure that most of the students are represented, it does nothing to protect the minority; indeed, it likely serves to intensify their offense.

The actual or perceived endorsement of the message, moreover, is established by factors beyond just the text of the policy. Once the student speaker is selected and the message composed, the invocation is then delivered to a large audience assembled as part of a regularly scheduled, school-sponsored function conducted on school property. The message is broadcast over the school's public address system, which remains subject to the control of school officials. It is fair to assume that the pregame ceremony is clothed in the traditional indicia of school sporting events, which generally include not just the team, but also cheerleaders and band members dressed in uniforms sporting the school name and mascot. The school's name is likely written in large print across the field and on banners and flags. The crowd will certainly include many who display the school colors and insignia on their school T-shirts, jackets, or hats and who may also be waving signs displaying the school name. It is in a setting such as this that "the board has chosen to permit" the elected student to rise and give the "statement or invocation."

In this context the members of the listening audience must perceive the pregame message as a public expression of the views of the majority of the student body delivered with the approval of the school administration. In cases involving state participation in a religious activity, one of the relevant questions is "whether an objective observer, acquainted with the text, legislative history, and implementation of the statute, would perceive it as a state endorsement of prayer in public schools." Regardless of the listener's support for, or objection to, the message, an objective Santa Fe High School student will unquestionably perceive the inevitable pregame prayer as stamped with her school's seal of approval.

The District next argues that its football policy is distinguishable from the graduation prayer in *Lee* because it does not coerce students to participate in religious observances. Its argument has two parts: first, that there is no impermissible government coercion because the pregame messages are the product of student choices; and second, that there is really no coercion at all because attendance at an extracurricular event, unlike a graduation ceremony, is voluntary.

Attendance at a high school football game, unlike showing up for class, is certainly not required in order to receive a diploma. Moreover, we may assume that the District is correct in arguing that the informal pressure to attend an athletic event is not as strong as a senior's desire to attend her own graduation ceremony.

There are some students, however, such as cheerleaders, members of the band, and, of course, the team members themselves, for whom seasonal commitments mandate their attendance, sometimes for class credit. The District also minimizes the importance to many students of attending and participating in extracurricular activities as part of a complete educational experience. As we noted in *Lee*, "law reaches past formalism." To assert that high school students do not feel immense social pressure, or have a truly genuine desire, to be involved in the extracurricular event that is American high school football is "formalistic in the extreme." We stressed in *Lee* the obvious observation that "adolescents are often susceptible to pressure from their peers towards conformity, and that the influence is strongest in matters of social convention." High school home football games are traditional gatherings of a school community; they bring together students and faculty as well as friends and family from years present and past to root for a common cause. Undoubtedly, the games are not important to some students, and they voluntarily choose not to attend. For many others, however, the choice between attending these games and avoiding personally offensive religious rituals is in no practical sense an easy one. The Constitution, moreover, demands that the school may not force this difficult choice upon these students for "it is a tenet of the First Amendment that the State cannot require one of its citizens to forfeit his or her rights and benefits as the price of resisting conformance to state-sponsored religious practice."

The policy is invalid on its face because it establishes an improper majoritarian election on religion, and unquestionably has the purpose and creates the perception of encouraging the delivery of prayer at a series of important school events.

CHIEF JUSTICE REHNQUIST, with whom JUSTICE SCALIA and JUSTICE THOMAS join, dissenting.

The Court distorts existing precedent to conclude that the school district's student-message program is invalid on its face under the Establishment Clause. But even more disturbing than its holding is the tone of the Court's opinion; it bristles with hostility to all things religious in public life. Neither the holding nor the tone of the opinion is faithful to the meaning of the Establishment Clause, when it is recalled that George Washington himself, at the request of the very Congress which passed the Bill of Rights, proclaimed a day of "public thanksgiving and prayer, to be observed by acknowledging with grateful hearts the many and signal favors of Almighty God."

Kennedy v. Bremerton School District

Supreme Court of the United States, 2022
142 S. Ct. 2407

JUSTICE GORSUCH delivered the opinion of the Court.

Joseph Kennedy lost his job as a high school football coach because he knelt at midfield after games to offer a quiet prayer of thanks. Mr. Kennedy prayed during a period when school employees were free to speak with a friend, call for a reservation at a restaurant, check email, or attend to other personal matters. He offered his prayers quietly while his students were otherwise occupied. Still, the Bremerton School District disciplined him anyway. It did so because it thought anything less could lead a reasonable observer to conclude (mistakenly) that it endorsed Mr. Kennedy's religious beliefs. That reasoning was misguided. Both the Free Exercise and Free Speech Clauses of the First Amendment protect expressions like Mr. Kennedy's. Nor does a proper understanding of the Amendment's Establishment Clause require the government to single out private religious speech for special disfavor. The Constitution and the best of our traditions counsel mutual respect and tolerance, not censorship and suppression, for religious and nonreligious views alike.

Joseph Kennedy began working as a football coach at Bremerton High School in 2008 after nearly two decades of service in the Marine Corps. Like many other football players and coaches across the country, Mr. Kennedy made it a practice to give "thanks through prayer on the playing field" at the conclusion of each game. In his prayers, Mr. Kennedy sought to express gratitude for "what the players had accomplished and for the opportunity to be part of their lives through the game of football." Mr. Kennedy offered his prayers after the players and coaches had shaken hands, by taking a knee at the 50-yard line and praying "quietly" for "approximately 30 seconds."

Initially, Mr. Kennedy prayed on his own. But over time, some players asked whether they could pray alongside him. Mr. Kennedy responded by saying, "This is a free country. You can do what you want." The number of players who joined Mr. Kennedy eventually grew to include most of the team, at least after some games. Sometimes team members invited opposing players to join. Other times Mr. Kennedy still prayed alone. Eventually, Mr. Kennedy began incorporating short motivational speeches with his prayer when others were present. Separately, the team at times engaged in pregame or postgame prayers in the locker room. It seems this practice was a "school tradition" that predated Mr. Kennedy's tenure. Mr. Kennedy explained that he "never told any student that it was important they participate in any religious activity." In particular, he "never pressured or encouraged any student to join" his postgame midfield prayers.

For over seven years, no one complained to the Bremerton School District about these practices. On September 17, the superintendent sent Mr. Kennedy a letter. In it, the superintendent identified "two problematic practices" in which Mr. Kennedy had engaged. First, Mr. Kennedy had provided "inspirational talk that included "overtly religious references" likely constituting "prayer" with the students "at midfield following the completion of games." Second, he had led "students and coaching staff in a prayer" in the locker-room tradition that "predated his involvement with the program."

After receiving the District's September 17 letter, Mr. Kennedy ended the tradition, predating him, of offering locker-room prayers. He also ended his practice of incorporating religious references or prayer into his postgame motivational talks to his team on the field.

On October 14, through counsel, Mr. Kennedy sent a letter to school officials informing them that, because of his "sincerely-held religious beliefs," he felt "compelled" to offer a "post-game personal prayer" of thanks at midfield. He asked the District to allow him to continue that "private religious expression" alone. On October 16, the District responded with another letter. The District acknowledged that Mr. Kennedy "had complied" with the "directives" in its September 17 letter. Yet instead of accommodating Mr. Kennedy's request to offer a brief prayer on the field while students were busy with other activities—whether heading to the locker room, boarding the bus, or perhaps singing the school fight song—the District issued an ultimatum. It forbade Mr. Kennedy from engaging in "any overt actions" that could "appear to a reasonable observer to endorse prayer while he is on duty as a District-paid coach." The District did so because it judged that anything less would lead it to violate the Establishment Clause.

After receiving this letter, Mr. Kennedy offered a brief prayer following the October 16 game. When he bowed his head at midfield after the game, "most Bremerton players were engaged in the traditional singing of the school fight song to the audience." Though Mr. Kennedy was alone when he began to pray, players from the other team and members of the community joined him before he finished his prayer. This event spurred media coverage of Mr. Kennedy's dilemma and a public response from the District.

After the October 23 game ended, Mr. Kennedy knelt at the 50-yard line, where "no one joined him," and bowed his head for a "brief, quiet prayer." After the final relevant football game on October 26, Mr. Kennedy again knelt alone to offer a brief prayer as the players engaged in postgame traditions. While he was praying, other adults gathered around him on the field.

Shortly after the October 26 game, the District placed Mr. Kennedy on paid administrative leave and prohibited him from participating, in any capacity, in football program activities. In a Q&A document provided to the public, the District admitted that it possessed no evidence that students have been directly coerced to pray with Kennedy. The Q&A also acknowledged that Mr. Kennedy had complied with the District's instruction to refrain from his "prior practices of leading players in a pre-game prayer in the locker room or leading players in a post-game prayer immediately following games." But the Q&A asserted that the District could not allow Mr. Kennedy to "engage in a public religious display." Otherwise, the District would "violate the Establishment Clause" because "reasonable students and attendees" might perceive the "district as endorsing religion."

Now before us, Mr. Kennedy renews his argument that the District's conduct violated both the Free Exercise and Free Speech Clauses of the First Amendment. These Clauses work in tandem. Where the Free Exercise Clause protects religious exercises, whether communicative or not, the Free Speech Clause provides overlapping protection for expressive religious activities. That the First Amendment doubly protects religious speech is no accident. It is a natural outgrowth of the framers' distrust of government attempts to regulate religion and suppress dissent.

Under this Court's precedents, a plaintiff bears certain burdens to demonstrate an infringement of his rights under the Free Exercise and Free Speech Clauses. If the plaintiff carries these burdens, the focus then shifts to the defendant to show that its actions were nonetheless justified and tailored consistent with the demands of our case law.

That Mr. Kennedy has discharged his burdens is effectively undisputed. No one questions that he seeks to engage in a sincerely motivated religious exercise.

Nor does anyone question that, in forbidding Mr. Kennedy's brief prayer, the District failed to act pursuant to a neutral and generally applicable rule. A government policy will not qualify as neutral if it is "specifically directed at religious practice."

When it comes to Mr. Kennedy's free speech claim, our precedents remind us that the First Amendment's protections extend to "teachers and students," neither of whom "shed their constitutional rights to freedom of speech or expression at the schoolhouse gate." *Tinker.*

To account for the complexity associated with the interplay between free speech rights and government employment, this Court's decisions in *Pickering*, *Garcetti*, and related cases suggest proceeding in two steps. The first step involves a threshold inquiry into the nature of the speech at issue. If a public employee speaks "pursuant to his or her official duties," this Court has said the Free Speech Clause generally will not shield the individual from an employer's control and discipline because that kind of speech is—for constitutional purposes at least—the government's own speech.

At the same time and at the other end of the spectrum, when an employee "speaks as a citizen addressing a matter of public concern," our cases indicate that the First Amendment may be implicated and courts should proceed to a second step. At this second step, our cases suggest that courts should attempt to engage in "a delicate balancing of the competing interests surrounding the speech and its consequences." Among other things, courts at this second step have sometimes considered whether an employee's speech interests are outweighed by "the interest of the State, as an employer, in promoting the efficiency of the public services it performs through its employees."

Applying these lessons here, it seems clear to us that Mr. Kennedy has demonstrated that his speech was private speech, not government speech. When Mr. Kennedy uttered the three prayers that resulted in his suspension, he was not engaged in speech "ordinarily within the scope" of his duties as a coach. He did not speak pursuant to government policy. He was not seeking to convey a government-created message. He was not instructing players, discussing strategy, encouraging better on-field performance, or engaged in any other speech the District paid him to produce as a coach.

Whether one views the case through the lens of the Free Exercise or Free Speech Clause, at this point the burden shifts to the District. Under the Free Exercise Clause, a government entity normally must satisfy at least "strict scrutiny," showing that its restrictions on the plaintiff's protected rights serve a compelling interest and are narrowly tailored to that end. See *Lukumi*. A similar standard generally obtains under the Free Speech Clause. See *Reed.* The District, however, asks us to apply to Mr. Kennedy's claims the more lenient second-step *Pickering-Garcetti* test, or alternatively intermediate scrutiny. Ultimately, however, it does not matter which standard we apply. The District cannot sustain its burden under any of them.

As we have seen, the District argues that its suspension of Mr. Kennedy was essential to avoid a violation of the Establishment Clause. On its account, Mr. Kennedy's prayers might have been protected by the Free Exercise and Free Speech Clauses. But his rights were in "direct tension" with the competing demands of the Establishment Clause. To resolve that clash, the District reasoned, Mr. Kennedy's rights had to "yield."

But how could that be? It is true that this Court and others often refer to the "Establishment Clause," the "Free Exercise Clause," and the "Free Speech Clause" as separate units. But the three Clauses appear in the same sentence of the same Amendment: "Congress shall make no law respecting an establishment of religion, or prohibiting the free exercise thereof; or abridging the freedom of speech." A natural reading of that sentence would seem to suggest the Clauses have "complementary" purposes, not warring ones where one Clause is always sure to prevail over the others.

To defend its approach, the District relied on *Lemon* and its progeny.

What the District and the Ninth Circuit overlooked, however, is that the "shortcomings" associated with this ambitious, abstract, and ahistorical approach to the Establishment Clause became so apparent that this Court long ago abandoned *Lemon* and its endorsement test offshoot.

In place of *Lemon* and the endorsement test, this Court has instructed that the Establishment Clause must be interpreted by "reference to historical practices and understandings." *Town of Greece; see also American Legion.*

To be sure, this Court has long held that government may not, consistent with a historically sensitive understanding of the Establishment Clause, "make a religious observance compulsory." *Zorach v. Clauson.* Government "may not coerce anyone to attend church," nor may it force citizens to engage in "a formal religious exercise," *Lee v. Weisman.* No doubt, too, coercion along these lines was among the foremost hallmarks of religious establishments the framers sought to prohibit when they adopted the First Amendment. Members of this Court have sometimes disagreed on what exactly qualifies as impermissible coercion in light of the original meaning of the Establishment Clause. But in this case Mr. Kennedy's private religious exercise did not come close to crossing any line one might imagine separating protected private expression from impermissible government coercion.

The absence of evidence of coercion in this record leaves the District to its final redoubt. Here, the District suggests that *any* visible religious conduct by a teacher or coach should be deemed—without more and as a matter of law—impermissibly coercive on students. In essence, the District asks us to adopt the view that the only acceptable government role models for students are those who eschew any visible religious expression.

Such a rule would be a sure sign that our Establishment Clause jurisprudence had gone off the rails. In the name of protecting religious liberty, the District would have us suppress it. Rather than respect the First Amendment's double protection for religious expression, it would have us preference secular activity. Not only could schools fire teachers for praying quietly over their lunch, for wearing a yarmulke to school, or for offering a midday prayer during a break before practice. Under the District's rule, a school would be required to do so. It is a rule that would defy this Court's traditional understanding that permitting private speech is not the same thing as coercing others to participate in it. See *Town of Greece*. It is a rule, too, that would undermine a long constitutional tradition under which learning how to tolerate diverse expressive activities has always been "part of learning how to live in a pluralistic society." We are aware of no historically sound understanding of the Establishment Clause that begins to make it necessary for government to be hostile to religion in this way. *Zorach v. Clauson*.

Meanwhile, this case looks very different from those in which this Court has found prayer involving public school students to be problematically coercive. In *Lee*, this Court held that school officials violated the Establishment Clause by including a clerical member who publicly recited prayers as part of an official school graduation ceremony because the school had in every practical sense compelled attendance and participation in a "religious exercise." In *Santa Fe Independent School Dist. v. Doe*, the Court held that a school district violated the Establishment Clause by broadcasting a prayer "over the public address system" before each football game. The Court observed that, while students generally were not required to attend games, attendance was required for "cheerleaders, members of the band, and, of course, the team members themselves." None of that is true here. The prayers for which Mr. Kennedy was disciplined were not publicly broadcast or recited to a captive audience. Students were not required or expected to participate. And, in fact, none of Mr. Kennedy's students did participate in any of the three October 2015 prayers that resulted in Mr. Kennedy's discipline.

Respect for religious expressions is indispensable to life in a free and diverse Republic—whether those expressions take place in a sanctuary or on a field, and whether they manifest through the spoken word or a bowed head. Here, a government entity sought to punish an individual for engaging in a brief, quiet, personal religious observance doubly protected by the Free Exercise and Free Speech Clauses of the First Amendment. And the only meaningful justification the government offered for its reprisal rested on a mistaken view that it had a duty to ferret out and suppress religious observances even as it allows comparable secular speech. The Constitution neither mandates nor tolerates that kind of discrimination. Mr. Kennedy is entitled to summary judgment on his First Amendment claims.

JUSTICE SOTOMAYOR, with whom JUSTICE BREYER and JUSTICE KAGAN join, dissenting.

This case is about whether a public school must permit a school official to kneel, bow his head, and say a prayer at the center of a school event. The Constitution does not authorize, let alone require, public schools to embrace this conduct. Since *Engel v. Vitale*, this Court consistently has recognized that school officials leading prayer is constitutionally impermissible. Official-led prayer strikes at the core of our constitutional protections for the religious liberty of students and their parents, as embodied in both the Establishment Clause and the Free Exercise Clause of the First Amendment.

The Court now charts a different path, yet again paying almost exclusive attention to the Free Exercise Clause's protection for individual religious exercise while giving short shrift to the Establishment Clause's prohibition on state establishment of religion. To the degree the Court portrays petitioner Joseph Kennedy's prayers as private and quiet, it misconstrues the facts. The record reveals that Kennedy had a longstanding practice of conducting demonstrative prayers on the 50-yard line of the football field. Kennedy consistently invited others to join his prayers and for years led student athletes in prayer at the same time and location. The Court ignores this history. The Court also ignores the severe disruption to school events caused by Kennedy's conduct, viewing it as irrelevant because the Bremerton School District (District) stated that it was suspending Kennedy to avoid it being viewed as endorsing religion. Under the Court's analysis, presumably this would be a different case if the District had cited Kennedy's repeated disruptions of school programming and violations of school policy regarding public access to the field as grounds for suspending him. As the District did not articulate those grounds, the Court assesses only the District's Establishment Clause concerns. It errs by assessing them divorced from the context and history of Kennedy's prayer practice.

Properly understood, this case is not about the limits on an individual's ability to engage in private prayer at work. This case is about whether a school district is required to allow one of its employees to incorporate a public, communicative display of the employee's personal religious beliefs into a school event, where that display is recognizable as part of a longstanding practice of the employee ministering religion to students as the public watched. A school district is not required to permit such conduct; in fact, the Establishment Clause prohibits it from doing so.

Kennedy's tradition of a 50-yard line prayer thus strikes at the heart of the Establishment Clause's concerns about endorsement. For students and community members at the game, Coach Kennedy was the face and the voice of the District during football games. The timing and location Kennedy selected for his prayers were "clothed in the traditional indicia of school sporting events." Kennedy spoke from the playing field, which was accessible only to students and school employees, not to the general public. Although the football game itself had ended, the football game events had not; Kennedy himself acknowledged that his responsibilities continued until the players went home.

Kennedy's prayer practice also implicated the coercion concerns at the center of this Court's Establishment Clause jurisprudence. This Court has recognized that students face immense social pressure. Students look up to their teachers and coaches as role models and seek their approval. Students also depend on this approval for tangible benefits. Players recognize that gaining the coach's approval may pay dividends small and large, from extra playing time to a stronger letter of recommendation to additional support in college athletic recruiting.

Photograph of J. Kennedy in prayer circle (Oct. 16, 2015).

Today's decision goes beyond merely misreading the record. The Court overrules *Lemon v. Kurtzman*, and calls into question decades of subsequent precedents that it deems "offshoots" of that decision. In the process, the Court rejects longstanding concerns surrounding government endorsement of religion and replaces the standard for reviewing such questions with a new "history and tradition" test. In addition, while the Court reaffirms that the Establishment Clause prohibits the government from coercing participation in religious exercise, it applies a nearly toothless version of the coercion analysis, failing to acknowledge the unique pressures faced by students when participating in school-sponsored activities. This decision does a disservice to schools and the young citizens they serve, as well as to our Nation's longstanding commitment to the separation of church and state. I respectfully dissent.

[Justice Thomas' and Justice Alito's concurring opinions are omitted.]

Points for Discussion

1. **One case, two fact patterns?** How does Justice Alito's rendition of the facts compare to Justice Sotomayor's? Whose rendition do you think more accurately characterizes the facts? Should it make a difference, in terms of the constitutional analysis, whose rendition is correct?

2. **When can a school limit a teacher's or coach's religious practice?** Can a school forbid a Jewish teacher from wearing a yarmulke to school? Can it forbid a Catholic teacher from wearing a large cross? Can a school insist that a teacher not say prayers out loud while class is in session? Can a school insist that a teacher not quote Bible verses? Can a school insist that a teacher not proselytize to her students?

3. **Is a moment of silence permissible?** In *Wallace v. Jaffree*, 472 U.S. 38 (1985), the Court struck down an Alabama law that authorized a period of silence "for meditation or voluntary prayer" in public schools. The Court held that the intent behind the law was to "return prayer" to public schools. The Court left open the possibility that a "moment of silence" policy that was not intended to encourage prayer could be constitutional: "The legislative intent to return prayer to the public schools is, of course, quite different from merely protecting every student's right to engage in voluntary prayer during an appropriate moment of silence during the schoolday."

4. **Ten Commandments displays and school release time.** You learned from reading the Ten Commandments cases that the Court held in *Stone v. Graham*, 449 U.S. 39 (1980), that a state could not require the posting of Ten Commandments displays on classroom walls. Why did the Court think this was unconstitutional? Should it be unconstitutional?

   On a different note, in *Zorach v. Clauson*, the Court upheld a New York City policy that permitted schools to release students during the day so they could receive religious instruction outside the school. Justice Douglas wrote the opinion for the Court which included this famous passage:

   > We are a religious people whose institutions presuppose a Supreme Being. We guarantee the freedom to worship as one chooses. We make room for as wide a variety of beliefs and creeds as the spiritual needs of man deem necessary. We sponsor an attitude on the part of government that shows no partiality to any one group and that lets each flourish according to the zeal of its adherents and the appeal of its dogma. When the state encourages religious instruction or cooperates

> with religious authorities by adjusting the schedule of public events to sectarian needs, it follows the best of our traditions. For it then respects the religious nature of our people and accommodates the public service to their spiritual needs.

Zorach contrasted with an earlier decision, *Illinois v. Board of Education*, 333 U.S. 203 (1948), which struck down a program that freed students from schoolwork so they could attend religious classes held inside the school buildings.

5. **Evolution and creationism.** In *Epperson v. Arkansas*, 393 U.S. 97 (1968), the Court struck down an Arkansas statute that made it unlawful for an instructor to teach evolution or to use a textbook that referred to this scientific theory. Although the law did not explicitly state its predominant religious purpose, the Court found that the statute "was a product of the upsurge of 'fundamentalist' religious fervor" that had long viewed evolutionary theory as contradicting the literal interpretation of the Bible. In *Edwards v. Aguillard*, 482 U.S. 578 (1987), the Court extended *Epperson* to strike down a Louisiana law that mandated balanced treatment for "Creation Science" and "Evolution Science." The Court observed, "The preeminent purpose of the Louisiana Legislature was clearly to advance the religious viewpoint that a supernatural being created humankind."

6. **The Scopes trial.** The first great showdown over the teaching of evolution in public schools was the trial of public school teacher John T. Scopes, who was charged with violating a Tennessee law prohibiting the teaching of evolution in public schools.

John T. Scopes

The case drew worldwide attention. It became known by the nickname "The Scopes Monkey Trial," a name coined by the famous *Baltimore Sun* journalist H.L. Mencken. The trial was one of the formative forces behind the creation of the American Civil Liberties Union, which undertook to pay for the litigation expenses of any public school teacher willing to challenge the anti-evolution law. The case featured two renowned "guest lawyers" who were brought in to serve as lead counsel for the opposing sides. The guest prosecutor was Williams Jennings Bryan, an American populist political leader who ran for president multiple times. Defending Scopes was Clarence Darrow, a legendary American defense lawyer from Chicago.

Clarence Darrow (L) and William Jennings Bryan (R)

Darrow and Bryan had at times been on the same side of issues on behalf of the working classes, but in this case, pitting science against religion, they were on opposite sides. In one of the strangest episodes in the history of American trials, Bryan took the witness stand as an expert on the Bible, subjecting himself to cross-examination by his opposing counsel, Darrow. It was one of the first "media trials," broadcast throughout the nation in the early days of radio. For a masterful nonfiction account of the trial, see Edward Larson, *Summer for the Gods: The Scopes Trial and America's Continuing Debate Over Science and Religion* (Harvard University Press 1998). The trial was later fictionalized and made into a play and a magnificent movie, "Inherit the Wind," starring Spencer Tracy, Frederic

March, and Gene Kelly. The cross-examination scene in the movie, which is drawn virtually verbatim from the actual trial transcript, may be the greatest courtroom examination scene in the history of American film.

You Be the Judge!
Does the recitation of the Pledge of Allegiance in schools violate the Establishment Clause?

In *Elk Grove Unified School District v. Newdow*, 542 U.S. 1 (2004), the Court heard a challenge to the recitation of the Pledge of Allegiance, which includes the phrase "one nation under God." The Court did not reach the merits, instead holding that the father of the child who had been exposed to the pledge at school did not have standing to litigate the case. Imagine that a new case is brought by a student who objects to school officials' practice of leading a recitation of the pledge as a violation of the Establishment Clause. The lawsuit points out that President Dwight Eisenhower, during the 1954 signing ceremony for the law adding "one nation under God" to the pledge, said: "From this day forward, the millions of our school children will daily proclaim in every city and town, every village and rural school house, the dedication of our Nation and our people to the Almighty." The student also relies on the famous statement in *West Virginia Board of Education v. Barnette*: "If there is any fixed star in our constitutional constellation, it is that no official, high or petty, can prescribe what shall be orthodox in politics, nationalism, religion, or other matters of opinion or force citizens to confess by word or act their faith therein." The school responds that the student is not coerced into participating in the pledge—indeed, it would violate *Barnette* to force the student to do so. The school argues that under current Establishment Clause principles, the ritual of starting a school day with a recitation of the Pledge of Allegiance, a ritual that occurs millions of times a year at public events of all sorts, cannot possibly be a violation of the Establishment Clause. If you were on the Supreme Court, how would you rule, and why?

E. Financial Support to Religion: From Bus Fares to Tuition Vouchers

This final section addresses government financial aid to religious institutions. While the relevant principles apply to economic support in any context, the vast bulk of cases dealing with the issue have involved support that benefits religious schools and universities.

Earlier in this chapter you read *Everson*, in which Justice Black proclaimed that "no tax in any amount, large or small, can be levied to support any religious activities or institutions" and that the wall between church and state must be "kept high and impregnable." Despite these bold assertions, Justice Black nevertheless held that New Jersey *could* reimburse parents for the bus fares paid to send their children to religious schools. Justice Black said the Establishment Clause required the government to be neutral toward religion, not hostile to it.

In subsequent years, the Court decided dozens of cases dealing with the constitutionality of government programs that provided support to parochial schools. The cases had mixed and sometimes seemingly conflicting results. The following landmark opinion offers a window into the Court's current views about taxpayer money being used to support religious education.

Zelman v. Simmons-Harris

Supreme Court of the United States, 2002
536 U.S. 639

CHIEF JUSTICE REHNQUIST delivered the opinion of the Court.

The State of Ohio has established a pilot program designed to provide educational choices to families with children who reside in the Cleveland City School District. The question presented is whether this program offends the Establishment Clause of the United States Constitution. We hold that it does not.

There are more than 75,000 children enrolled in the Cleveland City School District. The majority of these children are from low-income and minority families. Few of these families enjoy the means to send their children to any school other than an inner-city public school. For more than a generation, however, Cleveland's public schools have been among the worst performing public schools in the Nation. The district had failed to meet any of the 18 state standards for minimal acceptable performance. Only 1 in 10 ninth graders could pass a basic proficiency examination, and students at all levels performed at a dismal rate compared with students in other Ohio public schools. More than two-thirds of high school students either dropped or failed out before graduation. Of those students who managed to reach their senior year, one of every four still failed to graduate. Of those students who did graduate, few could read, write, or compute at levels comparable to their counterparts in other cities.

It is against this backdrop that Ohio enacted, among other initiatives, its Pilot Project Scholarship Program. The program provides two basic kinds of assistance to parents of children in a covered district. First, the program provides tuition aid for students in kindergarten through third grade, expanding each year through eighth grade, to attend a participating public or private school of their parent's choosing.

Second, the program provides tutorial aid for students who choose to remain enrolled in public school.

The tuition aid portion of the program is designed to provide educational choices to parents who reside in a covered district. Any private school, whether religious or nonreligious, may participate in the program and accept program students so long as the school is located within the boundaries of a covered district and meets statewide educational standards. Participating private schools must agree not to discriminate on the basis of race, religion, or ethnic background, or to "advocate or foster unlawful behavior or teach hatred of any person or group on the basis of race, ethnicity, national origin, or religion." Any public school located in a school district adjacent to the covered district may also participate in the program. Adjacent public schools are eligible to receive a $2,250 tuition grant for each program student accepted in addition to the full amount of per-pupil state funding attributable to each additional student. All participating schools, whether public or private, are required to accept students in accordance with rules and procedures established by the state superintendent.

The Establishment Clause of the First Amendment, applied to the States through the Fourteenth Amendment, prevents a State from enacting laws that have the "purpose" or "effect" of advancing or inhibiting religion. There is no dispute that the program challenged here was enacted for the valid secular purpose of providing educational assistance to poor children in a demonstrably failing public school system. Thus, the question presented is whether the Ohio program nonetheless has the forbidden "effect" of advancing or inhibiting religion.

To answer that question, our decisions have drawn a consistent distinction between government programs that provide aid directly to religious schools, and programs of true private choice, in which government aid reaches religious schools only as a result of the genuine and independent choices of private individuals. While our jurisprudence with respect to the constitutionality of direct aid programs has changed significantly over the past two decades, our jurisprudence with respect to true private choice programs has remained consistent and unbroken. Three times we have confronted Establishment Clause challenges to neutral government programs that provide aid directly to a broad class of individuals, who, in turn, direct the aid to religious schools or institutions of their own choosing. Three times we have rejected such challenge.

In *Mueller v. Allen,* 463 U.S. 388 (1983), we rejected an Establishment Clause challenge to a Minnesota program authorizing tax deductions for various educational expenses, including private school tuition costs, even though the great majority of the program's beneficiaries (96%) were parents of children in religious schools. We began by focusing on the class of beneficiaries, finding that because the class included "*all* parents," including parents with "children who attend nonsectarian private schools or sectarian private schools," the program was "not readily subject to challenge under the Establishment Clause." Then, viewing the program as a whole, we emphasized the principle of private choice, noting that public funds were made available to religious schools "only as a result of numerous, private choices of individual parents of school-age children." This, we said, ensured that "no imprimatur of state approval can be deemed to have been conferred on any particular religion, or on religion generally." That the program was one of true private choice, with no evidence that the State deliberately skewed incentives toward religious schools, was sufficient for the program to survive scrutiny under the Establishment Clause.

In *Witters v. Washington Department of Services for Blind*, 474 U.S. 481 (1986), we used identical reasoning to reject an Establishment Clause challenge to a vocational scholarship program that provided tuition aid to a student studying at a religious institution to become a pastor. Looking at the program as a whole, we observed that "any aid that ultimately flows to religious institutions does so only as a result of the genuinely independent and private choices of aid recipients." We further remarked that, as in *Mueller*, "the program is made available generally without regard to the sectarian-nonsectarian, or public-nonpublic nature of the institution benefited."

Finally, in *Zobrest v. Catalina Foothills School District*, 509 U.S. 1 (1993), we applied *Mueller* and *Witters* to reject an Establishment Clause challenge to a federal program that permitted sign-language interpreters to assist deaf children enrolled in religious schools. Reviewing our earlier decisions, we stated that "government programs that neutrally provide benefits to a broad class of citizens defined without reference to religion are not readily subject to an Establishment Clause challenge."

Mueller, Witters, and *Zobrest* thus make clear that where a government aid program is neutral with respect to religion, and provides assistance directly to a broad class of citizens who, in turn, direct government aid to religious schools wholly as a result of their own genuine and independent private choice, the program is not readily subject to challenge under the Establishment Clause. A program that shares these features permits government aid to reach religious institutions only by way of the deliberate choices of numerous individual recipients. The incidental advancement of a religious mission, or the perceived endorsement of a religious message, is reasonably attributable to the individual recipient, not to the government, whose role ends with the disbursement of benefits. It is precisely for these reasons that we have never found a program of true private choice to offend the Establishment Clause.

We believe that the program challenged here is a program of true private choice, consistent with *Mueller, Witters*, and *Zobrest*, and thus constitutional. As was true in those cases, the Ohio program is neutral in all respects toward religion. It is part of a general and multifaceted undertaking by the State of Ohio to provide educational opportunities to the children of a failed school district. It confers educational assistance directly to a broad class of individuals defined without reference to religion, *i.e.*, any parent of a school-age child who resides in the Cleveland City School District.

There also is no evidence that the program fails to provide genuine opportunities for Cleveland parents to select secular educational options for their school-age children. Cleveland schoolchildren enjoy a range of educational choices: They may remain in public school as before, remain in public school with publicly funded tutoring aid, obtain a scholarship and choose a religious school, obtain a scholarship and choose a nonreligious private school, enroll in a community school, or enroll in a magnet school. That 46 of the 56 private schools now participating in the program are religious schools does not condemn it as a violation of the Establishment Clause. The Establishment Clause question is whether Ohio is coercing parents into sending their children to religious schools, and that question must be answered by evaluating all options Ohio provides Cleveland schoolchildren, only one of which is to obtain a program scholarship and then choose a religious school.

Justice Souter speculates that because more private religious schools currently participate in the program, the program itself must somehow discourage the participation of private nonreligious schools. But Cleveland's preponderance of religiously affiliated private schools certainly did not arise as a result of the program; it is a phenomenon common to many American cities. To attribute constitutional significance to this figure, moreover, would lead to the absurd result that a neutral school-choice program might be permissible in some parts of Ohio, such as Columbus, where a lower percentage of private schools are religious schools,

Respondents and Justice Souter claim that even if we do not focus on the number of participating schools that are religious schools, we should attach constitutional significance to the fact that 96% of scholarship recipients have enrolled in religious schools. They claim that this alone proves parents lack genuine choice, even if no parent has ever said so. We need not consider this argument in detail, since it was flatly rejected in *Mueller*, where we found it irrelevant that 96% of parents taking deductions for tuition expenses paid tuition at religious schools. Indeed, we have recently found it irrelevant even to the constitutionality of a direct aid program that a vast majority of program benefits went to religious schools. The constitutionality of a neutral educational aid program simply does not turn on whether and why, in a particular area, at a particular time, most private schools are run by religious organizations, or most recipients choose to use the aid at a religious school.

In sum, the Ohio program is entirely neutral with respect to religion. It provides benefits directly to a wide spectrum of individuals, defined only by financial need and residence in a particular school district. It permits such individuals to exercise genuine choice among options public and private, secular and religious. The program is therefore a program of true private choice. In keeping with an unbroken line of decisions rejecting challenges to similar programs, we hold that the program does not offend the Establishment Clause.

JUSTICE SOUTER, with whom JUSTICE STEVENS, JUSTICE GINSBURG, and JUSTICE BREYER join, dissenting.

The applicability of the Establishment Clause to public funding of benefits to religious schools was settled in *Everson*, which inaugurated the modern era of establishment doctrine. The Court stated the principle in words from which there was no dissent: "No tax in any amount, large or small, can be levied to support any religious activities or institutions, whatever they may be called, or whatever form they may adopt to teach or practice religion." The Court has never in so many words repudiated this statement, let alone, in so many words, overruled *Everson*.

Today, however, the majority holds that the Establishment Clause is not offended by Ohio's Pilot Project Scholarship Program, under which students may be eligible to receive as much as $2,250 in the form of tuition vouchers transferable to religious schools. Public tax money will pay at a systemic level for teaching the covenant with Israel and Mosaic law in Jewish schools, the primacy of the Apostle Peter and the Papacy in Catholic schools, the truth of reformed Christianity in Protestant schools, and the revelation to the Prophet in Muslim schools, to speak only of major religious groupings in the Republic.

How can a Court consistently leave *Everson* on the books and approve the Ohio vouchers? The answer is that it cannot. It is only by ignoring *Everson* that the majority can claim to rest on traditional law in its invocation of neutral aid provisions and private choice to sanction the Ohio law.

JUSTICE BREYER, with whom JUSTICE STEVENS and JUSTICE SOUTER join, dissenting.

I write separately to emphasize the risk that publicly financed voucher programs pose in terms of religiously based social conflict. I do so because I believe that the Establishment Clause concern for protecting the Nation's social fabric from religious conflict poses an overriding obstacle to the implementation of this well-intentioned school voucher program.

With respect to government aid to private education, did not history show that efforts to obtain equivalent funding for the private education of children whose parents did not hold popular religious beliefs only exacerbated religious strife? As Justice Rutledge recognized: "Public money devoted to payment of religious costs, educational or other, brings the quest for more. It brings too the struggle of sect against sect for the larger share or for any." *Everson* (dissenting opinion).

The upshot is the development of constitutional doctrine that reads the Establishment Clause as avoiding religious strife, *not* by providing every religion with an *equal opportunity* (say, to secure state funding or to pray in the public schools), but by drawing fairly clear lines of *separation* between church and state—at least where the heartland of religious belief, such as primary religious education, is at issue. The principle underlying these cases—avoiding religiously based social conflict—remains of great concern. As religiously diverse as America had become when the Court decided its major 20th-century Establishment Clause cases, we are exponentially more diverse today.

Consider the voucher program here at issue. That program insists that the religious school accept students of all religions. Does that criterion treat fairly groups whose religion forbids them to do so? The program also insists that no participating school "advocate or foster unlawful behavior or teach hatred of any person or group on the basis of race, ethnicity, national origin, or religion." And it requires the State to "revoke the registration of any school if, after a hearing, the superintendent determines that the school is in violation" of the program's rules. As one amicus argues, "it is difficult to imagine a more divisive activity" than the appointment of state officials as referees to determine whether a particular religious doctrine "teaches hatred or advocates lawlessness." Efforts to respond to these problems not only will seriously entangle church and state, but also will promote division among religious groups, as one group or another fears (often legitimately) that it will receive unfair treatment at the hands of the government.

I concede that the Establishment Clause currently permits States to channel various forms of assistance to religious schools, for example, transportation costs for students, computers, and secular texts. School voucher programs differ, however, in both kind and degree from aid programs upheld in the past. They differ in kind because they direct financing to a core function of the church: the teaching of religious truths to young children. For that reason the constitutional demand for separation is of particular constitutional concern.

Vouchers also differ in degree. The aid programs recently upheld by the Court involved limited amounts of aid to religion. But the majority's analysis here appears to permit a considerable shift of taxpayer dollars from public secular schools to private religious schools. That fact, combined with the use to which these dollars will be put, exacerbates the conflict problem. State aid that takes the form of peripheral secular items, with prohibitions against diversion of funds to religious teaching, holds significantly less potential for social division. In this respect as well, the secular aid upheld in *Mitchell v. Helms*, 530 U.S. 793 (2000), differs dramatically from the present case. Although it was conceivable that minor amounts of money could have, contrary to the statute, found their way to the religious activities of the recipients, that case is at worst the camel's nose, while the litigation before us is the camel itself.

[Justice O'Connor's and Justice Thomas' concurring opinions are omitted, as is Justice Stevens' dissenting opinion.]

Points for Discussion

1. ***Zelman* and payments to parents.** In *Everson*, Justice Black allowed the government to reimburse parents for the transportation costs of sending their children to religious schools even though he said that the wall between church and state must be kept "high and impregnable" and that the "slightest breach" was intolerable. That may have seemed like a contradiction, but at least the breach Justice Black approved, reimbursement of bus fare, was truly small. Literally, pocket change. By contrast, the financial assistance at issue in *Zelman*, tuition assistance vouchers, was of a totally different magnitude. Does that mean that *Zelman* is inconsistent with *Everson*, or is it possible to reconcile the opinions? Can you make persuasive arguments either way?

2. **Must the government allow families to use tuition vouchers at religious schools?** *Zelman* did not say the government must allow families to use education vouchers at religious schools. It merely said the government *may* neutrally offer vouchers for private schools even if some families use the vouchers at religious schools. In the aftermath of the *Trinity Lutheran*, *Espinoza*, and *Carson* cases you read about in Chapter 18, may the government now offer tuition vouchers for private schools and not allow parents to use them at religious schools? *See, e.g.*, Erwin Chemerinsky & Barry P. McDonald, *Eviscerating a Healthy Church-State Separation*, 96 Wash. U. L. Rev. 1009 (2019).

3. **What about direct aid to religious schools?** In *Zelman*, the tuition vouchers were not given directly to religious schools but were instead distributed to parents who independently decided to use the vouchers at religious schools. But what about programs in which government aid flows directly to religious schools or to students already enrolled in the schools?

   The Court's jurisprudence in this latter context has been anything but consistent. In earlier years, when the justices leaned more toward the high separationist pole, the Court frequently, but not always, found aid to religious schools or their students to be unconstitutional. Reimbursements for transportation costs to get students to parochial schools were permitted but not transportation costs to take students on field trips. Lending textbooks was acceptable but not instructional equipment such as projectors or recording devices. In more recent years, as the justices have increasingly leaned toward the low separationist pole, the Court has become more accepting of aid to parochial schools and their students. In *Mitchell v. Helms*, 530 U.S. 793 (2000), for example, the Court upheld a government aid program that lent an array of educational materials and equipment to qualifying public and private schools, including religious schools. While a majority of the Court upheld this aid, the justices were sharply divided over the appropriate standards for evaluating such aid.

All the justices agreed that aid cannot be offered exclusively to parochial schools or their students. Instead, any aid had to be neutrally offered to a wide range of schools, as was the case in *Mitchell*. The justices also agreed that any distributed materials could not be inherently religious. Indeed, the regulatory regime in *Mitchell* required the materials and equipment to be "secular, neutral, and nonideological." But the justices split over whether aid was improper if it could be diverted for religious instruction. Some believed that aid was improper if it had the potential to be easily diverted, while others thought it was improper only if had been actually diverted. Justice Thomas, joined by three other justices, thought the focus on diversion was misguided and potentially boundless, noting that "lecterns, chalk, crayons, pens, paper, and paintbrushes" could all be diverted for religious instruction. If governmental aid does not have religious content and is distributed through a neutral process, Justice Thomas explained, "any use of that aid to indoctrinate cannot be attributed to the government and is thus not of constitutional concern."

The aid in *Mitchell* was also allocated based on the student enrollment in any given school. For Justice Thomas, that made it little different from the tuition vouchers offered in *Zelman*. The only difference was that the parents in *Mitchell* had previously decided to enroll their children in parochial schools instead of doing so after first being given a tuition voucher. "Although the presence of private choice is easier to see when aid literally passes through the hands of individuals," Justice Thomas explained, "there is no reason why the Establishment Clause requires such a form." By contrast, Justice O'Connor, whose opinion concurring in the judgment was joined by Justice Breyer, thought there was a stark difference between government aid reaching parochial schools indirectly through parents and aid given directly to the schools. If aid given directly to a parochial school is used for religious instruction, she said, "the reasonable observer would naturally perceive the aid program as *government* support for the advancement of religion."

While the precise legal parameters for evaluating aid programs to schools are still a work in progress, it is worth noting that any secular aid in *Mitchell* that might have been diverted for religious purposes would be tiny compared to the tuition vouchers at issue in *Zelman*. Indeed, in his dissent in *Zelman*, Justice Breyer described *Mitchell* as being "at worst the camel's nose," whereas *Zelman* was "the camel itself."

4. **Grants to religious universities.** Government grants to universities, including religious universities, can often involve very substantial sums. Yet the Court's decisions involving financial aid to religious colleges and universities have been far less demanding of separation of church and state than the decisions involving aid to elementary, middle, and high schools. The Court has generally allowed government to provide substantial financial grants to religious colleges and universities if those grants are part of general programs available across the board to all institutions of higher learning and the aid will be used for secular purposes. In contrast to the decisions involving lower schools, in which the Court has generally required that the reimbursement of costs go to parents, who then voluntarily choose to use the benefits for education of their children in religious schools, the decisions involving higher education have more willingly permitted direct financial grants to the colleges and universities themselves. *See Tilton v. Richardson*, 403 U.S. 672 (1971); *Hunt v. McNair*, 413 U.S. 734 (1973); *Roemer v. Board of Pub. Works of Md.*, 426 U.S. 736 (1976). Why would the Court be more willing to tolerate direct government aid to colleges and universities than to K–12 schools? Does the different treatment parallel the more rigorous high separationist principles that animate constitutional restrictions on religion in lower public schools, such as the heavy resistance to school prayer, in contrast to the willingness to tolerate government prayer in non-school settings, such as the legislative sessions in *Marsh* or *Town of Greece*?

5. **What about tax exemptions for religious institutions?** You have probably heard about church properties' being exempt from property taxes. How could that be? If the exemptions were only for religious institutions, they would be unconstitutional. But the Court has upheld tax exemptions when they are offered to a broad range of properties being used for religious, educational, or charitable purposes. For example, in *Walz v. Tax Commission*, 397 U.S. 664 (1970), the Court upheld a tax exemption program that included religious properties among "a broad class of property owned by nonprofit, quasi-public corporations which include hospitals, libraries, playgrounds, scientific, professional, historical, and patriotic groups." The Court noted that the government considered these groups "beneficial and stabilizing influences in community life."

6. **Is the "wall of separation" a metaphor or a myth?** The notion of a "wall of separation" between church and state has long held powerful sway as a metaphor for the meaning of the religion clauses. High separationists are particularly apt to draw on the metaphor. Plainly, however, more recent Supreme Court decisions have moved decisively toward the lower separationist pole. One might view this in two ways. To those who believe the wall of separation is what the Framers intended, and what the First Amendment should mean, low separationist decisions such as *American Legion*, *Town of Greece*, *Zelman*, and *Bremerton* represent an inappropriate crumbling of the wall. To those who find those same opinions

sound, both as to the Framers' intent and as modern constitutional law, however, the very notion of the "wall of separation" may be seen as a myth that never accurately reflected the authentic meaning of the religion clauses. Which view do you share?

A Comparative Perspective

The notion of separating church and state is also a core value of French society. "Laïcité," or secularism, is the term the French use to express this principle. While both the United States and France view separation of church and state as a vehicle for protecting religious liberty, scholars suggest that the primary focus of laïcité is to protect the state from the excesses of religion. This anti-clerical orientation traces back to the hostility toward the Catholic Church during the French Revolution. T. Jeremy Gunn, *Religious Freedom and Laïcité: A Comparison of the United States and France*, 2004 B.Y.U. L. Rev. 419, 420 n.2 (2004).

The impact of this different orientation can be seen in a series of French laws restricting the wearing of religious clothing in public schools. For example, in 2004 the French Parliament enacted a law that barred students from wearing clothing or accoutrements that "openly manifest a religious affiliation." The law had the effect of barring Jewish students from wearing yarmulkes, Catholic students from wearing large crosses, and Muslim girls from wearing hijabs. In 2023, the French education minister barred girls in public schools from wearing abayas, the loose-fitting dresses often worn by Muslim women.

After the 2004 law went into effect, Professor Steven Gey described how the French attitude toward religion and education varied from the American:

> In short, the main question is, "How does the government best foster a tradition of spiritual and intellectual liberty among its young citizens?" Does the government foster religious liberty best by deferring to the dictates of religious communities, or is the cause of religious liberty better served by government actions that affirmatively seek to provide space for young citizens to choose their own religious paths independent of the religious community in which they live or were raised? The French and American systems answer this question very differently. Recent actions by the French indicate that country's belief that liberty is best fostered through a system of rigorously secular education, in which the government provides the tools for students to make decisions about a range of issues, including those involving sensitive matters of religious faith. American courts, on the other hand, assume that a child comes to school with a preformed religious sensibility and that

schools should do nothing to foster the child's skeptical appraisal of his or her religious perspective.

Steven G. Gey, *Free Will, Religious Liberty, and a Partial Defense of the French Approach to Religious Expression in Public Schools*, 42 Hous. L Rev. 1, 4–5 (2005).

Which approach, the American or French, appeals to you?

Test Your Knowledge

To assess your understanding of the material in this chapter, click here to take a quiz.

Index

References are to pages.

FREEDOM OF SPEECH

SECONDARY EFFECTS DOCTRINE

SEDITION